Explori
Development

Exploring **Child** Development

Laura E. Berk
Illinois State University

Dedication

In gratitude to

Marla, Greg, Ani, Kendra, Judith, Shari, Miranda, and Isra

for leadership and collaboration in initiating The Art Station at Illinois State University

Vice President and Senior Publisher: Roth Wilkofsky
Managing Editor: Tom Pauken
Development Editor: Rachel Trapp-Gardner
Editorial Assistant: Kaylee Navarra
Manager, Content Producer: Amber Mackey
Team Lead/Senior Content Producer: Elizabeth Gale Napolitano
Program Management: Ann Pulido, Katharine Glynn
Supplements Manager: Judy Ashkenaz
Digital Studio Product Manager: Elissa Senra-Sargent
Senior Operations Specialist: Carol Melville, LSC
Rights and Permissions Manager: Ben Ferrini
Interior Design: Carol Somberg
Cover Design: Lumina Datamatics, Inc.
Full-Service Project Management: iEnergizer/Aptara®, Inc.
Electronic Page Makeup: Jeff Miller
Copyeditor and References Editor: Josephine Cepeda
Proofreader: Charles A. Hutchinson
Indexer: Linda Hallinger
Printer/Binder: LSC Communications, Kendallville, IN
Cover Printer: Lumina Datamatics LTD
Text Font: Times
Cover Photo: Joel Bergner, www.artolution.org

Library of Congress Cataloging-in-Publication Data

Names: Berk, Laura E., author.
Title: Exploring child development / Laura E. Berk, Illinois State University.
Description: Boston : Pearson, [2019]
Identifiers: LCCN 2017060785| ISBN 9780134893471 (pbk.) | ISBN 0134893476 (pbk.) | ISBN 9780134983844 (instructor's review edition) | ISBN 013498384X (instructor's review edition) | ISBN 9780134983752 (a la carte edition) | ISBN 0134983750 (a la carte edition)
Subjects: LCSH: Child development. | Child psychology.
Classification: LCC HQ767.9 .B4643 2019 | DDC 305.231—dc23 LC record available at https://lccn.loc.gov/2017060785

1 18

Student Edition
ISBN 10: 0-13-489347-6
ISBN 13: 978-0-13-489347-1

Instructor's Review Edition
ISBN 10: 0-13-498384-X
ISBN 13: 978-0-13-498384-4

À la Carte Edition
ISBN 10: 0-13-498375-0
ISBN 13: 978-0-13-498375-2

ABOUT THE AUTHOR

Laura E. Berk is a distinguished professor of psychology at Illinois State University, where she has taught child, adolescent, and lifespan development for more than three decades. She received her bachelor's degree in psychology from the University of California, Berkeley, and her master's and doctoral degrees in child development and educational psychology from the University of Chicago. She has been a visiting scholar at Cornell University, UCLA, Stanford University, and the University of South Australia.

Berk has published widely on the effects of school environments on children's development, the development of private speech, and the role of make-believe play in development. Her empirical studies have attracted the attention of the general public, leading to contributions to *Psychology Today* and *Scientific American.* She has also been featured on National Public Radio's *Morning Edition* and in *Parents Magazine, Wondertime,* and *Reader's Digest.*

Berk has served as a research editor of *Young Children*, a consulting editor for *Early Childhood Research Quarterly,* and as an associate editor of the *Journal of Cognitive Education and Psychology.* She is a frequent contributor to edited volumes, having written the article on social development in *The Child: An Encyclopedic Companion* and the article on Vygotsky in *The Encyclopedia of Cognitive Science.* She is coauthor of the chapter on make-believe play and self-regulation in the *Sage Handbook of Play in Early Childhood* and the chapter on psychologists writing textbooks in *Career Paths in Psychology: Where Your Degree Can Take You,* published by the American Psychological Association.

Berk's books include *Private Speech: From Social Interaction to Self-Regulation; Scaffolding Children's Learning: Vygotsky and Early Childhood Education; A Mandate for Playful Learning in Preschool: Presenting the Evidence;* and *Awakening Children's Minds: How Parents and Teachers Can Make a Difference.* In addition to *Exploring Child Development,* she is author of the best-selling texts *Child Development*, *Infants, Children, and Adolescents,* and *Development Through the Lifespan,* published by Pearson.

Berk is active in work for children's causes. She serves on the governing boards of the Illinois Network of Child Care Resource and Referral Agencies and of Artolution, an organization devoted to engaging children, youths, and families in community-based public art projects around the world as a means of promoting trauma relief and resilience. Berk has been designated a YWCA Woman of Distinction for service in education. She is a fellow of the American Psychological Association, Division 7: Developmental Psychology.

FEATURES AT A GLANCE

SOCIAL ISSUES

BIOLOGY AND ENVIRONMENT

CULTURAL INFLUENCES

APPLYING WHAT WE KNOW

CONTENTS

CHAPTER 6
Emotional and Social Development in Infancy and Toddlerhood 171

PART IV
EARLY CHILDHOOD: TWO TO SIX YEARS

CHAPTER 7
Physical and Cognitive Development in Early Childhood 202

CHAPTER 8 Emotional and Social Development in Early Childhood 245

PART V
MIDDLE CHILDHOOD: SIX TO ELEVEN YEARS

CHAPTER 9 Physical and Cognitive Development in Middle Childhood 280

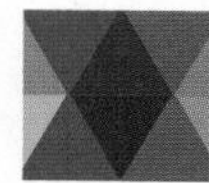

CHAPTER 10
Emotional and Social Development in Middle Childhood 320

A PERSONAL NOTE TO STUDENTS

My more than 30 years of teaching child development have brought me in contact with thousands of students like you—students with diverse college majors, future goals, interests, and needs. Some are affiliated with my own field, psychology, but many come from other related fields—education, sociology, anthropology, family studies, biology, social service, and nursing, to name just a few. Each semester, my students' aspirations have proved to be as varied as their fields of study. Many look toward careers in applied work—counseling, caregiving, teaching, nursing, social work, school psychology, and program administration. Most hope someday to become parents, whereas others are already parents who come with a desire to better understand and rear their children. And almost all arrive with a deep curiosity about how they themselves developed into the complex human beings they are today.

My goal in preparing *Exploring Child Development* is to provide a textbook that meets the instructional goals of your course as well as your personal interests and needs. To achieve these objectives, I have grounded this book in a carefully selected body of classic and current theory and research. In addition, the text highlights the interwoven contributions of biology and environment to the developing child. It also illustrates commonalities and differences among ethnic groups and cultures and discusses the broader social contexts in which children develop. I have provided a unique pedagogical program that will assist you in mastering information, integrating various aspects of development, critically examining controversial issues, applying what you have learned, and relating the information to real life.

I hope that learning about child development will be as rewarding for you as I have found it over the years. I would like to know what you think about both the field of child development and this book. I welcome your comments; please feel free to send them to me at berkexploringchild@gmail.com.

Laura E. Berk

PREFACE FOR INSTRUCTORS

In preparing *Exploring Child Development,* my goal is to provide students with a clear, efficient survey of the most important concepts and research findings in the field of child development. Each step of the way, I aim to make classic, contemporary, and cutting-edge theories and research accessible in a manageable and relevant way, with an especially strong emphasis on real-world applications. Chronologically organized, the text offers a solid introduction to the field in just 10 chapters and 353 pages of reading.

I hope that the text's combination of rich content with concise presentation will offer instructors unusual flexibility in designing their courses to meet both curricular and student needs. For example, *Exploring Child Development* is meant to ease adaptation of the course to the learning needs of beginning students. It is also intended to facilitate combining a text-based survey with supplementary readings, child observation, applied experiences, or service learning. And it is well-suited for courses of reduced duration—quarter systems, half semesters, summer sessions, or short terms. Furthermore, the text should serve well in professional courses for which a broad introduction to child development is a vital foundation.

TEXT PHILOSOPHY

The basic approach of this book has been shaped by my own professional and personal history as a teacher, researcher, and parent. It consists of seven philosophical ingredients that I regard as essential for students to emerge from a course with a thorough understanding of child development. Each theme is woven into every chapter:

1. **An understanding of the diverse array of theories in the field and the strengths and shortcomings of each.** The first chapter begins by emphasizing that only knowledge of multiple theories can do justice to the richness of child development. As I take up each age period and domain of development, I present a variety of theoretical perspectives, indicate how each highlights previously overlooked aspects of development, and discuss research that evaluates it. Consideration of contrasting theories also serves as the context for an evenhanded analysis of many controversial issues.

2. **An appreciation of research strategies for investigating child development.** To evaluate theories and research evidence, students must have a firm grounding in research methods and designs. In addition to a section in Chapter 1 covering basic research strategies and a section in Chapter 4 devoted to neurobiological methods, numerous studies are discussed in sufficient detail throughout the text for students to use what they have learned to critically assess the findings, conclusions, and implications of research.

3. **Knowledge of both the sequence of child development and the processes that underlie it.** Students are provided with discussion of the organized sequence of development along with processes of change. An understanding of *process*—how complex combinations of biological, psychological, and environmental factors produce development—has been the focus of most recent research. Accordingly, the text reflects this emphasis. But new information about the timetable of change has also emerged. Current evidence on the sequence and timing of development, along with its implications for process, is presented throughout the text.

4. **An appreciation of the impact of context and culture on child development.** A wealth of research indicates that children live in rich physical and social contexts that affect all domains of development. Throughout the text, students travel to distant parts of the world as I review a growing body of cross-cultural evidence. The text narrative also discusses many findings on socioeconomically and ethnically diverse children within the United States and on children with varying abilities and challenges. Besides highlighting the effects of immediate settings, such as family, neighborhood, and school, I make a concerted effort to underscore the influence of larger social structures—societal values, laws, and government policies and programs—on children's well-being.

5. **An understanding of the joint contributions of biology and environment to development.** The field recognizes more powerfully than ever before the joint roles of hereditary/constitutional and environmental factors—that these contributions to development combine in complex ways and cannot be separated in a simple manner. Chapter 2 provides an overview of how genetically based dispositions can be maintained as well as transformed by social contexts. It serves as an advance organizer for numerous additional examples discussed in subsequent chapters.

6. **A sense of the interdependency of all domains of development—physical, cognitive, emotional, and social.** Every chapter emphasizes an integrated approach to child development, illustrating how physical, cognitive, emotional, and social development are interwoven. Within the text narrative, and in the Ask Yourself questions at the end of major sections, students are referred to other sections of the text to deepen their grasp of relationships among various aspects of change.

7. **An appreciation of the interrelatedness of theory, research, and applications.** Throughout, I emphasize that theories of child development and the research stimulated by them provide the foundation for sound, effective practices with children. The links among theory, research, and applications are reinforced by an organizational format in which theory and research are presented first, followed by practical implications. In addition, a current focus in the field—harnessing knowledge of child development to shape social policies that

support children's needs—is reflected in every chapter. The text addresses the current condition of children in the United States and elsewhere in the world and shows how theory and research have combined with public interest to spark successful interventions.

TEXT ORGANIZATION

The chronological organization of this text assists students in thoroughly understanding each age period. It also eases the task of integrating the various domains of development because each is discussed in close proximity. At the same time, a chronologically organized book requires that theories covering several age periods be presented incrementally, so students must link the various parts together. To assist with this task, I frequently remind students of important earlier achievements before discussing new developments, cross-referencing to relevant text sections. Also, chapters devoted to the same developmental domain are similarly organized, making it easier for students to draw connections across age periods and construct an overall view of developmental change.

UP-TO-DATE COVERAGE

Child development is a fascinating and ever-changing field, with constantly emerging new discoveries and refinements in existing knowledge. *Exploring Child Development* represents this burgeoning contemporary research literature. Cutting-edge topics in every chapter underscore the text's major themes. Here is a sampling:

CHAPTER 1: Developmental neuroscience • Biology and Environment box on resilience • Cultural Influences box on immigrant youths

CHAPTER 2: Impact of poverty on child development • Neighborhood influences on children's physical and mental health • Epigenesis and the bidirectional relationship between heredity and environment

CHAPTER 3: Fetal brain development, sensory capacities, and behavior • Long-term consequences of maternal emotional stress during pregnancy • Interventions for preterm and low-birthweight infants

CHAPTER 4: Cultural variations in infant sleep practices, including Cultural Influences box on parent–infant cosleeping • Long-term consequences of malnutrition in infancy and toddlerhood • Impact of crawling and walking on perceptual and cognitive development

CHAPTER 5: Toddlers' symbolic understanding of words, photos, and videos • Contributions of high-quality child care to cognitive and social development • SES variations in early language development, with implications for young children's literacy skills and later school success

CHAPTER 6: Temperament and individual differences in susceptibility to the effects of good and poor parenting • Cultural variations in views of sensitive parenting, with implications for development of attachment • Interventions that promote attachment security

CHAPTER 7: Development of executive function skills in preschoolers, including the facilitating role of parental sensitivity and scaffolding • Cognitive attainments and social experiences that contribute to young children's theory of mind • Contributions of universal prekindergarten programs to school success

CHAPTER 8: Influence of parental communication on preschoolers' self-concept and understanding of emotion • Cultural variations in make-believe play • Contributions of language, theory of mind, and social experiences to moral understanding in early childhood

CHAPTER 9: Influence of physical fitness on executive function and academic achievement • Cognitive benefits of bilingualism • Academic achievement of U.S. students from an international perspective

CHAPTER 10: Cultural variations in school-age children's self-esteem • Development of racial and ethnic prejudice in middle childhood, including effective ways to reduce prejudice • Cultural Influences box on the impact of ethnic and political violence on children

PEDAGOGICAL FEATURES

Maintaining a highly accessible writing style—one that is lucid and engaging without being simplistic—is one of my major goals. I frequently converse with students, encouraging them to relate what they read to their own lives. In doing so, I aim to make the study of child development involving and pleasurable.

Chapter Introductions and Vignettes

To provide a preview of chapter content, I include an outline and overview in each chapter introduction. To help students construct a clear image of development and to enliven the text narrative, each chronological age division is unified by case examples woven throughout that set of chapters. For example, within the infancy and toddlerhood section, we look in on three children, observe dramatic changes and striking individual differences, and address the impact of family background, child-rearing practices, parents' and children's life experiences, and child-care quality on development. Besides a set of main characters who bring unity to each age period, many additional vignettes offer vivid examples of development and diversity.

CHAPTER 2 Genetic and Environmental Foundations

Heredity and environment combine in intricate ways, making members of this multigenerational extended family both alike and different in physical characteristics and behavior.

© WALTER HODGES/FLIRT/ALAMY STOCK PHOTO

WHAT'S AHEAD IN CHAPTER 2

Genetic Foundations
The Genetic Code • The Sex Cells • Sex Determination • Multiple Offspring • Patterns of Gene–Gene Interaction • Chromosomal Abnormalities

Reproductive Cho
Genetic Counselin
Diagnosis • Adop

■ **SOCIAL ISSUES** *The Pros and Cons of Reproductive Technologies*

Environmental Contexts for Development
The Family • Socioeconomic Status and

Understanding the Relationship Between Heredity and Environment
The Question, "How Much?" • The Question, "How?"

■ **BIOLOGY AND ENVIRONMENT** *The Tutsi*

"It's a girl!" announces the doctor, holding up the squalling newborn baby as her parents gaze with amazement at their miraculous creation.

"A girl! We've named her Sarah!" exclaims the proud father to eager relatives waiting for news of their new family member.

As we join these parents in thinking about how this wondrous being came into existence and imagining her future, we are struck by many questions. How could this baby, equipped with everything necessary for life outside the womb, have developed from the union of two tiny cells? What ensures that Sarah will, in due time, roll over, reach for objects, walk, talk, make friends, learn, imagine, and create—just like other typical children born before her? Why is she a girl and not a boy, dark-haired rather than blond, calm and patient rather than energetic and distractible? What difference will it make that Sarah is given a name and place in one family, community, nation, and culture rather than another?

To answer these questions, this chapter takes a close look at the foundations of development: heredity and environment. Because nature has prepared us for survival, all humans have features in common. Yet each of us is also unique. Think about several children you know well, and jot down the most obvious physical and behavioral similarities between them and their parents. Did you find that one child shows combined features of both parents, another resembles just one parent, whereas a third is not like either parent? These directly observable characteristics are called **phenotypes.** They depend in part on the individual's **genotype**—the complex blend of genetic information that determines our species and influences all our unique characteristics. Yet phenotypes are also affected by each person's lifelong history of experiences.

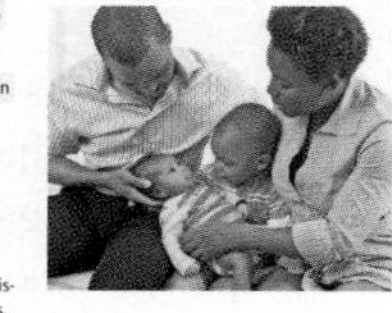

© LAURA DWIGHT PHOTOGRAPHY

We begin our discussion with a review of basic genetic principles that help explain similarities and differences among children in appearance and behavior. Then we turn to aspects of the environment that play powerful roles in children's lives. As our discussion proceeds, some findings may surprise you. For example, many people believe that when children inherit unfavorable characteristics, little can be done to help them. Others are convinced that the damage done to a child by a harmful environment can easily be corrected. As we will see, neither of these assumptions is true. Rather, heredity and environment continuously collaborate, each modifying the power of the other to influence the course of development.

Genetic Foundations

2.1 Explain what genes are and how they are transmitted from one generation to the next.
2.2 Describe various patterns of gene–gene interaction.
2.3 Describe major chromosomal abnormalities, and explain how they occur.

Within each of the trillions of cells in the human body (except red blood cells) is a control center, or *nucleus,* that contains rodlike structures called **chromosomes,** which store and transmit genetic information. Human chromosomes come in 23 matching pairs; an exception is the XY pair in males, which we will discuss shortly. Each member of a pair corresponds to the other in size, shape, and genetic functions. One chromosome is inherited from the mother and one from the father (see Figure 2.1).

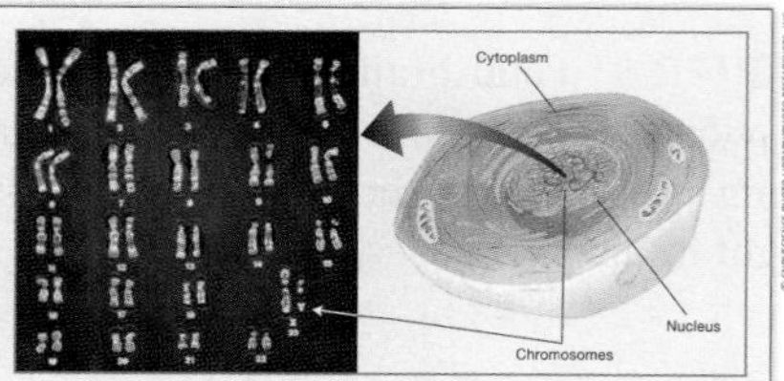

© CNRI/SCIENCE PHOTO LIBRARY/PHOTO RESEARCHERS, INC

FIGURE 2.1 A karyotype, or photograph, of human chromosomes. The 46 chromosomes shown on the left were isolated from a human cell, stained, greatly magnified, and arranged in pairs according to decreasing size of the upper "arm" of each chromosome. The twenty-third pair, XY, reveals that the cell donor is a genetic male. In a genetic female, this pair would be XX.

40

332 CHAPTER 10 Emotional and Social Development in Middle Childhood

- *A social world in which people are sorted into groups.* The more adults highlight group distinctions and the less interracial contact children experience, the more likely White children will express in-group favoritism and out-group prejudice (Aboud & Brown, 2013).

Reducing Prejudice. An effective way to reduce prejudice is through intergroup contact, in which racially and ethnically different children have equal status, work toward common goals, and become personally acquainted (Tropp & Page-Gould, 2015). Children assigned to cooperative learning groups with peers of diverse backgrounds show low levels of prejudice in their expressions of likability and in their behavior. For example, they form more cross-race friendships (Pettigrew & Tropp, 2006). Sharing thoughts and feelings with close, cross-race friends, in turn, reduces even subtle, unintentional prejudices (Turner, Hewstone, & Voci, 2007).

Long-term contact and collaboration among neighborhood, school, and community groups may be the best way to reduce prejudice (Rutland, Killen, & Abrams, 2010). School environments that expose children to broad ethnic diversity, that teach them to understand and value those differences, that directly address the damage caused by prejudice, and that emphasize moral values of justice and fairness prevent children from forming negative biases and lessen already acquired biases (Beelmann & Heinemann, 2014).

Finally, inducing children to view others' traits as changeable, by discussing with them the many possible influences on those traits, is helpful. The more children believe that people can change their personalities, the more they report liking and perceiving themselves as similar to members of disadvantaged outgroups. Furthermore, children who believe that human attributes are changeable spend more time volunteering to help people in need (Karafantis & Levy, 2004; Levy et al., 2016). Volunteering may, in turn, promote a view of others as changeable by helping children take the perspective of the underprivileged and appreciate the social conditions that lead to disadvantage.

© JOEL ARTISTA

▶ Palestinian and Israeli children and adolescents take a break from mural painting to sing and dance together. Intergroup contact, in which racially and ethnically different children have equal status, work toward common goals, and become personally acquainted, is an effective way to reduce prejudice.

ASK YOURSELF

CONNECT Cite examples of how older children's capacity to take more information into account enhances their emotional and moral understanding.

APPLY Ten-year-old Marla says her classmate Bernadette will never get good grades because she's lazy. Jane believes that Bernadette tries but can't concentrate because her parents are divorcing. Why is Marla more likely than Jane to develop prejudices?

REFLECT Did you attend an integrated elementary school? Why is school integration vital for reducing racial and ethnic prejudice?

Peer Relations

10.5 Describe changes in peer sociability and friendship in middle childhood.
10.6 Describe categories of peer acceptance and ways to help rejected children.

In middle childhood, the society of peers becomes an increasingly important context for development. The capacity for recursive perspective taking permits more sophisticated understanding of self and others, which, in turn, contributes to peer interaction. Compared with preschoolers, school-age children resolve conflicts more effectively, and prosocial acts such as sharing and helping increase. In line with these changes, aggression declines. But the drop is greatest for physical attacks (Côté et al., 2007). As we will see, verbal and relational aggression continue as children organize into peer groups.

Learning Objectives

In the text margins next to each main head, learning objectives guide students' reading and study.

End-of-Chapter Summaries

Comprehensive end-of-chapter summaries, organized according to the major divisions of each chapter, highlighting important terms, and illustrated with photos, remind students of key points in the text discussion. Learning objectives are included in the summary to encourage focused study.

Look and Listen

This active-learning feature presents students with opportunities to observe what real children say and do; speak with them or with professionals invested in their well-being; and inquire into community programs and practices that influence development. "Look and Listen" experiences are tied to relevant text sections, with the goal of making the study of development more authentic and meaningful.

Ask Yourself Questions

Active engagement with the subject matter is also supported by study questions at the end of each major section. Three types of questions prompt students to think about child development in diverse ways: **Connect** questions help students build an image of the whole child by integrating what they have learned across age periods and domains of development. **Apply** questions encourage application of knowledge to controversial issues and problems faced by children, parents, and professionals who work with them. **Reflect** questions personalize study of child development by asking students to reflect on their own development and life experiences.

Three Types of Thematic Boxes

Thematic boxes accentuate the philosophical themes of this book:

SOCIAL ISSUES boxes discuss the impact of social conditions on children and emphasize the need for sensitive social policies to ensure their well-being. Examples include: *Family Chaos Undermines Parents' and Children's Well-Being, A Cross-National Perspective on Health Care and Other Policies for Parents and Newborn Babies,* and *Magnet Schools: Equal Access to High-Quality Education.*

BIOLOGY AND ENVIRONMENT boxes highlight growing attention to the complex, bidirectional relationship between biology and environment. Examples include *The Tutsi Genocide and Epigenetic Transmission of Maternal Stress to Children, Transgender Children,* and *Bullies and Their Victims.*

CULTURAL INFLUENCES boxes deepen the attention to culture threaded throughout the text. They highlight both cross-cultural and multicultural variations in child development—for example, *Immigrant Youths: Adapting to a New Land, Why Are Children from Asian Cultures Advanced in Drawing Skills?,* and *The Flynn Effect: Massive Generational Gains in IQ.*

CHAPTER 3 Prenatal Development, Birth, and the Newborn Baby 99

APPLYING WHAT WE KNOW

Soothing a Crying Baby

METHOD	EXPLANATION
Talk softly or play rhythmic sounds.	Continuous, monotonous, rhythmic sounds (such as a clock ticking, a fan whirring, or peaceful music) are more effective than intermittent sounds.
Offer a pacifier.	Sucking helps babies control their own level of arousal.
Massage the baby's body.	Stroking the baby's torso and limbs with continuous, gentle motions relaxes the baby's muscles.
Swaddle the baby.	Restricting movement and increasing warmth often soothe a young infant.
Lift the baby to the shoulder and rock or walk.	This combination of physical contact, upright posture, and motion is an effective soothing technique, causing young infants to become quietly alert.
Take the baby for a short car ride or a walk in a baby carriage; swing the baby in a cradle.	Gentle, rhythmic motion of any kind helps lull the baby to sleep.
Combine several of the methods just listed.	Stimulating several of the baby's senses at once is often more effective than stimulating only one.
If these methods do not work, let the baby cry for a short period.	Occasionally, a baby responds well to just being put down and will, after a few minutes, fall asleep.

Sources: Dayton et al., 2015; Evanoo, 2007; St James-Roberts, 2012.

lose control (Barr et al., 2014). We will discuss a host of additional influences on child abuse in Chapter 8.

Sensory Capacities

On his visit to my class, Joshua looked wide-eyed at my bright pink blouse and turned to the sound of his mother's voice. During feedings, he lets Yolanda know through his sucking rhythm that he prefers the taste of breast milk to a bottle of plain water. Clearly, Joshua has some well-developed sensory capacities. In the following sections, we explore the newborn's responsiveness to touch, taste, smell, sound, and visual stimulation.

Touch. In our discussion of preterm infants, we saw that touch helps stimulate early physical growth. As we will see in Chapter 6, it is vital for emotional development as well. Therefore, it is not surprising that sensitivity to touch is well-developed at birth. Newborns even use touch to investigate their world. When small objects are placed in their palms, they can distinguish shape (prism versus cylinder) and texture (smooth versus rough), as indicated by their tendency to hold on longer to an object with an unfamiliar shape or texture than to a familiar object (Lejeune et al., 2012; Sann & Streri, 2007).

At birth, infants are highly sensitive to pain. If male newborns are circumcised without anesthetic, they often respond with a high-pitched, stressful cry and a dramatic rise in heart rate, blood pressure, palm sweating, pupil dilation, and muscle tension (Lehr et al., 2007; Warnock & Sandrin, 2004). Brain-imaging research suggests that because of central nervous system immaturity, preterm babies, particularly males, feel the pain of a medical injection especially intensely (Bartocci et al., 2006).

Certain local anesthetics for newborns ease the pain of these procedures. Offering a nipple that delivers a sweet liquid is also helpful, with breast milk being especially effective (Roman-

Applying What We Know Tables

In this feature, I summarize research-based applications on many issues, speaking directly to students as parents or future parents and to those pursuing different careers or areas of study, such as teaching, health care, counseling, or social work. The tables include *Supporting Early Language Learning, Regulating Screen Media Use,* and *Helping Children Adjust to Their Parents' Divorce.*

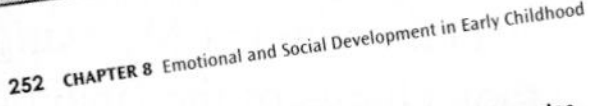

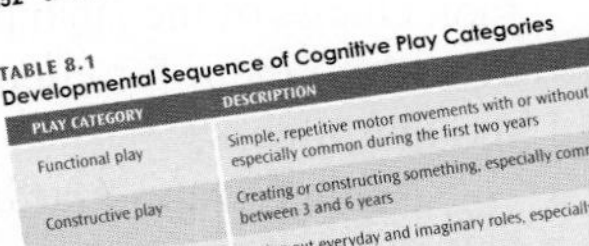

Milestones Tables

A Milestones table appears at the end of each age division of the text. The tables summarize major physical, cognitive, language, emotional, and social attainments, providing a convenient aid for reviewing the chronology of child development.

Art and Photo Program

Colorful graphics present concepts and research findings with clarity and attractiveness, thereby aiding student understanding and retention. Each photo has been carefully selected to complement text discussion and to represent the diversity of children around the world.

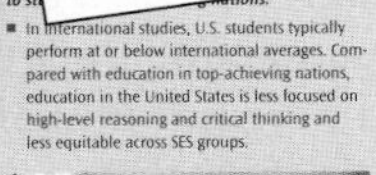

In-Text Key Terms with Definitions, End-of-Chapter Term List, and End-of-Book Glossary

In-text highlighting of key terms and definitions encourages students to review the central vocabulary of the field in greater depth by rereading related information. Key terms also appear in an end-of-chapter page-referenced term list and an end-of-book glossary.

ACKNOWLEDGMENTS

The dedicated contributions of many individuals helped make this text a reality and contributed to its supplements package.

REVIEWERS

An impressive cast of reviewers provided many helpful suggestions, constructive criticisms, as well as encouragement and enthusiasm for the organization and content of the text. I am grateful to each one of them:

J. Victor Ammons I, Kansas City Kansas Community College
Patricia A. Bellas, Irvine Valley College
Jennifer Bennett, University of New Mexico
Irene Bersola-Nguyen, California State University, Sacramento
Angela E. Beyer, San Joaquin Delta College
Nicole Evangelista Brandt, Columbus State Community College
Kelly Champion, Northern Illinois University
Melvin L. Chapman, Oakland Community College
Shaun-Adrián Choflá, Butte College
Kristee Davis, Olive-Harvey College
Melinda Day, Cañada College
Lisa Fozio-Thielk, Waubonsee Community College
Ofelia E. Garcia, Cabrillo College
Shinder Gill, California State University, Sacramento
Christine S. Hodges, Coastal Carolina University
Janet S. Holmes, Miami University
Nora Kametani, Nunez Community College
Megan K. Taylor Kuykendoll, Miami University
Joseph Lao, Hunter College of CUNY
Amy N. Madewell, Southeastern Oklahoma State University
Robert McDermid, Missouri Southern State University
Madhavi Menon, Nova Southeastern University
Angela M. Miller-Hargis, University of Cincinnati Blue Ash
Jennifer Montgomery, El Camino College
Hira Nair, Kansas City Kansas Community College
Susheela Narayanan, San Diego Mesa College
Randy H. Simonson, College of Southern Idaho
Joanne Stephenson, Union University
Ingrid M. Tiegel, Carthage College
Jennifer M. Weaver, Boise State University
Rob Weisskirch, California State University, Monterey Bay
Angela Williamson, Tarrant County College
Gina Wilson, Palomar College

EDITORIAL AND PRODUCTION TEAM

I cannot begin to express what a pleasure it has been, once again, to work with Tom Pauken, Managing Editor, who has worked with me on many editions of my other texts and returned to edit this new title. Tom's keen organizational skills, responsive day-to-day communication, careful review of manuscript, insightful suggestions, interest in the subject matter, sense of humor (at just the right moments), and steadfast dedication to my series at Pearson greatly enhanced the quality of *Exploring Child Development.* I look forward to working with Tom on future projects.

My sincere thanks, as well, to Roth Wilkofsky, Senior Publisher, for his enthusiasm for this new project, for overseeing the expert review process, and for paving the way toward efficient production in both print and Revel™. I have benefitted greatly from Roth's astute problem solving and encouragement, wide-ranging knowledge and experience, cordiality, and hospitality during visits to Pearson.

Liz Napolitano and Ann Pulido, Senior Production Managers, coordinated the complex production tasks, transforming my manuscript into a beautiful print text and Revel™ online learning system. Monica Moosang, Project Manager at Aptara, skillfully took charge of the final phase of production. I am deeply grateful to each of them for attention to detail, flexibility, efficiency, and thoughtfulness.

Rachel Trapp-Gardner, Assistant Editor and Development Editor for the text manuscript, has been nothing short of amazing. In addition to vetting the manuscript for accuracy and clarity, she assisted with preparation of online assessments and other pedagogical supplements.

The supplements package also benefited from the talents and dedication of several individuals. Judy Ashkenaz, Development Editor, wrote the Lecture Enhancements for the Instructor's Resource Manual and revised its chapter summaries and outlines. In addition, she oversaw the preparation of online assessments. Alan Swinkels, St. Edwards University, also contributed to online assessments and prepared an excellent Test Bank. Maria Henneberry and Phil Vandiver of Contemporary Visuals in Bloomington, IL, collaborated with me in producing the many unique and informative video segments that complement text content.

Special words of gratitude go to my family. My sons, David and Peter, grew up with my texts, passing from childhood to adolescence and then to adulthood as successive editions were written. David has a unique connection with the text's subject matter as an elementary school teacher. Peter is now an experienced attorney, and his vivacious and talented wife, Melissa is an accomplished linguist and university professor. All three continue to enrich my understanding through reflections on events and progress in their own lives. I thank my husband, Ken, for willingly making room in our lives for this immensely demanding endeavor.

Finally, as an expression of my appreciation to Illinois State University for its many years of support of my work as a teacher and author, all royalty proceeds from *Exploring Child Development* will be donated to The Art Station at Illinois State University, artstation.illinoisstate.edu. Initiated in 2017, The Art Station will provide educative and expressive visual arts experiences to children, adolescents, and their families in the surrounding community, with a special focus on reaching underserved and at-risk young people.

Laura E. Berk

REVEL™

REVEL is an immersive learning experience designed for the way today's students read, think, and learn. Designed in consultation with educators and students nationwide, REVEL is Pearson's newest, fully digital method of delivering course content.

REVEL for *Exploring Child Development* further enlivens the text with a wealth of author-overseen and -produced interactive media and assessments—all integrated within the narrative to provide opportunities for students to engage deeply with course content while reading. Greater student engagement leads to more thorough understanding of concepts and improved performance throughout the course.

To learn more about REVEL, visit www.pearsonhighered.com/REVEL

INSTRUCTOR RESOURCES

An array of high-quality instructor materials accompanies *Exploring Child Development.*

INSTRUCTOR'S RESOURCE MANUAL (IRM) The IRM can be used by first-time or experienced instructors to enrich classroom experiences. Each chapter includes a brief chapter summary; a chapter outline; lecture enhancements that present cutting-edge topics along with suggestions for using the content in class; and learning activities that provide "live" examples of research findings, discussion topics, and written assignments. Also included are model answers to the text's Ask Yourself questions and listings of available DVDs and streaming videos on relevant topics.

TEST BANK The Test Bank contains over 1,200 multiple-choice and essay questions, each of which is page-referenced to chapter content and classified by type as remember, apply, or understand.

PEARSON MYTEST This secure online environment allows instructors to easily create exams, study guide questions, and quizzes from any computer with an Internet connection.

POWERPOINT PRESENTATION The PowerPoint presentation provides outlines and illustrations of key topics for each chapter of the text.

"EXPLORATIONS IN CHILD DEVELOPMENT" DVD AND GUIDE Designed for classroom use, this DVD is over six hours in length and contains more than 50 narrated segments that illustrate theories, concepts, and milestones of child development. The DVD and Guide are available only to instructors who are confirmed adopters of the text.

ABOUT THE COVER IMAGE

The cover photo depicts a Syrian refugee child participating in a collaborative art project conducted by the international nonprofit organization Artolution, Inc. With family members, the child fled war-torn Syria, crossing the border into Jordan. Like nearly 50 million other refugee children worldwide, he left behind his home, school, and neighborhood and the security of a familiar, organized daily life.

Artolution projects provide children and youths who have faced trauma and social exclusion—including refugees and young people living in areas of violent conflict or extreme poverty—with collaborative opportunities to create community-based public art. Guided by professional artists and art educators, project participants join with one another to represent their past experiences, hopes, and dreams in murals, sculptures, dance, theater, and music—an educational and therapeutic process that promotes trauma relief and healing.

To learn more about the work of Artolution, visit www.artolution.org.

▶ This child paints a tricycle axle, to be installed as part of a sculpture made of discarded materials and collaboratively built by children residing in the Za'atari refugee camp in northern Jordan. The project was facilitated by artist Max Frieder, co-director of Artolution, and local artists. Za'atari houses over 83,000 refugees who have fled the violence of the Syrian civil war.

Artolution's Za'atari project was organized by the following partnering organizations: the Norwegian Refugee Council and the International Rescue Committee.

CHAPTER 1

History, Theory, and Research Strategies

© ELLEN B. SENISI

Kindergarten drummers delight in collaboratively exploring the rhythmic and tonal possibilities of their instruments. Chapter 1 will introduce you to a multiplicity of ways to think about and study child development.

WHAT'S AHEAD IN CHAPTER 1

Not long ago, I traveled from my Midwestern home to visit the small city in northern California where I spent my childhood. One Saturday morning, I visited the neighborhood where I grew up—a place I had not seen since I was 12 years old.

I stood at the entrance to my old schoolyard. Buildings and grounds that had looked large to me as a child now seemed strangely smaller. I peered through the window of my first-grade classroom. A table of computers and iPads rested against the far wall, where I once sat. On the school's grassy field, where I had played pick-up games of kickball with my friends, a city soccer-league game was under way, with a crowd of parents watching from the sidelines. I walked my old route home from school, the distance shrunken by my longer stride. I paused in front of my best friend Kathryn's house, where we once drew sidewalk pictures and produced plays in the garage.

As I walked, I reflected on early experiences that had contributed to who I am today: weekends helping my father in his downtown clothing shop, the year my mother studied to become a high school teacher, moments of companionship and rivalry with my sister and brother, and visits to my grandmother's house, where I became someone extra special.

Passing the homes of my childhood friends, I thought of what I knew about their present lives. Kathryn, star student and president of our sixth-grade class—today a successful corporate lawyer and board member of a foundation devoted to research on treating childhood cancer. Shy, withdrawn Phil, cruelly teased because of his cleft lip—now owner of a thriving chain of hardware stores and member of the city council. Julio, immigrant from Mexico who joined our class in third grade—today, director of an elementary school bilingual education program and parent of an adopted Mexican son. And finally, my next-door neighbor Rick, who struggled with reading, picked fights at recess, became a teenage parent, dropped out of high school, and moved from one low-paid job to another throughout his adult years.

As you begin this course in child development, perhaps you, too, wonder about some of the same questions that crossed my mind during that nostalgic neighborhood walk:

- In what ways are children's home, school, and neighborhood experiences the same today as they were in past generations, and in what ways are they different?
- How are young children's perceptions of the world similar to adults', and how are they different?
- What determines the features that humans have in common and those that make each of us unique—physically, mentally, and behaviorally?
- Why do some of us, like Kathryn and Rick, retain the same styles of responding that characterized us as children, whereas others, like Phil, change in essential ways?
- How do cultural changes—employed mothers, child care, divorce, smaller families, and new technologies—affect children's attributes?

LUMI IMAGES / ALAMY STOCK PHOTO

These are central questions addressed by **child development,** a field of study devoted to understanding constancy and change from conception through adolescence. Child development is part of a larger, interdisciplinary field known as **developmental science,** which includes all changes we experience throughout the lifespan (Lerner et al., 2014; Overton & Molenaar, 2015). Great diversity characterizes the interests and concerns of investigators who study development. But all have a common goal: to identify those factors that influence consistencies and changes in young people during the first two decades of life.

The Field of Child Development

1.1 Describe the field of child development, along with factors that stimulated its expansion.

1.2 Explain how child development is typically divided into domains and periods.

The questions just listed are not just of scientific interest. Each has *applied,* or practical, importance as well. Research about development has also been stimulated by social pressures to improve children's lives. For example, the beginning of public education in the early twentieth century led to a demand for knowledge about what and how to teach children of different ages. Pediatricians' interest in improving children's health required an understanding of physical growth, nutrition, and disease. The social service profession's desire to treat children's emotional and behavior problems and to help them cope with challenging life circumstances, such as the birth of a sibling, parental divorce, poverty, bullying in school, or the death of a loved one, required information about personality and social development. And parents have continually sought expert advice about child-rearing practices and experiences that would promote their children's development and well-being.

Our large storehouse of information about child development is *interdisciplinary.* It has grown through the combined efforts of people from many fields of study. Because of the need for solutions to everyday problems concerning children, researchers from psychology, sociology, anthropology, biology, and neuroscience have joined forces in research with professionals from education, family studies, medicine, public health, and social service, to name just a few. Together, they have created the field as it exists today—a body of knowledge that is not only scientifically important but also relevant and useful.

© ELLEN B. SENISI

▶ Child development research has great practical value. Findings on how children learn best in school have contributed to new approaches to education that emphasize exploration, discovery, and collaboration.

Domains of Development

To make the vast, interdisciplinary study of constancy and change more orderly and convenient, development is often divided into three broad domains: *physical, cognitive,* and *emotional and social.* Refer to Figure 1.1 for a description and illustration of each. Within each period from infancy through adolescence, we will consider the three domains in the order just mentioned. Yet the domains are not really distinct. Rather, they combine in an integrated, holistic fashion to yield the living, growing child.

Furthermore, each domain influences and is influenced by the others. For example, in Chapter 4 you will see that new motor capacities, such as reaching, sitting, crawling, and walking (physical), contribute greatly to infants' understanding of their surroundings (cognitive). When babies think and act more competently, adults stimulate them more with games, language, and expressions of delight at their new achievements (emotional and social). These enriched experiences, in turn, promote all aspects of development.

You will encounter instances of the interwoven nature of all domains on nearly every page of this book. In the margins of the text, you will find occasional *Look and Listen* activities—opportunities for you to see everyday illustrations of holistic development by observing what real children say and do or by attending to everyday influences on children. Through these experiences, I hope to make your study of development more authentic and meaningful.

Physical Development
Changes in body size, proportions, appearance, functioning of body systems, perceptual and motor capacities, and physical health

Cognitive Development
Changes in intellectual abilities, including attention, memory, academic and everyday knowledge, problem solving, imagination, creativity, and language

Emotional and Social Development
Changes in emotional communication, self-understanding, knowledge about other people, interpersonal skills, friendships, intimate relationships, and moral reasoning and behavior

FIGURE 1.1 Major domains of development. The three domains are not really distinct. Rather, they overlap and interact.

TABLE 1.1
Major Periods of Child Development

PERIOD	APPROXIMATE AGE RANGE	BRIEF DESCRIPTION
Prenatal	Conception to birth	The one-celled organism transforms into a human baby with remarkable capacities to adjust to life in the surrounding world.
Infancy and toddlerhood	Birth–2 years	Dramatic changes in the body and brain support the emergence of a wide array of motor, perceptual, and intellectual capacities; the beginnings of language; and first intimate ties to others. Infancy spans the first year; toddlerhood spans the second, during which children take their first independent steps, marking a shift to greater autonomy.
Early childhood	2–6 years	During the "play years," motor skills are refined, thought and language expand, make-believe play blossoms, and children become more self-controlled and self-sufficient. A sense of morality is evident, and children establish ties with peers.
Middle childhood	6–11 years	The school years are marked by improved athletic abilities; more logical thought processes; increased responsibilities; mastery of fundamental reading, writing, math, and other academic knowledge and skills; advances in self-understanding, morality, and friendship; and the beginnings of peer-group membership.
Adolescence	11–18 years	Puberty leads to an adult-sized body and sexual maturity. Thought becomes increasingly complex, abstract, and idealistic, and schooling is directed toward preparation for higher education and the world of work. Adolescents begin to establish autonomy from the family and to define personal values and goals.

Periods of Development

Besides distinguishing and integrating the three domains, another dilemma arises in discussing development: how to divide the flow of time into sensible, manageable parts. Researchers usually use the age periods described in Table 1.1, according to which I have organized this book. Each brings new capacities and social expectations that serve as important transitions in major theories.

With this introduction in mind, let's turn to basic issues that have captivated, puzzled, and sparked debate among child development theorists. Then our discussion will trace the emergence of the field and survey major theories. We will return to each contemporary theory in greater detail in later chapters.

Basic Issues

1.3 Identify three basic issues on which theories of child development take a stand.

Research on child development did not begin until the late nineteenth and early twentieth centuries. But ideas about how children grow and change have a much longer history. As these speculations combined with research, they inspired the construction of *theories* of development. A **theory** is an orderly, integrated set of statements that describes, explains, and predicts behavior. For example, a good theory of infant–caregiver attachment would (1) *describe* the behaviors of babies in the second half of the first year as they seek the affection and comfort of a familiar adult, (2) *explain* how and why infants develop this strong desire to bond with a caregiver, and (3) *predict* the consequences of this emotional bond for future relationships.

Theories are vital tools for two reasons. First, they provide organizing frameworks for our observations of children, *guiding and giving meaning* to what we see. Second, theories that are verified by research provide a sound basis for practical action. Once a theory helps us *understand* development, we are in a much better position *to know how to improve* the welfare and treatment of children.

As we will see, theories are influenced by the cultural values and belief systems of their times. But theories differ from mere opinion or belief: A theory's continued existence depends on *scientific verification.* Every theory must be tested using a fair set of research procedures agreed on by the scientific community, and its findings must endure, or be replicated over time.

Within the field of child development, many theories offer very different ideas about what children are like and how they change. The study of development provides no ultimate truth because investigators do not always agree on the meaning of what they see. Also, children are complex beings; they change physically, cognitively, emotionally, and socially. No single theory has explained all these aspects. But the existence of many theories helps advance knowledge as researchers try to support, contradict, and integrate these different points of view.

Although there are many theories, we can easily organize them by looking at the stand they take on three basic issues: (1) Is the course of development continuous or discontinuous? (2) Does one course of development characterize all children, or are there many possible courses? (3) What are the roles of genetic and environmental factors—nature and nurture—in development?

Continuous or Discontinuous Development?

A mother reported with amazement that her 20-month-old son Angelo had pushed a toy car across the floor while making a motorlike sound, "Brmmmm, brmmmm," for the first time. When he hit a nearby wall with a bang, Angelo exclaimed, "C'ash!"

"How come Angelo can pretend, but he couldn't a few months ago?" his mother asked. "And I wonder what 'Brmmmm, brmmmm' and 'Crash' mean to Angelo. Does he understand motor-like sounds and collision the same way I do?"

Angelo's mother has raised a puzzling issue about development: How can we best describe the differences in capacities among infants, children, adolescents, and adults? As Figure 1.2 illustrates, major theories recognize two possibilities.

One view holds that infants and preschoolers respond to the world in much the same way as adults do. The difference between the immature and mature being is simply one of *amount or complexity*. For example, little Angelo's thinking may be just as logical and well-organized as our own. Perhaps (as his mother reports) he can sort objects into simple categories, recognize whether he has more of one kind than another, and remember where he left his favorite toy at child care the week before. Angelo's only limitation may be that he cannot perform these skills with as much information and precision as adults can. If this is so, then changes in Angelo's thinking must be **continuous**—a process of gradually augmenting the same types of skills that were there to begin with.

According to a second view, infants and children have *unique ways of thinking, feeling, and behaving,* ones quite different from those of adults. If so, then development is **discontinuous**—a process in which new ways of understanding and responding to the world emerge at specific times. From this perspective, Angelo is not yet able to organize objects or remember and interpret experiences as we do. Instead, he will move through a series of developmental steps, each with distinct features, until he reaches the highest level of functioning.

Theories that accept the discontinuous perspective regard development as taking place in **stages**—*qualitative* changes in thinking, feeling, and behaving that characterize specific periods of development. In stage theories, development is like climbing a staircase, with each step corresponding to a more mature, reorganized way of functioning. The stage concept also assumes that people undergo periods of rapid transformation as they step up from one stage to the next. In other words, change is fairly sudden rather than gradual and ongoing.

Does development actually occur in a neat, orderly sequence of stages? This ambitious assumption has faced significant challenges. Later in this chapter, we will review some influential stage theories.

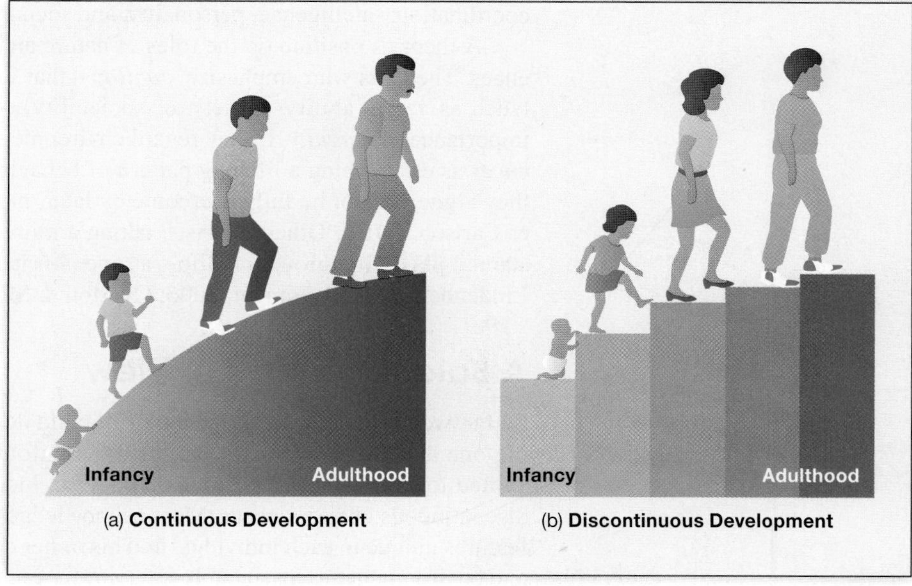

FIGURE 1.2 Is development continuous or discontinuous? (a) Some theorists believe that development is a smooth, continuous process. Children gradually add more of the same types of skills. (b) Other theorists think that development takes place in discontinuous stages. Children change rapidly as they step up to a new level and then change very little for a while. With each step, the child interprets and responds to the world in a reorganized, qualitatively different way. As we will see later, still other theorists believe that development is characterized by both continuous and discontinuous change.

Resilience

John and his best friend, Gary, grew up in a rundown, crime-ridden, inner-city neighborhood. By age 10, each had experienced years of family conflict followed by parental divorce. Reared from then on in mother-headed households, John and Gary rarely saw their fathers. Both dropped out of high school and were in and out of trouble with the police.

Then their paths diverged. By age 30, John had fathered two children with women he never married, had spent time in prison, was unemployed, and drank alcohol heavily. In contrast, Gary had returned to finish high school, had studied auto mechanics at a community college, and had become manager of a gas station and repair shop. Married with two children, he had saved his earnings and bought a home. He was happy, healthy, and well-adapted to life.

A wealth of evidence shows that environmental risks—poverty, negative family interactions, and parental divorce, job loss, mental illness, and drug abuse—predispose children to future problems (Masten, 2013). Why did Gary "beat the odds" and bounce back from adversity?

Research on **resilience**—the ability to adapt effectively in the face of threats to development—is receiving increased attention as investigators look for ways to protect young people from the damaging effects of stressful life conditions. This interest has been inspired by several long-term studies on the relationship of life stressors in childhood to competence and adjustment in adolescence and adulthood (Werner, 2013). In each study, some individuals were shielded from negative outcomes, whereas others had lasting problems. Four broad factors seemed to offer protection from the damaging effects of stressful life events.

Personal Characteristics

A child's genetically influenced characteristics can reduce exposure to risk or lead to experiences that compensate for early stressful events. High intelligence and socially valued talents (in music or athletics, for example) increase the chances that a child will have rewarding experiences in school and in the community that offset the impact of a stressful home life. Temperament is particularly powerful. Children who have easygoing, sociable dispositions and who can readily inhibit negative emotions and impulses tend to have an optimistic outlook on life and a special capacity to adapt to change—qualities that elicit positive responses from others. In contrast, emotionally reactive and irritable children often tax the patience of people around them (Wang & Deater-Deckard, 2013). For example, both John and Gary moved several times during their childhoods. Each time, John became anxious and angry, whereas Gary looked forward to making new friends.

▶ This teenager's close, affectionate relationship with his grandfather helps foster resilience. A strong bond with a competent, caring adult can shield children from the damaging effects of stressful life conditions.

A Warm Parental Relationship

A close relationship with at least one parent who provides warmth, appropriately high expectations, monitoring of the child's activities, and an organized home environment fosters resilience (Shonkoff & Garner, 2012; Taylor, 2010). But this factor (as well as the next one) is not independent of children's personal characteristics. Children who are self-controlled, socially responsive, and able to deal with change are easier to rear and more likely to enjoy positive relationships with parents and other people. At the same time, children develop more attractive dispositions as a result of parental warmth and attention (Luthar, Crossman, & Small, 2015).

Social Support Outside the Immediate Family

The most consistent asset of resilient children is a strong bond with a competent, caring adult. For children who do not have a close bond with either parent, a grandparent, aunt, uncle, or teacher who forms a special relationship with the child can promote resilience (Masten, 2013). Gary received support in adolescence from his grandfather, who listened to Gary's concerns and helped him solve problems.

Associations with rule-abiding peers who value academic achievement are also linked to resilience (Furman & Rose, 2015). Children who have positive relationships with adults are far more likely to establish these supportive peer ties.

Community Resources and Opportunities

Community supports—supervision offered by neighborhood adults, high-quality child-care centers and public schools, convenient and affordable health care and social services, libraries, and recreation centers—foster both parents' and children's well-being. In addition, engaging in extracurricular activities at school and in religious youth groups, scouting, and other organizations teaches important social skills, such as cooperation, leadership, and contributing to others' welfare. As participants acquire these competencies, they gain in self-reliance, self-esteem, and community commitment—attributes that help them overcome adversity (Leventhal, Dupéré, & Shuey, 2015). As a college student, Gary volunteered for Habitat for Humanity, joining a team building affordable housing in low-income neighborhoods. Community involvement offered Gary opportunities to form meaningful relationships, which further strengthened his resilience.

Research on resilience highlights the complex connections between heredity and environment. Armed with positive characteristics, which stem from native endowment, favorable rearing experiences, or both, children and adolescents can act to reduce stressful situations.

But when many risks pile up, they are increasingly difficult to overcome (Obradović et al., 2009). To fortify children against the negative effects of risk, interventions must not only reduce risks but also enhance children's protective relationships at home, in school, and in the community.

factors contributing to developmental change and the challenges of isolating the effects of each, more researchers are envisioning it from a *developmental systems perspective*—as a perpetually ongoing process that is molded by a complex network of genetic/biological, psychological, and social influences (Lerner, 2015). Our review of child development theories will conclude with current, influential systems theories.

ASK YOURSELF

CONNECT Provide an example of how one domain of development (physical, cognitive, or emotional/social) can affect development in another domain.

APPLY Anna, a high school counselor, devised a program that integrates classroom learning with vocational training to help adolescents at risk for school dropout stay in school and transition to work life. What is Anna's position on *stability versus plasticity* in development? Explain.

REFLECT Describe an aspect of your development that differs from a parent's or a grandparent's when he or she was your age. How might differing *contexts* be responsible?

Scientific Beginnings

1.4 Describe major early influences on the scientific study of child development.

Scientific study of child development evolved quickly in the late nineteenth and early twentieth centuries. Early observations of children were soon followed by improved methods and theories, contributing to the firm foundation on which the field rests today.

Darwin: Forefather of Scientific Child Study

British naturalist Charles Darwin (1809–1882) observed the infinite variation among plant and animal species. He also saw that within a species, no two individuals are exactly alike. From these observations, he constructed his famous *theory of evolution.*

The theory emphasized two related principles: *natural selection* and *survival of the fittest.* Darwin (1859/1936) explained that certain species survive in particular environments because they have characteristics that fit with, or are adapted to, their surroundings. Other species die off because they are less well-suited to their environments. Individuals within a species who best meet the environment's survival requirements live long enough to reproduce and pass their more beneficial characteristics to future generations. Darwin's emphasis on the adaptive value of physical characteristics and behavior found its way into important developmental theories.

During his explorations, Darwin discovered that early prenatal growth is strikingly similar in many species. Other scientists concluded from Darwin's observations that the development of the human child follows the same general plan as the evolution of the human species. Although this belief eventually proved inaccurate, efforts to chart parallels between child growth and human evolution prompted researchers to make careful observations of all aspects of children's behavior. As a result, scientific child study was born.

The Normative Period

G. Stanley Hall (1844–1924), one of the most influential American psychologists of the early twentieth century, is regarded as the founder of the child study movement (Cairns & Cairns, 2006). Inspired by Darwin's work, Hall and his student Arnold Gesell (1880–1961) devised theories based on evolutionary ideas. They regarded development as a *maturational process*—a genetically determined series of events that unfold automatically (Gesell, 1933; Hall, 1904).

Hall and Gesell are remembered less for their one-sided theories than for their intensive efforts to describe all aspects of child development. They launched the **normative approach,** in which measures of behavior are taken on large numbers of individuals, and age-related averages are computed to represent typical development. Using this procedure, Hall constructed elaborate questionnaires asking children of different ages almost everything they could tell about themselves—interests, fears, imaginary playmates, dreams, friendships, everyday knowledge, and more. Through careful observations and parent interviews, Gesell collected detailed normative information on the motor achievements, social behaviors, and personality characteristics of infants and children.

Gesell was also among the first to make knowledge about child development meaningful to parents by informing them of what to expect at each age. Along with Benjamin Spock's *Baby and Child Care,* Gesell's books became central to a rapidly expanding child development literature for parents.

The Mental Testing Movement

While Hall and Gesell were developing their theories and methods in the United States, French psychologist Alfred Binet (1857–1911) was also taking a normative approach, but for a different reason. In the early 1900s, Binet and his colleague Theodore Simon were asked by Paris school officials to find a way to identify children with learning problems for placement in special classes. To address these practical educational concerns, Binet and Simon constructed the first successful intelligence test.

In 1916, at Stanford University, Binet's test was adapted for use with English-speaking children. Since then, the English version has been known as the *Stanford-Binet Intelligence Scale.* Besides providing a score that successfully predicted school achievement, the Binet test sparked tremendous interest in individual differences in development. Comparisons of the scores of people who vary in gender, ethnicity, birth order, family background, and other characteristics became a major focus of research. And intelligence tests moved quickly to the forefront of the nature–nurture controversy.

Mid-Twentieth-Century Theories

1.5 Describe theories that influenced child development research in the mid-twentieth century.

In the mid-twentieth century, the study of child development expanded into a legitimate discipline. A variety of theories emerged, each of which still has followers today. In these theories, the European concern with the individual's inner thoughts and feelings contrasts sharply with the North American academic focus on scientific precision and concrete, observable behavior.

The Psychoanalytic Perspective

By the 1930s and 1940s, parents increasingly sought help from professionals to deal with emotional difficulties. The earlier normative movement had answered the question, What are children like? Now a new question had to be addressed: How and why do children become the way they are? To treat psychological problems, psychiatrists and social workers turned to an approach to personality development that emphasized each child's unique history.

According to the **psychoanalytic perspective,** children move through a series of stages in which they confront conflicts between biological drives and social expectations. How these conflicts are resolved determines the person's ability to learn, get along with others, and cope with anxiety. Among the many contributors to the psychoanalytic perspective, two were especially influential: Sigmund Freud, founder of the psychoanalytic movement, and Erik Erikson.

Freud's Theory. Freud (1856–1939), a Viennese physician, sought a cure for emotionally troubled adults by having them talk freely about painful events of their childhoods. Working with these recollections, he examined his patients' unconscious motivations and constructed his **psychosexual theory,** which emphasizes that how parents manage their child's sexual and aggressive drives in the first few years is crucial for healthy personality development.

In Freud's theory, three parts of the personality—id, ego, and superego—become integrated during five stages, summarized in Table 1.2 on page 10. The *id,* the largest portion of the mind, is the source of basic biological needs and desires. The *ego,* the conscious, rational part of personality, emerges in early infancy to redirect the id's impulses into acceptable behaviors. Between 3 and 6 years of age, the *superego,* or conscience, develops as parents insist that children conform to the values of society. Now the ego faces the increasingly complex task of reconciling the demands

TABLE 1.2
Freud's Psychosexual Stages and Erikson's Psychosocial Stages Compared

APPROXIMATE AGE	FREUD'S PSYCHOSEXUAL STAGE	ERIKSON'S PSYCHOSOCIAL STAGE
Birth–1 year	***Oral:*** If oral needs are not met through sucking from breast or bottle, the individual may develop such habits as thumb sucking, fingernail biting, overeating, or smoking.	***Basic trust versus mistrust:*** From warm, responsive care, infants gain a sense of trust, or confidence, that the world is good. Mistrust occurs if infants are neglected or handled harshly.
1–3 years	***Anal:*** Toddlers and preschoolers enjoy holding and releasing urine and feces. If parents toilet train before children are ready or make too few demands, conflicts about anal control may appear in the form of extreme orderliness or disorder.	***Autonomy versus shame and doubt:*** Using new mental and motor skills, children want to decide for themselves. Parents can foster autonomy by permitting reasonable free choice and not forcing or shaming the child.
3–6 years	***Phallic:*** As preschoolers take pleasure in genital stimulation, Freud's Oedipus conflict for boys and Electra conflict for girls arise: Children feel a sexual desire for the other-sex parent. To avoid punishment, they give up this desire and adopt the same-sex parent's characteristics and values. As a result, the superego is formed, and children feel guilty when they violate its standards.	***Initiative versus guilt:*** Through make-believe play, children gain insight into the person they can become. Initiative—a sense of ambition and responsibility—develops when parents support their child's sense of purpose. If parents demand too much self-control, children experience excessive guilt.
6–11 years	***Latency:*** Sexual instincts die down, and the superego strengthens as children acquire new social values from adults and same-sex peers.	**Industry versus inferiority:** At school, children learn to work and cooperate with others. Inferiority develops when negative experiences at home, at school, or with peers lead to feelings of incompetence.
Adolescence	***Genital:*** With puberty, sexual impulses reappear. Successful development during earlier stages leads to marriage, mature sexuality, and child rearing.	***Identity versus role confusion:*** By exploring values and vocational goals, young people form a personal identity. The negative outcome is confusion about future adult roles.
Early adulthood		***Intimacy versus isolation:*** Young adults establish intimate relationships. Because of earlier disappointments, some individuals cannot form close bonds and remain isolated.
Middle adulthood		***Generativity versus stagnation:*** Generativity means giving to the next generation through child rearing, caring for others, or productive work. The person who fails in these ways feels an absence of meaningful accomplishment.
Old age		***Integrity versus despair:*** Integrity results from feeling that life was worth living as it happened. Older people who are dissatisfied with their lives fear death.

▶ Erik Erikson

of the id, the external world, and conscience—for example, the id impulse to grab an attractive toy from a playmate versus the superego's warning that such behavior is wrong. According to Freud, the relations established among id, ego, and superego during the preschool years determine the individual's basic personality.

Freud (1938/1973) believed that during childhood, sexual impulses shift their focus from the oral to the anal to the genital regions of the body. In each stage, parents walk a fine line between permitting too much or too little gratification of their child's basic needs. If parents strike an appropriate balance, children grow into well-adjusted adults with the capacity for mature sexual behavior and investment in family life.

Freud's theory was the first to stress the influence of the early parent–child relationship on development. But his perspective was eventually criticized. First, it overemphasized the influence of sexual feelings in development. Second, because it was based on the problems of sexually repressed, well-to-do adults in nineteenth-century Victorian society, it did not apply in other cultures. Finally, Freud had not studied children directly.

Erikson's Theory. Several of Freud's followers improved on his vision. The most important was Erik Erikson (1902–1994), who expanded the picture of development at each stage. In his **psychosocial theory,** Erikson emphasized that in addition to mediating between id impulses and superego demands, the ego makes a positive contribution to development, acquiring attitudes and skills that make the individual an active, contributing member of society. A basic psychosocial conflict, which is resolved along a continuum from positive to negative, determines healthy or maladaptive outcomes at each stage. As Table 1.2 shows, Erikson's first five stages parallel Freud's stages, but Erikson added three adult stages.

Erikson pointed out that normal development must be understood in relation to each culture's life situation. For example, in the 1940s, he observed that Yurok Indians of the U.S. northwest coast deprived newborns of breastfeeding for the first 10 days, instead feeding them a thin soup. At age 6 months, infants were abruptly weaned, a practice that, from our cultural vantage point, might seem cruel. But Erikson explained that the Yurok lived in a world in which salmon filled the river just once a year, a circumstance requiring considerable self-restraint for survival. In this way, he showed that child rearing is responsive to the competencies valued and needed by an individual's society.

ANTONIA TOZER/GETTY IMAGES/AWL IMAGES RM

▶ A child of the Kazakh people of Mongolia learns from her grandfather how to train an eagle to hunt small animals, essential for the meat-based Kazakh diet. As Erikson recognized, this parenting practice is best understood in relation to the competencies valued and needed in Kazakh culture.

Contributions and Limitations of the Psychoanalytic Perspective. A special strength of the psychoanalytic perspective is its emphasis on understanding the individual's unique life history. Consistent with this view, psychoanalytic theorists accept the *clinical,* or *case study, method,* which synthesizes information from a variety of sources into a detailed picture of the personality of a single child. (We will discuss this method at the end of this chapter.) The psychoanalytic approach has also inspired a wealth of research on many aspects of emotional and social development, including infant–caregiver attachment, aggression, sibling relationships, child-rearing practices, morality, gender roles, and adolescent identity.

Despite its contributions, the psychoanalytic perspective is no longer in the mainstream of child development research. Psychoanalytic theorists were so strongly committed to in-depth study of individuals that they failed to consider other methods. In addition, many psychoanalytic ideas, such as psychosexual stages and ego functioning, are too vague to be tested empirically (Crain, 2010). Nevertheless, Erikson's broad outline of psychosocial change captures key, optimal personality attainments during each major period. We will return to it in later chapters.

Behaviorism and Social Learning Theory

As the psychoanalytic perspective gained in prominence, the study of development was also influenced by a very different perspective. According to **behaviorism,** directly observable events—stimuli and responses—are the appropriate focus of study. North American behaviorism began in the early twentieth century with the work of John Watson (1878–1958), who wanted to create an objective science of psychology.

Traditional Behaviorism. Watson was inspired by Russian physiologist Ivan Pavlov's studies of animal learning. Pavlov knew that dogs release saliva as an innate reflex when they are given food. But he noticed that his dogs were salivating before they tasted any food—when they saw the trainer who usually fed them. The dogs, Pavlov reasoned, must have learned to associate a neutral stimulus (the trainer) with another stimulus (food) that produces a reflexive response (salivation). Because of this association, the neutral stimulus alone could bring about a response resembling the reflex. Eager to test this idea, Pavlov successfully taught dogs to salivate at the sound of a bell by pairing it with the presentation of food. He had discovered *classical conditioning.*

In a historic experiment that applied classical conditioning to children's behavior, Watson taught Albert, an 11-month-old infant, to fear a neutral stimulus—a soft white rat—by presenting it several times with a sharp, loud sound, which naturally scared the baby. Little Albert, who at first had reached out eagerly to touch the furry rat, began to cry and retreat at the sight of it (Watson & Raynor, 1920). In fact, Albert's fear was so intense that researchers eventually challenged the ethics of studies like this one. Watson concluded that environment is the supreme force in development and that adults can mold children's behavior by carefully controlling stimulus–response associations. He viewed development as continuous—a gradual increase with age in the number and strength of these associations.

Another form of behaviorism is B. F. Skinner's (1904–1990) *operant conditioning theory.* Skinner showed that the frequency of a behavior can be increased by following it with a wide variety of *reinforcers,* such as food, praise, or a friendly smile, or decreased through *punishment,* such as disapproval or withdrawal of privileges. As a result of Skinner's work, operant conditioning became a broadly applied learning principle. We will consider these basic learning capacities further in Chapter 4.

Social Learning Theory. Psychologists wondered whether behaviorism might offer a more direct and effective explanation of the development of social behavior than the less precise concepts of psychoanalytic theory. This sparked approaches that built on the principles of conditioning, providing expanded views of how children acquire new responses.

Several kinds of **social learning theory** emerged. The most influential, devised by Albert Bandura (1925–), emphasizes *modeling,* also known as *imitation* or *observational learning,* as a powerful source of development. The baby who claps her hands after her mother does so, the child who angrily hits a playmate in the same way that he has been punished at home, and the teenager who wears the same clothes and hairstyle as her friends at school are all displaying observational learning. In his early work, Bandura found that diverse factors affect children's motivation to imitate: their own history of reinforcement or punishment for the behavior, the promise of future reinforcement or punishment, and even observations of the model being reinforced or punished.

▶ Social learning theory recognizes that children acquire many skills through modeling. By observing and imitating his father's behavior, this child learns an important skill.

Bandura's work continues to influence much research on social development. But today, his theory stresses the importance of *cognition,* or thinking. In fact, the most recent revision of Bandura's (1992, 2001, 2011) theory places such strong emphasis on how we think about ourselves and other people that he calls it a *social-cognitive* rather than a social learning approach.

In Bandura's revised view, children gradually become more selective in what they imitate. From watching others engage in self-praise and self-blame and through feedback about the worth of their own actions, children develop *personal standards* for behavior and *a sense of self-efficacy*—the belief that their own abilities and characteristics will help them succeed. These cognitions guide responses in particular situations (Bandura, 2011, 2016). For example, imagine a parent who often remarks, "I'm glad I kept working on that task, even though it was hard," and who encourages persistence by saying, "I know you can do a good job on that homework!" Soon the child starts to view herself as hardworking and high-achieving and selects people with these characteristics as models. In this way, as individuals acquire attitudes, values, and convictions about themselves, they control their own learning and behavior.

Contributions and Limitations of Behaviorism and Social Learning Theory. Behaviorism and social learning theory have been helpful in treating adjustment problems. **Applied behavior analysis** consists of careful observations of individual behavior and related environmental events, followed by systematic changes in those events based on procedures of conditioning and modeling. The goal is to eliminate undesirable behaviors and increase desirable responses. It has been used to relieve a wide range of difficulties in children and adults, ranging from poor time management and unwanted habits to serious problems, such as language delays, persistent aggression, and extreme fears (Heron, Hewar, & Cooper, 2013).

Nevertheless, behaviorism and social learning theory offer too narrow a view of important environmental influences, which extend beyond immediate reinforcement, punishment, and modeled behaviors to people's rich physical and social worlds. Behaviorism and social learning theory

One Course of Development or Many?

Stage theorists assume that people everywhere follow the same sequence of development. Yet the field of child development is becoming increasingly aware that children and adults live in distinct **contexts**—unique combinations of personal and environmental circumstances that can result in different paths of change. For example, a shy individual who fears social encounters develops in very different contexts from those of an outgoing agemate who readily seeks out other people. Children and adults in non-Western village societies have experiences in their families and communities that differ sharply from those of people in large Western cities (Kagan, 2013a; Mistry & Dutta, 2015). These different circumstances foster different cognitive capacities, social skills, and feelings about the self and others.

As you will see, contemporary theorists regard the contexts that shape development as many-layered and complex. On the personal side, these include heredity and biological makeup. On the environmental side, they include home, school, and neighborhood as well as circumstances more remote from people's everyday lives: community resources, societal values, and historical time period. Furthermore, new evidence is increasingly emphasizing *mutually influential relations* between individuals and their contexts: People not only are affected by but also contribute to the contexts in which they develop (Elder, Shanahan, & Jennings, 2015). Finally, researchers today are more conscious than ever before of cultural diversity in development.

Relative Influence of Nature and Nurture?

In addition to describing the course of child development, each theory takes a stand on a major question about its underlying causes: Are genetic or environmental factors more important? This is the age-old **nature–nurture controversy.** By *nature,* we mean the hereditary information we receive from our parents at the moment of conception. By *nurture,* we mean the complex forces of the physical and social world that influence our biological makeup and psychological experiences before and after birth.

Although all theories grant roles to both nature and nurture, they vary in emphasis. Consider the following questions: Is the older child's ability to think in more complex ways largely the result of a built-in timetable of growth, or is it primarily influenced by stimulation from parents and teachers? What accounts for the vast individual differences among children—in height, weight, physical coordination, intelligence, personality, and social skills? Is nature or nurture more responsible?

A theory's position on the roles of nature and nurture affects how it explains individual differences. Theorists who emphasize *stability*—that individuals who are high or low in a characteristic (such as verbal ability, anxiety, or sociability) will remain so at later ages—typically stress the importance of *heredity.* If they regard environment as important, they usually point to *early experiences* as establishing a lifelong pattern of behavior. Powerful negative events in the first few years, they argue, cannot be fully overcome by later, more positive ones (Bowlby, 1980; Sroufe, Coffino, & Carlson, 2010). Other theorists, taking a more optimistic view, see development as having substantial **plasticity** throughout life—as open to change in response to influential experiences (Baltes, Lindenberger, & Staudinger, 2006; Overton & Molenaar, 2015).

A Balanced Point of View

So far, we have discussed basic issues of child development in terms of extremes—solutions favoring one side or the other. As we trace the unfolding of the field, you will see that theorists have shifted toward balanced positions. Today, an increasing number believe that both continuous and discontinuous changes occur. Most acknowledge that development has both universal features and features unique to each individual and his or her contexts. And the current consensus is that heredity and environment are inseparably interwoven, each affecting the potential of the other to modify the child's traits and capacities (Lerner et al., 2014; Overton & Molenaar, 2015). We will discuss these new ideas about nature and nurture in Chapter 2.

Finally, as you will see later in this book, the relative impact of early and later experiences varies greatly from one domain of development to another and even—as the Biology and Environment box on the following page indicates—across individuals! Because of the complex network of have also been criticized for underestimating people's contributions to their own development. Bandura, in emphasizing cognition, is unique among theorists whose work grew out of the behaviorist tradition in granting children and adults an active role in their own learning.

Piaget's Cognitive-Developmental Theory

If one individual has influenced research on child development more than any other, it is Swiss cognitive theorist Jean Piaget (1896–1980). North American investigators did not grant Piaget's work much attention until the 1960s, mainly because his ideas were at odds with behaviorism (Watrin & Darwich, 2012). Piaget did not believe that children's learning depends on reinforcers, such as rewards from adults. According to his **cognitive-developmental theory,** children actively construct knowledge as they manipulate and explore their world.

Piaget's Stages. Piaget's view of development was greatly influenced by his early training in biology. Central to his theory is the biological concept of *adaptation* (Piaget, 1971). Just as structures of the body are adapted to fit with the environment, so structures of the mind develop to better fit with, or represent, the external world. In infancy and early childhood, Piaget claimed, children's understanding is different from adults'. For example, he believed that young babies do not realize that an object hidden from view continues to exist. He also concluded that preschoolers' thinking is full of faulty logic. For example, preschoolers commonly say that the amount of a liquid changes when it is poured into a different-shaped container. According to Piaget, children eventually revise these incorrect ideas in their ongoing efforts to achieve an *equilibrium,* or balance, between their cognitive structures and information they encounter in their everyday worlds.

▶ In Piaget's sensorimotor stage, babies learn by acting on the world. As this 1-year-old bangs a wooden spoon on a coffee can, he discovers that his movements have predictable effects on objects, and that objects influence one another in regular ways.

In Piaget's theory, as the brain develops and children's experiences expand, they move through four broad stages, each characterized by qualitatively distinct ways of thinking. Table 1.3 provides a brief description of Piaget's stages. Cognitive development begins in the *sensorimotor stage* with the baby's use of the senses and movements to explore the world. These action patterns evolve into the symbolic but illogical thinking of the preschooler in the *preoperational stage.* Then

TABLE 1.3
Piaget's Stages of Cognitive Development

STAGE	PERIOD OF DEVELOPMENT	DESCRIPTION
Sensorimotor	Birth–2 years	Infants "think" by acting on the world with their eyes, ears, hands, and mouth. As a result, they invent ways of solving sensorimotor problems, such as pulling a lever to hear the sound of a music box, finding hidden toys, and putting objects into and taking them out of containers.
Preoperational	2–7 years	Preschool children use symbols to represent their earlier sensorimotor discoveries. Development of language and make-believe play takes place. However, thinking lacks the logic of the two remaining stages.
Concrete operational	7–11 years	Children's reasoning becomes logical and better organized. School-age children understand that a certain amount of lemonade or play dough remains the same even after its appearance changes. They also organize objects into hierarchies of classes and subclasses. However, children think in a logical, organized fashion only when dealing with concrete information they can perceive directly.
Formal operational	11 years on	The capacity for abstract, systematic thinking enables adolescents, when faced with a problem, to start with a hypothesis, deduce testable inferences, and isolate and combine variables to see which inferences are confirmed. Adolescents can also evaluate the logic of verbal statements without referring to real-world circumstances.

▶ Jean Piaget

© ELLEN B. SENISI

In Piaget's preoperational stage, preschoolers represent their earlier sensorimotor discoveries with symbols, and language and make-believe play develop rapidly. These 4-year-olds use a variety of props to create an imaginary birthday party.

© UPPERCUT IMAGES/ALAMY

In Piaget's concrete operational stage, school-age children think in an organized, logical fashion about concrete objects. This 7-year-old understands that the amount of pie dough remains the same after he changes its shape from a ball to a flattened circle.

© JIM WEST/THE IMAGE WORKS

In Piaget's formal operational stage, adolescents think systematically and abstractly. These high school students participating in a robotics competition solve problems by generating hypotheses about procedures that might work and conducting systematic tests to observe their real-world consequences.

cognition is transformed into the more organized, logical reasoning of the school-age child in the *concrete operational stage.* Finally, in the *formal operational stage,* thought becomes the abstract, systematic reasoning system of the adolescent and adult.

Piaget devised special methods for investigating how children think. Early in his career, he carefully observed his three infant children and presented them with everyday problems, such as an attractive object that could be grasped, mouthed, kicked, or searched for. From their responses, Piaget derived his ideas about cognitive changes during the first two years. To study childhood and adolescent thought, Piaget adapted the clinical method of psychoanalysis, conducting open-ended *clinical interviews* in which a child's initial response to a task served as the basis for Piaget's next question.

Contributions and Limitations of Piaget's Theory. Piaget convinced the field that children are active learners whose minds consist of rich structures of knowledge. Besides investigating children's understanding of the physical world, Piaget explored their reasoning about the social world. His stages have sparked a wealth of research on children's conceptions of themselves, other people, and social relationships. In practical terms, Piaget's theory encouraged the development of educational philosophies and programs that emphasize discovery learning and direct contact with the environment.

Despite Piaget's overwhelming contributions, his theory has been challenged. Research indicates that Piaget underestimated the competencies of infants and preschoolers. When young children are given tasks scaled down in difficulty and relevant to their everyday experiences, their understanding appears closer to that of the older child and adult than Piaget assumed.

Furthermore, children's performance on Piagetian problems can be improved with training—findings that call into question Piaget's assumption that discovery learning rather than adult teaching is the best way to foster development (Klahr, Matlen, & Jirout, 2013). Critics also point out that Piaget's stagewise account pays insufficient attention to social and cultural influences on development and the resulting wide variation in thinking among children and adolescents of the same age.

ASK YOURSELF

CONNECT What aspect of behaviorism made it attractive to critics of psychoanalytic theory? How did Piaget's theory respond to a major limitation of behaviorism?

APPLY A 4-year-old becomes frightened of the dark and refuses to go to sleep at night. How would a psychoanalyst and a behaviorist differ in their views of how this problem developed?

REFLECT Illustrate Bandura's ideas by describing a personal experience in which you observed and received feedback from another person that strengthened your sense of self-efficacy.

Recent Theoretical Perspectives

New ways of understanding the developing child are constantly emerging—questioning, building on, and enhancing the discoveries of earlier theories. Today, a wealth of fresh approaches and research emphases is broadening our understanding of children's development.

1.6 Describe recent theoretical perspectives on child development.

Information Processing

In the 1970s and 1980s, researchers turned to the field of cognitive psychology for ways to understand the development of thinking. The design of digital computers that use mathematically specified steps to solve problems suggested to psychologists that the human mind might also be viewed as a symbol-manipulating system through which information flows—a perspective called **information processing.** From the time information is presented to the senses at *input* until it emerges as a behavioral response at *output,* information is actively coded, transformed, and organized.

Information-processing researchers often design flowcharts to map the precise steps individuals use to solve problems and complete tasks, much like the plans devised by programmers to get computers to perform a series of "mental operations." They seek to clarify how both task characteristics and cognitive limitations—for example, memory capacity or available knowledge—influence performance (Birney & Sternberg, 2011). To see the usefulness of this approach, let's look at an example.

In a study of problem solving, a researcher gave school-age children a pile of blocks varying in size, shape, and weight and asked them to build a bridge across a "river" that was too wide for any single block to span (Thornton, 1999). Whereas older children easily built successful bridges, only one 5-year-old did. Careful tracking of her efforts revealed that she repeatedly tried unsuccessful strategies, such as pushing two planks together and pressing down on their ends to hold them in place. But eventually, her experimentation triggered the idea of using the blocks as counterweights, as shown in Figure 1.3 on page 16. Her mistaken procedures helped her understand why the counterweight approach worked.

Some information-processing models, like the one just considered, track mastery of one or a few tasks. Others describe the human cognitive system as a whole (Gopnik & Tenenbaum, 2007; Ristic & Enns, 2015; Westermann et al., 2006). These general models are used as guides for asking questions about broad changes in thinking: Does a child's ability to solve problems become more organized and "planful" with age? What strategies do younger and older children use to remember new information, and how do those strategies affect children's recall?

Like Piaget's theory, the information-processing approach regards people as actively modifying their own thinking in response to environmental demands (Halford & Andrews, 2011; Munakata, 2006). However, the thought processes studied—perception, attention, memory, categorization of information, planning, problem solving, and comprehension of written and spoken prose—are typically viewed as similar at all ages but present to a lesser or greater extent. The view of development is one of continuous change.

Because information processing has provided precise accounts of how children and adults tackle many cognitive tasks, its findings have important implications for education. Currently, researchers are intensely interested in the development of an array of "executive" processes that enable children and adults to manage their thoughts, emotions, and actions. These capacities—variously labeled

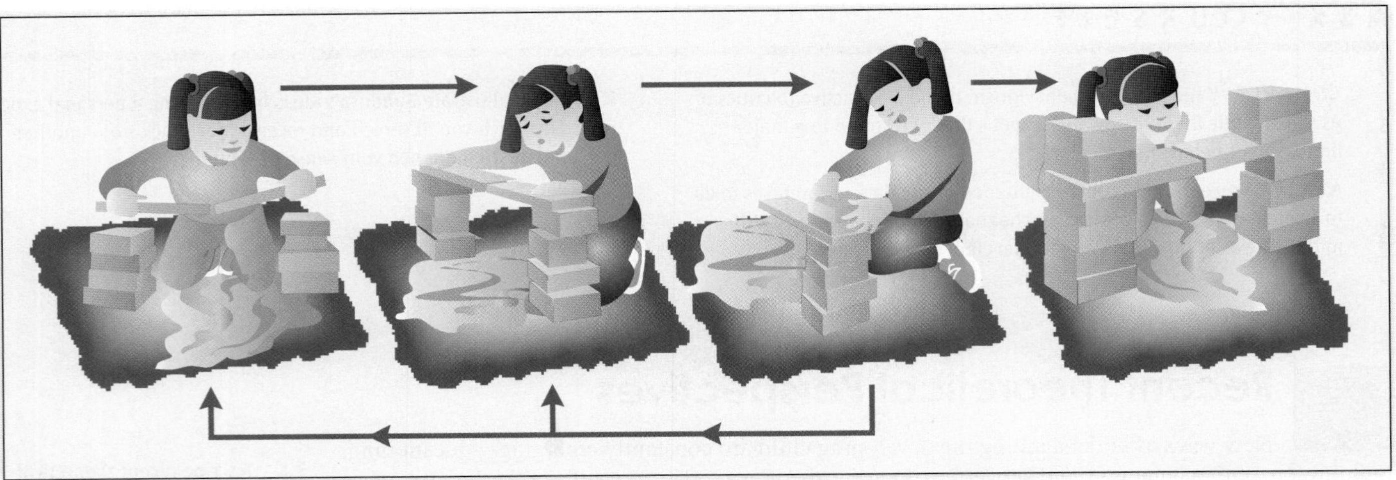

FIGURE 1.3 Information-processing flowchart showing the steps that a 5-year-old used to solve a bridge-building problem. Her task was to use blocks varying in size, shape, and weight, some of which were planklike, to construct a bridge across a "river" (painted on a floor mat) too wide for any single block to span. The child discovered how to counterweight and balance the bridge. The arrows reveal that, even after building a successful counterweight, she returned to earlier, unsuccessful strategies, which seemed to help her understand why the counterweight approach worked. (Based on Thornton, 1999.)

executive function, self-control, self-regulation, delay of gratification, and more—are essential for attaining our goals in challenging situations (Carlson, Zelazo, & Faja, 2013; Chevalier, 2015; Müller & Kerns, 2015). Executive processes are consistent predictors of academic achievement and socially competent behavior.

Nevertheless, information processing has fallen short in some respects. It has been better at analyzing thinking into its components than at putting them back together into a comprehensive theory. And it has had little to say about aspects of cognition that are not linear and logical, such as imagination and creativity.

Developmental Neuroscience

Over the past three decades, as information-processing research expanded, a new area of investigation arose called **developmental cognitive neuroscience.** It brings together researchers from psychology, biology, neuroscience, and medicine to study the relationship between changes in the brain and the developing child's cognitive processing and behavior patterns.

Improved methods for analyzing brain activity while children and adults perform various tasks have greatly enhanced knowledge of relationships between brain functioning and behavior (de Haan, 2015). Armed with these brain electrical-recording and imaging techniques (which we will consider in Chapter 4), neuroscientists are tackling questions like these: How does genetic makeup combine with specific experiences at various ages to influence growth and organization of the child's brain? What transformations in the brain make it harder for adolescents and adults than for children to acquire a second language?

A complementary new area, **developmental social neuroscience,** is devoted to studying the relationship between changes in the brain and emotional and social development (Baron-Cohen, Tager-Flusberg, & Lombardo, 2013). When researchers started to tap convenient neurobiological measures that are sensitive to psychological state, such as heart rate, blood pressure, and hormone levels detected in saliva, an explosion of social-neuroscience investigations followed.

Active areas of study include identification of the neural systems underlying infant gains in perception of facial expressions, risk-taking behavior in adolescence, and individual differences in impulsivity, sociability, anxiety, aggression, and depression. One particularly energetic focus is the negative impact of extreme adversity, such as early rearing in deprived orphanages, on brain development and cognitive, emotional, and social skills (Anderson & Beauchamp, 2013; Gunnar, Doom, & Esposito, 2015). Another research interest is uncovering the neurological bases of *autism*—the disrupted brain structures and networks that lead to the impaired social skills, language delays, and repetitive motor behavior of this disorder (Stoner et al., 2014). As these efforts illustrate, researchers are forging links between cognitive and social neuroscience, identifying brain systems that affect both domains of development.

Rapid progress in clarifying the types of experiences that support or undermine brain development at diverse ages is contributing to effective interventions for enhancing cognitive and social functioning. Today, researchers are examining the impact of various training and treatment techniques on both brain functioning and behavior (Johnson & de Haan, 2015). Although much remains to be discovered, developmental neuroscience is broadening our understanding of development and yielding major practical applications.

▶ A therapist encourages a 6-year-old with autism to master the alphabet and interact socially, giving her a high five for progress. Developmental social neuroscientists are intensely interested in identifying the neurological bases of autism and using those findings to devise effective interventions.

Nevertheless, neuroscience research has so captivated the field that it poses the risk that brain properties underlying child behavior will be granted undue importance over powerful environmental influences, such as parenting, education, and economic inequalities in families and communities. Although most neuroscientists are mindful of the complex interplay among heredity, individual experiences, and brain development, their findings have too often resulted in excessive emphasis being placed on biological processes (Kagan, 2013b).

Fortunately, an advantage of having many theories is that they encourage researchers to attend to previously neglected dimensions of people's lives. The final four perspectives we will discuss focus on *contexts* for development. The first of these views emphasizes that the environments to which humans have been exposed over their long evolutionary history influence the development of many capacities.

Ethology and Evolutionary Developmental Psychology

Ethology is concerned with the adaptive, or survival, value of behavior and its evolutionary history. Its roots can be traced to the work of Darwin. Two European zoologists, Konrad Lorenz and Niko Tinbergen, laid its modern foundations. Watching diverse animal species in their natural habitats, Lorenz and Tinbergen observed behavior patterns that promote survival. The best known of these is *imprinting,* the early following behavior of certain baby birds, such as geese, that ensures that the young will stay close to the mother and be fed and protected from danger. Imprinting takes place during an early, restricted period of development (Lorenz, 1952). If the mother goose is absent during this time but an object resembling her in important features is present, young goslings may imprint on it instead.

Observations of imprinting led to a major concept in child development: the *critical period.* It is a limited time span during which the child is biologically prepared to acquire certain adaptive behaviors but needs the support of a stimulating environment. Many researchers have investigated whether complex cognitive and social behaviors must be learned during certain time periods. For example, if children are deprived of adequate physical and social stimulation during their early years, will their intelligence, emotional responsiveness, and social skills be impaired?

▶ Ethology focuses on the adaptive, or survival, value of behavior and on similarities between human behavior and that of other species, especially our primate relatives. Observing this chimpanzee mother cuddling her infant helps us understand the human infant–caregiver relationship.

In later chapters, we will see that the term *sensitive period* applies better to child development than the strict notion of a critical period (Knudsen, 2004). A **sensitive period** is a time that is biologically optimal for certain capacities to emerge because the individual is especially responsive to environmental influences. However, its boundaries are less well-defined than those of a critical period. Development can occur later, but it is harder to induce.

Inspired by observations of imprinting, British psychoanalyst John Bowlby (1969) applied ethological theory to the understanding of the human infant–caregiver relationship. He argued that infant smiling, babbling, grasping, and crying are built-in social signals that encourage the caregiver to approach, care for, and interact with the baby. By keeping the parent near, these behaviors help ensure that the infant will be fed, protected from danger, and provided with stimulation and affection necessary for healthy growth. The development of attachment in humans is a lengthy process involving psychological changes that lead the baby to form a deep affectionate tie with the caregiver (Thompson, 2006). Bowlby believed that this bond has lifelong consequences for human relationships. In later chapters, we will consider research that evaluates this assumption.

Recently, investigators have extended the efforts of ethologists in an area of research called **evolutionary developmental psychology.** It seeks to understand the adaptive value of species-wide cognitive, emotional, and social competencies as those competencies change with age (King & Bjorklund, 2010; Lickliter & Honeycutt, 2013). Evolutionary developmental psychologists ask questions like these: What role does early helping behavior, observed in 18- to 24-month-olds, play in the development of cooperation, sharing, and volunteering, which are essential for human survival? Why do children play in gender-segregated groups? What do they learn from such play that might lead to adult gender-typed behaviors, such as male dominance and female investment in caregiving?

As these examples suggest, evolutionary psychologists are not just concerned with the genetic and biological roots of development. They recognize that humans' large brain and extended childhood resulted from the need to master an increasingly complex environment, so they are also interested in learning (Bjorklund, Causey, & Periss, 2009). In sum, evolutionary developmental psychology aims to understand the entire *person–environment system*. The next contextual perspective we will discuss, Vygotsky's sociocultural theory, serves as an excellent complement to the evolutionary viewpoint because it highlights social and cultural contexts for development.

Vygotsky's Sociocultural Theory

The field of child development has recently seen a dramatic increase in research demonstrating that development and culture are closely interwoven (Mistry & Dutta, 2015). The contributions of Russian psychologist Lev Vygotsky (1896–1934) and his followers have played a major role in this trend.

COURTESY OF JAMES V. WERTSCH/WASHINGTON UNIVERSITY IN ST. LOUIS

▶ According to Lev Vygotsky, shown here with his daughter, many cognitive processes and skills are socially transferred from more knowledgeable members of society to children. Vygotsky's sociocultural theory helps explain the wide cultural variation in cognitive competencies.

Vygotsky's (1934/1987) perspective, called **sociocultural theory,** focuses on how *culture*—the values, beliefs, customs, and skills of a social group—is transmitted to the next generation. According to Vygotsky, *social interaction*—in particular, cooperative dialogues with more knowledgeable members of society—is necessary for children to acquire the ways of thinking and behaving that make up a community's culture. Vygotsky believed that as adults and more expert peers help children master culturally meaningful activities, the communication between them becomes part of children's thinking. As children internalize the features of these dialogues, they use the language within them to guide their own thought and actions and to acquire new skills (Lourenço, 2012; Winsler, Fernyhough, & Montero, 2009). The young child instructing herself while working a puzzle, preparing a table for dinner, or solving a math problem has begun to produce the same kind of guiding comments that an adult previously used to help her master culturally important tasks.

Vygotsky's theory has been especially influential in the study of cognitive development. Whereas Piaget emphasized children's independent efforts to make sense of their world, Vygotsky viewed cognitive development as a *socially mediated process,* in which children depend on others' assistance as they tackle new challenges.

In Vygotsky's theory, children undergo certain stagewise changes. For example, when they acquire language, they gain in ability to participate in dialogues with others, and mastery of culturally valued competencies surges forward. When children enter school, they spend much time discussing language, literacy, and other academic concepts—experiences that induce them to reflect on their own thinking (Kozulin, 2003). As a result, they advance dramatically in reasoning and problem solving.

At the same time, Vygotsky stressed that dialogues with experts lead to continuous changes in thinking that vary greatly from culture to culture. Consistent with this view, cultures select tasks for their members, and social interaction surrounding those tasks leads to competencies essential for success in a particular culture. For example, in industrialized nations, teachers help people learn to read, drive a car, or use a computer. Among the Zinacanteco Indians of southern Mexico, adult experts guide young girls as they master complicated weaving techniques (Greenfield, 2004).

Research stimulated by Vygotsky's theory reveals that people in different cultures develop unique strengths. Nevertheless, Vygotsky's emphasis on culture and social experiences led him to neglect the biological side of development. And his focus on social transmission of knowledge meant that he placed less emphasis than other theories on children's capacity to shape their own development. Followers of Vygotsky stress that children actively participate in the social activities from which their development springs (Daniels, 2011; Rogoff, 2003). Contemporary sociocultural theorists grant the individual and society balanced, mutually influential roles.

▶ With her teacher's guidance, this Chinese child practices calligraphy. She acquires a culturally valued skill through interaction with an older, more experienced calligrapher.

Ecological Systems Theory

Urie Bronfenbrenner (1917–2005) is responsible for an approach that rose to the forefront of the field because it offers the most differentiated and complete account of contextual influences on development. **Ecological systems theory** views the child as developing within a complex *system* of relationships affected by multiple levels of the surrounding environment. Because the child's biologically influenced dispositions join with diverse environmental forces to mold development, Bronfenbrenner characterized his perspective as a *bioecological model* (Bronfenbrenner & Morris, 2006).

Bronfenbrenner envisioned the environment as a series of interrelated, nested structures that include but also extend beyond the home, school, and neighborhood settings in which children spend their everyday lives (see Figure 1.4). Each layer joins with the others to powerfully affect development.

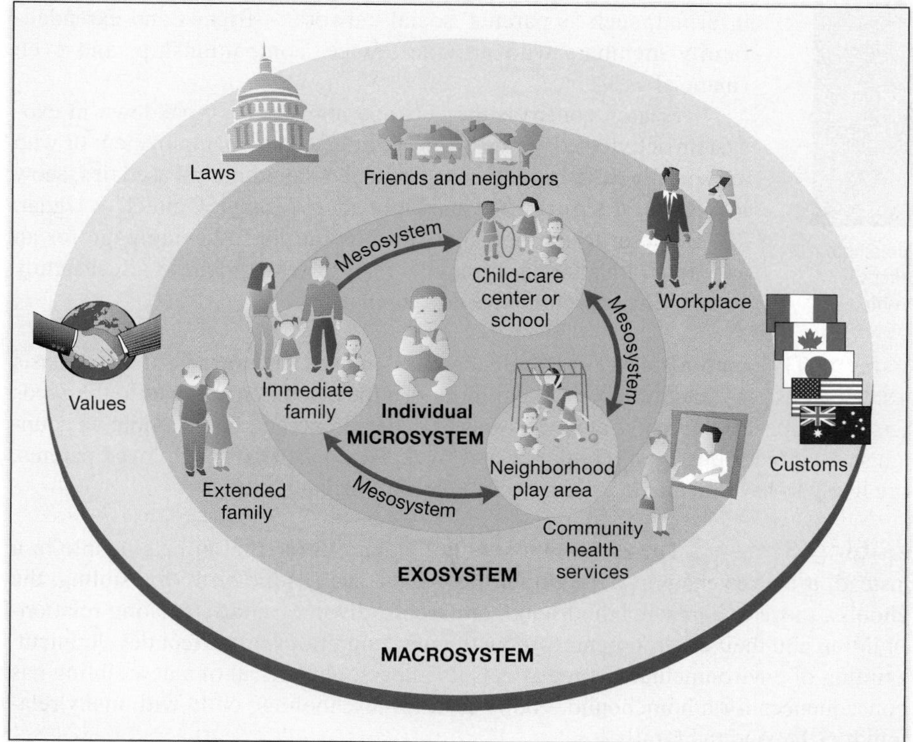

FIGURE 1.4 Structure of the environment in ecological systems theory. The *microsystem* concerns relations between the child and the immediate environment; the *mesosystem*, connections among immediate settings; the *exosystem*, social settings that affect but do not contain children; and the *macrosystem*, the values, laws, customs, and resources of the culture that affect activities and interactions at all inner layers. The *chronosystem* (not pictured) is not a specific context. Instead, it refers to the dynamic, ever-changing nature of the child's environment.

The Microsystem. The innermost level of the environment, the **microsystem,** consists of activities and interaction patterns in the child's immediate surroundings. Bronfenbrenner emphasized that to understand development at this level, we must keep in mind that all relationships are *bidirectional:* Adults affect children's behavior, but children's biologically and socially influenced characteristics—their physical attributes, personalities, and capacities—also affect adults' behavior. A friendly, attentive child is likely to evoke positive, patient reactions from parents, whereas an easily upset, emotionally negative child is more likely to receive impatience, restriction, and punishment (Streit et al., 2017). When these reciprocal interactions occur often over time, they have an enduring impact on development.

Third parties—other individuals in the microsystem—also affect the quality of any two-person relationship. If they are supportive, interaction is enhanced. For example, when parents encourage each other in their child-rearing roles, each engages in more effective parenting. In contrast, marital conflict is associated with inconsistent discipline and hostility toward children. In response, children often react with fear and anxiety or with anger and aggression, and the well-being of both parent and child suffers (Cummings & Davies, 2010; Low & Stocker, 2012).

The Mesosystem. The second level of Bronfenbrenner's model, the **mesosystem,** encompasses connections between microsystems. For example, a child's academic progress depends on parent involvement in school life and on the extent to which academic learning is carried over to the home (Wang & Sheikh-Khalil, 2014). Similarly, parent–child interaction at home is likely to affect caregiver–child interaction in the child-care setting, and vice versa. Each relationship is more likely to support development when there are links between home and child care, in the form of visits and cooperative exchanges of information.

© ELLEN B. SENISI

▶ A mother says good-bye to her son as she drops him off at preschool. The child's experiences at preschool (microsystem) and the mother's experiences at work (exosystem) affect the parent–child relationship.

The Exosystem. The **exosystem** consists of social settings that do not contain children but nevertheless affect experiences in immediate settings. These can be formal organizations, such as parents' workplaces, religious institutions, and community health and welfare services. Flexible work schedules, paid maternity and paternity leave, and sick leave for parents whose children are ill are examples of ways that work settings can support child rearing and, indirectly, enhance children's development. Exosystem supports can also be informal, such as parents' social networks—friends and extended-family members who provide advice, companionship, and even financial assistance.

Research confirms the negative impact of a breakdown in exosystem activities. Families who are affected by unemployment or who are socially isolated, with few personal or community-based ties, show increased rates of conflict and child abuse (Tomyr, Ouimet, & Ugnat, 2012). Refer to the Social Issues box on the following page for an additional illustration of the power of the exosystem to affect family functioning and children's development.

The Macrosystem. The outermost level of Bronfenbrenner's model, the **macrosystem,** consists of cultural values, laws, customs, and resources. The priority that the macrosystem gives to the needs of children affects the support they receive at inner levels of the environment. For example, in countries that set high standards for quality of child care and workplace benefits for employed parents, children are more likely to have favorable experiences in their immediate settings.

LOOK AND LISTEN

Ask a parent to explain his or her most worrisome child-rearing challenge. Describe one source of support at each level of Bronfenbrenner's bioecological model that could ease parental stress and promote child development.

An Ever-Changing System. The environment is not a static force that affects people in a uniform way. Instead, it is ever-changing. Important life events, such as the birth of a sibling, the beginning of school, a move to a new neighborhood, or parents' divorce, modify existing relationships between children and their environments, producing new conditions that affect development. In addition, the timing of environmental change affects its impact. The arrival of a new sibling has very different consequences for a homebound toddler than for a school-age child with many relationships and activities beyond the family.

SOCIAL ISSUES

Family Chaos Undermines Parents' and Children's Well-Being

▶ A chaotic home life interferes with warm, relaxed parent–child interaction and contributes to behavior problems. Exosystem influences, such as excessive workplace pressures, can trigger disorganized family routines.

All of us can recall days during our childhoods when family routines—regular mealtime, bedtime, homework time, and parent–child reading and playtime—were disrupted, perhaps because of a change in the parent's job, a family illness, or a busy season of after-school sports. In some families, however, absence of daily structure is nearly constant, yielding a chaotic home life that interferes with healthy development (Fiese & Winter, 2010). An organized family life provides a supportive context for warm, involved parent–child interaction, which is essential to both parents' and children's well-being.

Family chaos is linked to economic disadvantage—especially, single mothers with limited incomes struggling to juggle the challenges of transportation, shift jobs, unstable child-care arrangements, and other daily hassles. But chaos is not limited to such families. Across income levels and ethnic groups, employed mothers and fathers, but especially mothers, report more multitasking while caring for children—preparing dinner while helping with homework, or reading to children while checking work-related emails (Bianchi, 2011; Offer & Schneider, 2011). Mothers who frequently multitask experience greater psychological stress.

Parental multitasking disrupts family routines. For example, only about half of U.S. families report eating meals together regularly (Child Trends, 2013). Frequency of family meals is associated with wide-ranging positive outcomes—in childhood, enhanced language development and academic achievement, fewer behavior problems, and time spent sleeping; and in adolescence, reduced sexual risk taking, alcohol and drug use, and mental health problems. Shared mealtimes also increase the likelihood of a healthy diet and protect against obesity and adolescent eating disorders (Fiese & Schwartz, 2008; Lora et al., 2014). As these findings suggest, regular mealtimes are a general indicator of an organized family life and positive parent involvement.

But family chaos can prevail even when families do engage in joint activities. Disorganized family routines involving harsh or lax parental discipline and hostile, disrespectful communication are associated with child and adolescent adjustment difficulties (Fiese, Foley, & Spagnola, 2006; Milkie, Nomaguchi, & Denny, 2015). As family time becomes pressured and overwhelming, its orderly structure diminishes, and parental stress escalates while warm parent–child engagement disintegrates.

Diverse circumstances can trigger a pileup of limited parental emotional resources, breeding family chaos. In addition to *microsystem* and *mesosystem* influences (parents with mental health problems, parental separation and divorce, single parents with few or no supportive relationships), the *exosystem* is powerful: When family time is at the mercy of external forces—parents commuting several hours a day to and from work, child-care arrangements often failing, parents experiencing excessive workplace pressures—family routines are threatened.

Family chaos contributes to children's behavior problems, above and beyond its negative impact on parenting effectiveness (Fiese & Winter, 2010; Martin, Razza, & Brooks-Gunn, 2012). Chaotic surroundings induce in children a sense of being hassled and feelings of powerlessness, which lead to anxiety and low self-esteem.

Exosystem and macrosystem supports—including work settings with favorable family policies and high-quality child care that is affordable and reliable—can help prevent escalating demands on families that give way to chaos. In one community, a child-care center initiated a take-home dinner program. Busy parents could special-order a healthy, reasonably priced family meal, ready to go at day's end to aid in making the family dinner a routine that enhances children's development.

Bronfenbrenner called the temporal dimension of his model the **chronosystem** (the prefix *chrono* means "time"). Life changes can be imposed on the child, as in the examples just given. Alternatively, they can arise from within the child, since as children get older they select, modify, and create many of their own settings and experiences. How they do so depends on their physical, intellectual, and personality characteristics and their environmental opportunities. Therefore, in ecological systems theory, development is neither controlled by environmental circumstances nor driven solely by inner dispositions. Rather, children and their environments form a network of interdependent effects. Notice how our discussion of resilient children on page 7 illustrates this idea. You will see many more examples in later chapters.

▶ The dynamic systems perspective views the child's mind, body, and physical and social worlds as a continuously reorganizing, integrated system. In response to the physical and psychological changes of adolescence, this father and daughter must develop a new, more mature relationship.

Development as a Dynamic System

Today, researchers recognize both consistency and variability in children's development and want to do a better job of explaining variation. Consequently, a new wave of systems theorists is looking closely at how children, in interacting with their complex contexts, alter their own behavior to attain more advanced functioning. According to this **dynamic systems perspective,** the child's mind, body, and physical and social worlds form an integrated system that guides mastery of new skills. The system is *dynamic,* or constantly in motion. A change in any part of it—from brain growth to physical or social surroundings—disrupts the current organism–environment relationship. When this happens, the child actively reorganizes his or her behavior so the various components of the system work together as a functioning whole again, but in a more complex, effective way (Fischer & Bidell, 2006; Spencer, Perone, & Buss, 2011; Thelen & Smith, 2006).

Researchers adopting a dynamic systems perspective try to find out just how children attain new levels of organization by studying their behavior while they are in transition (Kloep et al., 2016; Thelen & Corbetta, 2002). For example, when presented with an attractive toy, how does a 3-month-old baby who engages in many, varied movements discover how to reach for it? On hearing a new word, how does a 2-year-old figure out the category of objects or events to which it refers? And how does a 5-year-old new to a kindergarten class form friendships, deciding whom to play with and whom to avoid?

Dynamic systems theorists acknowledge that a common human genetic heritage and basic regularities in children's physical and social worlds yield certain universal, broad outlines of development. But children's biological makeup, interests and goals, everyday tasks, and the people who support children in mastery of those tasks vary greatly, yielding wide individual differences in specific skills. Even when children master the same skills, such as walking, talking, or making new friends, they often do so in unique ways. And because children build competencies by engaging in real activities in real contexts, different skills vary in maturity within the same child. From this perspective, development cannot be characterized as a single line of change. As Figure 1.5 shows, it is more like a web of fibers branching out in many directions, each representing a different skill area that may undergo both continuous and stagewise transformations (Fischer & Bidell, 2006).

The dynamic systems view has been inspired by other scientific disciplines, especially biology and physics. It also draws on information-processing and contextual theories—evolutionary developmental psychology, sociocultural theory, and ecological systems theory. Dynamic systems research is still in its early stages. The perspective has been applied largely to children's motor and cognitive skills, but investigators have drawn on it to explain emotional and social development as well (Fogel & Garvey, 2007; Kunnen, 2012).

As dynamic systems research illustrates, today investigators are tracking and analyzing development in all its complexity. In doing so, they hope to move closer to an all-encompassing approach to understanding developmental change.

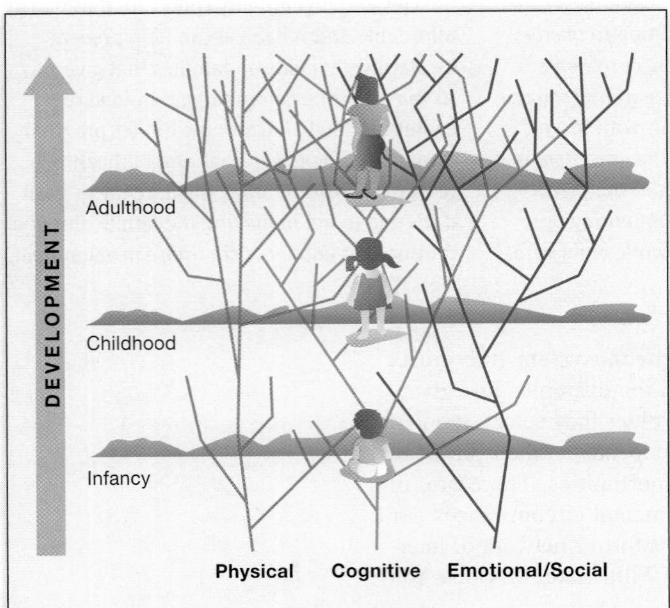

FIGURE 1.5 The dynamic systems view of development. Rather than envisioning a single line of stagewise or continuous change (refer to Figure 1.2 on page 5), dynamic systems theorists conceive of development as a web of fibers branching out in many directions. Each strand in the web represents a skill within the major domains of development—physical, cognitive, and emotional/social. The differing directions of the strands signify possible variations in paths and outcomes as the child masters skills necessary to participate in diverse contexts. The interconnections of the strands at each row of "hills" portray stagelike changes—periods of major transformation in which various skills work together as a functioning whole. As the web expands, skills become more numerous, complex, and effective. (Based on Fischer & Bidell, 2006.)

ASK YOURSELF

CONNECT Explain how each recent theoretical perspective views children as active contributors to their own development?

APPLY Mario wants to find out precisely how children of different ages recall stories. Desiree is interested in how adult–child communication in different cultures influences children's storytelling. Which theoretical perspective has Mario probably chosen? How about Desiree? Explain.

REFLECT To illustrate the chronosystem in ecological systems theory, select an important event from your childhood, such as a move to a new neighborhood, a class with an inspiring teacher, or parental divorce. How did the event affect you? How might its impact have differed had you been five years younger? How about five years older?

Comparing Theories

1.7 Identify the stand taken by each major theory on the three basic issues of child development.

In the preceding sections, we reviewed major theoretical perspectives in child development research that differ in many respects. First, they focus on different domains of development. Some, such as the psychoanalytic perspective and ethology, emphasize emotional and social development. Others, such as Piaget's cognitive-developmental theory, information processing, and Vygotsky's sociocultural theory, stress changes in thinking. The remaining approaches—behaviorism, social learning theory, evolutionary developmental psychology, ecological systems theory, and the dynamic systems perspective—encompass many aspects of children's functioning. Second, every theory contains a point of view about development. As we conclude our review of theoretical perspectives, identify the stand that each theory takes on the basic issues discussed at the beginning of this chapter. Then check your analysis against Table 1.4 on page 24.

Studying Development

1.8 Describe research methods commonly used to study child development.

1.9 Distinguish between correlational and experimental research designs, noting the strengths and limitations of each.

1.10 Describe designs for studying development, noting the strengths and limitations of each.

1.11 Discuss special ethical concerns that arise in research on children.

In every science, research usually begins with a *hypothesis*—a prediction drawn from a theory. Theories and hypotheses, however, merely initiate the many activities that result in sound evidence on child development. Conducting research according to scientifically accepted procedures involves many steps and choices. Investigators must decide which participants, and how many, to include. Then they must figure out what the participants will be asked to do and when, where, and how many times each will be seen. Finally, they must examine and draw conclusions from their data.

In the following sections, we look at research strategies commonly used to study child development. We begin with *research methods*—the specific activities of participants, such as being observed, responding to interviews, answering questionnaires, or taking tests. Then we turn to *research designs*—overall plans for research studies that permit the best possible test of the investigator's hypothesis. Finally, we discuss ethical issues involved in doing research on children.

Why learn about research strategies? There are two reasons. First, each of us must be a wise and critical consumer of knowledge. Knowing the strengths and limitations of various research strategies is important in separating dependable information from misleading results. Second, individuals who work directly with children or adults may be in a unique position to build bridges between research and practice by conducting studies, either on their own or in partnership with experienced investigators. Community agencies such as schools, mental health facilities, museums, and parks and recreation programs sometimes partner with researchers in designing, implementing, and evaluating interventions aimed at enhancing children's development (Tseng, Easton, & Supplee, 2017). To broaden these efforts, a basic understanding of the research process is essential.

LOOK AND LISTEN

Ask a teacher, counselor, social worker, or nurse to describe a question about development he or she would like researchers to address. After reading the rest of this chapter, recommend research strategies best suited to answering that question.

Common Research Methods

How does a researcher choose a basic approach to gathering information? Common methods include systematic observation, self-reports (such as questionnaires and interviews), clinical or case studies of a single individual, and ethnographies of the life circumstances of a specific group of children. Table 1.5 on page 25 summarizes the strengths and limitations of each.

TABLE 1.4
Stances of Major Theories on Basic Issues in Child Development

THEORY	CONTINUOUS OR DISCONTINUOUS DEVELOPMENT?	ONE COURSE OF DEVELOPMENT OR MANY?	RELATIVE INFLUENCE OF NATURE AND NURTURE?
Psychoanalytic perspective	*Discontinuous:* Psychosexual and psychosocial development takes place in stages.	*One course:* Stages are assumed to be universal.	*Both nature and nurture:* Innate impulses are channeled and controlled through child-rearing experiences. *Early experiences* set the course of later development.
Behaviorism and social learning theory	*Continuous:* Development involves an increase in learned behaviors.	*Many possible courses:* Behaviors reinforced and modeled may vary from child to child.	*Emphasis on nurture:* Development is the result of conditioning and modeling. *Both early and later experiences* are important.
Piaget's cognitive-developmental theory	*Discontinuous:* Cognitive development takes place in stages.	*One course:* Stages are assumed to be universal.	*Both nature and nurture:* Development occurs as the brain grows and children exercise their innate drive to discover reality in a generally stimulating environment. *Both early and later experiences* are important.
Information processing	*Continuous:* Children gradually improve in perception, attention, memory, and problem-solving skills.	*One course:* Changes studied characterize most or all children.	*Both nature and nurture:* Children are active, sense-making beings who modify their thinking as the brain grows and they confront new environmental demands. *Both early and later experiences* are important.
Ethology and evolutionary developmental psychology	*Both continuous and discontinuous:* Children and adults gradually develop a wider range of adaptive behaviors. Sensitive periods occur in which qualitatively distinct capacities emerge fairly suddenly.	*One course:* Adaptive behaviors and sensitive periods apply to all members of a species.	*Both nature and nurture:* Evolution and heredity influence behavior, and learning lends greater flexibility and adaptiveness to it. In sensitive periods, *early experiences* set the course of later development.
Vygotsky's sociocultural theory	*Both continuous and discontinuous:* Language acquisition and schooling lead to stagewise changes. Dialogues with more expert members of society also result in continuous changes that vary from culture to culture.	*Many possible courses:* Socially mediated changes in thought and behavior vary from culture to culture.	*Both nature and nurture:* Heredity, brain growth, and dialogues with more expert members of society jointly contribute to development. *Both early and later experiences* are important.
Ecological systems theory	*Not specified.*	*Many possible courses:* Biologically influenced dispositions join with environmental forces at multiple levels to mold development in unique ways.	*Both nature and nurture:* The individual's characteristics and the reactions of others affect each other in a bidirectional fashion. *Both early and later experiences* are important.
Dynamic systems perspective	*Both continuous and discontinuous:* Change in the system is always ongoing. Stagelike transformations occur as children reorganize their behavior so components of the system work as a functioning whole.	*Many possible courses:* Biological makeup, interests and goals, everyday tasks, and social experiences vary, yielding wide individual differences in specific skills.	*Both nature and nurture:* The child's mind, body, and physical and social surroundings form an integrated system that guides mastery of new skills. *Both early and later experiences* are important.

Systematic Observation. Observations of the behavior of children and adults can be made in different ways. One approach is to go into the field, or natural environment, and record the behavior of interest—a method called **naturalistic observation.**

A study aimed at finding out if teacher–child conversations about storybook characters' emotions can augment young children's socially competent behavior provides a good example (Grazzani et al., 2016). Observing 2- and 3-year-olds during free play and lunch periods at preschool, researchers recorded the number of times each child spontaneously used mental-state language (referred to others' desires, thoughts, or emotions) and helped, comforted, or shared with a classmate. Children who had participated in a series of storybook conversations, compared with those who had not, used more mental-state talk (suggesting greater awareness of others' viewpoints and feelings) and engaged in considerably more caring acts with peers. The great strength of naturalistic observation

TABLE 1.5
Strengths and Limitations of Common Research Methods

METHOD	DESCRIPTION	STRENGTHS	LIMITATIONS
SYSTEMATIC OBSERVATION			
Naturalistic observation	Observation of behavior in natural contexts.	Reflects participants' everyday lives.	Cannot control conditions under which participants are observed.
Structured observation	Observation of behavior in a laboratory, where conditions are the same for all participants.	Grants each participant an equal opportunity to display the behavior of interest. Permits study of behaviors rarely seen in everyday life.	May not yield observations typical of participants' behavior in everyday life.
SELF-REPORTS			
Clinical interview	Flexible interviewing procedure in which the investigator obtains a complete account of the participant's thoughts.	Comes as close as possible to the way participants think in everyday life. Great breadth and depth of information can be obtained in a short time.	May not result in accurate reporting of information. Flexible procedure makes comparing individuals' responses difficult.
Structured interview, questionnaires, and tests	Self-report instruments in which each participant is asked the same questions in the same way.	Permits comparisons of participants' responses and efficient data collection. Researchers can specify answer alternatives that participants might not think of in an open-ended interview.	Does not yield the same depth of information as a clinical interview. Responses are still subject to inaccurate reporting.
CLINICAL, OR CASE STUDY, METHOD			
	A full picture of one individual's psychological functioning, obtained by combining interviews, observations, and test scores.	Provides rich, descriptive insights into factors that affect development.	May be biased by researchers' theoretical preferences. Findings cannot be applied to individuals other than the participant.
ETHNOGRAPHY			
	Participant observation of a culture or distinct social group. By making extensive field notes, the researcher tries to capture the culture's unique values and social processes.	Provides a more complete description than can be derived from a single observational visit, interview, or questionnaire.	May be biased by researchers' values and theoretical preferences. Findings cannot be applied to individuals and settings other than the ones studied.

is that investigators can see directly the everyday behaviors they hope to explain.

Naturalistic observation also has a major limitation: Not all individuals have the same opportunity to display a particular behavior in everyday life. In the study just described, some children might have witnessed a peer needing more help or comfort than others or been exposed to more cues for positive social responses from their teachers. For these reasons, they might have displayed more caring.

Researchers commonly deal with this difficulty by making **structured observations,** in which the investigator sets up a laboratory situation that evokes the behavior of interest so that every participant has equal opportunity to display the response. In one such study, 2-year-olds' emotional reactions to harm that they thought they had caused were observed by asking each of them to take care of a rag doll that had been modified so its leg would fall off when the child picked it up. Researchers recorded children's facial expressions of sadness and concern for the injured doll, efforts to help the doll, and body tension—responses indicating worry, remorse, and a desire to make

▶ In naturalistic observation, the researcher goes into the field and records the behavior of interest. Here, a research assistant observes children at preschool. She may be focusing on their playmate choices, cooperation, helpfulness, or conflicts.

amends. In addition, mothers were asked to engage in brief conversations about emotions with their 2-year-olds (Garner, 2003). Children whose mothers more often explained the causes and consequences of emotion were more likely to express concern for the injured doll.

Systematic observation provides invaluable information on how children and adults actually behave, but it tells us little about the reasoning behind their responses. For this kind of information, researchers must turn to self-report techniques.

Self-Reports. Self-reports ask research participants to provide information on their perceptions, thoughts, abilities, feelings, attitudes, beliefs, and past experiences. They range from relatively unstructured interviews to highly structured interviews, questionnaires, and tests.

In a **clinical interview,** researchers use a flexible, conversational style to probe for the participant's point of view. In the following example, Piaget questioned a 5-year-old child about his understanding of dreams:

> *Where does the dream come from?*—I think you sleep so well that you dream.—*Does it come from us or from outside?*—From outside.—*When you are in bed and you dream, where is the dream?*—In my bed, under the blanket. I don't really know. If it was in my stomach, the bones would be in the way and I shouldn't see it.—*Is the dream there when you sleep?*—Yes, it is in the bed beside me. (Piaget, 1926/1930, pp. 97–98)

Although a researcher conducting clinical interviews with more than one participant would typically ask the same first question to establish a common task, individualized prompts are used to provide a fuller picture of each child's reasoning.

The clinical interview has two major strengths. First, it permits people to display their thoughts in terms that are as close as possible to the way they think in everyday life. Second, the clinical interview can provide a large amount of information in a fairly brief period (Sharp et al., 2013). For example, in an hour-long session, we can obtain a wide range of information on child rearing from a parent—much more than we could capture by observing for the same amount of time.

A major limitation of the clinical interview has to do with the accuracy with which people report their thoughts, feelings, and experiences. Some participants, wishing to please the interviewer, may make up answers that do not represent their actual thinking. When asked about past events, some may have trouble recalling exactly what happened. And because the clinical interview depends on verbal ability and expressiveness, it may underestimate the capacities of individuals who have difficulty putting their thoughts into words.

The clinical interview has also been criticized because of its flexibility. When questions are phrased differently for each participant, responses may reflect the manner of interviewing rather than real differences in the way people think about a topic. **Structured interviews** (including tests and questionnaires), in which each participant is asked the same set of questions in the same way, eliminate this problem. These instruments are also much more efficient. Answers are briefer, and researchers can obtain written responses from an entire group at the same time.

But structured interviews do not yield the same depth of information as a clinical interview. And they can still be affected by the problem of inaccurate reporting.

▶ Using the clinical, or case study, method, this researcher interacts with a 3-year-old during a home visit. Interviews and observations will contribute to an in-depth picture of this child's psychological functioning.

The Clinical, or Case Study, Method. An outgrowth of psychoanalytic theory, the **clinical, or case study, method** brings together a wide range of information on one child, including interviews, observations, and test scores. The aim is to obtain as complete a picture as possible of that individual's psychological functioning and the experiences that led up to it.

The clinical method is well-suited to studying the development of certain types of individuals who are few in number but vary widely in characteristics. For example, the method has been used to find out what contributes to the accomplishments of *prodigies*—extremely gifted children who attain adult competence in a field before age 10.

In one investigation, researchers conducted case studies of eight child prodigies nationally recognized for talents in such areas as art, music, and mathematics (Ruthsatz & Urbach, 2012). For example, one child started reading as an infant, took college-level classes beginning at age 8, and published a paper in a mathematics journal at 13. Across the eight cases, the investigators noticed interesting patterns, including above-average intelligence and exceptionally high scores on tests of memory and attention to detail. Several prodigies had relatives with autism, a condition that also involves intense attention to detail. Although child prodigies generally do not display the cognitive and social deficits of autism, the two groups may share an underlying genetic trait that affects the functioning of certain brain regions, heightening perception and attention.

The clinical method yields richly detailed case narratives that offer valuable insights into the many factors influencing development. Nevertheless, because information often is collected unsystematically and subjectively, researchers' theoretical preferences may bias their observations and interpretations. In addition, investigators cannot assume that their conclusions apply, or generalize, to anyone other than the child or children studied (Stanovich, 2013). Even when patterns emerge across cases, it is wise to confirm these with other research strategies.

Methods for Studying Culture. To study the impact of culture, researchers adjust the methods just considered or tap procedures specially devised for cross-cultural and multicultural research. Which approach investigators choose depends on their research goals.

Sometimes researchers are interested in characteristics that are believed to be universal but that vary in degree from one society to the next: Are parents warmer or more directive in some cultures than others? How strong are gender stereotypes in different nations? In each instance, several cultural groups will be compared, and all participants must be questioned or observed in the same way. Therefore, researchers draw on the observational and self-report procedures we have already considered, adapting them through translation so they can be understood in each cultural context. Still, investigators must be mindful of cultural differences in familiarity with being observed and with responding to self-report instruments, which can bias their findings (van de Vijver, 2011).

© KEITH DANNEMILLER/ALAMY STOCK PHOTO

A Western researcher works with Zinacantec Mayan children in Chiapas, Mexico, using the ethnographic method to gather information about how they learn through everyday activities.

At other times, researchers want to uncover the *cultural meanings* of children's and adults' behaviors by becoming as familiar as possible with their way of life. To achieve this goal, investigators rely on a method borrowed from the field of anthropology—**ethnography.** Like the clinical method, ethnographic research is a descriptive, qualitative technique. But instead of aiming to understand a single individual, it is directed toward understanding a culture or distinct social group through *participant observation.* Typically, the researcher spends months, and sometimes years, in the cultural community, participating in its daily life. Extensive field notes are gathered, consisting of a mix of observations, self-reports from members of the culture, and careful interpretations by the investigator (Case, Todd, & Kral, 2014). Later, these notes are put together into a description of the community that tries to capture its unique values and social processes.

In some ethnographies, investigators look at many aspects of experience, as one researcher did in describing what it is like to grow up in a small American town. Others focus on one or a few settings and issues—for example, youth resilience in an economically disadvantaged Alaskan-Native community (Peshkin, 1997; Rasmus, Allen, & Ford, 2014). Researchers may supplement traditional self-report and observational methods with ethnography if they suspect that unique meanings underlie cultural differences, as the Cultural Influences box on page 28 reveals.

Ethnographers strive to minimize their influence on the culture they are studying by becoming part of it. Nevertheless, as with clinical research, investigators' cultural values and theoretical commitments sometimes lead them to observe selectively or misinterpret what they see. Finally, the findings of ethnographic studies cannot be assumed to generalize beyond the people and settings in which the research was conducted.

CULTURAL INFLUENCES

Immigrant Youths: Adapting to a New Land

These Tibetan-American children march in an international immigrants parade in New York City. Cultural values that engender allegiance to family and community promote high achievement and protect many immigrant youths from involvement in risky behaviors.

Over the past several decades, increasing numbers of immigrants have come to North America, fleeing war and persecution in their homelands or seeking better life chances. Today, one-fourth of U.S. children and adolescents have foreign-born parents, mostly originating from Latin America, the Caribbean, Asia, and Africa. Although some move with their parents, nearly 90 percent of young people from immigrant families are U.S.-born citizens (Migration Policy Institute, 2015).

How well are these youths—now the fastest-growing sector of the U.S. youth population—adapting to their new country? To find out, researchers use multiple research methods: academic testing, questionnaires assessing psychological adjustment, and in-depth ethnographies.

Academic Achievement and Adjustment

Although educators and laypeople often assume that the transition to a new country has a negative impact on psychological well-being, many children of immigrant parents adapt amazingly well. Students who are first generation (foreign-born, immigrated with their parents) or second generation (American-born, with immigrant parents) often achieve in school as well as or better than students of native-born parents (Hao & Woo, 2012; Hernandez, Denton, & Blanchard, 2011). And compared with their agemates, adolescents from immigrant families are less likely to commit delinquent and violent acts, use drugs and alcohol, have early sex, miss school because of illness, or suffer from obesity (Saucier et al., 2002; Supple & Small, 2006).

These outcomes are strongest for Chinese, Filipino, Japanese, Korean, and East Indian youths, less dramatic for other ethnicities (Fuligni, 2004; Louie, 2001; Portes & Rumbaut, 2005). Variation in adjustment is greater among Mexican, Central American, and Southeast Asian (Hmong, Cambodian, Laotian, Thai, and Vietnamese) young people, who show elevated rates of school dropout, delinquency, teenage parenthood, and drug use (Gurrola, Ayón, & Moya Salas, 2016; Pong & Landale, 2012). Disparities in parental economic resources, education, English-language proficiency, and support of children contribute to these trends.

Still, many immigrant youths whose parents face considerable financial hardship and who speak little English are successful (Suárez-Orozco, Marks, & Abo-Zena, 2015). Factors other than income are responsible—notably, family values and strong ethnic-community ties.

Family and Ethnic-Community Influences

Ethnographies reveal that immigrant parents view education as the surest way to improve life chances (Feliciano & Lanuza, 2015). Aware of the challenges their children face, they typically emphasize trying hard. They remind their children that, because educational opportunities were not available in their native countries, they themselves are often limited to menial jobs.

Adolescents from these families internalize their parents' valuing of education, endorsing it more strongly than agemates with native-born parents. Because minority ethnicities usually stress allegiance to family and community over individual goals, immigrant young people feel a strong sense of obligation to their parents. They view school success as both their own and their parents' success and as an important way of repaying their parents for the hardships they have endured (van Geel & Vedder, 2011). Both family relationships and school achievement protect these youths from risky behaviors.

Immigrant parents of successful youths typically develop close ties to an ethnic community, which exerts additional control through a high consensus on values and constant monitoring of young people's activities. The following comments capture the power of these family and community forces:

> *A 16-year-old girl from Central America describes the supportive adults in her neighborhood:* They ask me if I need anything for school. If we go to a store and I see a notebook, they ask me if I want it. They give me advice, tell me that I should be careful of the friends I choose. They also tell me to stay in school to get prepared. They tell me I am smart. They give me encouragement. (Suárez-Orozco, Pimental, & Martin, 2009, p. 733)

> *A teenage boy from Mexico discusses the importance of family in his culture:* A really big part of the Hispanic population [is] being close to family, and the family being a priority all the time. I hate people who say, "Why do you want to go to a party where your family's at? Don't you want to get away from them?" You know, I don't really get tired of them. I've always been really close to them. That connection to my parents, that trust that you can talk to them, that makes me Mexican. (Bacallao & Smokowski, 2007, p. 62)

The experiences of well-adjusted immigrant youths are not problem-free. Many encounter racial and ethnic prejudices and experience tensions between family values and the new culture (Sirin et al., 2013). In the long term, however, family and community cohesion, supervision, and high expectations promote favorable outcomes.

ASK YOURSELF

CONNECT What strengths and limitations do the clinical, or case study, method and ethnography have in common?

APPLY A researcher wants to study the thoughts and feelings of children who have a parent on active duty in the military. Which method should she use? Why?

General Research Designs

In deciding on a research design, investigators choose a way of setting up a study that permits them to test their hypotheses with the greatest certainty possible. Two main types of designs are used in all research on human behavior: *correlational* and *experimental.*

Correlational Design.

In a **correlational design,** researchers gather information on individuals, generally in natural life circumstances, without altering their experiences. Then they look at relationships between participants' characteristics and their behavior or development. Suppose we want to answer the following questions: Do parents' styles of interacting with their children have any bearing on children's intelligence? How do child abuse and neglect affect children's feelings about themselves? In these and many other instances, the conditions of interest are difficult or impossible to arrange and control and must be studied as they currently exist.

Correlational studies have one major limitation: We cannot infer cause and effect. For example, if we were to find that parental interaction is related to children's intelligence, we would not know whether parents' behavior actually *causes* intellectual differences among children. In fact, the opposite is possible. The behaviors of highly intelligent children may be so attractive that they cause parents to interact more favorably. Or a third variable that we did not even consider, such as the amount of noise and distraction in the home, may cause changes in both parental interaction and children's intelligence.

In correlational studies and in other types of research designs, investigators often examine relationships by using a **correlation coefficient**—a number that describes how two measures, or variables, are associated with each other. We will encounter the correlation coefficient in discussing research findings throughout this book, so let's look at what it is and how it is interpreted. A correlation coefficient can range in value from +1.00 to –1.00. The *magnitude, or size, of the number* shows the *strength of the relationship.* A zero correlation indicates no relationship; the closer the value is to +1.00 or –1.00, the stronger the relationship (see Figure 1.6). For instance, a correlation of –.78 is high, –.52 is moderate, and –.18 is low. Note, however, that correlations of +.52 and –.52 are equally strong. The *sign of the number* (+ or –) refers to the *direction of the relationship.* A positive sign (+) means that as one variable *increases,* the other also *increases.* A negative sign (–) indicates that as one variable *increases,* the other *decreases.*

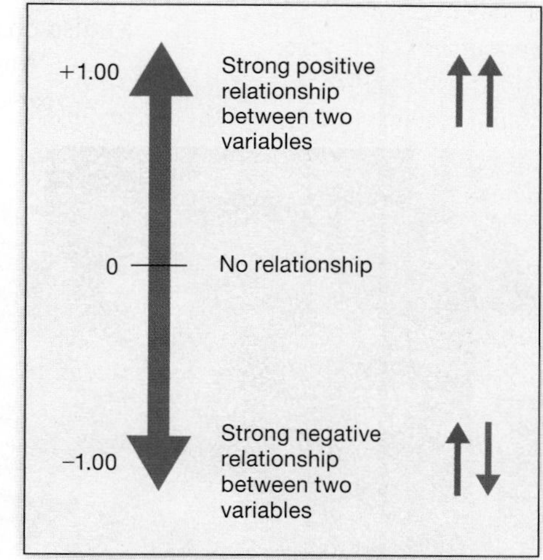

FIGURE 1.6 The meaning of correlation coefficients. The magnitude of the number indicates the *strength* of the relationship. The sign of the number (+ or –) indicates the *direction* of the relationship.

Let's look at some examples of how a correlation coefficient works. One researcher reported a +.55 correlation between a measure of maternal language stimulation and the size of 2-year-olds' vocabularies (Hoff, 2003). In another study, the extent to which mothers spoke harshly, interrupted, and controlled their 4-year-olds' play correlated negatively with children's compliance, at –.31 for boys and –.42 for girls (Smith et al., 2004).

Are you tempted to conclude from these correlations that maternal behaviors influenced children's responses? Although the researchers suspected this was so, they could not be sure of cause and effect. Can you think of other possible explanations? Finding a relationship in a correlational study suggests that tracking down its cause—using a more powerful experimental strategy, if possible—would be worthwhile.

Experimental Design

An **experimental design** permits inferences about cause and effect because researchers use an evenhanded procedure to assign people to two or more treatment conditions. In an experiment, the events and behaviors of interest are divided into two types: independent and dependent variables. The **independent variable** is the one the investigator expects to cause changes in another variable. The **dependent variable** is the one the investigator expects to be influenced by the independent variable. Cause-and-effect relationships can be detected because the researcher directly *controls* or *manipulates* changes in the independent variable by exposing participants to the treatment conditions. Then the researcher compares their performance on measures of the dependent variable.

In one *laboratory experiment,* researchers explored the impact of adults' angry interactions on children's adjustment (El-Sheikh, Cummings, & Reiter, 1996). They hypothesized that the way angry encounters end (independent variable) affects children's emotional reactions (dependent variable). Four- and 5-year-olds were brought one at a time to a laboratory, accompanied by their mothers. One group was exposed to an *unresolved-anger treatment,* in which two adult actors entered the room and argued but did not work out their disagreements. The other group witnessed a resolved-anger treatment, in which the adults ended their disputes by apologizing and compromising. When witnessing a follow-up adult conflict, children in the *resolved-anger treatment* showed fewer behavioral signs of distress, such as anxious facial expressions and seeking closeness to their mothers. The experiment revealed that anger resolution can reduce the stressful impact of adult conflict on children.

In experimental studies, investigators must control for participants' characteristics that could reduce the accuracy of their findings. In the study just described, if a greater number of children from homes high in parental conflict ended up in the unresolved-anger treatment, we could not tell what produced the results—the independent variable or the children's family backgrounds. To protect against this problem, researchers engage in **random assignment** of participants to treatment conditions. By using an unbiased procedure, such as drawing numbers out of a hat or flipping a coin, investigators increase the chances that participants' characteristics will be equally distributed across treatment groups.

Modified Experimental Designs: Field and Natural Experiments. Most experiments are conducted in laboratories, where researchers can achieve the maximum possible control over treatment conditions. But, as we have already indicated, findings obtained in laboratories may not always apply to everyday situations. In *field experiments,* investigators assign participants randomly to treatment conditions in natural settings. In the experiment just described, we can conclude that the emotional climate established by adults affects children's behavior in the laboratory. But does it also do so in daily life?

Another study helps answer this question. Ethnically diverse, poverty-stricken families with a 2-year-old child were randomly assigned to either a brief intervention condition, called the Family Check-Up, or a no-intervention control group. The intervention consisted of three home-based sessions in which a consultant gave parents feedback about their child-rearing practices and their child's adjustment, explored parents' willingness to improve, and offered follow-up sessions on parenting practices and other concerns (Brennan et al., 2013; Dishion et al., 2008; Shaw et al., 2016). Findings showed that families assigned to the Family Check-Up (but not controls) gained in positive parenting, which predicted a reduction in child problem behaviors and higher academic achievement when the children reached school age. Lessening of aggression was greatest for children living in neighborhoods with the deepest poverty.

▶ When researchers cannot randomly assign children to conditions in the real world, they sometimes conduct natural experiments using treatments that already exist. For example, the learning environments of different preschools might be compared to explore the impact of teacher–child interaction on language and literacy development.

Often researchers cannot randomly assign participants and manipulate conditions in the real world. Sometimes they compromise by conducting *natural,* or *quasi-, experiments,* comparing treatments that already exist, such as different family environments, child-care centers, or schools. These studies differ from correlational research only in that groups of participants are carefully chosen to ensure that their characteristics are as much alike as possible. In this way, investigators do their best to rule out alternative explanations for their treatment effects. But despite these efforts, natural experiments cannot achieve the precision and rigor of true experimental research.

TABLE 1.6
Strengths and Limitations of Research Designs

DESIGN	DESCRIPTION	STRENGTHS	LIMITATIONS
GENERAL			
Correlational	The investigator obtains information on participants without altering their experiences.	Permits study of relationships between variables.	Does not permit inferences about cause-and-effect relationships.
Experimental	Through random assignment of participants to treatment conditions, the investigator manipulates an independent variable and examines its effect on a dependent variable. Can be conducted in the laboratory or the natural environment.	Permits inferences about cause-and-effect relationships.	When conducted in the laboratory, findings may not generalize to the real world. In *field experiments,* control over the treatment is usually weaker than in the laboratory. In *natural,* or *quasi-, experiments,* lack of random assignment substantially reduces the precision of research.
DEVELOPMENTAL			
Longitudinal	The investigator studies the same group of participants repeatedly at different ages.	Permits study of common patterns and individual differences in development and relationships between early and later events and behaviors.	Age-related changes may be distorted because of participant dropout, practice effects, and cohort effects.
Cross-sectional	The investigator studies groups of participants differing in age at the same point in time.	More efficient than the longitudinal design. Not plagued by such problems as participant dropout and practice effects.	Does not permit study of individual developmental trends. Age differences may be distorted because of cohort effects.
Sequential	The investigator conducts several similar cross-sectional or longitudinal studies (called sequences). These might study participants over the same ages but in different years, or they might study participants over different ages but during the same years.	When the design includes longitudinal sequences, permits both longitudinal and cross-sectional comparisons. Also reveals cohort effects. Permits tracking of age-related changes more efficiently than the longitudinal design.	May have the same problems as longitudinal and cross-sectional strategies, but the design itself helps identify difficulties.

To help you compare correlational and experimental designs, Table 1.6 summarizes their strengths and limitations. It also includes an overview of designs for studying development, to which we turn next.

Designs for Studying Development

Scientists interested in child development require information about the way research participants change over time. To answer questions about development, they must extend correlational and experimental approaches to include measurements at different ages using longitudinal and cross-sectional designs.

The Longitudinal Design. In a **longitudinal design,** participants are studied repeatedly, and changes are noted as they get older. The time spanned may be relatively short (a few months to several years) or very long (a decade or even a lifetime). The longitudinal approach has two major strengths. First, because it tracks the performance of each person over time, researchers can identify common patterns as well as individual differences in development. Second, longitudinal studies permit investigators to examine relationships between early and later events and behaviors. Let's illustrate these ideas.

A group of researchers wondered whether children who display extreme personality styles—either angry and explosive or shy and withdrawn—retain the same dispositions when they become adults and, if so, what the consequences are for long-term adjustment. To answer these questions, the researchers delved into the archives of the Guidance Study, a well-known longitudinal investigation initiated in 1928 at the University of California, Berkeley, that continued for several decades (Caspi, Elder, & Bem, 1987, 1988).

Results revealed that between ages 8 and 30, a good number of individuals remained the same in personality style, whereas others changed substantially. When stability did occur, it appeared to be due to a "snowballing effect," in which children evoked responses from adults and peers that acted to maintain their dispositions. Explosive youngsters were likely to be treated with anger, whereas shy children were apt to be ignored. As a result, explosive children came to view others as hostile; shy children regarded them as unfriendly (Caspi & Roberts, 2001). Together, these factors led explosive children to sustain or increase their unruliness and shy children to continue to withdraw—patterns that tended to persist into adulthood and to negatively affect adjustment to marriage, parenting, and work life. Shy women, however, were an exception. Because a withdrawn, unassertive style was socially acceptable for women at that time, they showed no special adjustment problems.

Problems in Conducting Longitudinal Research. Despite their strengths, longitudinal investigations pose a number of problems. For example, participants may move away or drop out of the research for other reasons. This biases the sample so that it no longer represents the population to whom researchers would like to generalize their findings. Also, from repeated study, people may become more aware of their own thoughts, feelings, and actions and revise them in ways that have little to do with age-related change. In addition, they may become "test-wise." Their performance may improve as a result of *practice effects*—better test-taking skills and increased familiarity with the test—not because of factors commonly associated with development.

The most widely discussed threat to the accuracy of longitudinal findings is **cohort effects:** Individuals born in the same time period are influenced by a particular set of historical and cultural conditions. Results based on one cohort may not apply to people developing at other times. For example, consider the findings on female shyness described in the preceding section, which were gathered in the 1950s. Today's shy adolescent girls and young women tend to be poorly adjusted—a difference that may be due to changes in gender roles in Western societies. Shy adults, whether male or female, feel more anxious and depressed, have fewer social supports, are delayed in forming romantic partnerships, and do less well in educational and career attainment than their agemates (Karevold et al., 2012; Poole, Van Lieshout, & Schmidt, 2017; Schmidt et al., 2017). Similarly, a longitudinal study of social development would probably result in quite different findings if it were carried out in the first decade of the twenty-first century, around the time of World War II, or during the Great Depression of the 1930s.

SPENCER PLATT/GETTY IMAGES

▶ These refugees being helped ashore in Greece are among millions of Syrians who have been displaced by or have fled their country's civil war. Their lives have been dramatically altered by their wartime and migration experiences—a cohort effect deemed the largest humanitarian crisis of contemporary times.

Cohort effects don't just operate broadly on an entire generation. They also occur when specific experiences influence some children but not others in the same generation. For example, children who witnessed the terrorist attacks of September 11, 2001 (either because they were near Ground Zero or because they saw injury and death on TV), or who lost a parent in the disaster, were far more likely than other children to display persistent emotional problems, including intense fear, anxiety, and depression (Mullett-Hume et al., 2008; Rosen & Cohen, 2010).

The Cross-Sectional Design. The length of time it takes for many behaviors to change, even in limited longitudinal studies, has led researchers to turn to a more efficient strategy for studying development. In the **cross-sectional design,** groups of people differing in age are studied at the same point in time. Because participants are measured only once, researchers need not be concerned about such difficulties as participant dropout or practice effects.

A study in which students in grades 3, 6, 9, and 12 filled out a questionnaire about their sibling relationships provides a good illustration (Buhrmester & Furman, 1990). Findings revealed that sibling interaction was characterized by greater equality and less power assertion with age. Also, feelings of sibling companionship declined in adolescence. The researchers speculated that as later-born children become more competent and independent, they no longer need, and are probably less willing to accept, direction from older siblings. Also, as adolescents move from psychological dependence on the family to greater involvement with peers, they may have less time and emotional need to invest in siblings. Subsequent research has confirmed this age-related trend (Whiteman, Solmeyer, & McHale, 2015).

Problems in Conducting Cross-Sectional Research. Despite its convenience, cross-sectional research does not provide evidence about development at the level at which it actually occurs: the individual. For example, in the cross-sectional study of sibling relationships just discussed, comparisons are limited to age-group averages. We cannot tell if important individual differences exist. Indeed, longitudinal findings reveal that adolescents vary considerably in the changing quality of their sibling relationships. Although many become more distant, others become more supportive and intimate, and still others more rivalrous and antagonistic (Dirks et al., 2015; Kim et al., 2006; McHale, Updegraff, & Whiteman, 2012).

Cross-sectional studies—especially those that cover a wide age span—have another problem. Like longitudinal research, they can be threatened by cohort effects. For example, comparisons of 5-year-old cohorts and 10-year-old cohorts—groups born and reared in different years—may not really represent age-related changes. Instead, they may reflect unique experiences associated with the historical period in which the age groups were growing up.

Improving Developmental Designs

Researchers have devised ways of building on the strengths and minimizing the weaknesses of longitudinal and cross-sectional approaches. Several modified developmental designs have resulted.

Sequential Designs. To overcome some of the limitations of traditional developmental designs, investigators sometimes use **sequential designs,** in which they conduct several similar cross-sectional or longitudinal studies (called *sequences*). The sequences might study participants over the same ages but in different years, or they might study participants over different ages but during the same years. Figure 1.7 illustrates the first of these options. As it also reveals, some sequential designs combine longitudinal and cross-sectional strategies, an approach that has two advantages:

- We can find out whether cohort effects are operating by comparing participants of the same age who were born in different years. In Figure 1.7, for example, we can compare the three longitudinal samples at seventh, eighth, and ninth grades. If they do not differ, we can rule out cohort effects.

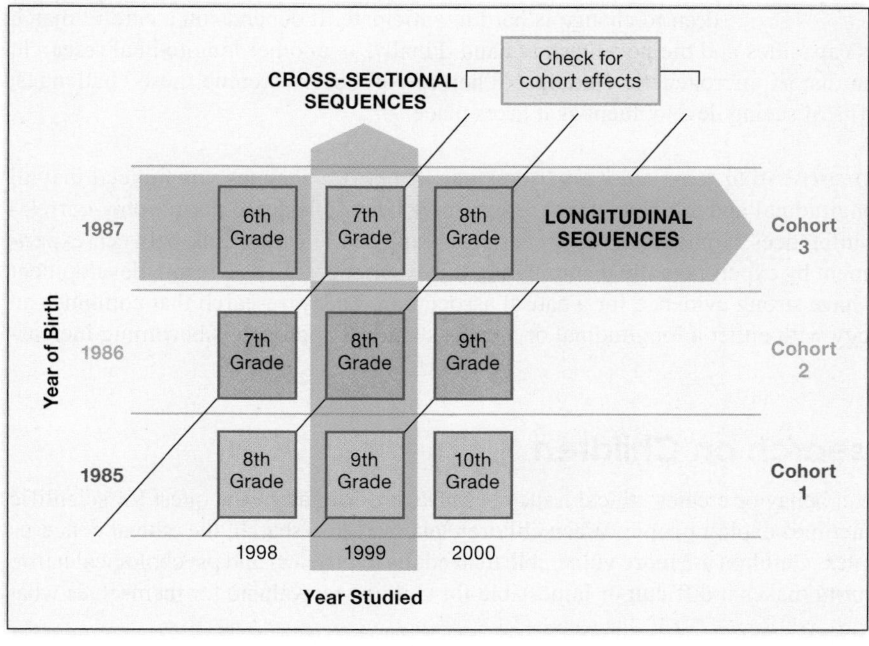

FIGURE 1.7 Example of a sequential design. Three cohorts, born in 1985 (blue), 1986 (orange), and 1987 (pink), are followed longitudinally for three years. Testing the cohorts in overlapping grades enables researchers to check for cohort effects by comparing participants born in different years when they reach the same grade (see diagonals). In a study using this design, same-grade adolescents who were members of different cohorts scored similarly on a questionnaire assessing family harmony, indicating no cohort effects. By following each cohort for just three years, the investigator could infer a developmental trend across five years, from sixth to tenth grade.

- We can make longitudinal and cross-sectional comparisons. If outcomes are similar in both, we can be especially confident about our findings.

In a study that used the design in Figure 1.7, researchers wanted to find out whether family harmony changed as teenagers experienced the dramatic physical and psychological changes of adolescence (Baer, 2002). A questionnaire assessing emotional bonding among family members was given to three adolescent cohorts, each born a year apart. In longitudinal follow-ups, each cohort again responded to the questionnaire during the following two years.

Findings for the three cohorts converged: All reported (1) a slight decline in family harmony with grade and (2) similar levels of family harmony as they reached the same grade, confirming that there were no cohort effects. Therefore, the researchers concluded that family closeness diminishes steadily from sixth to tenth grade. They noted, however, that the change is mild—not enough to threaten supportive family ties.

When sequential designs do uncover cohort effects, they help explain diversity in development. Yet to date, only a small number of sequential studies have been conducted.

▶ How do these first graders make use of manipulatives to master place value in arithmetic? A microgenetic design, which permits researchers to follow children's mastery of a challenging task, is uniquely suited to answering this question.

Microgenetic Design. In the examples of developmental research just discussed, observations of children are fairly widely spaced—once a year or every few years. When we observe only occasionally, we can describe development, but we cannot easily capture the processes that produce it.

The microgenetic design, an adaptation of the longitudinal approach, presents children with a novel task and follows their mastery over a series of closely spaced sessions. Within this "microcosm" of development, researchers observe how change occurs (Flynn & Siegler, 2007; Kuhn, 1995). The microgenetic design has been used to trace infants' mastery of motor skills, such as crawling and walking; the strategies children use to acquire new knowledge in reading, math, or science; and gains in social competence during childhood and adolescence (Adolph et al., 2012; Booker & Dunsmore, 2017; Laski & Siegler, 2014). Investigators try to conduct microgenetic research on participants who are in transition—ready to master the particular skill being studied.

Microgenetic studies are difficult to carry out. Researchers must pore over hours of recorded information, analyzing each participant's behavior many times. And the time required for children to change is hard to anticipate. It depends on a careful match between the child's capacities and the novel task at hand. Finally, as in other longitudinal research, practice effects can distort microgenetic findings. When researchers overcome these challenges, they reap the benefits of seeing development as it takes place.

Combining Experimental and Developmental Designs. Perhaps you noticed that all the examples of longitudinal and cross-sectional research we have considered permit only correlational, not causal, inferences. Sometimes researchers can explore the causal link between experiences and development by experimentally manipulating the experiences. If, as a result, development improves, then we have strong evidence for a causal association. Today, research that combines an experimental strategy with either a longitudinal or a cross-sectional approach is becoming increasingly common.

Ethics in Research on Children

Research into human behavior creates ethical issues because, unfortunately, the quest for scientific knowledge can sometimes exploit people. When children take part in research, the ethical concerns are especially complex. Children are more vulnerable than adults to physical and psychological harm. In addition, immaturity makes it difficult or impossible for children to evaluate for themselves what participation in research will mean. For these reasons, special ethical guidelines for research have been developed by the federal government, by funding agencies, and by research-oriented associations, such as the American Psychological Association (2017) and the Society for Research in Child Development (2007).

Table 1.7 presents a summary of children's basic research rights drawn from these guidelines. After examining them, read about the following research situations, each of which poses a serious ethical dilemma. What precautions do you think should be taken in each instance? Is either so threatening to children's well-being that it should not be carried out?

- In a study of moral development, an investigator wants to assess children's ability to resist temptation by videotaping their behavior without their knowledge. She promises 7-year-olds a prize for solving difficult puzzles but tells them not to look at a classmate's correct solutions, which are deliberately placed at the back of the room. Informing children ahead of time that cheating is being studied or that their behavior is being monitored will defeat the purpose of the study.
- A researcher is interviewing fifth graders about their experiences with bullying. One child describes frequent name-calling and derogatory comments by her older sister. Although the child is unhappy, she wants to handle the problem on her own. If the researcher alerts the girl's parents to provide protection and help, he will break his promise to keep participants' responses private.

TABLE 1.7
Children's Research Rights

RESEARCH RIGHT	DESCRIPTION
Protection from harm	Children have the right to be protected from physical or psychological harm in research. If in doubt about the harmful effects of research, investigators should seek the opinion of others. When harm seems possible, investigators should find other means for obtaining the desired information or abandon the research.
Informed consent	All participants, including children, have the right to have explained to them, in language appropriate to their level of understanding, all aspects of the research that may affect their willingness to participate. When children are participants, informed consent of parents as well as others who act on the child's behalf (such as school officials) should be obtained, preferably in writing, along with the child's written or verbal assent (agreement) for participation. Children, and the adults responsible for them, have the right to discontinue participation in the research at any time.
Privacy	Children have the right to concealment of their identity on all information collected in the course of research. They also have this right with respect to written reports and any informal discussions about the research.
Knowledge of results	Children and the adults responsible for them have the right to be informed of the results of research in language that is appropriate to their level of understanding.
Beneficial treatments	If experimental treatments believed to be beneficial are under investigation, participants in control groups have the right to alternative beneficial treatments (if available) or to the same treatment (if found to be effective) once the research is complete.

Sources: American Psychological Association, 2017; Society for Research in Child Development, 2007.

Virtually every organization that has devised ethical principles for research has concluded that conflicts arising in research situations do not have simple right-or-wrong answers. The ultimate responsibility for the ethical integrity of research lies with the investigator. But researchers are advised—and often required—to seek advice from others. Committees for this purpose, called *institutional review boards (IRBs),* exist in colleges, universities, and other institutions, which follow U.S. federal guidelines for the protection of human subjects. If any risks to the safety and welfare of participants outweigh the worth of the research, then preference is always given to the participants' interests.

The ethical principle of *informed consent* requires special interpretation when participants cannot fully appreciate the research goals and activities. Parental consent is meant to protect the safety of children. But as soon as they are old enough to appreciate the purpose of the research, and certainly by age 7, children's own informed *assent,* or agreement, should be obtained in addition to parental consent. Around age 7, changes in children's thinking permit them to better understand basic scientific principles and the needs of others. Researchers should respect and enhance these new capacities by giving children a full explanation of research activities in language they can understand (Birbeck & Drummond, 2015).

Extra care must be taken when telling children that the information they provide will be kept confidential and that they can end their participation at any time. Even adolescents may not understand, and sometimes do not believe, these promises (Bruzzese & Fisher, 2003). In certain ethnic minority communities, where deference to authority and meeting the needs of a guest (the researcher)

▶ Extra steps must be taken to protect children's research rights. Although this 8-year-old responds to the interviewer's questions, she may not know that she has the right to withdraw from the study at any time without negative consequences.

are highly valued, children and parents may be particularly likely to consent or assent when they would rather not do so (Fisher et al., 2002).

Careful attention to informed consent and assent helps resolve dilemmas about relaying children's responses to parents, teachers, or other authorities when those responses suggest that the child's welfare is at risk. Children can be told in advance that if they report that someone is harming them, the researcher will tell an appropriate adult to take action to ensure the child's safety (Jennifer & Cowie, 2009).

Finally, all ethical guidelines advise that special precautions be taken in the use of deception and concealment, as occurs when researchers observe people from behind one-way mirrors, give them false feedback about their performance, or do not tell them the truth about the real purpose of the research. When these procedures are used with adults, *debriefing,* in which the investigator provides a full account and justification of the activities, occurs after the research session is over. Debriefing should also be done with children, and it sometimes works well. But young children often lack the cognitive skills to understand the reasons for deceptive procedures and, despite explanations, even older children may leave the research situation questioning the honesty of adults. Ethical standards permit deception if investigators satisfy IRBs that such practices are necessary. Nevertheless, because deception may have serious emotional consequences for some children, many experts in research ethics believe that investigators should use it only if the risk of harm is minimal.

ASK YOURSELF

CONNECT Review the study of the Family Check-Up, described on page 30. Why is it ethically important for researchers to offer the intervention to the no-intervention control group after completion of the study? (Hint: Refer to Table 1.7 on page 35.)

APPLY A researcher compares children who attended summer leadership camps with those who attended athletic camps. She finds that those who attended the leadership camps are friendlier. Should the investigator tell parents that sending children to leadership camps will make them more sociable? Why or why not?

REFLECT Suppose a researcher asks you to enroll your baby in a 10-year longitudinal study. What factors would lead you to agree and to stay involved? Do your answers shed light on why longitudinal studies often have biased samples? Explain.

CHAPTER 1 SUMMARY

The Field of Child Development *(p. 2)*

1.1 ***Describe the field of child development, along with factors that stimulated its expansion.***

- **Child development** is a field devoted to understanding constancy and change from conception through adolescence. It is part of a larger interdisciplinary field known as **developmental science.** Research on child development has been stimulated by both scientific curiosity and social pressures to improve children's lives.

1.2 ***Explain how child development is typically divided into domains and periods.***

- Development is often divided into physical, cognitive, and emotional and social domains. These domains are not really distinct; rather, they combine in an integrated, holistic fashion.
- Researchers generally divide the flow of time into the following age periods: (1) prenatal (conception to birth), (2) infancy and toddlerhood (birth to 2 years), (3) early childhood (2 to 6 years), (4) middle childhood (6 to 11 years), and adolescence (11 to 18 years).

Basic Issues *(p. 4)*

1.3 ***Identify three basic issues on which theories of child development take a stand.***

- Each **theory** of child development takes a stand on three fundamental issues: (1) development as a **continuous** process or a series of **discontinuous stages;** (2) one course of development characterizing all children, or many possible courses, depending on **contexts;** (3) development influenced more by genetic or environmental factors (the **nature–nurture controversy**) and stable or characterized by substantial **plasticity.**

- Recent theories have shifted toward a balanced stand on these issues. And contemporary researchers realize that answers may vary across domains of development and even, as research on **resilience** illustrates, across individuals. More researchers are endorsing a developmental systems perspective, which views developmental change as shaped by a complex network of genetic/biological, psychological, and social influences.

Scientific Beginnings *(p. 8)*

1.4 ***Describe major early influences on the scientific study of child development.***

- Darwin's theory of evolution influenced important developmental theories and inspired scientific child study. In the early twentieth century, Hall and Gesell introduced the **normative approach,** which measured behaviors of large groups to yield descriptive facts about development.
- Binet and Simon constructed the first successful intelligence test, which sparked interest in individual differences in development.

Mid-Twentieth-Century Theories *(p. 9)*

1.5 ***Describe theories that influenced child development research in the mid-twentieth century.***

- In the 1930s and 1940s, psychiatrists and social workers turned to the **psychoanalytic perspective** for help in treating children's emotional problems. In Freud's **psychosexual theory,** the individual moves through five stages, during which three portions of the personality—id, ego, and superego—become integrated. Erikson's **psychosocial theory** expands Freud's theory, emphasizing the development of culturally relevant attitudes and skills and the lifespan nature of development.

ANTONIA TOZER/GETTY IMAGES/AWL IMAGES RM

- **Behaviorism** focuses on directly observable events (stimuli and responses). Pavlov's studies of animal learning led to the discovery of classical conditioning. B. F. Skinner's work led operant conditioning to become a broadly applied learning principle.
- A related approach, Albert Bandura's **social learning theory,** focuses on modeling as a major means of learning. Its most recent revision stresses the role of cognition, or thinking, in children's imitation and learning and is known as a social-cognitive approach.

© LAURA DWIGHT PHOTOGRAPHY

- Behaviorism and social learning theory gave rise to **applied behavior analysis,** in which procedures of conditioning and modeling are used to eliminate undesirable behaviors and increase desirable responses.
- Piaget's **cognitive-developmental theory** emphasizes that children actively construct knowledge as they move through four stages, beginning with the baby's sensorimotor action patterns and ending with the abstract, systematic reasoning system of the adolescent and adult. Piaget's work has stimulated a wealth of research on children's thinking and encouraged educational programs that emphasize children's discovery learning.

Recent Theoretical Perspectives *(p. 15)*

1.6 ***Describe recent theoretical perspectives on child development.***

- **Information processing** views the mind as a complex symbol-manipulating system through which information flows. Because this approach provides precise accounts of how children and adults tackle cognitive tasks, its findings have important implications for education.
- Researchers in **developmental cognitive neuroscience** study the relationship between changes in the brain and the developing child's cognitive processing and behavior patterns. Investigators in **developmental social neuroscience** are examining relationships between changes in the brain and emotional and social development.
- Four contemporary perspectives emphasize *contexts* for development. **Ethology** stresses the adaptive value of behavior and inspired the **sensitive period** concept. In **evolutionary developmental psychology,** which extends this emphasis, researchers seek to understand the adaptiveness of species-wide competencies as they change with age.
- Vygotsky's **sociocultural theory,** which focuses on how culture is transmitted from one generation to the next through social interaction, views cognitive development as a socially mediated process. Through cooperative dialogues with more expert members of society, children come to use language to guide their own thought and actions and acquire culturally relevant knowledge and skills.

© FLORESCO PRODUCTIONS/CORBIS

- The third perspective, **ecological systems theory,** views the child as developing within a complex system of relationships affected by multiple, nested layers of the surrounding environment—**microsystem, mesosystem, exosystem,** and **macrosystem.** The **chronosystem** represents the dynamic, ever-changing nature of individuals and their experiences.
- According to the **dynamic systems perspective,** the child's mind, body, and physical and social worlds form an integrated system that guides mastery of new skills. A change in any part of the system prompts the child to reorganize his or her behavior so the various components work together again, but in a more complex, effective way. The dynamic systems perspective aims to improve our understanding of variability in children's development.

Comparing Theories *(p. 23)*

1.7 ***Identify the stand taken by each major theory on the three basic issues of child development.***

- Theories vary in their focus on different domains of development and in their view of how development occurs. (For a full summary, see Table 1.4 on page 24.)

Studying Development *(p. 23)*

1.8 ***Describe research methods commonly used to study child development.***

- **Naturalistic observations,** gathered in everyday environments, permit researchers to see directly the everyday behaviors they hope to explain. **Structured observations,** which take place in laboratories, give every participant an equal opportunity to display the behaviors of interest.
- Self-report methods can be flexible and open-ended like the **clinical interview**. Alternatively, in **structured interviews**—including tests and questionnaires—each participant is asked the same questions in the same way. Investigators use the **clinical, or case study, method** to obtain an in-depth understanding of a single individual.
- Researchers have adapted observational and self-report methods to permit direct comparisons of cultures. To understand the unique values and social processes of a culture or distinct social group, researchers rely on **ethnography,** engaging in participant observation.

© KEITH DANNEMILLER/ALAMY STOCK PHOTO

1.9 ***Distinguish between correlational and experimental research designs, noting the strengths and limitations of each.***

- The **correlational design** examines relationships between variables without altering participants' experiences. A **correlation coefficient** is often used to measure the association between variables. Correlational studies can help identify relationships that are worth exploring with a more powerful experimental strategy.
- An **experimental design** permits inferences about cause and effect. Researchers manipulate an **independent variable** by exposing participants to two or more treatment conditions. Then they determine what effect this variable has on a **dependent variable. Random assignment** to treatment conditions reduces the chances that participants' characteristics will affect the accuracy of experimental findings.
- Field and natural, or quasi-, experiments compare treatments in natural environments. However, these approaches are less rigorous than laboratory experiments.

1.10 ***Describe designs for studying development, noting the strengths and limitations of each.***

- The **longitudinal design** permits researchers to identify common patterns as well as individual differences in development and to examine relationships between early and later events and behaviors. Longitudinal research poses several problems, including biased sampling, practice effects, and **cohort effects**—difficulty generalizing to children developing at other historical times.
- The **cross-sectional design** is a more efficient way to study development, but it is limited to comparisons of age-group averages and can be vulnerable to cohort effects.
- **Sequential designs** compare participants of the same age who were born in different years to determine whether cohort effects are operating. When sequential designs combine longitudinal and cross-sectional strategies, researchers can see if outcomes are similar, for added confidence in their findings.
- Combining experimental and developmental designs permits researchers to examine causal influences on development.

1.11 ***Discuss special ethical concerns that arise in research on children.***

- Because of their immaturity, children are especially vulnerable to harm and often cannot evaluate the risks and benefits of research participation. Ethical guidelines and institutional review boards help ensure that children's research rights are protected.
- Besides obtaining informed consent from parents and others who act on children's behalf, researchers should seek the informed assent of children 7 years and older. The use of deception in research with children is especially risky because it may undermine their basic faith in the honesty of adults.

IMPORTANT TERMS AND CONCEPTS

applied behavior analysis (p. 12)
behaviorism (p. 11)
child development (p. 2)
chronosystem (p. 21)
clinical interview (p. 26)
clinical, or case study, method (p. 26)
cognitive-developmental theory (p. 13)
cohort effects (p. 32)
contexts (p. 6)
continuous development (p. 5)
correlation coefficient (p. 29)
correlational design (p. 29)
cross-sectional design (p. 32)
dependent variable (p. 29)
developmental cognitive neuroscience (p. 16)
developmental science (p. 2)
developmental social neuroscience (p. 16)
discontinuous development (p. 5)
dynamic systems perspective (p. 22)
ecological systems theory (p. 19)
ethnography (p. 27)
ethology (p. 17)
evolutionary developmental psychology (p. 18)
exosystem (p. 20)
experimental design (p. 29)
independent variable (p. 29)
information processing (p. 15)
longitudinal design (p. 31)
macrosystem (p. 20)
mesosystem (p. 20)
microsystem (p. 20)
naturalistic observation (p. 24)
nature–nurture controversy (p. 6)
normative approach (p. 8)
plasticity (p. 6)
psychoanalytic perspective (p. 9)
psychosexual theory (p. 9)
psychosocial theory (p. 10)
random assignment (p. 30)
resilience (p. 7)
sensitive period (p. 17)
sequential designs (p. 33)
social learning theory (p. 12)
sociocultural theory (p. 18)
stage (p. 5)
structured interview (p. 26)
structured observation (p. 25)
theory (p. 4)

CHAPTER

2 Genetic and Environmental Foundations

Heredity and environment combine in intricate ways, making members of this multigenerational extended family both alike and different in physical characteristics and behavior.

© WALTER HODGES/FLIRT/ALAMY STOCK PHOTO

WHAT'S AHEAD IN CHAPTER 2

"It's a girl!" announces the doctor, holding up the squalling newborn baby as her parents gaze with amazement at their miraculous creation.

"A girl! We've named her Sarah!" exclaims the proud father to eager relatives waiting for news of their new family member.

As we join these parents in thinking about how this wondrous being came into existence and imagining her future, we are struck by many questions. How could this baby, equipped with everything necessary for life outside the womb, have developed from the union of two tiny cells? What ensures that Sarah will, in due time, roll over, reach for objects, walk, talk, make friends, learn, imagine, and create—just like other typical children born before her? Why is she a girl and not a boy, dark-haired rather than blond, calm and patient rather than energetic and distractible? What difference will it make that Sarah is given a name and place in one family, community, nation, and culture rather than another?

To answer these questions, this chapter takes a close look at the foundations of development: heredity and environment. Because nature has prepared us for survival, all humans have features in common. Yet each of us is also unique. Think about several children you know well, and jot down the most obvious physical and behavioral similarities between them and their parents. Did you find that one child shows combined features of both parents, another resembles just one parent, whereas a third is not like either parent? These directly observable characteristics are called **phenotypes.** They depend in part on the individual's **genotype**—the complex blend of genetic information that determines our species and influences all our unique characteristics. Yet phenotypes are also affected by each person's lifelong history of experiences.

© LAURA DWIGHT PHOTOGRAPHY

We begin our discussion with a review of basic genetic principles that help explain similarities and differences among children in appearance and behavior. Then we turn to aspects of the environment that play powerful roles in children's lives. As our discussion proceeds, some findings may surprise you. For example, many people believe that when children inherit unfavorable characteristics, little can be done to help them. Others are convinced that the damage done to a child by a harmful environment can easily be corrected. As we will see, neither of these assumptions is true. Rather, heredity and environment continuously collaborate, each modifying the power of the other to influence the course of development.

Genetic Foundations

2.1 Explain what genes are and how they are transmitted from one generation to the next.

2.2 Describe various patterns of gene–gene interaction.

2.3 Describe major chromosomal abnormalities, and explain how they occur.

Within each of the trillions of cells in the human body (except red blood cells) is a control center, or *nucleus,* that contains rodlike structures called **chromosomes,** which store and transmit genetic information. Human chromosomes come in 23 matching pairs; an exception is the XY pair in males, which we will discuss shortly. Each member of a pair corresponds to the other in size, shape, and genetic functions. One chromosome is inherited from the mother and one from the father (see Figure 2.1).

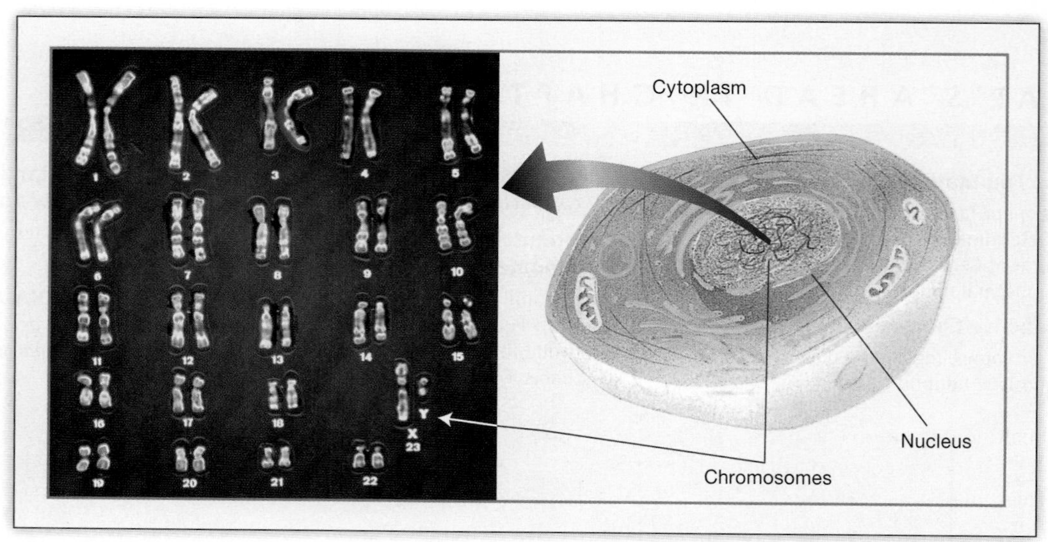

© CNRI/SCIENCE PHOTO LIBRARY/PHOTO RESEARCHERS, INC.

FIGURE 2.1 A karyotype, or photograph, of human chromosomes. The 46 chromosomes shown on the left were isolated from a human cell, stained, greatly magnified, and arranged in pairs according to decreasing size of the upper "arm" of each chromosome. The twenty-third pair, XY, reveals that the cell donor is a genetic male. In a genetic female, this pair would be XX.

The Genetic Code

Chromosomes are made up of a chemical substance called **deoxyribonucleic acid (DNA).** As Figure 2.2 shows, DNA is a long, double-stranded molecule that looks like a twisted ladder. Each rung of the ladder consists of a specific pair of chemical substances called *bases,* joined together between the two sides. It is this sequence of base pairs that provides genetic instructions. A **gene** is a segment of DNA along the length of the chromosome. Genes can be of different lengths—perhaps 100 to several thousand ladder rungs long. An estimated 19,000 to 20,000 **protein-coding genes,** which directly affect our body's characteristics, lie along the human chromosomes (Ezkuria et al., 2014). They send instructions for making a rich assortment of proteins to the *cytoplasm,* the area surrounding the cell nucleus. Proteins, which trigger chemical reactions throughout the body, are the biological foundation on which our characteristics are built. An additional 18,000 **regulator genes** modify the instructions given by protein-coding genes, greatly complicating their genetic impact (Pennisi, 2012).

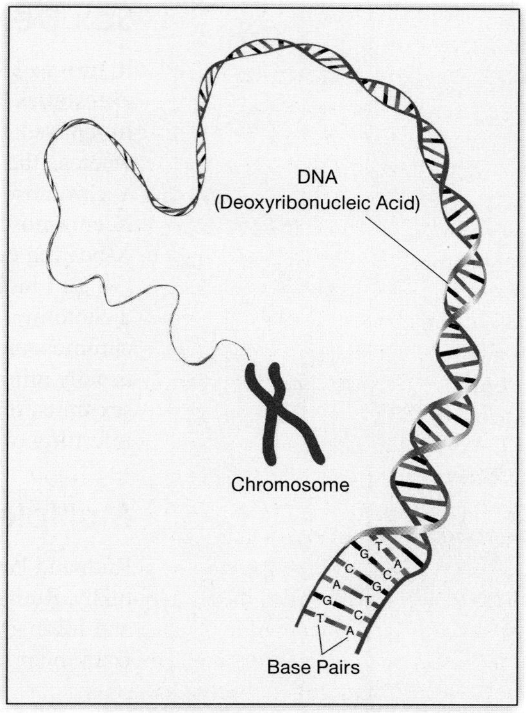

We share most of our DNA with other mammals, especially primates. About 95 percent of chimpanzee and human DNA is identical. And the genetic variation from one human to the next is even less: Individuals around the world are about 99.6 percent genetically identical (Tishkoff & Kidd, 2004). But many human DNA segments that appear like those of chimpanzees have undergone duplications and rearrangements with other segments. So in actuality, the species-specific genetic material responsible for the attributes that make us human, from our upright gait to our extraordinary language and cognitive capacities, is extensive (Preuss, 2012). Furthermore, it takes a change in only a single DNA base pair to influence human traits. And such tiny changes generally combine in unique ways across multiple genes, amplifying human variability.

FIGURE 2.2 DNA's ladderlike structure. A gene is a segment of DNA along the length of the chromosome, varying from perhaps 100 to several thousand ladder rungs long. The pairings of bases across the rungs of the ladder are very specific: Adenine (A) always appears with thymine (T), and cytosine (C) always appears with guanine (G).

How do humans, with far fewer genes than scientists once thought, manage to develop into such complex beings? The answer lies in the proteins our genes make, which break up and reassemble in staggering variety—about 10 to 20 million altogether. Simpler species have far fewer proteins. Furthermore, the communication system between the cell nucleus and cytoplasm, which fine-tunes gene activity, is more intricate in humans than in simpler organisms. Finally, within the cell, environmental factors modify gene expression. Many such effects are unique to humans and influence brain development (Hernando-Herraez et al., 2013). So even at this microscopic level, biological events of profound developmental significance are the result of *both* genetic and nongenetic forces.

The Sex Cells

New individuals are created when two special cells called **gametes,** or sex cells—the sperm and ovum—combine. A gamete contains only 23 chromosomes, half as many as a regular body cell. Gametes are formed through a cell division process called **meiosis,** which halves the number of chromosomes normally present in body cells. When sperm and ovum unite at conception, the resulting cell, called a **zygote,** will again have 46 chromosomes.

In meiosis, the chromosomes pair up and exchange segments, so that genes from one are replaced by genes from another. Then chance determines which member of each pair will gather with others and end up in the same gamete. These events make the likelihood extremely low—about 1 in 700 trillion—that nontwin siblings will be genetically identical (Gould & Keeton, 1996). The genetic variability produced by meiosis is adaptive: It increases the chances that at least some members of a species will cope with ever-changing environments and will survive.

In the male, the cells from which sperm arise are produced continuously throughout life, so a healthy man can father a child at any age after sexual maturity. The female is born with a bank of ova already present in her ovaries, though recent findings suggest that new ova may arise from ovarian stem cells later on (Virant-Klun, 2015). About 350 to 450 female sex cells will mature during a woman's childbearing years (Moore, Persaud, & Torchia, 2016a).

Sex Determination

Return to Figure 2.1 and note that 22 of the 23 pairs of chromosomes are matching pairs, called **autosomes** (meaning *not* sex chromosomes). The twenty-third pair consists of **sex chromosomes.** In females, this pair is called XX; in males, it is called XY. The X is a relatively long chromosome, whereas the Y is short and carries little genetic material. When gametes form in males, the X and Y chromosomes separate into different sperm cells. The gametes that form in females all carry an X chromosome. Therefore, the genetic sex of the new organism is determined by whether an X-bearing or a Y-bearing sperm fertilizes the ovum.

But biologists caution that human sexual diversity is much wider than a simple male–female dichotomy. As a result of variations in genes or chance events in development, some individuals' sex chromosomes do not match their sexual anatomy. An estimated 1 in every 100 people are affected, usually mildly but occasionally substantially (Ainsworth, 2015). The existence of people with intersex traits, many of whom go through life unaware of their condition unless they seek treatment for infertility or another medical issue, is redefining sex as a spectrum.

Multiple Offspring

Ruth and Peter, a couple I know well, tried for several years to have a child, without success. Eventually, Ruth's doctor prescribed a fertility drug, and twins—Jeannie and Jason—were born. Jeannie and Jason are **fraternal,** or **dizygotic, twins,** the most common type of multiple offspring, resulting from the release and fertilization of two ova. Genetically, they are no more alike than ordinary siblings. Older maternal age, fertility drugs, and in vitro fertilization are major causes of the dramatic rise in fraternal twinning and other multiple births in industrialized nations over the past several decades. Currently, fraternal twins account for 1 in about every 33 births in the United States (Martin et al., 2017).

© RAY EVANS/ALAMY STOCK PHOTO

These identical, or monozygotic, twins were created when a duplicating zygote separated into two clusters of cells, which developed into two individuals with the same genetic makeup.

Twins can also be created when a zygote that has started to duplicate separates into two clusters of cells that develop into two individuals. These are called **identical,** or **monozygotic, twins** because they have the same genetic makeup. The frequency of identical twins is the same around the world—about 1 in every 350 to 400 births (Kulkarni et al., 2013). Animal research has uncovered environmental influences that prompt this type of twinning, including temperature changes, variation in oxygen levels, and late fertilization of the ovum (Lashley, 2007). In a minority of cases, identical twinning runs in families, but this occurs so rarely that it is likely due to chance rather than heredity.

During their early years, children of single births often are healthier and develop more rapidly than twins. Jeannie and Jason, like most twins, were born several weeks prematurely and required special care in the hospital. When the twins came home, Ruth and Peter had to divide time between them. Perhaps because neither baby received as much attention as the average single infant, Jeannie and Jason walked and talked several months later than most children their age, though twins usually catch up in development by middle childhood (Lytton & Gallagher, 2002; Nan et al., 2013; Raz et al., 2016). Parental energies are further strained after the birth of triplets, whose early development is slower than that of twins (Feldman, Eidelman, & Rotenberg, 2004).

Patterns of Gene–Gene Interaction

Jeannie has her parents' dark, straight hair; Jason is curly-haired and blond. The way genes from each parent interact helps explain these outcomes. Recall that except for the XY pair in males, all chromosomes come in matching pairs. Two forms of each gene occur at the same place on the chromosomes, one inherited from the mother and one from the father. Each form of a gene is called an **allele.** If the alleles from both parents are alike, the child is **homozygous** and will display the inherited trait. If the alleles differ, then the child is **heterozygous,** and relationships between the alleles influence the phenotype.

Dominant–Recessive Pattern. In many heterozygous pairings, **dominant–recessive inheritance** occurs: Only one allele affects the child's characteristics. It is called *dominant;* the second allele, which has no effect, is called *recessive.* Hair color is an example. The allele for dark hair is dominant (we can represent it with a capital *D*), whereas the one for blond hair is recessive (symbolized by a lowercase *b*). A child who inherits a homozygous pair of dominant alleles *(DD)* and a child who inherits a heterozygous pair *(Db)* will both be dark-haired, even though their genotypes differ. Blond hair (like Jason's) can result only from having two recessive alleles *(bb).* Still, heterozygous individuals with just one recessive allele *(Db)* can pass that trait to their children. Therefore, they are called **carriers** of the trait.

Most recessive alleles—like those for blond hair, pattern baldness, or nearsightedness—are of little developmental importance. But some cause serious disabilities and diseases. One well-known recessive disorder is *phenylketonuria,* or *PKU,* which affects the way the body breaks down proteins contained in many foods. Infants born with two recessive alleles lack an enzyme that converts one of the basic amino acids that make up proteins (phenylalanine) into a byproduct essential for body functioning (tyrosine). Without this enzyme, phenylalanine quickly builds to toxic levels that damage the central nervous system, causing permanent intellectual disability.

Despite its potentially damaging effects, PKU illustrates that inheriting unfavorable genes does not always lead to an untreatable condition. All U.S. states require that each newborn be given a blood test for PKU. If the disease is found, doctors place the baby on a diet low in phenylalanine. Children who receive this treatment nevertheless show mild deficits in control of attention, memory, planning, decision making, and problem solving, because even small amounts of phenylalanine interfere with brain functioning (DeRoche & Welsh, 2008; Fonnesbeck et al., 2013; Jahja et al., 2014). But as long as dietary treatment begins early and continues, children with PKU usually attain an average level of intelligence and have a normal lifespan.

In dominant–recessive inheritance, if we know the genetic makeup of the parents, we can predict the percentage of children in a family who are likely to display or carry a trait. Figure 2.3 illustrates this for PKU. For a child to inherit the condition, each parent must have a recessive allele. But because of the action of regulator genes, children vary in the degree to which phenylalanine accumulates in their tissues and in the extent to which they respond to treatment.

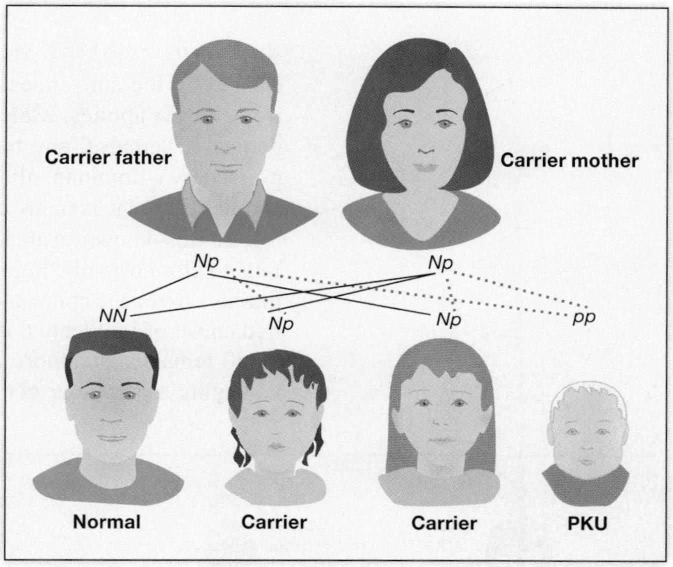

FIGURE 2.3 Dominant–recessive mode of inheritance, as illustrated by PKU. When both parents are heterozygous carriers of the abnormal, recessive allele *(p),* we can predict that 25 percent of their offspring are likely to inherit two normal alleles *(NN),* 50 percent are likely to be carriers of the disorder *(Np),* and 25 percent are likely to inherit the disorder *(pp).* Notice that the PKU-affected child, in contrast to his siblings, has light hair. The recessive gene for PKU affects more than one trait. It also leads to fair coloring.

Only rarely are serious diseases due to dominant alleles. Think about why this is so. Children who inherit the dominant allele always develop the disorder. They seldom live long enough to reproduce, so the harmful dominant allele is eliminated from the family's heredity in a single generation. Some dominant disorders, however, do persist. One is *Huntington disease,* a condition in which the central nervous system degenerates. Its symptoms usually do not appear until age 35 or later, after the person has passed the dominant allele to his or her children.

Incomplete-Dominance Pattern. In some heterozygous circumstances, the dominant–recessive relationship does not hold completely. Instead, we see **incomplete dominance inheritance,** in which both alleles are expressed in the phenotype, resulting in a combined trait, or one that is intermediate between the two.

The *sickle cell trait,* a heterozygous condition present in many Black Africans, provides an example. *Sickle cell anemia* occurs in full form when a child inherits two recessive alleles. They cause the usually round red blood cells to become sickle (crescent-moon) shaped, especially under low-oxygen conditions. The sickled cells clog the blood vessels and block the flow of blood, causing intense pain, swelling, and tissue damage. Despite medical advances that today allow 85 percent of affected children to survive to adulthood, North Americans with sickle cell anemia have an average life expectancy of only 55 years (Chakravorty & Williams, 2015). Heterozygous individuals are protected from the disease under most circumstances. However, when they experience oxygen deprivation—for example, at high altitudes or after intense physical exercise—the single recessive allele asserts itself, and a temporary, mild form of the illness occurs.

The sickle cell allele is common among Black Africans for a special reason. Carriers of it are more resistant to malaria than are individuals with two alleles for normal red blood cells. In Africa, where malaria is common, these carriers survived and reproduced more frequently than others, leading the gene to be maintained in the Black population. But in regions of the world where the risk of malaria is low, the frequency of the gene is declining. For example, only 8 percent of African Americans are carriers, compared with 20 percent of Black Africans (Centers for Disease Control and Prevention, 2016b).

X-Linked Pattern. Males and females have an equal chance of inheriting recessive disorders carried on the autosomes. But when a harmful allele is carried on the X chromosome, **X-linked inheritance** applies. Males are more likely to be affected because their sex chromosomes do not match. In females, any recessive allele on one X chromosome has a good chance of being suppressed by a dominant allele on the other X. But the Y chromosome is only about one-third as long and therefore lacks many corresponding genes to override those on the X.

A well-known example of X-linked inheritance is *hemophilia,* a disorder in which the blood fails to clot normally. Figure 2.4 shows its greater likelihood of inheritance by male children whose mothers carry the abnormal allele. Another example is *fragile X syndrome*, the most common inherited cause of intellectual disability. In this disorder, which affects about 1 in 2,000 males and 1 in 6,000 females, an abnormal repetition of a sequence of DNA bases occurs on the X chromosome, damaging a particular gene. In addition to cognitive impairments, the majority of individuals with fragile X syndrome suffer from attention deficits and high anxiety, and about 30 to 35 percent also have symptoms of autism (Wadell, Hagerman, & Hessl, 2013). Because the disorder is X-linked, males are more often affected.

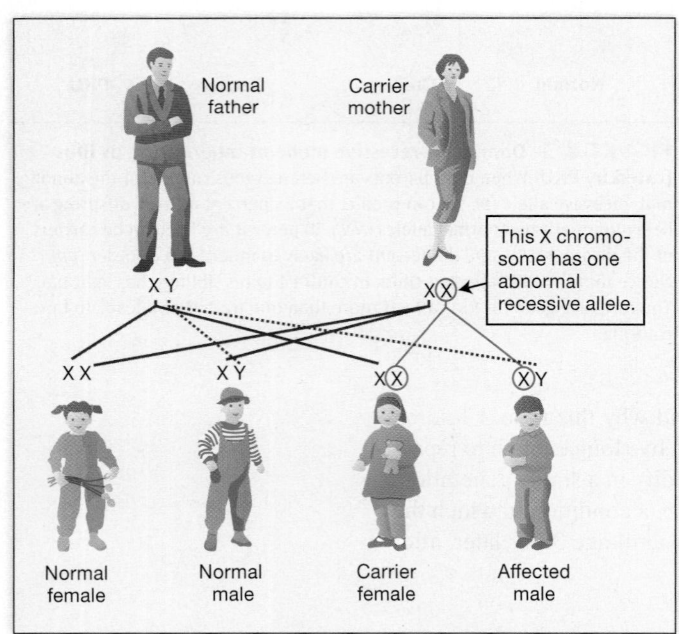

FIGURE 2.4 X-linked inheritance. In the example shown here, the allele on the father's X chromosome is normal. The mother has one normal and one abnormal recessive allele on her X chromosomes. By looking at the possible combinations of the parents' alleles, we can predict that 50 percent of these parents' male children are likely to have the disorder and 50 percent of their female children are likely to be carriers of it.

Besides X-linked disorders, many sex differences reveal the male to be at a disadvantage. Rates of miscarriage, infant and childhood deaths, birth defects, learning disabilities, behavior disorders, and intellectual disability all are higher for boys (Boyle et al., 2011; MacDorman & Gregory, 2015). It is possible that these sex differences can be traced to the genetic code. The female, with two X chromosomes, benefits from a greater variety of genes. Nature, however, seems to have adjusted for the male's disadvantage. Worldwide, about 103 boys are born for every 100 girls, and an even greater number of males are conceived (United Nations, 2017).

In cultures with strong gender-biased attitudes that induce expectant parents to prefer a male child, the male-to-female birth sex ratio is often much larger. In China, for example, the spread of ultrasound technology (which enables prenatal sex determination) and enforcement of a one-child family policy to control population growth—both of which began in the 1980s—led to a dramatic increase in sex-selective abortion. In 2015, China ended its one-child policy, substituting a two-child policy. Nevertheless, many Chinese couples continue to say they desire just one child (Basten & Jiang, 2015; Jiang, Li, & Sanchez-Barricarte, 2016). Today, China's birth sex ratio is 117 boys for every 100 girls—a gender imbalance with adverse social consequences, such as rising crime rates and male competition for marriage partners.

Genomic Imprinting. More than 1,000 human characteristics follow the rules of dominant–recessive and incomplete-dominance inheritance (National Center for Biotechnology Information, 2015). For these traits, whichever parent contributes a gene to the new individual, the gene responds similarly. Geneticists, however, have identified some exceptions. In **genomic imprinting,** alleles are imprinted, or chemically marked, within the ovum or sperm in such a way that one pair member (either the mother's or the father's) is silenced, leaving the other to be expressed regardless of its makeup (Perez, Rubinstein, & Dulac, 2016). The imprint is often temporary; it may be erased in the next generation.

The number of genes subjected to genomic imprinting is believed to be small—less than 1 percent. Nevertheless, these genes have a significant impact on brain development and physical health, as disruptions in imprinting reveal. For example, imprinting is involved in several childhood cancers and in *Prader-Willi syndrome,* a rare disorder with symptoms of intellectual disability, delays in language motor development, small stature, and severe obesity. Imprinting also may explain why children are more likely to develop diabetes if their father, rather than their mother, suffers from it, and why people with asthma or hay fever tend to have mothers, not fathers, with the illness (Ishida & Moore, 2013).

Mutation. Although less than 3 percent of pregnancies result in the birth of a baby with a hereditary abnormality, these children account for about 20 percent of infant deaths and contribute substantially to lifelong impaired physical and mental functioning (Martin et al., 2017). How are harmful genes created in the first place? The answer is **mutation,** a sudden but permanent change in a segment of DNA. A mutation may affect only one or two genes, or it may involve many genes, as in the chromosomal disorders we will discuss shortly. Some mutations occur spontaneously, simply by chance. Others are caused by hazardous environmental agents.

Ionizing (high-energy) radiation is an established cause of mutation. Women who receive repeated doses before conception are more likely to miscarry or give birth to children with hereditary defects. The incidence of genetic abnormalities, such as physical malformations and childhood cancer, is also higher in children whose fathers are exposed to radiation in their occupation. However, infrequent and mild exposure to radiation generally does not cause genetic damage (Adelstein, 2014). Rather, moderate to high doses over an extended time can impair DNA.

The examples just given illustrate *germline mutation,* which takes place in the cells that give rise to gametes. When the affected individual mates, the defective DNA is passed on to the next generation. In a second type, called *somatic mutation,* normal body cells mutate, an event that can occur at any time of life. The DNA defect appears in every cell derived from the affected body cell, eventually causing disease (such as cancer) or disability.

It is easy to see how disorders that run in families can result from germline mutation. But somatic mutation may be involved in these disorders as well. Some people harbor a genetic susceptibility that causes certain body cells to mutate easily in the presence of triggering events (Weiss, 2005). This helps explain why certain individuals develop serious illnesses (such as cancer) as a result of smoking, exposure to pollutants, or psychological stress, while others do not.

Although virtually all mutations that have been studied are harmful, some spontaneous ones (such as the sickle cell allele in malaria-ridden regions of the world) are necessary and desirable. By increasing genetic variation, they help individuals adapt to unexpected environmental challenges. Scientists, however, seldom go looking for mutations that contribute to favorable traits, such as an exceptional talent or sturdy immune system. They are far more concerned with identifying and eliminating unfavorable genes that threaten health and survival.

Polygenic Inheritance. So far, we have discussed patterns of gene–gene interaction in which people either display a particular trait or do not. These cut-and-dried individual differences are much easier to trace to their genetic origins than are characteristics that vary on a continuum among people, such as height, weight, intelligence, and personality. These traits are due to **polygenic inheritance,** in which many genes affect the characteristic in question. Polygenic inheritance is complex, and much about it is still unknown. In the final section of this chapter, we will discuss how researchers infer the influence of heredity on human attributes when they do not know the precise patterns of inheritance.

Chromosomal Abnormalities

Besides harmful recessive alleles, abnormalities of the chromosomes are a major cause of serious developmental problems. Most chromosomal defects result from mistakes during meiosis, when the ovum and sperm are formed. A chromosome pair does not separate properly or part of a chromosome breaks off. Because these errors involve far more DNA than problems due to single genes, they usually produce many physical and mental symptoms.

Down Syndrome. The most common chromosomal disorder, occurring in 1 out of every 700 live births, is *Down syndrome.* In 95 percent of cases, it results from a failure of the twenty-first pair of chromosomes to separate during meiosis, so the new individual receives three of these chromosomes rather than the normal two. For this reason, Down syndrome is sometimes called *trisomy 21.* In other, less frequent forms, an extra broken piece of a twenty-first chromosome is attached to another chromosome (called *translocation* pattern). Or an error occurs during early prenatal cell duplication, causing some but not all body cells to have the defective chromosomal makeup (called *mosaic* pattern) (U.S. Department of Health and Human Services, 2017b). Because the mosaic type involves less genetic material, symptoms may be less extreme.

An 8-year-old with Down syndrome, at right, plays with a typically developing classmate. Despite impaired intellectual development, this child benefits from exposure to stimulating environments and from opportunities to interact with peers.

The consequences of Down syndrome include intellectual disability, memory and speech problems, limited vocabulary, and slow motor development. Measures of electrical brain activity indicate that the brains of individuals with Down syndrome function in a less coordinated fashion than do the brains of typical individuals (Ahmadlou et al., 2013). The disorder is also associated with distinct physical features—a short, stocky build, a flattened face, a protruding tongue, almond-shaped eyes, and (in 50 percent of cases) an unusual crease running across the palm of the hand. In addition, infants with Down syndrome are often born with eye cataracts, hearing loss, and heart and intestinal defects (U.S. Department of Health and Human Services, 2017b).

Because of medical advances, life expectancy of individuals with Down syndrome has increased greatly: Today, it is about 60 years of age. However, about 70 percent of affected people who live past age 40 show symptoms of *Alzheimer's disease,* the most common form of dementia (Hartley et al., 2015). Genes on chromosome 21 are linked to this disorder.

Infants with Down syndrome smile less readily, show poor eye-to-eye contact, have weak muscle tone, and explore objects less persistently (Slonims & McConachie, 2006). But when parents encourage them to engage with their surroundings, children with Down syndrome develop more favorably. They also benefit from infant and preschool intervention programs, although emotional, social, and motor skills improve more than intellectual performance (Roizen, 2013). Clearly, environmental factors affect how well children with Down syndrome fare.

As Figure 2.5 shows, the risk of bearing a baby with Down syndrome, as well as other chromosomal abnormalities, rises dramatically with maternal age. But exactly why older mothers are more likely to release ova with meiotic errors is not yet known (Chiang, Schultz, & Lampson, 2012). In about 5 percent of cases, the extra genetic material originates with the father (Vranekovic et al., 2012).

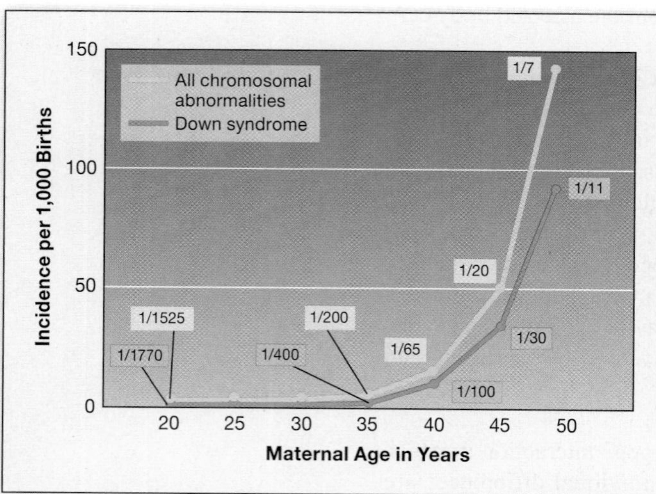

FIGURE 2.5 Risk of Down syndrome and all chromosomal abnormalities by maternal age. Risk rises sharply after age 35. (From R. L. Schonberg, 2012, "Birth Defects and Prenatal Diagnosis," from *Children with Disabilities,* 7th ed., M. L. Batshaw, N. J. Roizen, & G. R. Lotrecchiano, eds., p. 50. Baltimore: Paul H. Brookes Publishing Co., Inc. Adapted by permission.)

Abnormalities of the Sex Chromosomes. Other disorders of the autosomes usually disrupt development so severely that miscarriage occurs. When such babies are born, they rarely survive beyond early childhood. In contrast, sex chromosome disorders often are not recognized until adolescence when, in some deviations, puberty is delayed. The most common problems involve the presence of an extra chromosome (either X or Y) or the absence of one X in females.

Research has discredited a variety of myths about individuals with sex chromosome disorders. For example, males with *XYY syndrome* are not necessarily more aggressive and antisocial than XY males (Re & Birkhoff, 2015). And most children with sex chromosome disorders do not suffer from intellectual disability but, rather, have specific cognitive challenges. Verbal difficulties—for example, with reading and vocabulary—are common among girls with *triple X syndrome* and boys with *Klinefelter syndrome,* both of whom inherit an extra X chromosome. In contrast, girls with *Turner syndrome,* who are missing an X, have trouble with spatial relationships—for example, drawing pictures, following travel directions, and noticing changes in facial expressions (Otter et al., 2013; Ross et al., 2012; Temple & Shephard, 2012). Brain-imaging evidence confirms that adding to or subtracting from the usual number of X chromosomes alters the development of certain brain structures, yielding particular intellectual deficits (Hong et al., 2014).

ASK YOURSELF

CONNECT Referring to ecological systems theory (Chapter 1, pages 19–21), explain why parents of children with genetic disorders often experience increased stress. What factors, within and beyond the family, can help these parents support their children's development?

APPLY Gilbert's genetic makeup is homozygous for dark hair. Jan's is homozygous for blond hair. What proportion of their children are likely to be dark-haired? Explain.

REFLECT Provide illustrations from our discussion, and from individuals you know with genetic disorders, of environmental influences on development.

Reproductive Choices

2.4 Discuss counseling, medical procedures, and reproductive options that can assist prospective parents in having healthy children.

In the past, many couples with genetic disorders in their families chose not to bear a child at all rather than risk the birth of an abnormal baby. Today, genetic counseling and prenatal diagnosis help people make informed decisions about conceiving, carrying a pregnancy to term, or adopting a child.

Genetic Counseling and Prenatal Diagnosis

Genetic counseling is a communication process designed to help couples assess their chances of giving birth to a baby with a hereditary disorder and choose the best course of action in view of risks and family goals. Individuals likely to seek counseling are those who have had difficulties bearing children—for example, repeated miscarriages—or who know that genetic problems exist in their families.

In addition, adults who delay childbearing are often candidates because as maternal age rises beyond age 35, the rates of chromosomal abnormalities increase sharply. Older paternal age elevates risk of DNA mutations as well. After age 40, it is associated with increased incidence of several serious psychological disorders. These include *autism* (see page 16 in Chapter 1); *schizophrenia,* characterized by hallucinations, delusions, and irrational behavior; and *bipolar disorder,* marked by alternating periods of elation and depression (Zitzmann, 2013). But because younger parents have children in far higher numbers than older parents, they still bear the majority of babies with genetic defects. Therefore, some experts argue that parental needs, not age, should determine referral for genetic counseling (Berkowitz, Roberts, & Minkoff, 2006).

SOCIAL ISSUES

The Pros and Cons of Reproductive Technologies

Some people decide not to risk pregnancy because of a history of genetic disease. Many others—12 percent of all couples who try to conceive—discover that they are infertile (Chandra, Copen, & Stephen, 2013). And some never-married adults and lesbian and gay couples want to bear children. Today, increasing numbers of individuals are turning to alternative methods of conception—technologies that have become the subject of heated debate.

Donor Insemination and In Vitro Fertilization

Donor insemination—injection of sperm from an anonymous man into a woman—is often used to overcome male reproductive difficulties. It also permits women without a male partner to become pregnant. Donor insemination is 70 percent successful, resulting in about 40,000 deliveries and 52,000 newborn babies in the United States each year (Rossi, 2014).

In vitro fertilization is another commonly used reproductive technology. About 1 percent of all children in developed countries—65,000 babies in the United States—are conceived through this technique annually (Sunderam et al., 2015). A woman is given hormones that stimulate ripening of several ova. These are removed surgically and placed in a dish of nutrients, to which sperm are added. Once an ovum is fertilized and duplicates into several cells, it is injected into the woman's uterus.

By mixing and matching gametes, pregnancies can be brought about when either or both partners have a reproductive problem. Usually, in vitro fertilization is used to treat women whose fallopian tubes are permanently damaged. But a single sperm can now be injected directly into an ovum, thereby overcoming most male fertility problems. And a "sex sorter" method helps ensure that couples who carry X-linked diseases (which usually affect males) have a daughter. Nevertheless, the success of assisted reproduction declines steadily with age, from 55 percent in women ages 31 to 35 to 8 percent in women age 43 (Cetinkaya, Siano, & Benadiva, 2013; Gnoth et al., 2011).

Children conceived through these methods may be genetically unrelated to one or both of their parents. Does lack of genetic ties or secrecy interfere with parent–child relationships? Perhaps because of a strong desire for parenthood, caregiving is actually somewhat warmer for young children conceived through donor insemination or in vitro fertilization. Also, these children and adolescents are as well-adjusted as their naturally conceived counterparts (Punamäki, 2006; Wagenaar et al., 2011).

Although reproductive technologies have many benefits, serious questions have arisen about their use. In many countries, including the United States, doctors are not required to keep records of donor characteristics, though information about the child's genetic background might be critical in the case of serious disease (Murphy, 2013).

In vitro fertilization poses greater risks than natural conception to infant survival and healthy development. About 26 percent of in vitro procedures result in multiple births. Most are twins, but 3 percent are triplets and higher-order multiples. Consequently, among in vitro babies, the rate of low birth weight is nearly four times as high as in the general population (Kulkarni et al., 2013; Sunderam et al., 2015). Risk of pregnancy complications, miscarriage, and major birth defects also rises, due to the biological effects of in vitro techniques and the older age of many people seeking treatment.

Surrogate Motherhood

An even more controversial form of medically assisted conception is *surrogate motherhood*. In this procedure, in vitro fertilization may be used to impregnate a woman (called a surrogate) with a couple's fertilized ovum. Alternatively, sperm from a man whose partner is infertile may be used to inseminate the

If a family history of intellectual disability, psychological disorders, physical defects, or inherited diseases exists, the genetic counselor interviews the couple and prepares a *pedigree,* a picture of the family tree in which affected relatives are identified. The pedigree is used to estimate the likelihood of an affected child. For many disorders traceable to a single gene, molecular genetic testing using a sample of blood, saliva, or body tissue can reveal whether the parent is a carrier of the harmful allele.

Autism, schizophrenia, and bipolar disorder have each been linked to an array of DNA-sequence deviations (called *genetic markers)* distributed across multiple chromosomes. New *genomewide testing methods,* which look for these genetic markers, enable genetic counselors to estimate risk for these conditions. But estimates are generally low because the genetic markers are found in only a minority of affected people. Also, the genetic markers are not associated with mental illness every time they appear. Their expression—as we will illustrate at the end of this chapter—seems to depend on environmental conditions. Recently, geneticists have begun to identify rare repeats and deletions of DNA bases that are more consistently related to mental illness (Vissers, Gilissen, & Veltman, 2016). These discoveries may lead to more accurate prediction of the likelihood of passing a psychological disorder from parent to child.

surrogate, who agrees to turn the baby over to the father. The child is then adopted by his partner. In both cases, the surrogate is paid a fee for her childbearing services.

Most surrogate arrangements proceed smoothly, and the limited evidence available suggests that families usually function well and stay in touch with the surrogate, especially if she is genetically related to the child (Golombok et al., 2011, 2013; Jadva, Casey, & Golombok, 2012). The small number of children who have been studied are generally well-adjusted. Nevertheless, because surrogacy typically involves the wealthy as contractors for infants and the less economically advantaged as surrogates, it may promote exploitation of financially needy women.

Reproductive Frontiers

Experts are debating the ethics of other reproductive options. Doctors have used donor ova from younger women in combination with in vitro fertilization to help postmenopausal women become pregnant. Most recipients are in their forties, but some in their fifties and sixties, and a few in their early seventies, have given birth. These cases magnify health risks to mother and baby and bring children into the world whose parents may not live to see them reach adulthood.

Today, customers at donor banks can select ova or sperm on the basis of physical characteristics and even IQ. And scientists are devising ways to alter the DNA of human ova, sperm, and embryos to protect against hereditary disorders—techniques that could be used to engineer other desired characteristics. Many worry that these practices are dangerous steps toward "designer babies"—controlling offspring traits by manipulating genetic makeup.

Although reproductive technologies permit many barren adults to become parents, laws are needed to regulate such practices. In Australia, New Zealand, and Europe, in vitro gamete donors and applicants for the procedure must undergo highly regulated screening (Murphy, 2013). Denmark, France, and Italy prohibit in vitro fertilization for women past menopause. Pressure from those working in the field of assisted reproduction may soon lead to similar policies in the United States.

The ethical problems of surrogate motherhood are so complex that 13 U.S. states and the District of Columbia sharply restrict or ban the practice (Swain, 2014). Most European nations, along with Australia and Canada, allow only "altruistic" surrogacy, in which the surrogate has no financial gain. More research on how such children grow up, including later-appearing medical conditions and feelings about their origins, is important for weighing the pros and cons of these techniques.

AP IMAGES/HERALD & REVIEW, JIM BOWLING

▶ Fertility drugs and in vitro fertilization often lead to multiple births. These quadruplets are healthy, but babies born with the aid of reproductive technologies are at high risk for low birth weight and major birth defects.

When all the relevant hereditary information is in, genetic counselors help people consider appropriate options. These include taking a chance and conceiving, choosing from among a variety of reproductive technologies (see the Social Issues box above), or adopting a child.

If couples at risk for bearing a child with abnormalities decide to conceive, several **prenatal diagnostic methods**—medical procedures that permit detection of developmental problems before birth—are available (see Table 2.1 on page 50). Except for *maternal blood analysis,* however, prenatal diagnosis should not be used routinely because of injury risks to the developing organism.

Prenatal diagnosis has led to advances in fetal medicine. For example, by inserting a needle into the uterus, doctors can administer drugs to the fetus. Surgery has been performed to repair such problems as heart, lung, and diaphragm malformations, urinary tract obstructions, and neural defects (Nassr et al., 2017). Fetuses with blood disorders have been given blood transfusions. And those with immune deficiencies have received bone marrow transplants that succeeded in creating a normally functioning immune system (Deprest et al., 2010).

These techniques frequently result in complications, the most common being premature labor and miscarriage (Danzer & Johnson, 2014). Yet parents may be willing to try almost any option,

TABLE 2.1
Prenatal Diagnostic Methods

METHOD	DESCRIPTION
Amniocentesis	The most widely used technique. A hollow needle is inserted through the abdominal wall to obtain a sample of fluid in the uterus. Cells are examined for genetic defects. Can be performed by the 14th week after conception; 1 to 2 more weeks are required for test results. Small risk of miscarriage.
Chorionic villus sampling	A procedure that can be used if results are desired or needed very early in pregnancy. A thin tube is inserted into the uterus through the vagina, or a hollow needle is inserted through the abdominal wall. A small plug of tissue is removed from the end of one or more chorionic villi, the hairlike projections on the membrane surrounding the developing organism. Cells are examined for genetic defects. Can be performed at 9 weeks after conception; results are available within 24 hours. Entails a slightly greater risk of miscarriage than amniocentesis and is also associated with a small risk of limb deformities.
Fetoscopy	A small tube with a light source at one end is inserted into the uterus to inspect the fetus for defects of the limbs and face. Also allows a sample of fetal blood to be obtained, permitting diagnosis of such disorders as hemophilia and sickle cell anemia, as well as neural defects. Usually performed between 15 and 18 weeks after conception but can be done as early as 5 weeks. Entails some risk of miscarriage.
Ultrasound	High-frequency sound waves are beamed at the uterus; their reflection is translated into a picture on a video screen that reveals the size, shape, and placement of the fetus. By itself, permits assessment of fetal age, detection of multiple pregnancies, and identification of gross physical defects. Also used to guide amniocentesis, chorionic villus sampling, and fetoscopy. When used five or more times, may increase the chances of low birth weight.
Maternal blood analysis	By the second month of pregnancy, some of the developing organism's cells enter the maternal bloodstream. An elevated level of alpha-fetoprotein may indicate kidney disease, abnormal closure of the esophagus, or neural tube defects. Isolated cells can be examined for genetic defects.
Ultrafast magnetic resonance imaging (MRI)	Sometimes used as a supplement to ultrasound, where brain or other abnormalities are detected and MRI can provide greater diagnostic accuracy. Uses a scanner to magnetically record detailed pictures of fetal structures. The ultrafast technique overcomes image blurring due to fetal movements. No evidence of adverse effects.
Preimplantation genetic diagnosis	After in vitro fertilization and duplication of the zygote into a cluster of cells, one or two cells are removed and examined for genetic defects. Only if that sample is normal is the fertilized ovum implanted in the woman's uterus.

Sources: Akolekar et al., 2015; Griffin et al., 2017; Jokhi & Whitby, 2011; Kollmann et al., 2013; Moore, Persaud, & Torchia, 2016b.

even one with only a slim chance of success. Currently, the medical profession is struggling with how to help parents make informed decisions about fetal surgery.

Advances in *genetic engineering* also offer hope for correcting hereditary defects. As part of the Human Genome Project—an ambitious international research program—thousands of genes have been identified, including those involved in disorders of the heart, digestive, blood, eye, and nervous system and in many forms of cancer (National Institutes of Health, 2017). As a result, new treatments are being explored, such as *gene therapy*—correcting genetic abnormalities by delivering DNA carrying a functional gene to the cells. Testing of gene therapies for relieving symptoms of hemophilia and treating severe immune system dysfunction, leukemia, and several forms of cancer has been encouraging (Kaufmann et al., 2013). In another approach, called *proteomics,* scientists modify gene-specified proteins involved in biological aging and disease (Twyman, 2014). But genetic treatments are still some distance away for most single-gene defects and farther off for diseases involving multiple genes that combine in complex ways with each other and the environment.

Adoption

Adults who are infertile or likely to pass along a genetic disorder, same-sex couples, and single adults who want a family are turning to adoption in increasing numbers. Couples who have children by birth, too, sometimes choose to expand their families through adoption. Because the availability of healthy babies has diminished (fewer young unwed mothers give up their babies than in the past), Americans, and people in other Western nations, often seek to adopt internationally. But despite a dramatic rise in orphaned, abandoned, and voluntarily surrendered children worldwide, intercountry adoption has declined substantially, due to host-country and U.S. adoption policies. Rising numbers of children are being adopted from U.S. foster care (Jones & Placek, 2017). And more families are accepting children who are past infancy or who have known developmental problems.

▶ Adoption is one option for adults who are infertile or have a family history of genetic disorders. This couple, who adopted their daughters from China, can promote their children's adjustment by helping them learn about their birth heritage.

Adopted children and adolescents—whether or not born in their adoptive parents' country— tend to have more learning and emotional difficulties than other children, a difference that increases with the child's age at time of adoption (Askeland et al., 2017; Diamond et al., 2015; van den Dries et al., 2009). Various explanations exist for adoptees' more problematic childhoods. The biological mother may have been unable to care for the child because of problems believed to be partly genetic, such as alcoholism or severe depression, and may have passed this tendency to her offspring. Or perhaps she experienced stress, poor diet, or inadequate medical care during pregnancy—factors that can affect the child. Furthermore, children adopted after infancy often have a preadoptive history of conflict-ridden family relationships, lack of parental affection, neglect and abuse, or deprived institutional rearing. Finally, adoptive parents and children, who are genetically unrelated, are less alike in intelligence and personality than are biological relatives—differences that may threaten family harmony.

Despite these risks, most adopted children fare well, and those with preexisting problems who experience sensitive parenting usually make rapid progress (Arcus & Chambers, 2008; Juffer & van IJzendoorn, 2012). Overall, international adoptees develop much more favorably than birth siblings or institutionalized agemates who remain in their birth country (Christoffersen, 2012). And children with troubled family histories who are adopted at older ages generally improve in feelings of trust and affection for their adoptive parents as they come to feel loved and supported (Veríssimo & Salvaterra, 2006). As we will see in Chapter 4, however, later-adopted children—especially those with multiple early-life adversities—are more likely than their agemates to have persistent cognitive, emotional, and social problems.

By adolescence, adoptees' lives are often complicated by unresolved curiosity about their roots. As they try to integrate aspects of their birth family and their adoptive family into their emerging identity, teenagers face a challenging process of defining themselves. When parents have been warm, open, and supportive in their communication about adoption, their children typically forge a positive sense of self (Brodzinsky, 2011). And as long as their parents took steps to help them learn about their heritage in childhood, young people adopted into a different ethnic group or culture generally develop identities that are healthy blends of their birth and rearing backgrounds (Nickman et al., 2005; Thomas & Tessler, 2007). The decision to search for birth parents, however, is often postponed until early adulthood, when marriage and childbirth may trigger it.

ASK YOURSELF

CONNECT How does research on adoption reveal resilience? Which factor related to resilience (see Chapter 1, page 7) is central in positive outcomes for adoptees?

APPLY Imagine that you must counsel a couple considering in vitro fertilization using donor ova to overcome infertility. What medical and ethical risks would you raise?

REFLECT Suppose you are a carrier of fragile X syndrome and want to have children. Would you choose pregnancy, adoption, or surrogacy? If you became pregnant, would you opt for prenatal diagnosis? Explain your decisions.

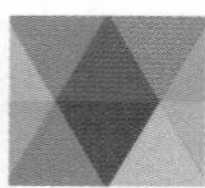

Environmental Contexts for Development

2.5 Describe family functioning from the perspective of ecological systems theory, along with aspects of the environment that support family well-being and development.

Just as complex as genetic inheritance is the surrounding environment—a many-layered set of influences that combine to help or hinder physical and psychological well-being. Jot down a brief description of events and people that have significantly influenced your development. Do the items on your list resemble those of my students, who mostly mention experiences that involve their families? This emphasis is not surprising, since the family is the first and longest-lasting context for development. Other influences that make most students' top 10 are friends, neighbors, school, workplace, and community and religious organizations.

Return to Bronfenbrenner's ecological systems theory, discussed in Chapter 1. It emphasizes that environments extending beyond the *microsystem*—the immediate settings just mentioned—powerfully affect development. Indeed, my students rarely mention one context, with an impact so pervasive that we seldom stop to think about it in our daily lives. This is the *macrosystem,* or broad social climate of society—its values and programs that support and protect children's development. All families need help in rearing children—through affordable housing and health care, safe neighborhoods, good schools, well-equipped recreational facilities, and high-quality child care and other services that permit them to meet both work and family responsibilities. And some families, because of poverty or special tragedies, need considerably more help than others.

In the following sections, we take up these contexts for development. Because they affect every age and aspect of change, we will return to them in later chapters. For now, our discussion emphasizes that environments, as well as heredity, can enhance or create risks for development.

The Family

In power and breadth of influence, no other microsystem context equals the family. The family creates unique bonds among people. Attachments to parents and siblings are usually lifelong and serve as models for relationships in the wider world. Within the family, children learn the language, skills, and social and moral values of their culture. And people of all ages turn to family members for information, assistance, and pleasurable interaction. Warm, gratifying family ties predict physical and psychological health throughout development (Khaleque & Rohner, 2012). In contrast, isolation or alienation from the family, especially from parents, is generally associated with developmental problems.

▶ The family is a network of interdependent relationships, in which each person's behavior influences that of others. As this family plays a game, warm, considerate parental communication encourages children's cooperation, which promotes further parental warmth and caring.

Contemporary researchers view the family as a network of interdependent relationships (Bronfenbrenner & Morris, 2006; Russell, 2014). Recall from ecological systems theory that *bidirectional influences* exist in which the behaviors of each family member affect those of others. Indeed, the very term *system* implies that the responses of family members are related. These system influences operate both directly and indirectly.

Direct Influences. The next time you have a chance to observe family members interacting, watch carefully. You are likely to see that kind, patient communication evokes cooperative, harmonious responses, whereas harshness and impatience engender angry, resistive behavior. Each of these reactions, in turn, forges a new link in the interactive chain. In the first instance, a positive message tends to follow; in the second, a negative or avoidant one is likely.

These observations fit with a wealth of research on the family system. Studies of families of diverse ethnicities show that when parents are firm but warm, children tend to comply with their requests. And when children cooperate, their parents are likely to be warm and gentle in the future. In contrast, children whose parents discipline harshly and impatiently are likely to refuse and rebel. And because children's misbehavior is stressful, parents may increase their use of punishment, leading to more unruliness by the child (Lorber & Egeland, 2011; Shaw, Hyde, & Brennan 2012). In each case, the behavior of one family member helps sustain a form of interaction in the other that either promotes or undermines children's psychological well-being.

LOOK AND LISTEN

Observe several parent–young child pairs in a supermarket or department store, where parents are likely to place limits on children's behavior. How does quality of parent communication seem to influence the child's response? How does the child's response affect the parent's subsequent interaction?

Indirect Influences. The impact of family relationships on development becomes even more complicated when we consider that interaction between any two members is affected by others present in the setting. Recall from Chapter 1 that Bronfenbrenner calls these indirect influences the effect of *third parties.*

Third parties can serve as supports for or barriers to development. For example, when a marital relationship is warm and considerate, mothers and fathers are more likely to engage in effective **coparenting,** mutually supporting each other's parenting behaviors. Such parents are warmer, praise and stimulate their children more, and nag and scold them less. Effective coparenting, in turn, fosters a positive marital relationship (Morrill et al., 2010). In contrast, parents whose marriage is tense and hostile often coparent ineptly. They interfere with each other's child-rearing efforts, are less responsive to children's needs, and are more likely to criticize, express anger, and punish (Palkovitz, Fagan, & Hull, 2013; Stroud et al., 2015).

Children who are chronically exposed to angry, unresolved parental conflict have serious behavior problems resulting from disrupted emotional security (Cummings & Miller-Graff, 2015). These include both *internalizing difficulties,* such as feeling anxious and fearful and trying to repair their parents' relationship, and *externalizing difficulties,* including anger and aggression (Goeke-Morey, Papp, & Cummings, 2013; Stroud et al., 2015). These child problems can further disrupt parents' relationship.

Adapting to Change. Think back to the *chronosystem* in Bronfenbrenner's theory (see pages 20–21 in Chapter 1). The interplay of forces within the family is dynamic and ever-changing as each member adapts to the development of other members.

For example, as children acquire new skills, parents adjust the way they treat their more competent youngsters. Consider the way a parent relates to a young infant as compared with a walking, talking toddler. During the first few months, parents spend much time feeding, bathing, and cuddling the baby. Within a year, things change dramatically. The 1-year-old points, shows, names objects, and explores the household cupboards. In response, parents devote more time to talking, playing games, and disciplining. These new ways of interacting, in turn, encourage the child's expanding motor, cognitive, and social skills.

Parents' development affects children as well. The rise in parent–child conflict that often occurs in early adolescence is not solely due to teenagers' striving for independence. This is a time when most parents have reached middle age and—conscious that their children will soon leave home and establish their own lives—are reconsidering their own commitments (Steinberg & Silk, 2002). While the adolescent presses for greater autonomy, the parent presses for more togetherness. This imbalance promotes friction, which parent and teenager gradually resolve by accommodating to changes in each other.

Historical time period also contributes to a dynamic family system. In recent decades, a declining birth rate, a high divorce rate, expansion of women's roles, increased acceptance of same-sex relationships, and postponement of parenthood have led to a smaller family size and a greater number of single parents, remarried parents, gay and lesbian parents, employed mothers, and dual-earner families. Clearly, families in industrialized nations have become more diverse than ever before. In later chapters, we will take up these family forms, examining how each affects family relationships and children's development. Nevertheless, some general patterns in family functioning do exist. In the United States and other industrialized nations, one important source of these consistencies is socioeconomic status.

Socioeconomic Status and Family Functioning

People in industrialized nations are stratified on the basis of what they do at work and how much they earn for doing it—factors that determine their social position and economic well-being. Researchers assess a family's standing on this continuum through an index called **socioeconomic status (SES),** which combines three related, but not completely overlapping, variables: (1) years of education and (2) the prestige of one's job and the skill it requires, both of which measure social status; and (3) income, which measures economic status. As SES rises and falls, parents and children face changing circumstances that profoundly affect family functioning.

SES is linked to timing of parenthood and to family size. People who work in skilled and semiskilled manual occupations (for example, construction workers, truck drivers, and custodians) tend to marry and have children earlier as well as give birth to more children than people in professional and technical occupations. The two groups also differ in child-rearing values and expectations. For example, when asked about personal qualities they desire for their children, lower-SES parents tend to emphasize external characteristics, such as obedience, politeness, neatness, and cleanliness. In contrast, higher-SES parents emphasize psychological traits, such as curiosity, happiness, self-direction, and cognitive and social maturity (Duncan & Magnuson, 2003; Hoff, Laursen, & Tardif, 2002).

These differences are reflected in family interaction. Parents higher in SES talk to, read to, and otherwise stimulate their infants and preschoolers more and grant them greater freedom to explore. With older children and adolescents, higher-SES parents use more warmth, explanations, and verbal praise; set higher academic and other developmental goals; and allow their children to make more decisions. Commands ("You do that because I told you to"), criticism, and physical punishment all occur more often in low-SES households (Bush & Peterson, 2008; Mandara et al., 2009).

Education contributes substantially to these variations. Higher-SES parents' interest in providing verbal stimulation, nurturing inner traits, and promoting academic achievement is supported by years of schooling, during which they learned to think about abstract, subjective ideas and, thus, to invest in their children's cognitive and social development (Mistry et al., 2008). At the same time, greater economic security enables parents to devote more time, energy, and material resources to fostering their children's psychological characteristics (Duncan, Magnuson, & Votruba-Drzal, 2015).

High levels of stress sparked by economic insecurity contribute to low-SES parents' reduced provision of stimulating interaction and activities as well as greater use of coercive discipline (Belsky, Schlomer, & Ellis, 2012; Conger & Donnellan, 2007). And because of limited education and low social status, many low-SES parents feel a sense of powerlessness in their relationships beyond the home. At work, for example, they must obey rules made by others in positions of authority. When they get home, they often expect the same unquestioning obedience from their children.

As early as the second year of life, higher SES is associated with enhanced cognitive and language development and with reduced incidence of behavior problems. And throughout childhood and adolescence, children from higher-SES families do better in school (Bradley & Corwyn, 2003; Hoff, 2013; Melby et al., 2008). As a result, they attain higher levels of education, which greatly enhances their opportunities for a prosperous adult life.

Poverty

When families slip into poverty, development is seriously threatened. In a TV documentary on childhood poverty, a PBS filmmaker explored the daily lives of several American children, along with the struggles of their families (Frontline, 2012). Asked what being poor is like, 10-year-old Kaylie replied, "We don't get three meals a day.... Sometimes we have cereal but no milk and have to eat it dry." Kaylie said she felt hungry much of the time, adding, "I'm afraid if we can't pay our bills, me and my brother will starve."

Kaylie lives with her 12-year-old brother Tyler and their mother, who suffers from depression and panic attacks and cannot work. The children sometimes gather discarded tin cans from around their rural neighborhood and sell them for a small amount. When money to pay rent ran out, the family moved from its small house to an extended-stay motel.

With family belongings piled haphazardly around her in the cramped motel room, Kaylie complained, "I have no friends, no places to play. I pass the time by." Kaylie and Tyler had few books and indoor games; no outdoor play equipment such as bicycles, bats and balls, and roller skates; and no scheduled leisure pursuits. Asked to imagine her future, Kaylie wasn't hopeful. "I see my future poor, on the streets, in a box, asking for money from everyone, stealing stuff.... I'd like to explore the world, but I'm never going to be able to do that."

Today, 13.5 percent of the U.S. population—43 million Americans—live in poverty. Among those hit hardest are parents under age 25 with young children. Poverty is also magnified among ethnic minorities and women. For example, 20 percent of U.S. children are poor, a rate that climbs to 29 percent for Hispanic children, 30 percent for Native-American children, and 33 percent for African-American children. For single mothers with preschool children, the poverty rate is close to 50 percent (Proctor, Semesga, & Kollar, 2016; U.S. Census Bureau, 2015).

As we will see later, government programs with insufficient resources to meet family needs are responsible for these disheartening statistics. The poverty rate is higher among children than any other age group. And of all Western nations, the United States has the highest percentage of extremely poor children. Nearly 9 percent of U.S. children live in deep poverty (at less than half the poverty threshold, the income level judged necessary for a minimum living standard). The earlier poverty begins, the deeper it is, and the longer it lasts, the more devastating are its effects. Children of poverty are more likely than other children to suffer from lifelong poor physical health, persistent deficits in cognitive development and academic achievement, high school dropout, mental illness, and impulsivity, aggression, and antisocial behavior (Duncan, Magnuson, & Votruba-Drzal, 2015; Yoshikawa, Aber, & Beardslee, 2012).

The constant stressors that accompany poverty gradually weaken the family system. Poor families have many daily hassles: loss of welfare and unemployment payments, basic services—phone, TV, electricity, hot water—being shut off because of inability to pay bills, and limited or uncertain access to food, to name just a few. When daily crises arise, family members become depressed, irritable, and distracted; hostile interactions increase; and children's development suffers (Conger & Donnellan, 2007; Kohen et al., 2008).

Negative outcomes are especially severe in single-parent families and in families who must live in rundown, overcrowded housing and dangerous neighborhoods—conditions that make everyday existence even more difficult while reducing social supports that help people cope with economic hardship (Leventhal, Dupéré, & Shuey, 2015). On average, poverty rates are higher, neighborhood disorganization greater, and community services scarcer in rural communities—like the one where Kaylie, Tyler, and their mother live—than in urban areas (Hicken et al., 2014; Vernon-Feagans & Cox, 2013). These circumstances heighten risks for disrupted family functioning and physical and psychological adjustment difficulties.

A related problem has reduced the life chances of substantial numbers of children: More than 3 percent—nearly 2.5 million—experienced homelessness in the most recently reported year (Bassuk et al., 2014). Most homeless families consist of women with children under age 5. Besides physical health problems (which affect the majority of homeless people), many homeless children suffer from developmental delays and chronic emotional stress due to harsh, insecure daily lives (Kilmer et al., 2012). Homeless children achieve less well than other poverty-stricken children because of poor school attendance, frequent moves from school to school, and poor physical and emotional health (Cutuli et al., 2010; National Coalition for the Homeless, 2012).

AP PHOTO/JOHN RAOUX

▶ Homelessness poses enormous challenges for maintaining positive family relationships and physical and mental health. This mother and her three young children prepare to move out of the motel room they share with her boyfriend and father.

Although gaps in overall health and achievement between poverty-stricken children and their economically better-off peers are substantial, a considerable number of children from financially stressed families are resilient, faring well. A host of interventions exist, all aimed at helping children and youths surmount the risks of poverty. Some address family functioning and parenting, while others directly target children's academic, emotional, and social skills. And more programs are recognizing that because poverty-stricken children often experience multiple adversities, they benefit most from multifaceted efforts that focus on family, parenting, and children's needs at once (Kagan, 2013a). We will discuss many such interventions later in this text.

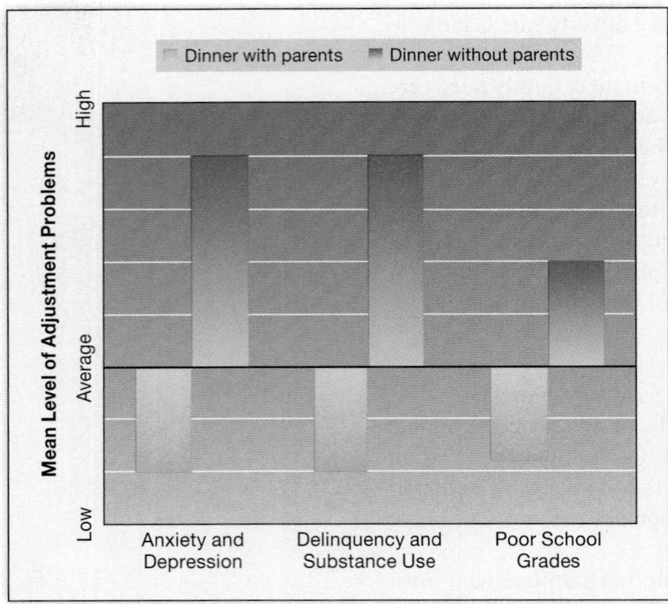

FIGURE 2.6 Relationship of regularly eating dinner with parents to affluent youths' adjustment problems. Compared with sixth graders who often ate dinner with their parents, those who rarely did so were far more likely to display anxiety and depression, delinquency and substance use, and poor school grades, even after many other aspects of parenting were controlled. In this study, frequent family mealtimes also protected low-SES youths from delinquency and substance use and from classroom learning problems. (Based on Luthar & Latendresse, 2005.)

Affluence

Despite their advanced education and great material wealth, affluent parents—those in prestigious and high-paying occupations—too often fail to engage in family interaction and parenting that promote favorable development. In several studies, researchers tracked the adjustment of youths growing up in wealthy suburbs. By seventh grade, many showed serious problems that worsened in high school (Luthar & Barkin, 2012; Racz, McMahon, & Luthar, 2011). Their school grades were poor, and they were more likely than youths in general to engage in alcohol and drug use, to commit delinquent acts, and to report high levels of anxiety and depression.

Why are so many affluent youths troubled? Compared to their better-adjusted counterparts, poorly adjusted affluent young people report less emotional closeness, less supervision, and fewer serious consequences for misbehaviors from their parents, who lead professionally and socially demanding lives. As a group, wealthy parents are nearly as physically and emotionally unavailable to their youngsters as parents coping with serious financial strain. At the same time, these parents often make excessive demands for achievement and are critical when their children perform less than perfectly (Luthar, Barkin, & Crossman, 2013). Adolescents whose parents value their accomplishments more than their character are more likely to have academic and emotional problems.

For both affluent and low-SES youths, a simple routine—eating dinner with parents—is associated with a reduction in adjustment difficulties, even after many other aspects of parenting are controlled (see Figure 2.6) (Luthar & Latendresse, 2005). Interventions that make wealthy parents aware of the high costs of a competitive lifestyle, weak involvement in children's lives, and unrealistically high expectations are badly needed.

Beyond the Family: Neighborhoods and Schools

As the concepts of *mesosystem* and *exosystem* in ecological systems theory make clear, connections between family and community are vital for psychological well-being. From our discussion of poverty, perhaps you can see why: In poverty-stricken areas, community life is often disrupted. Families move often, parks and playgrounds are in disarray, and community centers providing organized leisure-time activities do not exist. In poor urban neighborhoods, family violence, child abuse and neglect, child and youth internalizing and externalizing difficulties, and adult criminal behavior are widespread (Chen, Howard, & Brooks-Gunn, 2011; Dunn, Schaefer-McDaniel, & Ramsay, 2010; Ingoldsby et al., 2012; Lang et al., 2008). And in poor rural communities, family isolation and scarcity of supportive services are especially high (Vernon-Feagans & Cox, 2013). In contrast, strong family ties to the surrounding social context—as indicated by frequent contact with relatives and friends and regular church, synagogue, temple, or mosque attendance—reduce stress and enhance adjustment.

Neighborhoods. Neighborhoods offer resources and social ties that play an important part in children's development. In an experimental study of neighborhood mobility, low-SES families were randomly assigned vouchers to move out of public housing into neighborhoods varying widely in affluence. Compared with their peers who remained in poverty-stricken areas, children and youths who moved into low-poverty neighborhoods and remained there for at least several years showed substantially better physical and mental health and school achievement (Anderson & Leventhal, 2014; Leventhal & Brooks-Gunn, 2003; Leventhal & Dupéré, 2011). The ability of low-income families to integrate into the social life of their new neighborhoods was key to favorable outcomes.

RICHARD W. RODRIGUEZ/AP IMAGES FOR BOYS & GIRLS CLUBS OF AMERICA

▶ A 5-year-old enjoys working with volunteers at a community garden sponsored by the Boys & Girls Clubs of America. Neighborhood resources are especially important for the development of economically disadvantaged children and youths.

Neighborhood resources have a greater impact on economically disadvantaged than on well-to-do young people. Higher-SES families can afford to transport their children to lessons and entertainment and, if necessary, to better-quality schools in distant parts of the community. In low-income neighborhoods, in-school and after-school programs that substitute for lack of other resources by providing art, music, sports, and other enrichment activities are associated with improved academic performance and a reduction in emotional and behavior problems in elementary and middle school (Durlak, Weissberg, & Pachan, 2010; Kataoka & Vandell, 2013; Vandell, Reisner, & Pierce, 2007). Neighborhood organizations, such as religious youth groups and special interest clubs, contribute to favorable development in adolescence, including increased self-confidence, school achievement, and educational aspirations (Barnes et al., 2007).

Yet in dangerous, disorganized neighborhoods, high-quality activities for children and adolescents are scarce. Even when they are available, crime and social disorder limit young people's access, and parents overwhelmed by financial and other stressors are less likely to encourage their children to participate (Dearing et al., 2009).

LOOK AND LISTEN

Ask several parents to list their school-age children's regular lessons and other enrichment activities. Then inquire about home and neighborhood factors that either encourage or impede their children's participation.

The Better Beginnings, Better Futures Project of Ontario, Canada, is a government-sponsored initiative aimed at preventing the dire consequences of neighborhood poverty by building resilient capacities in children, families, and communities. Using neighborhood elementary schools as its base, Better Beginnings programs provided children ages 4 to 8 years with in-class, before- and after-school, and summer enrichment activities. Program staff also visited each child's parents regularly, informed them about community resources, and encouraged their involvement in the child's school and neighborhood life. And a community-wide component focused on improving neighborhood life, by offering leadership training and adult education programs and organizing special events and celebrations (Peters, 2005; Peters, Petrunka, & Arnold, 2003).

Longitudinal follow-ups as participants reached grades 3, 6, 9, and 12 revealed wide-ranging benefits compared with children and families living in impoverished neighborhoods without this set of programs (Peters et al., 2010; Worton et al., 2014). Among these were gains in children's academic achievement and social adjustment, a reduction in adolescent delinquency, and parent-reported improved family functioning, child-rearing practices, and sense of community connection.

Schools. Unlike the informal worlds of family and neighborhood, the school is a formal institution designed to transmit knowledge and skills needed to become productive members of society. Children and youths in the developed world spend much time in school—a total of about 14,000 hours, on average, by high school graduation. And today, because many children younger than age 5 attend "school-like" child-care centers or preschools, the impact of schooling begins earlier and is even more powerful than these figures suggest.

Schools are complex social systems that affect many aspects of development. Schools vary in their physical environments—space, equipment, and materials available for work and play. They also differ in their educational philosophies—whether teachers regard students as passive learners to be molded by adult instruction; as active, curious beings who determine their own learning; or as collaborative partners assisted by adult experts, who guide their mastery of new skills. The social life of schools varies as well—in the degree to which students cooperate and compete; in the extent to which students of different abilities, SES, and ethnic backgrounds learn together; and in whether they are safe, humane settings or riddled with peer harassment and violence. We will discuss these aspects of schooling in later chapters.

As with SES and family functioning, schooling and academic achievement contribute substantially to life chances and well-being. Furthermore, these contextual factors are interrelated: Children living in low-income and poverty-stricken neighborhoods are more likely to attend underfunded schools and experience poorer quality education. For these reasons, educational interventions aimed at upgrading the educational experiences and school performance of economically disadvantaged children are best begun in the early years (Crosnoe & Benner, 2015). But intervening at later periods to target specific educational problems is also helpful—for example, by providing high-quality vocational education to non-college-bound youths.

Students whose parents are involved in their education—through participating in school organizations, volunteering at school, attending parent–teacher conferences, and reinforcing school-based learning at home—show better academic achievement. And when followed up in early adulthood, their educational attainment is higher (Benner, Boyle, & Sadler, 2016). Higher-SES parents, whose backgrounds and values are similar to those of teachers, are more likely to sustain regular educational involvement. In contrast, low-SES and ethnic minority parents often feel uncomfortable about coming to school, and daily stressors reduce the energy they have to support their child's education (Grant & Ray, 2010). Teachers and administrators must take extra steps with low-SES and ethnic minority families to build supportive family–school ties.

The Cultural Context

Our discussion in Chapter 1 emphasized that child development can be fully understood only when viewed in its larger cultural context. In the following sections, we expand on this theme by taking up the role of the *macrosystem* in development. First, we discuss ways that cultural values and practices affect contexts for development. Then we consider how healthy development depends on laws and government programs that shield children from harm and foster their well-being.

Cultural Values and Practices. Cultures shape family interaction and community settings beyond the home—in short, all aspects of daily life. Many of us remain blind to aspects of our own cultural heritage until we see them in relation to the practices of others.

Consider the question, Who should be responsible for rearing young children? How would you answer it? Here are some common responses from my students: "If parents decide to have a baby, then they should be ready to care for it," "Most people are not happy about others intruding into family life." These statements reflect a widely held opinion in the United States—that the care and rearing of children, and paying for that care, are the duty of parents, and only parents. This view has a long history—one in which independence, self-reliance, and the privacy of family life emerged as central American values (Dodge & Haskins, 2015). It is one reason, among others, that the public has been slow to endorse government-supported benefits for all families, such as high-quality child care and paid employment leave for meeting family needs. It has also contributed to the large number of U.S. children who remain poor, even though their parents are employed (Gruendel & Aber, 2007; UNICEF, 2013).

▶ In Hispanic extended families, grandparents are especially likely to share actively in child rearing, reflecting the cultural ideal of familism. This grandmother enjoys a close relationship with her two grandchildren.

Although the culture as a whole may value independence and privacy, not all citizens share the same values. Some belong to **subcultures**—groups of people with beliefs and customs that differ from those of the larger culture. Many ethnic minority groups in the United States have cooperative family structures, which help protect their members from the harmful effects of poverty. For example, the African-American tradition of **extended-family households,** in which parent and child live with one or more adult relatives, is a vital feature of African-American family life that promotes resilience in children (Washington, Gleeson, & Rulison, 2013).

Active, involved extended families also characterize Asian, Native-American, and Hispanic subcultures. Within the extended family, grandparents play meaningful roles in guiding younger generations; adults who face employment, marital, or child-rearing difficulties receive assistance and emotional support; and caregiving is enhanced for children (Jones & Lindahl, 2011). In Hispanic extended families, grandparents are especially likely to share in child rearing—a collaborative parenting arrangement that has physical and emotional health benefits for grandparents, parents, and children alike (Goodman & Silverstein, 2006). A likely reason for such far-reaching effects is that intergenerational shared parenting is consistent with the Hispanic cultural ideal of *familism,* which places a particularly high priority on close, harmonious family bonds.

Our discussion so far reflects two broad sets of values on which cultures and subcultures are commonly compared: *collectivism* versus *individualism* (Triandis & Gelfand, 2012). In cultures that emphasize collectivism, people stress group goals over individual goals and value *interdependent* qualities, such as social harmony, obligations and responsibility to others, and collaborative endeavors. In cultures that emphasize individualism, people are largely concerned with their own personal needs and value *independence*—personal exploration, discovery, achievement, and choice in relationships. Although it is the most common basis for comparing cultures, the collectivism–individualism distinction is controversial because both sets of values exist, in varying mixtures, in most cultures (Taras et al., 2014). Nevertheless, consistent cross-national differences in collectivism–individualism remain: The United States is more individualistic than most Western European countries, which place greater weight on collectivism. These values affect a nation's approach to protecting the well-being of its children, families, and aging citizens.

Public Policies and Child Development. When widespread social problems arise, such as poverty, hunger, and disease, nations attempt to solve them through devising **public policies**—laws and government programs designed to improve current conditions. In the United States, public policies safeguarding children and youths have lagged behind policies in other developed nations. As Table 2.2 reveals, the United States does not rank well on important key measures of children's health and well-being.

TABLE 2.2
How Does the United States Compare to Other Nations on Indicators of Children's Health and Well-Being?

INDICATOR	U.S. RANK[a]	SOME COUNTRIES THE UNITED STATES TRAILS
Childhood poverty (among 20 economically advanced nations with similar standards of living)	20th	Canada, Iceland, Germany, United Kingdom, Norway, Sweden, Spain
Infant deaths in the first year of life (among 39 industrialized nations considered)	39th	Canada, Greece, Hungary, Ireland, Singapore, Spain
Teenage birth rate (among 20 industrialized nations considered)	20th	Australia, Canada, Czech Republic, Denmark, Hungary, Iceland, Poland, Slovakia
Public expenditure on education as a percentage of gross domestic product[b] (among 32 industrialized nations considered)	13th	Belgium, France, Iceland, New Zealand, Portugal, Spain, Sweden
Public expenditure on early childhood education as a percentage of gross domestic product[b] (among 34 industrialized nations considered)	21st	Austria, Germany, Italy, Netherlands, France, Sweden
Public expenditure on health as a percentage of total health expenditure, public plus private (among 35 industrialized nations considered)	35th	Austria, Australia, Canada, France, Hungary, Iceland, Switzerland, New Zealand

[a]1 = highest, or best, rank.
[b]Gross domestic product is the value of all goods and services produced by a nation during a specified time period. It provides an overall measure of a nation's wealth.

Sources: OECD, 2013, 2017; Sedgh et al., 2015; UNICEF, 2013; U.S. Census Bureau, 2017c.

AP IMAGES/SETH WENIG

▶ These students from low-income families benefit from participation in Upward Bound, a federally funded educational enrichment program. Public policies fostering children's development are vital both on humanitarian grounds and as an investment in the future.

The problems of children and youths extend beyond the indicators in the table. The Affordable Care Act, signed into law in 2010, extended government-supported health insurance to all children in low-income families. But expanded coverage for low-income adults, including parents, is not mandatory for the states, leaving millions of low-income parents without an affordable coverage option. Largely because uninsured parents lack knowledge of how to enroll their children, 11 percent of children eligible for the federally supported Children's Health Insurance Program (CHIP)—more than 5 million—do not receive coverage (Kaiser Family Foundation, 2015, 2017). Furthermore, the United States has been slow to move toward national standards and funding for child care. Affordable care is in short supply, and much of it is mediocre to poor in quality (Burchinal et al., 2015). In families affected by divorce, weak enforcement of child support payments heightens poverty in mother-headed households. And 7 percent of 16- to 24-year-olds who dropped out of high school have not returned to earn a diploma (U.S. Department of Education, 2016a).

Why have attempts to help children and youths been difficult to realize in the United States? Cultural values of self-reliance and privacy have made government hesitant to become involved in family matters. Furthermore, good social programs are expensive, and they must compete for a fair share of a country's economic resources. Children can easily remain unrecognized in this process because they cannot vote or speak out to protect their own interests (Ripple & Zigler, 2003). They must rely on the goodwill of others to become an important government priority.

Looking Toward the Future. Public policies aimed at fostering children's development can be justified on two grounds. The first is that children are the future—the parents, workers, and citizens of tomorrow. Investing in children yields valuable returns to a nation's quality of life. Second, child-oriented policies can be defended on humanitarian grounds—children's basic rights as human beings.

In 1989, the United Nations General Assembly, with the assistance of experts from many child-related fields, drew up the *Convention on the Rights of the Child,* a legal agreement among nations that commits each cooperating country to work toward guaranteeing environments that foster children's development, protect them from harm, and enhance their community participation and self-determination. Examples of rights include the highest attainable standard of health; an adequate standard of living; free and compulsory education; a happy, understanding, and loving family life; protection from all forms of abuse and neglect; and freedom of thought, conscience, and religion, subject to appropriate parental guidance and national law.

The United States played a key role in drawing up the Convention, yet it is the only country in the world whose legislature has not ratified it. American individualism has stood in the way (Scherrer, 2012). Opponents maintain that the Convention's provisions would shift the burden of child rearing from family to state.

Although the worrisome state of many children and families persists, efforts are being made to improve their condition. Throughout this text, we will discuss many successful programs that could be expanded. Also, growing awareness of the gap between what we know and what we do to better children's lives has led experts in child development to join with concerned citizens as advocates for more effective policies. As a result, influential interest groups devoted to the well-being of children have emerged.

In the United States, one of the most vigorous is the Children's Defense Fund (CDF), *www.childrensdefense.org*, a nonprofit organization that engages in public education and partners with other organizations, communities, and elected officials to improve policies for children.

Another energetic advocacy organization is the National Center for Children in Poverty, *www.nccp.org*, dedicated to advancing the economic security, health, and welfare of U.S. children in low-income families.

Besides strong advocacy, public policies that enhance development depend on research that documents needs and evaluates programs to spark improvements. Today, more researchers are collaborating with community and government agencies to enhance the social relevance of their investigations. They are also doing a better job of disseminating their findings in easily understandable, compelling ways, through reports to government officials, websites aimed at increasing public understanding, and collaborations with the media to ensure accurate and effective reporting (Shonkoff & Bales, 2011). In these ways, researchers are helping to create the sense of immediacy about the condition of children and families that is necessary to spur a society into action.

ASK YOURSELF

CONNECT How does poverty affect functioning of the family system, placing all domains of development at risk?

APPLY Check your local newspaper or one or two national news websites to see how often articles appear on the condition of children and families. Why is it important for researchers to communicate with the public about children's needs?

REFLECT Do you agree with the widespread American sentiment that government should not become involved in family life? Explain.

Understanding the Relationship Between Heredity and Environment

2.6 Explain the various ways heredity and environment may combine to influence complex traits.

Throughout this chapter, we have discussed a wide variety of genetic and environmental influences, each of which has the power to alter the course of development. Yet children who are born into the same family (and who therefore share both genes and environments) are often quite different in characteristics. We also know that some individuals are affected more than others by their homes, neighborhoods, and communities. In some cases, a child who is given many advantages nevertheless does poorly, while another, though exposed to unfavorable rearing conditions, does well. How do scientists explain the impact of heredity and environment when they seem to work in so many different ways?

Behavioral genetics is a field devoted to uncovering the contributions of nature and nurture to this diversity in human traits and abilities. Although they are making progress in identifying the multiple variations in DNA sequences associated with such complex traits as intelligence and personality, so far these genetic markers explain only a small amount of variation in human behavior, and a minority of cases of most psychological disorders (Plomin et al., 2016; Zhao & Castellanos, 2016). For the most part, scientists are still limited to investigating the impact of genes on complex characteristics indirectly.

Some believe that it is useful and possible to answer the question of *how much each factor contributes* to differences among people. A growing consensus, however, regards that question as unanswerable. These investigators believe that heredity and environment are inseparable (Lickliter & Honeycutt, 2015; Moore, 2013). The important question, they maintain, is *how nature and nurture work together.* Let's consider each position in turn.

The Question, "How Much?"

To infer the role of heredity in complex human characteristics, researchers use special methods, the most common being the *heritability estimate.* Let's look closely at the information this procedure yields, along with its limitations.

Heritability. **Heritability estimates** measure the extent to which individual differences in complex traits in a specific population are due to genetic factors. We will take a brief look at heritability findings on intelligence and personality here, returning to them in greater detail in later chapters. Heritability estimates are obtained from **kinship studies,** which compare the characteristics of family members. The most common type of kinship study compares identical twins, who share all their genes, with fraternal twins, who, on average, share only half. If people who are genetically more alike are also more similar in intelligence and personality, then the researcher assumes that heredity plays an important role.

Kinship studies of intelligence provide some of the most controversial findings in the field of developmental science. Some experts claim a strong genetic influence, whereas others believe that heredity is barely involved. Currently, most kinship findings support a moderate role for heredity. When many twin studies are examined, correlations between the scores of identical twins are consistently higher than those of fraternal twins. In a summary of more than 10,000 twin pairs of diverse ages, the correlation for intelligence was .85 for identical twins and .60 for fraternal twins (Plomin & Spinath, 2004; Plomin et al., 2016).

Researchers use a complex statistical procedure to compare these correlations, arriving at a heritability estimate ranging from 0 to 1.00. The typical overall value for intelligence is about .50 for child and adolescent twin samples in Western industrialized nations. This suggests that differences in genetic makeup explain half the variation in intelligence. However, heritability increases with age, from approximately .40 in childhood, to .55 in adolescence, to .65 in early adulthood (Haworth et al., 2010; Plomin et al., 2016). As we will see later, one explanation is that, compared to children, adolescents and adults exert greater personal control over their intellectual experiences—for example, how much time they spend reading or solving challenging problems. Adopted children's mental test scores are more strongly related to their biological parents' scores than to those of their adoptive parents, offering further support for the role of heredity (Petrill & Deater-Deckard, 2004).

JANEK SKARZYNSKI/AFP/GETTY IMAGES

▶ Kasia Ofmanski, of Warsaw, Poland, holds photos of Nina (right), the identical twin from whom she was mistakenly separated at birth, and Edyta (left), who was assumed to be her twin and who grew up with her. When the twins first met at age 17, Kasia exclaimed, "She's just like me." They found many similarities: Both were physically active, extroverted, and earned similar grades in school. Clearly heredity contributes to personality traits, but generalizing from twin evidence to the population is controversial.

Heritability research also reveals that genetic factors are important in personality. For frequently studied traits, such as sociability, anxiety, agreeableness, and activity level, heritability estimates obtained on child, adolescent, and young adult twins are moderate, in the .40s and .50s (Vukasović & Bratko, 2015). Unlike intelligence, however, heritability of personality does not increase with age (Turkheimer, Pettersson, & Horn, 2014).

Twin studies of schizophrenia, bipolar disorder, and autism generally yield high heritabilities, above .70. Heritabilities for antisocial behavior and major depression are considerably lower, in the .30s and .40s (Ronald & Hoekstra, 2014; Sullivan, Daly, & O'Donovan, 2012). Again, adoption studies are consistent with these results. Biological relatives of adoptees with schizophrenia, bipolar disorder, or autism are more likely than adoptive relatives to share the same disorder (Plomin, DeFries, & Knopik, 2013).

Limitations of Heritability. The accuracy of heritability estimates depends on the extent to which the twin pairs studied reflect genetic and environmental variation in the population. Within a population in which all people have very similar home, school, and community experiences, individual differences in intelligence and personality are assumed to be largely genetic, and heritability estimates should be close to 1.00. Conversely, the more environments vary, the more likely they are to account for individual differences, yielding lower heritability estimates. In twin studies, most twin pairs are reared together under highly similar conditions. Even when separated twins are available for study, social service agencies have often placed them in advantaged homes that are alike in many ways (Richardson & Norgate, 2006). Because the environments of most twin pairs are less diverse than those of the general population, heritability estimates are likely to exaggerate the role of heredity.

Heritability estimates can easily be misapplied. For example, high heritabilities have been used to suggest that ethnic differences in intelligence, such as the poorer performance of African-American children compared to European-American children, have a genetic basis (Jensen, 1969, 2001; Rushton, 2012). Yet heritabilities computed on mostly White twin samples do not explain test score differences between ethnic groups. We have already seen that large SES differences are involved. In Chapter 9, we will discuss research indicating that when African-American children are adopted into economically advantaged homes at an early age, their scores are well above average and substantially higher than those of children growing up in impoverished families.

Consistent with these findings, the heritability of children's intelligence increases as parental education and income increase—that is, as children grow up in conditions that allow them to make the most of their genetic endowment. In impoverished environments, children are prevented from realizing their potential. Consequently, enhancing these children's experiences through interventions—such as parent education and high-quality preschool or child care—has a greater impact on development (Bronfenbrenner & Morris, 2006; Phillips & Lowenstein, 2011).

The Question, "How?"

Today, most researchers view development as the result of a dynamic interplay between heredity and environment. How do nature and nurture work together? Several concepts shed light on this question.

Gene–Environment Interaction.

The first of these ideas is **gene–environment interaction,** which means that because of their genetic makeup, individuals differ in their responsiveness to qualities of the environment (Rutter, 2011). Gene–environment interaction can apply to any characteristic; it is illustrated for intelligence in Figure 2.7. Notice that when environments vary from extremely unstimulating to highly enriched, Ben's intelligence increases steadily, Linda's rises sharply and then falls off, and Ron's begins to increase only after the environment becomes modestly stimulating.

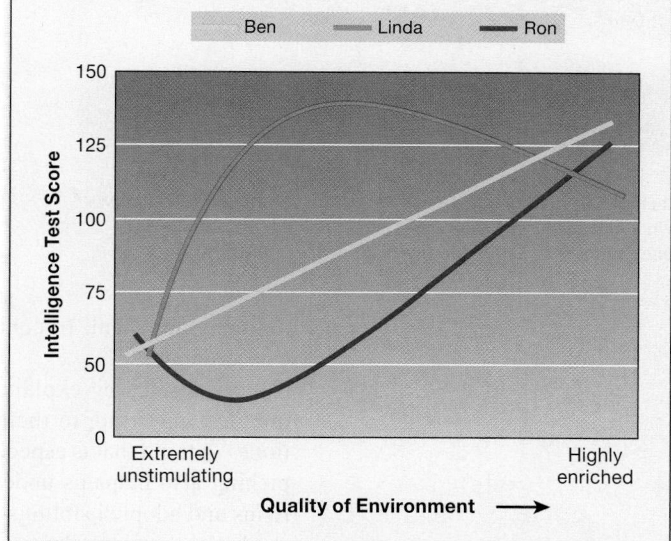

FIGURE 2.7 Gene–environment interaction, illustrated for intelligence by three children who differ in responsiveness to quality of the environment. As environments vary from extremely unstimulating to highly enriched, Ben's intelligence test score increases steadily, Linda's rises sharply and then falls off, and Ron's begins to increase only after the environment becomes modestly stimulating.

Gene–environment interaction highlights two important points. First, it shows that because each of us has a unique genetic makeup, we respond differently to the same environment. Second, sometimes different gene–environment combinations can make two people look the same! For example, if Linda is reared in a minimally stimulating environment, her score will be about 100—average for people in general. Ben and Ron can also obtain this score, but to do so, they must grow up in fairly enriched circumstances (Gottlieb, Wahlsten, & Lickliter, 2006).

Recently, researchers have made strides in identifying gene–environment interactions in personality development. In Chapter 6 we will see that young children with certain genes that increase their risk of an emotionally reactive temperament respond especially strongly to variations in parenting quality (Bakermans-Kranenburg & van IJzendoorn, 2015). When parenting is favorable, they gain control over their emotions and adjust as well or better than other children. But when parenting is unfavorable, they become increasingly irritable, difficult, and poorly adjusted, more so than children not at genetic risk.

Gene–Environment Correlation.

A major problem in trying to separate heredity and environment is that they are often correlated (Rutter, 2011; Scarr & McCartney, 1983). According to the concept of **gene–environment correlation,** our genes influence the environments to which we are exposed. The way this happens changes with age.

▶ These parents share their enthusiasm for outdoor sports with their children, who may have inherited the parents' athletic ability. When heredity and environment are correlated, the influence of one cannot be separated from the influence of the other.

Passive and Evocative Correlation. At younger ages, two types of gene–environment correlation are common. The first is called *passive* correlation because the child has no control over it. Early on, parents provide environments influenced by their own heredity. For example, parents who are good athletes emphasize outdoor activities and enroll their children in swimming and gymnastics. Besides being exposed to an "athletic environment," the children may have inherited their parents' athletic ability. As a result, they are likely to become good athletes for both genetic and environmental reasons.

The second type of gene–environment correlation is *evocative*. Children evoke responses that are influenced by the child's heredity, and these responses strengthen the child's original style. For example, a cooperative, attentive child probably receives more sensitive, patient interactions from parents than an inattentive, distractible child. In support of this idea, the more genetically alike siblings are, the more their parents treat them alike, in both warmth and negativity. Parents' treatment of identical twins is highly similar, whereas their treatment of fraternal twins and nontwin biological siblings is only moderately so (Reiss, 2003). Likewise, identical-twin pairs—who resemble each other more in sociability than fraternal twins do—tend to be more alike in the degree of friendliness they evoke from new playmates (DiLalla, Bersted, & John, 2015).

Active Correlation. At older ages, *active* gene–environment correlation becomes common. As children extend their experiences beyond the immediate family and are given the freedom to make more choices, they actively seek environments that fit with their genetic tendencies. The well-coordinated, muscular child spends more time at after-school sports, while the intellectually curious child is a familiar patron at her local library.

This tendency to actively choose environments that complement our heredity is called **niche-picking** (Scarr & McCartney, 1983). Infants and young children cannot do much niche-picking because adults select environments for them. In contrast, older children and adolescents are increasingly in charge of their environments.

Niche-picking explains why pairs of identical twins reared apart during childhood and later reunited may find, to their surprise, that they have similar hobbies, food preferences, and vocations—a trend that is especially marked when twins' environmental opportunities are similar. Niche-picking also helps us understand why identical twins become somewhat more alike, and fraternal twins and adopted siblings less alike, in intelligence with age (Bouchard, 2004). And niche-picking sheds light on why identical twin pairs—far more often than same-sex fraternal pairs—report similar stressful life events influenced by personal decisions and actions, such as failing a course or getting in trouble for drug-taking (Bemmels et al., 2008).

The influence of heredity and environment is not constant but changes over time. With age, genetic factors may become more important in influencing the environments we experience and choose for ourselves.

Environmental Influences on Gene Expression. Notice how, in the concepts just considered, heredity is granted priority. In gene–environment interaction, it affects responsiveness to particular environments. Similarly, gene–environment correlation is viewed as driven by genetics, in that children's genetic makeup causes them to receive, evoke, or seek experiences that actualize their hereditary tendencies (Rutter, 2011).

A growing number of researchers contend that heredity does not dictate children's experiences or development in a rigid way. For example, in a large Finnish adoption study, children with a genetic tendency for mental illness (based on having a biological mother diagnosed with schizophrenia) but who were being reared by healthy adoptive parents showed little mental illness. In contrast, schizophrenia and other psychological impairments piled up in adoptees whose biological and adoptive parents were both mentally ill (Tienari, Wahlberg, & Wynne, 2006; Tienari et al., 2003).

Furthermore, parents and other caring adults can *uncouple* unfavorable gene–environment correlations by providing children with positive experiences that modify the expression of heredity, yielding positive outcomes. In a study that tracked the development of 5-year-old identical twins, pair members tended to resemble each other in level of aggression. And the more aggression they displayed, the more maternal anger and criticism they received (a gene–environment correlation). Nevertheless, some mothers treated their twins differently. When followed up at age 7, twins who had been targets of more maternal negativity engaged in even more aggressive behavior. In contrast, their better-treated, genetically identical counterparts showed a reduction in disruptive acts (Caspi et al., 2004). Good parenting protected them from a spiraling, antisocial course of development.

Accumulating evidence reveals that the relationship between heredity and environment is *bidirectional:* Genes affect people's behavior and experiences, but their experiences and behavior also affect gene expression. This view of the relationship between heredity and environment, depicted in Figure 2.8, is called **epigenesis,** which means development resulting from ongoing, bidirectional exchanges between heredity and all levels of the environment (Cox, 2013; Gottlieb, 1998, 2007). Biologists are clarifying the precise mechanisms through which environment can alter gene expression without changing the DNA sequence—a field of research called *epigenetics.* One such mechanism is **methylation**—a biochemical process triggered by certain experiences, in which a set of chemical compounds (called a methyl group) lands on top of a gene and changes its impact, reducing or silencing its expression. Methylation levels can be measured, and they help explain why identical twins, though precisely the same in DNA sequencing, sometimes display strikingly different phenotypes with age.

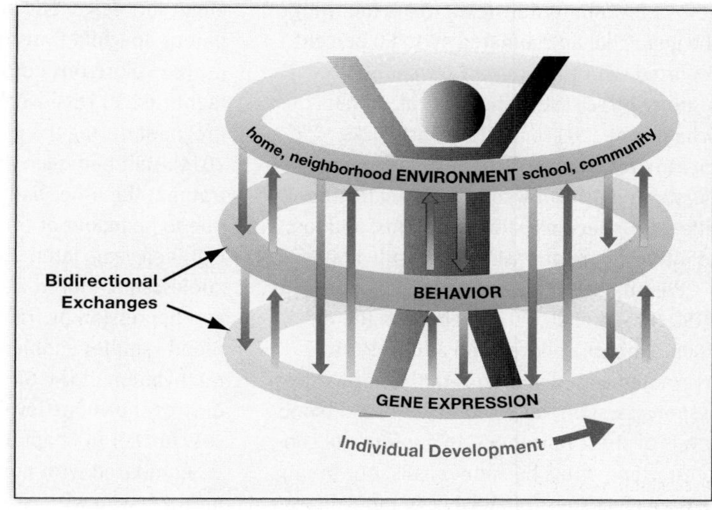

FIGURE 2.8 Epigenesis. Development takes place through ongoing, bidirectional exchanges between heredity and all levels of the environment. Genes affect behavior and experiences. Experiences and behavior also affect gene expression. (Based on Gottlieb, 2007.)

A case study of a pair of identical-twin adults offers an illustration. Researchers reported that they had been highly similar in personality throughout childhood. But after high school, one twin remained close to home, studied law, married, and had children, whereas the other left home, became a journalist, and traveled to war zones around the world, where she repeatedly encountered life-threatening situations. Assessed again in their forties, compared with the "law twin," the "war twin" engaged in more risky behaviors, including drinking and gambling (Kaminsky et al., 2007). DNA analyses revealed greater methylation of a gene known to affect impulse control in the "war twin" than in the "law twin"—a difference much larger than is typical for identical-twin pairs.

Environmental modification of gene expression can occur at any age, even prenatally. Recall our discussion of genomic imprinting on page 45. It is an epigenetic process occurring within the ovum or sperm, often involving methylation. And one way harmful prenatal environmental factors we will address in Chapter 3 may compromise development is through gene methylation (Markunas et al., 2014). As the Biology and Environment box on page 66 illustrates, severe maternal stress during pregnancy is linked to long-term impairment in children's capacity to manage stress, with gene methylation likely contributing to unfavorable outcomes. Furthermore, animal evidence indicates that some methylated genes are passed from parent to offspring at conception, thereby affecting development in subsequent generations (Grossniklaus et al., 2013).

We must keep in mind, however, that epigenetic processes also operate positively: Favorable rearing experiences alter gene expression in ways that enhance development! And some negative epigenetic modifications may be reversible through carefully designed interventions (van IJzendoorn, Bakermans-Kranenburg, & Ebstein, 2011). The concept of epigenesis reminds us that the genome is constantly in flux, both reflecting and affecting the individual's ever-changing environment.

BIOLOGY AND ENVIRONMENT

The Tutsi Genocide and Epigenetic Transmission of Maternal Stress to Children

In 1994, in a genocidal rampage against the Tutsi people of Rwanda, nearly 1 million people perished within a three-month period. The horror was so extreme that in surveys of Rwandans during the years following the genocide, an estimated 40 to 60 percent reported symptoms of *post-traumatic stress disorder (PTSD)* (Neugebauer et al., 2009; Schaal et al., 2011). In PTSD, flashbacks, nightmares, anxiety, irritability, angry outbursts, and difficulty concentrating lead to intense distress, physical symptoms, and loss of interest in relationships and daily life.

Parental PTSD is a strong predictor of child PTSD (Brand et al., 2011; Yehuda & Bierer, 2009). In both children and adults, PTSD is associated with disruptions in the body's stress response system, reflected in abnormal blood levels of stress hormones. In appropriate concentrations, stress hormones assist our brains in managing stress effectively. In individuals with PTSD, stress hormone levels are either too high or (more often) too low, contributing to persistently disturbed stress regulation.

Mounting evidence confirms that exposure to extreme adversity increases methylation of a chromosome-5 gene called GR, which plays a central role in stress-hormone regulation. Might this epigenetic process contribute to parent–to–child transmission of PTSD?

To explore this question, researchers identified 50 Tutsi women who had been pregnant during the genocide (Perroud et al., 2014). Half had been directly exposed to the trauma; the other half had not been exposed due to being out of the country at the time. Eighteen years later, the mothers and their adolescent children were assessed for PTSD and depression by trained psychologists. Blood samples enabled genetic testing for methylation of the GR gene and assessment of stress-hormone levels (which we will discuss further in Chapter 3).

Compared with non-exposed mothers, mothers who witnessed the genocidal carnage had substantially higher PTSD and depression scores, and children of the two groups of mothers differed similarly. Also, as Figure 2.9 reveals, exposed mothers and their children displayed stronger GR methylation. And consistent with methylation's dampening effect on gene expression, trauma-exposed mothers and their children had much lower stress-hormone levels than their non-exposed counterparts.

These findings are consistent with other evidence, in both animals and humans, indicating that prenatal exposure to the biological consequences of severe maternal stress can induce epigenetic changes, through methylation, that impair functioning of the body's stress response system (Daskalakis & Yehuda, 2014; Mueller & Bale, 2008). In the Tutsi mothers and children, the effects of genocidal trauma were long-lasting, evident in serious psychological disorders nearly two decades later.

As the researchers noted, more remains to be discovered about exactly how maternal trauma exposure compromised the Tutsi children's capacity to manage stress. Epigenetic processes, not just prenatally but also at later ages, may have been largely responsible. Alternatively, poor-quality parenting, resulting from maternal anxiety, irritability, anger, and depression, could have been the major influence. More likely, epigenetic changes, inept parenting, and other unfavorable environmental factors combined to place the Tutsi children at high risk for PTSD and depression. In Chapter 3, we will return to the impact of prenatal stress, including evidence showing that its negative impact can be lessened or prevented through social support.

JONATHAN TORGOVNIK/GETTY IMAGES REPORTAGE

This Rwandan mother gave birth shortly after the Tutsi genocide. Nine years later, she continues to suffer from PTSD caused by first-hand experience of atrocities, including repeated rape and loss of her mother, brother, and two sisters in the massacre. Her daughter's PTSD and depression might be the result of prenatal exposure to severe maternal stress, which can trigger epigenetic changes that disrupt the body's stress response system.

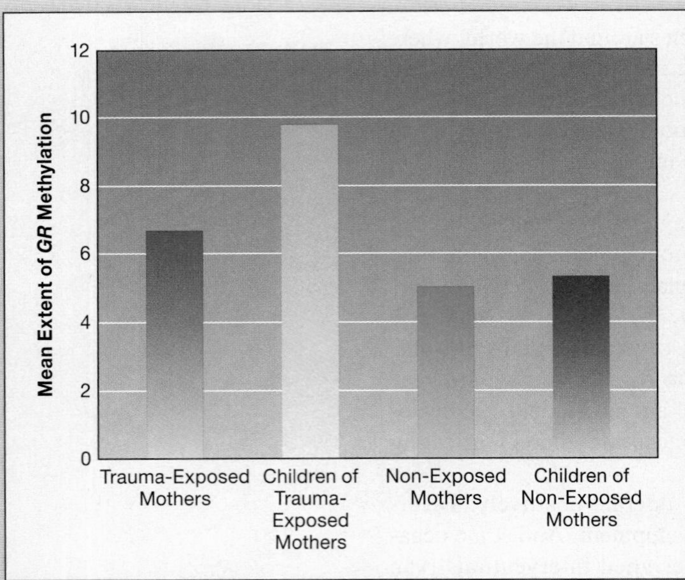

FIGURE 2.9 Methylation status of the *GR* gene in trauma-exposed and non-trauma-exposed Tutsi mothers and their children. Mothers who had been directly exposed to the Rwandan Tutsi genocide, as well as their children, showed elevated methylation of the *GR* gene, which is centrally involved in functioning of the body's stress response system. (Based on Perroud et al., 2014.)

Epigenetics is still an emerging field, and clarifying its mechanisms may prove to be even more complex than efforts to understand DNA sequence variations (Duncan, Pollastri, & Smoller, 2014). But from what we already know, one lesson is clear: Development is best understood as a series of complex exchanges between nature and nurture. Although people cannot be changed in any way we might desire, environments can modify genetic influences. The success of any attempt to improve development depends on the characteristics we want to change, the genetic makeup of the individual, and the type and timing of our intervention.

ASK YOURSELF

CONNECT Explain how each of the following concepts supports the conclusion that genetic influences on human characteristics are not constant but change over time: somatic mutation (page 45), niche-picking (page 64), and epigenesis (page 65).

APPLY Bianca's parents are accomplished musicians. At age 4, Bianca began taking piano lessons. By age 10, she was accompanying the school choir. At age 14, she asked to attend a special music high school. Explain how gene–environment correlation promoted Bianca's talent.

REFLECT What aspects of your own development—for example, interests, hobbies, college major, or vocational choice—are probably due to niche-picking? Explain.

CHAPTER 2 SUMMARY

Genetic Foundations *(p. 40)*

2.1 ***Explain what genes are and how they are transmitted from one generation to the next.***

- Each individual's **phenotype,** or directly observable characteristics, is a product of both **genotype** and environment. **Chromosomes,** rodlike structures within the cell nucleus, contain our hereditary endowment. Along their length are **genes,** segments of **deoxyribonucleic acid (DNA). Protein-coding genes** send instructions for making proteins to the cell's cytoplasm; **regulator genes** modify those instructions. A wide range of environmental factors also alter gene expression.
- **Gametes,** or sex cells, result from a cell division process called **meiosis,** which ensures that each individual receives a unique set of genes from each parent. Once sperm and ovum unite, the resulting **zygote** will then have the full complement of chromosomes.
- Genetic sex is determined by whether sperm containing an X-bearing or a Y-bearing chromosome fertilizes the ovum. **Fraternal,** or **dizygotic, twins** result when two ova are released from the mother's ovaries and each is fertilized. **Identical,** or **monozygotic, twins** develop when a zygote divides in two during the early stages of cell duplication.

© RAY EVANS/ALAMY STOCK PHOTO

2.2 ***Describe various patterns of gene–gene interaction.***

- Traits controlled by single genes follow **dominant–recessive** and **incomplete-dominance inheritance. Homozygous** individuals have two identical **alleles,** or forms of a gene. **Heterozygous** individuals, with one dominant and one recessive allele, are **carriers** of the recessive trait. In incomplete dominance, both alleles are expressed in the phenotype.
- **X-linked inheritance** applies when recessive disorders are carried on the X chromosome and, therefore, are more likely to affect males. In **genomic imprinting,** alleles are chemically marked within the ovum or sperm, silencing one pair member and leaving the other to be expressed, regardless of its makeup.
- Harmful genes arise from **mutation,** which can occur spontaneously or be caused by hazardous environmental agents. Germline mutation occurs in the cells that give rise to gametes; somatic mutation can occur in body cells at any time of life.
- Traits that vary on a continuum, such as intelligence and personality, result from **polygenic inheritance**—the effects of many genes.

2.3 ***Describe major chromosomal abnormalities, and explain how they occur.***

- Most chromosomal abnormalities result from errors during meiosis. The most common, Down syndrome, leads to intellectual disability and physical defects. **Sex chromosome** disorders are milder than defects of the **autosomes**.

Reproductive Choices *(p. 47)*

2.4 ***Discuss counseling, medical procedures, and reproductive options that can assist prospective parents in having healthy children.***

- **Genetic counseling** helps couples at risk for giving birth to children with genetic abnormalities consider reproductive options. **Prenatal diagnostic methods** allow early detection of developmental problems. Genetic engineering and gene therapy offer hope for treating hereditary disorders.

- Reproductive technologies, such as donor insemination, in vitro fertilization, and surrogate motherhood, enable individuals to become parents who otherwise would not, but they raise legal and ethical concerns.
- Many adults who cannot conceive or are likely to transmit a genetic disorder choose adoption. Although adopted children tend to have more learning and emotional problems than children in general, most fare well in the long run. Warm, sensitive parenting predicts favorable development.

Environmental Contexts for Development *(p. 52)*

2.5 ***Describe family functioning from the perspective of ecological systems theory, along with aspects of the environment that support family well-being and development.***

- The first and foremost context for child development is the family, a dynamic system characterized by bidirectional influences, in which each member's behaviors affect those of others. Both direct and indirect influences operate within the family system, which must continually adjust to new events and changes in its members. Warm, gratifying family ties, which foster effective **coparenting,** help ensure children's psychological health.
- **Socioeconomic status (SES)** profoundly affects family functioning. Higher-SES families tend to be smaller, to emphasize psychological traits, and to engage in warm, verbally stimulating interaction with children. Lower-SES families often stress external characteristics and use more commands, criticism, and physical punishment.
- Poverty and homelessness undermine effective parenting and pose serious threats to children's development. In affluent families, parental physical and emotional unavailability may impair youths' adjustment.
- Children benefit from supportive ties between the family and community, including stable, socially cohesive neighborhoods that provide constructive leisure and enrichment activities. High-quality schooling and parental involvement in children's education enhance academic achievement and educational attainment.
- The values and practices of cultures and **subcultures** affect all aspects of children's daily life. **Extended-family households,** which are common among many ethnic minorities, help protect family members from the negative effects of poverty and other stressful life conditions.
- Consistent cross-national differences in *collectivism–individualism* powerfully affect approaches to devising **public policies** to address social problems. Largely because of its strongly individualistic values, the United States lags behind other developed nations in policies safeguarding children and youths.

Understanding the Relationship Between Heredity and Environment *(p. 61)*

2.6 ***Explain the various ways heredity and environment may combine to influence complex traits.***

- **Behavioral genetics** examines the contributions of nature and nurture to the diversity in human traits and abilities. Some researchers use **kinship studies** to compute **heritability estimates,** which attempt to quantify the influence of genetic factors on such complex traits as intelligence and personality. However, the accuracy of this approach has been challenged.

- In **gene–environment interaction,** heredity influences each individual's responsiveness to qualities of the environment. **Gene–environment correlation** and **niche-picking** describe how children's genes affect the environments to which they are exposed.
- **Epigenesis** reminds us that development is best understood as a series of complex exchanges between heredity and all levels of the environment. Epigenetic research is uncovering biochemical processes—such as **methylation**—through which environment can modify gene expression.

IMPORTANT TERMS AND CONCEPTS

CHAPTER 3

Prenatal Development, Birth, and the Newborn Baby

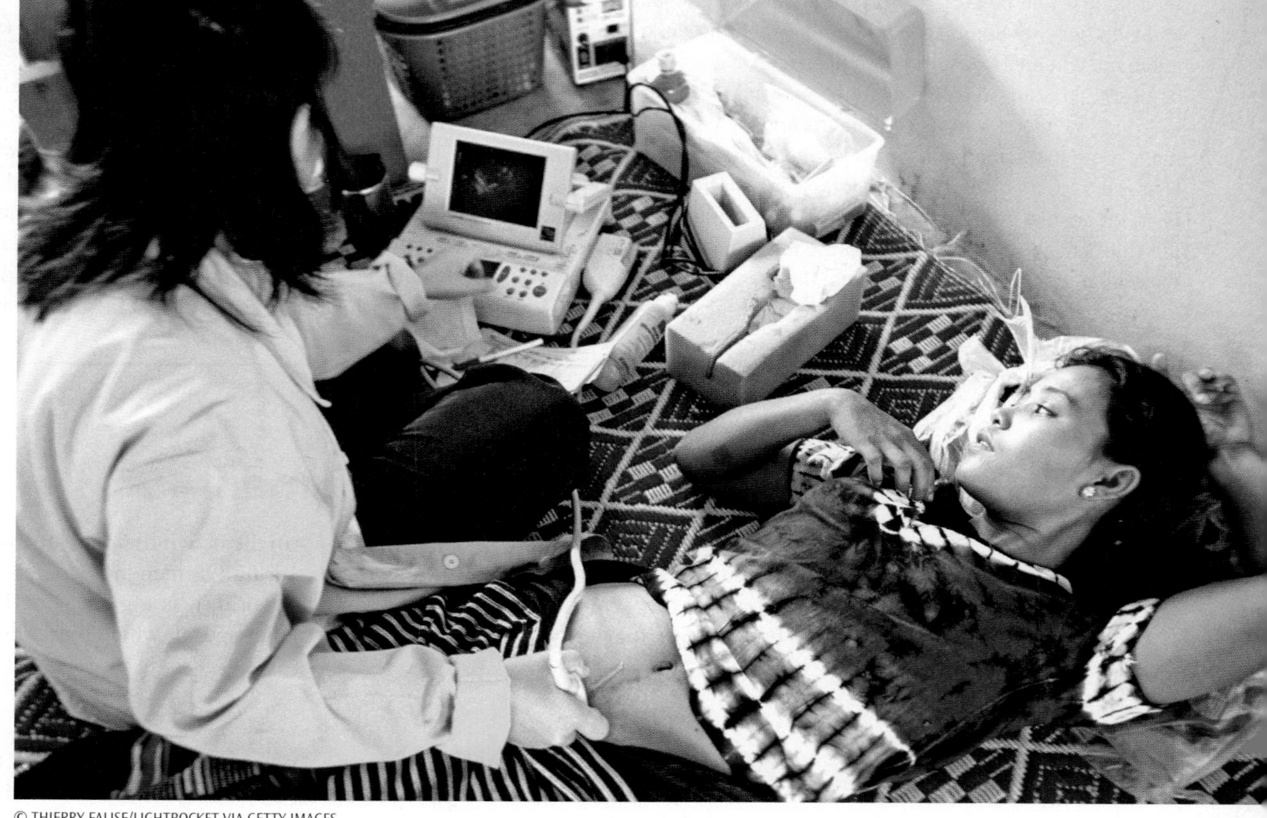

An expectant mother observes closely as a nurse uses a portable ultrasound device to check the health of her fetus. High-quality prenatal care provided at this field clinic along the Thai-Burmese border helps protect pregnant women from serious diseases that are common in the region.

WHAT'S AHEAD IN CHAPTER 3

One fall, Yolanda and Jay enrolled in an evening section of my child development course, when Yolanda was just two months pregnant. In their early thirties with their careers well under way, they had decided to have a baby. Both were full of questions: "How does the baby grow before birth?" "When is each organ formed?" "Has its heart begun to beat?" "Can it hear, feel, or sense our presence?"

Yolanda and Jay wanted to do everything possible to make sure their baby would be born healthy. Yolanda wondered about her diet and whether she should keep up her daily aerobic workout. And she asked me whether an aspirin for a headache, a glass of wine at dinner, or a few daily cups of coffee might be harmful.

In this chapter, we answer Yolanda and Jay's questions, along with many more that scientists have asked about the events before birth. First, we trace prenatal development, paying special attention to supports for healthy growth as well as to damaging influences that threaten the child's health and survival. Because the changes taking place during these nine months are so astounding, the prenatal environment can exert a powerful, lasting impact—for better or for worse—on physical and mental health. Next, we turn to the events of childbirth, including the choices available to women in industrialized nations about where and how to give birth.

ARIEL SKELLEY/GETTY IMAGES/BLEND IMAGES

Yolanda and Jay's son Joshua was strong, alert, and healthy at birth. But the birth process does not always go smoothly. We will consider the pros and cons of medical interventions, such as pain-relieving drugs and surgical deliveries, designed to ease a difficult birth and protect the health of mother and baby. Our discussion also addresses the development of infants born underweight or too early. We conclude with a close look at the remarkable capacities of newborns.

Prenatal Development

3.1 List the three periods of prenatal development, and describe the major milestones of each.

The sperm and ovum that unite to form the new individual are uniquely suited for the task of reproduction. The ovum is a tiny sphere, measuring 1⁄175 inch in diameter—the size of the period at the end of this sentence. But in its microscopic world, it is a giant—the largest cell in the human body, making it a perfect target for the much smaller sperm, which measure only 1⁄500 inch.

Conception

About once every 28 days, in the middle of a woman's menstrual cycle, an ovum bursts from one of her *ovaries,* two walnut-sized organs located deep inside her abdomen, and is drawn into one of two *fallopian tubes*—long, thin structures that lead to the hollow, softly lined uterus (see Figure 3.1). While the ovum is traveling, the spot on the ovary from which it was released, now called the *corpus luteum,* secretes hormones that prepare the lining of the uterus to receive a fertilized ovum. If pregnancy does not occur, the corpus luteum shrinks, and the lining of the uterus is discarded two weeks later with menstruation.

The male produces sperm in vast numbers—an average of 300 million a day—in the *testes,* two glands located in the *scrotum,* sacs that lie just behind the penis. Each sperm develops a tail that permits it to swim long distances, upstream in the female reproductive tract, through the *cervix* (opening of the uterus) and into the fallopian tube, where fertilization usually takes place. The journey is difficult: Only 300 to 500 reach their destination. Sperm live for up to six days and can lie in wait for the ovum, which survives for only one day after its release from the ovary. However, most conceptions result from intercourse occurring during a three-day period—on the day of ovulation or during the two days preceding it (Mu & Fehring, 2014).

With conception, the story of prenatal development begins to unfold. The vast changes that take place during the 38 weeks of pregnancy are usually divided into three periods: (1) the germinal period, (2) the period of the embryo, and (3) the period of the fetus. As we consider each, refer to Table 3.1 on page 72, which summarizes milestones of prenatal development.

Germinal Period

The **germinal period** lasts about two weeks, from fertilization and formation of the zygote until the tiny mass of cells drifts down and out of the fallopian tube and attaches itself to the wall of the

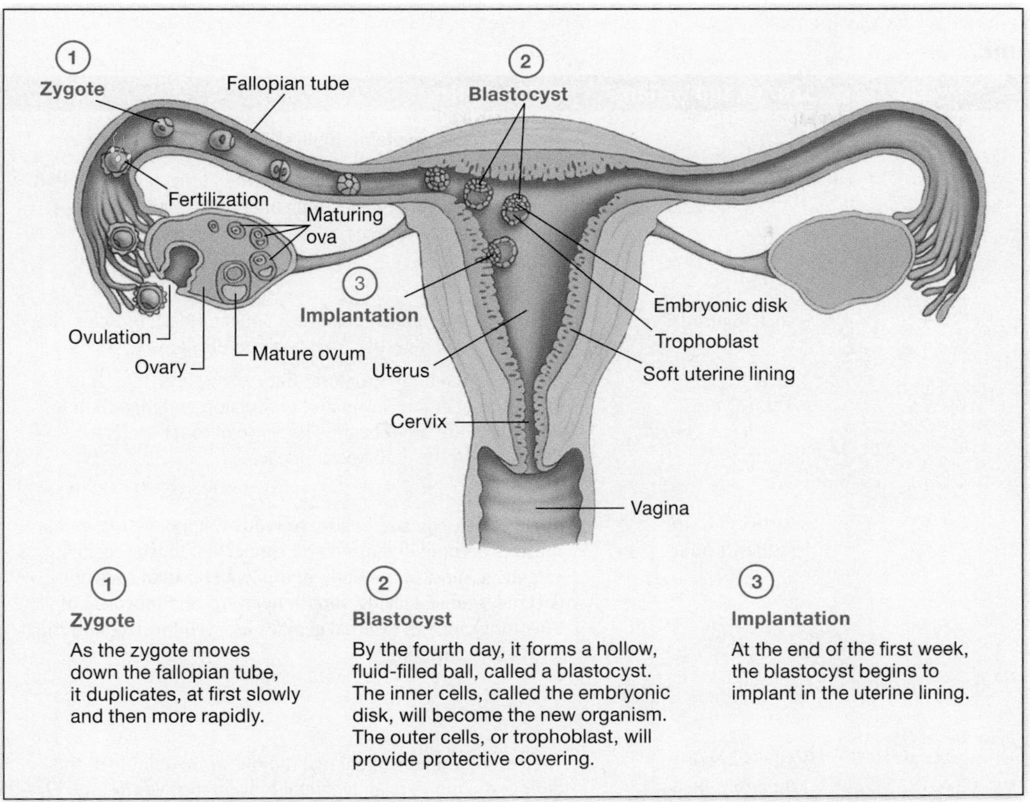

FIGURE 3.1 Female reproductive organs, showing fertilization, early cell duplication, and implantation. (From *Before We Are Born,* 9th ed., by K. L. Moore, T. V. N. Persaud, & M. G. Torchia, p. 33. Copyright © 2016 Elsevier, Inc.)

uterus. The zygote's first cell duplication is long and drawn out, taking about 30 hours. Gradually, new cells are added at a faster rate. By the fourth day, 60 to 70 cells exist that form a hollow, fluid-filled ball called a *blastocyst* (refer again to Figure 3.1). The cells on the inside of the blastocyst, called the *embryonic disk,* will become the new organism; the outer ring of cells, termed the *trophoblast,* will become the structures that provide protective covering and nourishment.

Implantation. Between the seventh and ninth days, **implantation** occurs: The blastocyst burrows deep into the uterine lining. Surrounded by the woman's nourishing blood, it starts to grow in earnest. At first, the trophoblast (protective outer layer) multiplies fastest. It forms a membrane, called the **amnion,** that encloses the developing organism in *amniotic fluid,* which helps keep the temperature of the prenatal world constant and provides a cushion against any jolts caused by the woman's movement. A *yolk sac* emerges that produces blood cells until the developing liver, spleen, and bone marrow are mature enough to take over this function (Moore, Persaud, & Torchia, 2016a).

As many as 30 percent of zygotes do not survive this period. In some, the sperm and ovum did not join properly. In others, cell duplication never begins. By preventing implantation in these cases, nature eliminates most prenatal abnormalities (Sadler, 2014).

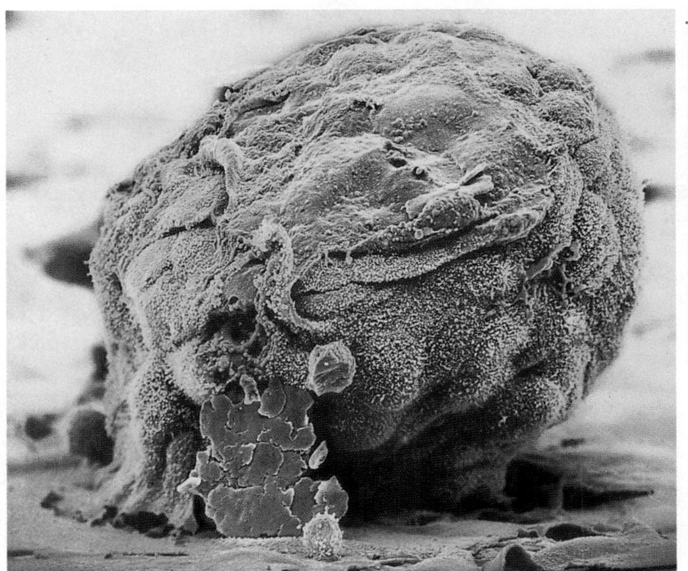

▶ **Germinal period: seventh to ninth day.** The fertilized ovum duplicates rapidly, forming a hollow ball of cells, or blastocyst, by the fourth day after fertilization. Here the blastocyst, magnified thousands of times, burrows into the uterine lining between the seventh and ninth days.

TABLE 3.1
Milestones of Prenatal Development

TRIMESTER	PRENATAL PERIOD	WEEKS	LENGTH AND WEIGHT	MAJOR EVENTS
First	Germinal	1		The one-celled zygote multiplies and forms a blastocyst.
		2		The blastocyst burrows into the uterine lining. Structures that feed and protect the developing organism begin to form—*amnion, chorion, yolk sac, placenta,* and *umbilical cord.*
	Embryo	3–4	¼ inch (6 mm)	A primitive brain and spinal cord appear. Heart, muscles, ribs, backbone, and digestive tract begin to develop.
		5–8	1 inch (2.5 cm); ⅐ ounce (4 g)	Many external body structures (face, arms, legs, toes, fingers) and internal organs form, and production and migration of neurons in the brain begin. The sense of touch starts to develop, and the embryo can move.
	Fetus	9–12	3 inches (7.6 cm); less than 1 ounce (28 g)	Rapid increase in size begins. Nervous system, organs, and muscles become organized and connected, touch sensitivity extends to most of the body, and new behavioral capacities (kicking, thumb sucking, mouth opening, and rehearsal of breathing) appear. External genitals are well-formed, and the fetus's sex is evident.
Second		13–24	12 inches (30 cm); 1.8 pounds (820 g)	The fetus continues to enlarge rapidly. In the middle of this period, the mother can feel fetal movements. Vernix and lanugo keep the fetus's skin from chapping in the amniotic fluid. Most of the brain's neurons are in place by 24 weeks. Eyes are sensitive to light, and the fetus reacts to sound.
Third		25–38	20 inches (50 cm); 7.5 pounds (3,400 g)	The fetus has a good chance of survival if born during this time. Size increases. Lungs mature. Rapid brain development, in neural connectivity and organization, enables sensory and behavioral capacities to expand. In the middle of this period, a layer of fat is added under the skin. Antibodies are transmitted from mother to fetus to protect against disease. Most fetuses rotate into an upside-down position in preparation for birth.

Source: Moore, Persaud, & Torchia, 2016a.

Photos (from top to bottom): © Claude Cortier/Photo Researchers, Inc.; © G. Moscoso/Photo Researchers, Inc.; © John Watney/Photo Researchers, Inc.; © James Stevenson/Photo Researchers, Inc.; © Lennart Nilsson, *A Child Is Born*/TT Nyhetsbyrån.

The Placenta and Umbilical Cord. By the end of the second week, cells of the trophoblast form another protective membrane—the **chorion,** which surrounds the amnion. From the chorion, tiny fingerlike *villi,* or blood vessels, emerge.[1] As these villi burrow into the uterine wall, the placenta starts to develop. By bringing the embryo's and mother's blood close together, the **placenta** permits food and oxygen to reach the developing organism and waste products to be carried away. A membrane forms that allows these substances to be exchanged but prevents the mother's and embryo's blood from mixing directly.

The placenta is connected to the developing organism by the **umbilical cord,** which first appears as a primitive body stalk and, during the course of pregnancy, grows to a length of 1 to 3

[1]Recall from Table 2.1 on page 50 that *chorionic villus sampling* is the prenatal diagnostic method that can be performed earliest, at nine weeks after conception.

feet. The umbilical cord contains one large vein that delivers blood loaded with nutrients and two arteries that remove waste products. The force of blood flowing through the cord keeps it firm, so it seldom tangles while the embryo, like a space-walking astronaut, floats freely in its fluid-filled chamber (Moore, Persaud, & Torchia, 2016a).

Period of the Embryo

The **period of the embryo** lasts from implantation through the eighth week of pregnancy. During these brief six weeks, the groundwork is laid for all body structures and internal organs.

Last Half of the First Month. In the first week of this period, the embryonic disk forms three layers of cells: (1) the *ectoderm,* which will become the nervous system and skin; (2) the *mesoderm,* from which will develop the muscles, skeleton, circulatory system, and other internal organs; and (3) the *endoderm,* which will become the digestive system, lungs, urinary tract, and glands. These three layers give rise to all parts of the body.

At first, the nervous system develops fastest. The ectoderm folds over to form the **neural tube,** or primitive spinal cord. At 3½ weeks, the top swells to form the brain. While the nervous system is developing, the heart begins to pump blood, and muscles, backbone, ribs, and digestive tract appear. At the end of the first month, the curled embryo—only ¼ inch long—consists of millions of organized groups of cells with specific functions.

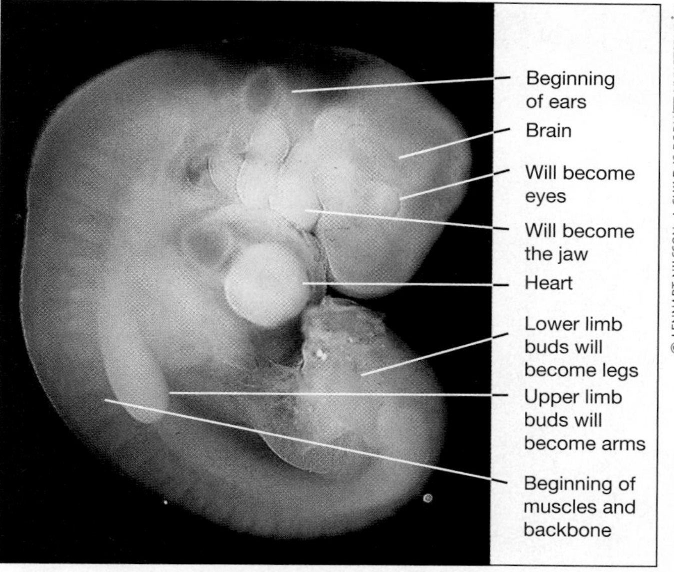

▶ **Period of the embryo: fourth week.** This 4-week-old embryo is only ¼-inch long, but many body structures have begun to form.

The Second Month. In the second month, growth continues rapidly. The eyes, ears, nose, jaw, and neck form. Tiny buds become arms, legs, fingers, and toes. Internal organs are more distinct: The intestines grow, the heart develops separate chambers, and the liver and spleen take over production of blood cells so that the yolk sac is no longer needed. Changing body proportions cause the embryo's posture to become more upright.

During the fifth week, production of *neurons* (nerve cells that store and transmit information) begins deep inside the neural tube at the astounding pace of more than 250,000 per minute (Jabès & Nelson, 2014). Once formed, neurons begin traveling along tiny threads to their permanent locations, where they will form the major parts of the brain.

By the end of this period, the embryo—about 1 inch long and ⅐ ounce in weight—can already sense its world. It responds to touch, particularly in the mouth area and on the soles of the feet. And it can move, although its tiny flutters are still too light to be felt by the mother (Moore, Persaud, & Torchia, 2016a).

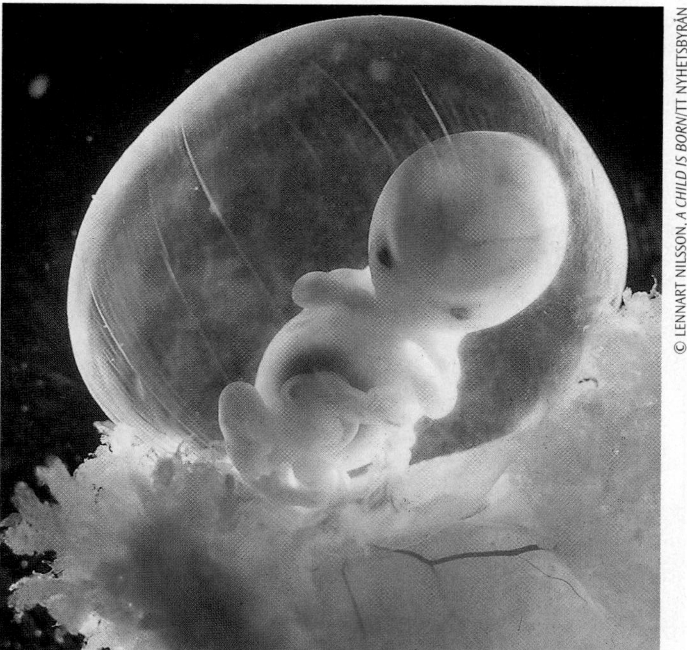

▶ **Period of the embryo: seventh week.** The embryo's posture is more upright. Body structures—eyes, nose, arms, legs, and internal organs—are more distinct. The embryo now responds to touch and can also move, although at less than one inch long and an ounce in weight, it is still too tiny to be felt by the mother.

Period of the Fetus

The **period of the fetus,** from the ninth week to the end of pregnancy, is the longest prenatal period. During this "growth and finishing" phase, the organism increases rapidly in size.

The Third Month. In the third month, the organs, muscles, and nervous system start to become organized and connected. Touch sensitivity extends to most of the body (Hepper, 2015). When the

Period of the fetus: eleventh week. The fetus grows rapidly. At 11 weeks, the brain and muscles are better connected. The fetus can kick, bend its arms, open and close its hands and mouth, and suck its thumb. Notice the yolk sac, which shrinks as the internal organs take over its function of producing blood cells.

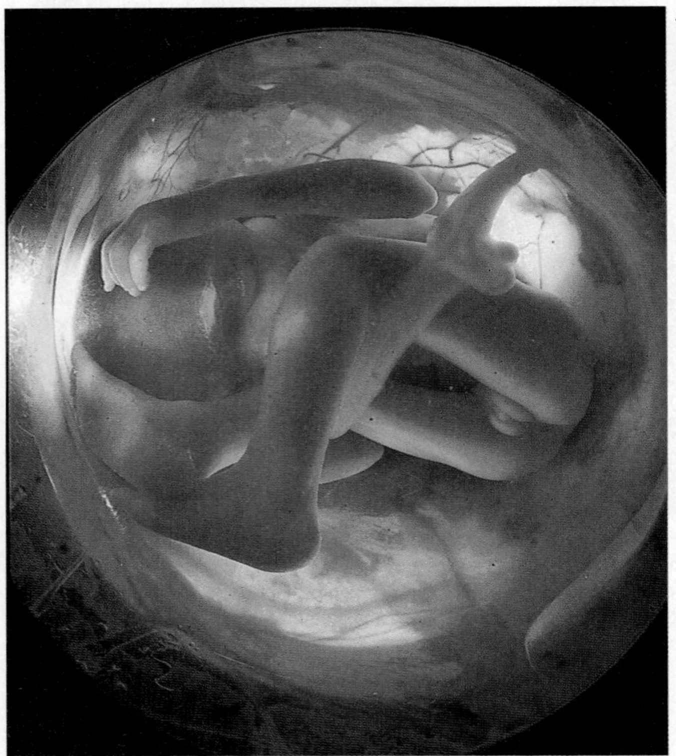

Period of the fetus: twenty-second week. This fetus is almost one foot long and weighs slightly more than one pound. Its movements can be felt easily by the mother and by other family members who place a hand on her abdomen. If born now, the fetus has a slim chance of survival.

brain signals, the fetus kicks, bends its arms, forms a fist, curls its toes, turns its head, opens its mouth, and even sucks its thumb, stretches, and yawns. The tiny lungs begin to expand and contract, rehearsing breathing movements.

By the twelfth week, the external genitals are well-formed, and the sex of the fetus can be detected with ultrasound (Sadler, 2014). Other finishing touches appear, such as fingernails, toenails, tooth buds, and eyelids. The heartbeat can now be heard through a stethoscope.

Prenatal development is sometimes divided into **trimesters,** or three equal time periods. At the end of the third month, the *first trimester* is complete.

The Second Trimester. By the middle of the second trimester, between 17 and 20 weeks, the new being has grown large enough for the mother to feel its movements. Already, the fetus is remarkably active, in motion nearly 30 percent of the time—which helps strengthen the joints and muscles (DiPietro, Costigan, & Voegtline, 2015). A white, cheeselike substance called **vernix** emerges on the skin, protecting it from chapping during the months spent bathing in the amniotic fluid. White, downy hair called **lanugo** appears over the entire body, helping the vernix stick to the skin.

At the end of the second trimester, many organs are well-developed, and most of the brain's billions of neurons are in place; few will be produced after this time. However, *glial cells,* which support and feed the neurons, continue to increase rapidly throughout the remainder of pregnancy, as well as after birth. Consequently, brain weight increases tenfold from the twentieth week until birth (Roelfsema et al., 2004). At the same time, neurons begin forming *synapses,* or connections, at a rapid pace.

Brain growth means new sensory and behavioral capacities. The 20-week-old fetus can be stimulated as well as irritated by sounds. And if a doctor looks inside the uterus using fetoscopy (see Table 2.1 on page 50), fetuses try to shield their eyes from the light with their hands, indicating that sight has begun to emerge (Moore, Persaud, & Torchia, 2016a). Still, a fetus born at this time cannot survive. Its lungs are immature, and the brain cannot yet control breathing movements or body temperature.

The Third Trimester. During the final trimester, a fetus born early has a chance for survival. The point at which the baby can first survive, called the **age of viability,** occurs sometime between 22 and 26 weeks (Moore, Persaud, & Torchia, 2016a). A baby born between the seventh and eighth months, however, usually needs oxygen assistance to breathe. Although the brain's respiratory center is now mature, tiny air sacs in the lungs are not yet ready to inflate and exchange carbon dioxide for oxygen.

The brain continues to make great strides. The *cerebral cortex,* seat of human intelligence, enlarges. As rapid gains in neural connectivity and organization continue, the fetus spends more time awake—11 percent of the time at 28 weeks, a figure that rises to 16 percent just before birth (DiPietro et al., 1996). Between 30 and 34 weeks, fetuses show rhythmic alternations between sleep and wakefulness that gradually increase in organization (Rivkees, 2003).

Around 36 weeks, synchrony between fetal heart rate and motor activity peaks: A rise in heart rate is usually followed within five seconds by a burst of motor activity (DiPietro et al., 2006; DiPietro, Costigan, & Voegtline, 2015). These are clear signs that coordinated neural networks are beginning to form in the brain.

The fetus also shows signs of developing temperament. In one study, more active fetuses during the third trimester became 1-year-olds who could better handle frustration and 2-year-olds who were more active as well as less fearful of unfamiliar adults and situations (DiPietro et al., 2002). Perhaps fetal activity is an indicator of healthy neurological development, which fosters adaptability in childhood.

The third trimester brings greater responsiveness to external stimulation. As we will see when we discuss newborn capacities, fetuses acquire taste and odor preferences from bathing in and swallowing amniotic fluid (its makeup is influenced by the mother's diet). Between 23 and 30 weeks, connections form between the cerebral cortex and brain regions involved in pain sensitivity. By this time, painkillers should be used in any surgical procedures (Lee et al., 2005). Around 28 weeks, fetuses blink their eyes in reaction to nearby sounds (Saffran, Werker, & Werner, 2006). And at 30 weeks, fetuses presented with a repeated auditory stimulus against the mother's abdomen initially react with a rise in heart rate, electrical brain-wave recordings, and body movements. Then responsiveness gradually declines, indicating *habituation* (adaptation) to the sound. If a new auditory stimulus is introduced, heart rate and brain waves recover to a high level, revealing that the fetus recognizes the new sound as distinct from the original stimulus (Hepper, Dornan, & Lynch, 2012; Muenssinger et al., 2013). This indicates that fetuses can remember for at least a brief period.

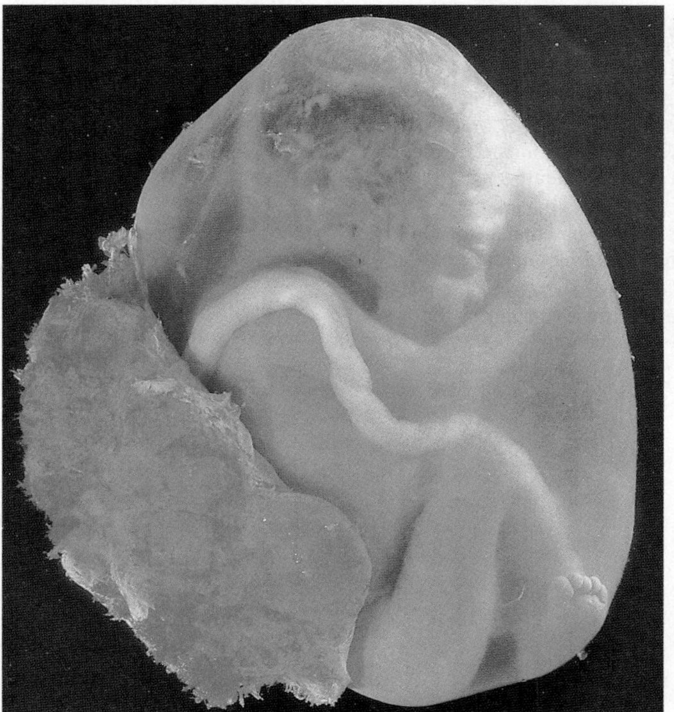

Period of the fetus: thirty-sixth week. This fetus fills the uterus. To nourish it, the umbilical cord and placenta have grown large. Notice the vernix (a cheeselike substance) on the skin, which protects it from chapping. The fetus has accumulated fat to aid temperature regulation after birth. In two more weeks, it will be full-term.

Within the next six weeks, fetuses distinguish the tone and rhythm of different voices and sounds—learning that will serve as a springboard for language development. They show systematic heart-rate and brain-wave changes in response to the mother's voice versus the father's or a stranger's, to their native language (English) versus a foreign language (Mandarin Chinese), and to a simple familiar melody versus an unfamiliar one (Granier-Deferre et al., 2003; Kisilevsky & Hains, 2011; Kisilevsky et al., 2009; Lecanuet et al., 1993; Lee & Kisilevsky, 2013; Voegtline et al., 2013). And in one clever study, mothers read aloud Dr. Seuss's lively book *The Cat in the Hat* each day during the last six weeks of pregnancy. After birth, their infants learned to turn on recordings of the mother's voice by sucking on nipples (DeCasper & Spence, 1986). They sucked hardest to hear *The Cat in the Hat*—the sound they had come to know while still in the womb.

In the final three months, the fetus gains more than 5 pounds and grows 7 inches. In the eighth month, a layer of fat is added to assist with temperature regulation. The fetus also receives antibodies from the mother's blood that protect against illnesses, since the newborn's immune system will not work well until several months after birth. In the last weeks, most fetuses assume an upside-down position, partly because of the shape of the uterus and partly because the head is heavier than the feet. Growth slows, and birth is about to take place.

ASK YOURSELF

CONNECT How is brain development related to fetal capacities and behavior? What implications do individual differences in fetal behavior have for infant temperament after birth?

APPLY Amy, two months pregnant, wonders how the embryo is being fed and what parts of the body have formed. "I don't look pregnant yet, so does that mean not much development has taken place?" she asks. How would you respond to Amy?

Prenatal Environmental Influences

3.2 Cite factors that influence the impact of teratogens, and discuss evidence on the impact of known or suspected teratogens.

3.3 Describe the impact of additional maternal factors on prenatal development.

3.4 Explain why early and regular health care is vital during the prenatal period.

Although the prenatal environment is far more constant than the world outside the womb, many factors can affect the embryo and fetus. Yolanda and Jay learned that parents—and society as a whole—can do a great deal to create a safe environment for development before birth.

Teratogens

The term **teratogen** (from the Greek word *teras,* meaning "malformation") refers to any environmental agent that causes damage during the prenatal period. The harm done by teratogens is not always simple and straightforward. It depends on the following factors:

- *Dose.* Larger doses over longer time periods usually have more negative effects.
- *Heredity.* The genetic makeup of the mother and the developing organism plays an important role. Some individuals are better able than others to withstand harmful environments.
- *Other negative influences.* The presence of several negative factors at once, such as additional teratogens, poor nutrition, and lack of medical care, can worsen the impact of a harmful agent.
- *Age.* The effects of teratogens vary with the age of the organism at time of exposure. To understand this last idea, think of the *sensitive period* concept—a limited time span in which a part of the body or a behavior is biologically prepared to develop rapidly. During that time, it is especially sensitive to its surroundings. If the environment is harmful, then damage occurs, and recovery is difficult and sometimes impossible.

Figure 3.2 summarizes prenatal sensitive periods. In the *germinal period,* before implantation, teratogens rarely have any impact. If they do, the tiny mass of cells is usually so damaged that it dies. The *embryonic period* is the time when serious defects are most likely to occur because the foundations for all body parts are being laid down. During the *fetal period,* teratogenic damage is usually minor. However, organs such as the brain, ears, eyes, teeth, and genitals can still be strongly affected.

The effects of teratogens go beyond immediate physical damage. Some health effects may show up years later. Growing evidence indicates that certain teratogens exert long-term effects epigenetically, by modifying gene expression (see page 66 in Chapter 2) (Markunas et al., 2014). Furthermore, delayed psychological consequences can occur indirectly, as a result of physical damage. For example, a defect resulting from drugs the mother took during pregnancy can affect others' reactions to the child as well as the child's ability to explore the environment. Over time, parent–child interaction, peer relations, and cognitive, emotional, and social development may suffer.

Prescription and Nonprescription Drugs. In the early 1960s, the world learned a tragic lesson about drugs and prenatal development. At that time, a sedative called *thalidomide* was widely available in Canada, Europe, and South America. When taken by mothers 4 to 6 weeks after conception, thalidomide produced gross deformities of the embryo's developing arms and legs and, less frequently, damage to the ears, heart, kidneys, and genitals. About 7,000 infants worldwide were affected (Moore, Persaud, & Torchia, 2016a). As children exposed to thalidomide grew older, many scored below average in intelligence. Perhaps the drug damaged the central nervous system directly. Or the child-rearing conditions of these youngsters with severe physical deformities may have impaired their intellectual development.

Another medication, a synthetic hormone called *diethylstilbestrol (DES),* was widely prescribed between 1945 and 1970 to prevent miscarriages. As daughters of these mothers reached adolescence and young adulthood, they showed unusually high rates of cancer of the vagina, malformations of the uterus, and infertility. Similarly, young men were at increased risk of genital abnormalities and cancer of the testes (Goodman, Schorge, & Greene, 2011; Reed & Fenton, 2013).

Currently, the most widely used potent teratogen is a vitamin A derivative called *isotretinoin,* which is prescribed to treat severe acne and taken by hundreds of thousands of women of childbearing age in industrialized nations. Exposure during the first trimester results in eye, ear, skull, brain, heart, and immune system abnormalities (Yook et al., 2012). U.S. regulations for prescribing isotretinoin require female users to commit to avoiding pregnancy by using two methods of birth control.

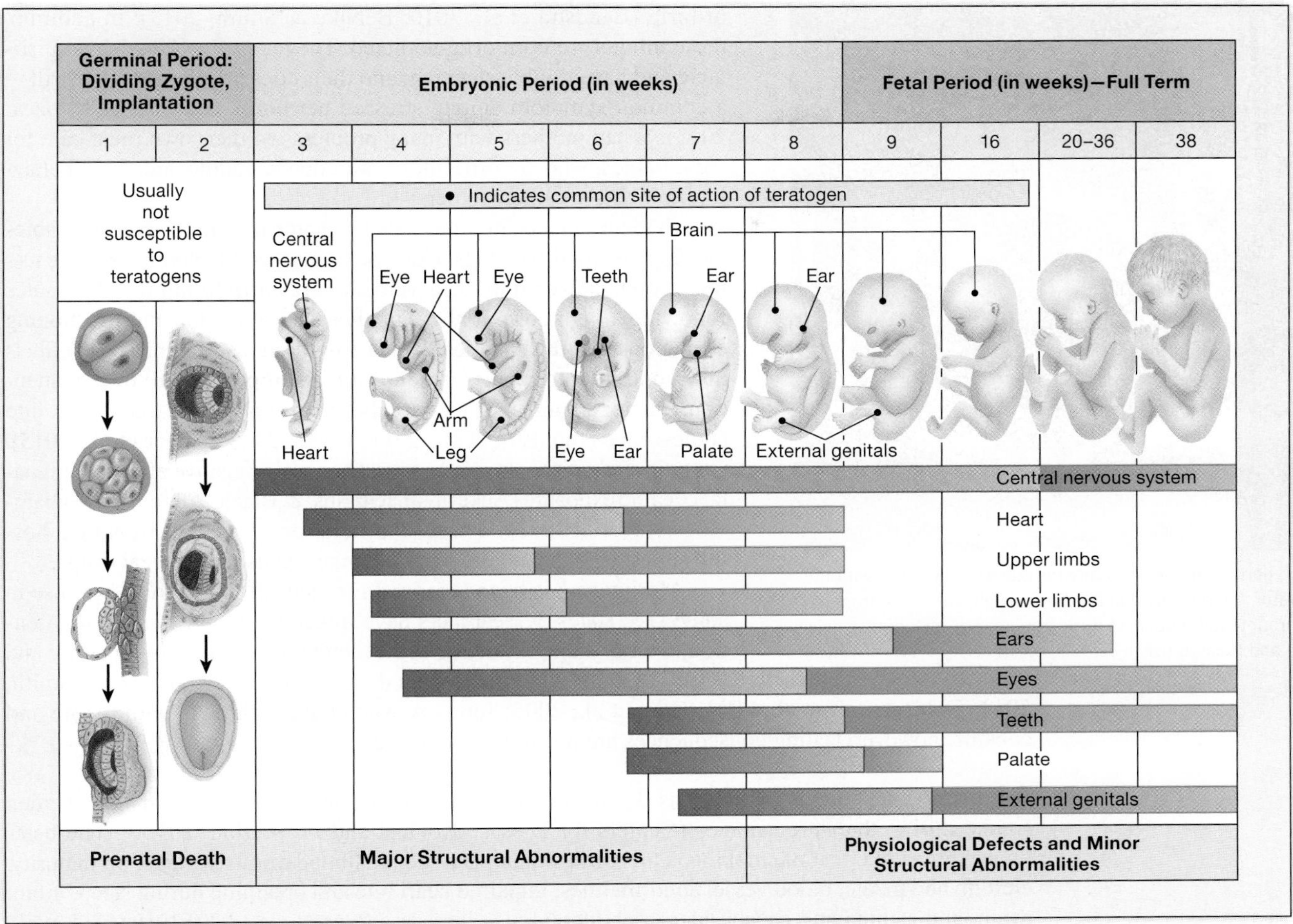

FIGURE 3.2 Sensitive periods in prenatal development. Each organ or structure has a sensitive period, during which its development may be disturbed. Blue horizontal bars indicate highly sensitive periods. Green horizontal bars indicate periods that are somewhat less sensitive to teratogens, although damage can occur. (Based on *Before We Are Born,* 9th ed., by K. L. Moore, T. V. N. Persaud, & M. G. Torchia, p. 313. Copyright © 2016 Elsevier, Inc.)

Any drug with a molecule small enough to penetrate the placental barrier can enter the embryonic or fetal bloodstream. Yet many pregnant women continue to take over-the-counter medications without consulting their doctors. Some research suggests that aspirin use is linked to brain damage leading to impaired motor control, inattention, and overactivity, though other research fails to confirm these findings (Barr et al., 1990; Kozer et al., 2003; Thompson et al., 2014; Tyler et al., 2012). Coffee, tea, cola, and cocoa contain another frequently consumed drug, caffeine. High doses increase the risk of low birth weight (Sengpiel et al., 2013). Persistent intake of antidepressant medication is associated with an elevated incidence of premature delivery, low birth weight, respiratory distress at birth, and delayed motor development, but contrary evidence exists (Grigoriadis et al., 2013; Huang et al., 2014; Robinson, 2015).

Because children's lives are involved, we must take findings like these seriously. At the same time, we cannot be sure that these drugs actually cause the problems just mentioned. Often mothers take more than one drug. If the embryo or fetus is injured, it is hard to tell which drug might be responsible or whether other factors correlated with drug taking are at fault. Until we have more information, the safest course of action is the one Yolanda took: Avoid drugs as far as possible.

Illegal Drugs. Nearly 6 percent of U.S. pregnant women take highly addictive, mood-altering drugs, such as cocaine or heroin (Substance Abuse and Mental Health Services Administration, 2016). Babies born to users are at risk for a wide variety of problems, including prematurity, low birth weight, brain abnormalities, physical defects, breathing difficulties, and death around the time

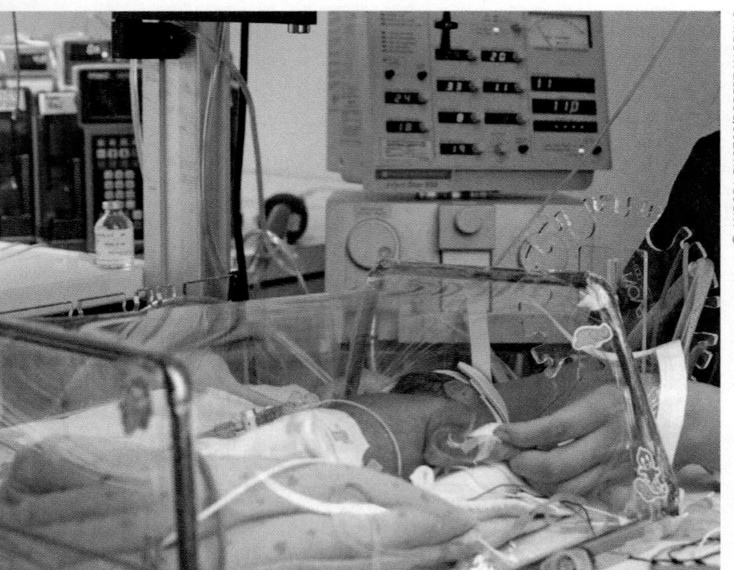
© AURORA PHOTOS/ROBERT HARDING

▶ This infant, born many weeks before his due date, breathes with the aid of a respirator. Prematurity and low birth weight can result from a variety of environmental influences during pregnancy, including maternal drug and tobacco use.

of birth (Bandstra et al., 2010; Behnke & Smith, 2013). In addition, these infants are born drug-addicted. They are often feverish and irritable and have trouble sleeping, and their cries are abnormally shrill—a common symptom among stressed newborns (Barthell & Mrozek, 2013). When mothers with many problems of their own must care for these babies, who are difficult to calm down, cuddle, and feed, behavior problems are likely to persist.

Evidence on cocaine suggests that some prenatally exposed babies develop lasting difficulties. Cocaine constricts the blood vessels, causing oxygen delivered to the developing organism to fall for 15 minutes following a high dose. It also can alter the production and functioning of neurons and the chemical balance in the fetus's brain. These effects may contribute to reports in some studies of perceptual, motor, attention, memory, language, and impulse-control problems that persist into adolescence (Bandstra et al., 2011; Coyle, 2013; Singer et al., 2015). Other investigations, however, reveal no major negative effects of prenatal cocaine exposure (Ackerman, Riggins, & Black, 2010; Buckingham-Howes et al., 2013). These contradictory findings illustrate how difficult it is to isolate the precise damage caused by illegal drugs.

Marijuana has been legalized for medical and recreational use in some U.S. states. Researchers have linked prenatal exposure to attention, memory, and academic achievement difficulties; impulsivity and overactivity; and depression as well as aggression in childhood and adolescence (Behnke & Smith, 2013; Goldschmidt et al., 2004; Gray et al., 2005; Jutras-Aswad et al., 2009). As with heroin and cocaine, however, lasting consequences are not well-established.

Tobacco. Although smoking has declined in Western nations, about 10 percent of U.S. women smoke during their pregnancies (Centers for Disease Control and Prevention, 2016c). The best-known prenatal effect of smoking is low birth weight. But the likelihood of miscarriage, prematurity, cleft lip and palate, blood vessel abnormalities, impaired heart rate and breathing during sleep, infant death, and asthma and cancer later in childhood also increases (Geerts et al., 2012; Havstad et al., 2012; Howell, Coles, & Kable, 2008; Mossey et al., 2009). The more cigarettes a mother smokes, the greater the chances that her baby will be affected. If a pregnant woman stops smoking at any time, she reduces the likelihood that her infant will be born underweight and suffer from future problems (Polakowski, Akinbami, & Mendola, 2009). The earlier she stops, the more beneficial the effects.

Newborns of smoking mothers are less attentive to sounds, display more muscle tension, are more excitable when touched and visually stimulated, and more often have colic (persistent crying). These findings suggest subtle negative effects on brain development (Espy et al., 2011; Law et al., 2003). Consistent with this view, prenatally exposed children and adolescents tend to have shorter attention spans, difficulties with impulsivity and overactivity, poorer memories, lower intelligence and achievement test scores, and higher levels of disruptive, aggressive behavior (Espy et al., 2011; Thakur et al., 2013).

Exactly how can smoking harm the fetus? Nicotine, the addictive substance in tobacco, constricts blood vessels, lessens blood flow to the uterus, and causes the placenta to grow abnormally. This reduces the transfer of nutrients, so the fetus gains weight poorly. Also, nicotine raises the concentration of carbon monoxide in the bloodstreams of both mother and fetus. Carbon monoxide displaces oxygen from red blood cells, damaging the central nervous system and slowing fetal body growth (Behnke & Smith, 2013). Other toxic chemicals in tobacco, such as cyanide and cadmium, contribute to its damaging effects.

From one-third to one-half of nonsmoking pregnant women are "passive smokers" because their husbands, relatives, or co-workers use cigarettes. Passive smoking is also related to low birth weight, infant death, childhood respiratory illnesses, and possible long-term attention, learning, and behavior problems (Best, 2009; Hawsawi, Bryant, & Goodfellow, 2015). Clearly, expectant mothers should avoid smoke-filled environments.

Alcohol. In his moving book *The Broken Cord,* Michael Dorris (1989), a Dartmouth College anthropology professor, described what it was like to rear his adopted son Adam, whose biological mother died of alcohol poisoning shortly after his birth. A Sioux Indian, Adam was born with **fetal alcohol spectrum disorder (FASD),** a term that encompasses a range of physical, mental, and behavioral outcomes caused by prenatal alcohol exposure. Children with FASD are given one of three diagnoses, which vary in severity:

1. **Fetal alcohol syndrome (FAS),** distinguished by (a) slow physical growth, (b) a pattern of three facial abnormalities (short eyelid openings; a thin upper lip; a smooth or flattened philtrum, or indentation running from the bottom of the nose to the center of the upper lip), and (c) brain injury, evident in a small head and impairment in at least three areas of functioning—for example, memory, language and communication, attention span and activity level (overactivity), planning and reasoning, motor coordination, or social skills. Other defects—of the eyes, ears, nose, throat, heart, genitals, urinary tract, or immune system—may also be present. Adam was diagnosed as having FAS. As is typical for this disorder, his mother drank heavily throughout pregnancy.
2. **Partial fetal alcohol syndrome (p-FAS),** characterized by (a) two of the three facial abnormalities just mentioned and (b) brain injury, again evident in at least three areas of impaired functioning. Mothers of children with p-FAS generally drank alcohol in smaller quantities, and children's defects vary with the timing and length of alcohol exposure. Research suggests that paternal alcohol use around the time of conception can alter gene expression, contributing to symptoms (Alati et al., 2013; Ouko et al., 2009).
3. **Alcohol-related neurodevelopmental disorder (ARND),** in which at least three areas of mental functioning are impaired, despite typical physical growth and absence of facial abnormalities. Again, prenatal alcohol exposure is less pervasive than in FAS (Mattson, Crocker, & Nguyen, 2012).

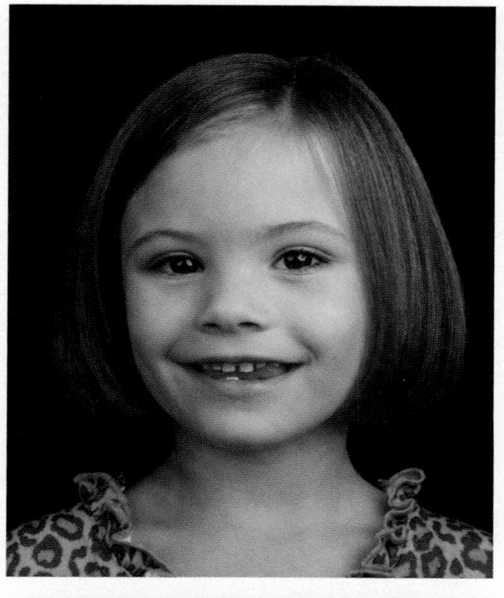

© SHUTTERSTOCK

© ELLEN B. SENISI

▶ Top photo: This 5-year-old's mother drank heavily during pregnancy. The child's widely spaced eyes, thin upper lip, and flattened philtrum are typical of fetal alcohol syndrome (FAS). Bottom photo: This 12-year-old has the small head and facial abnormalities of FAS. She also shows the cognitive impairments and slow growth that accompany the disorder.

Even when provided with enriched diets, FAS babies fail to catch up in physical size during childhood. Mental impairment associated with all three FASD diagnoses is also permanent: In his teens and twenties, Adam had trouble concentrating and suffered from poor judgment. For example, he would buy something and not wait for change or would wander off in the middle of a task. He died at age 23, after being hit by a car.

The more alcohol a pregnant woman consumes, the poorer the child's motor coordination, speed of information processing, reasoning, and intelligence and achievement test scores during the preschool and school years (Burden, Jacobson, & Jacobson, 2005; Mattson, Calarco, & Lang, 2006). In adolescence and early adulthood, FASD is associated with persisting attention and motor-coordination deficits, trouble with the law, inappropriate social and sexual behaviors, alcohol and drug abuse, and lasting mental health problems, including depression and high emotional reactivity to stress (Bertrand & Dang, 2012; Hellemans et al., 2010; Roszel, 2015).

Alcohol produces its devastating effects by interfering with production and migration of neurons in the primitive neural tube. Brain-imaging research reveals reduced brain size, damage to many brain structures, and abnormalities in brain functioning, including electrical and chemical activity involved in transferring messages from one part of the brain to another (de la Monte & Kril, 2014; Memo et al., 2013). Animal research reveals widespread epigenetic changes, including altered methylation of many genes, that contribute to deficits in brain functioning (Gupta & Shirasaka, 2016).

About 25 percent of U.S. mothers report drinking at some time during their pregnancies. As with heroin and cocaine, alcohol abuse is higher in poverty-stricken women. It is especially high among Native Americans, for whom the risk of a baby born with FAS is 20 to 25 times greater than for the rest of the U.S. population (Rentner, Dixon, & Lengel, 2012). How much alcohol is safe during pregnancy? Even mild drinking, less than one drink per day, is associated with reduced head size (a measure of brain development), slow body growth, and behavior problems (Flak et al., 2014; Martinez-Frias et al., 2004).

Radiation. Defects due to ionizing radiation were tragically apparent in children born to pregnant women who survived the bombing of Hiroshima and Nagasaki during World War II. Similar abnormalities surfaced in the nine months following the 1986 Chernobyl, Ukraine, nuclear power plant accident. After each disaster, the incidence of miscarriage and babies born with brain damage, physical deformities, and slow physical growth rose dramatically (Double et al., 2011; Schull, 2003).

Even when a radiation-exposed baby seems normal, problems may appear later. For example, even low-level radiation, resulting from industrial leakage or medical X-rays, can increase the risk of childhood cancer (Fushiki, 2013). In middle childhood, prenatally exposed Chernobyl children had abnormal brain-wave activity, lower intelligence test scores, and rates of language and emotional disorders two to three times greater than those of nonexposed children in the surrounding area (Loganovskaja & Loganovsky, 1999; Loganovsky et al., 2008).

Environmental Pollution. In industrialized nations, an astounding number of potentially dangerous chemicals are released into the environment. When 10 newborns were randomly selected from U.S. hospitals for analysis of umbilical cord blood, researchers uncovered a startling array of industrial contaminants—287 in all (Houlihan et al., 2005). They concluded that many babies are "born polluted" by chemicals that not only impair prenatal development but increase the chances of life-threatening diseases and health problems later on.

High levels of prenatal exposure to *mercury* disrupt production and migration of neurons, causing widespread brain damage (Caserta et al., 2013; Hubbs-Tait et al., 2005). Mercury in maternal seafood diets predicts deficits in speed of cognitive processing, attention, and memory during the school years (Boucher et al., 2010, 2012; Lam et al., 2013). Pregnant women are wise to avoid eating long-lived predatory fish, such as swordfish, albacore tuna, and shark, which are heavily contaminated with mercury.

OSLAN RAHMAN/AFP/GETTY IMAGES

▶ This pregnant woman wears a face mask as protection against Singapore's smog, which occasionally hits life-threatening levels. Prolonged exposure to polluted air poses serious risks to prenatal development.

For many years, *polychlorinated biphenyls (PCBs)* were used to insulate electrical equipment, until research showed that, like mercury, they entered waterways and the food supply. Prenatal exposure to high levels results in low birth weight, skin deformities, brain-wave abnormalities, and delayed cognitive development (Chen & Hsu, 1994; Chen et al., 1994). Even at low levels, PCBs are linked to reduced birth weights, smaller heads, persisting attention and memory difficulties, and lower intelligence test scores in childhood (Boucher, Muckle, & Bastien, 2009; Polanska, Jurewicz, & Hanke, 2013; Stewart et al., 2008).

Another teratogen, *lead,* is present in paint flaking off the walls of old buildings and in certain materials used in industrial occupations. High levels of prenatal lead exposure are related to prematurity, low birth weight, brain damage, and a wide variety of physical defects. Babies with low-level exposure show slightly poorer mental and motor development (Caserta et al., 2013; Jedrychowski et al., 2009).

Prenatal exposure to *dioxins*—toxic compounds resulting from incineration—is linked to thyroid abnormalities in infancy and to an increased incidence of breast and uterine cancers in women, perhaps through altering hormone levels (ten Tusscher & Koppe, 2004). Even tiny amounts of dioxin in the paternal bloodstream cause a dramatic change in the sex ratio of offspring: Affected men father nearly twice as many girls as boys (Ishihara et al., 2007). Dioxin seems to impair the fertility of Y-bearing sperm prior to conception.

Finally, persistent air pollution inflicts substantial prenatal harm. Exposure to traffic-related fumes and smog is associated with reduced infant head size, low birth weight, elevated infant death rates, impaired lung and immune-system functioning, and later respiratory illnesses (Proietti et al., 2013; Ritz et al., 2014).

Infectious Disease. In the mid-1960s, a worldwide epidemic of *rubella* (three-day, or German, measles) led to the birth of more than 20,000 American babies with serious defects and to 13,000 fetal and newborn deaths. Consistent with the sensitive period concept, more than 50 percent of infants whose mothers become ill during the embryonic period show deafness; eye deformities, including cataracts; heart, genital, urinary, intestinal, bone, and dental defects; and intellectual disability. Infection during the fetal period is less harmful, but low birth weight, hearing loss, and bone defects may still occur. The organ damage inflicted by prenatal rubella often leads to severe mental illness, diabetes, cardiovascular disease, and thyroid and immune-system dysfunction in adulthood (Duszak, 2009; Waldorf & McAdams, 2013). Routine vaccination in infancy and childhood has made new rubella outbreaks unlikely in industrialized nations. But over 100,000 cases of prenatal infection continue to occur each year, primarily in developing countries in Africa and Asia with weak or absent immunization programs (World Health Organization, 2017b).

The *human immunodeficiency virus (HIV),* which can lead to *acquired immune deficiency syndrome (AIDS),* a disease that destroys the immune system, has infected increasing numbers of women over the past three decades. In developing countries, where 95 percent of new infections occur, more than half affect women. In South Africa, for example, 30 percent of all pregnant women are HIV-positive (Burton, Giddy, & Stinson, 2015). Untreated HIV-infected expectant mothers pass the deadly virus to the developing organism 10 to 20 percent of the time.

AIDS progresses rapidly in infants, with most becoming ill by 6 months and, if untreated, dying by age 3 (Siberry, 2015). Antiretroviral drug therapy reduces prenatal transmission to less than 1 to 2 percent, and several babies born with HIV for whom aggressive retroviral treatment began within 2 days after birth appeared free of the disease (McNeil, 2014). However, these medications remain unavailable to at least one-third of HIV-infected pregnant women in developing countries (World Health Organization, 2017a).

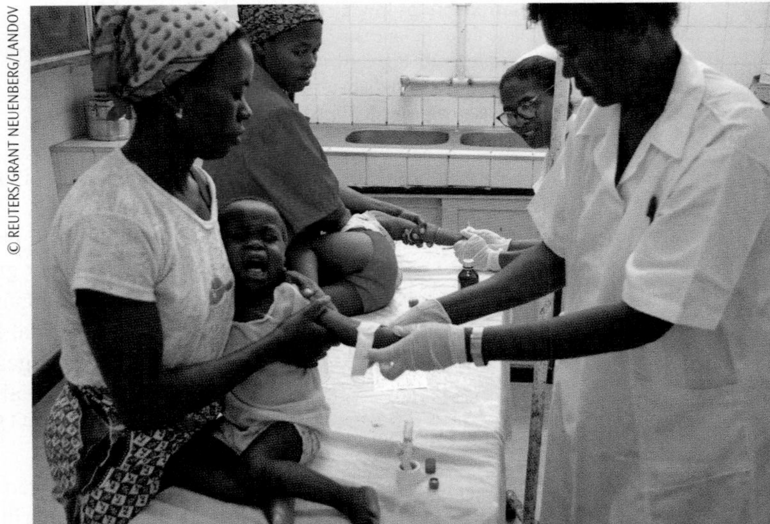

Babies are tested for the HIV virus in a clinic in Mozambique, Africa. Prenatal treatment with antiretroviral drugs reduces transmission of AIDS from mother to child to less than 1 to 2 percent.

The developing organism is especially sensitive to the family of herpes viruses, for which no broadly effective vaccine or treatment exists. Among these, *cytomegalovirus* (the most frequent prenatal infection, transmitted through respiratory or sexual contact) and *herpes simplex 2* (which is sexually transmitted) are especially dangerous. In both, the virus invades the mother's genital tract, infecting babies either during pregnancy or at birth.

Toxoplasmosis, caused by a parasite found in many animals, can affect pregnant women who have contact with the feces of infected cats, handle contaminated soil while gardening, or eat raw or undercooked meat. If the disease strikes during the first trimester, it is likely to cause eye and brain damage. Later infection is linked to mild visual and cognitive impairments (Wallon et al., 2013). Expectant mothers can avoid toxoplasmosis by having pet cats checked for the disease, turning over the care of litter boxes and the garden to other family members, and making sure that the meat they eat is well-cooked.

Other Maternal Factors

Besides avoiding teratogens, expectant parents can support prenatal development in other ways. In the following sections, we examine the influence of nutrition, emotional stress, blood type, and maternal age.

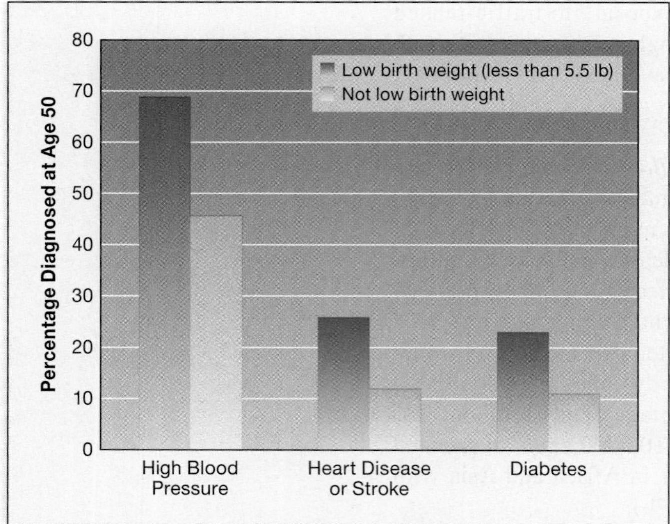

FIGURE 3.3 Relationship of low birth weight to disease risk in adulthood. In a follow-up of more than 2,000 U.S. births at age 50, low birth weight was associated with a greatly increased incidence of high blood pressure, heart disease, stroke, and diabetes after many other prenatal and postnatal health risks were controlled. (Based on Johnson & Schoeni, 2011.)

Nutrition. During the prenatal period, when children are growing more rapidly than at any other time, they depend totally on the mother for nutrients. A healthy diet that results in a weight gain of 25 to 30 pounds (10 to 13.5 kilograms) helps ensure the health of mother and baby.

Prenatal malnutrition can cause serious damage to the central nervous system. The poorer the mother's diet, the greater the loss in brain weight, especially if malnutrition occurred during the last trimester, when the brain is increasing rapidly in size. An inadequate diet during pregnancy can also distort the structure of the liver, kidney, pancreas, and cardiovascular system, predisposing the individual to later health problems. As Figure 3.3 illustrates, large-scale studies reveal a consistent link between low birth weight and high blood pressure, cardiovascular disease, and diabetes in adulthood (Johnson & Schoeni, 2011).

Many studies show that providing pregnant women with an adequate quantity of food has a substantial impact on the health of their newborn babies. Vitamin–mineral enrichment is also crucial. For example, taking a folic acid supplement around the time of conception reduces by more than 70 percent abnormalities of the neural tube, which result in birth defects of the brain and spinal cord. Folic acid supplementation early in pregnancy also lessens the risk of other physical defects, including cleft lip and palate, circulatory system and urinary tract abnormalities, and limb deformities. U.S. government guidelines recommend that all women of childbearing age consume 0.4 milligram of folic acid per day (Talaulikar & Arulkumaran, 2011). Because many U.S. pregnancies are unplanned, government regulations mandate that bread, flour, rice, pasta, and other grain products be fortified with folic acid.

Although prenatal malnutrition is highest in developing countries, it also occurs in the industrialized world. The U.S. Special Supplemental Food Program for Women, Infants, and Children (WIC), which provides food packages and nutrition education to low-income pregnant women, reaches about 90 percent of those who qualify because of their extremely low incomes (U.S. Department of Agriculture, 2015b). But many U.S. women who need nutrition intervention are not eligible for WIC.

Emotional Stress. When women experience severe emotional stress during pregnancy, especially during the first two trimesters, their babies are at risk for a wide variety of difficulties, including miscarriage, prematurity, low birth weight, infant respiratory and digestive illnesses, colic (persistent infant crying), sleep disturbances, and irritability during the child's first three years (Dunkel-Shetter & Lobel, 2012; Field, 2011; Lazinski, Shea, & Steiner, 2008). Prenatal stressors consistently found to impair later physical and psychological well-being include chronic strain due to poverty; major negative life events such as divorce or death of a family member; disasters such as earthquakes or terrorist attacks; and fears specific to pregnancy and childbirth, including persistent anxiety about the health and survival of the baby and oneself. It is important to note that mild to moderate occasional stress has no adverse impact.

How can severe maternal stress affect the developing organism? When we experience fear and anxiety, stress hormones released into our bloodstream—such as *epinephrine* (adrenaline) and *cortisol,* known as the "fight or flight" hormones—cause us to be "poised for action." Large amounts of blood are sent to parts of the body involved in the defensive response—the brain, the heart, and the muscles in the arms, legs, and trunk. Blood flow to other organs, including the uterus, is reduced. As a result, the fetus is deprived of a full supply of oxygen and nutrients.

Maternal stress hormones also cross the placenta, causing a dramatic rise in fetal stress hormones and, therefore, in fetal heart rate, blood pressure, blood glucose, and activity level (Kinsella & Monk, 2009; Weinstock, 2008). Excessive fetal stress is associated with structural alterations in the infant brain that are linked to mood disorders in later life (O'Donnell & Meaney, 2016). Infants and children of mothers who experienced severe prenatal anxiety display cortisol levels that are either abnormally high or abnormally low, both of which signal reduced physiological capacity to

SOCIAL ISSUES

The Nurse–Family Partnership: Reducing Maternal Stress and Enhancing Child Development Through Social Support

COURTESY OF NURSE–FAMILY PARTNERSHIP

▶ The Nurse–Family Partnership provides this first-time, low-income mother with regular home visits from a registered nurse. In follow-up research, children of home-visited mothers developed more favorably—cognitively, emotionally, and socially—than comparison children.

At age 17, Denise—an unemployed high-school dropout living with her disapproving parents—gave birth to Tara. Having no one to turn to for help during pregnancy and beyond, Denise felt overwhelmed and anxious much of the time. Tara was premature and cried uncontrollably, slept erratically, and suffered from frequent minor illnesses throughout her first year. When she reached school age, she had trouble keeping up academically, and her teachers described her as distractible, angry, and uncooperative.

The Nurse–Family Partnership—currently implemented in hundreds of counties across 43 U.S. states, in six tribal communities, in the U.S. Virgin Islands, and internationally in Australia, Canada, the Netherlands, and the United Kingdom—is a voluntary home visiting program for first-time, low-income expectant mothers like Denise. Its goals are to reduce pregnancy and birth complications, promote competent early caregiving, and improve family conditions, thereby protecting children from lasting adjustment difficulties.

A registered nurse visits the home weekly during the first month after enrollment, twice a month during the remainder of pregnancy and through the middle of the child's second year, and then monthly until age 2. In these sessions, the nurse provides the mother with intensive social support—a sympathetic ear; assistance in accessing health and other community services and the help of family members (especially fathers and grandmothers); and encouragement to finish high school, find work, and engage in future family planning.

To evaluate the program's effectiveness, researchers randomly assigned large samples of mothers at risk for high prenatal stress (due to teenage pregnancy, poverty, and other negative life conditions) to nurse-visiting or comparison conditions (just prenatal care, or prenatal care plus infant referral for developmental problems). Families were followed through their child's school-age years and, in one experiment, into adolescence (Kitzman et al., 2010; Olds et al., 2004, 2007; Rubin et al., 2011).

As kindergartners, Nurse–Family Partnership children obtained higher language and intelligence test scores. And at both ages 6 and 9, the children of home-visited mothers in the poorest mental health during pregnancy exceeded comparison children in academic achievement and displayed fewer behavior problems. Furthermore, from their baby's birth on, home-visited mothers were on a more favorable life course: They had fewer subsequent births, longer intervals between their first and second births, more frequent contact with the child's father, more stable intimate partnerships, less welfare dependence, and a greater sense of control over their lives. Perhaps for these reasons, adolescent children of home-visited mothers continued to be advantaged in academic achievement and reported less alcohol use and drug-taking than comparison-group agemates.

The Nurse–Family Partnership is highly cost-effective (Miller, 2015). For $1 spent, it saves more than five times as much in public spending on pregnancy complications, preterm births, and child and youth health, learning, and behavior problems.

manage stress. Recall from Chapter 2 that prenatal epigenetic changes (gene methylation) may be partly or largely responsible (Monk et al., 2016).

Maternal emotional stress during pregnancy is related to diverse, long-term negative behavioral outcomes, including anxiety, depression, short attention span, anger, aggression, overactivity, and lower intelligence test scores, above and beyond the impact of other risks, such as maternal smoking during pregnancy, low birth weight, postnatal maternal anxiety, and low SES (Coall et al., 2015; Monk, Georgieff, & Osterholm, 2013). Furthermore, similar to prenatal malnutrition, overwhelming the fetus with maternal stress hormones heightens susceptibility to later illness, including cardiovascular disease and diabetes in adulthood (Reynolds, 2013).

But stress-related prenatal complications are greatly reduced when mothers have partners, other family members, and friends who offer social support (Bloom et al., 2013; Luecken et al., 2013). The impact of social support is particularly strong for economically disadvantaged women, who often lead highly stressful lives (see the Social Issues box above).

LOOK AND LISTEN

List prenatal environmental factors that can compromise later academic performance and social adjustment. Ask several adults who hope someday to be parents to explain what they know about each factor. How great is their need for prenatal education?

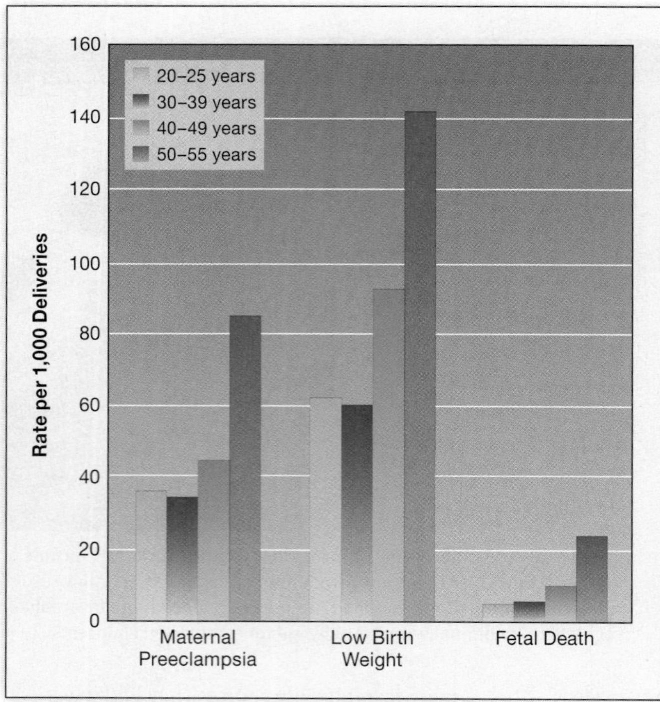

FIGURE 3.4 Relationship of maternal age to prenatal and birth complications. Complications increase after age 40, with a sharp rise between 50 and 55 years. See below for a description of preeclampsia. (Based on Salihu et al., 2003.)

Rh Factor Incompatibility. When inherited blood types of mother and fetus differ, serious problems sometimes result. The most common cause of these difficulties is **Rh factor incompatibility.** When the mother is Rh-negative (lacks the Rh blood protein) and the father is Rh-positive (has the protein), the baby may inherit the father's Rh-positive blood type. If even a little of a fetus's Rh-positive blood crosses the placenta into the Rh-negative mother's bloodstream, she begins to form antibodies to the foreign Rh protein. If these enter the fetus's system, they destroy red blood cells, reducing the oxygen supply to organs and tissues. Intellectual disability, miscarriage, heart damage, and infant death can occur.

It takes time for the mother to produce Rh antibodies, so firstborn children are rarely affected. The danger increases with each additional pregnancy. Fortunately, Rh incompatibility can be prevented in most cases. After the birth of each Rh-positive baby, Rh-negative mothers are routinely given a vaccine to prevent the buildup of antibodies.

Maternal Age. In Chapter 2, we noted that women who delay childbearing until their thirties or forties face increased risk of infertility, miscarriage, and babies with chromosomal defects. Are other pregnancy complications more common for older mothers? Research indicates that healthy women in their thirties have about the same rates as those in their twenties. Thereafter, as Figure 3.4 reveals, complication rates increase, with a sharp rise among women ages 50 to 55—an age at which, because of menopause (end of menstruation) and aging reproductive organs, few women can conceive naturally (Salihu et al., 2003; Usta & Nassar, 2008).

In the case of teenage mothers, does physical immaturity cause prenatal complications? Infants born to teenagers do have a higher rate of problems, but not directly because of maternal age (Ruedinger & Cox, 2012). Most pregnant teenagers come from low-income backgrounds, where stress, poor nutrition, and health problems are common.

© MARK PETERSON/REDUX

▶ Expectant mothers are invited to ask questions during a group prenatal care session. Ethnic minority mothers who receive culturally sensitive prenatal care engage in more health-promoting behaviors and have healthier newborns.

The Importance of Prenatal Health Care

Yolanda's pregnancy, like most others, was free of complications. But unexpected difficulties can arise, especially if mothers have health problems. For example, the 5 percent of pregnant women who have diabetes need careful monitoring. Extra glucose in the diabetic mother's bloodstream causes the fetus to grow larger than average, making pregnancy and birth problems more common. Maternal high blood glucose also compromises prenatal brain development: It is linked to poorer memory and learning in infancy and early childhood (Riggins et al., 2009). Another complication, experienced by 5 to 10 percent of pregnant women, is *preeclampsia* (sometimes called *toxemia*), in which blood pressure increases sharply and the face, hands, and feet swell in the last half of pregnancy. If untreated, preeclampsia can cause convulsions in the mother and fetal death (Vest & Cho, 2012). Usually, hospitalization, bed rest, and drugs can lower blood pressure to a safe level.

Unfortunately, 6 percent of pregnant women in the United States wait until after the first trimester to seek prenatal care or receive none at all. Inadequate care is far more common among adolescent and low-income, ethnic minority mothers. Their infants are three times as likely to be born underweight and five times as likely to die as are babies of mothers who receive early medical attention (Child Trends,

APPLYING WHAT WE KNOW

Do's and Don'ts for a Healthy Pregnancy

DO	DON'T
Do make sure that you have been vaccinated against infectious diseases that are dangerous to the embryo and fetus, such as rubella, before you get pregnant. Most vaccinations are not safe during pregnancy.	Don't take any drugs without consulting your doctor.
Do see a doctor as soon as you suspect that you are pregnant, and continue to get regular medical checkups throughout pregnancy.	Don't smoke. If you have already smoked during part of your pregnancy, cut down or, better yet, quit. If other members of your family smoke, ask them to quit or to smoke outside.
Do eat a well-balanced diet and take vitamin–mineral supplements, as prescribed by your doctor, both prior to and during pregnancy. Gain 25 to 30 pounds gradually.	Don't drink alcohol from the time you decide to get pregnant.
Do obtain literature from your doctor, library, or bookstore about prenatal development. Ask your doctor about anything that concerns you.	Don't engage in activities that might expose your embryo or fetus to environmental hazards, such as radiation or chemical pollutants. If you work in an occupation that involves these agents, ask for a safer assignment or a leave of absence.
Do keep physically fit through moderate exercise. If possible, join a special exercise class for expectant mothers.	Don't engage in activities that might expose your embryo or fetus to harmful infectious diseases, such as toxoplasmosis.
Do avoid emotional stress. If you are a single expectant mother, find a relative or friend on whom you can rely for emotional support.	Don't choose pregnancy as a time to go on a diet.
Do get plenty of rest. An overtired mother is at risk for pregnancy complications.	Don't gain too much weight during pregnancy. A very large weight gain is associated with complications.
Do enroll in a prenatal and childbirth education class with your partner or other companion. When parents know what to expect, the nine months before birth can be one of the most joyful times of life.	

2015c). Although government-sponsored health services for low-income pregnant women have expanded, some do not qualify and must pay for at least part of their care.

Besides financial hardship, *situational barriers* (difficulty finding a doctor, getting an appointment, and arranging transportation) and *personal barriers* (psychological stress, the demands of taking care of other young children) can prevent mothers from seeking prenatal care. Many also engage in high-risk behaviors, such as smoking and drug abuse, which they do not want to reveal to health professionals (Kitsantas, Gaffney, & Cheema, 2012). For these women assistance in making prenatal appointments, drop-in child-care centers, and free or low-cost transportation are vital.

Culturally sensitive health-care practices are also helpful. In a strategy called *group prenatal care,* after each medical checkup, trained leaders provided ethnic minority expectant mothers with a group discussion session that encouraged them to talk about important health issues. Compared to mothers receiving traditional brief appointments with little opportunity to ask questions, participants engaged in more health-promoting behaviors and gave birth to babies with a reduced incidence of prematurity and low birth weight (Tandon et al., 2012). Refer to Applying What We Know above, which lists "do's and don'ts" for a healthy pregnancy.

ASK YOURSELF

CONNECT Using what you learned about research strategies in Chapter 1, explain why it is difficult to determine the prenatal effects of many environmental agents, such as drugs and pollution.

APPLY Nora, pregnant for the first time, believes that a few cigarettes and a glass of wine a day won't be harmful. Provide Nora with research-based reasons for not smoking or drinking.

REFLECT If you had to choose five environmental influences to publicize in a campaign aimed at promoting healthy prenatal development, which ones would you choose, and why?

Childbirth

3.5 Describe the three stages of childbirth and the baby's adaptation to labor and delivery.

Yolanda and Jay agreed to return the following spring to share their experiences with my next class. Two-week-old Joshua came along as well. Their story revealed that the birth of a baby is one of the most dramatic and emotional events in human experience. Yolanda explained:

> By morning, we knew I was in labor. It was Thursday, so we went in for my usual weekly appointment. The doctor said, yes, the baby was on the way, but it would be a while. He told us to go home and relax and come to the hospital in three or four hours. We checked in at 3 in the afternoon; Joshua arrived at 2 o'clock the next morning. When, finally, I was ready to deliver, it went quickly; a half hour or so and some good hard pushes, and there he was! His face was red and puffy, and his head was misshapen, but I thought, "Our son! I can't believe he's really here."

Jay was also elated by Joshua's birth. "It was awesome, indescribable. I can't stop looking and smiling at him," Jay said, holding Joshua over his shoulder and patting and kissing him gently. In the following sections, we explore the experience of childbirth, from both the parents' and the baby's point of view.

The Stages of Childbirth

It is not surprising that childbirth is often referred to as labor. It is the hardest physical work a woman may ever do. A complex series of hormonal changes between mother and fetus initiates the process, which naturally divides into three stages (see Figure 3.5):

1. *Dilation and effacement of the cervix.* This is the longest stage of labor, lasting an average of 12 to 14 hours with a first birth and 4 to 6 hours with later births. Contractions of the uterus gradually become more frequent and powerful, causing the cervix, or uterine opening, to widen and thin to nothing, forming a clear channel from the uterus into the birth canal, or vagina.

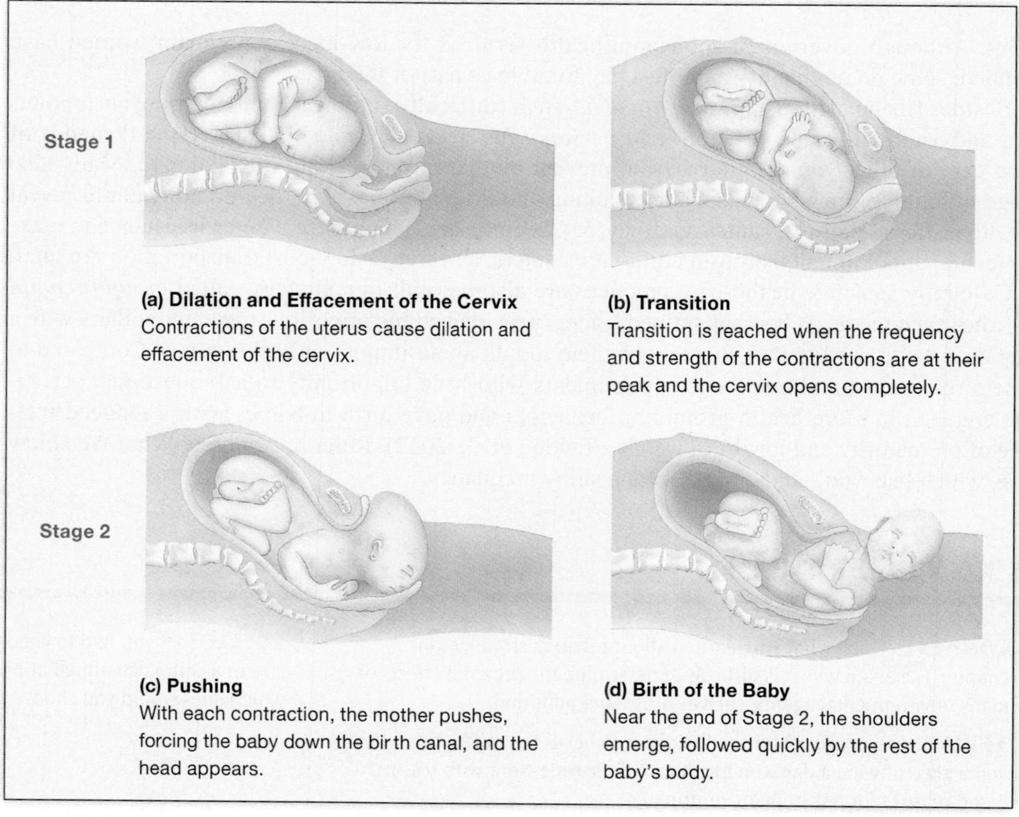

FIGURE 3.5 A normal birth. The first two stages of labor are depicted. In the third stage, the placenta is delivered.

2. *Delivery of the baby.* This stage is much shorter, lasting about 50 minutes for a first birth and 20 minutes in later births. Strong contractions of the uterus continue, but the mother also feels a natural urge to squeeze and push with her abdominal muscles. As she does so with each contraction, she forces the baby down and out.
3. *Delivery of the placenta.* Labor comes to an end with a few final contractions and pushes. These cause the placenta to separate from the wall of the uterus and be delivered in about 5 to 10 minutes.

The Baby's Adaptation to Labor and Delivery

At first glance, labor and delivery seem like a dangerous ordeal for the baby. The strong contractions exposed Joshua's head to a great deal of pressure, and they squeezed the placenta and the umbilical cord, temporarily reducing Joshua's supply of oxygen.

Fortunately, healthy babies are equipped to withstand these traumas. The force of the contractions intensifies the baby's production of stress hormones. Unlike during pregnancy, when excessive stress endangers the fetus, during childbirth high levels of infant cortisol and other stress hormones are adaptive. They help the baby withstand oxygen deprivation by sending a rich supply of blood to the brain and heart (Gluckman, Sizonenko, & Bassett, 1999). In addition, stress hormones prepare the baby to breathe by causing the lungs to absorb any remaining fluid and by expanding the bronchial tubes (passages leading to the lungs). Finally, stress hormones arouse the infant into alertness. Joshua was born wide awake, ready to interact with the surrounding world.

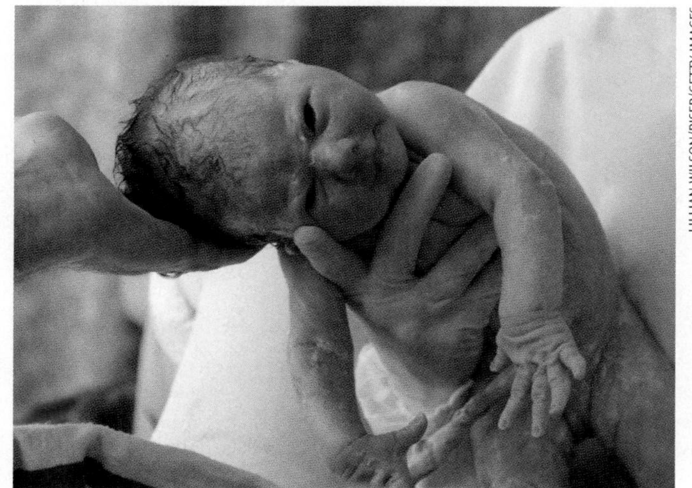

LILLIAN WILSON/RISER/GETTY IMAGES

▶ This newborn's body readily turns pink as she takes her first few breaths.

Assessing the Newborn's Physical Condition: The Apgar Scale

To assess the newborn's physical condition quickly, doctors and nurses use the **Apgar Scale.** As Table 3.2 shows, a rating of 0, 1, or 2 on each of five characteristics is made at 1 minute and again at 5 minutes after birth. A combined Apgar score of 7 or better indicates that the infant is in good physical condition. If the score is between 4 and 6, the baby needs assistance in establishing breathing and other vital signs. If the score is 3 or below, the infant is in serious danger and requires emergency medical attention (Apgar, 1953). Two Apgar ratings are given because some babies have trouble adjusting at first but do well after a few minutes.

TABLE 3.2
The Apgar Scale

	RATING		
SIGN[a]	***0***	***1***	***2***
Heart rate	No heartbeat	Under 100 beats per minute	100 to 140 beats per minute
Respiratory effort	No breathing for 60 seconds	Irregular, shallow breathing	Strong breathing and crying
Reflex irritability (sneezing, coughing, and grimacing)	No response	Weak reflexive response	Strong reflexive response
Muscle tone	Completely limp	Weak movements of arms and legs	Strong movements of arms and legs
Color[b]	Blue body, arms, and legs	Body pink with blue arms and legs	Body, arms, and legs completely pink

[a]To remember these signs, you may find it helpful to use a technique in which the original labels are reordered and renamed as follows: color = **A**ppearance; heart rate = **P**ulse; reflex irritability = **G**rimace; muscle tone = **A**ctivity; and respiratory effort = **R**espiration. Together, the first letters of the new labels spell **Apgar.**

[b]The skin tone of nonwhite babies makes it difficult to apply the "pink" color criterion. However, newborns of all races can be rated for pinkish glow resulting from the flow of oxygen through body tissues.

Source: Apgar, 1953.

Approaches to Childbirth

3.6 Describe natural childbirth and home delivery, noting benefits and concerns associated with each.

Childbirth practices, like other aspects of family life, are heavily influenced by culture. In many village and tribal societies, expectant mothers are well-acquainted with the childbirth process. For example, among the Mende of Sierra Leone, birth attendants, who are appointed by the village chief, visit mothers before and after birth to provide advice and practice traditional strategies during labor to quicken delivery, including massaging the abdomen and supporting the woman in a squatting position (Dorwie & Pacquiao, 2014).

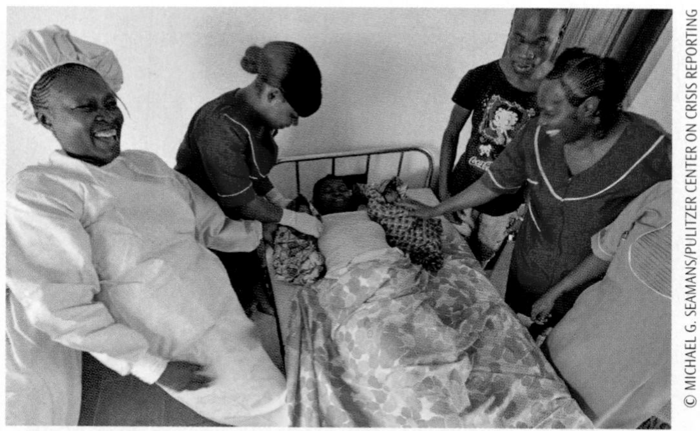

In Sierra Leone, a new mother rests comfortably after giving birth to twins. She had her first twin at home, assisted by village birth attendants. After complications arose, the birth attendants took her to a clinic, where they collaborated with nurses in delivering her second twin. Throughout, cultural practices remained a part of this birth experience.

In Western nations, childbirth has changed dramatically over the centuries. Before the late 1800s, birth usually took place at home and was a family-centered event. The industrial revolution brought greater crowding to cities, along with new health problems. As a result, childbirth moved from home to hospital, where the health of mothers and babies could be protected (Borst, 1995). Once doctors assumed responsibility for childbirth, women's knowledge of it declined, and relatives and friends no longer participated.

By the 1950s and 1960s, women had begun to question the medical procedures used during labor. Many felt that routine use of strong drugs and delivery instruments had robbed them of a precious experience and was often neither necessary nor safe for the baby. Gradually, a natural childbirth movement arose in Europe and spread to North America. Today, most hospitals offer birth centers that are family-centered and homelike and that encourage early contact between parents and baby.

Natural, or Prepared, Childbirth

Yolanda and Jay chose **natural,** or **prepared, childbirth**—a group of techniques aimed at reducing pain and medical intervention and making childbirth a rewarding experience. Most natural childbirth programs draw on methods developed by Grantly Dick-Read (1959) in England and Fernand Lamaze (1958) in France. These physicians recognized that cultural attitudes had taught women to fear the birth experience. An anxious, frightened woman in labor tenses her muscles, heightening the pain that usually accompanies strong contractions.

In a typical natural childbirth program, the expectant mother and a companion (a partner, relative, or friend) participate in three activities:

- *Classes.* Yolanda and Jay attended a series of classes in which they learned about the anatomy and physiology of labor and delivery. Knowledge about the birth process reduces a mother's fear.
- *Relaxation and breathing techniques.* During each class, Yolanda was taught relaxation and breathing exercises aimed at counteracting the pain of uterine contractions.
- *Labor coach.* Jay learned how to help Yolanda during childbirth by reminding her to relax and breathe, massaging her back, supporting her body, and offering encouragement and affection.

Social support is important to the success of natural childbirth. Mothers who are supported during labor and delivery—either by a *doula* (a Greek word referring to a trained lay birth attendant) or by a relative or friend with doula training—less often have instrument-assisted or cesarean (surgical) deliveries or need medication to control pain. Also, their babies' Apgar scores are higher, and they are more likely to be breastfeeding at a two-month follow-up (Campbell et al., 2006, 2007; Hodnett et al., 2012; McGrath & Kennell, 2008). Social support also makes Western hospital-birth customs more acceptable to women from cultures where assistance from family and community members is the norm.

Home Delivery

Home birth has always been popular in certain industrialized nations, such as England, the Netherlands, and Sweden. The number of American women choosing to have their babies at home rose during the 1970s and 1980s but remains small, at less than 1 percent (Martin et al., 2017). Although some home births are attended by doctors, many more are handled by *certified nurse–midwives,* who have degrees in nursing and additional training in childbirth management.

Is it just as safe to give birth at home as in a hospital? For healthy women without pregnancy complications who are assisted by a well-trained doctor or midwife, it seems so because complications rarely occur (Cheyney et al., 2014). However, if attendants are not carefully trained and prepared to handle emergencies, the likelihood of infant disability and death is high (Grünebaum et al., 2015). When mothers are at risk for any kind of complication, the appropriate place for labor and delivery is the hospital, where life-saving treatment is available.

ERSEN ROSS/BRAND X PICTURES/GETTY IMAGES

▶ After a home birth, the midwife and a lay attendant provide support to the new mother. For healthy women attended by a well-trained doctor or midwife, home birth is as safe as hospital birth.

Medical Interventions

3.7 List common medical interventions during childbirth, circumstances that justify their use, and any dangers associated with each.

Four-year-old Melinda walks with a halting gait and has difficulty keeping her balance. She has *cerebral palsy,* a general term for a variety of impairments in muscle coordination caused by brain damage before, during, or just after birth. One out of every 500 American children has cerebral palsy. For about 10 percent, including Melinda, the brain damage was caused by **anoxia,** or inadequate oxygen supply, during labor and delivery (Clark, Ghulmiyyah, & Hankins, 2008; McIntyre et al., 2013). Melinda was in **breech position,** turned so that the buttocks or feet would be delivered first, and the umbilical cord was wrapped around her neck. Her mother had gotten pregnant accidentally, was frightened and alone, and arrived at the hospital at the last minute. Had she come to the hospital earlier, doctors could have monitored Melinda's condition and delivered her surgically as soon as squeezing of the umbilical cord led to distress, thereby reducing the damage or preventing it entirely.

In cases like Melinda's, medical interventions are clearly justified. But in others, they can interfere with delivery and even pose new risks. In the following sections, we examine some commonly used medical procedures during childbirth.

Fetal Monitoring

Fetal monitors are electronic instruments that track the baby's heart rate during labor. An abnormal heartbeat pattern may indicate that the baby is in distress due to anoxia and needs to be delivered immediately. Continuous fetal monitoring, which is required in most U.S. hospitals, is used in over 85 percent of U.S. births (Ananth et al., 2013). The most popular type of monitor is strapped across the mother's abdomen throughout labor. A more accurate method involves threading a recording device through the cervix and placing it under the baby's scalp.

Fetal monitoring is a safe medical procedure that has saved the lives of many babies in high-risk situations. But in healthy pregnancies, it does not reduce the already low rates of infant brain damage and death. Furthermore, most infants have some heartbeat irregularities during labor, so critics worry that fetal monitors identify many babies as in danger who, in fact, are not. Monitoring is linked to an increase in the number of instrument and cesarean (surgical) deliveries, practices we will discuss shortly (Alfirevic, Devane, & Gyte, 2013). In addition, some women complain that the devices are uncomfortable and interfere with the normal course of labor.

Still, fetal monitors will probably continue to be used routinely in the United States, even though they are not necessary in most cases. Doctors fear that they will be sued for malpractice if an infant dies or is born with problems and they cannot show they did everything possible to protect the baby.

Labor and Delivery Medication

Some form of medication is used in more than 80 percent of U.S. births (Declercq et al., 2014). *Analgesics,* drugs used to relieve pain, may be given in mild doses during labor to help a mother relax. *Anesthetics* are a stronger type of painkiller that blocks sensation. Currently, the most common approach to controlling pain during labor is *epidural analgesia,* in which a regional pain-relieving drug is delivered continuously through a catheter into a small space in the lower spine. Because the mother retains the capacity to feel the pressure of the contractions and to move her trunk and legs, she is able to push during the second stage of labor.

Although pain-relieving drugs help women cope with childbirth and enable doctors to perform essential medical interventions, they also can cause problems. Epidural analgesia weakens uterine contractions. As a result, labor is prolonged, and the chances of cesarean (surgical) birth increase. And because drugs rapidly cross the placenta, exposed newborns are at risk for respiratory distress (Kumar et al., 2014). They also tend to be sleepy and withdrawn, to suck poorly during feedings, and to be irritable when awake (Eltzschig, Lieberman, & Camann, 2003; Platt, 2014). Although no confirmed long-term consequences for development exist, the negative impact of these drugs on the newborn's adjustment supports the current trend to limit their use.

Cesarean Delivery

In a **cesarean delivery,** the doctor makes an incision in the mother's abdomen and lifts the baby out of the uterus. Forty years ago, cesarean delivery was rare. Since then, cesarean rates have climbed internationally, reaching 16 percent in Finland, 26 percent in New Zealand, 28 percent in Canada, 31 percent in Germany, and 32 percent in Australia and the United States (Martin et al., 2017; OECD, 2017).

Cesareans have always been warranted by medical emergencies, such as Rh incompatibility and certain breech births, in which the baby risks head injury or anoxia (as in Melinda's case). But these factors do not explain the worldwide rise in cesarean deliveries. Instead, medical control over childbirth is largely responsible. Because many needless cesareans are performed, pregnant women should ask questions about the procedure when choosing a doctor. Although the operation itself is safe, mother and baby require more time for recovery. Anesthetic may have crossed the placenta, making cesarean newborns sleepy and unresponsive and putting them at increased risk for breathing difficulties (Ramachandrappa & Jain, 2008).

ASK YOURSELF

CONNECT How might natural childbirth positively affect the parent–newborn relationship? Explain how your answer illustrates bidirectional influences between parent and child, emphasized in ecological systems theory.

APPLY Sharon, a heavy smoker, has just arrived at the hospital in labor. Which medical intervention discussed in the preceding sections is her doctor justified in using? (For help in answering this question, review the prenatal effects of tobacco on page 78.)

REFLECT If you were an expectant parent, would you choose home birth? Why or why not?

Preterm and Low-Birth-Weight Infants

3.8 Describe risks associated with preterm birth and low birth weight, along with effective interventions.

The average newborn weighs 7½ pounds (3,400 grams). Babies born three weeks or more before the end of a full 38-week pregnancy or who weigh less than 5½ pounds (2,500 grams) have for many years been referred to as "premature." Birth weight is the best available predictor of infant survival and healthy development. Many newborns who weigh less than 3½ pounds (1,500 grams) experience difficulties that are not overcome, an effect that becomes stronger as length of pregnancy and birth weight decrease (Bolisetty et al., 2006; Wilson-Ching et al., 2013). Brain abnormalities, delayed physical growth, frequent illness, sensory impairments, poor motor coordination, inattention, overactivity, language delays, low intelligence test scores, deficits in school learning, and emotional and behavior problems are some of the difficulties that persist through childhood and adolescence and into adulthood (Hutchinson et al., 2013; Lawn et al., 2014; Lemola, 2015).

About 11 percent of American infants are born early, and 8 percent are born underweight. The two risk factors often co-occur and are highest among poverty-stricken women (Martin et al., 2017). These mothers, as noted earlier, are more likely to be under stress, undernourished, and exposed to other harmful environmental influences.

Recall from Chapter 2 that preterm and low birth weight are common in multiple births. Because space inside the uterus is restricted, multiples gain less weight than singletons in the second half of pregnancy.

Preterm versus Small-for-Date Infants

Although preterm and low-birth-weight infants face many obstacles to healthy development, most go on to lead normal lives; about half of those born at 23 to 24 weeks gestation and weighing only a couple of pounds have no disability. To better understand why some babies do better than others, researchers divide them into two groups. **Preterm infants** are born several weeks or more before their due date. Although they are small, their weight may still be appropriate, based on time spent in the uterus. **Small-for-date infants** are below their expected weight considering length of the pregnancy. Some small-for-date infants are actually full-term. Others are preterm infants who are especially underweight.

Small-for-date infants—especially those who are also preterm—usually have more serious problems. During the first year, they are more likely to die, catch infections, and show evidence of brain damage. By middle childhood, they have lower intelligence test scores, are less attentive, achieve more poorly in school, and are socially immature (Katz et al., 2013; Sullivan et al., 2008; Wilson-Ching et al., 2013). Small-for-date infants probably experienced inadequate nutrition before birth. Perhaps their mothers did not eat properly, the placenta did not function normally, or the babies themselves had defects that prevented them from growing as they should. Consequently, small-for-date infants are especially likely to suffer from neurological impairments that permanently weaken their capacity to manage stress (Osterholm, Hostinar, & Gunnar, 2012). Severe stress, in turn, heightens their susceptibility to later physical and psychological health problems.

Even among preterm newborns whose weight is appropriate for length of pregnancy, just 7 to 14 more days—from 34 to 35 or 36 weeks—greatly reduces rates of illness, costly medical procedures, lengthy hospital stays, and later cognitive delays (Ananth, Friedman, & Gyamfi-Bannerman, 2013; Morse et al., 2009). In longitudinal follow-ups of thousands of births, babies born even 1 or 2 weeks early showed slightly lower cognitive and language scores in kindergarten and reading and math scores in third grade than children who experienced a full-length prenatal period (Noble et al., 2012; Woythaler et al., 2015). These outcomes persisted even after controlling for other factors linked to achievement, such as birth weight and SES. Yet doctors often induce births several weeks preterm, under the misconception that these babies are developmentally "mature."

Consequences for Caregiving

The appearance and behavior of preterm babies—scrawny and thin-skinned, sleepy and unresponsive, irritable when briefly awake—can lead parents to be less sensitive in caring for them. Compared with full-term infants, preterm babies—especially those who are very ill at birth—are less often held close, touched, and talked to gently (Feldman, 2007). Distressed, emotionally reactive preterm infants are particularly susceptible to the effects of parenting quality: Among a sample of preterm 9-month-olds, the combination of infant negativity and angry or intrusive parenting yielded the highest rate of behavior problems at 2 years of age. But with warm, sensitive parenting, distressed preterm babies' rate of behavior problems was the lowest (Poehlmann et al., 2011).

When preterm infants are born to isolated, poverty-stricken mothers who cannot provide good nutrition, health care, and parenting, the likelihood of unfavorable outcomes increases. In contrast, parents with stable life circumstances and social supports usually can overcome the stress of caring for a preterm infant (Ment et al., 2003). In these cases, even sick preterm babies have a good chance of catching up in development by middle childhood.

These findings suggest that how well preterm infants develop has a great deal to do with the parent–child relationship. Consequently, interventions directed at supporting both sides of this tie are more likely to help these infants recover.

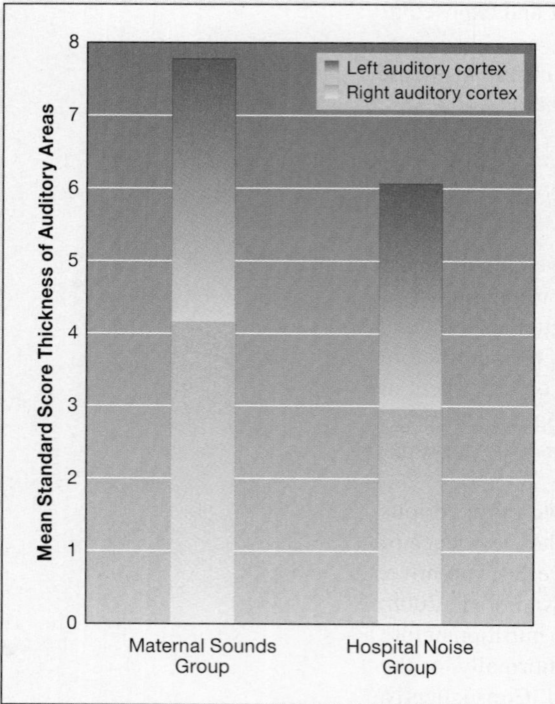

FIGURE 3.6 Listening to mother's voice and heartbeat enhances brain development in extremely preterm newborns. Infants born between the 25th and 32nd prenatal weeks were randomly assigned to hear either recordings of their mother's voice and heartbeat for several hours a day or routine, unpatterned hospital noise. After a month's exposure in the intensive care nursery, ultrasound measures showed that the left and right cerebral auditory areas were substantially thicker in the maternal sounds group than the hospital noise group. (Based on Webb et al., 2015.)

Interventions for Preterm Infants

A preterm baby is cared for in a special Plexiglas-enclosed bed called an *isolette.* Temperature is carefully controlled because these babies cannot yet regulate their own body temperature effectively. To help protect the baby from infection, air is filtered before it enters the isolette. When a preterm infant is fed through a stomach tube, breathes with the aid of a respirator, and receives medication through an intravenous needle, the isolette can be very isolating indeed! Physical needs that otherwise would lead to close contact and other human stimulation are met mechanically.

Special Infant Stimulation. In proper doses, certain kinds of stimulation can help preterm infants develop. In some intensive care nurseries, preterm babies rock in suspended hammocks or listen to soft music—experiences that promote faster weight gain, more predictable sleep patterns, and greater alertness (Arnon et al., 2006; Marshall-Baker, Lickliter, & Cooper, 1998). In one experiment, extremely preterm newborns, born between the 25th and 32nd prenatal weeks, were exposed either to recordings of their mother's voice and heartbeat for several hours each day or to routine hospital noise. At age 1 month, an ultrasound revealed that auditory areas of the brain had grown substantially larger in the maternal sounds group (see Figure 3.6) (Webb et al., 2015). Listening to womblike, familiar rhythmic maternal sounds, as opposed to the unpredictable din of hospital equipment, promoted brain development.

In baby animals, touching the skin releases certain brain chemicals that support physical growth—effects believed to occur in humans as well. When preterm infants were massaged several times each day in the hospital, they gained weight faster and, at the end of the first year, were advanced in cognitive and motor development over preterm babies not given this stimulation (Field, 2001; Field, Hernandez-Reif, & Freedman, 2004).

In developing countries where hospitalization is not always possible, skin-to-skin "kangaroo care" is the most readily available intervention for promoting the recovery of preterm babies. It involves placing the infant in a vertical position between the mother's breasts or next to the father's chest (under the parent's clothing) so the parent's body functions as a human incubator.

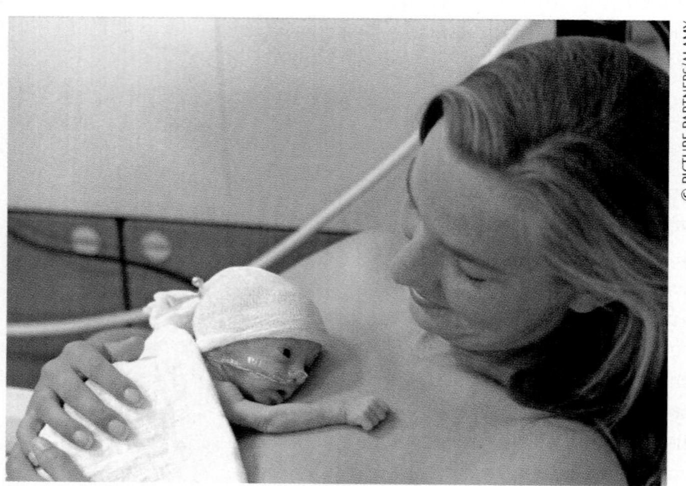

In Western nations, kangaroo care may be used to supplement hospital intensive care. Here, a U.S. mother engages in the technique with her fragile newborn.

Kangaroo skin-to-skin contact fosters improved oxygenation of the baby's body, temperature regulation, sleep, breastfeeding, alertness, and infant survival (Conde-Agudelo, Belizan, & Diaz-Rossello, 2011; Kaffashi et al., 2013). Mothers and fathers practicing it feel more confident about caring for their fragile babies, interact more sensitively and affectionately, and feel more attached to them (Dodd, 2005; Feldman, 2007).

Together, these factors may explain why preterm babies given many hours of kangaroo care in their early weeks, compared to those given little or no such care, develop more favorably during the first year and beyond. In one investigation that followed children born preterm until age 10, those who had experienced kangaroo care, compared with matched controls, displayed a more adaptive cortisol stress response, better organized sleep, more favorable mother–child interaction, and enhanced cognitive development

(Feldman, Rosenthal, & Eidelman, 2014). Because of its diverse benefits, most U.S. hospital nurseries now offer kangaroo care to parents and preterm newborns.

Training Parents in Infant Caregiving Skills. Interventions that support parents of preterm infants generally teach them how to recognize and respond to the baby's needs. For parents with adequate economic and personal resources to care for a preterm infant, just a few sessions of coaching are linked to enhanced parent–infant interaction, reduced infant crying and improved sleep, more rapid language development in the second year, and steady gains in mental test performance that equal those of full-term children by middle childhood (Achenbach, Howell, & Aoki, 1993; Newnham, Milgrom, & Skouteris, 2009).

When preterm infants live in stressed, economically disadvantaged households, long-term, intensive intervention is necessary (Guralnick, 2012). In the Infant Health and Development Program, preterm babies born into poverty received a comprehensive intervention. It combined medical follow-up, weekly parent training sessions, and cognitively stimulating child care from 1 to 3 years of age. More than four times as many intervention children as no-intervention controls (39 percent versus 9 percent) were within normal range at age 3 in intelligence, psychological adjustment, and physical growth (Bradley et al., 1994). In addition, mothers in the intervention group were more affectionate and more often encouraged play and cognitive mastery in their children—reasons their 3-year-olds may have been developing so favorably (McCarton, 1998).

At ages 5 and 8, children who had attended the child-care program regularly—for more than 350 days over the three-year period—continued to show better intellectual functioning. In contrast, children who attended only sporadically gained little or lost ground (Hill, Brooks-Gunn, & Waldfogel, 2003). These findings confirm that babies who are both preterm and economically disadvantaged require *intensive* intervention.

Nevertheless, even the best caregiving environments cannot always overcome the enormous biological risks associated with extreme preterm and low birth weight. A better course of action is prevention. The high rate of underweight babies in the United States—one of the worst in the industrialized world—could be greatly reduced by improving the health and social conditions described in the Social Issues box on page 94.

ASK YOURSELF

CONNECT List factors discussed in this chapter that increase the chances that an infant will be born underweight. How many of these factors could be prevented by better health care for expectant mothers?

APPLY Cecilia and Anna each gave birth to a 3-pound baby seven weeks preterm. Cecilia is single and on welfare. Anna and her partner are happily married and earn a good income. Plan an intervention appropriate for helping each baby develop.

REFLECT Many people object to the use of extraordinary medical measures to save extremely low-birth-weight babies because of their high risk for serious developmental problems. Do you agree or disagree? Explain.

The Newborn Baby's Capacities

Newborn infants have a remarkable set of capacities that are crucial for survival and for evoking adult attention and care. In relating to their physical and social worlds, babies are active from the very start.

3.9 Describe the newborn baby's reflexes and states of arousal, noting sleep characteristics and ways to soothe a crying baby.

3.10 Describe the newborn baby's sensory capacities.

Reflexes

A **reflex** is an inborn, automatic response to a particular form of stimulation. Reflexes are the newborn baby's most obvious organized patterns of behavior. As Jay placed Joshua on a table in my classroom, we saw several. When Jay bumped the side of the table, Joshua reacted with the *Moro (or "embracing") reflex*, flinging his arms wide and bringing them back toward his body. As Yolanda stroked Joshua's cheek, he turned his head in her direction, a response called the *rooting reflex*.

A Cross-National Perspective on Health Care and Other Policies for Parents and Newborn Babies

Infant mortality—the number of deaths in the first year of life per 1,000 live births—is an index used around the world to assess the overall health of a nation's children. Although the United States has the most up-to-date health-care technology in the world, it has made less progress in reducing infant deaths than many other countries. Over the past three decades, it has slipped in the international rankings, from seventh in the 1950s to thirty-ninth in 2015. Members of America's poor ethnic minorities are at greatest risk, with African-American infants more than twice as likely as White infants to die in the first year of life (U.S. Census Bureau, 2017c).

Neonatal mortality, the rate of death within the first month of life, accounts for 67 percent of the U.S. infant death rate. Two factors are largely responsible. The first is serious physical defects, most of which cannot be prevented. The percentage of babies born with physical defects is about the same in all ethnic and income groups. The second leading cause of neonatal mortality is low birth weight, which is largely preventable.

Widespread poverty and inadequate health-care programs for mothers and young children are largely responsible for these trends. In addition to providing government-sponsored health-care benefits to all citizens, each country in Figure 3.7 that outranks the United States in infant survival takes extra steps to make sure that pregnant mothers and babies have access to good nutrition, high-quality medical care, and social and economic supports that promote effective parenting.

For example, all Western European nations guarantee women a certain number of prenatal visits at very low or no cost. After a baby is born, a health professional routinely visits the home to provide counseling about infant care and to arrange continuing medical services.

Paid, job-protected employment leave is another vital societal intervention for new parents. Sweden has the most generous parental leave program in the world. Mothers can begin maternity leave 60 days prior to expected delivery and extend it to 6 weeks after birth; fathers are granted 2 weeks of birth leave. In addition, either parent can take full leave for 15 months at 80 percent of prior earnings, followed by an additional 3 months at a modest flat rate. Each parent is also entitled to another 18 months of unpaid leave. Even economically less well-off nations provide parental leave benefits. In Bulgaria, new mothers are granted 11 months paid leave, and fathers receive 3 weeks (Addati, Cassirer, & Gilchrist, 2014).

Yet in the United States, the federal government mandates *only 12 weeks of unpaid leave* for employees in companies with at least 50 workers. Most women, however, work in smaller businesses, and many of those who work in large enough companies cannot afford to take unpaid leave. And because of financial pressures, many new mothers who are eligible for unpaid work leave take far less than 12 weeks. Similarly, though paternal leave predicts fathers' increased involvement in infant care at the end of the first year, many fathers take little or none at all (Nepomnyaschy & Waldfogel, 2007).

In 2002, California became the first state to guarantee a mother or father paid leave—up to 6 weeks at half salary, regardless of the size of the company. Since then, Hawaii, New Jersey, New York, Rhode Island, Washington, Washington, DC, and the territory of Puerto Rico have passed similar legislation.

Nevertheless, 6 weeks of childbirth leave (the norm in the United States) is not enough. Leaves of 6 to 8 weeks or less are linked to increased maternal anxiety, depression, sense of role overload (conflict between work and family responsibilities), and negative interactions with the baby. A leave of 12 weeks or more predicts favorable maternal physical and mental health, supportive marital interaction, and sensitive caregiving (Aitken et al., 2015; Chatterji & Markowitz, 2012; Feldman, Sussman, & Zigler, 2004).

In countries with low infant mortality rates, expectant parents need not wonder how or where they will get health care and other resources to support their baby's development. The powerful impact of universal, high-quality health care, generous parental leave, and other social services on maternal and infant well-being provides strong justification for these policies.

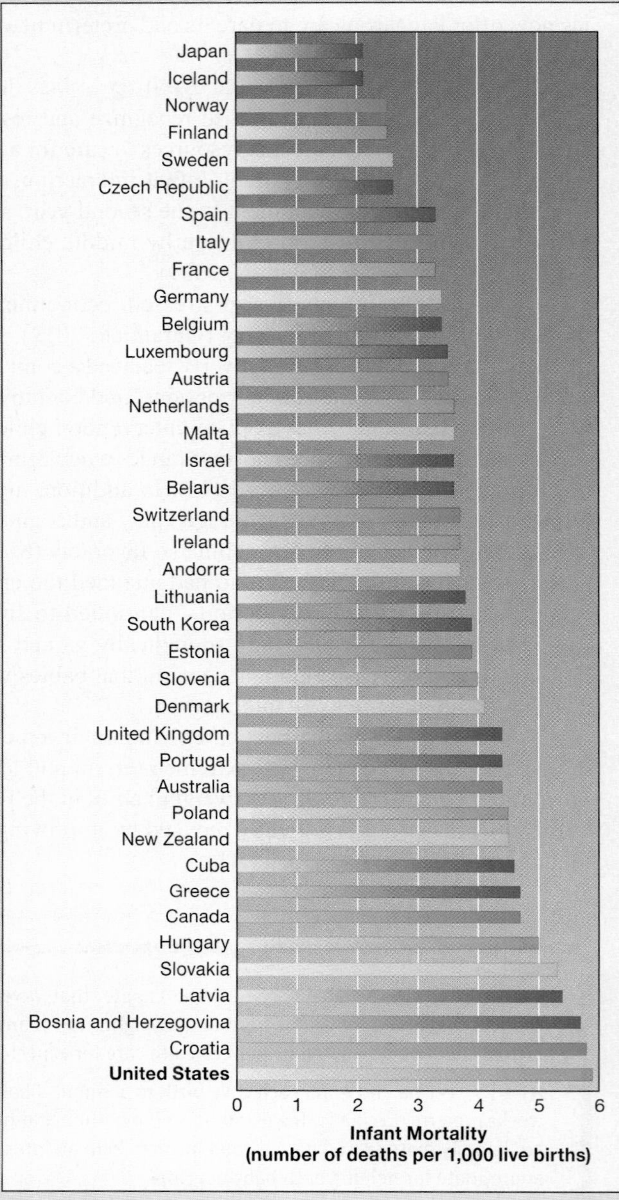

FIGURE 3.7 Infant mortality in 39 nations. Despite its advanced health-care technology, the United States ranks poorly. It is thirty-ninth in the world, with a death rate of 5.9 infants per 1,000 births. (Based on U.S. Census Bureau, 2017c.)

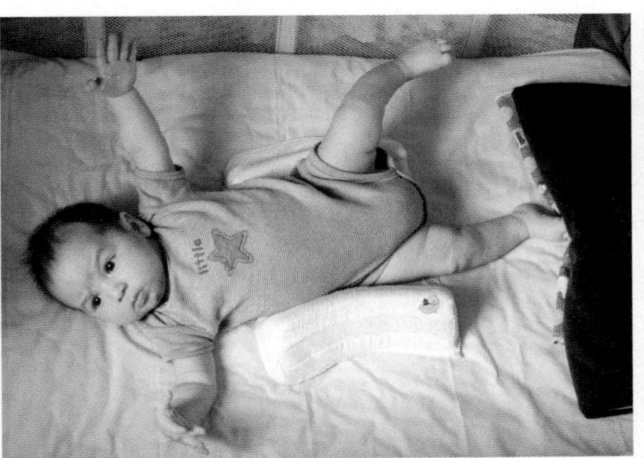

▶ In the Moro reflex, loss of support or a sudden loud sound causes the baby to arch his back, extend his legs, throw his arms outward, and then return them toward the body in an "embracing" motion.

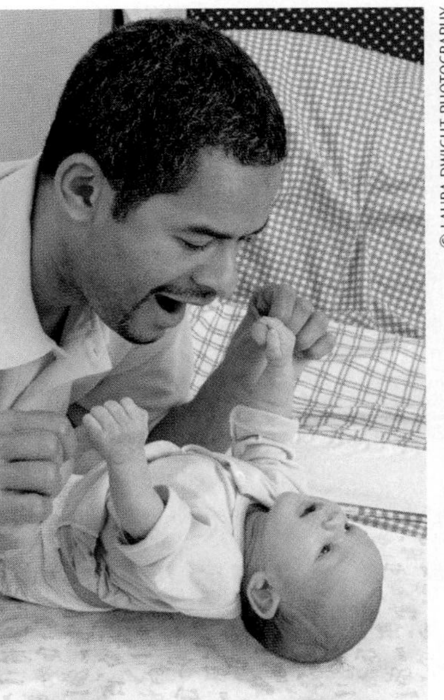

▶ The grasp reflex is so strong during the first week after birth that many infants can use it to support their entire weight.

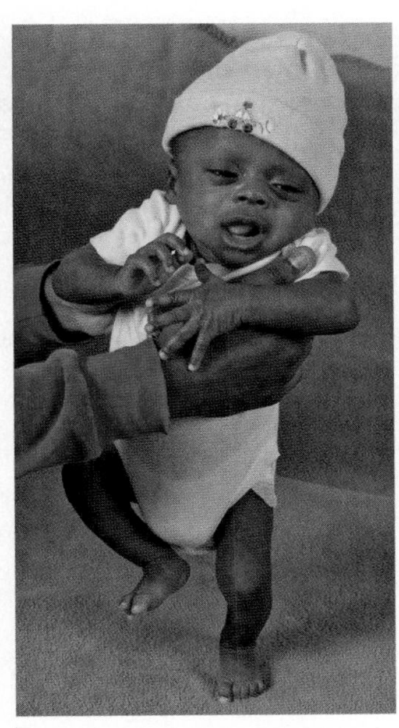

▶ When held upright under the arms, newborn babies show reflexive stepping movements.

Some reflexes have survival value. In our evolutionary past, when infants were carried about all day, the Moro reflex helped a baby who lost support to embrace and, along with the *grasp reflex*, regain its hold on the mother's body. The rooting reflex helps a breastfed baby find the mother's nipple. Babies display it only when hungry and touched by another person, not when they touch themselves (Rochat & Hespos, 1997). And without the *sucking reflex* enabling newborn feeding, our species would be unlikely to survive for a single generation!

Several reflexes help parents and infants establish gratifying interaction. A baby who successfully finds the nipple, sucks easily during feedings, and grasps when the hand is touched encourages parents to respond lovingly and feel competent as caregivers. Reflexes can also help caregivers comfort the baby. For example, on outings with Joshua, Yolanda brought along a pacifier. If he became fussy, sucking helped quiet him until she could feed, change, or hold him.

A few reflexes form the basis for complex motor skills that will develop later. For example, the *stepping reflex* looks like a primitive walking response. Around 2 months, it declines as infants increasingly relax their limbs, flexing their legs at the hip and knees when lowered onto a flat surface, which inhibits stepping. But if babies are held upright in the air, the reflex is clearly evident and persists, over time becoming integrated into independent walking (Barbu-Roth et al., 2015). Furthermore, when stepping is exercised regularly, babies make more reflexive stepping movements and are likely to walk several weeks earlier than if stepping is not practiced (Zelazo et al., 1993).

Most newborn reflexes disappear during the first six months (stepping is an exception), due to a gradual increase in voluntary control over behavior as the cerebral cortex develops. Pediatricians test reflexes carefully because reflexes can reveal the health of the baby's nervous system. Weak or absent reflexes, overly rigid or exaggerated reflexes, and reflexes that persist beyond the point in development when they should normally drop out can signal brain damage (Schott & Rossor, 2003).

States of Arousal

Throughout the day and night, newborn infants move in and out of five **states of arousal,** or degrees of sleep and wakefulness, described in Table 3.3 on page 96. Much to the relief of their fatigued parents, newborns spend the greatest amount of time asleep—about 16 to 18 hours a day.

However, striking individual differences in daily rhythms exist that affect parents' attitudes toward and interactions with the baby. A few newborns sleep for long periods, increasing the energy their well-rested parents have for sensitive, responsive care. Other babies cry a great deal, and their parents must exert great effort to soothe them. If these parents do not succeed, they may feel less competent and less positive toward their infant. Babies who spend more time alert probably receive

TABLE 3.3
Infant States of Arousal

STATE	DESCRIPTION	DAILY DURATION IN NEWBORN
Regular, or NREM, sleep	The infant is at full rest and shows little or no body activity. The eyelids are closed, no eye movements occur, the face is relaxed, and breathing is slow and regular.	8–9 hours
Irregular, or REM, sleep	Gentle limb movements, occasional stirring, and facial grimacing occur. Although the eyelids are closed, occasional rapid eye movements can be seen beneath them. Breathing is irregular.	8–9 hours
Drowsiness	The infant is either falling asleep or waking up. Body is less active than in irregular sleep but more active than in regular sleep. The eyes open and close; when open, they have a glazed look. Breathing is even but somewhat faster than in regular sleep.	Varies
Quiet alertness	The infant's body is relatively inactive, with eyes open and attentive. Breathing is even.	2–3 hours
Waking activity and crying	The infant shows frequent bursts of uncoordinated body activity. Breathing is very irregular. Face may be relaxed or tense and wrinkled. Crying may occur.	1–4 hours

Source: Wolff, 1966.

more social stimulation and opportunities to explore and, therefore, may have a slight advantage in cognitive development.

As with adults, sleep enhances babies' learning and memory. In one study, eye-blink responses and brain-wave recordings revealed that sleeping newborns readily learned that a tone would be followed by a puff of air to the eye (Fifer et al., 2010). Because young infants spend so much time sleeping, the capacity to learn about external stimuli during sleep may be essential for babies' adaptation to their surroundings.

Of the states listed in Table 3.3, the two extremes—sleep and crying—have been of greatest interest to researchers. Each tells us something about normal and abnormal early development.

Sleep. Observing Joshua as he slept, Yolanda and Jay wondered why his eyelids and body twitched and his rate of breathing varied. Sleep is made up of at least two states. During irregular, or **rapid-eye-movement (REM), sleep,** brain-wave activity is remarkably similar to that of the waking state. The eyes dart beneath the lids; heart rate, blood pressure, and breathing are uneven; and slight body movements occur. In contrast, during regular, or **non-rapid-eye-movement (NREM), sleep,** the body is almost motionless, and heart rate, breathing, and brain-wave activity are slow and even.

Like children and adults, newborns alternate between REM and NREM sleep, but they spend far more time in the REM state than they ever will again. REM sleep accounts for 50 percent of a newborn baby's sleep time. By 3 to 5 years, it has declined to an adultlike level of 20 percent (Louis et al., 1997).

The stimulation of REM sleep is vital for growth of the central nervous system (Tarullo, Balsam, & Fifer, 2011). Young infants seem to have a special need for this stimulation because they spend little time in an alert state, when they can get input from the environment. In support of this idea, the percentage of REM sleep is especially great in the fetus and in preterm babies, who are even less able than full-term newborns to take advantage of external stimulation (Peirano, Algarin, & Uauy, 2003).

Because newborns' normal sleep behavior is organized and patterned, observations of sleep states can help identify central nervous system abnormalities. In infants who are brain-damaged or who have experienced birth trauma, disturbed REM–NREM sleep cycles are often present. Babies with poor sleep organization are likely to be behaviorally disorganized and, therefore, to have difficulty learning and evoking caregiver interactions that enhance their development. In follow-ups during the preschool years, they show delayed motor, cognitive, and language development (Feldman, 2006; Holditch-Davis, Belyea, & Edwards, 2005; Weisman et al., 2011). And the brain-functioning problems that underlie newborn sleep irregularities may culminate in sudden infant death syndrome, a major cause of infant mortality (see the Biology and Environment box on the following page).

BIOLOGY AND ENVIRONMENT

The Mysterious Tragedy of Sudden Infant Death Syndrome

Millie awoke with a start one morning and looked at the clock. It was 7:30, and Sasha had missed both her night waking and her early morning feeding. Wondering if she was all right, Millie and her husband, Stuart, tiptoed into the room. Sasha lay still, curled up under her blanket. She had died silently during her sleep.

Sasha was a victim of **sudden infant death syndrome (SIDS),** the unexpected death, usually during the night, of an infant younger than 1 year of age that remains unexplained after thorough investigation. In industrialized nations, SIDS is the leading cause of infant mortality between 1 and 12 months, accounting for about 20 percent of these deaths in the United States (Centers for Disease Control and Prevention, 2017).

SIDS victims usually show physical problems from the beginning. Early medical records of SIDS babies reveal higher rates of prematurity and low birth weight, poor Apgar scores, and limp muscle tone. Abnormal heart rate and respiration and disturbances in sleep–wake activity and in REM–NREM cycles while asleep are also involved (Cornwell & Feigenbaum, 2006; Garcia, Koschnitzky, & Ramirez, 2013). At the time of death, many SIDS babies have a mild respiratory infection (Blood-Siegfried, 2009). This seems to increase the chances of respiratory failure in an already vulnerable baby.

Mounting evidence suggests that impaired brain functioning is a major contributor to SIDS. Between 2 and 4 months, when SIDS is most likely to occur, reflexes decline and are replaced by voluntary, learned responses. Neurological weaknesses may prevent SIDS babies from acquiring behaviors that replace defensive reflexes (Horne, 2017; Rubens & Sarnat, 2013). As a result, when breathing difficulties occur during sleep, these infants do not wake up, shift their position, or cry out for help. Instead, they simply give in to oxygen deprivation and death. In support of this interpretation, autopsies reveal that the brains of SIDS babies contain unusually low levels of serotonin (a brain chemical that assists with arousal when survival is threatened) as well as other abnormalities in centers that control breathing and arousal (Salomonis, 2014).

Several environmental factors are linked to SIDS. Maternal cigarette smoking, both during and after pregnancy, as well as smoking by other caregivers, doubles risk of the disorder. Babies exposed to cigarette smoke arouse less easily from sleep and have more respiratory infections (Blackwell et al., 2015). Prenatal abuse of drugs that depress central nervous system functioning (alcohol, opiates, and barbiturates) increases the risk of SIDS as much as fifteenfold (Hunt & Hauck, 2006).

BANANASTOCK/GETTY IMAGES PLUS/GETTY IMAGES

▶ Public education campaigns encouraging parents to put their infants on their backs to sleep have helped reduce the incidence of SIDS by more than half in many Western nations.

Infant sleep practices may also be involved. Infants who sleep on their stomachs rather than their backs and who are wrapped very warmly in clothing and blankets less often wake when their breathing is disturbed, especially if they suffer from biological vulnerabilities (Richardson, Walker, & Horne, 2008). In other cases, healthy babies sleeping face down on soft bedding may die from continually breathing their own exhaled breath—deaths due to accidental suffocation and therefore incorrectly classified as SIDS.

SIDS rates are especially high among poverty-stricken minorities (U.S. Department of Health and Human Services, 2015b). In these families, parental stress, substance abuse, reduced access to health care, and lack of knowledge about safe sleep practices are widespread.

The U.S. government's Safe to Sleep campaign encourages parents to create safe sleep environments and engage in other protective practices (National Institutes of Health, 2017). Recommendations include quitting smoking and drug taking, placing infants on their backs, using light sleep clothing, providing a firm sleep surface, and eliminating soft bedding. An estimated 20 percent of SIDS cases would be prevented if all infants had smoke-free homes. Dissemination of information to parents about putting infants down on their backs has cut the incidence of SIDS by more than half (Behm et al., 2012). Other protective measures are breastfeeding (discussed in Chapter 4) and pacifier use: Sleeping babies who suck arouse more easily in response to breathing and heart-rate irregularities (Alm et al., 2016).

When SIDS does occur, surviving family members require a great deal of help to overcome a sudden and unexpected death. As Millie commented six months after Sasha's death, "It's the worst crisis we've ever been through. What's helped us most are the comforting words of others who've experienced the same tragedy."

LAURA DWIGHT PHOTOGRAPHY

▶ To soothe his crying infant, this father rocks her gently while talking softly.

LOOK AND LISTEN

In a public setting, watch several parents soothe their crying infants. What techniques did the parents use, and how successful were they?

Crying. Crying is the first way that babies communicate, letting parents know they need food, comfort, or stimulation. The baby's cry is a complex stimulus that varies in intensity, from a whimper to a message of all-out distress (Wood, 2009). Most of the time, the strength of the cry, combined with the experiences leading up to it, helps guide parents toward its cause.

Young infants usually cry because of physical needs, most commonly hunger, but babies may also cry in response to temperature change when undressed, a sudden noise, or a painful stimulus. Newborns (as well as older babies up to age 6 months) often cry at the sound of another crying baby (Dondi, Simion, & Caltran, 1999; Geangu et al., 2010). Some researchers believe that this response reflects an inborn capacity to react to the suffering of others. Furthermore, crying typically increases during the early weeks, peaks at about 6 weeks, and then declines (Barr, 2001). Because this trend appears in many cultures with vastly different infant care practices, researchers believe that normal readjustments of the central nervous system underlie it.

The next time you hear an infant cry, notice your own reaction. The sound stimulates a sharp rise in blood cortisol, alertness, and feelings of discomfort in men and women, parents and nonparents alike (de Cock et al., 2015; Yong & Ruffman, 2014). This powerful response is probably innately programmed to ensure that babies receive the care they need to survive.

Soothing Crying Infants. Although parents do not always interpret their baby's cry correctly, their accuracy improves with experience. At the same time, they vary widely in responsiveness. Parents who are high in empathy (ability to take the perspective of others in distress) and who hold "child-centered" attitudes toward infant care (for example, believe that babies cannot be spoiled by being picked up) are more likely to respond quickly and sensitively (Cohen-Bendahan, van Doornen, & de Weerth, 2014; Leerkes, 2010).

Fortunately, there are many ways to soothe a crying baby when feeding and diaper changing do not work (see Applying What We Know on the following page). The technique that Western parents usually try first, lifting the baby to the shoulder and rocking or walking, is highly effective. Another common soothing method is swaddling—wrapping the baby snugly in a blanket. The Quechua, who live in the cold, high-altitude desert regions of Peru, dress young babies in layers of clothing and blankets that cover the head and body, a practice that reduces crying and promotes sleep (Tronick, Thomas, & Daltabuit, 1994). It also allows the baby to conserve energy for early growth in the harsh Peruvian highlands.

In many tribal and village societies and non-Western developed nations (such as Japan), babies are in physical contact with their caregivers almost continuously. Infants in these cultures show shorter bouts of crying than their American counterparts (Barr, 2001). When Western parents choose to practice "proximal care" by holding their babies extensively, the amount of crying in the early months is reduced by about one-third (St James-Roberts, 2012).

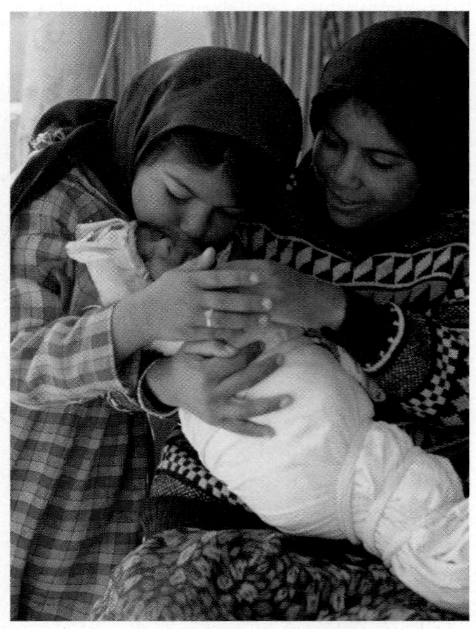
DAVID POOLE/ROBERT HARDING

▶ The Bedouin people of the Middle East tightly swaddle young infants, a practice that reduces crying and promotes sleep.

Abnormal Crying. Like reflexes and sleep patterns, the infant's cry offers a clue to central nervous system distress. The cries of brain-damaged babies and those who have experienced prenatal and birth complications are often shrill, piercing, and shorter in duration than those of healthy infants (Green, Irwin, & Gustafson, 2000). Even newborns with a fairly common problem—*colic,* or persistent crying—tend to have high-pitched, harsh-sounding cries. Although the cause of colic is unknown, certain newborns, who react especially strongly to unpleasant stimuli, are susceptible (St James-Roberts, 2007). Colic generally subsides between 3 and 6 months.

Most parents try to respond to a crying baby with extra care and attention, but sometimes the cry is so unpleasant and persistent that parents become frustrated, resentful, and angry. Preterm and ill babies are more likely to be abused by highly stressed parents, who sometimes mention a high-pitched, grating cry as one factor that caused them to

APPLYING WHAT WE KNOW

Soothing a Crying Baby

METHOD	EXPLANATION
Talk softly or play rhythmic sounds.	Continuous, monotonous, rhythmic sounds (such as a clock ticking, a fan whirring, or peaceful music) are more effective than intermittent sounds.
Offer a pacifier.	Sucking helps babies control their own level of arousal.
Massage the baby's body.	Stroking the baby's torso and limbs with continuous, gentle motions relaxes the baby's muscles.
Swaddle the baby.	Restricting movement and increasing warmth often soothe a young infant.
Lift the baby to the shoulder and rock or walk.	This combination of physical contact, upright posture, and motion is an effective soothing technique, causing young infants to become quietly alert.
Take the baby for a short car ride or a walk in a baby carriage; swing the baby in a cradle.	Gentle, rhythmic motion of any kind helps lull the baby to sleep.
Combine several of the methods just listed.	Stimulating several of the baby's senses at once is often more effective than stimulating only one.
If these methods do not work, let the baby cry for a short period.	Occasionally, a baby responds well to just being put down and will, after a few minutes, fall asleep.

Sources: Dayton et al., 2015; Evanoo, 2007; St James-Roberts, 2012.

lose control (Barr et al., 2014). We will discuss a host of additional influences on child abuse in Chapter 8.

Sensory Capacities

On his visit to my class, Joshua looked wide-eyed at my bright pink blouse and turned to the sound of his mother's voice. During feedings, he lets Yolanda know through his sucking rhythm that he prefers the taste of breast milk to a bottle of plain water. Clearly, Joshua has some well-developed sensory capacities. In the following sections, we explore the newborn's responsiveness to touch, taste, smell, sound, and visual stimulation.

Touch. In our discussion of preterm infants, we saw that touch helps stimulate early physical growth. As we will see in Chapter 6, it is vital for emotional development as well. Therefore, it is not surprising that sensitivity to touch is well-developed at birth. Newborns even use touch to investigate their world. When small objects are placed in their palms, they can distinguish shape (prism versus cylinder) and texture (smooth versus rough), as indicated by their tendency to hold on longer to an object with an unfamiliar shape or texture than to a familiar object (Lejeune et al., 2012; Sann & Streri, 2007).

At birth, infants are highly sensitive to pain. If male newborns are circumcised without anesthetic, they often respond with a high-pitched, stressful cry and a dramatic rise in heart rate, blood pressure, palm sweating, pupil dilation, and muscle tension (Lehr et al., 2007; Warnock & Sandrin, 2004). Brain-imaging research suggests that because of central nervous system immaturity, preterm babies, particularly males, feel the pain of a medical injection especially intensely (Bartocci et al., 2006).

Certain local anesthetics for newborns ease the pain of these procedures. Offering a nipple that delivers a sweet liquid is also helpful, with breast milk being especially effective (Roman-Rodriguez et al., 2014). And the smell of the milk of the baby's mother reduces infant distress to a routine blood-test heel stick more effectively than the odor of another mother's milk or of formula (Badiee, Asghari, & Mohammadizadeh, 2013; Nishitani et al., 2009). Combining sweet liquid with gentle holding by the parent lessens pain even more. Research on infant mammals indicates that physical touch releases *endorphins*—painkilling chemicals in the brain (Axelin, Salanterä, & Lehtonen, 2006).

Allowing a baby to endure severe pain overwhelms the nervous system with stress hormones (Walker, 2013). The result is heightened pain sensitivity, sleep disturbances, feeding problems, and difficulty calming down when upset.

Taste and Smell. Newborns can distinguish several basic tastes. Like adults, they relax their facial muscles in response to sweetness, purse their lips when the taste is sour, and show an archlike mouth opening when it is bitter. Similarly, certain odor preferences are present at birth. For example, the smell of bananas or chocolate causes a pleasant facial expression, whereas the odor of rotten eggs makes the infant frown (Steiner, 1979; Steiner et al., 2001). These reactions are important for survival: The food that best supports the infant's early growth is the sweet-tasting milk of the mother's breast. Not until 4 months do babies prefer a salty taste to plain water, a change that may prepare them to accept solid foods (Mennella & Beauchamp, 1998).

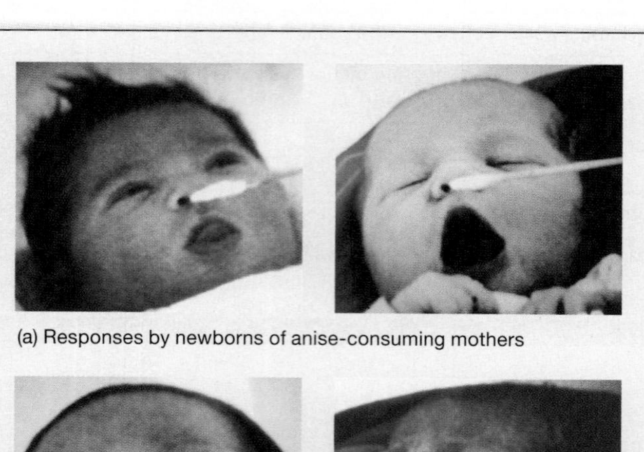

(a) Responses by newborns of anise-consuming mothers

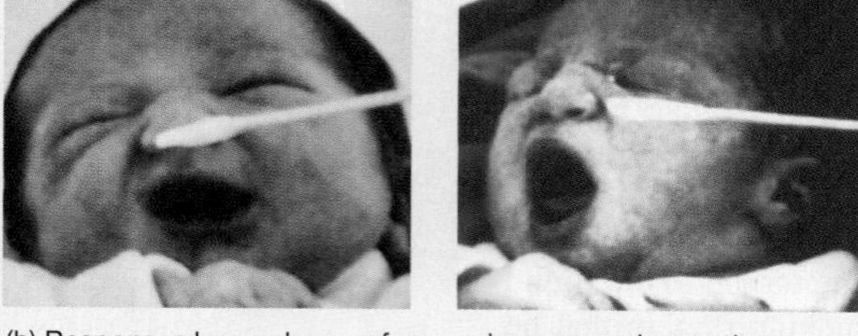

(b) Responses by newborns of non-anise-consuming mothers

FIGURE 3.8 Examples of facial expressions of newborns exposed to the odor of anise whose mothers' diets differed in anise-flavored foods during late pregnancy. (a) Babies of anise-consuming mothers spent more time turning toward the odor and sucking, licking, and chewing. (b) Babies of non-anise-consuming mothers more often turned away with a negative facial expression. (From B. Schaal, L. Marlier, & R. Soussignan, 2000, "Human Foetuses Learn Odours from Their Pregnant Mother's Diet," *Chemical Senses, 25,* p. 731. © 2000 Oxford University Press, Inc.; permission conveyed through Copyright Clearance Center, Inc.)

During pregnancy, the amniotic fluid is rich in tastes and smells that vary with the mother's diet—early experiences that influence newborns' preferences. In a study carried out in the Alsatian region of France, where anise is frequently used to flavor foods, researchers tested newborns for their reaction to the anise odor (Schaal, Marlier, & Soussignan, 2000). The mothers of some babies had regularly consumed anise during the last two weeks of pregnancy; the other mothers had never consumed it. When presented with the anise odor on the day of birth, the babies of non-anise-consuming mothers were far more likely to turn away with a negative facial expression (see Figure 3.8). These different reactions were still apparent four days later, even though all mothers had refrained from consuming anise during this time.

Young infants will readily learn to prefer a taste that at first evoked either a negative or a neutral response. Bottle-fed newborns allergic to cow's milk who are given a soy or other vegetable-based substitute (typically sour and bitter-tasting) soon prefer it to regular formula (Beauchamp & Mennella, 2011). This taste preference is still evident at ages 4 to 5 years, in more positive responses to foods with sour and bitter tastes than shown by agemates.

In mammals, including humans, the sense of smell—in addition to playing an important role in feeding—helps mothers and babies identify each other. At 2 to 4 days of age, breastfed babies prefer the odors of their own mother's breast and underarm to those of an unfamiliar lactating mother (Cernoch & Porter, 1985; Marin, Rapisardi, & Tani, 2015). And both breast- and bottle-fed 3- to 4-day-olds orient more to the smell of unfamiliar human milk than to formula milk, indicating that (even without postnatal exposure) the odor of human milk is more attractive to newborns (Marlier & Schaal, 2005). Newborns' dual attraction to the odors of their mother and of breast milk helps them locate an appropriate food source and, in the process, begin to distinguish their caregiver from other people.

Hearing. Newborn infants can hear a wide variety of sounds—sensitivity that improves greatly over the first few months (Johnson & Hannon, 2015). At birth, infants prefer complex sounds, such as noises and voices, to pure tones. And babies only a few days old can tell the difference between a variety of sound patterns: a series of tones arranged in ascending versus descending order; utterances with two versus three syllables; the stress patterns of words ("*ma*-ma" versus "ma-*ma*"); happy-sounding speech as opposed to speech with negative or neutral emotional qualities; and even two languages spoken by the same bilingual speaker, as long as those languages differ in their rhythmic features—for example, French versus Russian (Mastropieri & Turkewitz, 1999; Ramus, 2002; Sansavini, Bertoncini, & Giovanelli, 1997; Trehub, 2001; Winkler et al., 2009).

Young infants listen longer to human speech than structurally similar nonspeech sounds (Vouloumanos, 2010). And they make fine-grained distinctions among many speech sounds. Indeed, researchers have found only a few speech sounds across widely differing languages that newborns cannot discriminate (Jusczyk & Luce, 2002). These capacities reveal that the baby is marvelously prepared for the awesome task of acquiring language.

Immediately after birth, infants will also suck more on a nipple to hear a recording of their mother's voice than that of an unfamiliar woman and to hear their native language as opposed to a foreign language (Moon, Cooper, & Fifer, 1993; Spence & DeCasper, 1987). These preferences result from hearing the muffled sounds of the mother's voice before birth.

Vision. Vision is the least-developed of the newborn baby's senses. Visual structures in both the eye and the brain are not yet fully formed. For example, cells in the *retina,* the membrane lining the inside of the eye that captures light and transforms it into messages that are sent to the brain, are not as mature or densely packed as they will be in several months. The optic nerve that relays these messages, and visual centers in the brain that receive them, will not be adultlike for several years. And muscles of the *lens,* which permit us to adjust our visual focus to varying distances, are weak (Johnson & Hannon, 2015).

As a result, newborns cannot focus their eyes well, and their **visual acuity,** or fineness of discrimination, is limited. At birth, infants perceive objects at a distance of 20 feet about as clearly as adults do at 600 feet (Slater et al., 2010). In addition, unlike adults (who see nearby objects most clearly), newborn babies see unclearly across a wide range of distances (Banks, 1980; Hainline, 1998). Images such as the parent's face, even from close up, look quite blurred. Although newborns prefer to look at colored over gray stimuli, they are not yet good at discriminating colors. It will take about four months for color vision to become adultlike (Johnson & Hannon, 2015). Despite limited vision and slow, imprecise eye movements, newborns actively explore their visual world by scanning it for interesting sights and tracking moving objects.

ASK YOURSELF

CONNECT How do the diverse capacities of newborn babies contribute to their first social relationships? Provide as many examples as you can.

REFLECT Are newborns more competent than you thought they were before you read this chapter? Which of their capacities most surprised you?

The Transition to Parenthood

3.11 Describe typical changes in the family after the birth of a new baby, along with conditions that contribute to successful adjustment to parenthood.

The early weeks after a baby's arrival are full of profound changes. The mother needs to recover from childbirth. If she is breastfeeding, energies must be devoted to working out this intimate relationship. The father must become a part of this new threesome while supporting the mother in her recovery. At times, he may feel ambivalent about the baby, who constantly demands and gets the mother's attention. And as we will see in Chapter 6, siblings—especially those who are young and firstborn—understandably feel displaced. They sometimes react with jealousy and anger.

While all this is going on, the tiny infant demands to be fed, changed, and comforted at odd times of the day and night. The family schedule becomes irregular and uncertain, and parental sleep deprivation and consequent daytime fatigue are often major challenges (Insana & Montgomery-Downs, 2012). Financial responsibilities increase, and couples have less time to devote to each other.

For most new parents, however, the arrival of a baby—though often followed by mild declines in relationship and overall life satisfaction—does not cause significant marital strain. Marriages that are gratifying and supportive tend to remain so (Doss et al., 2009; Luhmann et al., 2012). But troubled marriages usually become more distressed after childbirth (Houts et al., 2008). And when

The arrival of a baby brings profound changes. For couples who have a positive, cooperative relationship, sufficient income, and social support, the stress of parenthood typically remains manageable, contributing to favorable development.

mothers lack partner support in parenting, they experience an especially difficult post-birth adjustment, with negative consequences for parent–infant interaction (Driver et al., 2012; McHale & Rotman, 2007; Moller, Hwang, & Wickberg, 2008). In contrast, sharing caregiving is associated with greater parental happiness and sensitivity to the baby.

About 40 percent of U.S. births are to single mothers. The majority are unplanned, to women in their twenties (Martin et al., 2017). Most of these mothers have incomes below the poverty level and experience a stressful transition to parenthood. Although many live with the baby's father or another partner, cohabiting relationships in the United States, compared with those in Western Europe, involve less commitment and cooperation (Guzzo, 2014). U.S. cohabiting couples are far more likely to break up, especially after an unplanned baby arrives. Single mothers often lack emotional and parenting support—strong predictors of psychological distress and infant caregiving difficulties (Keating-Lefler et al., 2004).

Special interventions are available to help parents adjust to life with a new baby. For those who are not high risk for problems, counselor-led parenting groups are highly effective (Gottman, Gottman, & Shapiro, 2010). High-risk parents struggling with poverty or the birth of a child with disabilities need more intensive interventions aimed at enhancing social support and parenting skills. Many low-income single mothers benefit from programs that focus on sustaining the father's involvement (Jones, Charles, & Benson, 2013). These parents also require tangible support—money, food, transportation, and affordable child care—to ease stress so they have the psychological resources to engage in sensitive, responsive care.

When parents' relationship is positive and cooperative, social support is available, and families have sufficient income, the stress caused by the birth of a baby remains manageable. These family conditions consistently contribute to favorable development—in infancy and beyond.

CHAPTER 3 SUMMARY

Prenatal Development *(p. 70)*

3.1 *List the three periods of prenatal development, and describe the major milestones of each.*

- The **germinal period** lasts about two weeks, from fertilization through **implantation** of the multicelled blastocyst in the uterine lining. Structures that will support prenatal growth begin to form, including the **placenta** and the **umbilical cord.**
- During the **period of the embryo,** weeks 2 through 8, the foundations for all body structures are laid down. The **neural tube** forms and the nervous system starts to develop. Other organs follow rapidly. By the end of this period, the embryo responds to touch and can move.
- The **period of the fetus,** lasting until the end of pregnancy, involves dramatic increase in body size and completion of physical structures. At the end of the second trimester, most of the brain's neurons are in place.
- The fetus reaches the **age of viability** at the beginning of the third trimester, between 22 and 26 weeks. The brain continues to develop rapidly, and new sensory and behavioral capacities emerge. Gradually the lungs mature, the fetus fills the uterus, and birth is near.

Prenatal Environmental Influences *(p. 76)*

3.2 *Cite factors that influence the impact of teratogens, and discuss evidence on the impact of known or suspected teratogens.*

- The impact of **teratogens** varies with amount and length of exposure, genetic makeup of mother and fetus, presence of other harmful agents, and age of the organism. The developing organism is especially vulnerable during the embryonic period. Certain teratogens exert long-term effects by modifying gene expression.
- The most widely used potent teratogen is isotretinoin, a drug used to treat severe acne. The prenatal impact of other commonly used medications, such as aspirin and caffeine, is hard to separate from other correlated factors.
- Babies born to users of cocaine or heroin are at risk for a wide variety of problems, including prematurity, low birth weight, brain abnormalities, physical defects, and breathing difficulties. However, lasting consequences are not well-established.
- Infants whose parents use tobacco are often born underweight, may have physical defects, and are at risk for long-term attention, learning, and behavior problems.

- Maternal alcohol consumption can lead to **fetal alcohol spectrum disorder (FASD). Fetal alcohol syndrome (FAS),** resulting from heavy drinking throughout pregnancy, involves slow physical growth, facial abnormalities, and mental impairments. Milder forms—**partial fetal alcohol syndrome (p-FAS)** and **alcohol-related neurodevelopmental disorder (ARND)**—affect children whose mothers consumed smaller quantities of alcohol.
- Prenatal exposure to high levels of ionizing radiation, mercury, PCBs, lead, and dioxins leads to physical malformations and severe brain damage. Low-level exposure has been linked to cognitive deficits and emotional and behavioral disorders. Persistent air pollution is associated with low birth weight and impaired lung and immune-system functioning.

OSLAN RAHMAN/AFP/GETTY IMAGES

- Among infectious diseases, rubella causes wide-ranging abnormalities. Babies with prenatally transmitted HIV rapidly develop AIDS, leading to brain damage and early death. Cytomegalovirus, herpes simplex 2, and toxoplasmosis can also be devastating to the embryo and fetus.

3.3 ***Describe the impact of additional maternal factors on prenatal development.***

- Prenatal malnutrition can lead to low birth weight and damage to the brain and other organs. Vitamin–mineral supplementation, including folic acid, can prevent prenatal and birth complications.
- Severe emotional stress is linked to pregnancy complications and structural alterations in the infants' and children's brains, resulting in impaired capacity to manage stress and susceptibility to later illness. These consequences can be reduced by providing the mother with social support.
- **Rh factor incompatibility**—an Rh-positive fetus developing within an Rh-negative mother—can lead to oxygen deprivation and infant death.
- Older mothers face increased risk of miscarriage, babies with chromosomal defects, and, after age 40, a rise in other pregnancy complications. Poor health and environmental risks associated with poverty explain higher rates of pregnancy complications in adolescent mothers.

3.4 ***Explain why early and regular health care is vital during the prenatal period.***

- Unexpected difficulties, such as preeclampsia, can arise, especially when pregnant women have preexisting health problems. Prenatal health care is especially crucial for women who are young and low-income.

Childbirth *(p. 86)*

3.5 ***Describe the three stages of childbirth and the baby's adaptation to labor and delivery.***

- In the first stage, contractions widen and thin the cervix. In the second stage, the mother feels an urge to push the baby down and out of the birth canal. In the final stage, the placenta is delivered.
- During labor, infants produce high levels of stress hormones, which help them withstand oxygen deprivation, clear the lungs for breathing, and arouse them into alertness at birth.
- The **Apgar Scale** helps doctors and nurses assess the baby's physical condition at birth.

Approaches to Childbirth *(p. 88)*

3.6 ***Describe natural childbirth and home delivery, noting benefits and concerns associated with each.***

- In **natural,** or **prepared, childbirth,** the expectant mother and a companion attend classes about labor and delivery, master relaxation and breathing techniques to counteract pain, and prepare for coaching during childbirth. Social support from a doula is linked to a reduction in birth complications and to higher Apgar scores.

ERSEN ROSS/BRAND X PICTURES/GETTY IMAGES

- Home birth is safe for healthy mothers who are assisted by a well-trained doctor or midwife, but mothers at risk for complications are safer giving birth in a hospital.

Medical Interventions *(p. 89)*

3.7 ***List common medical interventions during childbirth, circumstances that justify their use, and any dangers associated with each.***

- **Fetal monitors** help save the lives of many babies at risk for **anoxia** because of pregnancy and birth complications. When used routinely, however, they may identify infants as in danger who, in fact, are not.
- Use of analgesics and anesthetics to control pain, though necessary in complicated deliveries, can prolong labor and may have negative effects on newborn adjustment.
- **Cesarean delivery** is warranted by medical emergencies and in certain cases of **breech position**. However, many unnecessary cesareans are performed.

Preterm and Low-Birth-Weight Infants *(p. 90)*

3.8 ***Describe risks associated with preterm birth and low birth weight, along with effective interventions.***

- Low birth weight, most common in infants born to poverty-stricken women, is a major cause of neonatal and **infant mortality** and developmental problems. Compared with **preterm infants,** whose weight is appropriate for time spent in the uterus, **small-for-date infants** usually have longer-lasting difficulties.

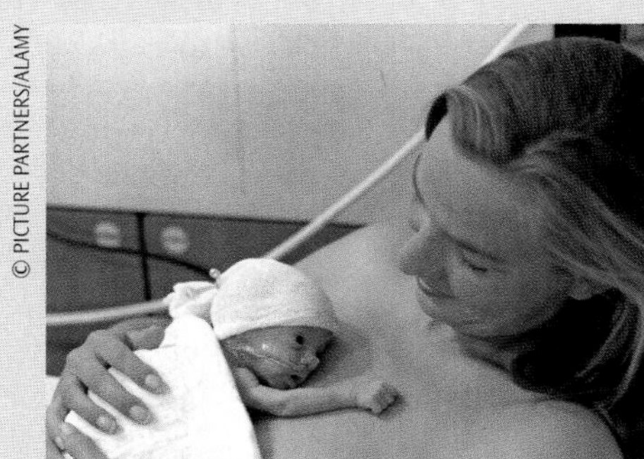
© PICTURE PARTNERS/ALAMY

- Some interventions provide special infant stimulation in the intensive care nursery. Others teach parents how to care for and interact with their babies. Preterm infants in stressed, low-income households need long-term, intensive intervention.

The Newborn Baby's Capacities *(p. 93)*

3.9 ***Describe the newborn baby's reflexes and states of arousal, noting sleep characteristics and ways to soothe a crying baby.***

- **Reflexes** are the newborn baby's most obvious organized patterns of behavior. Some have survival value, others help parents and infants establish gratifying interaction, and a few provide the foundation for complex motor skills.

- Newborns experience five **states of arousal** but spend most of their time asleep. Sleep includes at least two states, **rapid-eye-movement (REM) sleep** and **non-rapid-eye-movement (NREM) sleep.** Newborns spend about 50 percent of sleep time in REM sleep, which provides them with stimulation essential for central nervous system development.
- A crying baby stimulates strong feelings of discomfort in nearby adults. Once feeding and diaper changing have been tried, a highly effective soothing technique is lifting the baby to the shoulder and rocking and walking. Extensive parent–infant physical contact substantially reduces crying in the early months.

3.10 ***Describe the newborn baby's sensory capacities.***

- Newborns use touch to investigate their world, are sensitive to pain, prefer sweet tastes and smells, and orient toward the odor of their own mother's lactating breast.
- Newborns can distinguish a variety of sound patterns and prefer complex sounds. They are especially responsive to human speech, can detect the sounds of any human language, and prefer their mother's voice.
- Vision is the least developed of the newborn's senses. At birth, focusing ability, **visual acuity,** and color discrimination are limited. Nevertheless, newborn babies actively explore their visual world.

The Transition to Parenthood *(p. 101)*

3.11 ***Describe typical changes in the family after the birth of a new baby, along with conditions that contribute to successful adjustment to parenthood.***

- The new baby's arrival is exciting but stressful, as the mother recuperates and the family schedule becomes irregular and uncertain. Gratifying marriages tend to remain so after childbirth, but troubled marriages usually become more distressed. When parents have a positive relationship, share caregiving, and have access to social support and adequate income, adjustment problems are manageable.

IMPORTANT TERMS AND CONCEPTS

age of viability (p. 74)
alcohol-related neurodevelopmental disorder (ARND) (p. 79)
amnion (p. 71)
anoxia (p. 89)
Apgar Scale (p. 87)
breech position (p. 89)
cesarean delivery (p. 90)
chorion (p. 72)
fetal alcohol spectrum disorder (FASD) (p. 79)
fetal alcohol syndrome (FAS) (p. 79)
fetal monitors (p. 89)
germinal period (p. 70)
implantation (p. 71)
infant mortality (p. 94)
lanugo (p. 74)
natural, or prepared, childbirth (p. 88)
neural tube (p. 73)
non-rapid-eye-movement (NREM) sleep (p. 96)
partial fetal alcohol syndrome (p-FAS) (p. 79)
period of the embryo (p. 73)
period of the fetus (p. 73)
placenta (p. 72)
preterm infants (p. 91)
rapid-eye-movement (REM) sleep (p. 96)
reflex (p. 93)
Rh factor incompatibility (p. 84)
small-for-date infants (p. 91)
states of arousal (p. 95)
sudden infant death syndrome (SIDS) (p. 97)
teratogen (p. 76)
trimesters (p. 74)
umbilical cord (p. 72)
vernix (p. 74)
visual acuity (p. 101)

CHAPTER

4 Physical Development in Infancy and Toddlerhood

Beginning to walk frees this 14-month-old's hands for carrying objects, grants a whole new perspective on a tantalizing physical world to explore, and enables her to interact with caregivers in new ways—for example, by showing an object or giving a hug. In the first two years, motor, perceptual, cognitive, and social development mutually influence one another.

WHAT'S AHEAD IN CHAPTER 4

On a brilliant June morning, 16-month-old Caitlin emerged from her front door, ready for the short drive to the child-care home where she spent her weekdays while her mother, Carolyn, and her father, David, worked. Clutching a teddy bear in one hand and her mother's arm with the other, Caitlin descended the steps. "One! Two! Threeee!" Carolyn counted as she helped Caitlin down. "How much she's changed," Carolyn thought to herself, looking at the child who, not long ago, had been a newborn. With her first steps, Caitlin had passed from *infancy* to *toddlerhood*—a period spanning the second year of life. At first, Caitlin did, indeed, "toddle" with an awkward gait, tipping over frequently. But her face reflected the thrill of conquering a new skill.

As they walked toward the car, Carolyn and Caitlin spotted 3-year-old Eli and his father, Kevin, in the neighboring yard. Eli dashed toward them, waving a bright yellow envelope. Carolyn bent down to open the envelope and took out a card. It read, "Announcing the arrival of Grace Ann. Born: Cambodia. Age: 16 months." Carolyn turned to Kevin and Eli. "That's wonderful news! When can we see her?"

"Let's wait a few days," Kevin suggested. "Monica's taken Grace to the doctor this morning. She's underweight and malnourished." Kevin described Monica's first night with Grace in a hotel room in Phnom Penh. Grace lay on the bed, withdrawn and fearful. Eventually she fell asleep, gripping crackers in both hands.

Carolyn felt Caitlin's impatient tug at her sleeve. Off they drove to child care, where Vanessa had just dropped off her 18-month-old son, Timmy. Within moments, Caitlin and Timmy were in the sandbox, shoveling sand into plastic cups and buckets with the help of their caregiver, Ginette.

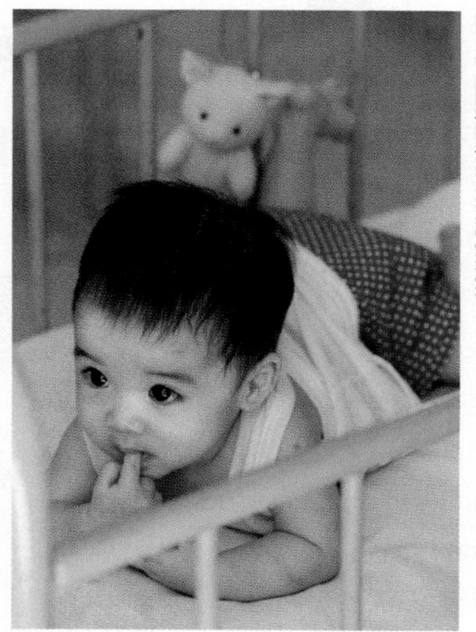
HOANG DINH NAM/AFP/GETTY IMAGES

A few weeks later, Grace joined Caitlin and Timmy at Ginette's child-care home. Although still unable to crawl or walk, she had grown taller and heavier, and her sad, vacant gaze had given way to a ready smile and an enthusiastic desire to imitate and explore. When Caitlin headed for the sandbox, Grace stretched out her arms, asking Ginette to carry her there, too. Soon Grace was pulling herself up at every opportunity. Finally, at age 18 months, she walked!

This chapter traces physical growth during the first two years. We will see how rapid changes in the infant's body and brain support learning, motor skills, and perceptual capacities. Caitlin, Grace, and Timmy will join us to illustrate individual differences and environmental influences on physical development.

Body Growth

4.1 Describe major changes in body growth over the first two years.

The next time you're walking in your neighborhood park or at the mall, note the contrast between infants' and toddlers' physical capabilities. One reason for the vast changes in what children can do over the first two years is that their bodies change enormously—faster than at any other time after birth.

Changes in Body Size and Muscle–Fat Makeup

By the end of the first year, a typical infant's height is about 32 inches—more than 50 percent greater than at birth. By 2 years, it is 75 percent greater (36 inches). Similarly, by 5 months of age, birth weight has doubled to about 15 pounds. At 1 year it has tripled to 22 pounds, and at 2 years it has quadrupled to about 30 pounds. Figure 4.1 illustrates this dramatic increase in body size.

One of the most obvious changes in infants' appearance is their transformation into round, plump babies by the middle of the first year. This early rise in "baby fat," which peaks at about 9 months, helps the small infant maintain a constant body temperature. In the second year, most toddlers slim down, a trend that continues into middle childhood (Fomon & Nelson, 2002). In contrast, muscle tissue increases very slowly during infancy and will not reach a peak until adolescence.

Changes in Body Proportions

As the child's overall size increases, different parts of the body grow at different rates. Two growth patterns describe these changes. The first is the **cephalocaudal trend**—from the Latin for "head to tail." During the prenatal period, the head develops more rapidly than the lower part of the body. At birth, the head takes up one-fourth of total body length, the legs only one-third. Notice how, in Figure 4.1, the lower portion of the body catches up. By age 2, the head accounts for only one-fifth and the legs for nearly one-half of total body length.

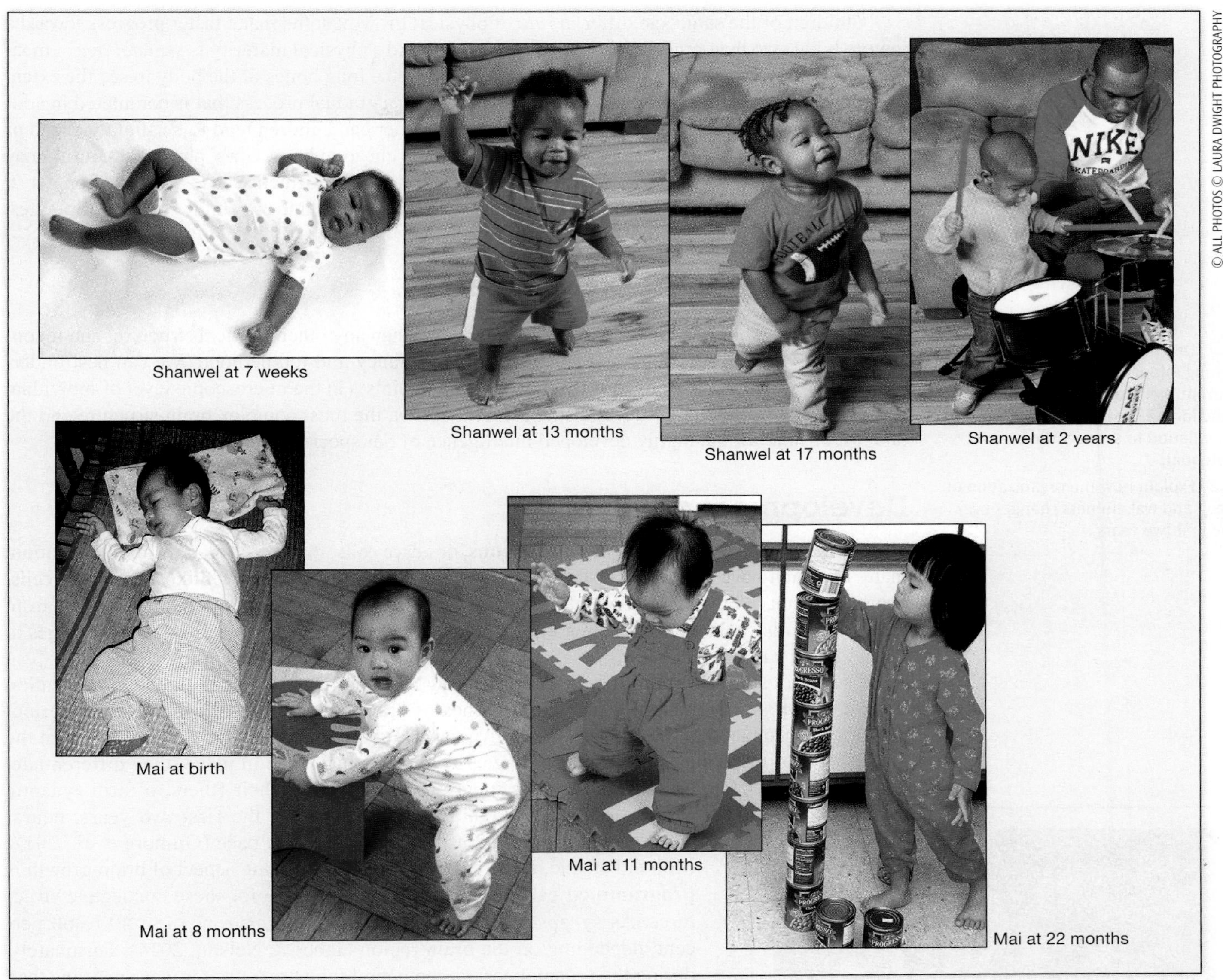

FIGURE 4.1 Body growth during the first two years. These photos depict the dramatic changes in body size and proportions during infancy and toddlerhood in two individuals—a boy, Shanwel, and a girl, Mai. In the first year, the head is quite large in proportion to the rest of the body, and height and weight gain are especially rapid. During the second year, the lower portion of the body catches up. Notice, also, how both children added "baby fat" in the early months of life and then slimmed down, a trend that continues into middle childhood.

In the second pattern, the **proximodistal trend,** growth proceeds, literally, from "near to far"—from the center of the body outward. In the prenatal period, the head, chest, and trunk grow first; then the arms and legs; and finally the hands and feet. During infancy and childhood, the arms and legs continue to grow somewhat ahead of the hands and feet.

Individual and Group Differences

In infancy, girls are slightly shorter and lighter than boys, with a higher ratio of fat to muscle. These small sex differences persist throughout early and middle childhood and are greatly magnified at adolescence. Ethnic differences in body size are apparent as well. Grace was below the *growth norms* (height and weight averages for children her age). Early malnutrition contributed, but even after substantial catch-up, Grace—as is typical for Asian children—remained below North American norms. In contrast, Timmy is slightly above average, as African-American children tend to be (Bogin, 2001).

Children of the same age differ in *rate* of physical growth; some make faster progress toward a mature body size than others. The best estimate of a child's physical maturity is *skeletal age,* a measure of bone development. It is determined by X-raying the long bones of the body to see the extent to which soft, pliable cartilage has hardened into bone—a gradual process that is completed in adolescence. When skeletal ages are examined, African-American children tend to be slightly ahead of European-American children, and girls are considerably ahead of boys. Girls' physical maturity may contribute to their greater resistance to harmful environmental influences. As noted in Chapter 2, girls experience fewer developmental problems and have lower infant and childhood mortality rates.

Brain Development

4.2 Describe brain development during infancy and toddlerhood, current methods of measuring brain functioning, and appropriate stimulation to support the brain's potential.

4.3 Explain how the organization of sleep and wakefulness changes over the first two years.

At birth, the brain is nearer to its adult size than any other physical structure, and it continues to develop at an astounding pace throughout infancy and toddlerhood. We can best understand brain growth by looking at it from two vantage points: (1) the microscopic level of individual brain cells and (2) the larger level of the cerebral cortex, the most complex brain structure and the one responsible for the highly developed intelligence of our species.

Development of Neurons

The human brain has 100 to 200 billion **neurons,** or nerve cells, that store and transmit information, many of which have thousands of direct connections with other neurons. Unlike other body cells, neurons are not tightly packed together. Between them are tiny gaps, or **synapses,** where fibers from different neurons come close together but do not touch (see Figure 4.2). Neurons send messages to one another by releasing chemicals called **neurotransmitters,** which cross the synapse.

The basic story of brain growth concerns how neurons form this elaborate communication system. Figure 4.3 summarizes major milestones of brain development. In the prenatal period, neurons are produced in the embryo's primitive neural tube. From there, they migrate to form the major parts of the brain (see Chapter 3, page 73). Once neurons are in place, they differentiate, establishing unique functions by extending their fibers to form synaptic connections with neighboring cells. During the first two years, neural fibers and synapses increase at an astounding pace (Gilmore et al., 2012; Moore, Persaud, & Torchia, 2016a). A surprising aspect of brain growth is **programmed cell death,** which makes space for these connective structures: As synapses form, many surrounding neurons die—40 to 60 percent, depending on the brain region (Jabès & Nelson, 2014). Fortunately, during the prenatal period, the neural tube produces far more neurons than the brain will ever need.

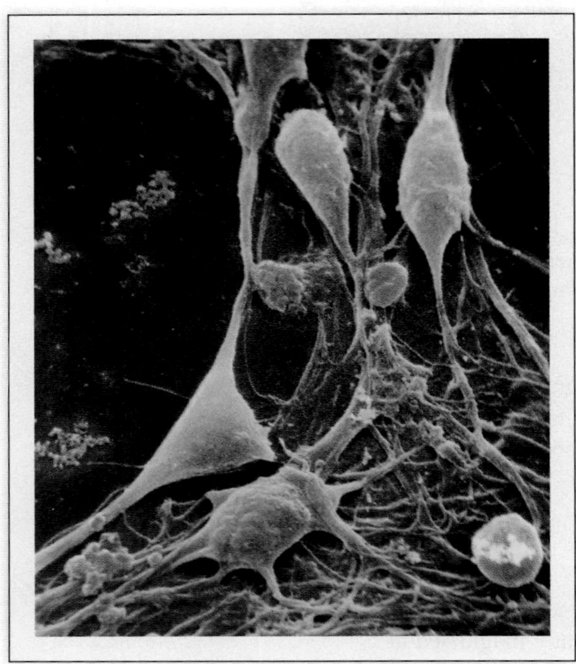

FIGURE 4.2 Neurons and their connective fibers. This photograph of several neurons, taken with the aid of a powerful microscope, shows the elaborate synaptic connections that form with neighboring cells.

As neurons form connections, *stimulation* becomes vital to their survival. Neurons that are stimulated by input from the surrounding environment continue to establish new synapses, forming increasingly elaborate systems of communication that support more complex abilities. At first, stimulation results in a massive overabundance of synapses, many of which serve identical functions, thereby ensuring that the child will acquire the motor, cognitive, and social skills that our species needs to survive. Neurons that are seldom stimulated soon lose their synapses, in a process called **synaptic pruning** that returns neurons not needed at the moment to an uncommitted state so they can support future development. In all, about 40 percent of synapses are pruned during childhood and adolescence to reach the adult level. For this process to advance, appropriate stimulation of the child's brain is vital during periods in which the formation of synapses is at its peak (Bryk & Fisher, 2012).

If few neurons are produced after the prenatal period, what causes the extraordinary increase in brain size during the first two years? About half the brain's volume is made up of **glial cells,** which are responsible for **myelination,**

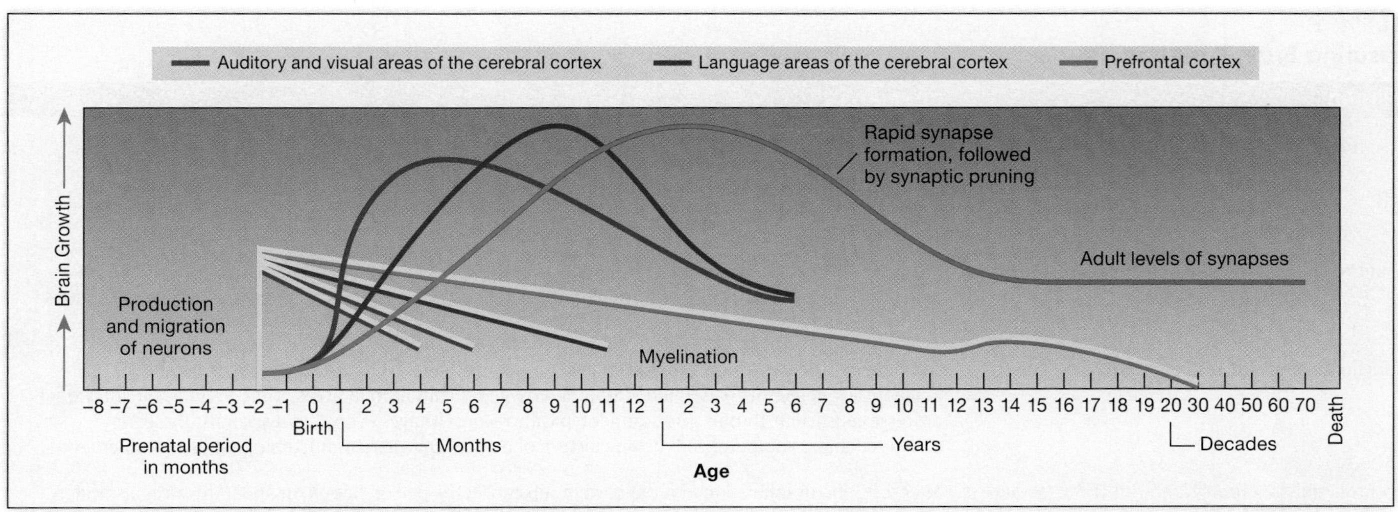

FIGURE 4.3 Major milestones of brain development. Formation of synapses is rapid during the first two years, especially in the auditory, visual, and language areas of the cerebral cortex. The prefrontal cortex, responsible for complex thought (see page 111), undergoes more extended synaptic growth. In each area, overproduction of synapses is followed by synaptic pruning. The prefrontal cortex is among the last regions to attain adult levels of synaptic connections—in mid- to late adolescence. Myelination occurs at a dramatic pace during the first two years, more slowly through childhood, followed by an acceleration at adolescence. The multiple yellow lines indicate that the timing of myelination varies among different brain areas. For example, neural fibers myelinate over a longer period in the language areas, and especially in the prefrontal cortex, than in the auditory and visual areas. (Based on Thompson & Nelson, 2001.)

the coating of neural fibers with an insulating fatty sheath (called *myelin*) that improves the efficiency of message transfer. Glial cells multiply rapidly from the end of pregnancy through the second year of life—a process that continues at a slower pace through middle childhood and accelerates again in adolescence. Gains in neural fibers and myelination account for the overall increase in size of the brain, from nearly 30 percent of its adult weight at birth to 70 percent by age 2 (Johnson, 2011). Growth is especially dramatic during the first year, when the brain more than doubles in size.

Brain development can be compared to molding a "living sculpture." First, neurons and synapses are overproduced. Then, cell death and synaptic pruning sculpt away excess building material to form the mature brain—a process jointly influenced by genetically programmed events and the child's experiences. The resulting "sculpture" is a set of interconnected regions, each with specific functions—much like countries on a globe that communicate with one another.

Measures of Brain Functioning

This "geography" of the brain permits researchers to study its developing organization and the activity of its regions (see Table 4.1 on page 110). Among these measures of brain functioning, the two most frequently used detect changes in *electrical activity* in the cerebral cortex. In an *electroencephalogram (EEG), brain-wave patterns* are examined for stability and organization—signs of mature cortical functioning. As the individual processes a particular stimulus, *event-related potentials (ERPs)* detect the general location of brain-wave activity—a technique often used to study preverbal infants' responsiveness to various stimuli, the impact of experience on specialization of specific cortical regions, and atypical brain functioning in individuals with learning and emotional problems (DeBoer, Scott, & Nelson, 2007; Gunnar & de Haan, 2009).

Neuroimaging techniques, which yield detailed, three-dimensional computerized pictures of the entire brain and its active areas, provide the most precise information about which brain regions are specialized for certain capacities and about abnormalities in brain functioning. The most promising of these methods is *functional magnetic resonance imaging (fMRI).* Unlike *positron emission tomography (PET),* fMRI does not depend on X-ray photography, which requires injection of a radioactive substance. Rather, when an individual is exposed to a stimulus, fMRI detects changes in blood flow and oxygen metabolism throughout the brain magnetically, yielding a colorful, moving picture of parts of the brain used to perform a given activity (see Figure 4.4a and b on page 110).

TABLE 4.1
Measuring Brain Functioning

METHOD	DESCRIPTION
Electroencephalogram (EEG)	Electrodes embedded in a head cap record electrical brain-wave activity in the brain's outer layers—the cerebral cortex. Researchers use an advanced tool called a geodesic sensor net (GSN) to hold interconnected electrodes (up to 128 for infants and 256 for children and adults) in place, yielding improved brain-wave detection.
Event-related potentials (ERPs)	Using the EEG, the frequency and amplitude of brain waves in response to particular stimuli (such as a picture, music, or speech) are recorded in the cerebral cortex. Enables identification of general regions of stimulus-induced activity.
Functional magnetic resonance imaging (fMRI)	While the person lies inside a tunnel-shaped apparatus that creates a magnetic field, a scanner magnetically detects increased blood flow and oxygen metabolism in areas of the brain as the individual processes particular stimuli. The scanner typically records images every 1 to 4 seconds; these are combined into a computerized moving picture of activity anywhere in the brain (not just its outer layers).
Positron emission tomography (PET)	After injection or inhalation of a radioactive substance, the person lies on an apparatus with a scanner that emits fine streams of X-rays, which detect increased blood flow and oxygen metabolism in areas of the brain as the person processes particular stimuli. As with fMRI, the result is a computerized image of activity anywhere in the brain.
Near-infrared spectroscopy (NIRS)	Using thin, flexible optical fibers attached to the scalp through a head cap, infrared (invisible) light is beamed at the brain; its absorption by areas of the cerebral cortex varies with changes in blood flow and oxygen metabolism as the individual processes particular stimuli. The result is a computerized moving picture of active areas in the cerebral cortex. Unlike fMRI and PET, NIRS is appropriate for infants and young children, who can move within a limited range during testing.

Because PET and fMRI require that the participant lie as motionless as possible for an extended time, they are not suitable for infants and young children. A neuroimaging technique that works well in infancy and early childhood is *near-infrared spectroscopy (NIRS)* (refer again to Table 4.1). Because the apparatus consists only of thin, flexible optical fibers attached to the scalp using a head cap, a baby can sit on the parent's lap and move during testing—as Figure 4.4c illustrates (Hespos et al., 2010). But unlike PET and fMRI, which map activity changes throughout the brain, NIRS examines only the functioning of the cerebral cortex.

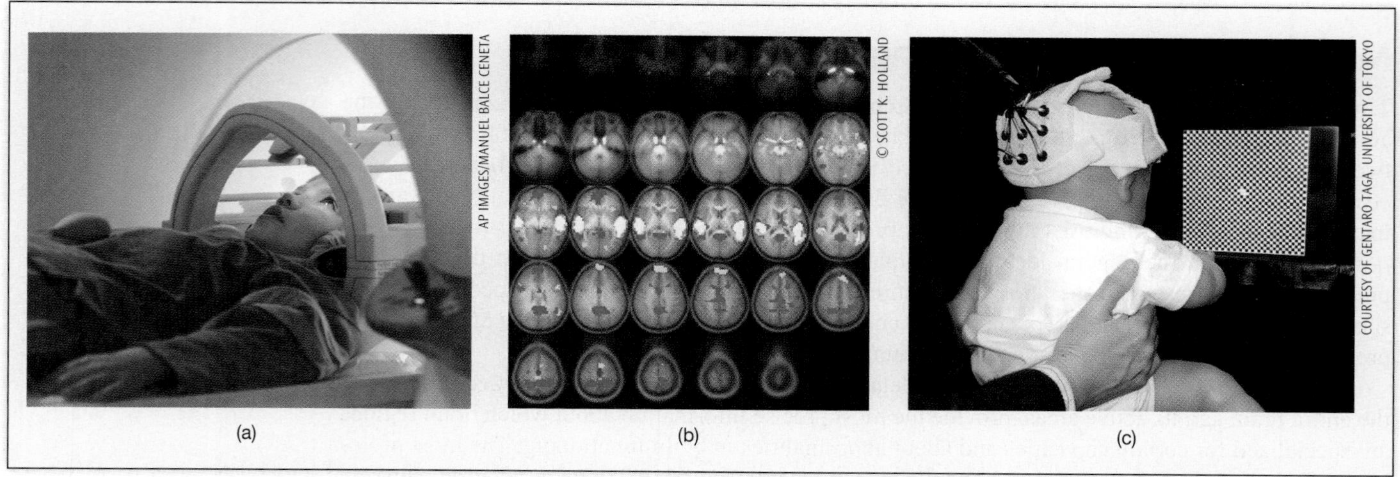

FIGURE 4.4 Functional magnetic resonance imaging (fMRI) and near-infrared spectroscopy (NIRS). (a) This 6-year-old is part of a study that uses fMRI to find out how his brain processes light and motion. (b) The fMRI image shows which areas of the child's brain are active while he views changing visual stimuli. (c) Here, NIRS is used to investigate a 2-month-old's response to a visual stimulus. During testing, the baby can move freely within a limited range. (Photo [c] from G. Taga, K. Asakawa, A. Maki, Y. Konishi, & H. Koisumi, 2003, "Brain Imaging in Awake Infants by Near-Infrared Optical Topography," *Proceedings of the National Academy of Sciences, 100,* p. 10723. Reprinted by permission.)

Like all research methods, the measures just reviewed have limitations. Even though a stimulus produces a consistent pattern of brain activity, investigators cannot be certain that an individual has processed it in a certain way (Kagan, 2013b). And a researcher who takes a change in brain activity as an indicator of information processing must make sure that the change was not due instead to hunger, boredom, fatigue, or body movements. Consequently, other methods must be combined with brain-wave and -imaging findings to clarify their meaning.

Development of the Cerebral Cortex

The **cerebral cortex** surrounds the rest of the brain, resembling half of a shelled walnut. It accounts for 85 percent of the brain's weight and contains the greatest number of neurons and synapses. Because the cerebral cortex is the last part of the brain to stop growing, it is sensitive to environmental influences for a much longer period than any other part of the brain.

Regions of the Cerebral Cortex. Figure 4.5 shows specific functions of regions of the cerebral cortex. The order in which cortical regions develop corresponds to the order in which various capacities emerge in the infant and growing child. For example, a burst of activity occurs in the auditory and visual cortexes and in areas responsible for body movement over the first year—a period of dramatic gains in auditory and visual perception and mastery of motor skills (Gilmore et al., 2012). Language areas are especially active from late infancy through the preschool years, when language development flourishes (Pujol et al., 2006).

The cortical regions with the most extended period of development are the *frontal lobes.* The **prefrontal cortex,** lying in front of areas controlling body movement, is responsible for complex thought—in particular, consciousness and various "executive" processes, including inhibition of impulses, integration of information, and memory, reasoning, planning, and problem-solving strategies. From age 2 months on, the prefrontal cortex functions more effectively. But it undergoes especially rapid myelination and formation and pruning of synapses during the preschool and school years, followed by another period of accelerated growth in adolescence, when it reaches an adult level of synaptic connections (Jabès & Nelson, 2014; Nelson, Thomas, & de Haan, 2006).

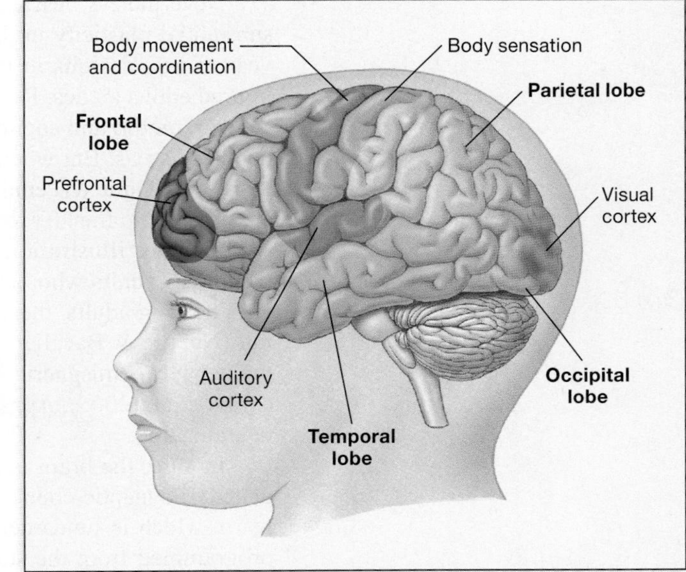

FIGURE 4.5 The left side of the human brain, showing the cerebral cortex. The cortex is divided into different lobes, each of which contains a variety of regions with specific functions. Some major regions are labeled here.

Lateralization and Plasticity of the Cortex. The cerebral cortex has two *hemispheres,* or sides, that differ in their functions. Some tasks are done mostly by the left hemisphere, others by the right. For example, each hemisphere receives sensory information from the side of the body opposite to it and controls only that side.[1] For most of us, the left hemisphere is largely responsible for verbal abilities (such as spoken and written language) and positive emotion (such as joy). The right hemisphere handles spatial abilities (judging distances, reading maps, and recognizing geometric shapes) and negative emotion (such as distress) (Banish & Heller, 1998; Nelson & Bosquet, 2000). In left-handed people, this pattern may be reversed or, more commonly, the cerebral cortex may be less clearly specialized than in right-handers.

Why does this specialization of the two hemispheres, called **lateralization,** occur? Studies using fMRI reveal that the left hemisphere is better at processing information in a sequential, analytic (piece-by-piece) way, a good approach for dealing with communicative information—both verbal (language) and emotional (a joyful smile). In contrast, the right hemisphere is specialized for processing information in a holistic, integrative manner, ideal for making sense of spatial

[1] The eyes are an exception. Messages from the right half of each retina go to the right hemisphere; messages from the left half of each retina go to the left hemisphere. Thus, visual information from both eyes is received by both hemispheres.

information and regulating negative emotion. A lateralized brain may have evolved because it enabled humans to cope more successfully with changing environmental demands (Falk, 2005). It permits a wider array of functions to be carried out effectively than if both sides processed information in exactly the same way.

Researchers study the timing of brain lateralization to learn more about **brain plasticity.** A highly *plastic* cerebral cortex, in which many areas are not yet committed to specific functions, has a high capacity for learning. And if a part of the cortex is damaged, other parts can take over tasks it would have handled. But once the hemispheres lateralize, damage to a specific region means that the abilities it controls cannot be recovered to the same extent or as easily as earlier.

At birth, the hemispheres have already begun to specialize. Most newborns show greater activation (detected with either ERP or NIRS) in the left hemisphere while listening to speech sounds or displaying a positive state of arousal. In contrast, the right hemisphere reacts more strongly to nonspeech sounds and to stimuli (such as a sour-tasting fluid) that evoke negative emotion (Hespos et al., 2010).

Nevertheless, research on children and adults who survived brain injuries offers evidence for substantial plasticity in the young brain. Among children with brain injuries sustained in the first year of life, deficits in language and spatial abilities were milder than those observed in brain-injured adults (Stiles, Reilly, & Levine, 2012; Stiles et al., 2008, 2009). As the children gained perceptual, motor, and cognitive experiences, other stimulated cortical structures compensated for the damaged areas. But when damage occurs to certain regions—for example, the prefrontal cortex—recovery is limited (Pennington, 2015). Because of its executive role in thinking, prefrontal abilities are difficult to transfer to other cortical areas.

Another illustration of how early experience greatly influences brain organization comes from deaf adults who, as infants and children, learned sign language (a spatial skill). Compared with hearing adults, these individuals depend more on the right hemisphere for language processing (Neville & Bavelier, 2002). Also, toddlers who are advanced in language development show greater left-hemispheric specialization for language than their more slowly developing agemates (Mills et al., 2005). Apparently, the very process of acquiring language and other skills promotes lateralization.

In sum, the brain is more plastic during the first few years than at later ages. An overabundance of synaptic connections supports brain plasticity and, therefore, young children's ability to learn, which is fundamental to their survival (Murphy & Corbett, 2009). Although the cortex is programmed from the start for hemispheric specialization, experience greatly influences the rate and success of its advancing organization.

Sensitive Periods in Brain Development

Animal studies confirm that early, extreme sensory deprivation results in permanent brain damage and loss of functions—findings that verify the existence of sensitive periods in brain development. For example, early, varied visual experiences must occur for the brain's visual centers to develop normally. If a 1-month-old kitten is deprived of light for just 3 or 4 days, these areas of the brain degenerate. If the kitten is kept in the dark during the fourth week of life and beyond, the damage is severe and permanent (Crair, Gillespie, & Stryker, 1998). And the general quality of the early environment affects overall brain growth. When animals reared from birth in physically and socially stimulating surroundings are compared with those reared in isolation, the brains of the stimulated animals are larger and show much denser synaptic connections (Sale, Berardi, & Maffei, 2009).

Human Evidence: Victims of Deprived Early Environments. For ethical reasons, we cannot deliberately deprive some infants of normal rearing experiences and observe the impact on their brains and competencies. Instead, we must turn to natural experiments, in which children were victims of deprived early environments that were later rectified. Such studies have revealed some parallels with the animal evidence just described. For example, when babies are born with cataracts in both eyes (clouded lenses, preventing clear visual images), those who have corrective surgery within 4 to 6 months show rapid improvement in vision, except for subtle aspects of face perception, which require early visual input to the right hemisphere to develop. The longer cataract surgery is postponed beyond infancy, the less complete the recovery in visual skills (Maurer & Lewis, 2013). And if surgery is delayed until adulthood, vision is severely and permanently impaired.

Studies of infants placed in orphanages who were later exposed to ordinary family rearing confirm the importance of a generally stimulating environment for psychological development. In one investigation, researchers followed the progress of a large sample of children transferred between birth and 3½ years from extremely deprived Romanian orphanages to adoptive families in Great Britain (Beckett et al., 2006; O'Connor et al., 2000; Rutter et al., 1998, 2004, 2010). On arrival, most were impaired in all domains of development. Cognitive catch-up was impressive for children adopted before 6 months, who attained average mental test scores in childhood and adolescence, performing as well as a comparison group of early-adopted British-born children.

But Romanian children who had been institutionalized for more than the first six months showed serious intellectual deficits. Although they improved in intelligence test scores during middle childhood and adolescence, they remained substantially below average. And most displayed at least three serious mental health problems, such as inattention, overactivity, unruly behavior, and autistic-like symptoms (social disinterest, stereotyped behavior) (Kreppner et al., 2007, 2010).

▶ This Romanian orphan receives little adult contact or stimulation. The longer he remains in this barren environment, the greater his risk of brain damage and lasting impairments in all domains of development.

Neurobiological findings indicate that early, prolonged institutionalization leads to a generalized decrease in size and activity in the cerebral cortex—especially the prefrontal cortex, which governs complex cognition and impulse control. Neural fibers connecting the prefrontal cortex with other brain structures involved in control of emotion are also reduced (Hodel et al., 2014; McLaughlin et al., 2014; Perego, Caputi, & Ogliari, 2016). And activation of the left cerebral hemisphere, governing positive emotion, is diminished relative to right cerebral activation, governing negative emotion (McLaughlin et al., 2011).

Additional evidence confirms that the chronic stress of early, deprived orphanage rearing disrupts the brain's capacity to manage stress. In another investigation, researchers followed the development of children who had spent their first eight months or more in Romanian institutions and were then adopted into Canadian homes (Gunnar & Cheatham, 2003; Gunnar et al., 2001). Compared with agemates adopted shortly after birth, these children showed extreme stress reactivity, as indicated by high concentrations of the stress hormone *cortisol* in their saliva. The longer the children spent in orphanage care, the higher their cortisol levels—even 6½ years after adoption.

In other research, orphanage children from diverse regions of the world who were later adopted by American families displayed abnormally low cortisol—a blunted physiological response that is also a sign of impaired capacity to manage stress (Koss et al., 2014; Loman & Gunnar, 2010). Persisting abnormally high or low cortisol levels are linked to later learning, emotional, and behavior problems, including both internalizing and externalizing difficulties.

Appropriate Stimulation. Unlike the orphanage children just described, Grace, whom Monica and Kevin had adopted from Cambodia at 16 months of age, showed favorable progress. Two years earlier, they had adopted Grace's older brother, Eli. When Eli was 2 years old, Monica and Kevin sent a letter to his biological mother, describing a bright, happy child. The next day, she tearfully asked an adoption agency to send her baby daughter to join Eli and his American family. Although Grace's early environment was very depleted, her biological mother's loving care—holding gently, speaking softly, playfully stimulating, and breastfeeding—likely prevented irreversible damage to her brain.

In the Bucharest Early Intervention Project, 136 institutionalized Romanian babies were randomized into conditions of either care as usual or transfer to high-quality foster families between 6 and 31 months of age. Specially trained social workers provided foster parents with counseling and support. Follow-ups between 2½ and 12 years revealed that the foster-care group exceeded the institutional-care group in intelligence test scores, language skills, emotional responsiveness, social skills, EEG and ERP assessments of brain development, and adaptive cortisol levels (Almas et al., 2016; McLaughlin et al., 2015). Consistent with an early sensitive period, on all measures, earlier foster placement predicted better outcomes.

In addition to impoverished environments, ones that overwhelm children with expectations beyond their current capacities interfere with the brain's potential. In recent years, expensive early learning centers as well as "educational" tablets and DVDs have become widespread. Within these contexts, infants are trained with letter and number flash cards and toddlers are given a full curriculum of reading, math, science, art, and more. There is no evidence that these programs yield smarter "superbabies" (Principe, 2011). To the contrary, trying to prime infants with stimulation for which they are not ready can cause them to withdraw, thereby threatening their interest in learning.

How, then, can we characterize appropriate stimulation during the early years? To answer this question, researchers distinguish between two types of brain development. The first, **experience-expectant brain growth,** refers to the young brain's rapidly developing organization, which depends on ordinary experiences—opportunities to explore the environment, interact with people, and hear language and other sounds. As a result of millions of years of evolution, the brains of all infants, toddlers, and young children *expect* to encounter these experiences and, if they do, grow normally. The second type of brain development, **experience-dependent brain growth,** occurs throughout our lives. It consists of additional growth and refinement of established brain structures as a result of specific learning experiences that vary widely across individuals and cultures (Greenough & Black, 1992). Reading and writing, playing computer games, weaving an intricate rug, and practicing the violin are examples. The brain of a violinist differs in certain ways from the brain of a poet because each has exercised different brain regions for a long time.

Too much emphasis on training at an early age–for example, drill on mastering the ABCs–can interfere with access to everyday experiences the young brain needs to grow optimally.

Experience-expectant brain development occurs early and naturally, as caregivers offer babies and preschoolers age-appropriate play materials and engage them in enjoyable daily routines—a shared meal, a bath before bed, a picture book to talk about, or a song to sing. The resulting growth provides the foundation for later-occurring, experience-dependent development (Belsky & de Haan, 2011). No evidence exists for a sensitive period in the first few years for mastering skills that depend on extensive training, such as reading, musical performance, or gymnastics. To the contrary, rushing early learning harms the brain by overwhelming its neural circuits, thereby reducing the brain's sensitivity to the everyday experiences it needs for a healthy start in life.

Changing States of Arousal

Rapid brain growth means that the organization of sleep and wakefulness changes substantially between birth and 2 years, and fussiness and crying also decline. The newborn baby takes round-the-clock naps that total about 16 to 18 hours. The average 2-year-old still needs 12 to 13 hours, but the sleep–wake pattern increasingly conforms to a night–day schedule. Most 6- to 9-month-olds take two daytime naps; by about 18 months, children generally need only one nap (Galland et al., 2012). Between ages 3 and 5, napping subsides.

These changing arousal patterns are due to brain development, but they are also affected by cultural beliefs and practices. Dutch parents, for example, view sleep regularity as far more important than U.S. parents do. And whereas U.S. parents regard a predictable sleep schedule as emerging naturally from within the child, Dutch parents believe that a schedule must be imposed, or the baby's development might suffer (Super & Harkness, 2010; Super et al., 1996). At age 6 months, Dutch babies are put to bed earlier and sleep, on average, 2 hours more per day than their U.S. agemates. Furthermore, as the Cultural Influences box on the following page reveals, isolating infants and toddlers in a separate room for sleep is rare around the world.

CULTURAL INFLUENCES

Cultural Variation in Infant Sleeping Arrangements

Western child-rearing advice from experts strongly encourages nighttime separation of baby from parent. For example, the most recent edition of Benjamin Spock's *Baby and Child Care* recommends that babies sleep in their own room by 3 months of age (Spock & Needlman, 2012). And the American Academy of Pediatrics (2016b) has issued a controversial warning that parent–infant bedsharing increases the risk of sudden infant death syndrome (SIDS) and accidental suffocation.

Yet parent–infant cosleeping—in the same room and often in the same bed—is the norm for approximately 90 percent of the world's population, in cultures as diverse as the Japanese, the rural Guatemalan Maya, and the Inuit of northwestern Canada. Japanese and Korean children usually lie next to their mothers throughout infancy and early childhood (Yang & Hahn, 2002). Among the Maya, mother–infant bedsharing is interrupted only by the birth of a new baby, when the older child is moved next to the father or to another bed in the same room (Morelli et al., 1992). Bedsharing is also common in U.S. ethnic minority families (McKenna & Volpe, 2007). African-American children, for example, frequently fall asleep with their parents and remain with them for part or all of the night (Buswell & Spatz, 2007).

Cultural values strongly influence infant sleeping arrangements. In one study, researchers interviewed Guatemalan Mayan mothers and American middle-SES mothers about their sleeping practices. Mayan mothers stressed the importance of promoting an *interdependent self,* explaining that cosleeping builds a close parent–child bond. In contrast, American mothers emphasized an *independent self,* mentioning their desire to instill early autonomy (Morelli et al., 1992).

Over the past several decades, cosleeping has increased in Western nations, including the United States. An estimated 11 percent of U.S. infants routinely bedshare, and an additional 30 to 35 percent sometimes do (Colson et al., 2013). Parents who support the practice say that it helps their baby sleep, makes breastfeeding more convenient, reduces infant distress, and provides valuable bonding time (McKenna & Volpe, 2007; Tikotzky et al., 2010).

ERIC LAFFORGUE/GAMMA-RAPHO VIA GETTY IMAGES

▶ This Vietnamese mother and child sleep together–a practice common in their culture and around the globe. Hard wooden sleeping surfaces protect cosleeping children from entrapment in soft bedding.

Babies who sleep with their parents breastfeed three times longer than infants who sleep alone (Huang et al., 2013). Because infants arouse to nurse more often when sleeping next to their mothers, some researchers believe that cosleeping may actually help safeguard babies at risk for SIDS. Consistent with this view, SIDS is rare in Asian nations where bedsharing is widespread, including Cambodia, China, Japan, Korea, Thailand, and Vietnam (McKenna, 2002; McKenna & McDade, 2005).

Critics warn that bedsharing will promote sleep and adjustment problems, especially excessive dependency. Yet in Western societies, bedsharing often emerges in response to children's sleep and emotional difficulties, rather than occurring as a consistent, intentional practice (Mileva-Seitz et al., 2017). In a study following children from the end of pregnancy through 18 years, young people who had regularly bedshared in the early years were no different from others in any aspect of adjustment (Okami, Weisner, & Olmstead, 2002).

A more serious concern is that infants might become trapped under the parent's body or in soft bedding and suffocate. Parents who are obese or who use alcohol, tobacco, or mood-altering drugs do pose a serious risk to bedsharing babies, as does the use of quilts and comforters or an overly soft mattress (Carpenter et al., 2013).

But with appropriate precautions, parents and infants can cosleep safely (Ball & Volpe, 2013). In cultures where cosleeping is widespread, parents and infants usually sleep together with light covering on hard surfaces, such as firm mattresses or wooden planks. Alternatively, babies sleep in a cradle or hammock next to the parents' bed. To protect against SIDS and other sleep-related deaths, the American Academy of Pediatrics (2016b) recommends that parents roomshare but not bedshare with their infant for the first year, placing the baby within easy view and reach on a separate surface designed for infants.

However, some researchers point out that placing too much emphasis on separate sleeping may have risky consequences—for example, inducing tired parents to avoid feeding their babies in bed in favor of using dangerously soft sofas (Bartick & Smith, 2014). Pediatricians are wise to discuss the safety of each infant's sleep environment with parents, while taking into account cultural values and motivations (Ward, 2015). Then they can work within that framework to create a safe sleep environment.

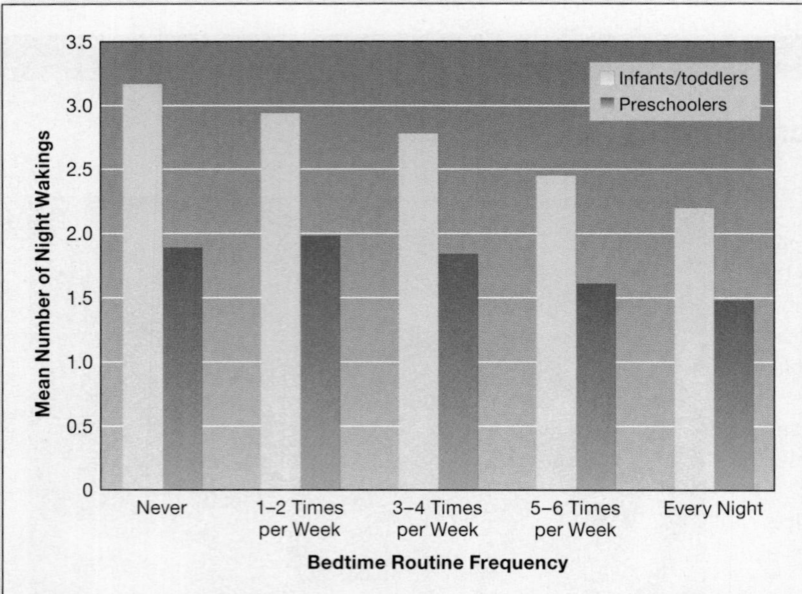

FIGURE 4.6 Relationship of bedtime routines to night-wakings in infancy/toddlerhood and the preschool years. In a large sample of mothers in 13 Western and Asian nations, the more consistently they used bedtime routines, the less often their infants, toddlers, and preschoolers woke during the night. Findings were similar for ease of falling asleep and amount of nighttime sleep. (From J. A. Mindell, A. M. Li, A. Sadeh, R. Kwon, & D. Y. T. Goh, 2015, "Bedtime Routines for Young Children: A Dose-Dependent Association with Sleep Outcomes," *Sleep, 38,* p. 720. Copyright © 2015 by permission of the Associated Professional Sleep Societies, LLC. Reprinted by permission.)

Motivated by demanding work schedules and other needs, many Western parents try to get their babies to sleep through the night as early as 3 to 4 months by offering an evening feeding. But infants who receive more milk or solid foods during the day are not less likely to wake, though they feed less at night (Brown & Harries, 2015). However, babies just a few weeks old—though they typically wake every two hours—have some capacity to resettle on their own (St James-Roberts et al., 2015). When infants awake and cry, parents who in the early weeks wait just a few minutes before initiating feeding, granting the baby an opportunity to settle and return to sleep, have infants who are more likely to sleep for longer nighttime periods at ages 3 and 6 months (St James-Roberts et al., 2017). Around 2 to 3 months, most Western infants begin sleeping for 4 to 5 hours at a stretch.

At the end of the first year, as REM sleep (the state that usually prompts waking) declines, infants approximate an adultlike sleep–wake schedule. But even after they sleep through the night, they continue to wake occasionally. In studies carried out in Australia, Israel, and the United States, night wakings increased around age 6 months and again between 1½ and 2 years (Armstrong, Quinn, & Dadds, 1994; Scher, Epstein, & Tirosh, 2004; Scher et al., 1995). As Chapter 6 will reveal, around the first year, infants are forming a clear-cut attachment to their familiar caregiver and begin protesting when he or she leaves. And the challenges of toddlerhood—the ability to range father from the caregiver and increased awareness of the self as separate from others—often prompt increased anxiety, evident in disturbed sleep and clinginess. In one study, young babies whose mothers were warm, sensitive, and available to them at bedtime slept more during the night (Philbrook & Teti, 2016). In turn, lower infant nighttime distress predicted greater maternal sensitivity in the following months.

Bedtime routines promote sleep as early as the first two years. In a study carried out in 13 Western and Asian nations, over 10,000 mothers reported on their bedtime practices and their newborn to 5-year-olds' sleep quality (Mindell et al., 2015). Consistently engaging in bedtime routines—for example, rocking and singing in infancy, storybook reading in toddlerhood and early childhood—was associated with falling asleep more readily, waking less often, and getting more nighttime sleep throughout the entire age range (see Figure 4.6).

Finally, beginning in infancy, restful sleep is vital for learning. For example, compared to 12-month-olds in a no-nap condition, those given an opportunity to nap displayed better memory, in that they imitated more adult actions with toys observed earlier that day (Konrad et al., 2016b). Similarly, 6-month-olds who slept well the previous night remembered more than babies who woke often (Konrad et al., 2016a). In addition to supporting memory storage, sleep enhanced toddlers' ability to solve a novel problem: figuring out how to efficiently navigate a tunnel to reach a caregiver waiting at the other end (Berger & Scher, 2017).

ASK YOURSELF

CONNECT Explain how either too little or too much stimulation can impair cognitive and emotional development in the early years.

APPLY Which infant enrichment program would you choose: one that emphasizes gentle talking and touching and social games, or one that includes reading and number drills and classical music lessons? Explain.

REFLECT What is your attitude toward parent–infant cosleeping? Is it influenced by your cultural background? Explain.

Influences on Early Physical Growth

Physical growth, like other aspects of development, results from a complex interplay between genetic and environmental factors. Heredity, nutrition, and emotional well-being all affect early growth.

4.4 Cite evidence that heredity and nutrition both contribute to early physical growth.

Heredity

Because identical twins are much more alike in body size than fraternal twins, we know that heredity is important in physical growth (Dubois et al., 2012). When diet and health are adequate, height and rate of physical growth are largely influenced by heredity. In fact, as long as negative environmental influences such as poor nutrition or illness are not severe, children and adolescents typically show *catch-up growth*—a return to a genetically influenced growth path once conditions improve.

Genetic makeup also affects body weight: Again, identical twins are far more similar than fraternal twins, and weights of adopted children correlate more strongly with those of their biological than of their adoptive parents (Elks et al., 2012; Kinnunen, Pietilainen, & Rissanen, 2006). At the same time, environment—in particular, nutrition—plays a vital role.

Nutrition

Nutrition is especially crucial for development in the first two years because the baby's brain and body are growing so rapidly. Pound for pound, an infant's energy needs are at least twice those of an adult. Twenty-five percent of infants' total caloric intake is devoted to growth, and babies need extra calories to keep rapidly developing organs functioning properly (Meyer, 2009).

Breastfeeding versus Bottle-Feeding. Babies need both enough food and the right kind of food. In early infancy, breastfeeding is ideally suited to their needs, and bottled formulas try to imitate it. Applying What We Know on page 118 summarizes major nutritional and health advantages of breastfeeding.

Because of these benefits, breastfed babies in poverty-stricken regions are much less likely to be malnourished and 6 to 14 times more likely to survive the first year of life. The World Health Organization recommends breastfeeding until age 2 years or longer, with solid foods added at 6 months. These practices, if widely followed, would save the lives of more than 800,000 infants annually (World Health Organization, 2017d). Even breastfeeding for just a few weeks offers some protection against respiratory and intestinal infections, which are devastating to young children in developing countries. Also, because a nursing mother is less likely to get pregnant, breastfeeding helps increase spacing between siblings, a major factor in reducing infant and childhood deaths in nations with widespread poverty. (Note, however, that breastfeeding is not a reliable method of birth control.)

Yet many mothers in the developing world do not know about these benefits. In Africa, the Middle East, and Latin America, most infants get some breastfeeding, but fewer than 40 percent are exclusively breastfed for the first six months, and one-third are fully weaned from the breast before 1 year (UNICEF, 2017b). In place of breast milk, mothers give their babies commercial formula or low-grade nutrients, such as highly diluted cow or goat milk. Contamination of these foods as a result of poor sanitation often leads to illness and infant death. The United Nations has encouraged all hospitals and maternity units in developing countries to promote breastfeeding as long as mothers do not have viral or bacterial infections (such as HIV or tuberculosis) that can be transmitted to the baby.

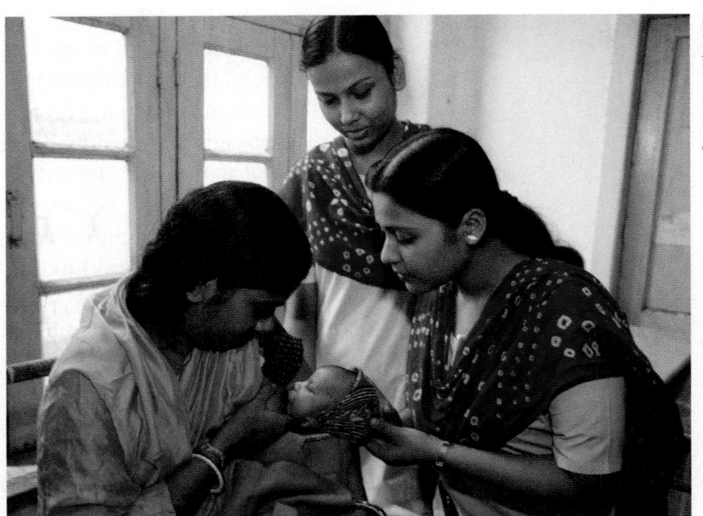

▶ Midwives in India support a mother as she learns to breastfeed her infant. Breastfeeding is especially important in developing countries, where it helps protect babies against life-threatening infections and early death.

APPLYING WHAT WE KNOW

Reasons to Breastfeed

NUTRITIONAL AND HEALTH ADVANTAGES	EXPLANATION
Provides the correct balance of fat and protein	Compared with the milk of other mammals, human milk is higher in fat and lower in protein. This balance, as well as the unique proteins and fats contained in human milk, is ideal for a rapidly myelinating nervous system.
Ensures nutritional completeness	A mother who breastfeeds need not add other foods to her infant's diet until the baby is 6 months old. The milks of all mammals are low in iron, but the iron contained in breast milk is much more easily absorbed by the baby's system. Consequently, bottle-fed infants need iron-fortified formula.
Helps ensure healthy physical growth	One-year-old breastfed babies are leaner (have a higher percentage of muscle to fat), a growth pattern that persists through the preschool years and that is associated with a reduction in later overweight and obesity.
Protects against many diseases	Breastfeeding transfers antibodies and other infection-fighting agents from mother to baby and enhances functioning of the immune system. Compared with bottle-fed infants, breastfed babies have far fewer allergic reactions and respiratory and intestinal illnesses. Breast milk also has anti-inflammatory effects, which reduce the severity of illness symptoms. Breastfeeding in the first four months (especially when exclusive) is linked to lower blood cholesterol levels in adulthood and, thereby, may help prevent cardiovascular disease.
Ensures digestibility	Because breastfed babies have a different kind of bacteria growing in their intestines than do bottle-fed infants, they rarely suffer from constipation or other gastrointestinal problems.
Smooths the transition to solid foods	Breastfed infants accept new solid foods more easily than do bottle-fed infants, perhaps because of their greater experience with a variety of flavors, which pass from the maternal diet into the mother's milk.

Sources: American Academy of Pediatrics, 2012; Druet et al., 2012; Owen et al., 2008; UNICEF, 2017b.

Partly as a result of the natural childbirth movement, breastfeeding has become more common in industrialized nations, especially among well-educated women. Today, 79 percent of American mothers begin breastfeeding after birth, but about half stop by 6 months (Centers for Disease Control and Prevention, 2014). Not surprisingly, mothers who return to work sooner wean their babies from the breast earlier (Smith & Forrester, 2013). But mothers who cannot be with their infants all the time can still combine breast- and bottle-feeding. The American Academy of Pediatrics (2012) advises exclusive breastfeeding for the first 6 months and inclusion of breast milk in the baby's diet until at least 1 year.

Women who do not breastfeed sometimes worry that they are depriving their baby of an experience essential for healthy psychological development. Yet breastfed and bottle-fed infants in industrialized nations do not differ in quality of the mother–infant relationship or in later emotional adjustment (Jansen, de Weerth, & Riksen-Walraven, 2008; Lind et al., 2014). A growing number of studies report a slight advantage in intelligence test scores for children and adolescents who were breastfed, after controlling for maternal intelligence, SES, and other factors (Bernard et al., 2017; Horta, Loret de Mola, & Victoria, 2015; Luby et al., 2016). Other studies, however, find no cognitive benefits (Walfisch et al., 2013).

Are Chubby Babies at Risk for Later Overweight and Obesity? From early infancy, Timmy was an enthusiastic eater who nursed vigorously and gained weight quickly. Vanessa wondered: Was she overfeeding Timmy and increasing his chances of becoming overweight?

Most chubby babies with nutritious diets thin out during toddlerhood and early childhood, as weight gain slows and they become more active. But recent evidence indicates a strengthening relationship between rapid weight gain in infancy and later obesity (Nanri et al., 2017). The trend may be due to the rise in overweight adults, who engage in unhealthy feeding practices in the first year. Their babies, some of whom may be genetically prone to overeat, establish an early pattern of excessive unhealthy food consumption that persists (Llewellyn & Wardle, 2015). Interviews with large, nationally representative samples of U.S. parents revealed that many routinely served their infants and toddlers french fries, pizza, candy, sugary fruit drinks, and soda (Miles & Siega-Riz, 2017; Siega-Riz et al., 2010). As many as one-fourth ate no fruits and vegetables.

How can parents prevent their infants from becoming overweight children and adults? One way is to breastfeed exclusively for the first six months, which is associated with slower early weight gain and 10 to 20 percent reduced obesity risk in later life (Koletzko et al., 2013). Another strategy is to avoid giving babies foods loaded with sugar, salt, and saturated fats. Once toddlers learn to walk, climb, and run, parents can also provide plenty of opportunities for energetic play.

Malnutrition

In developing countries and war-torn areas where food resources are limited, malnutrition is widespread. Malnutrition contributes to one-third of worldwide infant and early childhood deaths—about 3 million children annually. It is also responsible for growth stunting of nearly one-fourth of the world's children under age 5 (UNICEF, 2017c). The 8 percent who are severely affected suffer from two dietary diseases.

Marasmus is a wasted condition of the body caused by a diet low in all essential nutrients. It usually appears in the first year of life when a baby's mother is too malnourished to produce enough breast milk and bottle-feeding is also inadequate. Her starving baby becomes painfully thin and is in danger of dying.

Kwashiorkor is caused by an unbalanced diet very low in protein. The disease usually strikes after weaning, between 1 and 3 years of age. It is common in regions where children get just enough calories from starchy foods but little protein. The child's body responds by breaking down its own protein reserves, which causes swelling of the abdomen and limbs, hair loss, skin rash, and irritable, listless behavior.

Children who survive these extreme forms of malnutrition often suffer from lasting damage to the brain, heart, liver, pancreas, and other organs (Müller & Krawinkel, 2005; Spoelstra et al., 2012). When their diets do improve, they tend to gain excessive weight (Black et al., 2013). A malnourished body protects itself by establishing a low basal metabolism rate, which may endure after nutrition improves. Also, malnutrition may disrupt appetite control centers in the brain, causing the child to overeat when food becomes plentiful.

Animal evidence reveals that a severely deficient diet permanently reduces brain weight and alters the production of neurotransmitters (Haller, 2005). Children who experienced marasmus or kwashiorkor show poor fine-motor coordination, have difficulty paying attention, often display conduct problems, and score low on intelligence tests into adulthood (Galler et al., 2012; Venables & Raine, 2016; Waber et al., 2014). They also display a more intense stress response to fear-arousing situations, perhaps caused by the constant pain of hunger (Fernald & Grantham-McGregor, 1998).

The irritability and passivity of malnourished children compound the developmental consequences of poor diet. These behaviors may appear even when nutritional deprivation is only mild to moderate. Because government-supported supplementary food programs do not reach all families in need, an estimated 8 percent of U.S. children suffer from *food insecurity*—uncertain access to enough food for a healthy, active life. Food insecurity is especially high among single-parent families and low-income ethnic minority families (U.S. Department of Agriculture, 2016). Although few of these children have marasmus or kwashiorkor, their physical growth and ability to learn are still affected.

▶ *Top photo:* This baby of Niger, Africa, has marasmus, a wasted condition caused by a diet low in all essential nutrients. *Bottom photo:* The swollen abdomen of this toddler, also of Niger, is a symptom of kwashiorkor, which results from a diet very low in protein. If these children survive, they are likely to be growth stunted and to suffer from lasting organ damage and serious cognitive and emotional impairments.

ASK YOURSELF

CONNECT Explain why breastfeeding can have lifelong, favorable consequences for the development of babies born in poverty-stricken regions of the world.

APPLY Eight-month-old Shaun is well below average in height and painfully thin. What serious dietary disease does he likely have, and what types of intervention, in addition to dietary enrichment, can help restore his development?

REFLECT Imagine that you are the parent of a newborn baby. Describe feeding practices you would use, and ones you would avoid, to prevent overweight and obesity.

Learning Capacities

4.5 Describe infant learning capacities, the conditions under which they occur, and the unique value of each.

Learning refers to changes in behavior as the result of experience. Babies are capable of two basic forms of learning, which were introduced in Chapter 1: classical and operant conditioning. They also learn through their natural preference for novel stimulation. Finally, shortly after birth, babies learn by observing others; they can imitate the facial expressions and gestures of adults.

Classical Conditioning

Newborn reflexes, discussed in Chapter 3, make **classical conditioning** possible in the young infant. In this form of learning, a neutral stimulus is paired with a stimulus that leads to a reflexive response. Once the baby's nervous system makes the connection between the two stimuli, the neutral stimulus produces the behavior by itself. Classical conditioning helps infants recognize which events usually occur together in the everyday world, so they can anticipate what is about to happen next. As a result, the environment becomes more orderly and predictable. Let's take a closer look at the steps of classical conditioning.

As Carolyn settled down in the rocking chair to nurse Caitlin, she often stroked Caitlin's forehead. Soon Carolyn noticed that each time she did this, Caitlin made sucking movements. Caitlin had been classically conditioned. Figure 4.7 shows how it happened:

1. Before learning takes place, an **unconditioned stimulus (UCS)** must consistently produce a reflexive, or **unconditioned response (UCR).** In Caitlin's case, sweet breast milk (UCS) resulted in sucking (UCR).
2. To produce learning, a *neutral stimulus* that does not lead to the reflex is presented just before, or at about the same time as, the UCS. Carolyn stroked Caitlin's forehead as each nursing period began. The stroking (neutral stimulus) was paired with the taste of milk (UCS).
3. If learning has occurred, the neutral stimulus by itself produces a response similar to the reflexive response. The neutral stimulus is then called a **conditioned stimulus (CS),** and the response it elicits is called a **conditioned response (CR).** We know that Caitlin has been classically conditioned because stroking her forehead outside the feeding situation (CS) results in sucking (CR).

If the CS is presented alone enough times, without being paired with the UCS, the CR will no longer occur, an outcome called *extinction.* In other words, if Carolyn repeatedly strokes Caitlin's forehead without feeding her, Caitlin will gradually stop sucking in response to stroking.

Young infants can be classically conditioned most easily when the association between two stimuli has survival value. In the example just described, learning which stimuli regularly accompany feeding improves the infant's ability to get food and survive (Blass, Ganchrow, & Steiner, 1984).

In contrast, some responses, such as fear, are difficult to classically condition in young babies. Until infants have the motor skills to escape unpleasant events, they have no biological need to form these associations.

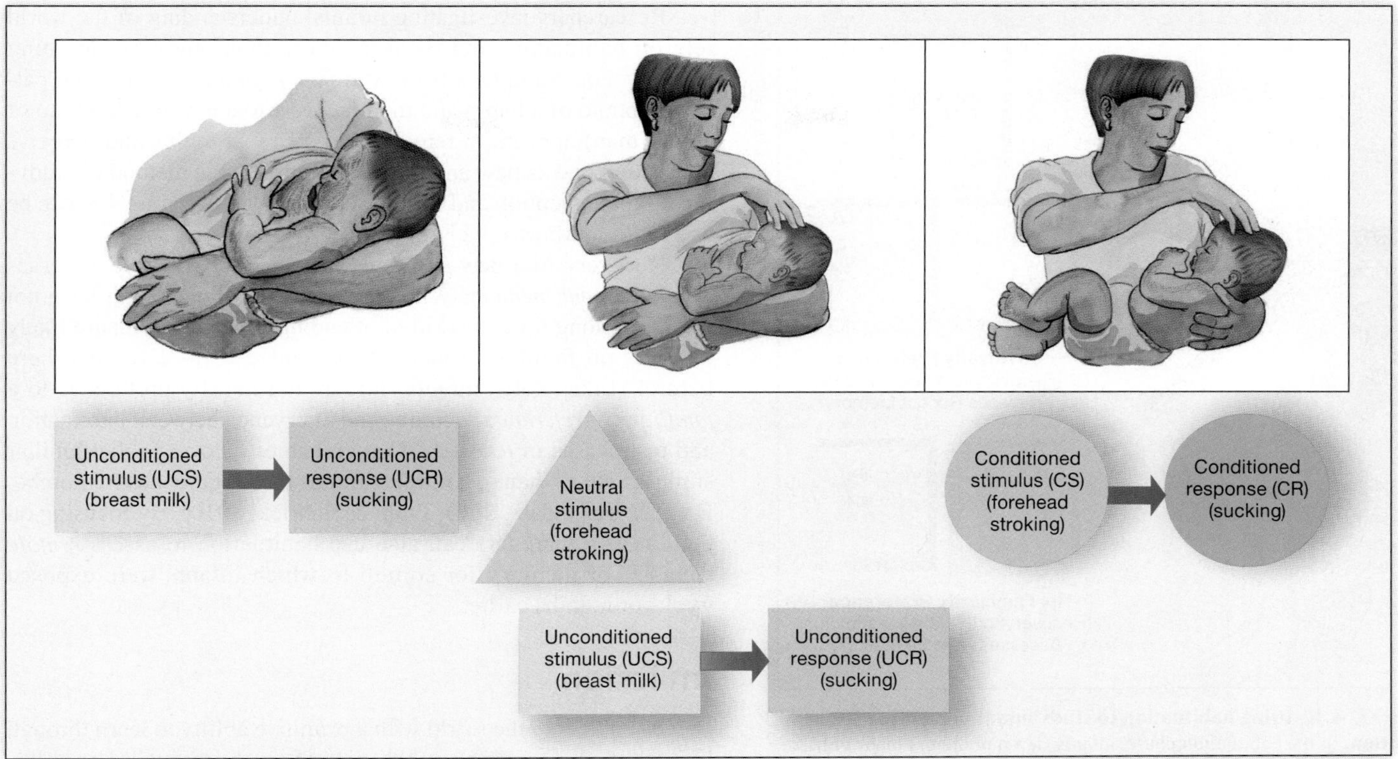

FIGURE 4.7 The steps of classical conditioning. This example shows how a mother classically conditioned her baby to make sucking movements by stroking the baby's forehead at the beginning of feedings.

Operant Conditioning

In classical conditioning, babies build expectations about stimulus events in the environment, but they do not influence the stimuli that occur. In **operant conditioning,** infants act, or *operate,* on the environment, and stimuli that follow their behavior change the probability that the behavior will occur again. A stimulus that increases the occurrence of a response is called a **reinforcer.** For example, sweet liquid *reinforces* the sucking response in newborns. Removing a desirable stimulus or presenting an unpleasant one to decrease the occurrence of a response is called **punishment.** A sour-tasting fluid *punishes* newborns' sucking response, causing them to stop sucking entirely.

Many stimuli besides food can serve as reinforcers of infant behavior. For example, newborns will suck faster on a nipple when their rate of sucking produces interesting sights and sounds, making operant conditioning a powerful tool for finding out what stimuli babies can perceive and which ones they prefer. Operant conditioning also plays a vital role in the formation of social relationships. When the baby gazes into the adult's eyes, the adult looks and smiles, and then the infant looks and smiles back. As the behavior of each partner reinforces the other, both continue their pleasurable interaction. In Chapter 6, we will see that this contingent responsiveness contributes to the development of infant–caregiver attachment.

Habituation

At birth, the human brain is set up to be attracted to novelty. Infants tend to respond more strongly to a new element that has entered their environment. **Habituation** refers to a gradual reduction in the strength of a response due to repetitive stimulation. Time spent looking at the stimulus, heart rate, respiration rate, and brain activity may all decline, indicating a loss of interest. Once this has occurred, a new stimulus—a change in the environment—causes responsiveness to return to a high level, an increase called **recovery.** Habituation and recovery make learning more efficient by focusing our attention on those aspects of the environment we know least about.

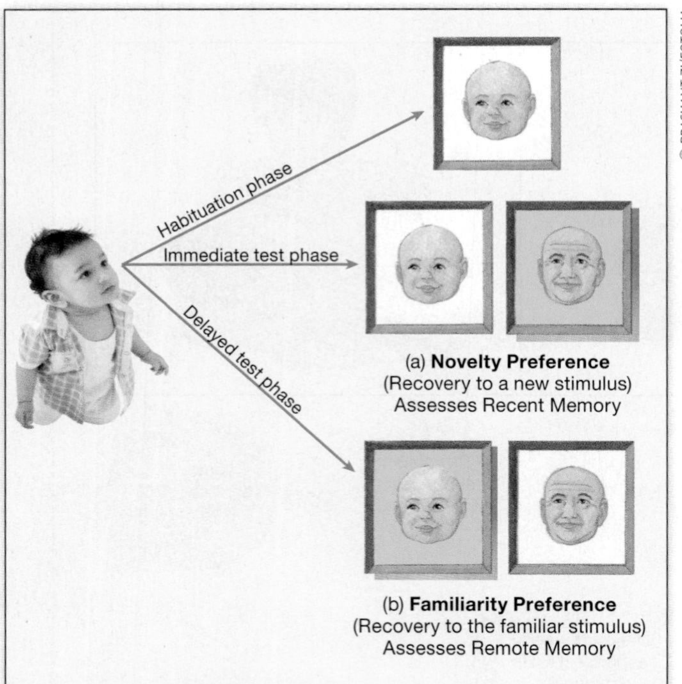

FIGURE 4.8 Using habituation to study infant perception and cognition. In the habituation phase, infants view a photo of a baby until their looking declines. In the test phase, infants are again shown the baby photo, but this time it appears alongside a photo of a bald-headed man. (a) When the test phase occurs soon after the habituation phase (within minutes, hours, or days, depending on the age of the infants), participants who remember the baby face and distinguish it from the man's face show a *novelty preference*; they recover to (spend more time looking at) the new stimulus. (b) When the test phase is delayed for weeks or months, infants who continue to remember the baby face shift to a *familiarity preference*; they recover to the familiar baby face rather than to the novel man's face.

Researchers investigating infants' understanding of the world rely on habituation and recovery more than any other learning capacity. For example, a baby who first *habituates* to a visual pattern (a photo of a baby) and then *recovers* to a new one (a photo of a bald man) appears to remember the first stimulus and perceive the second one as new and different from it. This method of studying infant perception and cognition, illustrated in Figure 4.8, can be used with newborns, including preterm infants.

Recovery to a new stimulus, or *novelty preference,* assesses infants' *recent memory.* When you return to a place you have not seen for a long time, instead of attending to novelty, you are likely to focus on familiar aspects: "I recognize that—I've been here before!" Like adults, infants shift from a novelty preference to a *familiarity preference* as more time intervenes between habituation and test phases in research. That is, babies recover to the familiar stimulus rather than to a novel stimulus (see Figure 4.8) (Colombo, Brez, & Curtindale, 2013; Flom & Bahrick, 2010). By focusing on that shift, researchers can also use habituation to assess *remote memory,* or memory for stimuli to which infants were exposed weeks or months earlier.

Imitation

Babies come into the world with a primitive ability to learn through **imitation**—by copying the behavior of another person. For example, Figure 4.9 shows a human newborn imitating two adult facial expressions (Meltzoff & Moore, 1977). The newborn's capacity to imitate extends to certain gestures, such as head and index-finger movements, and has been demonstrated in many ethnic groups and cultures (Meltzoff & Kuhl, 1994; Nagy et al., 2005). As the figure reveals, even newborn primates, including chimpanzees (our closest evolutionary relatives), imitate some behaviors (Ferrari et al., 2006; Myowa-Yamakoshi et al., 2004).

Nevertheless, some studies have failed to reproduce the human findings (see, for example, Anisfeld, 2005). And because newborn mouth and tongue movements occur with increased frequency to almost any arousing change in stimulation (such as lively music or flashing lights), some researchers argue that certain newborn "imitative" responses are actually mouthing—a common early exploratory response to interesting stimuli (Jones, 2009). Furthermore, imitation is harder to induce in babies 2 to 3 months old than just after birth. Therefore, skeptics believe that the newborn imitative capacity is little more than an automatic response that declines with age, much like a reflex (Keven & Aikins, 2017).

Others claim that newborns imitate a variety of facial expressions and head movements with effort and determination, even after short delays—when the adult is no longer demonstrating the behavior (Meltzoff & Williamson, 2013; Paukner, Ferrari, & Suomi, 2011). Furthermore, these investigators argue that imitation—unlike reflexes—does not decline. Human babies several months old often do not imitate an adult's behavior right away because they first try to play familiar social games—mutual gazing, cooing, smiling, and waving their arms. But when an adult models a gesture repeatedly, these infants soon get down to business and imitate (Meltzoff & Moore, 1994). Similarly, imitation declines in baby chimps around 9 weeks of age, when mother–baby mutual gazing and other face-to-face exchanges increase.

According to Andrew Meltzoff, newborns imitate much as older children and adults do—by actively trying to match body movements they *see* with ones they *feel* themselves make. With successive tries, they imitate a modeled gesture with greater accuracy (Meltzoff & Williamson, 2013).

Scientists have identified specialized cells in motor areas of the cerebral cortex in primates—called **mirror neurons**—that may underlie early imitative capacities. Mirror neurons fire identically when a primate hears or sees an action and when it carries out that action on its own (Ferrari &

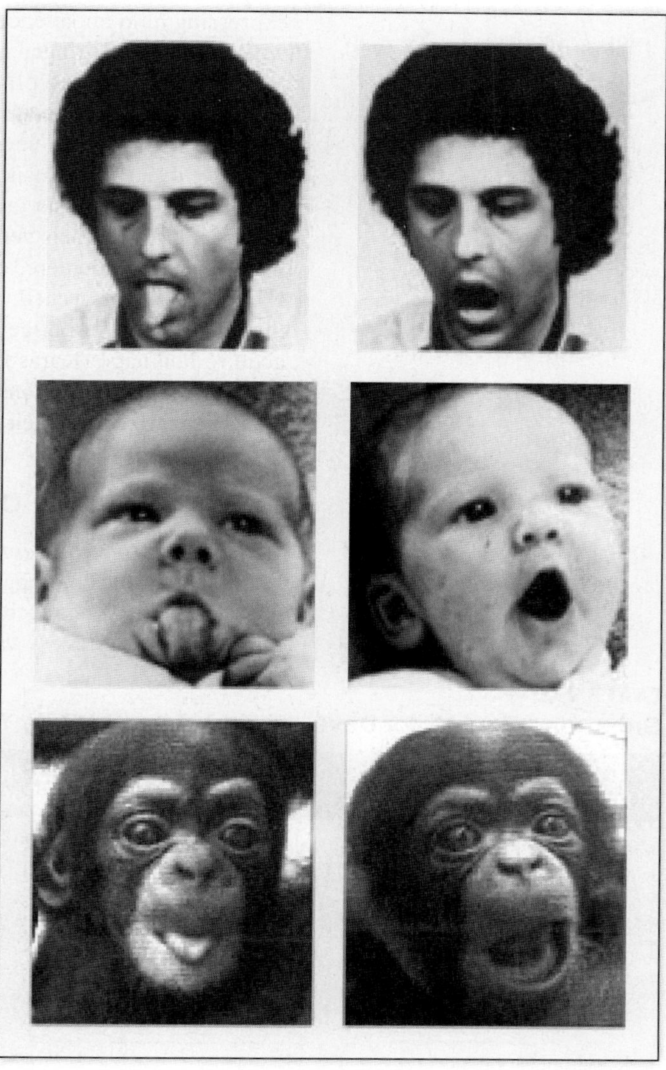

FIGURE 4.9 Imitation by human and chimpanzee newborns. The human infants in the middle row imitating (left) tongue protrusion and (right) mouth opening are 2 to 3 weeks old. The chimpanzee imitating both facial expressions is 2 weeks old. (From A. N. Meltzoff & M. K. Moore, 1977, "Imitation of Facial and Manual Gestures by Human Neonates," *Science, 198,* p. 75. Copyright © 1977 by AAAS. Reprinted with permission of the American Association for the Advancement of Science conveyed through Copyright Clearance Center, Inc., and Dr. Andrew Meltzoff. And from M. Myowa-Yamakoshi et al., 2004, "Imitation in Neonatal Chimpanzees [Pan Troglodytes]." *Developmental Science, 7,* p. 440. Copyright © 2004 by John Wiley & Sons. Reprinted with permission of John Wiley and Sons conveyed through Copyright Clearance Center, Inc.)

Coudé, 2011). Brain-imaging research reveals functioning neural-mirroring systems in human infants by the middle of the first year that enable them to observe another's behavior while simulating the behavior in their own brain (Shimada & Hiraki, 2006). These systems are believed to be the biological basis of a variety of interrelated, complex social abilities in addition to imitation, including empathic sharing of emotions and understanding others' intentions.

Still, Meltzoff's view of newborn imitation as a flexible, voluntary capacity remains controversial (Oostenbroek et al., 2013). Even researchers who believe that newborns can imitate agree that many opportunities to see oneself act, to watch others' responses, and to engage in imitative games with caregivers are required for infants to become proficient imitators (Marshall & Meltzoff, 2011). Consistent with this view, human neural-mirroring systems, though possibly functional at birth, undergo an extended period of development, likely supported by rich early social experiences (Ferrari et al., 2013). And as we will see in Chapter 5, the capacity to imitate expands over the first two years.

However limited it is at birth, imitation is a powerful means of learning. Using imitation, infants explore their social world, learning from other people. As they notice similarities between their own actions and those of others, they experience other people as "like me" and learn about themselves (Meltzoff & Williamson, 2013). Finally, caregivers take great pleasure in a baby who participates in imitative exchanges, which strengthens the parent–infant bond.

ASK YOURSELF

CONNECT Which learning capacities contribute to an infant's first social relationships? Explain, providing examples.

APPLY Nine-month-old Byron has a toy with large, colored push buttons on it. Each time he pushes a button, he hears a nursery tune. Which learning capacity is the manufacturer of this toy taking advantage of? What can Byron's play with the toy reveal about his perception of sound patterns?

Motor Development

4.6 Describe dynamic systems theory of motor development, along with factors that influence motor progress in the first two years.

Carolyn, Monica, and Vanessa each kept a baby book, filled with proud notations about when their children first held up their heads, reached for objects, sat by themselves, and walked alone. Parents are understandably excited about these new motor skills, which allow babies to master their bodies and the environment in new ways.

Babies' motor achievements have a powerful effect on their social relationships. When Caitlin crawled at 7½ months, Carolyn and David began to restrict her movements by saying no and expressing mild impatience. When she walked three days after her first birthday, the first "testing of wills" occurred (Biringen et al., 1995). Despite her mother's warnings, she sometimes pulled items from shelves that were off limits. "Don't do that!" Carolyn would say firmly, taking Caitlin's hand and redirecting her attention.

At the same time, newly walking babies more actively attend to and initiate social interaction (Clearfield, 2011; Karasik, Tamis-LeMonda, & Adolph, 2011). Caitlin frequently toddled over to her parents to express a greeting, give a hug, or show them objects of interest. Carolyn and David, in turn, increased their verbal responsiveness, expressions of affection, and playful activities. And when Caitlin encountered risky situations, such as a sloping walkway or a dangerous object, Carolyn and David intervened, combining emotional warnings with rich verbal and gestural information that helped Caitlin notice critical features of her surroundings, regulate her motor actions, and acquire language (Karasik et al., 2008). Caitlin's delight as she worked on new motor skills triggered pleasurable reactions in others, which encouraged her efforts further. Motor, social, cognitive, and language competencies developed together and supported one another.

The Sequence of Motor Development

Gross-motor development refers to control over actions that help infants get around in the environment, such as crawling, standing, and walking. *Fine-motor development* has to do with smaller movements, such as reaching and grasping. Table 4.2 shows the average age at which U.S. infants and toddlers achieve a variety of gross- and fine-motor skills. It also presents the age range

TABLE 4.2
Gross- and Fine-Motor Development in the First Two Years

MOTOR SKILL	AVERAGE AGE ACHIEVED	AGE RANGE IN WHICH 90 PERCENT OF INFANTS ACHIEVE THE SKILL
When held upright, holds head erect and steady	6 weeks	3 weeks–4 months
When prone, lifts self by arms	2 months	3 weeks–4 months
Rolls from side to back	2 months	3 weeks–5 months
Grasps cube	3 months, 3 weeks	2–7 months
Rolls from back to side	4½ months	2–7 months
Sits alone	7 months	5–9 months
Crawls	7 months	5–11 months
Pulls to stand	8 months	5–12 months
Plays pat-a-cake	9 months, 3 weeks	7–15 months
Stands alone	11 months	9–16 months
Walks alone	11 months, 3 weeks	9–17 months
Builds tower of two cubes	11 months, 3 weeks	10–19 months
Scribbles vigorously	14 months	10–21 months
Walks up stairs with help	16 months	12–23 months
Jumps in place	23 months, 2 weeks	17–30 months
Walks on tiptoe	25 months	16–30 months

Note: These milestones represent overall age trends. Individual differences exist in the precise age at which each milestone is attained.

Sources: Bayley, 1969, 1993, 2005.

during which most babies accomplish each skill, indicating large individual differences in *rate* of motor progress. Also, a baby who is a late reacher will not necessarily be a late crawler or walker. We would be concerned about a child's development only if many motor skills were seriously delayed.

Historically, researchers assumed that motor skills emerged in a fixed sequence governed by a built-in maturational timetable. This view has long been discredited. Rather, motor skills are interrelated. Each is a product of earlier motor attainments and a contributor to new ones. And children acquire motor skills in highly individual ways (Adolph & Robinson, 2013). For example, before her adoption, Grace spent most of her days lying in a hammock. Because she was rarely placed on her tummy and on firm surfaces that enabled her to move on her own, she did not try to crawl. As a result, she pulled to a stand and walked before she crawled!

Motor Skills as Dynamic Systems

According to **dynamic systems theory of motor development,** mastery of motor skills involves acquiring increasingly complex *systems of action.* When motor skills work as a system, separate abilities blend together, each cooperating with others to produce more effective ways of exploring and controlling the environment. For example, control of the head and upper chest combine into sitting with support. Kicking, rocking on all fours, and reaching combine to become crawling. Then crawling, standing, and stepping are united into walking (Adolph & Robinson, 2015; Thelen & Smith, 1998).

Each new skill is a joint product of four factors: (1) central nervous system development, (2) the body's movement capacities, (3) the goals the child has in mind, and (4) environmental supports for the skill. Change in any element makes the system less stable, so the child starts to explore and select new, more effective motor patterns.

The broader physical environment is also profoundly influential. Infants with stairs in their home learn to crawl up stairs at an earlier age and also more readily master a back-descent strategy—the safest but also the most challenging position because the baby must give up visual guidance of her goal and crawl backward (Berger, Theuring, & Adolph, 2007). And if children were reared on the moon, with its reduced gravity, they would prefer jumping to walking or running!

When a skill is first acquired, infants must refine it. For example, in learning to walk, toddlers practice six or more hours a day, traveling the length of 29 football fields! They fall, on average, 17 times per hour but rarely cry, returning to motion within a few seconds (Adolph et al., 2012). Gradually their small, unsteady steps change to a longer stride, their toes point to the front, and their legs become symmetrically coordinated. As movements are repeated thousands of times, they promote new synaptic connections in the brain that govern motor patterns.

LOOK AND LISTEN

Spend an hour observing a newly crawling or walking baby. Note the goals that motivate the baby to move, along with the baby's effort and motor experimentation. Describe parenting behaviors and features of the environment that promote mastery of the skill.

Dynamic Motor Systems in Action. To find out how infants acquire motor capacities, some studies have tracked babies from their first attempts at a skill until it became smooth and effortless. In one investigation, researchers held sounding toys alternately in front of infants' hands and feet, from the time they showed interest until they engaged in well-coordinated reaching and grasping (Galloway & Thelen, 2004). As Figure 4.10 illustrates, the infants violated the normative sequence of arm and hand control preceding leg and foot control, shown in Table 4.2. They first reached for the toys with their feet—as early as 8 weeks of age, at least a month before reaching with their hands!

Why did babies reach "feet first"? Because the hip joint constrains the legs to move less freely than the shoulder constrains the arms, infants could more easily control their leg movements. As these findings confirm, rather than following a strict sequence, the order in which motor skills develop depends on the anatomy of the body part being used, the surrounding environment, and the baby's efforts.

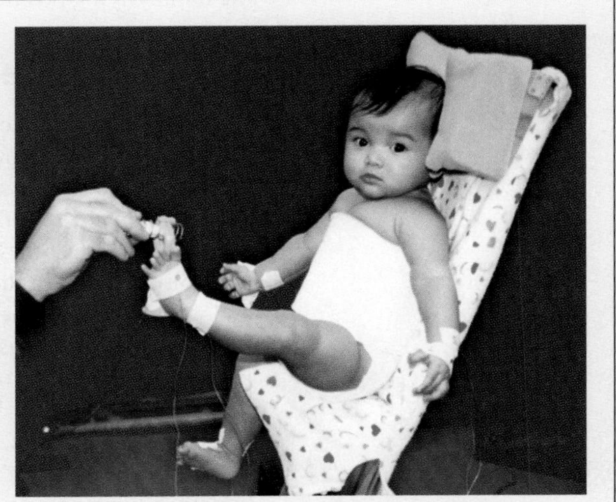

FIGURE 4.10 Reaching "feet first." When sounding toys were held in front of babies' hands and feet, they reached with their feet as early as 8 weeks of age, a month or more before they reached with their hands. This 2½-month-old skillfully explores an object with her foot.

© DON DESPAIN/ALAMY

This West Indian mother of Jamaica "walks" her baby up her body in a deliberate effort to promote early mastery of walking.

Furthermore, in building a more effective dynamic system, babies often use advances in one motor skill to support others. For example, beginning to walk frees the hands for carrying, and new walkers like to fetch distant objects and transport them. Observations of new walkers reveal that, surprisingly, they fall less often when carrying objects than when their hands are empty (Karasik et al., 2012). Toddlers integrate object carrying into their emerging "walking system," using it to improve their balance.

Cultural Variations in Motor Development. Cultural values and infant-rearing customs affect motor development. To ensure safety and ease toileting while parents work in the fields, mothers in rural northeastern China place infants on their backs in bags of sand (similar to kitty litter) for most of the day, continuing this practice into the second year. Compared with diapered infants in the same region, sandbag-reared babies are greatly delayed in sitting and walking (Mei, 1994). Among the Zinacanteco Indians of southern Mexico and the Gusii of Kenya, adults view babies who walk before they know enough to keep away from cooking fires and weaving looms as dangerous to themselves and disruptive to others (Greenfield, 1992). Zinacanteco and Gusii parents actively discourage infants' gross-motor progress.

In contrast, among the Kipsigis of Kenya and the West Indians of Jamaica, babies hold their heads up, sit alone, and walk considerably earlier than North American infants. In both societies, parents emphasize early motor maturity, practicing formal exercises to stimulate particular skills (Adolph, Karasik, & Tamis-LeMonda, 2010). In the first few months, babies are seated in holes dug in the ground, with rolled blankets to keep them upright. Walking is promoted by frequently bouncing infants on their feet (Hopkins & Westra, 1988; Super, 1981). As parents in these cultures support babies in upright postures and rarely put them down on the floor, their infants usually skip crawling—a motor skill regarded as crucial in Western nations!

Finally, because it decreases exposure to "tummy time," the current Western practice of having babies sleep on their backs to protect them from SIDS (see page 97 in Chapter 3) delays gross-motor milestones of rolling, sitting, and crawling (Scrutton, 2005). Regularly exposing infants to the tummy-lying position during waking hours prevents these delays.

Fine-Motor Development: Reaching and Grasping

Of all motor skills, reaching may play the greatest role in infant cognitive development. By grasping things, turning them over, and seeing what happens when they are released, infants learn a great deal about the sights, sounds, and feel of objects. Because certain gross-motor attainments vastly change infants' view of their surroundings, they promote manual coordination. When babies sit, and even more so when they stand and walk, they see the panorama of an entire room (Kretch, Franchak, & Adolph, 2014). In these positions, they focus mainly on the sights and sounds of nearby objects and want to explore them.

Reaching and grasping, like many other motor skills, start out as gross, diffuse activity and move toward mastery of fine movements. Figure 4.11 illustrates some milestones of reaching over the first nine months. Newborns make poorly coordinated swipes, called *prereaching,* toward an object in front of them, but they rarely contact the object. Like newborn reflexes, prereaching drops out around 7 weeks of age (von Hofsten, 2004). Yet these early behaviors suggest that babies are biologically prepared to coordinate hand with eye in the act of exploring.

Around 3 to 4 months, as infants develop the necessary eye, head, and shoulder control, reaching reappears as purposeful, forward arm movements in the presence of a nearby toy and gradually improves in accuracy (Bhat, Heathcock, & Galloway, 2005). By 5 to 6 months, infants reach for an object in a room that has been darkened during the reach by switching off the lights (McCarty &

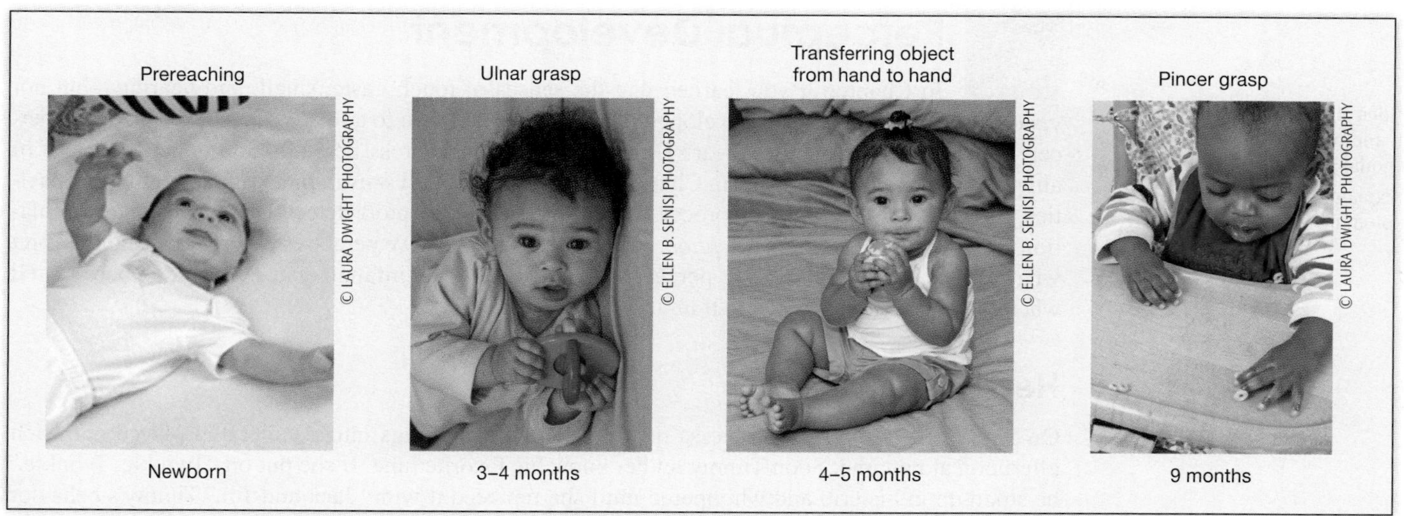

FIGURE 4.11 Some milestones of reaching and grasping. The average age at which each skill is attained is given. (Ages from Bayley, 1969; Rochat, 1989.)

Ashmead, 1999). Early on, vision is freed from the basic act of reaching so it can focus on more complex adjustments. During the next few months, infants become better at reaching with one arm (rather than both) and at reaching for moving objects—ones that spin, change direction, and move sideways, closer, or farther away (Fagard, Spelke, & von Hofsten, 2009; Wentworth, Benson, & Haith, 2000).

Once infants can reach, they modify their grasp. The newborn's grasp reflex is replaced by the *ulnar grasp,* a clumsy motion in which the fingers close against the palm. Still, even 4- to 5-month-olds modify their grasp to suit an object's size, shape, and texture (rigid versus soft)—a capacity that improves over the second half-year (Rocha et al., 2013; Witherington, 2005). Around 4 to 5 months, when infants begin to sit up, both hands become coordinated in exploring objects. Babies of this age can hold an object in one hand while the other scans it with the fingertips, and they frequently transfer objects from hand to hand (Rochat & Goubet, 1995). By the end of the first year, babies use the thumb and index finger opposably in a well-coordinated *pincer grasp.* Then the ability to manipulate objects greatly expands. The 1-year-old can pick up raisins and blades of grass, turn knobs, and open and close small boxes.

Between 8 and 11 months, reaching and grasping are well-practiced, so attention is released from the motor skill to events that occur before and after attaining the object. For example, 10-month-olds modify their reach to anticipate their next action, such as reaching for a ball faster when they intend to throw it than when they intend to push it down a narrow tube (Kayed & Van der Meer, 2009). Finally, the capacity to reach for and manipulate an object increases infants' attention to the way an adult reaches for and plays with that same object (Hauf, Aschersleben, & Prinz, 2007). As babies watch what others do, they broaden the range of actions that can be performed on various objects.

ASK YOURSELF

CONNECT Provide several examples of how motor development influences infants' and toddlers' social experiences. How do social experiences, in turn, influence motor development?

APPLY List everyday experiences that support mastery of reaching, grasping, sitting, and crawling. Why should caregivers place young infants in a variety of waking-time body positions?

REFLECT Do you favor early, systematic training of infants in motor skills such as crawling, walking, and stair climbing? Why or why not?

Perceptual Development

4.7 Identify changes in hearing, depth and pattern perception, and intermodal perception during infancy.

4.8 Explain differentiation theory of perceptual development.

In Chapter 3, you learned that the senses of touch, taste, smell, and hearing—but not vision—are remarkably well-developed at birth. Now let's turn to a related question: How does perception change over the first year? Our discussion will address hearing and vision, the focus of almost all research. Recall that in Chapter 3, we used the word *sensation* to talk about these capacities. It suggests a fairly passive process—what the baby's receptors detect when exposed to stimulation. Now we use the word *perception,* which is active: When we perceive, we organize and interpret what we see. As we review the perceptual achievements of infancy, you may find it hard to tell where perception leaves off and thinking begins.

Hearing

On Timmy's first birthday, Vanessa downloaded nursery songs into a tablet and played one each afternoon at naptime. Soon Timmy let her know his favorite tune. If she put on "Twinkle, Twinkle," he stood up in his crib and whimpered until she replaced it with "Jack and Jill." Timmy's behavior illustrates the greatest change in hearing over the first year of life: Babies start to organize sounds into complex patterns.

Between 4 and 7 months, infants display a sense of musical phrasing: They prefer Mozart minuets with pauses between phrases to those with awkward breaks (Krumhansl & Jusczyk, 1990). Around 6 to 7 months, they can distinguish tunes on the basis of variations in rhythmic patterns, including beat structure (duple or triple) and accent structure (emphasis on the first note of every beat unit or at other positions) (Hannon & Johnson, 2004). They are also sensitive to features conveying the purpose of familiar types of songs, preferring to listen to high-pitched playsongs (aimed at entertaining) and low-pitched lullabies (used to soothe) (Tsang & Conrad, 2010). As we will see next, 6- to 12-month-olds make comparable discriminations in human speech: They readily detect sound regularities.

Speech Perception. Recall from Chapter 3 that newborns can distinguish nearly all sounds in human languages and that they prefer listening to human speech over nonspeech sounds and to their native tongue rather than a foreign language. Brain-imaging evidence reveals that in young infants, discrimination of speech sounds activates both auditory and motor areas in the cerebral cortex (Kuhl et al., 2014). While perceiving speech sounds, babies seem to generate internal motor plans that prepare them for producing those sounds.

As infants listen to people talk, they learn to focus on meaningful sound variations. ERP brain-wave recordings reveal that around 5 months, infants become sensitive to the overall syllable stress rhythm of their own language (Weber et al., 2004). Between 6 and 8 months, they start to "screen out" sounds not used in their native tongue (Curtin & Werker, 2007). Bilingual infants do so in both their native languages, though slightly later, between 8 and 9 months, due to the challenges of processing the sounds of two languages. But once bilingual babies begin distinguishing native from nonnative sounds, they do so more rapidly and effectively than their monolingual agemates. Their richer linguistic experience seems to induce heightened sensitivity to the details of language sounds (Liu & Kager, 2015, 2016; Ramirez et al., 2017). As the Biology and Environment box on the following page explains, increased responsiveness to native-language sounds is part of a general "tuning" process in the second half of the first year—a possible sensitive period in which infants acquire a range of perceptual skills for picking up socially important information.

Soon after, infants focus on larger speech units that are critical to figuring out meaning. They recognize familiar words in spoken passages and listen longer to speech with clear clause and phrase boundaries (Johnson & Seidl, 2008; Jusczyk & Hohne, 1997; Soderstrom et al., 2003). Around 7 to 9 months, infants extend this sensitivity to speech structure to individual words: They begin to divide the speech stream into wordlike units (Jusczyk, 2002; MacWhinney, 2015).

Analyzing the Speech Stream. How do infants make such rapid progress in perceiving the structure of speech? Research shows that they have an impressive **statistical learning capacity.** By analyzing the speech stream for patterns—repeatedly occurring sequences of sounds—they

BIOLOGY AND ENVIRONMENT

"Tuning In" to Familiar Speech, Faces, and Music: A Sensitive Period for Culture-Specific Learning

To share experiences with members of their family and community, babies must become skilled at making perceptual discriminations that are meaningful in their culture. As we have seen, at first babies are sensitive to virtually all speech sounds, but around 6 months, they narrow their focus, limiting the distinctions they make to the language they hear and will soon learn.

The ability to perceive faces shows a similar **perceptual narrowing effect**—perceptual sensitivity that becomes increasingly attuned with age to information most often encountered. After habituating to one member of each pair of faces in Figure 4.12, 6-month-olds were shown the familiar face and the novel face side by side. For both pairs, they recovered to (looked longer at) the novel face, indicating that they could discriminate individual faces of both humans and monkeys equally well (Pascalis, de Haan, & Nelson, 2002). But at 9 months, infants no longer showed a novelty preference when viewing the monkey pair. Like adults, they could distinguish only the human faces. Similar findings emerge with sheep faces: Four- to 6-month-olds easily distinguish them, but 9- to 11-month-olds no longer do (Simpson et al., 2011).

This perceptual narrowing effect appears again in musical rhythm perception. Western adults are accustomed to the even-beat pattern of Western music—repetition of the same rhythmic structure in every measure of a tune—and easily notice rhythmic changes that disrupt this familiar beat. But present them with music that does not follow this typical Western rhythmic form—Baltic folk tunes, for example—and they fail to pick up on rhythmic-pattern deviations. In contrast, 6-month-olds can detect such disruptions in both Western and non-Western melodies. By 12 months, however, after added exposure to Western music, babies are no longer aware of deviations in foreign musical rhythms, although their sensitivity to Western rhythmic structure remains unchanged (Hannon & Trehub, 2005b).

Several weeks of regular interaction with a foreign-language speaker and of daily opportunities to listen to non-Western music fully restore 12-month-olds' sensitivity to wide-ranging speech sounds and music rhythms (Hannon & Trehub, 2005a; Kuhl, Tsao, & Liu, 2003). Similarly, 6-month-olds given three months of training in discriminating individual monkey faces, in which each image is labeled with a distinct name ("Carlos," "Iona") instead of the generic label "monkey," retain their ability to discriminate monkey faces at 9 months (Scott & Monesson, 2009). Adults given similar extensive experiences, by contrast, show little improvement in perceptual sensitivity.

Taken together, these findings suggest a heightened capacity—or sensitive period—in the second half of the first year, when babies are biologically prepared to "zero in" on socially meaningful perceptual distinctions. Notice how, between 6 and 12 months, learning is especially rapid across several domains (speech, faces, and music) and is easily modified by experience. This suggests a broad neurological change—perhaps a special time of experience-expectant brain growth (see page 114) in which babies analyze stimulation of all kinds in ways that prepare them to participate in their cultural community.

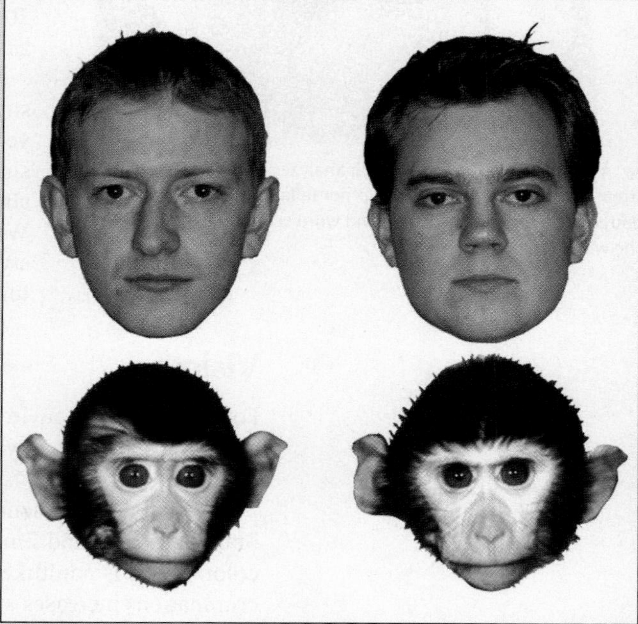

FIGURE 4.12 Discrimination of human and monkey faces. Which of these pairs is easiest for you to tell apart? After habituating to one of the photos in each pair, infants were shown the familiar and the novel face side by side. For both pairs, 6-month-olds recovered to (looked longer at) the novel face, indicating that they could discriminate human and monkey faces equally well. By 9 months, babies lost their ability to distinguish the monkey faces. Like adults, they showed a novelty preference only to human stimuli. (From O. Pascalis et al., 2002, "Is Face Processing Species-Specific During the First Year of Life?" *Science, 296,* p. 1322. Copyright © 2002 by AAAS. Republished with permission of American Association for the Advancement of Science conveyed through Copyright Clearance Center, Inc.)

© LAURA DWIGHT PHOTOGRAPHY

▶ A 6-month-old is a remarkable analyzer of the speech stream. While listening to her mother talk, she detects sound patterns, discriminating words and word sequences for which she will later learn meanings.

acquire a stock of speech structures for which they will later learn meanings, long before they start to talk around age 12 months.

For example, when presented with controlled sequences of nonsense syllables, babies as young as 5 months listen for statistical regularities: They distinguish syllables that often occur together (indicating that they belong to the same word) from syllables that seldom occur together (indicating a word boundary) (Johnson & Tyler, 2010). Consider the English word sequence *pretty#baby*. After listening to the speech stream for just one minute (about 60 words), babies can distinguish a word-internal syllable pair *(pretty)* from a word-external syllable pair *(ty#ba)*. They prefer to listen to new speech that preserves the word-internal pattern (Saffran & Thiessen, 2003).

Once infants locate words, they focus on the words and, around 7 to 8 months, start to identify regular syllable-stress patterns—for example, in English, that the onset of a strong syllable (*hap*-py, *rab*-bit) often signals a new word (Thiessen & Saffran, 2007). By 10 months, babies can detect words that start with weak syllables, such as "sur*prise,*" by listening for sound regularities before and after the words (Kooijman, Hagoort, & Cutler, 2009).

Infants' remarkable statistical learning capacity also extends to visual stimuli (Aslin & Newport, 2012; Altvater-Mackensen, Jessen, & Grossmann, 2017). Statistical learning seems to be a general capacity that infants use to analyze complex stimulation.

Finally, the more rapidly 10-month-olds detect words within the speech stream (as indicated by ERP recordings), the larger their vocabulary at age 2 years (Junge et al., 2012). Parents' speech to babies, which often contains single-word utterances followed by the same words embedded in the speech stream ("Doggie!" "See the big doggie?") aids word discrimination (Lew-Williams, Pelucchi, & Saffran, 2011). As we will see in Chapter 5, adults' style of communicating with infants greatly facilitates analysis of the structure of speech.

Vision

For exploring the environment, humans depend on vision more than any other sense. Although at first the baby's visual world is fragmented, it undergoes extraordinary changes during the first 7 to 8 months of life.

Visual development is supported by rapid maturation of the eye and visual centers in the cerebral cortex. Around 2 months, infants can focus on objects about as well as adults can, and their color vision is adultlike by 4 months (Johnson & Hannon, 2015). *Visual acuity* (fineness of discrimination) increases steadily, reaching 20/80 by 6 months and an adult level of about 20/20 by 4 years (Slater et al., 2010). Scanning the environment and tracking moving objects also improve over the first half-year as infants better control their eye movements and build an organized perceptual world (Johnson, Slemmer, & Amso, 2004).

As babies explore their visual field, they figure out the characteristics of objects and how they are arranged in space. To understand how they do so, let's examine the development of two aspects of vision: depth and pattern perception.

Depth Perception. *Depth perception* is the ability to judge the distance of objects from one another and from ourselves. It is important for understanding the layout of the environment and for guiding motor activity.

Figure 4.13 shows the *visual cliff,* designed by Eleanor Gibson and Richard Walk (1960) and used in the earliest studies of depth perception. It consists of a Plexiglas-covered table with a platform at the center, a "shallow" side with a checkerboard pattern just under the glass, and a "deep" side with a checkerboard several feet below the glass. The researchers found that crawling babies readily crossed the shallow side, but most avoided the deep side. They concluded that around the time infants crawl, most distinguish deep from shallow surfaces.

The visual cliff shows that crawling and avoidance of drop-offs are linked, but not how they are related or when depth perception first appears. Subsequent research has looked at babies' ability to detect specific depth cues, using methods that do not require that they crawl.

Motion is the first depth cue to which infants are sensitive. Babies 3 to 4 weeks old blink their eyes defensively when an object moves toward their face as if it is going to hit (Nánez & Yonas, 1994). *Binocular depth cues* arise because our two eyes have slightly different views of the visual field. Sensitivity to binocular cues emerges between 2 and 3 months and improves rapidly over the first year (Brown & Miracle, 2003). Finally, beginning at 3 to 4 months and strengthening between 5 and 7 months, babies display sensitivity to *pictorial depth cues*—the ones artists often use to make a painting look three-dimensional. Examples include receding lines that create the illusion of perspective, changes in texture (nearby textures are more detailed than faraway ones), and overlapping objects (an object partially hidden by another object is perceived to be more distant) (Kavšek, Yonas, & Granrud, 2012).

Why does perception of depth cues emerge in the order just described? Researchers speculate that motor development is involved. For example, control of the head during the early weeks of life may help babies notice motion and binocular cues. Around 5 to 6 months, the ability to turn, poke, and feel the surface of objects promotes perception of pictorial cues (Bushnell & Boudreau, 1993; Soska, Adolph, & Johnson, 2010). And as we will see next, one aspect of motor progress—independent movement—plays a vital role in refinement of depth perception.

© MARK RICHARDS/PHOTOEDIT

FIGURE 4.13 The visual cliff. Plexiglas covers the deep and shallow sides. By refusing to cross the deep side and showing a preference for the shallow side, this infant demonstrates the ability to perceive depth.

Independent Movement and Depth Perception. At 6 months, Timmy started crawling. "He's fearless!" exclaimed Vanessa. "If I put him down in the middle of my bed, he crawls right over the edge." Will Timmy become wary of the side of the bed as he becomes a more experienced crawler? Research suggests that he will.

From extensive everyday experience, babies gradually figure out how to use depth cues to detect the danger of falling. But because the loss of body control that leads to falling differs greatly for each body position, babies must undergo this learning separately for each posture (Adolph & Kretch, 2012). For example, infants with more crawling experience (regardless of when they started to crawl) are far more likely to refuse to cross the deep side of the visual cliff. And with increased walking experience, toddlers gradually figure out how to navigate slopes and uneven surfaces (Adolph et al., 2008; Kretch & Adolph, 2013). As babies discover how to avoid falling in different postures and situations, their understanding of depth expands.

Independent movement promotes other aspects of three-dimensional understanding. Seasoned crawlers are better than their inexperienced agemates at remembering object locations, finding hidden objects, and recognizing the identity of a previously viewed object from a new angle (Campos et al., 2000; Schwarzer, Freitag, & Schum, 2013). Why does crawling make such a difference? Compare your own experience of the environment when you are driven from one place to another with what you experience when you walk or drive yourself. When you move on your own, you are much more aware of landmarks and routes of travel, and you take more careful note of what things look like from different points of view. The same is true for infants.

© ELLEN B. SENISI

▶ As this 8-month-old becomes adept at crawling, his experience fosters three-dimensional understanding—for example, remembering object locations and how objects appear from different viewpoints.

Pattern Perception. Even newborns prefer to look at patterned rather than plain stimuli (Fantz, 1961). Because of their poor vision, very young babies cannot resolve the features in complex patterns, so they prefer to look at a checkerboard with large, bold squares than one with many small squares.

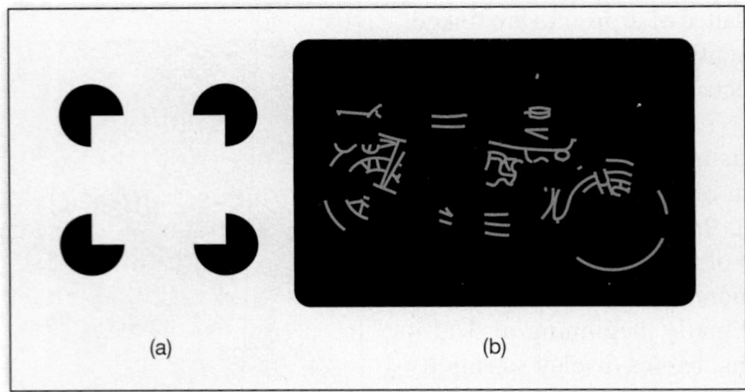

FIGURE 4.14 Subjective boundaries in visual patterns. (a) Do you perceive a square in the middle of the figure? By 4 months of age, infants do, too. (b) What does the image, missing two-thirds of its outline, look like to you? By 12 months, infants detect a motorcycle. After habituating to the incomplete motorcycle image, they were shown an intact motorcycle figure paired with a novel form. Twelve-month-olds recovered to (looked longer at) the novel figure, indicating that they recognized the motorcycle pattern on the basis of little visual information. (Adapted from Ghim, 1990; Rose, Jankowski, & Senior, 1997.)

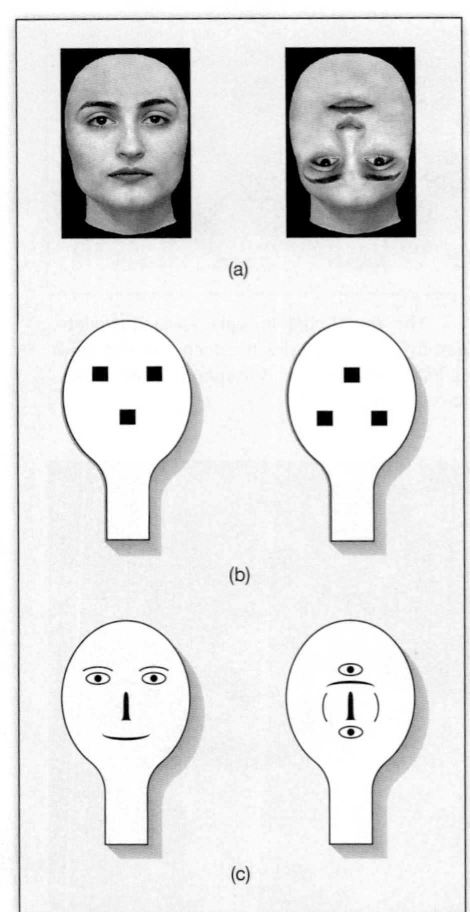

FIGURE 4.15 Early face perception. Newborns prefer to look at the photo of a face (a) and the simple pattern resembling a face (b) over the upside-down versions. (c) When the complex drawing of a face on the left and the equally complex, scrambled version on the right are moved across newborns' visual field, they follow the face longer. But if the two stimuli are stationary, infants show no preference for the face until around 2 months of age. (From Cassia, Turati, & Simion, 2004; Johnson, 1999; Mondloch et al., 1999.)

Around 2 months, when detection of fine-grained detail improves, infants spend more time looking at the more complex checkerboard (Gwiazda & Birch, 2001).

In the early weeks of life, infants respond to the separate parts of a pattern, staring at single high-contrast features, generally on the edges, and have difficulty shifting their gaze away toward other interesting stimuli (Hunnius & Geuze, 2004a, 2004b). At 2 to 3 months, when vision improves and infants can better control their scanning, they thoroughly explore a pattern's features, pausing briefly to look at each part (Bronson, 1994).

Once babies can take in all aspects of a pattern, they integrate the parts into a unified whole. Around 4 months, babies are so good at detecting pattern organization that they perceive subjective boundaries that are not really present. For example, they perceive a square in the center of Figure 4.14a, just as you do (Ghim, 1990). Older infants carry this sensitivity to subjective form further, applying it to complex, moving stimuli. For example, 9-month-olds look much longer at an organized series of blinking lights that resembles a human being walking than at an upside-down or scrambled version (Bertenthal, 1993). At 12 months, infants detect familiar objects represented by incomplete drawings, even when as much as two-thirds of the drawing is missing (see Figure 4.14b) (Rose, Jankowski, & Senior, 1997). As these findings reveal, infants' increasing knowledge of objects and actions supports pattern perception.

Face Perception. Infants' tendency to search for structure in a patterned stimulus also applies to face perception. Newborns prefer to look at photos and simplified drawings of faces with features arranged naturally (upright) rather than unnaturally (upside-down or sideways) (see Figure 4.15a) (Cassia, Turati, & Simion, 2004; Mondloch et al., 1999). They also track a facelike pattern moving across their visual field farther than they track other stimuli (Johnson, 1999). Yet another amazing capacity is newborns' tendency to look longer at both human and animal faces judged by adults as attractive—a preference that may be the origin of the widespread social bias favoring physically attractive people (Quinn et al., 2008; Slater et al., 2010).

Some researchers claim that these behaviors reflect a built-in capacity to orient toward members of one's own species, just as many newborn animals do (Slater et al., 2011). Others assert that newborns prefer any stimulus in which the most salient elements are arranged horizontally in the upper part of a pattern—like the "eyes" in Figure 4.15b (Cassia, Turati, & Simion, 2004). Another conjecture is that newborns are exposed to faces more often than to other stimuli—early experiences that could quickly "wire" the brain to detect faces and prefer attractive ones (Bukacha, Gauthier, & Tarr, 2006).

Although newborns respond to facelike structures, they cannot discriminate a stationary, complex facial pattern from other, equally complex patterns (see Figure 4.15c). But from repeated exposures to their mother's face, they quickly learn to prefer her face to that of an unfamiliar woman, although they mostly attend to its broad outlines (Bushnell, 2001). Around 2 months, when they can combine pattern elements into an organized whole, babies prefer a complex drawing of the human face to other equally complex stimulus arrangements (Dannemiller & Stephens, 1988). And they clearly prefer their mother's detailed facial features to those of another woman (Bartrip, Morton, & de Schonen, 2001).

Around 3 months, infants make fine distinctions among the features of different faces—for example, between photographs of two strangers, even when the faces are moderately similar (Farroni et al., 2007). At 5 months—and strengthening over the second half-year—infants perceive emotional expressions as meaningful wholes. They treat positive faces (happy and surprised) as different from negative ones (sad and fearful) (Bornstein & Arterberry, 2003). And by 7 months, they discriminate among a wider range of facial expressions, including happiness, surprise, sadness, fearfulness, and anger (Safar & Moulson, 2017; Witherington et al., 2010).

Experience influences face processing, leading babies to form group biases at a tender age. As early as 3 months, infants prefer and more easily discriminate among female faces than among male faces (Liu et al., 2015; Ramsey-Rennels & Langlois, 2006). The greater time spent with female adults explains this effect, since babies with a male primary caregiver prefer male faces. Furthermore, 3-month-olds exposed mostly to members of their own race prefer to look at the faces of members of that race, and between 6 and 9 months their ability to discriminate other-race faces weakens (Fassbender, Teubert, & Lohaus, 2016; Kelly et al., 2007, 2009). This own-race bias is absent in babies who have frequent contact with members of other races, and it can be reversed through exposure to racial diversity (Anzures et al., 2013; Heron-Delaney et al., 2011). Notice how early experience promotes *perceptual narrowing* with respect to gender and racial information, as discussed in the Biology and Environment box on page 129.

Development of areas specialized for face processing in the right cerebral hemisphere plus extensive face-to-face interaction with caregivers contribute to infants' refinement of face perception. Face identification continues to improve throughout childhood (Stiles et al., 2015). Not until ages 10 to 11 are children as adept as adults at rapidly and accurately discriminating highly similar faces encountered in everyday life.

Up to this point, we have considered the infant's sensory systems one by one. Now let's examine their coordination.

Intermodal Perception

Our world provides rich, continuous *intermodal stimulation*—simultaneous input from more than one *modality*, or sensory system. In **intermodal perception,** we make sense of these running streams of light, sound, tactile, odor, and taste information, perceiving them as integrated wholes. We know, for example, that an object's shape is the same whether we see it or touch it, that lip movements are closely coordinated with the sound of a voice, and that dropping a rigid object on a hard surface will cause a sharp, banging sound.

Infants perceive input from different sensory systems in a unified way by detecting *amodal sensory properties*—information that overlaps two or more sensory systems, such as rate, rhythm, duration, intensity, temporal synchrony (for vision and hearing), and texture and shape (for vision and touch). Consider the sight and sound of a bouncing ball or the face and voice of a speaking person. In each event, visual and auditory information occur simultaneously and with the same rate, rhythm, duration, and intensity.

Even newborns are impressive perceivers of amodal properties. After touching an object (such as a cylinder) placed in their palms, they recognize it visually, distinguishing it from a different-shaped object (Sann & Streri, 2007). And they require just one exposure to learn the association between the sight and sound of a toy, such as a rhythmically jangling rattle (Morrongiello, Fenwick, & Chance, 1998).

Within the first half-year, infants master a remarkable range of intermodal relationships. Three- to 5-month-olds can match faces with voices on the basis of lip–voice synchrony, emotional expression, and even age and gender of the speaker. Around 6

▶ This toddler exploring a tambourine readily detects amodal relations in the synchronous sounds and visual appearance of its metal jingles.

months, infants can perceive and remember the unique face–voice pairings of unfamiliar adults (Flom, 2013).

How does intermodal perception develop so quickly? Young infants seem biologically primed to focus on amodal information. Their detection of amodal relations—for example, the common tempo and rhythm in sights and sounds—precedes and provides the basis for detecting more specific intermodal matches, such as the relation between a particular person's face and the sound of her voice or between an object and its verbal label (Bahrick, 2010).

Intermodal sensitivity is crucial for perceptual development. In the first few months, when much stimulation is unfamiliar and confusing, it enables babies to notice meaningful correlations between sensory inputs and rapidly make sense of their surroundings.

LOOK AND LISTEN

While watching a parent and infant playing, list instances of parental intermodal stimulation and communication. What is the baby likely learning about people, objects, or language from each intermodal experience?

In addition to easing perception of the physical world, intermodal perception facilitates social and language processing. For example, as 3- to 4-month-olds gaze at an adult's face, they initially require both vocal and visual input to distinguish positive from negative emotional expressions (Flom & Bahrick, 2007). Only later do infants discriminate positive from negative emotion in each sensory modality—first in voices (around 5 months), then (from 6 months on) in faces (Bahrick, Hernandez-Reif, & Flom, 2005). Furthermore, in speaking to infants, parents often provide temporal synchrony between words, object motions, and touch—for example, saying "doll" while moving a doll and having it touch the infant. This greatly increases the chances that babies will remember the association between the word and the object (Gogate & Bahrick, 2001).

In sum, intermodal perception fosters all aspects of psychological development. When caregivers provide many concurrent sights, sounds, and touches, babies process more information and learn faster (Bahrick, 2010). Intermodal perception is yet another fundamental capacity that assists infants in their active efforts to build an orderly, predictable world.

Understanding Perceptual Development

Now that we have reviewed the development of infant perceptual capacities, how can we put together this diverse array of amazing achievements? Widely accepted answers come from the work of Eleanor and James Gibson. According to the Gibsons' **differentiation theory,** infants actively search for *invariant features* of the environment—those that remain stable—in a constantly changing perceptual world. In pattern perception, for example, young babies search for features that stand out and orient toward faces. Soon they explore a stimulus, noticing *stable relationships* among its features, detecting patterns. Similarly, infants analyze the speech stream for regularities, detecting words, word-order sequences, and—within words—syllable-stress patterns. The development of intermodal perception also reflects this principle (Bahrick & Lickliter, 2012). Babies seek out invariant relationships—first, amodal properties and later more detailed associations, such as unique voice–face matches.

The Gibsons described their theory as *differentiation* (where *differentiate* means "analyze" or "break down") because over time, the baby detects finer and finer invariant features among stimuli. So one way of understanding perceptual development is to think of it as a built-in tendency to seek order and consistency—a capacity that becomes increasingly fine-tuned with age (Gibson, 1970; Gibson, 1979).

Infants constantly look for ways in which the environment *affords possibilities for action* (Gibson, 2003). By exploring their surroundings, they figure out which objects can be grasped, squeezed, bounced, or stroked and which surfaces are safe to cross or present the possibility of falling. And from handling objects, babies become more aware of a variety of observable object properties (Perone et al., 2008). As a result, they differentiate the world in new ways and act more competently.

To illustrate, recall how infants' changing capabilities for independent movement affect their perception. When babies crawl, and again when they walk, they gradually realize that a sloping surface *affords the possibility of falling*. With added practice of each skill, they hesitate to crawl or walk down a risky incline. Experience in trying to keep their balance on various surfaces makes crawlers and walkers more aware of the consequences of their movements. Crawlers come to detect when surface slant places so much body weight on their arms that they will fall forward, and

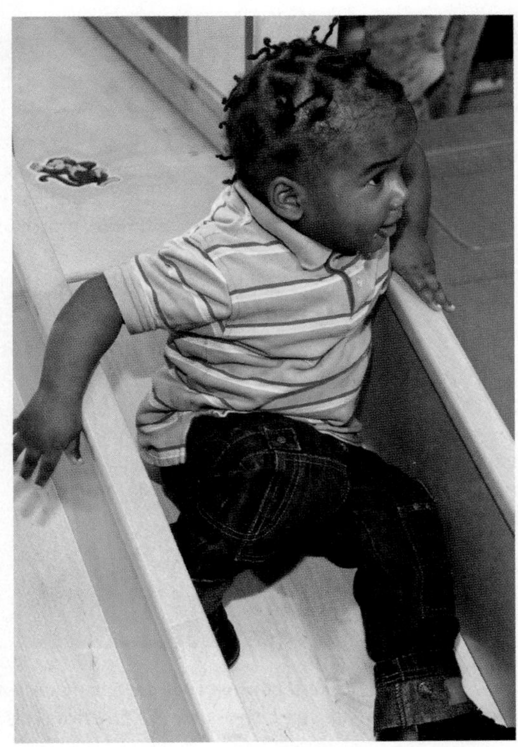

▶ Babies' changing motor skills tranform the way they perceive surfaces. Left photo: A 12-month-old who has just begun to walk proceeds feet-first down a steep incline, unaware of the high risk of falling. Right photo: An 18-month-old with extensive experience walking knows that it's best to sit and scoot down the incline.

walkers come to sense when an incline shifts body weight so their legs and feet can no longer hold them upright.

Infants do not transfer their learning about slopes or drop-offs from crawling to walking because the affordances for each posture are different (Adolph, Kretch, & LoBue, 2014). Learning takes time because newly crawling and walking babies cross many types of surfaces in their homes each day. As they experiment with balance and postural adjustments to accommodate each, they perceive surfaces in new ways that guide their movements. As a result, they act more competently.

As we conclude this chapter, it is only fair to note that some researchers believe that babies do more than make sense of experience by searching for invariant features and action possibilities: They also *impose meaning* on what they perceive, constructing categories of objects and events in the surrounding environment (Johnson & Hannon, 2015). We have seen the glimmerings of this *cognitive* point of view in this chapter. For example, older babies *interpret* a familiar face as a source of pleasure and affection and a pattern of blinking lights as a human being walking. This cognitive perspective also has merit in understanding the achievements of infancy. In fact, many researchers combine these two positions, regarding infant development as proceeding from a perceptual to a cognitive emphasis over the first year of life.

ASK YOURSELF

CONNECT Using examples, explain why intermodal perception is vital for infants' developing understanding of their physical and social worlds.

APPLY Ben, age 13 months, has just started to walk. Using the concept of affordances, explain why he is likely to step over risky drop-offs.

REFLECT Consider a new motor skill that you acquired. How do you think it changed your perceptual and cognitive capacities?

CHAPTER 4 SUMMARY

Body Growth *(p. 106)*

4.1 *Describe major changes in body growth over the first two years.*

- Height and weight gains are rapid during the first two years. Body fat rises quickly during the first nine months, whereas muscle development increases slowly. Body proportions change as growth follows the **cephalocaudal** and **proximodistal trends.**

Brain Development *(p. 108)*

4.2 *Describe brain development during infancy and toddlerhood, current methods of measuring brain functioning, and appropriate stimulation to support the brain's potential.*

- Early in development, the brain grows faster than any other organ of the body. Once **neurons** are in place, they rapidly form **synapses.** To communicate, neurons release chemicals called **neurotransmitters,** which cross synapses. **Programmed cell death** makes space for neural fibers and synapses. Seldom stimulated neurons lose their synapses in a process called **synaptic pruning. Glial cells,** responsible for **myelination,** multiply rapidly through the second year, contributing to large gains in brain weight.
- Measures of brain functioning include those that detect changes in electrical activity in the cerebral cortex (EEG, ERPs), neuroimaging techniques (PET, fMRI), and NIRS, an imaging technique suitable for infants and young children.
- The **cerebral cortex** is the largest, most complex brain structure and the last to stop growing. Its frontal lobes contain the **prefrontal cortex,** which is responsible for complex thought. Gradually, the hemispheres of the cerebral cortex specialize, a process called **lateralization.** But in the first few years of life, there is high **brain plasticity,** with many areas not yet committed to specific functions.
- Stimulation of the brain is essential during sensitive periods, when the brain is developing most rapidly. Prolonged early deprivation can disrupt development of the cerebral cortex, especially the prefrontal cortex, and interfere with the brain's capacity to manage stress, with long-term physical and psychological consequences.
- Appropriate early stimulation promotes **experience-expectant brain growth,** which depends on ordinary experiences. No evidence exists for a sensitive period in the first few years for **experience-dependent brain growth,** which relies on specific learning experiences.

4.3 *Explain how the organization of sleep and wakefulness changes over the first two years.*

- Infants' changing arousal patterns are affected by brain growth, but cultural beliefs and practices also contribute. Periods of sleep and wakefulness increasingly conform to a night–day schedule.
- Many Western parents try to get their babies to sleep through the night earlier than other parents throughout the world, who are more likely to sleep with their babies. Regular bedtime routines promote sleep.

Influences on Early Physical Growth *(p. 117)*

4.4 *Cite evidence that heredity and nutrition both contribute to early physical growth.*

- Twin and adoption studies reveal that heredity contributes to body size and rate of physical growth.
- Breast milk is ideally suited to infants' growth needs. Breastfeeding protects against disease and prevents malnutrition and infant death in poverty-stricken areas of the world.
- Most infants and toddlers can eat nutritious foods freely without risk of becoming overweight. However, the relationship between rapid weight gain in infancy and later obesity is strengthening, likely because of the rise in unhealthy parental feeding practices.
- **Marasmus** and **kwashiorkor,** two dietary diseases caused by malnutrition, affect many children in developing countries. If prolonged, they can permanently stunt body growth and brain development.

Learning Capacities *(p. 120)*

4.5 *Describe infant learning capacities, the conditions under which they occur, and the unique value of each.*

- **Classical conditioning** helps infants recognize which events usually occur together in the everyday world. Infants can be classically conditioned most easily when the pairing of an **unconditioned stimulus (UCS)** and a **conditioned stimulus (CS)** has survival value.
- In **operant conditioning,** infants act on the environment, and their behavior is followed by either **reinforcers,** which increase the occurrence of a preceding behavior, or **punishment,** which decreases the occurrence of a response. In young infants, interesting sights and sounds and pleasurable caregiver interaction serve as effective reinforcers.
- **Habituation** and **recovery** reveal that at birth, babies are attracted to novelty. Novelty preference (recovery to a novel stimulus) assesses recent memory, whereas familiarity preference (recovery to the familiar stimulus) assesses remote memory.
- Newborns have a primitive ability to imitate adults' facial expressions and gestures. **Imitation** is a powerful means of learning. Specialized cells called **mirror neurons** may underlie infants' capacity to imitate, which expands greatly over the first two years.

Motor Development *(p. 123)*

4.6 *Describe dynamic systems theory of motor development, along with factors that influence motor progress in the first two years.*

- According to **dynamic systems theory of motor development,** children acquire new motor skills by combining existing skills into increasingly complex systems of action. Each new skill is a joint product of central nervous system development, the body's movement possibilities, the child's goals, and environmental supports for the skill. Cultural values and infant-rearing customs also contribute to motor development.

- During the first year, infants perfect reaching and grasping. Reaching gradually becomes more accurate and flexible, and the clumsy ulnar grasp is transformed into a refined pincer grasp.

Perceptual Development *(p. 128)*

4.7 ***Identify changes in hearing, depth and pattern perception, and intermodal perception during infancy.***

- Infants organize sounds into increasingly complex patterns and, as part of the **perceptual narrowing effect,** begin to "screen out" sounds not used in their native language in the second half of the first year. An impressive **statistical learning capacity** enables babies to detect sound patterns, for which they will later learn meanings.
- Rapid maturation of the eye and visual centers in the brain supports the development of focusing, color discrimination, and visual acuity during the first half-year. Scanning the environment and tracking moving objects also improve.
- Research on depth perception reveals that responsiveness to motion cues develops first, followed by sensitivity to binocular and then to pictorial cues. Experience in independent movement enhances depth perception and other aspects of three-dimensional understanding.
- At first, babies stare at single, high-contrast features. Over time, they discriminate increasingly complex, meaningful patterns.
- Newborns prefer to look at and track simple, facelike stimuli, and they look longer at attractive faces. Around 2 months, infants prefer their mother's facial features; at 3 months, they distinguish the features of different faces; and by 7 months, they discriminate among a wide range of emotional expressions.
- From the start, infants are capable of **intermodal perception**—combining information across sensory modalities. Detection of amodal relations (such as common tempo or rhythm) provides the basis for detecting other intermodal matches.

4.8 ***Explain differentiation theory of perceptual development.***

- According to **differentiation theory,** perceptual development is a matter of detecting invariant features in a constantly changing perceptual world. Acting on the world plays a major role in perceptual differentiation. From a cognitive perspective, infants also impose meaning on what they perceive. Many researchers combine these two ideas.

IMPORTANT TERMS AND CONCEPTS

brain plasticity (p. 112)
cephalocaudal trend (p. 106)
cerebral cortex (p. 111)
classical conditioning (p. 120)
conditioned response (CR) (p. 120)
conditioned stimulus (CS) (p. 120)
differentiation theory (p. 134)
dynamic systems theory of motor development (p. 125)
experience-dependent brain growth (p. 114)
experience-expectant brain growth (p. 114)
glial cells (p. 108)
habituation (p. 121)
imitation (p. 122)
intermodal perception (p. 133)
kwashiorkor (p. 119)
lateralization (p. 111)
marasmus (p. 119)
mirror neurons (p. 122)
myelination (p. 108)
neurons (p. 108)
neurotransmitters (p. 108)
operant conditioning (p. 121)
perceptual narrowing effect (p. 129)
prefrontal cortex (p. 111)
programmed cell death (p. 108)
proximodistal trend (p. 107)
punishment (p. 121)
recovery (p. 121)
reinforcer (p. 121)
statistical learning capacity (p. 128)
synapses (p. 108)
synaptic pruning (p. 108)
unconditioned response (UCR) (p. 120)
unconditioned stimulus (UCS) (p. 120)

CHAPTER 5

Cognitive Development in Infancy and Toddlerhood

ROMONA ROBBINS PHOTOGRAPHY/GETTY IMAGES

A father encourages his child's curiosity and delight in discovery. With the sensitive support of caring adults, infants' and toddlers' cognition and language develop rapidly.

WHAT'S AHEAD IN CHAPTER 5

When Caitlin, Grace, and Timmy, each nearly 18 months old, gathered at Ginette's child-care home, the playroom was alive with activity. Grace dropped shapes through holes in a plastic box that Ginette held and adjusted so the harder ones would fall smoothly into place. Once a few shapes were inside, Grace grabbed the box and shook it, squealing with delight as the lid fell open and the shapes scattered around her. The clatter attracted Timmy, who picked up a shape, carried it to the railing at the top of the basement steps, and dropped it overboard, then followed with a teddy bear, a ball, his shoe, and a spoon.

As the toddlers experimented, I could see the beginnings of spoken language—a whole new way of influencing the world. "All gone baw!" Caitlin exclaimed as Timmy tossed the bright red ball down the basement steps. Later that day, Grace revealed the beginnings of make-believe. "Night-night," she said, putting her head down and closing her eyes.

Over the first two years, the small, reflexive newborn baby becomes a self-assertive, purposeful being who solves simple problems and starts to master the most amazing human ability: language. Parents wonder, how does all this happen so quickly? This question has also captivated researchers, yielding a wealth of findings along with vigorous debate over how to explain the astonishing pace of infant and toddler cognitive development.

© ELLEN B. SENISI

In this chapter, we take up three perspectives: Piaget's *cognitive-developmental theory, information processing,* and Vygotsky's *sociocultural theory.* We also consider the usefulness of tests that measure infants' and toddlers' intellectual progress. Finally, we look at the beginnings of language. We will see how toddlers' first words build on early cognitive attainments and how, very soon, new words and expressions greatly increase the speed and flexibility of thinking. Throughout development, cognition and language mutually support each other.

Piaget's Cognitive-Developmental Theory

5.1 Explain how, in Piaget's theory, schemes change over the course of development.

5.2 Describe major cognitive attainments of the sensorimotor stage.

5.3 Explain the implications of follow-up research on infant cognitive development for the accuracy of Piaget's sensorimotor stage.

Swiss theorist Jean Piaget inspired a vision of children as busy, motivated explorers whose thinking develops as they act directly on the environment. Influenced by his background in biology, Piaget believed that the child's mind forms and modifies psychological structures so they achieve a better fit with external reality. Recall from Chapter 1 that in Piaget's theory, children move through four stages between infancy and adolescence. During these stages, all aspects of cognition develop in an integrated fashion, changing in a similar way at about the same time.

Piaget's **sensorimotor stage** spans the first two years of life. Piaget believed that infants and toddlers "think" with their eyes, ears, hands, and other sensorimotor equipment. They cannot yet carry out many activities inside their heads. But by the end of toddlerhood, children can solve everyday practical problems and represent their experiences in speech, gesture, and play. To appreciate Piaget's view of how these vast changes take place, let's consider some important concepts.

Piaget's Ideas About Cognitive Change

According to Piaget, specific psychological structures—organized ways of making sense of experience called **schemes**—change with age. At first, schemes are sensorimotor action patterns. For example, at 6 months, Timmy dropped objects in a fairly rigid way, simply letting go of a rattle or teething ring and watching with interest. By 18 months, his "dropping scheme" had become deliberate and creative. In tossing objects down the basement stairs, he threw some in the air, bounced others off walls, released some gently and others forcefully. Soon, instead of just acting on objects, he will show evidence of thinking before he acts. For Piaget, this change marks the transition from sensorimotor to preoperational thought.

In Piaget's theory, two processes, *adaptation* and *organization,* account for changes in schemes.

Adaptation. The next time you have a chance, notice how infants and toddlers tirelessly repeat actions that lead to interesting effects. **Adaptation** involves building schemes through direct interaction with the environment. It consists of two complementary activities, *assimilation* and *accommodation.* During **assimilation,** we use our current schemes to interpret the external world. For example, when Timmy dropped objects, he was assimilating them to his sensorimotor "dropping

▶ In Piaget's theory, first schemes are sensorimotor action patterns. As this 12-month-old experiments with his dropping scheme, his behavior becomes more deliberate and varied.

scheme." In **accommodation,** we create new schemes or adjust old ones after noticing that our current ways of thinking do not capture the environment completely. When Timmy dropped objects in different ways, he modified his dropping scheme to take account of the varied properties of objects.

According to Piaget, the balance between assimilation and accommodation varies over time. When children are not changing much, they assimilate more than they accommodate—a steady, comfortable state that Piaget called cognitive *equilibrium.* During times of rapid cognitive change, children are in a state of *disequilibrium,* or cognitive discomfort. Realizing that new information does not match their current schemes, they shift from assimilation to accommodation. After modifying their schemes, they move back toward assimilation, exercising their newly changed structures until they are ready to be modified again.

Each time this back-and-forth movement between equilibrium and disequilibrium occurs, more effective schemes are produced. Because the times of greatest accommodation are the earliest ones, the sensorimotor stage is Piaget's most complex period of development.

Organization. Schemes also change through **organization,** a process that occurs internally, apart from direct contact with the environment. Once children form new schemes, they rearrange them, linking them with other schemes to create a strongly interconnected cognitive system. For example, eventually Timmy will relate "dropping" to "throwing" and to his developing understanding of "nearness" and "farness." According to Piaget, schemes truly reach equilibrium when they become part of a broad network of structures that can be jointly applied to the surrounding world (Piaget, 1936/1952).

In the following sections, we will first describe infant development as Piaget saw it, noting research that supports his observations. Then we will consider evidence demonstrating that in some ways, babies' cognitive competence is more advanced than Piaget believed.

The Sensorimotor Stage

The difference between the newborn baby and the 2-year-old child is so vast that Piaget divided the sensorimotor stage into six substages, summarized in Table 5.1. Piaget based this sequence on a

TABLE 5.1
Summary of Piaget's Sensorimotor Stage

SENSORIMOTOR SUBSTAGE	TYPICAL ADAPTIVE BEHAVIORS
1. Reflexive schemes (birth–1 month)	Newborn reflexes (see Chapter 3, pages 94, 96)
2. Primary circular reactions (1–4 months)	Simple motor habits centered around the infant's own body; limited anticipation of events
3. Secondary circular reactions (4–8 months)	Actions aimed at repeating interesting effects in the surrounding world; imitation of familiar behaviors
4. Coordination of secondary circular reactions (8–12 months)	Intentional, or goal-directed, behavior; ability to find a hidden object in the first location in which it is hidden (object permanence); improved anticipation of events; imitation of behaviors slightly different from those the infant usually performs
5. Tertiary circular reactions (12–18 months)	Exploration of the properties of objects by acting on them in novel ways; imitation of novel behaviors; ability to search in several locations for a hidden object (accurate A–B search)
6. Mental representation (18 months–2 years)	Internal depictions of objects and events, as indicated by sudden solutions to problems; ability to find an object that has been moved while out of sight (invisible displacement); deferred imitation; and make-believe play

very small sample: observations of his son and two daughters as he presented them with everyday problems (such as hidden objects) that helped reveal their understanding of the world.

According to Piaget, at birth infants know so little that they cannot explore purposefully. The **circular reaction** provides a special means of adapting their first schemes. It involves stumbling onto a new experience caused by the baby's own motor activity. The reaction is "circular" because, as the infant tries to repeat the event again and again, a sensorimotor response that first occurred by chance strengthens into a new scheme. Consider Caitlin, who at age 2 months accidentally made a smacking sound after a feeding. Intrigued, she tried to repeat it until, after a few days, she became quite expert at smacking her lips.

Infants' difficulty inhibiting new and interesting behaviors may underlie the circular reaction. This immaturity in inhibition seems to be adaptive, helping to ensure that new skills will not be interrupted before they strengthen (Carey & Markman, 1999). Piaget considered revisions in the circular reaction so important that, as Table 5.1 shows, he named the sensorimotor substages after them.

© LAURA DWIGHT PHOTOGRAPHY

▶ When this 4-month-old accidentally hits a toy hung in front of her, she repeatedly attempts to recapture this interesting effect. In the process, she forms a new "hitting scheme."

Repeating Chance Behaviors. Piaget saw newborn reflexes as the building blocks of sensorimotor intelligence. In Substage 1, babies suck, grasp, and look in much the same way, no matter what experiences they encounter. Around 1 month, as they enter Substage 2, infants start to gain voluntary control over their actions through the *primary circular reaction,* by repeating chance behaviors largely motivated by basic needs. This leads to some simple motor habits, such as sucking their fist or thumb. Babies also begin to vary their behavior in response to environmental demands. For example, they open their mouths differently for a nipple than for a spoon. And they start to anticipate events. When hungry, 3-month-old Timmy would stop crying as soon as Vanessa entered the room—a signal that feeding time was near.

During Substage 3, from 4 to 8 months, infants sit up and reach for and manipulate objects. These motor attainments strengthen the *secondary circular reaction,* through which babies try to repeat interesting events in the surrounding environment that are caused by their own actions. For example, 4-month-old Caitlin accidentally knocked a toy hung in front of her, producing a swinging motion. Over the next three days, Caitlin tried to repeat this effect, gradually forming a new "hitting" scheme.

Intentional Behavior. In Substage 4, 8- to 12-month-olds combine schemes into new, more complex action sequences. As a result, actions that lead to new schemes no longer have a random, hit-or-miss quality—*accidentally* bringing the thumb to the mouth or *happening* to hit the toy. Instead, 8- to 12-month-olds can engage in **intentional, or goal-directed, behavior,** coordinating schemes deliberately to solve simple problems. Consider Piaget's famous object-hiding task, in which he shows the baby an attractive toy and then hides it behind his hand or under a cover. Infants of this substage can find the object by coordinating two schemes—"pushing" aside the obstacle and "grasping" the toy. Piaget regarded these *means–end action sequences* as the foundation for all problem solving.

Retrieving hidden objects reveals that infants have begun to master **object permanence,** the understanding that objects continue to exist when out of sight. But this awareness is not yet complete. Babies still make the *A-not-B search error:* If they reach several times for an object at a first hiding place (A), then see it moved to a second (B), they still search for it in the first hiding place (A).

© LAURA DWIGHT PHOTOGRAPHY

▶ To find the toy hidden inside the pot, a 10-month-old engages in intentional, goal-directed behavior—the basis for all problem solving.

Infants in Substage 4, who can better anticipate events, sometimes use their capacity for intentional behavior to try to change those events. At

10 months, Timmy crawled after Vanessa when she put on her coat, whimpering to keep her from leaving. Also, babies can now imitate behaviors slightly different from those they usually perform. After watching someone else, they try to stir with a spoon or push a toy car (Piaget, 1945/1951).

In Substage 5, from 12 to 18 months, the *tertiary circular reaction,* in which toddlers repeat behaviors with variation, emerges. Recall how Timmy dropped objects over the basement steps, trying first this action, then that, then another. This deliberately exploratory approach makes 12- to 18-month-olds better problem solvers. For example, Grace figured out how to fit a shape through a hole in a container by turning and twisting it until it fell through and how to use a stick to get toys that were out of reach. According to Piaget, the capacity to experiment leads toddlers to look for a hidden toy in several locations, displaying an accurate A–B search. Their more flexible action patterns also permit them to imitate many more behaviors—stacking blocks, scribbling on paper, and making funny faces.

© LAURA DWIGHT PHOTOGRAPHY

▶ The capacity for mental representation enables this 20-month-old to engage in first acts of make-believe.

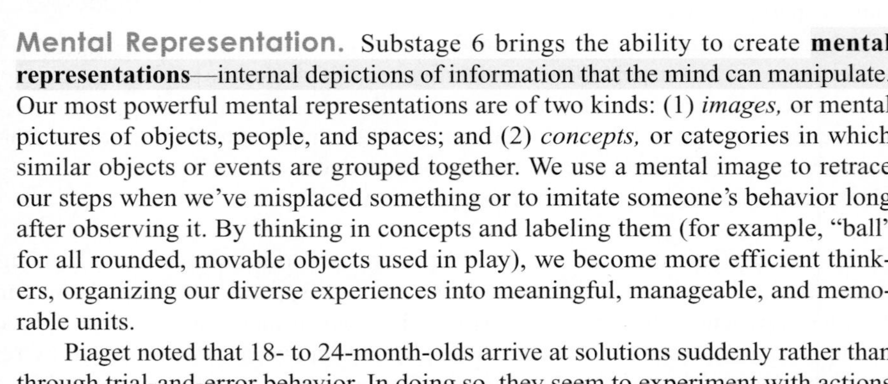

Mental Representation. Substage 6 brings the ability to create **mental representations**—internal depictions of information that the mind can manipulate. Our most powerful mental representations are of two kinds: (1) *images,* or mental pictures of objects, people, and spaces; and (2) *concepts,* or categories in which similar objects or events are grouped together. We use a mental image to retrace our steps when we've misplaced something or to imitate someone's behavior long after observing it. By thinking in concepts and labeling them (for example, "ball" for all rounded, movable objects used in play), we become more efficient thinkers, organizing our diverse experiences into meaningful, manageable, and memorable units.

Piaget noted that 18- to 24-month-olds arrive at solutions suddenly rather than through trial-and-error behavior. In doing so, they seem to experiment with actions inside their heads—evidence that they can mentally represent their experiences. For example, at 19 months, Grace—after bumping her new push toy against a wall—paused for a moment as if to "think," and then immediately turned the toy in a new direction. Representation enables older toddlers to solve advanced object permanence problems involving *invisible displacement*—finding a toy moved while out of sight, such as into a small box while under a cover. It also permits **deferred imitation**—the ability to remember and copy the behavior of models who are not present. And it makes possible **make-believe play,** in which children act out everyday and imaginary activities. As the sensorimotor stage draws to a close, mental symbols have become major instruments of thinking.

Follow-Up Research on Infant Cognitive Development

Many studies suggest that infants display a wide array of understandings earlier than Piaget believed. Recall the operant conditioning research reviewed in Chapter 4, in which newborns sucked vigorously on a nipple to gain access to interesting sights and sounds. This behavior, which closely resembles Piaget's secondary circular reaction, shows that infants explore and control the external world long before 4 to 8 months. In fact, they do so as soon as they are born.

To discover what infants know about hidden objects and other aspects of physical reality, researchers often use the **violation-of-expectation method.** They may *habituate* babies to a physical event (expose them to the event until their looking declines) to familiarize them with a situation in which their knowledge will be tested. Or they may simply show babies an *expected event* (one that is consistent with reality) and an *unexpected event* (a variation of the first event that violates reality). Heightened attention to the unexpected event suggests that the infant is "surprised" by a deviation from physical reality and, therefore, is aware of that aspect of the physical world.

The violation-of-expectation method is controversial. Some researchers believe that it indicates limited, implicit (nonconscious) awareness of physical events—not the full-blown, conscious understanding that was Piaget's focus in requiring infants to act on their surroundings, as in searching for hidden objects (Campos et al., 2008). Others maintain that the method reveals only babies' perceptual preference for novelty, not their knowledge of the physical world (Bremner, 2010; Bremner, Slater, & Johnson, 2015). Let's examine this debate in light of recent evidence.

Object Permanence. In a series of studies using the violation-of-expectation method, Renée Baillargeon and her collaborators claimed to have found evidence for object permanence in the first few months of life. Figure 5.1 explains and illustrates one of these studies, in which infants exposed to both an expected and an unexpected object-hiding event looked longer at the unexpected event (Aguiar & Baillargeon, 2002; Baillargeon & DeVos, 1991). Additional violation-of-expectation studies yielded similar results, indicating that infants look longer at a wide variety of unexpected events involving hidden objects (Wang, Baillargeon, & Paterson, 2005).

Another type of looking behavior suggests that young infants are aware that objects persist when out of view. Four- and 5-month-olds will track a ball's path of movement as it disappears and reappears from behind a barrier, even gazing ahead to where they expect it to emerge. As further support for such awareness, 5- to 9-month-olds more often engaged in such predictive tracking when a ball viewed on a computer screen gradually rolled behind a barrier than when it disappeared instantaneously or imploded (rapidly decreased in size) at the barrier's edge (Bertenthal, Gredebäck, & Boyer, 2013; Bertenthal, Longo, & Kenny, 2007). With age, babies are more likely to fixate on the predicted place of the ball's reappearance and wait for it—evidence of an increasingly secure grasp of object permanence.

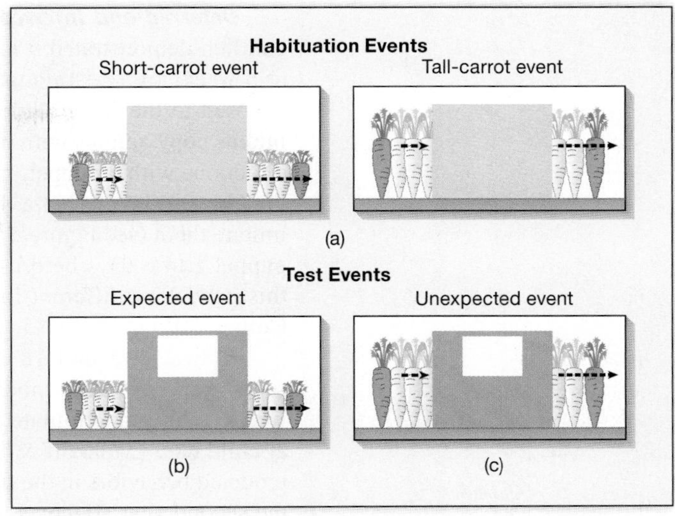

FIGURE 5.1 Testing young infants for understanding of object permanence using the violation-of-expectation method. (a) First, infants were habituated to two events: a short carrot and a tall carrot moving behind a yellow screen, on alternate trials. Next, the researchers presented two test events. The color of the screen was changed to help infants notice its window. (b) In the *expected event,* the carrot shorter than the window's lower edge moved behind the blue screen and reappeared on the other side. (c) In the *unexpected event,* the carrot taller than the window's lower edge moved behind the screen and did not appear in the window, but then emerged intact on the other side. Infants as young as 2½ to 3½ months looked longer at the *unexpected event,* suggesting that they had some understanding of object permanence. (Adapted from R. Baillargeon & J. DeVos, 1991, "Object Permanence in Young Infants: Further Evidence," *Child Development, 62,* p. 1230. © 1991, John Wiley and Sons. Reproduced with permission of John Wiley & Sons Ltd. conveyed through Copyright Clearance Center, Inc.)

If young infants do have some notion of object permanence, how do we explain Piaget's finding that even babies capable of reaching do not try to search for hidden objects before 8 months of age? Compared with looking reactions in violation-of-expectation tasks, searching for hidden objects is far more cognitively demanding: The baby must figure out where the hidden object is. Consistent with this idea, infants solve some object-hiding tasks before others. For example, 10-month-olds search for an object placed on a table and covered by a cloth before they search for an object that a hand deposits under a cloth (Moore & Meltzoff, 2008). Experience with partially hidden objects—common in infants' everyday lives—may help them grasp that a completely covered object has not been replaced by the cloth but, rather, continues to exist and can be retrieved.

Once 8- to 12-month-olds search for hidden objects, they make the A-not-B search error. Some research suggests that they do not attend closely when the hiding place moves from A to B (Ruffman & Langman, 2002). A more comprehensive explanation is that a complex, dynamic system of factors—having built a habit of reaching toward A, continuing to look at A, having the hiding place at B appear similar to the one at A, and maintaining a constant body posture—increases the chances that the baby will make the A-not-B search error. Disrupting any one of these factors increases 10-month-olds' accurate searching at B (Thelen et al., 2001). In addition, older infants are still perfecting reaching and grasping (Berger, 2010). If these motor skills are challenging, babies have little attention left to focus on inhibiting their habitual reach toward A.

LOOK AND LISTEN

Using an attractive toy and cloth, try several object-hiding tasks with 8- to 18-month-olds. Is their searching behavior consistent with research findings?

In sum, infants' understanding of object permanence becomes increasingly complex with age: They must distinguish the object from the barrier concealing it, keep track of the object's whereabouts, and use this knowledge to obtain the object (Bremner, Slater, & Johnson, 2015). Success at object search tasks coincides with rapid development of the frontal lobes of the cerebral cortex (Bell, 1998). Also crucial are a wide variety of experiences perceiving, acting on, and remembering objects.

Mental Representation. In Piaget's theory, before about 18 months of age, infants are unable to mentally represent experience. Yet 8- to 10-month-olds' ability to recall the location of hidden objects after delays of more than a minute, and 14-month-olds' recall after delays of a day or more, indicate that babies construct mental representations of objects and their whereabouts (McDonough, 1999; Moore & Meltzoff, 2004). And in studies of deferred imitation and problem solving, representational thought is evident even earlier.

Deferred and Inferred Imitation. Piaget studied deferred imitation by noting when his three children demonstrated it in their everyday behavior. Laboratory research suggests that it is present at 6 weeks of age! Infants who watched an unfamiliar adult's facial expression imitated it when exposed to the same adult the next day (Meltzoff & Moore, 1994). As motor capacities improve, infants copy actions with objects. In one study, an adult showed 6- and 9-month-olds a novel series of actions with a puppet: taking its glove off, shaking the glove to ring a bell inside, and replacing the glove. When tested a day later, infants who had seen the novel actions were far more likely to imitate them (see Figure 5.2). And when the adult paired a second, motionless puppet with the first puppet 1 to 6 days before the demonstration, 6- to 9-month-olds generalized the novel actions to this new, very different-looking puppet (Barr, Marrott, & Rovee-Collier, 2003; Giles & Rovee-Collier, 2011).

Between 12 and 18 months, toddlers use deferred imitation to enrich their sensorimotor schemes. They retain modeled behaviors for at least several months, copy the actions of peers as well as adults, and imitate across a change in context—for example, enact at home a behavior seen at child care (Meltzoff & Williamson, 2010; Patel, Gaylord, & Fagen, 2013). The ability to recall modeled behaviors in the order they occurred—evident as early as 6 months—also strengthens over the second year (Bauer, Larkina, & Deocampo, 2011; Rovee-Collier & Cuevas, 2009). And when toddlers imitate in correct sequence, they remember more behaviors.

Older infants and toddlers even imitate rationally, by *inferring* others' intentions! They are more likely to imitate purposeful than arbitrary behaviors on objects (Thoermer et al., 2013). And they adapt their imitative acts to a model's goals. If 12-month-olds see an adult perform an unusual action for fun (make a toy dog enter a miniature house by jumping through the chimney, even though its door is wide open), they copy the behavior. But if the adult engages in the odd behavior because she *must* (makes the dog go through the chimney after first trying the door and finding it locked), 12-month-olds typically imitate the more efficient action (putting the dog through the door) (Schwier et al., 2006).

Between 14 and 18 months, toddlers become increasingly adept at imitating actions an adult *tries* to produce, even if these are not fully realized (Bellagamba, Camaioni, & Colonnesi, 2006; Olineck & Poulin-Dubois, 2009). On one occasion, Ginette attempted to pour some raisins into a bag but missed, spilling them. A moment later, Grace began dropping the raisins into the bag, indicating that she had inferred Ginette's goal.

FIGURE 5.2 Testing infants for deferred imitation. After researchers performed a novel series of actions with a puppet, this 6-month-old imitated the actions a day later: (a) removing the glove; (b) shaking the glove to ring a bell inside. With age, gains in recall are evident in deferred imitation of others' behaviors over longer delays.

Problem Solving. As Piaget indicated, around 7 to 8 months, infants develop intentional means–end action sequences that they use to solve simple problems, such as pulling on a cloth to obtain a toy resting on its far end (Willatts, 1999). Out of these explorations of object-to-object relations, the capacity for tool use in problem solving—flexibly manipulating an object as a means to a goal—emerges (Keen, 2011).

For example, 12-month-olds who were repeatedly presented with a spoon oriented so its handle pointed toward their preferred hand (usually the right) adapted their preferred-hand grip when the spoon's handle was presented in the opposite orientation (to the left). As a result, they succeeded in transporting food to their mouths most of the time (McCarty & Keen, 2005). With age, babies increasingly adjusted their grip to fit the spoon's orientation in advance, planning ahead for what they wanted to do with the tool.

By 10 to 12 months, infants can *solve problems by analogy*—apply a solution strategy from one problem to other relevant problems. In one study, babies of this age were given three similar problems, each requiring them to overcome a barrier, grasp a string, and pull it to get an attractive toy. The problems differed in many aspects of their superficial features—texture and color of the string, barrier, and floor mat and type of toy (horse, doll, or car). For the first problem, the parent demonstrated the solution and encouraged the infant to imitate (Chen, Sanchez, & Campbell, 1997). Babies obtained the toy more readily with each additional problem.

These findings suggest that at the end of the first year, infants form flexible mental representations of how to use tools to get objects. They have some ability to move beyond trial-and-error experimentation, represent a solution mentally, and use it in new contexts.

Symbolic Understanding. One of the most momentous early attainments is the realization that words can be used to cue mental images of things not physically present—a symbolic capacity called **displaced reference** that emerges around the first birthday. It greatly enhances toddlers' capacity to learn about the world through communicating with others. Observations of 12- to 13-month-olds reveal that they respond to the label of an absent toy by looking at and gesturing toward the spot where it usually rests (Saylor, 2004). As memory and vocabulary improve, skill at displaced reference expands.

But at first, toddlers have difficulty using language to acquire new information about an absent object—an ability that is essential to learn from symbols. In one study, an adult taught 19- and 22-month-olds a name for a stuffed animal—"Lucy" for a frog. Then, with the frog out of sight, each toddler was told that some water had spilled, so "Lucy's all wet!" Finally, the adult showed the toddler three stuffed animals—a wet frog, a dry frog, and a pig—and said, "Get Lucy!" (Ganea et al., 2007). Although all the children remembered that Lucy was a frog, only the 22-month-olds identified the wet frog as Lucy. This capacity to use language as a flexible symbolic tool—to modify and enrich existing mental representations—improves into the preschool years.

A beginning awareness of the symbolic function of pictures also emerges in the first year, strengthening in the second. By 9 months, the majority of infants touch, rub, or pat a color photo of an object but rarely try to grasp it (Ziemer, Plumert, & Pick, 2012). These behaviors suggest that 9-month-olds do not mistake a picture for the real thing, though they may not yet comprehend it as a symbol. By the middle of the second year toddlers clearly treat pictures symbolically, as long as pictures strongly resemble real objects. After hearing a novel label ("blicket") applied to a color photo of an unfamiliar object, most 15- to 24-month-olds—when presented with both the real object and its picture and asked to indicate the "blicket"—gave a symbolic response (Ganea et al., 2009). They selected either the real object or both the object and its picture, not the picture alone.

▶ A 17-month-old points to a picture in a book, revealing her beginning awareness of the symbolic function of pictures. But pictures must be highly realistic for toddlers to treat them symbolically.

By the middle of the second year, toddlers often use pictures as vehicles for communicating with others and acquiring new knowledge. They point to, name, and talk about pictures, and they can apply something learned from a

SOCIAL ISSUES

Baby Learning from Screen Media: The Video Deficit Effect

© UK STOCK IMAGES LTD/ALAMY

▶ A 2-year-old looks puzzled by a video image. Perhaps she has difficulty grasping its meaning because onscreen characters do not converse with her directly, as adults in real life do.

Children first become TV and video viewers in early infancy, as they are exposed to programs watched by parents and older siblings or to ones specially aimed at baby viewers. U.S. parents report that 50 percent of 2-month-olds watch TV and videos, a figure that rises to 90 percent by 2 years of age. Smart phone and tablet use by children under age 2, who often view videos on these devices, is similar. Average screen time increases from 55 minutes per day at 6 months to just under 1½ hours per day at age 2 (Anand et al., 2014; Cespedes et al., 2014; Kabali et al., 2015). Although parents assume that babies learn from videos, research indicates that babies cannot take full advantage of them.

Initially, infants respond to videos of people as if viewing people directly—smiling, moving their arms and legs, and (by 6 months) imitating actions of a televised adult (Barr, Muentener, & Garcia, 2007). But when shown videos of attractive toys, 9-month-olds touch and grab at the screen, suggesting that they confuse the images with the real thing. By the middle of the second year, manual exploration declines in favor of pointing at the images (Pierroutsakos & Troseth, 2003). Nevertheless, toddlers have difficulty applying what they see on video to real situations.

In a series of studies, some 2-year-olds watched through a window while a live adult hid an object in an adjoining room, while others watched the same event on a video screen. Children in the direct viewing condition retrieved the toy easily; those in the video condition had difficulty (Troseth, 2003). This **video deficit effect**—poorer performance after viewing a video than a live demonstration—has also been found for 2-year-olds' deferred imitation, word learning, and means–end problem solving (Bellagamba et al., 2012; Hayne, Herbert, & Simcock, 2003; Krcmar, Grela, & Linn, 2007).

Toddlers seem to discount information on video as relevant to their everyday experiences because people do not look at and converse with them directly or establish a shared focus on objects, as their caregivers do. In one study, researchers gave some 2-year-olds an interactive video experience (using a two-way, closed-circuit video system). An adult on video interacted with the child for five minutes—calling the child by name, talking about the child's siblings and pets, waiting for the child to respond, and playing interactive games (Troseth, Saylor, & Archer, 2006). Compared with 2-year-olds who viewed the same adult in a noninteractive video, those in the interactive condition were far more successful in using a verbal cue from a person on video to retrieve a toy.

Around age 2½, the video deficit effect declines. The American Academy of Pediatrics (2016a) recommends against screen media exposure before 1½ to 2 years of age and, between 2 and 5 years, limiting it to 1 hour per day with parental coviewing. In support of this advice, amount of viewing is negatively related to toddlers' language progress (Zimmerman, Christakis, & Meltzoff, 2007). And 1- to 3-year-old heavy viewers tend to have attention, memory, and reading difficulties in the early school years (Christakis et al., 2004; Zimmerman & Christakis, 2005).

When toddlers do watch TV and video, it is likely to work best as a teaching tool when it is rich in social cues (Lauricella, Gola, & Calvert, 2011). These include use of familiar characters and close-ups in which the character looks directly at the camera, addresses questions to viewers, and pauses to invite a response.

book with realistic-looking pictures to real objects, and vice versa (Ganea, Ma, & DeLoache, 2011; Simcock, Garrity, & Barr, 2011).

Picture-rich environments in which caregivers frequently direct babies' attention to the link between pictures and real objects promote pictorial understanding. In a study carried out in a village community in Tanzania, Africa, where children receive no exposure to pictures before school entry, an adult taught 1½-year-olds a new name for an unfamiliar object during picture-book interaction (Walker, Walker, & Ganea, 2012). When later asked to pick the named object from a set of real objects, not until 3 years of age did the Tanzanian children perform as well as U.S. 15-month-olds.

How do infants and toddlers interpret another ever-present, pictorial medium—video? Refer to the Social Issues box above to find out.

Evaluation of the Sensorimotor Stage

Table 5.2 summarizes the remarkable cognitive attainments we have just considered. Compare this table with Piaget's description of the sensorimotor substages in Table 5.1 on page 140. You will see that infants anticipate events, actively search for hidden objects, master the A–B object search, flexibly vary their sensorimotor schemes, engage in make-believe play, and treat pictures and video images symbolically within Piaget's time frame. Yet other capacities—including secondary circular reactions, understanding of object properties, first signs of object permanence, deferred imitation, problem solving by analogy, and displaced reference of words—emerge earlier than Piaget expected.

These findings confirm that the cognitive attainments of infancy and toddlerhood do not develop together in the neat, stepwise fashion that Piaget assumed. They also show that infants comprehend a great deal before they are capable of the motor behaviors that Piaget assumed led to those understandings. How can we account for babies' amazing cognitive accomplishments?

Alternative Explanations. Unlike Piaget, who thought young babies construct all mental representations out of sensorimotor activity, most researchers now believe that infants have some built-in cognitive equipment for making sense of experience. But intense disagreement exists over the extent of this initial understanding. Researchers who lack confidence in the violation-of-expectation method argue that babies' cognitive starting point is limited (Bremner, Slater, & Johnson, 2015; Cohen, 2010; Kagan, 2013b). For example, some believe that newborns begin life with a set of biases for attending to certain information and with general-purpose learning procedures—such as powerful techniques for analyzing complex perceptual information (Bahrick, 2010; MacWhinney, 2015; Rakison, 2010). Together, these capacities enable infants to construct a wide variety of schemes.

Others, convinced by violation-of-expectation findings, believe that infants start out with impressive understandings. According to this **core knowledge perspective,** babies are born with a set of innate knowledge systems, or *core domains of thought.* Each of these prewired understandings permits a ready grasp of new, related information and therefore supports early, rapid development (Carey, 2009; Leslie, 2004; Spelke, 2016; Spelke & Kinzler, 2013). Core knowledge theorists argue that infants could not make sense of the complex stimulation around them without having been genetically "set up" in the course of evolution to comprehend its crucial aspects.

Researchers have conducted many studies of infants' *physical knowledge,* including object permanence, object solidity (that one object cannot move through another), and gravity (that an object will fall without support). Violation-of-expectation findings suggest that in the first few months, infants have some awareness of all these basic object properties and quickly build on this knowledge (Baillargeon et al., 2009, 2011). Core knowledge theorists also assume that an inherited foundation

TABLE 5.2
Some Cognitive Attainments of Infancy and Toddlerhood

AGE	COGNITIVE ATTAINMENTS
Birth–1 month	Secondary circular reactions using limited motor skills, such as sucking a nipple to gain access to interesting sights and sounds
1–4 months	Awareness of object permanence, object solidity, and gravity, as suggested by violation-of-expectation findings; deferred imitation of an adult's facial expression over a short delay (1 day)
4–8 months	Improved knowledge of object properties and basic numerical knowledge, as suggested by violation-of-expectation findings; deferred imitation of an adult's novel actions on objects over a short delay (1 to 3 days)
8–12 months	Ability to search for a hidden object; ability to solve simple problems by analogy to a previous problem
12–18 months	Ability to search for a hidden object when it is moved from one location to another (accurate A–B search); deferred imitation of an adult's novel actions on objects after long delays (at least several months) and across a change in situation (from child care to home); rational imitation, inferring the model's intentions; displaced reference of words
18 months–2 years	Ability to find an object moved while out of sight (invisible displacement); deferred imitation of actions an adult tries to produce, even if these are not fully realized; deferred imitation of everyday behaviors in make-believe play; strengthening awareness of pictures and video as symbols of reality

of *linguistic knowledge* enables swift language acquisition in early childhood—a possibility we will consider later in this chapter. Furthermore, these theorists argue, infants' early orientation toward people initiates rapid development of *psychological knowledge*—in particular, understanding of mental states, such as intentions, emotions, desires, and beliefs.

Research even suggests that infants have basic *numerical knowledge.* In the best-known study, 5-month-olds saw a screen raised to hide a single toy animal and then watched a hand place a second toy behind the screen. Finally, the screen was removed to reveal either one or two toys. If infants kept track of the two objects (requiring them to add one object to another), then they should look longer at the unexpected, one-toy display—which is what they did (see Figure 5.3) (Wynn, 1992). These findings and others suggest that babies can discriminate quantities up to three and use that knowledge to perform simple arithmetic—both addition and subtraction (in which two objects are covered and one object is removed) (Kobayashi, Hiraki, & Hasegawa, 2005; Walden et al., 2007; Wynn, Bloom, & Chiang, 2002).

Additional evidence suggests that 6-month-olds can distinguish among large sets of items, as long as the difference between those sets is very great—at least a factor of two. For example, they can tell the difference between 8 and 16 dots but not between 8 and 12 (Lipton & Spelke, 2003). Furthermore, 6-month-olds' factor-of-two discrimination capacity is similar across quantitative dimensions: It also applies to the area of spatial surfaces and the duration of tones (Brannon, Lutz, & Cordes, 2006; Lipton & Spelke, 2003; VanMarle & Wynn, 2006). Consequently, some researchers believe that in addition to making small-number discriminations, infants can represent approximate large-number values and that their ability to do so reflects a more general quantitative understanding.

But as with other violation-of-expectation results, this evidence is controversial. Skeptics question whether other aspects of object displays, rather than numerical sensitivity, are responsible for the findings (Bremner, Slater, & Johnson, 2015; Clearfield & Westfahl, 2006). Indisputable evidence for built-in core knowledge requires that it be demonstrated at birth or close to it—in the absence of relevant opportunities to learn. Yet findings on newborns' ability to process small and large numerical values are inconsistent (Coubart et al., 2014; Izard et al., 2009). And critics point

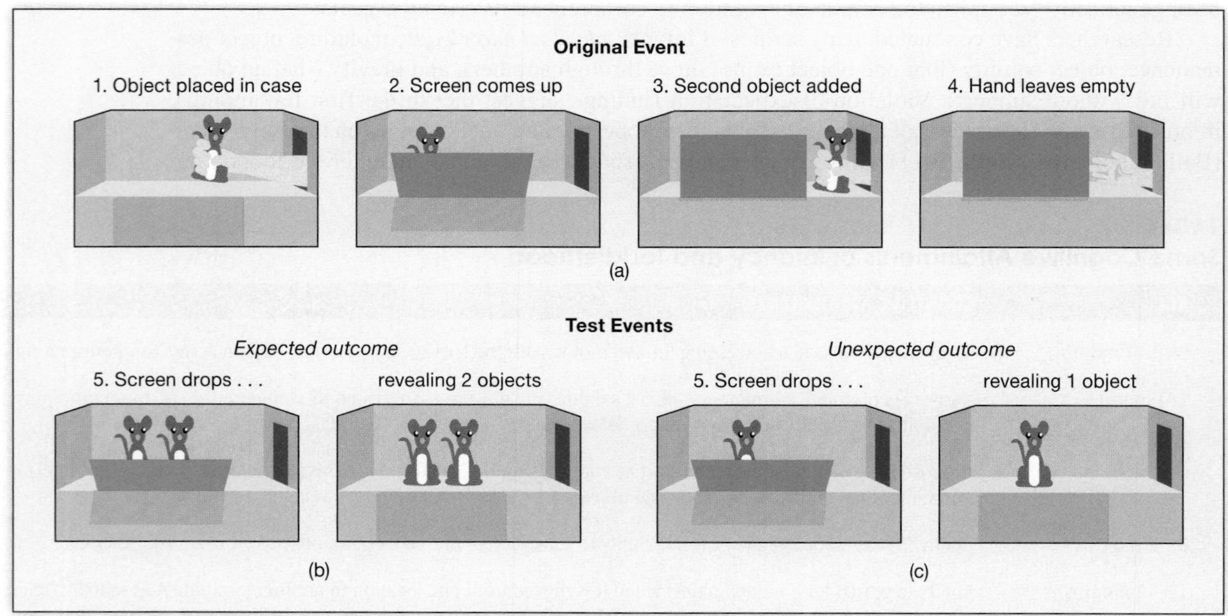

FIGURE 5.3 Testing infants for basic number concepts. (a) First, infants saw a screen raised in front of a toy animal. Then an identical toy was added behind the screen. Next, the researchers presented two outcomes. (b) In the *expected outcome,* the screen dropped to reveal two toy animals. (c) In the *unexpected outcome,* the screen dropped to reveal one toy animal. Five-month-olds shown the unexpected outcome looked longer than did 5-month-olds shown the expected outcome. The researchers concluded that infants can discriminate the quantities "one" and "two" and use that knowledge to perform simple addition: 1 + 1 = 2. A variation of this procedure suggested that 5-month-olds could also do simple subtraction: 2 – 1 = 1. (From K. Wynn, 1992, "Addition and Subtraction by Human Infants." *Nature, 358,* p. 749. © 1992 by Nature Publishing Group. Adapted with permission of Nature Publishing Group in the format "Republish in a book" via Copyright Clearance Center.)

out that claims for infants' number knowledge are surprising, in view of other research indicating that before 14 to 16 months, toddlers have difficulty making less-than and greater-than comparisons between small sets. Not until the preschool years do children add and subtract small sets correctly.

The core knowledge perspective, while emphasizing native endowment, acknowledges that experience is essential for children to extend this initial knowledge. But so far, it has said little about which experiences are most important in each core domain for advancing children's thinking. Despite these limitations, core knowledge investigators have sharpened the field's focus on clarifying the starting point for human cognition and on carefully tracking the changes that build on it.

Piaget's Legacy. Current research on infant cognition yields broad agreement on two issues. First, many cognitive changes of infancy are not abrupt and stagelike but gradual and continuous (Bjorklund, 2012). Second, rather than developing together, various aspects of infant cognition change unevenly because of the challenges posed by different types of tasks and infants' varying experiences with them. These ideas serve as the basis for another major approach to cognitive development—*information processing.*

Before turning to this alternative point of view, let's recognize Piaget's enormous contributions. Piaget's work inspired a wealth of research on infant cognition, including studies that challenged his theory. His observations also have been of great practical value. Teachers and caregivers continue to look to the sensorimotor stage for guidelines on how to create developmentally appropriate environments for infants and toddlers.

ASK YOURSELF

CONNECT Which of the capacities listed in Table 5.2 indicate that mental representation emerges earlier than Piaget believed?

APPLY Several times, after her father hid a teething biscuit under a red cup, 12-month-old Mimi retrieved it easily. Then Mimi's father hid the biscuit under a nearby yellow cup. Why did Mimi persist in searching for it under the red cup?

REFLECT What advice would you give the typical U.S. parent about permitting an infant or toddler to watch as much as 1 to 2 hours of TV or video per day? Explain.

Information Processing

5.4 Describe the information-processing view of cognitive development and the general structure of the information-processing system.

5.5 Describe changes in attention, memory, and categorization over the first two years.

5.6 Explain the strengths and limitations of the information-processing approach to early cognitive development.

Recall from Chapter 1 that information-processing researchers are not satisfied with general concepts, such as assimilation and accommodation, to describe how children think. Instead, they want to know exactly what individuals of different ages do when faced with a task or problem (Birney & Sternberg, 2011). Rather than providing a single, unified theory of cognitive development, they focus on many aspects of thinking—from attention, memory, and categorization skills to complex problem solving.

A General Model of Information Processing

Most information-processing researchers assume that we hold information in three parts of the mental system for processing: the *sensory register,* the *short-term memory store,* and the *long-term memory store* (see Figure 5.4 on page 150). As information flows through each, we can use *mental strategies* to operate on and transform it, increasing the chances that we will retain information, use it efficiently, and think flexibly, adapting it to changing circumstances. To understand this more clearly, let's look at each aspect of the mental system.

First, information enters the **sensory register,** where sights and sounds are represented directly and stored briefly. Look around you, and then close your eyes. An image of what you saw persists momentarily, but then it decays, or disappears, unless you use mental strategies to preserve it. For example, by *attending to* some information more carefully than to other information, you increase the chances that it will transfer to the next step of the information-processing system.

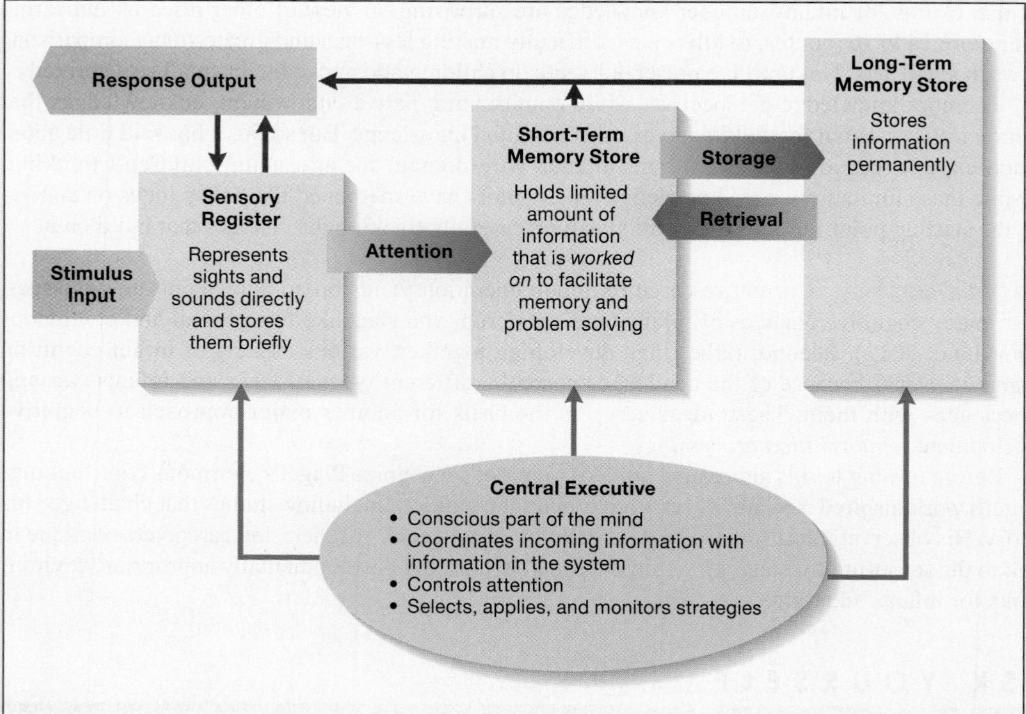

FIGURE 5.4 Model of the human information-processing system. Information flows through three parts of the mental system: the *sensory register,* the *short-term memory store,* and the *long-term memory store.* In each, mental strategies can be used to manipulate information, increasing the efficiency and flexibility of thinking and the chances that information will be retained. The *central executive* is the conscious, reflective part of the mental system. It coordinates incoming information with information already in the system, decides what to attend to, and oversees the use of strategies.

In the second part of the mind, the **short-term memory store,** we retain attended-to information briefly so we can actively "work on" it to reach our goals. One way of looking at the short-term store is in terms of its *basic capacity,* often referred to as *short-term memory:* how many pieces of information can be held at once for a few seconds. But most researchers endorse a contemporary view of the short-term store, which offers a more meaningful indicator of its capacity, called **working memory**—the number of items that can be briefly held in mind while also engaging in some effort to monitor or manipulate those items. Working memory can be thought of as a "mental workspace." From childhood on, researchers assess changes in its capacity by presenting individuals with lists of items (such as numerical digits or short sentences), asking them to work on the items (for example, repeat the digits backward or remember the final word of each sentence in correct order), and seeing how well they do.

The sensory register can take in a wide panorama of information. Short-term and working memory are far more restricted, though their capacity increases steadily from early childhood to early adulthood—on a verbatim digit-span task tapping short-term memory, from about two to seven items; and on working-memory tasks, from about two to five items (Cowan & Alloway, 2009). Still, individual differences are evident at all ages. By engaging in a variety of basic cognitive procedures, such as focusing attention on relevant items and repeating (rehearsing) them rapidly, we increase the chances that information will be retained and accessible to ongoing thinking.

To manage the cognitive system's activities, the **central executive** directs the flow of information, implementing the basic procedures just mentioned and also engaging in more sophisticated activities that enable complex, flexible thinking. For example, the central executive coordinates incoming information with information already in the system, and it selects, applies, and monitors strategies that facilitate memory storage, comprehension, reasoning, and problem solving. The central executive is the conscious, reflective part of our mental system.

The more effectively the central executive joins with working memory to process information, the better learned cognitive activities will be and the more *automatically* we can apply them. Consider the richness of your thinking while you automatically drive a car. **Automatic processes** are so well-learned that they require no space in working memory and, therefore, permit us to focus on other information while performing them. Furthermore, the more effectively we process information in working memory, the more likely it will transfer to the third, and largest, storage area—**long-term memory,** our permanent knowledge base, which has a massive capacity. In fact, we store so much in long-term memory that *retrieval*—getting information back from the system—can be problematic. To aid retrieval, we apply strategies, just as we do in memory storage. Information in long-term memory is *categorized* by its contents, much like a digital library reference system that enables us to retrieve items by following the same network of associations used to store them in the first place.

Information-processing researchers believe that several aspects of the cognitive system improve during childhood and adolescence: (1) the *basic capacity* of its stores, especially working memory; (2) the *speed* with which information is worked on; and (3) the *functioning of the central executive.* Together, these changes make possible more complex forms of thinking with age (Halford & Andrews, 2010).

Gains in working-memory capacity are due in part to brain development, but greater processing speed also contributes. Fast, fluent thinking frees working-memory resources to support storage and manipulation of additional information. Furthermore, researchers have become increasingly interested in studying the development of **executive function**—the diverse cognitive operations and strategies that enable us to achieve our goals in cognitively challenging situations. These include controlling attention by inhibiting impulses and irrelevant actions and by flexibly directing thought and behavior to suit the demands of a task; coordinating information in working memory; and planning—capacities governed by the prefrontal cortex and its elaborate connections to other brain regions (Chevalier, 2015). Measures of executive function predict important cognitive and social outcomes in childhood, adolescence, and adulthood, such as task persistence, self-control, academic achievement, and interpersonal acceptance (Carlson, Zelazo, & Faja, 2013; Müller & Kerns, 2015).

Gains in aspects of executive function are under way in the first two years. Dramatic strides will follow in childhood and adolescence.

Attention

Recall from Chapter 4 that around 2 to 3 months of age, infants visually explore objects and patterns more thoroughly (Frank, Amso, & Johnson, 2014). Besides attending to more aspects of the environment, infants gradually take in information more quickly. Preterm and newborn babies require a long time—about 3 to 4 minutes—to habituate and recover to novel visual stimuli. But by 4 or 5 months, they need as little as 5 to 10 seconds to take in a complex visual stimulus and recognize it as different from a previous one (Colombo, Kapa, & Curtindale, 2011).

Over the first year, infants mostly attend to novel and eye-catching events. In the second year, as toddlers become increasingly capable of intentional behavior (refer back to Piaget's Substage 4), attraction to novelty declines (but does not disappear) and *sustained attention* increases. A toddler who engages even in simple goal-directed behavior, such as stacking blocks or putting them in a container, must sustain attention to reach the goal (Ruff & Capozzoli, 2003). As plans and activities gradually become more complex, the duration of attention increases.

▶ By encouraging her toddler's goal-directed play, this mother promotes sustained attention.

Memory

Methods devised to assess infants' short-term memory, which require keeping in mind an increasingly longer sequence of very briefly presented visual stimuli, reveal that retention increases from one item at age 6 months to two to four items at 12 months (Oakes, Ross-Sheehy, & Luck, 2007).

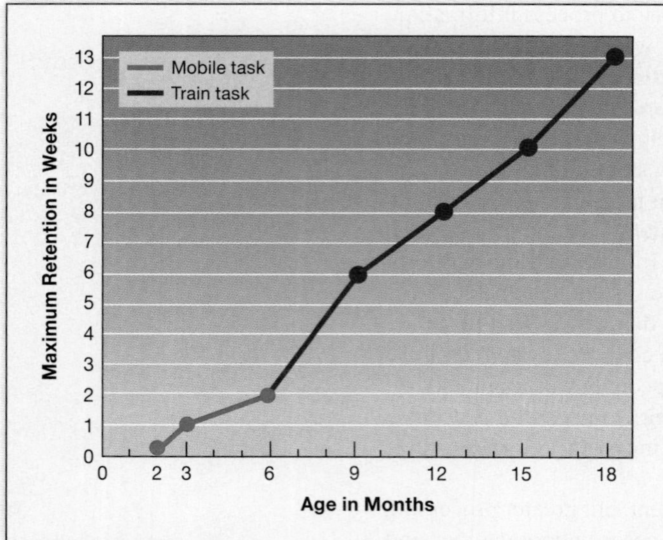

FIGURE 5.5 Increase in retention in two operant conditioning tasks from 2 to 18 months. Two- to 6-month-olds were trained to make a kicking response that turned a mobile. Six- to 18-month-olds were trained to press a lever that made a toy train move around a track. Six-month-olds learned both responses and retained them for an identical length of time, indicating that the tasks are comparable. Consequently, researchers could plot a single line tracking gains in retention from 2 to 18 months of age. The line shows that memory improves dramatically. (From C. Rovee-Collier & R. Barr, 2001, "Infant Learning and Memory," in G. Bremner & A. Fogel [Eds.], *Blackwell Handbook of Infant Development,* Oxford, UK: Blackwell, p. 150. © 2001, 2004 by Blackwell Publishing Ltd.)

Operant conditioning and habituation techniques, which grant babies more time to process information, provide windows into early long-term memory. Both methods show that retention of visual events improves greatly with age.

Using operant conditioning, researchers study infant memory by teaching 2- to 6-month-olds to move a mobile by kicking a foot tied to it with a long cord. Two-month-olds remember how to activate the mobile for 1 to 2 days after training, and 3-month-olds for one week. By 6 months, memory increases to two weeks (Rovee-Collier, 1999; Rovee-Collier & Bhatt, 1993). Around the middle of the first year, babies can manipulate switches or buttons to control stimulation. When 6- to 18-month-olds pressed a lever to make a toy train move around a track, duration of memory continued to increase with age; 13 weeks after training, 18-month-olds still remembered how to press the lever (see Figure 5.5) (Hartshorn et al., 1998).

Even after infants forget an operant response, they need only a brief prompt—an adult who shakes the mobile—to reinstate the memory (Hildreth & Rovee-Collier, 2002). And when 6-month-olds are given a chance to reactivate the response themselves for just a couple of minutes, their memory not only returns but extends dramatically, to about 17 weeks (Rovee-Collier & Cuevas, 2009). Perhaps permitting the baby to generate the previously learned behavior strengthens memory because it reexposes the child to more aspects of the original learning situation.

Habituation studies show that infants learn and retain a wide variety of information just by watching objects and events, sometimes for much longer time spans than in operant conditioning studies. Babies are especially captivated by the movements of objects and people. For example, 3- to 5-month-olds' retention of the unusual movements of objects (such as a metal nut swinging on the end of a string) persists for at least three months (Bahrick, Hernandez-Reif, & Pickens, 1997). By contrast, their memory for the faces of unfamiliar people and the features of objects is short-lived—only about 24 hours.

By 10 months, infants remember both novel actions and the features of objects involved in those actions equally well (Baumgartner & Oakes, 2011). This improved sensitivity to object appearance is fostered by infants' increasing ability to manipulate objects, which helps them learn about objects' observable properties.

So far, we have discussed only **recognition**—noticing when a stimulus is identical or similar to one previously experienced. It is the simplest form of memory: All babies have to do is indicate (by kicking, pressing a lever, or looking) whether a new stimulus is identical or similar to a previous one. **Recall** is more challenging because it involves remembering something not present. By the middle of the first year, infants are capable of recall, as indicated by their ability to find hidden objects and engage in deferred imitation. Recall, too, improves steadily with age (see pages 143–144).

The evidence as a whole indicates that infants' memory processing is remarkably similar to that of older children and adults: Babies have distinct short-term and long-term memories and display both recognition and recall. And they acquire information quickly and retain it over time, doing so more effectively with age (Howe, 2015). Yet a puzzling finding is that older children and adults no longer recall their earliest experiences! See the Biology and Environment box on the following page for a discussion of *infantile amnesia.*

Categorization

Even young infants can *categorize,* grouping similar objects and events into a single representation. Categorization reduces the enormous amount of new information infants encounter every day, helping them learn and remember.

Infantile Amnesia

If infants and toddlers recall many aspects of their everyday lives, how do we explain **infantile amnesia**—that most of us can retrieve few, if any, events that happened to us before age 2 to 3? The reason cannot be merely the passage of time because we can recall many personally meaningful one-time events from both the recent and the distant past: the day a sibling was born or a move to a new house—recollections known as **autobiographical memory.**

Several explanations of infantile amnesia exist. One theory credits brain development, pointing to the *hippocampus* (located just under the temporal lobes of the cerebral cortex), which plays a vital role in the formation of new memories. Though its overall structure is formed prenatally, the hippocampus continues to add new neurons well after birth. Integrating those neurons into existing neural circuits is believed to disrupt already stored early memories (Josselyn & Frankland, 2012). In support of this view, the decline in production of hippocampal neurons—in monkeys and rats as well as in humans—coincides with the ability to form stable, long-term memories of unique experiences.

Another conjecture is that older children and adults often use verbal means for storing information, whereas infants' and toddlers' memory processing is largely nonverbal—an incompatibility that may prevent long-term retention of early experiences. To test this idea, researchers sent two adults to the homes of 2- to 4-year-olds with an unusual toy that the children were likely to remember: the Magic Shrinking Machine, shown in Figure 5.6. One adult showed the child how, after inserting an object in an opening on top of the machine and turning a crank that activated flashing lights and musical sounds, the child could retrieve a smaller, identical object (discreetly dropped down a chute by the second adult) from behind a door on the front of the machine.

A day later, children's nonverbal memory—based on acting out the "shrinking" event and recognizing the "shrunken" objects in photos—was excellent. But children younger than age 3 had trouble describing features of the "shrinking" experience. Verbal recall increased sharply between ages 3 and 4, when infantile amnesia typically subsides (Simcock & Hayne, 2003). In a follow-up study, which assessed verbal recall 6 years later, only 19 percent—including just two children who had been younger than age 3—remembered the "shrinking" event (Jack, Simcock, & Hayne, 2012). Those who recalled were more likely to have conversed with a parent about the experience, which could have helped them gain verbal access to the memory.

These findings help reconcile infants' and toddlers' remarkable memory skills with infantile amnesia. During the first few years, children rely heavily on nonverbal memory techniques, such as visual images and motor actions. As language develops, their ability to use it to refer to preverbal memories requires support from adults. As children encode autobiographical events in verbal form, they use language-based cues to retrieve them, increasing the accessibility of these memories (Peterson, Warren, & Short, 2011).

Other evidence indicates that the advent of a clear self-image contributes to the end of infantile amnesia. For example, among children and adolescents, average age of earliest memory is around age 2 to 2½ (Howe, 2014; Tustin & Hayne, 2010). Though these recollections are sparse in information recalled, their timing coincides with the age at which toddlers display firmer self-awareness, reflected in pointing to themselves in photos and referring to themselves by name.

Very likely, both neurobiological change and social experience contribute to the decline of infantile amnesia. Brain development and adult–child interaction may jointly foster self-awareness, language, and improved memory, which enable children to talk with adults about significant past experiences (Howe, 2015). As a result, preschoolers begin to construct a long-lasting autobiographical narrative of their lives and enter into the history of their family and community.

(a)

(b)

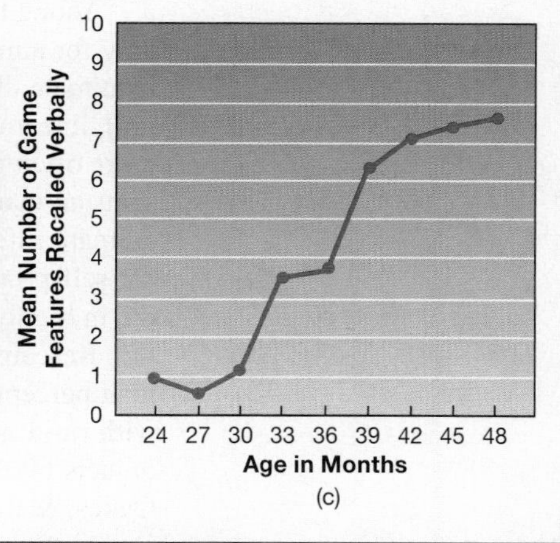

(c)

FIGURE 5.6 The Magic Shrinking Machine, used to test young children's verbal and nonverbal memory of an unusual event. After being shown how the machine worked, the child participated in selecting objects from a polka-dot bag, dropping them into the top of the machine (a), and turning a crank, which produced a "shrunken" object (b). When tested the next day, below 36 months, verbal recall was poor, based on the number of features recalled about the game (c). Recall improved between 36 and 48 months. (From G. Simcock & H. Hayne, 2003, "Age-Related Changes in Verbal and Nonverbal Memory During Early Childhood," *Developmental Psychology, 39,* pp. 807, 809. Copyright © 2003 by the American Psychological Association. *Photos:* Ross Coombes/Courtesy of Harlene Hayne.)

FIGURE 5.7 Investigating infant categorization using operant conditioning. Three-month-olds were taught to kick to move a mobile that was made of small blocks, all with the letter *A* on them. After a delay, kicking returned to a high level only if the babies were shown a mobile whose elements were labeled with the same form (the letter *A*). If the form was changed (from *A* to *2*), infants no longer kicked vigorously. While making the mobile move, the babies had grouped together its features. They associated the kicking response with the category *A* and, at later testing, distinguished it from the category *2*. (Bhatt, Rovee-Collier, & Weiner, 1994; Hayne, Rovee-Collier, & Perris, 1987.)

Creative variations of operant conditioning research with mobiles have been used to investigate infant categorization. One such study, of 3-month-olds, is described and illustrated in Figure 5.7. Similar investigations reveal that in the first few months, infants categorize stimuli on the basis of shape, size, and other physical properties (Wasserman & Rovee-Collier, 2001). By 6 months, they can categorize on the basis of two correlated features—for example, the shape and color of an alphabet letter (Bhatt et al., 2004). This ability to categorize using clusters of features prepares babies for acquiring many complex everyday categories.

Habituation has also been used to study infant categorization. Researchers show babies a series of pictures or toys belonging to one category and then see whether they recover to (look longer at) a picture that is not a member of the category or, in the case of toys, spend more time manipulating the out-of-category item. Findings reveal that by the second half of the first year, infants group familiar objects into an impressive array of categories—food items, furniture, birds, land animals, air animals, sea animals, plants, vehicles, kitchen utensils, and spatial location ("above" and "below," "on" and "in") (Bornstein, Arterberry, & Mash, 2010; Casasola & Park, 2013; Sloutsky, 2015). Besides organizing the physical world, infants of this age categorize their emotional and social worlds. They sort people and their voices by gender and age, distinguish emotional expressions, separate people's natural actions (walking) from other motions, and expect people (but not inanimate objects) to move spontaneously (Spelke, Phillips, & Woodward, 1995; see also Chapter 4, pages 132, 133).

Babies' earliest categories are based on similar overall appearance or prominent object part: legs for animals, wheels for vehicles. But as infants approach their first birthday, more categories appear to be based on subtle sets of features (Mandler, 2004; Quinn, 2008). Older infants can even make categorical distinctions when the perceptual contrast between two categories is minimal (birds versus airplanes).

Toddlers begin to categorize flexibly: When 14-month-olds are given four balls and four blocks, some made of soft rubber and some of rigid plastic, their sequence of object touching reveals that after classifying by shape, they can switch to classifying by material (soft versus hard) if an adult calls their attention to the new basis for grouping (Ellis & Oakes, 2006).

Young toddlers' play behaviors reveal that they know certain actions (drinking) are appropriate only for animals, not inanimate objects. By the end of the second year, their grasp of the animate–inanimate distinction expands. Nonlinear motions are typical of animates (a person or a dog jumping), linear motions of inanimates (a car or a table pushed along a surface). At 18 months, toddlers more often imitate a nonlinear motion with a toy that has animate-like parts (legs), even if it represents an inanimate (a bed). At 22 months, toddlers imitate a nonlinear motion only with toys in the animate category (a cat but not a bed) (Rakison, 2005). They seem to realize that whereas animates are self-propelled and therefore have varied paths of movement, inanimates move only when acted on, in highly restricted ways.

Researchers disagree on how toddlers gradually shift from categorizing on the basis of prominent perceptual features (objects with flapping wings and feathers belong to one category; objects with rigid wings and a smooth surface to another) to categorizing on a conceptual basis, grouping objects by their common function or behavior (birds versus airplanes, dogs versus cats) (Madole, Oakes, & Rakison, 2011; Mandler, 2004; Träuble & Pauen, 2011). But all acknowledge that exploration of objects and expanding knowledge of the world contribute. In addition, adult labeling of a set of objects with a consistently applied word—"Look at the car!" "Do you see the car?"—calls babies' attention to commonalities among objects, fostering categorization as early as 3 to 4 months of age (Althus & Plunkett, 2016; Ferry, Hespos, & Waxman, 2010). Toddlers' vocabulary growth, in turn, promotes categorization (Cohen & Brunt, 2009).

Evaluation of Information-Processing Findings

The information-processing perspective underscores the continuity of human thinking from infancy into adult life. Though infants' and toddlers' thinking is far from proficient, they think in ways that are remarkably similar to our own thinking. And their capacity to recall events and to categorize stimuli attests, once again, to their ability to mentally represent their experiences.

Information-processing research has contributed greatly to our view of infants and toddlers as sophisticated cognitive beings. But its central strength—analyzing cognition into its components, such as perception, attention, memory, and categorization—is also its greatest drawback: difficulty putting these components back together into a comprehensive theory.

One approach to overcoming this weakness has been to combine Piaget's theory with the information-processing approach, an effort we will explore in Chapter 9. A more recent trend has been the application of a *dynamic systems view* to early cognition. In this approach, researchers analyze each cognitive attainment to see how it results from a complex system of prior accomplishments and the child's current goals (Spencer, Perone, & Buss, 2011; Thelen & Smith, 2006). Once these ideas are fully tested, they may move the field closer to a more powerful view of how the minds of infants and children develop.

The Social Context of Early Cognitive Development

5.7 Explain how Vygotsky's concept of the zone of proximal development expands our understanding of early cognitive development.

Recall the description at the beginning of this chapter of Grace dropping shapes into a container. Notice that she learns about the toy with Ginette's support.

According to Vygotsky's sociocultural theory, complex mental activities have their origins in social interaction. Through joint activities with more mature members of their society, children master activities and think in ways that have meaning in their culture.

A special Vygotskian concept explains how this happens. The **zone of proximal** (or potential) **development** refers to a range of tasks that the child cannot yet handle alone but can do with the help of more skilled partners. To understand this idea, think about how a sensitive adult (such as Ginette) introduces a child to a new activity. The adult picks a task that the child can master but that is challenging enough that the child cannot do it by herself. As the adult guides and supports, the child joins in the interaction and picks up mental strategies. As her competence increases, the adult steps back, permitting the child to take more responsibility for the task (Mermelshtine, 2017). This form of teaching—known as *scaffolding*—promotes learning at all ages, and we will consider it further in Chapter 7.

Picture an adult helping a baby figure out how a jack-in-the-box works. In the early months, the adult demonstrates and, as the clown pops out, tries to capture the infant's attention by saying something like "See what happened!" By the end of the first year, when cognitive and motor skills have improved, the adult guides the baby's hand in turning the crank. During the second year, the adult helps from a distance using gestures and verbal prompts, such as pointing to the crank, making a turning motion, and verbally prompting, "Turn it!" This fine-tuned support is related to advanced play, language, and problem solving in toddlerhood and early childhood (Bornstein et al., 1992; Charman et al., 2001; Tamis-LeMonda & Bornstein, 1989).

As early as the first year, cultural variations in social experiences affect mental strategies. In the jack-in-the-box example, adults and children focus on a single activity. This strategy, common in Western middle-SES homes, is well-suited to lessons in which children master skills apart from the everyday

▶ By bringing the task within his son's zone of proximal development and adjusting his communication to suit the child's needs, this father transfers mental strategies to the child, promoting his cognitive development.

situations in which they will later use those skills. In contrast, infants and young children in Guatemalan Mayan, Native American, and other indigenous communities often attend to several events at once. For example, one 12-month-old skillfully put objects in a jar while watching a passing truck and blowing into a toy whistle (Chavajay & Rogoff, 1999; Correa-Chávez, Roberts, & Pérez, 2011).

Processing several competing events simultaneously may be vital in cultures where children largely learn through keen observation of others' ongoing activities. In a comparison of 18-month-olds from German middle-SES homes and Nso farming villages in Cameroon, the Nso toddlers copied far fewer adult-demonstrated actions on toys than did the German toddlers (Borchert et al., 2013). Nso caregivers rarely create such child-focused teaching situations. Rather they expect children to imitate adult behaviors without prompting. Nso children are motivated to do so because they want to be included in the major activities of their community.

Earlier we saw how infants and toddlers create new schemes by acting on the physical world (Piaget) and how certain skills become better developed as children represent their experiences more efficiently and meaningfully (information processing). Vygotsky adds a third dimension to our understanding by emphasizing that many aspects of cognitive development are socially mediated. The Cultural Influences box on the following page presents additional evidence for this idea, and we will see even more in the next section.

ASK YOURSELF

CONNECT List techniques that parents can use to *scaffold* development of categorization in infancy and toddlerhood, and explain why each is effective.

APPLY When Timmy was 18 months old, his mother stood behind him, helping him throw a large ball into a box. As his skill improved, she stepped back, letting him try on his own. Using Vygotsky's ideas, explain how Timmy's mother is supporting his cognitive development.

REFLECT Describe your earliest autobiographical memory. How old were you when the event occurred? Do your recollections fit with research on infantile amnesia?

Individual Differences in Early Mental Development

5.8 Describe the mental testing approach and the extent to which infant tests predict later performance.

5.9 Discuss environmental influences on early mental development, including home, child care, and early intervention for at-risk infants and toddlers.

At age 22 months, Timmy had only a handful of words in his vocabulary, played in a less mature way than Caitlin and Grace, and seemed restless and overactive. Worried about Timmy's progress, Vanessa arranged for a psychologist to give him one of many tests available for assessing mental development in infants and toddlers.

The cognitive theories we have just discussed try to explain the *process* of development—how children's thinking changes. Mental tests, in contrast, focus on *individual differences*: They measure variations in developmental progress, arriving at scores that *predict* future performance, such as later intelligence and academic achievement. This concern with prediction arose about a century ago, when French psychologist Alfred Binet designed the first successful intelligence test. It inspired the design of many new tests, including ones that measure intelligence at very early ages.

Infant and Toddler Intelligence Tests

Accurately measuring infants' intelligence is challenging because they cannot answer questions or follow directions. As a result, most infant tests emphasize perceptual and motor responses. But increasingly, tests are being developed that also tap early language, cognition, and social behavior, especially with older infants and toddlers.

One commonly used test, the *Bayley Scales of Infant and Toddler Development,* is suitable for children between 1 month and 3½ years. The most recent edition, the Bayley-III, has three main subtests: (1) the Cognitive Scale, which includes such items as attention to familiar and unfamiliar

CULTURAL INFLUENCES

Social Origins of Make-Believe Play

One of the activities my husband, Ken, used to do with our two young sons was to bake pineapple upside-down cake, a favorite treat. One day, as 4-year-old David stirred the batter, Ken poured some into a small bowl for 21-month-old Peter and handed him a spoon.

"Here's how you do it, Petey," instructed David, with a superior air. Peter watched as David stirred, then tried to copy. When it was time to pour the batter, Ken helped Peter hold and tip the small bowl.

"Time to bake it," said Ken.

"Bake it, bake it," repeated Peter, watching Ken slip the pan into the oven.

Several hours later, we observed one of Peter's earliest instances of make-believe play. He got his pail from the sandbox and, after filling it with a handful of sand, carried it into the kitchen. "Bake it, bake it," Peter called to Ken. Together, father and son placed the pretend cake in the oven.

Vygotsky believed that society provides children with opportunities to represent culturally meaningful activities in play. Make-believe, he claimed, is first learned under the guidance of experts (Meyers & Berk, 2014). In the example just described, Peter extended his capacity to represent daily events when Ken drew him into the baking task and helped him act it out in play.

In Western middle-SES families, make-believe is culturally cultivated and scaffolded by adults (Gaskins, 2014). Mothers, especially, offer toddlers a rich array of cues that they are pretending—looking and smiling at the child more, making more exaggerated movements, and using more "we" talk (acknowledging that pretending is a joint endeavor) than they do during the same real-life event (Lillard, 2007). These cues encourage toddlers to join in and probably facilitate their ability to distinguish pretend from real acts, which strengthens over the second and third years.

When adults participate, toddlers' make-believe is more elaborate (Keren et al., 2005). The more parents pretend with their toddlers, the more time their children devote to make-believe (Cote & Bornstein, 2009).

In some cultures, such as those of Indonesia and Mexico, where play is viewed as solely a child's activity and sibling caregiving is common, make-believe is more frequent and complex with older siblings than with mothers. As early as ages 3 to 4, children provide rich, challenging stimulation to their younger brothers and sisters, take these teaching responsibilities seriously, and adjust their playful interactions to the younger child's needs (Zukow-Goldring, 2002). In a study of Zinacanteco Indian children of southern Mexico, by age 8, sibling teachers were highly skilled at showing 2-year-olds how to play at everyday tasks, such as washing and cooking (Maynard, 2002). They often guided toddlers verbally and physically through the task and provided feedback.

As we will see in Chapter 7, make-believe play is an important means through which children enhance their cognitive and social skills (Nielsen, 2012). Vygotsky's theory, and the findings that support it, tells us that providing a stimulating physical environment is not enough to promote early cognitive development. In addition, toddlers must be invited and encouraged by more skilled members of their culture to participate in the social world around them. Parents and teachers can enhance early make-believe by playing often with toddlers, guiding and elaborating their make-believe themes.

FARZANA WAHIDY/AP IMAGES

▶ In cultures where sibling caregiving is common, make-believe play is more frequent and complex with older siblings than with mothers. These Afghan children play "wedding," dressing the youngest as a bride.

objects, looking for a fallen object, and pretend play; (2) the Language Scale, which assesses understanding and expression of language—for example, recognition of objects and people, following simple directions, and naming objects and pictures; and (3) the Motor Scale, which includes gross and fine motor skills, such as grasping, sitting, stacking blocks, and climbing stairs (Bayley, 2005).

Two additional Bayley-III scales depend on parental report: (4) the Social-Emotional Scale, which asks caregivers about such behaviors as ease of calming, social responsiveness, and imitation in play; and (5) the Adaptive Behavior Scale, which asks about adaptation to the demands of daily life, including communication, self-control, following rules, and getting along with others.

▶ A trained examiner administers a test based on the Bayley Scales of Infant Development to a 1-year-old sitting in her mother's lap. Compared with earlier editions, the Bayley-III Cognitive and Language Scales better predict preschool mental test performance.

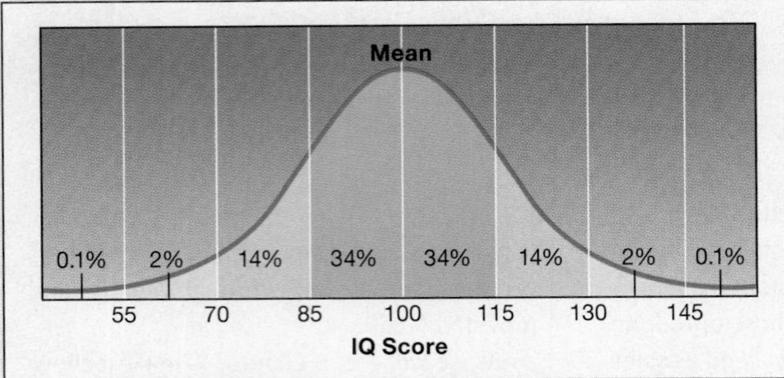

FIGURE 5.8 Normal distribution of intelligence test scores. To determine what percentage of same-age individuals in the population a person with a certain IQ outperformed, add the figures to the left of that IQ score. For example, an 8-year-old child with an IQ of 115 scored better than 84 percent of the population of 8-year-olds.

Computing Intelligence Test Scores. Intelligence tests for infants, children, and adults are scored in much the same way—by computing an **intelligence quotient (IQ),** which indicates the extent to which the raw score (number of items passed) deviates from the typical performance of same-age individuals. To make this comparison possible, test designers engage in **standardization**—giving the test to a large, representative sample and using the results as the *standard* for interpreting scores. The standardization sample for the Bayley-III included 1,700 infants, toddlers, and young preschoolers, reflecting the U.S. population in SES and ethnic diversity.

Within the standardization sample, performances at each age level form a **normal distribution,** in which most scores cluster around the mean, or average, with progressively fewer falling toward the extremes (see Figure 5.8). This *bell-shaped distribution* results whenever researchers measure individual differences in large samples. When intelligence tests are standardized, the mean IQ is set at 100. An individual's IQ is higher or lower than 100 by an amount that reflects how much his or her test performance deviates from the standardization-sample mean.

The IQ offers a way of finding out whether an individual is ahead, behind, or on time (average) in mental development compared with others of the same age. For example, if Timmy's score is 100, then he did better than 50 percent of his agemates. A child with an IQ of 85 did better than only 16 percent, whereas a child with an IQ of 130 outperformed 98 percent. The IQs of 96 percent of individuals fall between 70 and 130; only a few achieve higher or lower scores.

Predicting Later Performance from Infant Tests. Despite careful construction, most infant tests—including previous editions of the Bayley—predict later intelligence poorly. Infants and toddlers easily become distracted, fatigued, or bored during testing, so their scores often do not reflect their true abilities. And infant perceptual and motor items differ from the tasks given to older children, which increasingly emphasize verbal, conceptual, and problem-solving skills. In contrast, the Bayley-III Cognitive and Language Scales, which better dovetail with childhood tests, are good predictors of preschool mental test performance (Albers & Grieve, 2007).

Infant tests are somewhat better at making long-term predictions for extremely low-scoring babies. Today, they are largely used for *screening*—helping to identify for intervention babies who are likely to have developmental problems.

As an alternative to infant tests, some researchers have turned to information-processing measures, such as habituation, to assess early mental progress. Their findings show that speed of habituation and recovery to novel visual stimuli is among the best available infant predictors of IQ, from early childhood through early adulthood (Fagan, Holland, & Wheeler, 2007; Kavšek, 2004). Habituation and recovery seem to be an especially effective early index of intelligence because they assess memory as well as quickness and flexibility of thinking (Colombo et al., 2004). The consistency of these findings has prompted designers of the Bayley-III to include items that tap such cognitive skills as habituation, object permanence, and categorization.

Early Environment and Mental Development

In Chapter 2, we indicated that intelligence is a complex blend of hereditary and environmental influences. As we consider evidence on the relationship of environmental factors to infant and toddler mental test scores, you will encounter findings that highlight the role of heredity as well.

Home Environment. The **Home Observation for Measurement of the Environment (HOME)** is a checklist for gathering information about the quality of children's home lives through observation and parental interview (Caldwell & Bradley, 1994). The HOME Infant–Toddler Subscales are the most widely used home environment measure during the first three years (Rijlaarsdam et al., 2012).

Factors measured include an organized, stimulating physical setting and parental affection, involvement, and encouragement of new skills. Regardless of SES and ethnicity, each predicts better language and IQ scores in toddlerhood and early childhood across SES and ethnic groups (Bornstein, 2015; Fuligni, Han, & Brooks-Gunn, 2004; Linver, Martin, & Brooks-Gunn, 2004; Tong et al., 2007). The extent to which parents talk to infants and toddlers is particularly important. It contributes strongly to early language progress, which, in turn, predicts intelligence and academic achievement in elementary school (Hart & Risley, 1995; Hoff, 2013).

Yet we must interpret these correlational findings cautiously. Parents who are more intelligent may provide better experiences while also giving birth to brighter children, who evoke more stimulation from their parents. Research supports these influences, which refer to *gene–environment correlation* (see Chapter 2, pages 63–64) (Hadd & Rodgers, 2017; Saudino & Plomin, 1997). But parent–child shared heredity does not account for the entire association between home environment and mental test scores. Family living conditions—both HOME scores and affluence of the surrounding neighborhood—continue to predict children's IQ beyond the contribution of parental IQ and education (Chase-Lansdale et al., 1997; Klebanov et al., 1998).

How can the research summarized so far help us understand Vanessa's concern about Timmy's development? Ben, the psychologist who tested Timmy, found that he scored only slightly below average. Ben talked with Vanessa about her child-rearing practices and watched her play with Timmy. A single parent who worked long hours, Vanessa had little energy for Timmy at the end of the day. Ben also noticed that Vanessa, anxious about Timmy's progress, was intrusive: She interfered with his active behavior and bombarded him with directions: "That's enough ball play. Stack these blocks."

Children who experience intrusive parenting are likely to be distractible and withdrawn and do poorly on mental tests—negative outcomes that persist unless parenting improves (Clincy & Mills-Koonce, 2013; Rubin, Coplan, & Bowker, 2009). Ben coached Vanessa in how to interact sensitively with Timmy while assuring her that warm, responsive parenting that builds on toddlers' current capacities is a much better indicator of how children will do later than an early mental test score.

▶ A father plays actively and affectionately with his baby. Parental warmth, attention, and verbal communication predict better language and IQ scores in toddlerhood and early childhood.

Infant and Toddler Child Care. Today, about 60 percent of U.S. mothers with a child under age 2 are employed (U.S. Bureau of Labor Statistics, 2017). Child care for infants and toddlers has become common, and its quality—though not as influential as parenting—affects mental development.

Infants and young children exposed to poor-quality child care—whether they come from middle- or low-SES homes—score lower on measures of cognitive, language, academic, and social skills during the preschool, elementary, and secondary school years (Belsky et al., 2007b; Burchinal et al., 2015; Dearing, McCartney, & Taylor, 2009; NICHD Early Child Care Research Network, 2000b, 2001, 2003b, 2006; Vandell et al., 2010). In contrast, good child care can reduce the negative impact of a stressed, poverty-stricken home life, and it sustains the benefits of growing up in an economically advantaged family (Burchinal, Kainz, & Cai, 2011; McCartney et al., 2007). As Figure 5.9 on page 160 illustrates, the Early Childhood Longitudinal Study—consisting of a large sample of U.S. children diverse in SES and ethnicity followed from birth through the preschool years—confirmed the importance of continuous high-quality child care from infancy through the preschool years (Li et al., 2013).

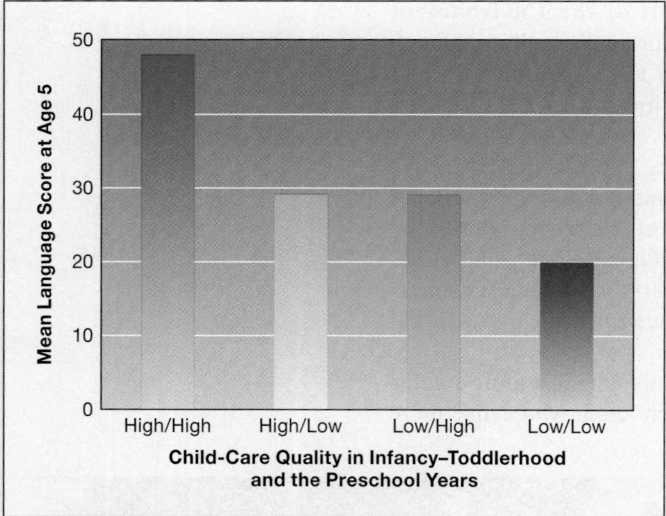

FIGURE 5.9 Relationship of child-care quality in infancy–toddlerhood and the preschool years to language development at age 5. When a nationally representative sample of more than 1,300 children was followed over the first five years, language scores were highest for those experiencing high-quality child care in both infancy–toddlerhood and the preschool years, intermediate for those experiencing high-quality care in just one of these periods, and lowest for those experiencing poor-quality care in both periods. Cognitive, literacy, and math scores also showed this pattern. (Based on Li et al., 2013.)

Unlike most European countries and Australia and New Zealand, where child care is nationally regulated and funded to ensure its quality, reports on U.S. child care raise serious concerns. Standards are set by the individual states and vary widely. In studies of quality, only 20 to 25 percent of U.S. child-care centers and family child-care homes provided infants and toddlers with sufficiently positive, stimulating experiences to promote healthy psychological development (NICHD Early Childhood Research Network, 2000a, 2004). Furthermore, the cost of child care in the United States is high: On average, full-time center-based care for one infant consumes 15 percent of the median income for couples and 50 percent for single parents (Child Care Aware, 2017). The cost of a family child-care home is about two-thirds of center-based care.

U.S. settings providing the very worst child care tend to serve middle-income families. These parents are especially likely to place their children in for-profit centers, where quality tends to be lowest. Economically disadvantaged children more often attend publicly subsidized, nonprofit centers, which are better equipped with learning materials and have smaller group sizes and more favorable teacher–child ratios (Johnson, Ryan, & Brooks-Gunn, 2012). Still, many low-income children experience substandard child care.

See Applying What We Know on the following page for signs of high-quality care for infants and toddlers, based on standards for **developmentally appropriate practice.** These standards, devised by the U.S. National Association for the Education of Young Children, specify program characteristics that serve young children's developmental and individual needs, based on both current research and consensus among experts.

LOOK AND LISTEN

Ask several employed parents of infants or toddlers to describe what they sought in a child-care setting, along with challenges they faced in finding child care. How knowledgeable are the parents about the ingredients of high-quality care?

Child care in the United States is affected by a macrosystem of individualistic values and weak government regulation and funding. In recent years, the U.S. federal government and some states have allocated additional funds to subsidize child-care costs, especially for low-income families (Matthews, 2014). Though far from meeting the need, this increase in resources has had a positive impact on child-care quality and accessibility.

Early Intervention for At-Risk Infants and Toddlers

Children living in persistent poverty are likely to show gradual declines in intelligence test scores and to achieve poorly when they reach school age (Schoon et al., 2012). These problems are largely due to stressful home environments that undermine children's ability to learn and increase the likelihood that they will remain poor as adults. A variety of intervention programs have been developed to break this tragic cycle of poverty. Although most begin during the preschool years (we will discuss these in Chapter 7), some start during infancy and continue through early childhood.

In center-based interventions, children attend an organized child-care or preschool program where they receive educational, nutritional, and health services, and their parents receive child-rearing and other social service supports. In home-based interventions, a skilled adult visits the home and works with parents, teaching them how to stimulate a young child's development. In most programs of either type, participating children score higher than untreated controls on mental tests by age 2. The earlier intervention begins, the longer it lasts, and the greater its scope and intensity, the better participants' cognitive and academic performance throughout childhood and adolescence (Ramey, Ramey, & Lanzi, 2006).

The Carolina Abecedarian Project illustrates these favorable outcomes. In the 1970s, more than 100 infants from poverty-stricken families, ranging in age from 3 weeks to 3 months, were randomly assigned to either a treatment group or a control group. Treatment infants were enrolled in full-time, year-round child care through the preschool years. There they received stimulation aimed at promoting motor, cognitive, language, and social skills and, after age 3, literacy and math concepts. Special emphasis was placed on rich, responsive adult–child verbal communication. All

APPLYING WHAT WE KNOW

Signs of Developmentally Appropriate Infant and Toddler Child Care

PROGRAM CHARACTERISTICS	SIGNS OF QUALITY
Physical setting	Indoor environment is clean, in good repair, well-lighted, well-ventilated, and not overcrowded. Fenced outdoor play space is available.
Toys and equipment	Play materials are age-appropriate and stored on low shelves within easy reach. Cribs, highchairs, infant seats, and child-sized tables and chairs are available. Outdoor equipment includes small riding toys, swings, slide, and sandbox.
Caregiver–child ratio	In child-care centers, caregiver–child ratio is no greater than 1 to 3 for infants and 1 to 6 for toddlers. Group size (number of children in one room) is no greater than 6 infants with 2 caregivers and 12 toddlers with 2 caregivers. In family child care, caregiver is responsible for no more than 6 children; within this group, no more than 2 are infants and toddlers.
Daily activities	Daily schedule includes times for active play, quiet play, naps, snacks, and meals. Atmosphere is warm and supportive, and children are never left unsupervised.
Interactions among adults and children	Caregivers respond promptly to infants' and toddlers' distress; hold them and talk, sing, and read to them; and interact with them in a manner that respects the individual child's interests and tolerance for stimulation. Staffing is consistent, so infants and toddlers can form relationships with particular caregivers.
Caregiver qualifications	Caregivers have some training in child development, first aid, and safety.
Relationships with parents	Parents are welcome anytime. Caregivers talk frequently with parents about children's behavior and development.
Licensing and accreditation	Child-care setting is licensed by the state. In the United States, voluntary accreditation by the National Association for the Education of Young Children, *www.naeyc.org/accreditation*, or the National Association for Family Child Care, *www.nafcc.org*, is evidence of an especially high-quality program.

Sources: Copple & Bredekamp, 2009.

children received nutrition and health services; the primary difference between treatment and controls was the intensive child-care experience.

By 12 months of age, treatment children scored higher in IQ, an advantage they sustained until last tested—at age 21. In addition, throughout their school years, treatment youths achieved higher scores in reading and math. These gains translated into reduced enrollment in special education, more years of schooling completed, higher rates of college enrollment and graduation, more consistent employment, and lower rates of adolescent parenthood (Campbell et al., 2001, 2002, 2012).

Recognition of the power of intervening as early as possible led the U.S. Congress to provide limited funding for services directed at infants and toddlers who already have serious developmental problems or who are at risk for problems because of poverty. Early Head Start, begun in 1995, currently has 1,000 sites serving about 110,000 low-income children and their families (Walker, 2014). An evaluation, conducted when children reached age 3, showed that Early Head Start led to warmer, more stimulating parenting, a reduction in harsh discipline, gains in cognitive and language development, and lessening of child aggression (Love, Chazan-Cohen, & Raikes, 2007; Love et al., 2005; Raikes et al., 2010). The strongest effects occurred at sites mixing center- and home-visiting services.

This Early Head Start program provides rich, educational experiences for toddlers plus parent education and family supports. The most favorable outcomes of Early Head Start result from mixing center- and home-visiting services.

By age 5, however, the benefits of Early Head Start had declined or disappeared, and a follow-up in fifth grade showed no persisting gains (U.S. Department of Health and Human Services, 2006; Vogel et al., 2010). One speculation is that more intentional educational experiences extending through the preschool years—as in the Abecedarian Project—would increase the lasting impact of Early Head Start (Barnett, 2011). Although Early Head Start is in need of refinement, it is a promising beginning at providing U.S. infants and toddlers living in poverty with publicly supported intervention.

ASK YOURSELF

CONNECT Using what you learned about brain development in Chapter 4, explain why it is best to initiate intervention for poverty-stricken children in the first two years rather than later.

APPLY Fifteen-month-old Manuel scored 115 on a mental test for infants and toddlers. His mother wants to know exactly what this means and what she should do to support his mental development. How would you respond?

REFLECT Suppose you were seeking a child-care setting for your baby. What would you want it to be like, and why?

Language Development

5.10 Describe theories of language development, and indicate the emphasis each places on innate abilities and environmental influences.

5.11 Describe major language milestones in the first two years, individual differences, and ways adults can support early language development.

Advances in perception and cognition during infancy pave the way for an extraordinary human achievement—language. In Chapter 4, we saw that by the second half of the first year, infants make dramatic progress in distinguishing the basic sounds of their language and in segmenting the flow of speech into word and phrase units. They also start to comprehend some words and, around 12 months of age, say their first word (MacWhinney, 2015). By age 6, children understand the meaning of about 14,000 words and speak in elaborate sentences.

How do infants and toddlers make such remarkable progress in launching these skills? To address this question, let's examine several prominent theories of language development.

Theories of Language Development

In the 1950s, researchers did not take seriously the idea that very young children might be able to figure out important properties of language. Children's regular and rapid attainment of language milestones suggested a process largely governed by maturation, inspiring the nativist perspective on language development. In recent years, new evidence has spawned the interactionist perspective, which emphasizes the joint roles of children's inner capacities and communicative experiences.

The Nativist Perspective. According to linguist Noam Chomsky's (1957) *nativist* theory, language is etched into the structure of the human brain. Focusing on grammar, Chomsky reasoned that the rules of sentence organization are too complex to be directly taught to or discovered by even a cognitively sophisticated young child. Rather, he proposed that all children have a **language acquisition device (LAD),** an innate system that contains a *universal grammar,* or set of rules common to all languages. It enables children, no matter which language they hear, to understand and speak in a rule-oriented fashion as soon as they pick up enough words.

Are children innately primed to acquire language? Recall from Chapter 4 that newborn babies are remarkably sensitive to speech sounds. And children everywhere attain major language milestones in a similar sequence (Parish-Morris, Golinkoff, & Hirsh-Pasek, 2013).

Furthermore, evidence that childhood is a *sensitive period* for language acquisition is consistent with Chomsky's idea of a biologically based language program. Researchers have examined the language competence of deaf adults who acquired their first language—American Sign Language (ASL), a gestural system just as complex as any spoken language—at different ages. The later learners, whose parents chose to educate them through the oral method, which relies on speech and lip-reading, did not acquire spoken language because of their profound deafness. Those who learned

ASL in adolescence or adulthood never became as proficient as those who learned in childhood (Mayberry, 2010; Singleton & Newport, 2004).

Nevertheless, Chomsky's theory has been contested on several grounds. First, researchers have had great difficulty specifying Chomsky's universal grammar. Critics doubt that one set of rules can account for the extraordinary variation in grammatical forms among the world's 5,000 to 8,000 languages. Second, children refine and generalize many grammatical forms gradually, engaging in much piecemeal learning and making errors along the way (Evans & Levinson, 2009; MacWhinney, 2015). As we will see in Chapter 9, complete mastery of some grammatical forms, such as the passive voice, is not achieved until well into middle childhood. This suggests that more experimentation and learning are involved than Chomsky assumed.

▶ Infants communicate from the very beginning of life. How will this child become a fluent speaker of her native language within just a few years? Theorists disagree sharply.

Finally, recall from Chapter 4 that for most people, language is housed largely in the left hemisphere of the cerebral cortex, consistent with Chomsky's notion of a brain prepared to process language. But our discussion also revealed that language areas in the cortex *develop* as children acquire language. Although the left hemisphere is biased for language processing, if it is injured in the early years, other regions take over (see page 112 in Chapter 4). Thus, left-hemispheric localization, though typical, is not necessary for effective language processing.

The Interactionist Perspective. Recent ideas about language development emphasize *interactions* between inner capacities and environmental influences. One type of interactionist theory applies the information-processing perspective to language development. A second type emphasizes social interaction.

Some information-processing theorists assume that children make sense of their complex language environments by applying powerful cognitive capacities of a general kind (MacWhinney, 2015; Saffran, 2009; Samuelson & McMurray, 2017). These theorists note that brain regions housing language also govern similar perceptual and cognitive abilities, such as the capacity to analyze musical and visual patterns (Saygin, Leech, & Dick, 2010).

Other theorists blend this information-processing view with Chomsky's nativist perspective. They argue that infants' capacity to analyze speech and other information is not sufficient to account for mastery of higher-level aspects of language, such as intricate grammatical structures (Aslin & Newport, 2012). They also point out that grammatical competence may depend more on specific brain structures than the other components of language. When 2- to 2½-year-olds and adults listened to short sentences—some grammatically correct, others with phrase-structure violations—both groups showed similarly distinct ERP brain-wave patterns for each sentence type in the left frontal and temporal lobes of the cerebral cortex (Oberecker & Friederici, 2006). This suggests that 2-year-olds process sentence structures using the same neural system as adults do. Furthermore, in studies of older children and adults with left-hemispheric brain damage, grammar is more impaired than other language functions (Curtiss & Schaeffer, 2005).

Still other interactionists emphasize that children's social skills and language experiences are centrally involved in language development. In this *social-interactionist* view, an active child strives to communicate, which cues her caregivers to provide appropriate language experiences. These experiences, in turn, help the child relate the content and structure of language to its social meanings (Bohannon & Bonvillian, 2013; Chapman, 2006).

Among social interactionists, disagreement continues over whether or not children are equipped with specialized language structures in the brain (Hsu, Chater, & Vitányi, 2013; Lidz, 2007; Tomasello, 2006). Nevertheless, as we chart the course of language development, we will encounter much support for their central premise—that children's social competencies and language experiences greatly affect their progress.

Getting Ready to Talk

Before babies say their first word, they make impressive language progress. They listen attentively to human speech, and they produce speechlike sounds. As adults, we can hardly help but respond.

Cooing and Babbling. Around 2 months, infants begin to make vowel-like noises, called **cooing** because of their pleasant "oo" quality. Gradually, consonants are added, and around 6 months, **babbling** appears, in which infants repeat consonant–vowel combinations. With age, they increasingly babble in long strings, such as "babababababa" or "nanananana," in an effort to gain control over producing particular sounds.

Babies everywhere (even those who are deaf) start babbling at about the same age and produce a similar range of early sounds. But for vocal babbling to develop further, infants must be able to hear human speech. In babies with hearing impairments, these speechlike sounds are greatly delayed and limited in diversity of sounds (Bass-Ringdahl, 2010). And deaf infants not exposed to sign language will stop babbling entirely (Oller, 2000).

Babies initially produce a limited number of sounds and then expand to a much broader range. Around 7 months, babbling starts to include many sounds of spoken languages (Goldstein & Schwade, 2008). And at 8 to 10 months, infants shift their gaze from the eyes to the mouth of an adult speaker and try to match the speaker's oral movements (de Boisferon et al., 2017; Diepstra et al., 2017). At about this time, infant babbling reflects the sound and intonation patterns of the child's language community—an attainment that predicts the timing of babies' first spoken words (Boysson-Bardies & Vihman, 1991; McGillion et al., 2017).

Deaf infants exposed to sign language from birth and hearing babies of deaf, signing parents produce babblelike hand motions with the rhythmic patterns of natural sign languages (Petitto et al., 2004; Petitto & Marentette, 1991). This sensitivity to language rhythm—evident in both spoken and signed babbling—supports both discovery and production of meaningful language units.

Becoming a Communicator. At birth, infants are prepared for some aspects of conversational behavior. For example, newborns initiate interaction through eye contact and terminate it by looking away. By 3 to 4 months, infants start to gaze in the same general direction adults are looking—a skill that becomes more accurate at 10 to 11 months, as babies realize that others' focus offers information about their communicative intentions (to talk about an object) or other goals (to obtain an object) (Brooks & Meltzoff, 2005; Senju, Csibra, & Johnson, 2008). This **joint attention,** in which the child attends to the same object or event as the caregiver, who often labels it, contributes greatly to early language development. Infants and toddlers who frequently experience it sustain attention longer, comprehend more language, produce meaningful gestures and words earlier, and show faster vocabulary development (Brooks & Meltzoff, 2008; Flom & Pick, 2003; Silvén, 2001).

TIINA & GEIR/CORBIS

▶ This baby uses a preverbal gesture to direct his father's attention. The father's verbal response ("I see that squirrel!") promotes the baby's transition to spoken language.

Around 3 months, interactions between caregivers and babies begin to include *give-and-take.* Infants and mothers mutually imitate the pitch, loudness, and duration of each other's sounds. Mothers take the lead, imitating about twice as often as 3-month-olds, who limit their imitations to a handful of sounds they find easier to produce (Gratier & Devouche, 2011). Between 4 and 6 months, imitation extends to social games, as in pat-a-cake and peekaboo. At first, the parent starts the game and the infant is an amused observer. By 12 months, infants participate actively, practicing the turn-taking pattern of human conversation.

At the end of the first year, babies use *preverbal gestures* to direct adults' attention, influence their behavior, and convey helpful information (Tomasello, Carpenter, & Liszkowski, 2007). For example, Caitlin held up a toy to show it, pointed to the cupboard when she wanted a cookie, and pointed at her mother's car keys lying on the floor. Carolyn responded to these gestures and also labeled them ("That's your bear!" "You want a cookie!" "Oh, there are my keys!"). In this way, toddlers learn that using language leads to desired results.

The more time caregivers and infants spend in joint play with objects, the earlier and more often babies use preverbal gestures (Salomo & Liszkowski, 2013). Soon toddlers integrate words with gestures, as in pointing to a toy while saying "give" (Capirci et al., 2005). The earlier toddlers form word–gesture combinations, the faster their vocabulary growth, the sooner they produce two-word utterances at the end of the second year, and the more complex their sentences at age 3½ (Huttenlocher et al., 2010; Rowe & Goldin-Meadow, 2009).

First Words

In the middle of the first year, infants begin to understand word meanings; for example, they respond to their own name (Mandel, Jusczyk, & Pisoni, 1995). And when 6-month-olds listened to the word "Mommy" or "Daddy" while viewing side-by-side videos of their parents, they looked longer at the video of the named parent (Tincoff & Jusczyk, 1999).

First recognizable spoken words, around 1 year, build on the sensorimotor foundations Piaget described and on categories children have formed. In a study tracking the first 10 words used by several hundred U.S. and Chinese (both Mandarin- and Cantonese-speaking) babies, important people ("Mama," "Dada"), common objects ("ball," "bread"), and sound effects ("woof-woof," "vroom") were mentioned most often. Action words ("hit," "grab," "hug") and social routines ("hi," "bye"), though also appearing in all three groups, were more often produced by Chinese than U.S. babies, and the Chinese babies also named more important people—differences we will consider shortly (Tardif et al., 2008).

When toddlers first learn words, they sometimes apply them too narrowly, an error called **underextension.** At 16 months, Caitlin used "bear" only to refer to the tattered bear she carried nearly constantly. As vocabulary expands, a more common error is **overextension**—applying a word to a wider collection of objects and events than is appropriate. For example, Grace used "car" for buses, trains, and trucks. Toddlers' overextensions reflect their sensitivity to categories (MacWhinney, 2005). They apply a new word to a group of similar experiences, often overextending deliberately because they have difficulty recalling or have not yet acquired a suitable word.

Overextensions illustrate another important feature of language development: the distinction between language *production* (the words and word combinations children use) and language *comprehension* (the language they understand). At all ages, comprehension develops ahead of production. Still, the two capacities are related. The speed and accuracy of toddlers' comprehension of spoken language increase dramatically over the second year. And toddlers who are faster and more accurate in comprehension show more rapid growth in words understood and produced over the following year (Fernald & Marchman, 2012). Quick comprehension frees space in working memory for picking up new words and using them to communicate.

The Two-Word Utterance Phase

Young toddlers add to their spoken vocabularies at a rate of one to three words per week. Because gains in word production between 18 and 24 months are so impressive (one or two words per day), many researchers concluded that toddlers undergo a *spurt in vocabulary*—a transition from a slower to a faster learning phase. In actuality, most children show a steady increase in rate of word learning that continues through the preschool years (Ganger & Brent, 2004).

Once toddlers produce 200 to 250 words, they start to combine two words: "Mommy shoe," "go car," "more cookie." These two-word utterances are called **telegraphic speech** because, like a telegram, they focus on high-content words, omitting smaller, less important ones ("can," "the," "to").

Two-word speech consists largely of simple formulas ("more + *X*," "eat + *X*"), with different words inserted in the "*X*" position. Toddlers rarely make gross grammatical errors, such as saying "chair my" instead of "my chair." But their word-order regularities are usually copies of adult word pairings, as when the parent says, "How about *more sandwich?*" This suggests that at first, young children rely on "concrete pieces of language" they often hear, gradually generalizing from those pieces to word-order and other grammatical rules (Bannard, Lieven, & Tomasello, 2009; MacWhinney, 2015). As we will see in Chapter 7, children master grammar steadily over the preschool years.

Individual and Cultural Differences

Although children typically produce their first word around their first birthday, the range is large, from 8 to 18 months—variation due to a complex blend of genetic and environmental influences. Earlier we saw that Timmy's spoken language was delayed, in part because of Vanessa's tense, directive communication with him. But Timmy is also a boy, and girls are slightly ahead of boys in early vocabulary growth (Frota et al., 2016; Van Hulle, Goldsmith, & Lemery, 2004). The most common explanation is girls' faster rate of physical maturation, which is believed to promote earlier development of the left cerebral hemisphere.

Temperament matters, too. For example, shy toddlers often wait until they understand a great deal before trying to speak. Once they do speak, their vocabularies increase rapidly, although they remain slightly behind their agemates (Spere et al., 2004).

Caregiver–child conversation—especially, the richness of adults' vocabularies—also plays a strong role (Huttenlocher et al., 2010). Commonly used words for objects appear early in toddlers' speech, and the more often their caregivers use a particular noun, the sooner young children produce it (Goodman, Dale, & Li, 2008). Mothers and fathers talk more to toddler-age girls than to boys, and parents converse less often with shy than with sociable children (Leaper, Anderson, & Sanders, 1998; Mascaro et al., 2017; Patterson & Fisher, 2002).

Compared to their higher-SES agemates, children from low-SES homes usually have smaller vocabularies. By 18 to 24 months, they are slower at word comprehension and have acquired 30 percent fewer words (Fernald, Marchman, & Weisleder, 2013). Limited parent–child conversation and book reading are major factors. On average, a middle-SES child is read to for 1,000 hours between 1 and 5 years, a low-SES child for only 25 hours (Neuman, 2003).

Rate of early vocabulary growth is a strong predictor of low-SES children's vocabulary size at kindergarten entry, which forecasts their later literacy skills and academic success (Rowe, Raudenbush, & Goldin-Meadow, 2012). Higher-SES toddlers who lag behind their agemates in word learning have more opportunities to catch up in early childhood.

Young children have distinct styles of early language learning. The vocabularies of Caitlin and Grace, like most toddlers, consisted mainly of words that refer to objects. A smaller number of toddlers produce many more social formulas and pronouns ("thank you," "done," "I want it") (Bates et al., 1994). The vocabularies of object-naming toddlers grow faster because all languages contain many more object labels than social phrases.

What accounts for a toddler's language style? Rapidly developing children with a vocabulary of many object words often have an especially active interest in exploration. They also eagerly imitate their parents' frequent naming of objects (Masur & Rodemaker, 1999). Toddlers who emphasize pronouns and social formulas tend to be highly sociable, and their parents more often use verbal routines ("How are you?" "It's no trouble") that support social relationships.

The two language styles are linked to culture. Object words (nouns) are particularly common in the vocabularies of English-speaking toddlers, but Chinese, Japanese, and Korean toddlers have more words for actions (verbs) and social routines. Mothers' speech in each culture reflects this difference (Chan, Brandone, & Tardif, 2009; Chan et al., 2011; Choi & Gopnik, 1995; Fernald & Morikawa, 1993). American mothers frequently label objects when interacting with their babies. Asian mothers, perhaps because of a cultural emphasis on the importance of group membership, emphasize actions and social routines. Also, in Mandarin, sentences often begin with verbs, making action words especially salient to Mandarin-speaking toddlers.

At what point should parents be concerned if their child talks very little or not at all? If a toddler's language is greatly delayed when compared with the typical ages at which children attain early language milestones, then parents should consult the child's doctor or a speech and language therapist. Late babbling may be a sign of slow language development that can be prevented with early intervention (Rowe, Raudenbush, & Goldin-Meadow, 2012). Some toddlers who do not follow simple directions or who, after age 2, have difficulty putting their thoughts into words may suffer from a hearing impairment or a language disorder that requires immediate treatment.

APPLYING WHAT WE KNOW

Supporting Early Language Learning

STRATEGY	CONSEQUENCE
Respond to coos and babbles with speech sounds and words.	Encourages experimentation with sounds that can later be blended into first words Provides experience with the turn-taking pattern of human conversation
Establish joint attention and comment on what child sees.	Predicts earlier onset of language and faster vocabulary development
Play social games, such as pat-a-cake and peekaboo.	Provides experience with the turn-taking pattern of human conversation
Engage toddlers in joint make-believe play.	Promotes all aspects of conversational dialogue
Engage toddlers in frequent conversations.	Predicts faster early language development and academic success during the school years
Read to toddlers often, engaging them in dialogues about picture books.	Provides exposure to many aspects of language, including vocabulary, grammar, communication skills, and information about written symbols and story structures

Supporting Early Language Development

Consistent with the interactionist view, a rich social environment builds on young children's natural readiness to acquire language. For a summary of how caregivers can consciously support early language development, see Applying What We Know above. Caregivers also do so unconsciously—through a special style of speech.

Adults in many cultures speak to babies in **infant-directed speech (IDS),** a form of communication made up of short sentences with high-pitched, exaggerated expression, clear pronunciation, distinct pauses between speech segments, clear gestures to support verbal meaning, and repetition of new words in a variety of contexts ("See the *ball,*" "The *ball* bounced!") (Fernald et al., 1989; O'Neill et al., 2005). Deaf parents use a similar style of communication when signing to their deaf babies (Masataka, 1996). From birth on, infants prefer IDS over other adult talk, and by 5 months they are more emotionally responsive to it (Aslin, Jusczyk, & Pisoni, 1998).

IDS builds on several communicative strategies we have already considered: joint attention, turn-taking, and caregivers' sensitivity to toddlers' preverbal gestures. In this example, Carolyn uses IDS with 18-month-old Caitlin:

Caitlin: "Go car."
Carolyn: "Yes, time to go in the car. Where's your jacket?"
Caitlin: *[Looks around, walks to the closet.]* "Dacket!" *[Points to her jacket.]*
Carolyn: "There's that jacket! *[Helps Caitlin into the jacket.]* On it goes! Let's zip up. *[Zips up the jacket.]* Now, say bye-bye to Grace and Timmy."
Caitlin: "Bye-bye, G-ace. Bye-bye, Te-te.
Carolyn: "Where's your bear?"
Caitlin: *[Looks around.]*
Carolyn: *[Pointing.]* "See? By the sofa." *[Caitlin gets the bear.]*

A mother speaks to her baby in short, clearly pronounced sentences with high-pitched, exaggerated intonation. This form of communication, called infant-directed speech, eases early language learning.

Parents constantly fine-tune the length and content of their utterances in IDS to fit children's needs—adjustments that foster both language comprehension and production (Ma et al., 2011;

Rowe, 2008). Furthermore, live interaction with a responsive adult is far better suited to spurring early language development than are media sources. After a month's regular exposure to a commercial video for babies that labeled common household objects, 12- to 18-month-olds did not add any more words to their vocabulary than non-viewing controls. Rather, toddlers in a comparison group whose parents spent time teaching them the words in everyday activities learned best (DeLoache et al., 2010). Consistent with these findings, a video format that allows an adult to interact responsively with a 2-year-old—as in a Skype session—is an effective context for acquiring new verbs (Roseberry, Hirsh-Pasek, & Golinkoff, 2014).

Similarly, toddlers are unable to learn words from a touch-screen tablet unless the program allows them to participate in specific, contingent interaction. For example, 2½-year-olds acquired names of objects in a tablet presentation only when their screen-touching enabled them to control the emergence of each object from a box and hear its spoken name, not when their touching merely advanced the screen and they watched as each object popped out of its box and was named (Kirkorian, Choi, & Pempek, 2016).

Do social experiences that promote language development remind you of those that strengthen cognitive development in general? IDS and reciprocal adult–child conversation create a *zone of proximal development* in which young children's language expands. In contrast, adult behaviors that are unresponsive to children's needs result in immature language skills (Cabrera, Shannon, & Tamis-LeMonda, 2007). In the next chapter, we will see that adult sensitivity supports infants' and toddlers' emotional and social development as well.

ASK YOURSELF

CONNECT Cognition and language are interrelated. List examples of how cognition fosters language development. Next, list examples of how language fosters cognitive development.

APPLY Fran frequently corrects her 17-month-old son Jeremy's attempts to talk and—fearing that he won't use words—refuses to respond to his gestures. How might Fran be contributing to Jeremy's slow language progress?

REFLECT Find an opportunity to speak to an infant or toddler. Did you use IDS? What features of your speech are likely to promote early language development, and why?

CHAPTER 5 SUMMARY

Piaget's Cognitive-Developmental Theory *(p. 139)*

5.1 ***Explain how, in Piaget's theory, schemes change over the course of development.***

- By acting on the environment, children move through four stages in which psychological structures, or **schemes,** achieve a better fit with external reality.
- Schemes change in two ways: through **adaptation,** which is made up of two complementary activities—**assimilation** and **accommodation**; and through **organization**.

5.2 ***Describe major cognitive attainments of the sensorimotor stage.***

- In the **sensorimotor stage,** the **circular reaction** provides a means of adapting first schemes, and the newborn's reflexes gradually transform into the flexible action patterns of the older infant. Eight- to 12-month-olds develop **intentional,** or **goal-directed, behavior** and begin to understand **object permanence.**

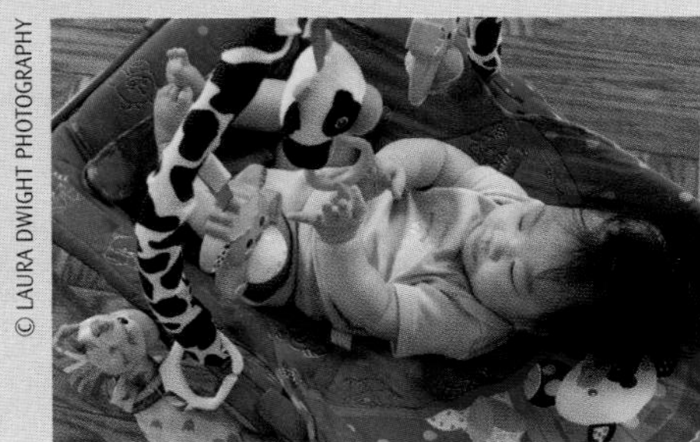
© LAURA DWIGHT PHOTOGRAPHY

- Between 18 and 24 months, **mental representation** is evident in sudden solutions to sensorimotor problems, mastery of object permanence problems involving invisible displacement, **deferred imitation,** and **make-believe play.**

5.3 ***Explain the implications of follow-up research on infant cognitive development for the accuracy of Piaget's sensorimotor stage.***

- Follow-up research suggests that infants display certain understandings earlier than Piaget believed. Some awareness of object permanence, as revealed by the **violation-of-expectation method** and object-tracking research, is evident in the first few months. Furthermore, young infants display deferred imitation, and by 10 to 12 months, they can solve problems by analogy—attainments that require mental representation.

- Around their first birthday, babies understand **displaced reference** of words. In the second year, toddlers treat realistic-looking pictures symbolically. Around 2½ years, the **video deficit effect** declines; children grasp the symbolic meaning of video.
- Researchers believe that newborns have more built-in equipment for making sense of their world than Piaget assumed, although they disagree on how much initial understanding infants have. According to the **core knowledge perspective,** infants are born with core domains of thought, including physical, psychological, linguistic, and numerical knowledge, that support early, rapid cognitive development.
- Broad agreement exists that many cognitive changes of infancy are continuous rather than stagelike and that aspects of cognition develop unevenly rather than in an integrated fashion.

Information Processing *(p. 149)*

5.4 ***Describe the information-processing view of cognitive development and the general structure of the information-processing system.***

- Most information-processing researchers assume that we hold information in three parts of the mental system for processing: the **sensory register,** the **short-term memory store,** and **long-term memory.** The **central executive** joins with **working memory**—our "mental workspace"—to process information effectively. **Automatic processes** permit us to focus on other information while performing them.
- Gains in **executive function**—impulse control, flexible thinking, coordinating information in working memory, and planning—in childhood predict important cognitive and social outcomes in adolescence and adulthood.

5.5 ***Describe changes in attention, memory, and categorization over the first two years.***

- With age, infants attend to more aspects of the environment and take information in more quickly. In the second year, attention to novelty declines and sustained attention improves.
- Young infants are capable of **recognition** memory. By the middle of the first year, they also engage in **recall.** Both recognition and recall improve steadily with age.
- Infants group stimuli into an expanding array of categories. In the second year, toddlers begin to categorize flexibly, switching their basis of object sorting, and their grasp of the animate–inanimate distinction expands. Gradually, they shift from a perceptual to a conceptual basis of categorizing.

5.6 ***Explain the strengths and limitations of the information-processing approach to early cognitive development.***

- Information-processing findings reveal remarkable similarities between babies' and adults' thinking. But information processing has not yet provided a broad, comprehensive theory of cognitive development.

The Social Context of Early Cognitive Development *(p. 155)*

5.7 ***Explain how Vygotsky's concept of the zone of proximal development expands our understanding of early cognitive development.***

- Vygotsky believed that infants master culturally meaningful tasks within the **zone of proximal development**—ones just ahead of their current capacities—through the support and guidance of more skilled partners. As early as the first year, cultural variations in social experiences affect mental strategies.

© JAMES SHAFFER/PHOTOEDIT

Individual Differences in Early Mental Development *(p. 156)*

5.8 ***Describe the mental testing approach and the extent to which infant tests predict later performance.***

- The mental testing approach measures individual differences in developmental progress in an effort to predict future performance. Scores are arrived at by computing an **intelligence quotient (IQ),** which compares an individual's test performance with that of a **standardization** sample of same-age individuals, whose scores form a **normal distribution.**
- Infant tests consisting largely of perceptual and motor responses predict later intelligence poorly. Speed of habituation and recovery to novel visual stimuli is one of the best predictors of future IQ.

5.9 ***Discuss environmental influences on early mental development, including home, child care, and early intervention for at-risk infants and toddlers.***

- Research with the **Home Observation for Measurement of the Environment (HOME)** shows that an organized, stimulating home environment and parental affection, involvement, and encouragement repeatedly predict higher mental test scores. The extent to which parents talk to infants and toddlers is especially influential.

© ROBERTO WESTBROOK/BLEND IMAGES/CORBIS

- Quality of infant and toddler child care predicts later cognitive, language, academic, and social skills. Standards for **developmentally appropriate practice** specify program characteristics that meet young children's developmental needs.
- Intensive intervention beginning in infancy and extending through early childhood can prevent the gradual declines in intelligence and the poor academic performance of many poverty-stricken children.

Language Development *(p. 162)*

5.10 ***Describe theories of language development, and indicate the emphasis each places on innate abilities and environmental influences.***

- Chomsky's nativist theory regards children as naturally endowed with a **language acquisition device (LAD).** Consistent with this perspective, children everywhere attain major language milestones in a similar sequence, and childhood is a sensitive period for language acquisition.
- Recent theories suggest that language development results from interactions between inner capacities and environmental influences. Some interactionists apply the information-processing perspective to language development. Others emphasize the importance of children's social skills and language experiences.

5.11 ***Describe major language milestones in the first two years, individual differences, and ways adults can support early language development.***

- Infants begin **cooing** at 2 months and **babbling** at about 6 months. At 10 to 11 months, their skill at establishing **joint attention** improves, and soon they use preverbal gestures. Adults can encourage language progress by playing turn-taking games, establishing joint attention and labeling what babies see, and labeling their preverbal gestures.
- Around 12 months, toddlers say their first word. Young children make errors of **underextension** and **overextension.** Once vocabulary reaches 200 to 250 words, two-word utterances called **telegraphic speech** appear. At all ages, language comprehension is ahead of production.

TIINA & GEIR/CORBIS

- Girls show faster language progress than boys, and shy toddlers may wait before trying to speak. Compared to their higher-SES agemates, toddlers from low-SES homes usually have smaller vocabularies, which forecast poorer literacy skills and academic performance at school entry. Most toddlers' early words consist mainly of names for objects. Some produce many more social formulas and pronouns, and their vocabularies grow more slowly.
- Adults in many cultures speak to young children in **infant-directed speech (IDS),** a simplified form of communication that is well-suited to their learning needs. Live interaction with a responsive adult is better suited to spurring language progress than are media sources, which are effective only if they permit specific, contingent interaction.

IMPORTANT TERMS AND CONCEPTS

accommodation (p. 140)
adaptation (p. 139)
assimilation (p. 139)
autobiographical memory (p. 153)
automatic processes (p. 151)
babbling (p. 164)
central executive (p. 150)
circular reaction (p. 141)
cooing (p. 164)
core knowledge perspective (p. 147)
deferred imitation (p. 142)
developmentally appropriate practice (p. 160)
displaced reference (p. 145)
executive function (p. 151)
Home Observation for Measurement of the Environment (HOME) (p. 159)
infant-directed speech (IDS) (p. 167)
infantile amnesia (p. 153)
intelligence quotient (IQ) (p. 158)
intentional, or goal-directed, behavior (p. 141)
joint attention (p. 164)
language acquisition device (LAD) (p. 162)
long-term memory (p. 151)
make-believe play (p. 142)
mental representation (p. 142)
normal distribution (p. 158)
object permanence (p. 141)
organization (p. 140)
overextension (p. 165)
recall (p. 152)
recognition (p. 152)
scheme (p. 139)
sensorimotor stage (p. 139)
sensory register (p. 149)
short-term memory store (p. 150)
standardization (p. 158)
telegraphic speech (p. 165)
underextension (p. 165)
video deficit effect (p. 146)
violation-of-expectation method (p. 142)
working memory (p. 150)
zone of proximal development (p. 155)

CHAPTER 6 Emotional and Social Development in Infancy and Toddlerhood

This mother has forged a close, affectionate bond with her son. Her warmth and sensitivity engender a sense of security in the baby–a vital foundation for all aspects of early development.

WHAT'S AHEAD IN CHAPTER 6

As Caitlin reached 8 months of age, her parents noticed that she had become more fearful. One evening, when Carolyn and David left her with a babysitter, she wailed as they headed for the door—an experience she had accepted easily a few weeks earlier. Caitlin and Timmy's caregiver Ginette also observed an increasing wariness of strangers. At the mail carrier's knock at the door, both infants clung to Ginette's legs, reaching out to be picked up.

At the same time, each baby seemed more willful. Removing an object from the hand produced little response at 5 months. But at 8 months, when Timmy's mother, Vanessa, took away a table knife he had managed to reach, Timmy burst into angry screams and could not be consoled or distracted.

All Monica and Kevin knew about Grace's first year was that she had been deeply loved by her destitute, homeless mother. Separation from her had left Grace in shock. At first she was extremely sad, turning away when Monica or Kevin picked her up. But as Grace's new parents held her close, spoke gently, and satisfied her craving for food, Grace returned their affection. Two weeks after her arrival, her despondency gave way to a sunny, easygoing disposition. As her second birthday approached, she pointed to herself, exclaiming "Gwace!" and laid claim to treasured possessions: "Gwace's teddy bear!"

Taken together, the children's reactions reflect two related aspects of personality development during the first two years: close ties to others and a sense of self. We begin with Erikson's psychosocial theory, which provides an overview of infant and toddler personality development. Then, as we chart the course of emotional development, we will discover why fear and anger became more apparent in Caitlin's and Timmy's range of emotions by the end of the first year. Our attention then turns to the origins and developmental consequences of individual differences in temperament.

BRITTNEY MCCHRISTY/GETTY IMAGES

Next, we take up attachment to the caregiver, the child's first affectionate tie. We will see how the feelings of security that grow out of this important bond support the child's exploration, self-awareness, and expanding social relationships. Finally, we consider how cognitive advances combine with social experiences to foster early self-development during the second year.

Erikson's Theory of Infant and Toddler Personality

6.1 Identify personality changes that take place during Erikson's stages of basic trust versus mistrust and autonomy versus shame and doubt.

Our discussion in Chapter 1 revealed that the psychoanalytic perspective is no longer in the mainstream of child development research. But one of its lasting contributions is its ability to capture the essence of personality during each period of development. The most influential psychoanalytic approach is Erik Erikson's *psychosocial theory*, summarized on pages 10–11. Let's look closely at his first two stages.

Basic Trust versus Mistrust

Erikson accepted Freud's emphasis on the importance of the parent–infant relationship during feeding, but he expanded and enriched Freud's view. A healthy outcome during infancy, Erikson believed, depends on the *quality* of caregiving: relieving discomfort promptly and sensitively, holding the infant gently, waiting patiently until the baby has had enough milk, and weaning when the infant shows less interest in breast or bottle.

Erikson recognized that many factors affect parental responsiveness—personal happiness, family conditions (for example, additional young children, social supports, financial well-being), and culturally valued child-rearing practices. But when the *balance of care* is sympathetic and loving, the psychological conflict of the first year—**basic trust versus mistrust**—is resolved on the positive side. The trusting infant expects the world to be good and gratifying, so he feels confident about venturing out to explore it. The mistrustful baby cannot count on the kindness and compassion of others, so she protects herself by withdrawing from people and things around her.

Autonomy versus Shame and Doubt

With the transition to toddlerhood, Freud viewed parents' manner of toilet training as decisive for psychological health. In Erikson's view, toilet training is only one of many influential experiences.

The familiar refrains of newly walking, talking toddlers—"No!" "Do it myself!"—reveal that they have entered a period of budding selfhood. The conflict of **autonomy versus shame and doubt** is resolved favorably when parents provide young children with suitable guidance and reasonable choices. A self-confident, secure 2-year-old has parents who do not criticize or attack him when he fails at new skills—using the toilet, eating with a spoon, or putting away toys. And they meet his assertions of independence with tolerance and understanding—for example, by giving him an extra five minutes to finish his play before leaving for the grocery store. In contrast, when parents are over- or undercontrolling, the outcome is a child who feels forced and shamed and who doubts his ability to control impulses and act competently on his own.

In sum, basic trust and autonomy grow out of warm, sensitive parenting and reasonable expectations for impulse control starting in the second year. If children emerge from the first few years without sufficient trust in caregivers and without a healthy sense of individuality, the seeds are sown for adjustment problems.

▶ On a visit to a science museum, a 2-year-old insists on exploring a flight simulator. As the mother supports her toddler's desire to "do it myself," she fosters a healthy sense of autonomy.

Emotional Development

Researchers have conducted careful observations to find out how babies convey their emotions and interpret those of others. They have discovered that emotions play powerful roles in organizing the attainments that Erikson regarded as so important: social relationships, exploration of the environment, and discovery of the self (Saarni et al., 2006).

6.2 Describe the development of basic emotions over the first year, noting the adaptive function of each.

6.3 Summarize changes during the first two years in understanding of others' emotions, expression of self-conscious emotions, and emotional self-regulation.

Basic Emotions

Basic emotions—happiness, interest, surprise, fear, anger, sadness, and disgust—are universal in humans and other primates and have a long evolutionary history of promoting survival. Do newborns express basic emotions?

Although signs of some emotions are present, babies' earliest emotional life consists of little more than two global arousal states: attraction to pleasant stimulation and withdrawal from unpleasant stimulation (Camras et al., 2003). Only gradually do emotions become clear, well-organized signals. The *dynamic systems perspective* helps us understand how this happens: Children coordinate separate skills into more effective, emotionally expressive systems as the central nervous system develops and the child's goals and experiences change (Camras & Shuster, 2013; Camras & Shutter, 2010).

Sensitive, contingent caregiver communication, in which parents selectively mirror aspects of the baby's diffuse emotional behavior, helps infants construct emotional expressions that more closely resemble those of adults (Gergely & Watson, 1999). With age, face, voice, and posture start to form organized patterns that vary meaningfully with environmental events. For example, 7-month-old Caitlin typically responded to her parents' playful interaction with a joyful face, pleasant babbling, and a relaxed posture, as if to say, "This is fun!" In contrast, an unresponsive parent often evokes a sad face, fussy sounds, and a drooping body (sending the message, "I'm despondent") or an angry face, crying, and "pick-me-up" gestures (as if to say, "Change this unpleasant event!") (Mesman, van IJzendoorn, & Bakermans-Kranenburg, 2009; Vieites & Reeb-Sutherland, 2017). Gradually, emotional expressions become well-organized and specific—and therefore provide more precise information about the baby's internal state.

Four basic emotions—happiness, anger, sadness, and fear—have received the most research attention. Let's see how they develop.

Happiness. Happiness—expressed first in blissful smiles and later through exuberant laughter—contributes to many aspects of development. When infants achieve new skills, they smile and laugh, displaying delight in motor and cognitive mastery. The baby's smile encourages caregivers to smile responsively and to be affectionate and stimulating, and then the baby smiles even more (Bigelow & Power, 2014). Happiness binds parent and baby into a warm, supportive relationship that fosters the infant's motor, cognitive, and social competencies.

During the early weeks, newborn babies smile when full, during REM sleep, and in response to gentle stroking of the skin, rocking, and a parent's soft, high-pitched voice. By the end of the first month, infants smile at dynamic, eye-catching sights, such as a bright object jumping suddenly across their field of vision. Between 6 and 10 weeks, the parent's communication evokes a broad grin called the **social smile** (Lavelli & Fogel, 2005). These changes parallel the development of infant perceptual capacities—in particular, sensitivity to visual patterns, including the human face (see Chapter 4).

Laughter, which typically appears around 3 to 4 months, reflects faster processing of information than smiling. But as with smiling, the first laughs occur in response to very active stimuli, such as the parent saying playfully, "I'm gonna get you!" and kissing the baby's tummy. As infants understand more about their world, they laugh at events with subtler elements of surprise, such as a silent game of peekaboo. Soon they pick up on parents' facial and vocal cues to humor (Mireault et al., 2015). From 5 to 7 months, in the presence of those cues, they increasingly find absurd events—such as an adult wearing a ball as a clown's nose—funny.

Babies just a few months old smile and laugh more when interacting with familiar people, a preference that strengthens the parent–child bond. And like adults, 10- to 12-month-olds have several smiles, which vary with context—a broad, "cheek-raised" smile in response to a parent's greeting; a reserved, muted smile for a friendly stranger; and a "mouth-open" smile during stimulating play (Messinger & Fogel, 2007). By the end of the first year, the smile has become a deliberate social signal.

Anger and Sadness. Newborn babies respond with generalized distress to a variety of unpleasant experiences, including hunger, changes in body temperature, and too much or too little stimulation. From 4 to 6 months into the second year, angry expressions increase in frequency and intensity (Braungart-Rieker, Hill-Soderlund, & Karrass, 2010). Older infants also react with anger in a wider range of situations—when an object is taken away, an expected pleasant event does not occur, the caregiver leaves for a brief time, or they are put down for a nap (Camras et al., 1992; Stenberg & Campos, 1990; Sullivan & Lewis, 2003).

Why do angry reactions increase with age? As infants become capable of intentional behavior (see Chapter 5), they want to control their own actions and the effects they produce (Mascolo & Fischer, 2007). Furthermore, older infants are better at identifying who caused them pain or removed a toy. Their anger is particularly intense when a caregiver from whom they have come to expect warm behavior causes discomfort. And increased parental limit setting once babies crawl and walk contributes to babies' angry responses (Roben et al., 2012). The rise in anger is also adaptive. Independent movement enables an angry infant to defend herself or overcome an obstacle to obtain a desired object. Finally, anger motivates caregivers to relieve the baby's distress.

Although expressions of sadness also occur in response to pain, removal of an object, and brief separations, they are less frequent than anger (Alessandri, Sullivan, & Lewis, 1990). But when caregiver–infant communication is seriously disrupted, infant sadness is common—a condition that impairs all aspects of development (see the Biology and Environment box on the following page).

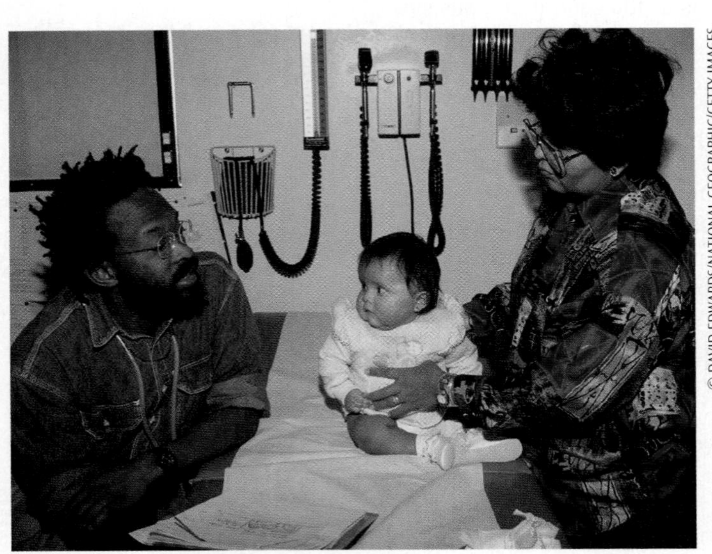

▶ Stranger anxiety appears in many infants after 6 months of age. This baby, though safe in her mother's arms, observes her doctor with cautious curiosity.

Fear. Like anger, fear rises from the second half of the first year into the second year (Braungart-Rieker, Hill-Soderland, & Karrass, 2010; Brooker et al., 2013). Older infants hesitate before playing with a new toy, and newly crawling infants soon back away from heights (see Chapter 4). But the most frequent expression of fear is to unfamiliar adults, a response called **stranger anxiety.** Many infants and toddlers are quite wary of strangers,

BIOLOGY AND ENVIRONMENT

Parental Depression and Child Development

About 8 to 10 percent of women experience chronic depression—mild to severe feelings of sadness, distress, and withdrawal that continue for months or years. In a similar percentage of mothers, depression emerges or strengthens after childbirth but fails to subside (Paulson & Bazemore, 2010). This is called *postpartum depression.*

Although it is less recognized and studied, fathers, too, experience chronic depression. About 5 percent of fathers report symptoms after the birth of a child (Gutierrez-Galve et al., 2015). Genetic makeup increases the risk of depressive illness, but social and cultural factors are also involved.

Maternal Depression

During Julia's pregnancy, her husband, Kyle, showed so little interest in the baby that Julia worried that having a child might be a mistake. Shortly after Lucy was born, Julia's mood plunged. She felt anxious and weepy, overwhelmed by Lucy's needs, and angry at loss of control over her own schedule. When Julia approached Kyle about her own fatigue and his unwillingness to help with the baby, he snapped that she was overreacting.

Julia's depressed mood quickly affected her baby. In the weeks after birth, infants of depressed mothers sleep poorly, are less attentive to their surroundings, and have elevated levels of the stress hormone cortisol (Fernandes et al., 2015; Goodman et al., 2011; Natsuaki et al., 2014). The more extreme the depression and the greater the number of stressors in a mother's life (such as marital discord, little or no social support, and poverty), the more the parent–child relationship suffers (Field, 2011; Vaever et al., 2015). By age 6 months, Lucy showed symptoms common in babies of depressed mothers—delays in motor and cognitive development, poor emotion regulation, an irritable mood, and attachment difficulties (Ibanez et al., 2015; Lefkovics, Baji, & Rigó, 2014; Vedova, 2014).

Depressed mothers view their babies negatively, which contributes to their inept caregiving (Lee & Hans, 2015). As their children get older, lack of warmth and involvement is often accompanied by inconsistent discipline—sometimes lax, at other times too forceful (Thomas et al., 2015). As we will see in later chapters, children who experience these maladaptive parenting practices often have serious adjustment problems. Some withdraw into a depressive mood themselves; others become impulsive and aggressive.

Paternal Depression

In a study of a large representative sample of British parents and babies, researchers assessed depressive symptoms of fathers shortly after birth and again the following year. Then they tracked the children's development into the preschool years (Ramchandani et al., 2008). Persistent paternal depression was, like maternal depression, a strong predictor of child behavior problems—especially overactivity, defiance, and aggression in boys.

Paternal depression is linked to frequent marital and father–child conflict as children grow older (Gutierrez-Galve et al., 2015). Over time, children subjected to parental negativity develop a pessimistic world view—one in which they lack self-confidence and perceive their parents and other people as threatening. Children who constantly feel in danger are especially likely to become overly aroused in stressful situations, easily losing control in the face of cognitive and social challenges (Sturge-Apple et al., 2008). Although children of depressed parents may inherit a tendency

▶ This father appears disengaged from his son. Disruptions in the parent–child relationship caused by paternal depression often lead to serious child behavior problems.

toward emotional and behavior problems, quality of parenting is a major factor in their adjustment.

Interventions

Early treatment is vital to prevent parental depression from interfering with the parent–child relationship. Julia's doctor referred her to a therapist, who helped Julia and Kyle with their marital problems. At times, antidepressant medication is prescribed.

In addition to alleviating parental depression, therapy that encourages depressed parents to engage in emotionally positive, responsive caregiving is vital for reducing developmental problems (Goodman et al., 2015). When a depressed parent does not respond easily to treatment, a warm relationship with the other parent or another caregiver can safeguard children's development.

although the reaction varies with temperament (some babies are generally more fearful), past experiences with strangers, and the current situation. When an unfamiliar adult picks up the infant, stranger anxiety is likely. But if the adult sits still while the baby moves around and a parent is nearby, infants often show positive and curious behavior (Horner, 1980). The stranger's style of interaction—expressing warmth, holding out an attractive toy, playing a familiar game, and approaching slowly rather than abruptly—reduces the baby's fear.

LOOK AND LISTEN

While observing an 8- to 18-month-old with his or her parent, gently approach the baby, offering a toy. Does the baby respond with stranger anxiety? To better understand the baby's behavior, ask the parent to describe his or her temperament and past experiences with strangers.

Cross-cultural research reveals that infant-rearing practices can modify stranger anxiety. Among the Efe hunters and gatherers of the Republic of Congo, where the maternal death rate is high, infant survival is safeguarded by a collective caregiving system in which, starting at birth, Efe babies are passed from one adult to another (Tronick, Morelli, & Ivey, 1992). Consequently, Efe infants show little stranger anxiety.

The rise in fear after age 6 months keeps newly mobile babies' enthusiasm for exploration in check. Once wariness develops, infants use the familiar caregiver as a **secure base,** or point from which to explore, venturing into the environment and then returning for emotional support. As part of this adaptive system, encounters with strangers lead to two conflicting tendencies: approach (indicated by interest and friendliness) and avoidance (indicated by fear). The infant's behavior is a balance between the two.

As toddlers discriminate more effectively between threatening and nonthreatening people and situations, stranger anxiety and other fears of the first two years decline. Fear also wanes as toddlers acquire more strategies for coping with it, as we will see when we discuss emotional self-regulation.

Understanding and Responding to the Emotions of Others

Infants' emotional expressions are closely tied to their ability to interpret the emotional cues of others. We have seen that in the first few months, babies match the feeling tone of the caregiver in face-to-face communication. Around 3 months, they become sensitive to the structure and timing of face-to-face interactions (see Chapter 5, page 164). When they gaze, smile, or vocalize, they now expect their social partner to respond in kind, and they reply with positive vocal and emotional reactions (Bigelow & Power, 2014; Markova & Legerstee, 2006). Recall from Chapter 4 (pages 122–123) that out of this early imitative communication, they start to view others as "like me"—an awareness believed to lay the foundation for understanding others' thoughts and feelings (Meltzoff, 2013).

At 4 to 5 months, infants distinguish positive from negative emotion in voices, and soon after, in facial expressions, gradually discriminating a wider range of emotions (see Chapter 4). Responding to emotional expressions as organized wholes indicates that these signals are becoming meaningful to babies. As skill at establishing joint attention improves, infants realize that an emotional expression not only has meaning but is also a meaningful reaction to a specific object or event (Thompson, 2015).

Once these understandings are in place, beginning at 8 to 10 months, infants engage in **social referencing**—actively seeking emotional information from a trusted person in an uncertain situation (Mumme et al., 2007). Many studies show that the caregiver's emotional expression (happy, angry, or fearful) influences whether a 1-year-old will be wary of strangers, play with a new toy, laugh at a humorous event, or cross the deep side of the visual cliff (see pages 174–175) (de Rosnay et al., 2006; Mireault et al., 2014; Stenberg, 2003; Striano & Rochat, 2000).

As toddlers start to appreciate that others' emotional reactions may differ from their own, social referencing allows them to compare their own and others' assessments of events. In one study, an adult showed 14- and 18-month-olds broccoli and crackers and acted delighted with one food but disgusted with the other (Repacholi & Gopnik, 1997). When asked to share the food, 18-month-olds offered the adult whichever food she appeared to like, regardless of their own preferences.

In sum, in social referencing, toddlers move beyond simply reacting to others' emotional messages. They use those messages to evaluate the safety and security of their surroundings, to guide their own actions, and to gather information about others' intentions and preferences.

Emergence of Self-Conscious Emotions

Besides basic emotions, humans are capable of a second, higher-order set of feelings, including guilt, shame, embarrassment, envy, and pride. These are called **self-conscious emotions** because each involves injury to or enhancement of our sense of self. We feel guilt when we have harmed someone and want to correct the wrongdoing. Envy arises when we desire something that another possesses, so we try to restore our sense of self-worth by securing that possession. When we are ashamed or embarrassed, we have negative feelings about our behavior, and we want to retreat so others will no longer notice our failings. In contrast, pride reflects delight in the self's achievements, and we are inclined to tell others what we have accomplished and to take on further challenges (Lewis, 2014).

Self-conscious emotions appear in the middle of the second year, as 18- to 24-month-olds become firmly aware of the self as a separate, unique individual. Toddlers show shame and embarrassment by lowering their eyes, hanging their head, and hiding their face with their hands. They show guiltlike reactions, too. After noticing Grace's unhappiness, 22-month-old Caitlin returned a toy she had grabbed and patted her upset playmate. Pride and envy also emerge around age 2 (Barrett, 2005; Garner, 2003; Lewis, 2014).

Besides self-awareness, self-conscious emotions require an additional ingredient: adult instruction in *when* to feel proud, ashamed, or guilty. Parents begin this tutoring early when they say, "Look how far you can throw that ball!" or "You should feel ashamed for grabbing that toy!" Self-conscious emotions play important roles in children's achievement-related and moral behaviors. The situations in which adults encourage these feelings vary from culture to culture. In Western nations, most children are taught to feel pride in personal achievement. In cultures such as China and Japan, which promote an interdependent self, calling attention to individual success evokes embarrassment and self-effacement. And violating cultural standards by failing to show concern for others—a parent, a teacher, or an employer—sparks intense shame (Lewis, 2014).

▶ This 2-year-old's older sister praises his success at tower building. To experience self-conscious emotions, such as pride, young children need self-awareness as well as instruction in when to feel proud of an accomplishment.

Beginnings of Emotional Self-Regulation

Besides expressing a wider range of emotions, infants and toddlers begin to manage their emotional experiences. **Emotional self-regulation** refers to the strategies we use to adjust our emotional state to a comfortable level of intensity so we can accomplish our goals (Thompson & Goodvin, 2007). When you remind yourself that an anxiety-provoking event will be over soon, suppress your anger at a friend's behavior, or decide not to see a scary horror film, you are engaging in emotional self-regulation.

Emotional self-regulation requires voluntary, effortful management of emotions. It improves rapidly during the first few years, as the result of a *dynamic system* of influences that include development of the prefrontal cortex and its networks of connections to brain areas involved in emotional reactivity and control; and support from caregivers, who help children manage intense emotion and, as cognitive and language skills improve, teach them strategies for doing so on their own (Rothbart, Posner, & Kieras, 2006; Thompson, 2015).

In the early months, infants are easily overwhelmed by intense emotion. They depend on soothing interventions of caregivers—being lifted to the shoulder, rocked, gently stroked, and talked to softly—for distraction and reorienting of attention.

More effective functioning of the prefrontal cortex increases the baby's tolerance for stimulation. Between 2 and 4 months, caregivers build on this capacity by initiating face-to-face play and attention to objects. In these interactions, parents arouse pleasure in the baby while adjusting the pace of their behavior so the infant does not become distressed (Kopp & Neufeld, 2003). As a result, the baby's tolerance for stimulation increases further.

From 3 months on, the ability to shift attention away from unpleasant events helps infants control distress (Ekas, Lickenbrock, & Braungart-Rieker, 2013). And crawling and walking, which permit babies to approach or retreat from various situations, contribute to more effective self-regulation in the second half of the first year.

Infants whose parents "read" and respond contingently and sympathetically to their emotional cues tend to be less fussy and fearful, to express more pleasurable emotion, to be more interested in exploration, and to be easier to soothe (Braungart-Rieker, Hill-Soderlund, & Karrass, 2010; Crockenberg & Leerkes, 2004). In contrast, parents who respond impatiently or angrily or who wait to intervene until the infant has become extremely agitated reinforce the baby's rapid rise to intense distress. Consequently, brain structures that buffer stress may fail to develop properly, resulting in an anxious, reactive child who has a reduced capacity for managing emotional problems (Blair & Raver, 2012; Frankel et al., 2015).

Caregivers also provide lessons in socially approved ways of expressing feelings. Beginning in the first few months, parents encourage infants to suppress negative emotion by imitating their expressions of interest, happiness, and surprise more often than their expressions of anger and sadness. Boys get more of this training than girls, in part because boys have a harder time regulating negative emotion (Else-Quest et al., 2006; Malatesta et al., 1986). As a result, the well-known sex difference—females as emotionally expressive and males as emotionally controlled—is promoted at a tender age.

Cultures that highly value social harmony place particular emphasis on socially appropriate emotional behavior while discouraging expression of individual feelings. Compared with Western parents, Chinese and Japanese parents, and parents in many non-Western village cultures, discourage the expression of strong emotion in babies. Nso mothers of rural Cameroon, for example, spend less time imitating infant social smiling than do German mothers, and Nso mothers are especially quick to quiet infant distress through soothing and breastfeeding. Chinese, Japanese, and Nso babies, in turn, smile, laugh, and cry less than their Western agemates (Friedlmeier, Corapci, & Cole, 2011; Gartstein et al., 2010; Kärtner, Holodynski, & Wörmann, 2013).

Toward the end of the second year, a vocabulary for talking about feelings—"happy," "love," "surprised," "scary," "yucky," "mad"—develops rapidly, but toddlers are not yet good at using language to manage their emotions. Temper tantrums tend to occur when an adult rejects their demands or they are otherwise frustrated, particularly when toddlers are fatigued or hungry (Mascolo & Fischer, 2007). When parents are sympathetic but set limits (by not giving in to tantrums), distract by offering acceptable alternatives, and later suggest better ways to solve the initial problem, children display more effective anger-regulation strategies and social skills during the preschool years (Lecuyer & Houck, 2006; Scrimgeour, Davis, & Buss, 2016).

ASK YOURSELF

CONNECT Why do children of depressed parents have difficulty regulating emotion (see page 175)? What implications do their weak self-regulatory skills have for their response to cognitive and social challenges?

APPLY At age 14 months, Reggie built a block tower and gleefully knocked it down. At age 2, he called to his mother and pointed proudly to his tall block tower. What explains this change in Reggie's emotional behavior?

REFLECT How do you typically manage negative emotion? How might your early experiences, gender, and cultural background have influenced your style of emotional self-regulation?

Temperament and Development

6.4 Explain the meaning of temperament and how it is measured.

6.5 Discuss the roles of heredity and environment in the stability of temperament, including the goodness-of-fit model.

From early infancy, Caitlin's sociability was unmistakable. She smiled and laughed while interacting with adults and, in her second year, readily approached other children. Meanwhile, Monica marveled at Grace's calm, relaxed disposition. At 19 months, she sat contentedly in a highchair through a two-hour family celebration at a restaurant. In contrast, Timmy was active and distractible. Vanessa found herself chasing him as he dropped one toy, moved on to the next, and climbed on chairs and tables.

When we describe one person as cheerful and "upbeat," another as active and energetic, and still others as calm, cautious, or prone to angry outbursts, we are referring to **temperament**—early-appearing, stable individual differences in reactivity and self-regulation. *Reactivity* refers to quickness and intensity of emotional arousal, attention, and motor activity. *Self-regulation,* as we have seen, refers to strategies that modify that reactivity (Rothbart, 2011; Rothbart & Bates, 2006). The psychological traits that make up temperament are believed to form the cornerstone of the adult personality.

In 1956, Alexander Thomas and Stella Chess initiated the New York Longitudinal Study, a groundbreaking investigation of the development of temperament that followed 141 children from early infancy well into adulthood. Results showed that temperament can increase a child's chances of experiencing psychological problems or, alternatively, protect a child from the negative effects of a highly stressful home life. At the same time, Thomas and Chess (1977) discovered that parenting practices can modify children's temperaments considerably.

These findings stimulated a growing body of research on temperament, including its stability, biological roots, and interaction with child-rearing experiences. Let's begin to explore these issues by looking at the structure, or makeup, of temperament and how it is measured.

The Structure of Temperament

Thomas and Chess's model of temperament inspired all others that followed. When detailed descriptions of infants' and children's behavior obtained from parent interviews were rated on nine dimensions of temperament, certain characteristics clustered together, yielding three types of children:

- The **easy child** (40 percent of the sample) quickly establishes regular routines in infancy, is generally cheerful, and adapts easily to new experiences.
- The **difficult child** (10 percent of the sample) is irregular in daily routines, is slow to accept new experiences, and tends to react negatively and intensely.
- The **slow-to-warm-up child** (15 percent of the sample) is inactive, shows mild, low-key reactions to environmental stimuli, is negative in mood, and adjusts slowly to new experiences.

Note that 35 percent of the children did not fit any of these categories. Instead, they showed unique blends of temperamental characteristics.

Difficult children are at high risk for adjustment problems—both anxious withdrawal and aggressive behavior in early and middle childhood (Bates, Wachs, & Emde, 1994; Ramos et al., 2005). Nevertheless, the difficult label has been criticized because judgments of child difficulty vary widely across caregivers and cultures. Although slow-to-warm-up children present fewer problems, they tend to show excessive fearfulness and slow, constricted behavior in the late preschool and school years, when they are expected to respond actively and quickly in classrooms and peer groups (Chess & Thomas, 1984; Schmitz et al., 1999).

Today, the most influential model of temperament is Mary Rothbart's, described in Table 6.1. It combines related traits proposed by Thomas and Chess and other researchers, yielding a concise list of six dimensions that represent the three underlying components included in the definition of temperament: (1) *emotion* ("fearful distress," "irritable distress," "positive affect"), (2) *attention* ("attention span/persistence"), and (3) *action* ("activity level"). Individuals differ not just in their reactivity on each dimension but also in the self-regulatory dimension of temperament, **effortful control**—the capacity to voluntarily suppress a dominant response in order to plan and execute a more adaptive response (Rothbart, 2011, 2015; Rothbart & Bates, 2006). Variations in effortful control are evident in how effectively a child can focus and shift attention, inhibit impulses, and manage negative emotion.

The capacity for effortful control in early childhood predicts favorable development and adjustment in diverse cultures, with some studies showing long-term effects into adolescence and adulthood (Chen & Schmidt, 2015). Positive outcomes include persistence, task mastery, academic achievement, cooperation, moral maturity (such as concern about wrongdoing and willingness to apologize), and social behaviors of cooperation, sharing, and helpfulness (Eisenberg, 2010; Kochanska & Aksan, 2006; Posner & Rothbart, 2007; Valiente, Lemery-Chalfant, & Swanson, 2010).

Turn back to page 151 in Chapter 5 to review the concept of executive function, and note its resemblance to effortful control. These converging concepts, which are

TABLE 6.1
Rothbart's Model of Temperament

DIMENSION	DESCRIPTION
REACTIVITY	
Activity level	Level of gross-motor activity
Attention span/persistence	Duration of orienting or interest
Fearful distress	Wariness and distress in response to intense or novel stimuli, including time to adjust to new situations
Irritable distress	Extent of fussing, crying, and distress when desires are frustrated
Positive affect	Frequency of expression of happiness and pleasure
SELF-REGULATION	
Effortful control	Capacity to voluntarily suppress a dominant, reactive response in order to plan and execute a more adaptive response In the first two years, called *orienting/regulation,* which refers to the capacity to engage in self-soothing, shift attention from unpleasant events, and sustain interest for an extended time

associated with similar positive outcomes, reveal that the same mental activities lead to effective regulation in both the cognitive and emotional/social domains.

Measuring Temperament

Temperament is often assessed through interviews or questionnaires given to parents. Behavior ratings by pediatricians, teachers, and others familiar with the child and laboratory observations by researchers have also been used. Parental reports are convenient and take advantage of parents' depth of knowledge about their child across many situations (Chen & Schmidt, 2015). Although information from parents has been criticized as being biased, parental reports are moderately related to researchers' observations of children's behavior (Majdandžić & van den Boom, 2007; Mangelsdorf, Schoppe, & Buur, 2000). And parent perceptions are useful for understanding how parents view and respond to their child.

Observations by researchers avoid the subjectivity of parental reports but can lead to other inaccuracies. In homes, observers find it hard to capture rare but important events, such as infants' response to frustration. And in the unfamiliar laboratory setting, fearful children may become too upset to complete the session (Rothbart, 2011). Still, researchers can better control children's experiences in the lab. And they can conveniently combine observations of behavior with neurobiological measures to gain insight into the biological bases of temperament.

Most neurobiological research has focused on children who fall at opposite extremes of the positive-affect and fearful-distress dimensions of temperament: **inhibited,** or **shy, children,** who react negatively to and withdraw from novel stimuli, and **uninhibited,** or **sociable, children,** who display positive emotion to and approach novel stimuli. As the Biology and Environment box on the following page reveals, biologically based reactivity differentiates children with inhibited and uninhibited temperaments.

Stability of Temperament

Young children who score low or high on attention span, irritability, sociability, shyness, or effortful control tend to respond similarly when assessed again several months to a few years later and, occasionally, even into the adult years (Casalin et al., 2012; Caspi et al., 2003; Kochanska & Knaack, 2003; Majdandžić & van den Boom, 2007; van den Akker et al., 2010). However, the overall stability of temperament is low in infancy and toddlerhood and only moderate from the preschool years on (Putnam, Samson, & Rothbart, 2000). A major reason is that temperament itself develops with age. To illustrate, let's look at irritability. Recall from Chapter 3 that the early months are a period of fussing and crying for most babies. As infants better regulate their attention and emotions, many who initially seemed irritable become calm and content.

Long-term prediction from early temperament is best achieved after age 3, when children's styles of responding are better established (Dyson et al., 2015; Roberts & DelVecchio, 2000). In line with this idea, between ages 2½ and 3, children improve substantially on a wide range of tasks requiring effortful control, such as waiting for a reward, succeeding at games like "Simon Says," and selectively attending to one stimulus while ignoring competing stimuli (Kochanska, Murray, & Harlan, 2000; Li-Grining, 2007). Researchers believe that around this time, areas in the prefrontal cortex involved in suppressing impulses develop rapidly (Rothbart, 2011).

Nevertheless, the ease with which children manage their reactivity depends on the type and strength of the reactive emotion. Compared to angry, irritable toddlers, fearful toddlers generally show greater improvement in effortful control by the preschool years (Bridgett et al., 2009; Kochanska & Knaack, 2003). Child rearing is also important in modifying reactivity. Young children with either fearful or irritable temperaments who experience patient, supportive parenting gain most in capacity to manage their emotions (Kim & Kochanska, 2012; Warren & Simmens, 2005). But if exposed to insensitive or unresponsive parenting, these emotionally negative children are especially likely to score low in effortful control.

In sum, many factors affect the extent to which a child's temperament remains stable, including development of the biological systems on which temperament is based, the child's capacity for effortful control, the success of her efforts, and child-rearing experiences. With these ideas in mind, let's turn to genetic and environmental contributions to temperament and personality.

BIOLOGY AND ENVIRONMENT

Development of Shyness and Sociability

Two 4-month-old babies, Larry and Mitch, visited the laboratory of Jerome Kagan, who observed their reactions to a variety of unfamiliar experiences. When exposed to new sights and sounds, such as a moving mobile decorated with colorful toys, Larry moved his arms and legs with agitation and cried. In contrast, Mitch remained relaxed and quiet, smiling and cooing.

As toddlers, Larry and Mitch returned to the lab, where they experienced several procedures designed to induce uncertainty. Electrodes were placed on their bodies and blood pressure cuffs on their arms to measure heart rate; toy robots, animals, and puppets moved before their eyes; and unfamiliar people behaved in unexpected ways. While Larry whimpered and quickly withdrew, Mitch watched with interest, laughed, and approached the toys and strangers.

On a third visit, at age 4½, Larry barely talked or smiled during an interview with an unfamiliar adult. In contrast, Mitch expressed pleasure at each new activity. In a playroom with two unfamiliar peers, Larry pulled back and watched, while Mitch made friends quickly.

In longitudinal research on several hundred European-American infants followed into adolescence, Kagan found that about 20 percent of 4-month-olds were, like Larry, easily upset by novelty; another 40 percent, like Mitch, were comfortable, even delighted, with new experiences. About 20 to 25 percent of these extreme groups retained their temperamental styles as they grew older (Kagan, 2003; Kagan et al., 2007). But most children's dispositions became less extreme over time. Genetic makeup and child-rearing experiences jointly influenced stability and change in temperament.

Neurobiological Correlates of Shyness and Sociability

Individual differences in arousal of the *amygdala,* an inner brain structure devoted to processing novelty and emotional information, contribute to these contrasting temperaments. In shy, inhibited children, novel stimuli easily excite the amygdala and its connections to the prefrontal cortex and the sympathetic nervous system, which prepares the body to act in the face of threat. In sociable, uninhibited children, the same level of stimulation evokes minimal neural excitation (Schwartz et al., 2012). And additional neurobiological responses mediated by the amygdala distinguish these two emotional styles:

- *Heart rate.* From the first few weeks of life, the heart rates of shy children are consistently higher than those of sociable children, and they speed up further in response to unfamiliar events (Schmidt et al., 2007; Snidman et al., 1995).
- *Cortisol.* Saliva concentrations of the stress hormone cortisol tend to be higher, and to rise more in response to a stressful event, in shy than in sociable children (Schmidt et al., 1999; Zimmermann & Stansbury, 2004).
- *Pupil dilation, blood pressure, and skin surface temperature.* Compared with sociable children, shy children show greater pupil dilation, rise in blood pressure, and cooling of the fingertips when faced with novelty (Kagan et al., 2007).

Furthermore, shy children show greater EEG activity in the right than in the left frontal lobe of the cerebral cortex, which is associated with negative emotional reactivity; sociable children show the opposite pattern (Fox et al., 2008). Neural activity in the amygdala, which is transmitted to the frontal lobes, probably contributes to these differences.

Child-Rearing Practices

According to Kagan, most extremely shy or sociable children inherit a physiology that biases them toward a particular temperamental style (Kagan et al., 2013c). Yet experience, too, has a powerful impact.

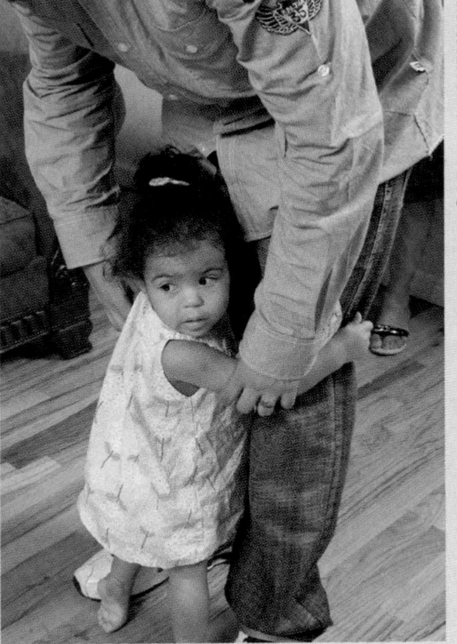

▶ A strong physiological response to uncertain situations prompts this toddler to cling to her father. With patient but insistent encouragement, her parents can help her overcome the urge to retreat.

Warm, supportive parenting reduces shy infants' and preschoolers' intense reactivity to novelty, whereas cold, intrusive parenting heightens anxiety (Davis & Buss, 2012; Kiel, Premo, & Buss, 2016). And if parents overprotect infants and young children who dislike novelty, they make it harder for the child to overcome an urge to retreat. Parents who make appropriate demands for their child to approach new experiences help shy youngsters develop strategies for regulating fear (Chronis-Tuscano et al., 2015).

When inhibition persists, it leads to excessive cautiousness, low self-esteem, and loneliness. In adolescence, it increases the risk of severe anxiety, depression, unrealistic worries about physical harm, and social phobia—intense fear of being humiliated in social situations (Kagan, 2013c; Karevold et al., 2012). For inhibited children to acquire effective social skills, parenting must be tailored to their temperaments—a theme we will encounter again in this and later chapters.

Genetic and Environmental Influences

Identical twins are more similar than fraternal twins across a wide range of temperamental and personality traits (Caspi & Shiner, 2006; Krueger & Johnson, 2008; Roisman & Fraley, 2006). In Chapter 2, we noted that heritability estimates derived from twin studies suggest a moderate role for genetic factors in temperament and personality: About half of individual differences have been attributed to differences in genetic makeup.

Although genetic influences on temperament are clear, environment is also powerful. Furthermore, heredity and environment often jointly contribute to temperament, since a child's approach to the world can be intensified or lessened by experience. To illustrate, let's begin by looking at ethnic and gender differences.

Ethnic and Gender Differences. Compared with European-American infants, Chinese and Japanese babies tend to be less active, irritable, vocal, more easily soothed when upset, and better at quieting themselves (Kagan, 2013c; Lewis, Ramsay, & Kawakami, 1993). East Asian babies are also more attentive and less distractible, and as 2-year-olds, they are more compliant and cooperative with adults and higher in effortful control—for example, able to wait longer to play with an attractive toy (Chen et al., 2003; Gartstein et al., 2006). At the same time, Chinese and Japanese babies are more fearful, displaying more anxiety in an unfamiliar playroom and when interacting with a stranger (Chen, Wang, & DeSouza, 2006).

These variations may have genetic roots, but they are supported by cultural beliefs and practices, yielding *gene–environment correlations* (see page 63 in Chapter 2). Japanese mothers usually say that babies come into the world as independent beings who must learn to rely on their parents through close physical contact. European-American mothers, in contrast, typically believe that they must wean the baby away from dependency toward autonomy. Consistent with these beliefs, Asian mothers interact gently, soothingly, and gesturally with their babies, whereas European-American mothers use a more active, stimulating, verbal approach (Kagan, 2010). Also, recall from our discussion of emotional self-regulation that Chinese and Japanese adults discourage babies from expressing strong emotion, which contributes further to their infants' tranquility.

▶ How will this mother respond to her daughter's anger and distress? With patience and support, emotionally reactive toddlers develop especially favorably. But when exposed to hostile, rejecting parenting, they fare worse than other children, quickly becoming aggressive and defiant.

Similarly, gender differences in temperament are evident as early as infancy, suggesting a genetic foundation. Boys are more active and daring, less fearful, more irritable when frustrated, and more impulsive—factors that contribute to their higher injury rates throughout childhood and adolescence. And girls' large advantage in effortful control undoubtedly contributes to their greater compliance and cooperativeness, better school performance, and lower incidence of behavior problems (Else-Quest, 2012; Olino et al., 2013). At the same time, parents more often encourage their young sons to be physically active and their daughters to seek help and physical closeness—through activities they encourage and through more positive reactions when their child exhibits temperamental traits consistent with gender stereotypes (Bryan & Dix, 2009; Hines, 2015).

Differential Susceptibility to Rearing Experiences. Earlier we mentioned findings indicating that emotionally reactive toddlers function worse than other children when exposed to inept parenting, yet benefit most from good parenting. Researchers have become increasingly interested in temperamental differences in children's susceptibility (or responsiveness) to environmental influences (Pluess & Belsky, 2011). Using molecular genetic testing, they are clarifying how these *gene–environment interactions* operate.

Consistently, young children with a chromosome 7 gene containing a certain repetition of base pairs called short 5-HTTLPR—which interferes with functioning of the inhibitory neurotransmitter serotonin and, thus, greatly increases the risk of self-regulation difficulties—are highly susceptible to effects of parenting quality. Those exposed to maladaptive parenting readily develop externalizing problems. But when parenting is kind and supportive, children with this gene fare exceedingly well in adjustment (Davies & Cicchetti, 2014; Kochanska et al., 2011, 2015; van IJzendoorn, Belsky, & Bakermans-Kranenburg, 2012). Among children without the 5-HTTLPR genotype, parenting—whether positive or negative—has minimal impact on externalizing symptoms.

As these outcomes reveal, young children with the short 5-HTTLPR gene show unusually high early *plasticity* (see page 6 in Chapter 1 to review). Because children with this "susceptibility attribute" fare better than other children when parenting is supportive, they are likely to benefit most from interventions aimed at promoting responsive child rearing.

Siblings' Unique Experiences. In families with several children, an additional influence on temperament is at work: When parents are asked to describe each of their children's personalities, they often look for differences between siblings: "She's a lot more active," "He's more sociable," "She's far more persistent." As a result, parents often regard siblings as more distinct than other observers do.

In a large study of 1- to 3-year-old twin pairs, parents rated identical twins as less alike in temperament than researchers' ratings indicated. And whereas researchers rated fraternal twins as moderately similar, parents viewed them as somewhat opposite in temperament (Saudino, 2003). This tendency to emphasize each child's unique qualities likely heightens parents' differential treatment of siblings.

Besides unique experiences within the family, siblings have distinct experiences with teachers, peers, and others in their community that affect personality development. And as we will see in Chapter 10, in middle childhood and adolescence, siblings often seek ways to differ from each other. For all these reasons, both identical and fraternal twins tend to become increasingly dissimilar in personality with age (Loehlin & Martin, 2001). In sum, temperament and personality can be understood only in terms of complex interdependencies between genetic and environmental factors.

Temperament and Child Rearing: The Goodness-of-Fit Model

Thomas and Chess (1977) proposed a **goodness-of-fit model** to explain how temperament and environment can together produce favorable outcomes. Goodness of fit involves creating child-rearing environments that recognize each child's temperament while simultaneously encouraging more adaptive functioning. If a child's disposition interferes with learning or getting along with others, adults must gently but consistently counteract the child's maladaptive style.

Difficult children (who withdraw from new experiences and react negatively and intensely) frequently experience parenting that fits poorly with their dispositions. As infants, they are less likely to receive sensitive caregiving. By the second year, their parents tend to resort to angry, punitive discipline, which undermines the development of effortful control. As the child reacts with defiance and disobedience, parents become increasingly stressed. As a result, they continue their coercive tactics and also discipline inconsistently, at times rewarding the child's noncompliance by giving in to it (Lee et al., 2012; Paulussen-Hoogeboom et al., 2007; Pesonen et al., 2008). These practices sustain and even increase the child's irritable, conflict-ridden style.

In contrast, when parents are positive and sensitive, which helps infants and toddlers—especially those who are emotionally reactive—regulate emotion, difficultness declines by age 2 or 3 (Raikes et al., 2007). In toddlerhood and childhood, parental sensitivity, support, clear expectations, and limits foster effortful control, also reducing the likelihood that difficultness will persist and lead to emotional and social difficulties (Cipriano & Stifter, 2010).

An effective match between rearing conditions and child temperament is best accomplished early, before unfavorable temperament–environment relationships produce maladjustment. The goodness-of-fit model reminds us that children have unique dispositions that adults must accept. Parents can neither take full credit for their children's virtues nor be blamed for all their faults. But parents can turn an environment that exaggerates a child's problems into one that builds on the child's strengths. As we will see next, goodness of fit is also at the heart of infant–caregiver attachment. This first intimate relationship grows out of interaction between parent and baby, to which the emotional styles of both partners contribute.

ASK YOURSELF

CONNECT Explain how findings on ethnic and gender differences in temperament illustrate gene–environment correlation, discussed on pages 63–64 in Chapter 2.

APPLY Mandy and Jeff are parents of 2-year-old inhibited Sam and 3-year-old irritable Maria. Explain the importance of effortful control to Mandy and Jeff, and suggest ways they can strengthen it in each of their children.

REFLECT How would you describe your temperament as a young child? Do you think your temperament has remained stable, or has it changed? What factors might be involved

Development of Attachment

6.6 Describe the development of attachment during the first two years.

6.7 Explain how researchers measure attachment security, the factors that affect it, and its implications for later development.

6.8 Describe infants' capacity for multiple attachments.

Attachment is the strong affectionate tie we have with special people in our lives that leads us to feel pleasure when we interact with them and to be comforted by their nearness in times of stress. By the second half-year, infants have become attached to familiar people who have responded to their needs. Consider how babies of this age single out their parents for special attention: When the parent enters the room, the baby breaks into a broad, friendly smile. When she picks him up, he pats her face, explores her hair, and snuggles against her. When he feels anxious or afraid, he crawls into her lap and clings closely.

Attachment has also been the subject of intense theoretical debate. Recall that the *psychoanalytic perspective* regards feeding as the central context in which caregivers and babies build this close emotional bond. *Behaviorism,* too, emphasizes the importance of feeding, but for different reasons. According to a well-known behaviorist explanation, infants learn to prefer the mother's soft caresses, warm smiles, and tender words because these events are paired with tension relief as she satisfies the baby's hunger.

Although feeding is an important context for building a close relationship, attachment does not depend on hunger satisfaction. In the 1950s, a famous experiment showed that rhesus monkeys reared with terry-cloth and wire-mesh "surrogate mothers" clung to the soft terry-cloth substitute, even though the wire-mesh "mother" held the bottle and infants had to climb onto it to be fed (Harlow & Zimmerman, 1959). Human infants, too, become attached to family members who seldom feed them, including fathers, siblings, and grandparents. And toddlers in Western cultures who sleep alone and experience frequent daytime separations from their parents sometimes develop strong emotional ties to cuddly objects, such as blankets and teddy bears, that play no role in infant feeding!

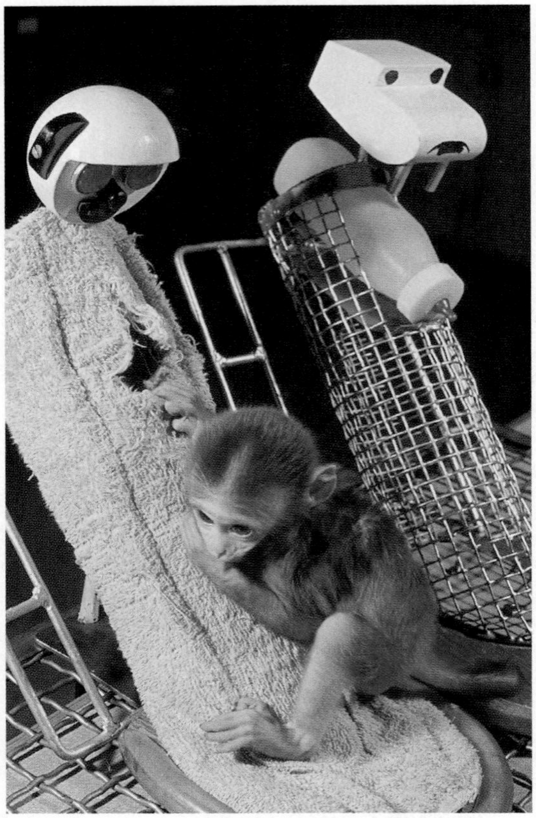

NINA LEEN/TIME LIFE PICTURES/GETTY IMAGES

▶ Baby monkeys reared with "surrogate mothers" preferred to cling to a soft terry-cloth "mother" over a wire-mesh "mother" holding a bottle—evidence that parent–infant attachment is based on more than satisfaction of hunger.

Bowlby's Ethological Theory

Today, **ethological theory of attachment,** which recognizes the infant's emotional tie to the caregiver as an evolved response that promotes survival, is the most widely accepted view. John Bowlby (1969), who first applied this perspective to the infant–caregiver bond, was inspired by Konrad Lorenz's studies of imprinting (see Chapter 1). Bowlby believed that the human infant, like the young of other animal species, is endowed with a set of built-in behaviors that help keep the parent nearby to protect the infant from danger and to provide support for exploring and mastering the environment. Contact with the parent also ensures that the baby will be fed, but Bowlby pointed out that feeding is not the basis for attachment. Rather, attachment can best be understood in an evolutionary context in which survival of the species—through ensuring both safety and competence—is of utmost importance.

According to Bowlby, the infant's relationship with the parent begins as a set of innate signals that call the adult to the baby's side. Over time, a true affectionate bond forms, supported by new cognitive and emotional capacities as well as by a history of warm, sensitive care. Attachment develops in four phases:

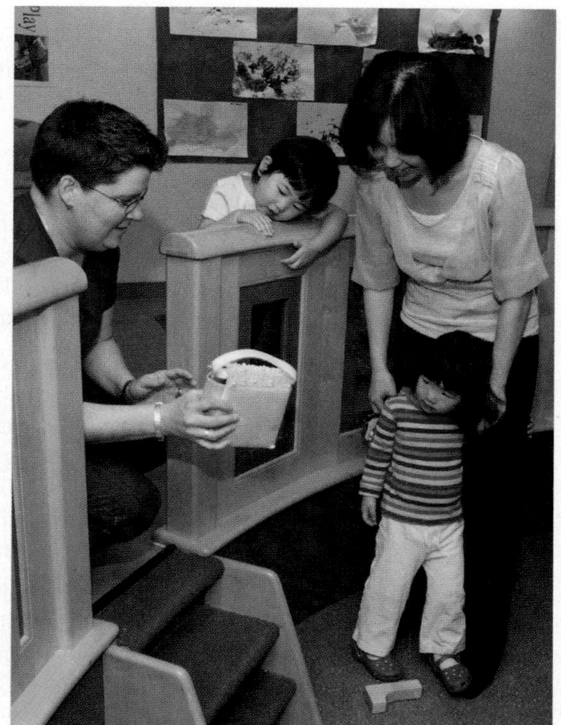

▶ With her teacher's enticement to play and an explanation that her mother will be back soon, this 2-year-old is likely to separate without tears. Her language and representational skills enable her to predict her mother's return, so separation anxiety declines.

1. *Preattachment phase (birth to 6 weeks).* Built-in signals—grasping, smiling, crying, and gazing into the adult's eyes—help bring newborn babies into close contact with other humans, who comfort them. Newborns prefer their own mother's smell, voice, and face (see Chapters 3 and 4). But they are not yet attached to her, since they do not mind being left with an unfamiliar adult.
2. *"Attachment-in-the-making" phase (6 weeks to 6–8 months).* Infants respond differently to a familiar caregiver than to a stranger. For example, at 4 months, Timmy smiled, laughed, and babbled more freely when interacting with his mother and quieted more quickly when she picked him up. As infants learn that their own actions affect the caregiver's behavior, they begin to develop a *sense of trust*—the expectation that the caregiver will respond when signaled—but they still do not protest when separated from her.
3. *"Clear-cut" attachment phase (6–8 months to 18 months–2 years).* Now attachment to the familiar caregiver is evident. Babies display **separation anxiety,** becoming upset when their trusted caregiver leaves. Like stranger anxiety (see page 174), separation anxiety does not always occur; it depends on infant temperament and the current situation. But in many cultures, separation anxiety increases between 6 and 15 months. Besides protesting the parent's departure, older infants and toddlers try hard to maintain her presence. They approach, follow, and climb on her in preference to others. And they use the familiar caregiver as a secure base from which to explore.
4. *Formation of a reciprocal relationship (18 months to 2 years and on).* Rapid growth in representation and language enables toddlers to understand some of the factors that influence the parent's coming and going and to predict her return. As a result, separation protest declines. Now children use requests and persuasion to alter the caregiver's goals. For example, at age 2, Caitlin asked Carolyn and David to read her a story before leaving her with a babysitter. The extra time with her parents, along with a better understanding of where they were going ("to have dinner with Uncle Sean") and when they would be back ("right after you go to sleep"), helped Caitlin withstand her parents' absence.

According to Bowlby (1980), out of their experiences during these four phases, children construct an enduring affectionate tie to the caregiver that they can use as a secure base in the parents' absence. This image serves as an **internal working model,** or set of expectations about the availability of attachment figures and their likelihood of providing support during times of stress. The internal working model becomes a vital part of personality, serving as a guide for all future close relationships (Bretherton & Munholland, 2008).

Consistent with these ideas, as early as the second year, toddlers seem to form attachment-related expectations about parental comfort and support. In several studies, securely attached 12- to 16-month-olds looked longer at a video of an unresponsive caregiver (inconsistent with their expectations) than a video of a responsive caregiver. Insecurely attached agemates, in contrast, either looked longer at the responsive caregiver or did not distinguish between the two (Johnson, Dweck, & Chen, 2007; Johnson et al., 2010). The researchers concluded that the toddlers' visual responses reflected "surprise" at caregiver behavior at odds with their own internal working model. With age, children continually revise and expand their internal working model as their cognitive, emotional, and social capacities increase and as they interact with parents and form other close bonds with adults, siblings, and friends.

Measuring the Security of Attachment

Although all family-reared babies become attached to a familiar caregiver, the quality of this relationship varies. A widely used laboratory procedure for assessing the quality of attachment between 1 and 2 years of age is the **Strange Situation.** Designed by Mary Ainsworth, it takes the baby through eight short episodes in which brief separations from and reunions with the parent occur (see Table 6.2).

Observing infants' responses to these episodes, researchers identified a secure attachment pattern and three patterns of insecurity (Ainsworth et al., 1978; Main & Solomon, 1990; Thompson, 2013). From the description at the beginning of this chapter, which of the following patterns do you think Grace displayed after adjusting to her adoptive family?

- **Secure attachment.** These infants use the parent as a secure base. When separated, they may or may not cry, but if they do, it is because the parent is absent and they prefer her to the stranger. When the parent returns, they convey clear pleasure—some expressing joy from a distance, others asking to be held until settling down to return to play—and crying is reduced immediately. About 60 percent of North American infants in middle-SES families show this pattern. In low-SES families, a smaller proportion of babies are secure, with higher proportions falling into the insecure patterns.
- **Insecure–avoidant attachment.** These infants seem unresponsive to the parent when she is present. When she leaves, they usually are not distressed, and they react to the stranger in much the same way as to the parent. During reunion, they avoid or are slow to greet the parent, and when picked up, they often fail to cling. About 15 percent of North American infants in middle-SES families show this pattern.
- **Insecure–resistant attachment.** Before separation, these infants seek closeness to the parent and often fail to explore. When the parent leaves, they are usually distressed, and on her return they combine clinginess with angry, resistive behavior (struggling when held, hitting and pushing). Many continue to cry after being picked up and cannot be comforted easily. About 10 percent of North American infants in middle-SES families show this pattern.
- **Disorganized/disoriented attachment.** This pattern reflects the greatest insecurity. At reunion, these infants show confused, contradictory behaviors—for example, looking away while the

TABLE 6.2
Episodes in the Strange Situation

EPISODE	EVENTS	ATTACHMENT BEHAVIOR OBSERVED
1	Researcher introduces parent and baby to playroom and then leaves.	
2	Parent is seated while baby plays with toys.	Parent as a secure base
3	Stranger enters, is seated, and talks to parent.	Reaction to unfamiliar adult
4	Parent leaves room. Stranger responds to baby and offers comfort if baby is upset.	Separation anxiety
5	Parent returns, greets baby, and offers comfort if necessary. Stranger leaves room.	Reaction to reunion
6	Parent leaves room.	Separation anxiety
7	Stranger enters room and offers comfort.	Ability to be soothed by stranger
8	Parent returns, greets baby, offers comfort if necessary, and tries to reinterest baby in toys.	Reaction to reunion

Note: Episode 1 lasts about 30 seconds; each of the remaining episodes lasts about 3 minutes. Separation episodes are cut short if the baby becomes very upset. Reunion episodes are extended if the baby needs more time to calm down and return to play.

Source: Ainsworth et al., 1978.

parent is holding them or approaching the parent with flat, depressed emotion. Most display a dazed facial expression, and a few cry out unexpectedly after having calmed down or display odd, frozen postures. About 15 percent of North American infants in middle-SES families show this pattern.

An alternative method, the **Attachment Q-Sort,** suitable for children between 1 and 5 years, depends on home observation (Waters et al., 1995). Either the parent or a highly trained observer sorts 90 behaviors—such as "Child greets mother with a big smile when she enters the room," "If mother moves very far, child follows along," and "Child uses mother's facial expressions as a good source of information when something looks risky or threatening"—into nine categories ranging from "highly descriptive" to "not at all descriptive" of the child. Then a score, ranging from high to low in security, is computed.

The Q-Sort responses of expert observers correspond well with babies' secure-base behavior in the Strange Situation, but parents' Q-Sorts do not (van IJzendoorn et al., 2004). Parents of insecure children, especially, may have difficulty accurately reporting their child's attachment behaviors.

Stability of Attachment

Research on the stability of attachment patterns between 1 and 2 years of age yields a wide range of findings. A close look at which babies stay the same and which ones change yields a more consistent picture.

Quality of attachment is usually secure and stable for middle-SES babies experiencing favorable life conditions. And infants who move from insecurity to security typically have well-adjusted mothers with positive family and friendship ties (Thompson, 2006, 2013). Perhaps many became parents before they were psychologically ready but, with social support, grew into the role. In contrast, in low-SES families with many daily stresses and little social support, attachment generally moves away from security or changes from one insecure pattern to another (Fish, 2004; Levendosky et al., 2011). In follow-ups extending from infancy to late adolescence and early adulthood, shifts from security to insecurity were associated with single parenthood, maternal depression, and poor family functioning and parenting quality, including child maltreatment (Booth-LaForce et al., 2014; Weinfield, Sroufe, & Egeland, 2000; Weinfield, Whaley, & Egeland, 2004).

These findings indicate that securely attached babies more often maintain their attachment status than insecure babies. The exception is disorganized/disoriented attachment, an insecure pattern that is either highly stable or consistently predicts later insecurity of another type (Groh et al., 2014; Weinfield, Whaley, & Egeland, 2004). Furthermore, adults with histories of attachment disorganization are at increased risk of having children who display disorganized/disoriented attachment (Raby et al., 2015). As you will soon see, many disorganized/disoriented infants and children experience extremely negative caregiving, which may disrupt emotional self-regulation so severely that confused, ambivalent feelings often persist, impairing child rearing of the next generation.

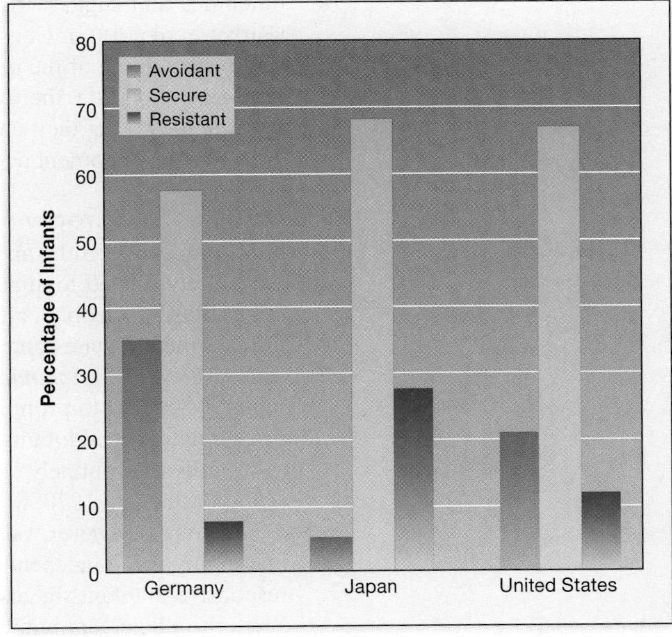

FIGURE 6.1 A cross-cultural comparison of infants' reactions in the Strange Situation. A high percentage of German babies seem avoidantly attached, whereas a substantial number of Japanese infants appear resistantly attached. Note that these responses may not reflect true insecurity. Instead, they are probably due to cultural differences in child-rearing practices. (Based on van IJzendoorn & Kroonenberg, 1988; van IJzendoorn & Sagi-Schwartz, 2008.)

Cultural Variations

Cross-cultural evidence indicates that attachment patterns may have to be interpreted differently in certain cultures. For example, as Figure 6.1 reveals, German infants show considerably more avoidant attachment than American babies do. But German parents value independence and encourage their infants to be nonclingy (Grossmann et al., 1985). In contrast, a study of infants of the Dogon people of Mali, Africa, revealed that none showed avoidant attachment to their mothers (True, Pisani, & Oumar, 2001). Even when grandmothers are primary caregivers (as they are with firstborn sons), Dogon mothers remain available to their babies, holding them close and nursing them promptly in response to hunger and distress.

Japanese infants, as well, rarely show avoidant attachment (refer again to Figure 6.1). Rather, many are resistantly attached, but this reaction may not represent true insecurity. Japanese mothers rarely leave their babies in others' care, so the Strange Situation probably induces greater stress in them than in babies who frequently experience maternal separations (Takahashi, 1990). Also, Japanese parents view the attention seeking that is part of resistant attachment as a normal indicator of infants' efforts to satisfy dependency and security needs (Rothbaum, Morelli, & Rusk, 2011). Despite these and other cultural variations, the secure pattern is still the most common attachment quality in all societies studied (van IJzendoorn & Sagi-Schwartz, 2008).

Factors That Affect Attachment Security

Researchers have looked closely at four important influences on attachment security: (1) early availability of a consistent caregiver, (2) quality of caregiving, (3) the baby's characteristics, and (4) family context, including parents' internal working models.

Early Availability of a Consistent Caregiver. Although adopted children who spent their first year or more in deprived Eastern European orphanages, where they had no opportunity to establish a close tie to a caregiver, are able to bond with their adoptive parents, they nevertheless show greatly elevated rates of attachment insecurity (Lionetti, Pastore, & Barone, 2015; Smyke et al., 2010; van den Dries et al., 2009). They are also at high risk for emotional and social difficulties. Many are indiscriminately friendly to unfamiliar adults; others are sad, anxious, and withdrawn (Bakermans-Kranenburg et al., 2011; O'Connor et al., 2003). These symptoms typically persist and are associated with wide-ranging mental health problems in middle childhood and adolescence, including cognitive impairments, inattention and overactivity, depression, and either social avoidance or aggressive behavior (Kreppner et al., 2010; Rutter et al., 2007, 2010).

Furthermore, as early as 7 months, institutionalized children show reduced ERP brain waves in response to facial expressions of emotion and have trouble discriminating such expressions—outcomes that suggest disrupted formation of neural structures involved in "reading" emotions (Parker et al., 2005). Consistent with these findings, in adopted children with longer institutional stays, the volume of the *amygdala* (see page 181) is atypically large (Tottenham et al., 2011). The larger the amygdala, the worse adopted children perform on tasks assessing understanding of emotion and the poorer their emotional self-regulation. Overall, the evidence indicates that fully normal emotional development depends on establishing a close tie with a caregiver early in life.

Quality of Caregiving. Dozens of studies report that **sensitive caregiving**—responding promptly, consistently, and appropriately to infants and holding them tenderly and carefully—is moderately related to attachment security in diverse cultures and SES groups (Belsky & Fearon, 2008; van IJzendoorn et al., 2004). Mothers of securely attached babies also frequently refer to their infants' mental states and motives: "You really *like* that swing." "Do you *remember* Grandma?" This *maternal mind-mindedness*—tendency to treat the baby as a person with inner thoughts and feelings—seems to promote sensitive caregiving (Meins, 2013; Meins et al., 2012). In contrast, insecurely attached infants tend to have mothers who engage in less physical contact, handle them awkwardly or "routinely," and are resentful and rejecting, particularly in response to infant distress (Ainsworth et al., 1978; McElwain & Booth-LaForce, 2006; Pederson & Moran, 1996).

Cultures, however, vary greatly in their view of sensitivity toward infants. In Western societies that highly value independence, sensitive caregiving follows the baby's lead by being contingently responsive to infant signals, "reading" the baby's mental states, and supporting exploration. In non-Western village communities and Asian cultures, caregiving that keeps the baby physically close, dampens emotional expressiveness, and teaches social appropriateness is deemed sensitive because it advances the child's connectedness to others and promotes social harmony (Morelli, 2015; Otto & Keller, 2014). Among the Gusii people of Kenya, for example, mothers are quick to quiet their infants and satisfy their physical needs, but they rarely interact playfully with them. Yet most Gusii infants are securely attached (LeVine et al., 1994). This suggests that security depends on attentive caregiving, not necessarily on contingent interaction. Puerto Rican mothers, who highly value obedience and socially appropriate behavior, often physically direct and limit their babies' actions—a caregiving style linked to attachment security in Puerto Rican culture (Carlson & Harwood, 2003). Yet typically in Western cultures, such physical control and restriction of exploration predict insecurity (Whipple, Bernier, & Mageau, 2011).

Compared with securely attached infants, avoidant babies tend to receive overstimulating, intrusive care. Their mothers might, for example, talk energetically to them while they are looking away or falling asleep. By avoiding the mother, these infants appear to be escaping from overwhelming interaction. Resistant infants often experience inconsistent care. Their mothers are unresponsive to infant signals, yet when the baby begins to explore, they interfere, shifting the infant's attention back to themselves. As a result, the baby is overly dependent as well as angry at the mother's lack of involvement (Cassidy & Berlin, 1994).

Highly inadequate caregiving is a powerful predictor of disruptions in attachment. Child abuse and neglect (topics we will consider in Chapter 8) are associated with all three forms of attachment insecurity. Among maltreated infants, disorganized/disoriented attachment is especially common (Cyr et al., 2010). Persistently depressed mothers, mothers with very low marital satisfaction, and parents suffering from a traumatic event, such as serious illness or loss of a loved one, also tend to promote the uncertain behaviors of this pattern (Campbell et al., 2004; Madigan et al., 2006). Some of these mothers engage in frightening, contradictory, and unpleasant behaviors, such as looking scared, teasing the baby, holding the baby stiffly at a distance, roughly pulling the baby by the arm, or seeking reassurance from the upset child (Hesse & Main, 2006; Solomon & George, 2011).

Infant Characteristics. Because attachment is the result of a *relationship* between two partners, infant characteristics should affect how easily it is established. Babies whose temperament is emotionally reactive are more likely to develop later insecure attachments (van IJzendoorn et al., 2004; Vaughn, Bost, & van IJzendoorn, 2008).

However, parental mental health and caregiving are involved. Babies with the short 5-HTTLPR gene, which is associated with emotional reactivity, are more likely than infants with a low-risk genotype to exhibit disorganized/disoriented attachment, but only when caregiving is insensitive (Spangler et al., 2009). In other research, mothers' experience of trauma was associated with attachment disorganization, but only in infants with a chromosome-11 gene having a certain repetition of DNA base pairs, called DRD4 7-repeat, which is linked to impulsive, overactive behavior (van IJzendoorn & Bakermans-Kranenburg, 2006). These babies, who face self-regulation challenges, were more susceptible to the negative impact of maternal adjustment problems.

Interventions that teach parents to interact sensitively with difficult-to-care-for babies enhance both sensitive caregiving and attachment security (van IJzendoorn & Bakermans-Kranenburg, 2015). One program that focused on both maternal sensitivity and effective discipline was particularly successful in reducing irritable distress and disruptive behavior in toddlers with the DRD4 7-repeat (Bakermans-Kranenburg et al., 2008a, 2008b). These findings suggest that the DRD4 7-repeat—like the short 5-HTTLPR gene—makes children more susceptible to the effects of both negative and positive parenting.

▶ Top photo: A father responds contingently to his baby's signals, "reading" the infant's joy and smiling exuberantly in return—a form of sensitivity common in Western societies. Bottom photo: In non-Western village communities and Asian cultures, parental sensitivity is expressed through physical closeness, calmness, and promptly meeting the infant's physical needs.

Family Circumstances. Shortly after Timmy's birth, his parents divorced and his father moved to a distant city. Anxious and distracted, Vanessa placed 2-month-old Timmy in Ginette's child-care home and began working 50-hour weeks to make ends meet. On days Vanessa stayed late at the office, a babysitter picked Timmy up, gave him dinner, and put him to bed. Once or twice a week, Vanessa retrieved Timmy from child care. As he neared his first birthday, Vanessa noticed that unlike the other children, who reached out, crawled, or ran to their parents, Timmy ignored her.

Timmy's behavior reflects a repeated finding: Job loss, a failing marriage, financial difficulties, or parental psychological problems (such as anxiety or depression) can undermine attachment indirectly by interfering with parental sensitivity. These stressors can also affect babies' sense of security directly, by altering the emotional climate of the family (for example, exposing them to angry adult interactions) or by disrupting familiar daily routines (Thompson, 2013). (See the Social Issues box on the following page to find out how child care affects attachment and child adjustment.) By reducing parental stress and improving parent–child communication, social support fosters attachment security (Moss et al., 2005). Ginette's sensitivity toward Timmy was helpful, as was the parenting advice Vanessa received from Ben, a psychologist. As Timmy turned 2, his relationship with his mother seemed warmer.

Parents' Internal Working Models. Parents bring to the family context their own history of attachment experiences, from which they construct internal working models that they apply to the bonds they establish with their children. Monica, who recalled her mother as tense and preoccupied, expressed regret that they had not had a closer relationship. Is her image of parenthood likely to affect Grace's attachment security?

To assess parents' internal working models, researchers ask them to evaluate childhood memories of attachment experiences (Main & Goldwyn, 1998). Parents who discuss their childhoods with objectivity and balance, regardless of whether their experiences were positive or negative, tend to behave sensitively and have securely attached children. In contrast, parents who dismiss the importance of early relationships or describe them in angry, confused ways usually have insecurely attached children and are less warm, sensitive, and encouraging of learning and mastery (Behrens, Hesse, & Main, 2007; McFarland-Piazza et al., 2012; Shafer et al., 2015).

But we must not assume any direct transfer of parents' childhood experiences to quality of attachment with their own children. Internal working models are *reconstructed memories* affected by many factors, including relationship experiences over the life course, personality, and current life satisfaction. Longitudinal research reveals that negative life events can weaken the link between an individual's own attachment security in infancy and a secure internal working model in adulthood. And insecurely attached babies who become adults with insecure internal working models often have lives that, based on self-reports in adulthood, are filled with family crises (Waters et al., 2000; Weinfield, Sroufe, & Egeland, 2000).

In sum, our early rearing experiences do not destine us to become either sensitive or insensitive parents (Bretherton & Munholland, 2008). Rather, the way we *view* our childhoods—our ability to come to terms with negative events, to integrate new information into our internal working models, and to look back on our own parents in an understanding, forgiving way—is far more influential in how we rear our children than the actual history of care we received.

Multiple Attachments

Babies develop attachments to a variety of familiar people—not just mothers but also fathers, grandparents, siblings, and professional caregivers. Although Bowlby (1969) believed that infants are predisposed to direct their attachment behaviors to a single special person, especially when they are distressed, his theory allows for these multiple attachments.

Fathers. When anxious or unhappy, most babies prefer to be comforted by their mother. But this preference typically declines over the second year. When babies are not distressed, they approach, vocalize to, and smile equally often at both parents, who respond similarly to these overtures (Bornstein, 2015; Parke, 2002).

SOCIAL ISSUES

Does Child Care in Infancy Threaten Attachment Security and Later Adjustment?

© ELLEN B. SENISI

▶ High-quality child care, with generous caregiver–child ratios, small group sizes, and knowledgeable caregivers, can be part of a system that promotes all aspects of development, including attachment security.

Are infants who experience daily separations from their employed parents and early placement in child care at risk for attachment insecurity and development problems? Evidence from the National Institute of Child Health and Development (NICHD) Study of Early Child Care—the largest longitudinal investigation of the effects of child care to date, which included more than 1,300 infants and their families—reveals that nonparental care by itself does not affect attachment quality (NICHD Early Child Care Research Network, 2001). Rather, the relationship between child care and emotional well-being depends on both family and child-care experiences.

Family Circumstances

We have seen that family conditions affect children's attachment security and later adjustment. The NICHD Study showed that parenting quality, based on a combination of maternal sensitivity and HOME scores (see page 159 in Chapter 5), exerts a more powerful impact on children's adjustment than does exposure to child care (NICHD Early Childhood Research Network, 1998; Watamura et al., 2011).

For employed parents, balancing work and caregiving can be stressful. Parents who feel overloaded by work and family pressures may respond less sensitively to their babies, thereby risking the infant's security.

Quality and Extent of Child Care

Nevertheless, poor-quality child care may contribute to a higher rate of insecure attachment. In the NICHD Study, when babies were exposed to combined home and child-care risk factors—insensitive caregiving at home along with insensitive caregiving in child care, long hours in child care, or more than one child-care arrangement—the rate of attachment insecurity increased. Overall, mother–child interaction was more favorable when children attended higher-quality child care and also spent fewer hours in child care (NICHD Early Child Care Research Network, 1997, 1999).

Furthermore, when these children reached age 3, a history of higher-quality child care predicted better social skills (NICHD Early Child Care Research Network, 2002). However, at ages 4½ to 5, children averaging more than 30 child-care hours per week displayed externalizing problems, especially defiance, disobedience, and aggression (NICHD Early Child Care Research Network, 2003a, 2006).

This does not necessarily mean that child care causes behavior problems. Rather, heavy exposure to substandard care, which is widespread in the United States, may promote these difficulties, especially when combined with family risk factors. A closer look at the NICHD participants during the preschool years revealed that those in both poor-quality home and child-care environments fared worst in problem behaviors, whereas those in both high-quality home and child-child care environments fared best. In between were preschoolers in high-quality child care but poor-quality homes (Watamura et al., 2011). These children benefited from the *protective influence* of high-quality child care.

Evidence from other industrialized nations confirms that full-time child care need not harm children's development. For example, amount of time spent in child care in Norway, which offers high-quality, government-subsidized center-based care, is unrelated to children's behavior problems (Zachrisson et al., 2013). And when family income drops, Norwegian children who don't attend child care show more behavior problems than children who do attend (Zachrisson & Dearing, 2015).

Conclusions

Taken together, research suggests that some infants may be at risk for attachment insecurity and adjustment problems due to inadequate child care, long hours in such care, and parental role overload. But it is inappropriate to use these findings to justify a reduction in child-care services. When family incomes are limited or mothers who want to work are forced to stay at home, children's emotional security is not promoted.

Instead, it makes sense to increase the availability of high-quality child care and to provide parents with paid employment leave (see page 94 in Chapter 3) and opportunities for part-time work. In the NICHD study, part-time (as opposed to full-time) employment during the baby's first year was associated with greater maternal sensitivity and a higher-quality home environment, which yielded more favorable development in early childhood (Brooks-Gunn, Han, & Waldfogel, 2010).

Fathers tend to engage in highly stimulating physical play with babies. This exciting play style helps infants and toddlers regulate emotion in intensely arousing situations.

Fathers' sensitive caregiving predicts attachment security, though somewhat less strongly than mothers' (Brown, Mangelsdorf, & Neff, 2012; Lucassen et al., 2011). But mothers and fathers in many cultures, including Australia, Canada, Germany, India, Israel, Italy, Japan, and the United States, tend to interact differently with their babies. Mothers devote more time to physical care and expressing affection, fathers to playful interaction (Freeman & Newland, 2010; Pleck, 2012).

Also, mothers and fathers tend to play differently. Mothers more often provide toys, talk to infants, and gently play conventional games like pat-a-cake and peekaboo. In contrast, fathers—especially with their infant sons—tend to engage in highly stimulating physical play with bursts of excitement (Feldman, 2003). As long as fathers are also sensitive, this stimulating, startling play style helps babies regulate emotion in intensely arousing situations, including novel physical environments and play with peers (Cabrera, Shannon, & Tamis-LeMonda, 2007; Hazen et al., 2010). Fathers' sensitive, challenging play with preschoolers is associated with favorable emotional and social adjustment from early childhood to early adulthood (Bureau et al., 2017; Grossmann et al., 2008). In contrast, paternal insensitivity during play is linked to preschoolers' attachment insecurity and externalizing problems, even after other factors linked to these outcomes (such as SES and parent-reported stress) have been controlled.

In cultures such as Japan, where long work hours prevent most fathers from sharing in infant caregiving, play may be an especially influential context in which fathers build secure attachments (Shwalb et al., 2004). In many Western nations, however, a strict division of parental roles—mother as caregiver, father as playmate—has changed over the past several decades in response to women's workforce participation and to cultural valuing of gender equality.

National surveys of thousands of U.S. married couples with children reveal that although their involvement continues to fall far short of mothers', today's fathers spend nearly three times as much time caring for children as fathers did in 1965 (see Figure 6.2) (Pew Research Center, 2015). Paternal availability to children is fairly similar across U.S. SES and ethnic groups, with one exception: Hispanic fathers spend more time engaged with their infants and young children, probably because of the particularly high value that Hispanic cultures place on family involvement (Cabrera, Aldoney, & Tamis-LeMonda, 2014; Hofferth, 2003).

A warm marital bond and supportive coparenting promote both parents' sensitivity and involvement and children's attachment security, but they are especially important for fathers (Brown et al., 2010; Sevigny & Loutzenhiser, 2010). And in studies carried out in many societies and ethnic groups, fathers' affectionate care of young children predicted later cognitive, emotional, and social competence as strongly as did mothers'—and occasionally more strongly (Rohner & Veneziano, 2001; Veneziano, 2003).

LOOK AND LISTEN

Observe parents at play with infants at home or a family gathering, describing both similarities and differences in mothers' and fathers' behaviors. Are your observations consistent with research findings?

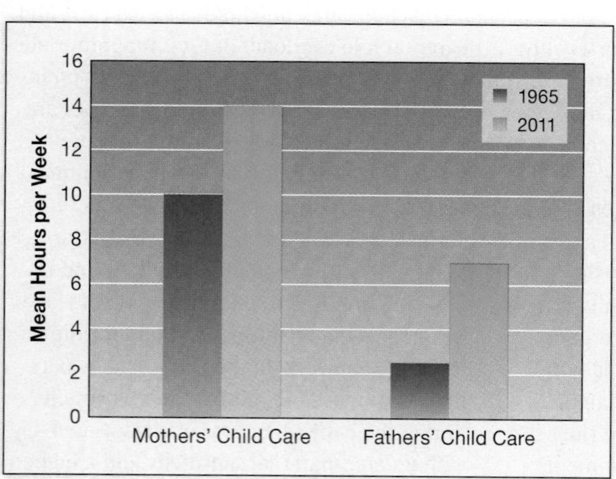

FIGURE 6.2 Average hours per week U.S. mothers and fathers reported devoting to caring for children in 1965 and 2011. In national surveys of thousands of married couples, mothers' time spent caring for children between birth and age 18 years increased moderately from 1965 to 2011. Though falling far short of mothers', fathers' time devoted to children rose nearly threefold. (Based on Pew Research Center, 2015.)

Siblings. Despite declines in family size, nearly 80 percent of U.S. children grow up with at least one sibling (U.S. Census Bureau, 2017b). The arrival of a new baby is a challenging experience for most preschoolers, who often display a temporary increase in aggressive behavior and become demanding, clingy, and less affectionate with their parents for a time. Attachment security may also decline, especially for children over age 2 (old enough to feel threatened and displaced) and for those with mothers under stress (Teti et al., 1996; Volling, 2012; Volling et al., 2017).

Yet resentment is only one feature of a rich emotional relationship that soon develops between siblings. Older children also show affection and concern when the infant cries. By the end of the first year, babies usually spend much time with older siblings and are comforted by the presence of a

APPLYING WHAT WE KNOW

Encouraging Affectionate Ties Between Infants and Their Preschool Siblings

SUGGESTION	DESCRIPTION
Spend extra time with the older child.	Parents can minimize the older child's feelings of being deprived of affection and attention by setting aside time to spend with her. Fathers can be especially helpful, planning outings with the preschooler and taking over care of the baby so the mother can be with the older child.
Handle sibling misbehavior with patience.	When parents respond patiently to the older sibling's misbehavior and demands for attention, these reactions are usually temporary. Parents can give the preschooler opportunities to feel proud of being more grown-up than the baby—for example, by encouraging the older child to assist with feeding, bathing, dressing, and offering toys, and showing appreciation for these efforts.
Discuss the baby's wants and needs.	By helping the older sibling understand the baby's point of view, parents can promote friendly, considerate behavior. They can say, for example, "He's so little that he just can't wait to be fed," or "He's trying to reach his rattle, and he can't."
Express positive emotion toward your partner and engage in effective coparenting.	When parents mutually support each other's parenting behavior, their good communication helps the older sibling cope adaptively with jealousy and conflict.

preschool-age brother or sister during short parental absences. Throughout childhood, children continue to treat older siblings as attachment figures, turning to them for comfort in stressful situations when parents are unavailable (Seibert & Kerns, 2009).

Nevertheless, individual differences in sibling relationships emerge early. Certain temperamental traits—high emotional reactivity or activity level—increase the chances of sibling conflict (Brody, Stoneman, & McCoy, 1994; Dunn, 1994). And maternal warmth toward both children is related to positive sibling interaction and to preschoolers' support of a distressed younger sibling (Volling, 2001; Volling & Belsky, 1992). In contrast, maternal harshness and lack of involvement are linked to antagonistic sibling relationships (Howe, Aquan-Assee, & Bukowski, 2001). However, older siblings who remain securely attached to their fathers after the baby's arrival are less likely to experience worsening conflict with their mothers and more likely to forge positive sibling ties later in the first year (Volling et al., 2017). A close father–child bond seems to support children in adjusting to siblinghood.

Finally, a good marriage is correlated with older preschool siblings' capacity to cope adaptively with jealousy and conflict (Volling, McElwain, & Miller, 2002). Perhaps good communication between parents serves as a model of effective problem solving. It may also foster a generally happy family environment, giving children less reason to feel jealous.

Refer to Applying What We Know above for ways to promote positive relationships between babies and their preschool siblings. Siblings offer a rich social context in which young children learn and practice a wide range of skills, including affectionate caring, conflict resolution, and control of hostile and envious feelings.

Attachment and Later Development

According to psychoanalytic and ethological theories, the inner feelings of affection and security that result from a healthy attachment relationship support all aspects of psychological development. Yet contrary evidence exists. In longitudinal research, secure infants generally fared better than insecure infants at later ages, but not always (Fearon et al., 2010; McCartney et al., 2004; Schneider, Atkinson, & Tardif, 2001; Stams, Juffer, & van IJzendoorn, 2002).

What accounts for this inconsistency? Mounting evidence indicates that *continuity of caregiving* determines whether attachment security is linked to later development (Lamb et al., 1985; Thompson, 2013). When researchers tracked a large sample of children from ages 1 to 3 years, those with histories of secure attachment followed by sensitive parenting scored highest in cognitive, emotional, and social outcomes. Those with histories of insecure attachment followed by insensitive parenting scored lowest, while those with mixed histories of attachment and maternal sensitivity scored in between (Belsky & Fearon, 2002).

In sum, a secure attachment in infancy launches the parent–child relationship on a positive path. An early warm parent–child tie, sustained over time, promotes many aspects of children's development: a more confident and complex self-concept, more advanced emotional understanding, greater effortful control, more effective social skills, a stronger sense of moral responsibility, and higher motivation to achieve in school (Drake, Belsky, & Fearon, 2014; Groh et al., 2014; Viddal et al., 2015). But the effects of early attachment security are *conditional*—dependent on the quality of the baby's future relationships. Finally, as we will see again in future chapters, attachment is just one of the complex influences on children's psychological development.

ASK YOURSELF

CONNECT Review research on emotional self-regulation on pages 177–178. How do the caregiving experiences of securely attached infants promote emotional self-regulation?

APPLY What attachment pattern did Timmy display when Vanessa arrived home from work, and what factors probably contributed to it?

REFLECT How would you characterize your internal working model? What factors, in addition to your relationship with your parents, might have influenced it?

Self-Development

6.9 Describe the development of self-awareness in infancy and toddlerhood, along with the emotional and social capacities it supports.

Infancy is a rich formative period for the development of both physical and social understanding. In Chapter 5, you learned that infants develop an appreciation of the permanence of objects. And in this chapter, we have seen that over the first year, infants recognize and respond appropriately to others' emotions and distinguish familiar from unfamiliar people. That both objects and people achieve an independent, stable existence for infants implies that knowledge of the self as a separate, permanent entity is also emerging.

Self-Awareness

After Caitlin's bath, Carolyn often held her in front of a mirror. As early as the first few months, Caitlin smiled and returned friendly behaviors to her image. At what age did she realize that the baby smiling back was herself?

Beginnings of Self-Awareness. Newborns' remarkable capacity for *intermodal perception* (see page 133 in Chapter 4) supports the beginnings of self-awareness (Rochat, 2013). As they feel their own touch, feel and watch their limbs move, and feel and hear themselves cry, babies experience intermodal matches that differentiate their own body from surrounding bodies and objects.

Over the first few months, infants distinguish their own visual image from other stimuli, but their self-awareness is limited. When shown two side-by-side video images of their kicking legs, one from their own perspective (camera behind the baby) and one from an observer's perspective (camera in front of the baby), 3-month-olds looked longer at the observer's view (Rochat, 1998). By 4 months, infants look and smile more at video images of others than at video images of themselves, indicating that they treat another person (as opposed to the self) as a social partner (Rochat & Striano, 2002).

This discrimination of one's own limb and facial movements from those of others in real-time video reflects an *implicit* awareness that the self is distinct from the surrounding world. Implicit self-awareness is also evident in young infants' social expectations—for example, in protest or withdrawal when face-to-face interaction with a responsive adult is disrupted (see page 173). These early signs of self-experience serve as the foundation for development of *explicit* self-awareness—understanding that the self is a unique object in a world of objects.

Explicit Self-Awareness. During the second year, toddlers become consciously aware of the self's physical features. In several studies, 9- to 28-month-olds were placed in front of a mirror. Then, under the pretext of wiping the baby's face, each mother rubbed red dye on her child's nose or forehead. Toddlers older than 18 to 20 months touched or rubbed their noses or foreheads, indicating awareness of their unique appearance (Bard et al., 2006; Lewis & Brooks-Gunn, 1979). Around age 2, **self-recognition**—identification of the self as a physically unique being—is well under way.Children point to themselves in photos and refer to themselves by name or with a personal pronoun ("I" or "me") (Lewis & Ramsay, 2004).

Nevertheless, toddlers make **scale errors,** attempting to do things that their body size makes impossible. For example, they will try to put on dolls' clothes, sit in a doll-sized chair, or walk through a doorway too narrow for them to pass through (Brownell, Zerwas, & Ramani, 2007; DeLoache et al., 2013). Possibly, toddlers lack an accurate understanding of their own body dimensions. Other evidence suggests that toddlers, in focusing intently on how they can act on objects, often ignore size information (Grzyb et al., 2017). Scale errors decline between ages 2 and 4.

This 20-month-old makes silly faces in a mirror, a playful response to her reflection that indicates she is aware of herself as a separate being and recognizes her unique physical features.

According to many theorists, self-awareness and self-recognition develop as infants and toddlers increasingly realize that their own actions cause objects and people to react in predictable ways (Nadel, Prepin, & Okanda, 2005; Rochat, 2013). For example, batting a mobile and seeing it swing in a pattern different from the infant's own actions informs the baby about the relation between self and physical world. Smiling and vocalizing at a caregiver who smiles and vocalizes back helps clarify the relation between self and social world. The contrast between these experiences helps young infants sense that they are separate from external reality. Furthermore, 18-month-olds who often establish joint attention with caregivers are advanced in mirror self-recognition (Nichols, Fox, & Mundy, 2005). Joint attention offers toddlers many opportunities to compare their own and others' reactions to objects and events, which may enhance their awareness of their own physical uniqueness.

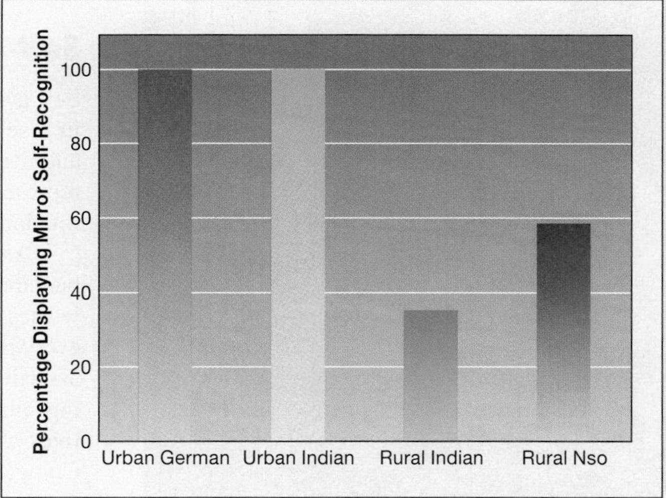

FIGURE 6.3 Mirror self-recognition at 19 months in four cultures. Urban middle-SES German and East Indian toddlers, whose mothers emphasized autonomous child-rearing goals, attained mirror self-recognition earlier than Nso toddlers of rural Cameroon and toddlers of rural East India, whose mothers emphasized relational child-rearing goals. (Based on Kärtner et al., 2012.)

Cultural variations exist in early self-development. In one investigation, urban middle-SES German and East Indian toddlers attained mirror self-recognition earlier than toddlers of non-Western farming communities, such as the Nso people of rural Cameroon and rural families of East India (see Figure 6.3) (Kärtner et al., 2012). Urban German and, to a lesser extent, urban East Indian mothers placed considerable emphasis on *autonomous child-rearing goals,* including promoting personal talents and interests and expressing one's own preferences, which strongly predicted earlier mirror self-recognition. In contrast, Nso and East Indian rural mothers valued *relational child-rearing goals*—doing what parents say and sharing with others. In related research, Nso toddlers, though delayed in mirror self-recognition, displayed an earlier capacity to comply with adult requests than did middle-SES urban Greek toddlers, whose mothers encouraged child autonomy (Keller et al., 2004).

Self-Awareness and Early Emotional and Social Development. Recall that self-conscious emotions depend on a strengthening sense of self. Self-awareness also leads to first efforts to understand another's perspective. Older toddlers draw on their advancing capacity to distinguish what happens to oneself from what happens to others to express first signs of **empathy**—the ability to understand another's emotional state and *feel with* that person, or respond emotionally in a similar way. For example, they communicate concern when others are distressed and may offer what they themselves find comforting—a hug, a reassuring comment, or a favorite doll or blanket (Hoffman, 2000; Moreno, Klute, & Robinson, 2008).

At the same time, toddlers demonstrate clearer awareness of how to upset others. One 18-month-old heard her mother talking to another adult about an older sibling: "Anny is really frightened of spiders" (Dunn, 1989). The innocent-looking toddler ran to the bedroom, returned with a toy spider, and pushed it in front of Anny's face!

Categorizing the Self

By the end of the second year, language becomes a powerful tool in self-development. Between 18 and 30 months, children develop a **categorical self** as they classify themselves and others on the basis of age ("baby," "boy," or "man"), sex ("boy" or "girl"), physical characteristics ("big," "strong"), and even goodness versus badness ("I a good girl." "Tommy mean!") and competencies ("Did it!" "I can't") (Stipek, Gralinski, & Kopp, 1990).

Toddlers use their limited understanding of these social categories to organize their own behavior. As early as 17 months, they select and play in a more involved way with toys that are stereotyped for their own gender—dolls and tea sets for girls, trucks and cars for boys. Their ability to label their own gender predicts a sharp rise in these play preferences over the next few months (Zosuls et al., 2009). Then parents encourage gender-typed behavior by responding more positively when toddlers display it (Hines, 2015). As we will see in Chapter 8, gender typing increases dramatically during early childhood.

Self-Control

Self-awareness also contributes to strengthening of effortful control. To behave in a self-controlled fashion, children must think of themselves as separate, autonomous beings who can direct their own actions. And they must have the representational and memory capacities to recall a caregiver's directive ("Caitlin, don't touch that light socket!") and apply it to their own behavior.

As these capacities emerge between 12 and 18 months, toddlers first become capable of **compliance.** They show clear awareness of caregivers' wishes and expectations and can obey simple requests and commands. And as every parent knows, they can also decide to do just the opposite! But for most, assertiveness and opposition occur alongside compliance with an eager, willing spirit, which suggests that the child is beginning to adopt the adult's directives as his own (Dix et al., 2007; Kochanska, Murray, & Harlan, 2000). Compliance quickly leads to toddlers' first consciencelike verbalizations—for example, correcting the self by saying "No, can't" before reaching for a cookie or jumping on the sofa.

SW PRODUCTIONS/PHOTODISC GREEN/GETTY IMAGES

▶ This father encourages compliance and the beginnings of self-control. The toddler joins in the task with an eager, willing spirit, which suggests he is adopting the adult's directive as his own.

Researchers often study the early emergence of self-control by giving children tasks that, like the situations just mentioned, require **delay of gratification**—waiting for an appropriate time and place to engage in a tempting act. Between ages 1½ and 4, children show an increasing capacity to wait before eating a treat, opening a present, or playing with a toy (Cole, LeDonne, & Tan, 2013; Vaughn, Kopp, & Krakow, 1984). Children who are advanced in development of attention, language, and suppressing negative emotion tend to be better at delaying gratification—findings that help explain why girls are typically more self-controlled than boys (Else-Quest, 2012).

Like effortful control in general, young children's capacity to delay gratification is influenced by quality of caregiving. Western toddlers and preschoolers

APPLYING WHAT WE KNOW

Helping Toddlers Develop Compliance and Self-Control

SUGGESTION	RATIONALE
Respond to the toddler with sensitivity and encouragement.	Toddlers whose parents are sensitive and supportive sometimes actively resist, but they are also more compliant and self-controlled.
Provide advance notice when the toddler must stop an enjoyable activity.	Toddlers find it more difficult to stop a pleasant activity that is already under way than to wait before engaging in a desired action.
Offer many prompts and reminders.	Toddlers' ability to remember and comply with rules is limited; they need continuous adult oversight and patient assistance.
Respond to self-controlled behavior with verbal and physical approval.	Praise and hugs reinforce appropriate behavior, increasing the likelihood that it will occur again.
Encourage selective and sustained attention (see Chapter 5, page 151).	Development of attention is related to self-control. Children who can shift attention from a captivating stimulus and focus on a less attractive alternative are better at controlling their impulses.
Support language development (see Chapter 5, page 167).	In the second year, children begin to use language to remind themselves of adult expectations and to delay gratification.
Gradually increase rules in a manner consistent with the toddler's developing capacities.	As cognition and language improve, toddlers can follow more rules related to safety, respect for people and property, family routines, manners, and simple chores.

who experience parental warmth and encouragement are more likely to be cooperative and to resist temptation. Recall that such parenting—which models patient, nonimpulsive behavior—is particularly important for emotionally reactive children (see pages 182–183). And Nso children of rural Cameroon are substantially ahead of their Western agemates in ability to delay gratification (Lamm et al., 2017). From an early age, Nso parents expect children to control their own emotions and behavior.

As self-control improves, parents gradually expand the rules they expect toddlers to follow, from safety and respect for property and people to family routines, manners, and simple chores (Gralinski & Kopp, 1993). Still, toddlers' control over their own actions depends on constant parental oversight and reminders. Several prompts ("Remember, we're going to go in just a minute") and gentle insistence were usually necessary to get Caitlin to stop playing so that she and her parents could go on an errand. Applying What We Know above summarizes ways to help toddlers develop compliance and self-control.

As the second year of life drew to a close, Carolyn, Monica, and Vanessa were delighted at their children's readiness to learn the rules of social life. As we will see in Chapter 8, advances in cognition and language, along with parental warmth and reasonable demands for maturity, lead preschoolers to make tremendous strides in this area.

ASK YOURSELF

CONNECT What type of early parenting fosters the development of emotional self-regulation, secure attachment, and self-control? Why, in each instance, is it effective?

APPLY Len, a caregiver of 1- and 2-year-olds, wonders whether toddlers recognize themselves. List signs of self-recognition in the second year that Len can observe.

REFLECT Do you think that the expression "the terrible twos"—commonly used to characterize toddler behavior—is an apt description? Explain.

CHAPTER 6 SUMMARY

Erikson's Theory of Infant and Toddler Personality *(p. 172)*

6.1 ***Identify personality changes that take place during Erikson's stages of basic trust versus mistrust and autonomy versus shame and doubt.***

- Warm, responsive caregiving leads infants to resolve Erikson's psychological conflict of **basic trust versus mistrust** on the positive side.
- During toddlerhood, **autonomy versus shame and doubt** is resolved favorably when parents provide appropriate guidance and reasonable choices.

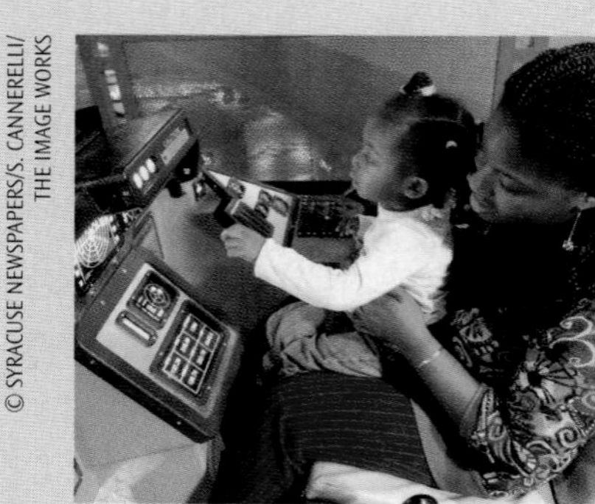

© SYRACUSE NEWSPAPERS/S. CANNERELLI/ THE IMAGE WORKS

Emotional Development *(p. 173)*

6.2 ***Describe the development of basic emotions over the first year, noting the adaptive function of each.***

- In the first half-year, **basic emotions** gradually become clear, well-organized signals. The **social smile** appears between 6 and 10 weeks, laughter around 3 to 4 months. Happiness strengthens the parent–child bond and both reflects and supports motor, cognitive, and social competencies.
- Anger and fear, especially in the form of **stranger anxiety,** increase in the second half-year as infants' cognitive and motor skills improve. Newly mobile babies use the familiar caregiver as a **secure base** from which to explore.

6.3 ***Summarize changes during the first two years in understanding of others' emotions, expression of self-conscious emotions, and emotional self-regulation.***

- As infants' ability to detect the meaning of emotional expressions improves, **social referencing** appears at 8 to 10 months. In the middle of the second year, toddlers realize that others' emotional reactions may differ from their own, and they use social referencing to gather information about others' intentions and preferences.
- During toddlerhood, self-awareness and adult instruction provide the foundation for **self-conscious emotions**. **Emotional self-regulation** emerges as the prefrontal cortex functions more effectively, as caregivers build on infants' increasing tolerance for stimulation, and as infants' ability to shift attention improves. When caregivers are emotionally sympathetic but set limits, toddlers display more effective anger-regulation strategies in the preschool years.

Temperament and Development *(p. 178)*

6.4 ***Explain the meaning of temperament and how it is measured.***

- Children differ greatly in **temperament**—early-appearing, stable individual differences in reactivity and self-regulation. The pioneering New York Longitudinal Study identified three patterns: the **easy child,** the **difficult child,** and the **slow-to-warm-up child.** Rothbart's influential model of temperament includes dimensions representing emotion, attention, and action, along with **effortful control,** the ability to regulate one's reactivity.
- Temperament is assessed through parental reports, behavior ratings by others familiar with the child, and laboratory observations. Most neurobiological research has focused on distinguishing **inhibited,** or **shy, children** from **uninhibited,** or **sociable, children.**

6.5 ***Discuss the roles of heredity and environment in the stability of temperament, including the goodness-of-fit model.***

- Temperament has low to moderate stability: It develops with age and can be modified by child-rearing experiences. Long-term prediction from early temperament is best achieved after age 3, when children improve substantially in effortful control.
- Ethnic and gender differences in temperament may have genetic foundations but are promoted by cultural beliefs and practices.
- Temperament affects differential susceptibility to rearing experiences. Children with the short 5-HTTLPR genotype, which heightens risk of self-regulation difficulties, function worse than other children when exposed to inept parenting and benefit most from good parenting. Parents tend to emphasize temperamental differences between siblings.
- According to the **goodness-of-fit model,** child-rearing conditions that recognize the child's temperament while encouraging more adaptive functioning promote favorable adjustment.

Development of Attachment *(p. 184)*

6.6 ***Describe the development of attachment during the first two years.***

- **Ethological theory,** the most widely accepted perspective on **attachment,** recognizes the infant's emotional tie to the caregiver as an evolved response that promotes survival. In early infancy, built-in signals help bring infants into close contact with other humans.

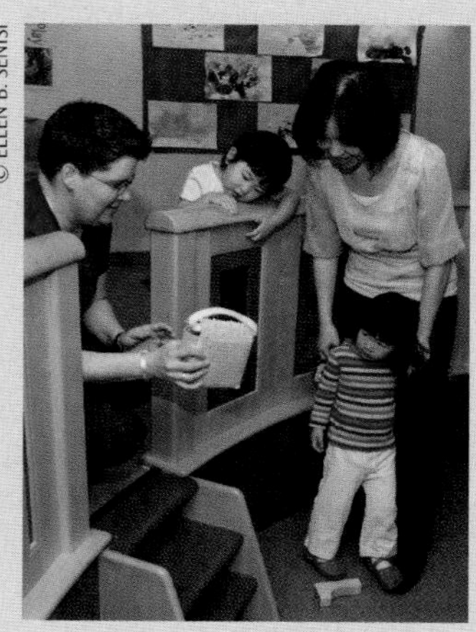

© ELLEN B. SENISI

- Around 6 to 8 months, **separation anxiety** and use of the caregiver as a secure base indicate the existence of a true attachment bond. As representation and language develop, separation protest declines. From early caregiving experiences, children construct an **internal working model** that guides future close relationships.

6.7 ***Explain how researchers measure attachment security, the factors that affect it, and its implications for later development.***

- Using the **Strange Situation,** a laboratory technique for assessing the quality of attachment between 1 and 2 years of age, researchers have identified four attachment patterns: **secure, insecure–avoidant, insecure–resistant,** and **disorganized/disoriented attachment.** The **Attachment Q-Sort,** based on home observations of children between ages 1 and 5, yields a score ranging from low to high in security.

- Securely attached babies with favorable life conditions more often maintain their attachment pattern than insecure babies. The disorganized/disoriented pattern shows greater stability than the other patterns. Cultural conditions must be considered in interpreting attachment patterns.
- Attachment security is influenced by early availability of a consistent caregiver, quality of caregiving, the fit between the baby's temperament and parenting practices, and family circumstances. **Sensitive caregiving** is moderately related to secure attachment.

© CHRISTOPHER HERWIG/ROBERT HARDING

- In Western cultures, sensitive caregiving includes responding contingently to infant signals and "reading" the baby's mental states. In non-Western village communities and Asian cultures, sensitive caregiving keeps the baby close and dampens emotional expressiveness.
- Continuity of caregiving is the crucial factor determining whether attachment security is linked to later development. If caregiving improves, children can recover from an insecure attachment history.

6.8 *Describe infants' capacity for multiple attachments.*

- Infants develop strong affectionate ties to fathers, who tend to engage in more exciting, physical play with babies than mothers do.
- Early in the first year, infants begin to build rich emotional relationships with siblings that combine rivalry and resentment with affection and sympathetic concern. Individual differences in quality of sibling relationships are influenced by temperament, parenting, and marital quality.

Self-Development *(p. 194)*

6.9 *Describe the development of self-awareness in infancy and toddlerhood, along with the emotional and social capacities it supports.*

- During the first few months, infants display an implicit awareness of the self as distinct from the surrounding world. In the middle of the second year, explicit awareness of the self's physical features emerges. Around age 2, **self-recognition** is clearly evident as toddlers identify themselves in photos and by name. However, **scale errors,** attempting to do things that their body size makes impossible, are common at this age.
- Self-awareness leads to toddlers' first efforts to appreciate another's perspective, including early signs of **empathy**. As language strengthens, children develop a **categorical self,** classifying themselves and others on the basis of social categories.

SW PRODUCTIONS/PHOTODISC GREEN/GETTY IMAGES

- Self-awareness also contributes to self-control. **Compliance** emerges between 12 and 18 months, followed by **delay of gratification,** which strengthens between 1½ and 4 years. Children who experience parental warmth and gentle encouragement are likely to be advanced in self-control.

IMPORTANT TERMS AND CONCEPTS

Development in Infancy and Toddlerhood

ELECTRA K. VASILELADOU/GETTY

BIRTH–6 MONTHS

Physical

- Height and weight increase rapidly. (106)
- Newborn reflexes decline. (95)
- Distinguishes basic tastes and odors; prefers sweet-tasting foods. (100)
- Responses can be classically and operantly conditioned. (120–121)
- Habituates to unchanging stimuli; recovers to novel stimuli. (121–122)
- Sleep is increasingly organized into a night–day schedule. (114)
- Holds head up, rolls over, and grasps objects. (124)
- Perceives auditory and visual stimuli as organized patterns. (128, 131–133)
- Shows sensitivity to motion, then binocular, and finally pictorial depth cues. (131)
- Recognizes and prefers human facial pattern; recognizes features of mother's face. (132–133)
- Masters a wide range of intermodal (visual, auditory, and tactile) relationships. (133–134)

Cognitive

- Engages in immediate and deferred imitation of adults' facial expressions. (122–123, 144)
- Repeats chance behaviors that lead to pleasurable and interesting results. (141)
- Has some awareness of many physical properties (including object permanence) and basic numerical knowledge. (143, 147–148)
- Visual search behavior and recognition memory for visual events improve. (130, 152)
- Attention becomes more efficient and flexible. (132, 151)
- Forms categories for familiar objects based on similar physical properties. (154)

Language

- Coos and, by end of this period, babbles. (164)
- Begins to establish joint attention with caregiver, who labels objects and events. (164)
- By end of this period, comprehends some word meanings. (165)

Emotional/Social

- Social smile and laughter emerge. (174)
- Matches feeling tone of caregiver in face-to-face communication; later, expects matched responses. (176)

TETRA IMAGES/ALAMY

- Emotional expressions become well-organized and meaningfully related to environmental events. (173)
- Regulates emotion by shifting attention and self-soothing. (99, 177)
- Smiles, laughs, and babbles more to caregiver than to a stranger. (185)
- Awareness of self as physically distinct from surroundings increases. (194)

7–12 MONTHS

Physical

- Sleep–wake pattern increasingly conforms to a night–day schedule. (119)
- Sits alone, crawls, and walks. (124)

© LAURA DWIGHT PHOTOGRAPHY

- Reaching and grasping improve in flexibility and accuracy; shows refined pincer grasp. (126–127)
- Discriminates among a wider range of facial expressions, including happiness, surprise, sadness, fearfulness, and anger. (133, 176)

Cognitive

- Engages in intentional, or goal-directed, behavior. (141)
- Finds object hidden in an initial location. (141)
- Recall memory improves, as indicated by gains in deferred imitation of adults' actions with objects. (143–144, 152)
- Tool use in problem solving emerges; solves simple problems by analogy to a previous problem. (145)
- Categorizes objects on the basis of subtle sets of features, even when the perceptual contrast between categories is minimal. (154)

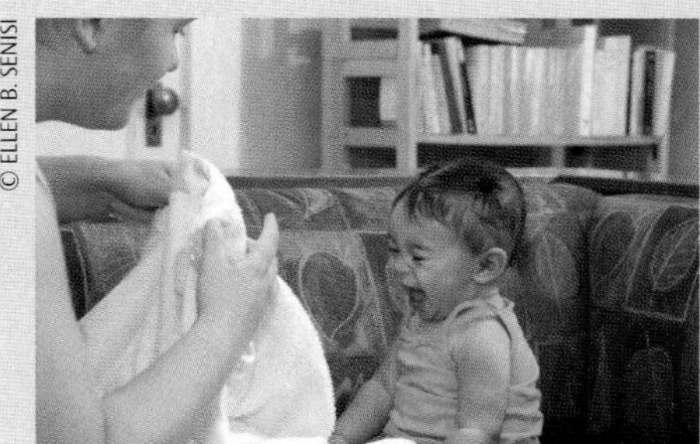

© ELLEN B. SENISI

Note: Numbers in parentheses indicate the page or pages on which each milestone is discussed.

Language

- Babbling expands to include many sounds of spoken languages and patterns of the child's language community. (164)
- Joint attention with caregiver becomes more accurate. (164)
- Takes turns in games, such as pat-a-cake and peekaboo. (164)
- Uses preverbal gestures (showing, pointing) to influence others' behavior and convey information. (164–165)
- Around end of this period, understands displaced reference of words and says first words. (145, 165)

Emotional/Social

- Smiling and laughter increase in frequency and expressiveness. (174)
- Anger and fear increase in frequency and intensity. (174–176)
- Stranger anxiety and separation anxiety appear. (174–176, 185)
- Uses caregiver as a secure base for exploration. (176, 185)
- Shows "clear-cut" attachment to familiar caregivers. (185)
- Increasingly detects the meaning of others' emotional expressions and engages in social referencing. (176)
- Regulates emotion by approaching and retreating from stimulation. (177)

13–18 MONTHS

Physical

- Height and weight gain are rapid, but not as great as in first year. (106)
- Walking is better coordinated. (124, 125)
- Manipulates small objects with improved coordination. (127)

Cognitive

- Explores the properties of objects by acting on them in novel ways. (142)
- Searches in several locations for a hidden object. (142)
- Engages in deferred imitation of adults' actions with objects over longer delays and across a change in context—for example, from child care to home. (144)
- Engages in deferred imitation of actions an adult tries to produce, even if not fully realized. (144)
- Sustained attention increases. (151)
- Recall memory improves further. (144, 152)

© LAURA DWIGHT PHOTOGRAPHY

- Sorts objects into categories. (154)
- Realizes that pictures can symbolize real objects. (145)

Language

- Steadily adds to vocabulary. (165)

Emotional/Social

- Realizes that others' emotional reactions may differ from one's own. (176)

DREAMPICTURES/VANESSA GAVALYA

- Complies with simple directives. (196)

19–24 MONTHS

Physical

- Walks up stairs with help, jumps, and walks on tiptoe. (124)

Cognitive

- Solves simple problems suddenly, through representation. (142)
- Finds a hidden object that has been moved while out of sight. (142)
- Engages in make-believe play, using simple actions experienced in everyday life. (142, 157)

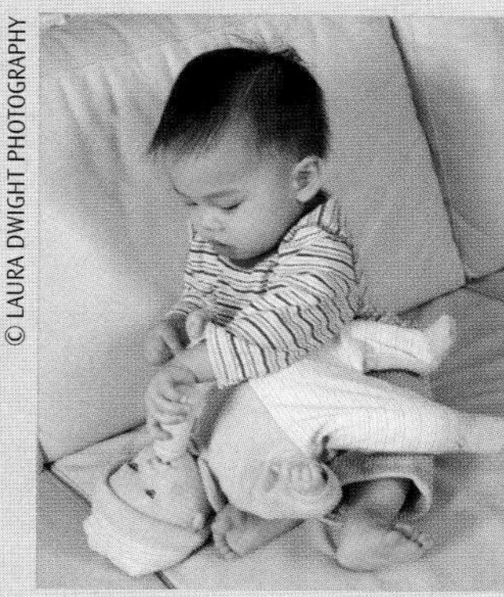

© LAURA DWIGHT PHOTOGRAPHY

- Categorizes objects conceptually, on the basis of common function or behavior. (154)
- Begins to use language as a flexible symbolic tool to modify existing mental representations. (145)

Language

- Produces 200 to 250 words. (165)
- Combines two words. (165)

Emotional/Social

- Self-conscious emotions (shame, embarrassment, guilt, envy, and pride) emerge. (177)
- Acquires a vocabulary for talking about feelings. (178)
- Begins to use language to assist with emotional self-regulation. (178)
- Begins to tolerate caregiver's absences more easily; separation anxiety declines. (185)
- Recognizes image of self and, by end of this period, uses own name or personal pronoun to refer to self. (195)
- Shows signs of empathy. (195–196)

© LAURA DWIGHT PHOTOGRAPHY

- Categorizes self and others on the basis of age, sex, physical characteristics, goodness and badness, and competencies. (196)
- Shows gender-stereotyped toy preferences. (196)
- Self-control, as indicated by delay of gratification, emerges. (196)

Note: Numbers in parentheses indicate the page or pages on which each milestone is discussed.

CHAPTER 7

Physical and Cognitive Development in Early Childhood

On an outing with 3- and 4-year-olds to a city pond, a teacher points out features of goldfish and responds to children's observations and questions. Language and knowledge of the world expand rapidly in early childhood, supported by rich conversations with adults and peers.

WHAT'S AHEAD IN CHAPTER 7

For more than a decade, my fourth-floor office window overlooked the preschool and kindergarten play yard of our university laboratory school. On mild fall and spring mornings, classroom doors swung open, and sand table, easels, and large blocks spilled out into a small courtyard. Alongside the building was a grassy area with jungle gyms, swings, a playhouse, and a flower garden planted by the children; beyond it, a circular path lined with tricycles and wagons. Each day, the setting was alive with activity.

The years from 2 to 6 are often called "the play years," since play blossoms during this time, becoming increasingly complex, flexible, and symbolic. Our discussion opens with the physical attainments of this period—body and brain growth and improvements in motor coordination. We pay special attention to genetic and environmental factors that support these changes and to their intimate connection with other domains of development.

Then we explore early childhood cognition, beginning with Piaget's preoperational stage. Recent research, along with Vygotsky's sociocultural theory and information processing, extends our understanding of preschoolers' cognitive competencies. Next, we address factors that contribute to individual differences in mental development—the home environment, the quality of preschool and child care, and the many hours young children devote to screen media. We conclude with the dramatic expansion of language in early childhood.

© ELLEN B. SENISI

PHYSICAL DEVELOPMENT

A Changing Body and Brain

7.1 Describe body growth and brain development during early childhood.

In early childhood, the rapid increase in body size of the first two years tapers off. On average, children add 2 to 3 inches in height and about 5 pounds in weight each year. Boys continue to be slightly larger than girls. As "baby fat" drops off further, children gradually become thinner, although girls retain somewhat more body fat than boys, who are slightly more muscular. As Figure 7.1 on page 204 shows, by age 5 the top-heavy, bowlegged, potbellied toddler has become a more streamlined, flat-tummied, longer-legged child with body proportions similar to those of adults. Consequently, posture and balance improve—changes that support gains in motor coordination.

Individual differences in body size are increasingly apparent in early childhood. Speeding around the bike path in the play yard, 5-year-old Darryl—at 48 inches tall and 55 pounds—towered over his kindergarten classmates. (The average North American 5-year-old boy is 43 inches tall and weighs 42 pounds.) Priti, an Asian-Indian child, was unusually small because of genetic factors linked to her cultural ancestry. Hal, a European-American child from a poverty-stricken home, was well below average for reasons we will discuss shortly.

Skeletal Growth

The skeletal changes of infancy continue throughout early childhood. Between ages 2 and 6, approximately 45 new *epiphyses,* or growth centers in which cartilage hardens into bone, emerge in various parts of the skeleton. X-rays of these growth centers enable doctors to estimate children's *skeletal age,* or progress toward physical maturity (see page 108 in Chapter 4)—information helpful in diagnosing growth disorders.

By the end of the preschool years, children start to lose their primary, or "baby," teeth. The age at which they do so is heavily influenced by heredity. For example, girls, who are ahead of boys in physical development, lose their primary teeth earlier. Environmental influences also matter: Prolonged malnutrition delays the appearance of permanent teeth, whereas overweight and obesity accelerate it (Costacurta et al., 2012; Heinrich-Weltzien et al., 2013).

Diseased baby teeth can affect the health of permanent teeth, so preventing decay in primary teeth is essential—by brushing consistently, avoiding sugary foods, drinking fluoridated water, and

FIGURE 7.1 Body growth during early childhood. During the preschool years, children grow more slowly than in infancy and toddlerhood. Wilson and Mariel's bodies became more streamlined, flat-tummied, and longer-legged. Boys continue to be slightly taller, heavier, and more muscular than girls. But generally, the two sexes are similar in body proportions and physical capacities.

getting topical fluoride treatments and sealants (plastic coatings that protect tooth surfaces). Another factor is exposure to tobacco smoke, which suppresses children's immune system, including the ability to fight bacteria responsible for tooth decay. Children in homes with regular smokers are at increased risk for decayed teeth (Hanioka et al., 2011; Wen et al., 2017).

An estimated 23 percent of U.S. preschoolers have tooth decay, a figure that rises to 50 percent in middle childhood and 60 percent by age 18. One-fourth of U.S. children living in poverty have untreated dental caries (U.S. Department of Health and Human Services, 2016b).

Brain Development

Between ages 2 and 6, the brain increases from 70 percent of its adult weight to 90 percent. By ages 4 to 5, many parts of the cerebral cortex have overproduced synapses. In some regions, such as the prefrontal cortex, the number of synapses is nearly double the adult value. Together, synaptic growth and myelination of neural fibers result in a high energy need. fMRI evidence reveals that energy metabolism in the cerebral cortex peaks around this age (Nelson, Thomas, & de Haan, 2006). *Synaptic pruning* follows: Neurons that are seldom stimulated lose their connective fibers, and the number of synapses gradually declines. Between ages 8 to 10, energy consumption of most cortical regions diminishes to near-adult levels (Lebel & Beaulieu, 2011). And cognitive capacities increasingly localize in distinct neural systems that become interconnected, resulting in networks of coordinated neural functioning that support children's advancing abilities (Bathelt et al., 2013; Markant & Thomas, 2013).

EEG, NIRS, and fMRI measures of neural activity reveal especially rapid growth from early to middle childhood in prefrontal-cortical areas devoted to executive function: inhibition, working memory, flexibility of thinking, and planning (Müller & Kerns, 2015). Furthermore, for most children, the left cerebral hemisphere is especially active between 3 and 6 years and then levels off. In contrast, activity in the right hemisphere increases steadily throughout early and middle childhood (Thatcher, Walker, & Giudice, 1987). In line with these developments, language skills (typically housed in the left hemisphere) expand at an astonishing pace in early childhood. In contrast, spatial skills (usually located in the right hemisphere), such as giving directions, drawing pictures, and reading maps, develop gradually over childhood and adolescence.

Differences in rate of development between the two hemispheres suggest that they are continuing to *lateralize* (specialize in cognitive functions). Let's take a closer look at brain lateralization in early childhood by focusing on handedness.

Handedness. Research on handedness, along with other evidence covered in Chapter 4, supports the joint contribution of nature and nurture to brain lateralization. By age 6 months, infants typically display a smoother, more efficient movement when reaching with their right than their left arm—an early tendency that may contribute to the right-handed bias of most children by the end of the first year (Nelson, Campbell, & Michel, 2013; Rönnqvist & Domellöf, 2006). Gradually, handedness extends to additional skills.

Handedness reflects the greater capacity of one side of the brain—the individual's **dominant cerebral hemisphere**—to carry out skilled motor action. Other important abilities are generally located on the dominant side as well. For right-handed people—in Western nations, 90 percent of the population—language is housed in the left hemisphere with hand control. For the left-handed 10 percent, language is occasionally located in the right hemisphere or, more often, shared between the hemispheres (Szaflarski et al., 2012). This indicates that the brains of left-handers tend to be less strongly lateralized than those of right-handers.

Heritability of left-handedness is weak to modest: Left-handed parents have only a mildly elevated chance of having left-handed children (Somers et al., 2015; Suzuki & Ando, 2014). This suggests a *genetic bias* favoring right-handedness that experiences can overcome, swaying children toward a left-hand preference.

Handedness involves practice. It is strongest for complex skills requiring extensive training, such as eating with utensils, writing, and engaging in athletic activities. And wide cultural differences exist. For example, in tribal and village cultures, rates of left-handedness are relatively high. But in one such society in New Guinea, individuals who had attended school in childhood were far more likely to be extremely right-handed—findings that highlight the role of experience (Geuze et al., 2012).

Although left-handedness is elevated among people with intellectual disabilities and mental illness, atypical brain lateralization is probably not responsible for these individuals' problems. Rather, early damage to the left hemisphere may have caused their disabilities while also leading to a shift in handedness. In support of this idea, left-handedness is associated with prenatal and birth difficulties that can result in brain damage, including severe maternal stress, prolonged labor, prematurity, Rh incompatibility, and breech delivery (Domellöf, Johansson, & Rönnqvist, 2011; Kurganskaya, 2011).

STANISLAV SOLNTSEV/13/OCEAN/CORBIS

▶ Genetic influences and parental acceptance may have contributed to this 5-year-old's left-handedness. Left-handed individuals show certain cognitive advantages, perhaps because their brains are less strongly lateralized than those of right-handers.

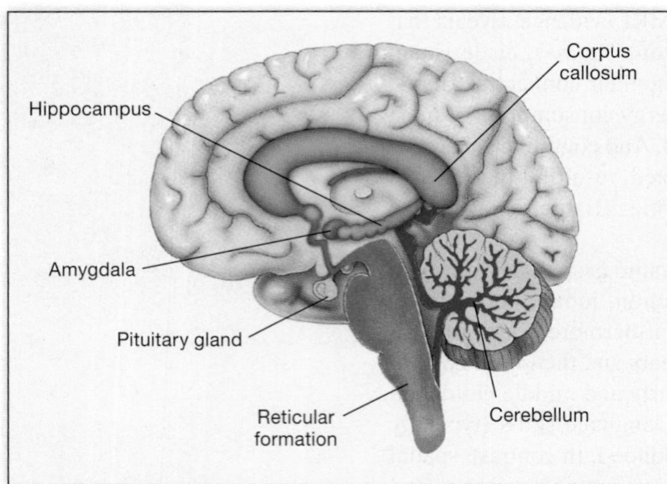

FIGURE 7.2 Cross-section of the human brain, showing the location of the cerebellum, the reticular formation, the amygdala, the hippocampus, and the corpus callosum. These structures undergo considerable development during early childhood. Also shown is the pituitary gland, which secretes hormones that control body growth (see page 207).

Most left-handers, however, have no developmental problems. In fact, they are slightly advantaged in speed and flexibility of thinking, and more likely than their right-handed agemates to develop outstanding verbal and mathematical talents (Beratis et al., 2013; Noroozian et al., 2012). More even distribution of cognitive functions across both brain hemispheres may be responsible.

Other Advances in Brain Development. Besides the cerebral cortex, several other areas of the brain make strides during early childhood (see Figure 7.2). All of these changes involve establishing links between parts of the brain, increasing the coordinated functioning of the central nervous system.

At the rear and base of the brain is the **cerebellum,** a structure that aids in balance and control of body movement. Fibers linking the cerebellum to the cerebral cortex grow and myelinate from birth through the preschool years, contributing to dramatic gains in motor coordination. Connections between the cerebellum and cerebral cortex also support thinking. Children with damage to the cerebellum usually display both motor and cognitive deficits, including problems with memory, planning, and language (Hoang et al., 2014; Noterdaeme et al., 2002).

The **reticular formation,** a structure in the brain stem that maintains alertness and consciousness, generates synapses and myelinates from infancy into the twenties (Sampaio & Truwit, 2001). Neurons in the reticular formation send out fibers to other brain regions. Many go to the prefrontal cortex, contributing to improvements in sustained, controlled attention.

An inner brain structure called the **amygdala** plays a central role in processing of novelty and emotional information. The amygdala is sensitive to facial emotional expressions, especially fear (Adolphs, 2010). It also enhances memory for emotionally salient events, thereby ensuring that information vital for survival—stimuli that signify danger or safety—will be retrieved on future occasions. Throughout childhood and adolescence, connections between the amygdala and the prefrontal cortex, which governs regulation of emotion, form and myelinate (Tottenham, Hare, & Casey, 2009).

▶ This child has been diagnosed with a rare condition in which part of the corpus callosum is absent. He has difficulty with tasks that have multiple steps and that require coordinated movements on both sides of the body. Here, a therapist helps him learn to tie shoes.

Also located in the inner brain, adjacent to the amygdala, is the **hippocampus,** which plays a vital role in memory and in images of space that help us find our way. It undergoes rapid synapse formation and myelination in the second half of the first year, when recall memory and independent movement emerge. Over the preschool and elementary school years, the hippocampus and surrounding areas of the cerebral cortex continue to develop swiftly, establishing connections with one another and with the prefrontal cortex and lateralizing toward greater right-sided activation (Hopf et al., 2013; Nelson, Thomas, & de Haan, 2006). These changes support the dramatic gains in memory and spatial understanding of early and middle childhood.

The **corpus callosum** is a large bundle of fibers connecting the two cerebral hemispheres. Production of synapses and myelination of the corpus callosum peak between 3 and 6 years, continuing at a slower pace through adolescence (Thompson et al., 2000). The corpus callosum supports smooth coordination of movements on both sides of the body and integration of many aspects of thinking, including perception, attention, memory, language, and problem solving. The more complex the task, the more essential is communication between the hemispheres.

Influences on Physical Growth and Health

7.2 Describe the effects of heredity, nutrition, and infectious disease on physical growth and health in early childhood.

7.3 Cite factors that increase the risk of unintentional injuries, and explain how childhood injuries can be prevented.

As we consider factors affecting growth and health in early childhood, you will encounter some familiar themes. Heredity remains important, but good nutrition, relative freedom from disease, and physical safety are also essential.

Heredity and Hormones

The impact of heredity on physical growth is evident throughout childhood. Children's physical size and rate of growth are related to those of their parents (Bogin, 2001). Genes influence growth by controlling the body's production of hormones. Figure 7.2 on page 206 shows the **pituitary gland,** located at the base of the brain, which plays a crucial role by releasing two hormones that induce growth.

The first, **growth hormone (GH),** is necessary for development of almost all body tissues. Without medical intervention, children who lack GH reach an average mature height of only 4 to 4½ feet. When treated early with injections of GH, such children show catch-up growth and then grow at a normal rate, becoming much taller than they would have without treatment (Bright, Mendoza, & Rosenfeld, 2009).

A second pituitary hormone, **thyroid-stimulating hormone (TSH),** prompts the thyroid gland in the neck to release *thyroxine,* which is necessary for brain development and for GH to have its full impact on body size. Infants born with inadequate thyroxine must receive it at once, or they will be intellectually disabled. Once the most rapid period of brain development is complete, children with too little thyroxine grow at a below-average rate, but the central nervous system is no longer affected (Donaldson & Jones, 2013). With prompt treatment, such children catch up in body growth and eventually reach normal size (Høybe et al., 2015).

Nutrition

With the transition to early childhood, many children become unpredictable, picky eaters. Preschoolers' appetites decline because their growth has slowed. And their wariness of new foods is adaptive. By sticking to familiar foods, they are less likely to swallow dangerous substances when adults are not around to protect them. With the transition to middle childhood, picky eating usually subsides (Birch & Fisher, 1995; Cardona Cano et al., 2015).

Though they eat less, preschoolers require a high-quality diet, including the same nutrients adults need. Children tend to imitate the food choices of people they admire, both adults and peers. Repeated, unpressured exposure to new foods also promotes acceptance (Lam, 2015). For example, serving broccoli or tofu increases children's liking for these healthy foods. In contrast, offering sweet fruit drinks or soft drinks promotes "milk avoidance" (Black et al., 2002).

Although children's healthy eating depends on a wholesome food environment, offering bribes—"Finish your vegetables, and you can have an extra cookie"—leads children to like the healthy food less and the treat more (Birch, Fisher, & Davison, 2003). In general, coercing children to eat results in withdrawal from food, whereas food restriction leads to excessive eating. In a study of nearly 5,000 Dutch 4-year-olds, the more mothers reported pressuring their child to eat, the greater the likelihood of an underweight child. And the more mothers reported restricting their child's eating, the greater the chances of an overweight or obese child (Jansen et al., 2012).

▶ This Mexican 3-year-old helps his mother prepare refried beans for dinner. Children tend to imitate the food preferences of those they admire—both adults and peers.

As indicated in earlier chapters, many children in the United States and in developing countries lack access to

LOOK AND LISTEN

Arrange to join a family with at least one preschooler for a meal, and closely observe parental mealtime practices. Are they likely to promote healthy eating habits? Explain.

sufficient high-quality food to support healthy growth. Five-year-old Hal rode a bus from a poor neighborhood to our laboratory preschool. His mother's welfare check barely covered her rent, let alone food. Hal's diet was deficient in protein and in essential vitamins and minerals. He was pale, inattentive, and disruptive at preschool. Throughout childhood and adolescence, a nutritionally deficient diet is associated with shorter stature, attention and memory difficulties, poorer intelligence and achievement test scores, and hyperactivity and aggression, even after family factors that might account for these relationships are controlled (Liu et al., 2004; Lukowski et al., 2010).

Infectious Disease

In well-nourished children, ordinary childhood illnesses have no effect on physical growth. But when children are undernourished, disease interacts with malnutrition in a vicious spiral, with potentially severe consequences.

Infectious Disease and Malnutrition. In developing countries, where many children live in poverty and do not receive routine immunizations, illnesses such as measles and chickenpox, which typically do not appear until after age 3, occur much earlier. Poor diet depresses the body's immune system, making children far more susceptible to disease. Of the 5.9 million annual deaths of children under age 5 worldwide, 98 percent are in developing countries and about half are due to infectious diseases (World Health Organization, 2015a).

Disease, in turn, contributes to malnutrition by reducing appetite and limiting the body's ability to absorb foods, especially in children with intestinal infections. In developing countries, widespread diarrhea, resulting from unsafe water and contaminated foods, leads to growth stunting and an estimated 1 million childhood deaths each year (Unger et al., 2014). Studies carried out in low-income countries reveal that the more persistent diarrhea is in early childhood, the shorter children are in height and the lower their intelligence test scores during the school years (Black, 2017; Pinkerton et al., 2016).

Most developmental impairments and deaths due to diarrhea can be prevented with nearly cost-free *oral rehydration therapy (ORT),* in which sick children are given a glucose, salt, and water solution that quickly replaces fluids the body loses. Since 1990, public health workers have taught nearly half the families in the developing world how to administer ORT. Also, low-cost supplements of zinc (essential for immune system functioning) substantially reduce the incidence of severe and prolonged diarrhea, especially when combined with ORT (Galvao et al., 2013).

Immunization. In the United States, routine childhood immunizations prevent an estimated 20 million illnesses and 40,000 deaths each year (Ventola, 2016). Yet about 17 percent of U.S. preschoolers lack essential immunizations. The rate rises to 22 percent for poverty-stricken preschoolers, many of whom do not receive full protection until ages 5 or 6, when it is required for school entry (Centers for Disease Control and Prevention, 2016d). In contrast, fewer than 10 percent of preschoolers lack immunizations in Australia, Denmark, and Norway, and fewer than 5 percent in Canada, the Netherlands, Sweden, and the United Kingdom (World Health Organization, 2017b).

Why does the United States lag behind these countries? Although the U.S. Affordable Care Act of 2010 greatly improved health insurance coverage for American children, many low-income children remain without coverage and, therefore, may not receive timely vaccinations. Beginning in 1994, all U.S. children whose parents were unable to pay were guaranteed free immunizations, a program that has led to gains in immunization rates.

Inability to afford vaccines is not the only cause of inadequate immunization. Parents with little education and with stressful daily lives often fail to schedule vaccination appointments (Falagas & Zarkadoulia, 2008). Some parents have been influenced by media reports—now widely discredited—suggesting a link between a mercury-based preservative used for decades in vaccines and a rise in the number of children diagnosed with autism. In fact, large-scale studies show no association (Hensley & Briars, 2010; Thompson et al., 2007). Still, as a precautionary measure, mercury-free versions of childhood vaccines are now available. Other parents have religious or philosophical objections—for example, the belief that children should develop immunities naturally.

In areas where many parents have refused to immunize their children, disease outbreaks have occurred, with life-threatening consequences (Salmon et al., 2015). Public education programs directed at increasing parental knowledge about the importance and safety of timely immunizations are badly needed. The Netherlands achieves its high child immunization rate by giving parents of every newborn baby a written schedule of when and where the child should be immunized (Lernout et al., 2013). If a parent does not bring the child at the specified time, a public health nurse goes to the home to ensure that the child remains in step with the schedule.

Childhood Injuries

Unintentional injuries are the leading cause of childhood mortality in industrialized nations. Although U.S. childhood injury fatalities have declined steadily over the past 35 years due to policies aimed at improving child safety, the United States ranks poorly among Western nations in these largely preventable events. About 35 percent of U.S. childhood deaths and 50 percent of adolescent deaths result from injuries, causing over 8,000 children to die annually (Child Trends, 2014b). Among the hundreds of thousands of injured children and youths who survive, many suffer pain, brain damage, and physical disabilities.

Auto and traffic accidents, suffocation, drowning, and poisoning are the most common injuries resulting in childhood deaths (Safe Kids Worldwide, 2015). Motor vehicle collisions are by far the most frequent overall source of injury. They rank as the second leading U.S. cause of mortality from birth to age 5 (after suffocation among infants and drowning among toddlers and preschoolers) and as the leading cause among school-age children and adolescents.

Factors Related to Childhood Injuries. The common view of childhood injuries as "accidental" suggests they are due to chance and cannot be prevented. In fact, these injuries occur within a complex *ecological system* of individual, family, community, and societal influences—and we can do something about them.

Because of their higher activity level and greater impulsivity and risk taking, boys are nearly twice as likely as girls to be injured, and their injuries are more severe (Merrick, 2016). Children with certain temperamental and personality characteristics—inattentiveness, overactivity, irritability, defiance, and aggression—are also at greater risk (Ordonana, Caspi, & Moffitt, 2008; Schwebel & Gaines, 2007).

Poverty, single parenthood, and low parental education are also strongly associated with injury (Dudani, Macpherson, & Tamim, 2010; Schwebel & Brezausek, 2007). Parents with many daily stressors often have little time or energy to monitor the safety of their children. And their homes and neighborhoods are likely to be noisy, crowded, and rundown, posing further risks.

Broad societal conditions also affect childhood injury. In developing countries, the rate of childhood death from injury is far greater than in developed nations (Kahn et al., 2015). Rapid population growth, overcrowding in cities, and heavy road traffic combined with weak safety measures are major causes. Safety devices, such as car safety seats and bicycle helmets, are neither readily available nor affordable.

Childhood injury rates are high in the United States because of extensive poverty, shortages of high-quality child care (to supervise children in their parents' absence), and a high rate of births to teenagers, who are not ready for parenthood (Child Trends, 2014a; Höllwarth, 2013). But U.S. children from economically advantaged families are also at greater risk for injury than children in other Western nations. This indicates that besides reducing poverty and teenage childbearing and upgrading the status of child care, additional steps are needed to ensure children's safety.

▶ Childhood injury rates are highest in areas with extensive poverty, lack of high-quality child care, and weak parental vigilance, as illustrated by these children's makeshift playground.

Preventing Childhood Injuries. Laws prevent many injuries by requiring car safety seats, child-resistant caps on medicine bottles, flameproof clothing, and fencing around backyard swimming pools. Communities can help by modifying their physical environments. Playgrounds, a common site of injury, can be covered with protective surfaces. Free, easily installed window guards can be given to families in high-rise apartment buildings to prevent falls. And media campaigns can inform parents and children about safety issues.

But even though they know better, many parents and children behave in ways that compromise safety. About 27 percent of U.S. parents fail to place their children in car safety seats, and nearly 75 percent of infant seats and 40 percent of child booster seats are improperly used (Macy et al., 2015). American parents, especially, seem willing to ignore familiar safety practices, perhaps because of the high value they place on individual rights and personal freedom.

Furthermore, many parents overestimate young children's knowledge of safety rules, engaging in too little monitoring of their access to hazards. And when parents teach safety rules to preschoolers, they frequently fail to explain the basis for the rules—despite evidence that explanations enhance children's retention, understanding, and compliance (Morrongiello, Ondejko, & Littlejohn, 2004; Morrongiello et al., 2014). Even with well-learned rules, preschoolers need supervision to ensure that they comply.

Interventions aimed at parents that highlight risk factors and that model and reinforce safety practices are effective in reducing childhood injuries (Kendrick et al., 2008). Attention must also be paid to family conditions that can prevent childhood injury: relieving crowding in the home, providing social supports to ease parental stress, and teaching parents to use effective discipline—a topic we will take up in Chapter 8.

ASK YOURSELF

CONNECT Using research on handedness, malnutrition, or unintentional injuries, show how physical growth and health in early childhood result from a complex interplay between heredity and environment.

APPLY One day, Leslie prepared a new snack to serve at preschool: celery stuffed with ricotta cheese. The first time she served it, few children touched it. How can Leslie encourage her students to accept the snack? What tactics should she avoid?

REFLECT Ask a parent or other family member whether, as a preschooler, you were a picky eater, suffered from many infectious diseases, or sustained any serious injuries. What factors might have been responsible?

Motor Development

7.4 Cite major milestones of gross- and fine-motor development, along with factors that affect motor progress, in early childhood.

Observe several 2- to 6-year-olds at play in a neighborhood park, preschool, or child-care center. You will see that an explosion of new motor skills occurs in early childhood. Preschoolers continue to integrate previously acquired skills into more complex, *dynamic systems.* Then they revise each new skill as their bodies grow larger and stronger, their central nervous systems develop, their environments present new challenges, and they set new goals.

Gross-Motor Development

As children's bodies become more streamlined and less top-heavy, their center of gravity shifts downward, toward the trunk. As a result, balance improves greatly, paving the way for new gross-motor skills. By age 2, children's gaits become smooth and rhythmic—secure enough that soon they leave the ground, at first by running and later by jumping, hopping, galloping, and skipping.

As children become steadier on their feet, their arms and torsos are freed to experiment with new skills—throwing and catching balls, steering tricycles, and swinging on horizontal bars and rings. Then upper- and lower-body skills combine into more refined actions. Five- and 6-year-olds

TABLE 7.1
Changes in Gross- and Fine-Motor Skills During Early Childhood

AGE	GROSS-MOTOR SKILLS	FINE-MOTOR SKILLS
2–3 years	Walks more rhythmically; hurried walk changes to run Jumps, hops, throws, and catches with rigid upper body Pushes riding toy with feet; little steering	Puts on and removes simple items of clothing Zips and unzips large zippers Uses spoon effectively
3–4 years	Walks up stairs, alternating feet, and down stairs, leading with one foot Jumps and hops, flexing upper body Throws and catches with slight involvement of upper body; still catches by trapping ball against chest Pedals and steers tricycle	Fastens and unfastens large buttons Serves self food without assistance Uses scissors Copies vertical line and circle Draws first picture of person, using tadpole image
4–5 years	Walks down stairs, alternating feet Runs more smoothly Gallops and skips with one foot Throws ball with increased body rotation and transfer of weight from one foot to the other; catches ball with hands Rides tricycle rapidly, steers smoothly	Uses fork effectively Cuts with scissors following line Copies triangle, cross, and some letters
5–6 years	Increases running speed to 12 feet per second Gallops more smoothly; engages in true skipping Displays mature throwing and catching pattern Rides bicycle with training wheels	Uses knife to cut soft food Ties shoes Draws person with six parts Copies some numbers and simple words

Sources: Cratty, 1986; Haywood & Getchell, 2014.

simultaneously steer and pedal a tricycle and flexibly move their whole body when throwing, catching, hopping, jumping, and skipping. By the end of the preschool years, all skills are performed with greater speed and endurance. Table 7.1 provides a closer look at gross-motor development in early childhood.

ELLEN B. SENISI

▶ As balance improves, preschoolers combine upper- and lower-body skills into more refined actions, such as walking on stilts.

Fine-Motor Development

Fine-motor skills, too, take a giant leap forward in the preschool years. As control of the hands and fingers improves, young children put puzzles together, build with small blocks, cut and paste, and improve in self-help skills—dressing and undressing, using a fork adeptly, and (at the end of early childhood) cutting food with a knife and tying shoes. Fine-motor progress is also apparent in drawings and first efforts to write.

Drawing. A variety of cognitive factors combine with fine-motor control in the development of children's artful representations (Golomb, 2004). These include the realization that pictures can serve as symbols, and improved planning and spatial understanding.

Typically, drawing progresses through the following sequence:

1. *Scribbles.* At first, children's gestures rather than the resulting scribbles contain the intended representation. For example, one 18-month-old made her crayon hop and, as it produced a series of dots, explained, "Rabbit goes hop-hop" (Winner, 1986).
2. *First representational forms.* Around age 3, children's scribbles start to become pictures. Few 3-year-olds spontaneously draw so others can tell what their picture

LOOK AND LISTEN

Visit a preschool, child-care center, or children's museum where artwork by 3- to 5-year-olds is plentiful. Note developmental progress in the drawings of human and animal figures and in the complexity of children's drawings.

represents. When adults draw with children and point out the resemblances between drawings and objects, preschoolers' pictures become more comprehensible and detailed (Braswell & Callanan, 2003).

A major milestone in drawing occurs when children use lines to represent the boundaries of objects, enabling 3- and 4-year-olds to draw their first picture of a person. Fine-motor and cognitive limitations lead preschoolers to reduce the figure to the simplest form that still looks human: the universal "tadpole" image, a circular shape with lines attached, shown on the left in Figure 7.3, evident in children from widely differing cultures (Gernhardt, Rübeling, & Keller, 2015). Four-year-olds add features, such as eyes, nose, mouth, hair, fingers, and feet.

Nevertheless, cultural values influence figure size and details. The tadpole self-depictions of children from non-Western village cultures are usually small, deemphasizing individuality in favor of interdependence with others (Gernhardt, Rübeling, & Keller, 2014; Rübeling, 2014). Those of Western urban children, in contrast, are usually large, fill out the page, and have prominent facial features, conveying a sense of independence and uniqueness.

3. *More realistic drawings.* Five- and 6-year-olds create more complex drawings, like the one on the right in Figure 7.3, containing more conventional human and animal figures, with the head and body differentiated. Older preschoolers' drawings contain perceptual distortions because they have just begun to represent depth. This free depiction of reality makes their artwork look fanciful and inventive.

In cultures that have rich artistic traditions and that highly value artistic competence, children create elaborate drawings that reflect cultural conventions. Adults encourage young children by guiding them in mastering basic drawing skills, modeling ways to draw, and discussing their pictures. Peers, as well, talk about one another's drawings and copy from one another's work (Boyatzis, 2000; Braswell, 2006). All of these practices enhance drawing progress. And as the Cultural Influences box on the following page reveals, they help explain why, from an early age, children in Asian cultures are advanced over Western children in drawing skills.

FIGURE 7.3 Examples of young children's drawings. The universal tadpolelike shape that children use to draw their first picture of a person is shown on the left. The tadpole soon becomes an anchor for details that sprout from the basic shape. By the end of the preschool years, children produce more complex, differentiated pictures like the one on the right, by a 5-year-old child. (*Left:* From H. Gardner, 1980, *Artful Scribbles: The Significance of Children's Drawings,* New York: Basic Books, p. 64. Copyright © 1980 by Howard Gardner. Reprinted by permission of Basic Books, a member of the Perseus Books Group, conveyed through Copyright Clearance Center. *Right:* © Children's Museum of the Arts New York, Permanent Collection.)

CULTURAL INFLUENCES

Why Are Children from Asian Cultures Advanced in Drawing Skills?

Children's drawings in Asian cultures, such as China, Japan, Korea, the Philippines, Taiwan, and Vietnam, reveal skills that are remarkably advanced over those of their Western agemates. What explains such early artistic ability?

To answer this question, researchers examined cultural influences on children's drawings, comparing China to the United States. Artistic models, teaching strategies, valuing of the visual arts, and expectations for children's artistic development have a notable impact on the art that children produce.

In China's 4,000-year-old artistic tradition, adults showed children how to draw, teaching the precise steps required to depict people, butterflies, fish, birds, and other images. When taught to paint, Chinese children follow prescribed brush strokes, at first copying their teacher's model. To learn to write, Chinese children must concentrate hard on the unique details of each Chinese character—a requirement that likely enhances their drawing ability. Chinese parents and teachers believe that children can be creative only after they have acquired a foundation of artistic knowledge and technique (Golomb, 2004). To that end, China has devised a national art curriculum with standards extending from age 3 through secondary school.

The United States, as well, has a rich artistic tradition, but its styles and conventions are enormously diverse compared with those of Asian cultures. Children everywhere try to imitate the art around them as a way to acquire their culture's "visual language." But American children face a daunting imitative task (Cohn, 2014). Furthermore, U.S. art education emphasizes independence—finding one's own style. Rather than promoting correct ways to draw, U.S. teachers emphasize imagination and self-expression.

▶ The complex drawings of these kindergartners in Shanghai, China, benefit from adult expectations that young children learn to draw well, careful teaching of artistic knowledge and technique, and the rich artistic tradition of Chinese culture.

Does the Chinese method of teaching drawing skills beginning in early childhood interfere with children's creativity? To find out, researchers followed a group of Chinese-American children of immigrant parents and a group of European-American children, all from middle-SES two-parent families, from ages 5 to 9. At two-year intervals, the children's human-figure drawings were rated for maturity and originality—inclusion of novel elements (Huntsinger et al., 2011). On each occasion, the Chinese-American children's drawings were more advanced and also more creative.

Interviews revealed that European-American parents more often provided their children with a rich variety of art materials, whereas Chinese-American parents more often enrolled their children in art lessons. The Chinese-American children also spent more time as preschoolers and kindergartners in focused practice of fine-motor skills, including drawing. And the more time they spent practicing, especially when their parents taught and modeled drawing at home, the more mature their drawing skills. Once they succeeded at drawing basic forms, they spontaneously added unusual details of their own.

In sum, even though young Chinese children are taught how to draw, their artistic products are original. Although Western children may come up with rich ideas about what to draw, until they acquire the necessary skills, they cannot implement those ideas. Cross-cultural research suggests that children benefit from adult guidance in learning to draw, just as they do in learning to talk.

Early Printing. At first, preschoolers do not distinguish between writing and drawing. Around age 4, writing shows some distinctive features of print, such as separate forms arranged in a line on the page. But children often include picturelike devices—for example, a circular shape to write "sun" (Ehri & Roberts, 2006). Only gradually, between ages 4 and 6, as they learn to name alphabet letters and link them with language sounds, do children realize that writing stands for language.

Preschoolers' first attempts to print often involve their name, generally using a single letter. "How do you make a *D?*" my older son, David, asked at age 3½. When I printed a large uppercase *D* for him to copy, he was quite satisfied with his backward, imperfect creation. By age 5, David printed his name clearly enough for others to read it, but, like many children, he continued to reverse some letters well into second grade. Until children start to read, they do not find it useful to distinguish between mirror-image forms, such as *b* and *d* or *p* and *q* (Bornstein & Arterberry, 1999).

Individual Differences in Motor Skills

Wide individual differences exist in the ages at which children reach motor milestones. A tall, muscular child tends to move more quickly and to acquire certain skills earlier than a short, stocky youngster. And as in other domains, parents and teachers probably provide more encouragement to children with biologically based motor-skill advantages.

Sex differences in motor skills are evident in early childhood. Boys are ahead of girls in skills that emphasize force and power. By age 5, they can broad-jump slightly farther, run slightly faster, and throw a ball about 5 feet farther. Girls have an edge in fine-motor skills and in certain gross-motor skills that require a combination of good balance and foot movement, such as hopping and skipping (Fischman, Moore, & Steele, 1992; Haywood & Getchell, 2014). Boys' greater muscle mass and, in the case of throwing, slightly longer forearms contribute to their skill advantages. And girls' greater overall physical maturity may be partly responsible for their better balance and precision of movement.

From an early age, boys and girls are usually encouraged into different physical activities. For example, fathers are more likely to play catch with their sons than with their daughters. Sex differences in motor skills increase with age, but they remain small throughout childhood (Greendorfer, Lewko, & Rosengren, 1996). This suggests that social pressures for boys, more than girls, to be active and physically skilled exaggerate small, genetically based sex differences.

Children master the gross-motor skills of early childhood through everyday play. Aside from throwing (where direct instruction is helpful), preschoolers exposed to gymnastics, tumbling, and other formal lessons do not make faster progress. When children have access to play spaces and equipment appropriate for running, climbing, jumping, and ball play and are encouraged to use them, they respond eagerly to these challenges. Similarly, fine-motor skills can be supported through richly equipped early childhood environments that include puzzles, construction sets, drawing, painting, sculpting, cutting, and pasting. And as the Cultural Influences box shows, adults who guide and support children in acquiring drawing skills foster artistic development.

ASK YOURSELF

APPLY Mabel and Chad want to do everything they can to support their 3-year-old daughter's motor development. What advice would you give them?

REFLECT Do you think that American children should be provided with systematic instruction in drawing skills beginning in early childhood, similar to the direct teaching Chinese children receive?

COGNITIVE DEVELOPMENT

One rainy morning, as I observed in our laboratory preschool, Leslie, the children's teacher, joined me at the back of the room. "Preschoolers' minds are such a blend of logic, fantasy, and faulty reasoning," Leslie reflected. "Every day, I'm startled by the maturity and originality of what they say and do. Yet at other times, their thinking seems limited and inflexible."

Leslie's comments sum up the puzzling contradictions of early childhood cognition. Hearing a loud thunderclap outside, 3-year-old Sammy exclaimed, "A magic man turned on the thunder!" Even after Leslie explained that thunder is caused by lightning, not by a person turning it on, Sammy persisted: "Then a magic lady did it."

In other respects, Sammy's thinking was surprisingly advanced. At snack time, he accurately counted, "One, two, three, four!" and then got four boxes of raisins, one for each child at his table.

But when his snack group included more than four children, Sammy's counting broke down. And after Priti dumped out her raisins, scattering them on the table, Sammy asked, "How come you got lots, and I only got this little bit?" He didn't realize that he had just as many raisins; his were simply all bunched up in a tiny red box.

While Priti washed her hands after snack, Sammy stuffed her remaining raisins back in the box and placed it in her cubby. When Priti returned and looked for her raisins, Sammy insisted, "You know where they are!" He failed to consider that Priti, who hadn't seen him move the raisins, would expect them to be where she had left them.

To understand Sammy's reasoning, we turn first to Piaget's and Vygotsky's theories along with evidence highlighting the strengths and limitations of each. Then we take up additional research on young children's cognition inspired by the information-processing perspective, address factors that contribute to individual differences in mental development, and conclude with the dramatic expansion of language in early childhood.

Piaget's Theory: The Preoperational Stage

As children move from the sensorimotor to the **preoperational stage,** which spans the years 2 to 7, the most obvious change is an extraordinary increase in representational, or symbolic, activity. Infants and toddlers' mental representations are impressive, but in early childhood, these capacities blossom.

7.5 Describe advances in mental representation, and limitations of thinking, during the preoperational stage.

7.6 Explain the implications of follow-up research on early childhood cognitive development for the accuracy of Piaget's preoperational stage.

Advances in Mental Representation

Piaget acknowledged that language is our most flexible means of mental representation. By detaching thought from action, it permits far more efficient thinking than was possible earlier. Despite the power of language, however, Piaget did not regard it as a major ingredient in childhood cognitive change. Instead, he believed that sensorimotor activity leads to internal images of experience, which children then label with words (Piaget, 1936/1952). In support of Piaget's view, recall from Chapter 5 that children's first words have a strong sensorimotor basis. Also, infants and toddlers acquire an impressive range of categories long before they use words to label them (see page 154). But as we will see, Piaget underestimated the power of language to spur children's cognition.

Make-Believe Play

Make-believe play is another example of the development of representation in early childhood. Piaget believed that through pretending, young children practice and strengthen newly acquired representational schemes. Drawing on his ideas, investigators have traced changes in preschoolers' make-believe play.

Development of Make-Believe. One day, Sammy's 20-month-old brother, Dwayne, visited the classroom. Dwayne picked up a toy telephone receiver, said, "Hi, Mommy," and then dropped it. Next, he found a cup and pretended to drink. Meanwhile, Sammy joined Vance and Priti in the block area for a space shuttle launch.

"That can be our control tower," Sammy suggested, pointing to a corner by a bookshelf. "Countdown!" he announced, speaking into his "walkie-talkie"—a small wooden block. "Five, six, two, four, one, blastoff!" Priti made a doll push a pretend button, and the rocket was off!

Comparing Dwayne's pretend play with Sammy's, we see three important changes in symbolic mastery:

- *Play detaches from the real-life conditions associated with it.* In early pretending, toddlers use only realistic objects—a toy telephone to talk into or a cup to drink from. Their earliest pretend acts usually imitate adults' actions and are not yet flexible. Children younger than age 2, for example, will pretend to drink from a cup but refuse to pretend a cup is a hat (Rakoczy, Tomasello, & Striano, 2005). They have trouble using an object (cup) that already has an obvious use as a symbol of another object (hat).

After age 2, children pretend with less realistic toys (a block for a telephone receiver). Gradually, they imagine objects and events without any support from the real world, as Sammy's imaginary control tower illustrates. And by age 3, they flexibly understand that an object (a yellow stick) may take on one fictional identity (a toothbrush) in one pretend game and another fictional identity (a carrot) in a different pretend game (Wyman, Rakoczy, & Tomasello, 2009).

- *Play becomes less self-centered.* At first, make-believe is directed toward the self—for example, Dwayne pretends to feed only himself. Soon, children direct pretend actions toward other objects, as when a child feeds a doll. Early in the third year, they become detached participants, making a doll feed itself or pushing a button to launch a rocket (McCune, 1993). Increasingly, preschoolers realize that agents and recipients of pretend actions can be independent of themselves.
- *Play includes more complex combinations of schemes.* Dwayne can pretend to drink from a cup, but he does not yet combine pouring and drinking. Later, children combine schemes with those of peers in **sociodramatic play,** the make-believe with others that is under way by the end of the second year and rapidly increases in complexity during early childhood (Kavanaugh, 2006). Already, Sammy and his classmates can create and coordinate several roles in an elaborate plot. By the end of early childhood, children have a sophisticated understanding of role relationships and story lines.

▶ Make-believe play increases in sophistication during the preschool years. Children pretend with less realistic toys and increasingly coordinate make-believe roles, such as school bus driver and passengers.

In sociodramatic play, children display awareness that make-believe is a representational activity—an understanding that strengthens over early childhood (Rakoczy, Tomasello, & Striano, 2004; Sobel, 2006). Listen closely to a group of preschoolers as they assign roles and negotiate make-believe plans: "You *pretend to be* the astronaut, I'll *act like* I'm operating the control tower!" In communicating about pretend, children think about their own and others' fanciful representations—evidence that they have begun to reason about people's mental activities, a topic we will return to later in this chapter.

Benefits of Make-Believe. Today, Piaget's view of make-believe as mere practice of representational schemes is regarded by many researchers as too limited. In their view, play not only reflects but also contributes to children's cognitive and social skills.

Preschoolers who devote more time to sociodramatic play are rated by observers as more socially competent a year later (Lindsey & Colwell, 2013). And make-believe predicts a wide variety of cognitive capacities, including executive function, memory, logical reasoning, language and literacy (including story comprehension and storytelling skills), imagination, creativity, and the ability to reflect on one's own thinking, regulate emotions, and take another's perspective (Berk & Meyers, 2013; Buchsbaum et al., 2012; Carlson & White, 2013; Melzer & Palermo, 2016; Mottweiler & Taylor, 2014; Nicolopoulou & Ilgaz, 2013; Roskos & Christie, 2013).

Critics, however, point out that the evidence just summarized is largely correlational, with too many studies failing to control all factors that might alternatively explain their findings (Lillard et al., 2013). In response, play investigators note that decades of research are consistent with a positive role for make-believe play in development and that new, carefully conducted research strengthens that conclusion (Berk, 2015; Carlson, White, & Davis-Unger, 2014). Furthermore, make-believe is difficult to study experimentally, by training children to engage in it. Besides alterations of reality, true make-believe *play* involves other qualities, including intrinsic motivation (doing it for fun, not to please an adult), positive emotion, and child control (Bergen, 2013).

LOOK AND LISTEN

Observe the make-believe play of several preschoolers at a family gathering, a preschool or child-care center, or in another community setting. Describe pretend acts that illustrate important developmental changes.

Finally, much make-believe takes place when adults are not around to observe it! For example, an estimated 25 to 45 percent of preschoolers and young school-age children spend much time creating imaginary companions—special fantasized friends endowed with humanlike qualities. Yet more than one-fourth of parents are unaware of their child's invisible friend (Taylor et al., 2004). Children with imaginary companions display more complex and imaginative make-believe play;

more often describe others in terms of their internal states, including desires, thoughts, and emotions; and are more sociable with peers (Bouldin, 2006; Davis, Meins, & Fernyhough, 2014; Gleason, 2013, 2017). Imaginary companions seem to offer children rich opportunities to enact events and practice social skills that might occur in real relationships.

Symbol–Real-World Relations

To make believe and draw—and to understand other forms of representation, such as photographs, models, and maps—preschoolers must realize that each symbol corresponds to something specific in everyday life. In Chapter 5, we saw that by the middle of the second year, children grasp the symbolic function of realistic-looking pictures and, around age 2½, of TV and video. When do children comprehend other challenging symbols—for example, three-dimensional models of real-world spaces?

In one study, 2½- and 3-year-olds watched an adult hide a small toy (Little Snoopy) in a scale model of a room and then were asked to retrieve it. Next, they had to find a larger toy (Big Snoopy) hidden in the room that the model represented. Not until age 3 could most children use the model as a guide to finding Big Snoopy in the real room (DeLoache, 1987). The 2½-year-olds did not realize that the model could be both *a toy room* and *a symbol of another room.* They had trouble with **dual representation**—viewing a symbolic object as both an object in its own right and a symbol. In support of this interpretation, when researchers made the model room less prominent as an object, by placing it behind a window and preventing children from touching it, more 2½-year-olds succeeded at the search task (DeLoache, 2002). Recall, also, that in make-believe play, 1½- to 2-year-olds cannot use an object that has an obvious use (cup) to stand for another object (hat).

When adults point out similarities between models and real-world spaces, 2½-year-olds perform better on the find-Snoopy task (Peralta de Mendoza & Salsa, 2003). Also, insight into one type of symbol–real-world relation promotes mastery of others. For example, children regard realistic-looking pictures as symbols early because a picture's primary purpose is to stand for something; it is not an interesting object in its own right (Simcock & DeLoache, 2006). And 3-year-olds who can use a model of a room to locate Big Snoopy readily transfer their understanding to a simple map (Marzolf & DeLoache, 1994). In sum, experiences with diverse symbols—picture books, photographs, drawings, make-believe, and maps—help preschoolers appreciate that one object can stand for another.

Limitations of Preoperational Thought

Aside from gains in representation, Piaget described preschoolers in terms of what they *cannot* understand. As the term *pre*operational suggests, he compared them to older, more competent school-age children. According to Piaget, young children are not capable of *operations*—mental representations of actions that obey logical rules. Rather, their thinking is rigid, limited to one aspect of a situation at a time, and strongly influenced by the way things appear at the moment.

FIGURE 7.4 Piaget's three-mountains problem. Each mountain is distinguished by its color and by its summit. One has a red cross, another a small house, and the third a snow-capped peak. Children at the preoperational stage respond egocentrically. They cannot select a picture that shows the mountains from the doll's perspective. Instead, they simply choose the photo that reflects their own vantage point.

Egocentrism.

For Piaget, the most fundamental deficiency of preoperational thinking is **egocentrism**—failure to distinguish others' symbolic viewpoints from one's own. He believed that when children first mentally represent the world, they tend to focus on their own viewpoint and simply assume that others perceive, think, and feel the same way they do.

Piaget's most convincing demonstration of egocentrism involves his *three-mountains problem,* described in Figure 7.4. He also regarded egocentrism as responsible for preoperational children's *animistic thinking*—the belief that inanimate objects have lifelike qualities, such as thoughts, wishes, feelings, and intentions (Piaget, 1926/1930). Recall Sammy's insistence that someone must have turned on the thunder. According to Piaget, because young children egocentrically assign human purposes to physical events, magical thinking is common during the preschool years.

Piaget argued that preschoolers' egocentric bias prevents them from *accommodating,* or reflecting on and revising their faulty reasoning in response to their physical and social worlds. To understand this shortcoming, let's consider some additional tasks that Piaget gave to children.

Inability to Conserve. Piaget's famous conservation tasks reveal a variety of deficiencies of preoperational thinking. **Conservation** refers to the idea that certain physical characteristics of objects remain the same, even when their outward appearance changes. At snack time, Priti and Sammy had identical boxes of raisins, but when Priti spread her raisins out on the table, Sammy was convinced that she had more.

In another conservation task involving liquid, the child is shown two identical tall glasses of water and asked if they contain equal amounts. Once the child agrees, the water in one glass is poured into a short, wide container. Then the child is asked whether the amount of water has changed. Preoperational children think the quantity has changed. They explain, "There is less now because the water is way down here" (that is, its level is so low) or, "There is more now because it is all spread out." Figure 7.5 illustrates other conservation tasks that you can try with children.

The inability to conserve highlights several related aspects of preoperational children's thinking. First, their understanding is *centered,* or characterized by **centration.** They focus on one aspect of a situation, neglecting other important features. In conservation of liquid, the child *centers* on the height of the water, failing to realize that changes in width compensate for changes in height. Second, children are easily distracted by the *perceptual appearance* of objects. Third, children treat the initial and final states of the water as unrelated events, ignoring the *dynamic transformation* (pouring of water) between them.

The most important illogical feature of preoperational thought is **irreversibility**—an inability to mentally go through a series of steps in a problem and then reverse direction, returning to the starting point. *Reversibility* is part of every logical operation. After Priti spills her raisins, Sammy cannot reverse by thinking, "I know that Priti doesn't have more raisins than I do. If we put them back in that little box, her raisins and my raisins would look just the same."

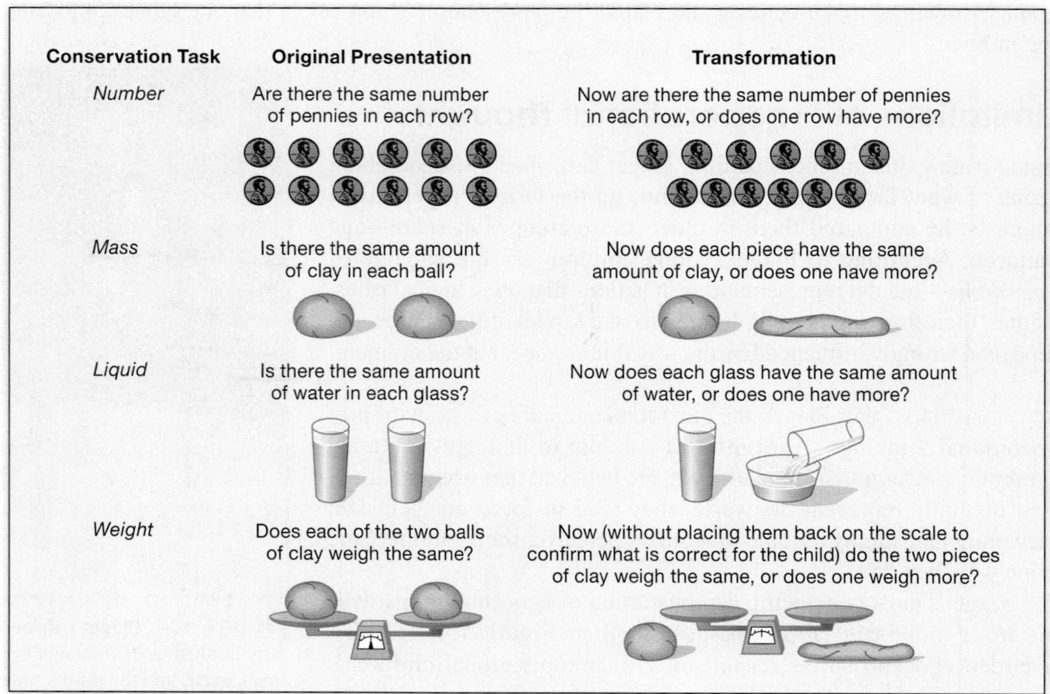

FIGURE 7.5 Some Piagetian conservation tasks. Children at the preoperational stage cannot yet conserve. These tasks are mastered gradually over the concrete operational stage. Children in Western nations typically acquire conservation of number, mass, and liquid sometime between 6 and 7 years and conservation of weight between 8 and 10 years.

Lack of Hierarchical Classification. Preoperational children have difficulty with **hierarchical classification**—the organization of objects into classes and subclasses on the basis of similarities and differences. Piaget's famous *class inclusion problem,* illustrated in Figure 7.6, demonstrates this limitation. Preoperational children center on the overriding feature, red. They do not think reversibly by moving from the whole class (flowers) to the parts (red and blue) and back again.

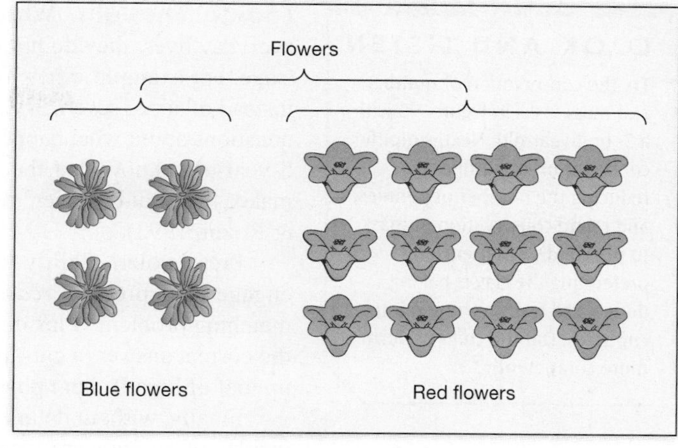

FIGURE 7.6 A Piagetian class inclusion problem. Children are shown 16 flowers, 4 of which are blue and 12 of which are red. Asked, "Are there more red flowers or flowers?" the preoperational child responds, "More red flowers," failing to realize that both red and blue flowers are included in the category "flowers."

Follow-Up Research on Preoperational Thought

Over the past three decades, researchers have challenged Piaget's view of preschoolers as cognitively deficient. Because many Piagetian problems contain unfamiliar elements or too many pieces of information for young children to handle at once, preschoolers' responses do not reflect their true abilities. Piaget also missed many naturally occurring instances of effective reasoning by preschoolers.

Egocentric, Animistic, and Magical Thinking. When researchers use simplified tasks with familiar objects, 3-year-olds show clear awareness of others' vantage points, such as recognizing how something appears to another person who is looking at it through a color filter (Moll & Meltzoff, 2011). Nonegocentric responses also appear in young children's everyday interactions. In Chapter 5, we saw that toddlers have already begun to infer others' intentions (see page 144). And in his later writings, Piaget (1945/1951) described preschoolers' egocentrism as a *tendency* rather than an inability. As we revisit the topic of perspective taking, we will see that it develops gradually throughout childhood and adolescence.

Piaget also overestimated preschoolers' animistic beliefs. By age 2½, children give psychological explanations ("he likes to" or "she wants to") for people and occasionally for other animals, but rarely for objects (Hickling & Wellman, 2001). In addition, preschoolers rarely attribute biological properties (like eating and growing) to robots, indicating that they are well aware that even a self-moving object with lifelike features is not alive. But unlike adults, they often say that robots have perceptual and psychological capacities—for example, seeing, thinking, and remembering (Jipson & Gelman, 2007; Subrahmanyam, Gelman, & Lafosse, 2002). These responses result from incomplete knowledge about certain objects, and they decline with age.

Similarly, preschoolers think that magic accounts for events they otherwise cannot explain—fairies, goblins, and, for Sammy, thunder. But their notions of magic are flexible and appropriate. For example, 3- and 4-year-olds are more likely to say that a magical process—wishing—caused an event (an object to appear in a box) when a person made the wish before the event occurred, the event is consistent with the wish (the wished-for object rather than another object appeared in the box), and no alternative causes were apparent (Woolley, Browne, & Boerger, 2006). These features of causality are the same ones preschoolers rely on in ordinary situations.

Between ages 4 and 8, as children gain familiarity with physical events and principles, their magical beliefs decline. They figure out who is behind Santa Claus and the Tooth Fairy, realize that magicians' feats are due to trickery, and say that characters and events in fantastical stories aren't real (Woolley & Cornelius, 2013; Woolley & Cox, 2007). Still, because children entertain the possibility that something they imagine might materialize, they may react with anxiety to scary stories, TV shows, and nightmares.

▶ Preschoolers distinguish between animate and inanimate and realize, for example, that a robot with lifelike features cannot eat or grow. But because of incomplete knowledge, they often claim that robots have perceptual and psychological capacities, such as seeing, thinking, and remembering.

LOOK AND LISTEN

Try the conservation of number and mass tasks in Figure 7.5 with a 3- or 4-year-old. Next, simplify conservation of number by reducing the number of pennies, and relate conservation of mass to the child's experience by pretending the clay is baking dough and transforming it into cupcakes. Did the child perform more competently?

Logical Thought. When preschoolers are given tasks that are simplified and relevant to their everyday lives, they do not display the illogical characteristics that Piaget saw in the preoperational stage. For example, when a conservation-of-number task is scaled down to include only three items instead of six or seven, 3-year-olds perform well (Gelman, 1972). And when asked carefully worded questions about what happens to a substance (such as sugar) after it is dissolved in water, most 3- to 5-year-olds know that the substance is conserved—that it continues to exist, can be tasted, and makes the liquid heavier, even though it is invisible in the water (Au, Sidle, & Rollins, 1993; Rosen & Rozin, 1993).

Preschoolers' ability to reason about transformations is evident on other problems. They can engage in impressive *reasoning by analogy* about physical changes. Presented with the picture-matching problem "Play dough is to cut-up play dough as apple is to … ?," even 3-year-olds choose the correct answer (a cut-up apple) from a set of alternatives, several of which (a bitten apple, a cut-up loaf of bread) share physical features with the right choice (Goswami, 1996).

Finally, without detailed biological or mechanical knowledge, preschoolers understand that the insides of animals are responsible for certain cause–effect sequences (such as willing oneself to move) that are impossible for nonliving things (Gelman, 2003). They seem to use illogical reasoning only when grappling with unfamiliar topics, too much information, or contradictory facts that they cannot reconcile.

Categorization. Despite their difficulty with Piagetian class inclusion tasks, preschoolers organize their everyday knowledge into nested categories at an early age. By the beginning of early childhood, children's categories include objects that go together because of their common function, behavior, or natural kind (animate versus inanimate), despite varying widely in perceptual features.

Indeed, 2- to 5-year-olds readily draw appropriate inferences about nonobservable characteristics shared by category members (Gopnik & Nazzi, 2003). For example, after being told that a bird has warm blood and that a stegosaurus (dinosaur) has cold blood, preschoolers infer that a pterodactyl (labeled a dinosaur) has cold blood, even though it closely resembles a bird.

▶ These 4-year-olds understand that a category ("dinosaurs") can be based on underlying characteristics ("cold-blooded"), not just on perceptual features such as upright posture and scaly skin.

Nevertheless, when most instances of a category have a certain perceptual property (such as long ears), preschoolers readily categorize on the basis of perceptual features. This indicates that they flexibly use different types of information to classify, depending on the situation (Rakison & Lawson, 2013). And past experiences influence the information they decide to use. Native-American 5-year-olds growing up on the Menominee Reservation in northern Wisconsin often use relations in the natural world to categorize animals—for example, grouping together wolves and eagles because of their shared forest habitat (Ross et al., 2003). European-American children, in contrast, mostly rely on the animals' common features.

During the second and third years, and perhaps earlier, children's categories differentiate. They form many *basic-level categories*—ones that are at an intermediate level of generality, such as "chairs," "tables," and "beds." By the third year, children easily move back and forth between basic-level categories and *general categories,* such as "furniture." And they break down basic-level categories into *subcategories,* such as "rocking chairs" and "desk chairs."

Preschoolers' rapidly expanding vocabularies and general knowledge support their impressive skill at categorizing, and they benefit greatly from conversations with adults, who frequently label and explain categories to them, especially during picture-book reading (Gelman & Kalish, 2006). In conversing about books, parents provide information that guides children's inferences about the structure of categories: "Penguins live at the South Pole, swim, catch fish, and have thick layers of fat and feathers that help them stay warm."

In sum, although preschoolers' category systems are less complex than those of older children and adults, they can classify hierarchically and on the basis of nonobvious properties. And they use logical, causal reasoning to identify the interrelated features that form the basis of a category and to classify new members.

Evaluation of the Preoperational Stage

Compare the cognitive attainments of early childhood, summarized in Table 7.2, with Piaget's description of the preoperational child on pages 215–219. The evidence as a whole indicates that Piaget was partly wrong and partly right about young children's cognitive capacities. That preschoolers can be trained to perform well on Piagetian problems also supports the idea that operational thought is not absent at one point in time and present at another (Ping & Goldin-Meadow, 2008). Over time, children rely on increasingly effective mental (as opposed to perceptual) approaches to solving problems.

Does a preoperational stage really exist? Some researchers no longer think so. Recall from Chapter 5 that according to the information-processing perspective, children work out their understanding of each type of task separately, and their thought processes are basically the same at all ages—just present to a greater or lesser extent.

Others think the stage concept is still valid, with modifications. For example, some *neo-Piagetian theorists* combine Piaget's stage approach with the information-processing emphasis on task-specific change (Case, 1998; Halford & Andrews, 2011). They believe that Piaget's strict stage definition must be transformed into a less tightly knit concept, one in which a related set of competencies develops over an extended period, depending on brain development and specific experiences. These investigators point to evidence that as long as the complexity of tasks and children's exposure to them are carefully controlled, children approach those tasks in similar, stage-consistent ways (Andrews & Halford, 2002; Case & Okamoto, 1996). For example, in drawing pictures, preschoolers depict objects separately, ignoring their spatial arrangement. In understanding stories, they grasp a single story line but have trouble with a main plot plus one or more subplots.

This flexible stage notion recognizes the unique qualities of early childhood thinking. At the same time, it provides a better account of why, as Leslie put it, "Preschoolers' minds are such a blend of logic, fantasy, and faulty reasoning."

TABLE 7.2
Some Cognitive Attainments of Early Childhood

APPROXIMATE AGE	COGNITIVE ATTAINMENTS
2–4 years © ELLEN B. SENISI	Shows a dramatic increase in representational activity, as reflected in the development of language, make-believe play, understanding of dual representation, and categorization Takes the perspective of others in simplified, familiar situations and in everyday, face-to-face communication Distinguishes animate beings from inanimate objects; prefers natural over supernatural explanations for events Grasps conservation, notices transformations, reverses thinking, and understands many cause-and-effect relationships in simplified, familiar situations Categorizes objects on the basis of common function, behavior, and natural kind as well as perceptual features, depending on context; uses inner causal features to categorize objects varying widely in external appearance Sorts familiar objects into hierarchically organized categories
4–7 years RYAN MCVAY/PHOTODISC/GETTY IMAGES	Becomes increasingly aware that make-believe and other thought processes are representational activities Replaces beliefs in magical creatures and events with plausible explanations Passes Piaget's conservation of number, mass, and liquid problems

ASK YOURSELF

CONNECT Select two of the following features of preoperational thought: egocentrism, a focus on perceptual appearances, difficulty reasoning about transformations, and lack of hierarchical classification. Present evidence indicating that preschoolers are more capable thinkers than Piaget assumed.

APPLY Three-year-old Will understands that his tricycle isn't alive and can't feel or move on its own. But at the beach, while watching the sun dip below the horizon, Will exclaimed, "The sun is tired. It's going to sleep!" What explains this apparent contradiction in Will's reasoning?

REFLECT Did you have an imaginary companion as a young child? If so, what was your companion like, and why did you create it?

Vygotsky's Sociocultural Theory

7.7 Describe Vygotsky's perspective on the social origins and developmental significance of children's private speech.

7.8 Describe Vygotsky's view of make-believe play, and evaluate his major ideas.

During early childhood, rapid expansion of language broadens preschoolers' participation in social dialogues with more knowledgeable individuals, who encourage them to master culturally important tasks. According to Vygotsky, soon children start to communicate with themselves in much the same way they converse with others. This greatly enhances their thinking and ability to control their own behavior.

Private Speech

Watch preschoolers as they play and explore the environment, and you will see that they frequently talk out loud to themselves. For example, as Sammy worked a puzzle, he said, "Where's the red piece? Now, a blue one. No, it doesn't fit. Try it here."

Piaget (1923/1926) called these utterances *egocentric speech,* reflecting his belief that young children have difficulty taking the perspectives of others. Their talk, he said, is often "talk for self" in which they express thoughts in whatever form they occur, regardless of whether a listener can understand. As egocentrism declines, so does this poorly adapted speech.

Vygotsky (1934/1987) disagreed with Piaget's conclusions. He maintained that language helps children think about their mental activities and select courses of action, thereby serving as the foundation for all higher cognitive processes, including controlled attention, deliberate memorization and recall, categorization, planning, problem solving, and self-reflection. In Vygotsky's view, children speak to themselves for self-guidance. As they get older and find tasks easier, their self-directed speech is internalized as silent, *inner speech*—the internal verbal dialogues we carry on while thinking and acting in everyday situations.

Because almost all studies support Vygotsky's perspective, children's self-directed speech is now called **private speech** instead of egocentric speech. Children use more of it when tasks are appropriately challenging (neither too easy nor too hard), after they make errors, or when they are confused about how to proceed. With age, as Vygotsky predicted, private speech goes underground, changing into whispers and silent lip movements. Furthermore, children who freely use private speech during a challenging activity are more attentive and involved and perform better than their less talkative agemates (Alarcón-Rubio, Sánchez-Medina, & Prieto-García, 2014; Benigno et al., 2011; Lidstone, Meins, & Fernyhough, 2010).

▶ A 4-year-old talks to herself as she draws. Research supports Vygotsky's theory that children use private speech to guide their thinking and behavior.

Social Origins of Early Childhood Cognition

Where does private speech come from? Recall from Chapter 5 that Vygotsky believed that children's learning takes place within the *zone of proximal development*—a range of tasks too difficult for the child to do alone but possible with the help of others. Consider the joint activity of Sammy and his mother as she helps him put together a difficult puzzle:

Sammy: I can't get this one in. *[Tries to insert a piece in the wrong place.]*
Mother: Which piece might go down here? *[Points to the bottom of the puzzle.]*
Sammy: His shoes. *[Looks for a piece resembling the clown's shoes, tries it, and it fits; then attempts another piece and looks at his mother.]*
Mother: Try turning it just a little. *[Gestures to show him.]*
Sammy: There! *[Puts in several more pieces while his mother watches.]*

Sammy's mother keeps the puzzle at a manageable level of difficulty. To do so, she engages in **scaffolding**—adjusting the support offered during a teaching session to fit the child's current level of performance. When the child has little notion of how to proceed, the adult uses direct instruction, breaking the task into manageable units and suggesting strategies. As the child's competence increases, effective scaffolders gradually and sensitively withdraw support, turning over responsibility to the child. Then children take the language of these dialogues, make it part of their private speech, and use this speech to organize their independent efforts.

Although preschoolers freely use private speech when alone or with others, they use more in the presence of others (McGonigle-Chalmers, Slater, & Smith, 2014). This suggests that some private speech retains a social purpose, perhaps as an indirect appeal for renewed scaffolding should the child need additional help. In several studies, children whose parents were effective scaffolders engaged in higher rates of private speech, were more likely to succeed when attempting challenging tasks on their own, and were advanced in overall cognitive development (Berk & Spuhl, 1995; Conner & Cross, 2003; Mulvaney et al., 2006).

Nevertheless, effective scaffolding can take different forms in different cultures. Unlike European-American parents, who emphasize independence by encouraging their children to think of ways to approach a task, Hmong immigrant parents from Southeast Asia—who highly value interdependence and child obedience—frequently tell their children what to do (for example, "Put this piece here, then this piece on top of it") (Stright, Herr, & Neitzel, 2009). Among European-American children, such directive scaffolding is associated with kindergartners' lack of self-control and behavior problems (Neitzel & Stright, 2003). Among the Hmong children, it predicted greater rule following, organization, and task completion.

Vygotsky's View of Make-Believe Play

Vygotsky (1933/1978) saw make-believe play as the ideal social context for fostering cognitive development in early childhood. As children create imaginary situations, they learn to follow internal ideas and social rules rather than impulses. For example, a child pretending to go to sleep follows the rules of bedtime behavior. A child imagining himself as a father conforms to the rules of parental behavior. According to Vygotsky, make-believe play is a unique, broadly influential zone of proximal development in which children try out a wide variety of challenging activities and acquire many new competencies.

Turn back to pages 216–217 to review evidence on the contribution of make-believe play to cognitive and social development. Pretending is also rich in private speech—a finding that supports its role in helping children bring action under the control of thought (Meyers & Berk, 2014). Preschoolers who spend more time engaged in sociodramatic play are better at inhibiting impulses, regulating emotion, and taking personal responsibility for following classroom rules (Elias & Berk, 2002; Kelly & Hammond, 2011; Lemche et al., 2003). These findings support the role of make-believe in children's increasing self-control.

Evaluation of Vygotsky's Theory

In granting social experience a fundamental role in cognitive development, Vygotsky's theory underscores the power of teaching and the wide cultural variation in children's cognitive skills. Nevertheless, his ideas have not gone unchallenged. In some cultures, verbal dialogues are not the only—or even the most important—means through which children learn. When Western parents scaffold,

CULTURAL INFLUENCES

Children in Village and Tribal Cultures Observe and Participate in Adult Work

In Western societies, schools equip children with the skills they need to become competent workers. In early childhood, middle-SES parents focus on preparing their children for school by engaging in child-focused conversations and play that enhance language, literacy, and other academic knowledge. In village and tribal cultures, children receive little or no schooling, spend their days in contact with adult work, and assume mature responsibilities in early childhood (Gaskins, 2014). Consequently, parents have little need to rely on conversation and play to teach children.

A study comparing 2- and 3-year-olds' daily lives in four cultures—two U.S. middle-SES suburbs, the Efe hunters and gatherers of the Republic of Congo, and a Mayan agricultural town in Guatemala—documented these differences (Morelli, Rogoff, & Angelillo, 2003). In the U.S. communities, young children had little access to adult work and spent much time conversing and playing with adults. The Efe and Mayan children spent their days close to—and frequently observing—adult work, which often took place in or near the Efe campsite or the Mayan family home.

An ethnography of a remote Mayan village in Yucatán, Mexico, shows that when young children are legitimate onlookers and participants in a daily life structured around adult work, their competencies differ from those of Western preschoolers (Gaskins, 1999; Gaskins, Haight, & Lancy, 2007). Yucatec Mayan adults are subsistence farmers. Men tend cornfields, aided by sons ages 8 and older. Women prepare meals, wash clothes, and care for the livestock and garden, assisted by daughters and by sons too young to work in the fields. Children join in these activities from the second year on. When not participating, they are expected to be self-sufficient.

© GAVRIEL JECAN/DANITA DELIMONT AGENT/ALAMY

▶ In a South-African village, a young child intently watches his mother grind grain. Children in village and tribal cultures observe and participate in the work of their community from an early age.

Young children make many nonwork decisions for themselves—how much to sleep and eat, what to wear, and even when to start school. As a result, Yucatec Mayan preschoolers are highly competent at self-care. In contrast, their make-believe play is limited; when it occurs, they usually imitate adult work. Otherwise, they watch others—for hours each day.

Yucatec Mayan parents rarely converse or play with preschoolers or scaffold their learning. Rather, when children imitate adult tasks, parents conclude that they are ready for more responsibility. Then they assign chores, selecting tasks the child can do with little help so that adult work is not disturbed. If a child cannot do a task, the adult takes over and the child observes, reengaging when able to contribute.

Expected to be autonomous and helpful, Yucatec Mayan children seldom ask others for something interesting to do. From an early age, they can sit quietly for long periods—through a lengthy religious service or a three-hour truck ride. And when an adult interrupts their activity and directs them to do a chore, they respond eagerly to the type of command that Western children frequently avoid or resent. By age 5, Yucatec Mayan children spontaneously take responsibility for tasks beyond those assigned.

their verbal communication resembles the teaching that occurs in school, where their children will spend years preparing for adult life. In cultures that place less emphasis on schooling and literacy, parents often expect children to take greater responsibility for acquiring new skills through keen observation and participation in community activities (Rogoff, Correa-Chávez, & Silva, 2011). See the Cultural Influences box above for research illustrating this difference.

To account for children's diverse ways of learning through involvement with others, Barbara Rogoff (2003) suggests the term **guided participation,** a broader concept than scaffolding. It refers to shared endeavors between more expert and less expert participants, without specifying the precise features of communication. Consequently, it allows for variations across situations and cultures.

Finally, Vygotsky's theory says little about how basic motor, perceptual, attention, memory, and problem-solving skills, discussed in Chapters 4 and 5, contribute to socially transmitted higher cognitive processes. For example, his theory does not address how these elementary capacities spark changes in children's social experiences, from which more advanced cognition springs (Daniels, 2011). Piaget paid far more attention than Vygotsky to the development of basic cognitive processes. It is intriguing to speculate about the broader theory that might exist today had Piaget and Vygotsky—the two twentieth-century giants of cognitive development—had a chance to meet and weave together their extraordinary accomplishments.

ASK YOURSELF

CONNECT Explain how Piaget's and Vygotsky's theories complement each other.

APPLY Tanisha sees her 5-year-old son, Toby, talking aloud to himself as he plays. She wonders whether she should discourage this behavior. How would you advise Tanisha?

REFLECT When do you use private speech? Does it serve a self-guiding function for you, as it does for children? Explain.

Information Processing

7.9 Describe changes in executive function and memory during early childhood.

7.10 Describe the young child's theory of mind.

7.11 Summarize children's literacy and mathematical knowledge during early childhood.

Recall from Chapter 5 that information processing focuses on cognitive operations and mental strategies that children use to transform stimuli flowing into their mental systems. As we have already seen, early childhood is a period of dramatic strides in mental representation. And the various components of *executive function*—inhibiting impulses and distracting stimuli, flexibly shifting attention depending on task demands, coordinating information in working memory, and planning—show impressive gains (Carlson, Zelazo, & Faja, 2013). Preschoolers also become more aware of their own mental life and begin to acquire academically relevant knowledge important for school success.

Executive Function

Control of attention improves substantially during early childhood, as studies of inhibition and flexible shifting reveal. As we will see, expansion of working memory supports these attainments. The components of executive function are closely interrelated in early childhood, and they contribute vitally to academic social skills (Shaul & Schwartz, 2014).

Inhibition. With age, preschoolers gain steadily in ability to inhibit impulses and keep their mind on a competing goal. Consider a task in which the child must tap once when the adult taps twice and tap twice when the adult taps once or must say "night" to a picture of the sun and "day" to a picture of the moon with stars. Whereas 3- and 4-year-olds make many errors, by ages 6 to 7 children find such tasks easy (Diamond, 2004; Montgomery & Koeltzow, 2010). They can resist the "pull" of their attention toward a dominant stimulus—a skill that predicts social maturity as well as reading and math achievement from kindergarten through high school (Blair & Razza, 2007; Duncan et al., 2007; Rhoades, Greenberg, & Domitrovich, 2009).

Flexible Shifting of Attention. In preschoolers and school-age children, ability to shift one's focus of attention, depending on what's important at the moment, is often studied through rule-use tasks (Zelazo et al., 2013). In this procedure, children are asked to switch the rules they use to sort picture cards in the face of conflicting cues. For example, a child might first be asked to sort pictures of boats and flowers using color rules, by placing all the blue boats and flowers in a box marked with a blue boat and all the red boats and flowers in a box marked with a red flower. Then the child is asked to switch to shape rules, placing all the boats (irrespective of color) into the box marked with the blue boat and all the flowers into the box marked with the red flower. Three-year-olds persist in sorting by color; not until age 4 do children succeed in switching rules (Zelazo, 2006). And when researchers increase the complexity of the rules—for example, requiring children to shift from color to shape rules only on a subset of picture cards with an added black border—most 6-year-olds have difficulty (Henning, Spinath, & Aschersleben, 2011).

As these findings confirm, flexible shifting improves greatly during the preschool years, with gains continuing in middle childhood. Note that inhibition contributes to preschoolers' flexible shifting (Kirkham, Cruess, & Diamond, 2003). To switch rules, children must inhibit attending to the previously relevant dimension while focusing on the dimension they had just ignored.

Working Memory. Gains in working memory contribute to control of attention. Greater working-memory capacity eases effort in keeping several rules in mind, ignoring ones not currently important, and flexibly shifting one's focus to new rules, thereby improving performance.

With age, the ability to hold and combine information in working memory becomes increasingly important in problem solving. In one study, both inhibition and working-memory scores predicted 2½- to 6-year-olds' solutions to a problem-solving task requiring multistep planning. But working memory was a stronger predictor for the 4- to 6-year-olds than for the younger children (Senn, Espy, & Kaufman, 2004). Older preschoolers were able to deploy their larger working memories to solve more challenging problems involving planning.

Planning. As the findings just described suggest, early childhood is a time of marked gains in *planning*—thinking out a sequence of acts ahead of time and performing them accordingly to reach a goal. Because successful planning requires that basic executive processes be integrated with other cognitive operations, it is regarded as a complex executive function activity (Müller & Kerns, 2015). As long as tasks are not too difficult, older preschoolers can follow a plan.

Consider a task, devised to resemble real-world planning, in which 3- to 5-year-olds were shown a doll named Molly, a camera, and a miniature zoo with a path, along which were three animal cages. The first and third cages had storage lockers next to them; the middle cage, with no locker, housed a kangaroo (see Figure 7.7). The children were told that Molly could follow the path only once and that she wanted to take a picture of the kangaroo. Then they were asked, "What locker could you leave the camera in so Molly can get it and take a photo of the kangaroo?" (McColgan & McCormack, 2008). Not until age 5 were children able to plan effectively, selecting the locker at the first cage.

On this and other planning tasks, young preschoolers have difficulty (McCormack & Atance, 2011). By the end of early childhood, children make strides in postponing action in favor of mapping out a sequence of future moves, evaluating the consequences of each, and adjusting their plan to fit task requirements.

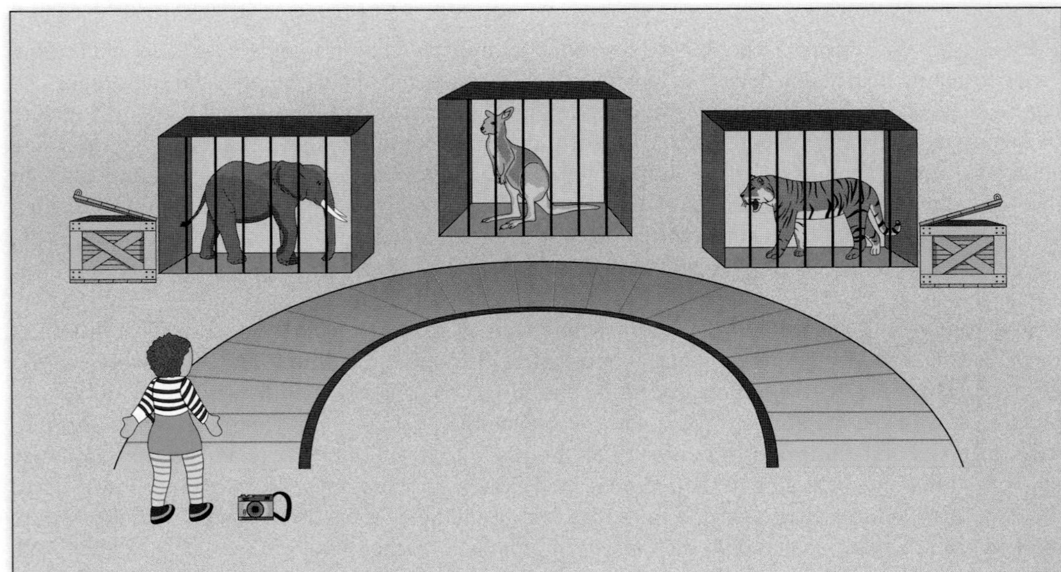

FIGURE 7.7 Miniature zoo used to assess children's planning. After having been told that Molly wanted to take a picture of the kangaroo but could follow the path only once, preschoolers were asked which locker the camera should be left in so Molly could get it and take the photo. Not until age 5 did children plan, more often selecting the first locker. (Based on McColgan & McCormack, 2008.)

Parenting and Development of Executive Function. Parental sensitivity and scaffolding foster preschoolers' executive function skills, as many investigations reveal (Carlson, Zelazo, & Faja, 2013). In one study, parental scaffolding of 2- and 3-year-olds while jointly solving a challenging puzzle predicted higher scores on diverse executive function tasks at age 4 (Hammond et al., 2012).

With respect to planning, children learn much from cultural tools that support it—directions for playing games, patterns for construction, recipes for cooking—especially when they collaborate with expert planners. When mothers were observed constructing a toy with their 4- to 7-year-olds, they often pointed out the usefulness of plans and how to implement specific steps: "Do you want to look at the picture and see what goes where? What piece do you need first?" After working with their mothers, younger children more often referred to the plan while building on their own (Gauvain, de la Ossa, & Hurtado-Ortiz, 2001). When parents encourage planning in everyday activities, from loading the dishwasher to packing for a vacation, they help children plan more effectively.

Poverty exerts a negative impact on executive function, in part through maladaptive parenting practices and chronic stress. In a sample diverse in SES and ethnicity, poverty-stricken mothers more often interacted harshly and intrusively with their 7- to 24-month-olds—parenting behaviors associated with children's elevated cortisol levels and with poor executive function scores during a follow-up at age 3 (Blair et al., 2011). As the authors noted, poverty and negative parenting undermined early stress regulation, promoting "reactive and inflexible rather than reflective and flexible forms of behavior and cognition" (p. 1980).

▶ A grandfather engages in scaffolding by breaking a challenging construction task into manageable units and suggesting strategies to his 3-year-old grandchild—support that consistently promotes diverse executive function skills.

Memory

Unlike infants and toddlers, preschoolers have the language skills to describe what they remember, and they can follow directions on memory tasks. As a result, memory becomes easier to study in early childhood.

Recognition and Recall. Show a young child a set of 10 pictures or toys. Then mix them up with some unfamiliar items, and ask the child to point to the ones in the original set. You will find that preschoolers' *recognition* memory—ability to tell whether a stimulus is the same as or similar to one they have seen before—is remarkably good. In fact, 4- and 5-year-olds perform nearly perfectly.

Now keep the items out of view, and ask the child to name the ones she saw. This more demanding task requires *recall*—generating a mental image of an absent stimulus. Young children's recall is much poorer than their recognition. At age 2, they can recall no more than one or two items, and at age 4 only about three or four (Perlmutter, 1984).

Improvement in recall in early childhood is strongly associated with language development, which greatly enhances long-lasting representations of past experiences (Melby-Lervag & Hulme, 2010). But even preschoolers with good language skills recall poorly because they are not skilled at using **memory strategies**—deliberate mental activities that improve our chances of remembering. Preschoolers do not yet *rehearse,* or repeat items over and over, to remember. Nor do they *organize,* intentionally grouping items that are alike (all the animals together, all the vehicles together) so they can easily retrieve those items by thinking of their similar characteristics—even after they are trained to do so (Bauer, 2013). Strategies tax the limited working memories of preschoolers, who have difficulty holding onto information and applying a strategy at the same time.

Memory for Everyday Experiences. Think about the difference between your recall of listlike information and your memory for everyday experiences—what researchers call **episodic memory.** In remembering everyday experiences, you recall information in context—linked to a particular time, place, or person. In remembering lists, you recall isolated pieces—information removed from the context in which it was first learned that has become part of your general knowledge base. Researchers call this type of memory **semantic memory.**

Between 3 and 6 years, children improve sharply in memory for relations among stimuli. For example, in a set of photos, they remember not just the animals they saw but their contexts, such as a bear emerging from a tunnel or a zebra tied to a tree (Lloyd, Doydum, & Newcombe, 2009). The capacity to bind together stimuli supports an increasingly rich episodic memory.

Memory for Routine Events. Like adults, preschoolers remember familiar, repeated events—what you do when you go to preschool or have dinner—in terms of **scripts,** general descriptions of what occurs and when it occurs in a particular situation. Young children's scripts begin as a structure of main acts. For example, when asked to tell what happens at a restaurant, a 3-year-old might say, "You go in, get the food, eat, and then pay." Although children's first scripts contain only a few acts, they are almost always recalled in correct sequence (Bauer, 2006, 2013). With age, scripts become more elaborate, as in this 5-year-old's account of going to a restaurant: "You go in. You can sit in a booth or at a table. Then you tell the waitress what you want. You eat. If you want dessert, you can have some. Then you pay and go home" (Hudson, Fivush, & Kuebli, 1992).

Scripts help children (and adults) organize and interpret routine experiences. Once formed, scripts can be used to predict what will happen in the future. Children rely on scripts in make-believe play and when listening to and telling stories. Scripts also support children's planning by helping them represent sequences of actions that lead to desired goals (Hudson & Mayhew, 2009).

Memory for One-Time Events. In Chapter 5, we considered a second type of episodic memory—*autobiographical memory,* or representations of personally meaningful, one-time events. As preschoolers' cognitive and conversational skills improve, their descriptions of special events become better organized and more detailed. A young preschooler simply reports, "I went camping." Older preschoolers include specifics: where and when the event happened and who was present. And with age, preschoolers increasingly include information about the event's personal significance (Bauer, 2013; Pathman et al., 2013). For example, they might say, "I *loved* sleeping all night in the tent."

Adults use two styles to elicit children's autobiographical narratives. In the *elaborative style,* they ask varied questions, add information to the child's statements, and volunteer their own recollections and evaluations of events. For example, after a trip to the zoo, the parent might say, "What was the first thing we did? Why weren't the parrots in their cages? I thought the lion was scary. What did you think?" In contrast, adults who use the *repetitive style* provide little information and keep repeating the same questions: "Do you remember the zoo? What did we do at the zoo?" Elaborative-style parents *scaffold* the autobiographical memories of their young children, who produce more organized and detailed personal stories when followed up later in childhood and in adolescence (Reese, 2002).

▶ As this toddler talks with his mother about past experiences, she responds in an elaborative style, asking varied questions and contributing her own recollections. Through such conversations, she enriches his autobiographical memory.

As children talk with adults about the past, they not only improve their autobiographical memory but also create a shared history that strengthens close relationships and self-understanding. Parents and preschoolers with secure attachment bonds engage in more elaborate reminiscing (Bost et al., 2006). And 5- and 6-year-olds of elaborative-style parents describe themselves in clearer, more consistent ways (Bird & Reese, 2006).

Girls tend to produce more organized and detailed personal narratives than boys. Compared with Asian children, Western children produce narratives with more talk about their own thoughts and emotions. These differences fit with variations in parent–child conversations. Parents reminisce in greater detail and talk more about the emotional significance of events with daughters (Fivush & Zaman, 2014). And cultural valuing of an interdependent self leads many Asian parents to discourage children from talking about themselves (Fivush & Wang, 2005).

The Young Child's Theory of Mind

As representation of the world, memory, and problem solving improve, children start to reflect on their own thought processes. They begin to construct a *theory of mind,* or coherent set of ideas about mental activities. This understanding is also called **metacognition,** or "thinking about thought" (the prefix *meta-* means "beyond" or "higher"). As adults, we have a complex appreciation of our inner mental worlds, which we use to interpret our own and others' behavior and to improve our performance on various tasks. How early are children aware of their mental lives, and how complete and accurate is their knowledge?

Awareness of Mental Life. At the end of the first year, babies view people as intentional beings who can share and influence one another's mental states, a milestone that opens the door to new forms of communication—joint attention, social referencing, preverbal gestures, and spoken language. As children approach age 2, they display a clearer grasp of others' emotions and desires, evident in their realization that people often differ from one another and from themselves in likes, dislikes, wants, needs, and wishes. As 2-year-olds' vocabularies expand, their first verbs include such mental-state words as *want, think, remember,* and *pretend* (Wellman, 2011). But 2- to 3-year-olds' verbal responses indicate that they assume people always behave in ways consistent with their *desires.* Not until age 4 do most realize that less obvious, more interpretive mental states, such as *beliefs,* also affect behavior.

Dramatic evidence for this advance comes from games that test whether preschoolers realize that *false beliefs*—ones that do not represent reality accurately—can guide people's actions. For example, show a child two small closed boxes—a familiar Band-Aid box and a plain, unmarked box (see Figure 7.8). Then say, "Pick the box you think has the Band-Aids in it." Children usually pick the marked container. Next, open the boxes and show the child that, contrary to her own belief, the marked one is empty and the unmarked one contains the Band-Aids. Finally, introduce the child to a hand puppet and explain, "Here's Pam. She has a cut, see? Where do you think she'll look for Band-Aids? Why would she look in there? Before you looked inside, did you think that the plain box contained Band-Aids? Why?" (Bartsch & Wellman, 1995). Only a handful of 3-year-olds can explain Pam's—and their own—false beliefs, but many 4-year-olds can.

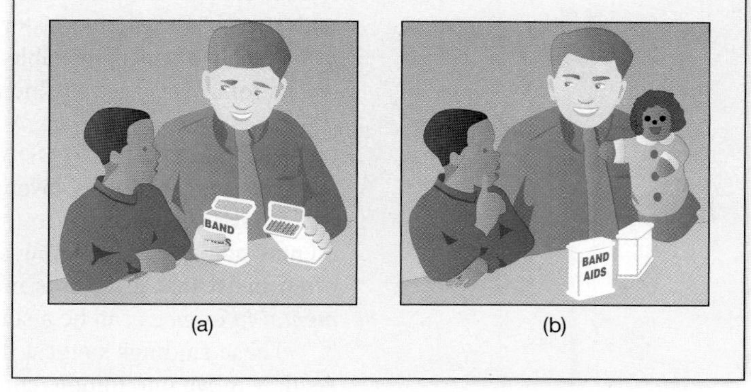

FIGURE 7.8 Example of a false-belief task. (a) An adult shows a child the contents of a Band-Aid box and of an unmarked box. The Band-Aids are in the unmarked container. (b) The adult introduces the child to a hand puppet named Pam and asks the child to predict where Pam would look for the Band-Aids and to explain Pam's behavior. The task reveals whether children understand that without having seen that the Band-Aids are in the unmarked container, Pam will hold a false belief.

Nevertheless, growing evidence suggests that toddlers have an *implicit* grasp of false belief, revealed by their nonverbal behaviors. Most 18-month-olds—after observing an adult reach for a box previously used for blocks that now contained a spoon—based their choice of how to help on her false belief about the contents of the box: They gave her a block rather than a spoon (Buttelmann et al., 2014). Still, researchers disagree sharply on the depth of toddlers' insights (Astington & Hughes, 2013; Carpendale & Lewis, 2015). They cannot explain the striking contrast between toddlers' success on nonverbal tasks and 3-year-olds' consistent failure on verbal assessments.

Among children of diverse cultural and SES backgrounds, *explicit* false-belief understanding strengthens after age 3½, becoming more secure between ages 4 and 6 (Wellman, 2012). During that time, it becomes a powerful tool for reflecting on the thoughts and emotions of oneself and others and a good predictor of social skills (Hughes, Ensor, & Marks, 2010).

Factors Contributing to Preschoolers' Theory of Mind. How do children develop a theory of mind at such a young age? Language, executive function, and social experiences contribute.

Many studies indicate that language ability strongly predicts preschoolers' false-belief understanding (Milligan, Astington, & Dack, 2007). Children who spontaneously use, or who are trained to use, mental-state words in conversation are especially likely to pass false-belief tasks (Hale & Tager-Flusberg, 2003; San Juan & Astington, 2012). Among the Quechua people of the Peruvian highlands, whose language lacks mental-state terms, children have difficulty with false-belief tasks for years after children in industrialized nations have mastered them (Vinden, 1996).

Several aspects of preschoolers' executive function—inhibition, flexible shifting of attention, and planning—predict mastery of false belief because they enhance children's ability to reflect on experiences and mental states (Benson et al., 2013; Müller et al., 2012; Powell & Carey, 2017). Inhibition is strongly related to false-belief understanding, perhaps because children must suppress an irrelevant response—the tendency to assume that others share their own knowledge and beliefs (Carlson, Moses, & Claxton, 2004).

Social experiences also make a difference. In longitudinal research, the maternal "mind-mindedness" experienced by securely attached babies (frequent commentary on their mental states) was positively associated with later performance on false-belief and other theory-of-mind tasks (Laranjo et al., 2010; Meins et al., 2003; Ruffman et al., 2006).

Also, preschoolers with siblings who are children (but not infants)—especially those with older siblings or two or more siblings—tend to be more aware of false beliefs because they are exposed to more family talk about varying thoughts, beliefs, and emotions (Devine & Hughes, 2018; Hughes et al., 2010; McAlister & Peterson, 2006, 2007). Similarly, preschool friends who often engage in mental-state talk—as children do during make-believe play—are advanced in false-belief understanding (de Rosnay & Hughes, 2006). These exchanges offer children extra opportunities to talk about their own and others' inner states.

Core knowledge theorists (see Chapter 5, page 147) believe that to profit from the social experiences just described, children must be biologically prepared to develop a theory of mind. Children with *autism,* for whom mastery of false belief is either greatly delayed or absent, are deficient in the brain mechanisms that enable humans to detect mental states. See the Biology and Environment box on the following page to find out more about the biological basis of reasoning about the mind.

Limitations of the Young Child's Understanding of Mental Life. Though surprisingly advanced, preschoolers' awareness of mental activities is far from complete. Children younger than age 6 pay little attention to the *process* of thinking. When asked about subtle distinctions between mental states, such as *know* and *forget,* they express confusion (Lyon & Flavell, 1994). And they often insist that all events must be directly observed to be known. They do not understand that *mental inferences* can be a source of knowledge (Miller, Hardin, & Montgomery, 2003).

These findings suggest that preschoolers view the mind as a passive container of information. As they move into middle childhood, they will increasingly see it as an active, constructive agent—a change we will consider further in Chapter 9.

Early Childhood Literacy

One week, Leslie's students created a make-believe grocery store. They placed empty food boxes on shelves in the classroom, labeled items with prices, and wrote checks at the cash register. A sign at the entrance announced the daily specials: "APLS BNS 5¢" ("apples bananas 5¢").

As their play reveals, preschoolers understand a great deal about written language long before they learn to read or write in conventional ways. This is not surprising: Children in industrialized nations live in a world filled with written symbols. Each day, they observe and participate in activities involving storybooks, calendars, lists, and signs. Children's active efforts to construct literacy knowledge through informal experiences are called **emergent literacy.**

Young preschoolers search for units of written language as they "read" memorized versions of stories and recognize familiar signs ("PIZZA"). But they do not yet understand the symbolic function of the elements of print (Bialystok & Martin, 2003). Many preschoolers think that a single letter stands for a whole word or that each letter in a person's signature represents a separate name. Children revise these ideas as their cognitive capacities improve, as they encounter writing in many contexts, and as adults help them with written communication. Gradually, they notice more features of written language and depict writing that varies in function, as in one child's horizontal line of letters to represent "a story" and vertical line to represent a "grocery list."

Eventually, children figure out that letters are parts of words and are linked to sounds in systematic ways, as 5- to 7-year-olds' invented spellings illustrate. At first, children rely on sounds in

BIOLOGY AND ENVIRONMENT

Autism and Theory of Mind

Michael stood at the water table in Leslie's classroom, repeatedly filling a plastic cup and dumping out its contents—dip–splash, dip–splash—until Leslie came over and redirected his actions. Without looking at Leslie's face, Michael moved to a new repetitive pursuit: pouring water from one cup into another and back again. As other children entered the play space and conversed, Michael hardly noticed.

Michael has *autism* (a term meaning "absorbed in the self"). Autism varies in severity along a continuum, called *autism spectrum disorder.* Michael's difficulties are substantial. Like other similarly affected children, by age 3 he displayed deficits in two core areas of functioning. First, he had only limited ability to engage in social interaction—evident in his difficulty with nonverbal communication, such as eye gaze, facial expressions, gestures, imitation, and give-and-take, and in his delayed and stereotyped language. Second, his interests were narrow and overly intense. For example, one day he sat for more than an hour spinning a toy Ferris wheel. And Michael showed another typical feature of autism: He engaged in much less make-believe play than other children (American Psychiatric Association, 2013; Tager-Flusberg, 2014).

Researchers agree that autism stems from abnormal brain functioning, usually due to genetic or prenatal environmental causes. Beginning in the first year, children with the disorder have larger-than-average brains, with the greatest excess in brain-region volume in the prefrontal cortex (Courchesne et al., 2011). This brain overgrowth is believed to result from lack of synaptic pruning, which accompanies typical development of cognitive, language, and communication skills. Furthermore, preschoolers with autism show a deficient left-hemispheric response to speech sounds (Eyler, Pierce, & Courchesne, 2012). Failure of the left hemisphere of the cerebral cortex to lateralize for language may underlie these children's language deficits.

The amygdala (see page 181 in Chapter 6) also grows abnormally large in childhood, followed by a greater than average reduction in size in adolescence and adulthood. This deviant growth pattern is believed to contribute to deficits in emotion processing involved in the disorder (Allely, Gillberg, & Wilson, 2014). fMRI studies reveal that autism is associated with weaker connections between the amygdala and the temporal lobes, which are important for interpreting facial expressions (Monk et al., 2010

▶ This child, who has autism, is barely aware of his teacher and classmates. Researchers disagree on whether the deficient emotional and social capacities of autism result from a basic impairment in ability to detect others' mental states, a deficit in executive function, or a style of information processing that focuses on parts rather than coherent wholes.

Mounting evidence reveals that children with autism are impaired in theory of mind. As early as the first two years, they show deficits in capacities believed to contribute to an understanding of mental life, including interest in observing people's actions, joint attention, and social referencing (Chawarska, Macari, & Shic, 2013; Warreyn, Roeyers, & De Groote, 2005). Long after they reach the intellectual level of an average 4-year-old, they have great difficulty with false belief. Most find it hard to attribute mental states to themselves or others (Hoogenhout & Malcolm-Smith, 2017).

Do these findings indicate that autism is due to impairment in an innate, core brain function that leaves the child unable to detect others' mental states and therefore deficient in human sociability? Some researchers think so (Baron-Cohen, 2011; Baron-Cohen & Belmonte, 2005). Others point out that individuals with general intellectual disability but not autism also do poorly on tasks assessing mental understanding (Yirmiya et al., 1998). This suggests that cognitive deficits are largely responsible.

One hypothesis with growing research support is that children with autism are impaired in executive function (Kimhi et al., 2014; Pugliese et al., 2016). This leaves them deficient in skills involved in flexible, goal-oriented thinking, including shifting attention to relevant aspects of a situation, inhibiting irrelevant responses, applying strategies, and generating plans (Robinson et al., 2009).

Another possibility is that children with autism display a peculiar style of information processing, preferring to process the parts of stimuli over coherent wholes (Booth & Happé, 2016). Deficits in thinking flexibly and in holistic processing of stimuli would each interfere with understanding the social world because social interaction requires quick integration of information from various sources and evaluation of alternative possibilities.

It is not clear which of these hypotheses is correct. Perhaps several biologically based deficits underlie the tragic social isolation of children like Michael.

© ELLEN B. SENISI

▶ Preschoolers acquire literacy knowledge by participating in everyday activities involving written symbols. These young chefs "write down" orders they need to fill.

the names of letters: "ADE LAFWTS KRMD NTU A LAVATR" ("eighty elephants crammed into a[n] elevator"). Over time, they grasp sound–letter correspondences (McGee & Richgels, 2012).

Literacy development builds on a broad foundation of spoken language and knowledge about the world (Dickinson, Golinkoff, & Hirsh-Pasek, 2010). **Phonological awareness**—the ability to reflect on and manipulate the sound structure of spoken language, as indicated by sensitivity to changes in sounds within words, to rhyming, and to incorrect pronunciation—is a strong predictor of emergent literacy knowledge and later reading and spelling achievement (Dickinson et al., 2003; Paris & Paris, 2006). When combined with sound–letter knowledge, it enables children to isolate speech segments and link them with their written symbols. Vocabulary and grammatical knowledge are also influential. And narrative competence, assessed by having preschoolers retell stories, fosters diverse language skills essential for literacy progress, including phonological awareness (Hipfner-Boucher et al., 2014). Coherent storytelling requires attention to large language structures, such as character, setting, problem, and resolution. This seems to support the smaller-scale analysis involved in awareness of sound structures.

The more informal literacy experiences young children have, the better their language and literacy skills (Dickinson & McCabe, 2001; Speece et al., 2004). Pointing out letter–sound correspondences and playing language–sound games enhance children's awareness of the sound structures of language and how they are represented in print (Ehri & Roberts, 2006). *Interactive reading,* in which adults discuss storybook content and vocabulary with preschoolers and reread books to deepen understanding, promotes many aspects of language and literacy development (Hood, Conlon, & Andrews, 2008; Storch & Whitehurst, 2001; Wasik, Hindman, & Snell, 2016). Each of these practices is linked to improved reading achievement in middle childhood.

Preschoolers from low-SES families have far fewer home and preschool language and literacy learning opportunities—a gap that translates into large differences in emergent literacy skills at kindergarten entry and into widening disparities in reading achievement during the school years (Cabell et al., 2013; Strang & Piasta, 2016). Providing low-SES parents with children's books, along with guidance in how to stimulate emergent literacy, greatly enhances literacy activities in the home (Huebner & Payne, 2010). And when teachers are shown how to engage in effective literacy instruction, low-SES preschoolers gain in emergent literacy skills included in their classroom experiences (Hilbert & Eis, 2014; Lonigan et al., 2013).

Early Childhood Mathematical Reasoning

Mathematical reasoning, like literacy, builds on informally acquired knowledge. Between 14 and 16 months, toddlers display a beginning grasp of **ordinality,** or order relationships between quantities—for example, that 3 is more than 2, and 2 is more than 1. In the early preschool years, children attach verbal labels (*lots, little, big, small*) to amounts and sizes. Sometime in the third year, they begin to count. By the time children turn 3, most can count a row of about five objects, although they do not yet know exactly what the words mean. But 2½- to 3½-year-olds realize that when a number label changes (for example, from *five* to *six*), the number of items should also change (Sarnecka & Gelman, 2004).

By age 3½ to 4, most children have mastered the meaning of numbers up to 10, count correctly, and grasp the vital principle of **cardinality**—that the last number in a counting sequence indicates the quantity of items in a set (Sarnecka & Wright, 2013). Mastery of cardinality increases the efficiency of children's counting.

Around age 4, children use counting to solve simple arithmetic problems. At first, their strategies are tied to the order of numbers as presented; to add 2 + 4, they count on from 2 (Bryant & Nunes, 2002). But soon they experiment with other strategies and eventually arrive at the most efficient, accurate approach—in this example, beginning with the higher digit. Around this time, children realize that subtraction cancels out addition. Knowing, for example, that 4 + 3 = 7, they can infer without counting that 7 – 3 = 4 (Rasmussen, Ho, & Bisanz, 2003). Grasping basic arithmetic rules facilitates rapid computation, and with enough practice, children recall answers automatically. Gradually, children extend their knowledge from smaller to larger numbers.

When adults provide many occasions for counting, comparing quantities, and talking about number concepts, children acquire these understandings sooner (Ginsburg, Lee, & Boyd, 2008). Preschoolers' math knowledge—especially, counting fluency, understanding of the cardinal value of number words, and ability to compare quantities—predicts math knowledge and skills at age 5 (Geary & VanMarle, 2016). Math proficiency at kindergarten entry, in turn, predicts math achievement years later, in elementary and secondary school (Duncan et al., 2007; Romano et al., 2010).

▶ Preschoolers "hop" a toy frog along a number line, measuring the length of each jump. Through informal exploration of number concepts, they construct basic understandings essential for learning math skills later on.

As with emergent literacy, children from low-SES families begin kindergarten with considerably less math knowledge than their economically advantaged agemates (DeFlorio & Beliakoff, 2015). Just a few sessions devoted to playing a number board game with an adult led to dramatic improvement in low-SES 4-year-olds' numerical understandings (Ramani, Siegler, & Hitti, 2012). And in an early childhood math curriculum called *Building Blocks,* materials that promote math concepts and skills through three types of media—computers, manipulatives, and print—enable teachers to weave math into many preschool daily activities (Clements et al., 2011). Compared with agemates randomly assigned to other preschool programs, low-SES preschoolers experiencing Building Blocks showed substantially greater year-end gains in math concepts and skills.

ASK YOURSELF

CONNECT Cite evidence on the development of preschoolers' executive function, memory, theory of mind, and literacy and mathematical understanding that is consistent with Vygotsky's sociocultural theory.

APPLY Lena wonders why her 4-year-old son Gregor's teacher provides extensive playtime in learning centers during each preschool day. Explain to Lena how adult-supported play can promote literacy and math skills essential for academic success.

REFLECT Describe informal experiences important for literacy and math development that you experienced while growing up.

Individual Differences in Mental Development

7.12 Describe early childhood intelligence tests and the impact of home, preschool and kindergarten programs, child care, and educational media on mental development.

Five-year-old Hal sat in a testing room while Sarah gave him an intelligence test. Some of Sarah's questions were *verbal.* For example, she showed Hal a picture of a shovel and said, "Tell me what this is"—an item measuring vocabulary. She tested his working memory by asking him to repeat lists of letters and numbers backward. To assess Hal's spatial reasoning, Sarah used *nonverbal* tasks: Hal copied designs with special blocks, figured out the pattern in a series of shapes, and indicated what a piece of paper folded and cut would look like when unfolded (Roid, 2003; Wechsler, 2012).

The questions Sarah asked Hal tap knowledge and skills that not all children have equal opportunity to learn. In Chapter 9, we will take up the hotly debated issue of *cultural bias* in mental testing. For now, keep in mind that intelligence tests do not sample all human abilities, and cultural and situational factors affect performance. Nevertheless, test scores remain important: By ages 6 to 7, they are good predictors of later IQ and academic achievement, which are related to adult vocational success. Let's see how the environments in which preschoolers spend their days—home, preschool, and child care—affect mental test performance.

Home Environment and Mental Development

A special version of the *Home Observation for Measurement of the Environment (HOME),* covered in Chapter 5, assesses aspects of 3- to 6-year-olds' home lives that foster intellectual growth. Research with the HOME early childhood subscales reveals that preschoolers who develop well intellectually have homes rich in educational toys and books. Their parents are warm and affectionate, stimulate language and academic knowledge, and arrange interesting outings. They also make reasonable demands for socially mature behavior—for example, that the child perform simple chores and behave courteously toward others. And these parents resolve conflicts with reason instead of physical force and punishment (Bradley & Caldwell, 1982; Espy, Molfese, & DiLalla, 2001; Roberts, Burchinal, & Durham, 1999).

When low-SES parents manage, despite life challenges, to obtain high HOME scores, their preschoolers do substantially better on tests of intelligence, language, and emergent literacy skills (Berger, Paxson, & Waldfogel, 2009; Mistry et al., 2008). In a study of African-American 3- and 4-year-olds from low-income families, HOME cognitive stimulation and emotional support subscales predicted reading achievement four years later (Zaslow et al., 2006). These findings highlight the vital contribution of home environmental quality to children's overall intellectual development.

Preschool, Kindergarten, and Child Care

Largely because of the rise in maternal employment, over the past several decades the number of young children enrolled in preschool or child care has steadily increased to more than 65 percent in the United States (U.S. Bureau of Labor Statistics, 2017). The line between preschool and child care is fuzzy. Parents often select a preschool as a child-care option. And in response to the needs of employed parents, many U.S. preschools, as well as most public school kindergartens, have increased their hours from half to full days (Child Trends, 2015b).

With age, preschoolers tend to shift from home-based to center-based programs. U.S. children of higher-income parents and of very-low-income parents are especially likely to be in preschools or child-care centers (Child Trends, 2015b). Many low-income working parents rely on care by relatives because they are not eligible for public preschool or government-subsidized child-care centers. A few states offer government-funded prekindergarten programs in public schools to all 4-year-olds. The goal of these universal prekindergartens is to ensure that as many children as possible, from all SES levels, enter kindergarten prepared to succeed.

Types of Preschool and Kindergarten. Preschool and kindergarten programs range along a continuum from child-centered to teacher-directed. In **child-centered programs,** teachers provide activities from which children select, and much learning takes place through play. In contrast, in **academic programs,** teachers structure children's learning, teaching letters, numbers, colors, shapes, and other academic skills through formal lessons, often using repetition and drill.

Despite evidence that extensive academic training undermines young children's motivation and emotional well-being, early childhood teachers have felt increased pressure to take this approach. Young children who spend much time in large-group, teacher-directed academic instruction and completing worksheets—as opposed to being actively engaged in learning centers—display more stress behaviors (such as wiggling and rocking), have less confidence in their abilities, prefer less challenging tasks, and are less advanced in motor, academic, language, and social skills at the end of the school year (Stipek, 2011; Stipek et al., 1995). Follow-ups reveal lasting effects through elementary school in poorer study habits and achievement (Burts et al., 1992; Hart et al., 1998, 2003; Stipek et al., 2017). These outcomes are strongest for low-SES children.

Although government spending for universal prekindergarten is controversial in the United States, in Western Europe such programs are widespread and child-centered in their daily activities. Enrolled preschoolers of all SES backgrounds show gains in cognitive and social development still evident in elementary and secondary school (Rindermann & Ceci, 2008; Waldfogel & Zhai, 2008). Findings on some U.S. universal prekindergarten programs that meet rigorous state standards of quality—especially, provision of rich teacher–child interactions and stimulating learning activities—reveal up to a one-year advantage in kindergarten and first-grade language, literacy, and math scores relative to those of children not enrolled (Gormley & Phillips, 2009; Weiland & Yoshikawa, 2013). Children from low-SES families benefit most.

As for the dramatic rise in full-day kindergartens, the longer school day is associated with better academic achievement through elementary school (Brownell et al., 2015; Cooper et al., 2010). But some evidence suggests that kindergartners in full-day as opposed to half-day classrooms have more behavior problems.

Early Intervention for At-Risk Preschoolers. In the 1960s, as part of the U.S. "War on Poverty," many intervention programs for low-SES preschoolers were initiated in an effort to address learning problems prior to school entry. The most extensive of these federal programs, **Project Head Start,** began in 1965. A typical Head Start center provides children with a year or two of preschool, along with nutritional and health services. Parent involvement is central to the Head Start philosophy. Parents serve on policy councils, contribute to program planning, work with children in classrooms, attend special programs on parenting and child development, and receive services directed at their own emotional, social, and vocational needs. Currently, Head Start serves about 915,000 children and their families across the nation (Office of Head Start, 2016).

Several decades of research have established the long-term benefits of preschool intervention. The most extensive study combined data from seven programs implemented by universities or research foundations. Results showed that poverty-stricken children who attended programs scored higher in IQ and achievement than no-intervention controls during the first 2 to 3 years of elementary school. After that, differences declined (Lazar & Darlington, 1982). But on real-life measures of school adjustment, children and adolescents who had received intervention remained ahead. They were less likely to be placed in special education or retained in grade, and a greater number graduated from high school.

A separate report on one program—the High/Scope Perry Preschool Project—revealed benefits lasting well into adulthood. Two years' exposure to cognitively enriching preschool was associated with increased employment and reduced pregnancy and delinquency rates in adolescence. At age 27, those who had attended preschool were more likely than their no-preschool counterparts to have earned both high school and college degrees, have higher incomes, be married, and own their own home—and less likely to have been involved with the criminal justice system. In the most recent follow-up, at age 40, the intervention group sustained its advantage on all these measures of life success (Schweinhart, 2010; Schweinhart et al., 2005).

Do effects on school adjustment of these excellent interventions generalize to Head Start and other community-based preschool interventions? Gains are similar, though not as strong because quality of services often does not equal that of model university-based programs (Barnett, 2011). But community-based interventions of high quality are associated with diverse real-life success outcomes, including higher rates of high school graduation and college enrollment and lower rates of school absenteeism, grade retention, and adolescent drug use and delinquency (Yoshikawa et al., 2013).

A consistent finding is that gains in IQ and achievement test scores from attending Head Start and other interventions quickly dissolve. In the Head Start Impact Study, a nationally representative sample of 5,000 Head Start–eligible 3- and 4-year-olds was randomly assigned to one year of Head Start or to a control group that could attend other types of preschool programs (Puma et al., 2012; U.S. Department of Health and Human Services, 2010). By year's end, Head Start 3-year-olds exceeded controls in vocabulary, emergent literacy, and math skills; Head Start 4-year-olds were ahead in vocabulary, emergent literacy, and color identification. But except for language skills, academic test-score advantages were no longer evident by the end of first grade. And Head Start graduates did not differ from controls on any achievement measures at the end of third grade.

What explains these disappointing results? Head Start programs vary considerably in quality, and children who attend typically enter inferior public schools in poverty-stricken neighborhoods, which undermine the benefits of preschool intervention (Ramey, Ramey, & Lanzi, 2006). In one evaluation of an inner-city Head Start program of especially high quality, achievement gains in math were still evident in middle school (Phillips, Gormley, & Anderson, 2016). And recall from Chapter 5 that when high-quality intervention begins in infancy, IQ gains are more likely to endure into adulthood (see pages 160–161).

A few supplementary programs have responded to the need to strengthen preschool intervention to augment its impact. One of the most widely implemented is *Head Start REDI* (Research-Based Developmentally Informed), an enrichment curriculum designed for integration into existing

▶ This teacher integrates Head Start REDI into her preschool classroom. By delivering extra educational enrichment, Head Start REDI yields greater gains in language, literacy, and social skills than typical Head Start classrooms.

Head Start classrooms. Before school begins, Head Start teachers—27 percent of whom do not have a bachelor's degree in early childhood education or a related field—take workshops in which they learn strategies for enhancing language, literacy, and social skills. Throughout the school year, they receive one-to-one mentoring from master teachers. Relative to typical Head Start classrooms, Head Start plus REDI yields higher year-end language, literacy, and social development scores—advantages still evident at the end of kindergarten (Bierman et al., 2008, 2014). REDI's impact on teaching quality is likely responsible.

Head Start is highly cost-effective when compared to the price of providing special education, treating criminal behavior, and supporting unemployed adults. Because of limited funding, however, only 46 percent of 3- and 4-year-olds living in poverty attend preschool, with Head Start serving only about half of these children (Barnett & Friedman-Krauss, 2017).

Child Care. We have seen that high-quality early intervention can enhance development. As noted in Chapter 5, however, much U.S. child care lacks quality. Preschoolers exposed to substandard care, especially for long hours, tend to score lower in cognitive and social skills and higher in teacher-rated behavior problems (Burchinal et al., 2015; NICHD Early Child Care Research Network, 2003b, 2006). Externalizing difficulties are especially likely to endure into the school years for economically advantaged children (Belsky et al., 2007; Huston, Bobbitt, & Bentley, 2015; Vandell et al., 2010). Children from low-income families more often attend publicly subsidized nonprofit child-care centers of better quality (see page 160 in Chapter 5), which may offset the negative impact of their stressful home lives.

In addition, good child care enhances cognitive, language, and social development, particularly for low-SES children—effects that persist into elementary school and, for academic achievement, into adolescence (Burchinal et al., 2015; Dearing, McCartney, & Taylor, 2009; Vandell et al., 2010). Applying What We Know on the following page summarizes characteristics of high-quality early childhood programs, based on standards for developmentally appropriate practice devised by the U.S. National Association for the Education of Young Children. These standards offer a set of worthy goals as the United States strives to upgrade child-care and educational services for young children.

Educational Media

Besides home and preschool, young children spend much time in another learning environment: screen media, including both television and computers. In the industrialized world, nearly all homes have at least one television set, and most have two or more. And more than 90 percent of U.S. children live in homes with one or more computers, most with a high-speed Internet connection (Rideout, Foehr, & Roberts, 2010; U.S. Census Bureau, 2016). About 70 percent of U.S. preschoolers have access to tablets and smartphones (Kabali et al., 2015).

Educational TV and Video. Sammy's favorite program, *Sesame Street,* uses lively visual and sound effects to stress basic literacy and number concepts and puppet and human characters to teach general knowledge, emotional and social understanding, and social skills. Today, *Sesame Street* is broadcast in more than 140 countries, making it the most widely viewed children's program in the world (Sesame Workshop, 2017).

Time devoted to watching children's educational programs, including *Sesame Street,* is associated with gains in early literacy and math skills and academic progress in elementary school (Ennemoser & Schneider, 2007; Mares & Pan, 2013). One study reported a link between preschool viewing of *Sesame Street* (and similar educational programs) and getting higher grades, reading more books, and placing more value on achievement in high school (Anderson et al., 2001).

Children's programs with slow-paced action and easy-to-follow narratives are associated with improved executive function, greater recall of program content, gains in vocabulary and reading

APPLYING WHAT WE KNOW

Signs of Developmentally Appropriate Early Childhood Programs

PROGRAM CHARACTERISTICS	SIGNS OF QUALITY
Physical setting	Classroom space is divided into richly equipped activity areas, including make-believe play, blocks, science, math, games and puzzles, books, art, and music. Fenced outdoor play space is equipped with swings, climbing equipment, tricycles, and sandbox.
Group size	In preschools and child-care centers, group size is no greater than 18 to 20 children with two teachers.
Teacher–child ratio	In preschools and child-care centers, teacher is responsible for no more than 8 to 10 children. In family child-care homes, caregiver is responsible for no more than 6 children.
Daily activities	Children select many of their own activities and learn through experiences relevant to their own lives, mainly in small groups or individually. Teachers facilitate children's involvement, accept individual differences, and adjust expectations to children's developing capacities.
Interactions between adults and children	Teachers move among groups and individuals, asking questions, offering suggestions, and adding more complex ideas. Teachers use positive guidance techniques, such as modeling and encouraging expected behavior and redirecting children to more acceptable activities.
Teacher qualifications	Teachers have college-level specialized preparation in early childhood development, early childhood education, or a related field.
Relationships with parents	Parents are encouraged to observe and participate. Teachers talk frequently with parents about children's behavior and development.
Licensing and accreditation	Preschool and child-care programs are licensed by the state. Voluntary accreditation by the National Association for the Education of Young Children, *www.naeyc.org/academy,* or the National Association for Family Child Care, *www.nafcc.org,* is evidence of an especially high-quality program.

Source: Copple & Bredekamp, 2009.

skills, and more elaborate make-believe play than programs presenting quick, disconnected bits of information (Lillard & Peterson, 2011; Linebarger & Piotrowski, 2010). Narratively structured educational programming eases processing demands, facilitating attention and freeing up space in working memory for applying program content to real-life situations.

At present, television remains the dominant form of youth media. The average U.S. 2- to 6-year-old watches TV programs and videos from 1½ to 2⅔ hours a day. In middle childhood, viewing time increases to an average of 3½ hours a day and then declines slightly in adolescence (Common Sense Media, 2013; Rideout, Foehr, & Roberts, 2010). An estimated three-fourths of preschoolers use tablets or smartphones—on average, for about 1 hour a day—mostly to view videos, use apps, or play games (Common Sense Media, 2013; Kabali et al., 2015). Use of mobile devices is increasing, though low-SES children have less access.

Low-SES children are more frequent TV viewers than their higher-SES agemates, perhaps because fewer alternative forms of entertainment are affordable for their parents. On the positive side, preschoolers in low-SES families watch as much educational programming as their economically advantaged agemates (Common Sense Media, 2013). But parents with limited education are more likely to engage in practices that heighten TV viewing of all kinds, including leaving the TV on all day and eating family meals in front of it (Rideout, Foehr, & Roberts, 2010).

About 35 percent of U.S. preschoolers and 45 percent of school-age children have a TV set in their bedroom, and a great many have their own mobile device, usually a tablet. These children spend from 40 to 90 minutes more per day watching programs, usually with no parental restrictions on what they view (Common Sense Media, 2013; Kabali et al., 2015).

Does extensive screen media use take children away from worthwhile activities? The more preschool and school-age children watch prime-time shows and cartoons, the less time they spend reading and interacting with others and the poorer their academic skills (Ennemoser & Schneider, 2007; Wright et al., 2001). Whereas educational media experiences can be beneficial, viewing entertainment media—especially heavy viewing—detracts from children's school success and social experiences.

© LAURA DWIGHT PHOTOGRAPHY

In a preschool computer-learning center, children jointly play a game aimed at strengthening math concepts and problem solving. They are likely to gain in both math and collaborative skills.

Learning with Computers. More than one-third of 2- to 4-year-olds use a computer regularly, although once again, preschoolers from higher-SES families have greater home access (Common Sense Media, 2013; Fletcher et al., 2014). Because computers can have rich educational benefits, most early childhood classrooms include computer-learning centers.

Computer literacy and math programs, including online storybooks, expand children's general knowledge and encourage diverse language, literacy, and arithmetic skills (Karemaker, Pitchford, & O'Malley, 2010; Li, Atkins, & Stanton, 2006). Kindergartners who use computers to draw or write produce more elaborate pictures and text and make fewer writing errors.

Simplified computer languages that children can use to make designs or build structures introduce them to programming skills. As long as adults support children's efforts, these activities promote problem solving and metacognition because children must plan and reflect on their thinking to get their programs to work (Resnick & Silverman, 2005; Tran & Subrahmanyam, 2013).

As with television, children spend much time using computers and other screen media for entertainment—especially game playing, which more than triples from early to middle childhood, when it consumes, on average, 1¼ hours per day. Boys are two to three times more likely than girls to be daily players (Common Sense Media, 2013; Rideout, Foehr, & Roberts, 2010). As we will see in Chapters 9 and 11, playing video games can have cognitive benefits. However, much TV and game media are rife with gender stereotypes and violence, a topic we will consider in the next chapter.

ASK YOURSELF

CONNECT Compare outcomes resulting from preschool intervention programs with those from interventions beginning in infancy (see pages 160–161 in Chapter 5). Which are more likely to lead to lasting cognitive gains? Explain.

APPLY Your senator has heard that IQ gains resulting from Head Start do not last, so he plans to vote against additional funding. Write a letter explaining why he should support Head Start.

REFLECT How much and what kinds of screen media use did you engage in as a child? How do you think your home media environment influenced your development?

Language Development

7.13 Trace the development of vocabulary, grammar, and conversational skills in early childhood.

7.14 Cite factors that support language learning in early childhood.

Language is intimately related to virtually all cognitive changes discussed in this chapter. Between ages 2 and 6, children make momentous advances. Their remarkable achievements, as well as their mistakes along the way, reveal their active, rule-oriented approach to mastering their native tongue.

Vocabulary

At age 2, Sammy had a spoken vocabulary of about 250 words. By age 6, he will comprehend around 10,000 words and produce several thousand (Byrnes & Wasik, 2009). To accomplish this feat, Sammy will learn about five new words each day. How do children build their vocabularies so quickly? Research shows that they can connect new words with their underlying concepts after only a brief encounter, a process called **fast-mapping.** But fast-mapping does not imply that children immediately acquire adultlike word meanings.

Types of Words. Children in many Western and non-Western language communities fast-map labels for objects especially rapidly because these refer to concepts that are easy to perceive (McDonough et al., 2011; Parish-Morris et al., 2010). Soon children add verbs (*go, run, broke*), which require more complex understandings of relationships between objects and actions (Scott & Fisher, 2012). Children learning Chinese, Japanese, and Korean—languages in which nouns are often omitted from adult sentences, while verbs are stressed—acquire verbs especially quickly (Chan et al., 2011; Ma et al., 2009). Gradually, preschoolers add modifiers (*red, round, sad*).

Strategies for Word Learning. Preschoolers figure out the meanings of new words by contrasting them with words they already know. How do they discover which concept each word picks out? One speculation is that early in vocabulary growth, children adopt a *mutual exclusivity bias*—assume that words refer to entirely separate (nonoverlapping) categories (Markman, 1992). Consistent with this idea, when 2-year-olds hear the labels for two distinct novel objects (for example, *clip* and *horn*), they assign each word correctly, to the whole object and not just a part of it (Waxman & Senghas, 1992).

Indeed, children's first several hundred nouns refer mostly to objects well-organized by shape. Learning nouns based on the perceptual property of shape heightens young children's attention to the distinctive shapes of other objects (Smith et al., 2002; Yoshida & Smith, 2003). This *shape bias* helps preschoolers master additional names of objects, and vocabulary accelerates.

Once the name of a whole object is familiar, on hearing a new name for the object, 2- and 3-year-olds set aside the mutual exclusivity assumption. For example, if the object (*bottle*) has a distinctively shaped part (*spout*), children readily apply the new label to it (Hansen & Markman, 2009). Still, mutual exclusivity and object shape cannot account for preschoolers' remarkably flexible responses when objects have more than one name. In these instances, children often call on other components of language.

For example, preschoolers discover many word meanings by observing how words are used in the structure of sentences (Gleitman et al., 2005; Naigles & Swenson, 2007). Consider an adult who says, "This is a *citron* one," while showing the child a yellow car. Two- and 3-year-olds conclude that a new word used as an adjective for a familiar object (car) refers to a property of that object (Imai & Haryu, 2004). As children hear the word in various sentence structures ("That lemon is bright *citron*"), they refine its meaning.

Young children also take advantage of rich social information that adults frequently provide, while drawing on their own expanding ability to infer others' intentions, desires, and perspectives. In one study, an adult performed an action on an object and then used a new label while looking back and forth between the child and the object, as if inviting the child to play. Two-year-olds concluded that the label referred to the action, not the object (Tomasello & Akhtar, 1995). By age 3, children can even use a speaker's recently expressed desire ("I really want to play with the *riff*") to figure out a word's meaning (Saylor & Troseth, 2006).

Furthermore, to fill in for words they have not yet learned, children as young as age 3 coin new words using ones they already know—"plant-man" for a gardener, "crayoner" for a child using crayons. Preschoolers also extend language meanings through metaphors based on concrete sensory comparisons: "Clouds are pillows," "Leaves are dancers." Once vocabulary and general knowledge expand, children also appreciate nonsensory comparisons: "Friends are like magnets," "Time flies by" (Keil, 1986; Özçaliskan, 2005). Metaphors permit young children to communicate in amazingly vivid and memorable ways.

According to one theory of vocabulary development, children draw on a *coalition* of cues—perceptual, social, and linguistic—which shift in importance with age (Golinkoff & Hirsh-Pasek, 2006, 2008).

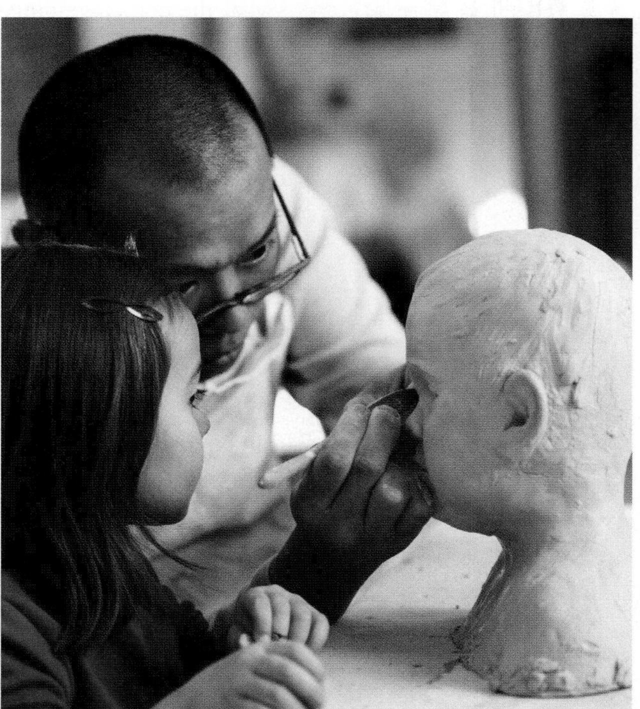

LAURIE AND CHARLES/GETTY IMAGES

▶ Young children rely on any useful information available to add to their vocabularies. As this child observes her father creating a sculpture, she attends to a variety of perceptual, social, and linguistic cues to grasp the meanings of unfamiliar words, such as *plaster, statue, base, form, sculpt, mold,* and *studio.*

Infants rely solely on perceptual features. Toddlers and young preschoolers, while still sensitive to perceptual features (such as object shape and physical action), increasingly attend to social cues—the speaker's direction of gaze, gestures, and expressions of intention and desire (Hollich, Hirsh-Pasek, & Golinkoff, 2000; Pruden et al., 2006). And as language develops further, linguistic cues—sentence structure and intonation (stress, pitch, and loudness)—play larger roles.

Preschoolers are most successful at figuring out new word meanings when several kinds of information are available (Parish-Morris, Golinkoff, & Hirsh-Pasek, 2013). Researchers have just begun to study the multiple cues that children use for different kinds of words and how their combined strategies change with development.

Grammar

Between ages 2 and 3, English-speaking children use simple sentences that follow a subject–verb–object word order. Children learning other languages adopt the word orders of the adult speech to which they are exposed.

Basic Rules. Toddlers' greater looking times at scenes that match sentences they hear reveal that they comprehend the meaning of basic grammatical structures that they cannot yet produce, such as "Big Bird is tickling Cookie Monster" or "What did the ball hit?" (Seidl, Hollich, & Jusczyk, 2003). First use of grammatical rules, however, is piecemeal—limited to just a few verbs. As children listen for familiar verbs in adults' speech, they expand their own utterances containing those verbs, relying on adult speech as their model (Gathercole, Sebastián, & Soto, 1999). Sammy, for example, added the preposition *with* to the verb *open* ("You open with scissors") because he often heard his parents say, "open with." But he failed to add *with* to the verb *hit* ("He hit me stick").

To test preschoolers' ability to generate novel sentences that conform to basic English grammar, researchers had them use a new verb in the subject–verb–object form after hearing it in a different construction, such as passive: "Ernie is getting *gorped* by the dog." When children were asked what the dog was doing, the percentage who could respond "He's *gorping* Ernie" rose steadily with age. But not until age 3½ to 4 could the majority of children apply the fundamental subject–verb–object structure broadly, to newly acquired verbs (Chan et al., 2010; Tomasello, 2006).

Once children form three-word sentences, they make small additions and changes to words that enable them to express meanings flexibly and efficiently. For example, they add *-ing* for ongoing actions (*playing*), add *-s* for plural (*cats*), use prepositions (*in* and *on*), and form various tenses of the verb *to be* (*is, are, were, has been, will*). English-speaking children master these grammatical markers in a regular sequence, starting with those that involve the simplest meanings and structures (Brown, 1973).

When preschoolers acquire these markers, they sometimes overextend the rules to words that are exceptions—a type of error called **overregularization.** "My toy car *breaked*" and "We each got two *foots*" are expressions that appear between ages 2 and 3 (Maratsos, 2000; Marcus, 1995).

Complex Structures. Gradually, preschoolers master more complex grammatical structures, although they do make mistakes. Question asking remains variable for several years. An analysis of one child's questions revealed that he inverted the subject and verb when asking certain questions ("What she will do?" "Why he can go?") but not others. The correct expressions were the ones he heard most often in his mother's speech (Rowland & Pine, 2000). And sometimes children produce errors in subject–verb agreement ("Where does the dogs play?") and subject case ("Where can me sit?") (Rowland, 2007).

Similarly, children have trouble with some passive sentences. When told, "The car is pushed by the truck," young preschoolers often make a toy car push a truck. By age 4½, they understand such expressions, whether they contain familiar or novel verbs (Dittmar et al., 2014). But full mastery of the passive form is not complete until the end of middle childhood.

Nevertheless, preschoolers' grasp of grammar is remarkable. By age 4 to 5, they form embedded sentences ("I think *he will come*"), tag questions ("Dad's going to be home soon, *isn't he?*"), and indirect objects ("He showed *his friend* the present") (Zukowski, 2013). As the preschool years draw to a close, children use most of the grammatical constructions of their language competently.

Evidence that grammatical development is an extended process has raised questions about Chomsky's nativist theory (to review, see pages 162–163 in Chapter 5). Some experts believe that grammar is a product of general cognitive development—children's tendency to search the environment for consistencies and patterns of all sorts. These *information-processing theorists* believe that children notice which words appear in the same positions in sentences and are combined in the same way with other words (Howell & Becker, 2013; MacWhinney, 2015; Tomasello, 2011). Over time, they group words into grammatical categories and use them appropriately in sentences.

Other theorists, while also focusing on how children process language, agree with the essence of Chomsky's theory—that the grammatical categories into which children group word meanings are innate, present at the outset (Pinker, 1999; Tien, 2013). Critics, however, point out that toddlers' two-word utterances do not reflect a flexible grasp of grammar and that preschoolers make many errors in their gradual mastery of grammar. In sum, controversy persists over whether a universal, built-in language acquisition device exists or whether children draw on general cognitive-processing procedures.

Conversation

Besides acquiring vocabulary and grammar, children must learn to engage in effective and appropriate communication. This practical, social side of language is called **pragmatics,** and preschoolers make considerable headway in mastering it.

As early as age 2, children are skilled conversationalists. In face-to-face interaction, they take turns and respond appropriately to their partners' remarks. With age, the number of turns over which children can sustain interaction, ability to maintain a topic over time, and responsiveness to queries requesting clarification increase (Comeau, Genesee, & Mendelson, 2010; Snow et al., 1996). By age 3, children can infer a speaker's intention when the speaker expresses it indirectly. For example, most know that an adult who, in response to an offer of cereal, says, "We have no milk," is declining the cereal (Schulze, Grassmann, & Tomasello, 2013). These surprisingly advanced abilities probably grow out of early interactive experiences.

© LAURA DWIGHT PHOTOGRAPHY

▶ These preschoolers likely use more assertive language when speaking for a male puppet than they would if speaking for a female puppet. In doing so, they reveal their early grasp of stereotypic features of social roles in their culture.

By age 4, children adjust their speech to fit the age, sex, and social status of their listeners. In acting out roles with hand puppets, they use more commands when playing socially dominant and male roles (teacher, doctor, father) but speak more politely and use more indirect requests when playing less dominant and female roles (student, patient, mother) (Anderson, 2000).

Preschoolers' conversations appear less mature in highly demanding situations in which they cannot see their listeners' reactions or rely on typical conversational aids, such as gestures or objects to talk about. When asked in a phone conversation what he received for his birthday, one 3-year-old held up a new toy and said, "This!" But 3- to 6-year-olds give more specific directions about how to solve a puzzle over the phone than in person, indicating that they realize that more verbal description is necessary on the phone (Cameron & Lee, 1997). Between ages 4 and 8, both conversing and giving directions over the phone improve greatly.

Supporting Language Learning in Early Childhood

As in toddlerhood, conversational give-and-take with adults is consistently related to preschoolers' language progress (Huttenlocher et al., 2010). And as noted in our discussion of early literacy, interactive book-reading is a powerful source of language learning.

In addition, sensitive, caring adults use specific techniques that promote early language skills. When children use words incorrectly or communicate unclearly, they give helpful, explicit feedback: "I can't tell which ball you want. Do you mean the large red one?" But they do not overcorrect, especially when children make grammatical mistakes. Criticism discourages children from freely using language in ways that lead to new skills.

Instead, adults generally provide indirect feedback about grammar by using two strategies, often in combination: **recasts**—restructuring inaccurate speech into correct form, and **expansions**—elaborating on children's speech, increasing its complexity (Bohannon & Stanowicz, 1988; Chouinard & Clark, 2003). For example, if a child says, "I gotted new red shoes," the parent might respond, "Yes, you got a pair of new red shoes." But these techniques do not consistently affect children's usage (Saxton, Bacley, & Gallaway, 2005; Strapp & Federico, 2000). Rather than eliminating errors, perhaps expansions and recasts model grammatical alternatives and encourage children to experiment with them.

Do the findings just described remind you once again of Vygotsky's theory? In language, as in other aspects of cognitive development, parents and teachers gently prompt children to take the next step forward. Children strive to master language because they want to connect with other people. Adults, in turn, respond to children's desire to become competent speakers by listening attentively, elaborating on what children say, modeling correct usage, and stimulating children to talk further. In the next chapter, we will see that this combination of warmth and encouragement of mature behavior is at the heart of early childhood emotional and social development as well.

ASK YOURSELF

CONNECT Explain how children's strategies for word learning support the interactionist perspective on language development, described on page 163 in Chapter 5.

APPLY Sammy's mother explained to him that the family would take a vacation in Miami. The next morning, Sammy announced, "I gotted my bags packed. When are we going to Your-ami?" What explains Sammy's errors?

CHAPTER 7 SUMMARY

PHYSICAL DEVELOPMENT

A Changing Body and Brain *(p. 203)*

7.1 ***Describe body growth and brain development during early childhood.***

- Gains in body size taper off in early childhood as children become longer and leaner. New epiphyses emerge in the skeleton, and by the end of the preschool years, children start to lose their primary teeth.
- Neural fibers in the brain continue to form synapses and to myelinate, followed by synaptic pruning and increasing localization of cognitive capacities in regions of the cerebral cortex. Prefrontal-cortical areas devoted to various aspects of executive function develop rapidly. The left cerebral hemisphere is especially active, supporting preschoolers' expanding language skills.
- Hand preference, reflecting an individual's **dominant cerebral hemisphere,** strengthens during early childhood. Research on handedness supports the joint contribution of nature and nurture to brain lateralization.
- Fibers linking the **cerebellum** to the cerebral cortex grow and myelinate, enhancing motor coordination and thinking. The **reticular formation,** responsible for alertness and consciousness; the **hippocampus,** which is vital in memory and spatial understanding; the **amygdala,** which plays a central role in processing novelty and emotional information; and the **corpus callosum,** connecting the two cerebral hemispheres, also form synapses and myelinate.

Influences on Physical Growth and Health *(p. 207)*

7.2 ***Describe the effects of heredity, nutrition, and infectious disease on physical growth and health in early childhood.***

- Heredity controls production and release of two hormones by the **pituitary gland: growth hormone (GH),** which is necessary for development of almost all body tissues, and **thyroid-stimulating hormone (TSH),** which affects brain development and body size.
- As growth rate slows, preschoolers' appetites decline, and they often become wary of new foods. Repeated, unpressured exposure to new foods promotes healthy, varied eating.

- Dietary deficiencies are associated with stunted physical growth, attention and memory difficulties, and academic and behavior problems. Disease—especially intestinal infections—also contributes to malnutrition.
- Immunization rates are lower in the United States than in other industrialized nations because many low-income children lack access to health care. Parental stress and misconceptions about vaccine safety also contribute.

7.3 *Cite factors that increase the risk of unintentional injuries, and explain how childhood injuries can be prevented.*

- Unintentional injuries are the leading cause of childhood mortality in industrialized nations. Victims are more likely to be boys; to be temperamentally inattentive, overactive, irritable, defiant, and aggressive; and to be growing up in poverty-stricken homes and neighborhoods.
- Effective injury prevention includes passing laws that promote child safety; creating safer environments; changing parent and child behaviors; and providing social supports to ease parental stress.

Motor Development *(p. 210)*

7.4 *Cite major milestones of gross- and fine-motor development, along with factors that affect motor progress, in early childhood.*

- As the child's center of gravity shifts toward the trunk, balance improves, paving the way for new gross-motor achievements. Preschoolers run, jump, hop, gallop, skip, throw, and catch, and generally become better coordinated.
- Improved control of the hands and fingers leads to dramatic gains in fine-motor skills. Preschoolers become self-sufficient at dressing and feeding.
- By age 3, children's scribbles become pictures. With age, drawings increase in complexity and realism, influenced by gains in children's cognitive and fine-motor capacities and by their culture's artistic traditions. Preschoolers also make progress in accurately printing alphabet letters.
- Body build and physical activities affect motor development. Sex differences favoring boys in force and power and girls in balance and fine movements are partly genetic, but social pressures exaggerate them. Children master the motor skills of early childhood through informal play experiences.

COGNITIVE DEVELOPMENT

Piaget's Theory: The Preoperational Stage *(p. 215)*

7.5 *Describe advances in mental representation, and limitations of thinking, during the preoperational stage.*

- Rapid advances in mental representation mark the beginning of Piaget's **preoperational stage.** Make-believe, which supports many aspects of development, becomes increasingly complex, evolving into **sociodramatic play** with peers. **Dual representation** improves rapidly over the third year as children realize that models, drawings, and simple maps correspond to circumstances in the real world.
- Preoperational children's cognitive limitations include **egocentrism, centration,** a focus on perceptual appearances, and **irreversibility.** As a result, they fail **conservation** and **hierarchical classification** tasks.

© ELLEN B. SENISI

7.6 *Explain the implications of follow-up research on early cognitive development for the accuracy of Piaget's preoperational stage.*

- When given simplified tasks relevant to their everyday lives, preschoolers are aware of others' perspectives, distinguish animate from inanimate objects, have flexible and appropriate notions of magic, reason by analogy about physical transformations, understand cause-and-effect relationships, and organize knowledge into hierarchical categories.
- Evidence that operational thinking develops gradually over the preschool years challenges Piaget's stage concept. Some theorists propose a more flexible view of stages.

Vygotsky's Sociocultural Theory *(p. 222)*

7.7 *Describe Vygotsky's perspective on the social origins and developmental significance of children's private speech.*

- Unlike Piaget, Vygotsky regarded language as the foundation for all higher cognitive processes. **Private speech,** or language used for self-guidance, emerges out of social communication as adults and more skilled peers help children master appropriately challenging tasks. Private speech is eventually internalized as silent, inner speech.
- **Scaffolding**—adjusting teaching support to fit children's current needs and suggesting strategies—promotes gains in children's thinking.

7.8 *Describe Vygotsky's view of make-believe play, and evaluate his major ideas.*

- Make-believe play is a vital zone of proximal development in early childhood.
- **Guided participation,** a broader concept than scaffolding, recognizes situational and cultural variations in shared endeavors between more expert and less expert participants.

Information Processing *(p. 225)*

7.9 *Describe changes in executive function and memory during early childhood.*

- Executive function improves markedly over the preschool years, contributing to academic and social skills. Preschoolers gain in inhibition, flexible shifting of attention, and working-memory capacity—executive function components that are closely interconnected and that contribute vitally to academic and social skills. Older preschoolers also improve in planning, a complex executive function activity.
- Parental sensitivity and scaffolding support preschoolers' executive function skills. Poverty exerts a negative impact through maladaptive parenting and chronic stress.

© LAURA DWIGHT PHOTOGRAPHY

- Young children's recognition memory is remarkably accurate, but their recall of listlike information is poor because they are not skilled at using **memory strategies**.
- **Episodic memory**—memory for everyday experiences—improves greatly in early childhood. Like adults, preschoolers remember recurring events as **scripts,** which become increasingly elaborate with age.
- As cognitive and conversational skills improve, children's autobiographical memories become more organized and detailed, especially when adults use an elaborative style in talking about the past.

7.10 *Describe the young child's theory of mind.*

- Preschoolers begin to construct a theory of mind, evidence of their capacity for **metacognition.** Between ages 4 and 6, explicit false-belief understanding becomes more secure, enhancing children's capacity to reflect on their own and others' thoughts and emotions. Language, executive function, and social experiences contribute.
- Preschoolers regard the mind as a passive container of information rather than as an active, constructive agent.

7.11 ***Summarize children's literacy and mathematical knowledge during early childhood.***

- Preschoolers' **emergent literacy** reveals that they revise their ideas about the meaning of print as their cognitive capacities improve, as they encounter writing in many contexts, and as adults help them with written communication. **Phonological awareness** is a strong predictor of emergent literacy knowledge and later spelling and reading achievement. Informal literacy experiences, including adult–child interactive storybook reading, foster literacy development.
- Toddlers display a beginning grasp of **ordinality.** By ages 3½ to 4, preschoolers understand **cardinality** and use counting to solve arithmetic problems, eventually arriving at the most efficient, accurate approach. Adults promote children's mathematical knowledge by providing many occasions for counting, comparing quantities, and talking about number concepts.

Individual Differences in Mental Development *(p. 233)*

7.12 ***Describe early childhood intelligence tests and the impact of home, preschool and kindergarten programs, child care, and educational media on mental development.***

- By ages 6 to 7, intelligence test scores are good predictors of later IQ and academic achievement. Children growing up in warm, stimulating homes with parents who make reasonable demands for mature behavior develop well intellectually.
- Preschool and kindergarten programs include both **child-centered programs,** in which much learning occurs through play, and **academic programs,** in which teachers structure children's learning. Emphasizing formal academic training undermines young children's motivation and negatively influences later achievement.
- **Project Head Start** is the most extensive U.S. federally funded preschool program for low-income children. Preschool intervention results in immediate IQ and achievement gains and long-term improvements in school adjustment.
- Enriching Head Start classrooms with Head Start REDI yields higher year-end language, literacy, and social skills that are still evident at the end of kindergarten. Good child care enhances cognitive, language, and social development, especially for low-SES children.

© LAURA DWIGHT PHOTOGRAPHY

- Children gain in diverse cognitive skills from educational TV programs, videos, and computer software. Programs with slow-paced action and easy-to-follow story lines foster executive function, vocabulary and reading skills, and elaborate make-believe play. Computer programs that introduce children to programming skills promote problem solving and metacognition. But heavy exposure to prime-time programs and cartoons is associated with poorer academic skills.

Language Development *(p. 238)*

7.13 ***Trace the development of vocabulary, grammar, and conversational skills in early childhood.***

- Supported by **fast-mapping,** preschoolers' vocabularies increase dramatically. Initially, they rely heavily on the perceptual cue of object shape to expand their vocabulary. With age, they increasingly draw on social and linguistic cues.
- Between ages 2 and 3, children adopt the basic word order of their language. As preschoolers gradually master grammatical rules, they sometimes overextend them in a type of error called **overregularization.** By the end of early childhood, children have acquired complex grammatical forms.
- **Pragmatics** is the practical, social side of language. Two-year-olds are already skilled conversationalists in face-to-face interaction. By age 4, children adapt their speech to their listener's age, sex, and social status.

7.14 ***Cite factors that support language learning in early childhood.***

- Conversational give-and-take with adults fosters language progress. Adults provide explicit feedback on the clarity of children's language and indirect feedback about grammar through **recasts** and **expansions.**

IMPORTANT TERMS AND CONCEPTS

CHAPTER

8 Emotional and Social Development in Early Childhood

During the preschool years, children make great strides in understanding the thoughts and feelings of others, and they build on these skills as they form first friendships—special relationships marked by attachment and common interests.

© LAURA DWIGHT PHOTOGRAPHY

WHAT'S AHEAD IN CHAPTER 8

As the children in Leslie's classroom moved through the preschool years, their personalities took on clearer definition. By age 3, they voiced firm likes and dislikes as well as new ideas about themselves. "Stop bothering me," Sammy said to Mark, who had reached for Sammy's beanbag as Sammy aimed it toward the mouth of a large clown face. "See, I'm great at this game," Sammy announced with confidence, an attitude that kept him trying, even though he missed most of the throws.

The children's conversations also revealed early notions about morality. Often they combined statements about right and wrong with forceful attempts to defend their own desires. "You're 'posed to share," stated Mark, grabbing the beanbag out of Sammy's hand.

"I was here first! Gimme it back," demanded Sammy, pushing Mark. The two boys struggled until Leslie intervened, provided an extra set of beanbags, and showed them how they could both play.

As the interaction between Sammy and Mark reveals, preschoolers quickly become complex social beings. Young children argue, grab, and push, but cooperative exchanges are far more frequent. Between ages 2 and 6, first friendships form, in which children converse, act out complementary roles, and learn that their own desires for companionship and toys are best met when they consider others' needs and interests.

The children's developing understanding of their social world was especially apparent in their growing attention to gender roles. While Priti and Karen cared for a sick baby doll in the housekeeping area, Sammy, Vance, and Mark transformed the block corner into a busy intersection. "Green light, go!" shouted police officer Sammy as Vance and Mark pushed large wooden cars and trucks across the floor. Already, the children preferred peers of their own gender, and their play themes mirrored their culture's gender stereotypes.

© LAURA DWIGHT PHOTOGRAPHY

This chapter is devoted to the many facets of early childhood emotional and social development. We begin with Erik Erikson's view of personality change in the preschool years. Then we consider children's concepts of themselves, their insights into their social and moral worlds, their gender typing, and their increasing ability to manage their emotional and social behaviors. Finally, we ask, What is effective child rearing? And we discuss the complex conditions that support good parenting or lead it to break down, including child abuse and neglect.

8.1 Identify personality changes that take place during Erikson's stage of initiative versus guilt.

Erikson's Theory: Initiative versus Guilt

According to Erikson (1950), once children have a sense of autonomy, they become less contrary than they were as toddlers. Their energies are freed for tackling the psychological conflict of the preschool years: **initiative versus guilt.** As the word *initiative* suggests, young children have a new sense of purposefulness. They are eager to tackle new tasks, join in activities with peers, and discover what they can do with the help of adults. They also make strides in conscience development.

Erikson regarded play as a means through which young children learn about themselves and their social world. Play creates a small social organization of children who try out meaningful roles and skills and who must cooperate to achieve common goals. Around the world, children act out family scenes and highly visible occupations—police officer, doctor, and nurse in Western societies, hut builder and spear maker among the Baka of West Africa (Gaskins, 2013).

Through patient, reasonable adult guidance and play experiences with peers, preschoolers acquire the moral and gender-role standards of their society. For Erikson, the negative outcome of early childhood is an overly strict superego, or conscience, that causes children to feel too much guilt because they have been threatened, criticized, and punished excessively by adults. When this happens, preschoolers' exuberant play and bold efforts to master new tasks break down.

As we will see, Erikson's image of initiative captures the diverse changes in young children's emotional and social lives. Early childhood is, indeed, a time when children develop a confident self-image, more effective control over their emotions, new social skills, the foundations of morality, and firm beliefs about gender, which they apply to themselves.

© ALVARO LEIVA/ROBERT HARDING WORLD IMAGERY

▶ A Guatemalan 3-year-old pretends to shell corn. By acting out family scenes and highly visible occupations, young children around the world develop a sense of initiative, gaining insight into what they can do and become in their culture.

Self-Understanding

8.2 Describe the development of self-concept and self-esteem in early childhood.

In Chapter 7, we noted that young children acquire a vocabulary for talking about their inner mental lives and refine their understanding of mental states. As self-awareness strengthens, preschoolers focus more intently on qualities that make the self unique. They begin to develop a **self-concept,** the set of attributes, abilities, attitudes, and values that an individual believes defines who he or she is.

Foundations of Self-Concept

Ask a 3- to 5-year-old to tell you about himself, and you are likely to hear something like this: "I'm Tommy. I'm 4 years old. I can wash my hair all by myself. I have a new Lego set, and I made this big, big tower." Preschoolers' self-concepts consist largely of observable characteristics, such as their name, physical appearance, possessions, and everyday behaviors (Harter, 2012).

By age 3½, children also describe themselves in terms of typical emotions and attitudes ("I'm happy when I play with my friends," "I don't like scary TV programs," "I usually do what Mommy says"), suggesting a beginning understanding of their unique psychological characteristics (Eder & Mangelsdorf, 1997). And by age 5, children's degree of agreement with such statements coincides with maternal reports of their personality traits, indicating that older preschoolers have a sense of their own timidity, agreeableness, and positive or negative affect (Brown et al., 2008). But most preschoolers do not yet say, "I'm helpful" or "I'm shy." Direct references to personality traits must wait for greater cognitive maturity.

A warm, sensitive parent–child relationship fosters a more positive, coherent early self-concept. Elaborative parent–child conversations focusing on children's thoughts, feelings, and subjective experiences about personally experienced events play an especially important role in early self-concept development. For example, when parents reminisce with preschoolers about times they successfully resolved upsetting feelings, 4- and 5-year-olds describe their emotional tendencies more favorably ("I'm not scared—not me!") (Goodvin & Romdall, 2013). By emphasizing the personal meaning of past events, conversations about internal states facilitate self-knowledge.

As early as age 2, parents use narratives of past events to impart rules, standards for behavior, and evaluative information about the child: "You added the milk when we made the mashed potatoes. That's a very important job!" (Nelson, 2003). These self-evaluative narratives are a major means through which caregivers imbue the young child's self-concept with personal values. In observational research on Irish-American families in Chicago and Chinese families in Taiwan, the Chinese parents frequently told preschoolers long stories about the child's misdeeds. In a warm, caring tone, they stressed the impact of the child's misbehavior on others ("You made Mama lose face"). Irish-American parents, in contrast, rarely dwelt on children's transgressions and, when they did, interpreted these acts positively ("He's got a lot of spunk!") (Miller, 2014; Miller et al., 1997, 2012). Consistent with these differences, the Chinese child's self-image emphasizes obligations to others, whereas the American child's is more autonomous.

As they talk about personally significant events and as their cognitive skills advance, preschoolers gradually come to view themselves as persisting over time—a change evident in their improved ability to anticipate their own future states and needs. By age 5, children better understand that their future preferences are likely to differ from their current ones. Most realize that when they grow up, they will prefer reading newspapers to reading picture books and drinking coffee to drinking grape juice (Bélanger et al., 2014). By the end of the preschool years, children can set aside their current state of mind and take a future perspective.

© LAURA DWIGHT PHOTOGRAPHY

This preschooler confidently prepares to slide down the pole of a playground jungle gym. Her high self-esteem contributes greatly to her initiative in mastering new skills.

Emergence of Self-Esteem

Another aspect of self-concept emerges in early childhood: **self-esteem,** the judgments we make about our own worth and the feelings associated with those judgments. These evaluations are among the most important aspects of self-development because they affect our emotional experiences, future behavior, and long-term psychological adjustment.

By age 4, preschoolers have several self-judgments—for example, about learning things in school, making friends, getting along with parents, and treating others kindly (Marsh, Ellis, & Craven, 2002). But because they have difficulty distinguishing between their desired and their actual competence, they usually rate their own ability as extremely high and underestimate task difficulty, as Sammy did when he asserted, despite his many misses, that he was great at beanbag throwing (Harter, 2012).

High self-esteem contributes greatly to preschoolers' initiative during a period in which they must master many new skills. By age 3, children whose parents patiently encourage while offering information about how to succeed are enthusiastic and highly motivated. In contrast, children whose parents criticize their worth and performance give up easily when faced with challenges and express shame and despondency after failing (Kelley, Brownell, & Campbell, 2000). Adults can avoid promoting these self-defeating reactions by adjusting their expectations to children's capacities, scaffolding children's attempts at difficult tasks (see Chapter 7, page 223), and pointing out effort and improvement in children's behavior.

Emotional Development

8.3 Identify changes in understanding and expressing emotion during early childhood, citing factors that influence those changes.

Gains in representation, language, and self-concept support emotional development in early childhood. Between ages 2 and 6, children attain a better understanding of their own and others' feelings, and emotional self-regulation improves. In addition, preschoolers more often experience self-conscious emotions and empathy, which contribute to their developing sense of morality.

Understanding Emotion

During the preschool years, children refer to causes, consequences, and behavioral signs of emotion (Thompson, Winer, & Goodvin, 2011). Over time, their understanding becomes more accurate and complex.

Three-year-olds tend to apply one label (such as *happy)* to all positive facial expressions of emotion and another to all negative expressions *(sad).* By ages 4 to 5, emotion labeling differentiates: Children use *happy, sad, angry, afraid,* and *surprised* accurately (Widen, 2013). Older preschoolers also correctly judge the causes of diverse basic emotions ("He's surprised because his mom's hair is pink," "He's sad because his goldfish died"). Their explanations tend to emphasize external factors over internal states, a balance that changes with age (Rieffe, Terwogt, & Cowan, 2005). In Chapter 7, we saw that after age 4, children appreciate that both desires and beliefs motivate behavior. Once these understandings are secure, children's grasp of how internal factors can trigger emotion expands.

▶ Warm, elaborative conversations in which parents label and explain emotions enhance preschoolers' emotional understanding.

Three- to 5-year-olds are good at inferring how others are feeling based on their behavior. For example, they can tell that a child who jumps up and down and claps his hands is probably happy and that a child who is tearful and withdrawn is sad (Widen & Russell, 2011). And they are beginning to realize that thinking and feeling are interconnected—that focusing on negative thoughts ("I broke my arm, so now I have to wear this itchy cast that makes it hard to play") is likely to make a person feel worse, but thinking positively ("Now I have a cool cast my friends can write their names on!") can help a person feel better (Bamford & Lagattuta, 2012). Furthermore, preschoolers come up with effective ways to relieve others' negative emotions, such as hugging to reduce sadness (Fabes et al., 1988). Overall, preschoolers have an impressive ability to interpret, predict, and change others' feelings.

The more parents label and explain emotions and express warmth when conversing with preschoolers, the more "emotion words" children use and the better developed their emotion understanding (Fivush & Haden, 2005). Discussions of negative experiences or disagreements are particularly helpful because they evoke more elaborative dialogues that validate children's feelings while helping them appreciate the emotional perspectives of others (Laible, 2011). In one study, mothers who explained emotions and negotiated and compromised during conflicts with their 2½-year-olds had children who, at age 3, were advanced in emotional understanding and used similar strategies to resolve disagreements (Laible & Thompson, 2002). Such dialogues seem to help children reflect on the causes and consequences of emotion while modeling mature communication skills.

Preschoolers' knowledge about emotion is related to friendly, considerate behavior, constructive responses to disputes with agemates, and perspective-taking ability (Garner & Estep, 2001; Hughes & Ensor, 2010; O'Brien et al., 2011). Also, preschoolers who refer to feelings when interacting with playmates are better liked by their peers (Fabes et al., 2001). Children seem to recognize that acknowledging others' emotions and explaining their own enhance the quality of relationships.

Emotional Self-Regulation

Language, along with preschoolers' growing emotion understanding, contributes to gains in *emotional self-regulation* (Thompson, 2015). By age 3 to 4, children verbalize a variety of strategies for alleviating negative emotion that they tailor to specific situations (Davis et al., 2010; Dennis & Kelemen, 2009). For example, they know they can restrict sensory input (cover their eyes or ears to block out a scary sight or sound), talk to themselves ("Mommy said she'll be back soon"), change their goals (decide that they don't want to play anyway after being excluded from a game), or repair a relationship ("stop fighting and share" to resolve a conflict with a peer). The effectiveness of preschoolers' recommended strategies improves with age.

As children use these strategies, emotional outbursts decline. Gains in executive function—in particular, inhibition and flexible shifting of attention—contribute greatly to managing emotion in early childhood. Three-year-olds who can distract themselves when upset and focus on how to handle their feelings tend to become cooperative school-age children with few problem behaviors (Gilliom et al., 2002).

Parents who are in tune with their own emotional experiences tend to be supportive of their preschoolers, offering suggestions and explanations of emotion-regulation strategies that strengthen children's capacity to handle stress (Meyer et al., 2014; Morris et al., 2011). In contrast, when parents rarely express positive emotion, dismiss children's feelings as unimportant, and fail to control their own anger, children's emotion regulation and psychological adjustment suffer (Hill et al., 2006; Thompson & Goodman, 2010).

Adult–child conversations that prepare children for difficult experiences by discussing what to expect and ways to handle anxiety also foster emotional self-regulation (Thompson & Goodman, 2010). Nevertheless, preschoolers' vivid imaginations and incomplete grasp of the distinction between fantasy and reality make fears common in early childhood. See Applying What We Know on page 250 for ways to help young children manage fears.

Self-Conscious Emotions

One morning in Leslie's classroom, a group of children crowded around for a bread-baking activity. Leslie asked them to wait patiently while she got a baking pan. But Sammy reached over to feel the dough, and the bowl tumbled off the table. When Leslie returned, Sammy looked at her, then covered his eyes with his hands and said, "I did something bad." He felt ashamed and guilty.

As their self-concepts develop, preschoolers become increasingly sensitive to praise and blame or to the possibility of such feedback. They more often experience *self-conscious emotions*—feelings that involve injury to or enhancement of their sense of self (see Chapter 6). By age 3, self-conscious emotions are clearly linked to self-evaluation (Lagattuta & Thompson, 2007; Lewis, 1995). But because preschoolers are still developing standards of excellence and conduct, they depend on the messages of parents, teachers, and others who matter to them to know *when* to feel proud, ashamed, or guilty, often viewing adult expectations as obligatory rules ("Dad said you're 'posed to take turns") (Thompson, Meyer, & McGinley, 2006).

APPLYING WHAT WE KNOW

Helping Children Manage Common Fears of Early Childhood

FEAR	SUGGESTION
Monsters, ghosts, and darkness	Reduce exposure to frightening stories and TV programs until the child is better able to understand that fantastical beings are not real. "Search" the child's room for monsters, showing him that none are there. Use a night-light, sit by the child's bed until he falls asleep, and tuck in a favorite toy for protection.
Preschool or child care	If the child resists going to preschool but seems content once there, the fear is probably separation. Provide a sense of warmth and caring while gently encouraging independence. If the child fears being at preschool, find out why—the teacher, the children, or a crowded, noisy environment. Provide support by accompanying the child and gradually lessening the amount of time you stay.
Animals	Do not force the child to approach a dog, cat, or other animal that arouses fear. Let the child move at her own pace. Demonstrate how to hold and pet the animal, showing that when treated gently, the animal is friendly. If the child is larger than the animal, emphasize this: "You're so big. That kitty is probably afraid of *you!*"
Intense fears	If a child's fear is intense, persists for a long time, interferes with daily activities, and cannot be reduced in any of the ways just suggested, it has reached the level of a *phobia.* Sometimes phobias are linked to family problems and require counseling. Other phobias diminish without treatment as the child's emotional self-regulation improves.

When parents repeatedly comment on the worth of the child and her performance ("That's a bad job!" "I thought you were a good girl!"), children experience self-conscious emotions intensely—more shame after failure, more pride after success. In contrast, when parents focus on how to improve performance ("You did it this way; now try it that way"), they induce moderate, more adaptive levels of shame and pride and greater persistence on difficult tasks (Kelley, Brownell, & Campbell, 2000).

Among Western children, intense shame is associated with feelings of personal inadequacy ("I'm stupid," "I'm a terrible person") and with maladjustment—withdrawal and depression as well as intense anger and aggression toward those who shamed them (Muris & Meesters, 2014). In contrast, guilt—when it occurs in appropriate circumstances and is neither excessive nor accompanied by shame—is related to good adjustment. Guilt helps children resist harmful impulses, and it motivates a misbehaving child to repair the damage and behave more considerately (Tangney, Stuewig, & Mashek, 2007). But overwhelming guilt—involving such high emotional distress that the child cannot make amends—is linked to depressive symptoms as early as age 3 (Luby et al., 2009).

Finally, the consequences of shame for children's adjustment may vary across cultures. People in Asian societies, who tend to define themselves in relation to their social group, view shame as an adaptive reminder of an interdependent self and of the importance of others' judgments (Friedlmeier, Corapci, & Cole, 2011).

Empathy and Sympathy

Empathy, another emotional capacity that becomes more common in early childhood, motivates **prosocial,** or **altruistic, behavior**—actions that benefit another person without any expected reward for the self (Eisenberg, Spinrad, & Knafo-Noam, 2015). Compared with toddlers, preschoolers rely more on words to communicate empathic feelings, a change that indicates a more reflective level of empathy. When a 4-year-old received a Christmas gift that she hadn't included on her list for Santa, she assumed it belonged to another little girl and pleaded with her parents, "We've got to give it back—Santa's made a big mistake. I think the girl's crying 'cause she didn't get her present!"

Yet for some children, empathizing—*feeling with* an upset adult or peer and responding emotionally in a similar way—does not yield acts of kindness and helpfulness but, instead, escalates into personal distress. In trying to reduce these negative feelings, the child focuses on his own anxiety rather than on the person in need. As a result, empathy does not lead to **sympathy**—feelings of concern or sorrow for another's plight.

Temperament plays a role in whether empathy prompts sympathetic, prosocial behavior or self-focused distress. Children who are sociable, assertive, and good at regulating emotion are more likely to help, share, and comfort others in distress (Eisenberg, Spinrad, & Knafo-Noam, 2015; Valiente et al., 2004). But poor emotion regulators less often display sympathetic concern and prosocial behavior.

Preschoolers' empathic concern strengthens in the context of a secure parent–child attachment relationship (Murphy & Laible, 2013). When parents respond to their preschoolers' feelings with empathy and sympathy, children react with concern to others' distress—a relationship that persists into adolescence and early adulthood (Michalik et al., 2007; Newton et al., 2014). Besides modeling empathy and sympathy, parents can teach children the importance of kindness and can intervene when they display inappropriate emotion—strategies that predict high levels of sympathetic responding (Eisenberg, 2003). In contrast, angry, punitive parenting can disrupt the development of empathy and sympathy at an early age.

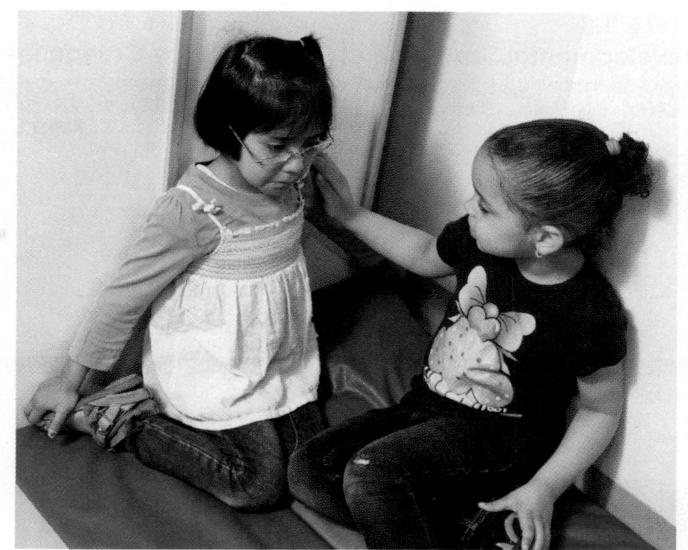

▶ As children's language skills and capacity to take the perspective of others improve, empathy also increases, motivating prosocial, or altruistic, behavior.

Peer Relations

8.4 Describe peer sociability and friendship in early childhood, along with cultural and parental influences on early peer relations.

As children become increasingly self-aware and better at communicating and understanding others' thoughts and feelings, their skill at interacting with peers improves rapidly. Peers provide young children with learning experiences they can get in no other way. Because peers interact on an equal footing, children must keep a conversation going, cooperate, and set goals in play. With peers, children form friendships—special relationships marked by attachment and common interests.

Advances in Peer Sociability

Mildred Parten (1932), one of the first to study peer sociability among 2- to 5-year-olds, noticed a dramatic rise with age in joint, interactive play. She concluded that social development proceeds in a three-step sequence. It begins with **nonsocial activity**—unoccupied, onlooker behavior and solitary play. Then it shifts to **parallel play,** in which a child plays near other children with similar materials but does not try to influence their behavior. At the highest level are two forms of true social interaction. In **associative play,** children engage in separate activities but exchange toys and comment on one another's behavior. Finally, in **cooperative play,** a more advanced type of interaction, children orient toward a common goal, such as acting out a make-believe theme.

Follow-Up Research on Peer Sociability. Longitudinal evidence indicates that these play forms emerge in the order suggested by Parten but that later-appearing ones do not replace earlier ones in a developmental sequence (Rubin, Bukowski, & Parker, 2006). Rather, all types coexist in early childhood.

During classroom free-play periods, preschoolers often transition from onlooker to parallel to cooperative play and back again (Robinson et al., 2003). They seem to use parallel play as a way station—a respite from the demands of complex social interaction and a crossroad to new activities. Also, both solitary and parallel play remain fairly stable from 3 to 6 years, accounting for as much of the child's play as cooperative interaction (Rubin, Fein, & Vandenberg, 1983).

We now understand that the *type,* not the amount, of solitary and parallel play changes during early childhood. In studies in Taiwan and the United States, researchers rated the *cognitive maturity* of nonsocial, parallel, and cooperative play, using the categories shown in Table 8.1 on page 252. Within each of Parten's play types, older children displayed more cognitively mature behavior than younger children (Pan, 1994; Rubin, Watson, & Jambor, 1978).

Often parents wonder whether a preschooler who spends much time playing alone is developing normally. But only *certain types* of nonsocial activity—aimless wandering, hovering near peers,

TABLE 8.1
Developmental Sequence of Cognitive Play Categories

PLAY CATEGORY	DESCRIPTION	EXAMPLES
Functional play	Simple, repetitive motor movements with or without objects, especially common during the first two years	Running around a room, rolling a car back and forth, kneading clay with no intent to make something
Constructive play	Creating or constructing something, especially common between 3 and 6 years	Making a house out of toy blocks, drawing a picture, putting together a puzzle
Make-believe play	Acting out everyday and imaginary roles, especially common between 2 and 6 years	Playing house, school, or police officer; acting out storybook or television characters

Source: Rubin, Fein, & Vandenberg, 1983.

© LAURA DWIGHT PHOTOGRAPHY

© LAURA DWIGHT PHOTOGRAPHY

▶ Top photo: Four-year-olds engage in parallel play. Bottom photo: Cooperative play develops later than parallel play, but preschool children continue to move back and forth between the two types of sociability, using parallel play as a respite from the complex demands of cooperation.

and functional play involving repetitive motor action—are cause for concern. Children who behave reticently, by watching peers without playing, are usually temperamentally inhibited—high in social fearfulness (Coplan & Ooi, 2014). And preschoolers who engage in solitary, repetitive behavior (banging blocks, making a doll jump up and down) tend to be immature, impulsive children who find it difficult to regulate anger and aggression (Coplan et al., 2001). Both reticent and impulsive children tend to experience peer ostracism (Coplan & Arbeau, 2008).

Other preschoolers with low rates of peer interaction simply like to play alone, and their solitary activities are positive and constructive. When they do play with peers, they show socially skilled behavior (Coplan & Armer, 2007). Still, a few preschoolers who engage in such age-appropriate solitary play—again, more often boys—are rebuffed by peers (Coplan et al., 2001, 2004). Perhaps because quiet play is inconsistent with the "masculine" gender role, boys who engage in it are at risk for negative peer reactions.

As noted in Chapter 7, *sociodramatic play*—an advanced form of cooperative play—becomes especially common over the preschool years. When researchers observed free-play periods in preschools, they found that girls participated more in sociodramatic play, whereas boys participated more in friendly, vigorous interactions called *rough-and-tumble play*. Each type of play was associated with expressions of positive emotion and predicted children's emotion understanding and self-regulation one year later (Lindsey & Colwell, 2013). Both sociodramatic play and rough-and-tumble play require children to exercise self-control and to respond to peers' verbal and nonverbal emotional cues. We will return to the topic of rough-and-tumble play in Chapter 9.

Cultural Variations. Peer sociability takes different forms, depending on the relative importance cultures place on group harmony as opposed to individual autonomy (Chen, 2012). For example, children in India generally play in large groups. Much of their behavior is imitative, occurs in unison, and involves close physical contact—a play style requiring high levels of cooperation. In a game called Bhatto Bhatto, children act out a script about a trip to the market, touching one another's elbows and hands as they pretend to cut and share a tasty vegetable (Roopnarine et al., 1994).

Cultural beliefs about the importance of play also affect early peer associations. Caregivers who view play as mere entertainment are less likely to provide props or to encourage pretending than those who value its cognitive and social benefits (Gaskins, 2014). Recall the description of children's daily lives in a Mayan village culture on page 224 in Chapter 7. When Mayan children do pretend, their play themes are *interpretive* of daily life—involving a limited number of scripts that reflect everyday roles and experiences. Children in industrialized, urban contexts more often engage in *inventive* play, generating make-believe scenarios unconstrained by actual experience (Gaskins, 2013). Perhaps Western-style sociodramatic play, with its elaborate materials and wide-ranging imaginative themes, is particularly important for social development in societies where the worlds of adults and children are distinct. It may be less crucial in village cultures where children participate in adult activities from an early age.

© JACOB MAENTZ/CORBIS

▶ Agta village children in the Philippines play a tug-of-war game. Large-group, highly cooperative play occurs more often in societies that value group harmony over individual autonomy.

First Friendships

As preschoolers interact, first friendships form that serve as important contexts for emotional and social development. Preschoolers understand that a friend is someone "who likes you," with whom you spend a lot of time playing, and with whom you share toys. But friendship does not yet have a long-term, enduring quality based on mutual trust (Damon, 1988a; Hartup, 2006). "Mark's my best friend," Sammy declared on days when the boys got along well. But when a dispute arose, he reversed himself: "Mark, you're not my friend!" Nevertheless, preschool friendships can be remarkably stable across early childhood, as long as peers remain in the same social group. In one study, nearly one-third mentioned the same best friends—the children they like to play with most—a year later (Dunn, 2004a; Eivers et al., 2012).

Already, interactions between preschoolers who mutually name each other as friends are especially positive, reflecting greater support and intimacy than do other peer relationships (Furman & Rose, 2015; Hartup, 2006). Preschool friends are more cooperative and emotionally expressive—talking, laughing, and looking at each other more often than nonfriends do.

As early as the preschool years, children with a mutual friendship are better adjusted and more socially competent (Shin et al., 2014). Furthermore, children entering kindergarten who have friends in their class or who readily make new friends adjust to school more favorably (Ladd, Birch, & Buhs, 1999; Proulx & Poulin, 2013). Perhaps the company of friends serves as a secure base from which to develop new relationships with classmates.

Peer Relations and School Readiness

The ease with which young children make new friends and are accepted by classmates predicts cooperative participation in classroom activities, task persistence, and academic skills in preschool, which carry over to better academic performance in kindergarten and the early school grades (Bell et al., 2016; Walker & Henderson, 2012; Ziv, 2013). Because social maturity in early childhood contributes to academic learning, readiness for kindergarten must be assessed in terms of not only academic skills but also social skills.

Young children's positive peer interactions occur most often in unstructured situations such as free play, making it important for preschools and kindergartens to provide space, time, materials, and adult scaffolding to support child-directed activities (Booren, Downer, & Vitiello, 2012; Shearer et al., 2016). Warm, responsive teacher–child interaction is also vital, especially for shy children and for impulsive, emotionally negative, and aggressive children, who are at high risk for social difficulties (Brendgen et al., 2011; Vitaro et al., 2012). Other indicators of program quality—small group sizes, generous teacher–child ratios, and developmentally appropriate daily activities (see page 237 in Chapter 7)—create classroom conditions that make positive teacher and peer relationships more likely.

© LAURA DWIGHT PHOTOGRAPHY

▶ Parents' play with children, especially same-sex children, contributes to social competence. By playing with his father as he would with a peer, this child acquires social skills that facilitate peer interaction.

Parental Influences on Early Peer Relations

Children first acquire skills for interacting with peers within the family. Preschoolers whose parents frequently arrange informal peer play activities tend to have larger peer networks and to be more socially skilled (Ladd, LeSieur, & Profilet, 1993). In providing play opportunities, parents show children how to initiate peer contacts. And parents' skillful suggestions for managing conflict, discouraging teasing, and entering a play group are associated with preschoolers' social competence and peer acceptance (Mize & Pettit, 2010; Parke et al., 2004).

Many parenting behaviors not directly aimed at promoting peer sociability nevertheless influence it. For example, secure attachments to parents are linked to more responsive, harmonious peer interaction, larger peer networks, and warmer, more supportive friendships during the preschool and school years (Laible, 2007; Lucas-Thompson & Clarke-Stewart, 2007; Seibert & Kerns, 2015). The sensitive, emotionally expressive communication that contributes to attachment security is likely responsible.

Warm, collaborative parent–child play seems particularly effective for promoting peer interaction skills. During play, parents interact with their child on a "level playing field," much as peers do. And perhaps because parents play more with children of their own sex, mothers' play is more strongly linked to daughters' competence, fathers' play to sons' competence (Lindsey & Mize, 2000; Pettit et al., 1998).

As we have seen, some preschoolers already have great difficulty with peer relations. In Leslie's classroom, Robbie was one of them. Wherever he happened to be, comments like "Robbie ruined our block tower" and "Robbie hit me for no reason" could be heard. As we take up moral development and aggression in the next section, you will learn more about how parenting contributed to Robbie's peer problems.

ASK YOURSELF

CONNECT How does emotional self-regulation affect the development of empathy and sympathy? Why are these emotional capacities vital for positive peer relations?

APPLY Three-year-old Ben lives in the country, with no other preschoolers nearby. His parents wonder whether it is worth driving Ben into town once a week to participate in a peer play group. What advice would you give Ben's parents, and why?

REFLECT What did your parents do that might have influenced your earliest peer relationships?

Foundations of Morality and Aggression

8.5 Identify the central features of psychoanalytic, social learning, and cognitive-developmental approaches to moral development.

8.6 Describe the development of aggression in early childhood, including family and media influences and effective approaches to reducing aggressive behavior.

Young children's behavior provides many examples of their budding moral sense. We have seen that they show empathic concern for others in distress and will try to help. They also expect others to act fairly, by dividing resources equally among peers (Geraci & Surian, 2011). As early as age 2, they use language to evaluate their own and others' actions: "I naughty. I wrote on the wall" or (after being hit by another child) "Connie not nice." And we have seen that children of this age share toys, help others, and cooperate in games—early indicators of considerate, prosocial attitudes.

Adults everywhere take note of this developing capacity to distinguish right from wrong. Some cultures have special terms for it. The Utku Indians of Hudson Bay say the child develops *ihuma* (reason). The Fijians believe that *vakayalo* (sense) appears. In response, parents hold children more responsible for their actions (Dunn, 2005). By the end of early childhood, children can state many moral rules: "Don't take someone's things without asking!" "Tell the truth!" In addition, they argue over matters of justice: "You sat there last time, so it's my turn." "It's not fair. He got more!"

All theories of moral development recognize that conscience begins to take shape in early childhood. And most agree that at first, the child's morality is *externally controlled* by adults. Gradually, it becomes regulated by *inner standards.* Truly moral individuals do not do the right thing just to conform to others' expectations. Rather, they have developed compassionate concerns and principles of good conduct, which they follow in many situations.

Each major theory of development emphasizes a different aspect of morality. Psychoanalytic theory stresses the *emotional side* of conscience development—in particular, identification and guilt as motivators of good conduct. Social learning theory focuses on how *moral behavior* is learned through reinforcement and modeling. Finally, the cognitive-developmental perspective emphasizes *thinking*—children's ability to reason about justice and fairness.

The Psychoanalytic Perspective

Recall that according to Freud, young children form a *superego,* or conscience, by adopting the same-sex parent's moral standards. Children obey the superego to avoid *guilt,* a painful emotion that arises each time they are tempted to misbehave. Moral development, Freud believed, is largely complete by 5 to 6 years of age.

Today, most researchers disagree with Freud's view of conscience development. In his theory, fear of punishment and loss of parental love motivate conscience formation and moral behavior. Yet children whose parents frequently use threats, commands, or physical force tend to violate standards often and feel little guilt, whereas parental warmth and responsiveness predict greater guilt following transgressions (Kochanska et al., 2005, 2008). And if a parent withdraws love after misbehavior—for example, refuses to speak to or states a dislike for the child—children often respond with high levels of self-blame and with impaired self-esteem, thinking "I'm no good" or "Nobody loves me." Eventually, to protect themselves from overwhelming guilt, these children may deny the emotion and, as a result, also develop a weak conscience (Kochanska, 1991; Rudy et al., 2014).

Inductive Discipline.

In contrast, conscience formation is promoted by a type of discipline called **induction,** in which an adult helps make the child aware of feelings by pointing out the effects of the child's misbehavior on others. For example, a parent might say, "She's crying because you won't give back her doll" (Hoffman, 2000). Preschoolers with warm parents who use induction are more likely to refrain from wrongdoing, confess and repair damage after misdeeds, and display prosocial behavior (Choe, Olson, & Sameroff, 2013; Volling, Mahoney, & Rauer, 2009).

The success of induction may lie in its power to motivate children's active commitment to moral standards. Induction gives children information about how to behave that they can use in future situations. By emphasizing the impact of the child's actions on others, it encourages empathy and sympathetic concern. And giving children reasons for changing their behavior encourages them to adopt moral standards because those standards make sense.

▶ A teacher uses inductive discipline to explain to a child the impact of her transgression on others, pointing out classmates' feelings. Induction encourages empathy, sympathetic concern, and commitment to moral standards.

In contrast, discipline that relies too heavily on threats of punishment or withdrawal of love makes children so anxious and frightened that they cannot think clearly enough to figure out what they should do. As a result, these practices do not get children to internalize moral rules and—as noted earlier—also interfere with empathy and prosocial responding (Eisenberg, Spinrad, & Knafo-Noam, 2015).

The Child's Contribution.

Although good discipline is crucial, children's characteristics affect the success of parenting techniques. Twin studies suggest a modest genetic contribution to empathy (Knafo et al., 2009). More empathic children evoke less power assertion and are more responsive to induction.

Temperament is also influential. Mild, patient tactics—requests, suggestions, and explanations—are sufficient to prompt guilt reactions in anxious, fearful preschoolers (Kochanska et al., 2002). But with fearless, impulsive children, gentle discipline has little impact. Power assertion also works poorly. It undermines children's effortful control, or capacity to regulate their emotional reactivity, which is linked to good conduct, empathy, sympathy, and prosocial behavior (Kochanska & Aksan, 2006). Parents of impulsive children can foster conscience development by ensuring a warm, harmonious relationship and combining firm correction of misbehavior with induction (Kochanska & Kim, 2014). When children are so low in anxiety that parental disapproval causes them little discomfort, a close parent–child bond motivates them to listen to parents as a means of preserving an affectionate, supportive relationship.

The Role of Guilt. Although little support exists for Freudian ideas about conscience development, Freud was correct that guilt motivates moral action. Inducing *empathy-based guilt*—expressions of personal responsibility and regret, such as "I'm sorry I hurt him"—by explaining that the child is harming someone and has disappointed the parent is particularly effective (Eisenberg, Eggum, & Edwards, 2010). Empathy-based guilt reactions are associated with stopping harmful actions, repairing damage caused by misdeeds, and engaging in future prosocial behavior.

But contrary to what Freud believed, guilt is not the only force that compels us to act morally. Nor is moral development complete by the end of early childhood. Rather, it is a gradual process that extends into adulthood.

Social Learning Theory

According to social learning theory, morality is acquired through modeling, just like any other set of responses.

Importance of Modeling. Many studies show that having helpful or generous models increases young children's prosocial responses. Models are most influential in the early years. In one study, toddlers' eager, willing imitation of their mothers' behavior predicted moral conduct (not cheating in a game) and guilt following transgressions at age 3 (Forman, Aksan, & Kochanska, 2004). At the end of early childhood, children who have had consistent exposure to caring adults tend to behave prosocially whether or not a model is present (Mussen & Eisenberg-Berg, 1977). They have internalized prosocial rules from repeated observations and encouragement by others.

At the same time, reinforcing young children with attention or praise appears unnecessary to induce them to help others. Most 2-year-olds will readily help an unfamiliar adult obtain an out-of-reach object, regardless of whether their parent encourages them (Warneken & Tomasello, 2013). And giving children material rewards for helping undermines their prosocial responding (Warneken & Tomasello, 2009). Children who are materially rewarded come to expect something in return for helping and, therefore, rarely help spontaneously, out of kindness to others.

Effects of Punishment. A sharp reprimand or physical force to restrain or move a child is justified when immediate obedience is necessary—for example, when a 3-year-old is about to run into the street. In fact, parents are most likely to use forceful methods under these conditions. But to foster long-term goals, such as acting kindly toward others, they tend to rely on warmth and reasoning (Kuczynski, 1984; Lansford et al., 2012). And in response to serious transgressions, such as lying and stealing, they often combine power assertion with reasoning (Grusec, 2006).

Frequent punishment promotes immediate compliance but not lasting changes in behavior. For example, Robbie's parents often punished by hitting, shouting, and criticizing. But as soon as they stopped punishing and turned away, Robbie—like most children subjected to corporal punishment—misbehaved again (Holden, Williamson, & Holland, 2014). The more harsh threats, angry physical control, and physical punishment children experience, the more likely they are to develop serious, lasting problems. These include weak internalization of moral rules; depression, aggression, antisocial behavior, and poor academic performance in childhood and adolescence; and depression, alcohol abuse, criminality, physical health problems, and family violence in adulthood (Afifi et al., 2013; Bender et al., 2007; Kochanska, Aksan, & Nichols, 2003).

Repeated harsh punishment has wide-ranging undesirable side effects:

- It models aggression.
- It induces a chronic sense of being personally threatened, which prompts children to focus on their own distress rather than respond sympathetically to others.
- It causes children to avoid the punitive parent, who, as a result, has little opportunity to teach desirable behaviors.
- By stopping children's misbehavior temporarily, it offers immediate relief to adults, who may then punish more often—a course of action that can spiral into serious abuse.
- Children, adolescents, and adults whose parents used *corporal punishment*—physical force that inflicts pain but not injury—are more accepting of it (Deater-Deckard et al., 2003; Vitrup & Holden, 2010). In this way, use of physical punishment may transfer to the next generation.

Although corporal punishment spans the SES spectrum, its frequency and harshness are elevated among less-educated, economically disadvantaged parents (Giles-Sims, Straus, & Sugarman, 1995; Lansford et al., 2009). And consistently, parents with conflict-ridden marriages and with mental health problems are more likely to be punitive and also to have hard-to-manage children (Berlin et al., 2009; Taylor et al., 2010). But even after controlling for child, parenting, and family characteristics that might otherwise account for the relationship, the link between physical punishment and later child and adolescent aggression remains (Lansford et al., 2011; Lee, Altschul, & Gershoff, 2015; MacKenzie et al., 2013).

Physical punishment affects children with certain temperaments more than others. In a longitudinal study extending from 15 months to 3 years, early corporal punishment was a stronger predictor of externalizing behavior in temperamentally difficult children (Mulvaney & Mebert, 2007). Similar findings emerged in a twin study in which physical punishment was most detrimental for children at high genetic risk for behavior problems (Boutwell et al., 2011).

Surveys of nationally representative samples of U.S. families reveal that although corporal punishment typically increases from infancy to age 5 and then declines, it is high at all ages (see Figure 8.1) (Gershoff et al., 2012; Straus & Stewart, 1999; Zolotor et al., 2011). More than one-third of physically punishing parents report having used a hard object, such as a brush or a belt.

A prevailing American belief is that corporal punishment, if implemented by caring parents, is harmless, perhaps even beneficial. But as the Cultural Influences box on page 258 reveals, this assumption is valid only under conditions of limited use in certain social contexts.

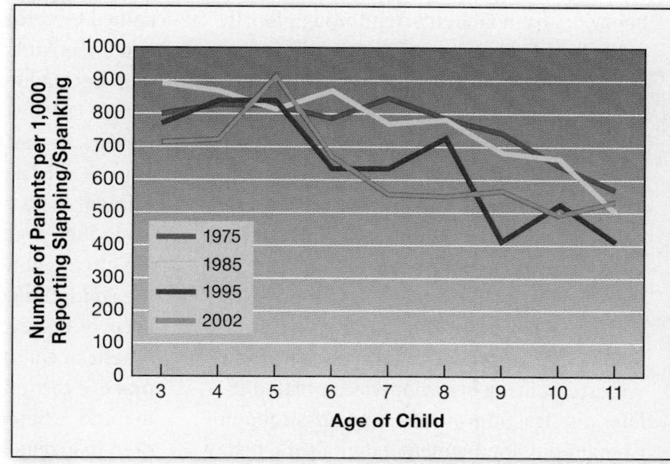

FIGURE 8.1 Prevalence of corporal punishment in early and middle childhood by year of survey. Five large surveys of U.S. parents show little change in use of corporal punishment over nearly three decades. Estimates are based on the number of parents per 1,000 reporting one or more instances of spanking or slapping their child during the past year. Rates are not shown for infants and toddlers, though other evidence indicates that 50 to 80 percent experience physical punishment. (From A. J. Zolotor, A. D. Theodore, D. K. Runyan, J. J. Chang, & A. L. Laskey, 2011, "Corporal Punishment and Physical Abuse: Population-Based Trends for Three- to 11-Year-Old Children in the United States," *Child Abuse Review, 20,* p. 61. Reprinted by permission of John Wiley & Sons, Ltd.)

Alternatives to Harsh Punishment. Alternatives to criticism, slaps, and spankings can reduce the side effects of punishment. A technique called **time out** involves removing children from the immediate setting—for example, by sending them to their rooms—until they are ready to act appropriately. When a child is out of control, a few minutes in time out can be enough to change behavior while also giving angry parents time to cool off (Morawska & Sanders, 2011). Another approach is *withdrawal of privileges,* such as watching a favorite TV program. Like time out, removing privileges allows parents to avoid using harsh techniques that can easily intensify into violence.

When parents do decide to use mild punishment, they can increase its effectiveness in three ways:

- *Consistency.* Permitting children to act inappropriately on some occasions but scolding them on others confuses them, and the unacceptable act persists (Acker & O'Leary, 1996).
- *A warm parent–child relationship.* Children of involved, caring parents find the interruption in parental affection that accompanies punishment especially unpleasant. They want to regain parental warmth and approval as quickly as possible.

CULTURAL INFLUENCES

Ethnic Differences in the Consequences of Physical Punishment

An impressive number of studies report ethnic variations in the consequences of physical punishment. In one longitudinal investigation, researchers followed several hundred families, collecting information from mothers on disciplinary strategies and from teachers on children's problem behaviors from kindergarten through fourth grade (Lansford et al., 2012). Regardless of ethnicity, reasoning was the most common approach to discipline, spanking the least common. But predictors and consequences of spanking differed by family ethnicity.

Among European-American families, externalizing behavior in kindergarten predicted parental physical punishment in first through third grades, which in turn led to more externalizing behavior by fourth grade. In contrast, among African-American families, kindergarten externalizing behavior was unrelated to later physical punishment, and physical punishment did not augment externalizing behavior (Lansford et al., 2012). The investigators concluded that European-American parents more often use physical discipline in reaction to challenging behaviors, causing those behaviors to escalate. African-American parents, in contrast, seem to use physical punishment to prevent child difficulties, thereby reducing its negative consequences.

Consistent with this interpretation, African-American and European-American parents report meting out physical punishment differently. In African-American families, such discipline is typically culturally approved, mild, delivered in a context of parental warmth, accompanied by verbal teaching, and aimed at helping children become responsible adults. European-American parents, in contrast, usually consider physical punishment to be wrong, so when they resort to it, they are often highly agitated and rejecting of the child (Dodge, McLoyd, & Lansford, 2006; LeCuyer et al., 2011). As a result, most African-American children may view spanking as a practice carried out with their best interests in mind, whereas European-American children may regard it as an act of aggression.

© LAURA DWIGHT PHOTOGRAPHY

In African-American families, physical discipline is often culturally approved, generally mild, and delivered in a context of parental warmth. As a result, children may view it as an effort to encourage maturity, not as an act of aggression.

In support of this view, when several thousand ethnically diverse children were followed from the preschool through the early school years, spanking was associated with a rise in behavior problems if parents were cold and rejecting, but not if they were warm and supportive (McLoyd & Smith, 2002). In another study, spanking predicted depressive symptoms only among a small number of African-American children whose mothers disapproved of the practice and, as a result, tended to use it when they were highly angry and frustrated (McLoyd et al., 2007).

These findings are not an endorsement of physical punishment. Other forms of discipline, including time out, withdrawal of privileges, and the positive parenting strategies listed on page 259, are far more effective.

In adolescence, ethnic differences in physical punishment fade: It is broadly associated with depression and misconduct among teenagers (Wang & Kenny, 2014). But it is noteworthy that the meaning and impact of physical discipline to children can vary sharply with its intensity level, context of warmth and support, and cultural approval.

- *Explanations.* Providing reasons for mild punishment helps children relate the misdeed to expectations for future behavior (Larzelere et al., 1996). This approach leads to a far greater reduction in misbehavior than using punishment alone.

Positive Relationships, Positive Parenting. The most effective forms of discipline encourage good conduct—by building a mutually respectful bond with the child, letting the child know ahead of time how to act, and acknowledging mature behavior ("You helped clear the dishes. That was kind"). When sensitivity, cooperation, and shared positive emotion are evident in joint activities between parents and preschoolers, children show firmer conscience development—expressing empathy after transgressions, playing fairly in games, and considering others' welfare (Kochanska et al., 2008; Thompson, 2014). Parent–child closeness leads children to heed parental demands because the child feels a sense of commitment to the relationship.

APPLYING WHAT WE KNOW

Positive Parenting

STRATEGY	EXPLANATION
Use transgressions as opportunities to teach.	When a child engages in harmful or unsafe behavior, intervene firmly, and then use induction, which motivates children to make amends and behave prosocially.
Reduce opportunities for misbehavior.	On a long car trip, bring back-seat activities that relieve children's restlessness. At the supermarket, converse with children and let them help with shopping. Children then learn to occupy themselves constructively when options are limited.
Provide reasons for rules.	When children appreciate that rules are rational, not arbitrary, they are more likely to strive to follow the rules.
Arrange for children to participate in family routines and duties.	By joining with adults in preparing a meal, clearing the table, or raking leaves, children develop a sense of responsible participation in family and community life and acquire many practical skills.
When children are obstinate, try compromising and problem solving.	When a child refuses to obey, express understanding of the child's feelings ("I know it's not fun to clean up"), suggest a compromise ("You put those away, I'll take care of these"), and help the child think of ways to avoid the problem in the future. Responding firmly but kindly and respectfully increases the likelihood of willing cooperation.
Encourage mature behavior.	Express confidence in children's capacity to learn and appreciation for effort and cooperation: "You gave that your best!" "Thanks for cleaning up on your own!" Adult encouragement fosters pride and satisfaction in succeeding, thereby inspiring children to improve further.

Sources: Berk, 2001; Grusec, 2006.

See Applying What We Know above for ways to parent positively. After experiencing a training program in these strategies, parents felt more confident about their ability to handle child-rearing challenges and were less approving of physical punishment (Durrant et al., 2014). When parents focus on promoting children's cooperation, problem solving, and consideration for others, they greatly reduce the need for punishment.

The Cognitive-Developmental Perspective

The psychoanalytic and social learning approaches to morality focus on how children acquire ready-made standards of good conduct from adults. In contrast, the cognitive-developmental perspective regards children as *active thinkers* about social rules. As early as the preschool years, children make moral judgments, deciding what is right or wrong on the basis of concepts they construct about justice and fairness (Gibbs, 2014; Helwig & Turiel, 2011).

Young children have some well-developed ideas about morality. As long as researchers emphasize people's intentions, 3-year-olds say that a person with bad intentions—someone who deliberately frightens, embarrasses, or otherwise hurts another—is more deserving of punishment than a well-intentioned person. They also protest when they see one person harming another (Helwig, Zelazo, & Wilson, 2001; Vaish, Missana, & Tomasello, 2011). Around age 4, children know that a person who expresses an insincere intention—saying, "I'll come over and help you rake leaves," while not intending to do so—is lying (Maas, 2008). And 4-year-olds approve of telling the truth and disapprove of lying, even when a lie remains undetected (Bussey, 1992).

Furthermore, preschoolers distinguish **moral imperatives,** which protect people's rights and welfare, from two other types of rules and expectations: **social conventions,** customs determined solely by consensus, such as table manners and politeness rituals (saying "please" and "thank you"); and **matters of personal choice,** such as choice of friends, hairstyle, and leisure activities, which do not violate rights and are up to the individual (Killen, Margie, & Sinno, 2006; Nucci & Gingo, 2011; Smetana, 2006). Interviews with 3- and 4-year-olds reveal that they consider moral violations (stealing an apple) as more wrong than violations of social conventions (eating ice cream with your fingers). And preschoolers' concern with personal choice, conveyed through statements like "I'm

© JEFF GREENBERG/PHOTOEDIT

▶ This preschooler understands that his choice of a toy is a matter of personal choice, distinct from moral imperatives and social conventions.

gonna wear *this* shirt," serves as the springboard for moral concepts of individual rights.

Young children's moral reasoning tends to be *rigid,* emphasizing salient features and consequences while neglecting other important information. For example, they have difficulty distinguishing between accidental and intentional transgressions (Killen et al., 2011). And they are more likely than older children to claim that stealing and lying are always wrong, even when a person has a morally sound reason for engaging in these acts (Lourenço, 2003). Furthermore, their explanations for why hitting others is wrong are simplistic and centered on physical harm: "When you get hit, it hurts, and you start to cry" (Nucci, 2009).

Children's commitment to the wrongness of moral transgressions builds on their early concern for others' welfare. With language and cognitive development—especially, in theory of mind and in understanding of emotion—older preschoolers start to reason morally by referring to others' perspectives and feelings. In several studies, understanding of false belief was associated with 4- and 5-year-olds' moral justifications that focused on the harmed individual's emotions and well-being (Dunn, Cutting, & Demetriou, 2000; Lane et al., 2010). But advances in theory of mind, though influencing preschoolers' explanations, are not sufficient to account for gains in moral understanding.

In addition, morally relevant social experiences are vital, contributing to gains in both theory of mind and moral understanding and to their integration (Killen & Smetana, 2015). Disputes with siblings and peers over rights, possessions, and property allow preschoolers to express emotions and perspectives, negotiate, compromise, and work out their first ideas about justice and fairness. Children also learn from warm, sensitive parental communication and from observing how adults respond to children's rule violations (Turiel & Killen, 2010). Children who are advanced in moral thinking tend to have parents who adapt their discussions about fighting, honesty, and ownership to what their children can understand, tell stories with moral implications, point out injustices, encourage prosocial behavior, and gently stimulate the child to think further (Dunn, 2014; Janssens & Deković, 1997).

Preschoolers and school-age children who verbally and physically assault others, often with little or no provocation, are delayed in moral reasoning (Ciu et al., 2016; Helwig & Turiel, 2004). Without special help, such children show long-term disruptions in moral development.

The Other Side of Morality: Development of Aggression

Beginning in late infancy, all children display aggression from time to time, and as opportunities to interact with siblings and peers increase, aggressive outbursts occur more often (Naerde et al., 2014). By the second year, aggressive acts with two distinct purposes emerge. Initially, the most common is **proactive** (or *instrumental*) **aggression,** in which children act to fulfill a need or desire—to obtain an object, privilege, space, or social reward, such as adult or peer attention—and unemotionally attack a person to achieve their goal. The other type, **reactive** (or *hostile*) **aggression,** is an angry, defensive response to provocation or a blocked goal and is meant to hurt another person (Eisner & Malti, 2015; Vitaro & Brendgen, 2012).

Proactive and reactive aggression come in three forms:

- **Physical aggression** harms others through physical injury—pushing, hitting, kicking, or punching others, or destroying another's property.
- **Verbal aggression** harms others through threats of physical aggression, name-calling, or hostile teasing.
- **Relational aggression** damages another's peer relationships through social exclusion, malicious gossip, or friendship manipulation.

Physical aggression rises sharply between ages 1 and 3 and then diminishes as verbal aggression replaces it (Alink et al., 2006; Vitaro & Brendgen, 2012). And proactive aggression declines as preschoolers' improved capacity to delay gratification enables them to resist grabbing others' possessions. But reactive aggression in verbal and relational forms tends to rise over early and middle childhood (Côté et al., 2007; Tremblay, 2000). Older children are better able to recognize malicious intentions and, as a result, more often retaliate in hostile ways.

By age 17 months, boys are more physically aggressive than girls—a difference found throughout childhood in many cultures (Baillargeon et al., 2007; Card et al., 2008). The sex difference is due in part to biology—in particular, to male sex hormones (androgens) and temperamental traits (activity level, irritability, impulsivity) on which boys exceed girls. Gender-role conformity is also important. For example, parents respond far more negatively to physical fighting in girls (Arnold, McWilliams, & Harvey-Arnold, 1998).

Although girls have a reputation for being both verbally and relationally more aggressive than boys, the sex difference is small (Crick, Ostrov, & Werner, 2006; Crick et al., 2006). Beginning in the preschool years, girls concentrate most of their aggressive acts in the relational category. Boys inflict harm in more variable ways. Physically and verbally aggressive boys also tend to be relationally aggressive (Card et al., 2008). Therefore, boys display overall rates of aggression that are much higher than girls'.

At the same time, girls more often use indirect relational tactics that—in disrupting intimate bonds especially important to girls—can be particularly mean. Whereas physical attacks are usually brief, acts of indirect relational aggression may extend for hours, weeks, or even months (Nelson, Robinson, & Hart, 2005; Underwood, 2003). In one instance, a 6-year-old girl formed a "pretty-girls club" and—for nearly an entire school year—convinced its members to exclude several classmates by saying they were "dirty and smelly."

▶ These preschoolers display proactive aggression, pushing and grabbing as they argue over a game. As children learn to compromise and share, and as their capacity to delay gratification improves, proactive aggression declines.

Children who are emotionally negative, impulsive, and disobedient and who score low in cognitive abilities—especially, language and executive function skills necessary for self-regulation—are at risk for early, high rates of physical or relational aggression (or both) that can persist. Persistent aggression, in turn, predicts later internalizing and externalizing difficulties and social skills deficits, including loneliness, anxiety, depression, peer relationship problems, and antisocial activity in middle childhood and adolescence (Eisner & Malti, 2015; Hay, 2017; Ostrov et al., 2013).

The Family as Training Ground for Aggressive Behavior. "I can't control him," Robbie's mother, Nadine, complained to Leslie one day. When Leslie asked if Robbie might be troubled by something happening at home, she discovered that his parents fought constantly and resorted to harsh, inconsistent discipline. Parental power assertion, critical remarks, physical punishment, and inconsistency are linked to aggression from early childhood through adolescence in many cultures, with most of these practices predicting both physical and relational forms (Côté et al., 2007; Gershoff et al., 2010; Kuppens et al., 2013; Nelson et al., 2013; Olson et al., 2011).

In families like Robbie's, anger and punitiveness quickly create a conflict-ridden family atmosphere and an "out-of-control" child. The pattern begins with forceful discipline, which occurs more often with stressful life experiences (such as economic hardship or an unhappy marriage), parental mental health problems, or a temperamentally difficult child (Baydar & Akcinar, 2017; Eisner & Malti, 2015). Typically, the parent threatens, criticizes, and punishes, and the child angrily resists until the parent "gives in," so the behaviors repeat and escalate.

These cycles generate anxiety and irritability among other family members, including siblings, who join in the hostile interactions. Destructive sibling conflict, in turn, spreads to peer relationships, contributing to poor impulse control and antisocial behavior by the early school years (Miller et al., 2012).

Boys are more likely than girls to be targets of harsh, inconsistent discipline because they are more active and impulsive and therefore harder to control. When children who are extreme in these characteristics are exposed to emotionally negative, inept parenting, their capacity for emotional self-regulation, empathic responding, and guilt after transgressions is seriously disrupted (Eisenberg, Eggum, & Edwards, 2010). Consequently, they lash out when disappointed, frustrated, or faced with a sad or fearful victim.

Children subjected to these family processes acquire a distorted view of the social world, often seeing hostile intent where it does not exist and, as a result, making many unprovoked attacks (Healy et al., 2015; Orbio de Castro et al., 2002). And some, who conclude that aggression "works" to access rewards and control others, callously use it to advance their own goals and are unconcerned about causing suffering in others—an aggressive style associated with later more severe conduct problems, violent behavior, and delinquency (Marsee & Frick, 2010).

LOOK AND LISTEN

Watch a half-hour of cartoons and a prime-time movie on TV, and tally the number of violent acts, including those that go unpunished. How often did violence, especially without consequences, occur in each type of program?

Media Violence and Aggression. In the United States, an estimated 60 percent of television programs contain violent scenes, often portraying repeated aggressive acts that go unpunished. TV victims of violence are rarely shown experiencing serious harm, and few programs condemn violence or depict other ways of solving problems (Calvert, 2015). Violent content is 10 percent above average in children's TV programs and videos, with cartoons being the most violent. And over the past several decades, violent video games have become increasingly realistic (Hartmann, Möller, & Krause, 2015). Many portray extreme, graphic violence.

Assessing the findings of thousands of studies, the overwhelming majority of researchers have concluded that violent screen media—including TV programs, movies, and video games—increase the likelihood of hostile thoughts and emotions and of verbally, physically, and relationally aggressive behavior (Anderson et al., 2015; Bushman, Gollwitzer, & Cruz, 2015; Bushman & Huesmann, 2012; Strasburger, Wilson, & Jordan, 2013). Although young people of all ages are susceptible, preschool and young school-age children may be especially likely to imitate screen media violence because they believe that much of it is real and accept what they see uncritically.

In addition to creating short-term difficulties in parent and peer relations, violent media fare can have lasting negative consequences. In several longitudinal studies, children's violent media exposure in childhood and adolescence predicted aggressive behavior in adulthood, after other factors linked to TV viewing (such as prior child and parent aggression, IQ, parent education, family income, and neighborhood crime) were controlled (Graber et al., 2006; Huesmann et al., 2003; Johnson et al., 2002). And in a longitudinal investigation of over 3,000 children and adolescents, violent video game play led to an increase in aggressive thoughts a year later, which in turn predicted a rise in aggressive behavior the following year (Gentile et al., 2014).

© ALEX SEGRE/ALAMY

▶ Watching TV violence increases the likelihood of hostile thoughts and emotions and aggressive behavior. Playing violent video and computer games has similar effects.

Aggressive children and adolescents have a greater appetite for violent media fare. And boys devote more time to violent media than girls, in part because of male-oriented themes of conquest and adventure. But even in nonaggressive children, violent TV sparks hostile thoughts and behavior (Anderson et al., 2015). Its impact is simply less intense.

Surveys of U.S. parents indicate that 20 to 30 percent of preschoolers and about half of school-age children experience no limits on TV, computer, or tablet use (Rideout & Hamel, 2006; Roberts, Foehr, & Rideout, 2005; Varnhagen, 2007). And parents often model excessive, inappropriate use of screen media. In observations of adults with children in fast-food restaurants, almost one-third of the adults spent the entire meal absorbed with mobile devices rather than engaged with children in their care (Radesky et al., 2014).

To help parents improve their preschoolers' "media diet," one group of researchers devised a year-long

APPLYING WHAT WE KNOW

Regulating Screen Media Use

STRATEGY	DESCRIPTION
Limit TV viewing and computer and tablet use.	Parents should provide clear rules limiting children's TV viewing and computer and tablet use and should stick to the rules. The TV or computer should not be used as a babysitter. Placing a TV or a computer in a child's bedroom substantially increases use and makes the child's activity hard to monitor.
Avoid using screen media as a reward.	When media access is used as a reward or withheld as a punishment, children become increasingly attracted to it.
When possible, watch TV and view online content with children, helping them understand what they see.	By raising questions about realism in media depictions, expressing disapproval of on-screen behavior, and encouraging discussion, adults help children understand and critically evaluate TV and online content.
Link TV and online content to everyday learning experiences.	Parents can extend TV and online learning in ways that encourage children to engage actively with their surroundings. For example, a program on animals might spark a trip to the zoo, a visit to the library for a book about animals, or new ways of observing and caring for the family pet.
Model good media practices.	Parents' media behavior influences children's behavior. Parents should avoid excessive media use, limit their own exposure to harmful content, and limit mobile device use during family interactions.

intervention in which they guided parents in replacing violent programs with age-appropriate educational and prosocial programs. Compared to a control group, children in intervention families displayed lower rates of externalizing behavior and improved social competence (Christakis et al., 2013). Applying What We Know above lists strategies parents can use to regulate children's screen media use.

Helping Children and Parents Control Aggression. Treatment for aggressive children is best begun early, before their behavior becomes well-practiced and difficult to change. Breaking the cycle of hostilities between family members and promoting effective ways of relating to others are crucial.

Leslie suggested that Robbie's parents enroll in a training program aimed at improving the parenting of children with conduct problems. In one approach, called *Incredible Years,* parents complete 18 weekly group sessions facilitated by two professionals, who teach positive parenting techniques for promoting children's academic, emotional, and social skills and for managing disruptive behaviors (Webster-Stratton & Reid, 2010). A special focus is positive parenting, including encouragement for prosocial behaviors.

Evaluations in which families with aggressive children were randomly assigned to either Incredible Years or control groups revealed that the program improved parenting and reduced child behavior problems. And the effects endure. In one long-term follow-up, 75 percent of young children with serious conduct problems whose parents participated in Incredible Years were well-adjusted as teenagers (Webster-Stratton, Rinaldi, & Reid, 2011).

At preschool, Leslie encouraged Robbie to talk about playmates' feelings and to express his own. As he increasingly took the perspective of others, empathized, and felt sympathetic concern, his lashing out at peers declined. Robbie also participated in a social problem-solving intervention. Throughout the school year, he met weekly with Leslie and a small group of classmates to act out common conflicts using puppets, discuss alternatives for settling disputes, and practice successful strategies. Preschoolers who receive such training show gains in emotional and social competence still present after entering kindergarten (Bierman & Powers, 2009; Moore et al., 2015).

Finally, relieving stressors that stem from economic disadvantage and neighborhood disorganization and providing families with social supports help prevent childhood aggression (Bugental, Corpuz, & Schwartz, 2012). When parents better cope with stressors in their own lives, interventions aimed at reducing children's aggression are more effective.

ASK YOURSELF

CONNECT What must parents do to foster conscience development in fearless, impulsive children? How does this illustrate the concept of goodness of fit (see page 183 in Chapter 6)?

APPLY Alice and Wayne want their two children to become morally mature, caring individuals. List some parenting practices they should use and some they should avoid.

REFLECT Which types of punishment for a misbehaving preschooler do you endorse, and which types do you reject? Why?

Gender Typing

8.7 Discuss biological and environmental influences on preschoolers' gender-stereotyped beliefs and behavior.

8.8 Describe and evaluate theories that explain the emergence of gender identity.

Gender typing refers to any association of objects, activities, roles, or traits with one sex or the other in ways that conform to cultural stereotypes (Blakemore, Berenbaum, & Liben, 2009). Already, the children in Leslie's classroom had acquired many gender-linked beliefs and preferences and tended to play with peers of their own sex.

Social learning theory, with its emphasis on modeling and reinforcement, and *cognitive-developmental theory,* with its focus on children as active thinkers about their social world, offer contemporary explanations of children's gender typing. As we will see, neither is adequate by itself. *Gender schema theory,* a third perspective that combines elements of both, has gained favor. In the following sections, we consider the early development of gender typing.

Early in the preschool years, gender typing is well under way. Girls tend to play with girls and are drawn to toys and activities that emphasize nurturance and cooperation.

Gender-Stereotyped Beliefs and Behavior

Recall from Chapter 6 that around age 2, children use such words as *boy, girl, lady,* and *man* appropriately. As soon as gender categories are established, young children's gender-typed learning accelerates.

Preschoolers associate toys, clothing, tools, household items, games, occupations, colors (pink and blue), and behaviors (physical and relational aggression) with one sex or the other (Banse et al., 2010; Giles & Heyman, 2005; Poulin-Dubois et al., 2002). And their actions reflect their beliefs, not only in play preferences but also in personality traits. As we have seen, boys tend to be more active, impulsive, assertive, and physically aggressive. Girls tend to be more fearful, dependent, emotionally sensitive, compliant, advanced in effortful control, and skilled at inflicting relational aggression (Else-Quest, 2012).

During early childhood, gender-stereotyped beliefs strengthen—so much so that many children apply them as blanket rules rather than as flexible guidelines (Halim et al., 2013; Trautner et al., 2005). When children were asked whether gender stereotypes could be violated, half or more of 3- and 4-year-olds answered "no" to clothing, hairstyle, and play with certain toys (Barbie dolls and G.I. Joes) (Blakemore, 2003). Furthermore, most 3- to 6-year-olds are firm about not wanting to be friends with a child who violates a gender stereotype (a boy who wears nail polish, a girl who plays with trucks) or to attend a school where such violations are allowed (Ruble et al., 2007).

These rigid, one-sided judgments are a joint product of gender stereotyping in the environment and young children's cognitive limitations. Most preschoolers do not yet realize that characteristics *associated with* being male or female—activities, toys, occupations, hairstyle, and clothing—do not *determine* a person's sex.

Biological Influences on Gender Typing

The sex differences in personality traits and behavior described earlier appear in many cultures around the world (Munroe & Romney, 2006). Certain ones—male activity level and physical aggression, female emotional sensitivity, and preference for same-sex playmates—are widespread among mammalian species (de Waal, 2001). According to an evolutionary perspective, the adult life of our male ancestors was largely oriented toward competing for mates, that of our female ancestors toward rearing children. Therefore, males became genetically primed for dominance and females for intimacy, responsiveness, and cooperativeness (Konner, 2010; Maccoby, 2002).

Experiments with nonhuman mammals reveal that prenatally administered androgens increase active play and aggression and suppress maternal caregiving in both males and females (Arnold, 2009). Research with humans shows similar patterns. Girls exposed prenatally to high levels of androgens, due to normal variation in hormone levels or to a genetic defect, show more "masculine" behavior—a preference for trucks and blocks over dolls, for active over quiet play, and for boys as playmates—even when parents encourage them to engage in gender-typical play (Berenbaum & Beltz, 2011; Hines, 2011). And boys with reduced prenatal androgen exposure, either because production by the testes is reduced or because body cells are androgen insensitive, tend to engage in "feminine" behaviors, including toy choices, play behaviors, and preference for girl playmates (Jürgensen et al., 2007; Lamminmaki et al., 2012).

Some researchers argue that biologically based sex differences, which affect children's play styles, cause children to seek out same-sex playmates whose interests and behaviors are compatible with their own (Maccoby, 1998; Mehta & Strough, 2009). Preschool girls like to play in pairs with other girls because they share a preference for quieter activities involving cooperative roles. Boys prefer larger-group play with other boys, due to a shared desire to run, climb, play-fight, and compete.

Research confirms that preschoolers are drawn to peers who engage in similar levels of gender-typed activities. But they also like to spend time with same-sex peers regardless of type of activity—perhaps because they expect a playmate who is like themselves in so basic a way to be more enjoyable (Martin et al., 2013). At age 4, children spend three times as much time with same-sex as with other-sex playmates. By age 6, this ratio has climbed to 11 to 1 (Martin & Fabes, 2001).

Environmental Influences on Gender Typing

A wealth of evidence reveals that environmental forces—at home, at school, with peers, and in the community—build on genetic influences to promote vigorous gender typing in early childhood.

Parents. Beginning at birth, parents have different expectations of sons than of daughters. Many parents prefer that their children play with "gender-appropriate" toys (Blakemore & Hill, 2008). And they tend to describe achievement, competition, and control of emotion as important for sons and warmth, polite behavior, and closely supervised activities as important for daughters (Brody, 1999; Turner & Gervai, 1995).

Parenting practices reflect these beliefs. Parents give their sons toys that stress action and competition (cars, tools, footballs) and their daughters toys that emphasize nurturance, cooperation, and physical attractiveness (dolls, tea sets, jewelry) (Leaper, 1994; Leaper & Friedman, 2007). Fathers of preschoolers report more physical activities (chasing, playing ball) with sons and more literacy activities (reading, storytelling) with daughters (Leavell et al., 2011). Furthermore, parents tend to react more positively when a son plays with cars and trucks, demands attention, runs and climbs, or tries to take toys from others. When interacting with daughters, parents more often direct play activities, provide help, encourage participation in household tasks, refer to emotions, and express approval and agreement (Clearfield & Nelson, 2006; Fagot & Hagan, 1991; Leaper, 2000).

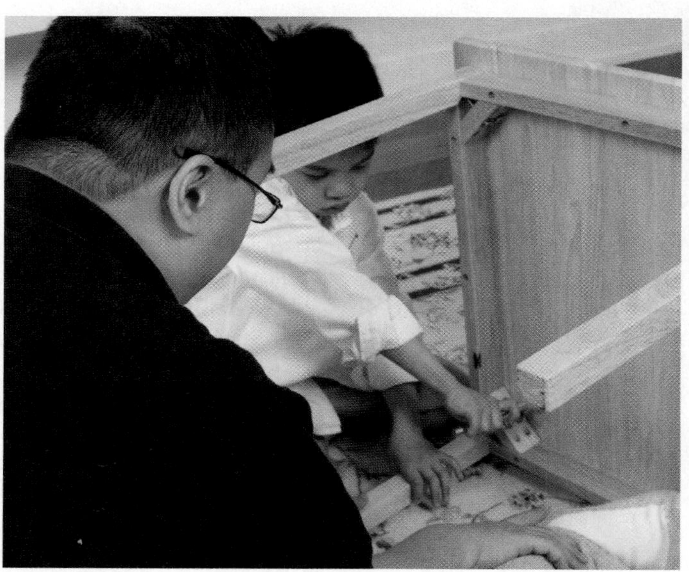

▶ This father teaches his son carpentry skills. Of the two sexes, boys are more gender-typed. Fathers, especially, promote "masculine" behavior in their sons by insisting that they conform to gender roles.

Parents also provide children with indirect cues about gender stereotypes through the language they use. In a study of picture book reading with toddlers and preschoolers, mothers frequently expressed *generic utterances,* which referred to nearly all same-sex individuals as alike, ignoring exceptions ("Boys can be sailors," "Most girls don't like trucks") (Gelman, Taylor, & Nguyen, 2004). Children readily picked up these expressions from their mother's speech, which their mothers often affirmed (Child: "Only boys can drive trucks," Mother: "Okay").

Of the two sexes, boys are more gender-typed. Fathers, especially, are more insistent that boys conform to gender roles. They place more pressure to achieve on sons and are less tolerant of sons' "cross-gender" behavior—more concerned when a boy acts like a "sissy" than when a girl acts like a "tomboy" (Blakemore & Hill, 2008; Wood, Desmarais, & Gugula, 2002).

Parents who hold nonstereotyped values have less gender-typed children (Tenenbaum & Leaper, 2002). Children of lesbian parents tend to be less gender-typed than their agemates of heterosexual or gay parents (Goldberg & Garcia, 2016; Goldberg, Kashy, & Smith, 2012). Lesbian mothers, due to their female gender and sexual minority status, may be especially accepting of "cross-gender" behavior in their children.

Teachers. Teachers often act in ways that extend gender-role learning. Several times, Leslie caught herself emphasizing gender distinctions when she called out, "Will the girls line up on one side and the boys on the other?" or pleaded, "Boys, I wish you'd quiet down like the girls!" These practices increase preschoolers' gender-stereotyped beliefs while reducing their liking for and willingness to play with other-sex peers (Hilliard & Liben, 2010).

Like parents, preschool teachers encourage girls to participate in adult-structured activities. Girls frequently cluster around the teacher, following directions, while boys are attracted to play areas where adults are minimally involved (Campbell, Shirley, & Candy, 2004). As a result, boys and girls engage in different social behaviors. Compliance and bids for help occur more often in adult-structured contexts; assertiveness, leadership, and creative use of materials in unstructured pursuits.

As early as kindergarten, teachers give more overall attention (both positive and negative) to boys than to girls—a difference evident in diverse countries, including China, England, and the United States. They praise boys more for their academic knowledge but also use more disapproval and controlling discipline with them (Chen & Rao, 2011; Davies, 2008; Swinson & Harrop, 2009). Teachers seem to expect boys to misbehave more often—a belief based partly on boys' actual behavior and partly on gender stereotypes.

In this preschool classroom, girls cluster around the teacher for instruction while boys play independently. As a result, children practice gender-typed behaviors—compliance and bids for attention by girls, assertiveness and leadership by boys.

Peers. Children's same-sex peers are a potent source of gender-role learning. By age 3, same-sex peers positively reinforce one another for gender-typed play by praising, imitating, or joining in. In contrast, when preschoolers engage in "cross-gender" activities—for example, when boys play with dolls or girls with cars and trucks—peers criticize them (Thorne, 1993). Boys are especially intolerant of cross-gender play in other boys.

Children also develop different styles of social influence in gender-segregated peer groups. To get their way in large-group play, boys often rely on commands, threats, and physical force. Girls' preference for playing in pairs leads to greater concern with a partner's needs, evident in girls' use of polite requests, persuasion, and acceptance. Girls soon find that gentle tactics succeed with other girls but not with boys, who ignore their courteous overtures (Leaper, 1994; Leaper, Tenenbaum, & Shaffer, 1999). Boys' unresponsiveness gives girls another reason to stop interacting with them.

Over time, children come to believe in the "correctness" of gender-segregated play and to perceive themselves as more similar to same-sex than other-sex peers, which further strengthens gender segregation and gender-stereotyped activities (Martin et al., 2011). As boys and girls separate, *in-group favoritism*—more positive evaluations of members of one's own gender—becomes another factor that sustains the separate social worlds of boys and girls. As a result, "two distinct subcultures" of knowledge, beliefs, interests, and behaviors form (Maccoby, 2002).

The Broader Social Environment. Finally, children's everyday environments present many examples of gender-typed behavior—in occupations, leisure activities, media portrayals, and achievements of men and women. Media stereotypes, which are especially prevalent in cartoons and video games, contribute to young children's biased beliefs about roles and behaviors suitable for males and females (Calvert, 2015; Leaper, 2013). As we will see next, children soon come to view not just their social surroundings but also themselves through a "gender-biased lens"—a perspective that can seriously restrict their interests and learning opportunities.

Gender Identity

As adults, each of us has a **gender identity**—an image of oneself as relatively masculine or feminine in characteristics. By middle childhood, researchers can measure gender identity by asking children to rate themselves on personality traits. A child or adult with a "masculine" identity scores high on traditionally masculine items (such as *ambitious, competitive,* and *self-sufficient*) and low on traditionally feminine items (such as *affectionate, cheerful,* and *soft-spoken*). Someone with a "feminine" identity does the reverse. And a substantial minority (especially females) have a gender identity called **androgyny,** scoring high on both masculine and feminine personality characteristics.

Gender identity is a good predictor of psychological adjustment. "Masculine" and androgynous children and adults have higher self-esteem than "feminine" individuals (DiDonato & Berenbaum, 2011; Harter, 2012). Also, androgynous individuals are more adaptable—able to show masculine independence or feminine sensitivity, depending on the situation (Huyck, 1996; Taylor & Hall, 1982). The existence of an androgynous identity demonstrates that children can acquire a mixture of positive qualities traditionally associated with each gender—an orientation that may best help them realize their potential.

Emergence of Gender Identity. How do children develop a gender identity? According to *social learning theory,* behavior comes before self-perceptions. Preschoolers first acquire gender-typed responses through modeling and reinforcement and only later organize these behaviors into gender-linked ideas about themselves. In contrast, *cognitive-developmental theory* maintains that self-perceptions come before behavior. Over the preschool years, children acquire **gender constancy**—a full understanding of the biologically based permanence of their gender, including the realization that sex remains the same even if clothing, hairstyle, and play activities change. Then children use this knowledge to guide their gender-related behavior.

Children younger than age 6 who watch an adult dress a doll in "other-gender" clothing typically insist that the doll's sex has also changed (Chauhan, Shastri, & Mohite, 2005; Fagot, 1985). Full attainment of gender constancy is strongly related to ability to pass Piagetian conservation tasks (DiLisi & Gallagher, 1991). Indeed, gender constancy tasks can be considered a type of conservation problem, in that children must conserve a person's sex despite a superficial change in his or her appearance.

Is cognitive-developmental theory correct that gender constancy is responsible for children's gender-typed behavior? Evidence for this assumption is weak. Some findings suggest that attaining gender constancy actually contributes to more flexible gender-role attitudes, perhaps because children then realize that engaging in gender-atypical behavior cannot cause their sex to change (Ruble et al., 2007). But overall, the impact of gender constancy on gender typing is not great. As research in the following section reveals, gender-role adoption is more powerfully affected by children's beliefs about how close the connection must be between their own gender and their behavior.

Gender Schema Theory. **Gender schema theory** is an information-processing approach that combines social learning and cognitive-developmental features. It explains how environmental pressures and children's cognitions work together to shape gender-role development (Martin & Halverson, 1987; Martin, Ruble, & Szkrybalo, 2002). At an early age, children pick up gender-stereotyped preferences and behaviors from others. At the same time, they organize their experiences into *gender schemas,* or masculine and feminine categories, that they use to interpret their

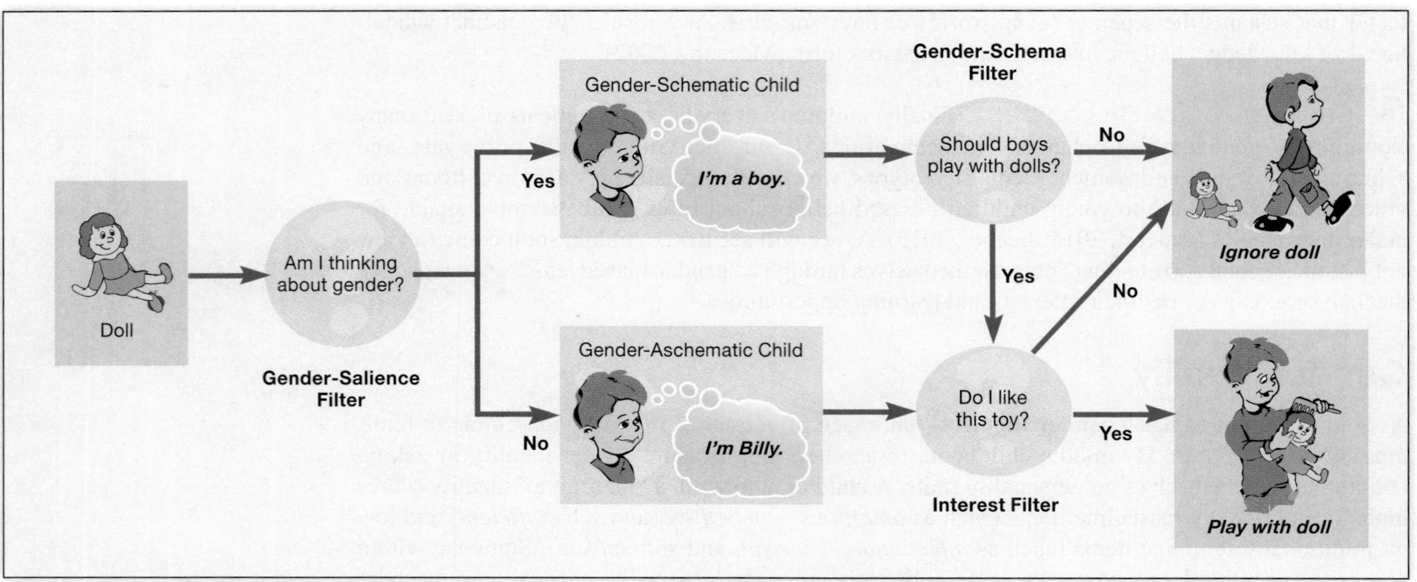

FIGURE 8.2 Cognitive pathways for gender-schematic and gender-aschematic children. In *gender-schematic children,* the gender-salience filter immediately makes gender highly relevant: Billy sees a doll and thinks, "I'm a boy. Should boys play with dolls?" Drawing on his experiences, he answers "yes" or "no." If he answers "yes" and the doll interests him, he plays with the doll. If he answers "no," he avoids the "gender-inappropriate" toy. *Gender-aschematic children* rarely view the world in gender-linked terms: Billy simply asks, "Do I like this toy?" and responds on the basis of his interests. (Reprinted by permission of Rebecca Bigler.)

world. As soon as preschoolers can label their own gender, they select gender schemas consistent with it ("Only boys can be doctors" or "Cooking is a girl's job") and apply those categories to themselves. Their self-perceptions then become gender-typed and serve as additional schemas that children use to process information and guide their own behavior.

We have seen that individual differences exist in the extent to which children endorse gender-typed views. Figure 8.2 shows different cognitive pathways for children who often apply gender schemas to their experiences and those who rarely do (Liben & Bigler, 2002). Consider Billy, who encounters a doll. If Billy is a *gender-schematic child,* his *gender-salience filter* immediately makes gender highly relevant. Drawing on his prior learning, he asks himself, "Should boys play with dolls?" If he answers "yes" and the toy interests him, he will explore it and learn more about it. If he answers "no," he will avoid the "gender-inappropriate" toy. But if Billy is a *gender-aschematic child*—one who seldom views the world in gender-linked terms—he simply asks himself, "Do I like this toy?" and responds on the basis of his interests.

Gender-schematic thinking is so powerful that when children see others behaving in "gender-inconsistent" ways, they often distort their memory to make it "gender-consistent." For example, when shown a picture of a male nurse, they may remember him as a doctor (Martin & Ruble, 2004). And because gender-schematic preschoolers typically conclude, "What I like, children of my own sex will also like," they often use their own preferences to add to their gender biases. For example, a girl who dislikes oysters may declare, "Only boys like oysters!" even though she has never actually been given information promoting such a stereotype. At least partly for this reason, young children's gender schemas contain both culturally standard and nonstandard ideas (Tenenbaum et al., 2010). Not until well into the school years do children's gender schemas fully resemble those of adults.

Gender identity involves self-perceptions that build on a core sense of one's own gender. A few children, however, express great discomfort with the sex they were assigned at birth and want to live as the other gender, saying so as early as the preschool years. For research on transgender children, refer to the Biology and Environment box on the following page.

Reducing Gender Stereotyping in Young Children

How can we help young children avoid developing gender schemas that restrict their behavior and learning opportunities? No easy recipe exists. Biology clearly affects children's gender typing, channeling boys, on average, toward active, competitive play and girls toward quieter, more intimate

BIOLOGY AND ENVIRONMENT

Transgender Children

Jacob, who began life as a girl named Mia, firmly insisted at age 2, "I am a boy!" in opposition to his parents' suggestion that he was merely "pretending." At preschool, he became increasingly angry at being identified as a girl. When his teacher asked him to write his name, he would print M-I-A but then vigorously cross it out. Gradually, his parents sensed the strength of his expressed identity. With guidance from a therapist, they began following his lead, providing boys' clothes, a short haircut, superhero action figures, and toy cars. At age 4, at his parents' suggestion, he affirmed that he wanted to change his name to Jacob and go to a different school, where he could start a new public life as a boy (Lemay, 2015). "I want to be a boy always," Jacob declared. His problematic behavior at home and school quickly subsided.

The number of transgender children, adolescents, and adults in Western nations, though few, has risen recently—perhaps because more stories like Jacob's are appearing in the media and because seeking treatment has become more acceptable. Individuals dissatisfied with their natal (birth) sex who strongly identify as the other sex experience substantial distress—a condition called *gender dysphoria.* Estimates based on adults in treatment suggest that 1 in 12,000 to 21,000 males and 1 in 30,000 to 48,000 females suffer from gender dysphoria (Zucker & Lawrence, 2009). In the general population, the prevalence of gender dysphoria may be considerably greater—according to one survey, perhaps as high as ½ of 1 percent (Conron et al., 2012). Many do not receive support from their families or from health professionals.

People who change gender in adulthood often trace the emergence of their gender dysphoria to early childhood. Although contributing factors are not well understood, the prenatal hormone environment seems to play a role. For example, genetic females known to have been exposed to high levels of prenatal androgens are more likely than other women to be transgender (Dessens, Slijper, & Drop, 2005). But many females prenatally exposed to high androgen levels, and many males exposed to low levels, do not express discomfort with their natal sex.

COURTESY OF MIMI LEMAY

▶ Jacob, who began life as a girl, changed his name and transitioned to living as a boy in early childhood. Transgender children whose parents support their desire to express their identified gender are more content and better-adjusted.

Although some studies claim that most cases of childhood gender dysphoria subside in adolescence and adulthood, their samples failed to distinguish between gender-dysphoric children and children who merely display gender-nonconforming behavior. Children who are severely troubled over the mismatch between their natal sex and core gender identity, who insist that they *are* the other gender, and who also engage in high levels of "other-gender" behavior generally experience persisting dysphoria (Ristori & Steensma, 2016; Steensma et al., 2011). These persisters are likely to transition mostly or entirely—as Jacob did—to their desired gender role.

Transgender preschoolers and school-age children are not pretending, confused, or delayed in gender understanding. When questioned about their peer preferences, gender-typed object choices, and gender identity, their responses are identical to those of nontransgender agemates who share their expressed gender (Fast & Olson, 2017; Olson, Key, & Eaton, 2015).

During early adolescence, gender dysphoria typically deepens as persisters encounter changes in their bodies and first feelings of sexual attraction (Leibowitz & de Vries, 2016). Some desire, and may be deemed eligible for, psychological and medical sex-change treatment, involving suppression of pubertal sex hormones, cross-sex hormone treatment after age 16, and surgery after age 18. Others go through a period of questioning, including hesitancy over invasive treatments, and take additional time to assess their feelings about transitioning physically (Steensma & Cohen-Kettenis, 2015). A number of these young people find their gender dysphoria so overwhelming that they eventually decide on treatment in their twenties and thirties.

Controversy exists over therapies for gender-dysphoric children. One approach is directed at lessening their cross-gender identity and behavior and increasing their comfort with their natal sex. These therapies, however, have yielded poor results (Adelson, 2012; Olson, 2016). Gender-dysphoric children react with heightened distress to efforts to suppress or deny their identified gender.

Increasing numbers of health professionals are convinced that therapies must be aimed at permitting children to follow their gender-identity inclinations and helping parents protect their children from the negative reactions of others. They are motivated by the tragic circumstances of many contemporary transgender adults, who experienced family rejection and social ostracism from childhood on and who face high rates of unemployment, poverty, homelessness, depression, and suicide (Byne et al., 2012; Di Ceglie, 2014; Haas, Rodgers, & Herman, 2014). Current evidence suggests that embracing transgender children's expressed identity leads to contented, better-adjusted children and adolescents. Follow-up research is needed to assess long-term outcomes in the coming generation of transgender adults.

interaction. At the same time, differential treatment of boys and girls begins at birth, amplifying biologically based tendencies and promoting many aspects of gender typing that are unrelated to human nature (Hines, 2015).

Because young children's cognitive limitations lead them to assume that cultural practices determine gender, adults are wise to try to delay preschoolers' exposure to gender-stereotyped messages. Parents and teachers can begin by limiting traditional gender roles in their own behavior and by providing children with nontraditional alternatives. For example, parents can take turns making dinner, bathing children, and driving the family car, and they can give their sons and daughters both trucks and dolls and both pink and blue clothing. Teachers can ensure that all children spend time in mixed-gender play activities and unstructured pursuits, as children's behavior tends to be less gender-typed in these contexts (Goble et al., 2012). Finally, adults can avoid using language that conveys gender stereotypes and can shield children from media presentations that do so.

Once children notice the vast array of gender stereotypes in their society, adults can point out exceptions. They can arrange for children to see men and women pursuing nontraditional careers and can explain that interests and skills, not sex, should determine a person's occupation. Research shows that such reasoning reduces children's gender-biased views. By middle childhood, children who hold flexible beliefs about what boys and girls can do are more likely to notice instances of gender discrimination (Brown & Bigler, 2004). And as we will see next, a rational approach to child rearing promotes healthy, adaptable functioning in many other areas as well.

ASK YOURSELF

CONNECT In addition to gender-stereotyped beliefs, what other aspects of preschoolers' social understanding tend to be rigid and one-sided?

APPLY List findings indicating that language and communication—between parents and children, between teachers and children, and between peers—powerfully affect children's gender typing. What recommendations would you make to counteract these influences?

REFLECT Would you describe your own gender identity as "masculine," "feminine," or androgynous? What biological and social factors might have influenced your gender identity?

Child Rearing and Emotional and Social Development

8.9 Describe the impact of child-rearing styles on development, and explain why authoritative parenting is effective.

8.10 Discuss the multiple origins of child maltreatment, its consequences for development, and prevention strategies.

We have seen how parents can foster children's competence—by building a parent–child relationship based on affection and cooperation, by modeling mature behavior, by using reasoning and inductive discipline, and by guiding and encouraging mastery of new skills. Now let's put these practices together into an overall view of effective parenting.

Styles of Child Rearing

Child-rearing styles are combinations of parenting behaviors that occur over a wide range of situations, creating an enduring child-rearing climate. In a landmark series of studies, Diana Baumrind (1971) gathered information on child rearing by watching parents interact with their preschoolers. Her findings, and those of others who have extended her work, reveal three features that consistently differentiate an effective style from less effective ones: (1) acceptance and involvement, (2) control, and (3) autonomy granting (Gray & Steinberg, 1999; Hart, Newell, & Olsen, 2003). Table 8.2 shows how child-rearing styles differ in these features.

Authoritative Child Rearing. The **authoritative child-rearing style**—the most successful approach—involves high acceptance and involvement, adaptive control techniques, and appropriate autonomy granting. Authoritative parents are warm, attentive, and sensitive, establishing an

TABLE 8.2
Features of Child-Rearing Styles

CHILD-REARING STYLE	ACCEPTANCE AND INVOLVEMENT	CONTROL	AUTONOMY GRANTING
Authoritative	Is warm, responsive, attentive, and sensitive to the child's needs	Engages in adaptive behavioral control: Makes reasonable demands for mature behavior and consistently enforces and explains them	Permits the child to make decisions in accord with readiness Encourages the child to express thoughts, feelings, and desires When parent and child disagree, engages in joint decision making when possible
Authoritarian	Is cold and rejecting and frequently degrades the child	Engages in coercive behavioral control: Makes excessive demands for mature behavior, uses force and punishment Often uses psychological control, withdrawing love and intruding on the child's individuality and attachment to parents	Makes decisions for the child Rarely listens to the child's point of view
Permissive	Is warm but overindulgent or inattentive	Is lax in behavioral control: Makes few or no demands for mature behavior	Permits the child to make many decisions before the child is ready
Uninvolved	Is emotionally detached and withdrawn	Is lax in behavioral control: Makes few or no demands for mature behavior	Is indifferent to the child's decision making and point of view

enjoyable, emotionally fulfilling parent–child relationship that draws the child into close connection. At the same time, authoritative parents exercise firm, reasonable control. They insist on mature behavior, give reasons for their expectations, and use disciplinary encounters as "teaching moments" to promote the child's self-regulation. Finally, authoritative parents engage in gradual, appropriate autonomy granting, allowing the child to make decisions in areas where he is ready to do so (Baumrind, 2013; Kuczynski & Lollis, 2002; Russell, Mize, & Bissaker, 2004).

Throughout childhood and adolescence, authoritative parenting is linked to many aspects of competence—an upbeat mood, self-control, task persistence, cooperativeness, high self-esteem, social and moral maturity, and favorable school performance (Amato & Fowler, 2002; Aunola, Stattin, & Nurmi, 2000; Gonzalez & Wolters, 2006; Jaffe, Gullone, & Hughes, 2010; Mackey, Arnold, & Pratt, 2001; Milevsky et al., 2007).

Authoritarian Child Rearing. The **authoritarian child-rearing style** is low in acceptance and involvement, high in coercive control, and low in autonomy granting. Authoritarian parents appear cold and rejecting. To exert control, they yell, command, criticize, and threaten, demanding unquestioning obedience. If the child resists, authoritarian parents resort to force and punishment.

Children of authoritarian parents are likely to be anxious, unhappy, and low in self-esteem and self-reliance. When frustrated, they tend to react with hostility and, like their parents, use force to get their way. Boys, especially, show high rates of anger and defiance. Although girls also engage in acting-out behavior, they are more likely to be dependent and overwhelmed by challenging tasks (Hart, Newell, & Olsen, 2003; Kakihara et al., 2010; Thompson, Hollis, & Richards, 2003). Children and adolescents exposed to the authoritarian style typically do poorly in school. However, because of their parents' concern with control, they tend to achieve better and to commit fewer antisocial acts than peers with undemanding parents—that is, those whose parents use one of the two styles we will consider next (Steinberg, Blatt-Eisengart, & Cauffman, 2006).

In addition to unwarranted direct control, authoritarian parents engage in a more subtle type called **psychological control,** in which they attempt to take advantage of children's psychological needs by intruding on and manipulating their verbal expressions, individuality, and attachments to parents. These parents frequently interrupt or put down the child's ideas, decisions, and choice of friends. When they are dissatisfied, they withdraw love, making their affection contingent on the child's compliance. Children subjected to psychological control exhibit adjustment problems involving both anxious, withdrawn behavior and defiance and aggression—especially the relational form, which (like parental psychological control) damages relationships through manipulation and exclusion (Barber, Stolz, & Olsen, 2005; Barber & Xia, 2013; Kuppens et al., 2013).

Permissive Child Rearing. The **permissive child-rearing style** is warm and accepting but uninvolved. Permissive parents are either overindulgent or inattentive and, thus, engage in little control. Instead of gradually granting autonomy, they allow children to make many of their own decisions at an age when they are not yet capable of doing so. Their children can eat meals and go to bed whenever they wish, can watch as much television as they want, and do not have to learn good manners or do any household chores. Although some permissive parents truly believe in this approach, many others simply lack confidence in their ability to influence their child's behavior (Oyserman et al., 2005).

Children of permissive parents tend to be impulsive, disobedient, and rebellious. They are also overly demanding and dependent on adults, and they show less persistence on tasks, poorer school achievement, and more antisocial behavior (Barber & Olsen, 1997; Steinberg, Blatt-Eisengart, & Cauffman, 2006).

Uninvolved Child Rearing. The **uninvolved child-rearing style** combines low acceptance and involvement with little control and general indifference to issues of autonomy. Often these parents are emotionally detached and depressed and so overwhelmed by life stress that they have little time and energy for children. At its extreme, uninvolved parenting is a form of child maltreatment called *neglect.* Especially when it begins early, it disrupts virtually all aspects of development (see Chapter 6, page 175). Even with less extreme parental disengagement, children and adolescents display many problems—poor emotional self-regulation, school achievement difficulties, depression, and antisocial behavior (Aunola, Stattin, & Nurmi, 2000; Schroeder et al., 2010).

What Makes Authoritative Child Rearing Effective?

Like all correlational findings, the association between authoritative parenting and children's competence is open to interpretation. Perhaps parents of well-adjusted children are authoritative because their children have especially cooperative dispositions. But although impulsive and emotionally negative children are more likely to evoke coercive, inconsistent discipline, extra warmth and firm control succeed in modifying these children's maladaptive styles (Cipriano & Stifter, 2010; Larzelere, Cox, & Mandara, 2013). With inhibited, fearful children, parents must suppress their tendency to be overprotective. Rather, inhibited children benefit from extra encouragement to be assertive and express their autonomy (Chronis-Tuscano et al., 2015).

The warmth and caring that authoritative parents accord their children are linked to favorable child functioning in many cultures and seem universally necessary (Khaleque & Rohner, 2002). And a variant of authoritativeness in which parents exert strong control—becoming directive but not coercive—yields just as favorable long-term outcomes as a more democratic approach (Baumrind, Larzelere, & Owens, 2010). Indeed, some children, because of their dispositions, require "heavier doses" of certain authoritative features.

In sum, authoritative child rearing seems to create a positive emotional context for parental influence in the following ways:

- Warm, involved parents who are secure in their expectations model caring concern as well as confident, self-controlled behavior.
- Children are far more likely to comply with and internalize control that appears fair and reasonable, not arbitrary.
- Authoritative parents appropriately make demands and grant autonomy. By conveying a sense of competence to their children, authoritative parents foster favorable self-esteem and cognitive and social maturity.
- Supportive aspects of the authoritative style, including parental acceptance, involvement, and rational control, are a powerful source of *resilience,* protecting children from the negative effects of family stress and poverty (Luthar, Crossman, & Small, 2015).

LOOK AND LISTEN

Ask several parents to explain their style of child rearing, inquiring about acceptance and involvement, control, and autonomy granting. Look, especially, for variations in amount and type of control over children's behavior along with parents' rationales.

Cultural Variations

Although authoritative parenting is broadly advantageous, ethnic minority parents often have distinct child-rearing beliefs and practices that reflect cultural values. Let's look at some examples.

Compared with Western parents, Chinese parents describe their parenting as more controlling. They are more directive in teaching and scheduling their children's time, as a way of fostering self-control and high achievement. Chinese parents may appear less warm than Western parents because they withhold praise, which they believe results in self-satisfied, poorly motivated children (Cheah & Li, 2010; Ng, Pomerantz, & Deng, 2014). Chinese parents report expressing affection and concern and using induction and other reasoning-oriented discipline as much as American parents do, but they more often shame a misbehaving child, withdraw love, and use physical punishment (Cheah et al., 2009; Chen, Sun, & Yu, 2017). When these practices become excessive, resulting in an authoritarian style high in psychological or coercive control, Chinese children display the same negative outcomes as Western children (Chan, 2010; Lee et al., 2012; Pong, Johnston, & Chen, 2010; Sorkhabi & Mandara, 2013).

In Hispanic families, Asian Pacific Island families, and Caribbean families of African or East Indian origin, firm insistence on respect for parental authority is paired with high parental warmth—a combination suited to promoting cognitive and social competence and family loyalty (Roopnarine, 2016; Tamis-LeMonda & McFadden, 2010). Hispanic fathers typically spend much time with their children and are warm and sensitive (Cabrera & Bradley, 2012).

Although wide variation exists, low-SES African-American parents tend to expect immediate obedience, regarding strictness as fostering self-control and vigilance in risky surroundings. African-American parents who use controlling strategies tend to have cognitively and socially competent children who view parental control as a sign of love and concern. And among African-American youths, controlling parenting, when combined with warmth and responsiveness, protects against delinquency and disruptive behaviors at school (Pezzella, Thornberry, & Smith, 2016; Roche, Ensminger, & Cherlin, 2007). Most African-American parents who use strict, "no-nonsense" discipline combine it with warmth and reasoning.

These cultural variations remind us that child-rearing styles must be viewed in their larger contexts. As we have seen, many factors contribute to good parenting: personal characteristics of both child and parent, SES, access to extended family and community supports, cultural values and practices, and public policies.

As we turn to the topic of child maltreatment, our discussion will underscore, once again, that effective child rearing is sustained not just by the desire of mothers and fathers to be good parents. Almost all want to be. Unfortunately, when vital supports for parenting break down, children—as well as parents—can suffer terribly.

In Caribbean families of African origins, respect for parental authority is paired with high parental warmth—a combination that promotes competence and family loyalty.

Child Maltreatment

Child maltreatment is as old as human history, but only in recent decades has the problem been widely acknowledged and studied. In the most recently reported year, about 700,000 U.S. children (10 out of every 1,000) were identified as victims (U.S. Department of Health and Human Services, 2017a). Because most cases go unreported, the true figures are much higher.

Child maltreatment takes the following forms:

- *Physical abuse:* Assaults, such as kicking, biting, shaking, punching, or stabbing, that inflict physical injury
- *Sexual abuse:* Fondling, intercourse, exhibitionism, commercial exploitation through prostitution or production of pornography, and other forms of sexual exploitation
- *Neglect:* Failure to meet a child's basic needs for food, clothing, medical attention, education, or supervision
- *Emotional abuse:* Acts that could cause serious emotional harm, including social isolation, repeated unreasonable demands, ridicule, humiliation, intimidation, or terrorizing

Neglect occurs in about 75 percent of reported cases, physical abuse in 17 percent, emotional abuse in 9 percent, and sexual abuse in 8 percent (U.S. Department of Health and Human Services, 2017a). But these figures are only approximate, as many children experience more than one form.

Parents commit 90 percent of abusive incidents. Other relatives account for about 5 percent, and the remainder are perpetrated by parents' unmarried partners, child-care providers, and other adults. Infants, toddlers, and preschoolers are at greatest risk for neglect, physical abuse, and emotional abuse. Sexual abuse is perpetrated more often against school-age and early adolescent children. But each type occurs at every age (Trocmé & Wolfe, 2002; U.S. Department of Health and Human Services, 2017a). Because many sexual abuse victims are identified in middle childhood, we will pay special attention to this form of maltreatment in Chapter 10.

The Family. Within the family, children whose characteristics make them more challenging to rear are more likely to become targets of abuse. These include premature or very sick babies and children who are temperamentally difficult, are inattentive and overactive, or have other developmental problems. Child factors, however, only slightly increase the risk of abuse (Jaudes & Mackey-Bilaver, 2008; Sidebotham et al., 2003). Whether such children are maltreated largely depends on parents' characteristics.

Maltreating parents are less skillful than other parents in handling discipline confrontations. They also suffer from biased thinking about their child. They often attribute their baby's crying or child's misdeeds to a stubborn or bad disposition, evaluate transgressions as worse than they are, and feel powerless in parenting—perspectives that lead them to move quickly toward physical force (Bugental & Happaney, 2004; Crouch et al., 2008).

© JEFF GREENBERG/PHOTOEDIT

▶ High parental stress, low income and education, and extreme household disorganization are often associated with child maltreatment. Abusive parents are more likely to live in rundown neighborhoods that offer few sources of social support.

Most parents have enough self-control not to respond with abuse to their child's misbehavior or developmental problems. Other factors combine with these conditions to prompt an extreme response. Abusive parents react to stressful situations with high emotional arousal. And low income, low education (less than a high school diploma), unemployment, alcohol and drug use, marital conflict, overcrowded living conditions, frequent moves, and extreme household disorganization are common in abusive and neglectful homes (Dakil et al., 2012; Wulczyn, 2009). These conditions increase the chances that parents will be too overwhelmed to meet basic child-rearing responsibilities or will vent their frustrations by lashing out at their children.

The Community. The majority of abusive and neglectful parents are isolated from both formal and informal social supports. Because of their life histories, many have learned to mistrust and avoid others and are poorly skilled at establishing and maintaining positive relationships. Also, maltreating parents are more likely to live in unstable, rundown neighborhoods that provide few links between family and community, such as parks, recreation centers, and religious institutions (Guterman et al., 2009; Tomyr, Ouimet, & Ugnat, 2012). They lack "lifelines" to others and have no one to turn to for help during stressful times.

The Larger Culture. Cultural values, laws, and customs profoundly affect the chances that child maltreatment will occur when parents feel overburdened. Societies that view violence as an appropriate way to solve problems set the stage for child abuse.

Although the United States has laws to protect children from maltreatment, widespread support exists for use of physical force with children (refer back to page 257). Twenty-three European countries have outlawed corporal punishment, a measure that dampens both physical discipline and abuse (duRivage et al., 2015; Zolotor & Puzia, 2010). Furthermore, all industrialized nations except the United States prohibit corporal punishment in schools. The U.S. Supreme Court has twice upheld the right of school officials to use corporal punishment. Fortunately, 31 U.S. states and the District of Columbia have passed laws that ban it.

Consequences of Child Maltreatment. The family circumstances of maltreated children impair the development of emotional self-regulation, empathy and sympathy, self-concept, social skills, and academic motivation. Over time, these youngsters show serious adjustment problems—cognitive deficits including impaired executive function, school failure, difficulties in processing emotional and social signals, peer relationship problems, severe depression, aggressive behavior, substance abuse, and violent crime (Cicchetti & Toth, 2015; Nikulina & Widom, 2013; Stronach et al., 2011).

Furthermore, the sense of abandonment conveyed by neglectful parenting and the humiliating, terrorizing behaviors of abusive adults result in low self-esteem, high anxiety, self-blame, and efforts to escape from extreme psychological pain—at times severe enough to lead to post-traumatic stress disorder (PTSD) and attempted suicide in adolescence (Nikulina, Widom, & Czaja, 2011; Wolfe, 2005). At school, maltreated children's noncompliance, poor motivation, and cognitive immaturity interfere with academic achievement, further undermining their chances for life success.

Finally, chronic abuse is associated with central nervous system damage, including abnormal EEG brain-wave activity; fMRI-detected reduced size and impaired functioning of the cerebral cortex, corpus callosum, cerebellum, and hippocampus; and atypical production of the stress hormone cortisol—initially too high but, after months of abuse, often too low. Over time, the massive trauma of persistent abuse seems to blunt children's normal physiological response to stress (Cicchetti & Toth, 2015; Jaffee & Christian, 2014). These effects increase the chances that cognitive and emotional problems will endure.

Preventing Child Maltreatment. Because child maltreatment is embedded in families, communities, and society as a whole, efforts to prevent it must be directed at each of these levels. Many approaches have been suggested, from teaching high-risk parents effective child-rearing strategies to developing broad social programs aimed at improving economic conditions and community services.

Providing social supports to families eases parental stress, sharply reducing child maltreatment. Parents Anonymous, a U.S. organization with affiliate programs around the world, helps child-abusing parents learn constructive parenting practices, largely through social supports. Its local chapters offer self-help group meetings, daily phone calls, and regular home visits to relieve social isolation and teach child-rearing skills.

Early intervention aimed at strengthening both child and parent competencies can prevent child maltreatment. Healthy Families America, a program that began in Hawaii and has spread to 430 sites across the United States and Canada, identifies families at risk for maltreatment during pregnancy or at birth. Each receives three years of home visitation, in which a trained worker helps parents manage crises, encourages effective child rearing, and puts parents in touch with community services (Healthy Families America, 2011). In evaluations, parents randomly assigned to Healthy Families home visitation, compared with no-intervention controls, more often engaged their child in developmentally supportive activities and used effective discipline strategies; less often displayed harsh, coercive tactics; and reported less parenting stress—factors that reduce the risk of child maltreatment (Green et al., 2014; LeCroy & Krysik, 2011). Another home-visiting program that prevents child abuse and neglect is the Nurse–Family Partnership, discussed on page 83 in Chapter 3 (Olds et al., 2009).

Even with intensive treatment, some adults persist in their abusive acts. An estimated 1,600 U.S. children, most of them infants and preschoolers, die from maltreatment annually (U.S. Department of Health and Human Services, 2017a). When parents are unlikely to change their behavior, the drastic step of separating parent from child and legally terminating parental rights is the only justifiable course of action.

Child maltreatment is a sad note on which to end our discussion of a period of childhood that is so full of excitement, awakening, and discovery. But there is reason to be optimistic. Great strides have been made over the past several decades in understanding and preventing child maltreatment.

▶ Each year, fourth to sixth graders across Los Angeles County enter a poster contest to celebrate Child Abuse Prevention Month. This recent winner urges parents not to commit acts of physical and emotional abuse. (Jonathan Chin, 0th Grade, Yaya Fine Art Studio, Temple City, CA. Courtesy ICAN Associates, Los Angeles County Inter-Agency Council on Child Abuse and Neglect, ican4kids.org)

ASK YOURSELF

CONNECT Which child-rearing style is most likely to be associated with inductive discipline, and why?

APPLY Chandra heard a news report about 10 severely neglected children, living in squalor in an inner-city tenement. She wondered, "Why would parents so mistreat their children?" How would you answer Chandra?

REFLECT How would you classify your parents' child-rearing styles? What factors might have influenced their approach to parenting?

CHAPTER 8 SUMMARY

Erikson's Theory: Initiative versus Guilt *(p. 246)*

8.1 ***Identify personality changes that take place during Erikson's stage of initiative versus guilt.***

- Preschoolers develop a new sense of purposefulness as they grapple with Erikson's psychological conflict of **initiative versus guilt.** A healthy sense of initiative depends on exploring the social world through play, forming a conscience, and experiencing supportive parenting.

© ALVARO LEIVA/ROBERT HARDING WORLD IMAGERY

Self-Understanding *(p. 247)*

8.2 ***Describe the development of self-concept and self-esteem in early childhood.***

- Preschoolers construct a **self-concept** consisting largely of observable characteristics and typical emotions and attitudes. A warm, sensitive parent–child relationship fosters a more positive, coherent early self-concept.
- Preschoolers' high **self-esteem** consists of several self-judgments and contributes to their sense of initiative.

Emotional Development *(p. 248)*

8.3 ***Identify changes in understanding and expressing emotion during early childhood, citing factors that influence those changes.***

- Preschoolers' impressive understanding of the causes, consequences, and behavioral signs of basic emotions is supported by cognitive and language development and conversations about feelings.
- By age 3 to 4, children are aware of various strategies for emotional self-regulation. Temperament and parental communication about coping strategies influence preschoolers' capacity to handle stress and negative emotion.
- As their self-concepts develop, preschoolers more often experience self-conscious emotions. They depend on feedback from parents and other adults to know when to feel these emotions.
- Empathy also becomes more common in early childhood. The extent to which empathy leads to **sympathy** and results in **prosocial,** or **altruistic, behavior** depends on temperament and parenting.

Peer Relations *(p. 251)*

8.4 ***Describe peer sociability and friendship in early childhood, along with cultural and parental influences on early peer relations.***

- During early childhood, peer interaction increases as children move from **nonsocial activity** to **parallel play,** then to **associative play** and **cooperative play.** Nevertheless, both solitary and parallel play remain common.
- Sociodramatic play seems especially important in societies where child and adult worlds are distinct. In cultures that highly value group harmony, play generally occurs in large groups and is highly cooperative.
- Interactions among preschool friends are unusually positive, but friendship does not yet have an enduring quality based on mutual trust. Early childhood social maturity contributes to school readiness and academic performance.
- Parents affect peer sociability by influencing their child's peer relations and through their child-rearing practices.

Foundations of Morality and Aggression *(p. 254)*

8.5 ***Identify the central features of psychoanalytic, social learning, and cognitive-developmental approaches to moral development.***

- Psychoanalytic theory stresses the emotional side of conscience development, especially identification and guilt as motivators of moral action. But contrary to Freud's view that morality develops out of fear of punishment and loss of parental love, conscience formation is promoted by **induction,** in which adults point out the effects of the child's misbehavior on others.
- Social learning theory focuses on how moral behavior is learned through modeling. Giving children material rewards undermines prosocial behavior.
- Alternatives to harsh punishment such as **time out** and withdrawal of privileges can help parents avoid undesirable side effects of punishment. Parents can increase the effectiveness of mild punishment by being consistent, maintaining a warm parent–child relationship, and offering explanations.
- The cognitive-developmental perspective views children as active thinkers about social rules. By age 4, children consider intentions in making moral judgments and disapprove of lying. Preschoolers also distinguish **moral imperatives** from **social conventions** and **matters of personal choice.** However, they tend to reason rigidly about morality, focusing on salient features such as physical harm.

© JEFF GREENBERG/PHOTOEDIT

8.6 Describe the development of aggression in early childhood, including family and media influences and effective approaches to reducing aggressive behavior.

- During early childhood, **proactive aggression** declines while **reactive aggression** increases. Proactive and reactive aggression come in three forms: **physical aggression** (more common in boys), **verbal aggression,** and **relational aggression.**
- Harsh, inconsistent discipline and a conflict-ridden family atmosphere promote children's aggression, as does media violence. Effective approaches to reducing aggressive behavior include training parents in effective child-rearing practices, teaching children conflict-resolution skills, helping parents cope with stressors in their own lives, and shielding children from violent media.

Gender Typing *(p. 264)*

8.7 Discuss biological and environmental influences on preschoolers' gender-stereotyped beliefs and behavior.

- **Gender typing** is well under way in early childhood. Preschoolers acquire a wide range of gender-stereotyped beliefs, often applying them rigidly.

© LAURA DWIGHT PHOTOGRAPHY

- Prenatal hormones contribute to boys' higher activity level and rougher play and to children's preference for same-sex playmates. But parents, teachers, and peers also encourage many gender-typed responses.

8.8 Describe and evaluate theories that explain the emergence of gender identity.

- Although most people have a traditional **gender identity,** some have an identity called **androgyny** consisting of both masculine and feminine characteristics. Masculine and androgynous identities are linked to better psychological adjustment.
- According to social learning theory, preschoolers first acquire gender-typed responses through modeling and reinforcement and then organize these behaviors into gender-linked ideas about themselves. Cognitive-developmental theory suggests that children must master **gender constancy** before developing gender-typed behavior, but evidence for this assumption is weak.
- **Gender schema theory** combines features of social learning and cognitive-developmental perspectives. As children acquire gender-typed preferences and behaviors, they form masculine and feminine categories, or gender schemas, that they apply to themselves and their world.
- A few children express great discomfort with the sex they were assigned at birth and, as early as the preschool years, express a desire to live as the other gender.

Child Rearing and Emotional and Social Development *(p. 270)*

8.9 Describe the impact of child-rearing styles on development, and explain why authoritative parenting is effective.

- Three features distinguish the major **child-rearing styles:** degree of (1) acceptance and involvement, (2) control, and (3) autonomy granting. Compared with the **authoritarian, permissive,** and **uninvolved** styles, the **authoritative style** promotes cognitive, emotional, and social competence. Warmth, reasonable (as opposed to coercive) control, and gradual autonomy granting account for the effectiveness of this style. **Psychological control,** which is associated with authoritarian parenting, contributes to adjustment problems.
- Although some ethnic groups effectively combine parental warmth with high levels of control, harsh and excessive control impairs academic and social competence.

© JANINE WIEDEL PHOTOLIBRARY/ALAMY

8.10 Discuss the multiple origins of child maltreatment, its consequences for development, and prevention strategies.

- Maltreating parents use ineffective discipline, hold a negatively biased view of their child, and feel powerless in parenting. Unmanageable parental stress and social isolation greatly increase the likelihood of abuse and neglect. Societal approval of corporal punishment promotes child abuse.
- Maltreated children are impaired in emotional self-regulation, empathy and sympathy, self-concept, social skills, and academic motivation. The trauma of repeated abuse is associated with central nervous system damage and serious, lasting adjustment problems. Successful prevention requires efforts at the family, community, and societal levels.

IMPORTANT TERMS AND CONCEPTS

androgyny (p. 267)
associative play (p. 251)
authoritarian child-rearing style (p. 271)
authoritative child-rearing style (p. 270)
child-rearing styles (p. 270)
cooperative play (p. 251)
gender constancy (p. 267)
gender identity (p. 267)
gender schema theory (p. 267)
gender typing (p. 264)
induction (p. 255)
initiative versus guilt (p. 246)
matters of personal choice (p. 259)
moral imperatives (p. 259)
nonsocial activity (p. 251)
parallel play (p. 251)
permissive child-rearing style (p. 272)
physical aggression (p. 260)
proactive aggression (p. 260)
prosocial, or altruistic, behavior (p. 250)
psychological control (p. 271)
reactive aggression (p. 260)
relational aggression (p. 260)
self-concept (p. 247)
self-esteem (p. 247)
social conventions (p. 259)
sympathy (p. 250)
time out (p. 257)
uninvolved child-rearing style (p. 272)
verbal aggression (p. 260)

Development in **Early Childhood**

D. HURST/ALAMY

2 YEARS

Physical

- Throughout early childhood, height and weight increase more slowly than in toddlerhood. (203)
- Balance improves; walks more rhythmically; hurried walk changes to run. (210)
- Jumps, hops, throws, and catches with rigid upper body. (211)
- Puts on and removes simple items of clothing. (211)
- Uses spoon effectively. (211)
- First drawings are gestural scribbles. (211)

Cognitive

- Make-believe becomes less dependent on realistic objects, less self-centered, and more complex; sociodramatic play increases. (215–216)
- Takes the perspective of others in simplified, familiar situations and in everyday interactions. (219, 229, 241)
- Recognition memory is well-developed. (227)
- Shows awareness of mental states, such as want, think, remember, and pretend. (229)
- Attaches verbal labels to amounts and sizes; begins to count. (232)

PEOPLEIMAGES.COM/GETTY IMAGES

Language

- Vocabulary increases rapidly. (238)
- Uses a coalition of cues—perceptual and, increasingly, social and linguistic—to figure out word meanings. (239–240)
- Speaks in simple sentences that follow basic word order of native language, gradually adding grammatical markers. (240)
- Displays effective conversational skills. (241)

Emotional/Social

- Understands causes, consequences, and behavioral signs of basic emotions. (248)

© ELLEN B. SENISI PHOTOGRAPHY

- Begins to develop self-concept and self-esteem. (247)
- Shows early signs of developing moral sense—verbal evaluations of own and others' actions and efforts to relieve others' distress. (254)
- May display proactive (instrumental) aggression. (260)
- Gender-stereotyped beliefs and behavior increase. (264)

3–4 YEARS

Physical

- Running, jumping, hopping, throwing, and catching become better coordinated. (211)
- Pedals and steers tricycle. (211)

© LAURA DWIGHT PHOTOGRAPHY

- Galloping and one-foot skipping appear. (211)
- Fastens and unfastens large buttons. (211)
- Uses scissors. (211)
- Uses fork effectively. (211)
- Draws first picture of a person, using tadpole image. (212)

Cognitive

- Understands the symbolic function of drawings and of models of real-world spaces. (212, 217)
- Grasps conservation, notices transformations, reverses thinking, and understands cause–effect sequences in simplified, familiar situations. (220)
- Organizes everyday knowledge into hierarchically organized categories. (220)
- Uses private speech to guide behavior during challenging tasks. (222)
- Gains in executive function, including inhibition, flexible shifting of attention, and working memory capacity. (225–226)
- Uses scripts to recall routine events. (228)
- Understands that beliefs can determine behavior. (229)
- Knows the meaning of numbers up to 10, counts correctly, and grasps cardinality. (232)

Note: Numbers in parentheses indicate the page or pages on which each milestone is discussed.

Language

- Aware of some meaningful features of written language. (230)

WAYNE ROYALTY FREE/ALAMY

- Coins new words based on known words; extends language meanings through metaphor. (239)
- Masters increasingly complex grammatical structures, occasionally overextending grammatical rules to exceptions. (240)
- Adjusts speech to fit the age, sex, and social status of listeners. (241)

Emotional/Social

- Describes self in terms of observable characteristics and typical emotions and attitudes. (247)
- Has several self-esteems, such as learning things in school, making friends, getting along with parents, and treating others kindly. (248)
- Emotional self-regulation improves. (249)
- Experiences self-conscious emotions more often. (249)
- Relies more on language to express empathy. (250)
- Proactive aggression declines, while reactive aggression (verbal and relational) increases. (261)
- Engages in associative and cooperative play with peers, in addition to parallel play. (251)

© LAURA DWIGHT PHOTOGRAPHY

- Forms first friendships, based on pleasurable play and sharing of toys. (253)
- Distinguishes truthfulness from lying. (259)
- Distinguishes moral imperatives from social conventions and matters of personal choice. (259–260)
- Preference for same-sex playmates strengthens. (265)

5–6 YEARS

Physical

- Starts to lose primary teeth. (203)
- Displays more efficient, flexible running, throwing, catching, hopping, jumping, skipping, and tricycle riding patterns. (210–211)
- Uses knife to cut soft foods. (211)
- Ties shoes. (211)
- Draws more complex pictures. (212)

© LAURA DWIGHT PHOTOGRAPHY

- Prints name; copies some numbers and simple words. (211, 214)

Cognitive

- Magical beliefs decline. (219)
- Gains further in executive function, including planning. (225–226)

© LAURA DWIGHT PHOTOGRAPHY

- Improves in recognition, recall, scripted memory, and autobiographical memory. (227–228)
- Understanding of false belief strengthens. (229)

Language

- Understands that letters and sounds are linked in systematic ways. (230, 232)
- Uses invented spellings. (230, 232)
- By age 6, comprehends about 10,000 words and produces several thousand. (238)
- Uses most grammatical constructions competently. (240)

Emotional/Social

- Improves in emotional understanding, including the ability to interpret, predict, and influence others' emotional reactions. (248)

© ELLEN B. SENISI

- Has acquired many morally relevant rules and behaviors. (256)
- Gender-stereotyped beliefs and behavior and preference for same-sex playmates continue to strengthen. (264–265)
- Understands gender constancy. (267)

Note: Numbers in parentheses indicate the page or pages on which each milestone is discussed.

CHAPTER

9 Physical and Cognitive Development in Middle Childhood

© LAURA DWIGHT PHOTOGRAPHY

During a first-grade math activity, students work together to take measurements and record data. An improved capacity to remember, reason, and reflect on one's thinking makes middle childhood a time of dramatic advances in academic learning and problem solving.

WHAT'S AHEAD IN CHAPTER 9

"I'm on my way, Mom!" hollered 10-year-old Joey as he stuffed the last bite of toast into his mouth, grabbed his backpack and helmet, dashed out the door, jumped on his bike, and headed down the street for school. Joey's 8-year-old sister Lizzie followed, pedaling furiously until she caught up with Joey.

"They're branching out," Rena, the children's mother and one of my colleagues at the university, commented to me over lunch that day as she described the children's expanding activities and relationships. Homework, household chores, soccer teams, music lessons, scouting, friends at school and in the neighborhood, and Joey's new paper route were all part of the children's routine. "It seems the basics are all there. Being a parent is still challenging, but it's more a matter of refinements—helping them become independent, competent, and productive individuals."

Joey and Lizzie have entered middle childhood—the years from 6 to 11. Around the world, children of this age are assigned new responsibilities. For children in industrialized nations, middle childhood is often called the "school years" because its onset is marked by the start of formal schooling. In village and tribal cultures, the school may be a field or a jungle. But universally, mature members of society guide children of this age period toward real-world tasks that increasingly resemble those they will perform as adults.

© LOVETHEPHOTO/ALAMY

By age 6, the brain has reached 90 percent of its adult weight, and the body continues to grow slowly. In this way, nature gives school-age children the mental powers to master challenging tasks as well as added time—before reaching physical maturity—to acquire fundamental knowledge and skills for life in a complex social world.

We begin by reviewing typical growth trends, gains in motor skills, and special health concerns. Then we return to Piaget's theory and the information-processing approach for an overview of cognitive changes. Next, we examine genetic and environmental contributions to IQ scores, which often influence important educational decisions. Our discussion continues with the further blossoming of language and the role of schools in children's learning and development.

PHYSICAL DEVELOPMENT

Body Growth

9.1 Describe major trends in body growth during middle childhood.

Physical growth during the school years continues at the slow, regular pace of early childhood. At age 6, the average North American child weighs about 45 pounds and is 3½ feet tall. Over the next few years, children will add about 2 to 3 inches in height and 5 pounds in weight each year (see Figure 9.1 on page 282). Between ages 6 and 8, girls are slightly shorter and lighter than boys. By age 9, this trend reverses as girls approach the dramatic adolescent growth spurt, which occurs two years earlier in girls than in boys.

Because the lower portion of the body is growing fastest, Joey and Lizzie appeared longer-legged than they had in early childhood. Girls continue to have slightly more body fat and boys more muscle. After age 8, girls begin accumulating fat at a faster rate, and they will add even more during adolescence (Hauspie & Roelants, 2012).

During middle childhood, the bones of the body lengthen and broaden. However, ligaments are not yet firmly attached to bones. This, combined with increasing muscle strength, gives children the unusual flexibility needed to perform cartwheels and handstands. As their bodies become stronger, many children experience a greater desire for physical exercise. Nighttime "growing pains"—stiffness and aches in the legs—are common as muscles adapt to an enlarging skeleton (Uziel et al., 2012).

Between ages 6 and 12, all 20 primary teeth are lost and replaced by permanent ones, with girls losing their teeth slightly earlier than boys. For a while, the permanent teeth seem too large. Gradually, growth of facial bones causes the face to lengthen and mouth to widen, accommodating the newly erupting teeth.

FIGURE 9.1 Body growth during middle childhood. Mai and Henry continue to display the slow, regular pattern of growth they showed in early childhood. Around age 9, girls begin to grow at a faster rate than boys as the adolescent growth spurt draws near.

Health Issues

9.2 Describe the causes and consequences of serious nutritional problems in middle childhood, giving special attention to obesity.

9.3 List factors that contribute to illness during the school years, and explain how these health problems can be reduced.

Children from economically advantaged homes, like Joey and Lizzie, are at their healthiest in middle childhood, full of energy and play. Growth in lung size permits more air to be exchanged with each breath, so children are better able to exercise vigorously without tiring. The cumulative effects of good nutrition, combined with rapid development of the body's immune system, offer greater protection against disease.

Not surprisingly, poverty continues to be a powerful predictor of ill health during middle childhood. Because economically disadvantaged U.S. families often lack health insurance, many children do not have regular access to a doctor. A substantial number also lack such basic necessities as regular meals.

Nutrition

Children need a well-balanced, plentiful diet to provide energy for learning and greater physical activity. With their increasing focus on friendships and new activities, many children spend little time at the table, and the number who eat meals with their families declines from age 9 on, with negative consequences for healthy eating (Hammons & Fiese, 2011).

School-age children report that they "feel better" and "focus better" after eating nutritious foods and that they feel sluggish, "like a blob," after eating junk foods. In a longitudinal study of nearly 14,000 U.S. children, a parent-reported diet high in sugar, fat, and processed food in early childhood predicted slightly lower IQ at age 8, after many factors that might otherwise account for this association were controlled (Northstone et al., 2012). Even mild nutritional deficits can affect cognitive functioning. Insufficient dietary iron and folate during the school years are related to poorer concentration and mental test performance (Arija et al., 2006; Low et al., 2013).

As we saw in earlier chapters, many poverty-stricken children in developing countries and in the United States suffer from serious and prolonged malnutrition. Unfortunately, malnutrition that persists from infancy or early childhood into the school years usually results in lasting physical, cognitive, and mental health problems (Liu et al., 2003; Schoenmaker et al., 2015).

Overweight and Obesity

Mona, a very heavy child in Lizzie's class, often watched from the sidelines during recess. When she did join in games, she was slow and clumsy. Most afternoons, she walked home from school alone while her schoolmates gathered in groups, talking, laughing, and chasing. At home, Mona sought comfort in high-calorie snacks.

Mona suffers from **obesity,** a greater-than-20-percent increase over healthy weight, based on *body mass index (BMI)*—a ratio of weight to height associated with body fat. A BMI above the 85th percentile for a child's age and sex is considered *overweight,* a BMI above the 95th percentile *obese.* During the past several decades, a rise in overweight and obesity has occurred in many Western nations. Today, 32 percent of U.S. children and adolescents are overweight, more than half of them extremely so: 17 percent are obese (Ogden et al., 2014, 2016; World Health Organization, 2015b).

Obesity rates have also risen in developing countries, as urbanization shifts the population toward sedentary lifestyles and diets high in meats and energy-dense refined foods (World Health Organization, 2015b). In China, for example, 25 percent of children are overweight and 9 percent obese, with two to three times as many boys as girls affected (Jia et al., 2017). In addition to lifestyle changes, a prevailing belief in Chinese culture that excess body fat signifies prosperity and health—carried over from a half-century ago, when famine caused millions of deaths—has contributed to this alarming upsurge. High valuing of sons may induce Chinese parents to offer boys especially generous portions of energy-dense foods.

Overweight rises with age, from 23 percent among U.S. preschoolers to 35 percent among school-age children and adolescents to an astronomical 69 percent among adults (Ogden et al., 2014). Overweight preschoolers are five times more likely than their normal-weight peers to be overweight at age 12, and few persistently overweight adolescents attain a normal weight in adulthood (Patton et al., 2011; Simmonds et al., 2016).

Causes of Obesity.

Identical twins are more likely than fraternal twins to resemble each other in BMI, and adopted children tend to resemble their biological parents (Min, Chiu, & Wang, 2013). Although heredity clearly contributes to children's risk, the importance of environment is apparent in the consistent relationship of low SES to overweight and obesity in industrialized nations, especially among ethnic minorities—in the United States, African-American, Hispanic, and Native-American children and adults (Ogden et al., 2014, 2016). Factors responsible include lack of knowledge about healthy diet; a tendency to buy high-fat, low-cost foods; and family stress, which can prompt overeating. Recall, also, that children who were undernourished in their early years are at risk for later excessive weight gain (see page 119 in Chapter 4).

Parental feeding practices also contribute. Overweight children are more likely to eat sugary and fatty foods, perhaps because these foods are plentiful in the diets offered by their parents, who also tend to be overweight (Kit, Ogden, & Flegal, 2014). Frequent eating out—which increases parents' and children's consumption of high-calorie fast foods—is linked to overweight.

Furthermore, some parents anxiously overfeed, interpreting almost all their child's discomforts as a desire for food. Other parents are overly controlling, restricting when, what, and how much

This 9-year-old, living in shelter housing with her mother, is at high risk for obesity. Home-life stressors, including poverty and single parenthood, contribute to overeating by impairing children's self-regulation.

their child eats and worrying about weight gain (Couch et al., 2014; Jansen et al., 2012). In each case, parents undermine children's ability to regulate their own food intake.

Because of these experiences, obese children soon develop maladaptive eating habits. They are more responsive than normal-weight individuals to external stimuli associated with food—taste, sight, smell, time of day, and food-related words—and less responsive to internal hunger cues (Temple et al., 2007). Furthermore, a stressful family life contributes to children's diminished self-regulatory capacity, amplifying uncontrolled eating (Evans, Fuller-Rowell, & Doan, 2012).

Another factor implicated in weight gain is insufficient sleep (Hakim, Kheirandish-Gozal, & Gozal, 2015). Reduced sleep may increase time available for eating while leaving children too fatigued for physical activity. It also disrupts the brain's regulation of hunger and metabolism.

The rise in childhood obesity is due in part to the many hours U.S. children devote to screen media. In a study that tracked children's TV viewing from ages 4 to 11, the more TV children watched, the more body fat they added (Proctor et al., 2003). TV and Internet ads encourage children to eat unhealthy snacks: The more ads they watch, the greater their consumption of high-calorie snack foods. Children permitted to have a TV in their bedroom—a practice linked to especially high TV viewing—are at even further risk for overweight (Borghese et al., 2015; Soos et al., 2014). And heavy viewing likely subtracts from time spent in physical exercise.

Growing evidence suggests that excessive food intake, especially unhealthy foods, may induce epigenetic modifications in expression of genes affecting metabolism and weight gain (Lopomo, Burgio, & Migliore, 2016). Alterations in gene expression may underlie the persistence of child and adolescent overweight and obesity into adulthood.

Consequences of Obesity. Obese children are at risk for lifelong health problems. Symptoms that begin to appear in the early school years—high blood pressure, high cholesterol levels, respiratory abnormalities, insulin resistance, and inflammatory reactions—are powerful predictors of heart disease, circulatory difficulties, type 2 diabetes, gallbladder disease, sleep and digestive disorders, many forms of cancer, and premature death. Furthermore, obesity has caused a dramatic rise in cases of diabetes in children, sometimes leading to early, severe complications, including stroke, kidney failure, and circulatory problems that heighten the risk of eventual blindness and leg amputation (Biro & Wien, 2010; Yanovski, 2015).

Unfortunately, physical appearance is a powerful predictor of social acceptance. In Western societies, both children and adults stereotype obese youngsters as unattractive, unhappy, self-doubting, deceitful, lazy, and less successful (Grant, Mizzi, & Anglim, 2016; Harrison, Rowlinson, & Hill, 2016; Penny & Haddock, 2007). In school, obese children and adolescents are often socially isolated. They report more emotional, social, and school difficulties, including peer teasing, rejection, victmization by bullies, and consequent low self-esteem (van Grieken et al., 2013; Stensland et al., 2015). They also tend to achieve less well than their healthy-weight agemates (Carey et al., 2015).

ARIEL SKELLEY/BLEND IMAGES/GETTY IMAGES

▶ A mother and son reinforce each other's efforts to lose weight and get in shape. The most effective interventions for childhood obesity focus on changing the whole family's behaviors, emphasizing fitness and healthy eating.

Persistent obesity from childhood into adolescence predicts serious psychological disorders, including severe anxiety and depression, defiance and aggression, and suicidal thoughts and behavior (Lopresti & Drummond, 2013; Puhl & Latner, 2007). These consequences combine with continuing discrimination to further impair physical health and to reduce life chances in close relationships and employment.

Treating Obesity. In Mona's case, the school nurse suggested that Mona and her obese mother enter a weight-loss program together. But Mona's mother, unhappily married for many years, had her own reasons for overeating and rejected this idea. Research reveals that 50 to 70 percent of parents judge their overweight or obese children to have a normal weight (Jones et al., 2011; McKee et al., 2016). Consistent with these findings, most obese children do not get any treatment.

The most effective interventions are family-based and focus on changing weight-related behaviors (Seburg et al., 2015). In one program, both parent and child revised eating patterns, exercised daily, and reinforced each other with praise and points for progress, which they exchanged for special activities and times together. The more weight parents lost, the more their children lost. Follow-ups after 5 and 10 years showed that children maintained their weight loss more effectively than adults—a finding that underscores the importance of early intervention (Epstein, Roemmich, & Raynor, 2001; Wrotniak et al., 2004). Monitoring dietary intake and physical activity is important. Small wireless sensors that sync with mobile devices, enabling individualized goal-setting and tracking of progress through game-like features, are effective (Calvert, 2015; Seburg et al., 2015). But these interventions work best when parents' and children's weight problems are not severe.

Because obesity is expected to rise further without broad prevention strategies, many U.S. states and cities have passed obesity-reduction legislation. Among measures taken are weight-related school screenings for all children, improved school nutrition standards, additional school recess time and physical education, and obesity awareness and weight-reduction programs as part of school curricula. A review of these school-based efforts reported impressive benefits (Waters et al., 2011). Obesity prevention in schools was more successful in reducing 6- to 12-year-olds' BMIs than programs delivered in other community settings, perhaps because schools are better able to provide long-term, comprehensive intervention.

LOOK AND LISTEN

Contact your state and city governments to find out about their childhood obesity-prevention legislation. Can policies be improved?

Illnesses

Children experience a somewhat higher rate of illness during the first two years of elementary school than later because of exposure to sick children and an immune system that is still developing. About 20 to 25 percent of U.S. children have chronic diseases and conditions (including physical disabilities) (Compas et al., 2012). By far the most common—accounting for about one-third of childhood chronic illness and the most frequent cause of school absence and childhood hospitalization—is *asthma,* in which the bronchial tubes (passages that connect the throat and lungs) are highly sensitive (Basinger, 2013). In response to a variety of stimuli, such as cold weather, infection, exercise, allergies, and emotional stress, they fill with mucus and contract, leading to coughing, wheezing, and serious breathing difficulties.

The prevalence of asthma in the United States has increased steadily over the past several decades, with nearly 8 percent of children affected. Although heredity contributes to asthma, environmental factors seem necessary to spark the illness. Boys, African-American children, and children who were born underweight, whose parents smoke, or who live in poverty are at greatest risk (Centers for Disease Control and Prevention, 2016a). For African-American and poverty-stricken children, pollution in inner-city areas (which triggers allergic reactions), stressful home lives, and lack of access to good health care are implicated. Childhood obesity is also related to asthma (Hampton, 2014). High levels of blood-circulating inflammatory substances associated with body fat and the pressure of excess weight on the chest wall may be responsible.

About 2 percent of U.S. children have more severe chronic illnesses, such as sickle cell anemia, diabetes, arthritis, cancer, and AIDS. Painful medical treatments, physical discomfort, and changes in appearance often disrupt the sick child's daily life, making it difficult to concentrate in school and separating the child from peers. As the illness worsens, family and child stress increases (Marin et al., 2009; Rodriguez, Dunn, & Compas, 2012). For these reasons, chronically ill children are at risk for academic, emotional, and social difficulties.

A strong link exists between good family functioning and child well-being for chronically ill children, just as it does for physically healthy children (Compas et al., 2012). Interventions that foster positive family relationships help parent and child cope with the disease and improve adjustment. These include health education, counseling, parent and peer support groups, and disease-specific summer camps, which teach children self-help skills and give parents time off from the demands of caring for an ill youngster.

Motor Development and Play

9.4 Cite major changes in motor development and play during middle childhood.

Gains in body size and muscle strength support improved motor coordination in middle childhood. And greater cognitive and social maturity enables older children to use their new motor skills in more complex ways. A major change in children's play takes place at this time.

© ZUMA PRESS, INC/ALAMY

▶ Improved physical flexibility, balance, agility, and force, along with more efficient information processing, promote gains in school-age children's gross-motor skills.

Gross-Motor Development

During the school years, running, jumping, hopping, and ball skills become more refined. Third to sixth graders burst into sprints as they race across the playground, jump quickly over rotating ropes, engage in intricate hopscotch patterns, kick and dribble soccer balls, bat at balls pitched by their classmates, and balance adeptly as they walk heel-to-toe across narrow ledges. These diverse skills reflect gains in four basic motor capacities:

- *Flexibility.* Compared with preschoolers, school-age children are physically more pliable and elastic, a difference evident as they swing bats, kick balls, jump over hurdles, and execute tumbling routines.
- *Balance.* Improved balance supports many athletic skills, including running, skipping, throwing, kicking, and the rapid changes of direction required in team sports.
- *Agility.* Quicker and more accurate movements are evident in the fancy footwork of dance and cheerleading and in the forward, backward, and sideways motions used to dodge opponents in tag and soccer.
- *Force.* Older children can throw and kick a ball harder and propel themselves farther off the ground when running and jumping than they could at earlier ages (Haywood & Getchell, 2014).

Along with body growth, more efficient information processing contributes greatly to improved motor performance. During middle childhood, the capacity to react only to relevant information increases. And steady gains in reaction time occur, including anticipatory responding to visual stimuli, such as a thrown ball or a turning jump rope (Debrabant et al., 2012; Kail, 2003). Ten-year-olds react twice as quickly as 5-year-olds.

Children's gross-motor activity not only benefits from but contributes to cognitive development. Physical fitness predicts improved executive function, memory, and academic achievement in middle childhood (Chaddock et al., 2011). Exercise-induced changes in the brain seem to be responsible: Brain-imaging research reveals that structures supporting attentional control and memory are larger, and myelination of neural fibers within them greater, in better-fit than in poorly-fit children (Chaddock et al., 2010a, 2010b; Chaddock-Heyman et al., 2014). Furthermore, children who are physically fit—and those assigned to a yearlong, one-hour-per-day school fitness program—activate these brain structures more effectively while performing executive function tasks (Chaddock et al., 2012; Chaddock-Heyman et al., 2013). Mounting evidence supports the role of vigorous exercise in optimal brain and cognitive functioning in childhood—a relationship that persists throughout the lifespan.

Fine-Motor Development

Fine-motor development also improves over the school years. By age 6, most children can print the alphabet, their first and last names, and the numbers from 1 to 10 with reasonable clarity. Their writing is large, however, because they make strokes using the entire arm rather than just the wrist and fingers. Children usually master uppercase letters first because their horizontal and vertical motions are easier to control than the small curves of the lowercase alphabet.

By the end of the preschool years, children can accurately copy many two-dimensional shapes, and they integrate these into their drawings. Some depth cues have also begun to appear, such as making distant objects smaller than near ones (Braine et al., 1993). Around 9 to 10 years, the third dimension is clearly evident through overlapping objects, diagonal placement, and converging lines. Furthermore, as Figure 9.2 shows, school-age children not only depict objects in considerable detail but also better relate them to one another as part of an organized whole (Case & Okamoto, 1996).

FIGURE 9.2 Increase in organization, detail, and depth cues in school-age children's drawings. Compare both drawings to the one by a 5-year-old in Figure 7.3 on page 212. In the drawing by an 8-year-old on the left, notice how all parts are depicted in relation to one another and with greater detail. Integration of depth cues increases dramatically over the school years, as shown in the drawing on the right, by an 11-year-old. Here, depth is indicated by overlapping objects, diagonal placement, and converging lines, as well as by making distant objects smaller than near ones.

Sex Differences

Sex differences in motor skills extend into middle childhood and, in some instances, become more pronounced. Girls have an edge in the fine-motor skills of handwriting and drawing and in gross-motor capacities that depend on balance and agility, such as hopping and skipping (Haywood & Getchell, 2014). But boys outperform girls on all other gross-motor skills, especially throwing and kicking.

School-age boys' genetic advantage in muscle mass is not large enough to account for their gross-motor superiority. Rather, experiences play a substantial role. Parents hold higher expectations for boys' athletic performance, and children readily absorb these messages. From first through twelfth grades, girls are less positive than boys about the value of sports and their own sports ability (Fredricks & Eccles, 2002; Noordstar et al., 2016). The more strongly girls believe that females are incompetent at sports (such as hockey or soccer), the lower they judge their own ability and the poorer they actually perform (Belcher et al., 2003; Chalabaev, Sarrazin, & Fontayne, 2009).

Educating parents about the minimal differences between school-age boys' and girls' physical capacities and sensitizing them to unfair biases against promotion of girls' athletic ability may help increase girls' self-confidence and participation in athletics. Greater emphasis on skill training for girls, along with increased attention to their athletic achievements, is also likely to help. As a positive sign, compared with a generation ago, many more girls now participate in individual and team sports, though their involvement continues to lag behind boys' (Bassett et al., 2015; Kanters et al., 2013).

Games with Rules

The physical activities of school-age children reflect an important advance in their play: Games with rules become common. Children around the world engage in an enormous variety of informally organized games, such as tag, hopscotch, and variants on popular sports. They have invented hundreds of other games, including red rover, statues, leapfrog, kick the can, and prisoner's base.

Gains in perspective taking—in particular, the ability to understand the roles of several players in a game—permit this transition to rule-oriented games. These play experiences, in turn, contribute greatly to emotional and social development. Child-invented games usually rely on simple physical skills and a sizable element of luck. As a result, they rarely become contests of individual ability. Instead, they permit children to try out different styles of cooperating, competing, winning, and losing with little personal risk. Also, in their efforts to organize a game, children discover why rules are necessary and which ones work well.

A group of boys gather in their schoolyard for a pick-up basketball game. Children in low-SES communities often play child-organized games, which serve as rich contexts for social learning.

School-age children today spend less time engaged in informal outdoor play—a change that reflects parental concern about neighborhood safety as well as time devoted to TV and other screen media. Another factor is the rise in adult-organized sports, such as Little League baseball and soccer and hockey leagues, which fill many hours that children from economically advantaged families used to devote to spontaneous play. Nearly half of U.S. children—60 percent of boys and 47 percent of girls—participate at some time between ages 5 and 18 (SFIA, 2015).

For most children, joining community athletic teams is associated with increased social skills and self-esteem (Cronin & Allen, 2015; Daniels & Leaper, 2006). Children who view themselves as good at sports are more likely to continue playing on teams in adolescence, which predicts greater particpation in sports and other physical fitness activities in adulthood (Kjønniksen, Anderssen, & Wold, 2009). In some cases, though, youth sports overemphasize competition and substitute adult control for children's experimentation with rules and strategies, setting the stage for emotional difficulties and early athletic dropout (Marholz et al., 2016; Wall & Côté, 2007).

In village societies and developing countries and in many low-SES communities in industrialized nations, children's informal sports and games remain widespread. In an ethnographic study in two communities—a refugee camp in Angola, Africa, and a Chicago public housing complex—the overwhelming majority of 6- to 12-year-olds engaged in child-organized games at least once a week, and half or more did so nearly every day. Play in each context reflected cultural values (Guest, 2013). In the Angolan community, games emphasized imitation of social roles, such as soccer moves of admired professional players. Games in Chicago, in contrast, were competitive and individualistic. In ballgames, for example, children often made sure peers noticed when they batted or fielded balls particularly well.

Rough-and-tumble play—which can be distinguished from aggression by its friendly quality—may have been important in our evolutionary past for developing fighting skill.

Shadows of Our Evolutionary Past

While watching children in your neighborhood park, notice how they sometimes wrestle, roll, hit, and run after one another, alternating roles while smiling and laughing. This friendly chasing and play-fighting is called **rough-and-tumble play.** It emerges in the preschool years and peaks in middle childhood (Pellegrini, 2006). Children in many cultures engage in it with peers whom they like especially well.

Children's rough-and-tumble play resembles the social behavior of many other young mammals. It is more common among boys, probably because prenatal exposure to androgens predisposes boys toward active play (see Chapter 8).

In our evolutionary past, rough-and-tumble play may have been important for developing fighting skill. Children seem to use play-fighting as a safe context to assess the strength of peers so they can refrain from challenging agemates with whom they are not well-matched physically (Fry, 2014; Roseth et al., 2007). Rough-and-tumble play offers lessons in how to handle combative interactions with restraint.

As children reach puberty, individual differences in strength become apparent, and rough-and-tumble play declines. When it does occur, its meaning changes: Adolescent boys' rough-and-tumble play is linked to aggression (Pellegrini, 2003). Unlike children, teenage rough-and-tumble players "cheat," hurting their opponent. In explanation, boys often say that they are retaliating, apparently to reestablish dominance. Thus, a play behavior that limits aggression in childhood becomes a context for hostility in adolescence.

Physical Education

Physical activity supports many aspects of children's development—physical health, self-esteem, and cognitive and social skills. Yet to devote more time to academic instruction, 42 U.S. states no longer require a daily recess in the elementary school grades. Although most U.S. states require some physical education, only six do so in every grade, and only one mandates at least 30 minutes per school day in elementary school and 45 minutes in middle and high school. Fewer than 30 percent of 6- to 17-year-olds engage in at least moderate-intensity activity for 60 minutes per day, including some vigorous activity (involving breathing hard and sweating) on three of those days—the U.S. government recommendations for good health (Society of Health and Physical Educators, 2016).

Many experts believe that schools should not only offer more physical education but also reduce the emphasis placed on competitive sports, which are unlikely to reach the least physically fit youngsters. Instead, programs should emphasize informal games and individual exercise—pursuits most likely to endure. Physically active children tend to become active adults who reap many benefits (Kjønniksen, Torsheim, & Wold, 2008). These include greater physical strength, resistance to many illnesses, enhanced psychological well-being, and a longer life.

ASK YOURSELF

CONNECT Select either obesity or asthma, and explain how both genetic and environmental factors contribute to it.

APPLY Nine-year-old Allison thinks she isn't good at sports, and she doesn't like physical education class. Suggest strategies her teacher can use to improve her pleasure and involvement in physical activity.

REFLECT Did you participate in adult-organized sports as a child? If so, what kind of climate for learning did coaches and parents create?

COGNITIVE DEVELOPMENT

"Finally!" 6-year-old Lizzie exclaimed the day Rena enrolled her in elementary school. "Now I get to go to real school, just like Joey!" Lizzie confidently walked into a combined kindergarten–first-grade class in her neighborhood school, ready for a more disciplined approach to learning. In a single morning, she and her classmates met in reading groups, wrote in journals, worked on addition and subtraction, and sorted leaves gathered for a science project. As Lizzie and Joey moved through the elementary school grades, they tackled increasingly complex projects and became more accomplished at reading, writing, math skills, and general knowledge of the world.

To understand the cognitive attainments of middle childhood, we turn to research inspired by Piaget's theory and the information-processing perspective. Then we look at expanding definitions of intelligence that help us appreciate individual differences. Our discussion continues with language, which blossoms further in these years. Finally, we consider the role of schools in children's development.

Piaget's Theory: The Concrete Operational Stage

9.5 Describe advances in thinking, and cognitive limitations, during the concrete operational stage.

9.6 Discuss follow-up research on concrete operational thought.

When Lizzie visited my child development class at age 4, Piaget's conservation problems confused her (see Chapter 7, page 218). For example, when water was poured from a tall, narrow container into a short, wide one, she insisted that the amount of water had changed. But when she returned at age 8, she found this task easy. "Of course it's the same!" she exclaimed. "The water's shorter, but it's also wider. Pour it back," she instructed the college student who was interviewing her about conservation of liquid. "You'll see, it's the same amount!"

Concrete Operational Thought

Lizzie has entered Piaget's **concrete operational stage,** which extends from about 7 to 11 years. Compared with early childhood, thought is more logical, flexible, and organized.

Conservation. The ability to pass *conservation tasks* provides clear evidence of *operations*—mental actions that obey logical rules. Notice how Lizzie is capable of *decentration,* focusing on several aspects of a problem and relating them, rather than centering on just one. She also demonstrates **reversibility,** the capacity to think through a series of steps and then mentally reverse direction, returning to the starting point. Recall from Chapter 7 that reversibility is part of every logical operation. It is solidly achieved in middle childhood.

© LAURA DWIGHT PHOTOGRAPHY

▶ An improved ability to categorize underlies children's interest in collecting objects during middle childhood. This 10-year-old sorts and organizes his extensive rock and mineral collection.

Classification. Between ages 7 and 10, children pass Piaget's *class inclusion problem* (see page 219 in Chapter 7). This indicates that they are better able to inhibit their habitual strategy of perceptually comparing the two specific categories (blue flowers and yellow flowers) in favor of relating each specific category to its less-obvious general category (Borst et al., 2013). School-age children's enhanced classification skills are evident in their enthusiasm for collecting treasured objects. At age 10, Joey spent hours sorting and resorting his baseball cards, grouping them first by league and team, then by playing position and batting average. He could separate the players into a variety of classes and subclasses and easily rearrange them.

Seriation. The ability to order items along a quantitative dimension, such as length or weight, is called **seriation.** To test for it, Piaget asked children to arrange sticks of different lengths from shortest to longest. Older preschoolers can put the sticks in a row, but they do so haphazardly, making many errors. In contrast, 6- to 7-year-olds create the series efficiently, moving in an orderly sequence from the smallest stick, to the next largest, and so on.

The concrete operational child can also seriate mentally, an ability called **transitive inference.** In a well-known transitive inference problem, Piaget showed children pairings of sticks of different colors. From observing that Stick *A* is longer than Stick *B* and Stick *B* is longer than Stick *C,* children must infer that *A* is longer than *C.* Like Piaget's class inclusion task, transitive inference requires children to integrate three relations at once—in this instance, *A–B, B–C,* and *A–C.* As long as they receive help in remembering the premises (*A–B* and *B–C*), 7- to 8-year-olds can grasp transitive inference (Wright, 2006). And when the task is made relevant to children's everyday experiences—for example, based on winners of races between pairs of cartoon characters—6-year-olds perform well (Wright, Robertson, & Hadfield, 2011).

Spatial Reasoning. Piaget found that school-age children's understanding of space is more accurate than that of preschoolers. To illustrate, let's consider children's **cognitive maps**—their mental representations of spaces such as a classroom, school, or neighborhood. Drawing or reading a map of a large-scale space (school or neighborhood) requires considerable perspective-taking skill. Because the entire space cannot be seen at once, children must infer its overall layout by relating its separate parts.

Preschoolers and young school-age children include *landmarks* on the maps they draw of a single room, but their arrangement is not always accurate. They do better when asked to place stickers showing the location of furniture and people on a map of the room. But if the map is rotated to a position other than the room's orientation, they have difficulty (Liben & Downs, 1993). Seven-year-olds are aided by the opportunity to walk through the room (Lehnung et al., 2003). As they experience landmarks from different vantage points, they form a more flexible mental representation.

With respect to large-scale outdoor environments, not until age 9 can many children accurately place stickers on a map to indicate landmarks. Children who spontaneously use strategies that help them align the map with their current location in the space—rotating the map or tracing their route on it—show better performance (Liben et al., 2013). Around this age, the maps children draw of large-scale spaces become better organized, showing landmarks along an *organized route of travel.* At the same time, children are able to give clear, well-organized directions for getting from one place to another.

At the end of middle childhood, most children can form an accurate *overall view of a large-scale space.* And they readily draw and read maps, even when the orientation of the map and the space it represents do not match (Liben, 2009). Ten- to 12-year-olds also grasp the notion of *scale*—the proportional relation between a space and its representation on a map (Liben, 2006).

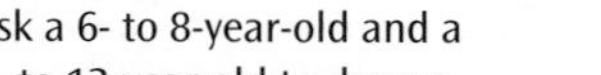

LOOK AND LISTEN

Ask a 6- to 8-year-old and a 9- to 12-year-old to draw a neighborhood map showing important landmarks, such as the school, a friend's house, or a shopping area. In what ways do the children's maps differ?

Limitations of Concrete Operational Thought

Concrete operational thinking suffers from one important limitation: Children think in an organized, logical fashion only when dealing with concrete information they can perceive directly. Their mental operations work poorly with abstract ideas—ones not apparent in the real world. Consider children's solutions to transitive inference problems. When shown pairs of sticks of unequal length, Lizzie easily engaged in transitive inference. But she had difficulty with a hypothetical version of this task: "Susan is taller than Sally, and Sally is taller than Mary. Who is the tallest?" Not until ages 11 or 12 can children typically solve this problem.

Children master concrete operational tasks step by step. For example, they usually grasp conservation of number first, followed by length, liquid, and mass, and then weight. This *continuum of acquisition* (or gradual mastery) of logical concepts is another indication of the limitations of concrete operational thinking. Rather than coming up with general logical principles that they apply to all relevant situations, school-age children seem to work out the logic of each problem separately.

Follow-Up Research on Concrete Operational Thought

According to Piaget, brain development combined with rich, varied experiences should lead children everywhere to reach the concrete operational stage at about the same time. Yet much evidence indicates that specific cultural and school practices have much to do with mastery of Piagetian tasks (Rogoff, 2003). And information-processing research helps explain the gradual mastery of logical concepts in middle childhood.

The Impact of Culture and Schooling. In village societies, conservation is often delayed. Among the Hausa of Nigeria, who live in small agricultural settlements and rarely send their children to school, even basic conservation tasks—number, length, and liquid—are not understood until age 11 or later (Fahrmeier, 1978). This suggests that participating in relevant everyday activities helps children master conservation and other Piagetian problems. Joey and Lizzie, for example, think of fairness in terms of equal distribution—a value emphasized in their culture. They frequently divide materials, such as Halloween treats or lemonade, equally among their friends. Because they often see the same quantity arranged in different ways, they grasp conservation early.

The experience of going to school promotes mastery of Piagetian tasks. When children of the same age are tested, those who have been in school longer do better on transitive inference problems (Artman & Cahan, 1993). Opportunities to seriate objects, learn about order relations, and remember the parts of complex problems are probably responsible. Yet certain informal nonschool experiences can also foster operational thought. Around ages 7 to 8, Zinacanteco Indian girls of southern Mexico, who learn to weave elaborately designed fabrics as an alternative to schooling, engage in mental transformations to figure out how a warp strung on a loom will turn out as woven cloth—reasoning expected at the concrete operational stage (Maynard &

▶ A Zinacanteco Indian girl of southern Mexico learns the centuries-old practice of backstrap weaving. Although Zinacanteco children might do poorly on Piaget's tasks, they are adept at the complex mental transformations involved in converting warp strung on a loom into woven cloth.

Greenfield, 2003). North American children of the same age, who do much better than Zinacanteco children on Piagetian tasks, have great difficulty with these weaving problems.

On the basis of such findings, some investigators have concluded that the forms of logic required by Piagetian tasks are heavily influenced by training, context, and cultural conditions. Does this view remind you of Vygotsky's sociocultural theory, discussed in earlier chapters?

An Information-Processing View of Concrete Operational Thought. The gradual mastery of logical concepts in middle childhood raises a familiar question about Piaget's theory: Is an abrupt stagewise transition to logical thought the best way to describe cognitive development in middle childhood?

Some *neo-Piagetian theorists* argue that the development of operational thinking can best be understood in terms of expansion of information-processing capacity rather than a sudden shift to a new stage. For example, Robbie Case (1996, 1998) proposed that, with brain development and practice, cognitive schemes are applied more rapidly, gradually demanding less attention and becoming automatic. This frees up space in working memory so children can focus on combining old schemes and generating new ones. For instance, as children's understanding that the height of a liquid changes after it is poured into a differently shaped container becomes routine, they notice that the width of the water changes as well. Soon they coordinate these observations, and they grasp conservation of liquid. Then, as this logical idea becomes well-practiced, children transfer it to more demanding tasks, such as weight.

Once the schemes of a Piagetian stage are sufficiently automatic, enough working memory is available to integrate them into an improved, broadly applicable representation. As a result, children transition from concrete operations to the complex, systematic reasoning of formal operational thought, which enables them to think effectively in a wider range of situations.

Case's theory, along with similar neo-Piagetian perspectives, helps explain why children's understandings appear in specific situations at different times rather than being mastered all at once (Andrews & Halford, 2011; Barrouillet & Gaillard, 2011a). First, different forms of the same logical insight, such as the various conservation tasks, vary in their processing demands, with those acquired later requiring more space in working memory. Second, children's experiences with different types of tasks vary widely, affecting their performance. Compared with Piaget's theory, neo-Piagetian approaches better account for unevenness in cognitive development.

Evaluation of the Concrete Operational Stage. Piaget was correct that school-age children approach many problems in more organized, rational ways than preschoolers. But disagreement continues over whether this difference is due to *continuous* improvement in logical skills or *discontinuous* restructuring of children's thinking (as Piaget's stage idea assumes). Many researchers think that both types of change may be involved (Andrews & Halford, 2011; Barrouillet & Gaillard, 2011b; Case, 1998; Mascolo & Fischer, 2015).

During the school years, children apply logical schemes to many more tasks. In the process, their thought seems to change qualitatively—toward a more comprehensive grasp of the underlying principles of logical thought. Piaget himself recognized this possibility in evidence for gradual mastery of conservation and other tasks. So perhaps some blend of Piagetian and information-processing ideas holds the greatest promise for explaining cognitive development in middle childhood.

ASK YOURSELF

CONNECT Explain how advances in perspective taking contribute to school-age children's improved ability to draw and use maps.

APPLY Nine-year-old Adrienne spends many hours helping her father build furniture in his woodworking shop. How might this experience facilitate Adrienne's advanced performance on Piagetian seriation problems?

REFLECT Which aspects of Piaget's description of the concrete operational child do you accept? Which do you doubt? Explain, citing research evidence.

Information Processing

9.7 Describe gains in executive function and memory in middle childhood, along with factors that influence children's progress.

9.8 Describe the school-age child's theory of mind and capacity to engage in self-regulation.

9.9 Discuss current perspectives on teaching reading and mathematics to elementary school children.

In contrast to Piaget's focus on overall cognitive change, the information-processing perspective examines separate aspects of thinking. As noted in our discussion of Case's theory, working-memory capacity continues to increase in middle childhood. And school-age children make strides in other facets of executive function, including control of attention and planning. Dramatic gains also occur in strategic memory and self-regulation.

Executive Function

The school years are a time of continued development of the prefrontal cortex, which increases its connections with more distant parts of the brain. Myelination of neural fibers rises steadily, especially in the prefrontal cortex and in the corpus callosum, which connects the two cerebral hemispheres (Giedd et al., 2009; Smit et al., 2012). As interconnectivity between the prefrontal cortex and other brain areas strengthens, the prefrontal cortex becomes a more effective "executive," overseeing the integrated functioning of neural networks.

Consequently, executive function undergoes marked improvement (Xu et al., 2013). Children handle increasingly difficult tasks that require the integration of working memory, inhibition, and flexible shifting of attention, which, in turn, support gains in planning, strategic thinking, and self-monitoring and self-correction of behavior.

Heritability evidence suggests considerable genetic contribution to executive function (Polderman et al., 2009; Young et al., 2009). And molecular genetic analyses are identifying specific genes related to severely deficient executive function components, such as inhibition and flexible thinking, which (as we will soon see) contribute to learning and behavior disorders, including attention-deficit hyperactivity disorder (ADHD) (refer to the Biology and Environment box on page 294).

But in both typically and atypically developing children, heredity combines with environmental contexts to influence executive function. As we turn now to the development of executive function components in middle childhood, our discussion will confirm once more that supportive home and school experiences are essential.

School-age children undergo marked gains in executive function. They can perform increasingly complex tasks—such as this science project on how floodplains are formed—that require the integration of working memory, inhibition, and flexible shifting of attention.

Inhibition and Flexible Shifting of Attention. School-age children become better at deliberately attending to relevant aspects of a task and inhibiting irrelevant responses. One way researchers study this increasing selectivity of attention is by introducing irrelevant stimuli into a task and seeing how well children attend to its central elements. Performance improves sharply between ages 6 and 10, with gains continuing throughout adolescence (Tabibi & Pfeffer, 2007; Vakil et al., 2009).

Older children are also better at flexibly shifting their attention in response to task requirements. When given rule-use tasks that require frequent switching of the rules used to sort picture cards containing conflicting cues (return to page 225 in Chapter 7 for an example), schoolchildren gain steadily with age in the complexity of rules they can keep in mind and in the speed and accuracy with which they shift between rules. Recall that flexible shifting benefits from gains in inhibition (enabling children to ignore rules not momentarily relevant) and expansion of working memory (helping children keep multiple rules in mind).

In sum, selectivity and flexibility of attention become better controlled and more efficient (Carlson, Zelazo, & Faja, 2013). Children adapt their attention more quickly in the face of increasingly complex distractors—skills that contribute to more organized, strategic approaches to challenging tasks.

Working Memory. As Case's theory emphasizes, working memory profits from increased efficiency of thinking. Time needed to process information on a wide variety of cognitive tasks declines rapidly between ages 6 and 12 in diverse cultures, likely due to myelination and enhanced

BIOLOGY AND ENVIRONMENT

Children with Attention-Deficit Hyperactivity Disorder

While the other fifth graders worked quietly at their desks, Calvin squirmed, dropped his pencil, looked out the window, and fiddled with his shoelaces. "Hey Joey," he yelled across the room, "wanna play ball after school?" But the other children weren't eager to play with Calvin, who was physically awkward and failed to follow the rules of the game. He had trouble taking turns at bat and, in the outfield, looked elsewhere when the ball came his way. Calvin's desk was a chaotic mess. He often lost pencils, books, and other school materials, and he had difficulty remembering assignments and due dates.

Symptoms of ADHD

Calvin is one of about 5 percent of U.S. school-age children with **attention-deficit hyperactivity disorder (ADHD)**, which involves inattention, impulsivity, and excessive motor activity resulting in academic and social problems (American Psychiatric Association, 2013; Goldstein, 2011). Boys are diagnosed two to three times as often as girls. However, many girls with ADHD seem to be overlooked, either because their symptoms are less flagrant or because of a gender bias: A difficult, disruptive boy is more likely to be referred for treatment (Owens, Cardoos, & Hinshaw, 2015).

Children with ADHD cannot stay focused on a task that requires mental effort for more than a few minutes. They often act impulsively, ignoring social rules and lashing out with hostility when frustrated. Many, though not all, are *hyperactive,* exhausting parents and teachers and irritating other children with their excessive motor activity. For a child to be diagnosed with ADHD, these symptoms must have appeared before age 12 as a persistent problem.

Because of their difficulty concentrating, children with ADHD score lower in IQ than other children, though the difference is mostly accounted for by a small subgroup with substantially below-average scores (Biederman et al., 2012). Researchers agree that deficient executive function underlies ADHD symptoms. Children with ADHD are impaired in ability to inhibit distracting behaviors and irrelevant information and score low in working-memory capacity (Antshel, Hier, & Barkley, 2015). Consequently, they have difficulty with sustained attention, planning, memory, reasoning, and problem solving in academic and social situations and often fail to manage frustration and intense emotion.

© ELLEN B. SENISI

▶ This child frequently engages in disruptive behaviors at school. Children with ADHD have great difficulty staying on task and often act impulsively, ignoring social rules.

Origins of ADHD

ADHD runs in families and is highly heritable: Identical twins share it more often than fraternal twins (Freitag et al., 2010). Children with ADHD show abnormal brain functioning, including reduced electrical and blood-flow activity and structural abnormalities in the prefrontal cortex and in other areas involved in attention, inhibition of behavior, and other aspects of motor control (Mackie et al., 2007). Also, the brains of children with ADHD grow more slowly and are about 3 percent smaller in overall volume, with a thinner cerebral cortex, than the brains of unaffected agemates (Narr et al., 2009; Shaw et al., 2007). Several genes that disrupt functioning of the neurotransmitters serotonin (involved in inhibition and self-control) and dopamine (required for effective cognitive processing) have been implicated in the disorder (Akutagava-Martins et al., 2013).

At the same time, ADHD is associated with environmental factors. Prenatal teratogens—such as tobacco, alcohol, illegal drugs, and environmental pollutants—are linked to inattention and hyperactivity. Furthermore, children with ADHD are more likely to have parents with psychological disorders and to come from homes where family stress is high (Law et al., 2014). These circumstances often intensify the child's preexisting difficulties.

Treating ADHD

Calvin's doctor eventually prescribed stimulant medication, the most common treatment for ADHD. These drugs seem to increase activity in the prefrontal cortex, thereby reducing impulsivity and hyperactivity and improving attention for most children who take them (Connor, 2015).

By itself, drug treatment is insufficient for helping children compensate for inattention and impulsivity in everyday situations. The most effective treatments combine medication with interventions that provide training in executive function skills (see page 295) and that model and reinforce appropriate academic and social behavior (Smith & Shapiro, 2015; Tamm, Nakonezny, & Hughes, 2014).

Family intervention is also vital. Inattentive, hyperactive children strain the patience of parents, who are likely to react punitively and inconsistently—a child-rearing style that strengthens defiant, aggressive behavior. In fact, in 50 to 75 percent of cases, these two sets of behavior problems occur together (Goldstein, 2011).

ADHD is usually a lifelong disorder. Adults with ADHD continue to need help in structuring their environments, regulating negative emotion, selecting appropriate careers, and understanding their condition as a biological deficit rather than a character flaw.

connectivity among regions of the cerebral cortex (Kail & Ferrer, 2007; Kail et al., 2013). A faster thinker can hold on to and operate on more information at once. Still, individual differences in working-memory capacity exist, and they are of particular concern because they predict intelligence test scores and academic achievement in many subjects (DeMarie & Lopez, 2014).

Observations of elementary school children with limited working memories revealed that they often failed at school assignments that made heavy memory demands (Alloway et al., 2009). They could not follow complex instructions, lost their place in tasks with multiple steps, and frequently gave up before finishing their work. The children struggled because they could not hold in mind sufficient information to complete assignments.

Children from poverty-stricken families are especially likely to score low on working-memory tasks. In one study, years of childhood spent in poverty predicted reduced working memory in early adulthood (Evans & Schamberg, 2009). Childhood neurobiological measures of stress—elevated blood pressure and stress hormone levels, including cortisol—largely explained this poverty–working-memory association. Chronic stress, as we saw in Chapter 4, can impair brain structure and function, especially in the prefrontal cortex and its connections with the hippocampus, which govern working-memory capacity.

Scaffolding in which parents and teachers modify tasks to reduce memory loads is essential for these children to learn. Effective approaches include communicating in short sentences with familiar vocabulary, repeating task instructions, breaking complex tasks into manageable parts, and encouraging children to use external memory aids—for example, lists of useful spellings while writing or number lines while doing math (Gathercole & Alloway, 2008).

Training Executive Function. Children's executive function skills can be improved through training, with benefits for both academic achievement and social competence (Müller & Kerns, 2015). To enhance control of attention and working memory, researchers often embed direct training in interactive computer games. In one investigation, 10-year-olds with learning difficulties who played a game providing working-memory training four times a week for eight weeks showed substantially greater improvement in working-memory capacity, IQ, and spelling and math achievement over agemates who played less often or did not play at all (Alloway, Bibile, & Lau, 2013). Gains were still evident eight months after the training ended.

▶ Fourth graders take a break from school work to meditate, a practice that requires focused attention and reflection. Mindfulness training such as meditation leads to gains in executive function, school grades, prosocial behavior, and positive peer relations.

Executive function can also be enhanced indirectly, by increasing children's participation in activities—such as exercise—known to promote it (see page 286). Another indirect method is *mindfulness training,* which—similar to meditation- and yoga-based exercises for adults—encourages children to focus attention on their current thoughts, feelings, and sensations, without judging them. For example, children might be asked to attend to their own breathing or to manipulate an object held behind their backs while noticing how it feels (Zelazo & Lyons, 2012). If their attention wanders, they are told to bring it back to the current moment. Mindfulness training leads to gains in executive function, school grades, prosocial behavior, and positive peer relations (Schonert-Reichl & Lawlor, 2010; Schonert-Reichl et al., 2015) The sustained attention and reflection that mindfulness requires seem to help children avoid snap judgments, distracting thoughts and emotions, and impulsive behavior.

Planning. Planning on multistep tasks improves over the school years. With age, children make decisions about what to do first and what to do next in a more orderly fashion. By the end of middle childhood, children engage in *advance planning*—evaluating an entire sequence of steps to see if it will get them to their goal (Tecwyn, Thorpe, & Chappell, 2014). Nine- and 10-year-olds can project ahead, predicting how early steps in their plan will affect success at later steps and adjust their overall plan accordingly.

As Chapter 7 revealed, children learn much about planning from collaborating with more-expert planners. With age, they take more responsibility in these joint endeavors, such as suggesting planning strategies and organizing task materials. The demands of school tasks—and parents' and teachers' explanations of how to plan—contribute to gains in planning.

Memory Strategies

As attention improves, so do *memory strategies,* deliberate mental activities we use to store and retain information. When Lizzie had a list of things to learn, such as the state capitals of the United States, she immediately used **rehearsal**—repeating the information to herself. Soon after, a second strategy becomes common: **organization**—grouping related items together (for example, all state capitals in the same part of the country), an approach that greatly improves recall (Schneider, 2002).

Perfecting memory strategies requires time and effort. Eight-year-old Lizzie rehearsed in a piecemeal fashion. After being given the word *cat* in a list of items, she said, "Cat, cat, cat." Ten-year-old Joey combined previous words with each new item, saying, "Desk, man, yard, cat, cat." This active, cumulative approach, in which neighboring words create contexts for each other that trigger recall, yields much better memory (Lehman & Hasselhorn, 2012). And whereas Lizzie often organized by everyday association (hat–head, carrot–rabbit), Joey grouped items *taxonomically,* based on common properties (clothing, food, animals), thus using fewer categories—an efficient procedure yielding dramatic memory gains (Bjorklund et al., 1994). Furthermore, Joey often combined several strategies—organizing items, stating category names, and rehearsing (Schwenck, Bjorklund, & Schneider, 2007). The more strategies children apply simultaneously, the better they remember.

By the end of middle childhood, children start to use **elaboration**—creating a relationship, or shared meaning, between two or more pieces of information that do not belong to the same category. For example, to learn the words *fish* and *pipe,* you might generate the verbal statement or mental image, "The fish is smoking a pipe" (Schneider & Pressley, 1997). This highly effective memory technique requires considerable effort and space in working memory. Because organization and elaboration combine items into *meaningful chunks,* they permit children to hold onto much more information and also to *retrieve* it easily by thinking of other items associated with it.

Knowledge and Memory

During middle childhood, children's general knowledge base, or *semantic memory,* grows larger and becomes organized into increasingly elaborate, hierarchically structured networks. This rapid growth of knowledge helps children use strategies and remember (Schneider, 2002). Knowing more about a topic makes new information more meaningful, so it is easier to store and retrieve.

To investigate this idea, researchers classified fourth graders as either experts or novices in knowledge of soccer and then gave both groups lists of soccer and nonsoccer items to learn. Experts remembered far more items on the soccer list (but not on the nonsoccer list) than novices. And during recall, the experts' listing of items was better organized, as indicated by clustering of items into categories (Schneider & Bjorklund, 1992). This superior organization at retrieval suggests that highly knowledgeable children organize information in their area of expertise with little or no effort. Consequently, experts can devote more working-memory resources to using recalled information for reasoning and problem solving.

But knowledge is not the only important factor in children's strategic memory processing. Children who are expert in an area are usually highly motivated. As a result, they not only acquire knowledge more quickly but also *actively use what they know* to add more. In contrast, academically unsuccessful children fail to ask how previously stored information can clarify new material. This, in turn, interferes with the development of a broad knowledge base (Schneider & Bjorklund, 1998). So extensive knowledge and use of memory strategies support each other.

Culture and Memory Strategies

A repeated finding is that people in village cultures who have little formal schooling do not use or benefit from instruction in memory strategies because they see no practical reason to use these techniques (Rogoff, 2003). Tasks requiring children to recall isolated pieces of information, which are common in classrooms, strongly motivate use of these techniques.

Societal modernization—indicated by the presence of books, writing tablets, electricity, radio, TV, and other economically advantageous resources in homes—is broadly associated with performance on cognitive tasks commonly given to children in industrialized nations. In an investigation in which researchers rated towns in Belize, Kenya, Nepal, and American Samoa for degree of modernization, Belize and American Samoa exceeded Kenya and Nepal (Gauvain & Munroe, 2009). Modernization predicted both extent of schooling and 5- to 9-year-olds' cognitive scores on a memory test plus an array of other measures.

In sum, the development of memory strategies is not just a product of a more competent information-processing system. It also depends on task demands, schooling, and cultural circumstances.

▶ Children in a shanty town on the outskirts of Lima use laptops provided by the Peruvian government. Societal modernization—access to contemporary resources for communication and literacy—is broadly associated with improved cognitive performance.

The School-Age Child's Theory of Mind

During middle childhood, children's *theory of mind,* or set of ideas about mental activities, becomes more elaborate and refined. Recall from Chapter 7 that this awareness of thought is often called *metacognition.* Children's improved ability to reflect on their own mental life is another reason that their thinking advances.

Unlike preschoolers, who view the mind as a passive container of information, older children regard it as an active, constructive agent that selects and transforms information (Astington & Hughes, 2013). Consequently, they have a much better understanding of cognitive processes and their impact on performance. For example, with age, elementary school children become increasingly aware of effective memory strategies and why they work (Alexander et al., 2003). They also grasp relationships between mental activities—for example, that remembering is crucial for understanding and that understanding strengthens memory (Schwanenflugel, Henderson, & Fabricius, 1998).

Furthermore, school-age children's understanding of sources of knowledge expands. They realize that people can extend their knowledge not just by directly observing events and talking to others but also by making *mental inferences* (Miller, Hardin, & Montgomery, 2003). This grasp of inference enables knowledge of *false belief* to expand. By age 7, children are aware that people form beliefs about other people's beliefs ("Joe believes that Andy believes the kitten is lost") and that these second-order beliefs can be wrong!

Appreciation of *second-order false belief* helps children pinpoint the reasons that another person arrived at a certain belief (Miller, 2009; Naito & Seki, 2009). Notice how it requires the ability to reason simultaneously about what two or more people are thinking, a form of perspective taking called **recursive thought.** We think recursively when we make such statements as "*Lisa believes that Jason believes* the letter is under his pillow, but that's *not what Jason really believes; he knows* the letter is in the desk."

The capacity for recursive thought greatly assists children in appreciating that people can harbor quite different interpretations of the same reality. For example, around ages 7 to 8, children realize that two people are likely to interpret the same event quite differently, regardless of the beliefs and biases they bring to the situation (Lalonde & Chandler, 2002). Indeed, school-age children's newfound awareness of varying viewpoints is so powerful that, at first, they overextend it (Lagattuta, Sayfan, & Blattman, 2010). They often overlook the fact that people with different past experiences sometimes agree!

As with other cognitive attainments, schooling contributes to a more reflective, process-oriented view of mental activities. In school, teachers often call attention to the workings of the mind by asking children to remember mental steps, share points of view with peers, and evaluate their own and others' reasoning.

Cognitive Self-Regulation

Although metacognition expands, school-age children frequently have difficulty putting what they know about thinking into action. They are not yet good at **cognitive self-regulation,** the process of continuously monitoring progress toward a goal, checking outcomes, and redirecting unsuccessful efforts. For example, Lizzie knows that she should group items when memorizing and reread a complicated paragraph to make sure she understands. But she does not always engage in these activities.

To study cognitive self-regulation, researchers sometimes look at the impact of children's awareness of memory strategies on how well they remember. By second grade, the more children know about memory strategies, the more they recall—a relationship that strengthens over middle childhood (DeMarie et al., 2004; Geurten, Catale, & Meulemans, 2015). And when children apply a strategy consistently, their knowledge of it strengthens, resulting in a bidirectional relationship between metacognition and strategy use that enhances self-regulation (Schlagmüller & Schneider, 2002).

Cognitive self-regulation develops gradually because monitoring and controlling task outcomes is highly demanding, requiring constant evaluation of effort and progress. Throughout elementary and secondary school, self-regulation predicts academic success (Schunk & Zimmerman, 2013). Students who do well in school know when they encounter obstacles to learning and take steps to address them—for example, by organizing the learning environment, reviewing confusing material, or seeking support from more-expert adults or peers.

Parents and teachers can foster self-regulation. In one study, researchers observed parents instructing their children on a problem-solving task during the summer before third grade. Parents who patiently pointed out important features of the task and suggested strategies had children who, in the classroom, more often discussed ways to approach problems and monitored their own performance (Stright et al., 2002). Explaining the effectiveness of strategies is particularly helpful because it provides a rationale for future action.

Children who acquire effective self-regulatory skills develop a sense of *academic self-efficacy*—confidence in their own ability, which supports future self-regulation (Fernandez-Rio et al., 2017). Unfortunately, some children receive messages from parents and teachers that seriously undermine their academic self-esteem and self-regulatory skills. We will consider these *learned-helpless* students in Chapter 10.

Applications of Information Processing to Academic Learning

Fundamental discoveries about the development of information processing have been applied to children's learning of reading and mathematics. Researchers are identifying the cognitive ingredients of skilled performance, tracing their development, and distinguishing good from poor learners by pinpointing differences in cognitive skills. They hope, as a result, to design teaching methods that will improve children's learning.

Reading. Reading makes use of many skills at once, taxing all aspects of our information-processing system. Joey and Lizzie must perceive single letters and letter combinations, translate them into speech sounds, recognize the visual appearance of many common words, hold chunks of text in working memory while interpreting their meaning, and combine the meanings of various parts of a text passage into an understandable whole. Because reading is so demanding, most or all of these skills must be done automatically. If one or more are poorly developed, they will compete for space in our limited working memories, and reading performance will decline.

As children make the transition from emergent literacy to conventional reading, *phonological awareness,* vocabulary growth, and narrative competence (see page 232 in Chapter 7) continue to facilitate their progress. Other information-processing skills also contribute. Gains in processing speed foster children's rapid conversion of visual symbols into sounds (Moll et al., 2014). Visual scanning and discrimination play important roles and improve with reading experience (Rayner, Pollatsek, & Starr, 2003). Performing these skills efficiently releases working memory for higher-level activities involved in comprehending the text's meaning.

Until recently, researchers were involved in an intense debate over which of two methods is best for teaching beginning reading. The *whole language approach* exposes children to text in its complete form—stories, poems, letters, posters, and lists. It assumes that by keeping reading whole and meaningful, children will be motivated to discover the specific skills they need. The *phonics approach*, in contrast, coaches children on the basic rules for translating written symbols into sounds before giving them complex reading material.

Many studies confirm that children learn best with a mixture of both approaches. In kindergarten, first, and second grades, teaching that includes phonics boosts reading scores, especially for children who lag behind in reading progress (Block, 2012; Brady, 2011). Learning letter–sound relationships enables children to *decode,* or decipher, words they have never seen before. Yet too much emphasis on basic skills may cause children to lose sight of the goal of reading: understanding. Children who read aloud fluently without registering meaning know little about effective metacognitive reading strategies—for example, that they must read more carefully if they will be tested than if they are reading for pleasure, that relating ideas in the text to personal experiences and general knowledge will deepen understanding, and that explaining a passage in their own words is a good way to assess comprehension. Teaching aimed at increasing awareness and use of reading strategies enhances reading performance from third grade on (Lonigan, 2015; McKeown & Beck, 2009).

Mathematics. Mathematics teaching in elementary school builds on and greatly enriches children's informal knowledge of number concepts and counting. Written notation systems and formal computational procedures enhance children's ability to represent numbers and compute. Over the early elementary school years, children acquire basic math facts through a combination of frequent practice, experimentation with diverse computational procedures (through which they discover faster, more accurate techniques), reasoning about number concepts, and teaching that conveys effective strategies. Eventually children retrieve answers automatically and apply this knowledge to more complex problems.

Arguments about how to teach mathematics resemble those in reading, pitting drill in computing against "number sense," or understanding. Again, a blend of both approaches is most beneficial (Fuson, 2009). In learning basic math, poorly performing students use cumbersome, error-prone techniques or try to retrieve answers from memory too soon. They have not sufficiently experimented with strategies to see which are most effective and to reorganize their observations in logical, efficient ways—for example, noticing that multiplication problems involving the number 2 (2 × 8) are equivalent to addition doubles (8 + 8) (Clements & Sarama, 2012).

This suggests that encouraging students to apply strategies and making sure they understand why certain strategies work well are essential for solid mastery of basic math. In one study, the more teachers emphasized conceptual knowledge, by having children actively construct meanings in word problems before practicing computation and memorizing math facts, the more children gained in math achievement from second to third grade (Staub & Stern, 2002). Children taught in this way draw on their solid knowledge of relationships between operations—for example, that the inverse of division is multiplication—to generate efficient, flexible procedures. And because they have been encouraged to estimate answers, if they go down the wrong track in computation, they are usually self-correcting. They also select math operations that are appropriate for problem contexts. They can solve a word problem ("Jesse spent \$3.45 for bananas, \$2.62 for bread, and \$3.55 for peanut butter. Can he pay for it all with a \$10 bill?") quickly through estimation instead of exact calculation (De Corte & Verschaffel, 2006).

In Asian countries, students receive a variety of supports for acquiring mathematical knowledge and often excel at math computation and reasoning. Use of the metric system helps Asian children grasp place value. The consistent structure of number words in Asian languages (*ten-two* for 12, *ten-three* for 13) also makes this idea clear (Miura & Okamoto, 2003). And because Asian number words are shorter and more quickly pronounced, more digits can be held in

▶ This fourth grader uses paper cut in different sizes to clarify the concept of fractions. The most effective math teaching combines frequent practice with instruction emphasizing conceptual understanding.

working memory at once, increasing speed of thinking. Furthermore, Chinese parents provide their preschoolers with extensive practice in counting and computation—experiences that contribute to the superiority of Chinese over U.S. children's math knowledge even before school entry (Siegler & Mu, 2008; Zhou et al., 2006). Finally, as we will see later in this chapter, compared with lessons in the United States, those in Asian classrooms devote more time to exploring math concepts and strategies and less to drill and repetition.

ASK YOURSELF

CONNECT Explain why gains in executive function are vital for mastery of reading and math in middle childhood.

APPLY Lizzie knows that if you have difficulty learning part of a task, you should devote extra attention to that part. But she plays each of her piano pieces from beginning to end instead of practicing the hard parts. What explains Lizzie's failure to engage in cognitive self-regulation?

REFLECT In your elementary school math education, how much emphasis was placed on computational drill and how much on understanding concepts? How do you think that balance affected your interest and performance in math?

Individual Differences in Mental Development

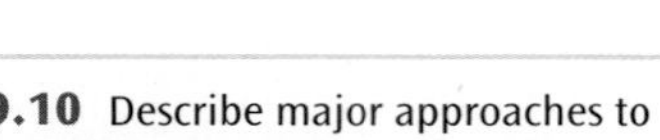

9.10 Describe major approaches to defining and measuring intelligence.

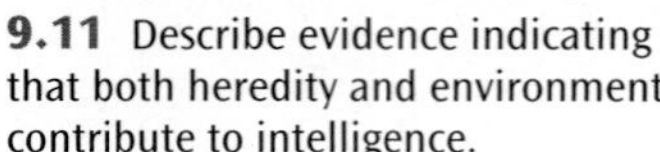

9.11 Describe evidence indicating that both heredity and environment contribute to intelligence.

Around age 6, IQ becomes more stable than it was at earlier ages, and it correlates moderately with academic achievement, typically around .50 to .60. And children with higher IQs are more likely to attain higher levels of education and enter more prestigious occupations in adulthood (Deary et al., 2007). Do intelligence tests accurately assess school-age children's ability to profit from academic instruction? Let's look closely at this controversial issue.

Defining and Measuring Intelligence

Virtually all intelligence tests provide an overall score (the IQ), which represents *general intelligence,* or reasoning ability, along with an array of separate scores measuring specific mental abilities. But intelligence is a collection of many capacities, not all of which are represented on currently available tests (Carroll, 2005; Sternberg, 2008). Test designers use a complicated statistical technique called *factor analysis* to identify the various abilities that intelligence tests measure. It identifies which sets of test items cluster together, meaning that test-takers who do well on one item in a cluster tend to do well on the others. Distinct clusters are called *factors,* each of which represents an ability. Figure 9.3 illustrates typical items on intelligence tests for children.

Although group-administered intelligence tests are available that permit large numbers of students to be tested at once, intelligence is most often assessed with *individually administered* tests, which are best suited for identifying highly intelligent children and diagnosing children with learning problems. During an individually administered test, a well-trained examiner not only considers the child's answers but also observes the child's behavior, noting such reactions as attention to and interest in the tasks and wariness of the adult. These observations provide insight into whether the test results accurately reflect the child's abilities. Two individual tests—the Stanford-Binet and the Wechsler—are used especially often.

The contemporary descendant of Alfred Binet's first successful intelligence test is the *Stanford-Binet Intelligence Scales,* Fifth Edition, for individuals from age 2 to adulthood. In addition to general intelligence, it assesses five intellectual factors: general knowledge, quantitative reasoning, visual–spatial processing, working memory, and basic information processing (such as speed of analyzing information). Each factor includes a verbal mode and a nonverbal mode of testing (Roid, 2003; Roid & Pomplun, 2012). The nonverbal mode is useful when assessing individuals with limited English, hearing impairments, or communication disorders. The knowledge and quantitative reasoning factors emphasize culturally loaded, fact-oriented information, such as

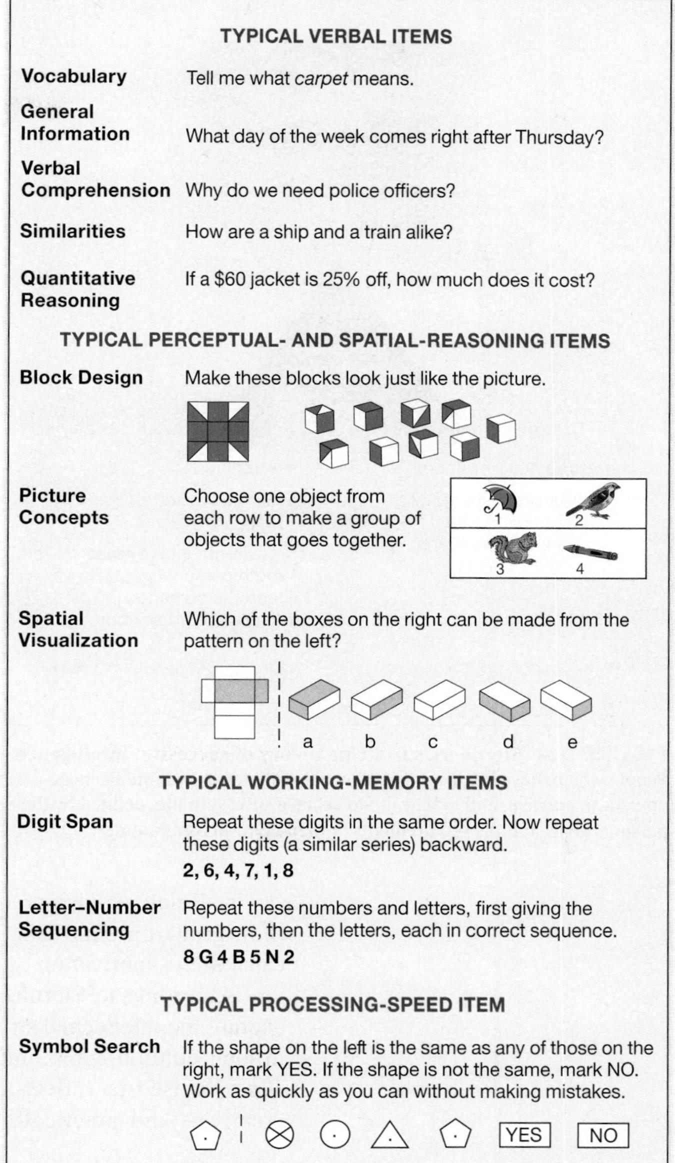

FIGURE 9.3 Test items like those on commonly used intelligence tests for children. The verbal items emphasize culturally loaded, fact-oriented information. The perceptual- and spatial-reasoning, working-memory, and processing-speed items emphasize aspects of information processing and are assumed to assess more biologically based skills.

vocabulary and arithmetic problems. In contrast, the visual–spatial processing, working-memory, and basic information-processing factors are assumed to be less culturally biased (see the spatial visualization item in Figure 9.3).

The *Wechsler Intelligence Scale for Children (WISC-V)* is the fifth edition of a widely used test for 6- through 16-year-olds. It measures general intelligence and an array of intellectual factors, five of which are recommended for a comprehensive evaluation of a child's intellectual ability: verbal comprehension, visual–spatial reasoning, fluid reasoning (tapping ability to apply rules in reasoning and to detect conceptual relationships among objects), working memory, and processing speed (Weiss et al., 2015). The WISC-V was designed to downplay culture-dependent information, which is emphasized on only one factor (verbal comprehension). The goal is to provide a test that is as "culture-fair" as possible.

Other Efforts to Define Intelligence

Some researchers have combined the mental-testing approach to defining intelligence with the information-processing approach. They believe that once we identify the processing skills that separate individuals who test well from those who test poorly, we will know more about how to intervene to improve performance.

Processing speed, assessed in terms of reaction time on diverse cognitive tasks, is moderately related to IQ (Coyle, 2013; Li et al., 2004). Individuals whose nervous systems function more efficiently, permitting them to take in more information and manipulate it quickly, have an edge in intellectual skills. And not surprisingly, executive function strongly predicts general intelligence (Brydges et al., 2012; Schweizer, Moosebrugger, & Goldhammer, 2006). We have seen that the components of executive function are vital for success on a great many cognitive tasks.

Individual differences in intelligence, however, are not entirely due to causes within the child. Throughout this book, we have seen how cultural and situational factors affect children's thinking. Robert Sternberg has devised a comprehensive theory that regards intelligence as a product of both inner and outer forces.

Sternberg's Triarchic Theory.

As Figure 9.4 on page 302 shows, Sternberg's (2008, 2011, 2013) **triarchic theory of successful intelligence** identifies three broad, interacting intelligences: (1) *analytical intelligence,* or information-processing skills; (2) *creative intelligence,* the capacity to solve novel problems; and (3) *practical intelligence,* application of intellectual skills in everyday situations. Intelligent behavior involves balancing all three intelligences to achieve success in life according to one's personal goals and the requirements of one's cultural community.

Analytical Intelligence. *Analytical intelligence* consists of the information-processing skills that underlie all intelligent acts: executive function, strategic thinking, knowledge acquisition, and cognitive self-regulation. But on intelligence tests, processing skills are used in only a few of their potential ways, resulting in far too narrow a view of intelligent behavior.

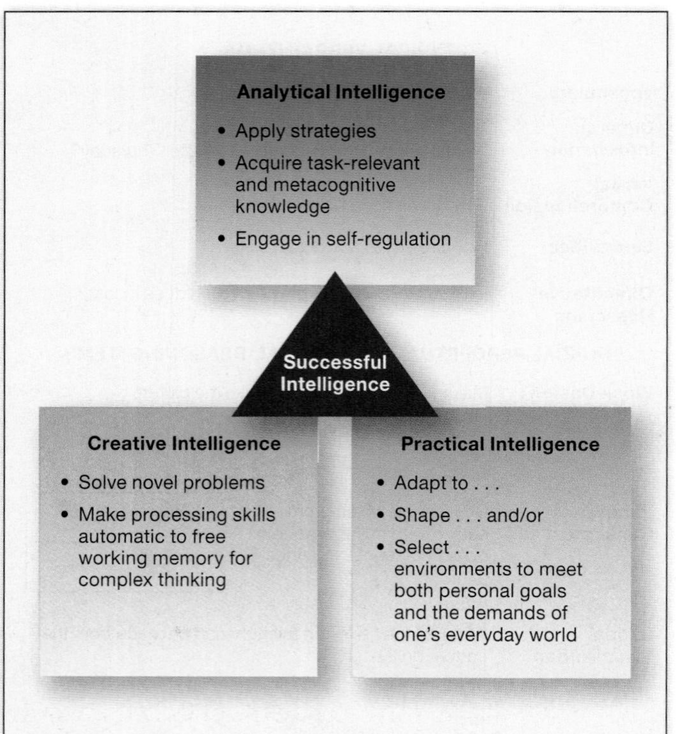

FIGURE 9.4 Sternberg's triarchic theory of successful intelligence. People who behave intelligently balance three interrelated intelligences—analytical, creative, and practical—to achieve success in life, defined by their personal goals and the requirements of their cultural communities.

Creative Intelligence. In any context, success depends not only on processing familiar information but also on generating useful solutions to new problems. People who are *creative* think more skillfully than others when faced with novelty. Given a new task, they apply their information-processing skills in exceptionally effective ways, rapidly making these skills automatic so that working memory is freed for more complex aspects of the situation.

Practical Intelligence. Finally, intelligence is a *practical,* goal-oriented activity aimed at *adapting to, shaping,* or *selecting environments.* Intelligent people skillfully *adapt* their thinking to fit with both their desires and the demands of their everyday worlds. When they cannot adapt to a situation, they try to *shape,* or change, it to meet their needs. If they cannot shape it, they *select* new contexts that better match their skills and goals. Practical intelligence reminds us that children with certain life histories do well on intelligence tests and adapt easily to the testing conditions. Others, with different backgrounds, may misinterpret or reject the testing context. Yet such children often display sophisticated abilities in daily life—for example, engaging in complex artistic activities or interacting skillfully with other people.

The triarchic theory highlights the limitations of current intelligence tests in assessing the complexity of intelligent behavior. For example, out-of-school, practical forms of intelligence are vital for life success and help explain why cultures vary widely in the behaviors they regard as intelligent (Sternberg, 2011). In villages in Kenya, children viewed as cognitively competent are highly knowledgeable about how to use herbal medicines to treat disease. Among the Yup'ik Eskimo people of central Alaska, intelligent youths are those with expert hunting, gathering, navigating, and fishing skills (Hein, Reich, & Grigorenko, 2015). And U.S. Cambodian, Filipino, Vietnamese, and Mexican immigrant parents asked to describe an intelligent first grader emphasized noncognitive capacities—motivation, self-management, and social skills (Okagaki & Sternberg, 1993).

According to Sternberg, intelligence tests, devised to predict achievement in school, do not capture the intellectual strengths that many children acquire through informal learning experiences in their cultural communities. But systematically measuring those strengths remains challenging. Tests devised to reflect the triarchic theory have not consistently yielded distinct analytical-, creative-, and practical-ability factors (Aljughaiman & Ayoub, 2012; Gubbels et al., 2016). Researchers are not sure whether these findings signify deficiencies in the triarchic theory or in available assessments.

© JEFF GREENBERG/ROBERT HARDING

▶ According to Gardner, people are capable of at least eight distinct intelligences. Through a project aimed at improving sea turtle nesting habitats, these children expand and enrich their naturalist intelligence.

Gardner's Theory of Multiple Intelligences. In yet another view of how information-processing skills underlie intelligent behavior, Howard Gardner's (1983, 1993, 2011) **theory of multiple intelligences** defines intelligence in terms of distinct sets of processing operations that permit individuals to engage in a wide range of culturally valued activities. Dismissing the idea of general intelligence, Gardner proposes at least eight independent intelligences (see Table 9.1).

Gardner believes that each intelligence has a unique neurological basis, a distinct course of development, and different expert, or "end-state," performances. At the same time, he emphasizes that a lengthy process of education is required to transform any raw potential into a mature social role (Gardner, 2011). Cultural values and learning opportunities affect the extent to which a child's intellectual strengths are realized and the ways they are expressed.

TABLE 9.1
Gardner's Multiple Intelligences

INTELLIGENCE	PROCESSING OPERATIONS	END-STATE PERFORMANCE POSSIBILITIES
Linguistic	Sensitivity to the sounds, rhythms, and meaning of words and the functions of language	Poet, journalist
Logico-mathematical	Sensitivity to, and capacity to detect, logical or numerical patterns; ability to handle long chains of logical reasoning	Mathematician
Musical	Ability to produce and appreciate pitch, rhythm (or melody), and aesthetic quality of the forms of musical expressiveness	Instrumentalist, composer
Spatial	Ability to perceive the visual–spatial world accurately, to perform transformations on those perceptions, and to re-create aspects of visual experience in the absence of relevant stimuli	Sculptor, navigator
Bodily-kinesthetic	Ability to use the body skillfully for expressive as well as goal-directed purposes; ability to handle objects skillfully	Dancer, athlete
Naturalist	Ability to recognize and classify all varieties of animals, minerals, and plants	Biologist
Interpersonal	Ability to detect and respond appropriately to the moods, temperaments, motivations, and intentions of others	Therapist, salesperson
Intrapersonal	Ability to discriminate complex inner feelings and to use them to guide one's own behavior; knowledge of one's own strengths, weaknesses, desires, and intelligences	Person with detailed, accurate self-knowledge

Sources: Gardner, 1983, 1993, 2011.

Gardner's list of abilities has yet to be firmly grounded in research. Neurological evidence for the independence of his abilities is weak. Some exceptionally gifted individuals have abilities that are broad rather than limited to a particular domain (Piirto, 2007). And research with mental tests suggests that several of Gardner's intelligences (linguistic, logico-mathematical, and spatial) have at least some features in common. Nevertheless, Gardner calls attention to several intelligences not tapped by IQ scores.

For example, his interpersonal and intrapersonal intelligences include a set of skills for accurately perceiving, reasoning about, and regulating emotion known as *emotional intelligence.* Among school-age children and adolescents, measures of emotional intelligence are positively associated with self-esteem, empathy, prosocial behavior, cooperation, leadership skills, and academic performance and negatively associated with internalizing and externalizing problems (Brackett, Rivers, & Salovey, 2011; Ferrando et al., 2011). These findings have increased teachers' awareness that coaching students in emotional abilities can improve their adjustment.

Explaining Individual and Group Differences in IQ

When we compare individuals in terms of academic achievement, years of education, and occupational status, it quickly becomes clear that certain sectors of the population are advantaged over others. In trying to explain these differences, researchers have compared the IQ scores of ethnic and SES groups. African-American children and adolescents score, on average, 10 to 12 IQ points below European-American children, although the difference has been shrinking over the past several decades (Nisbett, 2009; Nisbett et al., 2012). Hispanic children fall midway between African-American and European-American children, and Asian Americans score slightly higher than their White counterparts—about 3 points (Ceci, Rosenblum, & Kumpf, 1998).

The gap between middle- and low-SES children—about 9 points—accounts for some of the ethnic differences in IQ, but not all (Brooks-Gunn et al., 2003). Of course, IQ varies greatly *within* each ethnic and SES group, and minority top performers are typically indistinguishable from top performers in the White majority. Still, these group differences are large enough and of serious enough consequence that they cannot be ignored.

Beginning in the 1970s, the IQ nature–nurture controversy escalated after psychologist Arthur Jensen (1969) claimed that heredity is largely responsible for individual, ethnic, and SES variations in intelligence—a position others asserted as well (Herrnstein & Murray, 1994; Rushton & Jensen, 2006, 2010). These contentions prompted an outpouring of research studies and responses, including ethical challenges reflecting deep concern that the conclusions would fuel social prejudices. Let's look closely at some important evidence.

Nature and Nurture. In Chapter 2, we introduced the *heritability estimate.* The most powerful evidence on the heritability of IQ involves twin comparisons. The IQ scores of identical twins (who share all their genes) are more similar than those of fraternal twins (who are genetically no more alike than ordinary siblings). On the basis of this and other kinship evidence, researchers estimate that about half the differences in IQ among children and adolescents can be traced to their genetic makeup.

But heritabilities risk overestimating genetic influences and underestimating environmental influences (see page 62). And heritability estimates do not reveal the complex processes through which genes and experiences influence intelligence as children develop.

Adoption studies offer a wider range of information. When young children are adopted into caring, stimulating homes, their IQs rise substantially compared with the IQs of nonadopted children who remain in economically deprived families (Hunt, 2011). But adopted children benefit to varying degrees. In one investigation, children of two extreme groups of biological mothers—those with IQs below 95 and those with IQs above 120—were adopted at birth by parents who were well above average in income and education. During the school years, the children of the low-IQ biological mothers scored above average in IQ. But they did not do as well as children of high-IQ biological mothers placed in similar adoptive families (Loehlin, Horn, & Willerman, 1997). Adoption research confirms that heredity and environment jointly contribute to IQ.

Adoption studies also shed light on IQ differences between ethnic groups. In two investigations, African-American children adopted into economically well-off White homes during the first year of life scored high on intelligence tests, attaining mean IQs of 110 and 117 by middle childhood (Moore, 1986; Scarr & Weinberg, 1983). The IQ gains of these children, who were "reared in the culture of the tests and schools," are consistent with a wealth of evidence that poverty severely depresses the intelligence of ethnic minority children (Nisbett et al., 2012).

Dramatic gains in IQ from one generation to the next offer additional support for the conclusion that, given new experiences and opportunities, members of oppressed groups can move far beyond their current test performance. See the Cultural Influences box on the following page to learn about the Flynn effect.

▶ The majority of African-American children enter school speaking African-American English. Their home discourse differs from standard English, on which school learning is based.

Cultural Influences. A controversial question raised about ethnic differences in IQ has to do with whether they result from *test bias.* If a test samples knowledge and skills that not all groups of children have had equal opportunity to learn, or if the testing situation impairs the performance of some groups but not others, then the resulting score is a biased, or unfair, measure.

Some experts claim that because IQ predicts academic achievement equally well for majority and minority children, intelligence tests are fair to both groups. The tests, they say, represent success in the common culture (Edwards & Oakland, 2006). Others believe that lack of exposure to certain communication styles and knowledge, along with negative stereotypes about the test-taker's ethnic group, can undermine children's performance (McKown, 2013; Sternberg, 2005).

Language and Communication Styles. Ethnic minority families often foster unique language skills that do not match the expectations of most classrooms and testing situations. African-American English is a complex, rule-governed dialect

CULTURAL INFLUENCES

The Flynn Effect: Massive Generational Gains in IQ

After gathering IQ scores from diverse nations that had either military mental testing or frequent testing of other large, representative samples, James Flynn (1999, 2007) reported a finding so consistent and intriguing that it became known as the **Flynn effect:** IQs have increased steadily from one generation to the next. Evidence for the Flynn effect now exists for 30 nations (Nisbett et al., 2012). This dramatic *secular trend* in intelligence test performance holds for industrialized and developing nations, both genders, and individuals varying in ethnicity and SES (Ang, Rodgers, & Wänström, 2010; Rodgers & Wänström, 2007). Gains are greatest on tests of spatial reasoning—tasks often assumed to be "culture-fair" and, therefore, mostly genetically based.

The amount of increase depends on extent of societal modernization (see page 297 to review). Among European and North American nations that modernized by the early twentieth century, IQ gains have been about 3 points per decade (Flynn, 2007). IQ has continued to increment at that pace in England and the United States, but gains have slowed in certain nations with especially favorable economic and social conditions, such as Norway and Sweden (Schneider, 2006; Sundet, Barlaug, & Torjussen, 2004).

Among nations that modernized later, around the mid-twentieth century (such as Argentina), IQ gains tend to be larger, as much as 5 to 6 points per decade (Flynn & Rossi-Casé, 2011). And nations that began to modernize in the late twentieth century (Caribbean countries, Kenya, Sudan) show even greater increments, especially in spatial reasoning (Daley et al., 2003; Khaleefa, Sulman, & Lynn, 2009). The degree of societal modernity possible today is far greater than it was a century ago.

Diverse aspects of modernization probably underlie the better reasoning ability of each successive generation. These include improved education, health, and technology (TV, computers, the Internet); more cognitively demanding jobs and leisure activities (reading, chess, video games); a generally more stimulating world; and greater test-taking motivation.

As developing nations continue to advance in IQ, they are projected to catch up with the industrialized world by the end of the twenty-first century (Nisbett et al., 2012). Large, environmentally induced gains in IQ over time present a major challenge to the assumption that ethnic variations in IQ are genetic.

▶ Dramatic generational gains in IQ may result, in part, from greater participation by each successive generation in cognitively stimulating leisure activities.

used by most African Americans in the United States (Craig & Washington, 2006). Nevertheless, it is often inaccurately viewed as a deficient form of standard American English rather than as different from it.

The majority of African-American children entering school speak African-American English, though they vary in the extent to which they use it. Greater users, who tend to come from low-SES families, quickly learn that the language they bring from home is devalued in school. Teachers frequently try to "correct" their use of African-American English forms, replacing these with standard English (Washington & Thomas-Tate, 2009). Because their home discourse is distinctly different from the linguistic knowledge required to learn to read, children who speak mostly African-American English generally progress slowly in reading and achieve poorly (Charity, Scarborough, & Griffin, 2004).

Many African-American children learn to flexibly shift between African-American English and standard English by third grade. But those who continue to speak mostly their African-American dialect through the later grades—the majority of whom live in poverty and therefore have few opportunities outside of school for exposure to standard English—fall further behind in reading and in overall achievement (Washington & Thomas-Tate, 2009). These children have a special need for school programs that facilitate mastery of standard English while respecting their home language in the classroom.

Research also reveals that many ethnic minority parents without extensive education prefer a *collaborative style of communication* when completing tasks with children. They work together in a coordinated, fluid way, each focused on the same aspect of the problem—a pattern of adult–child engagement observed in Native-American, Canadian Inuit, Hispanic, and Guatemalan Mayan cultures (Chavajay & Rogoff, 2002; Crago, Annahatak, & Ningiuruvik, 1993; Paradise & Rogoff, 2009). With increasing education, parents establish a *hierarchical style of communication,* like that of classrooms and tests. The parent directs each child to carry out an aspect of the task, and children work independently (Greenfield, Suzuki, & Rothstein-Fish, 2006). This sharp discontinuity between home and school communication practices likely contributes to low-SES minority children's lower IQs and school performance.

Knowledge. Many researchers argue that IQ scores are affected by specific information acquired as part of majority-culture upbringing. In one study, researchers assessed African-American and European-American community college students' familiarity with vocabulary taken from items on an intelligence test. When verbal comprehension, similarities, and analogies items depended on words that the European-American students knew better, they scored higher than African-Americans. When the same types of items involved words that the two groups knew equally well, the two groups did not differ (Fagan & Holland, 2007). Prior knowledge, not reasoning ability, fully explained ethnic differences in performance.

Even nonverbal test items, such as spatial reasoning, depend on learning opportunities. For example, among children, adolescents, and adults alike, playing video games that require fast responding and mental rotation of visual images increases success on spatial test items (Uttal et al., 2013). Low-income minority children may lack opportunities to use games and objects that promote certain intellectual skills.

Furthermore, the sheer amount of time children spend in school predicts IQ. In comparisons of children of the same age who are in different grades, those who have been in school longer score higher in verbal intelligence—a difference that increases as the children advance further in school (Bedard & Dhuey, 2006). Taken together, these findings indicate that children's exposure to the knowledge and ways of thinking valued in classrooms has a sizable impact on their intelligence test performance.

Stereotypes. Imagine trying to succeed at an activity when the prevailing attitude is that members of your group are incompetent. **Stereotype threat**—the fear of being judged on the basis of a negative stereotype—can trigger anxiety that interferes with performance. Mounting evidence confirms that stereotype threat undermines test taking in children and adults (McKown & Strambler, 2009). For example, researchers gave African-American, Hispanic-American, and European-American 6- to 10-year-olds verbal tasks. Some children were told that the tasks were "not a test." Others were told they were "a test of how good children are at school problems"—a statement designed to induce stereotype threat in the ethnic minority children. Among children who were aware of ethnic stereotypes (such as "Black people aren't smart"), African Americans and Hispanics performed far worse in the "test" condition than in the "not a test" condition (McKown & Weinstein, 2003). European-American children, in contrast, performed similarly in both conditions.

From third grade on, children become increasingly conscious of ethnic stereotypes. By early adolescence, many low-SES minority students start to say doing well in school is not important to them (Killen, Rutland, & Ruck, 2011). Self-protective disengagement, sparked by stereotype threat, may be responsible. This weakening of motivation can have serious, long-term consequences. Research shows that self-discipline—effort and delay of gratification—predicts school performance, as measured by report card grades, better than IQ does (Duckworth, Quinn, & Tsukayama, 2012).

Reducing Cultural Bias in Testing. Although not all experts agree, many acknowledge that IQ scores can underestimate the intelligence of children from ethnic minority groups. A special concern exists about incorrectly labeling minority children as slow learners and assigning them to remedial classes, which are far less stimulating than regular school experiences. To avoid this danger, test scores need to be combined with assessments of children's adaptive behavior—their ability to cope with the demands of their everyday environments. The child who does poorly on an intelligence test yet plays a complex game on the playground or figures out how to rewire a broken TV is unlikely to be intellectually deficient.

In addition, flexible testing procedures enhance minority children's performance. In an approach called **dynamic assessment,** an innovation consistent with Vygotsky's zone of proximal development, the adult introduces purposeful teaching into the testing situation to find out what the child can attain with social support (Robinson-Zañartu & Carlson, 2013).

Research shows that children's receptivity to teaching and capacity to transfer what they have learned to novel problems contribute substantially to gains in test performance (Haywood & Lidz, 2007). In one study, first graders diverse in SES and ethnicity participated in dynamic assessment in which they were asked to solve a series of unfamiliar math equations that increased in difficulty, such as __ + 1 = 4 (easier) and 3 + 6 = 5 + ___ (difficult). When a child could not solve an equation, an adult provided increasingly explicit teaching. Beyond static IQ-like measures of children's verbal, math, and reasoning abilities, performance during dynamic assessment strongly predicted end-of-year scores on a test of math story problems, which children usually find highly challenging (Seethaler et al., 2012). Dynamic assessment seemed to evoke skills and understandings that children readily applied to a very different and demanding type of math.

Although their initial scores are lower, low-SES ethnic minority children show gains after dynamic assessment that are just as large as those of their cultural-majority agemates (Stevenson, Heiser, & Resing, 2016). In view of its many problems, should intelligence testing be suspended? Most experts reject this solution. Without testing, important educational decisions would be based only on subjective impressions, perhaps increasing discriminatory placement of minority children. Intelligence tests are useful when interpreted carefully by psychologists and educators who are sensitive to cultural influences on test performance. And despite their limitations, IQ scores continue to be useful measures of school learning potential for the majority of Western children.

▶ This teacher uses dynamic assessment, tailoring instruction to students' individual needs—an approach that reveals what each child can learn with social support.

ASK YOURSELF

CONNECT Explain how dynamic assessment is consistent with Vygotsky's zone of proximal development and with scaffolding. (See Chapter 7, page 223.)

APPLY Josefina, a Hispanic fourth grader, does well on homework assignments. But when her teacher announces, "It's time for a test to see how much you've learned," Josefina usually does poorly. How might stereotype threat explain this inconsistency?

REFLECT Do you think that intelligence tests are culturally biased? What observations and evidence influenced your conclusions?

Language Development

9.12 Describe changes in school-age children's vocabulary, grammar, and pragmatics, and cite the advantages of bilingualism for development.

Vocabulary, grammar, and pragmatics continue to develop in middle childhood, though less obviously than at earlier ages. In addition, children's attitude toward language undergoes a fundamental shift: They develop language awareness.

Vocabulary and Grammar

During the elementary school years, vocabulary increases fourfold, eventually reaching comprehension of 40,000 words. On average, children learn about 20 new words each day, a rate of growth greater than in early childhood. In addition to the word-learning strategies discussed in Chapter 7, school-age children add to their vocabularies by analyzing the structure of complex words. From *happy* and *decide,* they quickly derive the meanings of *happiness* and *decision* (Larsen & Nippold, 2007). They also figure out many more word meanings from context (Nagy & Scott, 2000).

As at younger ages, children benefit from conversing with more-expert speakers. But because written language contains a far more diverse and complex vocabulary than spoken language, reading contributes enormously to vocabulary growth. By second to third grade, reading comprehension and reading habits strongly predict later vocabulary size into high school (Cain & Oakhill, 2011). And as we saw earlier in this chapter, vocabulary growth, in turn, fosters reading progress.

As their knowledge becomes better organized, older school-age children think about and use words more precisely: In addition to the verb *fall,* for example, they also use *topple, tumble,* and *plummet*. Word definitions also illustrate this change. Five- and 6-year-olds offer concrete descriptions referring to functions or appearance—*knife:* "when you're cutting carrots." By the end of elementary school, synonyms and explanations of categorical relationships appear—for example, *knife:* "something you could cut with. A saw is like a knife. It could also be a weapon" (Uccelli & Pan, 2013). This advance reflects older children's ability to deal with word meanings on an entirely verbal plane. They can add new words to their vocabulary simply by being given a definition.

LOOK AND LISTEN

Record examples of 8- to 10-year-olds' humor, or examine storybooks for humor aimed at second through fourth graders. Does it require a grasp of the multiple meanings of words?

School-age children's more reflective and analytical approach to language permits them to appreciate the multiple meanings of words—to recognize, for example, that many words, such as *cool* or *neat,* have psychological as well as physical meanings: "Cool shirt!" or "Neat movie!" This grasp of double meanings permits 8- to 10-year-olds to comprehend subtle metaphors, such as "sharp as a tack" and "spilling the beans" (Nippold, Taylor, & Baker, 1996; Wellman & Hickling, 1994). It also leads to a change in children's humor. Riddles and puns that alternate between different meanings of a key word are common: "Hey, did you take a bath?" "Why, is one missing?"

Mastery of complex grammatical constructions also improves. For example, English-speaking children use the passive voice more frequently, and they more often extend it from an abbreviated form ("It broke") into full statements ("The glass was broken by Mary") (Tomasello, 2006). Another grammatical achievement of middle childhood is advanced understanding of infinitive phrases—the difference between "John is eager to please" and "John is easy to please" (Berman, 2007; Chomsky, 1969). Like gains in vocabulary, appreciation of these subtle grammatical distinctions is supported by an improved ability to analyze and reflect on language.

Pragmatics

A more advanced theory of mind—in particular, the capacity for recursive thought—enables children to understand and use increasingly indirect expressions of meaning. Around age 8, children begin to grasp irony and sarcasm (Glenright & Pexman, 2010). After Rena prepared a dish for dinner that Joey didn't like, he quipped sarcastically, "Oh boy, my favorite!" Notice how this remark requires the speaker to consider at least two perspectives simultaneously—in Joey's case, his mother's desire to serve a particular dish despite his objection, expressed through a critical comment with a double meaning.

Furthermore, as a result of improved memory and ability to take the perspective of listeners, children's narratives increase in organization, detail, and expressiveness. A typical 4- or 5-year-old's narrative states what happened: "We went to the lake. We fished and waited. Paul caught a huge catfish." Six- and 7-year-olds add orienting information (time, place, participants) and connectives ("next," "then," "so," "finally") that lend coherence to the story. Gradually, narratives lengthen into a *classic form* in which events not only build to a high point but resolve: "After Paul reeled in the catfish, Dad cleaned and cooked it. Then we ate it all up!" And evaluative comments rise dramatically, becoming common by ages 8 to 9: "The catfish tasted great. Paul was so proud!" (Melzi & Schick, 2013; Ukrainetz et al., 2005).

▶ In families who regularly eat meals together, children are advanced in language and literacy development. Mealtimes offer many opportunities to relate complex, extended personal stories.

Because children pick up the narrative styles of significant adults in their lives, their narratives vary widely across cultures. For example, instead of the *topic-focused style* of most European-American children, who describe an experience from beginning to end, African-American children often use a *topic-associating style* in which they blend several similar experiences. One 9-year-old related having a tooth pulled, then described seeing her sister's tooth pulled, next told how she had removed one of her own baby teeth, and concluded, "I'm a pullin-teeth expert . . . call me, and I'll be over" (McCabe, 1997, p. 164). Like adults in their families and communities, African-American children are more attuned to keeping their listeners interested than to relating a linear sequence of events. They often embellish their narratives by including fictional elements and many references to characters' motives and intentions (Gorman et al., 2011). As a result, their narratives are usually longer and more complex than those of White children.

The ability to generate clear oral narratives enhances reading comprehension and prepares children for producing longer, more explicit written narratives. In families who regularly eat meals together, children are advanced in language and literacy development (Snow & Beals, 2006). Mealtimes offer many opportunities to relate personal stories.

Learning Two Languages

Throughout the world, many children grow up *bilingual,* and some acquire more than two languages. An estimated 22 percent of U.S. children—11.2 million in all—speak a language other than English at home (U.S. Census Bureau, 2017a).

Bilingual Development. Children can become bilingual in two ways: (1) by acquiring both languages at the same time in early childhood or (2) by learning a second language after acquiring the first. Children of bilingual parents who teach them both languages in infancy and early childhood separate the language systems early on and attain early language milestones according to a typical timetable (Hoff et al., 2012). When preschool and school-age children from immigrant families acquire a second language after they already speak the language of their cultural heritage, the time required to master the second language to the level of native-speaking agemates varies greatly, from 1 to 5 or more years (MacWhinney, 2015; Páez & Hunter, 2015). Influential factors include child motivation, knowledge of the first language (which supports mastery of the second), and quality of communication and of literacy experiences in both languages at home and at school.

As with first-language development, a *sensitive period* for second-language development exists. Mastery must begin sometime in childhood for most second-language learners to attain full proficiency (Hakuta, Bialystok, & Wiley, 2003). But a precise age cutoff for a decline in second-language learning has not been established. Rather, a continuous age-related decrease from childhood to adulthood occurs.

Children who become fluent in two languages develop denser synaptic connections in areas of the left hemisphere devoted to language. And compared to monolinguals, bilinguals show greater activity in these areas and in the prefrontal cortex during linguistic tasks, likely due to the high executive-processing demands of controlling two languages (Costa & Sebastián-Gallés, 2014). Because both languages are always active, bilingual speakers must continuously decide which one to use in particular social situations, resisting attention to the other.

This increase in executive processing has diverse cognitive benefits as bilinguals acquire more efficient executive function skills and apply them to other tasks (Bialystok, 2015). Bilingual children and adults outperform others on tests of inhibition, sustained and selective attention, flexible shifting, analytical reasoning, concept formation, and false-belief understanding (Bialystok, Craik, & Luk, 2012; Carlson & Meltzoff, 2008). They are also advanced in certain aspects of language awareness, such as detection of errors in grammar, meaning, and conventions of conversation (responding politely, relevantly, and informatively). And children transfer their phonological awareness skills in one language to the other, especially if the two languages share phonological features and letter–sound correspondences, as Spanish and English do (Bialystok, 2013; Siegal, Iozzi, & Surian, 2009). These capacities, as noted earlier, enhance reading achievement.

Bilingual Education. The advantages of bilingualism provide strong justification for bilingual education programs in schools. In Canada, about 10 percent of elementary school students are enrolled in *language immersion programs,* in which English-speaking children are taught entirely in French for several years (Lepage & Corbeil, 2016). This strategy succeeds in developing children who are proficient in both languages and who, by grade 6, achieve as well as their counterparts in the regular English program (Genesee & Jared, 2008; Lyster & Genesee, 2012).

In the United States, fierce disagreement exists over how best to educate dual language learning children. Some believe that time spent communicating in the child's native tongue detracts from

© CHRISTINA KENNEDY/PHOTOEDIT

▶ The child on the left, a native Spanish speaker, benefits from an English–Spanish bilingual classroom, which sustains her native language while she masters English. And her native-English-speaking classmate has the opportunity to begin learning Spanish!

English-language achievement. Other educators, committed to developing minority children's native language while fostering mastery of English, note that providing instruction in the native tongue lets minority children know that their heritage is respected. It also prevents inadequate proficiency in both languages. Minority children who gradually lose facility in the first language as a result of being taught only the second end up limited in both languages for a time (McCabe et al., 2013). This leads to severe academic difficulties and is believed to contribute to the high rates of school failure and dropout among low-SES Hispanic young people, who make up over 70 percent of the U.S. language-minority population.

At present, public opinion and educational practice favor English-only instruction. Many U.S. states have passed laws declaring English to be their official language, creating conditions in which schools have no obligation to teach minority students in languages other than English (Wright, 2013). Yet in classrooms where both languages are integrated into the curriculum, minority children are more involved in learning and acquire the second language more easily—gains that result in better academic achievement. In contrast, when teachers speak only in a language that children can barely understand, minority children display frustration, boredom, and escalating academic difficulties (Paradis, Genesee, & Crago, 2011).

Supporters of U.S. English-only education often point to the success of Canadian language immersion programs, in which classroom lessons are conducted in the second language. But Canadian parents enroll their children in immersion classrooms voluntarily, and students in those programs are native speakers of the dominant language of their region. Furthermore, teaching in the child's native language is merely delayed, not ruled out. For U.S. non-English-speaking minority children, whose native languages are not valued by the larger society, a different strategy is necessary—one that promotes children's native language and literacy skills while they learn English.

ASK YOURSELF

CONNECT How can bilingual education promote ethnic minority children's cognitive and academic development?

APPLY After soccer practice, 10-year-old Shana remarked, "I'm wiped out!" Megan, her 5-year-old sister, responded, "What did'ya wipe out?" Explain Shana's and Megan's different understandings.

REFLECT Considering research on bilingualism, what changes would you make in your second-language learning, and why?

9.13 Describe the influence of educational philosophies on children's motivation and academic achievement.

9.14 Discuss the role of teacher–student interaction and grouping practices in academic achievement.

9.15 Describe conditions that promote successful placement of children with learning difficulties in regular classrooms.

9.16 Describe the characteristics of gifted children and efforts to meet their educational needs.

9.17 Discuss factors that lead U.S. students to fall behind in academic achievement compared to students in top-achieving nations.

Learning in School

Evidence cited throughout this chapter indicates that schools are vital forces in children's cognitive development. How do schools exert such a powerful influence? Research looking at schools as complex social systems, varying in educational philosophies, teacher–student relationships, and larger cultural context, provides important insights. As you read about these topics, refer to Applying What We Know on the following page, which summarizes characteristics of high-quality education in elementary school.

Educational Philosophies

Teachers' educational philosophies play a major role in children's learning. Two philosophical approaches have received most research attention. They differ in what children are taught, the way they are believed to learn, and how their progress is evaluated.

APPLYING WHAT WE KNOW

Signs of High-Quality Education in Elementary School

CLASSROOM CHARACTERISTICS	SIGNS OF QUALITY
Physical setting	Space is divided into richly equipped activity centers—for reading, writing, playing math or language games, exploring science, working on construction projects, using computers, and engaging in other academic pursuits. Spaces are used flexibly for individual and small-group activities and whole-class gatherings.
Curriculum	The curriculum helps children both achieve academic standards and make sense of their learning. Subjects are integrated so that children apply knowledge in one area to others. The curriculum is implemented through activities responsive to children's interests, ideas, and everyday lives, including their cultural backgrounds.
Daily activities	Teachers provide challenging activities that include opportunities for small-group and independent work. Groupings vary in size and makeup of children, depending on the activity and on children's learning needs. Teachers encourage cooperative learning and guide children in attaining it.
Interactions between teachers and children	Teachers foster each child's progress and use intellectually engaging strategies, including posing problems, asking thought-provoking questions, discussing ideas, and adding complexity to tasks. They also demonstrate, explain, coach, and assist in other ways, depending on each child's learning needs.
Evaluations of progress	Teachers regularly evaluate children's progress through written observations and work samples, which they use to enhance and individualize teaching. They help children reflect on their work and decide how to improve it. They also seek information and perspectives from parents on how well children are learning and include parents' views in evaluations.
Relationship with parents	Teachers forge partnerships with parents. They hold periodic conferences and encourage parents to visit the classroom anytime, to observe and volunteer.

Source: Copple & Bredekamp, 2009; National Association for the Education of Young Children, 2017.

Traditional versus Constructivist Classrooms. In a **traditional classroom,** the teacher is the sole authority for knowledge, rules, and decision making. Students are relatively passive—listening, responding when called on, and completing teacher-assigned tasks. Their progress is evaluated by how well they keep pace with a uniform set of standards for their grade.

A **constructivist classroom,** in contrast, encourages students to *construct* their own knowledge. Although constructivist approaches vary, many are grounded in Piaget's theory, which views children as active agents who reflect on and coordinate their own thoughts rather than absorbing those of others. A glance inside a constructivist classroom reveals richly equipped learning centers, small groups and individuals solving self-chosen problems, and a teacher who guides and supports in response to children's needs. Students are evaluated by considering their progress in relation to their own prior development.

In the 1960s and early 1970s, constructivist classrooms gained in popularity in the United States. Then, as concern arose over the academic progress of children and youths, classrooms returned to traditional instruction—a style that became increasingly pronounced as a result of the 2001 No Child Left Behind Act, followed by its 2015 replacement, the Every Student Succeeds Act. These policies, by placing heavy pressure on teachers and school administrators to improve achievement test scores, have narrowed the curricular focus in many schools to preparing students to take such tests (Kew et al., 2012).

Although older elementary school children in traditional classrooms have a slight edge in achievement test scores, constructivist settings are associated with many other benefits—gains in critical thinking, greater social and moral maturity, and more positive attitudes toward school (DeVries, 2001; Rathunde & Csikszentmihalyi, 2005; Walberg, 1986). And as noted in Chapter 7, when teacher-directed instruction is emphasized in preschool and kindergarten, it undermines motivation and achievement, especially in low-SES children.

Recent Philosophical Directions. Recent approaches to education, grounded in Vygotsky's sociocultural theory, capitalize on the rich social context of the classroom to spur children's learning.

In these **social-constructivist classrooms,** children participate in a wide range of challenging activities with teachers and peers, with whom they jointly construct understandings. As children acquire knowledge and strategies through working together, they become competent, contributing members of their classroom community and advance in cognitive and social development (Bodrova & Leong, 2007; Lourenço, 2012). Vygotsky's emphasis on the social origins of complex mental activities has inspired the following educational themes:

- *Teachers and children as partners in learning.* A classroom rich in both teacher–child and child–child collaboration transfers culturally valued ways of thinking to children.
- *Experiences with many types of symbolic communication in meaningful activities.* As children master reading, writing, and mathematics, they become aware of their culture's communication systems, reflect on their own thinking, and bring it under voluntary control. Can you identify research presented earlier in this chapter that supports this theme?
- *Teaching adapted to each child's zone of proximal development.* Assistance that both responds to current understandings and encourages children to take the next step helps ensure that each child makes the best progress possible.

© LAURA DWIGHT PHOTOGRAPHY

▶ Fourth graders work together to complete an assignment. Cooperative learning enhances children's complex reasoning skills as well as their enjoyment of learning and academic achievement.

According to Vygotsky, besides teachers, more-expert peers can spur children's learning, as long as they adjust the help they provide to fit the less mature child's zone of proximal development. Mounting evidence confirms that peer collaboration promotes development under certain conditions. A crucial factor is **cooperative learning,** in which small groups of classmates work toward common goals—by considering one another's ideas, appropriately challenging one another, providing sufficient explanations to correct misunderstandings, and resolving differences of opinion on the basis of reasons and evidence. When teachers explain, model, and have children role-play how to work together effectively, cooperative learning results in more complex reasoning, greater enjoyment of learning, and achievement gains across a wide range of subjects (Jadallah et al., 2011; Slavin, 2015).

Teacher–Student Interaction and Grouping Practices

Elementary school students describe good teachers as caring, helpful, and stimulating—behaviors associated with gains in motivation, achievement, and positive peer relations (Hughes & Kwok, 2006, 2007; O'Connor & McCartney, 2007). But too many U.S. teachers—especially those in schools with many students from low-income families—emphasize repetitive drill over higher-level thinking, such as grappling with ideas and applying knowledge to new situations (Valli, Croninger, & Buese, 2012).

Of course, teachers do not interact in the same way with all children. Well-behaved, high-achieving students typically get more encouragement and praise, whereas unruly students have more conflicts with teachers and receive more criticism from them (Henricsson & Rydell, 2004). Warm, low-conflict teacher–student relationships have an especially strong impact on the academic self-esteem, achievement, and social behavior of low-SES minority students and other children at risk for learning difficulties (Hughes, 2011; Hughes et al., 2012; Spilt et al., 2012). But overall, higher-SES students—who tend to be higher-achieving and to have fewer learning and behavior problems—have more sensitive and supportive relationships with teachers (Jerome, Hamre, & Pianta, 2009).

Unfortunately, once teachers' attitudes toward students are established, they can become more extreme than is warranted by students' behavior. Of special concern are **educational self-fulfilling prophecies:** Children may adopt teachers' positive or negative views and start to live up to them. This effect is especially strong when teachers emphasize competition and publicly compare children, regularly favoring the best students (Weinstein, 2002).

Low-achieving students are especially sensitive to self-fulfilling prophecies, which can be beneficial when teachers believe in them (McKown, Gregory, & Weinstein, 2010). But biased teacher

SOCIAL ISSUES

Magnet Schools: Equal Access to High-Quality Education

Each school-day morning, Emma leaves her affluent suburban neighborhood, riding a school bus 20 miles to a magnet school in an impoverished, mostly Hispanic inner-city neighborhood. In her fifth-grade class, she settles into a science project with her friend, Maricela, who lives in the local neighborhood. For the first hour of the day, the children use a thermometer, ice water, and a stopwatch to determine which of several materials is the best insulator, recording and graphing their data. Throughout the school, which specializes in innovative math and science teaching, students diverse in SES and ethnicity learn side-by-side.

Despite the 1954 U.S. Supreme Court *Brown v. Board of Education* decision ordering schools to desegregate, school integration receded over the 1990s as federal courts canceled their integration orders and returned this authority to states and cities. Since 2000, the racial divide in American education has improved only modestly (Stroub & Richards, 2013). When minority students attend ethnically mixed schools, they typically do so with other minorities.

U.S. schools in inner-city, low-income neighborhoods are vastly disadvantaged in educational opportunities, largely because public education is primarily supported by local property taxes. Consequently, in inner-city segregated neighborhoods, dilapidated school buildings; inexperienced teachers; outdated, poor-quality educational resources; and school cultures that fail to encourage strong teaching are widespread (Condron, 2013). The negative impact on student achievement is severe.

© ODESSA AMERICAN, EDYTA BLASZCZYK/AP IMAGES

▶ A magnet-school teacher receives hugs from her first-grade students at a party celebrating news that she is a finalist for Texas Elementary Teacher of the Year. Magnet schools typically attract students diverse in ethnicity and SES because of their rich academic offerings and innovative teaching.

Magnet schools offer a solution. In addition to the usual curriculum, they emphasize a specific area of interest—such as performing arts, math and science, or technology. Families outside the school neighborhood are attracted to magnet schools (hence the name) by their rich academic offerings. Often magnets are located in low-income, minority areas, where they serve the neighborhood student population. Other students, who apply and are admitted by lottery, are bussed in—many from well-to-do city and suburban neighborhoods. In another model, all students—including those in the surrounding neighborhood—must apply. In either case, magnet schools are voluntarily desegregated.

A Connecticut study comparing students enrolled in magnet schools with those whose lottery numbers were not drawn and who therefore attended other city schools confirmed that the magnet students showed greater gains in reading and math achievement over a two-year period (Bifulco, Cobb, & Bell, 2009). These outcomes were strongest for low-SES, ethnic minority students.

By high school, the higher-achieving peer environments of ethnically diverse schools encourage more students to pursue higher education (Franklin, 2012). In sum, magnet schools are a promising approach to overcoming the negative forces of SES and ethnic isolation in American schools.

judgments are usually slanted in a negative direction. In one study, African-American and Hispanic elementary school students taught by high-bias teachers (who expected them to do poorly) showed substantially lower end-of-year achievement than their counterparts taught by low-bias teachers (McKown & Weinstein, 2008). Recall our discussion of *stereotype threat.* A child in the position of confirming a negative stereotype may respond with especially intense anxiety and reduced motivation, amplifying a negative self-fulfilling prophecy.

In many schools, students are assigned to *homogeneous* groups or classes in which children of similar ability levels are taught together. Homogeneous grouping can be a potent source of self-fulfilling prophecies. Low-group students—who are more likely to be low-SES, minority, and male—get more drill on basic facts and skills, engage in less discussion, and progress at a slower pace. Gradually, they decline in self-esteem and motivation and fall further behind in achievement (Lleras & Rangel, 2009; Worthy, Hungerford-Kresser, & Hampton, 2009).

Widespread SES and ethnic segregation in U.S. schools consigns large numbers of low-SES, minority students to a form of schoolwide homogeneous grouping. Refer to the Social Issues: Education box above to find out how magnet schools foster heterogeneous learning contexts, thereby reducing achievement differences between SES and ethnic groups.

Teaching Children with Special Needs

We have seen that effective teachers flexibly adjust their teaching strategies to accommodate students with a wide range of characteristics. These adjustments are especially challenging at the very low and high ends of the ability distribution. How do schools serve children with special learning needs?

Children with Learning Difficulties. U.S. legislation mandates that schools place children who require special supports for learning in the "least restrictive" (as close to normal as possible) environments that meet their educational needs. In **inclusive classrooms,** students with learning difficulties learn alongside typical students in the regular educational setting for all or part of the school day—a practice designed to prepare them for participation in society and to combat prejudices against individuals with disabilities. Largely as the result of parental pressures, an increasing number of students experience *full inclusion*—full-time placement in regular classrooms.

Students with *mild intellectual disability* are sometimes integrated into inclusive classrooms. Typically, their IQs fall between 55 and 70, and they also show problems in adaptive behavior, or skills of everyday living (American Psychiatric Association, 2013). But the largest number designated for inclusion—5 to 10 percent of school-age children—have **learning disabilities,** great difficulty with one or more specific aspects of learning, usually reading. As a result, they do not progress academically at an appropriate rate, even when more intensive instruction is provided in the regular classroom. Often the deficits of students with learning disabilities express themselves in other ways—for example, as deficiencies in processing speed and executive function (Cornoldi et al., 2014). Their problems cannot be traced to any obvious physical or emotional difficulty or to environmental disadvantage. Instead, deficits in brain functioning are involved (Swanson, Harris, & Graham, 2014). In many instances, the cause is unknown.

© ELLEN B. SENISI

▶ In this inclusive first-grade classroom, a teacher encourages special-needs students' active participation. They are likely to do well if they receive support from a special education teacher and if their regular classroom teacher promotes positive peer relations.

Although some students benefit academically from inclusion, many do not. Achievement gains depend on both the severity of the disability and the support services available (Downing, 2010). Furthermore, children with disabilities are often rejected by regular-classroom peers. Students with intellectual disability are overwhelmed by the social skills of their classmates; they cannot interact adeptly in a conversation or game. And the processing deficits of some students with learning disabilities lead to problems in social awareness and responsiveness (Nowicki, Brown, & Stepien, 2014).

Does this mean that students with special needs cannot be served in regular classrooms? Not necessarily. Often these children do best when they receive instruction in a resource room for part of the day and in the regular classroom for the remainder (McLeskey & Waldron, 2011). In the resource room, a special education teacher works with students on an individual and small-group basis. Then, depending on their progress, children join typically developing classmates for different subjects and amounts of time.

Special steps must be taken to promote peer relations in inclusive classrooms. Peer tutoring experiences in which teachers guide typical students in supporting the academic progress of classmates with learning difficulties lead to friendly interaction, improved peer acceptance, and achievement gains (Mastropieri et al., 2013). And when teachers prepare their class for the arrival of a student with special needs, inclusion may foster emotional sensitivity and prosocial behavior among regular classmates.

Gifted Children. Some children are **gifted,** displaying exceptional intellectual strengths. An IQ score above 130 is the standard definition of giftedness based on intelligence test performance (Pfeiffer & Yermish, 2014). High-IQ children have an exceptional capacity to solve challenging academic problems. Yet recognition that intelligence tests do not sample the entire range of human mental skills has led to an expanded conception of giftedness.

Creativity and Talent. **Creativity** is the ability to produce work that is *original* yet *appropriate*—something others have not thought of that is useful in some way (Kaufman & Sternberg, 2007). A child with high potential for creativity can be designated as gifted. Tests of creative capacity tap **divergent thinking**—the generation of multiple and unusual possibilities when faced with a task or problem. Divergent thinking contrasts sharply with **convergent thinking,** which involves arriving at a single correct answer and is emphasized on intelligence tests (Guilford, 1985).

Because highly creative children (like high-IQ children) are often better at some tasks than others, a variety of tests of divergent thinking are available (Runco, 1992; Torrance, 1988). A verbal measure might ask children to name uses for common objects (such as a newspaper). A figural measure might ask them to create drawings based on a circular motif (see Figure 9.5). A "real-world problem" measure requires students to suggest solutions to everyday problems. Responses can be scored for the number of ideas generated and their originality.

FIGURE 9.5 Responses of an 8-year-old who scored high on a figural measure of divergent thinking. This child was asked to make as many pictures as she could from the circles on the page. The titles she gave her drawings, from left to right, are as follows: "Dracula," "one-eyed monster," "pumpkin," "Hula-Hoop," "poster," "wheelchair," "earth," "stop-light," "planet," "movie camera," "sad face," "picture," "beach ball," "the letter O," "car," "glasses." Tests of divergent thinking tap only one of the complex cognitive contributions to creativity. (Reprinted by permission of Laura E. Berk.)

Yet critics point out that these measures tap only one of the complex cognitive contributions to creativity (Plucker & Makel, 2010). Also involved are defining new and important problems, evaluating divergent ideas, choosing the most promising, and calling on relevant knowledge to understand and solve problems (Lubart, Georgsdottir, & Besançon, 2009).

Consider these ingredients, and you will see why people usually demonstrate creativity in only one or a few related areas. Partly for this reason, definitions of giftedness have been extended to include **talent**—outstanding performance in a specific field. Case studies reveal that excellence in such endeavors as creative writing, mathematics, science, music, visual arts, athletics, and leadership has roots in specialized interests and skills that first appear in childhood (Sobotnik, Worrell, & Olszewski-Kubilius, 2016). Highly talented children are biologically prepared to master their domain of interest, and they display a passion for doing so.

But talent must be nurtured. Studies of the backgrounds of talented children and highly accomplished adults often reveal warm, sensitive parents who provide a stimulating home life, are devoted to developing their child's abilities, and provide models of hard work. These parents are reasonably demanding but not overly ambitious (Witte et al., 2015). They arrange for caring teachers while the child is young and for more rigorous master teachers as the child's talent develops.

Although most are well-adjusted, many gifted children and adolescents experience social isolation, partly because of their highly driven, independent styles and partly because they enjoy solitude, which is necessary to develop their talents (Pfeiffer & Yermish, 2014). Still, gifted children desire gratifying peer relationships, and some try to become better-liked by hiding their abilities (Reis, 2004).

Finally, whereas many talented youths become experts in their fields, few become highly creative. Rapidly mastering an existing field requires different skills than innovating in that field. The world, however, needs both experts and creators.

Educating the Gifted. Debate about the effectiveness of school programs for the gifted typically focuses on factors irrelevant to giftedness—whether to provide enrichment in regular classrooms, pull children out for special instruction (the most common practice), or advance brighter students to a higher grade. Overall, gifted children fare well within each of these models, as long as special activities promote problem solving, critical thinking, and creativity (Guignard & Lubart, 2006).

Gardner's theory of multiple intelligences has inspired several model programs that provide enrichment to all students in diverse disciplines. Meaningful activities, each tapping a specific intelligence or set of intelligences, serve as contexts for assessing strengths and weaknesses and, on that basis, teaching new knowledge and original thinking (Gardner, 2000; Hoerr, 2004). For example, linguistic intelligence might be fostered through storytelling or playwriting; spatial intelligence through drawing, sculpting, or taking apart and reassembling objects; and kinesthetic intelligence through dance or pantomime.

Evidence is still needed on how well these programs nurture children's talents and creativity. But they have already succeeded in one way—by highlighting the strengths of some students who previously had been considered unexceptional or even at risk for school failure (Ford, 2012). Consequently, they may be especially useful in identifying talented low-SES, ethnic minority children, who are underrepresented in school programs for the gifted.

	Country	Average Math Achievement Score
High-Performing Nations	Singapore	571
	China (Hong Kong)	554
	Taiwan	548
	China (Macao)	547
	Japan	536
	Korea	529
	Switzerland	526
	Estonia	521
	Canada	518
	Netherlands	516
	Finland	514
	Denmark	513
	Belgium	513
	Slovenia	512
	Germany	508
	Poland	505
	Ireland	505
	Norway	504
Intermediate-Performing Nations	Austria	501
	France	499
	New Zealand	497
	Sweden	496
	United Kingdom	496
	Australia	495
	Portugal	495
	Russia	494
	Czech Republic	494
International Average = 492	Italy	491
	Iceland	489
	Spain	489
	Luxembourg	487
	Latvia	483
	Hungary	480
	Slovak Republic	479
	Israel	473
	United States	**470**
Low-Performing Nations	Greece	455
	Romania	442
	Turkey	417
	Mexico	407

FIGURE 9.6 Average mathematics scores of 15-year-olds by country. The Programme for International Student Assessment measures achievement in many nations around the world. In recent comparisons of countries' performance, the United States performed below the international average in math; in reading and science, its performance was about average. (Adapted from Programme for International Student Assessment, 2017.)

How Well-Educated Are U.S. Children?

Our discussion of schooling has largely focused on how teachers can support the education of children. Yet many factors—both within and outside schools—affect children's learning. Societal values, school resources, quality of teaching, and parental encouragement all play important roles. These multiple influences are especially apparent when schooling is examined in cross-cultural perspective.

In international studies of reading, mathematics, and science achievement, young people in China, Korea, and Japan are consistently top performers. Among Western nations, Canada, Finland, the Netherlands, and Switzerland are also in the top tier. But U.S. students typically perform at or below the international averages (see Figure 9.6) (Programme for International Student Assessment, 2017).

Why do U.S. students fall behind in academic accomplishment? According to international comparisons, instruction in the United States is less challenging, more focused on absorbing facts, and less focused on high-level reasoning and critical thinking than in other countries. Furthermore, countries with large socioeconomic inequalities (such as the United States) rank lower in achievement, in part because low-SES children tend to live in less favorable family and neighborhood contexts (Condron, 2013). But the United States is also far less equitable than top-achieving countries in the quality of education it provides its low-SES and ethnic minority students. U.S. teachers, for example, vary much more in training, salaries, and teaching conditions.

Finland is a case in point. Its nationally mandated curricula, teaching practices, and assessments are aimed at cultivating initiative, problem solving, and creativity. Finnish teachers are highly trained: They must complete several years of graduate-level education at government expense (Ripley, 2013). And Finnish education is grounded in equal opportunity for all—a policy that has nearly eliminated SES variations in achievement, despite an influx of immigrant students from low-income families into Finnish schools over the past two decades.

In-depth research on learning environments in Asian nations, such as Japan, Korea, and Taiwan, also highlights social forces that foster strong student learning. Among these is cultural valuing of effort. Whereas American parents and teachers tend to regard native ability as the key to academic success, Japanese, Korean, and Taiwanese parents and teachers believe that all children can succeed as long as they try hard. Asian children, influenced by interdependent values, typically view striving to achieve as a moral obligation—part of their responsibility to family and community (Hau & Ho, 2010).

As in Finland, all students in Japan, Korea, and Taiwan receive the same nationally mandated, high-quality instruction, delivered by teachers who are well-prepared and far better paid than U.S. teachers (Kang & Hong, 2008; U.S. Department of Education, 2016a).

The Finnish and Asian examples underscore the need for American families, schools, and the larger society to work together to upgrade education. Recommended strategies, verified by research, include:

- supporting parents in attaining economic security, creating stimulating home learning environments, and monitoring their children's academic progress
- investing in high-quality preschool education, so every child arrives at school ready to learn
- strengthening teacher education
- providing intellectually challenging, relevant instruction with real-world applications
- vigorously pursuing school improvements that reduce the large inequities in quality of education between SES and ethnic groups.

© OLIVIER MORIN/AFP/GETTY IMAGES

▶ A Finnish teacher passes out materials to her second-grade students. Finland's teachers are highly trained, and their education system—designed to cultivate initiative, problem solving, and creativity in all students—has nearly eliminated SES variations in achievement.

ASK YOURSELF

CONNECT Review research on child-rearing styles on pages 270–272 in Chapter 8. What style do gifted children who realize their potential typically experience? Explain.

APPLY Sandy wonders why her daughter Mira's teacher often has students work on assignments in small, cooperative groups. Explain the benefits of this approach to Sandy.

REFLECT What grouping practices were used in your elementary education—homogeneous, heterogeneous, or a combination? What impact do you think those practices had on your motivation and achievement?

CHAPTER 9 SUMMARY

PHYSICAL DEVELOPMENT

Body Growth *(p. 281)*

9.1 ***Describe major trends in body growth during middle childhood.***

- During middle childhood, physical growth continues at a slow, regular pace. Bones lengthen and broaden, and permanent teeth replace the primary teeth. By age 9, girls overtake boys in physical size.

Health Issues *(p. 282)*

9.2 ***Describe the causes and consequences of serious nutritional problems in middle childhood, giving special attention to obesity.***

- School-age children report feeling poorly after eating junk foods. Even mild nutritional deficits can affect cognitive functioning.
- Overweight and **obesity** have increased dramatically in both industrialized and developing nations. Although heredity contributes to obesity, parental feeding practices, maladaptive eating habits, family stress, reduced sleep, lack of exercise, and unhealthy diets are powerful influences. Obesity leads to serious physical health and adjustment problems.
- The most effective approaches to treating childhood obesity are family-based interventions aimed at changing parents' and children's eating patterns and lifestyles.

ARIEL SKELLEY/BLEND IMAGES/GETTY IMAGES

9.3 ***List factors that contribute to illness during the school years, and explain how these health problems can be reduced.***

- Children experience more illnesses during the first two years of elementary school than later because of exposure to sick children and an immature immune system.
- The most common chronic illness is asthma. It occurs more often among African-American and poverty-stricken children, as well as obese children.
- Children with severe chronic illnesses are at risk for academic, emotional, and social difficulties, but positive family relationships improve adjustment.

Motor Development and Play *(p. 285)*

9.4 ***Cite major changes in motor development and play during middle childhood.***

- Gains in flexibility, balance, agility, and force, along with more efficient information processing, contribute to school-age children's improved gross-motor performance.
- Fine-motor development also improves. By age 6, children print letters and numbers with reasonable clarity. During the school years, drawings increase in organization, detail, and representation of depth.
- Although girls outperform boys in fine-motor skills, boys outperform girls in all gross-motor skills except those requiring balance and agility. Parents' higher expectations for boys' athletic performance play a substantial role.
- Games with rules become common during the school years, contributing to emotional and social development. Children, especially boys, also engage in **rough-and-tumble play**—play-fighting that, in our evolutionary past, likely contributed to development of fighting skill.
- Most U.S. school-age children are not active enough for good health, in part because of cutbacks in recess and physical education.

COGNITIVE DEVELOPMENT

Piaget's Theory: The Concrete Operational Stage *(p. 289)*

9.5 ***Describe advances in thinking, and cognitive limitations, during the concrete operational stage.***

- In the **concrete operational stage,** children's thought becomes more logical, flexible, and organized. Mastery of conservation demonstrates decentration and **reversibility** in thinking.
- School-age children are also better at hierarchical classification and **seriation,** including **transitive inference.** Their spatial reasoning improves, evident in their ability to generate **cognitive maps** representing familiar large-scale spaces.
- Concrete operational thought is limited in that children do not come up with general logical principles. They master concrete operational tasks step by step.

9.6 ***Discuss follow-up research on concrete operational thought.***

- Specific cultural practices, especially those associated with schooling, promote children's mastery of Piagetian tasks.

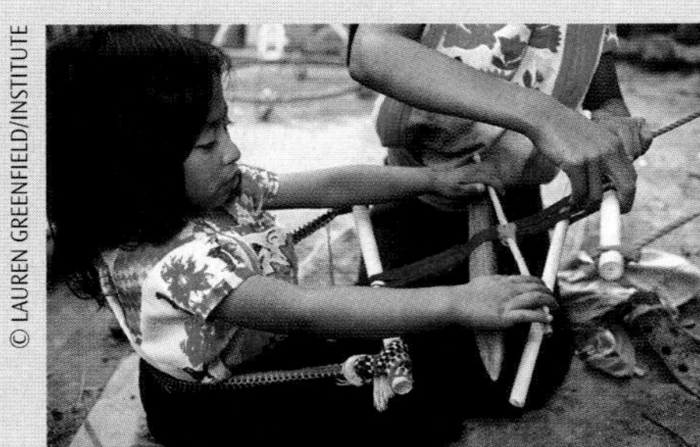

© LAUREN GREENFIELD/INSTITUTE

- Some researchers attribute the gradual development of operational thought to expansion of information-processing capacity. Case's neo-Piagetian theory proposes that with brain development and practice, cognitive schemes become more automatic, freeing up space in working memory for combining old schemes and generating new ones that are integrated into improved, broadly applicable representations.

Information Processing *(p. 293)*

9.7 ***Describe gains in executive function and memory in middle childhood, along with factors that influence children's progress.***

- As the prefrontal cortex continues to develop, children make great strides in executive function, enabling them to handle increasingly complex tasks that require integration of working memory, inhibition, and flexible shifting of attention. Planning on multistep tasks also improves.
- Heredity and environmental factors, including home and school experiences, combine to influence children's executive-function skills. Deficits in executive function underlie symptoms of **attention-deficit hyperactivity disorder (ADHD).**
- Memory strategies also improve. **Rehearsal** appears first, followed by **organization** and then **elaboration.** With age, children combine memory strategies.
- Development of children's general knowledge base, or semantic memory, facilitates strategic memory processing, as does their motivation to use what they know. Societal modernization is broadly associated with cognitive performance, including on memory tasks.

9.8 ***Describe the school-age child's theory of mind and capacity to engage in self-regulation.***

- School-age children regard the mind as an active, constructive agent, yielding a better understanding of cognitive processes, including mental inference and second-order false belief, which requires **recursive thought**. **Cognitive self-regulation** develops gradually, improving with adult instruction in strategy use.

9.9 ***Discuss current perspectives on teaching reading and mathematics to elementary school children.***

- Skilled reading draws on all aspects of the information-processing system. A combination of whole language and phonics is most effective for teaching beginning reading. Teaching that blends practice in basic skills with conceptual understanding also is best in mathematics.

Individual Differences in Mental Development *(p. 300)*

9.10 ***Describe major approaches to defining and measuring intelligence.***

- In middle childhood, IQ becomes more stable and correlates moderately with academic achievement. Most intelligence tests yield an overall score as well as scores for separate intellectual factors. Processing speed and executive function predict IQ.
- Sternberg's **triarchic theory of successful intelligence** identifies three broad, interacting intelligences: analytical intelligence (information-processing skills), creative intelligence (capacity to solve novel problems), and practical intelligence (application of intellectual skills in everyday situations).

© JEFF GREENBERG/ROBERT HARDING

- Gardner's **theory of multiple intelligences** identifies at least eight distinct mental abilities. It has stimulated efforts to define, measure, and foster emotional intelligence.

9.11 ***Describe evidence indicating that both heredity and environment contribute to intelligence.***

- Heritability estimates and adoption research indicate that intelligence is a product of both heredity and environment. Adoption studies suggest that environmental factors underlie ethnic differences in IQ. The **Flynn effect,** steady generational gains in IQ in many nations, is closely associated with extent of societal modernization.
- IQ scores are affected by culturally influenced language and communication styles and knowledge. **Stereotype threat** triggers anxiety that interferes with test performance. **Dynamic assessment** helps many minority children perform more competently on mental tests.

Language Development *(p. 307)*

9.12 ***Describe changes in school-age children's vocabulary, grammar, and pragmatics, and cite the advantages of bilingualism for development.***

- Language awareness contributes to language progress. School-age children have a more precise and flexible understanding of word meanings and use more complex grammatical constructions. Narratives increase in organization, detail, and expressiveness.
- Mastery of a second language must begin in childhood for full proficiency to occur. Bilingualism has positive consequences for executive function, various other cognitive skills, and aspects of language awareness.

© CHRISTINA KENNEDY/PHOTOEDIT

Learning in School *(p. 310)*

9.13 ***Describe the influence of educational philosophies on children's motivation and academic achievement.***

- Older students in **traditional classrooms** have a slight edge in achievement test scores over those in **constructivist classrooms,** who gain in critical thinking, social and moral maturity, and positive attitudes toward school.
- Students in **social-constructivist classrooms** benefit from working collaboratively on meaningful activities and from teaching adapted to each child's zone of proximal development. Teacher support for **cooperative learning** promotes complex reasoning and achievement gains.

© LAURA DWIGHT PHOTOGRAPHY

9.14 ***Discuss the role of teacher–student interaction and grouping practices in academic achievement.***

- Caring, helpful, and stimulating teaching fosters children's motivation, achievement, and peer relations. **Educational self-fulfilling prophecies** have a greater impact on low than high achievers. Homogeneous grouping can induce self-fulfilling prophecies in low-group students, who decline in self-esteem and achievement.

9.15 ***Describe conditions that promote successful placement of children with learning difficulties in regular classrooms.***

- The success of **inclusive classrooms** for students with mild intellectual disability and **learning disabilities** depends on meeting individual learning needs and promoting positive peer relations.

9.16 ***Describe the characteristics of gifted children and efforts to meet their educational needs.***

- **Giftedness** includes high IQ, **creativity,** and **talent.** Tests of creativity that tap **divergent thinking** focus on only one of the ingredients of creativity. Highly talented children generally have parents and teachers who nurture their exceptional abilities.

9.17 ***Discuss factors that lead U.S. students to fall behind in academic achievement compared to students in top-achieving nations.***

- In international studies, U.S. students typically perform at or below international averages. Compared with education in top-achieving nations, education in the United States is less focused on high-level reasoning and critical thinking and less equitable across SES groups.

© OLIVIER MORIN/AFP/GETTY IMAGES

IMPORTANT TERMS AND CONCEPTS

attention-deficit hyperactivity disorder (ADHD) (p. 294)
cognitive maps (p. 290)
cognitive self-regulation (p. 298)
concrete operational stage (p. 290)
constructivist classroom (p. 311)
convergent thinking (p. 315)
cooperative learning (p. 312)
creativity (p. 315)
divergent thinking (p. 315)
dynamic assessment (p. 307)
educational self-fulfilling prophecies (p. 312)
elaboration (p. 296)
Flynn effect (p. 305)
gifted (p. 314)
inclusive classrooms (p. 314)
learning disabilities (p. 314)
obesity (p. 283)
organization (p. 296)
recursive thought (p. 296)
rehearsal (p. 296)
reversibility (p. 290)
rough-and-tumble play (p. 288)
seriation (p. 290)
social-constructivist classroom (p. 312)
stereotype threat (p. 306)
talent (p. 315)
theory of multiple intelligences (p. 302)
traditional classroom (p. 311)
transitive inference (p. 290)
triarchic theory of successful intelligence (p. 301)

CHAPTER 10 Emotional and Social Development in Middle Childhood

Having fled their war-torn homeland of Syria, school-age friends nestle together in a barren refugee camp. In middle childhood, trust—mutual kindness and assistance—becomes a defining feature of friendship. For children experiencing the dislocation and losses of war, friends can serve as a source of resilience.

WHAT'S AHEAD IN CHAPTER 10

One afternoon as school dismissed, Joey urgently tapped his best friend Terry on the shoulder. "Gotta talk to you," Joey pleaded. "Everything was going great until I got that word—*porcupine,*" Joey went on, referring to the fifth-grade spelling bee that day. "Just my luck! *P-o-r-k,* that's how I spelled it! I can't believe it. I *know* I'm one of the best spellers in our class, better than that stuck-up Belinda Brown. I knocked myself out studying those spelling lists. Then *she* got all the easy words. If I *had* to lose, why couldn't it be to a nice person?"

Joey's conversation reflects new emotional and social capacities. By entering the spelling bee, he shows *industriousness,* the energetic pursuit of meaningful achievement in his culture—a major change of middle childhood. Joey's social understanding has also expanded: He can size up strengths, weaknesses, and personality characteristics. Furthermore, friendship means something different to Joey than it did earlier: He counts on his best friend, Terry, for understanding and emotional support.

For an overview of the personality changes of middle childhood, we return to Erikson's theory. Then we look at children's views of themselves and of others, their moral understanding, and their peer relationships. Each increases in complexity as children reason more effectively and spend more time in school and with agemates.

© ELLEN B. SENISI

Despite changing parent–child relationships, the family remains powerfully influential in middle childhood. Today, family structures are more diverse than ever before. Through Joey and his younger sister Lizzie's experiences with parental divorce, we will see that family functioning is far more important than family structure in ensuring children's well-being. Finally, we look at some common emotional problems of middle childhood.

Erikson's Theory: Industry versus Inferiority

10.1 Identify personality changes that take place during Erikson's stage of industry versus inferiority.

According to Erikson (1950), children whose previous experiences have been positive enter middle childhood prepared to focus their energies on realistic accomplishment. Erikson believed that the combination of adult expectations and children's drive toward mastery sets the stage for the psychological conflict of middle childhood, **industry versus inferiority,** which is resolved positively when experiences lead children to develop a sense of competence at useful skills and tasks. In cultures everywhere, adults respond to children's improved physical and cognitive capacities by making new demands, and children are ready to benefit from those challenges.

In most of the world, the transition to middle childhood is marked by the beginning of formal schooling, where children discover their own and others' unique capacities, learn the value of division of labor, and develop a sense of moral commitment and responsibility. The danger at this stage is *inferiority,* reflected in the pessimism of children who lack confidence in their ability to do things well. This sense of inadequacy can develop when family life has not prepared children for school life or when teachers and peers destroy children's self-confidence with negative responses.

Erikson's sense of industry combines several developments of middle childhood: a positive but realistic self-concept, pride in accomplishment, moral responsibility, and cooperative participation with agemates. How do these aspects of self and social relationships change over the school years?

ECO IMAGES/GETTY IMAGES

▶ The industriousness of middle childhood involves responding to new expectations for realistic accomplishment. In the informal, encouraging atmosphere of this classroom in India, children come to view themselves as responsible, capable, and cooperative.

Self-Understanding

10.2 Describe school-age children's self-concept and self-esteem, and discuss factors that affect their achievement-related attributions.

In middle childhood, children begin to describe themselves in terms of psychological traits, compare their own characteristics with those of their peers, and speculate about the causes of their strengths and weaknesses. These transformations in self-understanding have a major impact on self-esteem.

Self-Concept

During the school years, children refine their self-concept, organizing their observations of behaviors and internal states into general dispositions. A major change takes place between ages 8 and 11, as the following self-description by a fourth grader illustrates:

> I'm pretty popular, at least with the girls who I spend time with, but not with the super-popular girls who think they are cooler than everyone else. With my friends, I know what it takes to be liked, so I'm nice to people and helpful and can keep secrets. . . . Sometimes, if I get in a bad mood I'll say something that can be a little mean and then I'm ashamed of myself. At school, I'm feeling pretty smart in certain subjects like language arts and social studies. . . . But I'm feeling pretty dumb in math and science, especially when I see how well a lot of the other kids are doing. I now understand that I can be both smart and dumb, you aren't just one or the other. (Harter, 2012, p. 59)

Instead of specific behaviors, this child emphasizes competencies: "smart in certain subjects like language arts and social studies." She also describes her personality, mentioning both positive and negative traits: "helpful" and "can keep secrets" but sometimes "a little mean." Older school-age children are far less likely than younger children to describe themselves in extreme, all-or-none ways (Harter, 2012).

These qualified, trait-based self-descriptions result from cognitive advances—specifically, the ability to combine typical experiences and behaviors into psychological dispositions. Children also become better at *perspective taking*—inferring others' attitudes toward themselves—and incorporate those attitudes into their self-definitions.

These capacities, along with more experiences in which children are evaluated against agemates, prompt **social comparisons**—judgments of their appearance, abilities, and behavior in relation to those of others. Notice, in the introduction to this chapter, Joey's observation that he is "one of the best spellers" in his class. Similarly, our fourth grader's self-description mentions feeling "smart" at some subjects but not at others, especially when she sees "how well a lot of the other kids are doing." Whereas 4- to 6-year-olds can compare their own performance to that of a single peer, older children can compare multiple individuals, including themselves (Harter, 2012).

Parental support for self-development continues to be vitally important. School-age children with a history of elaborative parent–child conversations about past experiences construct rich, positive narratives about the self and therefore have more complex, favorable, and coherent self-concepts (Baddeley & Singer, 2015). Children also look to more people beyond the family for information about themselves as they enter a wider range of school and community settings. And self-descriptions now include frequent reference to social groups: "I'm a Boy Scout, a paper boy, and a Prairie City soccer player," said Joey. As children move into adolescence, although parents and other adults remain influential, self-concept is increasingly vested in feedback from close friends (Oosterwegel & Oppenheimer, 1993).

But recall that the content of self-concept varies from culture to culture. In earlier chapters, we noted that Asian parents stress harmonious interdependence, whereas Western parents emphasize independence and self-assertion. When asked to recall personally significant past experiences (their last birthday, a time their parent scolded them), U.S. school-age children gave longer accounts including more personal preferences, interests, skills, and opinions. Chinese children, in contrast, more often referred to social interactions and to others. Similarly, in their self-descriptions, U.S. children listed more personal attributes ("I'm smart," "I like hockey"), Chinese children more attributes involving group membership and relationships ("I'm in second grade," "My friends are crazy about me") (Wang, 2006; Wang, Shao, & Li, 2010).

Self-Esteem

To study school-age children's self-esteem, researchers ask them to indicate the extent to which statements such as "I'm good at reading" or "I'm usually the one chosen for games" are true of themselves. By ages 6 to 7, children in diverse Western cultures have formed at least four broad self-evaluations: academic competence, social competence, physical/athletic competence, and physical appearance. Within these are more refined categories that become increasingly distinct with age (Marsh, 1990; Marsh & Ayotte, 2003; Van den Bergh & De Rycke, 2003). Furthermore, the capacity to view the self in terms of stable dispositions permits school-age children to combine their separate self-evaluations into a general psychological image of themselves—an overall sense of self-esteem (Harter, 2012). As a result, self-esteem takes on the hierarchical structure shown in Figure 10.1.

Children attach greater importance to certain self-evaluations than to others. Although individual differences exist, during childhood and adolescence, perceived physical appearance correlates more strongly with overall self-worth than does any other self-esteem factor (Baudson, Weber, & Freund, 2016; O'Dea, 2012). Emphasis on appearance—in the media, by parents and peers, and in society—has major implications for young people's overall satisfaction with themselves.

Self-esteem generally remains high during elementary school but becomes more realistic and nuanced as children evaluate themselves in various areas (Marsh, Craven, & Debus, 1998; Wigfield et al., 1997). These changes occur as children receive more competence-related feedback, as their performances are increasingly judged in relation to those of others, and as they become cognitively capable of social comparison (Harter, 2012).

Influences on Self-Esteem

From middle childhood on, individual differences in self-esteem become increasingly stable (Trzesniewski, Donnellan, & Robins, 2003). And positive relationships among self-esteem, valuing of various activities, and success at those activities emerge and strengthen. What social influences might lead self-esteem to be high for some children and low for others?

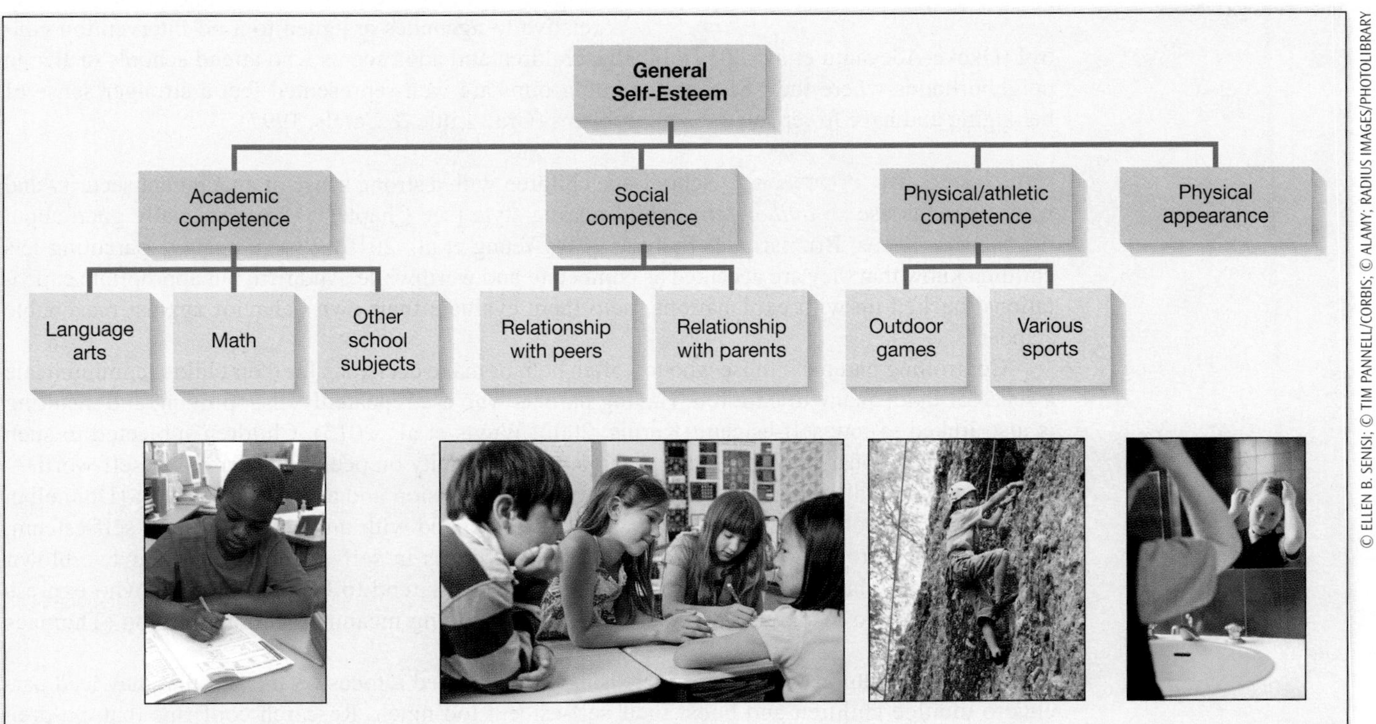

FIGURE 10.1 Hierarchical structure of self-esteem in the mid-elementary school years. From their experiences in different settings, children form at least four separate self-esteems: academic competence, social competence, physical/athletic competence, and physical appearance. These differentiate into additional self-evaluations and combine to form a general sense of self-esteem.

Culture, Gender, and Ethnicity. An especially strong emphasis on social comparison in school may explain why Chinese and Japanese children, despite their higher academic achievement, score lower than U.S. children in self-esteem—a difference that widens with age (Harter, 2012; Twenge & Crocker, 2002). And because their cultures value social harmony, Asian children tend to be reserved in positive self-judgments but generous in praise of others (Falbo et al., 1997).

Gender-stereotyped expectations also affect self-esteem. In one study, the more 5- to 8-year-old girls talked with friends about the way people look, watched TV shows focusing on physical appearance, and perceived their friends as valuing thinness, the greater their dissatisfaction with their physical self and the lower their overall self-esteem a year later (Dohnt & Tiggemann, 2006). In another investigation, being overweight was more strongly linked to negative body image for third-grade girls than for boys (Shriver et al., 2013). By the end of middle childhood, girls feel less confident than boys about their physical appearance and athletic abilities. In academic self-judgments, girls score higher in language arts self-esteem, whereas boys have higher math and science self-esteem—even when children of equal skill levels are compared (Jacobs et al., 2002; Kurtz-Costes et al., 2008). At the same time, girls exceed boys in self-esteem dimensions of close friendship and social acceptance.

AP IMAGES/THE DAY, SEAN D. ELLIOT

▶ Children learn African drumming skills at a community center during Kwanzaa, a holiday honoring their African heritage. A stronger sense of ethnic pride may contribute to slightly higher self-esteem among African-American children compared with their European-American agemates.

Compared with their European-American agemates, African-American children tend to have slightly higher self-esteem, possibly because of warm extended families and a stronger sense of ethnic pride (Gray-Little & Hafdahl, 2000). Consistent with this interpretation, African-American 7- to 10-year-olds randomly assigned to a 10-session, small-group program celebrating African-American family life and culture gained in self-esteem relative to agemates assigned to a no-intervention control (Okeke-Adeyanju et al., 2014). Finally, children and adolescents who attend schools or live in neighborhoods where their SES and ethnic groups are well-represented feel a stronger sense of belonging and have fewer self-esteem problems (Gray-Little & Carels, 1997).

Child-Rearing Practices. School-age children with a strong sense of attachment security and whose parents use an *authoritative* child-rearing style (see Chapter 8) feel especially good about themselves (Kerns, Brumariu, & Seibert, 2011; Yeung et al., 2016). Warm, positive parenting lets children know that they are accepted as competent and worthwhile. And firm but appropriate expectations, backed up with explanations, help them evaluate their own behavior against reasonable standards.

Controlling parents—those who too often help or make decisions for their child—communicate a sense of inadequacy to children. Having parents who are repeatedly disapproving and insulting is also linked to low self-esteem (Kernis, 2002; Wuyts et al., 2015). Children subjected to such parenting need constant reassurance, and many rely heavily on peers to affirm their self-worth—a risk factor for adjustment difficulties, including aggression and antisocial behavior (Donnellan et al., 2005). In contrast, indulgent parenting is associated with unrealistically high self-esteem. These children are vulnerable to temporary, sharp drops in self-esteem when their overblown self-images are challenged (Thomaes et al., 2013). They tend to lash out at peers who express disapproval and to display adjustment problems, including meanness and aggression (Thomaes et al., 2008).

American cultural values have increasingly emphasized a focus on the self that may lead parents to indulge children and boost their self-esteem too much. Research confirms that children do not benefit from compliments ("You're terrific") that have no basis in real accomplishment (Wentzel & Brophy, 2014). Rather, the best way to foster a positive, secure self-image is to encourage children to strive for worthwhile goals. Over time, a bidirectional relationship emerges: Achievement fosters self-esteem, which contributes to further effort and gains in performance (Marsh et al., 2005).

What can adults do to promote, and to avoid undermining, this mutually supportive relationship between motivation and self-esteem? Answers come from research on the precise content of adults' messages to children in achievement situations.

Achievement-Related Attributions. *Attributions* are our common, everyday explanations for the causes of behavior. Notice how Joey, in talking about the spelling bee at the beginning of this chapter, attributes his disappointing performance to *luck* (Belinda got all the easy words) and his usual success to *ability* (he *knows* he's a better speller than Belinda). Joey also appreciates that *effort* matters: "I knocked myself out studying those spelling lists."

The combination of improved reasoning skills and frequent evaluative feedback permits 10- to 12-year-olds to separate all these variables in explaining performance. Those who are high in academic self-esteem and motivation make **mastery-oriented attributions,** crediting their successes to ability—a characteristic they can improve through trying hard and can count on when faced with new challenges. And they attribute failure to factors that can be changed or controlled, such as insufficient effort or a difficult task (Dweck & Molden, 2013). Whether these children succeed or fail, they take an industrious, persistent approach to learning.

In contrast, children who develop **learned helplessness** attribute their failures, not their successes, to ability. When they succeed, they conclude that external factors, such as luck, are responsible. Unlike their mastery-oriented counterparts, they believe that ability is fixed and cannot be improved by trying hard (Dweck & Molden, 2013). When a task is difficult, these children experience an anxious loss of control—in Erikson's terms, a pervasive sense of inferiority. They give up without really trying.

Children's attributions affect their goals. Mastery-oriented children seek information on how best to increase their ability through effort. Hence, their performance improves over time (Dweck & Molden, 2013). In contrast, learned-helpless children focus on obtaining positive and avoiding negative evaluations of their fragile sense of ability. Gradually, their ability ceases to predict how well they do (Pomerantz & Saxon, 2001). Because they fail to connect effort with success, learned-helpless children do not develop the metacognitive and self-regulatory skills necessary for high achievement (see Chapter 9). Lack of effective learning strategies, reduced persistence, and a sense of loss of control sustain one another in a vicious cycle.

Influences on Achievement-Related Attributions. Adult communication plays a key role in the different attributions of mastery-oriented and learned-helpless children. Children with a learned-helpless style often have parents who believe that their child is not very capable. When the child fails, the parent might say, "You can't do that, can you? It's okay if you quit" (Hokoda & Fincham, 1995). Similarly, students with unsupportive teachers often regard their performance as externally controlled (by their teachers or by luck), withdraw from learning activities, decline in achievement, and come to doubt their ability (Skinner, Zimmer-Gembeck, & Connell, 1998).

When a child succeeds, adults can offer **person praise,** which emphasizes the child's traits ("You're so smart!"), or **process praise,** which emphasizes behavior and effort ("You figured it out!"). Children—especially those with low self-esteem—feel more shame following failure if they previously received person praise, less shame if they previously received process praise or no praise at all (Brummelman, Crocker, &

▶ When adults offer process praise emphasizing behavior and effort, children learn that persistence builds competence. Teacher remarks, such as "You found a good way to solve that problem!" will foster a mastery-oriented approach in this student.

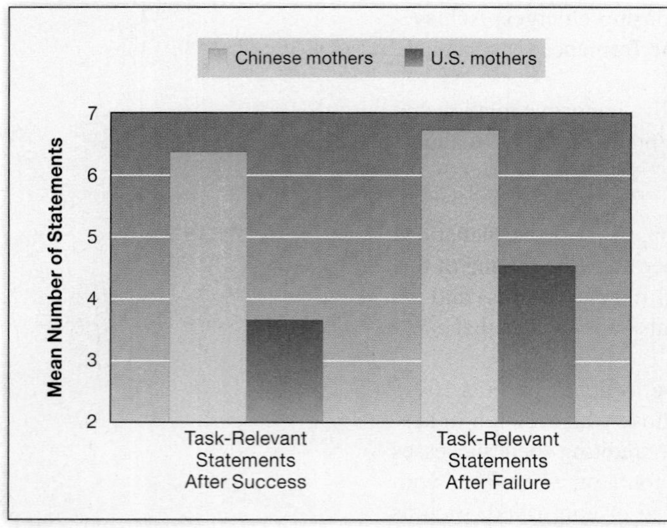

FIGURE 10.2 Chinese and U.S. mothers' task-relevant statements in response to their fourth-grade child's success or failure on puzzle tasks. Observations revealed that regardless of whether their child had just succeeded or failed, Chinese mothers were more likely than U.S. mothers to make task-relevant statements aimed at ensuring that the child exerted high effort. (Based on Ng, Pomerantz, & Lam, 2007)

Bushman, 2016). Consistent with a learned-helpless orientation, person praise teaches children that abilities are fixed, which leads them to question their competence and retreat from challenges (Pomerantz & Kempner, 2013). In contrast, process praise—consistent with a mastery orientation—implies that competence develops through effort (Pomerantz, Grolnick, & Price, 2013).

For some children, performance is especially likely to be undermined by adult feedback. Despite their higher achievement, girls more often than boys attribute poor performance to lack of ability. When girls do not do well, they tend to receive messages from teachers and parents that their ability is at fault, and negative stereotypes (for example, that girls are weak at math) undermine their interest and effort (Gunderson et al., 2012; Robinson-Cimpian et al., 2014). And as Chapter 9 revealed, low-SES ethnic minority students often receive less favorable feedback from teachers, especially when assigned to homogeneous groups of poorly achieving students.

Finally, cultural values influence children's views about success and failure. Asian parents and teachers are more likely than their American counterparts to view effort as key to achievement (Mok, Kennedy, & Moore, 2011; Qu & Pomerantz, 2015). Asians also attend more to failure than to success because failure indicates where corrective action is needed. Americans, in contrast, focus more on success because it enhances self-esteem. Observations of U.S. and Chinese mothers' responses to their fourth and fifth graders' puzzle solutions revealed that the U.S. mothers offered more praise after success, whereas the Chinese mothers more often pointed out the child's inadequate performance. And Chinese mothers made more task-relevant statements aimed at ensuring that children exerted sufficient effort ("You concentrated on it," "You only got 6 out of 12") (see Figure 10.2) (Ng, Pomerantz, & Lam, 2007). When children continued with the task after mothers left the room, the Chinese children showed greater gains in performance.

LOOK AND LISTEN

Observe a school-age child working on a challenging homework assignment under the guidance of a parent or other adult. What features of the adult's communication likely foster mastery-oriented attributions? How about learned helplessness? Explain.

Fostering a Mastery-Oriented Approach. An intervention called *attribution retraining* encourages children with learned helplessness to believe that they can overcome failure by exerting more effort and using more effective strategies. Children are given tasks difficult enough that they will experience some failure, followed by repeated feedback that helps them revise their attributions: "You can do it if you try harder." After they succeed, children are given process praise—"Your strategies worked," "You really tried hard on that one"—so that they attribute their success to both effort and effective strategies, not chance. Another approach is to encourage low-effort students to focus less on grades and more on mastering a task for its own sake and on individual improvement (Wentzel & Brophy, 2014). Instruction in effective strategies and self-regulation is also vital, to compensate for development lost in this area and to ensure that renewed effort pays off (Berkeley, Mastropieri, & Scruggs, 2011). For a summary of ways to foster mastery orientation, consult Applying What We Know on the following page.

ASK YOURSELF

CONNECT What cognitive changes, described in Chapter 9, support the transition to a self-concept emphasizing competencies, personality traits, and social comparisons?

APPLY Should parents try to promote children's self-esteem by telling them they're "smart" or "wonderful"? Are children harmed if they do not feel good about everything they do? Explain.

REFLECT Recall your own attributions for academic successes and failures when you were in elementary school. What are those attributions like now? What messages from others may have contributed to your attributions?

APPLYING WHAT WE KNOW

Fostering a Mastery-Oriented Approach to Learning

STRATEGY	DESCRIPTION
Provision of tasks	Select tasks that are meaningful, responsive to a diversity of student interests, and appropriately matched to current competence so that the child is challenged but not overwhelmed.
Parent and teacher encouragement	Communicate warmth, confidence in the child's abilities, the value of achievement, and the importance of effort in success. Resist praising children's personal qualities, focusing instead on their competent behavior, sustained effort, and successful strategies. Model high effort in overcoming failure. *For teachers:* Communicate often with parents, suggesting ways to foster children's effort and progress. *For parents:* Monitor schoolwork; provide scaffolded assistance that promotes knowledge of effective strategies and self-regulation.
Performance evaluations	Make evaluations private; avoid publicizing success or failure through wall posters, stars, privileges for "smart" children, or prizes for "best" performance. Emphasize individual progress and self-improvement. Provide accurate, constructive feedback to children about their performance.
School environment	Provide for cooperative learning and peer tutoring, in which children assist one another; avoid ability grouping, which makes evaluations of children's progress public. Accommodate individual and cultural differences in learning styles. Create an atmosphere that sends a clear message that all students can learn.

Sources: Wentzel & Brophy, 2014; Wigfield et al., 2006.

Emotional Development

10.3 Cite changes in self-conscious emotions, emotional understanding, and emotional self-regulation in middle childhood.

Greater self-awareness and social sensitivity support advances in emotional competence in middle childhood. Gains take place in experience of self-conscious emotions, emotional understanding, and emotional self-regulation.

Self-Conscious Emotions

As school-age children integrate social expectations into their self-concepts, self-conscious emotions of pride and guilt become clearly governed by personal responsibility. Children experience pride in a new accomplishment and guilt over a transgression, even when no adult is present (Harter, 2012). Also, children no longer report guilt for any mishap, as they did earlier, but only for intentional wrongdoing, such as ignoring responsibilities, cheating, or lying (Ferguson, Stegge, & Damhuis, 1991). These changes reflect the older child's more mature sense of morality, addressed later in this chapter.

Pride motivates children to take on further challenges, whereas guilt prompts them to make amends and to strive for self-improvement. But in Chapter 8 we noted that excessive guilt is linked to depressive symptoms. And harsh, insensitive reprimands from adults ("Everyone else can do it! Why can't you?") can lead to intense shame, which is particularly destructive, yielding both internalizing and externalizing problems (see page 250).

Emotional Understanding

School-age children's understanding of mental activity means that, unlike preschoolers, they are likely to explain emotion by referring to internal states, such as happy or sad thoughts, rather than to

AP IMAGES/THE EVANSVILLE COURIER & PRESS, JASON CLARK

▶ Third graders help prepare meal packages to be sent to Africa to feed children in need. Gains in emotional understanding and perspective taking enable children to respond with empathy to people's general life condition.

external events (Flavell, Flavell, & Green, 2001). Also, between ages 6 and 12, children become more aware of circumstances likely to spark mixed emotions, each of which may be positive or negative and may differ in intensity (Pons et al., 2003; Zadjel et al., 2013). For example, Joey reflected, "I was very happy that I got a birthday present from my grandma but a little sad that I didn't get just what I wanted."

Appreciating mixed emotions helps children realize that people's expressions may not reflect their true feelings (Misailidi, 2006). It also fosters awareness of self-conscious emotions. For example, between ages 6 and 7, children improve in ability to distinguish pride from happiness and surprise (Tracy, Robins, & Lagattuta, 2005). And 8- and 9-year-olds understand that pride combines two sources of happiness—joy in accomplishment and joy that a significant person recognized that accomplishment (Harter, 1999).

As with self-understanding, gains in emotional understanding are supported by cognitive development and social experiences, especially adults' sensitivity to children's feelings and willingness to discuss emotions. These factors lead to a rise in empathy as well. As children move closer to adolescence, advances in perspective taking permit an empathic response not just to people's immediate distress but also to their general life condition (Hoffman, 2000). As Joey and Lizzie imagined how people who are chronically ill or hungry feel and evoked those emotions in themselves, they gave part of their allowance to charity and joined in fundraising projects through school and scouting.

Emotional Self-Regulation

In Chapter 8, we saw that emotional understanding, along with parents' teaching of emotion-regulation strategies, contributes to young children's ability to manage emotions. These factors continue to play important roles during middle childhood, a period of rapid gains in emotional self-regulation (Zalewski et al., 2011).

By age 10, most children shift adaptively between two general strategies for managing emotion. In **problem-centered coping,** they appraise the situation as changeable, identify the difficulty, and decide what to do about it. If problem solving does not work, they engage in **emotion-centered coping,** which is internal, private, and aimed at controlling distress when little can be done about an outcome (Kliewer, Fearnow, & Miller, 1996; Lazarus & Lazarus, 1994). For example, when faced with an anxiety-provoking test or an angry friend, older school-age children view problem solving and seeking social support as the best strategies. But when outcomes are beyond their control—after receiving a bad grade—they opt for distraction or try to redefine the situation: "Things could be worse. There'll be another test." School-age children's improved ability to appraise situations and reflect on thoughts and feelings means that, compared with preschoolers, they more often use these internal strategies to manage emotion (Brenner & Salovey, 1997).

Furthermore, through interacting with parents, teachers, and peers, school-age children become more knowledgeable about socially approved ways to display negative emotion. They increasingly prefer verbal expression ("Please stop pushing and wait your turn") to crying, sulking, or aggression (Waters & Thompson, 2014). Young school-age children justify these more mature displays of emotion by mentioning avoidance of punishment or adult approval, but by third grade, they begin to emphasize concern for others' feelings. Children with this awareness are rated as especially helpful, cooperative, and socially responsive by teachers and as better-liked by peers (McDowell & Parke, 2000).

When emotional self-regulation has developed well, school-age children acquire a sense of *emotional self-efficacy*—a feeling of being in control of their emotional experience (Thompson & Goodman, 2010). This fosters a favorable self-image and an optimistic outlook, which further help children face emotional challenges. As at younger ages, school-age children whose parents respond sensitively and helpfully when the child is distressed are emotionally well-regulated—generally upbeat in mood and also empathic and prosocial. In contrast, poorly regulated children often experience hostile, dismissive parental reactions to distress (Morris et al., 2007; Vinik, Almas, & Grusec, 2011). These children are overwhelmed by negative emotion, a response that interferes with empathy and prosocial behavior.

Moral Development

10.4 Describe changes in moral understanding during middle childhood, including children's understanding of diversity and inequality.

Recall from Chapter 8 that preschoolers pick up many morally relevant behaviors through modeling and reinforcement. By middle childhood, they have had time to internalize rules for good conduct: "It's good to help others in trouble" or "It's wrong to take something that doesn't belong to you." This change leads children to become considerably more independent and trustworthy.

In Chapter 8, we also saw that children do not just copy their morality from others. As the cognitive-developmental approach emphasizes, they actively think about right and wrong. An expanding social world, the capacity to consider more information when reasoning, and gains in recursive perspective taking lead moral understanding to advance greatly in middle childhood.

Moral and Social-Conventional Understanding

During the school years, children construct a flexible appreciation of moral rules. They take into account an increasing number of variables—not just the action and its immediate impact, but also the actor's intentions and the context of his behavior (Killen & Smetana, 2015). For example, between ages 7 and 11, children say it is acceptable to hit another child in certain situations—in self-defense, to protect someone else from serious bodily injury, or to prevent the other child from hurting herself (Jambon & Smetana, 2014). Older children focus less on the actor's transgression (hitting) and more on the aim of her behavior (trying to prevent harm).

Similarly, by ages 7 to 8, children no longer say that truth telling is always good and lying is always bad but consider prosocial and antisocial intentions and context. They evaluate certain types of truthfulness very negatively—for example, blunt statements, particularly in public contexts where they are especially likely to have negative social consequences (telling a classmate that you don't like her drawing) (Ma et al., 2011).

Although both Chinese and Canadian schoolchildren consider lying about antisocial acts "very naughty," Chinese children more often rate lying favorably when the intention is modesty, as when a student who has thoughtfully picked up litter from the playground says, "I didn't do it" (Cameron et al., 2012; Lee et al., 2001). Similarly, Chinese children are more likely to favor lying to support the group at the expense of the individual (saying you're sick so, as a poor singer, you won't harm your class's chances of winning a singing competition). In contrast, Canadian children more often favor lying to support the individual at the expense of the group (claiming that a friend who is a poor speller is actually a good speller because the friend wants to participate in a spelling competition) (Fu et al., 2007; Lau et al., 2012).

Notice how these judgments require *recursive* perspective taking: Children must consider simultaneously the viewpoints of two or more people—the person who lies and the recipients of the lie. Appreciation of second-order false belief, which depends on recursive thought (see page 297 in Chapter 9), is related to gains in moral judgment in middle childhood. In one study, researchers gave children a morally relevant second-order false-belief task: A child, while helping her teacher clean up, accidently throws out a bag containing a treasured cupcake belonging to a classmate who is out of the room (Fu et al., 2014). School-age children who reasoned accurately about the helper's belief about the bag's contents (trash) and the cupcake owner's belief about the cupcake's location (in a bag in the classroom) assigned less blame to the helper. Using their recursive capacity, these children inferred that *the cupcake owner would understand that the helper thought the bag had trash in it.*

As children construct more advanced ideas about justice, they clarify and link moral imperatives and social conventions. School-age children distinguish social conventions with a clear *purpose* (not running in school hallways to prevent injuries) from ones with no obvious justification (crossing a "forbidden" line on the playground) (Buchanan-Barrow & Barrett, 1998). They regard violations of purposeful social conventions as closer to moral transgressions.

▶ New York City schoolchildren participate in the People's Climate March, which advocates for global action to prevent climate change. Children's grasp of personal choice enhances moral understanding, including freedom of speech.

Understanding Individual Rights

When children challenge adult authority, they typically do so within the personal domain (Nucci, 2005). As their grasp of moral imperatives and social conventions strengthens, so does their conviction that certain choices, such as hairstyle, friends, and leisure activities, are up to the individual.

Notions of personal choice, in turn, enhance children's moral understanding. As early as age 6, children view freedom of speech and religion as individual rights, even if laws exist that deny those rights (Helwig, 2006). And they regard laws that discriminate against individuals—for example, denying certain people access to medical care or education—as wrong and worthy of violating (Helwig & Jasiobedzka, 2001). In justifying their responses, children appeal to personal privileges and, by the end of middle childhood, to the importance of individual rights for maintaining a fair society.

At the same time, older school-age children place limits on individual choice. Fourth graders faced with conflicting moral and personal concerns—such as whether or not to befriend a classmate of a different race or gender—typically decide in favor of kindness and fairness (Killen et al., 2002). High-quality friendships may play an important role in facilitating children's moral sensibilities (McDonald et al., 2014). The cooperativeness, responsiveness, and empathic understanding between good friends promotes concern for others' rights and welfare, while also highlighting the circumstances in which some transgressions ought to be forgiven.

Culture and Moral Understanding

Children and adolescents in diverse cultures use similar criteria to reason about moral, social-conventional, and personal concerns (Nucci, 2005, 2009). For example, Chinese young people, whose culture places a high value on respect for adult authority, nevertheless say that adults have no right to interfere in children's personal matters, such as how they spend free time (Hasebe, Nucci, & Nucci, 2004). A Colombian child illustrated this passionate defense of personal control when asked if a teacher has the right to tell a student where to sit during circle time. In the absence of a moral reason from the teacher, the child declared, "She should be able to sit wherever she wants" (Ardila-Rey & Killen, 2001, p. 249).

Furthermore, when a directive is fair and caring, such as telling children to share candy or to return lost money to its owner, school-age children view it as right, regardless of who states it—even a child with no authority. And even in Korean culture, which promotes children's deference to adults, 7- to 11-year-olds evaluate negatively a teacher's or principal's order to engage in immoral acts, such as stealing or refusing to share (Kim, 1998). In sum, children everywhere seem to realize that higher principles, independent of rule and authority, must prevail when people's personal rights and welfare are at stake.

Understanding Diversity and Inequality

By the early school years, children absorb societal attitudes about race and ethnicity, associating power and privilege with White people and poverty and inferior status with people of color. They do not necessarily acquire these views directly from parents or friends, whose attitudes may differ from their own (Aboud & Doyle, 1996; Pahlke, Bigler, & Suizzo, 2012). Rather, children seem to pick up mainstream beliefs from implicit messages in the media and elsewhere in their environments. Powerful sources include social contexts that present a world sorted into groups, such as racial and ethnic segregation in schools and communities.

In-Group and Out-Group Biases: Development of Prejudice. Studies in diverse Western nations confirm that by ages 5 to 6, White children generally evaluate their own racial group favorably and other racial groups less favorably or negatively. *In-group favoritism* emerges first; children simply prefer their own group, generalizing from self to similar others (Buttelmann & Böhm, 2014; Dunham, Baron, & Carey, 2011; Nesdale et al., 2004).

The ease with which a trivial group label supplied by an adult can induce in-group favoritism is striking. In one study, European-American 5-year-olds were told that they were members of a group based on T-shirt color. Although no information was provided about group status and the children never met any group members, they still displayed vigorous in-group favoritism (Dunham, Baron, & Carey, 2011). When shown photos of unfamiliar agemates wearing either an in-group or an out-group T-shirt, the children claimed to like members of their own group better, gave them more resources, and engaged in positively biased recall of group members' behavior.

Out-group prejudice requires a more challenging social comparison between in-group and out-group. But it does not take long for White children to acquire negative attitudes toward ethnic minority out-groups when such attitudes are encouraged by circumstances in their environments. When White Canadian 4- to 7-year-olds living in a White community and attending nearly all-White schools sorted positive and negative adjectives into boxes labeled as belonging to a White child and a Black child, out-group prejudice emerged at age 5 (Corenblum, 2003). Unfortunately, many minority children show a reverse pattern: *out-group favoritism,* in which they assign positive characteristics to the privileged White majority and negative characteristics to their own group (Averhart & Bigler, 1997; Newheiser et al., 2014).

But recall that with age, children pay more attention to inner traits. The capacity to classify the social world in multiple ways enables school-age children to understand that people can be both "the same" and "different"—those who look different need not think, feel, or act differently. Consequently, voicing of negative attitudes toward minorities declines after age 7 or 8 (Aboud, 2008; Raabe & Beelmann, 2011). Around this time, both majority and minority children express in-group favoritism, and White children's prejudice against out-group members often weakens (Nesdale et al., 2004; Ruble et al., 2004).

Yet even in children aware of the injustice of discrimination, prejudice often operates unintentionally and without awareness—as it does in many adults (Dunham, Baron, & Banaji, 2006). Consider a study in which U.S. children and adults were shown pictures of computer-generated racially ambiguous faces displaying happy and angry expressions and asked to classify them by race. White participants more often categorized happy faces as White and angry faces as African American or Asian. These implicit biases were evident across all ages tested—as early as 3 or 4. In contrast, African-American participants did not show any racial biases in their responses (Dunham, Chen, & Banaji, 2013). The absence of any in-group favoritism (classifying happy faces as Black) suggests an early-emerging, implicit sensitivity to prevailing racial attitudes among African Americans.

The extent to which children hold racial and ethnic biases varies, depending on the following personal and situational factors:

- *A fixed view of personality traits.* Children who believe that people's personality traits are fixed rather than changeable often judge others as either "good" or "bad." Ignoring motives and circumstances, they readily form prejudices based on limited information. For example, they might infer that "a new child at school who tells a lie to get other kids to like her" is simply "a bad kid" (Levy & Dweck, 1999).
- *Overly high self-esteem.* Children (and adults) with very high self-esteem are more likely to hold racial and ethnic prejudices (Baumeister et al., 2003; Bigler, 2013). These individuals seem to belittle disadvantaged people or groups to justify their own extremely favorable, yet insecure, self-evaluations. Children who say their own ethnicity makes them feel especially "good"—and thus perhaps socially superior—are more likely to display in-group favoritism and out-group prejudice (Pfeifer et al., 2007).

- *A social world in which people are sorted into groups.* The more adults highlight group distinctions and the less interracial contact children experience, the more likely White children will express in-group favoritism and out-group prejudice (Aboud & Brown, 2013).

Reducing Prejudice. An effective way to reduce prejudice is through intergroup contact, in which racially and ethnically different children have equal status, work toward common goals, and become personally acquainted (Tropp & Page-Gould, 2015). Children assigned to cooperative learning groups with peers of diverse backgrounds show low levels of prejudice in their expressions of likability and in their behavior. For example, they form more cross-race friendships (Pettigrew & Tropp, 2006). Sharing thoughts and feelings with close, cross-race friends, in turn, reduces even subtle, unintentional prejudices (Turner, Hewstone, & Voci, 2007).

© JOEL ARTISTA

▶ Palestinian and Israeli children and adolescents take a break from mural painting to sing and dance together. Intergroup contact, in which racially and ethnically different children have equal status, work toward common goals, and become personally acquainted, is an effective way to reduce prejudice.

Long-term contact and collaboration among neighborhood, school, and community groups may be the best way to reduce prejudice (Rutland, Killen, & Abrams, 2010). School environments that expose children to broad ethnic diversity, that teach them to understand and value those differences, that directly address the damage caused by prejudice, and that emphasize moral values of justice and fairness prevent children from forming negative biases and lessen already acquired biases (Beelmann & Heinemann, 2014).

Finally, inducing children to view others' traits as changeable, by discussing with them the many possible influences on those traits, is helpful. The more children believe that people can change their personalities, the more they report liking and perceiving themselves as similar to members of disadvantaged out-groups. Furthermore, children who believe that human attributes are changeable spend more time volunteering to help people in need (Karafantis & Levy, 2004; Levy et al., 2016). Volunteering may, in turn, promote a view of others as changeable by helping children take the perspective of the underprivileged and appreciate the social conditions that lead to disadvantage.

ASK YOURSELF

CONNECT Cite examples of how older children's capacity to take more information into account enhances their emotional and moral understanding.

APPLY Ten-year-old Marla says her classmate Bernadette will never get good grades because she's lazy. Jane believes that Bernadette tries but can't concentrate because her parents are divorcing. Why is Marla more likely than Jane to develop prejudices?

REFLECT Did you attend an integrated elementary school? Why is school integration vital for reducing racial and ethnic prejudice?

Peer Relations

10.5 Describe changes in peer sociability and friendship in middle childhood.

10.6 Describe categories of peer acceptance and ways to help rejected children.

In middle childhood, the society of peers becomes an increasingly important context for development. The capacity for recursive perspective taking permits more sophisticated understanding of self and others, which, in turn, contributes to peer interaction. Compared with preschoolers, school-age children resolve conflicts more effectively, and prosocial acts such as sharing and helping increase. In line with these changes, aggression declines. But the drop is greatest for physical attacks (Côté et al., 2007). As we will see, verbal and relational aggression continue as children organize into peer groups.

Peer Groups

▶ Peer groups first form in middle childhood. These boys have probably established a peer-group structure of leaders and followers as they gather for a soccer game. Their relaxed body language and similar dress suggest a strong sense of group belonging.

By the end of middle childhood, children display a strong desire for group belonging. They form **peer groups,** collectives that generate unique values and standards for behavior and a social structure of leaders and followers. Peer groups organize on the basis of proximity (being in the same classroom) and similarity in sex, ethnicity, academic achievement, popularity, and aggression (Rubin et al., 2013).

The practices of these informal groups lead to a "peer culture" that typically involves a specialized vocabulary, dress code, and place to "hang out." These customs bind peers together, creating a sense of group identity. Within the group, children acquire many social skills—cooperation, leadership, followership, and loyalty to collective goals.

Most school-age children believe a group is wrong to exclude a peer on the basis of unconventional appearance or behavior—a view that strengthens with age (Killen, Crystal, & Watanabe, 2002). Nevertheless, children do exclude, often using relationally aggressive tactics. Peer groups—at the instigation of their leaders, who can be skillfully aggressive—frequently oust no longer "respected" children. Some of these castouts, whose own previous behavior toward outsiders reduces their chances of being included elsewhere, turn to other low-status peers with poor social skills (Farmer et al., 2010). Socially anxious children, when ousted, often become increasingly peer-avoidant and thus more isolated (Buhs, Ladd, & Herald-Brown, 2010). In either case, opportunities to acquire socially competent behavior diminish.

School-age children's desire for group membership can also be satisfied through formal group ties such as scouting, 4-H, and religious youth groups. Adult involvement holds in check the negative behaviors associated with children's informal peer groups. And through working on joint projects and helping in their communities, children gain in social and moral maturity (Vandell et al., 2015).

Friendships

Whereas peer groups provide children with insight into larger social structures, friendships contribute to the development of trust and sensitivity. During the school years, friendship becomes more complex and psychologically based. Consider the following 8-year-old's ideas:

> *Why is Shelly your best friend?* Because she helps me when I'm sad, and she shares. . . . *How come you like Shelly better than anyone else?* She's done the most for me. She never disagrees, she never eats in front of me, she never walks away when I'm crying, and she helps me with my homework. . . . *How do you get someone to like you?* . . . If you're nice to [your friends], they'll be nice to you. (Damon, 1988b, pp. 80–81)

As these responses show, friendship has become a mutually agreed-on relationship in which children like each other's personal qualities and respond to one another's needs and desires. And once a friendship forms, *trust* becomes its defining feature (Hartup & Abecassis, 2004). Older children regard violations of trust, such as not helping when others need help, breaking promises, and gossiping behind the other's back, as serious breaches of friendship.

Because of these features, school-age children's friendships are more selective. Whereas preschoolers say they have lots of friends, by age 8 or 9, children name only a handful of good friends. Girls, who demand greater closeness than boys, are more exclusive in their friendships.

School-age children tend to select friends similar to themselves in age, sex, race, ethnicity, and SES. Friends also resemble one another in personality (sociability, inattention/hyperactivity, aggression, depression), peer popularity, academic achievement, and prosocial behavior (Rubin et al., 2013). But friendship opportunities encouraged by children's environments also affect their choices.

LOOK AND LISTEN

Ask an 8- to 11-year-old to tell you what he or she looks for in a best friend. Is *trust* centrally important? Does the child mention personality traits, just as school-age children do in describing themselves?

© KLAUS-PETER WOLF/ROBERT HARDING

▶ School-age children tend to select friends who are similar to themselves in personality and academic achievement. Their friendships are fairly stable: These boys are likely to remain friends for at least a full school year.

Children whose parents have cross-race friends form more cross-race friendships (Pahlke, Bigler, & Suizzo, 2012). And as noted earlier, in integrated classrooms with mixed-race collaborative learning groups, students develop more cross-race friendships.

Over middle childhood, high-quality friendships remain fairly stable. About 50 to 70 percent endure over a school year, and some last for several years. Gains in friendship support—including compromise, sharing of thoughts and feelings, and prosocial behavior—contribute to this stability (Berndt, 2004; Furman & Rose, 2015).

Through friendships, children learn the importance of emotional commitment. They come to realize that close relationships can survive disagreements if friends are secure in their liking for each other and resolve disputes in ways that meet both partners' needs. Yet the impact of friendships on children's development depends on the nature of those friends. Children who bring kindness and compassion to their friendships strengthen each other's prosocial tendencies.

But when aggressive children make friends, the relationship is often riddled with hostile exchanges and is at risk for breakup, especially when just one member of the pair is aggressive. And within these close ties, children's aggressive tendencies worsen (Henneberger, Coffman, & Gest, 2017; Salmivalli, 2010). Aggressive girls' friendships are high in exchange of private feelings but also full of jealousy, conflict, and betrayal. Aggressive boys' friendships involve frequent expressions of anger, coercive statements, physical attacks, and enticements to rule-breaking behavior (Rubin et al., 2013; Werner & Crick, 2004). As we will see next, aggressive children often acquire negative reputations in the wider world of peers.

Peer Acceptance

Peer acceptance refers to likability—the extent to which a child is viewed by a group of agemates, such as classmates, as a worthy social partner. Unlike friendship, likability is not a mutual relationship but a one-sided perspective, involving the group's view of an individual. Nevertheless, better-accepted children tend to be socially competent and, as a result, have more friends and more positive relationships with them (Mayeux, Houser, & Dyches, 2011).

To assess peer acceptance, researchers usually use self-reports that measure *social preferences*—for example, asking children to identify classmates whom they "like most" or "like least" (Cillessen, 2009). These self-reports yield five general categories of peer acceptance:

- **Popular children,** who get many positive votes (are well-liked)
- **Rejected children,** who get many negative votes (are disliked)
- **Controversial children,** who receive many votes, both positive and negative (are both liked and disliked)
- **Neglected children,** who are seldom mentioned, either positively or negatively
- *Average children,* who receive average numbers of positive and negative votes and account for about one-third of children in a typical elementary school classroom

Another approach assesses *perceived popularity*—children's judgments of whom most of their classmates admire. Only moderate correspondence exists between the classmates children perceive as popular (believe are admired by many others) and those classified as popular based on peer preferences (receive many "like most" ratings) (Mayeux, Houser, & Dyches, 2011).

Peer acceptance is a powerful predictor of psychological adjustment. Rejected children, especially, are anxious, unhappy, disruptive, and low in self-esteem. Both teachers and parents rate them as having a wide range of emotional and social problems. Peer rejection in middle childhood is also strongly associated with poor school performance, absenteeism, dropping out, substance use, depression, antisocial behavior, and delinquency in adolescence and with criminality in adulthood (Ladd, 2005; Rubin et al., 2013).

However, earlier influences—children's characteristics combined with parenting practices—may largely explain the link between peer acceptance and adjustment. School-age children with peer-relationship problems are more likely to have weak emotional self-regulation skills and to have experienced family stress due to low income and insensitive parenting, including coercive discipline (Blair et al., 2014; Trentacosta & Shaw, 2009). Nevertheless, as we will see, rejected children evoke reactions from peers that contribute to their unfavorable development.

Determinants of Peer Acceptance. Why is one child liked while another is rejected? A wealth of research reveals that social behavior plays a powerful role.

Popular Children. **Popular-prosocial children** are both well-liked (socially preferred) and admired (high in perceived popularity). They combine academic and social competence, performing well in school and communicating with peers in friendly and cooperative ways (Cillessen & Bellmore, 2004; Mayeux, Houser, & Dyches, 2011).

But other popular children are admired for their socially adept yet belligerent behavior. **Popular-antisocial children** include "tough" boys—athletically skilled but poor students who cause trouble and defy adult authority—and relationally aggressive boys and girls who enhance their own status by ignoring, excluding, and spreading rumors about other children (Rose, Swenson, & Waller, 2004; Vaillancourt & Hymel, 2006). Despite their aggressiveness, peers often view these youths as "cool," perhaps because of their athletic abilities and sophisticated but devious social skills. But with age, peers like these high-status, aggressive youths less and less, eventually rejecting them.

Rejected Children. Rejected children display a wide range of negative social behaviors. The largest subtype, **rejected-aggressive children,** show high rates of conflict, physical and relational aggression, and hyperactive, inattentive, and impulsive behavior (Dodge, Coie, & Lynam, 2006; Rubin et al., 2013). Compared with popular-antisocial children, they are more extremely antagonistic.

In contrast, **rejected-withdrawn children** are passive and socially awkward. Overwhelmed by social anxiety, they hold negative expectations about interactions with peers and worry about being scorned and attacked (Rubin et al., 2013; Troop-Gordon & Asher, 2005).

As rejected children are excluded, their classroom participation declines, their feelings of loneliness rise, their academic achievement falters, and they want to avoid school (Buhs, Ladd, & Herald-Brown, 2010; Gooren et al., 2011). Most have few friends, and some have none—a circumstance that predicts severe adjustment difficulties (Ladd et al., 2011; Pedersen et al., 2007).

Both types of rejected children are at risk for peer harassment (Craig et al., 2016). But as the Biology and Environment box on page 336 reveals, rejected-aggressive children also act as bullies, and rejected-withdrawn children are especially likely to be victimized.

LOOK AND LISTEN

Contact a nearby elementary school or a school district to find out what practices are in place to prevent bullying. Inquire about a written antibullying policy, and request a copy.

Controversial and Neglected Children. Consistent with the mixed peer opinion they engender, controversial children display a blend of positive and negative social behaviors. They are hostile and disruptive, but they also engage in positive, prosocial acts. Even though some peers dislike them, they have qualities that protect them from social exclusion. They have many friends and are happy with their peer relationships (de Bruyn & Cillessen, 2006). But like their popular-antisocial and rejected-aggressive counterparts, they often bully others and engage in calculated relational aggression to sustain their dominance (Putallaz et al., 2007).

Perhaps the most surprising finding on peer acceptance is that neglected children, once thought to be in need of treatment, are usually well-adjusted. Although they engage in low rates of interaction, most are just as socially skilled as average children and do not report feeling unhappy about their social life. When they want to, they can break away from their usual pattern of playing alone, cooperating well with peers and forming positive, stable friendships (Ladd & Burgess, 1999; Ladd et al., 2011). Neglected, socially competent children remind us that an outgoing, gregarious personality style is not the only path to emotional well-being.

BIOLOGY AND ENVIRONMENT

Bullies and Their Victims

Follow the activities of aggressive children over a school day, and you will see that they reserve their hostilities for certain peers. A particularly destructive form of interaction is **peer victimization,** in which certain children become targets of verbal and physical attacks or other forms of abuse. What sustains these repeated assault–retreat cycles?

About 20 percent of children are bullies, while 25 percent are repeatedly victimized. Most bullies who engage in face-to-face physical and verbal attacks are boys, but a considerable number of girls bombard vulnerable classmates with verbal and relational hostility (Cook et al., 2010).

As bullies move into adolescence, an increasing number attack through electronic means. About 20 to 40 percent of youths have experienced "cyberbullying" through text messages, e-mail, social media sites, or other electronic tools (Kowalski & Limber, 2013). Compared with face-to-face bullying, gender differences in cyberbullying are less pronounced; the indirectness of online aggression may lead girls to prefer it (Menesini & Spiel, 2012). Girls more often cyberbully with words, whereas boys typically distribute embarrassing photos or videos. Victims are far less likely to report cyberbullying to parents or adults at school. In many instances, the cyberbully's identity is unknown to the victim and audience.

Many bullies are disliked, or become so, because of their cruelty. But a substantial number are socially powerful youngsters who are broadly admired by peers. These high-status bullies often target already-peer-rejected children, whom classmates are unlikely to defend (Veenstra et al., 2010). Peers rarely intervene to help victims, and about 20 to 30 percent of onlookers actually encourage bullies, even joining in (Salmivalli & Voeten, 2004).

Bullying occurs more often in schools where many students judge bullying behavior to be "OK" (Guerra, Williams, & Sadek, 2011). Indeed, bullies and the peers who assist them typically display overly high self-esteem, pride in their acts, and indifference to harm done to their victims (Hymel et al., 2010).

© JOHN BIRDSALL/THE IMAGE WORKS

▶ Bullies and the peers who assist them typically display overly high self-esteem, pride in their acts, and indifference to the harm done to their victims. Chronic victims are often easy targets—physically weak, passive, and inhibited.

Chronic victims tend to be passive when active behavior is expected. Biologically based traits—an inhibited temperament and a frail physical appearance—contribute. But victims also have histories of resistant attachment, overly controlling child rearing, and maternal overprotection—parenting that prompts anxiety, low self-esteem, and dependency, resulting in a fearful demeanor that marks these children as vulnerable (Snyder et al., 2003).

Like persistent child abuse, victimization is linked to impaired production of cortisol, suggesting a disrupted physiological response to stress (Vaillancourt, Hymel, & McDougall, 2013). Persistent traditional bullying and cyberbullying are related to declining self-esteem, classroom and school participation, and academic achievement and rising anxiety, depression, and suicidal thoughts (Ladd, Ettekal, & Kochenderfer-Ladd, 2017; Menesini, Calussi, & Nocentini, 2012; van den Eijnden et al., 2014). Repeated cyber-attacks directed at causing widespread damage to the victim's reputation—for example, circulating malicious photos or videos on cell phones or social media sites—magnify these effects.

Aggression and victimization are not polar opposites. One-third to one-half of victims are also aggressive, meting out physical, relational, or cyberhostilities. Bullies usually respond by abusing them again—a cycle that sustains their victim status (Cooley, Fite, & Pederson, 2017). Among rejected children, these bully/victims are the most despised. They often have histories of extremely maladaptive parenting, including child abuse. This combination of highly negative home and peer experiences places them at severe risk for maladjustment (Kowalski, Limber, & Agatston, 2008).

Interventions that change victimized children's negative opinions of themselves and that teach them to respond in nonreinforcing ways to their attackers are helpful. Another way to assist victimized children is to help them form and maintain a gratifying, supportive friendship (Cuadros & Berger, 2016). When children have a close friend to whom they can turn for help, bullying episodes usually end quickly.

Although modifying victimized children's behavior can help, the best way to reduce bullying is to promote prosocial attitudes and behaviors. Effective approaches include developing school and community codes against both traditional bullying and cyberbullying; teaching child bystanders to intervene; strengthening parental oversight of children's use of cell phones, computers, and the Internet; and increasing adult supervision of high-bullying areas in schools, such as hallways, lunchroom, and schoolyard (Fite et al., 2013).

The U.S. Department of Health and Human Services manages an antibullying website, *www.stopbullying.gov*, that raises awareness of the harmfulness of bullying and provides information on prevention.

Helping Rejected Children. A variety of interventions exist to improve the peer relations and psychological adjustment of rejected children. Most involve coaching, modeling, and reinforcing positive social skills, such as how to initiate interaction with a peer, cooperate in play, and respond to another child with friendly emotion and approval. Several of these programs have produced lasting gains in social competence and peer acceptance (Asher & Rose, 1997; DeRosier, 2007). Combining social-skills training with other treatments increases its effectiveness. Rejected children are often poor students, whose low academic self-esteem magnifies their negative interactions with teachers and classmates. Intensive academic tutoring improves both school achievement and social acceptance (O'Neill et al., 1997).

Another approach focuses on training in perspective taking and in solving social problems. One eleven-session intervention involved teaching rejected-aggressive children to recognize others' feelings and resolve conflicts constructively within their best friendships, which are typically of low quality (see page 334) (Salvas et al., 2016). Relative to no-intervention controls, participants gained in friendship quality and declined in aggressive behavior.

But many rejected-aggressive children are unaware of their poor social skills and do not take responsibility for their social failures (Lynch et al., 2016; Mrug, Hoza, & Gerdes, 2001). Rejected-withdrawn children, in contrast, are likely to develop a *learned-helpless* approach to peer difficulties—concluding, after repeated rebuffs, that they will never be liked (Wichmann, Coplan, & Daniels, 2004). Both types of children need help attributing their peer difficulties to internal, changeable causes.

As rejected children gain in social skills, teachers must encourage peers to alter their negative opinions. Accepted children often selectively recall rejected classmates' negative acts while overlooking their positive ones (Mikami, Lerner, & Lun, 2010). Consequently, even in the face of contrary evidence, rejected children's negative reputations tend to persist. Teachers' praise and expressions of liking can modify peer judgments (De Laet et al., 2014).

Finally, because rejected children's socially incompetent behaviors often originate in harsh, authoritarian parenting, interventions focusing on the child alone may not be sufficient. If parent–child interaction does not change, children may soon return to their old behavior patterns.

Gender Typing

Children's understanding of gender roles broadens in middle childhood, and their gender identities (views of themselves as relatively masculine or feminine) change as well. We will see how gender stereotypes influence children's attitudes, behaviors, peer relations, and self-perceptions.

10.7 Discuss changes in gender-stereotyped beliefs and gender identity during middle childhood.

Gender-Stereotyped Beliefs

Research in many countries reveals that stereotyping of personality traits increases steadily in middle childhood, becoming adultlike around age 11 (Best, 2001; Heyman & Legare, 2004). For example, children regard "tough," "aggressive," "rational," and "dominant" as masculine and "gentle," "sympathetic," and "dependent" as feminine.

Children derive these distinctions from observing gender differences in behavior as well as from adult treatment. When helping a child with a task, for example, parents (especially fathers) behave in a more mastery-oriented fashion with sons, setting higher standards, explaining concepts, and pointing out important features of tasks—particularly during gender-typed pursuits, such as science activities (Tenenbaum & Leaper, 2003; Tenenbaum et al., 2005).

Furthermore, elementary school teachers tend to stereotype girls who display "feminine" behavior as diligent and compliant and boys who display "masculine" behavior as lazy and troublesome (Heyder & Kessels, 2015). These perceptions may contribute to boys' reduced academic engagement and lower school grades relative to girls'. At the same time, when teachers are presented with a boy and a girl who are equally successful at math, they tend to see the girl as having to work harder (Robinson-Cimpian et al., 2014). As we saw in our discussion of achievement-related attributions, this downrating of girls' ability negatively affects their performance.

Also in line with adult stereotypes, school-age children often regard reading, spelling, art, and music as subjects girls are good at and mathematics, athletics, and mechanical skills as subjects boys are good at (Cvencek, Meltzoff, & Greenwald, 2011; Eccles, Jacobs, & Harold, 1990). These attitudes influence children's preferences for and sense of competence at various subjects.

An encouraging sign is that in several investigations carried out in Canada, France, and the United States, a majority of elementary and secondary students disagreed with the idea that math is a "masculine" subject (Kurtz-Costes et al., 2014; Martinot, Bagès, & Désert, 2012; Plante, Théoret, & Favreau, 2009; Rowley et al., 2007). And although school-age children are aware of many stereotypes, they also develop a more open-minded view of what males and females *can do.* The ability to classify flexibly contributes to this change. School-age children realize that a person's sex is not a certain predictor of his or her personality traits, activities, and behavior (Halim & Ruble, 2010). Similarly, by the end of middle childhood, most children regard gender typing as socially rather than biologically influenced (Taylor, Rhodes, & Gelman, 2009).

Nevertheless, acknowledging that people *can* cross gender lines does not mean that children always *approve* of doing so. In one longitudinal study, between ages 7 and 13, children generally became more open-minded about girls being offered the same opportunities as boys (Crouter et al., 2007). This increasing flexibility, however, was less pronounced among boys and among children whose parents held more traditional gender attitudes. Furthermore, many children take a harsh view of certain violations—boys playing with dolls and wearing girls' clothing, girls acting noisily and roughly (Blakemore, 2003). They are especially intolerant when boys engage in these "cross-gender" acts.

© TAMPA BAY TIMES/CHRIS ZUPPA/THE IMAGE WORKS

An 8-year-old launches the rocket she made in her school's Young Astronaut Club. Whereas school-age boys usually stick to "masculine" pursuits, girls experiment with a wider range of options.

Gender Identity and Behavior

Children who were more strongly gender-typed relative to their agemates in early childhood usually remain so in middle childhood (Golombok et al., 2008). Nevertheless, overall changes do occur, with boys' and girls' gender identities following different paths.

From third to sixth grade, boys tend to strengthen their identification with "masculine" personality traits, whereas girls' identification with "feminine" traits declines. Girls are more *androgynous,* often describing themselves as having some "other-gender" characteristics (Serbin, Powlishta, & Gulko, 1993). And whereas boys usually stick to "masculine" pursuits, many girls experiment with a wider range of options—from cooking and sewing to sports and science projects—and consider traditionally male future work roles (Liben & Bigler, 2002).

These changes are due to a mixture of cognitive and social forces. School-age children of both sexes are aware that society attaches greater prestige to "masculine" characteristics. For example, they rate "masculine" occupations as having higher status than "feminine" occupations and an unfamiliar job as higher in status when portrayed with a male worker than a female worker (Liben, Bigler, & Krogh, 2001; Weisgram, Bigler, & Liben, 2010). Messages from adults and peers are also influential. In Chapter 8, we saw that parents (especially fathers) are more disapproving when sons, as opposed to daughters, cross gender lines. Similarly, a tomboyish girl can interact with boys without losing the approval of her female peers, but a boy who hangs out with girls is likely to be ridiculed and rejected.

As school-age children make social comparisons and characterize themselves in terms of stable dispositions, their gender identity expands to include the following self-evaluations, which greatly affect their adjustment:

- *Gender typicality*—the degree to which the child feels similar to, or "fits in" socially with, others of the same gender.
- *Gender contentedness*—the degree to which the child feels comfortable with his or her gender assignment.
- *Felt pressure to conform to gender roles*—the degree to which the child feels parents and peers disapprove of his or her gender-related traits.

In a longitudinal study of third through seventh graders, gender-typical and gender-contented children gained in self-esteem over the following year, whereas gender-atypical and gender-discontented children declined in self-worth. Furthermore, *gender-atypical* children, especially those who report *intense pressure to conform to gender roles,* experience serious adjustment difficulties—withdrawal, sadness, disappointment, and anxiety (Corby, Hodges, & Perry, 2007; Yunger, Carver, & Perry, 2004). Clearly, school-age children who experience rejection because of their gender-atypical traits suffer profoundly.

More experts are advocating interventions that help parents and peers become more accepting of children's gender-atypical interests and behaviors (Bigler, 2007; Conway, 2007; Hill et al., 2010). Return to page 269 in Chapter 8 to review related evidence on gender-dysphoric children, along with the best therapeutic approach to help them.

ASK YOURSELF

CONNECT Describe similarities in development of self-concept, attitudes toward racial and ethnic minorities, and gender-stereotyped beliefs in middle childhood.

APPLY What changes in parent–child and teacher–child relationships are likely to help rejected children?

REFLECT As a school-age child, did you have classmates you would classify as popular-antisocial? What were they like, and why do you think peers admired them?

Family Influences

10.8 Discuss changes in parent–child communication and sibling relationships in middle childhood?

10.9 Explain how children fare in lesbian and gay families and in never-married, single-parent families.

10.10 Cite factors that influence children's adjustment to divorce and blended family arrangements.

10.11 Discuss how maternal employment and life in dual-earner families affect school-age children.

As children move into school, peer, and community contexts, the parent–child relationship changes. At the same time, children's well-being continues to depend on the quality of family interaction. In the following sections, we will see that contemporary diversity in family life—more lesbian and gay parents who are open about their sexual orientation, more never-married parents, and high rates of divorce, remarriage, maternal employment, and dual-earner families—has reshaped the family system. As we consider this array of family forms, note how children's well-being, in each instance, is promoted by supportive ties between family and community and by favorable public policies.

Parent–Child Relationships

In middle childhood, the amount of time children spend with parents declines dramatically. Children's growing independence means that parents must deal with new issues. "I've struggled with how many chores to assign, how much allowance to give, whether their friends are good influences, and what to do about problems at school," Rena remarked. "And then there's the challenge of keeping track of them when they're out—or even when they're home and I'm not there to see what's going on."

Despite these new concerns, child rearing becomes easier for parents who established an authoritative style during the early years. Reasoning is more effective with school-age children because of their greater capacity for logical thinking and their increased respect for parents' expert knowledge. And children of parents who engage in joint decision making when possible are more likely to listen to parents' perspectives in situations where compliance is vital (Russell, Mize, & Bissaker, 2004).

As children demonstrate that they can manage daily activities and responsibilities, parents gradually shift control from adult to child—a change associated with favorable academic achievement and high-quality peer relationships (Wang & Fletcher, 2016). Parents do not let go entirely but, rather, engage in **coregulation,** a form of supervision in which they exercise general oversight while letting children take charge of moment-by-moment decision making. Coregulation grows out of a warm, cooperative parent–child relationship based on give-and-take. Parents must guide and monitor from a distance and effectively communicate expectations when they are with their children. And children must inform parents of their whereabouts, activities, and problems so parents can intervene when necessary (Collins, Madsen, & Susman-Stillman, 2002). Coregulation supports and protects children while preparing them for adolescence, when they will make many important decisions themselves.

As at younger ages, mothers tend to spend more time than fathers with school-age children, although many fathers are highly involved (Pew Research Center, 2015). Both parents, however, tend to devote more time to children of their own sex (Lam, McHale, & Crouter, 2012).

Although school-age children often press for greater independence, they know they need their parents' support. A positive parent–child relationship is linked to improved emotional self-regulation in children, reducing the negative impact of stressful events (Brumariu, Kerns, & Seibert, 2012; Hazel et al., 2014). School-age children often turn to parents for affection, advice, affirmation of self-worth, and assistance with everyday problems.

Siblings

Sibling rivalry tends to increase in middle childhood. As children participate in a wider range of activities, parents often compare siblings' traits and accomplishments. The child who gets less parental affection, more disapproval, or fewer material resources is likely to be resentful and show poorer adjustment (Dunn, 2004b; McHale, Updegraff, & Whiteman, 2012).

For same-sex siblings who are close in age, parental comparisons are more frequent, resulting in more antagonism. This effect is particularly strong when parents are under stress (Jenkins, Rasbash, & O'Connor, 2003). Parents whose energies are drained become less careful about being fair. Perhaps because fathers, overall, spend less time with children than mothers, children react especially intensely when fathers prefer one child (Kolak & Volling, 2011).

▶ An older sister helps her 6-year-old brother with homework. Although sibling rivalry tends to increase in middle childhood, siblings also provide each other with emotional support and help with difficult tasks.

To reduce rivalry, siblings often strive to be different from one another (McHale, Updegraff, & Whiteman, 2012). For example, two brothers I know deliberately selected different athletic pursuits and musical instruments. Parents can limit the effects of rivalry by refraining from comparing children, but some feedback about their competencies is inevitable. As siblings strive to win recognition for their own uniqueness, they shape important aspects of each other's development.

Although conflict rises, school-age siblings continue to rely on each other for companionship and support. But for siblings to reap these benefits, parental encouragement of warm, considerate sibling ties is vital. The more positive the sibling relationship, the more siblings resolve disagreements constructively, provide each other with various forms of assistance, and contribute to resilience in the face of major stressors, such as parental divorce (Conger, Stocker, & McGuire, 2009; Soli, McHale, & Feinberg, 2009).

When siblings get along well, the older sibling's academic and social competence tends to "rub off on" the younger sibling, fostering more favorable achievement and peer relations. And both older and younger siblings benefit in empathy and prosocial behavior (Brody & Murry, 2001; Lam, Solmeyer, & McHale, 2012; Padilla-Walker, Harper, & Jensen, 2010). But destructive sibling conflict is associated with negative outcomes, including conflict-ridden peer relationships, anxiety, depressed mood, and later substance use and delinquency (Kim et al., 2007; Ostrov, Crick, & Stauffacher, 2006; Pike & Oliver, 2016). Child conduct problems, in turn, predict worsening of sibling-relationship quality over time.

Only Children

Although sibling relationships bring many benefits, they are not essential for healthy development. Contrary to popular belief, only children are not spoiled, and in some respects, they are advantaged. U.S. children growing up in one-child and multichild families do not differ in self-rated personality traits (Mottus, Indus, & Allik, 2008). And compared to children with siblings, only children are higher in self-esteem, do better in school, and attain higher levels of education. One reason may be that only children have somewhat closer relationships with parents, who can invest more time in their child's educational experiences (Falbo, 2012). However, only children tend to be less well-accepted in the peer group, perhaps because they have not had opportunities to learn effective conflict-resolution strategies through sibling interactions (Kitzmann, Cohen, & Lockwood, 2002).

Favorable development also characterizes only children in China, where a one-child family policy was enforced in urban areas for more than three decades, until it was abolished in 2015. Compared with agemates who have siblings, Chinese only children are slightly advantaged in cognitive development and academic achievement. They also report fewer emotional symptoms (such as anxiety, depression, or hostility), perhaps because government disapproval led to tension in families with more than one child (Falbo, 2012; Falbo & Hooper, 2015). Chinese mothers usually ensure that their children have regular contact with first cousins (who are considered siblings). Perhaps as a result, Chinese only children do not differ from agemates with siblings in social skills and peer acceptance (Hart, Newell, & Olsen, 2003).

Lesbian and Gay Families

According to recent estimates, about 20 to 35 percent of lesbian couples and 5 to 15 percent of gay couples are parents, most through previous heterosexual marriages, some through adoption, and a growing number through reproductive technologies (Brewster, Tillman, & Jokinen-Gordon, 2014; Gates, 2013). In the past, because of laws assuming that lesbians and gay men could not be adequate parents, those who divorced a heterosexual partner lost custody of their children. Today, child custody and adoption by sexual minority parents are legal in all U.S. states and in many other industrialized nations.

Most research on families headed by same-sex couples is limited to volunteer samples. Findings indicate that lesbian and gay parents are as committed to and effective at child rearing as heterosexual parents and sometimes more so (Bos, 2013). Also, whether born to or adopted by their parents or conceived through donor insemination, children in lesbian and gay families do not differ from the children of heterosexual parents in mental health, peer relations, gender-role behavior, quality of life, or sexual orientation (Bos & Sandfort, 2010; Goldberg, 2010; Patterson, 2013; van Gelderen et al., 2012).

To surmount the potential bias associated with volunteer samples, some researchers take advantage of large, nationally representative data banks to study lesbian and gay families. Findings confirm that children with same-sex and other-sex parents develop similarly, and that children's adjustment is linked to factors other than parental sexual orientation (Moore & Stambolis-Ruhstorfer, 2013). For example, close parent–child relationships predict better peer relations and a reduction in adolescent delinquency, whereas family transitions (such as parental divorce or remarriage) predict academic difficulties, regardless of family form (Potter, 2012; Russell & Muraco, 2013).

When extended-family members withhold acceptance, lesbian and gay parents often build "families of choice" through friends, who assume the roles of relatives (Frost, Meyer, & Schwartz, 2016). Usually, however, parents of sexual minorities cannot endure a permanent rift. With time, extended family relationships become more positive and supportive.

A major concern of lesbian and gay parents is that their children will be stigmatized by their parents' sexual orientation. Peer teasing and disapproval are problems for some children of sexual minority parents. Close parent–child relationships, supportive school environments, and connections with other lesbian and gay families protect children from the negative effects of these experiences (Bos, 2013). Overall, lesbian and gay families can be distinguished from other families mainly by issues related to living in discriminatory contexts.

▶ Lesbian and gay parents are as committed to and effective at child rearing as heterosexual parents, and the children of same-sex and other-sex parents develop similarly.

Never-Married, Single-Parent Families

Today, about 40 percent of U.S. births are to single mothers, more than double the percentage in 1980. Whereas teenage parenthood has declined steadily since 1990, births to single adult women have increased, with a particularly sharp rise during the first decade of the twenty-first century (Martin et al., 2017).

A growing number of nonmarital births are to cohabiting couples. But these relationships—common among young adults with low education and income—are often unstable (Guzzo, 2014). In addition, more than 12 percent of U.S. children live with a single parent who has never married and does not have a partner. Of these parents, about 90 percent are mothers, 10 percent fathers (Martin et al., 2017).

Single motherhood is especially prevalent among African-American young women, who are considerably more likely than White women to give birth outside of marriage and less likely to live with the baby's father. As a result, more than half of births to Black mothers in their twenties are to women without a partner, compared with about 14 percent of births to White women (Child Trends, 2015a; Martin et al., 2017). Job loss, persisting unemployment, and consequent inability of many Black men to support a family have contributed to the number of African-American never-married, single-mother families.

Never-married African-American mothers tap the extended family, especially their own mothers and sometimes male relatives, for help in rearing their children (Anderson, 2012). Compared with their White counterparts, low-SES African-American women tend to marry later—within a decade after birth of the first child—but not necessarily to the child's biological father (Dixon, 2009; Wu, Bumpass, & Musick, 2001).

Still, for low-SES women, never-married parenthood generally increases financial hardship; about half live in poverty. Many children in single-mother homes display adjustment problems associated with economic disadvantage (Lamb, 2012; Mather, 2010). Furthermore, children of never-married mothers who lack a father's consistent warmth and involvement show less favorable cognitive development and engage in more antisocial behavior than children in low-SES, first-marriage families—problems that make life more difficult for mothers (Waldfogel, Craigie, & Brooks-Gunn, 2010). But marriage to the child's biological father benefits children only when the father is a reliable source of economic and emotional support. For example, adolescents who feel close to their nonresident father fare better in school performance and emotional and social adjustment than do those in two-parent homes where a close father tie is lacking (Booth, Scott, & King, 2010).

Unfortunately, most unwed fathers—who usually have little education and are doing poorly financially—gradually spend less and less time with their children (Lerman, 2010). Strengthening parenting skills, social support, education, and employment opportunities for low-SES parents would greatly enhance the well-being of unmarried mothers and their children.

Divorce

Children's interactions with parents and siblings are affected by other aspects of family life. When Joey was 8 and Lizzie 5, their father, Drake, moved out. During the preceding months, Joey began pushing, hitting, taunting, and calling Lizzie names—fighting that coincided with Rena and her husband's growing marital unhappiness.

Between 1960 and 1985, divorce rates in Western nations rose dramatically before stabilizing in most countries. The United States has experienced a decline in divorce over the past twenty years, largely due to a rise in age at first marriage and a drop in marriage rates. However, this decrease largely applies to well-educated, financially secure families. As Figure 10.3 shows, individuals with less education experience substantially greater marital instability (Lundberg & Pollak, 2015). Because educational and economic disadvantage increases family fragility, divorce rates are higher among African Americans, Hispanic Americans, and Native Americans than among European Americans (Raley, Sweeny, & Wondra, 2015).

Among developed nations, the United States has one of the highest divorce rates. Of the estimated 42 to 45 percent of American marriages that end in divorce, half involve children. More than one-fourth of U.S. children live in divorced, single-parent households. Although most reside with their mothers, the percentage in father-headed households has increased steadily, to about 17 percent (Grall, 2016).

Children of divorce spend an average of five years in a single-parent home. About 10 percent of U.S. children live with one parent (usually their mother) and a married or cohabiting stepparent (Kreider & Ellis, 2011). Many of these children eventually experience a third major change—the end of their parent's second marriage or cohabiting partnership.

These figures reveal that divorce is a transition that leads to a variety of new living arrangements, accompanied by changes in housing, income, and family roles and responsibilities. Although divorce is stressful for children and increases the risk of adjustment problems, most adjust favorably (Greene et al., 2012; Lamb, 2012). How well children fare depends on many factors: the custodial parent's psychological health and financial resources, the child's characteristics, and social supports within the family and surrounding community.

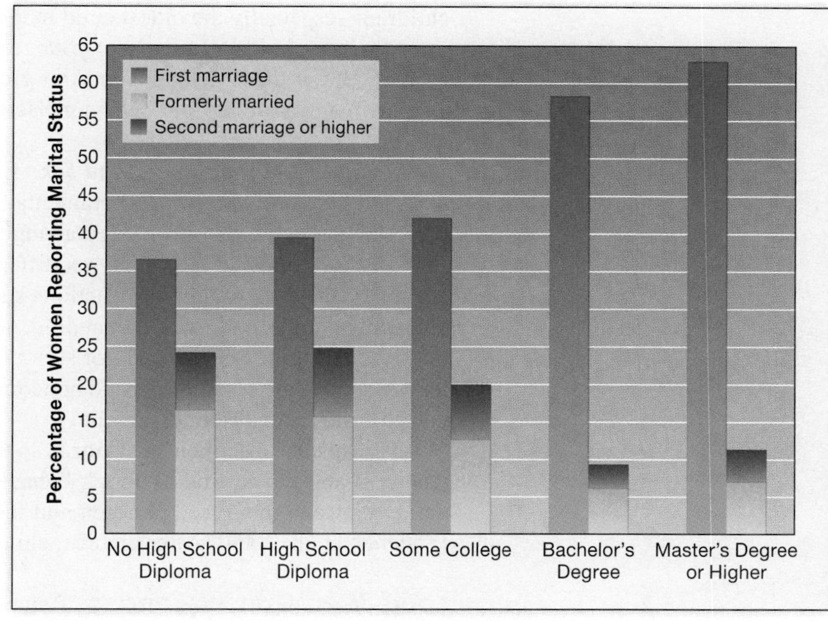

FIGURE 10.3 Divorce rates among U.S. women by level of education. A survey of over 10,000 U.S. women between ages 15 and 44 revealed that increased education is linked to marital stability, whereas limited education is linked to divorce, remarriage, and subsequent divorce. (Based on Lundberg & Pollak, 2015.)

Immediate Consequences. "Things were the worst after Drake and I decided to separate," Rena reflected. "We fought over division of our belongings and custody of the children, and the kids suffered. Sobbing, Lizzie told me she was 'sorry she made Daddy go away.' Joey kicked and threw things at home and didn't do his work at school. We had to sell the house, and I needed a better-paying job."

Family conflict often rises in newly divorced households as parents try to settle disputes over children and possessions. Once one parent moves out, additional events threaten supportive parent–child interaction. Mother-headed households typically experience a sharp drop in income. In the United States, nearly 30 percent of divorced mothers with young children live in poverty, and many more are low-income, getting less than the full amount of child support from the absent father or none at all (Grall, 2016).

The transition from marriage to divorce typically leads to high maternal stress, depression, and anxiety and to a disorganized family life (Williams & Dunne-Bryant, 2006). "Meals and bedtimes were at all hours, the house didn't get cleaned, and I stopped taking Joey and Lizzie on weekend outings," said Rena. As children react with distress and anger to their less secure home lives, discipline may become harsh and inconsistent. Over time, contact with noncustodial fathers—and quality of the father–child relationship—often decreases, particularly when parental conflict is high (Troilo & Coleman, 2012). Fathers who see their children only occasionally are inclined to be permissive and indulgent, making the mother's task of managing the child even more difficult.

The more parents argue and fail to provide children with warmth, involvement, and consistent guidance, the poorer children's adjustment. About 20 to 25 percent of children in divorced families display severe problems, compared with about 10 percent in nondivorced families (Golombok & Tasker, 2015; Lansford, 2009). At the same time, reactions vary with children's age, temperament, and sex.

Children's Age. Preschool and young school-age children often blame themselves for a marital breakup and fear that both parents may abandon them. Although older children have the cognitive maturity to understand that they are not responsible for their parents' divorce, many react strongly, declining in school performance, becoming unruly, and escaping into undesirable peer activities, especially when family conflict is high (Kleinsorge & Covitz, 2012; Lansford et al., 2006). Some children—especially the oldest child in the family—display more mature behavior, willingly taking on extra household tasks, care of younger siblings, and emotional support of a depressed, anxious mother. But if these demands are too great, these children may eventually become resentful and engage in angry, acting-out behavior (Hetherington & Kelly, 2002).

Children's Temperament and Sex. Exposure to stressful life events and inadequate parenting magnifies the problems of temperamentally difficult children (see Chapter 6). In contrast, easy children are less often targets of parental anger and also cope more effectively with adversity.

These findings help explain sex differences in response to divorce. Girls sometimes respond as Lizzie did, with internalizing reactions such as crying, self-criticism, and withdrawal. More often, children of both sexes show demanding, attention-getting behavior. But in mother-custody families, boys are at slightly greater risk for serious adjustment problems (Amato, 2010). Recall from Chapter 8 that boys are more active and noncompliant—behaviors that increase with exposure to parental conflict and inconsistent discipline.

Perhaps because their behavior is so unruly, boys receive less emotional support from mothers, teachers, and peers. And as Joey's behavior toward Lizzie illustrates, the cycles of coercive interaction between distressed children and their divorced mothers soon spread to sibling relationships (Sheehan et al., 2004). After divorce, children who are challenging to rear generally get worse.

Long-Term Consequences. Rena eventually found better-paying work and gained control over the daily operation of the household. After several meetings with a counselor, Rena and Drake realized the harmful impact of their quarreling on Joey and Lizzie. Drake visited regularly and handled Joey's unruliness with firmness and consistency. Soon Joey's school performance improved, his behavior problems subsided, and both children seemed calmer and happier.

Most children show improved adjustment by two years after divorce. Yet overall, children and adolescents of divorced parents continue to score slightly lower than children of continuously married parents in academic achievement, self-esteem, and social competence (Lansford, 2009; Weaver & Schofield, 2015). And divorce is linked to problems with adolescent sexuality and development of intimate ties. Young people who experienced parental divorce—especially more than once—display higher rates of early sexual activity and adolescent parenthood. Some show other lasting difficulties—reduced educational attainment, troubled romantic relationships and marriages, and divorce in adulthood (Amato, 2010).

The overriding factor in positive adjustment following divorce is effective parenting—shielding the child from family conflict and using authoritative child rearing (Lamb, 2012). Parent-training programs can help custodial parents support their children's development. One eleven-session parent-training intervention for mothers of school-age children yielded improved parent–child relationships and child coping skills, with effects persisting for six years (Velez et al., 2011).

▶ Regular contact with both parents and effective coparenting—supporting each other in their child-rearing roles—greatly improve adjustment in children of divorce.

Where the custodial parent is the mother, regular contact with fathers is important. The more paternal contact and the warmer the father–child relationship, the less children react with internalizing and externalizing problems (Elam et al., 2016). A few studies report that outcomes for children are slightly better when the father is the custodial parent (Clarke-Stewart & Hayward, 1996; Guttman & Lazar, 1998; McLanahan, 1999). Fathers' greater economic security and image of authority may help them engage in effective parenting. At the same time, single mothers tend to provide children with more warmth, monitoring, and supervision than fathers (Coles, 2015). In most investigations, children in mother-custody and father-custody homes do not differ on any measure of psychological well-being.

APPLYING WHAT WE KNOW

Helping Children Adjust to Their Parents' Divorce

SUGGESTION	EXPLANATION
Shield children from conflict.	Witnessing intense parental conflict is very damaging to children. If one parent insists on expressing hostility, children fare better if the other parent does not respond in kind.
Provide children with as much continuity, familiarity, and predictability as possible.	Children adjust better during the period surrounding divorce when their lives have some stability—for example, the same school, bedroom, babysitter, playmates, and daily schedule.
Explain the divorce, and tell children what to expect.	Children may develop fears of abandonment if they are not prepared for their parents' separation. They should be told that their parents will not be living together anymore, which parent will be moving out, and when they will be able to see that parent. If possible, parents should explain the divorce together, providing a reason that each child can understand and assuring children that they are not to blame.
Emphasize the permanence of the divorce.	Fantasies of parents getting back together can prevent children from accepting the reality of their current life. Children should be told that the divorce is final and that they cannot change this fact.
Respond sympathetically to children's feelings.	Children need supportive, understanding responses to their feelings of sadness, fear, and anger. For children to adjust well, their painful emotions must be acknowledged, not denied or avoided.
Engage in authoritative parenting.	Authoritative parenting—providing affection and acceptance, reasonable demands for mature behavior, and consistent, rational discipline—greatly reduces children's risk of maladjustment following divorce.
Promote a continuing relationship with both parents.	When parents disentangle their lingering hostility toward the former spouse from the child's need for a continuing relationship with the other parent, children adjust well.

Although divorce is painful for children, remaining in an intact but high-conflict family is much worse than making the transition to a low-conflict, single-parent household (Lamb, 2012; Strohschein, 2005). Divorcing parents who manage to engage in *effective coparenting* (see page 53 in Chapter 2), supporting each other in their child-rearing roles, greatly improve their children's chances of growing up competent, stable, and happy (Lamb, 2012).

Divorce Mediation, Joint Custody, and Child Support. Community-based services exist to help families of divorce through this difficult time. One approach is *divorce mediation,* a series of meetings between divorcing adults and a trained professional aimed at reducing family conflict, including legal battles over property division and child custody. Mediation increases out-of-court settlements, cooperation and involvement of both parents in child rearing, and parents' and children's feelings of well-being (Douglas, 2006).

Joint custody, which grants parents equal say in important decisions about the child's upbringing, is becoming increasingly common. Children usually reside with one parent and see the other on a fixed schedule, similar to the typical sole-custody situation. In other cases, parents share physical custody, and children move between homes. Joint-custody parents report little conflict—fortunately so, since the success of the arrangement depends on effective coparenting (Bauserman, 2012). And their children tend to be better-adjusted than children in sole-maternal-custody homes (Baude, Pearson, & Drapeau, 2016; Bauserman, 2002).

Finally, many single-parent families depend on child support from the noncustodial parent to relieve financial strain. All U.S. states have procedures for withholding wages from parents who fail to make these payments. Noncustodial fathers who have generous visitation schedules are more likely to pay child support regularly (Amato & Sobolewski, 2004). And increases in paternal contact and in child support over time predict better coparenting relationships (Hofferth, Forry, & Peters, 2010). Applying What We Know above summarizes ways to help children adjust to their parents' divorce.

Blended Families

"If you get married to Wendell, and Daddy gets married to Carol," Lizzie wondered aloud to Rena, "then I'll have two sisters and one more brother. And let's see, how many grandmothers and grandfathers? A lot!" exclaimed Lizzie.

About 60 percent of divorced parents remarry within a few years. Others cohabit with a partner outside of marriage. Parent, stepparent, and children form a new family structure called the **blended,** or **reconstituted, family.** For some children, this expanded family network is positive, bringing greater adult attention. But children in blended families usually have more adjustment problems than children in stable, first-marriage families (Pryor, 2014). Switching to stepparents' new rules and expectations can be stressful, and children often view steprelatives as intruders. How well they adapt is, again, related to the quality of family functioning. This depends on which parent forms a new relationship, the complexity of blended-family relationships, and the child's age and sex.

Mother–Stepfather Families. Because mothers generally retain custody of children, the most common form of blended family is a mother–stepfather arrangement. Boys tend to adjust quickly, welcoming a stepfather who is warm and who refrains from exerting his authority too quickly (Visher, Visher, & Pasley, 2003). Stepfathers who marry rather than cohabit are more involved in parenting, perhaps because men who choose to marry a mother with children are more interested in and skilled at child rearing (Hofferth & Anderson, 2003). Girls, however, often react with sulky, resistant behavior when a new stepfather disrupts the close tie they have established with their mother (Pryor, 2014).

But age affects these findings. Older school-age children and adolescents of both sexes display more irresponsible, acting-out behavior than their peers not in stepfamilies (Hetherington & Stanley-Hagan, 2000; Robertson, 2008). If parents are warmer and more involved with their biological children than with their stepchildren, older children are more likely to notice and challenge unfair treatment. And adolescents often view the new stepparent as a threat to their freedom, especially if they experienced little parental monitoring in the single-parent family. But when teenagers have affectionate, cooperative relationships with their mothers, many develop good relations with their stepfathers—a circumstance linked to more favorable adolescent well-being (King, 2009; Jensen et al., 2017).

Father–Stepmother Families. Remarriage of noncustodial fathers often leads to reduced contact with their biological children, especially when fathers remarry quickly, before they have established postdivorce parent–child routines (Dunn, 2002; Juby et al., 2007). When fathers have custody, children typically react negatively to remarriage. One reason is that children living with fathers often start out with more problems. Perhaps the biological mother could no longer handle the difficult child (usually a boy), so the father and his new partner are faced with the child's behavior problems. In other instances, the father has custody because of a very close relationship with the child, and his remarriage disrupts this bond (Buchanan, Maccoby, & Dornbusch, 1996).

Girls, especially, have a hard time getting along with their stepmothers, either because the remarriage threatens the girl's bond with her father or because she becomes entangled in loyalty conflicts between the two mother figures. But the longer girls live in father–stepmother households, the more positive their interaction with stepmothers becomes (King, 2007). With time and patience, children of both genders benefit from the support of a second mother figure.

Support for Blended Families. Parenting education and couples counseling can help parents and children adapt to the complexities of blended families. Effective approaches encourage stepparents to move into their new roles gradually by first building a warm relationship with the child, which makes more active parenting possible (Pasley & Garneau, 2012). Counselors can offer couples guidance in effective coparenting to limit loyalty conflicts and provide consistency in child rearing. And tempering parents' unrealistic expectations for children's rapid adjustment—by pointing out that building a unified blended family often takes years—makes it easier for families to endure the transition and succeed.

Unfortunately, the divorce rate for second marriages is higher than for first marriages. Parents with antisocial tendencies and poor child-rearing skills are particularly likely to have several divorces and remarriages, and their children have greater adjustment difficulties (Amato, 2010). These families usually require prolonged, intensive therapy.

Maternal Employment and Dual-Earner Families

Today, whether single or married, three-fourths of U.S. mothers with school-age children are employed (U.S. Bureau of Labor Statistics, 2017). In previous chapters, we saw that the impact of maternal employment on early development depends on the quality of child care and the parent–child relationship. The same is true in middle childhood.

Maternal Employment and Child Development. When employed mothers remain committed to parenting, children develop favorably, displaying higher self-esteem and less gender-stereotyped beliefs. Girls, especially, perceive women's roles as involving more freedom of choice and satisfaction and are more career-oriented (Hoffman, 2000). Furthermore, stable maternal employment begun in early childhood is linked to higher achievement and fewer behavior problems in elementary school, especially for children of low-income mothers (Lombardi & Coley, 2013, 2014; Lucas-Thompson, Goldberg, & Prause, 2010). Employed mothers who feel economically more secure are more likely to engage in warmer, more involved parenting.

In dual-earner households, maternal employment often leads fathers to take on greater child-rearing responsibilities. Paternal involvement in childhood and adolescence is associated with higher achievement, more mature social behavior, and a flexible view of gender roles; and in adulthood with generally better mental health (Bornstein, 2015; Lamb & Lewis, 2013).

But when employment places heavy demands on parents' schedules or is stressful for other reasons, children are at risk for lower-quality parenting, poorer cognitive development, and increased behavior problems (Li et al., 2014; Strazdins et al., 2006, 2013). In contrast, part-time employment and flexible work schedules are associated with good child adjustment (Buehler & O'Brian, 2011; Youn, Leon, & Lee, 2012). By preventing role overload, these arrangements help parents meet children's needs.

Child Care for School-Age Children. High-quality child care is vital for children's well-being, even in middle childhood. An estimated 4.5 million 5- to 14-year-olds in the United States are **self-care children,** who regularly look after themselves for some period of time after school (Laughlin, 2013). Self-care increases with age and also with SES, perhaps because of the greater safety of higher-income neighborhoods. But when lower-SES parents lack alternatives to self-care, their children spend more hours on their own (Casper & Smith, 2002).

Younger school-age children who spend many hours in self-care have more adjustment difficulties (Vandell & Posner, 1999). As children become old enough to look after themselves, those whose parents engage in authoritative child rearing, monitor their activities through telephone calls, and assign regular after-school chores appear responsible and well-adjusted (Coley, Morris, & Hernandez, 2004; Vandell et al., 2006). In contrast, children left to their own devices are more likely to bend to peer pressures and engage in antisocial behavior.

Throughout middle childhood, attending after-school programs with well-trained and supportive staffs, generous adult–child ratios, and skill-building activities is linked to good school performance and emotional and social adjustment (Durlak, Weissberg, & Pachan, 2010; Kantaoka & Vandell, 2013). Low-SES children who participate in programs offering academic assistance and enrichment activities (scouting, music and art lessons, clubs) show special benefits. They exceed their self-care

▶ High-quality after-school programs with enrichment activities yield academic and social benefits, especially for low-SES children.

counterparts in classroom work habits, academic achievement, and prosocial behavior and display fewer behavior problems (Lauer et al., 2006; Vandell et al., 2006).

Yet good after-care is in especially short supply in low-income neighborhoods (Greenberg, 2013). A special need exists for programs in these areas that provide safe environments, warm relationships with adults, and enjoyable, goal-oriented activities.

ASK YOURSELF

CONNECT How does each level in Bronfenbrenner's ecological systems theory—microsystem, mesosystem, exosystem, and macrosystem—contribute to effects of parents' employment on children's development?

APPLY Steve and Marissa are in the midst of an acrimonious divorce. Their 9-year-old son Dennis has become hostile and defiant. How can Steve and Marissa help Dennis adjust?

REFLECT What after-school child-care arrangements did you experience in elementary school? How do you think they influenced your development?

Some Common Problems of Development

10.12 Cite common fears and anxieties of middle childhood, and discuss their impact on children's adjustment.

10.13 Discuss factors related to child sexual abuse, its consequences for children's development, and its prevention and treatment.

10.14 Cite factors that foster resilience in middle childhood.

We have considered a variety of stressful experiences that place children at risk for future problems. Next, we address two more areas of concern: school-age children's fears and anxieties and the consequences of child sexual abuse. Finally, we sum up factors that help children cope effectively with stress.

Fears and Anxieties

Although fears of the dark, thunder and lightning, and supernatural beings persist into middle childhood, older children's anxieties are also directed toward new concerns. As children begin to understand the realities of the wider world, the possibility of personal harm (being robbed, stabbed, or shot) and media events (war and disasters) often trouble them. Other common worries include academic failure, physical injuries, separation from parents, parents' health, the possibility of dying, and peer rejection (Muris & Field, 2011; Weems & Costa, 2005).

As long as fears are not too intense, most children handle them constructively, and they decline with age (Gullone, 2000; Muris & Field, 2011). But about 5 percent of school-age children develop an intense, unmanageable fear called a **phobia.** Children with inhibited temperaments are at high risk (Ollendick, King, & Muris, 2002).

Some children with phobias and other anxieties develop *school refusal*—severe apprehension about attending school, often accompanied by physical complaints such as dizziness, nausea, and stomachaches (Wimmer, 2013). About one-third of children with school refusal are 5- to 7-year-olds for whom the real fear is maternal separation (Elliott, 1999). Family therapy helps these children, whose difficulty can often be traced to parental overprotection.

Most cases of school refusal appear around ages 11 to 13, in children who usually find a particular aspect of school frightening—an overcritical teacher, a school bully, or too much parental pressure to achieve. A change in school environment or parenting practices may be needed. Firm insistence that the child return to school, along with training in how to cope with difficult situations, is also helpful (Kearney, Spear, & Mihalas, 2014).

Severe childhood anxiety may arise from harsh living conditions. In inner-city ghettos and in war-torn areas of the world, children live in the midst of constant danger and deprivation. As the Cultural Influences box on the following page reveals, they are at risk for long-term difficulties. Finally, as we saw in our discussion of child abuse in Chapter 8, too often violence and other destructive acts become part of adult–child relationships. During middle childhood, child sexual abuse increases.

CULTURAL INFLUENCES

Impact of Ethnic and Political Violence on Children

Around the world, many children live with armed conflict, terrorism, and other acts of violence stemming from ethnic and political tensions. Some children participate in fighting, either because they are forced or because they want to please adults. Others are kidnapped, assaulted, and tortured. Child bystanders often come under direct fire and may be killed or physically maimed. And many watch in horror as family members, friends, and neighbors flee, are wounded, or die. An estimated 250 million children live in conflict-ridden, poor countries. In the past decade, wars have left 25 million homeless, 6 million physically disabled, and more than 1 million separated from their parents (Masten et al., 2015; UNICEF, 2017a).

The greater children's exposure to life-threatening experiences, the more likely they are to display symptoms of post-traumatic stress disorder (PTSD)—extreme fear and anxiety, terrifying intrusive memories, depression, irritability, anger, aggression, and a pessimistic view of the future (Dimitry, 2012; Eisenberg & Silver, 2011). These outcomes appear to be culturally universal, emerging among children in every war zone studied—from Bosnia, Rwanda, and the Sudan to the West Bank, Gaza, Iraq, Afghanistan, and Syria.

Parental affection and reassurance are the best protection against lasting problems. When parents offer security, discuss traumatic experiences sympathetically, and serve as role models of calm emotional strength, most children can withstand even extreme war-related violence. Parenting interventions delivered in war-torn regions that foster positive child-rearing behaviors enhance children's well-being (Murphy et al., 2017). But programs must also address parents' wartime stressors, fostering their resilience so they can parent more effectively.

Children separated from their parents, who are at greatest risk for maladjustment, must rely on help from their communities. Orphans in Eritrea who were placed in residential settings where they could form a close emotional tie with an adult showed less emotional stress five years later than orphans placed in impersonal settings (Wolff & Fesseha, 1999). Yet most orphanages in war zones offer children little emotional support (Wessells, 2017). Education and recreation programs are powerful safeguards, too, providing children with consistency in their lives along with teacher and peer supports.

GETTY IMAGES/PAULA BRONSTEIN/STRINGER

▶ Rohingya children who fled violence in Myanmar attend school in a refugee camp in Bangladesh. By providing meaningful activities and consistency in severely stressful environments, education helps protect children from lasting adjustment problems.

With the September 11, 2001, terrorist attacks on the World Trade Center, some U.S. children experienced extreme wartime violence firsthand. Most children, however, learned about the attacks indirectly—from the media or from caregivers or peers. Both direct and indirect exposure triggered child and adolescent distress, but extended exposure—having a family member affected or repeatedly witnessing the attacks on TV—resulted in more severe symptoms (Agronick et al., 2007; Rosen & Cohen, 2010). During the following months, distress reactions declined, though more slowly for children with preexisting adjustment problems.

Unlike many war-traumatized children in the developing world, students in New York's Public School 31, who watched from their classroom windows as the towers collapsed, received immediate intervention—a therapeutic "trauma curriculum" in which they expressed their emotions through writing, drawing, and discussion and participated in experiences aimed at helping them manage stress and restore trust and tolerance. Evaluations of similar school-based interventions in war-torn regions reveal that they are highly effective in lessening child and adolescent PTSD symptoms (Peltonen & Punamäki, 2010; Qouta et al., 2012).

When wartime drains families and communities of resources, international organizations must step in and help children. The Children and War Foundation, *www.childrenandwar.org*, offers programs and manuals that train local personnel in how to promote children's adaptive coping.

Child Sexual Abuse

Until recently, child sexual abuse was considered rare, and adults often dismissed children's claims of abuse. In the 1970s, efforts by professionals and media attention led to recognition of child sexual abuse as a serious and widespread problem. About 57,000 cases in the United States were confirmed in the most recently reported year (U.S. Department of Health and Human Services, 2017a).

Characteristics of Abusers and Victims. Sexual abuse is committed against children of both sexes, but more often against girls. Most cases are reported in middle childhood, but for some victims, abuse begins early in life and continues for many years (Collin-Vézina, Daigneault, & Hébert, 2013).

In the vast majority of cases, the abuser is male, often a parent or someone the parent knows well—a father, stepfather, live-in boyfriend, uncle, or older brother (Olafson, 2011). If the abuser is a nonrelative, the person is usually someone the child has come to know and trust, such as a teacher, caregiver, clergy member, or family friend (Sullivan et al., 2011). The Internet and mobile phones have become avenues through which some perpetrators commit sexual abuse—for example, by exposing children and adolescents to pornography and online sexual advances as a way of "grooming" them for sexual acts offline (Kloess, Beech, & Harkins, 2014).

Many offenders blame the abuse on the willing participation of a seductive youngster. Yet children are not capable of making a deliberate, informed decision to enter into a sexual relationship! Even adolescents are not free to say yes or no. Rather, the responsibility lies with abusers, who tend to have characteristics that predispose them toward sexual exploitation of children. They have great difficulty controlling their impulses and may suffer from psychological disorders, including alcohol and drug abuse. Often they pick out children who are unlikely to defend themselves or to be believed—those who are physically weak, emotionally deprived, socially isolated, or affected by disabilities (Collin-Vézina, Daigneault, & Hébert, 2013).

Reported cases are linked to poverty and marital instability. Children who live in homes with a constantly changing cast of characters—repeated marriages, separations, and new partners—are especially vulnerable (Murray, Nguyen, & Cohen, 2014). But children in economically advantaged, stable homes are also victims, although their abuse is more likely to escape detection.

Consequences. The adjustment problems of child sexual abuse victims—including anxiety, depression, low self-esteem, mistrust of adults, and anger and hostility—are often severe and can persist for years after the abusive episodes. Younger children frequently react with sleep difficulties, loss of appetite, and generalized fearfulness. Adolescents may run away and show suicidal reactions, eating disorders (including weight gain and obesity), substance abuse, and delinquency. At all ages, persistent abuse accompanied by force, violence, and a close relationship to the perpetrator (incest) has a more severe impact, and is especially likely to result in post-traumatic stress disorder (PTSD) and to have lasting effects on mental health. And repeated sexual abuse, like physical abuse, is associated with central nervous system damage (Easton & Kong, 2017; Gaskill & Perry, 2012).

Sexually abused children frequently display precocious sexual knowledge and behavior. In adolescence, abused young people often engage in risky sexual behaviors, and as adults, they are more likely to be perpetrators and victims of sexually aggressive acts and to be arrested for sex crimes. Furthermore, women who were sexually abused are likely to choose partners who abuse them and their children, and they often engage in irresponsible and coercive parenting, including child abuse and neglect (Collin-Vézina, Daigneault, & Hébert, 2013; Krahé & Berger, 2017; Trickett, Noll, & Putnam, 2011). In these ways, the harmful impact of sexual abuse is transmitted to the next generation.

Prevention and Treatment. Because child sexual abuse typically appears in the midst of other serious family problems, specialized trauma-focused therapy with both children and parents is usually needed (Saunders, 2012). The best way to reduce the suffering of victims is to prevent sexual abuse from continuing. Today, courts are prosecuting abusers more vigorously and taking children's testimony more seriously.

Educational programs that teach children to recognize inappropriate sexual advances and identify sources of help reduce the risk of abuse (Finkelhor, 2009; Morris et al., 2017). Yet because of controversies over educating children about sexual abuse, few schools offer these interventions. New Zealand is the only country with a national, school-based prevention program targeting sexual abuse. In Keeping Ourselves Safe, children and adolescents learn that abusers are rarely strangers. Parent involvement ensures that home and school collaborate in teaching children self-protection skills. Evaluations reveal that virtually all New Zealand parents and children support the program and that it has helped many children avoid or report abuse (Sanders, 2006).

Fostering Resilience in Middle Childhood

Throughout middle childhood—and other periods of development—children encounter challenging and sometimes threatening situations that require them to cope with stress. In this and the previous chapter, we have considered such topics as chronic illness, learning disabilities, achievement expectations, divorce, harsh living conditions and wartime trauma, and sexual abuse. Each taxes children's coping resources, creating serious risks for development.

Nevertheless, only a modest relationship exists between stressful life experiences and psychological disturbance in childhood (Masten, 2014). In our earlier discussions of poverty, troubled family lives, and birth complications, we noted that some children manage to surmount their negative impact. The same is true for school difficulties, family transitions, the experience of war, and child maltreatment. Recall from Chapter 1 that four broad factors protect against maladjustment: (1) the child's personal characteristics, including an easygoing temperament and a mastery-oriented approach to new situations; (2) a warm parental relationship; (3) an adult outside the immediate family who offers a support system; and (4) community resources, such as good schools, social services, and youth organizations and recreation centers.

Often just one or a few of these ingredients account for why one child is resilient and another is not. Usually, however, personal and environmental factors are interconnected: Each resource favoring resilience strengthens others. For example, safe, stable neighborhoods with family-friendly community services reduce parents' daily hassles and stress, thereby promoting good parenting (Chen, Howard, & Brooks-Gunn, 2011). In contrast, unfavorable home, school, and neighborhood experiences increase the chances that children will act in ways that expose them to further hardship.

Several highly effective school-based social and emotional learning programs promote children's resilience by increasing academic motivation, social competence, and supportive relationships (Durlak et al., 2011). Among these is the 4Rs (Reading, Writing, Respect, and Resolution) Program, which provides elementary school students with weekly lessons in emotional and social understanding and skills. Topics include managing anger, responding with empathy, being assertive, resolving social conflicts, and standing up against prejudice and bullying. High-quality children's literature, selected for relevance to program themes, complements each lesson. Discussion, writing, and role-playing of the stories deepen students' understanding.

An evaluation of 4Rs in New York City public schools revealed that relative to controls, participating children became less depressed, less aggressive, more attentive, and more socially competent (Aber et al., 2011). In unsafe neighborhoods, 4Rs transforms schools into places of safety and mutual respect, where learning can occur.

Programs like 4Rs recognize that *resilience* is not a preexisting attribute but rather a capacity that develops, enabling children to use internal and external resources to cope with adversity (Luthar, Crossman, & Small, 2015). Throughout our discussion, we have seen how families, schools, communities, and society as a whole can enhance or undermine school-age children's developing sense of competence. Young people whose childhood experiences helped them learn to control impulses, overcome obstacles, strive for self-direction, and respond considerately and sympathetically to others meet the challenges of the next period—adolescence—quite well.

ASK YOURSELF

CONNECT Explain how factors that promote resilience contribute to favorable adjustment following divorce.

APPLY Claire told her 6-year-old daughter never to talk to or take candy from strangers. Why is Claire's warning unlikely to protect her daughter from sexual abuse?

REFLECT Describe a challenging time during your childhood. What aspects of the experience increased stress? What resources helped you cope with adversity?

CHAPTER 10 SUMMARY

Erikson's Theory: Industry versus Inferiority *(p. 321)*

10.1 ***Identify personality changes that take place during Erikson's stage of industry versus inferiority.***

- Children who successfully resolve Erikson's psychological conflict of **industry versus inferiority** develop a positive but realistic self-concept, pride in their accomplishments, a sense of moral responsibility, and cooperative participation with agemates.

ECO IMAGES/GETTY IMAGES

Self-Understanding *(p. 322)*

10.2 ***Describe school-age children's self-concept and self-esteem, and discuss factors that affect their achievement-related attributions.***

- As school-age children gain in perspective-taking skills, their self-concepts increasingly include competencies, personality traits, and **social comparisons.** Although parental support remains vital, children increasingly look to more people beyond the family for information about themselves.
- Self-esteem differentiates further and becomes hierarchically organized and more realistic. Cultural forces, gender-stereotyped expectations, and child-rearing practices contribute to variations in self-esteem. Authoritative parenting is linked to favorable self-esteem.
- Children who hold **mastery-oriented attributions** believe ability can be improved by trying hard and attribute failure to controllable factors, such as insufficient effort. Children who receive negative feedback about their ability are likely to develop **learned helplessness,** attributing success to external factors, such as luck, and failure to low ability.
- **Process praise,** which emphasizes behavior and effort, encourages mastery-oriented attributions, whereas **person praise,** which focuses on fixed abilities, is linked to learned helplessness. Cultural valuing of effort also promotes a mastery-oriented approach.

Emotional Development *(p. 327)*

10.3 ***Cite changes in self-conscious emotions, emotional understanding, and emotional self-regulation in middle childhood.***

- Self-conscious emotions of pride and guilt become clearly governed by personal responsibility. Intense shame is particularly destructive, yielding both internalizing and externalizing problems.
- School-age children develop an appreciation of mixed emotions. Empathy increases and includes sensitivity to both people's immediate distress and their general life condition.
- By age 10, most children shift adaptively between **problem-centered coping** and **emotion-centered coping** to regulate emotion. Children who acquire a sense of emotional self-efficacy are upbeat, empathic, and prosocial.

Moral Development *(p. 329)*

10.4 ***Describe changes in moral understanding during middle childhood, including children's understanding of diversity and inequality.***

- By middle childhood, children have internalized rules for good conduct. They construct a flexible appreciation of moral rules based on intentions and context and develop a better understanding of personal choice and individual rights.

© JIM WEST/ALAMY

- School-age children absorb societal attitudes about race and ethnicity. With age, they pay more attention to inner traits, although implicit racial biases may persist. Children most likely to hold biases believe that personality traits are fixed, have inflated self-esteem, and live in a social world that highlights group differences. Long-term intergroup contact is most effective at reducing prejudice.

Peer Relations *(p. 332)*

10.5 ***Describe changes in peer sociability and friendship in middle childhood.***

- Peer interaction becomes more prosocial, and physical aggression declines. By the end of middle childhood, children organize into **peer groups.**

© BJARKI REYR MR/ALAMY

- Friendships develop into mutual relationships based on trust. Children tend to select friends similar to themselves in multiple ways.

10.6 ***Describe categories of peer acceptance and ways to help rejected children.***

- On measures of **peer acceptance, popular children** are well-liked; **rejected children** are disliked; **controversial children** are both liked and disliked; **neglected children** arouse little reaction, positive or negative; and average children receive average numbers of positive and negative votes.
- **Popular-prosocial children** combine academic and social competence, while **popular-antisocial children** are aggressive but admired. **Rejected-aggressive children** are especially high in conflict and hostility; in contrast, **rejected-withdrawn children** are passive, socially awkward, and frequent targets of **peer victimization.**
- Coaching in social skills, academic tutoring, and training in perspective taking and solving social problems can help rejected children gain in social competence and peer acceptance. Intervening to improve the quality of parent–child interaction is often necessary.

Gender Typing *(p. 337)*

10.7 ***Discuss changes in gender-stereotyped beliefs and gender identity during middle childhood.***

- School-age children extend their awareness of gender stereotypes to personality traits and academic subjects. But they also broaden their view of what males and females can do.

- Boys strengthen their identification with "masculine traits," whereas girls often describe themselves as having some "other-gender" characteristics. Gender identity includes self-evaluations of gender typicality, gender contentedness, and felt pressure to conform to gender roles—each of which affects adjustment.

Family Influences *(p. 339)*

10.8 ***Discuss changes in parent–child communication and sibling relationships in middle childhood.***

- Despite declines in time spent with parents, **coregulation** allows parents to exercise general oversight over children, who increasingly make their own decisions.
- Sibling rivalry tends to increase with participation in a wider range of activities and more frequent parental comparisons. Compared to children with siblings, only children are higher in self-esteem, school performance, and educational attainment.

10.9 ***Explain how children fare in lesbian and gay families and in never-married, single-parent families.***

- Lesbian and gay parents are as effective at child rearing as heterosexual parents, and their children are as well-adjusted as those reared by heterosexual parents.
- Never-married parenthood generally increases financial hardship for low-SES mothers and their children. Children of never-married mothers who lack a father's warmth and involvement show less favorable cognitive development and engage in more antisocial behavior than children in low-SES, first-marriage families.

10.10 ***Cite factors that influence children's adjustment to divorce and blended family arrangements.***

- Marital breakup is often stressful for children. Individual differences are affected by parental psychological health, financial resources, child characteristics (age, temperament, and sex), and social supports. Divorce is linked to early sexual activity, adolescent parenthood, and long-term relationship difficulties.
- The overriding factor in positive adjustment following divorce is effective parenting and both parents' continued involvement. Divorce mediation can foster parental conflict resolution in the period surrounding divorce. The success of joint custody depends on effective coparenting.

© BURGER/PHANIE/THE IMAGE WORKS

- In **blended, or reconstituted, families,** girls, older children, and children in father–stepmother families tend to have more adjustment problems. Stepparents who move into their roles gradually help children adjust.

10.11 ***Discuss how maternal employment and life in dual-earner families affect school-age children.***

- When employed mothers remain committed to parenting, children display higher self-esteem, less gender-stereotyped beliefs, better achievement, and fewer behavior problems. In dual-earner families, the father's willingness to take on child-rearing responsibilities is associated with favorable development.
- Authoritative child rearing, parental monitoring, and regular after-school chores lead **self-care children** to be responsible and well-adjusted. Good after-school programs also aid school performance and emotional and social adjustment, especially for low-SES children.

Some Common Problems of Development *(p. 348)*

10.12 ***Cite common fears and anxieties of middle childhood, and discuss their impact on children's adjustment.***

- School-age children's fears include physical harm, media events, academic failure, parents' health, the possibility of dying, and peer rejection. Children with inhibited temperaments are at higher risk of developing **phobias.** Harsh living conditions can also cause severe anxiety.

10.13 ***Discuss factors related to child sexual abuse, its consequences for children's development, and its prevention and treatment.***

- Child sexual abuse is typically committed by male family members, more often against girls than boys. Abusers have characteristics that predispose them toward sexual exploitation of children. Reported cases are strongly associated with poverty and marital instability. Abused children often have severe adjustment problems.
- Treatment typically requires therapy with both children and parents. Educational programs that teach children to recognize inappropriate sexual advances and identify sources of help reduce the risk of sexual abuse.

10.14 ***Cite factors that foster resilience in middle childhood.***

- Only a modest relationship exists between stressful life experiences and psychological disturbance in childhood. Children's personal characteristics, supportive adults, authoritative parenting, and community resources predict resilience.

© SIMON A. THALMANN/ KELLOGG COMMUNITY COLLEGE

IMPORTANT TERMS AND CONCEPTS

blended, or reconstituted, families (p. 346)
controversial children (p. 334)
coregulation (p. 339)
emotion-centered coping (p. 328)
industry versus inferiority (p. 321)
learned helplessness (p. 325)
mastery-oriented attributions (p. 325)
neglected children (p. 334)
peer acceptance (p. 334)
peer group (p. 333)
peer victimization (p. 336)
person praise (p. 325)
phobia (p. 348)
popular-antisocial children (p. 335)
popular children (p. 334)
popular-prosocial children (p. 335)
problem-centered coping (p. 328)
process praise (p. 325)
rejected-aggressive children (p. 335)
rejected children (p. 324)
rejected-withdrawn children (p. 335)
self-care children (p. 347)
social comparisons (p. 322)

Development in **Middle Childhood**

6–8 YEARS

Physical

- Slow gains in height and weight continue. (281)
- Permanent teeth gradually replace primary teeth. (281)
- Prints an increasing number of uppercase, then lowercase, alphabet letters. (286)
- Drawings become more organized and detailed and include some depth cues. (286–287)
- Games with rules and rough-and-tumble play become common. (287)

PHOTO AND CO/PHOTODISC/GETTY IMAGES

Cognitive

- Thought becomes more logical, as shown by the ability to pass Piagetian conservation, class inclusion, and seriation problems. (290)

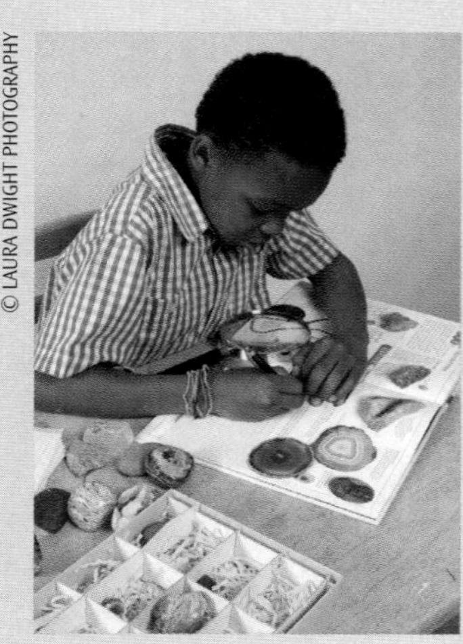
© LAURA DWIGHT PHOTOGRAPHY

- Improves dramatically in speed of information processing. (293, 295)
- Gains further in executive function, with marked improvements in inhibition, flexible shifting of attention, working memory capacity, and planning on multistep tasks. (293, 295)
- Uses memory strategies of rehearsal and then organization. (296)
- Views the mind as an active, constructive agent, capable of transforming information. (297)
- Awareness of memory strategies and of the impact of psychological factors, such as mental inferences, on performance improves. (297)
- Understands second-order false belief; capable of recursive thought. (297)
- Uses informal knowledge of number concepts and counting to master increasingly complex mathematical skills. (299)

Language

- Vocabulary increases rapidly throughout middle childhood, eventually reaching comprehension of 40,000 words. (307)
- Word definitions are concrete, referring to functions and appearance. (308)
- Transitions from emergent literacy to conventional reading. (298)

IMAGE SOURCE/ALAMY

- Language awareness develops. (307)
- Understands and uses increasingly subtle, indirect expressions of meaning, such as irony and sarcasm. (308)
- Narratives increase in organization, detail, and expressiveness. (308)

Emotional/Social

- Self-concept begins to include personality traits, competencies, and social comparisons. (322)
- Self-esteem differentiates, becomes hierarchically organized, and adjusts to a more realistic level. (323)
- Self-conscious emotions of pride and guilt are governed by personal responsibility. (327)
- Recognizes that individuals can experience mixed emotions and that their expressions may not reflect their true feelings. (328)

© LAURA DWIGHT PHOTOGRAPHY

- Gains in understanding of self-conscious emotions. (328)
- Empathy increases. (328)
- Becomes more independent and trustworthy. (329)
- Constructs a flexible appreciation of moral rules, considering prosocial and antisocial intentions and the context of the behavior. (329)
- Physical aggression declines; verbal and relational aggression continue. (332)
- Resolves conflicts more effectively. (332)

9–11 YEARS

Physical

- Adolescent growth spurt begins two years earlier in girls than in boys. (281)
- Executes gross-motor movements of running, jumping, hopping, and ball skills more quickly and with better coordination. (286)

Note: Numbers in parentheses indicate the page or pages on which each milestone is discussed.

STEVE SKJOLD/ALAMY

- Ability to represent depth in drawings expands. (286–287)

Cognitive

- Continues to master concrete operational tasks in a step-by-step fashion. (291)
- Spatial reasoning improves; readily draws and reads maps of large-scale spaces and grasps the notion of scale. (290–291)

ANTHONY BRADSHAW/PHOTODISC/GETTY IMAGES

- Continues to improve in speed of information processing. (293, 295)
- Continues to gain in executive function. (293, 295)
- Uses memory strategies of rehearsal and organization more effectively. (296)
- Applies several memory strategies simultaneously; begins to use elaboration. (296)
- General knowledge base (semantic memory) grows larger and becomes better organized. (296)
- Theory of mind becomes more elaborate and refined. (297)
- Cognitive self-regulation improves. (298)

Language

- Thinks about and uses words more precisely; word definitions emphasize synonyms and categorical relations. (308)
- Grasps multiple meanings of words, as reflected in comprehension of metaphors and humor. (308)
- Continues to master complex grammatical constructions. (308)

KALI9/GETTY IMAGES

- Narratives lengthen, become more coherent, and include more evaluative comments. (308)

Emotional/Social

- Self-esteem remains high but continues to become more realistic and nuanced. (323)
- Distinguishes ability, effort, and external factors (such as luck) in attributions for success and failure. (325)
- Empathic responding extends to general life conditions. (328)
- Shifts adaptively between problem-centered and emotion-centered strategies in regulating emotion. (328)
- Clarifies and links moral imperatives and social conventions. (330)
- Convictions about matters of personal choice strengthen, and understanding of individual rights expands. (330)
- Voicing of outgroup prejudice toward minorities declines. (331)
- Friendships become more selective and are based on mutual trust. (333)
- Peer groups emerge. (333)

DAVID ROTH/THE IMAGE BANK/GETTY IMAGES

- Becomes aware of more gender stereotypes, including personality traits and achievement, but has a flexible appreciation of what males and females can do. (337–338)
- Gender identity expands to include self-evaluations of typicality, contentedness, and felt pressure to conform. (338–339)
- Sibling rivalry tends to increase. (340)

GOGO IMAGES CORPORATION/ALAMY

Note: Numbers in parentheses indicate the page or pages on which each milestone is discussed.

GLOSSARY

A

academic programs Preschool and kindergarten programs in which teachers structure children's learning, teaching academic skills through formal lessons that often involve repetition and drill. Distinguished from *child-centered programs.* (p. 234)

accommodation In Piaget's theory, the part of adaptation in which new schemes are created and old ones adjusted to produce a better fit with the environment. Distinguished from *assimilation.* (p. 140)

adaptation In Piaget's theory, the process of building schemes through direct interaction with the environment. Consists of two complementary activities: *assimilation* and *accommodation.* (p. 139)

age of viability The point at which the baby can first survive if born early, occurring sometime between 22 and 26 weeks. (p. 74)

alcohol-related neurodevelopmental disorder (ARND) The least severe form of fetal alcohol spectrum disorder, involving brain injury but with typical physical growth and absence of facial abnormalities. Distinguished from *fetal alcohol syndrome (FAS)* and *partial fetal alcohol syndrome (p-FAS).* (p. 79)

allele Each of two forms of a gene located at the same place on corresponding pairs of chromosomes. (p. 43)

amnion The inner membrane that encloses the developing organism in amniotic fluid, which helps keep the temperature of the prenatal world constant and provides a cushion against jolts caused by the woman's movements. (p. 71)

amygdala An inner-brain structure that plays a central role in processing of novelty and emotional information. (p. 206)

androgyny The gender identity held by individuals who score high on both traditionally masculine and traditionally feminine personality characteristics. (p. 267)

anoxia Inadequate oxygen supply. (p. 89)

Apgar Scale A rating system used to assess a newborn baby's physical condition immediately after birth on the basis of five characteristics: heart rate, respiratory effort, reflex irritability, muscle tone, and color. (p. 87)

applied behavior analysis Careful observations of individual behavior and related environmental events, followed by systematic changes in those events based on procedures of conditioning and modeling. The goal is to eliminate undesirable behaviors and increase desirable responses. (p. 12)

assimilation In Piaget's theory, the part of adaptation in which current schemes are used to interpret the external world. Distinguished from *accommodation.* (p. 139)

associative play A form of social interaction in which children engage in separate activities but exchange toys and comment on one another's behavior. Distinguished from *nonsocial activity, parallel play,* and *cooperative play.* (p. 251)

attachment The strong affectionate tie we have with special people in our lives, which leads us to feel pleasure when interacting with them and to be comforted by their nearness in times of stress. (p. 184)

Attachment Q-Sort A method for assessing the quality of attachment in children between 1 and 5 years of age through home observations of a variety of attachment-related behaviors. (p. 187)

attention-deficit hyperactivity disorder (ADHD) A childhood disorder involving inattention, impulsivity, and excessive motor activity, resulting in academic and social problems. (p. 294)

authoritarian child-rearing style A child-rearing style that is low in acceptance and involvement, high in coercive and psychological control, and low in autonomy granting. Distinguished from *authoritative, permissive,* and *uninvolved child-rearing styles.* (p. 271)

authoritative child-rearing style A child-rearing style that is high acceptance and involvement, adaptive control techniques, and appropriate autonomy granting. Distinguished from *authoritarian, permissive,* and *uninvolved child-rearing styles.* (p. 270)

autobiographical memory Long-lasting recollections of personally meaningful one-time events from both the recent and the distant past. (p. 153)

automatic processes Cognitive activities that are so well-learned that they require no space in working memory and, therefore, permit an individual to focus on other information while performing them. (p. 151)

autonomy versus shame and doubt In Erikson's theory, the psychological conflict of toddlerhood, which is resolved favorably when parents provide young children with suitable guidance and reasonable choices. (p. 173)

autosomes The 22 matching pairs of chromosomes in each human cell. (p. 42)

B

babbling Infants' repetition of consonant–vowel combinations, beginning around 6 months of age. (p. 164)

basic emotions Emotions such as happiness, interest, surprise, fear, anger, sadness, and disgust that are universal in humans and other primates and have a long evolutionary history of promoting survival. (p. 173)

basic trust versus mistrust In Erikson's theory, the psychological conflict of infancy, which is resolved positively when the balance of care is sympathetic and loving. (p. 172)

behavioral genetics A field devoted to uncovering the contributions of nature and nurture to the diversity of human traits and abilities. (p. 61)

behaviorism An approach that regards directly observable events—stimuli and responses—as the appropriate focus of study and views the development of behavior as taking place through classical and operant conditioning. (p. 11)

blended, or reconstituted, family A family structure resulting from remarriage or cohabitation that includes parent, child, and steprelatives. (p. 346)

brain plasticity The capacity of various parts of the cerebral cortex to take over functions of damaged regions. Declines as hemispheres of the cerebral cortex lateralize. (p. 112)

breech position A position of the baby in the uterus that would cause the buttocks or feet to be delivered first. (p. 89)

C

cardinality The mathematical principle specifying that the last number in a counting sequence indicates the quantity of items in the set. (p. 233)

carriers Heterozygous individuals who can pass a recessive trait to their offspring. (p. 43)

categorical self Classification of the self on the basis of prominent ways in which people differ, such as age, sex, physical characteristics, goodness versus badness, and competencies. Develops between 18 and 30 months. (p. 196)

central executive In information processing, the conscious, reflective part of our mental system that directs the flow of information, coordinating incoming information with information already in the system and selecting, applying, and monitoring strategies that facilitate memory storage, comprehension, reasoning, and problem solving. (p. 150)

centration In Piaget's theory, the tendency of preoperational children to focus on one aspect of a situation while neglecting other important features. (p. 218)

cephalocaudal trend An organized pattern of physical growth that proceeds from the upper to the lower part of the body ("head to tail"). Distinguished from *proximodistal trend.* (p. 106)

cerebellum A structure at the rear and base of the brain that aids in balance and control of body movement. (p. 206)

cerebral cortex The largest, most complex structure of the human brain, which contains the greatest number of neurons and synapses and accounts for the highly developed intelligence of the human species. (p. 111)

cesarean delivery A surgical birth, in which the doctor makes an incision in the mother's abdomen and lifts the baby out of the uterus. (p. 90)

child-centered programs Preschool and kindergarten programs in which teachers provide a variety of activities from which children select, and much learning takes place through play. Distinguished from *academic programs.* (p. 234)

child development A field of study devoted to understanding constancy and change from conception through adolescence. (p. 2)

child-rearing styles Combinations of parenting behaviors that occur over a wide range of situations, creating an enduring child-rearing climate. (p. 270)

chorion The outer membrane that surrounds the amnion, forming a protective covering around the developing organism. It sends out tiny fingerlike villi, from which the placenta begins to develop. (p. 72)

chromosomes Rodlike structures in the cell nucleus that store and transmit genetic information. (p. 40)

chronosystem In ecological systems theory, the temporal dimension of the environment, in which life changes can either be imposed externally or, alternatively, can arise from within the child. Distinguished from *microsystem, mesosystem, exosystem,* and *macrosystem.* (p. 21)

circular reaction In Piaget's theory, a means of building schemes in which infants try to repeat a chance event caused by their own motor activity. (p. 141)

classical conditioning A form of learning that involves associating a neutral stimulus with a stimulus that leads to a reflexive response. Once the nervous system makes the connection between the two stimuli, the neutral stimulus alone produces the behavior. (p. 120)

clinical interview An interview method in which the researcher uses a flexible, conversational style to probe for the participant's point of view. Distinguished from *structured interview.* (p. 26)

clinical, or case study, method A research method in which the aim is to obtain as complete a picture as possible of one child's psychological functioning and the experiences that led up to it by bringing together interview data, observations, and test scores. (p. 26)

cognitive-developmental theory Piaget's view that children actively construct knowledge as they manipulate and explore their world and that cognitive development takes place in stages. (p. 13)

cognitive maps Mental representations of familiar spaces, such as a classroom, school, or neighborhood. (p. 290)

cognitive self-regulation The process of continuously monitoring progress toward a goal, checking outcomes, and redirecting unsuccessful efforts. (p. 298)

cohort effects The effects of cultural–historical change on the accuracy of longitudinal and cross-sectional research findings. Results based on one cohort—individuals developing in the same time period, who are influenced by particular historical and cultural conditions—may not apply to other cohorts. (p. 32)

compliance Voluntary obedience to requests and commands. (p. 196)

concrete operational stage Piaget's third stage of cognitive development, extending from about 7 to 11 years, during which thought becomes logical, flexible, and organized in its application to concrete information, but the capacity for abstract thinking is not yet present. (p. 290)

conditioned response (CR) In classical conditioning, a new response elicited by a conditioned stimulus (CS) that is similar to the unconditioned, or reflexive, response (UCR). (p. 120)

conditioned stimulus (CS) In classical conditioning, a neutral stimulus that, through pairing with an unconditioned stimulus (UCS), leads to a new, conditioned response. (CR). (p. 120)

conservation The understanding that certain physical characteristics of objects remain the same, even when their outward appearance changes. (p. 218)

constructivist classroom A classroom grounded in Piaget's view of children as active agents who construct their own knowledge. Features include richly equipped learning centers, small groups and individuals solving self-chosen problems, a teacher who guides and supports in response to children's needs, and evaluation based on individual students' progress in relation to their own prior development. Distinguished from *traditional* and *social-constructivist classrooms.* (p. 324)

contexts Unique combinations of personal and environmental circumstances that can result in different paths of development. (p. 6)

continuous development The view that development is a process of gradually augmenting the same types of skills that were there to begin with. Distinguished from *discontinuous development.* (p. 5)

controversial children Children who receive many votes, both positive and negative, on self-report measures of peer acceptance, indicating that they are both liked and disliked. Distinguished from *popular, neglected,* and *rejected children.* (p. 334)

convergent thinking The type of cognition emphasized on intelligence tests, which involves arriving at a single correct answer to a problem. Distinguished from *divergent thinking.* (p. 315)

cooing Pleasant vowel-like noises made by infants beginning around 2 months of age. (p. 164)

cooperative learning Collaboration on a task by a small group of classmates who work toward common goals by considering one another's ideas, appropriately challenging one another, providing sufficient explanations to correct misunderstandings, and resolving differences of opinion on the basis of reasons and evidence. (p. 312)

cooperative play A form of social interaction in which children orient toward a common goal, such as acting out a make-believe theme. Distinguished from *nonsocial activity, parallel play,* and *associative play.* (p. 251)

coparenting Parents' mutual support of each other's parenting behaviors. (p. 53)

coregulation A form of supervision in which parents exercise general oversight while letting children take charge of moment-by-moment decision making. (p. 339)

core knowledge perspective A perspective that states that infants are born with a set of innate knowledge systems, or core domains of thought, each of which permits a ready grasp of new, related information and therefore supports early, rapid development of certain aspects of cognition. (p. 147)

corpus callosum The large bundle of fibers connecting the two hemispheres of the cerebral cortex. Supports smooth coordination of movements on both sides of the body and integration of many aspects of thinking. (p. 206)

correlational design A research design in which investigators gather information on individuals without altering their experiences and then examine relationships between participants' characteristics and their behavior or development. Does not permit inferences about cause and effect. (p. 29)

correlation coefficient A number, ranging from +1.00 to –1.00, that describes the strength and direction of the relationship between two variables. (p. 29)

creativity The ability to produce work that is original yet appropriate—something others have not thought of that is useful in some way. (p. 315)

cross-sectional design A research design in which groups of participants differing in age are studied at the same point in time. Distinguished from *longitudinal design.* (p. 32)

D

deferred imitation The ability to remember and copy the behavior of models who are not present. (p. 142)

delay of gratification The ability to wait for an appropriate time and place to engage in a tempting act. (p. 196)

deoxyribonucleic acid (DNA) Long, double-stranded molecules that make up chromosomes. (p. 41)

dependent variable The variable the researcher expects to be influenced by the independent variable in an experiment. Distinguished from *independent variable.* (p. 29)

developmental cognitive neuroscience An area of investigation that brings together researchers from psychology, biology, neuroscience, and medicine to study the relationship between changes in the brain and the developing child's cognitive processing and behavior patterns. (p. 16)

developmentally appropriate practice A set of standards devised by the U.S. National Association for the Education of Young Children, specifying program characteristics that serve young children's developmental and individual needs, based on current research and consensus among experts. (p. 160)

developmental science An interdisciplinary field devoted to understanding constancy and change throughout the lifespan. (p. 2)

developmental social neuroscience A field devoted to studying the relationship between changes in the brain and emotional and social development. (p. 16)

differentiation theory The view that perceptual development involves the detection of increasingly fine-grained, invariant features in the environment. (p. 134)

difficult child A child whose temperament is characterized by irregularity in daily routines, slowness in accepting new experiences, and a tendency to react negatively and intensely. Distinguished from *easy child* and *slow-to-warm-up child.* (p. 179)

discontinuous development The view that development is a process in which new ways of understanding and responding to the world emerge at specific times. Distinguished from *continuous development.* (p. 5)

disorganized/disoriented attachment The attachment pattern reflecting the greatest insecurity, characterizing infants who show confused, contradictory responses when reunited with the parent after a separation. Distinguished from *secure, insecure-avoidant,* and *insecure-resistant attachment.* (p. 186)

displaced reference The realization that words can be used to cue mental images of things that are not physically present. (p. 145)

divergent thinking The type of thinking associated with creativity, which involves generating multiple and unusual possibilities when faced with a task or problem. Distinguished from *convergent thinking.* (p. 315)

dominant cerebral hemisphere The hemisphere of the cerebral cortex responsible for skilled motor action and other important abilities. In right-handed individuals, the left hemisphere is dominant; in left-handed individuals, motor and language skills are often shared between the hemispheres. (p. 205)

dominant–recessive inheritance A pattern of inheritance in which, under heterozygous conditions, only one allele, called dominant, affects the child's characteristics. The second allele, which has no effect, is called recessive. (p. 43)

dual representation The ability to view a symbolic object as both an object in its own right and a symbol. (p. 217)

dynamic assessment An approach to testing consistent with Vygotsky's zone of proximal development, in which purposeful teaching is introduced into the testing situation to find out what the child can attain with social support. (p. 307)

dynamic systems perspective A view that regards the child's mind, body, and physical and social worlds as a dynamic, integrated system. A change in any part of the system leads the child to reorganize his or her behavior so the various components work together again, but in a more complex, effective way. (p. 22)

dynamic systems theory of motor development A theory that views mastery of motor skills as a process of acquiring increasingly complex systems of action, in which separate abilities blend together, each cooperating with others to produce more effective ways of exploring and controlling the environment. Each new skill is a joint product of central nervous system development, the body's movement capacities, the child's goals, and environmental supports for the skill. (p. 125)

E

easy child A child whose temperament is characterized by quick establishment of regular routines in infancy, general cheerfulness, and easy adaptation to new experiences. Distinguished from *difficult child* and *slow-to-warm-up child.* (p. 179)

ecological systems theory Bronfenbrenner's approach, which views the child as developing within a complex system of relationships affected by multiple levels of the surrounding environment, from immediate settings of family and school to broad cultural values and programs. (p. 19)

educational self-fulfilling prophecies Teachers' positive or negative views of individual children, who tend to adopt and start to live up to those views. (p. 312)

effortful control The self-regulatory dimension of temperament, involving the capacity to voluntarily suppress a dominant response in order to plan and execute a more adaptive response. (p. 179)

egocentrism Failure to distinguish others' symbolic viewpoints from one's own. (p. 217)

elaboration A memory strategy that involves creating a relationship, or shared meaning, between two or more pieces of information that do not belong to the same category. (p. 296)

emergent literacy Children's active efforts to construct literacy knowledge through informal experiences. (p. 230)

emotional self-regulation Strategies for adjusting our emotional state to a comfortable level of intensity so we can accomplish our goals. (p. 177)

emotion-centered coping A strategy for managing emotion that is internal, private, and aimed at controlling distress when little can be done about an outcome. Distinguished from *problem-centered coping.* (p. 328)

empathy The ability to understand another's emotional state and *feel with* that person, or respond emotionally in a similar way. (p. 196)

epigenesis Development resulting from ongoing, bidirectional exchanges between heredity and all levels of the environment. (p. 65)

episodic memory Memory for everyday experiences. Distinguished from *semantic memory.* (p. 227)

ethnography A research method in which the researcher attempts to understand a culture or a distinct social group through participant observation—spending months, and sometimes years, in the cultural community, participating in its daily life and gathering field notes. (p. 27)

ethological theory of attachment Bowlby's theory, the most widely accepted view of attachment, which recognizes the infant's emotional tie to the caregiver as an evolved response that promotes survival. (p. 184)

ethology An approach concerned with the adaptive, or survival, value of behavior and its evolutionary history. (p. 17)

evolutionary developmental psychology An area of research that seeks to understand the adaptive value of species-wide cognitive, emotional, and social competencies as those competencies change with age. (p. 18)

executive function The diverse cognitive operations and strategies that enable us to achieve our goals in cognitively challenging situations. These include controlling attention by inhibiting impulses and irrelevant actions and by flexibly directing thought and behavior to suit the demands of a task; coordinating information in working memory; and planning. (p. 151)

exosystem In ecological systems theory, the level of the environment consisting of social settings that do not contain children but nevertheless affect experiences in immediate settings. Distinguished from *microsystem, mesosystem, macrosystem,* and *chronosystem.* (p. 20)

expansions Adult responses that elaborate on children's speech, increasing its complexity. (p. 242)

experience-dependent brain growth Growth and refinement of established brain structures as a result of specific learning experiences that vary widely across individuals and cultures. Distinguished from *experience-expectant brain growth.* (p. 114)

experience-expectant brain growth The young brain's rapidly developing organization, which depends on ordinary experiences—opportunities to explore the environment, interact with people, and hear language and other sounds. Distinguished from *experience-dependent brain growth.* (p. 114)

experimental design A research design in which investigators randomly assign participants to two or more treatment conditions and then study the effect that manipulating an independent variable has on a dependent variable. Permits inferences about cause and effect. (p. 29)

extended-family households Households in which parent and child live with one or more adult relatives. (p. 59)

F

fast-mapping Children's ability to connect new words with their underlying concepts after only a brief encounter. (p. 238)

fetal alcohol spectrum disorder (FASD) A range of physical, mental, and behavioral outcomes caused by prenatal alcohol exposure, including *fetal alcohol syndrome (FAS), partial fetal alcohol syndrome (p-FAS),* and *alcohol-related neurodevelopmental disorder (ARND).* (p. 79)

fetal alcohol syndrome (FAS) The most severe form of fetal alcohol spectrum disorder, distinguished by slow physical growth, facial abnormalities, and brain injury. Usually affects children whose mothers drank heavily throughout pregnancy. Distinguished from *partial fetal alcohol* *syndrome (p-FAS)* and *alcohol-related neurodevelopmental disorder (ARND).* (p. 79)

fetal monitors Electronic instruments that track the baby's heart rate during labor. (p. 89)

Flynn effect The steady increase in IQ from one generation to the next. (p. 305)

fraternal, or dizygotic, twins Twins resulting from the release and fertilization of two ova. They are genetically no more alike than ordinary siblings. Distinguished from *identical,* or *monozygotic, twins.* (p. 42)

G

gametes The sex cells, or sperm and ovum, which contain half as many chromosomes as regular body cells. (p. 41)

gender constancy A full understanding of the biologically based permanence of one's gender, including the realization that sex remains the same even if clothing, hairstyle, and play activities change. (p. 267)

gender identity An image of oneself as relatively masculine or feminine in characteristics. (p. 267)

gender schema theory An information-processing approach to gender typing that combines social learning and cognitive-developmental features to explain how environmental pressures and children's cognitions work together to shape gender-role development. (p. 267)

gender typing Any association of objects, roles, or traits with one sex or the other in ways that conform to cultural stereotypes. (p. 264)

gene A segment of DNA along the length of the chromosome containing instructions for making proteins that contribute to body growth and functioning. (p. 41)

gene–environment correlation The idea that individuals' genes influence the environments to which they are exposed. (p. 63)

gene–environment interaction The view that because of their genetic makeup, individuals differ in their responsiveness to qualities of the environment. (p. 63)

genetic counseling A communication process designed to help couples assess their chances of giving birth to a baby with a hereditary disorder and choose the best course of action in view of risks and family goals. (p. 47)

genomic imprinting A pattern of inheritance in which alleles are imprinted, or chemically marked, in such a way that one pair member is activated, regardless of its makeup. (p. 45)

genotype An individual's genetic makeup. Distinguished from *phenotype.* (p. 40)

germinal period The two-week period from fertilization and formation of the zygote until the tiny mass of cells drifts down and out of the fallopian tube and attaches itself to the wall of the uterus. (p. 70)

gifted Displaying exceptional intellectual strengths, such as high IQ, high potential for creativity, or specialized talent. (p. 314)

glial cells Cells that are responsible for myelination of neural fibers, which improves the efficiency of message transfer. (p. 108)

goodness-of-fit model A model proposed by Thomas and Chess to explain how favorable outcomes depend on an effective match, or good fit, between a child's temperament and the child-rearing environment. (p. 183)

growth hormone (GH) A pituitary hormone that affects the development of almost all body tissues. (p. 207)

guided participation Shared endeavors between more expert and less expert participants, without specifying the precise features of communication, thereby allowing for variations across situations and cultures. A broader concept than *scaffolding.* (p. 224)

H

habituation A gradual reduction in the strength of a response due to repetitive stimulation. (p. 121)

heritability estimate A statistic that measures the extent to which individual differences in complex traits, such as intelligence or personality, in a specific population are due to genetic factors. (p. 62)

heterozygous Having two different alleles at the same place on a pair of chromosomes. Distinguished from *homozygous.* (p. 43)

hierarchical classification The organization of objects into classes and subclasses on the basis of similarities and differences. (p. 219)

hippocampus An inner-brain structure that plays a vital role in memory and in images of space that help us find our way. (p. 206)

Home Observation for Measurement of the Environment (HOME) A checklist for gathering information about the quality of children's home lives through observation and parental interview. (p. 159)

homozygous Having two identical alleles at the same place on a pair of chromosomes. Distinguished from *heterozygous.* (p. 43)

I

identical, or monozygotic, twins Twins that result when a zygote that has started to duplicate separates into two clusters of cells with the same genetic makeup, which develop into two individuals. Distinguished from *fraternal,* or *dizygotic, twins.* (p. 42)

imitation Learning by copying the behavior of another person. (p. 122)

implantation Attachment of the blastocyst to the uterine lining, which occurs seven to nine days after fertilization. (p. 71)

inclusive classrooms Classrooms in which students with learning difficulties learn alongside typical students in the regular educational setting for all or part of the school day—a practice designed to prepare them for participation in society and to combat prejudices against individuals with disabilities. (p. 314)

incomplete dominance inheritance A pattern of inheritance in which both alleles are expressed in the phenotype, resulting in a combined trait, or one that is intermediate between the two. (p. 43)

independent variable In an experiment, the variable the investigator expects to cause changes in another variable and that the researcher manipulates by randomly assigning participants to different treatment conditions. Distinguished from *dependent variable.* (p. 29)

induction A type of discipline in which an adult helps make the child aware of feelings by pointing out the effects of the child's misbehavior on others. (p. 255)

industry versus inferiority In Erikson's theory, the psychological conflict of middle childhood, which is resolved positively when experiences lead children to develop a sense of competence at useful skills and tasks. (p. 321)

infant-directed speech (IDS) A form of communication used by adults to speak to babies, consisting of short sentences with high-pitched, exaggerated expression, clear pronunciation, distinct pauses between speech segments, clear gestures to support verbal meaning, and repetition of new words in a variety of contexts. (p. 167)

infantile amnesia The inability of most older children and adults to retrieve events that happened before age 2 to 3. (p. 153)

infant mortality The number of deaths in the first year of life per 1,000 live births. (p. 94)

information processing A perspective that views the human mind as a symbol-manipulating system through which information flows and that regards cognitive development as a continuous process. (p. 15)

inhibited, or shy, children Children whose temperament is such that they react negatively to and withdraw from novel stimuli. Distinguished from *uninhibited,* or *sociable, children.* (p. 180)

initiative versus guilt In Erikson's theory, the psychological conflict of early childhood, which is resolved positively through play experiences that foster a healthy sense of initiative and through development of a superego, or conscience, that is not overly strict and guilt-ridden. (p. 246)

insecure–avoidant attachment The attachment pattern characterizing infants who seem unresponsive to the parent when she is present, are usually not distressed by parental separation, react to the stranger in much the same way as to the parent, avoid or are slow to greet the parent when she returns, and when picked up, often fail to cling. Distinguished from *secure, insecure–resistant,* and *disorganized/disoriented attachment.* (p. 186)

insecure–resistant attachment The attachment pattern characterizing infants who seek closeness to the parent and fail to explore before separation, are usually distressed when the parent leaves, and combine clinginess with angry, resistive behavior when the parent returns. Distinguished from *secure, insecure–avoidant,* and *disorganized/disoriented attachment.* (p. 186)

intelligence quotient (IQ) A score that permits an individual's performance on an intelligence test to be compared to the performances of other individuals of the same age. (p. 158)

intentional, or goal-directed, behavior A sequence of actions in which schemes are deliberately coordinated to solve a problem. (p. 141)

intermodal perception The process of making sense of simultaneous input from more than one modality, or sensory system, perceiving these separate streams of information as an integrated whole. (p. 133)

internal working model A set of expectations about the availability of attachment figures and their likelihood of providing support in times of stress. It becomes a vital part of personality, serving as a guide for all future close relationships. (p. 185)

irreversibility The inability to mentally go through a series of steps in a problem and then reverse direction, returning to the starting point. Distinguished from *reversibility.* (p. 218)

J

joint attention A state in which the child attends to the same object or event as the caregiver, who often labels it. Contributes to early language development. (p. 164)

K

kinship studies Studies that compare the characteristics of family members to determine the importance of heredity in complex human characteristics. (p. 62)

kwashiorkor A disease caused by an unbalanced diet very low in protein that usually appears after weaning, between 1 and 3 years of age. Symptoms include an enlarged belly, swollen feet, hair loss, skin rash, and irritable, listless behavior. (p. 119)

L

language acquisition device (LAD) In Chomsky's theory, an innate system containing a universal grammar, or set of rules common to all languages, that enables children, no matter which language they hear, to understand and speak in a rule-oriented fashion as soon as they pick up enough words. (p. 162)

lanugo White, downy hair that covers the entire body of the fetus, helping the vernix stick to the skin. (p. 74)

lateralization Specialization of functions in the two hemispheres of the cerebral cortex. (p. 111)

learned helplessness Attribution of success to external factors, such as luck, and failure to low ability, which is fixed and cannot be improved by trying hard. Distinguished from *mastery-oriented attributions.* (p. 325)

learning disabilities Great difficulty with one or more specific aspects of learning, usually reading, resulting in slower than appropriate academic progress, even when more intensive instruction is provided. (p. 314)

longitudinal design A research design in which participants are studied repeatedly, and changes are noted as they get older. Distinguished from *cross-sectional design.* (p. 35)

long-term memory In information processing, the largest storage area in memory, containing our permanent knowledge base. (p. 151)

M

macrosystem In ecological systems theory, the outermost level of the environment, consisting of cultural values, laws, customs, and resources that influence children's experiences and interactions at inner levels. Distinguished from *microsystem, mesosystem, exosystem,* and *chronosystem.* (p. 20)

make-believe play A type of play in which children act out everyday and imaginary activities. (p. 142)

marasmus A wasted condition of the body caused by a diet low in all essential nutrients, which usually appears in the first year of life when the mother is too malnourished to produce enough breast milk and bottle-feeding is also inadequate. (p. 119)

mastery-oriented attributions Attributions that credit success to ability, which can be improved through effort, and failure to factors that can be changed or controlled, such as insufficient effort or a difficult task. Distinguished from *learned helplessness.* (p. 325)

matters of personal choice Concerns such as choice of friends, hairstyle, and leisure activities, which do not violate rights and are up to the individual. Distinguished from *moral imperatives* and *social conventions.* (p. 259)

meiosis The process of cell division through which gametes are formed and in which the number of chromosomes normally present in each cell is halved. (p. 41)

memory strategies Deliberate mental activities that improve the likelihood of remembering. (p. 227)

mental representations Internal depictions of information that the mind can manipulate, including images and concepts. (p. 142)

mesosystem In ecological systems theory, the second level of the environment, encompassing connections between the child's microsystems, or immediate settings. Distinguished from *microsystem, exosystem, macrosystem,* and *chronosystem.* (p. 20)

metacognition Thinking about thought; a theory of mind, or coherent set of ideas about mental activities. (p. 229)

methylation A biochemical process triggered by certain experiences, in which a set of chemical compounds (called a methyl group) lands on top of a gene and changes its impact, reducing or silencing its expression. (p. 65)

microsystem In ecological systems theory, the innermost level of the environment, consisting of activities and interaction patterns in the child's immediate surroundings. Distinguished from *mesosystem, exosystem, macrosystem,* and *chronosystem.* (p. 20)

mirror neurons Specialized cells in motor areas of the cerebral cortex in primates that may underlie early imitative capacities by firing identically when a primate hears or sees an action and when it carries out the action on its own. (p. 122)

moral imperatives Rules and expectations that protect people's rights and welfare. Distinguished from *social conventions* and *matters of personal choice.* (p. 259)

mutation A sudden but permanent change in a segment of DNA. (p. 45)

myelination The coating of neural fibers with an insulating fatty sheath, called myelin, that improves the efficiency of message transfer. (p. 108)

N

naturalistic observation A research method in which the investigator goes into the field, or natural environment, and records the behavior of interest. Distinguished from *structured observation.* (p. 24)

natural, or prepared, childbirth A group of techniques aimed at reducing pain and medical intervention and making childbirth a rewarding experience. (p. 88)

nature–nurture controversy Disagreement among theorists about whether genetic or environmental factors are more important influences on development. (p. 6)

neglected children Children who are seldom mentioned, either positively or negatively, on self-report measures of peer acceptance. Distinguished from *popular, rejected,* and *controversial children.* (p. 334)

neural tube During the period of the embryo, the primitive spinal cord that develops from the ectoderm, the top of which swells to form the brain. (p. 73)

neurons Nerve cells that store and transmit information. (p. 108)

neurotransmitters Chemicals released by neurons that cross the synapse to send messages to other neurons. (p. 108)

niche-picking A type of gene–environment correlation in which individuals actively choose environments that complement their heredity. (p. 64)

non-rapid-eye-movement (NREM) sleep A "regular" sleep state during which the body is almost motionless and heart rate, breathing, and brain-wave activity are slow and even. Distinguished from *rapid-eye-movement (REM) sleep.* (p. 96)

nonsocial activity Unoccupied, onlooker behavior and solitary play. Distinguished from *parallel, associative,* and *cooperative play.* (p. 251)

normal distribution The bell-shaped distribution that results when researchers measure individual differences in large samples. Most scores cluster around the mean, or average, with progressively fewer falling toward the extremes. (p. 158)

normative approach An approach in which measures of behavior are taken on large numbers of individuals, and age-related averages are computed to represent typical development. (p. 8)

O

obesity A greater-than-20-percent increase over healthy weight, based on body mass index (BMI), a ratio of weight to height associated with body fat. (p. 283)

object permanence The understanding that objects continue to exist when out of sight. (p.141)

operant conditioning A form of learning in which a spontaneous behavior is followed by a stimulus that changes the probability that the behavior will occur again. (p. 121)

ordinality The mathematical principle specifying order relationships (more than and less than) between quantities. (p. 232)

organization In Piaget's theory, the internal rearrangement and linking of schemes to create a strongly interconnected cognitive system. In information processing, a memory strategy that involves grouping related items together to improve recall. (pp. 140, 296)

overextension An early vocabulary error in which young children apply a word too broadly, to a wider collection of objects and events than is appropriate. Distinguished from *underextension.* (p. 165)

overregularization Overextension of regular grammatical rules to words that are exceptions. (p. 240)

P

parallel play A form of limited social participation in which a child plays near other children with similar materials but does not try to influence their behavior. Distinguished from *nonsocial activity, associative play,* and *cooperative play.* (p. 251)

partial fetal alcohol syndrome (p-FAS) A form of fetal alcohol spectrum disorder characterized by facial abnormalities and brain injury, but less severe than fetal alcohol syndrome. Usually affects children whose mothers drank alcohol in smaller quantities during pregnancy. Distinguished from *fetal alcohol syndrome (FAS)* and *alcohol-related neurodevelopmental disorder (ARND).* (p. 79)

peer acceptance Likability, or the extent to which a child is viewed by a group of agemates as a worthy social partner. (p. 334)

peer groups Collectives of peers who generate unique values and standards for behavior and a social structure of leaders and followers. (p. 333)

peer victimization A destructive form of peer interaction in which certain children become frequent targets of verbal and physical attacks or other forms of abuse. (p. 336)

perceptual narrowing effect Perceptual sensitivity that becomes increasingly attuned with age to information most often encountered. (p. 129)

period of the embryo The six-week period from implantation through the eighth week of pregnancy, during which the groundwork is laid for all body structures and internal organs. (p. 73)

period of the fetus The longest prenatal period, from the ninth week to the end of pregnancy. During this "growth and finishing" phase, the organism increases rapidly in size. (p. 73)

permissive child-rearing style A child-rearing style that is warm and accepting but uninvolved, lax in control (either overindulgent or inattentive), and lenient rather than appropriate in autonomy granting. Distinguished from *authoritative, authoritarian,* and *uninvolved child-rearing styles.* (p. 272)

person praise Praise that emphasizes a child's traits, such as "You're so smart!" Distinguished from *process praise.* (p. 325)

phenotype An individual's directly observable physical and behavioral characteristics, which are determined by both genetic and environmental factors. Distinguished from *genotype.* (p. 40)

phobia An intense, unmanageable fear that leads to persistent avoidance of the feared situation. (p. 348)

phonological awareness The ability to reflect on and manipulate the sound structure of spoken language, as indicated by sensitivity to changes in sounds within words, to rhyming, and to incorrect pronunciation. A strong predictor of emergent literacy knowledge and later reading and spelling achievement. (p. 232)

physical aggression A form of aggression that harms others through physical injury to themselves or their property. Distinguished from *verbal aggression* and *relational aggression.* (p. 260)

pituitary gland A gland located at the base of the brain that releases hormones that induce physical growth. (p. 207)

placenta The organ that permits exchange of food and oxygen to reach the developing organism and waste products to be carried away, while also preventing the mother's and embryo's blood from mixing directly. (p. 72)

plasticity Development as open to change in response to influential experiences. (p. 6)

polygenic inheritance A pattern of inheritance in which many genes influence a characteristic. (p. 45)

popular-antisocial children A subgroup of popular children who are admired for their socially adept yet belligerent behavior. Includes "tough" boys—athletically skilled but poor students who cause trouble and defy authority—and relationally aggressive boys and girls who enhance their own status by ignoring, excluding, and spreading rumors about other children. Distinguished from *popular-prosocial children.* (p. 335)

popular children Children who receive many positive votes on self-report measures of peer acceptance, indicating they are well-liked. Distinguished from *rejected, controversial,* and *neglected children.* (p. 334)

popular-prosocial children A subgroup of popular children who combine academic and social competence and are both well-liked and admired. Distinguished from *popular-antisocial children.* (p. 335)

pragmatics The practical, social side of language, concerned with how to engage in effective and appropriate communication. (p. 241)

prefrontal cortex The region of the cerebral cortex, lying in front of areas controlling body movement, that is responsible for thought—in particular, consciousness, inhibition of impulses, integration of information, and memory, reasoning, planning, and problem-solving strategies. (p. 111)

prenatal diagnostic methods Medical procedures that permit detection of developmental problems before birth. (p. 49)

preoperational stage Piaget's second stage of cognitive development, extending from about 2 to 7 years of age, in which children undergo an extraordinary increase in representational, or symbolic, activity, although thought is not yet logical. (p. 215)

preterm infants Infants born several weeks or more before their due date. (p. 91)

private speech Self-directed speech that children use to plan and guide their own behavior. (p. 222)

proactive aggression A type of aggression in which children act to fulfill a need or desire—to obtain an object, privilege, space, or social reward, such as adult or peer attention—and unemotionally attack a person to achieve their goal. Also called instrumental aggression. Distinguished from *reactive aggression.* (p. 260)

problem-centered coping A strategy for managing emotion that involves appraising the situation as changeable, identifying the difficulty, and deciding what to do about it. Distinguished from *emotion-centered coping.* (p. 328)

process praise Praise that emphasizes behavior and effort, such as "You figured it out!" Distinguished from *person praise.* (p. 325)

programmed cell death An aspect of brain growth in which, as synapses form, many surrounding neurons die, making space for these connective structures. (p. 108)

Project Head Start The most extensive U.S. federally funded preschool program, which provides low-SES children with a year or two of preschool education, along with nutritional and health services, and encourages parent involvement in children's learning and development. (p. 235)

prosocial, or altruistic, behavior Actions that benefit another person without any expected reward for the self. (p. 250)

protein-coding genes Genes that directly affect our body's characteristics by sending instructions for making a rich assortment of proteins to the cytoplasm surrounding the cell nucleus. (p. 41)

proximodistal trend An organized pattern of physical growth that proceeds from the center of the body outward ("near to far"). Distinguished from *cephalocaudal trend.* (p. 107)

psychoanalytic perspective An approach to personality development introduced by Freud that assumes children move through a series of stages in which they confront conflicts between biological drives and social expectations. How these conflicts are resolved determines the child's ability to learn, to get along with others, and to cope with anxiety. (p. 9)

psychological control Parental behaviors that intrude on and manipulate children's verbal expressions, individuality, and attachments to parents. (p. 271)

psychosexual theory Freud's theory, which emphasizes that how parents manage children's sexual and aggressive drives in the first few years is crucial for healthy personality development. (p. 9)

psychosocial theory Erikson's theory, which emphasizes that in each Freudian stage, individuals not only develop a unique personality but also acquire attitudes and skills that make them active, contributing members of their society. (p. 10)

public policies Laws and government programs designed to improve current conditions. (p. 59)

punishment In operant conditioning, removal of a desirable stimulus or presentation of an unpleasant one to decrease the occurrence of a response. (p. 121)

R

random assignment An unbiased procedure for assigning participants to treatment conditions in an experiment, such as drawing numbers out of a hat or flipping a coin. Increases the chances that participants' characteristics will be equally distributed across treatment groups. (p. 30)

rapid-eye-movement (REM) sleep An irregular sleep state in which brain-wave activity is similar to that of the waking state. Distinguished from *non-rapid-eye-movement (NREM) sleep.* (p. 96)

reactive aggression An angry, defensive response to provocation or a blocked goal, which is meant to hurt another person. Also called *hostile aggression.* Distinguished from *proactive aggression.* (p. 260)

recall A type of memory that involves remembering something that is not present. Distinguished from *recognition.* (p. 152)

recasts Adult responses that restructure children's grammatically inaccurate speech into correct form. (p. 242)

recognition A type of memory that involves noticing when a stimulus is identical or similar to one previously experienced. Distinguished from *recall.* (p. 152)

recovery Following habituation, an increase in responsiveness to a new stimulus. (p. 121)

recursive thought A form of perspective taking that involves the ability to view a situation from at least two perspectives—that is, to reason simultaneously about what two or more people are thinking. (p. 297)

reflex An inborn, automatic response to a particular form of stimulation. (p. 93)

regulator genes Genes that modify the instructions given by protein-coding genes, greatly complicating their genetic impact. (p. 41)

rehearsal A memory strategy that involves repeating information to oneself. (p. 296)

reinforcer In operant conditioning, a stimulus that increases the occurrence of a response. (p. 121)

rejected-aggressive children A subgroup of rejected children who show high rates of conflict, physical and relational aggression, and hyperactive, inattentive, and impulsive behavior. Distinguished from *rejected-withdrawn children.* (p. 335)

rejected children Children who receive many negative votes on self-report measures of peer acceptance, indicating they are actively disliked. Distinguished from *popular, controversial,* and *neglected children.* (p. 334)

rejected-withdrawn children A subgroup of rejected children who are passive and socially awkward. Distinguished from *rejected-aggressive children.* (p. 335)

relational aggression A form of aggression that damages another's peer relationships through social exclusion, malicious gossip, or friendship manipulation. Distinguished from *physical aggression* and *verbal aggression.* (p. 260)

resilience The ability to adapt effectively in the face of threats to development. (p. 7)

reticular formation A structure in the brain stem that maintains alertness and consciousness. (p. 206)

reversibility The capacity to think through a series of steps in a problem and then mentally reverse direction, returning to the starting point. Distinguished from *irreversibility.* (p. 290)

Rh factor incompatibility A condition that arises when the Rh protein is present in the fetus's blood but not in the mother's, causing the mother to build up antibodies. If these enter the fetus's system, they destroy red blood cells, reducing the oxygen supply to organs and tissues. Intellectual disability, miscarriage, heart damage, and infant death can occur. (p. 84)

rough-and-tumble play A form of peer interaction involving friendly chasing and play-fighting that emerges in the preschool years and peaks in middle childhood. In our evolutionary past, it may have been important for developing fighting skill. (p. 288)

S

scaffolding Adjusting the support offered during a teaching session to fit the child's current level of performance. As competence increases, effective scaffolders gradually and sensitively withdraw support, turning over responsibility to the learner. (p. 223)

scale errors Toddlers' attempts to do things that their body size makes impossible, such as trying to put on dolls' clothes, sit in a doll-sized chair, or walk through a door too narrow to pass through. (p. 195)

schemes In Piaget's theory, specific psychological structures, or organized ways of making sense of experience, that change with age. (p. 139)

scripts General descriptions of what occurs and when it occurs in a particular situation, used to organize and interpret routine experiences. (p. 228)

secure attachment The attachment pattern characterizing infants who use the parent as a secure base from which to explore, may be distressed by separation from the parent, but convey clear pleasure and are easily comforted when the parent returns. Distinguished from *insecure–avoidant, insecure–resistant,* and *disorganized/disoriented attachment.* (p. 186)

secure base The familiar caregiver as a point from which the baby explores, venturing into the environment and then returning for emotional support. (p. 176)

self-care children Children who regularly look after themselves for some period of time after school. (p. 347)

self-concept The set of attributes, abilities, attitudes, and values that an individual believes defines who he or she is. (p. 247)

self-conscious emotions Emotions involving injury to or enhancement of the sense of self, including guilt, shame, embarrassment, envy, and pride. (p. 176)

self-esteem An aspect of self-concept that involves judgments about one's own worth and the feelings associated with those judgments. (p. 247)

self-recognition Identification of the self as a physically unique being. (p. 195)

semantic memory Memory for information removed from the context in which it was first learned that has become part of an individual's general knowledge base. Distinguished from *episodic memory.* (p. 228)

sensitive caregiving Caregiving that involves responding promptly, consistently, and appropriately to infants and holding them tenderly and carefully. (p. 188)

sensitive period A time that is biologically optimal for certain capacities to emerge because the individual is especially responsive to environmental influences. Development can occur later, but it is harder to induce. (p. 17)

sensorimotor stage Piaget's first stage, spanning the first two years of life, during which infants and toddlers "think" with their eyes, ears, hands, and other sensorimotor equipment. (p. 139)

sensory register The part of the information-processing system in which sights and sounds are represented directly and stored briefly. (p. 149)

separation anxiety An infant's distressed reaction to the departure of the trusted caregiver. (p. 185)

seriation The ability to order items along a quantitative dimension, such as length or weight. (p. 290)

sequential designs Developmental designs in which investigators conduct several similar cross-sectional or longitudinal studies (called *sequences*) at varying times, sometimes combining longitudinal and cross-sectional strategies. (p. 33)

sex chromosomes The twenty-third pair of chromosomes, which determines the sex of the individual. In females, it is called *XX;* in males, *XY.* (p. 42)

short-term memory store The part of the mind in which attended-to information is retained briefly so we can actively "work on" it to reach our goals. (p. 150)

slow-to-warm-up child A child whose temperament is characterized by inactivity; mild, low-key reactions to environmental stimuli; negative mood; and slow adjustment to new experiences. Distinguished from *easy child* and *difficult child.* (p. 179)

small-for-date infants Infants whose birth weight is below their expected weight considering length of the pregnancy. Some are full-term; others are preterm infants who are especially underweight. (p. 91)

social comparisons Judgments of one's own appearance, abilities, and behavior in relation to those of others. (p. 322)

social-constructivist classroom A classroom grounded in Vygotsky's sociocultural theory, in which children participate in a wide range of challenging activities with teachers and peers, with whom they jointly construct understandings. Distinguished from *traditional* and *constructivist classrooms.* (p. 312)

social conventions Customs determined solely by consensus within a society, such as table manners and politeness rituals. Distinguished from *moral imperatives* and *matters of personal choice.* (p. 259)

social learning theory An approach that emphasizes *modeling,* also known as *imitation* or *observational learning,* as a powerful source of development. (p. 12)

social referencing Actively seeking emotional information from a trusted person in an uncertain situation. (p. 176)

social smile The infant's broad grin, evoked by the parent's communication, that first appears between 6 and 10 weeks of age. (p. 174)

sociocultural theory Vygotsky's theory, in which children acquire the ways of thinking and behaving that make up their community's culture through *social interaction*—in particular, cooperative dialogues with more knowledgeable members of society. (p. 18)

sociodramatic play The make-believe with others that is under way by the end of the second year and increases rapidly in complexity during early childhood. (p. 216)

socioeconomic status (SES) A measure of an individual's or a family's social position and economic well-being that combines three related, but not completely overlapping, variables: years of education, the prestige of one's job and the skill it requires, and income. (p. 54)

stages Qualitative changes in thinking, feeling, and behaving that characterize specific periods of development. (p. 5)

standardization The practice of giving a newly constructed test to a large, representative sample and using the results as the standard for interpreting individual scores. (p. 158)

states of arousal Different degrees of sleep and wakefulness. (p. 95)

statistical learning capacity Infants' capacity to analyze the speech stream for patterns—repeatedly occurring sequences of sounds—through which they acquire a stock of speech structures for which they will later learn meanings. (p. 128)

stereotype threat The fear of being judged on the basis of a negative stereotype, which can trigger anxiety that interferes with performance. (p. 306)

stranger anxiety The infant's expression of fear in response to unfamiliar adults, which appears in many infants in the second half of the first year. (p. 174)

Strange Situation A laboratory procedure used to assess the quality of attachment between 1 and 2 years of age by observing the baby's response to eight short episodes involving brief separations from and reunions with the caregiver in an unfamiliar playroom. (p. 186)

structured interview An interview method in which the researcher asks each participant the same set of questions in the same way. Distinguished from *clinical interview.* (p. 26)

structured observation A research method in which the investigator sets up a laboratory situation that evokes the behavior of interest so that every participant has equal opportunity to display the response. Distinguished from *naturalistic observation.* (p. 25)

subcultures Groups of people with beliefs and customs that differ from those of the larger culture. (p. 58)

sudden infant death syndrome (SIDS) The unexpected death, usually during the night, of an infant younger than 1 year of age that remains unexplained after thorough investigation. (p. 97)

sympathy Feelings of concern or sorrow for another's plight. (p. 250)

synapses The gaps between neurons, across which chemical messages are sent. (p. 108)

synaptic pruning A process in which neurons that are seldom stimulated lose their synapses and are returned to an uncommitted state so they can support future development. (p. 108)

T

talent Outstanding performance in a specific field. (p. 315)

telegraphic speech Toddlers' two-word utterances that, like a telegram, focus on high-content words while omitting smaller, less important words. (p. 165)

temperament Early-appearing, stable individual differences in reactivity (quickness and intensity of emotional arousal, attention, and motor activity) and self-regulation (strategies that modify that reactivity). (p. 178)

teratogen Any environmental agent that causes damage during the prenatal period. (p. 76)

theory An orderly, integrated set of statements that describes, explains, and predicts behavior. (p. 4)

theory of multiple intelligences Gardner's theory, which identifies at least eight independent intelligences—linguistic, logico-mathematical, musical, spatial, bodily-kinesthetic, naturalist, interpersonal, and intrapersonal—defined in terms of distinct sets of processing operations that permit individuals to engage in a wide range of culturally valued activities. (p. 302)

thyroid-stimulating hormone (TSH) A pituitary hormone that prompts the thyroid gland to release *thyroxine,* which is necessary for brain development and for growth hormone to have its full impact on body size. (p. 207)

time out A form of mild punishment that involves removing children from the immediate setting until they are ready to act appropriately. (p. 257)

traditional classroom A classroom in which the teacher is the sole authority for knowledge, rules, and decision making and students are relatively passive learners whose progress is evaluated by how well they keep pace with a uniform set of standards for their grade. Distinguished from *constructivist* and *social-constructivist classrooms.* (p. 311)

transitive inference The ability to seriate, or order items along a quantitative dimension, mentally. (p. 290)

triarchic theory of successful intelligence Sternberg's theory, in which intelligent behavior involves balancing three broad, interacting intelligences—analytical, creative, and practical—to achieve success in life according to one's personal goals and the requirements of one's cultural community. (p. 301)

trimesters Three equal time periods, each lasting three months, into which prenatal development is sometimes divided. (p. 74)

U

umbilical cord The long cord connecting the developing organism to the placenta that delivers nutrients and removes waste products. (p. 72)

unconditioned response (UCR) In classical conditioning, a reflexive response that is consistently produced by an unconditioned stimulus (UCS). Distinguished from *conditioned response.* (p. 120)

unconditioned stimulus (UCS) In classical conditioning, a stimulus that consistently produces a reflexive response. Distinguished from *conditioned stimulus.* (p. 120)

underextension An early vocabulary error in which young children apply a word too narrowly, to a smaller number of objects and events than is appropriate. Distinguished from *overextension.* (p. 165)

uninhibited, or sociable, children Children whose temperament is such that they display positive emotion to and approach novel stimuli. Distinguished from *inhibited,* or *shy, children.* (p. 180)

uninvolved child-rearing style A child-rearing style that combines low acceptance and involvement with little control and general indifference to issues of autonomy. Distinguished from *authoritative, authoritarian,* and *permissive child-rearing styles.* (p. 272)

V

verbal aggression A type of aggression that harms others through threats of physical aggression, name-calling, or hostile teasing. Distinguished from *physical aggression* and *relational aggression.* (p. 260)

vernix A white, cheeselike substance that covers the fetus, preventing the skin from chapping due to constant exposure to amniotic fluid. (p. 74)

video deficit effect In toddlers, poorer performance on tasks after watching a video than after seeing a live demonstration. (p. 146)

violation-of-expectation method A method in which researchers show babies an expected event (one that is consistent with reality) and an unexpected event (a variation of the first event that violates reality). Heightened attention to the unexpected event suggests that the infant is "surprised" by a deviation from physical reality and, therefore, is aware of that aspect of the physical world. (p. 142)

visual acuity Fineness of visual discrimination. (p. 101)

W

working memory The number of items that can be briefly held in mind while also engaging in some effort to monitor or manipulate those items—a "mental workspace" that we use to accomplish many activities in daily life. A contemporary view of the short-term memory store. (p. 150)

X

X-linked inheritance A pattern of inheritance in which a harmful allele is carried on the X chromosome, so that males are more likely than females to be affected. (p. 44)

Z

zone of proximal development In Vygotsky's theory, a range of tasks too difficult for a child to handle alone but possible with the help of more skilled partners. (p. 155)

zygote The newly fertilized cell formed by the union of sperm and ovum at conception. (p. 41)

REFERENCES

A

Aber, L., Brown, J. L., Jones, S. M., Berg, J., & Torrente, C. (2011). School-based strategies to prevent violence, trauma, and psychopathology: The challenges of going to scale. *Development and Psychopathology, 23,* 411–421.

Aboud, F. E. (2008). A social-cognitive developmental theory of prejudice. In S. M. Quintana & C. McKown (Eds.), *Handbook of race, racism, and the developing child* (pp. 55–71). Hoboken, NJ: Wiley.

Aboud, F. E., & Brown, C. S. (2013). Positive and negative intergroup contact among children and its effect on attitudes. In G. Hodson & M. Hewstone (Eds.), *Advances in intergroup contact* (pp. 176–199). New York: Psychology Press.

Aboud, F. E., & Doyle, A. (1996). Parental and peer influences on children's racial attitudes. *International Journal of Intercultural Relations, 20,* 371–383.

Achenbach, T. M., Howell, C. T., & Aoki, M. F. (1993). Nine-year outcome of the Vermont Intervention Program for low birth weight infants, *Pediatrics, 91,* 45–55.

Acker, M. M., & O'Leary, S. G. (1996). Inconsistency of mothers' feedback and toddlers' misbehavior and negative affect. *Journal of Abnormal Child Psychology, 24,* 703–714.

Ackerman, J. P., Riggins, T., & Black, M. M. (2010). A review of the effects of prenatal cocaine exposure among school-aged children. *Pediatrics, 125,* 554–565.

Addati, L., Cassirer, N., & Gilchrist, K. (2014). *Maternity and paternity at work: Law and practice across the world.* Geneva, Switzerland: International Labour Organization.

Adelson, S. L. (2012). Practice parameter on gay, lesbian, or bisexual sexual orientation, gender nonconformity, and gender discordance in children and adolescents. *Journal of the American Academy of Child and Adolescent Psychiatry, 51,* 957–974.

Adelstein, S. J. (2014). Radiation risk. In S. T. Treves (Ed.), *Pediatric nuclear medicine and molecular imaging* (pp. 675–682). New York: Springer Science + Business.

Adolph, K. E., Cole, W. G., Komati, M., Garciaguirre, J. S., Badaly, D., Lingeman, J. M., et al. (2012). How do you learn to walk? Thousands of steps and hundreds of falls per day. *Psychological Science, 23,* 1387–1394.

Adolph, K. E., Karasik, L. B., & Tamis-LeMonda, C. S. (2010). Motor skill. In M. H. Bornstein (Ed.), *Handbook of cultural developmental science* (pp. 61–88). New York: Psychology Press.

Adolph, K. E., & Kretch, K. S. (2012). Infants on the edge: Beyond the visual cliff. In A. Slater & P. Quinn (Eds.), *Developmental psychology: Revisiting the classic studies* (pp. 36–55). London: Sage.

Adolph, K. E., Kretch, K. S., & LoBue, V. (2014). Fear of heights in infants? *Current Directions in Psychological Science, 23,* 60–66.

Adolph, K. E., & Robinson, S. R. (2013). The road to walking: What learning to walk tells us about development. In P. Zelazo (Ed.), *Oxford handbook of developmental psychology* (pp. 403–443). New York: Oxford University Press.

Adolph, K. E., & Robinson, S. R. (2015). Perceptual development. In L. S. Liben & U. Müller (Eds.), *Handbook of child psychology and developmental science: Vol. 2. Cognitive processes* (7th ed., pp. 113–157). Hoboken, NJ: Wiley.

Adolph, K. E., Tamis-LeMonda, C. S., Ishak, S., Karasik, L. B., & Lobo, S. A. (2008). Locomotor experience and use of social information are posture specific. *Developmental Psychology, 44,* 1705–1714.

Adolphs, R. (2010). What does the amygdala contribute to social cognition? *Annals of the New York Academy of Sciences, 119,* 42–61.

Afifi, T. O., Mota, M., MacMillan, H. L., & Sareen, J. (2013). Harsh physical punishment in childhood and adult physical health. *Pediatrics, 132,* e333–e340.

Agronick, G., Stueve, A., Vargo, S., & O'Donnell, L. (2007). New York City young adults' psychological reactions to 9/11: Findings from the Reach for Health longitudinal study. *American Journal of Community Psychology, 39,* 79–90.

Aguiar, A., & Baillargeon, R. (2002). Developments in young infants' reasoning about occluded objects. *Cognitive Psychology, 45,* 267–336.

Ahmadlou, M., Gharib, M., Hemmti, S., Vameghi, R., & Sajedi, F. (2013). Disrupted small-world brain network in children with Down syndrome. *Clinical Neurophysiology, 124,* 1755–1764.

Ainsworth, C. (2015). Sex redefined. *Nature, 518,* 288–291.

Ainsworth, M. D. S., Blehar, M. C., Waters, E., & Wall, S. (1978). *Patterns of attachment.* Hillsdale, NJ: Erlbaum.

Aitken, Z., Garrett, C. C., Hewitt, B., Keogh, L., Hocking, J. S., & Kavanagh, A. M. (2015). The maternal health outcomes of paid maternity leave: A systematic review. *Social Science and Medicine, 130,* 32–41.

Akolekar, R., Beta, J., Picciarelli, G., Ogilive, C., & D'Antonio, F. (2015). Procedure-related risk of miscarriage following amniocentesis and chorionic villus sampling: A systematic review and meta-analysis. *Ultrasound in Obstetrics and Gynecology, 45,* 16–26.

Akutagava-Martins, G. C., Salatino-Oliveira, A., Kieling, C. C., Rohde, L. A., & Hutz, M. H. (2013). Genetics of attention-deficit/hyperactivity disorder: Current findings and future directions. *Expert Review of Neurotherapeutics, 13,* 435–445.

Alarcón-Rubio, D., Sánchez-Medina, J. A., & Prieto-Garcia, J. R. (2014). Executive function and verbal self-regulation in childhood: Developmental linkages between partially internalized private speech and cognitive flexibility. *Early Childhood Research Quarterly, 29,* 95–105.

Alati, R., Smith, G. D., Lewis, S. J., Sayal, K., Draper, E. S., Golding, J., et al. (2013). Effect of prenatal alcohol exposure on childhood academic outcomes: Contrasting maternal and paternal associations in the ALSPAC Study. *PLOS ONE, 8*(10), e74844.

Albers, C. A., & Grieve, A. J. (2007). Test review: Bayley, N. (2006). Bayley Scales of Infant and Toddler Development–Third Edition. San Antonio, TX: Harcourt Assessment. *Journal of Psychoeducational Assessment, 25,* 180–190.

Alessandri, S. M., Sullivan, M. W., & Lewis, M. (1990). Violation of expectancy and frustration in early infancy. *Developmental Psychology, 26,* 738–744.

Alexander, J. M., Fabricius, W. V., Fleming, V. M., Zwahr, M., & Brown, S. A. (2003). The development of metacognitive causal explanations. *Learning and Individual Differences, 13,* 227–238.

Alfirevic, Z., Devane, D., & Gyte, G. M. L. (2013). Continuous cardiotocography (CTG) as a form of electronic fetal monitoring (EFM) for fetal assessment during labour. *Cochrane Database of Systematic Reviews,* Issue 5, Art. No.: CD006066.

Alink, L. R. A., Mesman, J., van Zeijl, J., Stolk, M. N., Juffer, F., & Koot, H. M. (2006). The early childhood aggression curve: Development of physical aggression in 10- to 50-month-old children. *Child Development, 77,* 954–966.

Aljughaiman, A. M., & Ayoub, A. E. A. (2012). The effect of an enrichment program on developing analytical, creative, and practical abilities of elementary gifted students. *Journal for the Education of the Gifted, 35,* 153–174.

Allely, C. S., Gillberg, C., & Wilson, P. (2014). Neurobiological abnormalities in the first few years of life in individuals later diagnosed with autism spectrum disorder: A review of recent data. *Behavioural Neurology.* Retrieved from www.hindawi.com/journals/bn/2014/210780

Alloway, T. P., Bibile, V., & Lau, G. (2013). Computerized working memory training: Can it lead to gains in cognitive skills in students? *Computers in Human Behavior, 29,* 632–638.

Alloway, T. P., Gathercole, S. E., Kirkwood, H., & Elliott, J. (2009). The cognitive and behavioral characteristics of children with low working memory. *Child Development, 80,* 606–621.

Almas, A. N., Degnan, K. A., Nelson, C. A., & Zeanah, C. H. (2016). IQ at age 12 following a history of institutional care: Findings from the Bucharest Early Intervention Project. *Developmental Psychology, 52,* 1858–1866.

Alm, B., Wennergren, G., Mölborg, P., & Lagercrantz, H. (2016). Breastfeeding and dummy use have a protective effect on sudden infant death syndrome. *Acta Paediatrica, 105*, 31–38.

Althaus, N., & Plunkett, K. (2016). Categorization in infancy: Labeling induces a persisting focus on commonalities. *Developmental Science, 19,* 770–780.

Altvater-Mackensen, N., Jessen, S., & Grossmann, T. (2017). Brain responses reveal that infants' face discrimination is guided by statistical learning from distributional information. *Developmental Science, 20*: 12393.

Amato, P. R. (2010). Research on divorce: Continuing trends and new developments. *Journal of Marriage and Family, 72,* 650–666.

Amato, P. R., & Fowler, F. (2002). Parenting practices, child adjustment, and family diversity. *Journal of Marriage and the Family, 64,* 703–716.

Amato, P. R., & Sobolewski, J. M. (2004). The effects of divorce on fathers and children: Nonresidential fathers and stepfathers. In M. E. Lamb (Ed.), *The role of the father in child development* (4th ed., pp. 341–367). Hoboken, NJ: Wiley.

American Academy of Pediatrics. (2012). Breastfeeding and the use of human milk. *Pediatrics, 129,* e827–e841.

American Academy of Pediatrics. (2016a). Media and young minds. *Pediatrics, 138,* e20162591.

American Academy of Pediatrics. (2016b). SIDS and other sleep-related infant deaths: Updated 2016 recommendations for a safe infant sleeping environment. *Pediatrics, 138,* e20162938.

American Psychiatric Association. (2013). *Diagnostic and statistical manual of mental disorders* (5th ed.). Arlington, VA: Author.

American Psychological Association. (2017). *Ethical principles of psychologists and code of conduct.* Retrieved from www.apa.org/ethics/code

Anand, V., Downs, S. M., Bauer, N. S., & Carroll, A. E. (2014). Prevalence of infant television viewing and maternal depression symptoms. *Journal of Developmental and Behavioral Pediatrics, 35,* 216–224.

Ananth, C. V., Chauhan, S. P., Chen, H.-Y., & D'Alton, M. E. (2013). Electronic fetal monitoring in the United States: Temporal trends and adverse perinatal outcomes. *Obstetrics and Gynecology, 121,* 927–933.

Ananth, C. V., Friedman, A. M., & Gyamfi-Bannerman, C. (2013). Epidemiology of moderate preterm, late preterm and early term delivery. *Clinics in Perinatology, 40,* 601–610.

Anderson, C. A., Bushman, B. J., Donnerstein, E. I., Hummer, T. A., & Warburton, W. (2015). SPSSI research summary on media violence. *Analyses of Social Issues and Public Policy, 15,* 4–19.

Anderson, C. M. (2012). The diversity, strengths, and challenges of single-parent households. In F. Walsh (Ed.), *Normal family processes: Growing diversity and complexity* (4th ed., pp. 128–148). New York: Guilford.

Anderson, D. M., Huston, A. C., Schmitt, K. L., Linebarger, D. L., & Wright, J. C. (2001). Early childhood television viewing and adolescent behavior. *Monographs of the Society for Research in Child Development, 66*(1, Serial No. 264).

Anderson, E. (2000). Exploring register knowledge: The value of "controlled improvisation." In L. Menn & N. B. Ratner (Eds.), *Methods for studying language production* (pp. 225–248). Mahwah, NJ: Erlbaum.

Anderson, S., & Leventhal, T. (2014). Exposure to neighborhood affluence and poverty in childhood and adolescence and academic achievement and behavior. *Applied Developmental Science, 18,* 123–138.

Anderson, V., & Beauchamp, M. H. (2013). A theoretical model of developmental social neuroscience. In V. Anderson & M. H. Beauchamp (Eds.), *Developmental social neuroscience and childhood brain insult: Theory and practice* (pp. 3–20). New York: Guilford.

Andrews, G., & Halford, G. S. (2002). A cognitive complexity metric applied to cognitive development. *Cognitive Psychology, 45,* 475–506.

Andrews, G., & Halford, G. S. (2011). Recent advances in relational complexity theory and its application to cognitive development. In P. Barrouillet & V. Gaillard (Eds.), *Cognitive development and working memory: A dialogue between neo-Piagetian and cognitive approaches* (pp. 47–68). Hove, UK: Psychology Press.

Ang, S., Rodgers, J. L., & Wänström, L. (2010). The Flynn effect within subgroups in the U.S.: Gender, race, income, education, and urbanization differences in the NLSY-Children data. *Intelligence, 38,* 367–384.

Anisfeld, M. (2005). No compelling evidence to dispute Piaget's timetable of the development of representational imitation in infancy. In S. Hurley & N. Chater (Eds.), *Perspectives on imitation: From neuroscience to social science: Vol. 2. Imitation, human development, and culture* (pp. 107–131). Cambridge, MA: MIT Press.

Antshel, K. M., Hier, B. O., & Barkley, R. A. (2015). Executive functioning theory and ADHD. In S. Goldstein & J. A. Naglieri (Eds.), *Handbook of executive functioning* (pp. 107–120). New York: Springer Science + Business Media.

Anzures, G., Quinn, P. C., Pascalis, O., Slater, A. M., Tanaka, J. W., & Lee, K. (2013). Developmental origins of the other-race effect. *Current Directions in Psychological Science, 22,* 173–178.

Apgar, V. (1953). A proposal for a new method of evaluation in the newborn infant. *Current Research in Anesthesia and Analgesia, 32,* 260–267.

Arcus, D., & Chambers, P. (2008). Childhood risks associated with adoption. In T. P. Gullotta & G. M. Blau (Eds.), *Family influences on childhood behavior and development* (pp. 117–142). New York: Routledge.

Ardila-Rey, A., & Killen, M. (2001). Middle-class Colombian children's evaluations of personal, moral, and social-conventional interactions in the classroom. *International Journal of Behavioral Development, 25,* 246–255.

Arija, V., Esparó, G., Fernández-Ballart, J., Murphy, M. M., Biarnés, E., & Canals, J. (2006). Nutritional status and performance in test of verbal and non-verbal intelligence in 6 year old children. *Intelligence, 34,* 141–149.

Armstrong, K. L., Quinn, R. A., & Dadds, M. R. (1994). The sleep patterns of normal children. *Medical Journal of Australia, 161,* 202–206.

Arnold, A. P. (2009). The organizational–activational hypothesis as the foundation for a unified theory of sexual differentiation of all mammalian tissues. *Hormones and Behavior, 55,* 570–578.

Arnold, D. H., McWilliams, L., & Harvey-Arnold, E. (1998). Teacher discipline and child misbehavior in daycare: Untangling causality with correlational data. *Developmental Psychology, 34,* 276–287.

Arnon, S., Shapsa, A., Forman, L., Regev, R., Bauer, S., & Litmanovitz, I. (2006). Live music is beneficial to preterm infants in the neonatal intensive care unit. *Birth, 33,* 131–136.

Artman, L., & Cahan, S. (1993). Schooling and the development of transitive inference. *Developmental Psychology, 29,* 753–759.

Asher, S. R., & Rose, A. J. (1997). Promoting children's social-emotional adjustment with peers. In P. Salovey & D. J. Sluyter (Eds.), *Emotional development and emotional intelligence* (pp. 193–195). New York: Basic Books.

Askeland, K. G., Hysing, M., La Greca, A. M., Aarø, L. E., Tell, G. S., & Siverstsen, B. (2017). Mental health in internationally adopted adolescents: A meta-analysis. *Psychiatry, 56,* 203–213.

Aslin, R. N., Jusczyk, P. W., & Pisoni, D. B. (1998). Speech and auditory processing during infancy: Constraints on and precursors to language. In D. Kuhn & R. S. Siegler (Eds.), *Handbook of child psychology: Vol. 2. Cognition, perception, and language* (5th ed., pp. 147–198). New York: Wiley.

Aslin, R. N., & Newport, E. L. (2012). Statistical learning: From acquiring specific items to forming general rules. *Psychological Science, 21,* 170–176.

Astington, J. W., & Hughes, C. (2013). Theory of mind: Self-reflection and social understanding. In S. M. Carlson, P. D. Zelazo, & S. Faja (Eds.), *Oxford handbook of developmental psychology: Vol. 2. Self and other* (pp. 398–424). New York: Oxford University Press.

Au, T. K., Sidle, A. L., & Rollins, K. B. (1993). Developing an intuitive understanding of conservation and contamination: Invisible particles as a plausible mechanism. *Developmental Psychology, 29,* 286–299.

Aunola, K., Stattin, H., & Nurmi, J.-E. (2000). Parenting styles and adolescents' achievement strategies. *Journal of Adolescence, 23,* 205–222.

Averhart, C. J., & Bigler, R. S. (1997). Shades of meaning: Skin tone, racial attitudes, and constructive memory in African-American children. *Journal of Experimental Child Psychology, 67,* 368–388.

Axelin, A., Salanterä, S., & Lehtonen, L. (2006). "Facilitated tucking by parents" in pain management of preterm infants—A randomized crossover trial. *Early Human Development*, 82, 241–247.

B

Bacallao, M. L., & Smokowski, P. R. (2007). The costs of getting ahead: Mexican family system changes after immigration. *Family Relations, 56,* 52–66.

Baddeley, J., & Singer, J. A. (2015). Charting the life story's path: Narrative identity across the life span. In J. D. Clandinin (Ed.), *Handbook of narrative inquiry: Mapping a methodology* (pp. 177–202). Thousand Oaks, CA: Sage.

Badiee, Z., Asghari, M., & Mohammadizadeh, M. (2013). The calming effect of maternal breast milk odor on premature infants. *Pediatrics and Neonatology, 54,* 322–325.

Baer, J. (2002). Is family cohesion a risk or protective factor during adolescent development? *Journal of Marriage and Family, 64,* 668–675.

Bahrick, L. E. (2010). Intermodal perception and selective attention to intersensory redundancy: Implications for typical social development and autism. In G. Bremner & T. D. Wachs (Eds.), *Wiley-Blackwell handbook of infant development: Vol. 1. Basic research* (2nd ed., pp. 120–166). Oxford, UK: Wiley-Blackwell.

Bahrick, L. E., Hernandez-Reif, M., & Flom, R. (2005). The development of infant learning about specific face–voice relations. *Developmental Psychology, 41,* 541–552.

Bahrick, L. E., Hernandez-Reif, M., & Pickens, J. N. (1997). The effect of retrieval cues on visual preferences and memory in infancy: Evidence for a four-phase attention function. *Journal of Experimental Child Psychology, 67,* 1–20.

Bahrick, L. E., & Lickliter, R. (2012). The role of intersensory redundancy in early perceptual, cognitive, and social development. In A. J. Bremner, D. J. Lewkowicz, & C. Spence (Eds.), *Multisensory development* (pp. 183–206). Oxford, UK: Oxford University Press.

Baillargeon, R., & DeVos, J. (1991). Object permanence in young infants: Further evidence. *Child Development, 62,* 1227–1246.

Baillargeon, R., Li, J., Gertner, Y., & Wu, D. (2011). How do infants reason about physical events? In U. Goswami (Ed.), *Wiley-Blackwell handbook of childhood cognitive development* (2nd ed., pp. 11–48). Chichester, UK: Wiley-Blackwell.

Baillargeon, R., Li, J., Ng, W., & Yuan, S. (2009). An account of infants' physical reasoning. In A. Woodward & A. Needham (Eds.), *Learning and the infant mind* (pp. 66–116). New York: Oxford University Press.

Baillargeon, R. H., Zoccolillo, M., Keenan, K., Côté, S., Pérusse, D., Wu, H.-X., & Boivin, M. (2007). Gender differences in physical aggression: A prospective population-based survey of children before and after 2 years of age. *Developmental Psychology, 43,* 13–26.

Bakermans-Kranenburg, M. J., Steele, H., Zeanah, C. H., Muhamedrahimov, R. J., Vorria, P., & Dobrova-Krol, N. A. (2011). Attachment and emotional development in institutional care: Characteristics and catch up. In R. B. McCall, M. H. van IJzendoorn, F. Juffer, C. J. Groark, & V. K. Groza (Eds.), Children without permanent parents: Research, practice, and policy. *Monographs of the Society for Research in Child Development, 76*(4, Serial No. 301), 62–91.

Bakermans-Kranenburg, M. J., & van IJzendoorn, M. H. (2015). The hidden efficacy of interventions: Gene × environment experiments from a differential susceptibility perspective. *Annual Review of Psychology, 66,* 381–409.

Bakermans-Kranenburg, M. J., van IJzendoorn, M. H., Mesman, J., Alink, L. R. A., & Juffer, F. (2008a). Effects of an attachment-based intervention on daily cortisol moderated by dopamine receptor D4: A randomized control trial on 1- to 3-year-olds screened for externalizing behavior. *Development and Psychopathology, 20,* 805–820.

Bakermans-Kranenburg, M. J., van IJzendoorn, M. H., Pijlman, F. T. A., Mesman, J., & Juffer, F. (2008b). Experimental evidence for differential sensitivity: Dopamine D4 receptor polymorphism (DRD4 VNTR) moderates intervention effects on toddlers' externalizing behavior in a randomized control trial. *Developmental Psychology, 44,* 293–300.

Ball, H. L., & Volpe, L. E. (2013). Sudden infant death syndrome (SIDS) risk reduction and infant sleep location—moving the discussion forward. *Social Science and Medicine, 79,* 84–91.

Baltes, P. B., Lindenberger, U., & Staudinger, U. M. (2006). Life span theory in developmental psychology. In R. M. Lerner (Ed.), *Handbook of child psychology: Vol. 1. Theoretical models of human development* (6th ed., pp. 569–664). Hoboken, NJ: Wiley.

Bamford, C., & Lagattuta, K. H. (2012). Looking on the bright side: Children's knowledge about the benefits of positive versus negative thinking. *Child Development, 83,* 667–682.

Bandstra, E. S., Morrow, C. E., Accornero, V. H., Mansoor, E., Xue, L., & Anthony, J. C. (2011). Estimated effects of in utero cocaine exposure on language development through early adolescence. *Neurotoxicology and Teratology, 33,* 25–35.

Bandstra, E. S., Morrow, C. E., Mansoor, E., & Accornero, V. H. (2010). Prenatal drug exposure: Infant and toddler outcomes. *Journal of Addictive Diseases, 29,* 245–258.

Bandura, A. (1992). Perceived self-efficacy in cognitive development and functioning. *Educational Psychologist, 28,* 117–148.

Bandura, A. (2001). Social cognitive theory: An agentic perspective. *Annual Review of Psychology, 52,* 1–26.

Bandura, A. (2011). Social cognitive theory. In P. A. M. Van Lange, A. W. Kruglanski, & E. T. Higgins (Eds.), *Handbook of theories of social psychology* (Vol. 1, pp. 349–373). Thousand Oaks, CA: Sage.

Bandura, A. (2016). The power of observational learning through social modeling. In R. J. Sternberg, S. T. Fiske, & D. J. Foss (Eds.), *Scientists making a difference: One hundred eminent behavioral and brain scientists talk about their most important contributions* (pp. 235–239). New York: Cambridge University Press.

Banish, M. T., & Heller, W. (1998). Evolving perspectives on lateralization of function. *Current Directions in Psychological Science, 7,* 1–2.

Banks, M. S. (1980). The development of visual accommodation during early infancy. *Child Development, 51,* 646–666.

Bannard, C., Lieven, E., & Tomasello, M. (2009). Modeling children's early grammatical knowledge. *Proceedings of the National Academy of Sciences, 106,* 17284–17289.

Banse, R., Gawronski, B., Rebetez, C., Gutt, H., & Morton, J. B. (2010). The development of spontaneous gender stereotyping in childhood: Relations to stereotype knowledge and stereotype flexibility. *Developmental Science, 13,* 298–306.

Barber, B. K., & Olsen, J. A. (1997). Socialization in context: Connection, regulation, and autonomy in the family, school, and neighborhood, and with peers. *Journal of Adolescent Research, 12,* 287–315.

Barber, B. K., Stolz, H. E., & Olsen, J. A. (2005). Parental support, psychological control, and behavioral control: Assessing relevance across time, culture, and method. *Monographs of the Society for Research in Child Development, 70*(4, Serial No. 282).

Barber, B. K., & Xia, M. (2013). The centrality of control to parenting and its effects. In R. E. Larzelere, A. S. Morris, & A. W. Harrist (Eds.), *Authoritative parenting: Synthesizing nurturance and discipline for optimal child development* (pp. 61–88). Washington, DC: American Psychological Association.

Barbu-Roth, M., Anderson, D. I., Streeter, R. J., Combrouze, M., Park, J., Schultz, B., et al. (2015). Why does infant stepping disappear and can it be stimulated by optic flow? *Child Development, 86,* 441–455.

Bard, K. A., Todd, B. K., Bernier, C., Love, J., & Leavens, D. A. (2006). Self-awareness in human and chimpanzee infants: What is measured and what is meant by the mark and mirror test? *Infancy, 9,* 191–219.

Barnes, J., Katz, I., Korbin, J. E., & O'Brien, M. (2007). *Children and families in communities: Theory, research, policy and practice*. Hoboken, NJ: Wiley.

Barnett, W. S. (2011). Effectiveness of early educational intervention. *Science, 333,* 975–978.

Barnett, W. S., & Friedman-Krauss, A. H. (2016). *State(s) of Head Start.* New Brunswick, NJ: National Institute for Early Education Research (NIEER), Rutgers University. Retrieved from nieer.org/wp-content/uploads/2016/12/HS_Full_Reduced.pdf

Baron-Cohen, S. (2011). What is theory of mind, and is it impaired in ASC? In S. Bolte & J. Hallmayer (Eds.), *Autism spectrum conditions: FAQs on autism, Asperger syndrome, and atypical autism answered by international experts* (pp. 136–138). Cambridge, MA: Hogrefe Publishing.

Baron-Cohen, S., & Belmonte, M. K. (2005). Autism: A window onto the development of the social and the analytic brain. *Annual Review of Neuroscience, 28,* 109–126.

Baron-Cohen, S., Tager-Flusberg, H., & Lombardo, M. V. (Eds.). (2013). *Understanding other minds: Perspectives from developmental social neuroscience*. New York: Oxford University Press.

Barr, H. M., Streissguth, A. P., Darby, B. L., & Sampson, P. D. (1990). Prenatal exposure to alcohol, caffeine, tobacco, and aspirin: Effects on fine and gross motor performance in 4-year-old children. *Developmental Psychology, 26,* 339–348.

Barr, R., Marrott, H., & Rovee-Collier, C. (2003). The role of sensory preconditioning in memory retrieval by preverbal infants. *Learning and Behavior, 31,* 111–123.

Barr, R., Muentener, P., & Garcia, A. (2007). Age-related changes in deferred imitation from television by 6- to 18-month-olds. *Developmental Science, 10,* 10–921.

Barr, R. G. (2001). "Colic" is something infants do, rather than a condition they "have": A developmental approach to crying phenomena patterns, pacification and (patho)genesis. In R. G. Barr, I. St James-Roberts, & M. R. Keefe (Eds.), *New evidence on unexplained infant crying* (pp. 87–104). St. Louis: Johnson & Johnson Pediatric Institute.

Barr, R. G., Fairbrother, N., Pauwels, J., Green, J., Chen, M., & Brant, R. (2014). Maternal frustration, emotional and behavioural responses to prolonged infant crying. *Infant Behavior and Development, 37,* 652–664.

Barrett, K. C. (2005). The origins of social emotions and self-regulation in toddlerhood: New evidence. *Cognition and Emotion, 19,* 953–979.

Barrouillet, P., & Gaillard, V. (2011a). Advances and issues: Some thoughts about controversial questions. In P. Barrouillet & V. Gaillard (Eds.), *Cognitive development and working memory: A dialogue between neo-Piagetian and cognitive approaches* (pp. 263–271). Hove, UK: Psychology Press.

Barrouillet, P., & Gaillard, V. (Eds.). (2011b). *Cognitive development and working memory: A dialogue between neo-Piagetian and cognitive approaches.* Hove, UK: Psychology Press.

Barthell, J. E., & Mrozek, J. D. (2013). Neonatal drug withdrawal. *Minnesota Medicine, 96,* 48–50.

Bartick, M., & Smith, L. J. (2014). Speaking out on safe sleep: Evidence-based infant sleep recommendations. *Breastfeeding Medicine, 9,* 417–422.

Bartocci, M., Berggvist, L. L., Lagercrantz, H., & Anand, K. J. (2006). Pain activates cortical areas in the preterm newborn brain. *Pain, 122,* 109–117.

Bartrip, J., Morton, J., & de Schonen, S. (2001). Responses to mother's face in 3-week- to 5-month-old infants. *British Journal of Developmental Psychology, 19,* 219–232.

Bartsch, K., & Wellman, H. (1995). *Children talk about the mind.* New York: Oxford University Press.

Basinger, B. (2013). Low-income and minority children with asthma. In L. Rubin & J. Merrick (Eds.), *Environmental health disparities with children: Asthma, obesity and food* (pp. 61–72). Hauppauge, NY: Nova Science.

Bassett, D. R., John, D., Conger, S. A., Fitzhugh, E. C., & Coe, D. P. (2015). Trends in physical activity and sedentary behaviors of United States youth. *Journal of Physical Activity & Health, 12,* 1102–1111.

Bass-Ringdahl, S. M. (2010). The relationship of audibility and the development of canonical babbling in young children with hearing impairment. *Journal of Deaf Studies and Deaf Education, 15,* 287–310.

Bassuk, E. L., DeCandia, C. J., Beach, C. A., & Berman, F. (2014). *America's youngest outcasts: A report card on child homelessness.* Waltham, MA: National Center on Family Homelessness.

Basten, S., & Jiang, Q. (2015). Fertility in China: An uncertain future. *Population Studies, 69,* S97–S105.

Bates, E., Marchman, V., Thal, D., Fenson, L., Dale, P., Reznick, J. S., Reilly, J., & Hartung, J. (1994). Developmental and stylistic variation in the composition of early vocabulary. *Journal of Child Language, 21,* 85–123.

Bates, J. E., Wachs, T. D., & Emde, R. N. (1994). Toward practical uses for biological concepts. In J. E. Bates & T. D. Wachs (Eds.), *Temperament: Individual differences at the interface of biology and behavior* (pp. 275–306). Washington, DC: American Psychological Association.

Bathelt, J., O'Reilly, H., Clayden, J. D., Cross, J. H., & de Haan, M. (2013). Functional brain network organization of children between 2 and 5 years derived from reconstructed activity of cortical sources of high-density EEG recordings. *NeuroImage, 82,* 595–604.

Baude, A., Pearson, J., & Drapeau, S. (2016). Child adjustment in joint physical custody versus sole custody: A meta-analytic review. *Journal of Divorce and Remarriage, 57,* 338–360.

Baudson, T. G., Weber, K. E., & Freund, P. A. (2016). More than only skin deep: Appearance self-concept predicts most of secondary school students' self-esteem. *Frontiers in Psychology, 7,* Article ID: 1568.

Bauer, P. J. (2006). Event memory. In D. Kuhn & R. Siegler (Eds.), *Handbook of child psychology: Vol. 2. Cognition, perception, and language* (6th ed., pp. 373–425). Hoboken, NJ: Wiley.

Bauer, P. J. (2013). Memory. In S. M. Carlson, P. D. Zelazo, & S. Faja (Eds.), *Oxford handbook of developmental psychology: Vol. 1. Body and mind* (pp. 505–541). New York: Oxford University Press.

Bauer, P. J., Larkina, M., & Deocampo, J. (2011). Early memory development. In U. Goswami (Ed.), *Wiley-Blackwell handbook of childhood cognitive development* (2nd ed., pp. 153–179). Chichester, UK: Wiley-Blackwell.

Baumeister, R. F., Campbell, J. D., Krueger, J. I., & Vohs, K. D. (2003). Does high self-esteem cause better performance, interpersonal success, happiness, or healthier lifestyles? *Psychological Science in the Public Interest, 4*(1), 1–44.

Baumgartner, H. A., & Oakes, L. M. (2011). Infants' developing sensitivity to object function: Attention to features and feature correlations. *Journal of Cognition and Development, 12,* 275–298.

Baumrind, D. (1971). Current patterns of parental authority. *Developmental Psychology Monograph, 4*(No. 1, Pt. 2).

Baumrind, D. (2013). Authoritative parenting revisited: History and current status. In R. E. Larzelere, A. S. Morris, & A. W. Harrist (Eds.), *Authoritative parenting: Synthesizing nurturance and discipline for optimal child development* (pp. 11–34). Washington, DC: American Psychological Association.

Baumrind, D., Lazelere, R. E., & Owens, E. B. (2010). Effects of preschool parents' power assertive patterns and practices on adolescent development. *Parenting, 10,* 157–201.

Bauserman, R. (2002). Child adjustment in joint-custody versus sole-custody arrangements: A meta-analytic review. *Journal of Family Psychology, 16,* 91–102.

Bauserman, R. (2012). A meta-analysis of parental satisfaction, adjustment, and conflict in joint custody and sole custody following divorce. *Journal of Divorce & Remarriage, 53,* 464–488.

Baydar, N., & Akcinar, B. (2017). Reciprocal relations between the trajectories of mothers' harsh discipline, responsiveness and aggression in early childhood. *Journal of Abnormal Child Psychology, 45.* Retrieved from doi.org/10.1007/s10802-017-0280-y.

Bayley, N. (1969). *Bayley Scales of Infant Development.* New York: Psychological Corporation.

Bayley, N. (1993). *Bayley Scales of Infant Development* (2nd ed.). San Antonio, TX: Psychological Corporation.

Bayley, N. (2005). *Bayley Scales of Infant and Toddler Development* (3rd ed.). San Antonio, TX: Harcourt Assessment.

Beauchamp, G. K., & Mennella, J. A. (2011). Flavor perception in human infants: Development and functional significance. *Digestion, 83*(Suppl. 1), 1–6.

Beckett, C., Maughan, B., Rutter, M., Castle, J., Colvert, E., & Groothues, C. (2006). Do the effects of early severe deprivation on cognition persist into early adolescence? Findings from the English and Romanian adoptees study. *Child Development, 77,* 696–711.

Bedard, K., & Dhuey, E. (2006). The persistence of early childhood maturity: International evidence of long-run age effects. *Quarterly Journal of Economics, 121,* 1437–1472.

Beelmann, A., & Heinemann, K. S. (2014). Preventing prejudice and improving intergroup attitudes: A meta-analysis of child and adolescent training programs. *Journal of Applied Developmental Psychology, 35,* 10–24.

Behm, I., Kabir, Z., Connolly, G. N., & Alpert, H. R. (2012). Increasing prevalence of smoke-free homes and decreasing rates of sudden infant death syndrome in the United States: An ecological association study. *Tobacco Control, 21,* 6–11.

Behnke, M., & Smith, V. C. (2013). Prenatal substance abuse: Short- and long-term effects on the exposed fetus. *Pediatrics, 131,* e1009–1024.

Behrens, K. Y., Hesse, E., & Main, M. (2007). Mothers' attachment status as determined by the Adult Attachment Interview predicts their 6-year-olds' reunion responses: A study conducted in Japan. *Developmental Psychology, 43*(6), 1553–1567.

Bélanger, M. J., Atance, C. M., Varghese, A. L., Nguyen, V., & Vendetti, C. (2014). What will I like best when I'm all grown up? Preschoolers' understanding of future preferences. *Child Development, 85,* 2419–2431.

Belcher, D., Lee, A., Solmon, M., & Harrison, L. (2003). The influence of gender-related beliefs and conceptions of ability on women learning the hockey wrist shot. *Research Quarterly for Exercise and Sport, 74,* 183–192.

Bell, E. R., Greenfield, D. B., Bulotsky-Shearer, R. J., & Carter, T. M. (2016). Peer play as a context for identifying profiles of children and examining rates of growth in academic readiness for children enrolled in Head Start. *Journal of Educational Psychology, 108,* 740–745.

Bell, M. A. (1998). Frontal lobe function during infancy: Implications for the development of cognition and attention. In J. E. Richards (Ed.), *Cognitive neuroscience of attention: A developmental perspective* (pp. 327–362). Mahwah, NJ: Erlbaum.

Bellagamba, F., Camaioni, L., & Colonnesi, C. (2006). Change in children's understanding of others' intentional actions. *Developmental Science, 9,* 182–188.

Bellagamba, F., Laghi, F., Lonigro, A., & Pace, C. S. (2012). Re-enactment of intended acts from a video presentation by 18- and 24-month-old children. *Cognitive Processes, 13,* 381–386.

Belsky, J., & de Haan, M. (2011). Parenting and children's brain development: The end of the beginning. *Journal of Child Psychology and Psychiatry, 52,* 409–428.

Belsky, J., & Fearon, R. M. P. (2002). Early attachment security, subsequent maternal sensitivity, and later child development: Does continuity in development depend on caregiving? *Attachment and Human Development, 4,* 361–387.

Belsky, J., & Fearon, R. M. P. (2008). Precursors of attachment security. In J. Cassidy & P. R. Shaver (Eds.), *Handbook of attachment: Theory, research, and clinical applications* (2nd ed., pp. 295–316). New York: Guilford.

Belsky, J., Schlomer, G. L., & Ellis, B. J. (2012). Beyond cumulative risk: Distinguishing harshness and unpredictability as determinants of parenting and early life history strategy. *Developmental Psychology, 48,* 662–673.

Belsky, J., Vandell, D. L., Burchinal, M., Clarke-Stewart, K. A., McCartney, K., & Owen, M. T. (2007). Are there long-term effects of early child care? *Child Development, 78,* 681–701.

Bemmels, H. R., Burt, A., Legrand, L. N., Iacono, W. G., & McGue, M. (2008). The heritability of life events: An adolescent twin and adoption study. *Twin Research and Human Genetics, 11,* 257–265.

Bender, H. L., Allen, J. P., McElhaney, K. B., Antonishak, J., Moore, C. M., Kelly, H. L., & Davis, S. M. (2007). Use of harsh physical discipline and developmental outcomes in adolescence. *Development and Psychopathology, 19,* 227–242.

Benigno, J. P., Byrd, D. L., McNamara, P. H., Berg, W. K., & Farrar, M. J. (2011). Talking through transitions: Microgenetic changes in preschoolers' private speech. *Child Language Teaching and Therapy, 27,* 269–285.

Benner, A. D., Boyle, A., & Sadler, S. (2016). Parental involvement and adolescents' educational success: The roles of prior achievement and socioeconomic status. *Journal of Youth and Adolescence, 45,* 1053–1064.

Benson, J. E., Sabbagh, M. A., Carlson, S. M., & Zelazo, P. D. (2013). Individual differences in executive functioning predict preschoolers' improvement from theory-of-mind training. *Developmental Psychology, 49,* 1615–1627.

Beratis, I. N., Rabavilas, A. D., Kyprianou, M., Papadimitriou, G. N., & Papageorgiou, C. (2013). Investigation of the link between higher order cognitive functions and handedness. *Journal of Clinical and Experimental Neuropsychology, 35,* 393–403.

Berenbaum, S. A., & Beltz, A. M. (2011). Sexual differentiation in human behavior: Effects of prenatal and pubertal organizational hormones. *Frontiers in Neuroendocrinology, 32,* 183–200.

Bergen, D. (2013). Does pretend play matter? Searching for evidence: Comment on Lillard et al. (2013). *Psychological Bulletin, 139,* 45–48.

Berger, L. M., Paxson, C., & Waldfogel, J. (2009). Income and child development. *Children and Youth Services Review, 31,* 978–989.

Berger, S. E. (2010). Locomotor expertise predicts infants' perseverative errors. *Developmental Psychology, 46,* 326–336.

Berger, S. E., & Scher, A. (2017). Naps improve new walkers' locomotor problem solving. *Journal of Experimental Child Psychology, 162,* 292–300.

Berger, S. E., Theuring, C., & Adolph, K. E. (2007). How and when infants learn to climb stairs. *Infant Behavior and Development, 30,* 36–49.

Berk, L. E. (2001). *Awakening children's minds: How parents and teachers can make a difference.* New York: Oxford University Press.

Berk, L. E. (2015). Make-believe play and children's self-regulation. *Speaking about … Psychology On-Demand Webinars.* Hoboken, NJ: Pearson Education. Retrieved from www.pearsoned.com/events-and-webinars/higher-education-events-and-webinars/speaking-about-webinars/on-demand-webinars/psychology

Berk, L. E., & Meyers, A. B. (2013). The role of make-believe play in the development of executive function: Status of research and future directions. *American Journal of Play, 6,* 98–110.

Berk, L. E., & Spuhl, S. (1995). Maternal interaction, private speech, and task performance in preschool children. *Early Childhood Research Quarterly, 10,* 145–169.

Berkeley, S., Mastropieri, M. A., & Scruggs, T. E. (2011). Reading comprehension strategy instruction and attribution retraining for secondary students with learning and other mild disabilities. *Journal of Learning Disabilities, 44,* 18–31.

Berkowitz, R. L., Roberts, J., & Minkoff, H. (2006). Challenging the strategy of maternal age-based prenatal genetic counseling. *JAMA, 295,* 1446–1448.

Berlin, L. J., Ipsa, J. M., Fine, M. A., Malone, P. S., Brooks-Gunn, J., Brady-Smith, C., et al. (2009). Correlates and consequences of spanking and verbal punishment for low-income White, African-American, and Mexican-American toddlers. *Child Development, 80,* 1403–1420.

Berman, R. A. (2007). Developing linguistic knowledge and language use across adolescence. In K. Hirsh-Pasek & R. M. Golinkoff (Eds.), *Action meets word: How children learn verbs* (pp. 347–367). New York: Oxford University Press.

Bernard, J. Y., Armand, M., Peyre, H., Garcia, C., Forhan, A., De Agostini, M., et al. (2017). Breastfeeding, polyunsaturated fatty acid levels in colostrum and child intelligence quotient at age 5–6 years. *Journal of Pediatrics, 183,* 43–50.

Berndt, T. J. (2004). Children's friendships: Shifts over a half-century in perspectives on their development and effects. *Merrill-Palmer Quarterly, 50,* 206–223.

Bertenthal, B. I. (1993). Infants' perception of biomechanical motions: Intrinsic image and knowledge-based constraints. In C. Granrud (Ed.), *Visual perception and cognition in infancy* (pp. 175–214). Hillsdale, NJ: Erlbaum.

Bertenthal, B. I., Gredebäck, G., & Boyer, T. W. (2013). Differential contributions of development and learning to infants' knowledge of object continuity and discontinuity. *Child Development, 84,* 413–421.

Bertenthal, B. I., Longo, M. R., & Kenny, S. (2007). Phenomenal permanence and the development of predictive tracking in infancy. *Child Development, 78,* 350–363.

Bertrand, J., & Dang, E. P. (2012). Fetal alcohol spectrum disorders: Review of teratogenicity, diagnosis and treatment issues. In D. Hollar (Ed.), *Handbook of children with special health care needs* (pp. 231–258). New York: Springer Science + Business Media.

Best, D. (2009). From the American Academy of Pediatrics: Technical report—secondhand and prenatal tobacco smoke exposure. *Pediatrics, 124,* e1017–e1044.

Best, D. L. (2001). Gender concepts: Convergence in cross-cultural research and methodologies. *Cross-cultural Research: The Journal of Comparative Social Science, 35,* 23–43.

Bhat, A., Heathcock, J., & Galloway, J. C. (2005). Toy-oriented changes in hand and joint kinematics during the emergence of purposeful reaching. *Infant Behavior and Development, 28,* 445–465.

Bhatt, R. S., Rovee-Collier, C., & Weiner, S. (1994). Developmental changes in the interface between perception and memory retrieval. *Developmental Psychology, 30,* 151–162.

Bhatt, R. S., Wilk, A., Hill, D., & Rovee-Collier, C. (2004). Correlated attributes and categorization in the first half-year of life. *Developmental Psychobiology, 44,* 103–115.

Bialystok, E. (2013). The impact of bilingualism on language and literacy development. In T. K. Bhatia & W. C. Ritchie (Eds.), *Handbook of bilingualism and multilingualism* (pp. 624–648). Chichester, UK: Wiley-Blackwell.

Bialystok, E. (2015). Bilingualism and the development of executive function: The role of attention. *Child Development Perspectives, 9,* 117–121.

Bialystok, E., Craik, F. I. M., & Luk, G. (2012). Bilingualism: Consequences for mind and brain. *Trends in Cognitive Sciences, 16,* 240–250.

Bialystok, E., & Martin, M. M. (2003). Notation to symbol: Development in children's understanding of print. *Journal of Experimental Child Psychology, 86,* 223–243.

Bianchi, S. M. (2011). Family change and time allocation in American families. *Annals of the American Academy of Political and Social Science, 638,* 21–44.

Biederman, J., Fried, R., Petty, C., Mahoney, L., & Faraone, S. V. (2012). An examination of the impact of attention-deficit hyperactivity disorder on IQ: A large controlled family-based analysis. *Canadian Journal of Psychiatry, 57,* 608–616.

Bierman, K. L., Domitrovich, C. E., Nix, R. L., Gest, S. D., Welsh, J. A., Greenberg, M. T., et al. (2008). Promoting academic and social-emotional school readiness: The Head Start REDI program. *Child Development, 79,* 1802–1817.

Bierman, K. L., Nix, R. L., Heinrichs, B. S., Domitrovich, C. E., Gest, S. D., Welsh, J. A., et al. (2014). Effects of Head Start REDI on children's outcomes 1 year later in different kindergarten contexts. *Child Development, 85,* 140–159.

Bierman, K. L., & Powers, L. M. (2009). Social skills training to improve peer relations. In K. H. Rubin, W. M. Bukowski, & B. Laursen (Eds.), *Handbook of peer interactions, relationships, and groups* (pp. 603–621). New York: Guilford Press.

Bifulco, R., Cobb, C. D., & Bell, C. (2009). Can interdistrict choice boost student achievement? The case of Connecticut's interdistrict magnet school program. *Educational Evaluation and Policy Analysis, 31,* 323–345.

Bigelow, A. E., & Power, M. (2014). Effects of maternal responsiveness on infant responsiveness and behavior in the still-face task. *Infancy, 19,* 558–584.

Bigler, R. S. (2007, June). Personal communication.

Bigler, R. S. (2013). Understanding and reducing social stereotyping and prejudice among children. In M. Banaji & S. A. Gelman (Eds.), *Navigating the social world: What infants, children, and other species can teach us* (pp. 327–33). New York: Oxford University Press.

Birbeck, D., & Drummond, M. (2015). Research methods and ethics working with young children. In O. N. Saracho (Ed.), *Handbook of research methods in early childhood education: Vol. 2. Review of research methodologies* (pp. 607–632). Charlotte, NC: IAP Information Age Publishing.

Birch, L. L., & Fisher, J. A. (1995). Appetite and eating behavior in children. *Pediatric Clinics of North America, 42,* 931–953.

Birch, L. L., Fisher, J. O., & Davison, K. K. (2003). Learning to overeat: Maternal use of restrictive feeding practices promotes girls' eating in the absence of hunger. *American Journal of Clinical Nutrition, 78,* 215–220.

Bird, A., & Reese, E. (2006). Emotional reminiscing and the development of an autobiographical self. *Developmental Psychology, 42,* 613–626.

Biringen, Z., Emde, R. N., Campos, J. J., & Appelbaum, M. I. (1995). Affective reorganization in the infant, the mother, and the dyad: The role of upright locomotion and its timing. *Child Development, 66,* 499–514.

Birney, D. P., & Sternberg, R. J. (2011). The development of cognitive abilities. In M. H. Bornstein & M. E. Lamb (Eds.), *Developmental science: An advanced textbook* (6th ed., pp. 353–388). New York: Psychology Press.

Biro, F. M., & Wien, M. (2010). Childhood obesity and adult morbidities. *American Journal of Clinical Nutrition, 91,* 1499S–1505S.

Bjorklund, D. F. (2012). *Children's thinking* (5th ed.). Belmont, CA: Wadsworth Cengage Learning.

Bjorklund, D. F., Causey, K., & Periss, V. (2009). The evolution and development of human social cognition. In P. Kappeler & J. Silk (Eds.), *Mind the gap: Racing the origins of human universals* (pp. 351–371). Berlin: Springer Verlag.

Bjorklund, D. F., Schneider, W., Cassel, W. S., & Ashley, E. (1994). Training and extension of a memory strategy: Evidence for utilization deficiencies in high- and low-IQ children. *Child Development, 65,* 951–965.

Black, R. E. (2017). Patterns of growth in early childhood and infectious disease and nutritional determinants. *Nestle Nutrition Institute Workshop Series, 87,* 63–72.

Black, R. E., Victora, C. G., Walker, S. P., Bhutta, Z. A., Christian, P., de Onis, M., et al. (2013). Maternal and child undernutrition and overweight in low-income and middle-income countries. *Lancet, 382,* 427–451.

Black, R. E., Williams, S. M., Jones, I. E., & Goulding, A. (2002). Children who avoid drinking cow milk have low dietary calcium intakes and poor bone health. *American Journal of Clinical Nutrition, 76,* 675–680.

Blackwell, C., Moscovis, S., Hall, S., Burns, C., & Scott, R. J. (2015). Exploring the risk factors for sudden infant deaths and their role in inflammatory responses to infection. *Frontiers in Immunology, 6*(44), 1–8.

Blair, B. L., Perry, N. B., O'Brien, M., Calkins, S. D., Keane, S. P., & Shanahan, L. (2014). The indirect effects of maternal emotion socialization on friendship quality in middle childhood. *Developmental Psychology, 50,* 566–576.

Blair, C., Grander, D. A., Willoughby, M., Mills-Koonce, R., Cox, M., Greenberg, M. T., et al. (2011). Salivary cortisol mediates effects of poverty and parenting on executive functions in early childhood. *Child Development, 82,* 1970–1984.

Blair, C., & Raver, C. C. (2012). Child development in the context of adversity: Experiential canalization of brain and behavior. *American Psychologist, 67,* 309–318.

Blair, C., & Razza, R. P. (2007). Relating effortful control, executive function, and false belief understanding to emerging math and literacy ability in kindergarten. *Developmental Psychology, 78,* 647–663.

Blakemore, J. E. O. (2003). Children's beliefs about violating gender norms: Boys shouldn't look like girls, and girls shouldn't act like boys. *Sex Roles, 48,* 411–419.

Blakemore, J. E. O., Berenbaum, S. A., & Liben, L. S. (2009). *Gender development.* New York: Psychology Press.

Blakemore, J. E. O., & Hill, C. A. (2008). The Child Gender Socialization Scale: A measure to compare traditional and feminist parents. *Sex Roles, 58,* 192–207.

Blass, E. M., Ganchrow, J. R., & Steiner, J. E. (1984). Classical conditioning in newborn humans 2–48 hours of age. *Infant Behavior and Development, 7,* 223–235.

Block, C. C. (2012). Proven and promising reading instruction. In J. S. Carlson & J. R. Levin (Eds.), *Instructional strategies for improving students' learning* (pp. 3–41). Charlotte, NC: Information Age Publishing.

Blood-Siegfried, J. (2009). The role of infection and inflammation in sudden infant death syndrome. *Immunopharmacology and Immunotoxicology, 31,* 516– 523.

Bloom, T., Glass, N., Curry, M. A., Hernandez, R., & Houck, G. (2013). Maternal stress exposures, reactions, and priorities for stress reduction among low-income, urban women. *Journal of Midwifery and Women's Health, 58,* 167–174.

Bodrova, E., & Leong, D. J. (2007). *Tools of the mind: The Vygotskian approach to early childhood education* (2nd ed.). Upper Saddle River, NJ: Merrill/Prentice Hall.

Bogin, B. (2001). *The growth of humanity.* New York: Wiley-Liss.

Bohannon, J. N., III, & Bonvillian, J. D. (2013). Theoretical approaches to language acquisition. In J. B. Gleason & N. B. Ratner (Eds.), *The development of language* (8th ed., pp. 190–240). Upper Saddle River, NJ: Pearson.

Bohannon, J. N., III, & Stanowicz, L. (1988). The issue of negative evidence: Adult responses to children's language errors. *Developmental Psychology, 24,* 684–689.

Bolisetty, S., Bajuk, B., Me, A.-L., Vincent, T., Sutton, L., & Lui, K. (2006). Preterm outcome table (POT): A simple tool to aid counselling parents of very preterm infants. *Australian and New Zealand Journal of Obstetrics and Gynaecology, 46,* 189–192.

Booker, J. A., & Dunsmore, J. C. (2017). Affective social competence in adolescence: Current findings and future directions. *Social Development, 26,* 3–20.

Booren, L. M., Downer, J. T., & Vitiello, V. E. (2012). Observations of children's interactions with teachers, peers, and tasks across preschool classroom activity settings. *Early Education and Development, 23,* 517–538.

Booth, A., Scott, M. E., & King, V. (2010). Father residence and adolescent problem behavior: Are youth always better off in two-parent families? *Journal of Family Issues, 31,* 585–605.

Booth, R. D., L., & Happé, F. G. E. (2016). Evidence of reduced global processing in autism spectrum disorder. *Journal of Autism and Developmental Disorders, 46,* ISSN 1573-3472.

Booth-LaForce, C., Groh, A. M., Burchinal, M. R., Roisman, G. I., Owen, M. T., & Cox, M. J. (2014). Caregiving and contextual sources of continuity and change in attachment security from infancy to late adolescence. In C. Booth-LaForce & G. I. Roisman (Eds.), The Adult Attachment Interview: Psychometrics, stability and change from infancy, and developmental origins. *Monographs of the Society for Research in Child Development, 79*(3, Serial No. 314), 67–84.

Borchert, S., Lamm, B., Graf, F., & Knopf, M. (2013). Deferred imitation in 18-month-olds from two cultural contexts: The case of Cameroonian Nso farmer and German-middle class infants. *Infant Behavior and Development, 36,* 717–727.

Borghese, M. M., Tremblay, M. S., Katzmarzyk, P. T., Tudor-Locke, C., Schuna, J. M., Jr., Leduc, G., et al. (2015). Mediating role of television time, diet patterns, physical activity and sleep duration in the association between television in the bedroom and adiposity in 10-year-old children. *International Journal of Behavioral Nutrition and Physical Activity, 12,* Article ID: 60.

Bornstein, M. H. (2015). Children's parents. In M. H. Bornstein & T. Leventhal (Eds.), *Handbook of child psychology and developmental science: Vol. 4. Ecological settings and processes* (7th ed., pp. 55–132). Hoboken, NJ: Wiley.

Bornstein, M. H., & Arterberry, M. E. (1999). Perceptual development. In M. H. Bornstein & M. E. Lamb

(Eds.), *Developmental psychology: An advanced textbook* (pp. 231–274). Mahwah, NJ: Erlbaum.

Bornstein, M. H., & Arterberry, M. E. (2003). Recognition, discrimination, and categorization of smiling by 5-month-old infants. *Developmental Science, 6,* 585–599.

Bornstein, M. H., Arterberry, M. E., & Mash, C. (2010). Infant object categorization transcends object–context relations. *Infant Behavior and Development, 33,* 7–15.

Bornstein, M. H., Vibbert, M., Tal, J., & O'Donnell, K. (1992). Toddler language and play in the second year: Stability, covariation, and influences of parenting. *First Language, 12,* 323–338.

Borst, C. G. (1995). *Catching babies: The professionalization of childbirth, 1870–1920.* Cambridge, MA: Harvard University Press.

Borst, G., Poirel, N., Pineau, A., Cassotti, M., & Houdé, O. (2013). Inhibitory control efficiency in a Piaget-like class-inclusion task in school-age children and adults: A developmental negative priming study. *Developmental Psychology, 49,* 1366–1374.

Bos, H. (2013). Lesbian-mother families formed through donor insemination. In A. E. Goldberg & K. R. Allen (Eds.), *LGBT-parent families: Innovations in research and implications for practice* (pp. 21–37). New York: Springer.

Bos, H. M. W., & Sandfort, T. G. M. (2010). Children's gender identity in lesbian and heterosexual two-parent families. *Sex Roles, 62,* 114–126.

Bost, K. K., Shin, N., McBride, B. A., Brown, G. L., Vaughn, B. E., & Coppola, G. (2006). Maternal secure base scripts, children's attachment security, and mother–child narrative styles. *Attachment and Human Development, 8,* 241–260.

Bouchard, T. J. (2004). Genetic influence on human psychological traits: A survey. *Current Directions in Psychological Science, 13,* 148–151.

Boucher, O., Bastien, C. H., Saint-Amour, D., Dewailly, E., Ayotte, P., Jacobson, J. L., Jacobson, et al. (2010). Prenatal exposure to methylmercury and PCBs affects distinct stages of information processing: An event-related potential study with Inuit children. *Neurotoxicology, 31,* 373–384.

Boucher, O., Jacobson, S. W., Plusquellec, P., Dewailly, E., Ayotte, P., Forget-Dubois, N., et al. (2012). Prenatal methylmercury, postnatal lead exposure, and evidence of attention deficit/hyperactivity disorder among Inuit children in Arctic Québec. *Environmental Health Perspectives, 120,* 1456–1461.

Boucher, O., Muckle, G., & Bastien, C. H. (2009). Prenatal exposure to polychlorinated biphenyls: A neuropsychologic analysis. *Environmental Health Perspectives, 117,* 7–16.

Bouldin, P. (2006). An investigation of the fantasy predisposition and fantasy style of children with imaginary companions. *Journal of Genetic Psychology, 167,* 17–29.

Boutwell, B. B., Franklin, C. A., Barnes, J. C., & Beaver, K. M. (2011). Physical punishment and childhood aggression: The role of gender and gene–environment interplay. *Aggressive Behavior, 37,* 559–568.

Bowlby, J. (1969). *Attachment and loss: Vol. 1. Attachment.* New York: Basic Books.

Bowlby, J. (1980). *Attachment and loss: Vol. 3. Loss: Sadness and depression.* New York: Basic Books.

Boyatzis, C. J. (2000). The artistic evolution of mommy: A longitudinal case study of symbolic and social processes. In C. J. Boyatzis & M. W. Watson (Eds.), *Symbolic and social constraints on the development of children's artistic style* (pp. 5–29). San Francisco: Jossey-Bass.

Boyle, C. A., Boulet, S., Schieve, L. A., Cohen, R. A., Blumberg, S. J., Yeargin-Allsopp, M., et al. (2011). Trends in the prevalence of developmental disabilities in U.S. children, 1997–2008. *Pediatrics, 127,* 1034–1042.

Boysson-Bardies, B. de, & Vihman, M. M. (1991). Adaptation to language: Evidence from Safar babbling and first words in four languages. *Language, 67,* 297–319.

Brackett, M. A., Rivers, S. E., & Salovey, P. (2011). Emotional intelligence: Implications for personal, social, academic, and workplace success. *Social and Personality Compass, 5,* 88–103.

Bradley, R. H., & Caldwell, B. M. (1982). The consistency of the home environment and its relation to child development. *International Journal of Behavioral Development, 5,* 445–465.

Bradley, R. H., & Corwyn, R. F. (2003). Age and ethnic variations in family process mediators of SES. In M. H. Bornstein & R. H. Bradley (Eds.), *Socioeconomic status, parenting, and child development* (pp. 161–188). Mahwah, NJ: Erlbaum.

Bradley, R. H., Whiteside, L., Mundfrom, D. J., Casey, P. H., Kelleher, K. J., & Pope, S. K. (1994). Early indications of resilience and their relation to experiences in the home environments of low birthweight, premature children living in poverty. *Child Development, 65,* 346–360.

Brady, S. A. (2011). Efficacy of phonics teaching for reading outcomes: Indications from post-NRP research. In S. A. Brady, D. Braze, & C. A. Fowler (Eds.), *Explaining individual differences in reading: Theory and evidence* (pp. 69–96). New York: Psychology Press.

Braine, L. G., Schauble, L., Kugelmass, S., & Winter, A. (1993). Representation of depth by children: Spatial strategies and lateral biases. *Developmental Psychology, 29,* 466–479.

Brand, S. R., Schechter, J. C., Hammen, C. L., Brocque, R. L., & Brennan, P. A. (2011). Do adolescent offspring of women with PTSD experience higher levels of chronic and episodic stress? *Journal of Trauma and Stress, 24,* 399–404.

Brannon, E. M., Lutz, D. J., & Cordes, S. (2006). The development of area discrimination and its implications for number representation in infancy. *Developmental Science, 9,* F59–F64.

Braswell, G. S. (2006). Sociocultural contexts for the early development of semiotic production. *Psychological Bulletin, 132,* 877–894.

Braswell, G. S., & Callanan, M. A. (2003). Learning to draw recognizable graphic representations during mother–child interactions. *Merrill-Palmer Quarterly, 49,* 471–494.

Braungart-Rieker, J. M., Hill-Soderlund, A. L., & Karrass, J. (2010). Fear and anger reactivity trajectories from 4 to 16 months: The roles of temperament, regulation, and maternal sensitivity. *Developmental Psychology, 46,* 791–804.

Bremner, J. G. (2010). Cognitive development: Knowledge of the physical world. In J. G. Bremner & T. D. Wachs (Eds.), *Wiley-Blackwell handbook of infant development: Vol. 1. Basic research* (2nd ed., pp. 204–242). Oxford, UK: Wiley-Blackwell.

Bremner, J. G., Slater, A. M., & Johnson, S. P. (2015). Perception of object persistence: The origins of object permanence in infancy. *Child Development Perspectives, 9,* 7–13.

Brendgen, M., Boivin, M., Dionne, G., Barker, E. D., Vitaro, F., Girard, A., et al. (2011). Gene–environment processes linking aggression, peer victimization, and the teacher–child relationship. *Child Development, 82,* 2021–2036.

Brennan, L. M., Shelleby, E. C., Shaw, D. S., Gardner, F., Dishion, T. J., & Wilson, M. (2013). Indirect effects of the family check-up on school-age academic achievement through improvements in parenting in early childhood. *Journal of Educational Psychology, 105,* 762–773.

Brenner, E., & Salovey, P. (1997). Emotional regulation during childhood: Developmental, interpersonal, and individual considerations. In P. Salovey & D. Sluyter (Eds.), *Emotional literacy and emotional development* (pp. 168–192). New York: Basic Books.

Bretherton, I., & Munholland, K. A. (2008). Internal working models in attachment relationships. In J. Cassidy & P. R. Shaver (Eds.), *Handbook of attachment: Theory, research, and clinical applications* (2nd ed., pp. 102–127). New York: Guilford.

Brewster, K. L., Tillman, K. H., & Jokinen-Gordon, H. (2014). Demographic characteristics of lesbian parents in the United States. *Population Research and Policy Review, 33,* 485–502.

Bridgett, D. J., Gartstein, M. A., Putnam, S. P., McKay, T., Iddins, R., Robertson, C., et al. (2009). Maternal and contextual influences and the effect of temperament development during infancy on parenting in toddlerhood. *Infant Behavior and Development, 32,* 103–116.

Bright, G. M., Mendoza, J. R., & Rosenfeld, R. G. (2009). Recombinant human insulin-like growth factor-1 treatment: Ready for primetime. *Endocrinology and Metabolism Clinics of North America, 38,* 625–638.

Brody, G. H., & Murry, V. M. (2001). Sibling socialization of competence in rural, single-parent African American families. *Journal of Marriage and Family, 63,* 996–1008.

Brody, G. H., Stoneman, Z., & McCoy, J. K. (1994). Forecasting sibling relationships in early adolescence from child temperaments and family processes in middle childhood. *Child Development, 65,* 771–784.

Brody, L. (1999). *Gender, emotion, and the family.* Cambridge, MA: Harvard University Press.

Brodzinsky, D. M. (2011). Children's understanding of adoption: Developmental and clinical implications. *Professional Psychology: Research and Practice, 42,* 200–207.

Bronfenbrenner, U., & Morris, P. A. (2006). The bioecological model of human development. In R. M. Lerner (Ed.), *Handbook of child psychology: Vol. 1. Theoretical models of human development* (6th ed., pp. 297–342). Hoboken, NJ: Wiley.

Bronson, G. W. (1994). Infants' transitions toward adultlike scanning. *Child Development, 65,* 1243–1261.

Brooker, R. J., Buss, K. A., Lemery-Chalfant, K., Aksan, N., Davidson, R. J., & Goldsmith, H. H. (2013). The development of stranger fear in infancy and toddlerhood: Normative development, individual differences, antecedents, and outcomes. *Developmental Science, 16,* 864–878.

Brooks, R., & Meltzoff, A. N. (2005). The development of gaze following and its relation to language. *Developmental Science, 8,* 535–543.

Brooks, R., & Meltzoff, A. N. (2008). Infant gaze following and pointing predict accelerated vocabulary growth through two years of age: A longitudinal, growth curve modeling study. *Journal of Child Language, 35,* 207–220.

Brooks-Gunn, J., Han, W.-J., & Waldfogel, J. (2010). First-year maternal employment and child development in the first 7 years. *Monographs of the Society for Research in Child Development, 75*(No. 2, Serial No. 296), 59–69.

Brooks-Gunn, J., Klebanov, P. K., Smith, J., Duncan, G. J., & Lee, K. (2003). The Black–White test score gap in young children. Contributions of test and family characteristics. *Applied Developmental Science, 7,* 239–252.

Brown, A., & Harries, V. (2015). Infant sleep and night feeding patterns during later infancy: Association with breastfeeding frequency, daytime complementary food intake, and infant weight. *Breastfeeding Medicine, 10,* 246–252.

Brown, A. M., & Miracle, J. A. (2003). Early binocular vision in human infants: Limitations on the generality of the superposition hypothesis. *Vision Research, 43,* 1563–1574.

Brown, B. B., Herman, M., Hamm, J. V., & Heck, D. (2008). Ethnicity and image: Correlates of minority adolescents' affiliation with individual-based versus ethnically defined peer crowds. *Child Development, 79,* 529–546.

Brown, C. S., & Bigler, R. S. (2004). Children's perceptions of gender discrimination. *Developmental Psychology, 40,* 714–726.

Brown, G. L., Mangelsdorf, S. C., & Neff, C. (2012). Father involvement, paternal sensitivity, and father–child attachment security in the first 3 years. *Journal of Family Psychology, 26,* 421–430.

Brown, G. L., Schoppe-Sullivan, S. J., Mangelsdorf, S. C., & Neff, C. (2010). Observed and reported supportive coparenting as predictors of infant–mother and infant–father attachment security. *Early Child Development and Care, 180,* 121–137.

Brown, R. W. (1973). *A first language: The early stages.* Cambridge, MA: Harvard University Press.

Brownell, C. A., Zerwas, S., & Ramani, G. B. (2007). "So big": The development of body self-awareness in toddlers. *Child Development, 78,* 1426–1440.

Brownell, M. D., Nickel, N. C., Chateau, D., Martens, P. J., Taylor, C., Crockett, L., et al. (2015). Long-term benefits of full-day kindergarten: A longitudinal study. *Early Child Development and Care, 185,* 291–316.

Brumariu, L. E., Kerns, K. A., & Seibert, A. (2012). Mother–child attachment, emotion regulation, and anxiety symptoms in middle childhood. *Personal Relationships, 19,* 569–585.

Brummelman, E., Crocker, J., & Bushman, B. J. (2016). The praise paradox: When and why praise backfires in children with low self-esteem. *Child Development Perspectives, 10,* 111–115.

Bruzzese, J.-M., & Fisher, C. B. (2003). Assessing and enhancing the research consent capacity of children and youth. *Applied Developmental Science, 7,* 13–26.

Bryan, A. E., & Dix, T. (2009). Mothers' emotions and behavioral support during interactions with toddlers: The role of child temperament. *Social Development, 18,* 647–670.

Bryant, P., & Nunes, T. (2002). Children's understanding of mathematics. In U. Goswami (Ed.), *Blackwell handbook of childhood cognitive development* (pp. 412–439). Malden, MA: Blackwell.

Brydges, C. R., Reid, C. L., Fox, A. M., & Anderson, M. (2012). A unitary executive function predicts intelligence in children. *Intelligence, 40,* 458–469.

Bryk, R. L., & Fisher, P. A. (2012). Training the brain: Practical applications of neural plasticity from the intersection of cognitive neuroscience, developmental psychology, and prevention science. *American Psychologist, 67,* 87–100.

Buchanan, C. M., Maccoby, E. E., & Dornbusch, S. M. (1996). *Adolescents after divorce.* Cambridge, MA: Harvard University Press.

Buchanan-Barrow, E., & Barrett, M. (1998). Children's rule discrimination within the context of the school. *British Journal of Developmental Psychology, 16,* 539–551.

Buchsbaum, D., Dridgers, S., Weisberg, D. S., & Gopnik, A. (2012). The power of possibility: Causal learning, counterfactual reasoning, and pretend play. *Philosophical Transactions of the Royal Society B, 367,* 2202–2212.

Buckingham-Howes, S., Berger, S. S., Scaletti, L. A., & Black, M. M. (2013). Systematic review of prenatal cocaine exposure and adolescent development. *Pediatrics, 131,* e1917–1936.

Buehler, C., & O'Brien, M. (2011). Mothers' part-time employment: Associations with mother and family well-being. *Journal of Family Psychology, 25,* 895–906.

Bugental, D. B., Corpuz, R., & Schwartz, A. (2012). Preventing children's aggression: Outcomes of an early intervention. *Developmental Psychology, 48,* 1443–1449.

Bugental, D. B., & Happaney, K. (2004). Predicting infant maltreatment in low-income families: The interactive effects of maternal attributions and child status at birth. *Developmental Psychology, 40,* 234–243.

Buhrmester, D., & Furman, W. (1990). Perceptions of sibling relationships during middle childhood and adolescence. *Child Development, 61,* 1387–1398.

Buhs, E. S., Ladd, G. W., & Herald-Brown, S. L. (2010). Victimization and exclusion: Links to peer rejection, classroom engagement, and achievement. In S. R. Jimerson, S. M. Swearer, & D. L. Espelage (Eds.), *Handbook of bullying in schools: An international perspective* (pp. 163–172). New York: Routledge.

Bukacha, C. M., Gauthier, S., & Tarr, M. J. (2006). Beyond faces and modularity: The power of an expertise framework. *Trends in Cognitive Sciences, 10,* 159–166.

Burchinal, M., Kainz, K., & Cai, Y. (2011). How well do our measures of quality predict child outcomes? A meta-analysis and coordinated analysis of data from large-scale studies of early childhood settings. In M. Zeslow (Ed.), *Reasons to take stock and strengthen our measures of quality* (pp. 11–31). Baltimore, MD: Paul H. Brookes.

Burchinal, M., Magnuson, K., Powell, D., & Hong, S. S. (2015). Early childcare and education. In M. H. Bornstein & T. Leventhal (Eds.), *Handbook of child psychology and developmental science: Vol. 4. Ecological settings and processes* (7th ed., pp. 223–267). Hoboken, NJ: Wiley.

Burden, M. J., Jacobson, S. W., & Jacobson, J. L. (2005). Relation of prenatal alcohol exposure to cognitive processing speed and efficiency in childhood. *Alcoholism: Clinical and Experimental Research, 29,* 1473–1483.

Bureau, J.-F., Martin, J., Yurkowski, K., Schmiedel, S., Quan, J., Moss, E., et al. (2017). Correlates of child–father and child–mother attachment in the preschool years. *Attachment & Human Development, 19,* 130–150.

Burton, R., Giddy, J., & Stinson, K. (2015). Prevention of mother-to-child transmission in South Africa: An ever-changing landscape. *Obstetric Medicine, 8,* 5–12.

Burts, D.C., Hart, C. H., Charlesworth, R., Fleege, P. O., Mosely, J., & Thomasson, R. H. (1992). Observed activities and stress behaviors of children in developmentally appropriate and inappropriate kindergarten classrooms. *Early Childhood Research Quarterly, 7,* 297–318.

Bush, K. R., & Peterson, G. W. (2008). Family influences on child development. In T. P. Gullotta & G. M. Blau (Eds.), *Handbook of child behavioral issues: Evidence-based approaches to prevention and treatment* (pp. 43–67). New York: Routledge.

Bushman, B. J., Gollwitzer, M., & Cruz, C. (2015). There is broad consensus: Media researchers agree that violent media increase aggression in children, and pediatricians and parents concur. *Psychology of Popular Media Culture, 4,* 200–214.

Bushman, B. J., & Huesmann, L. R. (2012). Effects of violent media on aggression. In D. G. Singer & J. L. Singer (Eds.), *Handbook of children and the media* (2nd ed., pp. 231–248). Thousand Oaks, CA: Sage.

Bushnell, E. W., & Boudreau, J. P. (1993). Motor development and the mind: The potential role of motor abilities as a determinant of aspects of perceptual development. *Child Development, 64,* 1005–1021.

Bushnell, I. W. R. (2001). Mother's face recognition in newborn infants: Learning and memory. *Infant and Child Development, 10,* 67–74.

Bussey, K. (1992). Lying and truthfulness: Children's definitions, standards, and evaluative reactions. *Child Development, 63,* 129–137.

Buswell, S. D., & Spatz, D. L. (2007). Parent–infant co-sleeping and its relationship to breastfeeding. *Journal of Pediatric Health Care, 21,* 22–28.

Buttelmann, D., & Böhm, R. (2014). The ontogeny of the motivation that underlies in-group bias. *Psychological Science, 25,* 921–927.

Buttelmann, D., Over, H., Carpenter, M., & Tomasello, M. (2014). Eighteen-month-olds understand false beliefs in an unexpected-contents task. *Journal of Experimental Child Psychology, 119,* 120–126.

Byne, W., Bradley, S. J., Coleman, E., Eyler, A. E., Green, R., Menvielle, E. J., et al. (2012). Report of the American Psychiatric Association Task Force on Treatment of Gender Identity Disorder. *Archives of Sexual Behavior, 41,* 759–796.

Byrnes, J. P., & Wasik, B. A. (2009). *Language and literacy development: What educators need to know.* New York: Guilford.

C

Cabell, S. Q., Justice, L. M., Logan, J. A. R., & Konold, T. R. (2013). Emergent literacy profiles among prekindergarten children from low-SES backgrounds: Longitudinal considerations. *Early Childhood Research Quarterly, 28,* 608–620.

Cabrera, N. J., Aldoney, D., & Tamis-LeMonda, C. S. (2014). Latino fathers. In N. J. Cabrera & C. S. Tamis-LeMonda (Eds.), *Handbook of father involvement: Multidisciplinary perspectives* (2nd ed., pp. 244–250). New York: Routledge.

Cabrera, N. J., & Bradley, R. H. (2012). Latino fathers and their children. *Child Development Perspectives, 6,* 232–238.

Cabrera, N. J., Shannon, J. D., & Tamis-LeMonda, C. (2007). Fathers' influence on their children's cognitive and emotional development: From toddlers to pre-K. *Applied Developmental Science, 11,* 208–213.

Cain, K., & Oakhill, J. (2011). Matthew effects in young readers: Reading comprehension and reading experience aid vocabulary development. *Journal of Learning Disabilities, 44,* 431–443.

Cairns, R. B., & Cairns, B. D. (2006). The making of developmental psychology. In R. M. Lerner (Ed.), *Handbook of child psychology: Vol. 1. Theoretical models of human development* (6th ed., pp. 89–165). Hoboken, NJ: Wiley.

Caldwell, B. M., & Bradley, R. H. (1994). Environmental issues in developmental follow-up research. In S. L. Friedman & H. C. Haywood (Eds.), *Developmental follow-up* (pp. 235–256). San Diego: Academic Press.

Calvert, S. L. (2015). Children and digital media. In M. H. Bornstein & T. Leventhal (Eds.), *Handbook of cultural developmental science: Vol. 4. Ecological settings and processes* (pp. 299–322). New York: Psychology Press.

Cameron, C. A., Lau, C., Fu, G., & Lee, K. (2012). Development of children's moral evaluations of modesty and self-promotion in diverse cultural settings. *Journal of Moral Education, 41,* 61–78.

Cameron, C. A., & Lee, K. (1997). The development of children's telephone communication. *Journal of Applied Developmental Psychology, 18,* 55–70.

Campbell, A., Shirley, L., & Candy, J. (2004). A longitudinal study of gender-related cognition and behaviour. *Developmental Science, 7,* 1–9.

Campbell, D. A., Lake, M. F., Falk, M., & Backstrand, J. R. (2006). A randomized control trial of continuous support in labor by a lay doula. *Journal of Obstetrics and Gynecology and Neonatal Nursing, 35,* 456–464.

Campbell, D. A., Scott, K. D., Klaus, M. H., & Falk, M. (2007). Female relatives or friends trained as labor doulas: Outcomes at 6 to 8 weeks postpartum. *Birth, 34,* 220–227.

Campbell, F. A., Pungello, E. P., Kainz, K., Burchinal, M., Pan, Y., Wasik, B. H., et al. (2012). Adult outcomes as a function of an early childhood educational program: An Abecedarian Project follow-up. *Developmental Psychology, 48,* 1033–1043.

Campbell, F. A., Pungello, E. P., Miller-Johnson, S., Burchinal, M., & Ramey, C. T. (2001). The development of cognitive and academic abilities: Growth curves from an early childhood educational experiment. *Developmental Psychology, 37,* 231–242.

Campbell, F. A., Ramey, C. T., Pungello, E. P., Sparling, J., & Miller-Johnson, S. (2002). Early childhood education: Young adult outcomes from the Abecedarian Project. *Applied Developmental Science, 6,* 42–57.

Campbell, S. B., Brownell, C. A., Hungerford, A., Spieker, S. J., Mohan, R., & Blessing, J. S. (2004). The course of maternal depressive symptoms and maternal sensitivity as predictors of attachment security at 36 months. *Development and Psychopathology, 16,* 231–252.

Campos, J. J., Anderson, D. I., Barbu-Roth, M. A., Hubbard, E. M., Hertenstein, J. J., & Witherington, D. (2000). Travel broadens the mind. *Infancy, 1,* 149–219.

Campos, J. J., Witherington, D., Anderson, D. I., Frankel, C. I., Uchiyama, I., & Barbu-Roth, M. (2008). Rediscovering development in infancy. *Child Development, 79,* 1625–1632.

Camras, L. A., Oster, H., Campos, J. J., & Bakeman, R. (2003). Emotional facial expressions in European-American, Japanese, and Chinese infants. *Annals of the New York Academy of Sciences, 1000,* 1–17.

Camras, L. A., Oster, H., Campos, J. J., Miyake, K., & Bradshaw, D. (1992). Japanese and American infants' responses to arm restraint. *Developmental Psychology, 28,* 578–583.

Camras, L. A., & Shuster, M. M. (2013). Current emotion research in developmental psychology. *Emotion Review, 5,* 321–329.

Camras, L. A., & Shutter, J. M. (2010). Emotional facial expressions in infancy. *Emotion Review, 2,* 120–129.

Capirci, O., Contaldo, A., Caselli, M. C., & Volterra, V. (2005). From action to language through gesture. *Gesture, 5,* 155–177.

Card, N. A., Stucky, B. D., Sawalani, G. M., & Little, T. D. (2008). Direct and indirect aggression during childhood and adolescence: A meta-analytic review of gender differences, intercorrelations, and relations to maladjustment. *Child Development, 79,* 1185–1229.

Cardona Cano, S., Tiemeier, H., Van Hoeken, D., Tharner, A., Jaddoe, V. W., Hofman, A., et al. (2015). Trajectories of picky eating during childhood: A general population study. *International Journal of Eating Disorders, 48,* 570–579.

Carey, F. R., Singh, G. K., Brown, H. S., III, & Wilkinson, A. V. (2015). Educational outcomes associated with childhood obesity in the United States: Cross-sectional results from the 2011–2012 National Survey of Children's Health. *International Journal of Behavioral Nutrition and Physical Activity, 12*(Suppl. 1): S3.

Carey, S. (2009). *The origins of concepts.* Oxford, UK: Oxford University Press.

Carey, S., & Markman, E. M. (1999). Cognitive development. In B. M. Bly & D. E. Rumelhart (Eds.), *Cognitive science* (pp. 201–254). San Diego: Academic Press.

Carlson, S. M., & Meltzoff, A. N. (2008). Bilingual experience and executive functioning in young children. *Developmental Science, 11,* 282–298.

Carlson, S. M., Moses, L. J., & Claxton, S. J. (2004). Individual differences in executive functioning and theory of mind: An investigation of inhibitory control and planning ability. *Journal of Experimental Child Psychology, 87,* 299–319.

Carlson, S. M., & White, R. E. (2013). Executive function, pretend play, and imagination. In R. E. White & S. M. Carlson (Eds.), *Oxford handbook of the development of imagination* (pp. 161–174). New York: Oxford University Press.

Carlson, S. M., White, R. E., & Davis-Unger, A. (2014). Evidence for a relation between executive function and pretense representation in preschool children. *Cognitive Development, 29,* 1–16.

Carlson, S. M., Zelazo, P. D., & Faja, S. (2013). Executive function. In P. D. Zelazo (Ed.), *Oxford handbook of developmental psychology: Vol. 1. Body and mind* (pp. 706–743). New York: Oxford University Press.

Carlson, V. J., & Harwood, R. L. (2003). Attachment, culture, and the caregiving system: The cultural patterning of everyday experiences among Anglo and Puerto Rican mother–infant pairs. *Infant Mental Health Journal, 24,* 53–73.

Carpendale, J. I. M., & Lewis, C. (2015). The development of social understanding. In L. S. Liben & U. Müller (Eds.), *Handbook of child psychology and developmental science: Vol. 2. Cognitive processes* (pp. 381–424). Hoboken, NJ: Wiley.

Carpenter, R., McGarvey, C., Mitchell, E. A., Tappin, D. M., Vennemann, M. M., Smuk, M., & Carpenter, J. R. (2013). Bed sharing when parents do not smoke: Is there a risk of SIDS? An individual level analysis of five major case-control studies. *British Medical Journal, 3,* e002299.

Carroll, J. B. (2005). The three-stratum theory of cognitive abilities. In D. P. Flanagan & P. L. Harrison (Eds.), *Contemporary intellectual assessment: Theories, tests, and issues* (2nd ed., pp. 69–76). New York: Guilford.

Casalin, S., Luyten, P., Vliegen, N., & Meurs, P. (2012). The structure and stability of temperament from infancy to toddlerhood: A one-year prospective study. *Infant Behavior and Development, 35,* 94–108.

Casasola, M., & Park, Y. (2013). Developmental changes in infant spatial categorization: When more is best and when less is enough. *Child Development, 84,* 1004–1019.

Case, A. D., Todd, N. R., & Kral, M. J. (2014). Ethnography in community psychology: Promises and tensions. *American Journal of Community Psychology, 54,* 60–71.

Case, R. (1996). Introduction: Reconceptualizing the nature of children's conceptual structures and their development in middle childhood. In R. Case & Y. Okamoto (Eds.), The role of central conceptual structures in the development of children's thought. *Monographs of the Society for Research in Child Development, 246*(61, Serial No. 246), pp. 1–26.

Case, R. (1998). The development of central conceptual structures. In D. Kuhn & R. Siegler (Eds.), *Handbook of child psychology: Vol. 2. Cognition, perception, and language* (5th ed., pp. 745–800). New York: Wiley.

Case, R., & Okamoto, Y. (Eds.). (1996). The role of central conceptual structures in the development of children's thought. *Monographs of the Society for Research in Child Development, 61*(1–2, Serial No. 246).

Caserta, D., Graziano, A., Lo Monte, G., Bordi, G., & Moscarini, M. (2013). Heavy metals and placental fetal–maternal barrier: A mini-review on the major concerns. *European Review for Medical and Pharmacological Sciences, 17,* 2198–2206.

Casper, L. M., & Smith, K. E. (2002). Dispelling the myths: Self-care, class, and race. *Journal of Family Issues, 23,* 716–727.

Caspi, A., Elder, G. H., Jr., & Bem, D. J. (1987). Moving against the world: Life-course patterns of explosive children. *Developmental Psychology, 23,* 308–313.

Caspi, A., Elder, G. H., Jr., & Bem, D. J. (1988). Moving away from the world: Life-course patterns of shy children. *Developmental Psychology, 24,* 824–831.

Caspi, A., Harrington, H., Milne, B., Amell, J. W., Theodore, R. F., & Moffitt, T. E. (2003). Children's behavioral styles at age 3 are linked to their adult personality traits at age 26. *Journal of Personality, 71,* 495–513.

Caspi, A., Moffitt, T. E., Morgan, J., Rutter, M., Taylor, A., Kim-Cohen, J., & Polo-Tomas, M. (2004). Maternal expressed emotion predicts children's antisocial behavior problems: Using monozygotic-twin differences to identify environmental effects on behavioral development. *Developmental Psychology, 40,* 149–161.

Caspi, A., & Roberts, B. W. (2001). Personality development across the life course: The argument for change and continuity. *Psychological Inquiry, 12,* 49–66.

Caspi, A., & Shiner, R. L. (2006). Personality development. In N. Eisenberg (Ed.), *Handbook of child psychology: Vol. 3. Social, emotional, and personality development* (6th ed., pp. 300–365). Hoboken, NJ: Wiley.

Cassia, V. M., Turati, C., & Simion, F. (2004). Can a nonspecific bias toward top-heavy patterns explain newborns' face preference? *Psychological Science, 15,* 379–383.

Cassidy, J., & Berlin, L. J. (1994). The insecure/ambivalent pattern of attachment: Theory and research. *Child Development, 65,* 971–991.

Ceci, S. J., Rosenblum, T. B., & Kumpf, M. (1998). The shrinking gap between high- and low-scoring groups: Current trends and possible causes. In U. Neisser (Ed.), *The rising curve* (pp. 287–302). Washington, DC: American Psychological Association.

Centers for Disease Control and Prevention. (2014). *Breastfeeding report card: United States/2014.* Retrieved from www.cdc.gov/breastfeeding/pdf/2014breastfeedingreportcard.pdf

Centers for Disease Control and Prevention. (2016a). *Asthma surveillance data.* Retrieved from www.cdc.gov/asthma/asthmadata.htm

Centers for Disease Control and Prevention. (2016b). *Sickle cell disease: Data and statistics.* Retrieved from www.cdc.gov/ncbddd/sicklecell/data.html

Centers for Disease Control and Prevention. (2016c). *Tobacco use and pregnancy.* Retrieved from www.cdc.gov/reproductivehealth/maternalinfanthealth/tobaccousepregnancy/index.htm

Centers for Disease Control and Prevention. (2016d). *2015 childhood combined 7-vaccine series coverage report.* Retrieved from www.cdc.gov/vaccines/imz-managers/coverage/childvaxview/data-reports/7-series/index.html

Centers for Disease Control and Prevention. (2017). *Sudden expected infant death and sudden infant death syndrome.* Retrieved from www.cdc.gov/sids/data.htm

Cernoch, J. M., & Porter, R. H. (1985). Recognition of maternal axillary odors by infants. *Child Development 56,* 1593–1598.

Cespedes, E. M., Gillman, M. W., Kleinman, D., Rifas-Shiman, S. L., Redline, S., & Taveras, E. M. (2014). Television viewing, bedroom television, and sleep duration from infancy to mid-childhood. *Pediatrics, 133,* e1163–1171.

Cetinkaya, M. B., Siano, L. J., & Benadiva, C. (2013). Reproductive outcome of women 43 years and beyond undergoing ART treatment with their own oocytes in two Connecticut university programs. *Journal of Assisted Reproductive Genetics, 30,* 673–678.

Chaddock, L., Erickson, K. I., Prakash, R. S., Kim, J. S., Voss, M. W., Van Patter, M., et al. (2010a). A neuroimaging investigation of the association between aerobic fitness and hippocampal volume and memory performance in preadolescent children. *Brain Research, 1358,* 172–183.

Chaddock, L., Erickson, K. I., Prakash, R. S., VanPatter, M., Voss, M. V., Pontifex, M. B., et al. (2010b). Basal ganglia volume is associated with aerobic fitness in preadolescent children. *Developmental Neuroscience, 32,* 249–256.

Chaddock, L., Erickson, K. I., Prakash, R. S., Voss, M. V., VanPatter, M., Pontifex, M. B., et al. (2012). A functional MRI investigation of the association between childhood aerobic fitness and neurocognitive control. *Biological Psychology, 89,* 260–268.

Chaddock, L., Pontifex, M. B., Hillman, C. H., & Kramer, A. F. (2011). A review of the relation of aerobic fitness and physical activity to brain structure and function in children. *Journal of the International Neuropsychological Society, 17,* 1–11.

Chaddock-Heyman, L., Erickson, K. I., Holtrop, J. L., Voss, M W., Pontifex, M. B., Raine, L. B., et al. (2014). Aerobic fitness is associated with greater white matter integrity in children. *Frontiers in Human Neuroscience, 8,* 584.

Chaddock-Heyman, L., Erickson, K. I., Voss, M. W., Knecht, A. M., Pontifex, M. B., Castelli, D. M., et al. (2013). The effects of physical activity on functional MRI activation associated with cognitive control in children: A randomized controlled intervention. *Frontiers in Human Neuroscience, 7,* 72.

Chakravorty, S., & Williams, T. N. (2015). Sickle cell disease: A neglected chronic disease of increasing global health importance. *Archives of Disease in Childhood, 100,* 48–53.

Chalabaev, A., Sarrazin, P., & Fontayne, P. (2009). Stereotype endorsement and perceived ability as mediators of the girls' gender orientation–soccer performance relationship. *Psychology of Sport and Exercise, 10,* 297–299.

Chan, A., Meints, K., Lieven, E., & Tomasello, M. (2010). Young children's comprehension of English SVO word order revisited: Testing the same children in act-out and intermodal preferential looking tasks. *Cognitive Development, 25,* 30–45.

Chan, C. C. Y., Brandone, A. C., & Tardif, T. (2009). Culture, context, or behavioral control? English- and Mandarin-speaking mothers' use of nouns and verbs in joint book reading. *Journal of Cross-Cultural Psychology, 40,* 584–602.

Chan, C. C. Y., Tardif, T., Chen, J., Pulverman, R. B., Zhu, L., & Meng, X. (2011). English- and Chinese-learning infants map novel labels to objects and actions differently. *Developmental Psychology, 47,* 1459–1471.

Chan, S. M. (2010). Aggressive behaviour in early elementary school children: Relations to authoritarian parenting, children's negative emotionality and coping strategies. *Early Child Development and Care, 180,* 1253–1269.

Chandra, A., Copen, C. E., & Stephen, E. H. (2013). Infertility and impaired fecundity in the United States, 1982–2010: Data from the National Survey of Family Growth. *National Health Statistics Reports,* No. 67. Retrieved from www.cdc.gov/nchs/data/nhsr/nhsr067.pdf

Chapman, R. S. (2006). Children's language learning: An interactionist perspective. In R. Paul (Ed.), *Language disorders from a developmental perspective* (pp. 1–53). Mahwah, NJ: Erlbaum.

Charity, A. H., Scarborough, H. S., & Griffin, D. M. (2004). Familiarity with school English in African American children and its relation to early reading achievement. *Child Development, 75,* 1340–1356.

Charman, T., Baron-Cohen, S., Swettenham, J., Baird, G., Cox, A., & Drew, A. (2001). Testing joint attention, imitation, and play as infancy precursors to language and theory of mind. *Cognitive Development, 15,* 481–49.

Chase-Lansdale, P. L., Gordon, R., Brooks-Gunn, J., & Klebanov, P. K. (1997). Neighborhood and family influences on the intellectual and behavioral competence of preschool and early school-age children. In J. Brooks-Gunn, G. Duncan, & J. L. Aber (Eds.), *Neighborhood poverty: Context and consequences for development* (pp. 79–118). New York: Russell Sage Foundation.

Chatterji, P., & Markowitz, S. (2012). Family leave after childbirth and the mental health of new mothers. *Journal of Mental Health Policy and Economics, 15,* 61–76.

Chauhan, G. S., Shastri, J., & Mohite, P. (2005). Development of gender constancy in preschoolers. *Psychological Studies, 50,* 62–71.

Chavajay, P., & Rogoff, B. (1999). Cultural variation in management of attention by children and their caregivers. *Developmental Psychology, 35,* 1079–1090.

Chavajay, P., & Rogoff, B. (2002). Schooling and traditional collaborative social organization of problem solving by Mayan mothers and children. *Developmental Psychology, 38,* 55–66.

Chawarska, K., Macari, S., & Shic, F. (2013). Decreased spontaneous attention to social scenes in 6-month-old infants later diagnosed with autism spectrum disorders. *Biological Psychiatry, 74,* 195–203.

Cheah, C. S. L., Leung, C. Y. Y., Tahseen, M., & Schultz, D. (2009). Authoritative parenting among immigrant Chinese mothers of preschoolers. *Journal of Family Psychology, 23,* 311–320.

Cheah, C. S. L., & Li, J. (2010). Parenting of young immigrant Chinese children: Challenges facing their social-emotional and intellectual development. In E. L. Grigorenko & R. Takanishi (Eds.), *Immigration, diversity, and education* (pp. 225–241). New York: Routledge.

Chen, E. S. L., & Rao, N. (2011). Gender socialization in Chinese kindergartens: Teachers' contributions. *Sex Roles, 64,* 103–116.

Chen, J. J., Howard, K. S., & Brooks-Gunn, J. (2011). How do neighborhoods matter across the life span? In K. L. Fingerman, C. A. Berg, J. Smith, & T. C. Antonucci (Eds.), *Handbook of life-span development* (pp. 805–836). New York: Springer.

Chen, J. J., Sun, P., & Yu, Z. (2017). A comparative study on parenting of preschool children between the Chinese in China and Chinese immigrants in the United States. *Journal of Family Issues, 38,* 1267–1287.

Chen, R. (2012). Institutional characteristics and college student dropout risks: A multilevel event history analysis. *Research in Higher Education, 53,* 487–505.

Chen, X. (2012). Culture, peer interaction, and socioemotional development. *Child Development Perspectives, 6,* 27–34.

Chen, X., Rubin, K. H., Liu, M., Chen, H., Wang, L., Li, D., et al. (2003). Compliance in Chinese and Canadian toddlers: A cross-cultural study. *International Journal of Behavioral Development, 27,* 428–436.

Chen, X., & Schmidt, L. A. (2015). Temperament and personality. In M. E. Lamb (Ed.), *Handbook of child psychology and developmental science: Vol. 3. Socioemotional processes* (7th ed., pp. 152–200). Hoboken, NJ: Wiley.

Chen, X., Wang, L., & DeSouza, A. (2006). Temperament, socioemotional functioning, and peer relationships in Chinese and North American children. In X. Chen, D. C. French, & B. H. Schneider (Eds.), *Peer relationships in cultural context* (pp. 123–147). New York: Cambridge University Press.

Chen, Y.-C., Yu, M.-L., Rogan, W., Gladen, B., & Hsu, C.-C. (1994). A 6-year follow-up of behavior and activity disorders in the Taiwan Yu-cheng children. *American Journal of Public Health, 84,* 415–421.

Chen, Y.-J., & Hsu, C.-C. (1994). Effects of prenatal exposure to PCBs on the neurological function of children: A neuropsychological and neurophysiological study. *Developmental Medicine and Child Neurology, 36,* 312–320.

Chen, Z., Sanchez, R. P., & Campbell, T. (1997). From beyond to within their grasp: The rudiments of analogical problem solving in 10- to 13-month-olds. *Developmental Psychology, 33,* 790–801.

Chess, S., & Thomas, A. (1984). *Origins and evolution of behavior disorders.* New York: Brunner/Mazel.

Chevalier, N. (2015). The development of executive function: Toward more optimal coordination of control with age. *Child Development Perspectives, 9,* 239–244.

Cheyney, M., Bovbjerg, M., Everson, C., Gordon, W., Hannibal, D., & Vedam, S. (2014). Outcomes of care for 16,924 planned home births in the United States: The Midwives Alliance of North America Statistics Project, 2004 to 2009. *Journal of Midwifery and Women's Health, 59,* 17–27.

Chiang, T., Schultz, R. M., & Lampson, M. A. (2012). Meiotic origins of maternal age-related aneuploidy. *Biology of Reproduction, 86,* 1–7.

Child Care Aware. (2017). *Parents and the high cost of child care: 2016 report.* Retrieved from usa.childcareaware.org

Child Trends. (2013). *Family meals.* Retrieved from www.childtrends.org/wp-content/uploads/2012/09/96_Family_Meals.pdf

Child Trends. (2014a). *Births to unmarried women.* Retrieved from www.childtrends.org/?indicators=births-to-unmarried-women

Child Trends. (2014b). *Unintentional injuries: Indicators on children and youth.* Retrieved from www.childtrends.org/wp-content/uploads/2014/08/122_Unintentional_Injuries.pdf

Child Trends. (2015a). *Births to unmarried women.* Retrieved from www.childtrends.org/wp-content/uploads/2015/03/75_Births_to_Unmarried_Women.pdf

Child Trends. (2015b). *Full-day kindergarten.* Retrieved from www.childtrends.org/?indicators=full-day-kindergarten

Child Trends. (2015c). *Late or no prenatal care.* Retrieved from www.childtrends.org/wp-content/uploads/2014/07/25_Prenatal_Care.pdf

Choe, D. E., Olson, S. L., & Sameroff, A. J. (2013). The interplay of externalizing problems and physical discipline and inductive discipline during childhood. *Developmental Psychology, 49,* 2029–2039.

Choi, S., & Gopnik, A. (1995). Early acquisition of verbs in Korean: A cross-linguistic study. *Journal of Child Language, 22,* 497–529.

Chomsky, C. (1969). *The acquisition of syntax in children from five to ten.* Cambridge, MA: MIT Press.

Chomsky, N. (1957). *Syntactic structures.* The Hague: Mouton.

Chouinard, M. M., & Clark, E. V. (2003). Adult reformulations of child errors as negative evidence. *Journal of Child Language, 30,* 637–669.

Christakis, D. A., Garrison, M. M., Herrenkohl, T., Haggerty, K., Rivara, F. P., Zhou, C., & Liekweg, K. (2013). Modifying media content for preschool children: A randomized controlled trial. *Pediatrics, 131,* 431–438.

Christakis, D. A., Zimmerman, F. J., DiGiuseppe, D. L., & McCarty, C. A. (2004). Early television exposure and subsequent attentional problems in children. *Pediatrics, 113,* 708–713.

Christoffersen, M. N. (2012). A study of adopted children, their environment, and development: A systematic review. *Adoption Quarterly, 15,* 220–237.

Chronis-Tuscano, A., Rubin, K., O'Brien, K. A., Coplan, R. J., Thoma, S. R., Dougherty, L. R., et al. (2015). Preliminary evaluation of a multimodal early intervention program for behaviorally inhibited preschoolers. *Journal of Consulting and Clinical Psychology, 83,* 534–540.

Cicchetti, D., & Toth, S. L. (2015). Child maltreatment. In M. E. Lamb (Ed.), *Handbook of child psychology and developmental science: Vol. 3. Socioemotional processes* (7th ed., pp. 513–563). Hoboken, NJ: Wiley.

Cillessen, A. H. N. (2009). Sociometric methods. In K. H. Rubin & W. M. Bukowski (Eds.), *Handbook of peer interactions, relationships, and groups* (pp. 82–99). New York: Guilford.

Cillessen, A. H. N., & Bellmore, A. D. (2004). Social skills and interpersonal perception in early and middle childhood. In P. K. Smith & C. H. Hart (Eds.), *Blackwell handbook of childhood social development* (pp. 355–374). Malden, MA: Blackwell.

Cipriano, E. A., & Stifter, C. A. (2010). Predicting preschool effortful control from toddler temperament and parenting behavior. *Journal of Applied Developmental Psychology, 31,* 221–230.

Ciu, L., Colasante, T., Malti, T., Ribeaud, D., & Eisner, M. P. (2016). Dual trajectories of reactive and proactive aggression from mid-childhood to early adolescence: Relations to sensation seeking, risk taking, and moral reasoning. *Journal of Abnormal Child Psychology*, 44, 663–675.

Clark, S. M., Ghulmiyyah, L. M., & Hankins, G. D. (2008). Antenatal antecedents and the impact of obstetric care in the etiology of cerebral palsy. *Clinical Obstetrics and Gynecology, 51,* 775–786.

Clarke-Stewart, K. A., & Hayward, C. (1996). Advantages of father custody and contact for the psychological well-being of school-age children. *Journal of Applied Developmental Psychology, 17,* 239–270.

Clearfield, M. W. (2011). Learning to walk changes infants' social interactions. *Infant Behavior and Development, 34,* 15–25.

Clearfield, M. W., & Nelson, N. M. (2006). Sex differences in mothers' speech and play behavior with 6-, 9-, and 14-month-old infants. *Sex Roles, 54,* 127–137.

Clearfield, M. W., & Westfahl, S. M.-C. (2006). Familiarization in infants' perception of addition problems. *Journal of Cognition and Development, 7,* 27–43.

Clements, D. H., & Sarama, J. (2012). Learning and teaching early and elementary mathematics. In J. S. Carlson & J. R. Levin (Eds.), *Instructional strategies for improving students' learning* (pp. 205–212). Charlotte, NC: Information Age Publishing.

Clements, D. H., Sarama, J., Spitler, M. E., Lange, A. A., & Wolfe, C. B. (2011). Mathematics learned by young children in an intervention based on learning trajectories: A large-scale cluster randomized trial. *Journal for Research in Mathematics Education, 42,* 127–166.

Clincy, A. R., & Mills-Koonce, W. R. (2013). Trajectories of intrusive parenting during infancy and toddlerhood as predictors of rural, low-income African American boys' school-related outcomes. *American Journal of Orthopsychiatry, 83,* 194–206.

Coall, D. A., Callan, A. C., Dickins, T. E., & Chisholm, J. S. (2015). Evolution and prenatal development: An evolutionary perspective. In M. E. Lamb (Ed.), *Handbook of child psychology and developmental science: Vol. 3. Socioemotional processes* (7th ed., pp. 57–105). Hoboken, NJ: Wiley.

Cohen, L. B. (2010). A bottom-up approach to infant perception and cognition: A summary of evidence and discussion of issues. In S. P. Johnson (Ed.), *Neoconstructivism: The new science of cognitive development* (pp. 335–346). New York: Oxford University Press.

Cohen, L. B., & Brunt, J. (2009). Early word learning and categorization: Methodological issues and recent empirical evidence. In J. Colombo, P. McCardle, & L. Freund (Eds.), *Infant pathways to language: Methods, models, and research disorders* (pp. 245–266). New York: Psychology Press.

Cohen-Bendahan, C. C. C., van Doornen, L. J. P., & de Weerth, C. (2014). Young adults' reactions to infant crying. *Infant Behavior and Development, 37,* 33–43.

Cohn, N. (2014). Framing "I can't draw": The influence of cultural frames on the development of drawing. *Culture and Psychology, 20,* 102–117.

Cole, P. M., LeDonne, E. N., & Tan, P. Z. (2013). A longitudinal examination of maternal emotions in relation to young children's developing self-regulation. *Parenting: Science and Practice, 13,* 113–132.

Coles, R. L. (2015). Single-father families: A review of the literature. *Journal of Family Theory & Review, 7,* 144–166.

Coley, R. L., Morris, J. E., & Hernandez, D. (2004). Out-of-school care and problem behavior trajectories among low-income adolescents: Individual, family, and neighborhood characteristics as added risks. *Child Development, 75,* 948–965.

Collins, W. A., Madsen, S. D., & Susman-Stillman, A. (2002). Parenting during middle childhood. In M. H. Bornstein (Ed.), *Handbook of parenting: Vol. 1* (2nd ed., pp. 73–101). Mahwah, NJ: Erlbaum.

Collin-Vézina, D., Daigneault, I., & Hébert, M. (2013). Lessons learned from child sexual abuse research: Prevalence, outcomes, and preventive strategies. *Child and Adolescent Psychiatry and Mental Health, 7,* 1–9.

Colombo, J., Brez, C. C., & Curtindale, L. M. (2013). Infant perception and cognition. In R. M. Lerner, M. A. Easterbrooks, & J. Mistry (Eds.), *Handbook of psychology: Vol. 6. Developmental psychology* (pp. 61–89). Hoboken, NJ: Wiley.

Colombo, J., Kapa, L., & Curtindale, L. (2011). Varieties of attention in infancy. In L. M. Oakes, C. H. Cashon, M. Casasola, & D. Rakison (Eds.), *Infant perception and cognition* (pp. 3–25). New York: Oxford University Press.

Colombo, J., Shaddy, D. J., Richman, W. A., Maikranz, J. M., & Blaga, O. M. (2004). The developmental course of habituation in infancy and preschool outcome. *Infancy, 5,* 1–38.

Colson, E. R., Willinger, M., Rybin, D., Heeren, T., Smith, L. A., Lister, G., et al. (2013). Trends and factors associated with infant bed sharing, 1993–2010. The National Infant Sleep Position Study. *JAMA Pediatrics, 167,* 1032–1037.

Comeau, L., Genesee, F., & Mendelson, M. (2010). A comparison of bilingual and monolingual children's conversational repairs. *First Language, 30,* 354–374.

Common Sense Media. (2013). *Zero to eight: Children's media use in America 2013.* San Francisco: Author. Retrieved from www.commonsensemedia.org/research/zero-to-eight-childrens-media-use-in-america-2013

Compas, B. E., Jaser, S. S., Dunn, M. J., & Rodriguez, E. M. (2012). Coping with chronic illness in childhood and adolescence. *Annual Review of Clinical Psychology, 8,* 455–480.

Conde-Agudelo, A., Belizan, J. M., and Diaz-Rossello, J. (2011). Kangaroo mother care to reduce morbidity and mortality in low birthweight infants. *Cochrane Database of Systematic Reviews,* Issue 3, Art. No.: CD002771.

Condron, D. J. (2013). Affluence, inequality, and educational achievement: A structural analysis of 97 jurisdictions, across the globe. *Sociological Spectrum, 33,* 73–97.

Conger, K. J., Stocker, C., & McGuire, S. (2009). Sibling socialization: The effects of stressful life events and experiences. In L. Kramer & K. J. Conger (Eds.), *Siblings as agents of socialization: New directions for child and adolescent development* (No. 126, pp. 44–60). San Francisco: Jossey-Bass.

Conger, R. D., & Donnellan, M. B. (2007). An interactionist perspective on the socioeconomic context of human development. *Annual Review of Psychology, 58,* 175–199.

Conner, D. B., & Cross, D. R. (2003). Longitudinal analysis of the presence, efficacy, and stability of maternal scaffolding during informal problem-solving interactions. *British Journal of Developmental Psychology, 21,* 315–334.

Connor, D. F. (2015). Stimulant and nonstimulant medications for childhood ADHD. In R. A. Barkley (Ed.), *Attention-deficit hyperactivity disorder: A handbook for diagnosis and treatment* (4th ed., pp. 666–685). New York: Guilford.

Conron, K. J., Scott, G., Stowell, G. S., & Landers, S. J. (2012). Transgender health in Massachusetts: Results from a household probability sample of adults. *American Journal of Public Health, 102,* 118–122.

Conway, L. (2007, April 5). Drop the Barbie: Ken Zucker's reparatist treatment of gender-variant children. *Trans News Updates*. Retrieved from ai.eecs.umich.edu/people/conway/TS/News/Drop%20the%20Barbie.htm

Cook, C. R., Williams, K. R., Guerra, N. G., & Kim, T. E. (2010). Variability in the prevalence of bullying and victimization: A cross-national and methodological analysis. In S. R. Jimerson, S. M. Swearer, & D. L. Espelage (Eds.), *Handbook of bullying in schools: An international perspective* (pp. 347–362). New York: Routledge.

Cooley, J. L., Fite, P. J., & Pederson, C. A. (2017). Bidirectional associations between peer victimization and functions of aggression in middle childhood: Further evaluation across informants and academic years. *Journal of Abnormal Child Psychology, 45.* Retrieved from doi.org/10.1007/s10802-017-0283-8

Cooper, H., Batts, A., Patall, E. A., & Dent, A. L. (2010). Effects of full-day kindergarten on academic achievement and social development. *Review of Educational Research, 80,* 54–70.

Coplan, R. J., & Arbeau, K. A. (2008). The stresses of a "brave new world": Shyness and school adjustment in kindergarten. *Journal of Research in Childhood Education, 22,* 377–389.

Coplan, R. J., & Armer, M. (2007). A "multitude" of solitude: A closer look at social withdrawal and nonsocial play in early childhood. *Child Development Perspectives, 1,* 26–32.

Coplan, R. J., Gavinsky-Molina, M. H., Lagace Seguin, D., & Wichmann, C. (2001). When girls versus boys play alone: Gender differences in the associates of nonsocial play in kindergarten. *Developmental Psychology, 37,* 464–474.

Coplan, R. J., & Ooi, L. (2014). The causes and consequences of "playing alone" in childhood. In R. J. Coplan & J. C. Bowker (Eds.), *The handbook of solitude: Psychological perspectives on social isolation, social withdrawal, and being alone* (pp. 111–128). Chichester, UK: Wiley-Blackwell.

Coplan, R. J., Prakash, K., O'Neil, K., & Armer, M. (2004). Do you "want" to play? Distinguishing between conflicted shyness and social disinterest in early childhood. *Developmental Psychology, 40,* 244–258.

Copple, C., & Bredekamp, S. (2009). *Developmentally appropriate practice in early childhood programs* (3rd ed.). Washington, DC: National Association for the Education of Young Children.

Corby, B. C., Hodges, E. V., & Perry, D. G. (2007). Gender identity and adjustment in Black, Hispanic, and White preadolescents. *Developmental Psychology, 26,* 261–266.

Corenblum, B. (2003). What children remember about ingroup and outgroup peers: Effects of stereotypes on children's processing of information about group members. *Journal of Experimental Child Psychology, 86,* 32–66.

Cornoldi, C., Giofré, D., Orsini, A., & Pezzuti, L. (2014). Differences in the intellectual profile of children with intellectual vs. learning disability. *Research in Developmental Disabilities, 35,* 2224–2230.

Cornwell, A. C., & Feigenbaum, P. (2006). Sleep biological rhythms in normal infants and those at high risk for SIDS. *Chronobiology International, 23,* 935–961.

Correa-Chávez, M., Roberts, A. L. D., & Perez, M. M. (2011). Cultural patterns in children's learning through keen observation and participation in their communities. In J. B. Benson (Ed.), *Advances in child development and behavior* (Vol. 40, pp. 209–241). San Diego, CA: Elsevier Academic Press.

Costa, A., & Sebastián-Gallés, N. (2014). How does the bilingual experience sculpt the brain? *Nature Reviews Neuroscience, 15,* 336–345.

Costacurta, M., Sicuro, L., Di Renzo, L., & Condo, R. (2012). Childhood obesity and skeletal-dental maturity. *European Journal of Paediatric Dentistry, 13,* 128–132.

Cote, L. R., & Bornstein, M. H. (2009). Child and mother play in three U.S. cultural groups: Comparisons and associations. *Journal of Family Psychology, 23,* 355–363.

Côté, S. M., Vaillancourt, T., Barker, E. D., Nagin, D., & Tremblay, R. E. (2007). The joint development of physical and indirect aggression: Predictors of continuity and change during childhood. *Development and Psychopathology, 19,* 37–55.

Coubart, A., Izard, V., Spelke, E. S., Marie, J., & Streri, A. (2014). Dissociation between small and large numerosities in newborn infants. *Developmental Science, 17,* 11–22.

Couch, S. C., Glanz, K., Zhou, C., Sallis, J. F., & Saelens, B. E. (2014). Home food environment in relation to children's diet quality and weight status. *Journal of the Academy of Nutrition and Dietetics, 114,* 1569–1579.

Courchesne, E., Mouton, P. R., Calhoun, M. E., Semendeferi, K., Ahrens-Barbeau, C., Hallet, M. J., et al. (2011). Neuron number and size in prefrontal cortex of children with autism. *JAMA, 306,* 2001–2010.

Cowan, N., & Alloway, T. P. (2009). Development of working memory in childhood. In M. L. Courage & N. Cowan (Eds.), *Development of memory in infancy and childhood* (pp. 303–342). Hove, UK: Psychology Press.

Cox, B. D. (2013). The past and future of epigenesis in psychology. *New Ideas in Psychology, 31,* 351–354.

Coyle, J. T. (2013). Brain structural alterations induced by fetal exposure to cocaine persist into adolescence and affect behavior. *JAMA Psychiatry, 70,* 1113–1114.

Crago, M. B., Annahatak, B., & Ningiuruvik, L. (1993). Changing patterns of language socialization in Inuit homes. *Anthropology and Education Quarterly, 24,* 205–223.

Craig, H. K., & Washington, J. A. (2006). *Malik goes to school: Examining the language skills of African American students from preschool–5th grade.* Mahwah, NJ: Erlbaum.

Craig, J. T., Gregus, S. J., Elledge, C., Pastrana, F. A., & Cavell, T. A. (2016). Preliminary investigation of the relation between lunchroom peer acceptance and peer victimization. *Journal of Applied Developmental Psychology, 43,* 101–111.

Crain, W. (2010). *Theories of development: Concepts and applications* (6th ed.). Upper Saddle River, NJ: Pearson.

Crair, M. C., Gillespie, D. C., & Stryker, M. P. (1998). The role of visual experience in the development of columns in cat visual cortex. *Science, 279,* 566–570.

Cratty, B. J. (1986). *Perceptual and motor development in infants and children* (3rd ed.), Englewood Cliffs, NJ: Prentice-Hall.

Crick, N. R., Ostrov, J. M., Burr, J. E., Cullerton-Sen, C., Jansen-Yeh, E., & Ralston, P. (2006). A longitudinal study of relational and physical aggression in preschool. *Journal of Applied Developmental Psychology, 27,* 254–268.

Crick, N. R., Ostrov, J. M., & Werner, N. E. (2006). A longitudinal study of relational aggression, physical aggression, and social-psychological adjustment. *Journal of Abnormal Child Psychology, 34,* 131–142.

Crockenberg, S., & Leerkes, E. (2004). Infant and maternal behaviors regulate infant reactivity to novelty at 6 months. *Developmental Psychology, 40,* 1123–1132.

Cronin, L. D., & Allen, J. B. (2015). Developmental experiences and well-being in sport: The importance of the coaching climate. *Sport Psychologist, 29,* 62–71.

Crosnoe, R., & Benner, A. D. (2015). Children at school. In M. H. Bornstein & T. Leventhal (Eds.), *Handbook of child psychology and developmental science: Vol. 4. Ecological settings and processes* (7th ed., pp. 268–304). Hoboken, NJ: Wiley.

Crouch, J. L., Skowronski, J. J., Milner, J. S., & Harris, B. (2008). Parental responses to infant crying: The influence of child physical abuse risk and hostile priming. *Child Abuse and Neglect, 32,* 702–710.

Crouter, A. C., Whiteman, S. D., McHale, S. M., & Osgood, D. W. (2007). Development of gender attitude traditionality across middle childhood and adolescence. *Child Development, 78,* 911–926.

Cuadros, O., & Berger, C. (2016). The protective role of friendship quality on the wellbeing of adolescents victimized by peers. *Journal of Youth and Adolescence, 45,* 1877–1888.

Cummings, E. M., & Davies, P. T. (2010). *Marital conflict and children: An emotional security perspective.* New York: Guilford.

Cummings, E. M., & Miller-Graff, L. E. (2015). Emotional security theory: An emerging theoretical model for youths' psychological and physiological responses across multiple developmental contexts. *Current Directions in Psychological Science, 24,* 208–213.

Curtin, S., & Werker, J. F. (2007). The perceptual foundations of phonological development. In G. Gaskell (Ed.), *Oxford handbook of psycholinguistics* (pp. 579–599). Oxford, UK: Oxford University Press.

Curtiss, S., & Schaeffer, J. (2005). Syntactic development in children with hemispherectomy: The I-, D-, and C-systems. *Brain and Language, 94,* 147–166.

Cutuli, J. J., Herbers, J. E., Rinaldi, M., Masten, A. S., & Oberg, C. N. (2010). Asthma and behavior in homeless 4- to 7-year-olds. *Pediatrics, 125,* e145–e151.

Cvencek, D., Meltzoff, A. N., & Greenwald, A. G. (2011). Math–gender stereotypes in elementary school children. *Child Development, 82,* 766–779.

Cyr, C., Euser, E. M., Bakermans-Kranenburg, M. J., & van IJzendoorn, M. H. (2010). Attachment security and disorganization in maltreating and high-risk families: Implications for developmental theory. *Development and Psychopathology, 14,* 843–860.

D

Dakil, S. R., Cox, M., Lin, H., & Flores, G. (2012). Physical abuse in U.S. children: Risk factors and deficiencies in referrals to support services. *Journal of Aggression, Maltreatment, and Trauma, 21,* 555–569.

Daley, T. C., Whaley, S. E., Sigman, M. D., Espinosa, M. P., & Neumann, C. (2003). IQ on the rise: The Flynn effect in rural Kenyan children. *Psychological Science, 14,* 215–219.

Damon, W. (1988a). *The moral child.* New York: Free Press.

Damon, W. (1988b). *Self-understanding in childhood and adolescence.* New York: Cambridge University Press.

Daniels, E., & Leaper, C. (2006). A longitudinal investigation of sport participation, peer acceptance, and self-esteem among adolescent girls and boys. *Sex Roles, 55,* 875–880.

Daniels, H. (2011). Vygotsky and psychology. In U. Goswami (Ed.), *The Wiley-Blackwell handbook of childhood cognitive development* (2nd ed., pp. 673–696). Malden, MA: Wiley-Blackwell.

Dannemiller, J. L., & Stephens, B. R. (1988). A critical test of infant pattern preference models. *Child Development, 59,* 210–216.

Danzer, E., & Johnson, M. P. (2014). Fetal surgery for neural tube defects. *Seminars in Fetal and Neonatal Medicine, 19,* 2–8.

Darwin, C. (1936). *On the origin of species by means of natural selection.* New York: Modern Library. (Original work published 1859)

Daskalakis, N., & Yehuda, R. (2014). Site-specific methylation changes in the glucocorticoid receptor exon 1F promoter in relation to life adversity: Systematic review of contributing factors. *Frontiers in Neuroscience, 8.* Retrieved from journal.frontiersin.org/article/10.3389/fnins.2014.00369/full

Davies, J. (2008). Differential teacher positive and negative interactions with male and female pupils in the primary school setting. *Educational and Child Psychology, 25,* 17–26.

Davies, P. T., & Cicchetti, D. (2014). How and why does the 5-HTTLPR gene moderate associations between maternal unresponsiveness and children's disruptive problems? *Child Development, 85,* 484–500.

Davis, E. L., & Buss, K. A. (2012). Moderators of the relation between shyness and behavior with peers: Cortisol dysregulation and maternal emotion socialization. *Social Development, 21,* 801–820.

Davis, E. L., Levine, L. J., Lench, H. C., & Quas, J. A. (2010). Metacognitive emotion regulation: Children's awareness that changing thoughts and goals can alleviate negative emotions. *Emotion, 10,* 498–510.

Davis, P. E., Meins, E., & Fernyhough, C. (2014). Children with imaginary companions focus on mental characteristics when describing their real-life friends. *Infant and Child Development, 23,* 622–633.

Dayton, C. J., Walsh, T. B., Oh, W., & Volling, B. (2015). Hush now baby: Mothers' and fathers' strategies for soothing their infants and associated parenting outcomes. *Journal of Pediatric Health Care, 29,* 145–155.

Dearing, E., McCartney, K., & Taylor, B. A. (2009). Does higher quality early child care promote low-income children's math and reading achievement in middle childhood? *Child Development, 80,* 1329–1349.

Dearing, E., Wimer, C., Simpkins, S. D., Lund, T., Bouffard, S. M., Caronongan, P., & Kreider, H. (2009). Do neighborhood and home contexts help explain why low-income children miss opportunities to participate in activities outside of school? *Developmental Psychology, 45,* 1545–1562.

Deary, I. J., Strand, S., Smith, P., & Fernandes, C. (2007). Intelligence and educational achievement. *Intelligence, 35,* 13–21.

Deater-Deckard, K., Lansford, J. E., Dodge, K. A., Pettit, G. S., & Bates, J. E. (2003). The development of attitudes about physical punishment: An 8-year longitudinal study. *Journal of Family Psychology, 17,* 351–360.

DeBoer, T., Scott, L. S., & Nelson, C. A. (2007). Methods for acquiring and analyzing infant event-related potentials. In M. de Haan (Ed.), *Infant EEG and event-related potentials* (pp. 5–37). New York: Psychology Press.

de Boisferon, A., Tift, A. H., Minar, N. J., Lewkowicz, D. J. (2017). Selective attention to a talker's mouth in infancy: Role of audiovisual temporal synchrony and linguistic experience. *Developmental Science, 20,* e12381.

Debrabant, J., Gheysen, F., Vingerhoets, G., & Van Waelvelde, H. (2012). Age-related differences in predictive response timing in children: Evidence from regularly relative to irregularly paced reaction time performance. *Human Movement Science, 31,* 801–810.

de Bruyn, E. H., & Cillessen, A. H. N. (2006). Popularity in early adolescence: Prosocial and antisocial subtypes. *Journal of Adolescent Research, 21,* 607–627.

DeCasper, A. J., & Spence, M. J. (1986). Prenatal maternal speech influences newborns' perception of speech sounds. *Infant Behavior and Development, 9,* 133–150.

Declercq, E. R., Sakala, C., Corry, M. P., Applebaum, S., & Herrlich, A. (2014). Major survey findings of

Listening to Mothers (SM) III: Pregnancy and Birth. *Journal of Perinatal Education, 23,* 9–16.

de Cock, E. S. A., Henrichs, J., Rijk, C. H. A. M., & van Bakel, H. J. A. (2015). Baby please stop crying: An experimental approach to infant crying, affect, and expected parent self-efficacy. *Journal of Reproductive and Infant Psychology, 33,* 414–425.

De Corte, E., & Verschaffel, L. (2006). Mathematical thinking and learning. In K. A. Renninger & I. E. Sigel (Eds.), *Handbook of child psychology: Vol. 4. Child psychology in practice* (6th ed., pp. 103–152). Hoboken, NJ: Wiley.

DeFlorio, L., & Beliakoff, A. (2015). Socioeconomic status and preschoolers' mathematical knowledge: The contribution of home activities and parent beliefs. *Early Education and Development, 25,* 319–341.

de Haan, M. (2015). Neuroscientific methods with children. In P. D. Zelazo (Ed.), *Oxford handbook of developmental psychology: Vol. 1. Body and mind* (pp. 683–712). New York: Oxford University Press.

De Laet, S. Doumen, S., Vervoort, E., Colpin, H., Van Leeuwen, K., Goossens, L., & Verschueren, K. (2014). Transactional links between teacher–child relationship quality and perceived versus sociometric popularity: A three-wave longitudinal study. *Child Development, 85,* 1647–1662.

de la Monte, S. M., & Kril, J. J. (2014). Human alcohol-related neuropathology. *Acta Neuropathologica, 127,* 71–90.

DeLoache, J. S. (1987). Rapid change in symbolic functioning of very young children. *Science, 238,* 1556–1557.

DeLoache, J. S. (2002). The symbol-mindedness of young children. In W. Hartup & R. A. Weinberg (Eds.), *Minnesota symposia on child psychology* (Vol. 32, pp. 73–101). Mahwah, NJ: Erlbaum.

DeLoache, J. S., Chiong, C., Sherman, K., Islam, N., Vanderborght, M., Troseth, G. L., et al. (2010). Do babies learn from baby media? *Psychological Science, 21,* 1570–1574.

DeLoache, J. S., LoBue, V., Vanderborght, M., & Chiong, C. (2013). On the validity and robustness of the scale error phenomenon in early childhood. *Infant Behavior and Development, 36,* 63–70.

DeMarie, D., & Lopez, L. M. (2014). Memory in schools. In P. J. Bauer & R. Fivush (Eds.), *Wiley handbook on the development of children's memory* (Vol. 2, pp. 836–864). Malden, MA: Wiley-Blackwell.

DeMarie, D., Miller, P. H., Ferron, J., & Cunningham, W. R. (2004). Path analysis tests of theoretical models of children's memory performance. *Journal of Cognition and Development, 5,* 461–492.

Dennis, T. A., & Kelemen, D. A. (2009). Preschool children's views on emotion regulation: Functional associations and implications for social–emotional adjustment. *International Journal of Behavioral Development, 33,* 243–252.

Deprest, J. A., Devlieger, R., Srisupundit, K., Beck, V., Sandaite, I., Rusconi, S., et al. (2010). Fetal surgery is a clinical reality. *Seminars in Fetal and Neonatal Medicine, 15,* 58–67.

DeRoche, K., & Welsh, M. (2008). Twenty-five years of research on neurocognitive outcomes in early-treated phenylketonuria: Intelligence and executive function. *Developmental Neuropsychology, 33,* 474–504.

DeRosier, M. E. (2007). Peer-rejected and bullied children: A safe schools initiative for elementary school students. In J. E. Zins, M. J. Elias, & C. A. Maher (Eds.), *Bullying, victimization, and peer harassment* (pp. 257–276). New York: Haworth.

de Rosnay, M., Copper, P. J., Tsigaras, N., & Murray, L. (2006). Transmission of social anxiety from mother to infant: An experimental study using a social referencing paradigm. *Behavior Research and Therapy, 44,* 1165–1175.

de Rosnay, M., & Hughes, C. (2006). Conversation and theory of mind: Do children talk their way to socio-cognitive understanding? *British Journal of Developmental Psychology, 24,* 7–37.

Dessens, A. B., Slijper, F. M. E., & Drop, S. L. S. (2005). Gender dysphoria and gender change in chromosomal females with congenital adrenal hyperplasia. *Archives of Sexual Behavior, 34,* 389–397.

Devine, R. T., & Hughes, C. (2018). Family correlates of false belief understanding in early childhood: A meta-analysis. *Child Development, 89*: 12682.

DeVries, R. (2001). Constructivist education in preschool and elementary school: The sociomoral atmosphere as the first educational goal. In S. L. Golbeck (Ed.), *Psychological perspectives on early childhood education* (pp. 153–180). Mahwah, NJ: Erlbaum.

de Waal, F. B. M. (2001). *Tree of origin.* Cambridge, MA: Harvard University Press.

Diamond, A. (2004). Normal development of prefrontal cortex from birth to young adulthood: Cognitive functions, anatomy, and biochemistry. In D. T. Stuff & R. T. Knight (Eds.), *Principles of frontal lobe function* (pp. 466–503). New York: Oxford University Press.

Diamond, G., Senecky, Y., Reichman, H., Inbar, D., & Chodick, G. (2015). Parental perception of developmental vulnerability after inter-country adoption: A 10-year follow-up study: Longitudinal study after inter-country adoption. *International Journal of Disabilities and Human Development, 14,* 75–80.

Diamond, L. M., Bonner, S. B., & Dickenson, J. (2015). The development of sexuality. In M. E. Lamb (Ed.), *Handbook of child psychology and developmental science: Vol. 3. Socioemotional processes* (7th ed., pp. 888–931). Hoboken, NJ: Wiley.

Di Ceglie, D. (2014). Care for gender-dysphoric children. In B. P. C. Kreukels, T. D. Steensma, & A. L. C. deVries (Eds.), *Gender dysphoria and disorders of sex development: Progress in care and knowledge* (pp. 151–169). New York: Springer Science + Business Media.

Dickinson, D. K., Golinkoff, R. M., & Hirsh-Pasek, K. (2010). Speaking out for language: Why language is central to reading development. *Educational Researcher, 39,* 305–310.

Dickinson, D. K., & McCabe, A. (2001). Bringing it all together: The multiple origins, skills, and environmental supports of early literacy. *Learning Disabilities Research and Practice, 16,* 186–202.

Dickinson, D. K., McCabe, A., Anastasopoulos, L., Peisner-Feinberg, E. S., & Poe, M. D. (2003). The comprehensive language approach to early literacy: The interrelationships among vocabulary, phonological sensitivity, and print knowledge among preschool-age children. *Journal of Educational Psychology, 95,* 465–481.

Dick-Read, G. (1959). *Childbirth without fear.* New York: Harper & Row.

DiDonato, M. D., & Berenbaum, S. A. (2011). The benefits and drawbacks of gender typing: How different dimensions are related to psychological adjustment. *Archives of Sexual Behavior, 40,* 457–463.

Diepstra, H., Trehub, S. E., Eriks-Brophy, A., van Lieshout, P. H. H. M. (2017). Imitation of non-speech oral gestures by 8-month-old infants. *Language and Speech, 60,* 154–166.

DiLalla, L. F., Bersted, K., & John, S. G. (2015). Evidence of reactive gene–environment correlation in preschoolers' prosocial play with unfamiliar peers. *Developmental Psychology, 51,* 1464–1475.

DiLisi, R., & Gallagher, A. M. (1991). Understanding of gender stability and constancy in Argentinian children. *Merrill-Palmer Quarterly, 37,* 483–502.

Dimitry, L. (2012) A systematic review on the mental health of children and adolescents in areas of armed conflict in the Middle East. *Child: Care, Health and Development, 38,* 153–161.

DiPietro, J. A., Bornstein, M. H., Costigan, K. A., Pressman, E. K., Hahn, C.-S., & Painter, K. (2002). What does fetal movement predict about behavior during the first two years of life? *Developmental Psychobiology, 40,* 358–371.

DiPietro, J. A., Caulfield, L. E., Irizarry, R. A., Chen, P., Merialdi, M., & Zavaleta, N. (2006). Prenatal development of intrafetal and maternal–fetal synchrony. *Behavioral Neuroscience, 120,* 687–701.

DiPietro, J. A., Costigan, K. A., & Voegtline, K. M. (2015). Studies in fetal behavior: Revisited, renewed, and reimagined. *Monographs of the Society for Research in Child Development, 80*(3, Serial No. 318).

DiPietro, J. A., Hodgson, D. M., Costigan, K. A., & Hilton, S. C. (1996). Fetal neurobehavioral development. *Child Development, 67,* 2553–2567.

Dirks, M. A., Persram, R., Recchia, H. A., & Howe, N. (2015). Sibling relationships as sources of risk and resilience in the development and maintenance of internalizing and externalizing problems during childhood and adolescence. *Clinical Psychology Review, 42,* 145–155.

Dishion, T. J., Shaw, D., Connell, A., Gardner, F., Weaver, C., & Wilson, M. (2008). The Family Check-Up with high-risk indigent families: Preventing problem behavior by increasing parents' positive behavior support in early childhood. *Child Development, 79,* 1395–1414.

Dittmar, M., Abbot-Smith, K., Lieven, E., & Tomasello, M. (2014). Familiar verbs are not always easier than novel verbs: How German preschool children comprehend active and passive sentences. *Cognitive Science, 38,* 128–151.

Dix, T., Stewart, A. D., Gershoff, E. T., & Day, W. H. (2007). Autonomy and children's reactions to being controlled: Evidence that both compliance and defiance may be positive markers in early development. *Child Development, 78,* 1204–1221.

Dixon, P. (2009). Marriage among African Americans: What does the research reveal? *Journal of African American Studies, 13,* 29–46.

Dodd, V. L. (2005). Implications of kangaroo care for growth and development in preterm infants. *Journal of Obstetric, Gynecologic and Neonatal Nursing, 34,* 218–232.

Dodge, K. A., Coie, J. D., & Lynam, D. (2006). Aggression and antisocial behavior in youth. In N. Eisenberg (Ed.), *Handbook of child psychology: Vol. 3. Social, emotional, and personality development* (6th ed., pp. 719–788). New York: Wiley.

Dodge, K. A., & Haskins, R. (2015). Children and government. In M. H. Bornstein & T. Leventhal (Eds.), *Handbook of child psychology and developmental science: Vol. 4. Ecological settings and processes* (7th ed., pp. 654–703). Hoboken, NJ: Wiley.

Dodge, K. A., McLoyd, V. C., & Lansford, J. E. (2006). The cultural context of physically disciplining children. In V. C. McLoyd, N. E. Hill, & K. A. Dodge (Eds.), *African-American family life: Ecological and cultural diversity* (pp. 245–263). New York: Guilford.

Dohnt, H., & Tiggemann, M. (2006). The contribution of peer and media influences to the development of body satisfaction and self-esteem in young girls: A prospective study. *Developmental Psychology, 42,* 929–936.

Domellöf, E., Johansson, A., & Rönnqvist, L. (2011). Handedness in preterm born children: A systematic review and meta-analysis. *Neuropsychologia, 49,* 2299–2310.

Donaldson, M., & Jones, J. (2013). Optimizing outcome in congenital hypothyroidism: Current opinions on best practice in initial assessment and subsequent management. *Journal of Clinical Research in Pediatric Endocrinology, 5*(Suppl. 12), 13–22.

Dondi, M., Simion, F., & Caltran, G. (1999). Can newborns discriminate between their own cry and the cry of another newborn infant? *Developmental Psychology, 35,* 418–426.

Donnellan, M. B., Trzesniewski, K. H., Robins, R. W., Moffitt, T. E., & Caspi, A. (2005). Low self-esteem is related to aggression, antisocial behavior, and delinquency. *Psychological Science, 16,* 328–335.

Dorris, M. (1989). *The broken cord.* New York: Harper & Row.

Dorwie, F. M., & Pacquiao, D. F. (2014). Practices of traditional birth attendants in Sierra Leone and perceptions by mothers and health professionals familiar with their care. *Journal of Transcultural Nursing, 25,* 33–41.

Doss, B. D., Rhoades, G. K., Stanley, S. M., & Markman, H. J. (2009). The effect of the transition to parenthood on relationship quality: An 8-year prospective study. *Journal of Personality and Social Psychology, 96,* 601–619.

Double, E. B., Mabuchi, K., Cullings, H. M., Preston, D. L., Kodama, K., Shimizu, Y., et al. (2011). Long-term radiation-related health effects in a unique human population: Lessons learned from the atomic bomb survivors of Hiroshima and Nagasaki. *Disaster Medicine and Public Health Preparedness, 5* (Suppl. 1), S122–S133.

Douglas, E. M. (2006). *Mending broken families: Social policies for divorced families.* Lanham, MD: Rowman & Littlefield.

Downing, J. E. (2010). *Academic instruction for students with moderate and severe intellectual disabilities.* Thousand Oaks, CA: Corwin.

Drake, K., Belsky, J., & Fearon, R. M. P. (2014). From early attachment to engagement with learning in school: The role of self-regulation and persistence. *Developmental Psychology, 50,* 1350–1361.

Driver, J., Tabares, A., Shapiro, A. F., & Gottman, J. M. (2012). Couple interaction in happy and unhappy marriages: Gottman Laboratory studies. In F. Walsh (Ed.), *Normal family processes: Growing diversity and complexity* (pp. 57–77). New York: Guilford.

Druet, C., Stettler, N., Sharp, S., Simmons, R. K., Cooper, C., Smith, G. D., et al. (2012). Prediction of childhood obesity by infancy weight gain: An individual-level meta-analysis. *Paediatric and Perinatal Epidemiology, 26,* 19–26.

Dubois, L., Kyvik, K. O., Girard, M., Tatone-Tokuda, F., Pérusse, D., Hjelmborg, J., et al. (2012). Genetic and environmental contributions to weight, height, and BMI from birth to 19 years of age: An international study of over 12,000 twin pairs. *PLOS ONE, 7*(2), e30153.

Duckworth, A. L., Quinn, P. D., & Tsukayama, E. (2012). What No Child Left Behind leaves behind: The roles of IQ and self-control in predicting standardized achievement test scores and report card grades. *Journal of Educational Psychology, 104,* 439–451.

Dudani, A., Macpherson, A., & Tamim, H. (2010). Childhood behavior problems and unintentional injury: A longitudinal, population-based study. *Journal of Developmental and Behavioral Pediatrics, 31,* 276–285.

Duncan, G. J., Dowsett, C. J., Claessens, A., Magnuson, K., Huston, A. C., Klebanov, P., et al. (2007). School readiness and later achievement. *Developmental Psychology, 43,* 1428–1446.

Duncan, G. J., & Magnuson, K. A. (2003). Off with Hollingshead: Socioeconomic resources, parenting, and child development. In M. H. Bornstein & R. H. Bradley (Eds.), *Socioeconomic status, parenting, and child development* (pp. 83–106). Mahwah, NJ: Erlbaum.

Duncan, G. J., Magnuson, K., & Votruba-Drzal, E. (2015). Children and socioeconomic status. In M. H. Bornstein & T. Leventhal (Eds.), *Handbook of child psychology and developmental science: Vol. 4. Ecological settings and processes* (7th ed., pp. 534–573). Hoboken, NJ: Wiley.

Duncan, L. E., Pollastri, A. R., & Smoller, J. W. (2014). Mind the gap: Why many geneticists and psychological scientists have discrepant views about gene–environment interaction (G×E) research. *American Psychologist, 69,* 249–268.

Dunham, Y., Baron, A. S., & Banaji, M. R. (2006). From American city to Japanese village: A cross-cultural investigation of implicit race attitudes. *Child Development, 77,* 1268–1281.

Dunham, Y., Baron, A. S., & Carey, S. (2011). Consequences of "minimal" group affiliations in children. *Child Development, 82,* 793–811.

Dunham, Y., Chen, E. E., & Banaji, M. R. (2013). Two signatures of implicit intergroup attitudes: Developmental invariance and early enculturation. *Psychological Science, 24,* 860–868.

Dunkel-Shetter, C., & Lobel, M. (2012). Pregnancy and birth: A multilevel analysis of stress and birth weight. In T. A. Revenson, A. Baum, & J. Singer (Eds.), *Handbook of health psychology* (2nd ed., pp. 431–463). London: Psychology Press.

Dunn, J. (1989). Siblings and the development of social understanding in early childhood. In P. G. Zukow (Ed.), *Sibling interaction across cultures* (pp. 106–116). New York: Springer-Verlag.

Dunn, J. (1994). Temperament, siblings, and the development of relationships. In W. B. Carey & S. C. McDevitt (Eds.), *Prevention and early intervention* (pp. 50–58). New York: Brunner/Mazel.

Dunn, J. (2002). The adjustment of children in stepfamilies: Lessons from community studies. *Child and Adolescent Mental Health, 7,* 154–161.

Dunn, J. (2004a). *Children's friendships: The beginnings of intimacy.* Oxford, UK: Blackwell.

Dunn, J. (2004b). Sibling relationships. In P. K. Smith & C. H. Hart (Eds.), *Handbook of childhood social development* (pp. 223–237). Malden, MA: Blackwell.

Dunn, J. (2005). Moral development in early childhood and social interaction in the family. In M. Killen & J. G. Smetana (Eds.), *Handbook of moral development* (pp. 331–350). Mahwah, NJ: Erlbaum.

Dunn, J. (2014). Moral development in early childhood and social interaction in the family. In M. Killen & J. G. Smetana (Eds.), *Handbook of moral development* (2nd ed., pp. 135–159). New York: Psychology Press.

Dunn, J., Cutting, A. L., & Demetriou, H. (2000). Moral sensibility, understanding others, and children's friendship interactions in the preschool period. *British Journal of Developmental Psychology, 18,* 159–177.

Dunn, J. R., Schaefer-McDaniel, N. J., & Ramsay, J. T. (2010). Neighborhood chaos and children's development: Questions and contradictions. In G. W. Evans & T. D. Wachs (Eds.), *Chaos and its influence on children's development: An ecological perspective* (pp. 173–189). Washington, DC: American Psychological Association.

duRivage, N., Keyes, K., Leray, E., Pez, O., Bilfoi, A., Koç, C., et al. (2015). Parental use of corporal punishment in Europe: Intersection between public health and policy. *PLOS ONE, 10*(2), e0118059.

Durlak, J. A., Weissberg, R. P., Dymnicki, A. B., Taylor, R. D., & Schellinger, K. B. (2011). The impact of enhancing students' social and emotional learning: A meta-analysis of school-based universal interventions. *Child Development, 82,* 405–432.

Durlak, J. A., Weissberg, R. P., & Pachan, M. (2010). A meta-analysis of after-school programs that seek to promote personal and social skills of children and adolescents. *American Journal of Community Psychology, 45,* 294–309.

Durrant, J. E., Plateau, D. P., Ateah, C., Stewart-Tufescu, A., Jones, A., Ly, G., et al. (2014). Preventing punitive violence: Preliminary data on the Positive Discipline in Everyday Parenting (PDEP) Program. *Canadian Journal of Community Mental Health, 33,* 109–125.

Duszak, R. S. (2009). Congenital rubella syndrome—major review. *Optometry, 80,* 36–43.

Dweck, C. S., & Molden, D. C. (2013). Self-theories: Their impact on competence motivation and acquisition. In A. J. Elliott & C. J. Dweck (Eds.), *Handbook of confidence and motivation* (pp. 122–140). New York: Guilford.

Dyson, M. W., Olino, T. M., Durbin, C. E., Goldsmith, H. H., Bufferd, S. J., Miller, A. R., & Klein, D. N. (2015). The structural and rank-order stability of temperament in young children based on a laboratory-observational measure. *Psychological Assessment, 27,* 1388–1401.

E

Easton, S., & Kong, J. (2017). Mental health indicators fifty years later: A population-based study of men with histories of child sexual abuse. *Child Abuse & Neglect, 63,* 273–283.

Eccles, J. S., Jacobs, J. E., & Harold, R. D. (1990). Gender-role stereotypes, expectancy effects, and parents' role in the socialization of gender differences in self-perceptions and skill acquisition. *Journal of Social Issues, 46,* 183–201.

Eder, R. A., & Mangelsdorf, S. C. (1997). The emotional basis of early personality development: Implications for the emergent self-concept. In R. Hogan, J. Johnson, & S. Briggs (Eds.), *Handbook of personality psychology* (pp. 209–240). San Diego, CA: Academic Press.

Edwards, O. W., & Oakland, T. D. (2006). Factorial invariance of Woodcock-Johnson III scores for African Americans and Caucasian Americans. *Journal of Psychoeducational Assessment, 24,* 358–366.

Ehri, L. C., & Roberts, T. (2006). The roots of learning to read and write: Acquisition of letters and phonemic awareness. In D. K. Dikinson & S. B. Neuman (Eds.), *Handbook of early literacy research* (Vol. 2, pp. 113–131). New York: Guildford.

Eisenberg, N. (2003). Prosocial behavior, empathy, and sympathy. In M. H. Bornstein & L. Davidson (Eds.), *Well-being: Positive development across the life course* (pp. 253–265). Mahwah, NJ: Erlbaum.

Eisenberg, N. (2010). Empathy-related responding: Links with self-regulation, moral judgment, and moral behavior. In M. Mikulincer & P. R. Shaver (Eds.), *Prosocial motives, emotions, and behavior: The better angels of our nature* (pp. 129–148). Washington, DC: American Psychological Association.

Eisenberg, N., Eggum, N. D., & Edwards, A. (2010). Empathy-related responding and moral development. In W. F. Arsenio & E. A. Lemerise (Eds.), *Emotions, aggression, and morality in children* (pp. 115–135). Washington, DC: American Psychological Association.

Eisenberg, N., & Silver, R. C. (2011). Growing up in the shadow of terrorism. *American Psychologist, 66,* 468–481.

Eisenberg, N., Spinrad, T. L., & Knafo-Noam, A. (2015). Prosocial development. In M. E. Lamb (Ed.), *Handbook of child psychology and developmental science: Vol. 3. Socioemotional processes* (7th ed., pp. 610–656). Hoboken, NJ: Wiley.

Eisner, M. P., & Malti, T. (2015). Aggressive and violent behavior. In M. E. Lamb (Ed.), *Handbook of child psychology and developmental science: Vol. 3. Socioemotional processes* (7th ed., pp. 794–841). Hoboken, NJ: Wiley.

Eivers, A. R., Brendgen, M., Vitaro, F., & Borge, A. I. H. (2012). Concurrent and longitudinal links between children's and their friends' antisocial and prosocial behavior in preschool. *Early Childhood Research Quarterly, 27,* 137–146.

Ekas, N. V., Lickenbrock, D. M., & Braungart-Rieker, J. M. (2013). Developmental trajectories of emotion regulation across infancy: Do age and the social partner influence temporal patterns? *Infancy, 18,* 729–754.

Elam, K. K., Sandler, I., Wolchik, S., & Tein, J.-Y. (2016). Non-residential father–child involvement, interparental conflict and mental health of children following divorce: A person-centered approach. *Journal of Youth and Adolescence, 45,* 581–593.

Elder, G. H., Jr., Shanahan, M. J., & Jennings, J. A. (2015). Human development in time and place. In M. H. Bornstein & T. Leventhal (Eds.), *Handbook of child psychology: Vol. 4. Ecological settings and processes* (7th ed., pp. 6–54). Hoboken, NJ: Wiley.

Elias, C. L., & Berk, L. E. (2002). Self-regulation in young children: Is there a role for sociodramatic play? *Early Childhood Research Quarterly, 17,* 1–17.

Elliott, J. G. (1999). School refusal: Issues of conceptualization, assessment, and treatment. *Journal of Child Psychology and Psychiatry and Allied Disciplines, 40,* 1001–1012.

Ellis, A. E., & Oakes, L. M. (2006). Infants flexibly use different dimensions to categorize objects. *Developmental Psychology, 42,* 1000–1011.

Elks, C. E., den Hoed, M., Zhao, J. H., Sharp, S. J., Wareham, N. J., Loo, R. J., & Ong, K. K. (2012). Variability in the heritability of body mass index: A systematic review and meta-regression. *Frontiers in Endocrinology, 3,* 29.

Else-Quest, N. M. (2012). Gender differences in temperament. In M. Zentner & R. L. Shiner (Eds.), *Handbook of temperament* (pp. 479–496). New York: Guilford.

Else-Quest, N. M., Hyde, J. S., Goldsmith, H. H., & Van Hulle, C. A. (2006). Gender differences in temperament: A meta-analysis. *Psychological Bulletin, 132,* 33–72.

El-Sheikh, M., Cummings, E. M., & Reiter, S. (1996). Preschoolers' responses to ongoing interadult conflict: The role of prior exposure to resolved versus unresolved arguments. *Journal of Abnormal Child Psychology, 24,* 665–679.

Eltzschig, H. K., Lieberman, E. S., & Camann, W. R. (2003). Regional anesthesia and analgesia for labor and delivery. *New England Journal of Medicine, 384,* 319–332.

Ennemoser, M., & Schneider, W. (2007). Relations of television viewing and reading: Findings from a 4-year longitudinal study. *Journal of Educational Psychology, 99,* 349–368.

Epstein, L. H., Roemmich, J. N., & Raynor, H. A. (2001). Behavioral therapy in the treatment of pediatric obesity. *Pediatric Clinics of North America*, 48, 981–983.

Erikson, E. H. (1950). *Childhood and society.* New York: Norton.

Espy, K. A., Fang, H., Johnson, C., Stopp, C., & Wiebe, S. A. (2011). Prenatal tobacco exposure: Developmental outcomes in the neonatal period. *Developmental Psychology, 47,* 153–156.

Espy, K. A., Molfese, V. J., & DiLalla, L. F. (2001). Effects of environmental measures on intelligence in young children: Growth curve modeling of longitudinal data. *Merrill-Palmer Quarterly, 47,* 42–73.

Evanoo, G. (2007). Infant crying: A clinical conundrum. *Journal of Pediatric Health Care, 21,* 333–338.

Evans, G. W., Fuller-Rowell, T. E., & Doan, S. N. (2012). Childhood cumulative risk and obesity: The mediating role of self-regulatory ability. *Pediatrics, 129,* e68–e73.

Evans, G. W., & Schamberg, M A. (2009). Childhood poverty, chronic stress, and adult working memory. *Proceedings of the National Academy of Sciences, 106,* 6545–6549.

Evans, N., & Levinson, S. C. (2009). The myth of language universals: Language diversity and its importance for cognitive science. *Behavioral and Brain Sciences, 32,* 429–492.

Eyler, L. T., Pierce, K., & Courchesne, E. (2012). A failure of left temporal cortex to specialize for language is an early emerging and fundamental property of autism. *Brain, 135,* 949–960.

Ezkurdia, I., Juan, D., Rodriguez, J. M., Frankish, A., Diekhans, M., Harrow, J., et al. (2014). Multiple evidence strands suggest that there may be as few as 19,000 human protein-coding genes. *Human Molecular Genetics, 23,* 5866–5878.

F

Fabes, R. A., Eisenberg, N., Hanish, L. D., & Spinrad, T. L. (2001). Preschoolers' spontaneous emotion vocabulary: Relations to likeability. *Early Education and Development, 12,* 11–27.

Fabes, R. A., Eisenberg, N., McCormick, S. E., & Wilson, M. S. (1988). Preschoolers' attributions of the situational determinants of others' naturally occurring emotions. *Developmental Psychology, 24,* 376–385.

Fagan, J. F., & Holland, C. R. (2007). Racial equality in intelligence: Predictions from a theory of intelligence as processing. *Intelligence, 35,* 319–334.

Fagan, J. F., Holland, C. R., & Wheeler, K. (2007). The prediction, from infancy, of adult IQ and achievement. *Intelligence, 35,* 225–231.

Fagard, J., Spelke, E., & von Hofsten, C. (2009). Reaching and grasping a moving object in 6-, 8-, and 10-month-old infants: Laterality and performance. *Infant Behavior and Development, 32,* 137–146.

Fagot, B. I. (1985). Changes in thinking about early sex role development. *Developmental Review, 5,* 83–98.

Fagot, B. I., & Hagan, R. I. (1991). Observations of parent reactions to sex-stereotyped behaviors: Age and sex effects. *Child Development, 62,* 617–628.

Fahrmeier, E. D. (1978). The development of concrete operations among the Hausa. *Journal of Cross-Cultural Psychology, 9,* 23–44.

Falagas, M. E., & Zarkadoulia, E. (2008). Factors associated with suboptimal compliance to vaccinations in children in developed countries: A systematic review. *Current Medical Research and Opinion, 24,* 1719–1741.

Falbo, T. (2012). Only children: An updated review. *Journal of Individual Psychology, 68,* 38–49.

Falbo, T., & Hooper, S. Y. (2015). China's only children and psychopathology: A quantitative synthesis. *American Journal of Orthopsychiatry, 85,* 259–274.

Falbo, T., Poston, D. L., Jr., Triscari, R. S., & Zhang, X. (1997). Self-enhancing illusions among Chinese schoolchildren. *Journal of Cross-Cultural Psychology, 28,* 172–191.

Falk, D. (2005). Brain lateralization in primates and its evolution in hominids. *American Journal of Physical Anthropology, 30,* 107–125.

Fantz, R. L. (1961, May). The origin of form perception. *Scientific American, 204*(5), 66–72.

Farmer, T. W., Irvin, M. J., Leung, M.-C., Hall, C. M., Hutchins, B. C., & McDonough, E. (2010). Social preference, social prominence, and group membership in late elementary school: Homophilic concentration and peer affiliation configurations. *Social Psychology of Education, 13,* 271–293.

Farroni, T., Massaccesi, S., Menon, E., & Johnson, M. H. (2007). Direct gaze modulates face recognition in young infants. *Cognition, 102,* 396–404.

Fassbender, I., Teubert, M., & Lohaus, A. (2016). The development of preferences for own-race versus other-race faces in 3-, 6- and 9-month-old Caucasian infants. *European Journal of Developmental Psychology, 13,* 152–165.

Fast, A. A., & Olson, K. R. (2017). Gender development in transgender preschool children. *Child Development, 88:* 12758.

Fearon, R. P., Bakermans-Kranenburg, M. J., Lapsley, A., & Roisman, G. I. (2010). The significance of insecure attachment and disorganization in the development of children's externalizing behavior: A meta-analytic study. *Child Development, 81,* 435–456.

Feldman, R. (2003). Infant–mother and infant–father synchrony: The coregulation of positive arousal. *Infant Mental Health Journal, 24,* 1–23.

Feldman, R. (2006). From biological rhythms to social rhythms: Physiological precursors of mother–infant synchrony. *Developmental Psychology, 42,* 175–188.

Feldman, R. (2007). Maternal versus child risk and the development of parent–child and family relationships in five high-risk populations. *Development and Psychopathology, 19,* 293–312.

Feldman, R., Eidelman, A. I., & Rotenberg, N. (2004). Parenting stress, infant emotion regulation, maternal sensitivity, and the cognitive development of triplets: A model for parent and child influences in a unique ecology. *Child Development, 75,* 1774–1791.

Feldman, R., Rosenthal, Z., & Eidelman, A. (2014). Maternal–preterm skin-to-skin contact enhances child physiologic organization and cognitive control across the first 10 years of life. *Biological Psychiatry, 75,* 56–64.

Feldman, R., Sussman, A. L., & Zigler, E. (2004). Parental leave and work adaptation at the transition to parenthood: Individual, marital, and social correlates. *Applied Developmental Psychology, 25,* 459–479.

Feliciano, C., & Lanuza, Y. R. (2015). The immigrant advantage in adolescent educational expectations. *International Migration Review, 50,* 758–792.

Ferguson, T. J., Stegge, H., & Damhuis, I. (1991). Children's understanding of guilt and shame. *Child Development, 62,* 827–839.

Fernald, A., & Marchman, V. A. (2012). Individual differences in lexical processing at 18 months predict vocabulary growth in typically developing and late-talking toddlers. *Child Development, 82,* 203–222.

Fernald, A., Marchman, V. A., & Weisleder, A. (2013). SES differences in language processing skill and vocabulary are evident at 18 months. *Developmental Science, 16,* 234–248.

Fernald, A., & Morikawa, H. (1993). Common themes and cultural variations in Japanese and American mothers' speech to infants. *Child Development, 64,* 637–656.

Fernald, A., Taeschner, T., Dunn, J., Papousek, M., Boyssen-Bardies, B., & Fukui, I. (1989). A cross-language study of prosodic modifications in mothers' and fathers' speech to preverbal infants. *Journal of Child Language, 16,* 477–502.

Fernald, L. C., & Grantham-McGregor, S. M. (1998). Stress response in school-age children who have been growth-retarded since early childhood. *American Journal of Clinical Nutrition, 68,* 691–698.

Fernandes, M., Stein, A., Srinivasan, K., Menezes, G., & Ramchandani, P. J. (2015). Foetal exposure to maternal depression predicts cortisol responses in infants: Findings from rural South India. *Child: Care, Health and Development, 41,* 677–686.

Fernandez-Rio, J., Cecchini, J. A., Ménde-Gimenez, A., Mendez-Alonso, D., & Prieto, J. A. (2017). Self-regulation, cooperative learning, and academic self-efficacy: Interactions to prevent school failure. *Frontiers, in Psychology, 8,* Article ID: 22.

Ferrando, M., Prieto, M. D., Almeida, L. S., Ferándiz, C., Bermejo, R., López-Pina, J. A., et al. (2011). Trait emotional intelligence and academic performance: Controlling for the effects of IQ, personality, and self-concept. *Journal of Psychoeducational Assessment, 29,* 150–159.

Ferrari, P. F., & Coudé, G. (2011). Mirror neurons and imitation from a developmental and evolutionary perspective. In A. Vilain, C. Abry, J.-L. Schwartz, & J. Vauclair (Eds.), *Primate communication and human language* (pp. 121–138). Amsterdam, Netherlands: John Benjamins.

Ferrari, P. F., Tramacere, A., Simpson, E. A., & Iriki, A. (2013). Mirror neurons through the lens of epigenetics. *Trends in Cognitive Sciences, 17,* 450–457.

Ferrari, P. F., Visalberghi E., Paukner A., Fogassi L., Ruggiero A., Suomi, S. (2006). Neonatal imitation in rhesus macaques. *PLOS Biology, 4,* e302.

Ferry, A. L., Hespos, S. J., & Waxman, S. R. (2010). Categorization in 3- and 4-month-old infants: An advantage of words over tones. *Child Development, 81,* 472–479.

Field, T. (2001). Massage therapy facilitates weight gain in preterm infants. *Current Directions in Psychological Science, 10,* 51–54.

Field, T. (2011). Prenatal depression effects on early development: A review. *Infant Behavior and Development, 34,* 1–14.

Field, T., Hernandez-Reif, M., & Freedman, J. (2004). Stimulation programs for preterm infants. *Social Policy Report of the Society for Research in Child Development, 18*(1).

Fiese, B. H., Foley, K. P., & Spagnola, M. (2006). Routine and ritual elements in family mealtimes: Contexts for child well-being and family identity. *New Directions for Child and Adolescent Development, 111,* 67–90.

Fiese, B. H., & Schwartz, M. (2008). Reclaiming the family table: Mealtimes and child health and well-being. *Social Policy Report of the Society for Research in Child Development, 22*(4), 3–18.

Fiese, B. H., & Winter, M. A. (2010). The dynamics of family chaos and its relation to children's socioemotional well-being. In G. W. Evans & T. D. Wachs (Eds.), *Chaos and its influence on children's development: An ecological perspective* (pp. 49–66). Washington, DC: American Psychological Association.

Fifer, W. P., Byrd, D. L., Kaku, M., Eigsti, I. M., Isler, J. R., Grose-Fifer, J., et al. (2010). Newborn infants learn during sleep. *Proceedings of the National Academy of Sciences, 107,* 10320–10323.

Finkelhor, D. (2009). The prevention of childhood sexual abuse. *Future of Children, 19,* 169–194.

Fischer, K. W., & Bidell, T. R. (2006). Dynamic development of action and thought. In R. M. Lerner (Ed.), *Handbook of child psychology: Vol. 1. Theoretical models of human development* (6th ed., pp. 313–399). Hoboken, NJ: Wiley.

Fischman, M. G., Moore, J. B., & Steele, K. H. (1992). Children's one-hand catching as a function of age, gender, and ball location. *Research Quarterly for Exercise and Sport, 63,* 349–355.

Fish, M. (2004). Attachment in infancy and preschool in low socioeconomic status rural Appalachian children: Stability and change and relations to preschool and kindergarten competence. *Development and Psychopathology, 16,* 293–312.

Fisher, C. B., Hoagwood, K., Boyce, C., Duster, T., Frank, D. A., & Grisso, T. (2002). Research ethics for mental health science involving ethnic minority children and youths. *American Psychologist, 57,* 1024–1040.

Fite, P. J., Williford, A., Cooley, J. L., DePaolis, K., Rubens, S. L., & Vernberg, E. M. (2013). Patterns of victimization locations in elementary school children: Effects of grade level and gender. *Child and Youth Care Forum, 42,* 585–597.

Fivush, R., & Haden, C. A. (2005). Parent–child reminiscing and the construction of a subjective self. In B. D. Homer & C. S. Tamis-LeMonda (Eds.), *The development of social cognition and communication* (pp. 315–336). Mahwah, NJ: Erlbaum.

Fivush, R., & Wang, Q. (2005). Emotion talk in mother–child conversations of the shared past: The effects of culture, gender, and event valence. *Journal of Cognition and Development, 6,* 489–506.

Fivush, R., & Zaman, W. (2014). Gender, subjective perspective, and autobiographical consciousness. In P. J. Bauer & R. Fivush (Eds.), *Wiley handbook on the development of children's memory* (pp. 586–604). Hoboken, NJ: Wiley-Blackwell.

Flak, A. L., Su, S., Bertrand, J., Denny, C. H., Kesmodel, U. S., & Cogswell, M. E. (2014). The association of mild, moderate, and binge prenatal alcohol exposure and child neuropsychological outcomes: A meta-analysis. *Alcoholism: Clinical and Experimental Research, 38,* 214–226.

Flavell, J. H., Flavell, E. R., & Green, F. L. (2001). Development of children's understanding of connections between thinking and feeling. *Psychological Science, 12,* 430–432.

Fletcher, E. N., Whitaker, R. C., Marino, A. J., & Anderson, S. E. (2014). Screen time at home and school among low-income children attending Head Start. *Child Indicators Research, 7,* 421–436.

Flom, R. (2013). Intersensory perception of faces and voices in infants. In P. Belin, S. Campanella, & T. Ethofer (Eds.), *Integrating face and voice in person perception* (pp. 71–93). New York: Springer.

Flom, R., & Bahrick, L. E. (2007). The development of infant discrimination of affect in multimodal and unimodal stimulation: The role of intersensory redundancy. *Developmental Psychology, 43,* 238–252.

Flom, R., & Bahrick, L. E. (2010). The effects of intersensory redundancy on attention and memory: Infants' long-term memory for orientation in audiovisual events. *Developmental Psychology, 46,* 428–436.

Flom, R., & Pick, A. D. (2003). Verbal encouragement and joint attention in 18-month-old infants. *Infant Behavior and Development, 26,* 121–134.

Flynn, E., & Siegler, R. (2007). Measuring change: Current trends and future directions in microgenetic research. *Infant and Child Development, 16,* 135–149.

Flynn, J. R. (1999). Searching for justice: The discovery of IQ gains over time. *American Psychologist, 54,* 5–20.

Flynn, J. R. (2007). *What is intelligence? Beyond the Flynn effect.* New York: Cambridge University Press.

Flynn, J. R., & Rossi-Casé, L. (2011). Modern women match men on Raven's Progressive Matrices. *Personality and Individual Differences, 50,* 799–803.

Fogel, A., & Garvey, A. (2007). Alive communication. *Infant Behavior and Development, 30,* 251–257.

Fomon, S. J., & Nelson, S. E. (2002). Body composition of the male and female reference infants. *Annual Review of Nutrition, 22,* 1–17.

Fonnesbeck, C. J., McPheeters, M. L., Krishnaswami, S., Lindegren, M. L., & Reimschisel, T. (2013). Estimating the probability of IQ impairment from blood phenylalanine for phenylketonuria patients: A hierarchical meta-analysis. *Journal of Inherited Metabolic Disease, 36,* 757–766.

Ford, D. Y. (2012). Gifted and talented education: History, issues, and recommendations. In K. R. Harris, S. Graham, T. Urdan, S. Graham, J. M. Royer, & M. Zeidner (Eds.), *APA educational psychology handbook: Vol. 2. Individual differences and cultural contextual factors* (pp. 83–110). Washington, DC: American Psychological Association.

Forman, D. R., Aksan, N., & Kochanska, G. (2004). Toddlers' responsive imitation predicts preschool-age conscience. *Psychological Science, 15,* 699–704.

Fox, N. A., Henderson, H. A., Pérez-Edgar, K., & White, L. K. (2008). The biology of temperament: An integrative approach. In C. A. Nelson & M. Luciana (Eds.), *Handbook of developmental cognitive neuroscience* (2nd ed., pp. 839–853). Cambridge, MA: MIT Press.

Frank, M. C., Amso, D., & Johnson, S. P. (2014). Visual search and attention to faces during early infancy. *Journal of Experimental Child Psychology, 118,* 13–26.

Frankel, L. A., Umemura, T., Jacobvitz, D., & Hazen, N. (2015). Marital conflict and parental responses to infant negative emotions: Relations with toddler emotional regulation. *Infant Behavior and Development, 40,* 73–83.

Franklin, V. P. (2012). "The teachers' unions strike back?" No need to wait for "Superman": Magnet schools have brought success to urban public school students for over 30 years. In D. T. Slaughter-Defoe, H. C. Stevenson, E. G. Arrington, & D. J. Johnson (Eds.), *Black educational choice: Assessing the private and public alternatives to traditional K–12 public schools* (pp. 217–220). Santa Barbara, CA: Praeger.

Fredricks, J. A., & Eccles, J. S. (2002). Children's competence and value beliefs from childhood through adolescence: Growth trajectories in two male-sex-typed domains. *Developmental Psychology, 38,* 519–533.

Freeman, H., & Newland, L. A. (2010). New directions in father attachment. *Early Child Development and Care, 180,* 1–8.

Freitag, C. M., Rohde, L. A., Lempp, T., & Romanos, M. (2010). Phenotypic and measurement influences on heritability estimates in childhood ADHD. *European Child and Adolescent Psychiatry, 19,* 311–323.

Freud, S. (1973). *An outline of psychoanalysis.* London: Hogarth. (Original work published 1938)

Friedlmeier, W., Corapci, F., & Cole, P. M. (2011). Socialization of emotions in cross-cultural perspective. *Social and Personality Psychology Compass, 5,* 410–427.

Frontline. (2012). *Poor kids.* Retrieved from www.pbs.org/wgbh/pages/frontline/poor-kids

Frost, D. M., Meyer, I. H., & Schwartz, S. (2016). Social support networks among diverse sexual minority populations. *American Journal of Orthopsychiatry, 86,* 91–102.

Frota, S., Butler, J., Correia, S., Severino, C., Vicente, S., & Vigário, M. (2016). Infant communicative development assessed with the European Portuguese MacArthur–Bates Communicative Development Inventories short forms. *First Language, 36,* 525–545.

Fry, D. P. (2014). Environment of evolutionary adaptedness, rough-and-tumble play, and the selection of restraint in human aggression. In D. Narvaez, K. Valentino, A. Fuentes, J. J. McKenna, & P. Gray (Eds.), *Ancestral landscapes in human evolution: Culture, childrearing and social wellbeing* (pp. 169–188). New York: Oxford University Press.

Fu, G., Xiao, W. S., Killen, M., & Lee, K. (2014). Moral judgment and its relation to second-order theory of mind. *Developmental Psychology, 50,* 2085–2092.

Fu, G., Xu, F., Cameron, C. A., Heyman, G., & Lee, K. (2007). Cross-cultural differences in children's choices, categorizations, and evaluations of truths and lies. *Developmental Psychology, 43,* 278–293.

Fuligni, A. J. (2004). The adaptation and acculturation of children from immigrant families. In U. P. Gielen & J. Roopnarine (Eds.), *Childhood and adolescence: Cross-cultural perspectives* (pp. 297–318). Westport, CT: Praeger.

Fuligni, A. S., Han, W.-J., & Brooks-Gunn, J. (2004). The Infant-Toddler HOME in the 2nd and 3rd years of life. *Parenting: Science and Practice, 4,* 139–159.

Furman, W., & Rose, A. J. (2015). Friendships, romantic relationships, and peer relationships. In M. E. Lamb (Ed.), *Handbook of child psychology and developmental science: Vol. 3. Socioemotional processes* (7th ed., pp. 932–974). Hoboken, NJ: Wiley.

Fushiki, S. (2013). Radiation hazards in children—lessons from Chernobyl, Three Mile Island and Fukushima. *Brain & Development, 35,* 220–227.

Fuson, K. C. (2009). Avoiding misinterpretations of Piaget and Vygotsky: Mathematical teaching without learning, learning without teaching, or helpful learning-path teaching? *Cognitive Development, 24,* 343–361.

G

Galland, B. C., Taylor, B. J., Elder, D. E., & Herbison, P. (2012). Normal sleep patterns in infants and children: A systematic review. *Sleep Medicine Reviews, 16,* 213–222.

Galler, J. R., Bryce, C. P., Waber, D. P., Hock, R. S., Harrison, R., Eaglesfield, G. D., et al. (2012). Infant malnutrition predicts conduct problems in adolescents. *Nutritional Neuroscience, 15,* 186–192.

Galloway, J., & Thelen, E. (2004). Feet first: Object exploration in young infants. *Infant Behavior and Development, 27,* 107–112.

Galvao, T. F., Thees, M. F., Pontes, R. F., Silva, M. T., & Pereira, M. G. (2013). Zinc supplementation for treating diarrhea in children: A systematic review and meta-analysis. *Pan American Journal of Public Health, 33,* 370–377.

Ganea, P. A., Allen, M. L., Butler, L., Carey, S., & DeLoache, J. S. (2009). Toddlers' referential understanding of pictures. *Journal of Experimental Child Psychology, 104,* 283–295.

Ganea, P. A., Ma, L., & DeLoache, J. S. (2011). Young children's learning and transfer of biological information from picture books to real animals. *Child Development, 82,* 1421–1433.

Ganea, P. A., Shutts, K., Spelke, E., & DeLoache, J. S. (2007). Thinking of things unseen: Infants' use of language to update object representations. *Psychological Science, 8,* 734–739.

Ganger, J., & Brent, M. R. (2004). Reexamining the vocabulary spurt. *Developmental Psychology, 40,* 621–632.

Garcia, A. J., Koschnitzky, J. E., & Ramirez, J. M. (2013). The physiological determinants of sudden infant death syndrome. *Respiratory Physiology and Neurobiology, 189,* 288–300.

Gardner, H. (1980). *Artful scribbles: The significance of children's drawings.* New York: Basic Books.

Gardner, H. (1983). *Frames of mind: The theory of multiple intelligences.* New York: Basic Books.

Gardner, H. (1993). *Multiple intelligences: The theory in practice.* New York: Basic Books.

Gardner, H. (2011). The theory of multiple intelligences. In M. A. Gernsbacher, R. W. Pew, L. M. Hough, & J. R. Pomerantz (Eds.), *Psychology and the real world: Essays illustrating fundamental contributions to society* (pp. 122–130). New York: Worth.

Gardner, H. E. (2000). *Intelligence reframed: Multiple intelligences for the twenty-first century.* New York: Basic Books.

Garner, P. W. (2003). Child and family correlates of toddlers' emotional and behavioral responses to a mishap. *Infant Mental Health Journal, 24,* 580–596.

Garner, P. W., & Estep, K. (2001). Emotional competence, emotion socialization, and young children's peer-related social competence. *Early Education and Development, 12,* 29–48.

Gartstein, M. A., Gonzalez, C., Carranza, J. A., Ahadi, S. A., Ye, R., Rothbart, M. K., & Yang, S. W. (2006). Studying cross-cultural differences in the development of infant temperament: People's Republic of China, the United States of America, and Spain. *Child Psychiatry and Human Development, 37,* 145–161.

Gartstein, M. A., Slobodskaya, H. R., Zylicz, P. O., Gosztyla, D., & Nakagawa, A. (2010). A cross-cultural evaluation of temperament: Japan, USA, Poland and Russia. *International Journal of Psychology and Psychological Therapy, 10,* 55–75.

Gaskill, R. L., & Perry, B. D. (2012). Child sexual abuse, traumatic experiences, and their impact on the developing brain. In P. Goodyear-Brown (Ed.), *Handbook of child sexual abuse: Identification, assessment, and treatment* (pp. 29–47). Hoboken, NJ: Wiley.

Gaskins, S. (1999). Children's daily lives in a Mayan village: A case study of culturally constructed roles and activities. In R. Göncü (Ed.), *Children's engagement in the world: Sociocultural perspectives* (pp. 25–61). Cambridge, UK: Cambridge University Press.

Gaskins, S. (2013). Pretend play as culturally constructed activity. In M. Taylor (Ed.), *Oxford handbook on the development of the imagination* (pp. 224–251). Oxford, UK: Oxford University Press.

Gaskins, S. (2014). Children's play as cultural activity. In L. Brooker, M. Blaise, & S. Edwards (Eds.), *Sage handbook of play and learning in early childhood* (pp. 31–42). London: Sage.

Gaskins, S., Haight, W., & Lancy, D. F. (2007). The cultural construction of play. In A. Göncü & S. Gaskins (Eds.), *Play and development: Evolutionary, sociocultural, and functional perspectives* (pp. 179–202). Mahwah, NJ: Erlbaum.

Gates, G. J. (2013). *LGBT parenting in the United States.* Los Angeles: Williams Institute, UCLA School of Law. Retrieved from http://williamsinstitute.law.ucla.edu/wp-content/uploads/LGBT-Parenting.pdf

Gathercole, S. E., & Alloway, T. P. (2008). Working memory and classroom learning. In S. K. Thurman & C. A. Fiorello (Eds.), *Applied cognitive research in K–3 classrooms* (pp. 17–40). New York: Routledge/Taylor & Francis Group.

Gathercole, V., Sebastián, E., & Soto, P. (1999). The early acquisition of Spanish verb morphology: Across-the-board or piecemeal knowledge? *International Journal of Bilingualism, 3,* 133–182.

Gauvain, M., de la Ossa, J. L., & Hurtado-Ortiz, M. T. (2001). Parental guidance as children learn to use cultural tools: The case of pictorial plans. *Cognitive Development, 16,* 551–575.

Gauvain, M., & Munroe, R. L. (2009). Contributions of societal modernity to cognitive development: A comparison of four cultures. *Child Development, 80,* 1628–1642.

Geangu, E., Benga, O., Stahl, D., & Striano, T. (2010). Contagious crying beyond the first days of life. *Infant Behavior and Development, 33,* 279–288.

Geary, D. C., & VanMarle, K. (2016). Young children's core symbolic and nonsymbolic quantitative knowledge in the prediction of later mathematics achievement. *Developmental Psychology, 52,* 2130–2144.

Geerts, C. C., Bots, M. L., van der Ent, C. K., Grobbee, D. E., & Uiterwaal, C. S. (2012). Parental smoking and vascular damage in their 5-year-old children. *Pediatrics, 129,* 45–54.

Gelman, R. (1972). Logical capacity of very young children: Number invariance rules. *Child Development, 43,* 75–90.

Gelman, S. A. (2003). *The essential child.* New York: Oxford University Press.

Gelman, S. A., & Kalish, C. W. (2006). Conceptual development. In D. Kuhn & R. Siegler (Eds.), *Handbook of child psychology: Vol. 2. Cognition, perception, and language* (6th ed., pp. 687–733). Hoboken, NJ: Wiley.

Gelman, S. A., Taylor, M. G., & Nguyen, S. P. (2004). Mother–child conversations about gender. *Monographs of the Society for Research in Child Development, 69*(1, Serial No. 275), 1–127.

Genesee, F., & Jared, D. (2008). Literacy development in early French immersion programs. *Canadian Psychology, 49,* 140–147.

Gentile, D. A., Li, D., Khoo, A., Prot, S., & Anderson, C. A. (2014). Mediators and moderators of long-term effects of violent video games on aggressive behavior. *JAMA Pediatrics, 168,* 450–457.

Geraci, A., & Surian, L. (2011). The developmental roots of fairness: Infants' reactions to equal and unequal distributions of resources. *Developmental Science, 14,* 1012–1020.

Gergely, G., & Watson, J. (1999). Early socioemotional development: Contingency perception and the social-biofeedback model. In P. Rochat (Ed.), *Early social cognition: Understanding others in the first months of life* (pp. 101–136). Mahwah, NJ: Erlbaum.

Gernhardt, A., Rübeling, H., & Keller, H. (2014). Self- and family conceptions of Turkish migrant, native German, and native Turkish children: A comparison of children's drawings. *International Journal of Intercultural Relations, 40,* 154–166.

Gernhardt, A., Rübeling, H., & Keller, H. (2015). Cultural perspectives on children's tadpole drawings: At the interface between representation and production. *Frontiers in Psychology, 6,* Article ID: 812.

Gershoff, E. T., Grogan-Kaylor, A., Lansford, J. E., Chang, L., Zelli, A., Deater-Deckard, K., et al. (2010). Parent discipline practices in an international sample: Associations with child behaviors and moderation by perceived normativeness. *Child Development, 81,* 487–502.

Gershoff, E. T., Lansford, J. E., Sexton, H. R., Davis-Kean, P., & Sameroff, A. J. (2012). Longitudinal links between spanking and children's externalizing behaviors in a national sample of White, Black, Hispanic, and Asian American families. *Child Development, 83,* 838–843.

Gesell, A. (1933). Maturation and patterning of behavior. In C. Murchison (Ed.), *A handbook of child psychology* (2nd ed., pp. 209–235). Worcester, MA: Clark University Press.

Geurten, M., Catale, C., & Meuklmans, T. (2015). When children's knowledge of memory improves children's performance in memory. *Applied Cognitive Psychology, 29,* 244–252.

Geuze, R. H., Schaafsma, S. M., Lust, J. M., Bouma, A., Schiefenhovel, W., Groothuis, T. G. G., et al. (2012). Plasticity of lateralization: Schooling predicts hand preference but not hand skill asymmetry in a non-industrial society. *Neuropsychologia, 50,* 612–620.

Ghim, H. R. (1990). Evidence for perceptual organization in infants: Perception of subjective contours by young infants. *Infant Behavior and Development, 13,* 221–248.

Gibbs, J. C. (2010). Beyond the conventionally moral. *Journal of Applied Developmental Psychology, 31,* 106–108.

Gibbs, J. C. (2014). *Moral development and reality: Beyond the theories of Kohlberg, Hoffman, and Haidt* (3rd ed.). New York: Oxford University Press.

Gibson, E. J. (1970). The development of perception as an adaptive process. *American Scientist, 58,* 98–107.

Gibson, E. J. (2003). The world is so full of a number of things: On specification and perceptual learning. *Ecological Psychology, 15,* 283–287.

Gibson, E. J., & Walk, R. D. (1960). The "visual cliff." *Scientific American, 202,* 64–71.

Gibson, J. J. (1979). *The ecological approach to visual perception.* Boston: Houghton Mifflin.

Giedd, J. N., Lalonde, F. M., Celano, M. J., White, S. L., Wallace, G. L., Lee, N. R., et al. (2009). Anatomical brain magnetic resonance imaging of typically developing children and adolescents. *Journal of the American Academy of Child and Adolescent Psychiatry, 48,* 465–470.

Giles, A., & Rovee-Collier, C. (2011). Infant long-term memory for associations formed during mere exposure. *Infant Behavior and Development, 34,* 327–338.

Giles, J. W., & Heyman, G. D. (2005). Young children's beliefs about the relationship between gender and aggressive behavior. *Child Development, 76,* 107–121.

Giles-Sims, J., Straus, M. A., & Sugarman, D. B. (1995). Child, maternal, and family characteristics associated with spanking. *Family Relations, 44,* 170–176.

Gilliom, M., Shaw, D. S., Beck, J. E., Schonberg, M. A., & Lukon, J. L. (2002). Anger regulation in disadvantaged preschool boys: Strategies, antecedents, and the development of self-control. *Developmental Psychology, 38,* 222–235.

Gilmore, J. H., Shi, F., Woolson, S. L., Knickmeyer, R. C., Short, S. J., Lin, W., et al. (2012). Longitudinal development of cortical and subcortical gray matter from birth to 2 years. *Cerebral Cortex, 22,* 2478–2485.

Ginsburg, H. P., Lee, J. S., & Boyd, J. S. (2008). Mathematics education for young children: What it is and how to promote it. *Social Policy Report of the Society for Research in Child Development, 22*(1).

Gleason, T. R. (2013). Imaginary relationships. In M. Taylor (Ed.), *Oxford handbook of the development of imagination* (pp. 251–271). New York: Oxford University Press.

Gleason, T. R. (2017). The psychological significance of play with imaginary companions in early childhood. *Learning and Behavior, 45*, 432–440.

Gleitman, L. R., Cassidy, K., Nappa, R., Papfragou, A., & Trueswell, J. C. (2005). Hard words. *Language Learning and Development, 1,* 23–64.

Glenright, M., & Pexman, P. M. (2010). Development of children's ability to distinguish sarcasm and verbal irony. *Journal of Child Language, 37,* 429–451.

Gluckman, P. D., Sizonenko, S. V., & Bassett, N. S. (1999). The transition from fetus to neonate—an endocrine perspective. *Acta Paediatrica Supplement, 88*(428), 7–11.

Gnoth, C., Maxrath, B., Skonieczny, T., Friol, K., Godehardt, E., & Tigges, J. (2011). Final ART success rates: A 10 years survey. *Human Reproduction, 26,* 2239–2246.

Goble, P., Martin, C. L., Hanish, L. D., & Fabes, R. A. (2012). Children's gender-typed activity choices across preschool social contexts. *Sex Roles, 67,* 435–451.

Goeke-Morey, M. C., Papp, L. M., & Cummings, E. M. (2013). Changes in marital conflict and youths' responses across childhood and adolescence: A test of sensitization. *Development and Psychopathology, 25,* 241–251.

Gogate, L. J., & Bahrick, L. E. (2001). Intersensory redundancy and 7-month-old infants' memory for arbitrary syllable–object relations. *Infancy, 2,* 219–231.

Goldberg, A. E. (2010). *Lesbian and gay parents and their children: Research on the family life cycle.* Washington, DC: American Psychological Association.

Goldberg, A. E., & Garcia, R. L. (2016). Gender-typed behavior over time in children with lesbian, gay, and heterosexual parents. *Journal of Family Psychology, 30,* 854–865.

Goldberg, A. E., Kashy, D. A., & Smith, J. Z. (2012). Gender-typed play behavior in early childhood: Adopted children with lesbian, gay, and heterosexual parents. *Sex Roles, 67,* 503–513.

Goldschmidt, L., Richardson, G. A., Cornelius, M. D., & Day, N. L. (2004). Prenatal marijuana and alcohol exposure and academic achievement at age 10. *Neurotoxicology and Teratology, 26,* 521–532.

Goldstein, M. H., & Schwade, J. A. (2008). Social feedback to infants' babbling facilitates rapid phonological learning. *Psychological Science, 19,* 515–523.

Goldstein, S. (2011). Attention-deficit/hyperactivity disorder. In S. Goldstein & C. R. Reynolds (Eds.), *Handbook of neurodevelopmental and genetic disorders in children* (2nd ed., pp. 131–150). New York: Guilford.

Golinkoff, R. M., & Hirsh-Pasek, K. (2006). Baby wordsmith: From associationist to social sophisticate. *Current Directions in Psychological Science, 15,* 30–33.

Golinkoff, R. M., & Hirsh-Pasek, K. (2008). How toddlers begin to learn verbs. *Trends in Cognitive Sciences, 12,* 397–403.

Golomb, C. (2004). *The child's creation of a pictorial world* (2nd ed.). Mahwah, NJ: Erlbaum.

Golombok, S., Blake, L., Casey, P., Roman, G., & Jadva, V. (2013). Children born through reproductive donation: A longitudinal study of psychological adjustment. *Journal of Child Psychology and Psychiatry, 54,* 653–660.

Golombok, S., Readings, J., Blake, L., Casey, P., Mellish, L., Marks, A., & Jadva, V. (2011). Children conceived by gamete donation: Psychological adjustment and mother–child relationships at age 7. *Journal of Family Psychology, 25,* 230–239.

Golombok, S., Rust, J., Zervoulis, K., Croudace, T., Golding, J., & Hines, M. (2008). Developmental trajectories of sex-typed behavior in boys and girls: A longitudinal general population study of children aged 2.5–8 years. *Child Development, 79,* 1583–1593.

Golombok, S., & Tasker, F. (2015). Socioemotional development in changing families. In M. E. Lamb (Ed.), *Handbook of child psychology and developmental science: Vol. 3. Socioemotional processes* (7th ed., pp. 419–463). Hoboken, NJ: Wiley.

Gonzalez, A.-L., & Wolters, C. A. (2006). The relation between perceived parenting practices and achievement motivation in mathematics. *Journal of Research in Childhood Education, 21,* 203–217.

Goodman, A., Schorge, J., & Greene, M. F. (2011). The long-term effects of in utero exposures—the DES story. *New England Journal of Medicine, 364,* 2083–2084.

Goodman, C., & Silverstein, M. (2006). Grandmothers raising grandchildren: Ethnic and racial differences in well-being among custodial and coparenting families. *Journal of Family Issues, 27,* 1605–1626.

Goodman, J., Dale, P., & Li, P. (2008). Does frequency count? Parental input and the acquisition of vocabulary. *Journal of Child Language, 35,* 515–531.

Goodman, J. H., Prager, J., Goldstein, R., & Freeman, M. (2015). Perinatal dyadic psychotherapy for postpartum depression: A randomized controlled pilot trial. *Archives of Women's Mental Health, 18,* 493–506.

Goodman, S. H., Rouse, M. H., Long, Q., Shuang, J., & Brand, S. R. (2011). Deconstructing antenatal depression: What is it that matters for neonatal behavioral functioning? *Infant Mental Health Journal, 32,* 339–361.

Goodvin, R., & Romdall, L. (2013). Associations of mother–child reminiscing about negative past events, coping, and self-concept in early childhood. *Infant and Child Development, 22,* 383–400.

Gooren, E. M. J. C., Pol, A. C., Stegge, H., Terwogt, M. M., & Koot, H. M. (2011). The development of conduct problems and depressive symptoms in early elementary school children: The role of peer rejection. *Journal of Clinical Child and Adolescent Psychology, 40,* 245–253.

Gopnik, A., & Nazzi, T. (2003). Words, kinds, and causal powers: A theory theory perspective on early naming and categorization. In D. H. Rakison & L. M. Oakes (Eds.), *Early category and concept development* (p. 303–329). New York: Oxford University Press.

Gopnik, A., & Tenenbaum, J. B. (2007). Bayesian networks, Bayesian learning and cognitive development. *Developmental Science, 10,* 281–287.

Gorman, B. K., Fiestas, C. E., Peña, E. D., & Clark, M. R. (2011). Creative and stylistic devices employed by children during a storybook narrative task: A cross-cultural study. *Language, Speech, and Hearing Services in Schools, 42,* 167–181.

Gormley, W. T., Jr., & Phillips, D. (2009). *The effects of pre-K on child development: Lessons from Oklahoma.* Washington, DC: National Summit on Early Childhood Education, Georgetown University.

Goswami, U. (1996). Analogical reasoning and cognitive development. In H. Reese (Ed.), *Advances in child development and behavior* (Vol. 26, pp. 91–138). New York: Academic Press.

Gottlieb, G. (1998). Normally occurring environmental and behavioral influences on gene activity: From central dogma to probabilistic epigenesis. *Psychological Review, 105,* 792–802.

Gottlieb, G. (2007). Probabilistic epigenesis. *Developmental Science, 10,* 1–11.

Gottlieb, G., Wahlsten, D., & Lickliter, R. (2006). The significance of biology for human development: A developmental psychobiological systems view. In R. M. Lerner (Ed.), *Handbook of child psychology: Vol. 1. Theoretical models of human development* (6th ed., pp. 210–257). Hoboken, NJ: Wiley.

Gottman, J. M., Gottman, J. S., & Shapiro, A. (2010). A new couples approach to interventions for the transition to parenthood. In M. S. Schulz, M. K. Pruett, P. K. Kerig, & R. D. Parke (Eds.), *Strengthening couple relationships for optimal child development* (pp. 165–179). Washington, DC: American Psychological Association.

Gould, J. L., & Keeton, W. T. (1996). *Biological science* (6th ed.). New York: Norton.

Graber, J. A., Brooks-Gunn, J., & Warren, M. P. (2006). Pubertal effects on adjustment in girls: Moving from demonstrating effects to identifying pathways. *Journal of Youth and Adolescence, 35,* 413–423.

Graber, J. A., Nichols, T., Lynne, S. D., Brooks-Gunn, J., & Botwin, G. J. (2006). A longitudinal examination of family, friend, and media influences on competent versus problem behaviors among urban minority youth. *Applied Developmental Science, 10,* 75–85.

Gralinski, J. H., & Kopp, C. B. (1993). Everyday rules for behavior: Mothers' requests to young children. *Developmental Psychology, 29,* 573–584.

Grall, T. (2016). Custodial mothers and fathers and their child support: 2013. *Current Population Reports,* P60–255. Retrieved from www.census.gov/content/dam/Census/library/publications/2016/demo/P60-255.pdf

Granier-Deferre, C., Bassereau, S., Ribeiro, A., Jacquet, A.-Y., & Lecanuet, J.-P. (2003). *Cardiac "orienting" response in fetuses and babies following in utero melody-learning.* Paper presented at the 11th European Conference on Developmental Psychology, Milan, Italy.

Grant, K. B., & Ray, J. A. (2010). *Home, school, and community collaboration: Culturally responsive family involvement.* Thousand Oaks, CA: Sage Publications.

Grant, S. L., Mizzi, T., & Anglim, J. (2016). 'Fat, four-eyed and female' 30 years later: A replication of Harris, Harris, and Bochner's (1982) early study of obesity stereotypes. *Australian Journal of Psychology, 68,* 290–300.

Gratier, M., & Devouche, E. (2011). Imitation and repetition of prosodic contour in vocal interaction at 3 months. *Developmental Psychology, 47,* 67–76.

Gray, K. A., Day, N. L., Leech, S., & Richardson, G. A. (2005). Prenatal marijuana exposure: Effect on child depressive symptoms at ten years of age. *Neurotoxicology and Teratology, 27,* 439–448.

Gray, M. R., & Steinberg, L. (1999). Unpacking authoritative parenting: Reassessing a multidimensional construct. *Journal of Marriage and the Family, 61,* 574–587.

Gray-Little, B., & Carels, R. (1997). The effects of racial and socioeconomic consonance on self-esteem and achievement in elementary, junior high, and high school students. *Journal of Research on Adolescence, 7,* 109–131.

Gray-Little, B., & Hafdahl, A. R. (2000). Factors influencing racial comparisons of self-esteem: A quantitative review. *Psychological Bulletin, 126,* 26–54.

Grazzani, I., Ornaghi, V., Agliati, A., & Brazzelli, E. (2016). How to foster toddlers' mental-state talk, emotion understanding, and prosocial behavior: A conversation-based intervention at nursery school. *Infancy, 21,* 199–227.

Green, B. L., Tarte, J. M., Harrison, P. M., Nygren, M., & Sanders, M. B. (2014). Results from a randomized trial of the Healthy Families Oregon accredited statewide program: Early program impacts on parenting. *Children and Youth Services Review, 44,* 288–298.

Green, G. E., Irwin, J. R., & Gustafson, G. E. (2000). Acoustic cry analysis, neonatal status and long-term developmental outcomes. In R. G. Barr, B. Hopkins, & J. A. Green (Eds.), *Crying as a sign, a symptom, and a signal* (pp. 137–156). Cambridge, UK: Cambridge University Press.

Greenberg, J. P. (2013). Determinants of after-school programming for school-age immigrant children. *Children and Schools, 35,* 101–111.

Greendorfer, S. L., Lewko, J. H., & Rosengren, K. S. (1996). Family and gender-based socialization of children and adolescents. In F. L. Smoll & R. E. Smith (Eds.), *Children and youth in sport: A biopsychological perspective* (pp. 89–111). Dubuque, IA: Brown & Benchmark.

Greene, S. M., Anderson, E. R., Forgatch, M. S., DeGarmo, D. S., & Hetherington, E. M. (2012). Risk and resilience after divorce. In F. Walsh (Ed.), *Normal family processes: Growing diversity and complexity* (4th ed., pp. 102–127). New York: Guilford.

Greenfield, P. (1992, June). *Notes and references for developmental psychology.* Conference on Making Basic Texts in Psychology More Culture-Inclusive and Culture-Sensitive, Western Washington University, Bellingham, WA.

Greenfield, P. M. (2004). *Weaving generations together: Evolving creativity in the Maya of Chiapas.* Santa Fe, NM: School of American Research.

Greenfield, P. M., Suzuki, L. K., & Rothstein-Fish, C. (2006). Cultural pathways through human development. In K. A. Renninger & I. E. Sigel (Eds.), *Handbook of child psychology: Vol. 4. Child psychology in practice* (6th ed., pp. 655–699). Hoboken, NJ: Wiley.

Greenough, W. T., & Black, J. E. (1992). Induction of brain structure by experience: Substrates for cognitive development. In M. R. Gunnar & C. A. Nelson (Eds.), *Minnesota Symposia on Child Psychology* (pp. 155–200). Hillsdale, NJ: Erlbaum.

Griffin, D. K., Fishel, S., Gordon, T., Yaron, Y., Grifo, J., Hourvitz, A., et al. (2017). Continuing to deliver: The evidence for pre-implantation genetic screening. *British Medical Journal, 356,* j752.

Grigoriadis, S., VonderPorten, E. H., Mamisashvili, L., Eady, A., Tomlinson, G., Dennis, C. L., et al. (2013). The effect of prenatal antidepressant exposure on neonatal adaptation: A systematic review and meta-analysis. *Journal of Clinical Psychiatry, 74,* e309–320.

Groh, A. M., Roisman, G. I., Booth-LaForce, C., Fraley, R. C., Owen, M. T., Cox, M. J., et al. (2014). Stability of attachment security from infancy to late adolescence. In C. Booth-LaForce & G. I. Roisman (Eds.), The Adult Attachment Interview: Psychometrics, stability and change from infancy, and developmental origins. *Monographs of the Society for Research in Child Development, 79*(3, Serial No. 314), 51–68.

Grossmann, K., Grossmann, K. E., Kindler, H., & Zimmermann, P. (2008). A wider view of attachment and exploration: The influence of mothers and fathers on the development of psychological security from infancy to young adulthood. In J. Cassidy & P. R. Shaver (Eds.), *Handbook of attachment: Theory, research, and clinical applications* (2nd ed., pp. 880–905). New York: Guilford.

Grossmann, K., Grossmann, K. E., Spangler, G., Suess, G., & Unzner, L. (1985). Maternal sensitivity and newborns' orientation responses as related to quality of attachment in Northern Germany. In I. Bretherton & E. Waters (Eds.), Growing points of attachment theory and research. *Monographs of the Society for Research in Child Development, 50*(1–2, Serial No. 209).

Grossniklaus, H. E., Nickerson, J. M., Edelhauser, H. F., Bergman, L. A. M. K., & Berglin, L. (2013). Anatomic alterations in aging and age-related diseases of the eye. *Investigative Ophthalmology and Visual Science, 54,* 23–27.

Gruendel, J., & Aber, J. L. (2007). Bridging the gap between research and child policy change: The role of strategic communications in policy advocacy. In J. L. Aber, S. J. Bishop-Josef, S. M. Jones, K. T. McLearn, & D. Phillips (Eds.), *Child development and social policy: Knowledge for action* (pp. 43–58). Washington, DC: American Psychological Association.

Grünebaum, A., McCullough, L. B., Brent, R. L., Arabin, B., Levene, M. I., & Chervenak, F. A. (2015). Perinatal risks of planned home births in the United States. *American Journal of Obstetrics and Gynecology, 212*(350), e1–e6.

Grusec, J. E. (2006). The development of moral behavior and conscience from a socialization perspective. In M. Killen & J. Smetana (Eds.), *Handbook of moral development* (pp. 243–265). Philadelphia: Erlbaum.

Grzyb, B. J., Cangelosi, A., Cattani, A., & Floccia, C. (2017). Decreased attention to object size information in scale errors performers. *Infant Behavior and Development, 47,* 72–82.

Gubbels, J., Segers, E., Keuning, J., & Verhoeven, L. (2016). The Aurora-a Battery as an assessment of triarchic intellectual abilities in upper primary grades. *Gifted Child Quarterly, 60,* 226–238.

Guerra, N. G., Williams, K. R., & Sadek, S. (2011). Understanding bullying and victimization during childhood and adolescence: A mixed methods study. *Child Development, 82,* 295–310.

Guest, A. M. (2013). Cultures of play during middle childhood: Interpretive perspectives from two distinct marginalized communities. *Sport, Education and Society, 18,* 167–183.

Guignard, J.-H., & Lubart, T. (2006). Is it reasonable to be creative? In J. C. Kaufman & J. Baer (Eds.), *Creativity and reason in cognitive development* (pp. 269–281). New York: Cambridge University Press.

Guilford, J. P. (1985). The structure-of-intellect model. In B. B. Wolman (Ed.), *Handbook of intelligence* (pp. 225–266). New York: Wiley.

Gullone, E. (2000). The development of normal fear: A century of research. *Clinical Psychology Review, 20,* 429–451.

Gunderson, E. A., Ramirez, G., Levine, S. C., & Beilock, S. L. (2012). The role of parents and teachers in the development of gender-related math attitudes. *Sex Roles, 66,* 153–166.

Gunnar, M. R., & Cheatham, C. L. (2003). Brain and behavior interfaces: Stress and the developing brain. *Infant Mental Health Journal, 24,* 195–211.

Gunnar, M. R., & de Haan, M. (2009). Methods in social neuroscience: Issues in studying development. In M. de Haan & M. R. Gunnar (Eds.), *Handbook of developmental social neuroscience* (pp. 13–37). New York: Guilford.

Gunnar, M. R., Doom, J. R., & Esposito, E. A. (2015). Psychoneuroendocrinology of stress: Normative development and individual differences. In M. E. Lamb (Eds.), *Handbook of child psychology and developmental science: Vol. 3. Socioemotional processes* (pp. 106–151). Hoboken, NJ: Wiley.

Gunnar, M. R., Morison, S. J., Chisholm, K., & Schuder, M. (2001). Salivary cortisol levels in children adopted from Romanian orphanages. *Development and Psychopathology, 13,* 611–628.

Gupta, K. K., & Shirasaka, T. (2016). An update on fetal alcohol syndrome—pathogenesis, risks, and treatment. *Alcoholism: Clinical and Experimental Research, 40,* 1594–1602.

Guralnick, M. J. (2012). Preventive interventions for preterm children: Effectiveness and developmental mechanisms. *Journal of Developmental and Behavioral Pediatrics, 33,* 352–364.

Gurrola, M., Ayón, C., & Moya Salas, L. (2016). Mexican adolescents' education and hopes in an anti-immigrant environment: The perspectives of first- and second-generation youth and parents. *Journal of Family Issues, 37,* 494–519.

Guterman, N. B., Lee, S. J., Taylor, C. A., & Rathouz, P. J. (2009). Parental perceptions of neighborhood processes, stress, personal control, and risk for physical child abuse and neglect. *Child Abuse and Neglect, 33,* 897–906.

Gutierrez-Galve, L., Stein, A., Hanington, L., Heron, J., & Ramchandani, P. (2015). Paternal depression in the postnatal period and child development: Mediators and moderators. *Pediatrics, 135,* e339–e347.

Guttman, J., & Lazar, A. (1998). Mother's or father's custody: Does it matter for social adjustment? *Educational Psychology: An International Journal of Experimental Educational Psychology, 18,* 225–234.

Guzzo, K. B. (2014). Trends in cohabitation outcomes: Compositional changes and engagement among never-married young adults. *Journal of Marriage and Family, 76,* 826–842.

Gwiazda, J., & Birch, E. E. (2001). Perceptual development: Vision. In E. B. Goldstein (Ed.), *Blackwell handbook of perception* (pp. 636–668). Oxford, UK: Blackwell.

H

Haas, A. P., Rodgers, P. L., & Herman, J. L. (2014). *Suicide attempts among transgender and gender non-conforming adults.* Los Angeles: The Williams Institute, UCLA School of Law.

Hadd, A. R., & Rodgers, J. L. (2017). Intelligence, income, and education as potential influences on a child's home environment: A (maternal) sibling-comparison design. *Developmental Psychology, 53,* 1286–1299.

Hainline, L. (1998). The development of basic visual abilities. In A. Slater (Ed.), *Perceptual development: Visual, auditory, and speech perception in infancy* (pp. 37–44). Hove, UK: Psychology Press.

Hakim, F., Kheirandish-Gozal, L., & Gozal, D. (2015). Obesity and altered sleep: A pathway to metabolic derangements in children? *Seminars in Pediatric Neurology, 22,* 77–85.

Hakuta, K., Bialystok, E., & Wiley, E. (2003). Critical evidence: A test of the critical-period hypothesis for second-language acquisitions. *Psychological Science, 14,* 31–38.

Hale, C. M., & Tager-Flusberg, H. (2003). The influence of language on theory of mind: A training study. *Developmental Science, 6,* 346–359.

Halford, G. S., & Andrews, G. (2010). Information-processing models of cognitive development. In J. G. Bremner & T. D. Wachs (Eds.), *Wiley-Blackwell handbook of infant development: Vol. 1. Basic research* (2nd ed., pp. 698–722). Oxford, UK: Wiley-Blackwell.

Halford, G. S., & Andrews, G. (2011). Information-processing models of cognitive development. In U. Goswami (Ed.), *Wiley-Blackwell handbook of childhood cognitive development* (2nd ed., pp. 697–722). Hoboken, NJ: Wiley-Blackwell.

Halim, M. L., & Ruble, D. (2010). Gender identity and stereotyping in early and middle childhood. In J. C. Chrisler & D. R. McCreary (Eds.), *Handbook of gender research in psychology* (pp. 495–525). New York: Springer.

Halim, M. L., Ruble, D., Tamis-LeMonda, C., & Shrout, P. E. (2013). Rigidity in gender-typed behaviors in early childhood: A longitudinal study of ethnic minority children. *Child Development, 84,* 1269–1284.

Hall, G. S. (1904). *Adolescence.* New York: Appleton.

Haller, J. (2005). Vitamins and brain function. In H. R. Lieberman, R. B. Kanarek, & C. Prasad (2005). *Nutritional neuroscience* (pp. 207–233). Philadelphia: Taylor & Francis.

Hammond, S. I., Müller, U., Carpendale, J. I. M., Bibok, M. B., & Lieberman-Finestone, D. (2012). The effects of parental scaffolding on preschoolers' executive function. *Developmental Psychology, 48,* 271–281.

Hammons, A. J., & Fiese, B. H. (2011). Is frequency of shared family meals related to the nutritional health of children and adolescents? *Pediatrics, 127,* e1565–e1574.

Hampton, T. (2014). Studies probe links between childhood asthma and obesity. *JAMA, 311,* 1718–1719.

Hanioka, T., Ojima, M., Tanaka, K., & Yamamoto, M. (2011). Does secondhand smoke affect the development of dental caries in children? A systematic review. *International Journal of Environmental Research and Public Health, 8,* 1503–1509.

Hannon, E. E., & Johnson, S. P. (2004). Infants use meter to categorize rhythms and melodies: Implications for musical structure learning. *Cognitive Psychology, 50,* 354–377.

Hannon, E. E., & Trehub, S. E. (2005a). Metrical categories in infancy and adulthood. *Psychological Science, 16,* 48–55.

Hannon, E. E., & Trehub, S. E. (2005b). Tuning in to musical rhythms: Infants learn more readily than adults. *Proceedings of the National Academy of Sciences, 102,* 12639–12643.

Hansen, M. B., & Markman, E. M. (2009). Children's use of mutual exclusivity to learn labels for parts of objects. *Developmental Psychology, 45,* 592–596.

Hao, L., & Woo, H. S. (2012). Distinct trajectories in the transition to adulthood: Are children of immigrants advantaged? *Child Development, 83,* 1623–1639.

Harlow, H. F., & Zimmerman, R. (1959). Affectional responses in the infant monkey. *Science, 130,* 421–432.

Harrison, S., Rowlinson, M., & Hill, A. J. (2016). 'No fat friend of mine': Young children's responses to overweight and disability. *Body Image, 18,* 65–73.

Hart, B., & Risley, T. R. (1995). *Meaningful differences in the everyday experience of young American children.* Baltimore, MD: Paul H. Brookes.

Hart, C. H., Burts, D. C., Durland, M. A., Charlesworth, R., DeWolf, M., & Fleege, P. O. (1998). Stress behaviors and activity type participation of preschoolers in more and less developmentally appropriate classrooms: SES and sex differences. *Journal of Research in Childhood Education, 13,* 176–196.

Hart, C. H., Newell, L. D., & Olsen, S. F. (2003). Parenting skills and social–communicative competence in childhood. In J. O. Greene & B. R. Burleson (Eds.), *Handbook of communication and social interaction skills* (pp. 753–797). Mahwah, NJ: Erlbaum.

Harter, S. (1999). *The construction of self: A developmental perspective.* New York: Guilford.

Harter, S. (2012). *The construction of the self: Developmental and sociocultural foundations* (2nd ed.). New York: Guilford.

Hartley, D., Blumenthal, T., Carrillo, M., DiPaolo, G., Esralew, L., Gardiner, K., et al. (2015). Down syndrome and Alzheimer's disease: Common pathways, common goals. *Alzheimer's and Dementia, 11,* 700–709.

Hartmann, T., Möller, I., & Krause, C. (2015). Factors underlying male and female use of violent video games. *New Media and Society, 17,* 1761–1776.

Hartshorn, K., Rovee-Collier, C., Gerhardstein, P., Bhatt, R. S., Wondoloski, T. L., Klein, P., et al. (1998). The ontogeny of long-term memory over the first year-and-a-half of life. *Developmental Psychobiology, 32,* 69–89.

Hartup, W. W. (2006). Relationships in early and middle childhood. In A. L. Vangelisti & D. Perlman (Eds.), *Cambridge handbook of personal relationships* (pp. 177–190). New York: Cambridge University Press.

Hartup, W. W., & Abecassis, M. (2004). Friends and enemies. In P. K. Smith & C. H. Hart (Eds.), *Blackwell handbook of childhood social development* (pp. 285–306). Malden, MA: Blackwell.

Hasebe, Y., Nucci, L., & Nucci, M. S. (2004). Parental control of the personal domain and adolescent symptoms of psychopathology: A cross-national study in the United States and Japan. *Child Development, 75,* 815–828.

Hau, K.-T., & Ho, I. T. (2010). Chinese students' motivation and achievement. In M. H. Bond (Ed.), *Oxford handbook of Chinese psychology* (pp. 187–204). New York: Oxford University Press.

Hauf, P., Aschersleben, G., & Prinz, W. (2007). Baby do–baby see! How action production influences action perception in infants. *Cognitive Development, 22,* 16–32.

Hauspie, R., & Roelants, M. (2012). Adolescent growth. In N. Cameron & R. Bogin (Eds.), *Human growth and development* (2nd ed., pp. 57–79). London: Elsevier.

Havstad, S. L., Johnson, D. D., Zoratti, E. M., Ezell, J. M., Woodcroft, K., Ownby, D. R., et al. (2012). Tobacco smoke exposure and allergic sensitization in children: A propensity score analysis. *Respirology, 17,* 1068–1072.

Haworth, C. M. A., Wright, M. J., Luciano, M., Martin, N. G., de Geus, E. J. C., van Beijsterveldt, C. E. M., et al. (2010). The heritability of general cognitive ability increases linearly from childhood to young adulthood. *Molecular Psychiatry, 15,* 1112–1120.

Hawsawi, A. M., Bryant, L. O., & Goodfellow, L. T. (2015). Association between exposure to secondhand smoke during pregnancy and low birthweight: A narrative review. *Respiratory Care, 60,* 135–140.

Hay, D. (2017). The early development of human aggression. *Child Development Perspectives, 11,* 102–106.

Hayne, H., Herbert, J., & Simcock, G. (2003). Imitation from television by 24- and 30-month-olds. *Developmental Science, 6,* 254–261.

Hayne, H., Rovee-Collier, C., & Perris, E. E. (1987). Categorization and memory retrieval by three-month-olds. *Child Development, 58,* 750–767.

Haywood, H. C., & Lidz, C. S. (2007). *Dynamic assessment in practice.* New York: Cambridge University Press.

Haywood, K., & Getchell, N. (2014). *Life span motor development* (6th ed.). Champaign, IL: Human Kinetics.

Hazel, N. A., Oppenheimer, C. W., Young, J. R., & Technow, J. R. (2014). Parent relationship quality buffers against the effect of peer stressors on depressive symptoms from middle childhood to adolescence. *Developmental Psychology, 50,* 2115–2123.

Hazen, N. L., McFarland, L., Jacobvitz, D., & Boyd-Soisson, E. (2010). Fathers' frightening behaviours and sensitivity with infants: Relations with fathers' attachment representations, father–infant attachment, and children's later outcomes. *Early Child Development and Care, 180,* 51–69.

Healthy Families America. (2011). *Healthy Families America FAQ.* Retrieved from www.healthyfamiliesamerica.org/about_us/faq.shtml

Healy, S. J., Murray, L., Cooper, P. J., Hughes, C., & Halligan, S. J. (2015). A longitudinal investigation of maternal influences on the development of child hostile attributions and aggression. *Journal of Clinical Child and Adolescent Psychology, 44,* 80–92.

Hein, S., Reich, J., & Grigorenko, E. (2015). Cultural manifestation of intelligence in formal and informal learning environments during childhood. In L. A. Jensen (Ed.), *Oxford handbook of human development and culture* (pp. 214–229). New York: Oxford University Press.

Heinrich-Weltzien, R., Zorn, C., Monse, B., & Kromeyer-Hauschild, K. (2013). Relationship between malnutrition and the number of permanent teeth in Filipino 10- to 13-year-olds. *BioMed Research International, 2013,* Article ID: 205950.

Hellemans, K. G., Sliwowska, J. H., Verma, P., & Weinberg, J. (2010). Prenatal alcohol exposure: Fetal programming and later life vulnerability to stress, expression and anxiety disorders. *Neuroscience and Biobehavioral Reviews, 34,* 791–807.

Helwig, C. C. (2006). Rights, civil liberties, and democracy across cultures. In M. Killen & J. G. Smetana (Eds.), *Handbook of moral development* (pp. 185–210). Philadelphia: Erlbaum.

Helwig, C. C., & Jasiobedzka, U. (2001). The relation between law and morality: Children's reasoning about socially beneficial and unjust laws. *Child Development, 72,* 1382–1393.

Helwig, C. C., & Turiel, E. (2004). Children's social and moral reasoning. In P. K. Smith & C. H. Hart (Eds.), *Blackwell handbook of childhood social development* (pp. 476–490). Malden, MA: Blackwell.

Helwig, C. C., & Turiel, E. (2011). Children's social and moral reasoning. In P. K. Smith & C. H. Hart (Eds.), *The Wiley-Blackwell handbook of childhood social development* (2nd ed., pp. 567–583). Chichester, UK: John Wiley & Sons.

Helwig, C. C., Zelazo, P. D., & Wilson, M. (2001). Children's judgments of psychological harm in normal and canonical situations. *Child Development, 72,* 66–81.

Henneberger, A. K., Coffman, D. L., & Gest, S. D. (2017). The effect of having aggressive friends on aggressive behavior in childhood: Using propensity scores to strengthen causal inference. *Social Development, 26,* 295–309.

Henning, A., Spinath, F. M., & Aschersleben, G. (2011). The link between preschoolers' executive function and theory of mind and the role of epistemic states. *Journal of Experimental Psychology, 108,* 513–531.

Henricsson, L., & Rydell, A.-M. (2004). Elementary school children with behavior problems: Teacher–child relations and self-perception. A prospective study. *Merrill-Palmer Quarterly, 50,* 111–138.

Hensley, E., & Briars, L. (2010). Closer look at autism and the measles-mumps-rubella vaccine. *Journal of the American Pharmacists Association, 50,* 736–741.

Hepper, P. (2015). Behavior during the prenatal period: Adaptive for development and survival. *Child Development Perspectives, 9,* 38–43.

Hepper, P. G., Dornan, J., & Lynch, C. (2012). Sex differences in fetal habituation. *Developmental Science, 15,* 373–383.

Hernandez, D. J., Denton, N. A., & Blanchard, V. L. (2011). Children in the United States of America: A statistical portrait by race-ethnicity, immigrant origins, and language. *Annals of the American Academy of Political and Social Science, 633,* 102–127.

Hernando-Herraez, I., Prado-Martinez, J., Garg, P., Fernandez-Callejo, M., Heyn, H., Hvilsom, C., et al. (2013). Dynamics of DNA methylation in recent human and great ape evolution. *PLOS Genetics, 9*(9), e1003763.

Heron, T. E., Hewar, W. L., & Cooper, J. O. (2013). *Applied behavior analysis.* Upper Saddle River, NJ: Pearson.

Heron-Delaney, M., Anzures, G., Herbert, J. S., Quinn, P. C., Slater, A. M., Tanaka, J. W., et al. (2011). Perceptual training prevents the emergence of the other race effect during infancy. *PLOS ONE, 6*(5), 231–255.

Herrnstein, R. J., & Murray, C. (1994). *The bell curve.* New York: Free Press.

Hespos, S. J., Ferry, A. L., Cannistraci, C. J., Gore, J., & Park, S. (2010). Using optical imaging to investigate functional cortical activity in human infants. In A. W. Roe (Ed.), *Imaging the brain with optical methods* (pp. 159–176). New York: Springer Science + Business Media.

Hesse, E., & Main, M. (2006). Frightening, threatening, and dissociative parental behavior in low-risk samples: Description, discussion, and interpretations. *Development and Psychopathology, 18,* 309–343.

Hetherington, E. M., & Kelly, J. (2002). *For better or for worse: Divorce reconsidered.* New York: Norton.

Hetherington, E. M., & Stanley-Hagan, M. (2000). Diversity among stepfamilies. In D. H. Demo, K. R. Allen, & M. A. Fine (Eds.), *Handbook of family diversity* (pp. 173–196). New York: Oxford University Press.

Heyder, A., & Kessels, U. (2015). Do teachers equate male and masculine with lower academic engagement? How students' gender enactment triggers gender stereotypes at school. *Social Psychology of Education, 18,* 467–485.

Heyman, G. D., & Legare, C. H. (2004). Children's beliefs about gender differences in the academic and social domains. *Sex Roles, 50,* 227–239.

Hicken, B. L., Smith, D., Luptak, M., & Hill, R. D. (2014). Health and aging in rural America. In J. Warren & K. B. Smalley (Eds.), *Rural public health: Best practices and preventive models* (pp. 241–254). New York: Springer.

Hickling, A. K., & Wellman, H. M. (2001). The emergence of children's causal explanations and theories: Evidence from everyday conversation. *Developmental Psychology, 37,* 668–683.

Hilbert, D. D., & Eis, S. D. (2014). Early intervention for emergent literacy development in a collaborative community pre-kindergarten. *Early Childhood Education Journal, 42,* 105–113.

Hildreth, K., & Rovee-Collier, C. (2002). Forgetting functions of reactivated memories over the first year of life. *Developmental Psychobiology, 41,* 277–288.

Hill, A. L., Degnan, K. A., Calkins, S. D., & Keane, S. P. (2006). Profiles of externalizing behavior problems for boys and girls across preschool: The roles of emotion regulation and inattention. *Developmental Psychology, 42,* 913–928.

Hill, D. B., Menvielle, E., Sica, K. M., & Johnson, A. (2010). An affirmative intervention for families with gender variant children: Parental ratings of child mental health and gender. *Journal of Sex and Marital Therapy, 36,* 6–23.

Hill, J. L., Brooks-Gunn, J., & Waldfogel, J. (2003). Sustained effects of high participation in an early intervention for low-birth-weight premature infants. *Developmental Psychology, 39,* 730–744.

Hilliard, L. J., & Liben, L. S. (2010). Differing levels of gender salience in preschool classrooms: Effects on children's gender attitudes and intergroup bias. *Child Development, 81,* 1787–1798.

Hines, M. (2011). Prenatal endocrine influences on sexual orientation and on sexually differentiated childhood behavior. *Neuroendocrinology, 32,* 170–182.

Hines, M. (2015). Gendered development. In M. E. Lamb (Ed.), *Handbook of child psychology and developmental science: Vol. 3. Socioemotional processes* (7th ed., pp. 842–887). Hoboken, NJ: Wiley.

Hipfner-Boucher, K., Milburn, T., Weitzman, E., Greenberg, J., Pelletier, J., & Girolametto, L. (2014). Relationships between preschoolers' oral language and phonological awareness. *First Language, 34,* 178–197.

Hoang, D. H., Pagnier, A., Guichardet, K., Dubois-Teklali, F., Schiff, I., Lyard, G., et al. (2014). Cognitive disorders in pediatric medulloblastoma: What neuroimaging has to offer. *Journal of Neurosurgery, 14,* 136–144.

Hodel, A. S., Hunt, R. H., Cowell, R. A., Van Den Heuvel, S. E., Gunnar, M. R., & Thomas, K. M. (2014). Duration of early adversity and structural brain development in post-institutionalized adolescents. *NeuroImage, 105,* 112–119.

Hodnett, E. D., Gates, S., Hofmeyr, G. J., & Sakala, C. (2012). Continuous support for women during childbirth. *Cochrane Database of Systematic Reviews,* Issue 7, Art. No.: CD003766.

Hoerr, T. (2004). How MI informs teaching at New City School. *Teachers College Record, 106,* 40–48.

Hoff, E. (2003). The specificity of environmental influence: Socioeconomic status affects early vocabulary development via maternal speech. *Child Development, 74,* 1368–1378.

Hoff, E. (2013). Interpreting the early language trajectories of children from low-SES and language minority homes: Implications for closing achievement gaps. *Developmental Psychology, 49,* 4–14.

Hoff, E., Core, C., Place, S., Rumiche, R., Senor, M., & Parra, M. (2012). Dual language exposure and early bilingual development. *Journal of Child Language, 39,* 1–27.

Hoff, E., Laursen, B., & Tardif, T. (2002). Socioeconomic status and parenting. In M. H. Bornstein (Ed.), *Handbook of parenting* (pp. 231–252). Mahwah, NJ: Erlbaum.

Hofferth, S. L. (2003). Race/ethnic differences in father involvement in two-parent families: Culture, context, or economy? *Journal of Family Issues, 24,* 185–216.

Hofferth, S. L., & Anderson, K. G. (2003). Are all dads equal? Biology versus marriage as a basis for paternal investment. *Journal of Marriage and Family, 65,* 213–232.

Hofferth, S. L., Forry, N. D., & Peters, H. E. (2010). Child support, father–child contact, and preteens' involvement with nonresidential fathers: Racial/ethnic differences. *Journal of Family Economic Issues, 31,* 14–32.

Hoffman, L. W. (2000). Maternal employment: Effects of social context. In R. D. Taylor & M. C. Wang (Eds.), *Resilience across contexts: Family, work, culture, and community* (pp. 147–176). Mahwah, NJ: Erlbaum.

Hoffman, M. L. (2000). *Empathy and moral development.* New York: Cambridge University Press.

Hokoda, A., & Fincham, F. D. (1995). Origins of children's helpless and mastery achievement patterns in the family. *Journal of Educational Psychology, 87,* 375–385.

Holden, G. W., Williamson, P. A., & Holland, G. W. O. (2014). Eavesdropping on the family: A pilot investigation of corporal punishment in the home. *Journal of Family Psychology, 28,* 401–406.

Holditch-Davis, D., Belyea, M., & Edwards, L. J. (2005). Prediction of 3-year developmental outcomes from sleep development over the preterm period. *Infant Behavior and Development, 79,* 49–58.

Hollich, G. J., Hirsh-Pasek, K., & Golinkoff, R. M. (2000). Breaking the language barrier: An emergentist coalition model for the origins of word learning. *Monographs of the Society for Research in Child Development, 65*(3, Serial No. 262).

Höllwarth, M. E. (2013). Prevention of unintentional injuries: A global role for pediatricians. *Pediatrics, 132,* 4–7.

Hong, D. S., Hoeft, F., Marzelli, M. J., Lepage, J.-F., Roeltgen, D., Ross, J., et al. (2014). Influence of the X-chromosome on neuroanatomy: Evidence from Turner and Klinefelter syndromes. *Journal of Neuroscience, 34,* 3509–3516.

Hood, M., Conlon, E., & Andrews, G. (2008). Preschool home literacy practices and children's literacy development: A longitudinal analysis. *Journal of Educational Psychology, 100,* 252–271.

Hoogenhout, M., & Malcolm-Smith, S. (2017). Theory of mind predicts severity level in autism. *Autism, 21,* 242–252.

Hopf, L., Quraan, M. A., Cheung, M. J., Taylor, M. J., Ryan, J. D., & Moses, S. N. (2013). Hippocampal lateralization and memory in children and adults. *Journal of the International Neuropsychological Society, 19,* 1042–1052.

Hopkins, B., & Westra, T. (1988). Maternal handling and motor development: An intracultural study. *Genetic, Social and General Psychology Monographs, 14,* 377–420.

Horne, R. S. C. (2017). Sleep disorders in newborns and infants. In S. Nevsimalová & O. Bruni (Eds.), *Sleep disorders in children* (pp. 129–153). Cham, Switzerland: Springer International.

Horner, T. M. (1980). Two methods of studying stranger reactivity in infants: A review. *Journal of Child Psychology and Psychiatry, 21,* 203–219.

Horta, B. L., Loret de Mola, C., & Victoria, C. G. (2015). Breastfeeding and intelligence: A systematic review and meta-analysis. *Acta Paediatrica, 104,* 14–19.

Houlihan, J., Kropp, T., Wiles, R., Gray, S., & Campbell, C. (2005). *Body burden: The pollution in newborns.* Washington, DC: Environmental Working Group.

Houts, R. M., Barnett-Walker, K. C., Paley, B., & Cox, M. J. (2008). Patterns of couple interaction during the transition to parenthood. *Personal Relationships, 15,* 103–122.

Howe, M. L. (2014). The co-emergence of self and autobiographical memory: An adaptive view of early memory. In P. J. Bauer & R. Fivush (Eds.), *Wiley handbook on the development of children's memory* (pp. 545–567). Hoboken, NJ: Wiley-Blackwell.

Howe, M. L. (2015). Memory development. In L. S. Liben & U. Müller (Eds.), *Handbook of child psychology and developmental science: Vol. 2. Cognitive processes* (7th ed., pp. 203–249). Hoboken, NJ: Wiley.

Howe, N., Aquan-Assee, J., & Bukowski, W. M. (2001). Predicting sibling relations over time: Synchrony between maternal management styles and sibling relationship quality. *Merrill-Palmer Quarterly, 47,* 121–141.

Howell, K. K., Coles, C. D., & Kable, J. A. (2008). The medical and developmental consequences of prenatal drug exposure. In J. Brick (Ed.), *Handbook of the medical consequences of alcohol and drug abuse* (2nd ed., pp. 219–249). New York: Haworth Press.

Howell, S. R., & Becker, S. (2013). Grammar from the lexicon: Evidence from neural network simulations of language acquisition. In D. Bittner & N. Ruhlig (Eds.), *Lexical bootstrapping: The role of lexis and semantics in child language* (pp. 245–264). Berlin: Walter de Gruyter.

Høybe, C., Cohen, P., Hoffman, A. R., Ross, R., Biller, B. M., & Christiansen, J. S. (2015). Status of long-acting-growth hormone preparations—2015. *Growth Hormone & IGF Research, 25,* 201–206.

Hsu, A. S., Chater, N., & Vitányi, P. (2013). Language learning from positive evidence, reconsidered: A simplicity-based approach. *Topics in Cognitive Science, 5,* 35–55.

Huang, H., Coleman, S., Bridge, J. A., Yonkers, K., & Katon, W. (2014). A meta-analysis of the relationship between antidepressant use in pregnancy and the risk of preterm birth and low birth weight. *General Hospital Psychiatry, 36,* 13–18.

Huang, Y., Hauck, F. R. F., Signore, C., Yu, A., Raju, T. N. K., Huang, T. T.-K., et al. (2013). Influence of bedsharing activity on breastfeeding duration among U.S. mothers. *JAMA Pediatrics, 167,* 1038–1044.

Hubbs-Tait, L., Nation, J. R., Krebs, N. F., & Bellinger, D. C. (2005). Neurotoxicants, micronurtrients, and social environments: Individual and combined effects on children's development. *Psychological Science in the Public Interest, 6,* 57–121.

Hudson, J. A., Fivush, R., & Kuebli, J. (1992). Scripts and episodes: The development of event memory. *Applied Cognitive Psychology, 6,* 483–505.

Hudson, J. A., & Mayhew, E. M. Y. (2009). The development of memory for recurring events. In M. L. Courage & N. Cowan (Eds.), *The development of memory in infancy and childhood* (pp. 69–91). Hove, UK: Psychology Press.

Huebner, C. E., & Payne, K. (2010). Home support for emergent literacy: Follow-up of a community-based implementation of dialogic reading. *Journal of Applied Developmental Psychology, 31,* 195–201.

Huesmann, L. R., Moise-Titus, J., Podolski, C. & Eron, L. D. (2003). Longitudinal relations between children's exposure to TV violence and their aggressive and violent behavior in young adulthood: 1977–1992. *Developmental Psychology, 39,* 201–221.

Hughes, C., & Ensor, R. (2010). Do early social cognition and executive function predict individual differences in preschoolers' prosocial and antisocial behavior? In B. W. Sokol, U. Müller, J. I. M. Carpendale, A. R. Young, & G. Iarocci (Eds.), *Social interaction and the development of social understanding and executive functions* (pp. 418–441). New York: Oxford University Press.

Hughes, C., Ensor, R., & Marks, A. (2010). Individual differences in false belief understanding are stable from 3 to 6 years of age and predict children's mental state talk with school friends. *Journal of Experimental Child Psychology, 108,* 96–112.

Hughes, C., Marks, A., Ensor, R., & Lecce, S. (2010). A longitudinal study of conflict and inner state talk in children's conversations with mothers and younger siblings. *Social Development, 19,* 822–837.

Hughes, J. N. (2011). Longitudinal effects of teacher and student perceptions of teacher–student relationship qualities on academic adjustment. *Elementary School Journal, 112,* 38–60.

Hughes, J. N., & Kwok, O. (2006). Classroom engagement mediates the effect of teacher–student support on elementary students' peer acceptance. *Journal of School Psychology, 43,* 465–480.

Hughes, J. N., & Kwok, O. (2007). Influence of student–teacher and parent–teacher relationships on lower achieving readers' engagement and achievement in the primary grades. *Journal of Educational Psychology, 99,* 39–51.

Hughes, J. N., Wu, J.-Y., Kwok, O., Villarreal, V., & Johnson, A. Y. (2012). Indirect effects of child reports of teacher–student relationship on achievement. *Journal of Educational Psychology, 104,* 350–365.

Hunnius, S., & Geuze, R. H. (2004a). Developmental changes in visual scanning of dynamic faces and abstract stimuli in infants: A longitudinal study. *Infancy, 6,* 231–255.

Hunnius, S., & Geuze, R. H. (2004b). Gaze shifting in infancy: A longitudinal study using dynamic faces and abstract stimuli. *Infant Behavior and Development, 27,* 397–416.

Hunt, C. E., & Hauck, F. R. (2006). Sudden infant death syndrome. *Canadian Medical Association Journal, 174,* 1861–1869.

Hunt, E. (2011). *Human intelligence.* New York: Cambridge University Press.

Huntsinger, C., Jose, P. E., Krieg, D. B., & Luo, Z. (2011). Cultural differences in Chinese American and European American children's drawing skills over time. *Early Childhood Research Quarterly, 26,* 134–145.

Huston, A. C., Bobbitt, K. C., & Bentley, A. (2015). Time spent in child care: How and why does it affect social development? *Developmental Psychology, 51,* 621–634.

Hutchinson, E. A., De Luca, C. R., Doyle, L. W., Roberts, G., & Anderson, P. J. (2013). School-age outcomes of extremely preterm or extremely low birth weight children. *Pediatrics, 131,* e1053–1061.

Huttenlocher, J., Waterfall, H., Veasilyeva, M., Vevea, J., & Hedges, L. (2010). Sources of variability in children's language growth. *Cognitive Psychology, 61,* 343–365.

Huyck, M. H. (1996). Continuities and discontinuities in gender identity in midlife. In V. L. Bengtson (Ed.), *Adulthood and aging* (pp. 98–121). New York: Springer-Verlag.

Hymel, S., Schonert-Reichl, K. A., Bonanno, R. A., Vaillancourt, T., & Henderson, N. R. (2010). Bullying and morality: Understanding how good kids can behave badly. In S. Jimerson, S. M. Swearer, & D. L. Espelage (Eds.), *Handbook of bullying in schools: An international perspective* (pp. 101–118). New York: Routledge.

I

Ibanez, G., Bernard, J. Y., Rondet, C., Peyre, H., Forhan, A., Kaminski, M., & Saurel-Cubizolles, M.-J. (2015). Effects of antenatal maternal depression and anxiety on children's early cognitive development: A prospective cohort study. *PLOS ONE, 10*(8), e0135849.

Imai, M., & Haryu, E. (2004). The nature of word-learning biases and their roles for lexical development: From a cross-linguistic perspective. In D. G. Hall & S. R. Waxman (Eds.), *Weaving a lexicon* (pp. 411–444). Cambridge, MA: MIT Press.

Ingoldsby, E. M., Shelleby, E., Lane, T., & Shaw, D. S. (2012). Extrafamilial contexts and children's conduct problems. In V. Maholmes & R. B. King (Eds.), *Oxford handbook of poverty and child development* (pp. 404–422). New York: Oxford University Press.

Insana, S. P., & Montgomery-Downs, H. E. (2012). Sleep and sleepiness among first-time postpartum parents: A field- and laboratory-based multimethod assessment. *Developmental Psychobiology, 55,* 361–372.

Ishida, M., & Moore, G. E. (2013). The role of imprinted genes in humans. *Molecular Aspects of Medicine, 34,* 826–840.

Ishihara, K., Warita, K., Tanida, T., Sugawara, T., Kitagawa, H., & Hoshi, N. (2007). Does paternal exposure to 2, 3, 7, 8-tetrachlorodibenzo-p-dioxin (TCDD) affect the sex ratio of offspring? *Journal of Veterinary Medical Science, 69,* 347–352.

Izard, V., Sann, C., Spelke, E. S., & Streri, A. (2009). Newborn infants perceive abstract numbers. *Proceedings of the National Academy of Sciences, 106,* 10382–10385.

J

Jabès, A., & Nelson, C. A. (2014). Neuroscience and child well-being. In A. Ben-Arieh, F. Casas, I. Frønes, & J. E. Korbin (Eds.), *Handbook of child well-being: Vol. 1* (pp. 219–247) Dordrecht, Germany: Springer Reference.

Jack, F., Simcock, G., & Hayne, G. (2012). Magic memories: Young children's verbal recall after a 6-year delay. *Child Development, 83,* 159–172.

Jacobs, J. E., Lanza, S., Osgood, D. W., Eccles, J. S., & Wigfield, A. (2002). Changes in children's self-competence and values: Gender and domain differences across grades one through twelve. *Child Development, 73,* 509–527.

Jadallah, M., Anderson, R. C., Nguyen-Jahiel, K., Miller, B. W., Kim, I.-H., Kuo, L.-J., et al. (2011). Influence of a teacher's scaffolding moves during child-led small-group discussions. *American Educational Research Journal, 48,* 194–230.

Jadva, V., Casey, P., & Golombok, S. (2012). Surrogacy families 10 years on: Relationship with the surrogate, decisions over disclosure and children's understanding of their surrogacy origins. *Human Reproduction, 27,* 3008–3014.

Jaffe, M., Gullone, E., & Hughes, E. K. (2010). The roles of temperamental dispositions and perceived parenting behaviours in the use of two emotion regulation strategies in late childhood. *Journal of Applied Developmental Psychology, 31,* 47–59.

Jaffee, S. R., & Christian, C. W. (2014). The biological embedding of child abuse and neglect: Implications for policy and practice. *Society for Research in Child Development Social Policy Report, 28*(1).

Jahja, R., Huijbregts, S. C. J., de Sonneville, L. M. J., van der Meere, J. J., & van Spronsen, F. J. (2014). Neurocognitive evidence for revision of treatment targets and guidelines for phenylketonuria. *Journal of Pediatrics, 164,* 895–899.

Jambon, M., & Smetana, J. G. (2014). Moral complexity in middle childhood: Children's evaluations of necessary harm. *Developmental Psychology, 50,* 22–33.

Jansen, J., de Weerth, C., & Riksen-Walraven, J. M. (2008). Breastfeeding and the mother–infant relationship. *Developmental Review, 28,* 503–521.

Jansen, P. W., Roza, S. J., Jaddoe, V. W. V., Mackenbach, J. D., Raat, H., Hofman, A., et al. (2012). Children's eating behavior, feeding practices of parents and weight problems in early childhood: Results from the population-based Generation R Study. *International Journal of Behavioral Nutrition and Physical Activity, 9,* 130–138.

Janssens, J. M. A. M., & Deković, M. (1997). Child rearing, prosocial moral reasoning, and prosocial behaviour. *International Journal of Behavioral Development, 20,* 509–527.

Jaudes, P. K., & Mackey-Bilaver, L. (2008). Do chronic conditions increase young children's risk of being maltreated? *Child Abuse and Neglect, 32,* 671–681.

Jedrychowski, W., Perera, F. P., Jankowski, J., Mrozek-Budzyn, D., Mroz, E., Flak, E., et al. (2009). Very low prenatal exposure to lead and mental development of children in infancy and early childhood. *Neuroepidemiology, 32,* 270–278.

Jenkins, J. M., Rasbash, J., & O'Connor, T. G. (2003). The role of the shared family context in differential parenting. *Developmental Psychology, 39,* 99–113.

Jennifer, D., & Cowie, H. (2009). Engaging children and young people actively in research. In K. Bryan (Ed.), *Communication in healthcare* (pp. 135–163). New York: Peter Lang.

Jensen, A. R. (1969). How much can we boost IQ and scholastic achievement? *Harvard Educational Review, 39,* 1–123.

Jensen, A. R. (2001). Spearman's hypothesis. In J. M. Collis & S. Messick (Eds.), *Intelligence and personality: Bridging the gap in theory and measurement* (pp. 3–24). Mahwah, NJ: Erlbaum.

Jensen, T. M., Lippold, M. A., Mills-Koonce, R., & Fosco, G. M. (2017). Stepfamily relationship quality and children's internalizing and externalizing problems. *Family Process, 56,* 12284.

Jerome, E. M., Hamre, B. K., & Pianta, R. C. (2009). Teacher–child relationships from kindergarten to sixth grade: Early childhood predictors of teacher-perceived conflict and closeness. *Social Development, 18,* 915–945.

Jia, P., Xue, H., Zhang, J., & Wang, Y. (2017). Time trend and demographic and geographic disparities in childhood obesity prevalence in China–evidence from twenty years of longitudinal data. *International Journal of Environmental Research and Public Health, 14,* 369.

Jiang, Q., Li, Y., & Sánchez-Barricarte, J. J. (2016). Fertility intention, son preference, and second childbirth: Survey findings from Shaanxi Province of China. *Social Indicators Research, 125,* 935–953.

Jipson, J. L., & Gelman, S. A. (2007). Robots and rodents: Children's inferences about living and nonliving kinds. *Child Development, 78,* 1675–1688.

Johnson, A. D., Ryan, R. M., & Brooks-Gunn, J. (2012). Child-care subsidies: Do they impact the quality of care children experience? *Child Development, 83,* 1444–1461.

Johnson, E. K., & Seidl, A. (2008). Clause segmentation by 6-month-old infants: A crosslinguistic perspective. *Infancy, 13,* 440–455.

Johnson, E. K., & Tyler, M. D. (2010). Testing the limits of statistical learning for word segmentation. *Developmental Science, 13,* 339–345.

Johnson, J. G., Cohen, P., Smailes, E. M., Kasen, S., & Brook, J. S. (2002). Television viewing and aggressive behavior during adolescence and adulthood. *Science, 295,* 2468–2471.

Johnson, M. H. (1999). Ontogenetic constraints on neural and behavioral plasticity: Evidence from imprinting and face processing. *Canadian Journal of Experimental Psychology, 55,* 77–90.

Johnson, M. H. (2011). Developmental neuroscience, psychophysiology, and genetics. In M H. Bornstein & M. E. Lamb (Eds.), *Developmental science: An advanced textbook* (6th ed., pp. 187–222). Mahwah, NJ: Erlbaum.

Johnson, M. H., & de Haan, M. (2015). *Developmental cognitive neuroscience: An introduction* (4th ed.). Chichester, UK: Wiley-Blackwell.

Johnson, R. C., & Schoeni, R. F. (2011). Early-life origins of adult disease: National longitudinal population-based study of the United States. *American Journal of Public Health, 101,* 2317–2324.

Johnson, S. C., Dweck, C. S., & Chen, F. S. (2007). Evidence for infants' internal working models of attachment. *Psychological Science, 18,* 501–502.

Johnson, S. C., Dweck, C., Chen, F. S., Stern, H. L., Ok, S.-J., & Barth, M. (2010). At the intersection of social and cognitive development: Internal working models of attachment in infancy. *Cognitive Science, 34,* 807–825.

Johnson, S. P., & Hannon, E. E. (2015). Perceptual development. In L. S. Liben & U. Müller (Eds.), *Handbook of child psychology and developmental science: Vol. 2. Cognitive processes* (7th ed., pp. 63–112). Hoboken, NJ: Wiley.

Johnson, S. P., Slemmer, J. A., & Amso, D. (2004). Where infants look determines how they see: Eye movements and object perception performance in 3-month-olds. *Infancy, 6,* 185–201.

Jokhi, R. P., & Whitby, E. H. (2011). Magnetic resonance imaging of the fetus. *Developmental Medicine and Child Neurology, 53,* 18–28.

Jones, A., Charles, P., & Benson, K. (2013). A model for supporting at-risk couples during the transition to parenthood. *Families in Society, 94,* 166–173.

Jones, A. R., Parkinson, K. N., Drewett, R. F., Hyland, R. M., Pearce, M. S., & Adamson, A. J. (2011). Parental perceptions of weight status in children: The Gateshead Millennium Study. *International Journal of Obesity, 35,* 953–962.

Jones, D. J., & Lindahl, K. M. (2011). Coparenting in extended kinship systems: African American, Hispanic, Asian heritage, and Native American families. In J. P. McHale & K. M. Lindahl (Eds.), *Coparenting* (pp. 61–79). Washington, DC: American Psychological Association.

Jones, J., & Placek, P. (2017). *Adoption by the numbers.* Washington, DC: National Council for Adoption. Retrieved from www.adoptioncouncil.org/files/large/249e5e967173624

Jones, S. (2009). The development of imitation in infancy. *Philosophical Transactions of the Royal Society B, 364,* 2325–2335.

Josselyn, S. A., & Frankland, P. W. (2012). Infantile amnesia: A neurogenic hypothesis. *Learning and Memory, 19,* 423–433.

Juby, H., Billette, J.-M., Laplante, B., & Le Bourdais, C. (2007). Nonresident fathers and children: Parents' new unions and frequency of contact. *Journal of Family Issues, 28,* 1220–1245.

Juffer, F., & van IJzendoorn, M. H. (2012). Review of meta-analytical studies on the physical, emotional, and cognitive outcomes of intercountry adoptees. In J. L. Gibbons & K. S. Rotabi (Eds.), *Intercountry adoption: Policies, practices, and outcomes* (pp. 175–186). Burlington, VT: Ashgate Publishing.

Junge, C., Kooijman, V., Hagoort, P., & Cutler, A. (2012). Rapid recognition at 10 months as a predictor of language development. *Developmental Science, 15,* 463–473.

Jürgensen, M., Hiort, O., Holterhus, P.-M., & Thyen, U. (2007). Gender role behavior in children with XY karyotype and disorders of sex development. *Hormones and Behavior, 51,* 443–453.

Jusczyk, P. W. (2002). Some critical developments in acquiring native language sound organization. *Annals of Otology, Rhinology and Laryngology, 189,* 11–15.

Jusczyk, P. W., & Hohne, E. A. (1997). Infants' memory for spoken words. *Science, 277,* 1984–1986.

Jusczyk, P. W., & Luce, P. A. (2002). Speech perception. In H. Pashler & S. Yantis (Eds.), *Stevens' handbook of experimental psychology: Vol. 1. Sensation and perception* (3rd ed., pp. 493–536). New York: Wiley.

Jutras-Aswad, D., DiNieri, J. A., Harkany, T., & Hurd, Y. L. (2009). Neurobiological consequences of maternal cannabis on human fetal development and its neuropsychiatric outcome. *European Archives of Psychiatry and Clinical Neuroscience, 259,* 395–412.

K

Kabali, H. K., Irigoyen, M. M., Nunez-Davis, R., Budacki, J. G., Mohanty, S. H., Leister, K. P., & Bonner, Jr., R. L. (2015). Exposure and use of mobile media devices by young children. *Pediatrics, 136,* 1044–1050.

Kaffashi, F., Scher, M. S., Ludington-Hoe, S. M., & Loparo, K. A. (2013). An analysis of the kangaroo care intervention using neonatal EEG complexity: A preliminary study. *Clinical Neurophysiology, 124,* 238–246.

Kagan, J. (2003). Behavioral inhibition as a temperamental category. In R. J. Davidson, K. R. Scherer, & H. H. Goldsmith (Eds.), *Handbook of affective science* (pp. 320–331). New York: Oxford University Press.

Kagan, J. (2010). Emotions and temperament. In M. H. Bornstein (Ed.), *Handbook of cultural developmental science* (pp. 175-194). New York: Psychology Press.

Kagan, J. (2013a). Contextualizing experience. *Developmental Review, 33,* 273–278.

Kagan, J. (2013b). Equal time for psychological and biological contributions to human variation. *Review of General Psychology, 17,* 351–357.

Kagan, J. (2013c). Temperamental contributions to inhibited and uninhibited profiles. In P. D. Zelazo (Ed.), *The Oxford handbook of developmental psychology* (pp. 142–164). New York: Oxford University Press.

Kagan, J., Snidman, N., Kahn, V., & Towsley, S. (2007). The preservation of two infant temperaments into adolescence. *Monographs of the Society for Research in Child Development, 72*(2, Serial No. 287).

Kahn, U. R., Sengoelge, M., Zia, N., Razzak, J. A., Hasselberg, M., & Laflamme, L. (2015). Country level economic disparities in child injury mortality. *Archives of Disease in Childhood, 100,* s29–s33.

Kail, R. V. (2003). Information processing and memory. In M. H. Bornstein, L. Davidson, C. L. M. Keyes, K. A. Moore, and the Center for Child Well-Being (Eds.), *Well-being: Positive development across the life course* (pp. 269–280). Mahwah, NJ: Erlbaum.

Kail, R. V., & Ferrer, E. F. (2007). Processing speed in childhood and adolescence: Longitudinal models for examining developmental change. *Child Development, 78,* 1760–1770.

Kail, R. V., McBride-Chang, C., Ferrer, E., Cho, J.-R., & Shu, H. (2013). Cultural differences in the development of processing speed. *Developmental Science, 16,* 476–483.

Kaiser Family Foundation. (2015). *How will the uninsured fare under the Affordable Care Act?* Retrieved from www.kff.org/health-reform/fact-sheet/how-will-the-uninsured-fare-under-the-affordable-care-act

Kaiser Family Foundation. (2017). *Where are states today? Medicaid and CHIP eligibility levels for children, pregnant women, and adults.* Retrieved from www.kff.org/medicaid/fact-sheet/where-are-states-today-medicaid-and-chip

Kakihara, F., Tilton-Weaver, L., Kerr, M., & Stattin, H. (2010). The relationship of parental control to youth adjustment: Do youths' feelings about their parents play a role? *Journal of Youth and Adolescence, 39,* 1442–1456.

Kaminsky, Z., Petronis, A., Wang, S.-C., Levine, B., Ghaffar, O., Floden, D., et al. (2007). Epigenetics of personality traits: An illustrative study of identical twins discordant for risk-taking behavior. *Twin Research and Human Genetics, 11,* 1–11.

Kang, N. H., & Hong, M. (2008). Achieving excellence in teacher workforce and equity in learning opportunities in South Korea. *Educational Researcher, 37,* 200–207.

Kantaoka, S., & Vandell, D. L. (2013). Quality of afterschool activities and relative change in adolescent functioning over two years. *Applied Developmental Science, 17,* 123–134.

Kanters, M. A., Bocarro, J. N., Edwards, M., Casper, J., & Floyd, M. F. (2013). School sport participation under two school sport policies: Comparisons by race/ethnicity, gender, and socioeconomic status. *Annals of Behavioral Medicine, 45*(Suppl. 1), S113–S121.

Karafantis, D. M., & Levy, S. R. (2004). The role of children's lay theories about the malleability of human attributes in beliefs about and volunteering for disadvantaged groups. *Child Development, 75,* 236–250.

Karasik, L. B., Adolph, K. E., Tamis-LeMonda, C. S., & Zuckerman, A. L. (2012). Carry on: Spontaneous object carrying in 13-month-old crawling and walking infants. *Developmental Psychology, 48,* 389–397.

Karasik, L. B., Tamis-LeMonda, C. S., & Adolph, K. E. (2011). Transition from crawling to walking affects infants' social actions with objects. *Child Development, 82,* 1199–1209.

Karasik, L. B., Tamis-LeMonda, C. S., Adolph, K. E., & Dimitroupoulou, K. A. (2008). How mothers encourage and discourage infants' motor actions. *Infancy, 13,* 366–392.

Karemaker, A., Pitchford, N., & O'Malley, C. (2010). Enhanced recognition of written words and enjoyment of reading in struggling beginner readers through whole-word multimedia software. *Computers and Education, 54,* 199–208.

Karevold, E., Ystrom, E., Coplan, R. J., Sanson, A. V., & Mathiesen, K. S. (2012). A prospective longitudinal study of shyness from infancy to adolescence: Stability, age-related changes, and prediction of socio-emotional functioning. *Journal of Abnormal Child Psychology, 40,* 1167–1177.

Kärtner, J., Holodynski, M., & Wörmann, V. (2013). Parental ethnotheories, social practice and the culture-specific development of social smiling in infants. *Mind, Culture, and Activity, 20,* 79–95.

Kärtner, J., Keller, H., Chaudhary, N., & Yovsi, R. D. (2012). The development of mirror self-recognition in different sociocultural contexts. *Monographs of the Society for Research in Child Development, 77*(4, Serial No. 305).

Kataoka, S., & Vandell, D. L. (2013). Quality of afterschool activities and relative change in adolescent functioning over two years. *Applied Developmental Science, 17,* 123–134.

Katz, J., Lee, A. C. C., Lawn, J. E., Cousens, S., Blencowe, H., Ezzati, M., et al. (2013). Mortality risk in preterm and small-for-gestational-age infants in low-income and middle-income countries: A pooled country analysis. *Lancet, 382,* 417–425.

Kaufman, J. C., & Sternberg, R. J. (2007, July/August). Resource review: Creativity. *Change, 39,* 55–58.

Kaufmann, K. B., Büning, H., Galy, A., Schambach, A., & Grez, M. (2013). Gene therapy on the move. *EMBO Molecular Medicine, 5,* 1642–1661.

Kavanaugh, R. D. (2006). Pretend play. In B. Spodek & O. N. Saracho (Eds.), *Handbook of research on the education of young children* (2nd ed., pp. 269–278). Mahwah, NJ: Erlbaum.

Kavšek, M. (2004). Predicting later IQ from infant visual habituation and dishabituation: A meta-analysis. *Journal of Applied Developmental Psychology, 25,* 369–393.

Kavšek, M., Yonas, A., & Granrud, C. E. (2012). Infants' sensitivity to pictorial depth cues: A review and meta-analysis. *Infant Behavior and Development, 35,* 109–128.

Kayed, N. S., & Van der Meer, A. L. H. (2009). A longitudinal study of prospective control in catching by full-term and preterm infants. *Experimental Brain Research, 194,* 245–258.

Kearney, C. A., Spear, M., & Mihalas, S. (2014). School refusal behavior. In L. Grossman & S. Walfish (Eds.), *Translating psychological research into practice* (pp. 83–88). New York: Springer.

Keating-Lefler, R., Hudson, D. B., Campbell-Grossman, C., Fleck, M. O., & Westfall, J. (2004). Needs, concerns, and social support of single, low-income mothers. *Issues in Mental Health Nursing, 25,* 381–401.

Keen, R. (2011). The development of problem solving in young children: A critical cognitive skill. *Annual Review of Psychology, 62,* 1–24.

Keil, F. C. (1986). Conceptual domains and the acquisition of metaphor. *Cognitive Development, 1,* 73–96.

Keller, H., Borke, Y. J., Kärtner, J., Jensen, H., & Papaligoura, Z. (2004). Developmental consequences of early parenting experiences: Self-recognition and self-regulation in three cultural communities. *Child Development, 75,* 1745–1760.

Kelley, S. A., Brownell, C. A., & Campbell, S. B. (2000). Mastery motivation and self-evaluative affect in toddlers: Longitudinal relations with maternal behavior. *Child Development, 71,* 1061–1071.

Kelly, D. J., Liu, S., Ge, L., Quinn, P. C., Slater, A. M., Lee, K., Liu, Q., & Pascalis, O. (2007). Cross-race preferences for same-race faces extend beyond the African versus Caucasian contrast in 3-month-old infants. *Infancy, 11,* 87–95.

Kelly, D. J., Quinn, P. C., Slater, A. M., Lee, K., Ge, L., & Pascalis, O. (2009). Development of the other-race effect during infancy: Evidence toward universality? *Journal of Experimental Child Psychology, 104,* 105–114.

Kelly, R., & Hammond, S. (2011). The relationship between symbolic play and executive function in young children. *Australasian Journal of Early Childhood, 36*(2), 21–27.

Kendrick, D., Barlow, J., Hampshire, A., Stewart-Brown, S., & Polnay, L. (2008). Parenting interventions and the prevention of unintentional injuries in childhood: Systematic review and meta-analysis. *Child: Care, Health and Development, 34,* 682–695.

Keren, M., Feldman, R., Namdari-Weinbaum, I., Spitzer, S., & Tyano, S. (2005). Relations between parents' interactive style in dyadic and triadic play and toddlers' symbolic capacity. *American Journal of Orthopsychiatry, 75,* 599–607.

Kernis, M. H. (2002). Self-esteem as a multifaceted construct. In T. M. Brinthaupt & R. P. Lipka (Eds.), *Understanding early adolescent self and identity* (pp. 57–88). Albany: State University of New York Press.

Kerns, K. A., Brumariu, L. E., & Seibert, A. (2011). Multi-method assessment of mother–child attachment: Links to parenting and child depressive symptoms in middle childhood. *Attachment and Human Development, 13,* 315–333.

Keven, N., & Akins, K. A. (2017, September). Neonatal imitation in context: Sensory-motor development in the perinatal period. *Behavioral and Brain Sciences, 40,* 1–107.

Kew, K., Ivory, G., Muniz, M. M., & Quiz, F. Z. (2012). No Child Left Behind as school reform: Intended and unintended consequences. In M. A. Acker-Hocevar, J. Ballenger, W. A. Place, & G. Ivory (Eds.), *Snapshots of school leadership in the 21st century: Perils and promises of leading for social justice, school improvement, and democratic community* (pp. 13–30). Charlotte, NC: IAP Information Age Publishing.

Khaleefa, O., Sulman, A., & Lynn, R. (2009). An increase of intelligence in Sudan, 1987–2007. *Journal of Biosocial Science, 41,* 279–283.

Khaleque, A., & Rohner, R. P. (2002). Perceived parental acceptance–rejection and psychological adjustment: A meta-analysis of cross cultural and intracultural studies. *Journal of Marriage and Family, 64,* 54–64.

Khaleque, A., & Rohner, R. P. (2012). Pancultural associations between perceived parental acceptance and psychological adjustment of children and adults: A meta-analytic review of worldwide research. *Journal of Cross-Cultural Psychology, 43,* 784–800.

Kiel, E. J., Premo, J. E., & Buss, K. A. (2016). Maternal encouragement to approach novelty: A curvilinear relation to change in anxiety for inhibited toddlers. *Journal of Abnormal Child Psychology, 44,* 433–444.

Killen, M., Crystal, D., & Watanabe, H. (2002). The individual and the group: Japanese and American children's evaluations of peer exclusion, tolerance of difference, and prescriptions for conformity. *Child Development, 73,* 1788–1802.

Killen, M., Lee-Kim, J., McGlothlin, H., & Stangor, C. (2002). How children and adolescents evaluate gender and racial exclusion. *Monographs of the Society for Research in Child Development, 67*(4, Serial No. 271).

Killen, M., Margie, N. G., & Sinno, S. (2006). Morality in the context of intergroup relationships. In M. Killen & J. G. Smetana (Eds.), *Handbook of moral development* (pp. 155–183). Mahwah, NJ: Erlbaum.

Killen, M., Mulvey, K. L., Richardson, C., Jampol, N., & Woodward, A. (2011). The accidental transgressor: Morally relevant theory of mind. *Cognition, 119,* 197–215.

Killen, M., Rutland, A., & Ruck, M. (2011). Promoting equity, tolerance, and justice in childhood. *Society for Research in Child Development Social Policy Report, 25*(4).

Killen, M., & Smetana, J. G. (2015). Origins and development of morality. In M. E. Lamb (Ed.), *Handbook of child psychology and developmental science: Vol. 3. Socioemotional processes* (pp. 701–749). Hoboken, NJ: Wiley.

Kilmer, R. P., Cook, J. R., Crusto, C., Strater, K. P., & Haber, M. G. (2012). Understanding the ecology and development of children and families experiencing homelessness: Implications for practice, supportive services, and policy. *American Journal of Orthopsychiatry, 82,* 389–401.

Kim, J. M. (1998). Korean children's concepts of adult and peer authority and moral reasoning. *Developmental Psychology, 34,* 947–955.

Kim, J.-Y., McHale, S. M., Crouter, A. C., & Osgood, D. W. (2007). Longitudinal linkages between sibling relationships and adjustment from middle childhood through adolescence. *Developmental Psychology, 43,* 960–973.

Kim, J.-Y., McHale, S. M., Osgood, D. W., & Crouter, A. C. (2006). Longitudinal course and family correlates of sibling relationships from childhood through adolescence. *Child Development, 77,* 1746–1761.

Kim, S., & Kochanska, G. (2012). Child temperament moderates effects of parent–child mutuality on self-regulation: A relationship-based path for emotionally negative infants. *Child Development, 83,* 1275–1289.

Kimhi, Y., Shoam-Kugelmas, D., Agam Ben-Artzi, G., Ben-Moshe, I., & Bauminger-Zviely, N. (2014). Theory of mind and executive function in preschoolers with typical development versus intellectually able preschoolers with autism spectrum disorder. *Journal of Autism and Developmental Disorders, 44,* 2341–2354.

King, A. C., & Bjorklund, D. F. (2010). Evolutionary developmental psychology. *Psicothema, 22,* 22–27.

King, V. (2007). When children have two mothers: Relationships with nonresident mothers, stepmothers, and fathers. *Journal of Marriage and Family, 69,* 1178–1193.

King, V. (2009). Stepfamily formation: Implications for adolescent ties to mothers, nonresident fathers, and stepfathers. *Journal of Marriage and Family, 71,* 954–968.

Kinnunen, M.-L., Pietilainen, K., & Rissanen, A. (2006). Body size and overweight from birth to adulthood. In L. Pulkkinen & J. Kaprio (Eds.), *Socioemotional development and health from adolescence to adulthood* (pp. 95–107). New York: Cambridge University Press.

Kinsella, M. T., & Monk, C. (2009). Impact of maternal stress, depression and anxiety on fetal neurobehavioral development. *Clinical Obstetrics and Gynecology, 52,* 425–440.

Kirkham, N. Z., Cruess, L., & Diamond, A. (2003). Helping children apply their knowledge to their behavior on a dimension-switching task. *Developmental Science, 6,* 449–476.

Kirkorian, H. L., Choi, K., & Pempek, T. A. (2016). Toddlers word learning from contingent and non-contingent video on touch screens. *Child Development, 87,* 405–413.

Kisilevsky, B. S., & Hains, S. M. J. (2011). Onset and maturation of fetal heart rate response to the mother's voice over late gestation. *Developmental Science, 14,* 214–223.

Kisilevsky, B. S., Hains, S. M. J., Brown, C. A., Lee, C. T., Cowperthwaite, B., & Stutzman, S. S. (2009). Fetal sensitivity to properties of maternal speech and language. *Infant Behavior and Development, 32,* 59–71.

Kit, B. K., Ogden, C. L., & Flegal, K. M. (2014). Epidemiology of obesity. In W. Ahrens & I. Pigeot (Eds.), *Handbook of epidemiology* (2nd ed., pp. 2229–2262). New York: Springer Science + Business Media.

Kitsantas, P., Gaffney, K. F., & Cheema, J. (2012). Life stressors and barriers to timely prenatal care for women with high-risk pregnancies residing in rural and nonrural areas. *Women's Health Issues, 22,* e455–e460.

Kitzman, H. J., Olds, D. L., Cole, R. E., Hanks, C. A., Anson, E. A., Arcoleo, K. J., et al. (2010). Enduring effects of prenatal and infancy home visiting by nurses on children: Follow-up of a randomized trial among children at age 12 years. *Archives of Pediatric and Adolescent Medicine, 164,* 412–418.

Kitzmann, K. M., Cohen, R., & Lockwood, R. L. (2002). Are only children missing out? Comparison of the peer-related social competence of only children and siblings. *Journal of Social and Personal Relationships, 19,* 299–316.

Kjønniksen, L., Anderssen, N., & Wold, B. (2009). Organized youth sport as a predictor of physical activity in adulthood. *Scandinavian Journal of Medicine and Science in Sports, 19,* 646–654.

Kjønniksen, L., Torsheim, T., & Wold, B. (2008). Tracking of leisure-time physical activity during adolescence and young adulthood: A 10-year longitudinal study. *International Journal of Behavioral Nutrition and Physical Activity, 5,* 69.

Klahr, D., Matlen, B., & Jirout, J. (2013). Children as scientific thinkers. In G. J. Feist & M. E. Gorman (Eds.), *Handbook of the psychology of science* (pp. 223–247). New York: Springer.

Klebanov, P. K., Brooks-Gunn, J., McCarton, C., & McCormick, M. C. (1998). The contribution of neighborhood and family income to developmental test scores over the first three years of life. *Child Development, 69,* 1420–1436.

Kleinsorge, C., & Covitz, L. M. (2012). Impact of divorce on children: Developmental considerations. *Pediatrics in Review, 33,* 147–155.

Kliewer, W., Fearnow, M. D., & Miller, P. A. (1996). Coping socialization in middle childhood: Tests of maternal and paternal influences. *Child Development, 67,* 2339–2357.

Kloep, M., Hendry, L. B., Taylor, R., & Stuart-Hamilton, I. (2016). *Development from adolescence to early adulthood: A dynamic systemic approach to transitions and transformations*. New York: Psychology Press.

Kloess, J. A., Beech, A. R., & Harkins, L. (2014). Online child sexual exploitation: Prevalence, process, and offender characteristics. *Trauma, Violence, & Abuse, 15,* 126–139.

Knafo, A., Zahn-Waxler, C., Davidov, M., Hulle, C. V., Robinson, J. L., & Rhee, S. H. (2009). Empathy in early childhood: Genetic, environmental, and affective contributions. In O. Vilarroya, S. Altran, A. Navarro, K. Ochsner, & A. Tobena (Eds.), *Values, empathy, and fairness across social barriers* (pp. 103–114). New York: New York Academy of Sciences.

Knudsen, E. I. (2004). Sensitive periods in the development of the brain and behavior. *Journal of Cognitive Neuroscience, 16,* 1412–1425.

Kobayashi, T., Hiraki, K., & Hasegawa, T. (2005). Auditory-visual intermodal matching of small numerosities in 6-month-old infants. *Developmental Science, 8,* 409–419.

Kochanska, G. (1991). Socialization and temperament in the development of guilt and conscience. *Child Development, 62,* 1379–1392.

Kochanska, G., & Aksan, N. (2006). Children's conscience and self-regulation. *Journal of Personality, 74,* 1587–1617.

Kochanska, G., Aksan, N., & Nichols, K. E. (2003). Maternal power assertion in discipline and moral discourse contexts: Commonalities, differences, and implications for children's moral conduct and cognition. *Developmental Psychology, 39,* 949–963.

Kochanska, G., Aksan, N., Prisco, T. R., & Adams, E. E. (2008). Mother–child and father–child mutually responsive orientation in the first 2 years and children's outcomes at preschool age: Mechanisms of influence. *Child Development, 79,* 30–44.

Kochanska, G., Boldt, L. J., Kim, S., Yoon, J. E., & Philibert, R. A. (2015). Developmental interplay between children's biobehavioral risk and the parenting environment from toddler to school age: Prediction of socialization outcomes in preadolescence. *Development and Psychopathology, 27,* 775–790.

Kochanska, G., Forman, D. R., Aksan, N., & Dunbar, S. B. (2005). Pathways to conscience: Early mother–child mutually responsive orientation and children's moral emotion, conduct, and cognition. *Journal of Child Psychology and Psychiatry, 46,* 19–34.

Kochanska, G., Gross, J. N., Lin, M.-H., & Nichols, K. E. (2002). Guilt in young children: Development, determinants, and relations with broader system standards. *Child Development, 73,* 461–482.

Kochanska, G., & Kim, S. (2014). A complex interplay among the parent–child relationship, effortful control, and internalized rule-compatible conduct in young children: Evidence from two studies. *Developmental Psychology, 50,* 8–21.

Kochanska, G., Kim, S., Barry, R. A., & Philibert, R. A. (2011). Children's genotypes interact with maternal responsive care in predicting children's competence: Diathesis-stress or differential susceptibility? *Development and Psychopathology, 23,* 605–616.

Kochanska, G., & Knaack, A. (2003). Effortful control as a personality characteristic of young children: Antecedents, correlates, and consequences. *Journal of Personality, 71,* 1087–1112.

Kochanska, G., Murray, K. T., & Harlan, E. T. (2000). Effortful control in early childhood: Continuity and change, antecedents, and implications for social development. *Developmental Psychology, 36,* 220–232.

Kohen, D. E., Leventhal, T., Dahinten, V. S., & McIntosh, C. N. (2008). Neighborhood disadvantage: Pathways of effects for young children. *Child Development, 79,* 156–169.

Kolak, A. M., & Volling, B. L. (2011). Sibling jealousy in early childhood: Longitudinal links to sibling relationship quality. *Infant and Child Development, 20,* 213–226.

Koletzko, B., Beyer, J., Brands, B., Demmelmair, H., Grote, V., Haile, G., et al. (2013). Early influences of nutrition on postnatal growth. *Nestlé Nutrition Institute Workshop Series, 71,* 11–27.

Kollmann, M., Haeusler, M., Haas, J., Csapo, B., Lang, U., & Klaritsch, P. (2013). Procedure-related complications after genetic amniocentesis and chorionic villus sampling. *Ultraschall in der Medizen, 34,* 345–348.

Konner, M. (2010). *The evolution of childhood: Relationships, emotion, mind.* Cambridge, MA: Harvard University Press.

Konrad, C., Herbert, J. S., Schneider, S., & Seehagen, S. (2016a). The relationship between prior night's sleep and measures of infant imitation. *Developmental Psychobiology, 58,* 450–461.

Konrad, C., Seehagen, S., Schneider, S., & Herbert, J. S. (2016b). Naps promote flexible memory retrieval in 12-month-old infants. *Developmental Psychobiology, 58,* 866–874.

Kooijman, V., Hagoort, P., & Cutler, A. (2009). Prosodic structure in early word segmentation: ERP evidence from Dutch ten-month-olds. *Infancy, 14,* 591–612.

Kopp, C. B., & Neufeld, S. J. (2003). Emotional development during infancy. In R. Davidson, K. R. Scherer, & H. H. Goldsmith (Eds.), *Handbook of affective sciences* (pp. 347–374). Oxford, UK: Oxford University Press.

Koss, K. J., Hostinar, C. E., Donzella, B., & Gunnar, M. R. (2014). Social deprivation and the HPA axis in early deprivation. *Psychoneuroendocrinology, 50,* 1–13.

Kowalski, R. M., & Limber, S. P. (2013). Psychological, physical, and academic correlates of cyberbullying and traditional bullying. *Journal of Adolescent Health, 53,* S13–S20.

Kowalski, R. M., Limber, S. P., & Agatston, P. W. (2008). *Cyber bullying: Bullying in the digital age*. Malden, MA: Blackwell.

Kozer, E., Costei, A. M., Boskovic, R., Nulman, I., Nikfar, S., & Koren, G. (2003). Effects of aspirin consumption during pregnancy on pregnancy outcomes: Meta-analysis. *Birth Defects Research, Part B, Developmental and Reproductive Toxicology, 68,* 70–84.

Kozulin, A. (Ed.). (2003). *Vygotsky's educational theory in cultural context.* Cambridge, UK: Cambridge University Press.

Krahé, B., & Berger, A. (2017). Gendered pathways from child sexual abuse to sexual aggression victimization and perpetration in adolescence and young adulthood. *Child Abuse & Neglect, 63,* 261–272.

Krcmar, M., Grela, B., & Linn, K. (2007). Can toddlers learn vocabulary from television? An experimental approach. *Media Psychology, 10,* 41–63.

Kreider, R. M., & Ellis, R. (2011). Living arrangements of children: 2009. *Current Population Reports,* P70–126. Retrieved from www.census.gov/prod/2011pubs/p70-126.pdf

Kreppner, J. M., Kumsta, R., Rutter, M., Beckett, C., Castle, J., Stevens, S., et al. (2010). Developmental course of deprivation specific psychological patterns: Early manifestations, persistence to age 15, and clinical features. *Monographs of the Society for Research in Child Development, 75*(1, Serial No. 295), 79–101.

Kreppner, J. M., Rutter, M., Beckett, C., Castle, J., Colvert, E., Groothues, C., Hawkins, A., & O'Connor, T. G. (2007). Normality and impairment following profound early institutional deprivation: A longitudinal follow-up into early adolescence. *Developmental Psychology, 43,* 931–946.

Kretch, K. S., & Adolph, K. E. (2013). Cliff or step? Posture-specific learning at the edge of a drop-off. *Child Development, 84,* 226–240.

Kretch, K. S., Franchak, J. M., & Adolph, K. E. (2014). Crawling and walking infants see the world differently. *Child Development, 85,* 1503–1518.

Krueger, R. F., & Johnson, W. (2008). Behavior genetics and personality. In L. Q. Pervin, O. P. John, & R. W. Robins (Eds.), *Handbook of personality: Theory and research* (3rd ed., pp. 287–310). New York: Guilford.

Krumhansl, C. L., & Jusczyk, P. W. (1990). Infants' perception of phrase structure in music. *Psychological Science, 1,* 70–73.

Kuczynski, L. (1984). Socialization goals and mother–child interaction: Strategies for long-term and short-term compliance. *Developmental Psychology, 20,* 1061–1073.

Kuczynski, L., & Lollis, S. (2002). Four foundations for a dynamic model of parenting. In J. R. M. Gerris (Ed.), *Dynamics of parenting.* Hillsdale, NJ: Erlbaum.

Kuhl, P. K., Ramirez, R. R., Bosseler, A., Lin, J. L., & Imada, T. (2014). Infants' brain responses to speech suggest analysis by synthesis. *Proceedings of the National Academy of Sciences, 111,* 11238–11245.

Kuhl, P. K., Tsao, F.-M., & Liu, H.-M. (2003). Foreign language experience in infancy: Effects of short-term exposure and social interaction on phonetic learning. *Proceedings of the National Academy of Sciences, 100,* 9096–9101.

Kuhn, D. (1995). Microgenetic study of change: What has it told us? *Psychological Science, 6,* 133–139.

Kulkarni, A. D., Jamieson, D. J., Jones, H. W., Jr., Kissin, D. M., Gallo, M. F., Macaluso, M., et al. (2013). Fertility treatments and multiple births in the United States. *New England Journal of Medicine, 369,* 2218–2225.

Kumar, M., Chandra, S., Ijaz, Z., & Senthilselvan, A. (2014). Epidural analgesia in labour and neonatal respiratory distress: A case-control study. *Archives of Disease in Childhood—Fetal and Neonatal Edition, 99,* F116–F119.

Kunnen, S. E. (2012). *A dynamic systems approach to adolescent development.* London: Routledge.

Kuppens, S., Laurent, L., Heyvaert, M., & Onghena, P. (2013). Associations between parental control and relational aggression in children and adolescents: A multilevel and sequential meta-analysis. *Developmental Psychology, 49,* 1697–1712.

Kurganskaya, M. E. (2011). Manual asymmetry in children is related to parameters of early development and familial sinistrality. *Human Physiology, 37,* 654–657.

Kurtz-Costes, B., Copping, K. E., Rowley, S. J., & Kinlaw, C. R. (2014). Gender and age differences in awareness and endorsement of gender stereotypes. *European Journal of Psychology and Education, 29,* 603–618.

Kurtz-Costes, B., Rowley, S. J., Harris-Britt, A., & Woods, T. A. (2008). Gender stereotypes about mathematics and science and self-perceptions of ability in late childhood and early adolescence. *Merrill-Palmer Quarterly, 54,* 386–409.

L

Ladd, G. W. (2005). *Children's peer relationships and social competence: A century of progress.* New Haven, CT: Yale University Press.

Ladd, G. W., Birch, S. H., & Buhs, E. S. (1999). Children's social and scholastic lives in kindergarten: Related spheres of influence? *Child Development, 70,* 1373–1400.

Ladd, G. W., & Burgess, K. B. (1999). Charting the relationship trajectories of aggressive, withdrawn, and aggressive/withdrawn children during early grade school. *Child Development, 70,* 910–929.

Ladd, G. W., Ettekal, I., & Kochenderfer-Ladd, B. (2017). Peer victimization trajectories from kindergarten through high school: Differential pathways for children's school engagement. *Journal of Educational Psychology, 109,* 826–841.

Ladd, G. W., Kochenderfer-Ladd, B., Eggum, N. D., Kochel, K. P., & McConnell, E. M. (2011). Characterizing and comparing the friendships of anxious-solitary and unsociable preadolescents. *Child Development, 82,* 1434–1453.

Ladd, G. W., LeSieur, K., & Profilet, S. M. (1993). Direct parental influences on young children's peer relations. In S. Duck (Ed.), *Learning about relationships* (Vol. 2, pp. 152–183). London: Sage.

Lagattuta, K. H., Sayfan, L., & Blattman, A. J. (2010). Forgetting common ground: Six- to seven-year-olds have an overinterpretive theory of mind. *Developmental Psychology, 46,* 1417–1432.

Lagattuta, K. H., & Thompson, R. A. (2007). The development of self-conscious emotions: Cognitive processes and social influences. In J. L. Tracy, R. W. Robins, & J. P. Tangney (Eds.), *The self-conscious emotions: Theory and research* (pp. 91–113). New York: Guilford.

Laible, D. (2007). Attachment with parents and peers in late adolescence: Links with emotional competence and social behavior. *Personality and Individual Differences, 43,* 1185–1197.

Laible, D. (2011). Does it matter if preschool children and mothers discuss positive vs. negative events during reminiscing? Links with mother-reported attachment, family emotional climate, and socioemotional development. *Social Development, 20,* 394–411.

Laible, D., & Thompson, R. A. (2002). Mother–child conflict in the toddler years: Lessons in emotion, morality, and relationships. *Child Development, 73,* 1187–1203.

Lalonde, C. E., & Chandler, M. J. (2002). Children's understanding of interpretation. *New Ideas in Psychology, 20,* 163–198.

Lam, C. B., McHale, S. M., & Crouter, A. C. (2012). Parent–child shared time from middle childhood to late adolescence: Developmental course and adjustment correlates. *Child Development, 83,* 2089–2103.

Lam, C. B., Solmeyer, A. R., & McHale, S. M. (2012). Sibling relationships and empathy across the transition to adolescence. *Journal of Youth and Adolescence, 41,* 1657–1670.

Lam, H. S., Kwok, K. M., Chan, P. H., So, H. K., Li, A. M., Ng, P. C., et al. (2013). Long term neurocognitive impact of low dose prenatal methylmercury exposure in Hong Kong. *Environment International, 54,* 59–64.

Lam, J. (2015). Picky eating in children. *Frontiers in Pediatrics, 3,* 41.

Lamaze, F. (1958). *Painless childbirth.* London: Burke.

Lamb, M. E. (2012). Mothers, fathers, families, and circumstances: Factors affecting children's adjustment. *Applied Developmental Science, 16,* 98–111.

Lamb, M. E., & Lewis, C. (2013). Father–child relationships. In N. J. Cabrera & C. S. Tamis-LeMonda (Eds.), *Handbook of father involvement* (2nd ed., pp. 119–134). New York: Routledge.

Lamb, M. E., Thompson, R. A., Gardner, W., Charnov, E. L., & Connell, J. P. (1985). Infant–mother attachment: The origins and developmental significance of individual differences in the Strange Situation: Its study and biological interpretation. *Behavioral and Brain Sciences, 7,* 127–147.

Lamm, B., Keller, H., Teiser, J., Gudi, H., Yovsi, R. D., Freitag, C., et al. (2017). Waiting for the second treat: Developing culture-specific modes of self-regulation. *Child Development, 88,* 12847.

Lamminmaki, A., Hines, M., Kuiri-Hanninen, T., Kilpelainen, L., Dunkel, L., & Sankilampi, U. (2012). Testosterone measured in infancy predicts subsequent sex-typed behavior in boys and girls. *Hormones and Behavior, 61,* 611–616.

Lane, J. D., Wellman, H. N., Olson, S. L., Labounty, J., & Kerr, D. C. R. (2010). Theory of mind and emotion understanding predict moral development in early childhood. *British Journal of Developmental Psychology, 28,* 871–889.

Lansford, J. E. (2009). Parental divorce and children's adjustment. *Perspectives on Psychological Science, 4,* 140–152.

Lansford, J. E., Criss, M. M., Dodge, K. A., Shaw, D. S., Pettit, G. S., & Bates, J. E. (2009). Trajectories of physical discipline: Early childhood antecedents and developmental outcomes. *Child Development, 80,* 1385–1402.

Lansford, J. E., Criss, M. M., Laird, R. D., Shaw, D. S., Pettit, G. S., Bates, J. E., & Dodge, K. A. (2011). Reciprocal relations between parents' physical discipline and children's externalizing behavior during middle childhood and adolescence. *Development and Psychopathology, 23,* 225–238.

Lansford, J. E., Malone, P. S., Castellino, D. R., Dodge, K. A., Pettit, G., & Bates, J. E. (2006). Trajectories of internalizing, externalizing, and grades for children who have and have not experienced their parents' divorce or separation. *Journal of Family Psychology, 20,* 292–301.

Lansford, J. E., Wagner, L. B., Bates, J. E., Dodge, K. A., & Pettit, G. S. (2012). Parental reasoning, denying privileges, yelling, and spanking: Ethnic differences and associations with child externalizing behavior. *Parenting: Science and Practice, 12,* 42–56.

Laranjo, J., Bernier, A., Meins, E., & Carlson, S. M. (2010). Early manifestations of children's theory of mind: The roles of maternal mind-mindedness and infant security of attachment. *Infancy, 15,* 300–323.

Larsen, J. A., & Nippold, M. A. (2007). Morphological analysis in school-age children: Dynamic assessment of a word learning strategy. *Language, Speech, and Hearing Services in Schools, 38,* 201–212.

Larzelere, R. E., Cox, R. B., Jr., & Mandara, J. (2013). Responding to misbehavior in young children: How authoritative parents enhance reasoning with firm control. In R. E. Larzelere, A. S. Morris, & A. W. Harrist (Eds.), *Authoritative parenting: Synthesizing nurturance and discipline for optimal child development* (pp. 89–111). Washington, DC: American Psychological Association.

Larzelere, R. E., Schneider, W. N., Larson, D. B., & Pike, P. L. (1996). The effects of discipline responses in delaying toddler misbehavior recurrences. *Child and Family Behavior Therapy, 18,* 35–57.

Lashley, F. R. (2007). *Essentials of clinical genetics in nursing practice*. New York: Springer.

Laski, E. V., & Siegler, R. S. (2014). Learning from number board games: You learn what you encode. *Developmental Psychology, 50,* 853–864.

Lau, Y. L., Cameron, C. A., Chieh, K. M., O'Leary, J., Fu, G., & Lee, K. (2012). Cultural differences in moral justifications enhance understanding of Chinese and Canadian children's moral decisions. *Journal of Cross-Cultural Psychology, 44,* 461–477.

Lauer, P. A., Akiba, M., Wilkerson, S. B., Apthorp, H. S., Snow, D., & Martin-Glenn, M. (2006). Out-of-school time programs: A meta-analysis of effects for at-risk students. *Review of Educational Research, 76,* 275–313.

Laughlin, L. (2013). *Who's minding the kids? Child care arrangements: Spring 2011. Current Population Reports,* P70–135. Retrieved from www.census.gov/prod/2013pubs/p70-135.pdf

Lauricella, A. R., Gola, A. A. H., & Calvert, S. L. (2011). Toddlers' learning from socially meaningful video characters. *Media Psychology, 14,* 216–232.

Lavelli, M., & Fogel, A. (2005). Developmental changes in the relationship between the infant's attention and emotion during early face-to-face communication: The 2-month transition. *Developmental Psychology, 41,* 265–280.

Law, E. C., Sideridis, G. D., Prock, L. A., & Sheridan, M. A. (2014). Attention-deficit/hyperactivity disorder in young children: Predictors of diagnostic stability. *Pediatrics, 133,* 659–667.

Law, K. L., Stroud, L. R., Niaura, R., LaGasse, L. L., Giu, J., & Lester, B. M. (2003). Smoking during pregnancy and newborn neurobehavior. *Pediatrics, 111,* 1318–1323.

Lawn, J. E., Blencowe, H., Oza, S., You, D., Lee, A. C., Waiswa, P., et al. (2014). Every newborn: Progress, priorities, and potential beyond survival. *Lancet, 12,* 189–205.

Lazar, I., & Darlington, R. (1982). Lasting effects of early education: A report from the Consortium for Longitudinal Studies. *Monographs of the Society for Research in Child Development, 47*(2–3, Serial No. 195).

Lazarus, R. S., & Lazarus, B. N. (1994). *Passion and reason.* New York: Oxford University Press.

Lazinski, M. J., Shea, A. K., & Steiner, M. (2008). Effects of maternal prenatal stress on offspring development: A commentary. *Archives of Women's Mental Health, 11,* 363–375.

Leaper, C. (1994). Exploring the correlates and consequences of gender segregation: Social relationships in childhood, adolescence, and adulthood. In C. Leaper (Ed.), *New directions for child development* (No. 65, pp. 67–86). San Francisco: Jossey-Bass.

Leaper, C. (2000). Gender, affiliation, assertion, and the interactive context of parent–child play. *Developmental Psychology, 36,* 381–393.

Leaper, C. (2013). Gender development during childhood. In P. D. Zelazo (Ed.), *Oxford handbook of developmental psychology: Vol. 2. Self and other* (pp. 326–377). New York: Oxford University Press.

Leaper, C., Anderson, K. J., & Sanders, P. (1998). Moderators of gender effects on parents' talk to their children: A meta-analysis. *Developmental Psychology, 34,* 3–27.

Leaper, C., & Friedman, C. K. (2007). The socialization of gender. In J. E. Grusec & P. D. Hastings (Eds.), *Handbook of socialization: Theory and research* (pp. 561–587). New York: Guilford.

Leaper, C., Tenenbaum, H. R., & Shaffer, T. G. (1999). Communication patterns of African-American girls and boys from low-income, urban backgrounds. *Child Development, 70,* 1489–1503.

Leavell, A. S., Tamis-LeMonda, C. S., Ruble, D. N., Zosuls, K. M, & Cabrera, N. J. (2011). African American, White, and Latino fathers' activities with their sons and daughters in early childhood. *Sex Roles, 66,* 53–65.

Lebel, C., & Beaulieu, C. (2011). Longitudinal development of human brain wiring continues from childhood into adulthood. *Journal of Neuroscience, 31,* 10937–10947.

Lecanuet, J.-P., Granier-Deferre, C., Jacquet, A.-Y., Capponi, I., & Ledru, L. (1993). Prenatal discrimination of a male and female voice uttering the same sentence. *Early Development and Parenting, 2,* 217–228.

LeCroy, C. W., & Krysik, J. (2011). Randomized trial of the Healthy Families Arizona home visiting program. *Children and Youth Services Review, 33,* 1761–1766.

LeCuyer, E., & Houck, G. M. (2006). Maternal limit-setting in toddlerhood: Socialization strategies for the development of self-regulation. *Infant Mental Health Journal, 27,* 344–370.

LeCuyer, E. A., Christensen, J. J., Kearney, M. H., & Kitzman, H. J. (2011). African American mothers' self-described discipline strategies with young children. *Issues in Comprehensive Pediatric Nursing, 34,* 144–162.

Lee, E. H., Zhou, Q., Eisenberg, N., & Wang, Y. (2012). Bidirectional relations between temperament and parenting styles in Chinese children. *International Journal of Behavioral Development, 37,* 57–67.

Lee, G. Y., & Kisilevsky, B. S. (2013). Fetuses respond to father's voice but prefer mother's voice after birth. *Developmental Psychobiology, 56,* 1–11.

Lee, H. Y., & Hans, S. L. (2015). Prenatal depression and young low-income mothers' perception of their children from pregnancy through early childhood. *Infant Behavior and Development, 40,* 183–192.

Lee, K., Xu, F., Fu, G., Cameron, C. A., & Chen, S. (2001). Taiwan and Mainland Chinese and Canadian children's categorization and evaluation of lie and truth-telling: A modesty effect. *British Journal of Developmental Psychology, 19,* 525–542.

Lee, S. J., Altschul, I., & Gershoff, E. T. (2015). Wait until your father gets home? Mothers' and fathers' spanking and development of child aggression. *Child and Youth Services Review, 52,* 158–166.

Lee, S. J., Ralston, H. J., Partridge, J. C., & Rosen, M. A. (2005). Fetal pain: A systematic multidisciplinary review of the evidence. *JAMA, 294,* 947–954.

Lee, S. L., Morrow-Howell, N., Jonson-Reid, M., & McCrary, S. (2012). The effect of the Experience Corps® program on student reading outcomes. *Education and Urban Society, 44,* 97–118.

Leerkes, E. M. (2010). Predictors of maternal sensitivity to infant distress. *Parenting: Science and Practice, 10,* 219–239.

Lefkovics, E., Baji, I., & Rigó, J. (2014). Impact of maternal depression on pregnancies and on early attachment. *Infant Mental Health Journal, 35,* 354–365.

Lehman, M., & Hasselhorn, M. (2012). Rehearsal dynamics in elementary school children. *Journal of Experimental Child Psychology, 111,* 552–560.

Lehnung, M., Leplow, B., Ekroll, V., Herzog, A., Mehdorn, M., & Ferstl, R. (2003). The role of locomotion in the acquisition and transfer of spatial knowledge in children. *Scandinavian Journal of Psychology, 44,* 79–86.

Lehr, V. T., Zeskind, P. S., Ofenstein, J. P., Cepeda, E., Warrier, I., & Aranda, J. V. (2007). Neonatal facial coding system scores and spectral characteristics of infant crying during newborn circumcision. *Clinical Journal of Pain, 23,* 417–424.

Leibowitz, S., & de Vries, A. L. C. (2016). Gender dysphoria in adolescence. *International Review of Psychiatry, 28,* 21–35.

Lejeune, F., Marcus, L., Berne-Audeoud, F., Streri, A., Debillon, T., & Gentaz, E. (2012). Intermanual transfer of shapes in preterm human infants from 33 to 34 + 6 weeks postconceptional age. *Child Development, 83,* 794–800.

Lemay, M. (2015, February 26). *A letter to my son Jacob on his 5th birthday.* Retrieved from www.boston.com/life/moms/2015/02/26/letter-son-jacob-his-birthday/a2Jynr9Jhc3W8VQ9lVFx8N/story.html

Lemche, E., Lennertz, I., Orthmann, C., Ari, A., Grote, K., Hafker, J., & Klann-Delius, G. (2003). Emotion-regulatory process in evoked play narratives: Their relation with mental representations and family interactions. *Praxis der Kinderpsychologie und Kinderpsychiatrie, 52,* 156–171.

Lemola, S. (2015). Long-term outcomes of very preterm birth: Mechanisms and interventions. *European Psychologist, 20,* 128–137.

Lepage, J.-F., & Corbeil, J.-P. (2016). *The evolution of English–French bilingualism in Canada from 1961–2011.* Retrieved from www.statcan.gc.ca/pub/75-006-x/2013001/article/11795-eng.pdf

Lerman, R. I. (2010). Capabilities and contributions of unwed fathers. *Future of Children, 20,* 63–85.

Lerner, R. M. (2015). Preface. In W. F. Overton & P. C. Molenaar (Eds.), *Handbook of child psychology and developmental science: Vol. 1. Theory and method* (pp. xv–xxi). Hoboken, NJ: Wiley.

Lerner, R. M., Agans, J. P., DeSouza, L. M., & Hershberg, R. M. (2014). Developmental science in 2025: A predictive review. *Research in Human Development, 11,* 255–272.

Lernout, T., Theeten, H., Hens, N., Braeckman, T., Roelants, M., Hoppenbrouwers, K., & Van Damme, P. (2013). Timeliness of infant vaccination and factors related with delay in Flanders, Belgium. *Vaccine, 32,* 284–289.

Leslie, A. M. (2004). Who's for learning? *Developmental Science, 7,* 417–419.

Levendosky, A. A., Bogat, G. A., Huth-Bocks, A. C., Rosenblum, K., & von Eye, A. (2011). The effects of domestic violence on the stability of attachment from infancy to preschool. *Journal of Clinical Child and Adolescent Psychology, 40,* 398–410.

Leventhal, T., & Brooks-Gunn, J. (2003). Children and youth in neighborhood contexts. *Current Directions in Psychological Science, 12,* 27–31.

Leventhal, T., & Dupéré, V. (2011). Moving to opportunity: Does long-term exposure to "low-poverty" neighborhoods make a difference for adolescents? *Social Science and Medicine, 73,* 737–743.

Leventhal, T., Dupéré, V., & Shuey, E. A. (2015). Children in neighborhoods. In M. H. Bornstein & T. Leventhal (Eds.), *Handbook of child psychology: Vol. 4. Ecological settings and processes* (7th ed., pp. 493–533). Hoboken, NJ: Wiley.

LeVine, R. A., Dixon, S., LeVine, S., Richman, A., Leiderman, P. H., Keefer, C. H., & Brazelton, T. B. (1994). *Child care and culture: Lessons from Africa.* New York: Cambridge University Press.

Levy, S. R., & Dweck, C. S. (1999). The impact of children's static vs. dynamic conceptions of people on stereotype formation. *Child Development, 70,* 1163–1180.

Levy, S. R., Lytle, A., Shin, J. E., & Hughes, J. M. (2016). Understanding and reducing racial and ethnic prejudice among children and adolescents. In T. D. Nelson (Ed.), *Handbook of prejudice, stereotyping, and discrimination* (2nd ed., pp. 455–483). New York: Psychology Press.

Lewis, M. (1995). Embarrassment: The emotion of self-exposure and evaluation. In J. P. Tangney & K. W. Fischer (Eds.), *Self-conscious emotions* (pp. 198–218). New York: Guilford.

Lewis, M. (2014). *The rise of consciousness and the development of emotional life.* New York: Guilford.

Lewis, M., & Brooks-Gunn, J. (1979). *Social cognition and the acquisition of self.* New York: Plenum.

Lewis, M., & Ramsay, D. (2004). Development of self-recognition, personal pronoun use, and pretend play during the 2nd year. *Child Development, 75,* 1821–1831.

Lewis, M., Ramsay, D. S., & Kawakami, K. (1993). Differences between Japanese infants and Caucasian American infants in behavioral and cortisol response to inoculation. *Child Development, 64,* 1722–1731.

Lew-Williams, C., Pelucchi, B., & Saffran, J. R. (2011). Isolated words enhance statistical language learning in infancy. *Developmental Science, 14,* 1323–1329.

Li, J., Johnson, S. E., Han, W., Andrews, S., Kendall, G., Strazdins, L., & Dockery, A. (2014). Parents' nonstandard work schedules and child well-being: A critical review of the literature. *Journal of Primary Prevention, 35,* 53–73.

Li, S.-C., Lindenberger, U., Hommel, B., Aschersleben, G., Prinz, W., & Baltes, P. B. (2004). Transformation in the couplings among intellectual abilities and constituent cognitive processes across the life span. *Psychological Science, 15,* 155–163.

Li, W., Farkas, G., Duncan, G. J., Burchinal, M. R., & Vandell, D. L. (2013). Timing of high-quality child care and cognitive, language, and preacademic development. *Developmental Psychology, 49,* 1440–1451.

Li, X., Atkins, M. S., & Stanton, B. (2006). Effects of home and school computer use on school readiness and cognitive development among Head Start children: A randomized control trial. *Merrill-Palmer Quarterly, 52,* 239–263.

Liben, L. S. (2006). Education for spatial thinking. In K. A. Renninger & I. E. Sigel (Eds.), *Handbook of child psychology: Vol. 4. Child psychology in practice* (6th ed., pp. 197–247). Hoboken, NJ: Wiley.

Liben, L. S. (2009). The road to understanding maps. *Current Directions in Psychological Science, 18,* 310–315.

Liben, L. S., & Bigler, R. S. (2002). The developmental course of gender differentiation: Conceptualizing, measuring, and evaluating constructs and pathways. *Monographs of the Society for Research in Child Development, 6*(4, Serial No. 271).

Liben, L. S., Bigler, R. S., & Krogh, H. R. (2001). Pink and blue collar jobs: Children's judgments of job status and job aspirations in relation to sex of worker. *Journal of Experimental Child Psychology, 79,* 346–363.

Liben, L. S., & Downs, R. M. (1993). Understanding person–space–map relations: Cartographic and developmental perspectives. *Developmental Psychology, 29,* 739–752.

Liben, L. S., Myers, L. J., Christensen, A. E., & Bower, C. A. (2013). Environmental-scale map use in middle childhood: Links to spatial skills, strategies, and gender. *Child Development, 84,* 2047–2063.

Lickliter, R., & Honeycutt, H. (2013). A developmental evolutionary framework for psychology. *Review of General Psychology, 17,* 184–189.

Lickliter, R., & Honeycutt, H. (2015). Biology, development, and human systems. In W. F. Overton & P. C. M. Molenaar (Eds.), *Handbook of child psychology and developmental science: Vol. 1. Theory and method* (7th ed., pp. 162–207). Hoboken, NJ: Wiley.

Lidstone, J. S. M., Meins, E., & Fernyhough, C. (2010). The roles of private speech and inner speech in planning during middle childhood: Evidence from a dual task paradigm. *Journal of Experimental Child Psychology, 107,* 438–451.

Lidz, J. (2007). The abstract nature of syntactic representations. In E. Hoff & M. Shatz (Eds.), *Blackwell handbook of language development* (pp. 277–303). Malden, MA: Blackwell.

Li-Grining, C. P. (2007). Effortful control among low-income preschoolers in three cities: Stability, change, and individual differences. *Developmental Psychology, 43,* 208–221.

Lillard, A. (2007). *Montessori: The science behind the genius.* New York: Oxford University Press.

Lillard, A. S., Lerner, M. D., Hopkins, E. J., Dore, R. A., Smith, E. D., & Palmquist, C. M. (2013). The impact of pretend play on children's development: A review of the evidence. *Psychological Bulletin, 139,* 1–34.

Lillard, A. S., & Peterson, J. (2011). The immediate impact of different types of television on young children's executive function. *Pediatrics, 128,* 644–649.

Lind, J. N., Li, R., Perrine, C. G., & Shieve, L. A. (2014). Breastfeeding and later psychosocial development of children at 6 years of age. *Pediatrics, 134,* S36–S41.

Lindsey, E. W., & Colwell, M. J. (2013). Pretend and physical play: Links to preschoolers' affective social competence. *Merrill-Palmer Quarterly, 59,* 330–360.

Lindsey, E. W., & Mize, J. (2000). Parent–child physical and pretense play: Links to children's social competence. *Merrill-Palmer Quarterly, 46,* 565–591.

Linebarger, D. L., & Piotrowski, J. T. (2010). Structure and strategies in children's educational television: The roles of program type and learning strategies in children's learning. *Child Development, 81,* 1582–1597.

Linver, M. R., Martin, A., & Brooks-Gunn, J. (2004). Measuring infants' home environment: The IT-HOME for infants between birth and 12 months in four national data sets. *Parenting: Science and Practice, 4,* 115–137.

Lionetti, F., Pastore, M., & Barone, L. (2015). Attachment in institutionalized children: A review and meta-analysis. *Child Abuse and Neglect, 42,* 135–145.

Lipton, J. S., & Spelke, E. S. (2003). Origins of number sense: Large-number discrimination in human infants. *Psychological Science, 14,* 396–401.

Liu, J., Raine, A., Venables, P. H., Dalais, C., & Mednick, S. A. (2003). Malnutrition at age 3 years and lower cognitive ability at age 11 years. *Archives of Paediatric and Adolescent Medicine, 157,* 593–600.

Liu, J., Raine, A., Venables, P. H., & Mednick, S. A. (2004). Malnutrition at age 3 years and externalizing behavior problems at age 8, 11, and 17 years. *American Journal of Psychiatry, 161,* 2006–2013.

Liu, L., & Kager, R. (2015). Understanding phonological acquisition through phonetic perception: The influence of exposure and acoustic salience. *Phonological Studies, 18,* 51–58.

Liu, L., & Kager, R. (2016). Perception of a native vowel contrast by Dutch monolingual and bilingual infants: A bilingual perceptual lead. *International Journal of Bilingualism, 20,* 335–345.

Liu, R. T., & Mustanski, B. (2012). Suicidal ideation and self-harm in lesbian, gay, bisexual, and transgender youth. *American Journal of Preventive Medicine, 42,* 221–228.

Liu, S., Xiao, N. G., Quinn, P. C., Zhu, D., Ge, L., Pascalis, O., & Lee, K. (2015). Asian infants show preference for own-race but not other-race female faces: The role of infant caregiving arrangements. *Frontiers in Psychology, 6,* Article ID: 593.

Lleras, C., & Rangel, C. (2009). Ability grouping practices in elementary school and African American/Hispanic achievement. *American Journal of Education, 115,* 279–304.

Llewellyn, C., & Wardle, J. (2015). Behavioral susceptibility to obesity: Gene–environment interplay in the development of weight. *Physiology & Behavior, 152,* 494–501.

Lloyd, M. E., Doydum, A. O., & Newcombe, N. S. (2009). Memory binding in early childhood: Evidence for a retrieval deficit. *Child Development, 80,* 1321–1328.

Loehlin, J. C., Horn, J. M., & Willerman, L. (1997). Heredity, environment, and IQ in the Texas Adoption Project. In R. J. Sternberg & E. L. Grigorenko (Eds.), *Intelligence, heredity, and environment* (pp. 105–125). New York: Cambridge University Press.

Loehlin, J. C., & Martin, N. G. (2001). Age changes in personality traits and their heritabilities during the adult years: Evidence from Australian twin registry samples. *Personality and Individual Differences, 30,* 1147–1160.

Loganovskaja, T. K., & Loganovsky, K. N. (1999). EEG, cognitive and psychopathological abnormalities in children irradiated in utero. *International Journal of Psychophysiology, 34,* 211–224.

Loganovsky, K. N., Loganovskaja, T. K., Nechayev, S. Y., Antipchuk, Y. Y., & Bomko, M. A. (2008). Disrupted development of the dominant hemisphere following prenatal irradiation. *Journal of Neuropsychiatry and Clinical Neurosciences, 20,* 274–291.

Loman, M. M., & Gunnar, M. R. (2010). Early experience and the development of stress reactivity and regulation in children. *Neuroscience and Biobehavioral Reviews, 34,* 867–876.

Lombardi, C. M., & Coley, R. L. (2013). Low-income mothers' employment experiences: Prospective links with young children's development. *Family Relations, 62,* 514–528.

Lombardi, C. M., & Coley, R. L. (2014). Early maternal employment and children's school readiness in contemporary families. *Developmental Psychology, 50,* 2071–2084.

Lonigan, C. J. (2015). Literacy development. In L. S. Liben & U. Müller (Eds.), *Handbook of child psychology and developmental science: Vol. 2. Cognitive processes* (7th ed., pp. 763–805). Hoboken, NJ: Wiley.

Lonigan, C. J., Purpura, D. J., Wilson, S. B., Walker, J., & Clancy-Menchetti, J. (2013). Evaluating the components of an emergent literacy intervention for preschool children at risk for reading difficulties. *Journal of Experimental Child Psychology, 114,* 111–130.

Lopomo, A., Burgio, E., & Migliore, L. (2016). Epigenetics of obesity. *Progress in Molecular Biology and Translational Science, 140,* 151–184.

Lopresti, A. L., & Drummond, P. D. (2013). Obesity and psychiatric disorders: Commonalities in dysregulated biological pathways and their implications for treatment. *Progress in Neuro-Psychopharmacology & Biological Psychiatry, 45,* 92–99.

Lora, K. R., Sisson, S. B., DeGrace, B. W., & Morris, A. S. (2014). Frequency of family meals and 6–11-year-old children's social behaviors. *Journal of Family Psychology, 28,* 577–582.

Lorber, M. F., & Egeland, B. (2011). Parenting and infant difficulty: Testing a mutual exacerbation hypothesis to predict early onset conduct problems. *Child Development, 82,* 2006–2020.

Lorenz, K. (1952). *King Solomon's ring.* New York: Crowell.

Louie, V. (2001). Parents' aspirations and investment: The role of social class in the educational experiences of 1.5- and second generation Chinese Americans. *Harvard Educational Review, 71,* 438–474.

Louis, J., Cannard, C., Bastuji, H., & Challemel, M. J. (1997). Sleep ontogenesis revisited: A longitudinal 24-hour home polygraphic study on 15 normal infants during the first two years of life. *Sleep, 20,* 323–333.

Lourenço, O. (2003). Making sense of Turiel's dispute with Kohlberg: The case of the child's moral competence. *New Ideas in Psychology, 21,* 43–68.

Lourenço, O. (2012). Piaget and Vygotsky: Many resemblances, and a crucial difference. *New Ideas in Psychology, 30,* 281–295.

Love, J. M., Chazan-Cohen, R., & Raikes, H. (2007). Forty years of research knowledge and use: From Head Start to Early Head Start and beyond. In. J. L. Aber, S. J. Bishop-Josef, S. M. Jones, K. T. McLearn, & D. Phillips (Eds.), *Child development and social policy: Knowledge for action* (pp. 79–95). Washington, DC: American Psychological Association.

Love, J. M., Kisker, E. E., Ross, C., Raikes, H., Constantine, J., Boller, K., & Brooks-Gunn, J. (2005). The effectiveness of Early Head Start for 3-year-old children and their parents: Lessons for policy and programs. *Developmental Psychology, 41,* 885–901.

Low, M., Farrell, A., Biggs, B., & Pasricha, S. (2013). Effects of daily iron supplementation in primary-school-aged children: Systematic review and meta-analysis of randomized controlled trials. *Canadian Medical Association Journal, 185,* E791–E802.

Low, S. M., & Stocker, C. (2012). Family functioning and children's adjustment: Associations among parents' depressed mood, marital hostility, parent–child hostility, and children's adjustment. *Journal of Family Psychology, 19,* 394–403.

Lubart, T. I., Georgsdottir, A., & Besançon, M. (2009). The nature of creative giftedness and talent. In T. Balchin, B. Hymer, & D. J. Matthews (Eds.), *The Routledge international companion to gifted education* (pp. 42–49). New York: Routledge.

Luby, J. L., Belden, A., Sullivan, J., Hayen, R., McCadney, A., & Spitznagel, E. (2009). Shame and guilt in preschool depression: Evidence for elevations in self-conscious emotions in depression as early as age 3. *Journal of Child Psychology and Psychiatry, 50,* 1156–1166.

Luby, J. L., Belden, A. C., Whalen, D., Harms, M. P., & Barch, D. M. (2016). Breastfeeding and childhood IQ: The mediating role of gray matter volume. *Journal of the American Academy of Child and Adolescent Psychiatry, 55,* 367–375.

Lucassen, N., Tharner, A., Van IJzendoorn, M. H., Bakermans-Kranenburg, M. J., Volling, B. L., Verhulst, F. C., et al. (2011). The association between paternal sensitivity and infant–father attachment security: A meta-analysis of three decades of research. *Journal of Family Psychology, 25,* 986–992.

Lucas-Thompson, R., & Clarke-Stewart, K. A. (2007). Forecasting friendship: How marital quality, maternal mood, and attachment security are linked to children's peer relationships. *Journal of Applied Developmental Psychology, 28,* 499–514.

Lucas-Thompson, R. G., Goldberg, W. A., & Prause, J. (2010). Maternal work early in the lives of children and its distal associations with achievement and behavior problems: A meta-analysis. *Psychological Bulletin, 136,* 915–942.

Luecken, L. J., Lin, B., Coburn, S. S., MacKinnon, D. P., Gonzales, N. A., & Crnic, K. A. (2013). Prenatal stress, partner support, and infant cortisol reactivity in low-income Mexican American families. *Psychoneuroendocrinology, 38,* 3092–3101.

Luhmann, M., Hofmann, W., Eid, M., & Lucas, R. E. (2012). Subjective well-being and adaptation to life events: A meta-analysis. *Journal of Personality and Social Psychology, 102,* 592–615.

Lukowski, A. F., Koss, M., Burden, M. J., Jonides, J., Nelson, C. A., Kaciroti, N., et al. (2010). Iron deficiency in infancy and neurocognitive functioning at 19 years: Evidence of long-term deficits in executive function and recognition memory. *Nutritional Neuroscience, 13,* 54–70.

Lundberg, S., & Pollak, R. A. (2015). The evolving role of marriage: 1950–2010. *Future of Children, 25*(2), 29–50.

Luthar, S. S., & Barkin, S. H. (2012). Are affluent youths truly "at risk"? Vulnerability and resilience across three diverse samples. *Development and Psychopathology, 24,* 429–449.

Luthar, S. S., Barkin, S., & Crossman, E. J. (2013). "I can, therefore I must": Fragility in the upper-middle classes. *Development and Psychopathology, 25,* 1529–1549.

Luthar, S. S., Crossman, E. J., & Small, P. J. (2015). Resilience and adversity. In M. E. Lamb (Ed.), *Handbook of child psychology and developmental science: Vol. 3. Socioemotional processes* (7th ed., pp. 247–286). Hoboken, NJ: Wiley.

Luthar, S. S., & Latendresse, S. J. (2005). Comparable "risks" at the socioeconomic status extremes: Preadolescents' perceptions of parenting. *Development and Psychopathology, 17,* 207–230.

Lynch, R. J., Kistner, J. A., Stephens, H. F., & David-Ferdon, C. (2016). Positively biased self-perceptions of peer acceptance and subtypes of aggression in children. *Aggressive Behavior, 42,* 82–96.

Lyon, T. D., & Flavell, J. H. (1994). Young children's understanding of "remember" and "forget." *Child Development, 65,* 1357–1371.

Lyster, R., & Genesee, F. (2012). Immersion education. In Carol A. Chapelle (Ed.), *Encyclopedia of applied linguistics* (pp. 2608–2614). Hoboken, NJ: Wiley.

Lytton, H., & Gallagher, L. (2002). Parenting twins and the genetics of parenting. In M. H. Bornstein (Ed.), *Handbook of parenting* (Vol. 1, pp. 227–253). Mahwah, NJ: Erlbaum.

M

Ma, F., Xu, F., Heyman, G. D., & Lee, K. (2011). Chinese children's evaluations of white lies: Weighing the consequences for recipients. *Journal of Experimental Child Psychology, 108,* 308–321.

Ma, W., Golinkoff, R. M., Hirsh-Pasek, K., McDonough, C., & Tardif, T. (2009). Imagine that! Imageability predicts the age of acquisition of verbs in Chinese children. *Journal of Child Language, 36,* 405–423.

Maas, F. K. (2008). Children's understanding of promising, lying, and false belief. *Journal of General Psychology, 13,* 301–321.

Maccoby, E. E. (1998). *The two sexes: Growing up apart, coming together.* Cambridge, MA: Belknap.

Maccoby, E. E. (2002). Gender and group process: A developmental perspective. *Current Directions in Psychological Science, 11,* 54–58.

MacDorman, M. F., & Gregory, E. C. W. (2015). Fetal and perinatal mortality: United States, 2013. *National Vital Statistics Reports, 64*(8). Retrieved from www.cdc.gov/nchs/data/nvsr/nvsr64/nvsr64_08.pdf

MacKenzie, M. J., Nicklas, E., Waldfogel, J., & Brooks-Gunn, J. (2013). Spanking and child development across the first decade of life. *Pediatrics, 132,* e1118–e1125. Retrieved from http://pediatrics.aappublications.org/content/132/5/e1118

Mackey, K., Arnold, M. L., & Pratt, M. W. (2001). Adolescents' stories of decision making in more and less authoritative families: Representing the voices of parents in narrative. *Journal of Adolescent Research, 16,* 243–268.

Mackie, S., Show, P., Lenroot, R., Pierson, R., Greenstein, D. K., & Nugent, T. F., III. (2007). Cerebellar development and clinical outcome in attention deficit hyperactivity disorder. *American Journal of Psychiatry, 164,* 647–655.

MacWhinney, B. (2005). Language development. In M. H. Bornstein & M. E. Lamb (Eds.), *Developmental science: An advanced textbook* (5th ed., pp. 359–387). Mahwah, NJ: Erlbaum.

MacWhinney, B. (2015). Language development. In L. S. Liben & U. Müller (Eds.), *Handbook of child psychology and developmental science: Vol. 2. Cognitive processes* (7th ed., pp. 296–338). Hoboken, NJ: Wiley.

Macy, M. L., Butchart, A. T., Singer, D C., Gebremariam, A., Clark, S. J., & Davis, M. M. (2015). Looking back on rear-facing car seats: Surveying U.S. parents in 2011 and 2013. *Academic Pediatrics, 15,* 526–533.

Madigan, S., Bakermans-Kranenburg, M. J., van IJzendoorn, M. H., Moran, G., Pederson, D. R., & Benoit, D. (2006). Unresolved states of mind, anomalous parental behavior, and disorganized attachment: A review and meta-analysis of a transmission gap. *Attachment and Human Development, 8,* 89–111.

Madole, K. L., Oakes, L. M., & Rakison, D. H. (2011). Information-processing approaches to infants' developing representation of dynamic features. In L. M. Oakes, C. H. Cashon, M. Casasola, & D. Rakison (Eds.), *Infant perception and cognition* (153–178). New York: Oxford University Press.

Main, M., & Goldwyn, R. (1998). *Adult attachment classification system.* London: University College.

Main, M., & Solomon, J. (1990). Procedures for identifying infants as disorganized/disoriented during the Ainsworth Strange Situation. In M. Greenberg, D. Cicchetti, & M. Cummings (Eds.), *Attachment in the preschool years: Theory, research, and intervention* (pp. 121–160). Chicago: University of Chicago Press.

Majdandžić, M., & van den Boom, D. C. (2007). Multimethod longitudinal assessment of temperament in early childhood. *Journal of Personality, 75,* 12.

Malatesta, C. Z., Grigoryev, P., Lamb, C., Albin, M., & Culver, C. (1986). Emotion socialization and expressive development in preterm and full-term infants. *Child Development, 57,* 316–330.

Mandara, J., Varner, F., Greene, N., & Richman, S. (2009). Intergenerational family predictors of the Black–White achievement gap. *Journal of Educational Psychology, 101,* 867–878.

Mandel, D. R., Jusczyk, P. W., & Pisoni, D. B. (1995). Infants' recognition of the sound patterns of their own names. *Psychological Science, 6,* 314–317.

Mandler, J. M. (2004). Thought before language. *Trends in Cognitive Sciences, 8,* 508–513.

Mangelsdorf, S. C., Schoppe, S. J., & Buur, H. (2000). The meaning of parental reports: A contextual approach to the study of temperament and behavior problems. In V. J. Molfese & D. L. Molfese (Eds.), *Temperament and personality across the life span* (pp. 121–140). Mahwah, NJ: Erlbaum.

Maratsos, M. (2000). More overregularizations after all: New data and discussion on Marcus, Pinker, Ullman, Hollander, Rosen, & Xu. *Journal of Child Language, 27,* 183–212.

Marcus, G. F. (1995). Children's overregularization of English plurals: A quantitative analysis. *Journal of Child Language, 22,* 447–459.

Mares, M.-L., & Pan, Z. (2013). Effects of *Sesame Street*: A meta-analysis of children's learning in 15 countries. *Journal of Applied Developmental Psychology, 34,* 140–151.

Marholz, O., Gómez-López, M., Martín, I., Garrido, R., Garcia-Mas, A., & Chirosa, L. J. (2016). Role played by the coach in the adolescent players' commitment. *Studia Psychologica, 58,* 184–198.

Marin, M. M., Rapisardi, G., & Tani, F. (2015). Two-day-old newborn infants recognize their mother by her axillary odour. *Acta Paediatrica, 104,* 237–240.

Marin, T. J., Chen, E., Munch, T., & Miller, G. (2009). Double exposure to acute stress and chronic family stress is associated with immune changes in children with asthma. *Psychosomatic Medicine, 71,* 378–384.

Markant, J. C., & Thomas, K. M. (2013). Postnatal brain development. In P. D. Zelazo (Ed.), *Oxford handbook of developmental psychology: Vol. 1. Body and mind* (pp. 129–163). New York: Oxford University Press.

Markman, E. M. (1992). Constraints on word learning: Speculations about their nature, origins, and domain specificity. In M. R. Gunnar & M. P. Maratsos (Eds.), *Minnesota Symposia on Child Psychology* (Vol. 25, pp. 59–101). Hillsdale, NJ: Erlbaum.

Markova, G., & Legerstee, M. (2006). Contingency, imitation, and affect sharing: Foundations of infants' social awareness. *Developmental Psychology, 42,* 132–141.

Markunas, C. A., Xu, Z., Harlid, S., Wade, P. A., Lie, R. T., Taylor, J. A., & Wilcox, A. J. (2014). Identification of DNA methylation changes in newborns related to maternal smoking during pregnancy. *Environmental Health Perspectives, 10,* 1147–1153.

Marlier, L., & Schaal, B. (2005). Human newborns prefer human milk: Conspecific milk odor is attractive without postnatal exposure. *Child Development, 76,* 155–168.

Marsee, M. A., & Frick, P. J. (2010). Callous-unemotional traits and aggression in youth. In W. F. Arsenio & E. A. Lemerise (Eds.), *Emotions, aggression, and morality in children: Bridging development and psychopathology* (pp. 137–156). Washington, DC: American Psychological Association.

Marsh, H. W. (1990). The structure of academic self-concept: The Marsh/Shavelson model. *Journal of Educational Psychology, 82,* 623–636.

Marsh, H. W., & Ayotte, V. (2003). Do multiple dimensions of self-concept become more differentiated with age? The differential distinctiveness hypothesis. *Journal of Educational Psychology, 95,* 687–706.

Marsh, H. W., Craven, R., & Debus, R. (1998). Structure, stability, and development of young children's self-concepts: A multicohort–multioccasion study. *Child Development, 69,* 1030–1053.

Marsh, H. W., Ellis, L. A., & Craven, R. G. (2002). How do preschool children feel about themselves? Unraveling measurement and multidimensional self-concept structure. *Developmental Psychology, 38,* 376–393.

Marsh, H. W., Trautwein, U., Lüdtke, O., Koller, O., & Baumert, J. (2005). Academic self-concept, interest, grades, and standardized test scores: Reciprocal effects models of causal ordering. *Child Development, 76,* 397–416.

Marshall, P. J., & Meltzoff, A. N. (2011). Neural mirroring systems: Exploring the EEG mu rhythm in human infancy. *Developmental Cognitive Neuroscience, 1,* 110–123.

Marshall-Baker, A., Lickliter, R., & Cooper, R. P. (1998). Prolonged exposure to a visual pattern may promote behavioral organization in preterm infants. *Journal of Perinatal and Neonatal Nursing, 12,* 50–62.

Martin, A., Razza, R. A., & Brooks-Gunn, J. (2012). Specifying the links between household chaos and preschool children's development. *Early Child Development and Care, 182,* 1247–1263.

Martin, C. L., & Fabes, R. A. (2001). The stability and consequences of young children's same-sex peer interactions. *Developmental Psychology, 37,* 431–446.

Martin, C. L., Fabes, R. A., Hanish, L., Leonard, S., & Dinella, L. M. (2011). Experienced and expected similarity to same-gender peers: Moving toward a comprehensive model of gender segregation. *Sex Roles, 65,* 421–434.

Martin, C. L., & Halverson, C. F. (1987). The role of cognition in sex role acquisition. In D. B. Carter (Ed.), *Current conceptions of sex roles and sex typing: Theory and research* (pp. 123–137). New York: Praeger.

Martin, C. L., Kornienko, O., Schaefer, D. R., Hanish, L. D., Fabes, R. A., & Goble, P. (2013). The role of sex of peers and gender-typed activities in young children's peer affiliative networks: A longitudinal analysis of selection and influence. *Child Development, 84,* 921–937.

Martin, C. L., & Ruble, D. (2004). Children's search for gender cues: Cognitive perspectives on gender development. *Current Directions in Psychological Science, 13,* 67–70.

Martin, C. L., Ruble, D. N., & Szkrybalo, J. (2002). Cognitive theories of early gender development. *Psychological Bulletin, 128,* 903–933.

Martin, J. A., Hamilton, B. E., Osterman, J. K., Driscoll, A. K., & Mathews, T. J. (2017). Births: Final data for 2015. *National Vital Statistics Reports*, *66*(1). Retrieved from www.cdc.gov/nchs/data/nvsr/nvsr66/nvsr66_01.pdf

Martinez-Frias, M. L., Bermejo, E., Rodríguez Pinilla, E., & Frías, J. L. (2004). Risk for congenital anomalies associated with different sporadic and daily doses of alcohol consumption during pregnancy: A case-control study. *Birth Defects Research, Part A, Clinical and Molecular Teratology, 70,* 194–200.

Martinot, D., Bagès, C., & Désert, M. (2012). French children's awareness of gender stereotypes about mathematics and reading: When girls improve their reputation in math. *Sex Roles, 66,* 210–219.

Marzolf, D. P., & DeLoache, J. S. (1994). Transfer in young children's understanding of spatial representations. *Child Development, 65,* 1–15.

Masataka, N. (1996). Perception of motherese in a signed language by 6-month-old deaf infants. *Developmental Psychology, 32,* 874–879.

Mascolo, M. F., & Fischer, K. W. (2007). The codevelopment of self and sociomoral emotions during the toddler years. In C. A. Brownell & C. B. Kopp (Eds.), *Socioemotional development in the toddler years: Transitions and transformations* (pp. 66–99). New York: Guilford.

Mascolo, M. F., & Fischer, K. W. (2015). Dynamic development of thinking, feeling, and acting. In W. F. Overton & P. C. Molenaar (Eds.), *Handbook of child psychology and developmental science: Vol. 1. Theory and method* (pp. 113–121). Hoboken, NJ: Wiley.

Mascro, J., Rentscher, K. E., Hackett, P. D., Mehl, M. R., & Rilling, J. K. (2017). Child gender influences paternal behavior, language, and brain function. *Behavioral Neuroscience, 13,* 262–273.

Masten, A. (2013). Risk and resilience in development. In P. D. Zelazo (Ed.), *Oxford handbook of developmental psychology: Vol. 2. Self and other* (pp. 579–607). New York: Oxford University Press.

Masten, A. S. (2014). Global perspectives on resilience in children and youth. *Child Development, 85,* 6–20.

Masten, A. S., Narayan, A. J., Silverman, W. K., & Osofsky, J. D. (2015). Children in war and disaster. In M. H. Bornstein & T. Leventhal (Eds.), *Handbook of child psychology and developmental science: Vol. 4. Ecological settings and processes* (7th ed., pp. 704–745). Hoboken, NJ: Wiley.

Mastropieri, D., & Turkewitz, G. (1999). Prenatal experience and neonatal responsiveness to vocal expression of emotion. *Developmental Psychobiology, 35,* 204–214.

Mastropieri, M. A., Scruggs, T. E., Guckert, M., Thompson, C. C., & Weiss, M. P. (2013). Inclusion and learning disabilities: Will the past be prologue? In J. P. Bakken, F. E. Oblakor, & A. Rotatori (Eds.), *Advances in special education* (Vol. 25, pp. 1–17). Bingley, UK: Emerald Group Publishing.

Masur, E. F., & Rodemaker, J. E. (1999). Mothers' and infants' spontaneous vocal, verbal, and action imitation during the second year. *Merrill-Palmer Quarterly, 45,* 392–412.

Mather, M. (2010, May). *U.S. children in single-mother families* (PRB Data Brief). Washington, DC: Population Reference Bureau.

Matthews, H. (2014, January 14). *A billion dollar boost or child care and early learning.* CLASP: Policy solutions that work for low-income people. Retrieved from www.clasp.org/issues/child-care-and-early-education/in-focus/a-billion-dollar-boost-for-child-care-and-early-learning

Mattson, S. N., Calarco, K. E., & Lang, A. R. (2006). Focused and shifting attention in children with heavy prenatal alcohol exposure. *Neuropsychology, 20,* 361–369.

Mattson, S. N., Crocker, N., & Nguyen, T. T. (2012). Fetal alcohol spectrum disorders: Neuropsychological and behavioral features. *Neuropsychological Review, 21,* 81–101.

Maurer, D., & Lewis, T. (2013). Human visual plasticity: Lessons from children treated for congenital cataracts. In J. K. E. Steeves & L. R. Harris (Eds.), *Plasticity in sensory systems* (pp. 75–93). New York: Cambridge University Press.

Mayberry, R. I. (2010). Early language acquisition and adult language ability: What sign language reveals about the critical period for language. In M. Marshark & P. E. Spencer (Eds.), *Oxford handbook of deaf studies, language, and education* (Vol. 2, pp. 281–291). New York: Oxford University Press.

Mayeux, L., Houser, J. J., & Dyches, K. D. (2011). Social acceptance and popularity: Two distinct forms of peer status. In A. H. N. Cillessen, D. Schwartz, & L. Mayeux (Eds.), *Popularity in the peer system* (pp. 79–102). New York: Guilford.

Maynard, A. E. (2002). Cultural teaching: The development of teaching skills in Maya sibling interactions. *Child Development, 73,* 969–982.

Maynard, A. E., & Greenfield, P. M. (2003). Implicit cognitive development in cultural tools and children: Lessons from Maya Mexico. *Cognitive Development, 18,* 489–510.

McAlister, A., & Peterson, C. C. (2006). Mental playmates: Siblings, executive functioning and theory of mind. *British Journal of Developmental Psychology, 24,* 733–751.

McAlister, A., & Peterson, C. C. (2007). A longitudinal study of child siblings and theory of mind development. *Cognitive Development, 22,* 258–270.

McCabe, A. (1997). Developmental and cross-cultural aspects of children's narration. In M. Bamberg (Ed.), *Narrative development: Six approaches* (pp. 137–174). Mahwah, NJ: Erlbaum.

McCabe, A., Tamis-LeMonda, C. S., Bornstein, M. H., Cates, C. B., Golinkoff, R., Guerra, A. W., et al. (2013). Multilingual children: Beyond myths and toward best practices. *Society for Research in Child Development Social Policy Report, 27*(4).

McCartney, K., Dearing, E., Taylor, B., & Bub, K. (2007). Quality child care supports the achievement of low-income children: Direct and indirect pathways through caregiving and the home environment. *Journal of Applied Developmental Psychology, 28,* 411–426.

McCartney, K., Owen, M., Booth, C., Clarke-Stewart, A., & Vandell, D. (2004). Testing a maternal attachment model of behavior problems in early childhood. *Journal of Child Psychology and Psychiatry, 45,* 765–778.

McCarton, C. (1998). Behavioral outcomes in low birth weight infants. *Pediatrics, 102,* 1293–1297.

McCarty, M. E., & Ashmead, D. H. (1999). Visual control of reaching and grasping in infants. *Developmental Psychology, 35,* 620–631.

McCarty, M. E., & Keen, R. (2005). Facilitating problem solving performance among 9- and 12-month-old infants. *Journal of Cognition and Development, 6,* 209–228.

McColgan, K. L., & McCormack, T. (2008). Searching and planning: Young children's reasoning about past and future event sequences. *Child Development, 79,* 1477–1479.

McCormack, T., & Atance, C. M. (2011). Planning in young children: A review and synthesis. *Developmental Review, 31,* 1–31.

McCune, L. (1993). The development of play as the development of consciousness. In M. H. Bornstein & A. O'Reilly (Eds.), *New directions for child development* (No. 59, pp. 67–79). San Francisco: Jossey-Bass.

McDonald, K., Malti, T., Killen, M., & Rubin, K. (2014). Best friends' discussion of social dilemmas. *Journal of Youth and Adolescence, 43,* 233–244.

McDonough, C., Song, L., Hirsh-Pasek, K., & Golinkoff, R. M. (2011). An image is worth a thousand words: Why nouns tend to dominate verbs in early word learning. *Developmental Science, 14,* 181–189.

McDonough, L. (1999). Early declarative memory for location. *British Journal of Developmental Psychology, 17,* 381–402.

McDowell, D. J., & Parke, R. D. (2000). Differential knowledge of display rules for positive and negative emotions: Influences from parents, influences on peers. *Social Development, 9,* 415–432.

McElwain, N. L., & Booth-LaForce, C. (2006). Maternal sensitivity to infant distress and nondistress as predictors of infant–mother attachment security. *Journal of Family Psychology, 20,* 247–255.

McFarland-Piazza, L., Hazen, N., Jacobvitz, D., & Boyd-Soisson, E. (2012). The development of father–child attachment: Associations between adult attachment representations, recollections of childhood experiences and caregiving. *Early Child Development and Care, 182,* 701–721.

McGee, L. M., & Richgels, D. J. (2012). *Literacy's beginnings: Supporting young readers and writers* (6th ed.). Boston: Allyn and Bacon.

McGillion, M., Herbert, J. S., Pine, J., Vihman, M., dePaolis, R., Keren-Portnoy, T., & Matthews, D. (2017). What paves the way to conventional language? The predictive value of babble, pointing, and socioeconomic status. *Child Development, 88,* 156–166.

McGonigle-Chalmers, M., Slater, H., & Smith, A. (2014). Rethinking private speech in preschoolers: The effects of social presence. *Developmental Psychology, 50,* 829–836.

McGrath, S. K., & Kennell, J. H. (2008). A randomized controlled trial of continuous labor support for middle-class couples: Effect on cesarean delivery rates. *Birth, 35,* 92–97.

McHale, J. P., & Rotman, T. (2007). Is seeing believing? Expectant parents' outlooks on coparenting and later coparenting solidarity. *Infant Behavior and Development, 30,* 63–81.

McHale, S. M., Updegraff, K. A., & Whiteman, S. D. (2012). Sibling relationships and influences in childhood and adolescence. *Journal of Marriage and Family, 74,* 913–930.

McIntyre, S., Blair, E., Badawi, N., Keogh, J., & Nelson, K. B. (2013). Antecedents of cerebral palsy and perinatal death in term and late preterm singletons. *Obstetrics and Gynecology, 122,* 869–877.

McKee, C., Long, L., Southward, L. H., Walker, B., & McCown, J. (2016). The role of parental misconception of child's body weight in childhood obesity. *Journal of Pediatric Nursing, 31,* 196–203.

McKenna, J. J. (2002, September/October). Breast-feeding and bedsharing still useful (and important) after all these years. *Mothering, 114.* Retrieved from www.mothering.com/articles/new_baby/sleep/mckenna.html

McKenna, J. J., & McDade, T. (2005). Why babies should never sleep alone: A review of the co-sleeping controversy in relation to SIDS, bedsharing, and breastfeeding. *Paediatric Respiratory Reviews, 6,* 134–152.

McKenna, J. J., & Volpe, L. E. (2007). Sleeping with baby: An Internet-based sampling of parental experiences, choices, perceptions, and interpretations in a Western industrialized context. *Infant and Child Development, 16,* 359–385.

McKeown, M. G., & Beck, I. L. (2009). The role of metacognition in understanding and supporting reading comprehension. In D. J. Hacker, J. Dunlosky, & A. C. Graesser (Eds.), *Handbook of metacognition in education* (pp. 7–25). New York: Routledge.

McKown, C. (2013). Social equity theory and racial ethnic achievement gaps. *Child Development, 84,* 1120–1136.

McKown, C., Gregory, A., & Weinstein, R. S. (2010). Expectations, stereotypes, and self-fulfilling prophecies in classroom and school life. In J. L. Meece & J. S. Eccles (Eds.), *Handbook of research on schools, schooling and human development* (pp. 256–274). New York: Routledge.

McKown, C., & Strambler, M. J. (2009). Developmental antecedents and social and academic consequences of stereotype-consciousness in middle childhood. *Child Development, 80,* 1643–1659.

McKown, C., & Weinstein, R. S. (2003). The development and consequences of stereotype consciousness in middle childhood. *Child Development, 74,* 498–515.

McKown, C., & Weinstein, R. S. (2008). Teacher expectations, classroom context, and the achievement gap. *Journal of School Psychology, 46,* 235–261.

McLanahan, S. (1999). Father absence and the welfare of children. In E. M. Hetherington (Ed.), *Coping with divorce, single parenting, and remarriage: A risk and resiliency perspective* (pp. 117–145). Mahwah, NJ: Erlbaum.

McLaughlin, K. A., Fox, N. A., Zeanah, C. H., & Nelson, C. A. (2011). Adverse rearing environments and neural development in children: The development of frontal electroencephalogram asymmetry. *Biological Psychiatry, 70,* 1008–1015.

McLaughlin, K. A., Sheridan, M. A., Tibu, F., Fox, N. A., Zeanah, C. H., & Nelson, C. H., III. (2015). Causal effects of the early caregiving environment on development of stress response systems in children. *Proceedings of the National Academy of Sciences, 112,* 5637–5642.

McLaughlin, K. A., Sheridan, M. A., Winter, W., Fox, N. A., Zeanah, C. H., Nelson, C. H., III, et al. (2014). Widespread reductions in cortical thickness following severe early-life deprivation: A neurodevelopmental pathway to attention-deficit hyperactivity disorder. *Biological Psychiatry, 76,* 629–638.

McLeskey, J., & Waldron, N. L. (2011). Educational programs for elementary students with learning disabilities: Can they be both effective and inclusive? *Learning Disabilities: Research and Practice, 26,* 48–57.

McLoyd, V. C., Kaplan, R., Hardaway, C. R., & Wood, D. (2007). Does endorsement of physical discipline matter? Assessing moderating influences on the maternal and child psychological correlates of physical discipline in African-American families. *Journal of Family Psychology, 21,* 165–175.

McLoyd, V. C., & Smith, J. (2002). Physical discipline and behavior problems in African-American, European-American, and Hispanic children: Emotional support as a moderator. *Journal of Marriage and Family, 64,* 40–53.

McNeil, D. G., Jr. (2014, March 5). Early treatment is found to clear H.I.V. in a 2nd baby. *New York Times,* p. A1.

Mehta, C. M., & Strough, J. (2009). Sex segregation in friendships and normative contexts across the life span. *Developmental Review, 29,* 21–220.

Mei, J. (1994). The Northern Chinese custom of rearing babies in sandbags: Implications for motor and intellectual development. In J. H. A. van Rossum & J. I. Laszlo (Eds.), *Motor development: Aspects of normal and delayed development* (pp. 41–48). Amsterdam, Netherlands: VU Uitgeverij.

Meins, E. (2013). Sensitive attunement to infants' internal states: Operationalizing the construct of mind-mindedness. *Attachment & Human Development, 15,* 524–544.

Meins, E., Fernyhough, C., de Rosnay, M., Arnott, B., Leekam, S. R., & Turner, M. (2012). Mind-mindedness as a multidimensional construct: Appropriate and nonattuned mind-related comments independently predict infant–mother attachment in a socially diverse sample. *Infancy, 17,* 393–415.

Meins, E., Fernyhough, C., Wainwright, R., Clark-Carter, D., Gupta, M. D., Fradley, E., & Tucker, M. (2003). Pathways to understanding mind: Construct validity and predictive validity of maternal mind-mindedness. *Child Development, 74,* 1194–1211.

Melby, J. N., Conger, R. D., Fang, S., Wichrama, K. A. S., & Conger, K. J. (2008). Adolescent family experiences and educational attainment during early adulthood. *Developmental Psychology, 44,* 1519–1536.

Melby-Lervag, M., & Hulme, C. (2010). Serial and free recall in children can be improved by training: Evidence for the importance of phonological and semantic representations in immediate memory tasks. *Psychological Science, 21,* 1694–1700.

Meltzoff, A. (2013). Origins of social cognition: Bidirectional self-other mapping and the "like-me" hypothesis. In M. Banaji & S. A. Gelman (Eds.), *Navigating the social world: What infants, children, and other species can teach us* (pp. 139–144). New York: Oxford University Press.

Meltzoff, A. N., & Kuhl, P. K. (1994). Faces and speech: Intermodal processing of biologically relevant signals in infants and adults. In D. J. Lewkowicz & R. Lickliter (Eds.), *The development of intersensory perception* (pp. 335–369). Hillsdale, NJ: Erlbaum.

Meltzoff, A. N., & Moore, M. K. (1977). Imitation of facial and manual gestures by human neonates. *Science, 198,* 75–78.

Meltzoff, A. N., & Moore, M. K. (1994). Imitation, memory, and the representation of persons. *Infant Behavior and Development, 17,* 83–99.

Meltzoff, A. N., & Williamson, R. A. (2010). The importance of imitation for theories of social-cognitive development. In J. G. Bremner & T. D. Wachs (Eds.), *Wiley-Blackwell handbook of infant development* (2nd ed., pp. 345–364). Oxford, UK: Wiley-Blackwell.

Meltzoff, A. N., & Williamson, R. A. (2013). Imitation: Social, cognitive, and theoretical perspectives. In P. D. Zelazo (Ed.), *Oxford handbook of developmental psychology: Vol. 1. Body and mind* (pp. 651–682). New York: Oxford University Press.

Melzer, D. K., & Palermo, C. O. (2016). 'Mommy, you are the princess and I am the queen': How preschool children's initiation and language use during pretend play relate to complexity. *Infant and Child Development, 25,* 221–230.

Melzi, G., & Schick, A. R. (2013). Language and literacy in the school years. In J. B. Gleason & N. B. Ratner (Eds.), *Development of language* (8th ed., pp. 329–365). Upper Saddle River, NJ: Pearson.

Memo, L., Gnoato, E., Caminiti, S., Pichini, S., & Tarani, L. (2013). Fetal alcohol spectrum disorders and fetal alcohol syndrome: The state of the art and new diagnostic tools. *Early Human Development, 89*(S1), S40–S43.

Menesini, E., Calussi, P., & Nocentini, A. (2012). Cyberbullying and traditional bullying: Unique, additive, and synergistic effects on psychological health symptoms. In L. Qing, D. Cross, & P. K. Smith (Eds.), *Cyberbullying in the global playground: Research from international perspectives* (pp. 245–262). Malden, MA: Wiley-Blackwell.

Menesini, E., & Spiel, C. (2012). Introduction: Cyberbullying: Development, consequences, risk and protective factors. *European Journal of Developmental Psychology, 9,* 163–167.

Mennella, J. A., & Beauchamp, G. K. (1998). Early flavor experiences: Research update. *Nutrition Reviews, 56,* 205–211.

Ment, L. R., Vohr, B., Allan, W., Katz, K. H., Schneider, K. C., Westerveld, M., Cuncan, C. C., & Makuch, R. W. (2003). Change in cognitive function over time in very low-birth-weight infants. *JAMA, 289,* 705–711.

Mermelshtine, R. (2017). Parent–child learning interactions: A review of the literature on scaffolding. *British Journal of Educational Psychology, 87,* 241–254.

Merrick, J. (2016). Unintentional injuries in childhood and years of potential life lost. *International Journal of Child and Adolescent Health, 9,* 277–278.

Mesman, J., van IJzendoorn, M. H., & Bakermans-Kranenburg, M. J. (2009). The many faces of the still-face paradigm: A review and meta-analysis. *Developmental Review, 29,* 120–162.

Messinger, D. S., & Fogel, A. (2007). The interactive development of social smiling. In R. Kail (Ed.), *Advances in child development and behavior* (Vol. 35, pp. 327–366). Oxford, UK: Elsevier.

Meyer, R. (2009). Infant feeding in the first year. 1: Feeding practices in the first six months of life. *Journal of Family Health Care, 19,* 13–16.

Meyer, S., Raikes, H. A., Virmani, E. A., Waters, S., & Thompson, R. A. (2014). Parent emotion representations and the socialization of emotion regulation in the family. *International Journal of Behavioral Development, 38,* 164–173.

Meyers, A. B., & Berk, L. E. (2014). Make-believe play and self-regulation. In L. Brooker, M. Blaise, & S. Edwards (Eds.), *Sage handbook of play and learning in early childhood* (pp. 43–55). London: Sage.

Michalik, N. M., Eisenberg, N., Spinrad, T. L., Ladd, B., Thompson, M., & Valiente, C. (2007). Longitudinal relations among parental emotional expressivity and sympathy and prosocial behavior in adolescence. *Social Development, 16,* 286–309.

Migration Policy Institute. (2015). *Children in U.S. Immigrant families*. Retrieved from www.migrationpolicy.org/programs/data-hub/charts/children-immigrant-families

Mikami, A. Y., Lerner, M. D., & Lun, J. (2010). Social context influences on children's rejection by their peers. *Child Development Perspectives, 4,* 123–130.

Miles, G., & Siega-Riz, M. (2017). Trends in food and beverage consumption among infants and toddlers: 2005–2012. *Pediatrics, 139*, e20163290.

Mileva-Seitz, V. R., Bakermans-Kranenburg, M. J., Battaini, C., & Luijk, M. P. C. M. (2017). Parent–child bed-sharing: The good, the bad, and the burden of evidence. *Sleep Medicine Reviews, 32*, 4–27.

Milevsky, A., Schlechter, M., Netter, S., & Keehn, D. (2007). Maternal and paternal parenting styles in adolescents: Associations with self-esteem, depression, and life satisfaction. *Journal of Child and Family Studies, 16,* 39–47.

Milkie, M. A., Nomaguchi, K. M., & Denny, K. E. (2015). Does the amount of time mothers spend with children or adolescents matter? *Journal of Marriage and Family, 77,* 355–372.

Miller, L. E., Grabell, A., Thomas, A., Bermann, E., & Grahgam-Bermann, S. A. (2012). The associations between community violence, television violence, parent–child aggression, and aggression in sibling relationships of a sample of preschoolers. *Psychology of Violence, 2,* 165–178.

Miller, P. H. (2009). *Theories of developmental psychology* (5th ed.). New York: Worth.

Miller, P. J. (2014). Entries into meaning: Socialization via narrative in the early years. In M. J. Gelfand, C.-Y. Chiu, & Y.-Y. Hong (Eds.), *Advances in culture and psychology* (Vol. 4, pp. 124–176). New York: Oxford University Press.

Miller, P. J., Fung, H., Lin, S., Chen, E. C., & Boldt, B. R. (2012). How socialization happens on the ground: Narrative practices as alternate socializing pathways in Taiwanese and European-American families. *Monographs of the Society for Research in Child Development, 77*(1, Serial No. 302).

Miller, P. J., Wiley, A. R., Fung, H., & Liang, C. H. (1997). Personal storytelling as a medium of socialization in Chinese and American families. *Child Development, 68,* 557–568.

Miller, S. A., Hardin, C. A., & Montgomery, D. E. (2003). Young children's understanding of the conditions for knowledge acquisition. *Journal of Cognition and Development, 4,* 325–356.

Miller, T. R. (2015). Projected outcomes of Nurse–Family Partnership home visitation during 1996–2013, USA. *Prevention Science, 16,* 765–777.

Milligan, K., Astington, J. W., & Dack, L. A. (2007). Language and theory of mind: Meta-analysis of the relation between language ability and falsebelief understanding. *Child Development, 78,* 622–646.

Mills, D., Plunkett, K., Prat, C., & Schafer, G. (2005). Watching the infant brain learn words: Effects of language and experience. *Cognitive Development, 20,* 19–31.

Min, J., Chiu, D. T., & Wang, T. (2013). Variation in the heritability of body mass index based on diverse twin studies: A systematic review. *Obesity Review, 14,* 871–882.

Mindell, J. A., Li, A. M., Sadeh, A., Kwon, R., & Goh, D. Y. T. (2015). Bedtime routines for young children: A dose-dependent association with sleep outcomes. *Sleep, 38,* 717–722.

Mireault, G. C., Crockenberg, S. C., Sparrow, J. E., Cousineau, K., Pettinato, C., & Woodard, K. (2015). Laughing matters: Infant humor in the context of parental affect. *Journal of Experimental Child Psychology, 136,* 30–41.

Mireault, G. C., Crockenberg, S. C., Sparrow, J. E., Pettinato, C. A., Woodard, K. C., & Malzac, K. (2014). Social looking, social referencing and humor perception in 6- and 12-month-olds. *Infant Behavior and Development, 37,* 536–545.

Misailidi, P. (2006). Young children's display rule knowledge: Understanding the distinction between apparent and real emotions and the motives underlying the use of display rules. *Social Behavior and Personality, 34,* 1285–1296.

Mistry, J., & Dutta, R. (2015). Human development and culture. In W. F. Overton & P. C. Molenaar (Eds.), *Handbook of child psychology and developmental science: Vol. 1. Theory and method* (pp. 369–406). Hoboken, NJ: Wiley.

Mistry, R. S., Biesanz, J. C., Chien, N., Howes, C., & Benner, A. D. (2008). Socioeconomic status, parental investments, and the cognitive and behavioral outcomes of low-income children from immigrant and native households. *Early Childhood Research Quarterly, 23,* 193–212.

Miura, I. T., & Okamoto, Y. (2003). Language supports for mathematics understanding and performance. In A. J. Baroody & A. Dowker (Eds.), *The development of arithmetic concepts and skills* (pp. 229–242). Mahwah, NJ: Erlbaum.

Mize, J., & Pettit, G. S. (2010). The mother–child playgroup as socialisation context: A short-term longitudinal study of mother–child–peer relationship dynamics. *Early Child Development and Care, 180,* 1271–1284.

Mok, M. M. C., Kennedy, K. J., & Moore, P. J. (2011). Academic attribution of secondary students: Gender, year level and achievement level. *Educational Psychology, 31,* 87–104.

Moll, H., & Meltzoff, A. N. (2011). How does it look? Level 2 perspective-taking at 36 months of age. *Child Development, 82,* 661–673.

Moll, K., Ramus, F., Bartling, J., Bruder, J., Kunze, S., Neuhoff, N., et al. (2014). Cognitive mechanisms underlying reading and spelling development in five European orthographies. *Learning and Instruction, 29,* 65–77.

Moller, K., Hwang, C. P., & Wickberg, B. (2008). Couple relationship and transition to parenthood: Does workload at home matter? *Journal of Reproductive and Infant Psychology, 26,* 57–68.

Mondloch, C. J., Lewis, T., Budreau, D. R., Maurer, D., Dannemillier, J. L., Stephens, B. R., & Kleiner-Gathercoal, K. A. (1999). Face perception during early infancy. *Psychological Science, 10,* 419–422.

Monk, C., Feng, T., Lee, S., Krupska, I., Champagne, F. A., & Tycko, B. (2016). Distress during pregnancy: Epigenetic regulation of placenta glucocorticoid-related genes and fetal neurobehavior. *American Journal of Psychiatry, 173,* 705–713.

Monk, C., Georgieff, M. K., & Osterholm, E. A. (2013). Research review: Maternal prenatal distress and poor nutrition—mutually influencing risk factors affecting infant neurocognitive development. *Journal of Child Psychology and Psychiatry, 54,* 115–130.

Monk, C., Sloan, R., Myers, M. M., Ellman, L., Werner, E., Jeon, J., et al. (2010). Neural circuitry of emotional face processing in autism spectrum disorders. *Journal of Psychiatry and Neuroscience, 35,* 105–114.

Montgomery, D. E., & Koeltzow, T. E. (2010). A review of the day–night task: The Stroop paradigm and interference control in young children. *Developmental Review, 30,* 308–330.

Moon, C., Cooper, R. P., & Fifer, W. P. (1993). Two-day-old infants prefer their native language. *Infant Behavior and Development, 16,* 495–500.

Moore, D. S. (2013). Behavioral genetics, genetics, and epigenetics. In P. D. Zelazo (Ed.), *Oxford handbook of developmental psychology: Vol. 1. Body and mind* (pp. 91–128). New York: Oxford University Press.

Moore, E. G. J. (1986). Family socialization and the IQ test performance of traditionally and transracially adopted Black children. *Developmental Psychology, 22,* 317–326.

Moore, J. A., Cooper, B. R., Domitrovich, C. E., Morgan, N. R., Cleveland, M. J., Shah, H., et al. (2015). Effects of exposure to an enhanced preschool program on the social-emotional functioning of at-risk children. *Early Childhood Research Quarterly, 32,* 127–138.

Moore, K. L., Persaud, T. V. N., & Torchia, M. G. (2016a). *Before we are born: Essentials of embryology and birth defects* (9th ed.). Philadelphia: Elsevier.

Moore, K. L., Persaud, T. V. N., & Torchia, M. G. (2016b). *The developing human: Clinically oriented embryology.* Philadelphia: Elsevier.

Moore, M. K., & Meltzoff, A. N. (2004). Object permanence after a 24-hr delay and leaving the locale of disappearance: The role of memory, space, and identity. *Developmental Psychology, 40,* 606–620.

Moore, M. K., & Meltzoff, A. N. (2008). Factors affecting infants' manual search for occluded objects and the genesis of object permanence. *Infant Behavior and Development, 31,* 168–180.

Moore, M. R., & Stambolis-Ruhstorfer, M. (2013). LGBT sexuality and families at the start of the twenty-first century. *Annual Review of Sociology, 39,* 491–507.

Morawska, A., & Sanders, M. (2011). Parental use of time out revisited: A useful or harmful parenting strategy? *Journal of Child and Family Studies, 20,* 1–8.

Morelli, G. (2015). The evolution of attachment theory and cultures of human attachment in infancy and early childhood. In L. A. Jensen (Ed.), *Oxford handbook of human development and culture: An interdisciplinary perspective* (pp. 149–164). New York: Oxford University Press.

Morelli, G., Rogoff, B., Oppenheim, D., & Goldsmith, D. (1992). Cultural variation in infants' sleeping arrangements: Questions of independence. *Developmental Psychology, 28,* 604–613.

Morelli, G. A., Rogoff, B., & Angelillo, C. (2003). Cultural variation in young children's access to work or involvement in specialized child-focused activities. *International Journal of Behavioral Development, 27,* 264–274.

Moreno, A. J., Klute, M. M., & Robinson, J. L. (2008). Relational and individual resources as predictors of empathy in early childhood. *Social Development, 17,* 613–637.

Morrill, M. I., Hines, D. A., Mahmood, S., & Córdova, J. V. (2010). Pathways between marriage and parenting for wives and husbands: The role of coparenting. *Family Process, 49,* 59–73.

Morris, A. S., Silk, J. S., Morris, M. D. S., & Steinberg, L. (2011). The influence of mother–child emotion regulation strategies on children's expression of anger and sadness. *Developmental Psychology, 47,* 213–225.

Morris, A. S., Silk, J. S., Steinberg, L., Myers, S. S., & Robinson, L. R. (2007). The role of the family context in the development of emotion regulation. *Social Development, 16,* 362–388.

Morris, M. C., Douros, C. D., Janecek, K., Freeman, R., Mielock, A., & Garber, J. (2017). Community-level moderators of a school-based childhood sexual assault prevention program. *Child Abuse & Neglect, 63,* 295–306.

Morrongiello, B. A., Fenwick, K. D., & Chance, G. (1998). Crossmodal learning in newborn infants: Inferences about properties of auditory-visual events. *Infant Behavior and Development, 21,* 543–554.

Morrongiello, B. A., Ondejko, L., & Littlejohn, A. (2004). Understanding toddlers' in-home injuries: I. Context, correlates, and determinants. *Journal of Pediatric Psychology, 29,* 415–431.

Morrongiello, B. A., Widdifield, R., Munroe, K., & Zdzieborski, D. (2014). Parents teaching young children home safety rules: Implications for childhood injury risk. *Journal of Applied Developmental Psychology, 35,* 254–261.

Morse, S. B., Zheng, H., Tang, Y., & Roth, J. (2009). Early school-age outcomes of late preterm infants. *Pediatrics, 123,* e622–e629.

Moss, E., Cyr, C., Bureau, J.-F., Tarabulsy, G. M., & Dubois-Comtois, K. (2005). Stability of attachment during the preschool period. *Developmental Psychology, 41,* 773–783.

Mossey, P. A., Little, J., Munger, R. G., Dixon, M. J., & Shaw, W. C. (2009). Cleft lip and palate. *Lancet, 374,* 1773–1785.

Mottus, R., Indus, K., & Allik, J. (2008). Accuracy of only children stereotype. *Journal of Research in Personality, 42,* 1047–1052.

Mottweiler, C. M., & Taylor, M. (2014). Elaborated role play and creativity in preschool age children. *Psychology of Aesthetics, Creativity, and the Arts, 8,* 277–286.

Mrug, S., Hoza, B., & Gerdes, A. C. (2001). Children with attention-deficit/hyperactivity disorder: Peer relationships and peer-oriented interventions. In D. W. Nangle & C. A. Erdley (Eds.), *The role of friendship in psychological adjustment* (pp. 51–77). San Francisco: Jossey-Bass.

Mu, Q., & Fehring, R. J. (2014). Efficacy of achieving pregnancy with fertility-focused intercourse. *American Journal of Maternal Child Nursing, 39,* 35–40.

Mueller, B. R., & Bale, T. L. (2008). Sex-specific programming of offspring emotionality after stress early in pregnancy. *Journal of Neuroscience, 28,* 9055–9065.

Muenssinger, J., Matuz, T., Schleger, F., Kiefer-Schmidt, I., Goelz, R., Wacker-Gussmann, A., et al. (2013). Auditory habituation in the fetus and neonate: An fMEG study. *Developmental Science, 16,* 287–295.

Müller, O., & Krawinkel, M. (2005). Malnutrition and health in developing countries. *Canadian Medical Association Journal, 173,* 279–286.

Müller, U., & Kerns, K. (2015). The development of executive function. In L. S. Liben & U. Müller (Eds.), *Handbook of child psychology and developmental science: Vol. 2. Cognitive processes* (7th ed., pp. 571–623). Hoboken, NJ: Wiley.

Müller, U., Liebermann-Finestone, D. P., Carpendale, J. I. M., Hammond, S. I., & Bibok, M. B. (2012). Knowing minds, controlling actions: The developmental relations between theory of mind and executive function from 2 to 4 years of age. *Journal of Experimental Child Psychology, 111,* 331–348.

Mullett-Hume, E., Anshel, D., Guevara, V., & Cloitre, M. (2008). Cumulative trauma and posttraumatic stress disorder among children exposed to the 9/11 World Trade Center attack. *American Journal of Orthopsychiatry, 78,* 103–108.

Mulvaney, M. K., McCartney, K., Bub, K. L., & Marshall, N. L. (2006). Determinants of dyadic scaffolding and cognitive outcomes in first graders. *Parenting: Science and Practice, 6,* 297–310.

Mulvaney, M. K., & Mebert, C. J. (2007). Parental corporal punishment predicts behavior problems in early childhood. *Journal of Family Psychology, 21,* 389–397.

Mumme, D. L., Bushnell, E. W., DiCorcia, J. A., & Lariviere, L. A. (2007). Infants' use of gaze cues to interpret others' actions and emotional reactions. In R. Flom, K. Lee, & D. Muir (Eds.), *Gaze-following: Its development and significance* (pp. 143–170). Mahwah, NJ: Erlbaum.

Munakata, Y. (2006). Information processing approaches to development. In D. Kuhn & R. S. Siegler (Eds.), *Handbook of child psychology: Vol. 3. Cognition, perception, and language* (6th ed., pp. 426–463). Hoboken, NJ: Wiley.

Munroe, R. L., & Romney, A. K. (2006). Gender and age differences in same-sex aggregation and social behavior. *Journal of Cross-Cultural Psychology, 37,* 3–19.

Muris, P., & Field, A. P. (2011). The "normal" development of fear. In W. K. Silverman & A. P. Field (Eds.), *Anxiety disorders in children and adolescents* (2nd ed., pp. 76–89). Cambridge, UK: Cambridge University Press.

Muris, P., & Meesters, C. (2014). Small or big in the eyes of the other: On the developmental psychopathology of self-conscious emotions as shame, guilt, and pride. *Clinical Child and Family Psychology Review, 17,* 19–40.

Murphy, J. B. (2013). Access to in vitro fertilization deserves increased regulation in the United States. *Journal of Sex and Marital Therapy, 39,* 85–92.

Murphy, K. M., Rodrigues, K., Costigan, J., & Annan, J. (2017). Raising children in conflict: An integrative model of parenting in war. *Peace and Conflict: Journal of Peace Psychology, 23,* 46–57.

Murphy, T. H., & Corbett, D. (2009). Plasticity during recovery: From synapse to behaviour. *Nature Reviews Neuroscience, 10,* 861–872.

Murphy, T. P., & Laible, D. J. (2013). The influence of attachment security on preschool children's empathic concern. *International Journal of Behavioral Development, 37,* 436–440.

Murray, L. K., Nguyen, A., & Cohen, J. A. (2014). Child sexual abuse. *Pediatric Clinics of North America, 23,* 321–337.

Mussen, P., & Eisenberg-Berg, N. (1977). *Roots of caring, sharing, and helping.* San Francisco: Freeman.

Myowa-Yamakoshi, M., Tomonaga, M., Tanaka, M., & Matsuzawa, T. (2004). Imitation in neonatal chimpanzees *(Pan troglodytes). Developmental Science, 7,* 437–442.

N

Nadel, J., Prepin, K., & Okanda, M. (2005). Experiencing contingency and agency: First step toward self-understanding in making a mind? *Interaction Studies, 6,* 447–462.

Naerde, A., Ogden, T., Janson, H., & Zachrisson, H. D. (2014). Normative development of physical aggression from 8 to 26 months. *Developmental Psychology, 6,* 1710–1720.

Nagy, E., Compagne, H., Orvos, H., Pal, A., Molnar, P., & Janszky, I. (2005). Index finger movement imitation by human neonates: Motivation, learning, and left-hand preference. *Pediatric Research, 58,* 749–753.

Nagy, W. E., & Scott, J. A. (2000). Vocabulary processes. In M. L. Kamil & P. B. Mosenthal (Eds.), *Handbook of reading research* (Vol. 3, pp. 269–284). Mahwah, NJ: Erlbaum.

Naigles, L. R., & Swenson, L. D. (2007). Syntactic supports for word learning. In E. Hoff & M. Shatz (Eds.), *Blackwell handbook of language development* (pp. 212–231). Malden, MA: Blackwell.

Naito, M., & Seki, Y. (2009). The relationship between second-order false belief and display rules reasoning: Integration of cognitive and affective social understanding. *Developmental Science, 12,* 150–164.

Nan, C., Piek, J., Warner, C., Mellers, D., Krone, R. E., Barrett, T., & Zeegers, M. P. (2013). Trajectories and predictors of developmental skills in healthy twins up to 24 months of age. *Infant Behavior and Development, 36,* 670–678.

Nánez, J., Sr., & Yonas, A. (1994). Effects of luminance and texture motion on infant defensive reactions to optical collision. *Infant Behavior and Development, 17,* 165–174.

Nanri, H., Shirasawa, T., Ochiai, H., Nomoto, S., Hoshino, H., & Kokaze, A. (2017). Rapid weight gain during infancy and early childhood is related to higher anthropometric measurements in preadolescence. *Child: Care, Health and Development, 43,* 435–440.

Narr, K. L., Woods, R. P., Lin J., Kim, J., Phillips, O. R., Del'Homme, M., et al. (2009). Widespread cortical thinning is a robust anatomical marker for attention-deficit/hyperactivity disorder. *Journal of the American Academy of Child and Adolescent Psychiatry, 48,* 1014–1022.

Nassr, A. A., Erfani, H., Fisher, J. E., Ogunleye, O. K., Espinosa, J., Belfort, M. A., et al. (2017). Fetal interventional procedures and surgeries: A practical approach. *Journal of Perinatal Medicine, 45.*

National Association for the Education of Young Children. (2017). *DAP in the early primary grades.* Retrieved from www.naeyc.org/dap/primary

National Center for Biotechnology Information. (2015). *Online Mendelian inheritance in man.* Retrieved from www.omim.org

National Coalition for the Homeless. (2012). *Education of homeless children and youth.* Retrieved from www.nationalhomeless.org/factsheets/education.html

National Institutes of Health. (2017). *Safe to sleep.* Retrieved from https://www.nichd.nih.gov/sts/Pages/default.aspx

Natsuaki, M. N., Shaw, D. S., Neiderhiser, J. M., Ganiban, J. M., Harold, G. T., Reiss, D., et al. (2014). Raised by depressed parents: Is it an environmental risk? *Clinical Child and Family Psychology Review, 17,* 357–367.

Neitzel, C., & Stright, A. D. (2003). Mothers' scaffolding of children's problem solving: Establishing a foundation of academic self-regulatory competence. *Journal of Family Psychology, 17,* 147–159.

Nelson, C. A., & Bosquet, M. (2000). Neurobiology of fetal and infant development: Implications for infant mental health. In C. H. Zeanah, Jr. (Ed.), *Handbook of infant mental health* (2nd ed., pp. 37–59). New York: Guilford.

Nelson, C. A., Fox, N. A., & Zeanah, C. H. (2014). *Romania's abandoned children: Deprivation, brain development, and the struggle for recovery.* Cambridge, MA: Harvard University Press.

Nelson, C. A., Thomas, K. M., & de Haan, M. (2006). Neural bases of cognitive development. In D. Kuhn & R. Siegler (Eds.), *Handbook of child psychology: Vol. 2. Cognition, perception, and language* (6th ed., pp. 3–57). Hoboken, NJ: Wiley.

Nelson, D. A., Robinson, C. C., & Hart, C. H. (2005). Relational and physical aggression of preschool-age children: Peer status linkages across informants. *Early Education and Development, 16,* 115–139.

Nelson, D. A., Yang, C., Coyne, S. M., Olsen, J. A., & Hart, C. H. (2013). Parental psychological control dimensions: Connections with Russian preschoolers' physical and relational aggression. *Journal of Applied Developmental Psychology, 34,* 1–8.

Nelson, E. L., Campbell, J. M., & Michel, G. F. (2013). Unimanual to bimanual: Tracking the development of handedness from 6 to 24 months. *Infant Behavior and Development, 36,* 181–188.

Nelson, K. (2003). Narrative and the emergence of a consciousness of self. In G. D. Fireman & T. E. McVay, Jr. (Eds.), *Narrative and consciousness: Literature, psychology, and the brain* (pp. 17–36). London: Oxford University Press.

Nepomnyaschy, L., & Waldfogel, J. (2007). Paternity leave and fathers' involvement with their young children. *Community, Work and Family, 10,* 427–453.

Nesdale, D., Durkin, K., Maas, A., & Griffiths, J. (2004). Group status, outgroup ethnicity, and children's ethnic attitudes. *Applied Developmental Psychology, 25,* 237–251.

Neugebauer, R., Fisher, P. W., Turner, J. B., Yamabe, S., Sarsfield, J. A., & Stehling-Ariza, T. (2009). Post-traumatic stress reactions among Rwandan children and adolescents in the early aftermath of genocide. *International Journal of Epidemiology, 38,* 1033–1045.

Neuman, S. B. (2003). From rhetoric to reality: The case for high-quality compensatory prekindergarten programs. *Phi Delta Kappan, 85*(4), 286–291.

Neville, H. J., & Bavelier, D. (2002). Human brain plasticity: Evidence from sensory deprivation and altered language experience. In M. A. Hofman, G. J. Boer, A. J. G. D. Holtmaat, E. J. W. van Someren, J. Berhaagen, & D. F. Swaab (Eds.), *Plasticity in the adult brain: From genes to neurotherapy* (pp. 177–188). Amsterdam: Elsevier Science.

Newheiser, A., Dunham, Y., Merrill, A., Hoosain, L., & Olson, K. R. (2014). Preference for high status predicts implicit outgroup bias among children from low-status groups. *Developmental Psychology, 50,* 1081–1090.

Newnham, C. A., Milgrom, J., & Skouteris, H. (2009). Effectiveness of a modified mother–infant transaction program on outcomes for preterm infants from 3 to 24 months of age. *Infant Behavior and Development, 32,* 17–26.

Newton, E. K., Laible, D., Carlo, G., Steele, J. S., & McGinley, M. (2014). Do sensitive parents foster kind children, or vice versa? Bidirectional influences between children's prosocial behavior and parental sensitivity. *Developmental Psychology, 50,* 1808–1816.

Ng, F. F., Pomerantz, E. M., & Deng, C. (2014). Why are Chinese mothers more controlling than American mothers?: "My child is my report card." *Child Development, 85,* 355–369.

Ng, F. F., Pomerantz, E. M., & Lam, S. (2007). European American and Chinese parents' responses to children's success and failure: Implications for children's responses. *Developmental Psychology, 43,* 1239–1255.

NICHD (National Institute of Child Health and Human Development) Early Child Care Research Network. (1997). The effects of infant child care on infant–mother attachment security: Results of the NICHD Study of Early Child Care. *Child Development, 68,* 860–879.

NICHD (National Institute of Child Health and Human Development) Early Child Care Research Network. (1998). Relations between family predictors and child outcomes: Are they weaker for children in child care? *Developmental Psychology, 34,* 1119–1128.

NICHD (National Institute of Child Health and Human Development) Early Child Care Research Network. (1999). Child care and mother–child interaction in the first 3 years of life. *Developmental Psychology, 35,* 1399–1413.

NICHD (National Institute of Child Health and Human Development) Early Child Care Research Network. (2000a). Characteristics and quality of child care for toddlers and preschoolers. *Applied Developmental Science, 4,* 116–135.

NICHD (National Institute of Child Health and Human Development) Early Child Care Research Network.

(2000b). The relation of child care to cognitive and language development. *Child Development, 71,* 960–980.

NICHD (National Institute of Child Health and Human Development) Early Child Care Research Network. (2001). Before Head Start: Income and ethnicity, family characteristics, child care experiences, and child development. *Early Education and Development, 12,* 545–575.

NICHD (National Institute of Child Health and Human Development) Early Child Care Research Network. (2002). The interaction of child care and family risk in relation to child development at 24 and 36 months. *Applied Developmental Science, 6,* 144–156.

NICHD (National Institute of Child Health and Human Development) Early Child Care Research Network. (2003a). Does amount of time spent in child care predict socioemotional adjustment during the transition to kindergarten? *Child Development, 74,* 976–1005.

NICHD (National Institute of Child Health and Human Development) Early Child Care Research Network. (2003b). Does quality of child care affect child outcomes at age 4½? *Developmental Psychology, 39,* 451–469.

NICHD (National Institute of Child Health and Human Development) Early Child Care Research Network. (2004). Trajectories of physical aggression from toddlerhood to middle childhood. *Monographs of the Society for Research in Child Development, 69*(4, Serial No. 278).

NICHD (National Institute of Child Health and Human Development) Early Child Care Research Network. (2006). Child-care effect sizes for the NICHD Study of Early Child Care and Youth Development. *American Psychologist, 61,* 99–116.

Nichols, K. E., Fox, N., & Mundy, P. (2005). Joint attention, self-recognition, and neurocognitive function in toddlers. *Infancy, 7,* 35–51.

Nickman, S. L., Rosenfeld, A. A., Fine, P., MacIntyre, J. C., Pilowsky, D. J., & Howe, R. A. (2005). Children in adoptive families: Overview and update. *Journal of the American Academy of Child and Adolescent Psychiatry, 44,* 987–995.

Nicolopoulou, A., & Ilgaz, H. (2013). What do we know about pretend play and narrative development? A response to Lillard, Lerner, Hopkins, Dore, Smith, and Palmquist on "The impact of pretend play on children's development: A review of the evidence." *American Journal of Play, 6,* 55–81.

Nielsen, M. (2012). Imitation, pretend play, and childhood: Essential elements in the evolution of human culture? *Journal of Comparative Psychology, 126,* 170–181.

Nikulina, V., & Widom, C. S. (2013). Child maltreatment and executive functioning in middle adulthood: A prospective examination. *Neuropsychology, 27,* 417–427.

Nikulina, V., Widom, C. S., & Czaja, S. (2011). The role of childhood neglect and childhood poverty in predicting academic achievement and crime in adulthood. *American Journal of Community Psychology, 48,* 309–321.

Nippold, M. A., Taylor, C. L., & Baker, J. M. (1996). Idiom understanding in Australian youth: A cross-cultural comparison. *Journal of Speech and Hearing Research, 39,* 442–447.

Nisbett, R. E. (2009). *Intelligence and how to get it.* New York: Norton.

Nisbett, R. E., Aronson, J., Blair, C., Dickens, W., Flynn, J., Halpern, D. F., et al. (2012). Intelligence: New findings and theoretical developments. *American Psychologist, 67,* 130–159.

Nishitani, S., Miyamura, T., Tagawa, M., Sumi, M., Takase, R., Doi, H., et al. (2009). The calming effect of a maternal breast milk odor on the human newborn infant. *Neuroscience Research, 63,* 66–71.

Noble, K. G., Fifer, W. P., Rauh, V. A., Nomura, Y., & Andrews, H. F. (2012). Academic achievement varies with gestational age among children born at term. *Pediatrics, 130,* e257–e264.

Noordstar, J. J., van der Net, J., Jak, S., Helders, P. J. M., & Jongmans, M. J. (2016). Global self-esteem, perceived athletic competence, and physical activity in children: A longitudinal cohort study. *Psychology of Sport and Exercise, 22,* 83–90.

Noroozian, M., Shadloo, B., Shakiba, A., & Panahi, P. (2012). Educational achievement and other controversial issues in left-handedness: A neuropsychological and psychiatric view. In T. Dutta & M. K. Mandal (Eds.), *Bias in human behavior* (pp. 41–82). Hauppauge, NY: Nova Science.

Northstone, K., Joinson, C., Emmett, P., Ness, A., & Paus, T. (2012). Are dietary patterns in childhood associated with IQ at 8 years of age? A population-based cohort study. *Journal of Epidemiological Community Health, 66,* 624–628.

Noterdaeme, M., Mildenberger, K., Minow, F., & Amorosa, H. (2002). Evaluation of neuromotor deficits in children with autism and children with a specific speech and language disorder. *European Child and Adolescent Psychiatry, 11,* 219–225.

Nowicki, E. A., Brown, J., & Stepien, M. (2014). Children's thoughts on the social exclusion of peers with intellectual or learning disabilities. *Journal of Intellectual Disability Research, 58,* 346–357.

Nucci, L. (2009). *Nice is not enough: Facilitating moral development.* Upper Saddle River, NJ: Prentice Hall.

Nucci, L. P. (2005). Culture, context, and the psychological sources of human rights concepts. In W. Edelstein & G. Nunner-Winkler (Eds.), *Morality in context* (pp. 365–394). Amsterdam, Netherlands: Elsevier.

Nucci, L. P., & Gingo, M. (2011). The development of moral reasoning. In U. Goswami (Ed.), *The Wiley-Blackwell handbook of childhood cognitive development* (2nd ed., pp. 420–444). Hoboken, NJ: Wiley.

O

Oakes, L. M., Ross-Sheehy, S., & Luck, S. J. (2007). The development of visual short-term memory in infancy. In L. M. Oakes & P. J. Bauer (Eds.), *Short- and -long-term memory in infancy and early childhood* (pp. 75–102). New York: Oxford University Press.

Oberecker, R., & Friederici, A. D. (2006). Syntactic event-related potential components in 24-month-olds' sentence comprehension. *NeuroReport, 17,* 1017–1021.

Obradović, J., Long, J. D., Cutuli, J. J., Chan, C. K., Hinz, E., Heistad, D., & Masten, A. S. (2009). Academic achievement of homeless and highly mobile children in an urban school district: Longitudinal evidence on risk, growth, and resilience. *Development and Psychopathology, 21,* 493–518.

O'Brien, M., Weaver, J. M., Nelson, J. A., Calkins, S. D., Leerkes, E. M., & Marcovitch, S. (2011). Longitudinal associations between children's understanding of emotions and theory of mind. *Cognition and Emotion, 25,* 1074–1086.

O'Connor, E., & McCartney, K. (2007). Examining teacher–child relationships and achievement as part of an ecological model of development. *American Educational Research Journal, 44,* 340–369.

O'Connor, T. G., Marvin, R. S., Rutter, M., Olrich, J. T., Britner, P. A., & the English and Romanian Adoptees Study Team. (2003). Child–parent attachment following early institutional deprivation. *Development and Psychopathology, 15,* 19–38.

O'Connor, T. G., Rutter, M., Beckett, C., Keaveney, L., Dreppner, J. M., & the English and Romanian Adoptees Study Team. (2000). The effects of global severe privation on cognitive competence: Extension and longitudinal follow-up. *Child Development, 71,* 376–390.

O'Dea, J. A. (2012). Body image and self-esteem. In T. F. Cash (Ed.), *Encyclopedia of body image and human appearance* (pp. 141–147). London: Elsevier.

O'Donnell, K. J., & Meaney, M. J. (2016). Fetal origins of mental health: The developmental origins of health and disease hypothesis. *American Journal of Psychiatry, 174,* 319–327.

OECD (Organisation for Economic Cooperation and Development). (2013). *Education at a glance 2013: OECD indicators.* Retrieved from www.oecd.org/edu/eag2013%20(eng)—FINAL%2020%20June%202013.pdf

OECD (Organisation for Economic Cooperation and Development). (2017). *OECD Health statistics 2017.* Retrieved from www.oecd.org/els/health-systems/health-data.htm

Offer, S., & Schneider, B. (2011). Revisiting the gender gap in time-use patterns: Multitasking and well-being among mothers and fathers in dual-earner families. *American Sociological Review, 76,* 809–833.

Office of Head Start. (2016). *Head Start program facts: Fiscal year 2016.* Retrieved from eclkc.ohs.acf.hhs.gov/sites/default/files/pdf/hs-program-fact-sheet-2016.pdf

Ogden, C. L., Carroll, M. D., Kit, B. K., & Flegal, K. M. (2014). Prevalence of childhood and adult obesity. *JAMA, 311,* 806–814.

Ogden, C. L., Carroll, M. D., Lawman, H. G., Frayar, C. D., Kruszon-Moran, D., Kit, B. K., & Flegal, K. M. (2016). Trends in obesity prevalence among children and adolescents in the United States, 1988–1994 through 2013–2014. *JAMA, 315,* 2292–2299.

Okagaki, L., & Sternberg, R. J. (1993). Parental beliefs and children's school performance. *Child Development, 64,* 36–56.

Okami, P., Weisner, T., & Olmstead, R. (2002). Outcome correlates of parent–child bedsharing: An eighteen-year longitudinal study. *Developmental and Behavioral Pediatrics, 23,* 244–253.

Okeke-Adeyanju, N., Taylor, L., Craig, A. B., Smith, R. E., Thomas, A., Boyle, A. E., et al. (2014). Celebrating the strengths of Black youth: Increasing self-esteem and implications for prevention. *Journal of Primary Prevention, 35,* 357–369.

Olafson, E. (2011). Child sexual abuse: Demography, impact, and interventions. *Journal of Child and Adolescent Trauma, 4,* 8–21.

Olds, D. L., Eckenrode, J., Henderson, C., Kitzman, H., Cole, R., Luckey, D., et al. (2009). Preventing child abuse and neglect with home visiting by nurses. In K. A. Dodge & D. L. Coleman (Eds.), *Preventing child maltreatment* (pp. 29–54). New York: Guilford.

Olds, D. L., Kitzman, H., Cole, R., Robinson, J., Sidora, K., Luckey, D. W., et al. (2004). Effects of nurse home-visiting on maternal life course and child development: Age 6 follow-up results of a randomized trial. *Pediatrics, 114,* 1550–1559.

Olds, D. L., Kitzman, H., Hanks, C., Cole, R., Anson, E., Sidora-Arcoleo, K., et al. (2007). Effects of nurse home visiting on maternal and child functioning: Age-9 follow-up of a randomized trial. *Pediatrics, 120,* e832–e845.

Olineck, K. M., & Poulin-Dubois, D. (2009). Infants' understanding of intention from 10 to 14 months: Interrelations among violation of expectancy and imitation tasks. *Infant Behavior and Development, 32,* 404–415.

Olino, T. M., Durbin, C. E., Klein, D. N., Hayden, E. P., & Dyson, M. W. (2013). Gender differences in young children's temperamental traits: Comparisons across observational and parent-report methods. *Journal of Personality, 81,* 119–129.

Ollendick, T. H., King, N. J., & Muris, P. (2002). Fears and phobias in children: Phenomenology, epidemiology, and aetiology. *Child and Adolescent Mental Health, 7,* 98–106.

Oller, D. K. (2000). *The emergence of the speech capacity.* Mahwah, NJ: Erlbaum.

Olson, K. R. (2016). Prepubescent transgender children: What we do and do not know. *Journal of the American Academy of Child and Adolescent Psychiatry, 55,* 155–156.

Olson, K. R., Key, A. C., & Eaton, N. R. (2015). Gender cognition in transgender children. *Psychological Science, 26,* 467–474.

Olson, S. L., Lopez-Duran, N., Lunkenheimer, E. S., Chang, H., & Sameroff, A. J. (2011). Individual differences in the development of early peer aggression: Integrating contributions of self-regulation, theory of mind, and parenting. *Development and Psychopathology, 23,* 253–266.

O'Neill, M., Bard, K. A., Kinnell, M., & Fluck, M. (2005). Maternal gestures with 20-month-old infants in two contexts. *Developmental Science, 8,* 352–359.

O'Neill, R., Welsh, M., Parke, R. D., Wang, S., & Strand, C. (1997). A longitudinal assessment of the academic correlates of early peer acceptance and rejection. *Journal of Clinical Child Psychology, 26,* 290–303.

Oostenbroek, J., Slaughter, V., Nielsen, M., & Suddendorf, T. (2013). Why the confusion around neonatal imitation? A review. *Journal of Reproductive and Infant Psychology, 31,* 328–341.

Oosterwegel, A., & Oppenheimer, L. (1993). *The self-system: Developmental changes between and within self-concepts.* Hillsdale, NJ: Erlbaum.

Orbio de Castro, B., Veerman, J. W., Koops, W., Bosch, J. D., & Monshouwer, H. J. (2002). Hostile attribution of intent and aggressive behavior: A meta-analysis. *Child Development, 73,* 916–934.

Ordonana, J. R., Caspi, A., & Moffitt, T. E. (2008). Unintentional injuries in a twin study of preschool children: Environmental, not genetic risk factors. *Journal of Pediatric Psychology, 33,* 185–194.

Osterholm, E. A., Hostinar, C. E., & Gunnar, M. R. (2012). Alterations in stress responses of the hypothalamic-pituitary-adrenal axis in small for gestational age infants. *Psychoneuroendocrinology, 37,* 1719–1725.

Ostrov, J. M., Crick, N. R., & Stauffacher, K. (2006). Relational aggression in sibling and peer relationships during early childhood. *Applied Developmental Psychology, 27,* 241–253.

Ostrov, J. M., Murray-Close, D., Godleski, S. A., & Hart, E. J. (2013). Prospective associations between forms and functions of aggression and social and affective processes during early childhood. *Journal of Experimental Child Psychology, 116,* 19–36.

Otter, M., Schrander-Stempel, C. T. R. M., Didden, R., & Curfs, L. M. G. (2013). The psychiatric phenotype in triple X syndrome: New hypotheses illustrated in two cases. *Developmental Neurorehabilitation, 15,* 233–238.

Otto, H., & Keller, H. (Eds.). (2014). *Different faces of attachment: Cultural variation of a universal human need.* Cambridge, UK: Cambridge University Press.

Ouko, L. A., Shantikumar, K., Knezovich, J., Haycock, P., Schnugh, D. J., & Ramsay, M. (2009). Effect of alcohol consumption on CpG methylation in the differentially methylated regions of H19 and IG-DMR in male gametes: Implications for fetal alcohol spectrum disorders. *Alcoholism, Clinical and Experimental Research, 33,* 1615–1627.

Overton, W. F., & Molenaar, P. C. M. (2015). Concepts, theory, and method in developmental science: A view of the issues. In W. F. Overton & P. C. Molenaar (Eds.), *Handbook of child psychology and developmental science: Vol. 1. Theory and method* (pp. 1–8). Hoboken, NJ: Wiley.

Owen, C. G., Whincup, P. H., Kaye, S. J., Martin, R. M., Smith, G. D., Cook, D. G., et al. (2008). Does initial breastfeeding lead to lower blood cholesterol in adult life? A quantitative review of the evidence. *American Journal of Clinical Nutrition, 88,* 305–314.

Owens, E. B., Cardoos, S. L., & Hinshaw, S. P. (2015). Developmental progression and gender differences among individuals with ADHD. In R. A. Barkley (Ed.), *Attention-deficit hyperactivity disorder: A handbook for diagnosis and treatment* (pp. 223–255). New York: Guilford Press.

Oyserman, D., Bybee, D., Mowbray, C., & Hart-Johnson, T. (2005). When mothers have serious mental health problems: Parenting as a proximal mediator. *Journal of Adolescence, 28,* 443–463.

Özçaliskan, S. (2005). On learning to draw the distinction between physical and metaphorical motion: Is metaphor an early emerging cognitive and linguistic capacity? *Journal of Child Language, 32,* 291–318.

P

Padilla-Walker, L. M., Harper, J. M., & Jensen, A. C. (2010). Self-regulation as mediators between parenting and adolescents' prosocial behaviors. *Journal of Research on Adolescence, 22,* 400–408.

Páez, M., & Hunter, C. (2015). Bilingualism and language learning for immigrant-origin children and youth. In C. Suárez-Orozco, M. Abo-Zena, & A. K. Marks (Eds.), *Transitions: The development of children of immigrants* (pp. 165–183). New York: New York University Press.

Pahlke, E., Bigler, R. S., & Suizzo, M.-A. (2012). Relations between colorblind socialization and children's racial bias: Evidence from European American mothers and their preschool children. *Child Development, 83,* 1164–1179.

Palkovitz, R., Fagan, J., & Hull, J. (2013). Coparenting and children's well-being. In N. Cabrera and C. S. LeMonda (Eds.), *Handbook of father involvement: Multidisciplinary perspectives* (2nd ed., pp. 202–219). New York: Routledge.

Pan, H. W. (1994). Children's play in Taiwan. In J. L. Roopnarine, J. E. Johnson, & F. H. Hooper (Eds.), *Children's play in diverse cultures* (pp. 31–50). Albany, NY: SUNY Press.

Paradis, J., Genesee, F., & Crago, M. B. (2011). *Dual language development and disorders: A handbook on bilingualism and learning* (2nd ed.). Baltimore, MD: Brookes.

Paradise, R., & Rogoff, B. (2009). Side by side: Learning by observing and pitching in. *Ethos, 27,* 102–138.

Paris, S. G., & Paris, A. H. (2006). Assessments of early reading. In K. A. Renninger & I. E. Sigel (Eds.), *Handbook of child psychology: Vol. 4. Child psychology in practice* (6th ed., pp. 48–74). Hoboken, NJ: Wiley.

Parish-Morris, J., Golinkoff, R. M., & Hirsh-Pasek, K. (2013). From coo to code: A brief story of language development. In P. D. Zelazo (Ed.), *Oxford handbook of developmental psychology: Vol. 1. Body and mind* (pp. 867–908). New York: Oxford University Press.

Parish-Morris, J., Pruden, S., Ma, W., Hirsh-Pasek, K., & Golinkoff, R. M. (2010). A world of relations: Relational words. In B. Malt & P. Wolf (Eds.), *Words and the mind: How words capture human experience* (pp. 219–242). New York: Oxford University Press.

Parke, R. D. (2002). Fathers and families. In M. H. Bornstein (Ed.), *Handbook of parenting*: Vol. 3 (2nd ed., pp. 27–73). Mahwah, NJ: Erlbaum.

Parke, R. D., Simpkins, S. D., McDowell, D. J., Kim, M., Killian, C., Dennis, J., Flyr, M. L., Wild, M., & Rah, Y. (2004). Relative contributions of families and peers to children's social development. In P. K. Smith & C. H. Hart (Eds.), *Blackwell handbook of childhood social development* (pp. 156–177). Malden, MA: Blackwell.

Parker, J. G., Low, C. M., Walker, A. R., & Gamm, B. K. (2005). Friendship jealousy in young adolescents: Individual differences and links to sex, self-esteem, aggression, and social adjustment. *Developmental Psychology, 41,* 235–250.

Parten, M. (1932). Social participation among preschool children. *Journal of Abnormal and Social Psychology, 27,* 243–269.

Pascalis, O., de Haan, M., & Nelson, C. A. (2002). Is face processing species-specific during the first year of life? *Science, 296,* 1321–1323.

Pasley, K., & Garneau, C. (2012). Remarriage and stepfamily life. In F. Walsh (Ed.), *Normal family processes: Growing diversity and complexity* (4th ed., pp. 149–171). New York: Guilford.

Patel, S., Gaylord, S., & Fagen, J. (2013). Generalization of deferred imitation in 6-, 9-, and 12-month-old infants using visual and auditory memory contexts. *Infant Behavior and Development, 36,* 25–31.

Pathman, T., Larkina, M., Burch, M. M., & Bauer, P. J. (2013). Young children's memory for the times of personal past events. *Journal of Cognition and Development, 14,* 120–140.

Patterson, C. J. (2013). Family lives of lesbian and gay adults. In G. W. Peterson & K. R. Bush (Eds.), *Handbook of marriage and family* (pp. 659–681). New York: Springer.

Patterson, G. R., & Fisher, P. A. (2002). Recent developments in our understanding of parenting: Bidirectional effects, causal models, and the search for parsimony. In M. H. Bornstein (Ed.), *Handbook of parenting* (Vol. 5, pp. 59–88). Mahwah, NJ: Erlbaum.

Patton, G. C., Coffey, C., Carlin, J. B., Sawyer, S. M., Williams, J., Olsson, C. A., et al. (2011). Overweight and obesity between adolescence and young adulthood: A 10-year prospective cohort study. *Journal of Adolescent Health, 48,* 275–280.

Paukner, A., Ferrari, P. F., & Suomi, S. J. (2011). Delayed imitation of lipsmacking gestures by infant rhesus macaques (*Macaca mulatta*). *PLOS ONE 6*(12), e28848.

Paulson, J. F., & Bazemore, S. D. (2010). Prenatal and postpartum depression in fathers and its association with maternal depression: A metal-analysis. *JAMA, 303,* 1961–1969.

Paulussen-Hoogeboom, M. C., Stams, G. J. J. M., Hermanns, J. M. A., & Peetsma, T. T. D. (2007). Child negative emotionality and parenting from infancy to preschool: A meta-analytic review. *Developmental Psychology, 43,* 438–453.

Pedersen, S., Vitaro, F., Barker, E. D., & Anne, I. H. (2007). The timing of middle-childhood peer rejection and friendship: Linking early behavior to early adolescent adjustment. *Child Development, 78,* 1037–1051.

Pederson, D. R., & Moran, G. (1996). Expressions of the attachment relationship outside of the Strange Situation. *Child Development, 67,* 915–927.

Peirano, P., Algarin, C., & Uauy, R. (2003). Sleep–wake states and their regulatory mechanisms throughout early human development. *Journal of Pediatrics, 43,* S70–S79.

Pellegrini, A. D. (2003). Perceptions and functions of play and real fighting in early adolescence. *Child Development, 74,* 1522–1533.

Pellegrini, A. D. (2006). The development and function of rough-and-tumble play in childhood and adolescence: A sexual selection theory. In A. Göncü & S. Gaskins (Eds.), *Play and development: Evolutionary, sociocultural, and functional perspectives* (pp. 77–98). Mahwah, NJ: Erlbaum.

Peltonen, K., & Punamäki, R.-L. (2010). Preventive interventions among children exposed to trauma of armed conflict: A literature review. *Aggressive Behavior, 36,* 95–116.

Pennington, B. F. (2015). Atypical cognitive development. In L. S. Liben & U. Müller (Eds.), *Handbook of child psychology and developmental science: Vol. 2. Cognitive processes* (7th ed., pp. 995–1042). Hoboken, NJ: Wiley.

Pennisi, E. (2012). ENCODE Project writes eulogy for junk DNA. *Science, 337,* 1160–1161.

Penny, H., & Haddock, G. (2007). Anti-fat prejudice among children: The 'mere proximity' effect in 5–10 year olds. *Journal of Experimental Social Psychology, 43,* 678–683.

Peralta de Mendoza, O. A., & Salsa, A. M. (2003). Instruction in early comprehension and use of a symbol–referent relation. *Cognitive Development, 18,* 269–284.

Perego, G., Caputi, M., & Ogliari, A. (2016). Neurobiological correlates of psychosocial deprivation in children: A systematic review of neuroscientific contributions. *Child and Youth Care Forum, 45,* 329–352.

Perez, J. D., Rubinstein, N. D., & Dulac, C. (2016). New perspectives on genomic imprinting, an essential and multifaceted mode of epigenetic control in the developing and adult brain. *Annual Review of Neuroscience, 39,* 347–384.

Perlmutter, M. (1984). Continuities and discontinuities in early human memory: Paradigms, processes, and performances. In R. V. Kail, Jr., & N. R. Spear (Eds.), *Comparative perspectives on the development of memory* (pp. 253–287). Hillsdale, NJ: Erlbaum.

Perone, S., Madole, K. L., Ross-Sheehy, S., Carey, M., & Oakes, L. M. (2008). The relation between infants' activity with objects and attention to object appearance. *Developmental Psychology, 44,* 1242–1248.

Perroud, N., Rutembesa, E., Paoloni-Giacobino, A., Mutabaruka, J., Mutesa, L., Stenz, L., et al. (2014). The Tutsi genocide and transgenerational transmission of maternal stress: Epigenetics and biology of the HPA axis. *World Journal of Biological Psychiatry, 15,* 334–345.

Peshkin, A. (1997). *Places of memory: Whiteman's schools and Native American communities.* Mahwah, NJ: Erlbaum.

Pesonen, A.-K., Räikkönen, K., Heinonen, K., & Komsi, N. (2008). A transactional model of temperamental development: Evidence of a relationship between child temperament and maternal stress over five years. *Social Development, 17,* 326–340.

Peters, R. D. (2005). A community-based approach to promoting resilience in young children, their families, and their neighborhoods. In R. D. Paters, B. Leadbeater, & R. J. McMahon (Eds.), *Resilience in children, families, and communities: Linking context to practice and policy* (pp. 157–176). New York: Kluwer Academic.

Peters, R. D., Bradshaw, A. J., Petrunka, K., Nelson, G., Herry, Y., Craig, W. M., et al. (2010). The Better Beginnings, Better Futures Project: Findings from grade 3 to grade 9. *Monographs of the Society for Research in Child Development, 75*(3, Serial No. 297).

Peters, R. D., Petrunka, K., & Arnold, R. (2003). The Better Beginnings, Better Futures Project: A universal, comprehensive, community-based prevention approach for primary school children and their families. *Journal of Clinical Child and Adolescent Psychology, 32,* 215–227.

Peterson, C., Warren, K. L., & Short, M. M. (2011). Infantile amnesia across the years: A 2-year follow-up of children's earliest memories. *Child Development, 82,* 1092–1105.

Petitto, L. A., Holowka, S., Sergio, L. E., Levy, B., & Ostry, D. J. (2004). Baby hands that move to the rhythm of language: Hearing babies acquiring sign languages babble silently on the hands. *Cognition, 93,* 43–73.

Petitto, L. A., & Marentette, P. F. (1991). Babbling in the manual mode: Evidence for the ontogeny of language. *Science, 251,* 1493–1496.

Petrill, S. A., & Deater-Deckard, K. (2004). The heritability of general cognitive ability: A within family adoption design. *Intelligence, 32,* 403–409.

Pettigrew, T. F., & Tropp, L. R. (2006). A meta-analytic test of intergroup contact theory. *Journal of Personality and Social Psychology, 90,* 751–783.

Pettit, G. S., Brown, E. G., Mize, J., & Lindsey, E. (1998). Mothers' and fathers' socializing behaviors in three contexts: Links with children's peer competence. *Merrill-Palmer Quarterly, 44,* 173–193.

Pew Research Center. (2015). *Modern parenthood: Roles of moms and dads converge as they balance work and family.* Retrieved from www.pewsocialtrends.org/2013/03/14/modern-parenthood-roles-of-moms-and-dads-converge-as-they-balance-work-and-family

Pezzella, F. S., Thornberry, T. P., & Smith, C. A. (2016). Race socialization and parenting styles: Links to delinquency for African American and White adolescents. *Youth Violence and Juvenile Justice, 14,* 448–467.

Pfeifer, J. H., Ruble, D. N., Bachman, M. A., Alvarez, J. M., Cameron, J. A., & Fuligni, A. J. (2007). Social identities and intergroup bias in immigrant and nonimmigrant children. *Developmental Psychology, 43,* 496–507.

Pfeiffer, S. I., & Yermish, A. (2014). Gifted children. In L. Grossman & S. Walfish (Eds.), *Translating psychological research into practice* (pp. 57–64). New York: Springer.

Philbrook, L. E., & Teti, D. M. (2016). Bidirectional associations between bedtime parenting and infant sleep: Parenting quality, parenting practices, and their interaction. *Journal of Family Psychology, 30,* 431–441.

Phillips, D. A., & Lowenstein, A. E. (2011). Early care, education, and child development. *Annual Review of Psychology, 62,* 483–500.

Phillips, D., Gormley, W., & Anderson, S. (2016). The effects of Tulsa's CAP Head Start program on middle-school academic outcomes and progress. *Developmental Psychology, 52,* 1247–1261.

Piaget, J. (1926). *The language and thought of the child.* New York: Harcourt, Brace & World. (Original work published 1923)

Piaget, J. (1930). *The child's conception of the world.* New York: Harcourt, Brace, & World. (Original work published 1926)

Piaget, J. (1951). *Play, dreams, and imitation in childhood.* New York: Norton. (Original work published 1945)

Piaget, J. (1952). *The origins of intelligence in children.* New York: International Universities Press. (Original work published 1936)

Piaget, J. (1971). *Biology and knowledge.* Chicago: University of Chicago Press.

Pierroutsakos, S. L., & Troseth, G. L. (2003). Video verité: Infants' manual investigation of objects on video. *Infant Behavior and Development, 26,* 183–199.

Piirto, J. (2007). *Talented children and adults* (3rd ed.). Waco, TX: Prufrock Press.

Pike, A., & Oliver, B. R. (2016). Child behavior and sibling relationship quality: A cross-lagged analysis. *Journal of Family Psychology, 31,* 250–255.

Ping, R. M., & Goldin-Meadow, S. (2008). Hands in the air: Using ungrounded iconic gestures to teach children conservation of quantity. *Developmental Psychology, 44,* 1277–1287.

Pinker, S. (1999). *Words and rules: The ingredients of language.* New York: Basic Books.

Pinkerton, R., Oriá, R. B., Lima, A. A., Rogawski, E. T., Oriá, M. O., Patrick, P. D., et al. (2016). Early childhood diarrhea predicts cognitive delays in later childhood independently of malnutrition. *American Journal of Tropical Medicine and Hygiene, 95,* 1004–1010.

Plante, I., Théoret, M., & Favreau, O. E. (2009). Student gender stereotypes: Contrasting the perceived maleness and femaleness of mathematics and language. *Educational Psychology, 29,* 385–405.

Platt, M. P. W. (2014). Neonatology and obstetric anaesthesia. *Archives of Disease in Childhood—Fetal and Neonatal Edition, 99,* F98.

Pleck, J. H. (2012). Integrating father involvement in parenting research. *Parenting: Science and Practice, 12,* 243–253.

Plomin, R., DeFries, J. C., & Knopik, V. S. (2013). *Behavioral genetics* (6th ed.). New York: Worth.

Plomin, R., DeFries, J. C., Knopik, V. S., & Neiderhiser, J. M. (2016). Top 10 replicated findings from behavioral genetics. *Psychological Science, 11,* 3–23.

Plomin, R., & Spinath, F. M. (2004). Intelligence: Genetics, genes, and genomics. *Journal of Personality and Social Psychology, 86,* 112–129.

Plucker, J. A., & Makel, M. C. (2010). Assessment of creativity. In J. C. Kaufman & R. J. Sternberg (Eds.), *Cambridge handbook of creativity* (pp. 48–73). New York: Cambridge University Press.

Pluess, M., & Belsky, J. (2011). Prenatal programming of postnatal plasticity? *Development and Psychopathology, 23,* 29–38.

Poehlmann, J., Schwichtenberg, A. J. M., Shlafer, R. J., Hahn, E., Bianchi, J.-P., & Warner, R. (2011). Emerging self-regulation in toddlers born preterm or low birth weight: Differential susceptibility to parenting. *Developmental and Psychopathology, 23,* 177–193.

Polakowski, L. L., Akinbami, L. J., & Mendola, P. (2009). Prenatal smoking cessation and the risk of delivering preterm and small-for-gestational-age newborns. *Obstetrics and Gynecology, 114,* 318–325.

Polanska, K., Jurewicz, J., & Hanke, W. (2013). Review of current evidence on the impact of pesticides, polychlorinated biphenyls and selected metals on attention deficit/hyperactivity disorder in children. *International Journal of Occupational Medicine and Environmental Health, 26,* 16–38.

Polderman, T. J. C., de Geus, J. C., Hoekstra, R. A., Bartels, M., van Leeuwen, M., Verhulst, F. C., et al. (2009). Attention problems, inhibitory control, and intelligence index overlapping genetic factors: A study in 9-, 12-, and 18-year-old twins. *Neuropsychology, 23,* 381–391.

Pomerantz, E. M., Grolnick, W. S., & Price, C. E. (2013). The role of parents in how children approach achievement: A dynamic process perspective. In A. J. Elliott & C. J. Dweck (Eds.), *Handbook of confidence and motivation* (pp. 259–278). New York: Guilford.

Pomerantz, E. M., & Kempner, S. G. (2013). Mothers' daily person and process praise: Implications for children's theory of intelligence and motivation. *Developmental Psychology, 13,* 2040–2046.

Pomerantz, E. M., & Saxon, J. L. (2001). Conceptions of ability as stable and self-evaluative processes: A longitudinal examination. *Child Development, 72,* 152–173.

Pong, S., Johnston, J., & Chen, V. (2010). Authoritarian parenting and Asian adolescent school performance. *International Journal of Behavioral Development, 34,* 62–72.

Pong, S., & Landale, N. S. (2012). Academic achievement of legal immigrants' children: The roles of parents' pre- and postmigration characteristics in origin-group differences. *Child Development, 83,* 1543–1559.

Pons, F., Lawson, J., Harris, P. L., & de Rosnay, M. (2003). Individual differences in children's emotion understanding: Effects of age and language. *Scandinavian Journal of Psychology, 44,* 347–353.

Poole, K. L., Van Lieshout, R. J., & Schmidt, L. A. (2017). Exploring relations between shyness and social anxiety disorder: The role of sociability. *Personality and Individual Differences, 110,* 55–59.

Portes, A., & Rumbaut, R. G. (2005). Introduction: The second generation and the Children of Immigrants Longitudinal Study. *Ethnic and Racial Studies, 28,* 983–999.

Posner, M. I., & Rothbart, M. K. (2007). Temperament and learning. In M. I. Posner & M. K. Rothbart (Eds.), *Educating the human brain* (pp. 121–146). Washington, DC: American Psychological Association.

Potter, D. (2012). Same-sex parent families and children's academic achievement. *Journal of Marriage and Family, 74,* 556–571.

Poulin-Dubois, D., Serbin, L. A., Eichstedt, J. A., Sen, M. G., & Beissel, C. F. (2002). Men don't put on make-up: Toddlers' knowledge of the gender stereotyping of household activities. *Social Development, 11,* 166–181.

Powell, L. J., & Carey, L. J. (2017). Executive function depletion in children and its impact on theory of mind. *Cognition, 164,* 150–162.

Preuss, T. M. (2012). Human brain evolution: From gene discovery to phenotype discovery. *Proceedings of the National Academy of Sciences, 109*(Suppl. 1), 10709–10716.

Principe, G. F. (2011). *Your brain on childhood: The unexpected side effects of classrooms, ballparks, family rooms, and the minivan.* Amherst, NY: Prometheus Books.

Proctor, B. D., Semega, J. L., & Kollar, M. A. (2016). Income and poverty in the United States: 2016. *Current Population Reports,* P60–259. Retrieved from www.census.gov/content/dam/Census/library/publications/2016/demo/p60-256.pdf

Proctor, M. H., Moore, L. L., Gao, D., Cupples, L. A., Bradlee, M. L., Hood, M. Y., & Ellison, R. C. (2003). Television viewing and change in body fat from preschool to early adolescence: The Framingham Children's Study. *International Journal of Obesity, 27,* 827–833.

Programme for International Student Assessment. (2017). *PISA data explorer: 2015 results.* Retrieved from http://www.oecd.org/pisa/data

Proietti, E., Röösli, M., Frey, U., & Latzin, P. (2013). Air pollution during pregnancy and neonatal outcome: A review. *Journal of Aerosol Medicine and Pulmonary Drug Delivery, 26,* 9–23.

Proulx, M., & Poulin, F. (2013). Stability and change in kindergartners' friendships: Examination of links with social functioning. *Social Development, 22,* 111–125.

Pruden, S. M., Hirsh-Pasek, K., Golinkoff, R. M., & Hennon, E. A. (2006). The birth of words: Ten-month-olds learn words through perceptual salience. *Child Development, 77,* 266–280.

Pryor, J. (2014). *Stepfamilies: A global perspective on research, policy, and practice.* New York: Routledge.

Pugliese, C. E., Anthony, L. G., Strang, J. F., Dudley, K., Wallace, G. L., Naiman, D. Q., et al. (2016). Longitudinal examination of adaptive behavior in autism spectrum disorders: Influence of executive function. *Journal of Autism and Developmental Disorders, 13,* 467–477.

Puhl, R. M., & Latner, J. D. (2007). Stigma, obesity, and the health of the nation's children. *Psychological Bulletin, 133,* 557–580.

Pujol, J., Soriano-Mas, C., Ortiz, H., Sebastián-Gallés, N., Losilla, J. M., & Deus, J. (2006). Myelination of language-related areas in the developing brain. *Neurology, 66,* 339–343.

Puma, M., Bell, S., Cook, R., Heid, C., Broene, P., Jenkins, F., et al. (2012). *Third grade follow-up to the Head Start Impact Study final report* (OPRE Report #2012-45b). Washington, DC: U.S. Department of Health and Human Services.

Punamaki, R. L. (2006). Ante- and perinatal factors and child characteristics predicting parenting experience among formerly infertile couples during the child's first year: A controlled study. *Journal of Family Psychology, 20,* 670–679.

Putallaz, M., Grimes, C. L., Foster, K. J., Kupersmidt, J. B., Coie, J. D., & Dearing, K. (2007). Overt and relational aggression and victimization: Multiple perspectives within the school setting. *Journal of School Psychology, 45,* 523–547.

Putnam, S. P., Sanson, A. V., & Rothbart, M. K. (2000). Child temperament and parenting. In V. J. Molfese & D. L. Molfese (Eds.), *Temperament and personality across the life span* (pp. 255–277). Mahwah, NJ: Erlbaum.

Q

Qouta, S. R., Palosaari, E., Diab, M., & Punamäki, R.-L. (2012). Intervention effectiveness among war-affected children: A cluster randomized controlled trial on improving mental health. *Journal of Traumatic Stress, 25,* 288–298.

Qu, Y., & Pomerantz, E. M. (2015). Divergent school trajectories in early adolescence in the United States and China: An examination of underlying mechanisms. *Journal of Youth and Adolescence, 44,* 2095–2109.

Quinn, P. C. (2008). In defense of core competencies, quantitative change, and continuity. *Child Development, 79,* 1633–1638.

Quinn, P. C., Kelly, D. J., Lee, K., Pascalis, O., & Slater, A. (2008). Preference for attractive faces extends beyond conspecifics. *Developmental Science, 11,* 76–83.

R

Raabe, T., & Beelmann, A. (2011). Development of ethnic, racial, and national prejudice in childhood and adolescence: A multinational meta-analysis of age differences. *Child Development, 82,* 1715–1737.

Raby, K. L., Steele, R. D., Carlson, E. A., & Sroufe, L. (2015). Continuities and changes in infant attachment patterns across two generations. *Attachment & Human Development, 17,* 414–428.

Racz, S. J., McMahon, R. J., & Luthar, S. S. (2011). Risky behavior in affluent youth: Examining the co-occurrence and consequences of multiple problem behaviors. *Journal of Child and Family Studies, 20,* 120–128.

Radesky, J. S., Kistin, C. J., Zuckerman, B., Nitzberg, K., Gross, J., Kaplan-Sanoff, M., et al. (2014). Patterns of mobile device use by caregivers and children during meals in fast food restaurants. *Pediatrics, 133,* e843–e849.

Raikes, H. A., Robinson, J. L., Bradley, R. H., Raikes, H. H., & Ayoub, C. C. (2007). Developmental trends in self-regulation among low-income toddlers. *Social Development, 16,* 128–149.

Raikes, H. H., Chazan-Cohen, R., Love, J. M., & Brooks-Gunn, J. (2010). Early Head Start impacts at age 3 and a description of the age 5 follow-up study. In A. J. Reynolds, A. J. Rolnick, M. M. Englund, & J. Temple (Eds.), *Childhood programs and practices in the first decade of life: A human capital integration* (pp. 99–118). New York: Cambridge University Press.

Rakison, D. H. (2005). Developing knowledge of objects' motion properties in infancy. *Cognition, 96,* 183–214.

Rakison, D. H. (2010). Perceptual categorization and concepts. In J. G. Bremner & T. D. Wachs (Eds.), *Wiley-Blackwell handbook of infant development* (2nd ed., pp. 243–270). Oxford, UK: Wiley-Blackwell.

Rakison, D. H., & Lawson, C. A. (2013). Categorization. In P. D. Zelazo (Ed.), *Oxford handbook of developmental psychology: Vol. 1. Body and mind* (pp. 591–627). New York: Oxford University Press.

Rakoczy, H., Tomasello, M., & Striano, T. (2004). Young children know that trying is not pretending: A test of the "behaving-as-if" construal of children's early concept of pretense. *Developmental Psychology, 40,* 388–399.

Rakoczy, H., Tomasello, M., & Striano, T. (2005). How children turn objects into symbols: A cultural learning account. In L. Namy (Ed.), *Symbol use and symbol representation* (pp. 67–97). New York: Erlbaum.

Raley, R. K., Sweeney, M. M., & Wondra, D. (2015). The growing racial and ethnic divide in U.S. marriage patterns. *Future of Children, 25,* 89–105.

Ramachandrappa, A., & Jain, L. (2008). Elective cesarean section: Its impact on neonatal respiratory outcome. *Clinics in Perinatology, 35,* 373–393.

Ramani, G. B., Siegler, R. S., & Hitti, A. (2012). Taking it to the classroom: Number board games as a small group learning activity. *Journal of Educational Psychology, 104,* 661–672.

Ramchandani, P. G., Stein, A., O'Connor, T. G., Heron, J., Murray, L., & Evans, J. (2008). Depression in men in the postnatal period and later child psychopathology: A population cohort study. *Journal of the American Academy of Child and Adolescent Psychiatry, 47,* 390–398.

Ramey, C. T., Ramey, S. L., & Lanzi, R. G. (2006). Children's health and education. In K. A. Renninger & I. E. Sigel (Eds.), *Handbook of child psychology: Vol. 4. Child psychology in practice* (6th ed., pp. 864–892). Hoboken, NJ: Wiley.

Ramirez, N. F., Ramirez, R. R., Clarke, M., Taulu, S., & Kuhl, P. K. (2017). Speech discrimination in 11-month-old bilingual and monolingual infants: A magnetoencephalography study. *Developmental Science, 20,* e12427.

Ramos, M. C., Guerin, D. W., Gottfried, A. W., Bathurst, K., & Oliver, P. H. (2005). Family conflict and children's behavior problems: The moderating role of child temperament. *Structural Equation Modeling, 12,* 278–298.

Ramsey-Rennels, J. L., & Langlois, J. H. (2006). Differential processing of female and male faces. *Current Directions in Psychological Science, 15,* 59–62.

Ramus, F. (2002). Language discrimination by newborns: Teasing apart phonotactic, rhythmic, and intonational cues. *Annual Review of Language Acquisition, 2,* 85–115.

Rasmus, S., Allen, J., & Ford, T. (2014). "Where I have to learn the ways how to live:" Youth resilience in a Yup'ik village in Alaska. *Transcultural Psychiatry, 51,* 735–756.

Rasmussen, C., Ho, E., & Bisanz, J. (2003). Use of the mathematical principle of inversion in young children. *Journal of Experimental Child Psychology, 85,* 89–102.

Rathunde, K., & Csikszentmihalyi, M. (2005). The social context of middle school: Teachers, friends, and activities in Montessori and traditional school environments. *Elementary School Journal, 106,* 59–79.

Rayner, K., Pollatsek, A., & Starr, M. S. (2003). Reading. In A. F. Healy & R. W. Proctor (Eds.), *Handbook of psychology: Experimental psychology* (Vol. 4, pp. 549–574). New York: Wiley.

Raz, S., Piercy, J. C., Heitzer, A. M., Peters, B. N., Newman, J. B, DeBastos, A. K., et al. (2016). Neuropsychological functioning in preterm-born twins and singletons at preschool age. *Journal of the International Neuropsychological Society, 22,* 865–877.

Reed, C. E., & Fenton, S. E. (2013). Exposure to diethylstilbestrol during sensitive life stages: A legacy of heritable health effects. *Birth Defects Research. Part C, Embryo Today: Reviews, 99,* 134–146.

Reese, E. (2002). A model of the origins of autobiographical memory. In J. W. Fagen & H. Hayne (Eds.), *Progress in Infancy Research* (Vol. 2, pp. 215–60). Mahwah, NJ: Erlbaum.

Reis, S. M. (2004). We can't change what we don't recognize: Understanding the special needs of gifted females. In S. Baum (Ed.), *Twice-exceptional and special populations of gifted students* (pp. 67–80). Thousand Oaks, CA: Corwin Press.

Reiss, D. (2003). Child effects on family systems: Behavioral genetic strategies. In A. C. Crouter & A. Booth (Eds.), *Children's influence on family dynamics: The neglected side of family relationships* (pp. 3–36). Mahwah, NJ: Erlbaum.

Rentner, T. L., Dixon, L. D., & Lengel, L. (2012). Critiquing fetal alcohol syndrome health communication campaigns targeted to American Indians. *Journal of Health Communication, 17,* 6–21.

Repacholi, B. M., & Gopnik, A. (1997). Early reasoning about desires: Evidence from 14- and 18-month-olds. *Developmental Psychology, 33,* 12–21.

Resnick, M., & Silverman, B. (2005). *Some reflections on designing construction kits for kids.* Proceedings of the Conference on Interaction Design and Children, Boulder, CO.

Reynolds, R. M. (2013). Programming effects of glucocorticoids. *Clinical Obstetrics and Gynecology, 56,* 602–609.

Rhoades, B. L., Greenberg, M. T., & Domitrovich, C. E. (2009). The contribution of inhibitory control to preschoolers' social-emotional competence. *Journal of Applied Developmental Psychology, 30,* 310–320.

Richardson, H. L., Walker, A. M., & Horne, R. S. C. (2008). Sleep position alters arousal processes maximally at the high-risk age for sudden infant death syndrome. *Journal of Sleep Research, 17,* 450–457.

Richardson, K., & Norgate, S. H. (2006). A critical analysis of IQ studies of adopted children. *Human Development, 49,* 339–350.

Rideout, V., & Hamel, E. (2006). *The media family: Electronic media in the lives of infants, toddlers, preschoolers and their parents.* Menlo Park, CA: Henry J. Kaiser Family Foundation.

Rideout, V. J., Foehr, U. G., & Roberts, D. F. (2010). *Generation M2: Media in the lives of 8- to 18-year-olds.* Menlo Park. CA: Henry J. Kaiser Family Foundation.

Rieffe, C., Terwogt, M. M., & Cowan, R. (2005). Children's understanding of mental states as causes of emotions. *Infant and Child Development, 14,* 259–272.

Riggins, T., Miller, N. C., Bauer, P., Georgieff, M. K., & Nelson, C. A. (2009). Consequences of low neonatal iron status due to maternal diabetes mellitus on explicit memory performance in childhood. *Developmental Neuropsychology, 34,* 762–779.

Rijlaarsdam, J., Stevens, G. W. J. M., van der Ende, J., Arends, L. R., Hofman, A., Jaddoe, V. W. V., et al. (2012). A brief observational instrument for the assessment of infant home environment: Development and psychometric testing. *International Journal of Methods in Psychiatric Research, 21,* 195–204.

Rindermann, H., & Ceci, S. J. (2008). *Education policy and country outcomes in international cognitive competence studies.* Graz, Austria: Institute of Psychology, Karl-Franzens-University Graz.

Ripley, A. (2013). *The smartest kids in the world: And how they got that way.* New York: Simon and Schuster.

Ripple, C. H., & Zigler, E. (2003). Research, policy, and the federal role in prevention initiatives for children. *American Psychologist, 58,* 482–490.

Ristic, J., & Enns, J. T. (2015). Attentional development. In L. S. Liben & U. Müller (Eds.), *Handbook of child psychology and developmental science: Vol. 2. Cognitive processes* (pp. 158–202). Hoboken, NJ: Wiley.

Ristori, J., & Steensma, T. D. (2016). Gender dysphoria in childhood. *International Review of Psychiatry, 28,* 13–20.

Ritz, B., Oiu, J., Lee, P. C., Lurmann, F., Penfold, B., Erin Weiss, R., et al. (2014). Prenatal air pollution exposure and ultrasound measures of fetal growth in Los Angeles, California. *Environmental Research, 130,* 7–13.

Rivkees, S. A. (2003). Developing circadian rhythmicity in infants. *Pediatrics, 112,* 373–381.

Roben, C. K. P., Bass, A. J., Moore, G. A., Murray-Kolb, L., Tan, P. Z., Gilmore, R. O., et al. (2012). Let me go: The influences of crawling experience and temperament on the development of anger expression. *Infancy, 17,* 558–577.

Roberts, B. W., & DelVecchio, W. E. (2000). The rank-order consistency of personality traits from childhood to old age: A quantitative review of longitudinal studies. *Psychological Bulletin, 126,* 3–25.

Roberts, D. F., Foehr, U. G., & Rideout, V. (2005). *Generation M: Media in the lives of 8–18 year olds.* Menlo Park, CA: Henry J. Kaiser Family Foundation.

Roberts, J. E., Burchinal, M. R., & Durham, M. (1999). Parents' report of vocabulary and grammatical development of American preschoolers: Child and environment associations. *Child Development, 70,* 92–106.

Robertson, J. (2008). Stepfathers in families. In J. Pryor (Ed.), *International handbook of stepfamilies: Policy and practice in legal, research, and clinical environments* (pp. 125–150). Hoboken, NJ: Wiley.

Robinson, C. C., Anderson, G. T., Porter, C. L., Hart, C. H., & Wouden-Miller, M. (2003). Sequential transition patterns of preschoolers' social interactions during child-initiated play: Is parallel-aware play a bi-directional bridge to other play states? *Early Childhood Research Quarterly, 18,* 3–21.

Robinson, G. E. (2015). Controversies about the use of antidepressants in pregnancy. *Journal of Nervous and Mental Disease, 203,* 159–163.

Robinson, S., Goddard, L., Dritschel, B., Wisley, M., & Howlin, P. (2009). Executive functions in children with autism spectrum disorders. *Brain and Cognition, 71,* 362–368.

Robinson-Cimpian, J. P., Lubienski, S. T., Ganley, C. M., & Copur-Gencturk, Y. (2014). Teachers' perceptions of students' mathematics proficiency may exacerbate early gender gaps in achievement. *Developmental Psychology, 50,* 1262–1281.

Robinson-Zañartu, C., & Carlson, J. (2013). Dynamic assessment. In K. F. Geisinger (Ed.), *APA handbook of testing and assessment in psychology: Vol. 3. Testing and assessment in school psychology and education* (pp. 149–168). Washington, DC: American Psychological Association.

Rocha, N. A. C. F., de Campos, A. C., Silva, F. P. dos Santos, & Tudella, E. (2013). Adaptive actions of young infants in the task of reaching for objects. *Developmental Psychobiology, 55,* 275–282.

Rochat, P. (1989). Object manipulation and exploration in 2- to 5-month-old infants. *Developmental Psychology, 25,* 871–884.

Rochat, P. (1998). Self-perception and action in infancy. *Experimental Brain Research, 123,* 102–109.

Rochat, P. (2013). Self-conceptualizing in development. In P. Zelazo (Ed.), *Oxford handbook of developmental psychology* (Vol. 2, pp. 378–397). New York: Oxford University Press.

Rochat, P., & Goubet, N. (1995). Development of sitting and reaching in 5- to 6-month-old infants. *Infant Behavior and Development, 18,* 53–68.

Rochat, P., & Hespos, S. J. (1997). Differential rooting responses by neonates: Evidence for an early sense of self. *Early Development and Parenting, 6,* 105–112.

Rochat, P., & Striano, T. (2002). Who's in the mirror? Self–other discrimination in specular images by four- and nine-month-old infants. *Infant and Child Development, 11,* 289–303.

Roche, K. M., Ensminger, M. E., & Cherlin, A. J. (2007). Variations in parenting and adolescent outcomes among African American and Latino families living in low-income, urban areas. *Journal of Family Issues, 28,* 882–909.

Rodgers, J. L., & Wänström, L. (2007). Identification of a Flynn effect in the NLSY: Moving from the center to the boundaries. *Intelligence, 35,* 187–196.

Rodriguez, E. M., Dunn, M. J., & Compas, B. E. (2012). Cancer-related sources of stress for children with cancer and their parents. *Journal of Pediatric Psychology, 37,* 185–197.

Roelfsema, N. M., Hop, W. C., Boito, S. M., & Wladimiroff, J. W. (2004). Three-dimensional sonographic measurement of normal fetal brain volume during the second half of pregnancy. *American Journal of Obstetrics and Gynecology, 190,* 275–280.

Rogoff, B. (2003). *The cultural nature of human development.* New York: Oxford University Press.

Rogoff, B., Correa-Chávez, M., & Silva, K. G. (2011). Cultural variation in children's attention and learning. In M. A. Gernsbacher, R. W. Pew, L. M. Hough, & J. R. Pomerantz (Eds.), *Psychology and the real world: Essays illustrating fundamental contributions to society* (pp. 154–163). New York: Worth.

Rohner, R. P., & Veneziano, R. A. (2001). The importance of father love: History and contemporary evidence. *Review of General Psychology, 5,* 382–405.

Roid, G. (2003). *The Stanford-Binet Intelligence Scales, Fifth Edition, interpretive manual.* Itasca, IL: Riverside Publishing.

Roid, G. H., & Pomplun, M. (2012). The Stanford-Binet Intelligence Scales, Fifth Edition. In D. P. Flanagan & P. L. Harrison (Eds.), *Contemporary intellectual assessment: Theories, tests and issues* (pp. 249–268). New York: Guilford.

Roisman, R., & Fraley, C. (2006). The limits of genetic influence: A behavior-genetic analysis of infant–caregiver relationship quality and temperament. *Child Development, 77,* 1656–1667.

Roizen, N. J. (2013). Down syndrome. In M. L. Matshaw, N. J. Roizen, & G. R. Lotrecchiano (Eds.), *Children with disabilities* (pp. 307–318). Baltimore: Paul H. Brookes.

Romano, E., Babchishin, L., Pagani, L. S., & Kohen, D. (2010). School readiness and later achievement: Replication and extension using a nationwide Canadian survey. *Developmental Psychology, 46,* 995–1007.

Roman-Rodriguez, C. F., Toussaint, T., Sherlock, D. J., Fogel, J., & Hsu, C.-D. (2014). Preemptive penile ring block with sucrose analgesia reduces pain response to neonatal circumcision. *Urology, 83,* 893–898.

Ronald, A., & Hoekstra, R. (2014). Progress in understanding the causes of autism spectrum disorders and autistic traits: Twin studies from 1977 to the present day. In S. H. Rhee & A. Ronald (Eds.), *Advances in Behavior Genetics* (Vol. 2, pp. 33–65). New York: Springer.

Rönnqvist, L., & Domellöf, E. (2006). Quantitative assessment of right and left reaching movements in infants: A longitudinal study from 6 to 36 months. *Developmental Psychobiology, 48,* 444–459.

Roopnarine, J. L. (2016). Family socialization practices and childhood development in Caribbean cultural communities. In J. L. Roopnarine & D. Chadee (Eds.), *Caribbean psychology: Indigenous contributions to a global discipline* (pp. 71–96). Washington, DC: American Psychological Association.

Roopnarine, J. L., Hossain, Z., Gill, P., & Brophy, H. (1994). Play in the East Indian context. In J. L. Roopnarine, J. E. Johnson, & F. H. Hooper (Eds.),

Children's play in diverse cultures (pp. 9–30). Albany: State University of New York Press.

Rose, A. J., Swenson, L. P., & Waller, E. M. (2004). Overt and relational aggression and perceived popularity: Developmental differences in concurrent and prospective relations. *Developmental Psychology, 40,* 378–387.

Rose, S. A., Jankowski, J. J., & Senior, G. J. (1997). Infants' recognition of contour-deleted figures. *Journal of Experimental Psychology: Human Perception and Performance, 23,* 1206–1216.

Roseberry, S., Hirsh-Pasek, K., & Golinkoff, R. M. (2014). Skype me! Socially contingent interactions help toddlers learn language. *Child Development, 85,* 956–970.

Rosen, A. B., & Rozin, P. (1993). Now you see it, now you don't: The preschool child's conception of invisible particles in the context of dissolving. *Developmental Psychology, 29,* 300–311.

Rosen, C. S., & Cohen, M. (2010). Subgroups of New York City children at high risk of PTSD after the September 11 attacks: A signal detection analysis. *Psychiatric Services, 61,* 64–69.

Roseth, C. J., Pellegrini, A. D., Bohn, C. M., van Ryzin, M., & Vance, N. (2007). Preschoolers' aggression, affiliation, and social dominance relationships: An observational, longitudinal study. *Journal of School Psychology, 45,* 479–497.

Roskos, K. A., & Christie, J. F. (2013). Gaining ground in understanding the play–literacy relationship. *American Journal of Play, 6,* 82–97.

Ross, C. E., & Mirowsky, J. (2012). The sense of personal control: Social structural causes and emotional consequences. In C. S. Aneschensel, J. C. Phelan, & A. Bierman (Eds.), *Handbook of the sociology of mental health* (2nd ed., pp. 379–402). New York: Springer.

Ross, J. L., Roeltgen, D. P., Kushner, H., Zinn, A. R., Reiss, A., Bardsley, M. Z., et al. (2012). Behavioral and social phenotypes in boys with 47, XYY syndrome or 47, XXY Klinefelter syndrome. *Pediatrics, 129,* 769–778.

Ross, N., Medin, D. L., Coley, J. D., & Atran, S. (2003). Cultural and experiential differences in the development of folkbiological induction. *Cognitive Development, 18,* 25–47.

Rossi, B. V. (2014). Donor insemination. In J. M. Goldfarb (Ed.), *Third-party reproduction* (pp. 133–142). New York: Springer.

Roszel, E. L. (2015). Central nervous system deficits in fetal alcohol spectrum disorder. *Nurse Practitioner, 40*(4), 24–33.

Rothbart, M. K. (2011). *Becoming who we are: Temperament and personality in development.* New York: Guilford.

Rothbart, M. K. (2015). The role of temperament in conceptualizations of mental disorder. In B. Probst (Ed.), *Critical thinking in clinical assessment and diagnosis* (pp. 133–149). Cham, Switzerland: Springer International Publishing.

Rothbart, M. K., & Bates, J. E. (2006). Temperament. In N. Eisenberg (Ed.), *Handbook of child psychology: Vol. 3. Social, emotional, and personality development* (6th ed., pp. 99–166). Hoboken, NJ: Wiley.

Rothbart, M. K., Posner, M. I., & Kieras, J. (2006). Temperament, attention, and the development of self-regulation. In K. McCartney & D. Phillips (Eds.), *Blackwell handbook of early childhood development* (pp. 338–357). Malden, MA: Blackwell.

Rothbaum, F., Morelli, G., & Rusk, N. (2011). Attachment, learning, and coping: The interplay of cultural similarities and differences. In M. J. Gelfand, C.-Y. Chiu, & Y.-Y. Horng (Eds.), *Advances in culture and psychology* (pp. 153–215). Oxford, UK: Oxford University Press.

Rovee-Collier, C. K. (1999). The development of infant memory. *Current Directions in Psychological Science, 8,* 80–85.

Rovee-Collier, C. K., & Barr, R. (2001). Infant learning and memory. In G. Bremner & A. Fogel (Eds.), *Blackwell handbook of infant development* (pp. 139–168). Oxford, UK: Blackwell.

Rovee-Collier, C. K., & Bhatt, R. S. (1993). Evidence of long-term memory in infancy. *Annals of Child Development, 9,* 1–45.

Rovee-Collier, C., & Cuevas, K. (2009). The development of infant memory. In M. Courage & N. Cowan (Eds.), *The development of memory in infancy and childhood* (pp. 11–41). Hove, UK: Psychology Press.

Rowe, M. L. (2008). Child-directed speech: Relation to socioeconomic status, knowledge of child development and child vocabulary skill. *Journal of Child Language, 35,* 185–205.

Rowe, M. L., & Goldin-Meadow, S. (2009). Early gesture selectively predicts later language learning. *Developmental Science, 12,* 182–187.

Rowe, M. L., Raudenbush, S. W., & Goldin-Meadow, S. (2012). The pace of vocabulary growth helps predict later vocabulary skill. *Child Development, 83,* 508–525.

Rowland, C. F. (2007). Explaining errors in children's questions. *Cognition, 104,* 106–134.

Rowland, C. F., & Pine, J. M. (2000). Subject-auxiliary inversion errors and wh-question acquisition: "What children do know?" *Journal of Child Language, 27,* 157–181.

Rowley, S. J., Kurtz-Costes, B., Mistry, R., & Feagans, L. (2007). Social status as a predictor of race and gender stereotypes in late childhood and early adolescence. *Social Development, 16,* 150–168.

Rübeling, H. (2014). "Zeichnen und Malen im Kinderlltag: Angebote und Einstellungen [Drawing and painting in children's everyday life: Offers and attitudes]." In A. Gernhrdt, R. Balakrishnon, & H. Drexler (Eds.), *Kinder Zechnen Ihre Wlt—Entwicklung und Kultur [Children Draw Their World—Development and Culture]* (pp. 41–45). Berlin, Germany: das netz.

Rubens, D., & Sarnat, H. B. (2013). Sudden infant death syndrome: An update and new perspectives of etiology. *Handbook of Clinical Neurology, 112,* 867–874.

Rubin, D. M., O'Reilly, A. L., Luan, X., Dai, D., Localio, A. R., et al. (2011). Variation in pregnancy outcomes following statewide implementation of a prenatal home visitation program. *Archives of Pediatrics and Adolescent Medicine, 165,* 198–204.

Rubin, K. H., Bowker, J. C., McDonald, K. L., & Menzer, M. (2013). Peer relationships in childhood. In P. D. Zelazo (Ed.), *Oxford handbook of developmental psychology: Vol. 2. Self and other* (pp. 242–275). New York: Oxford University Press.

Rubin, K. H., Bukowski, W. M., & Parker, J. G. (2006). Peer interactions, relationships, and groups. In N. Eisenberg (Ed.), *Handbook of child psychology: Vol. 3. Social, emotional, and personality development* (6th ed., pp. 571–645). Hoboken, NJ: Wiley.

Rubin, K. H., Coplan, R. J., & Bowker, J. C. (2009). Social withdrawal in childhood. *Annual Review of Psychology, 60,* 141–171.

Rubin, K. H., Fein, G. G., & Vandenberg, B. (1983). Play. In E. M. Hetherington (Ed.), *Handbook of child psychology: Vol. 4. Socialization, personality, and social development* (4th ed., pp. 693–744). New York: Wiley.

Rubin, K. H., Watson, K. S., & Jambor, T. W. (1978). Free-play behaviors in preschool and kindergarten children. *Child Development, 49,* 539–536.

Ruble, D. N., Alvarez, J., Bachman, M., Cameron, J., Fuligni, A., García Coll, C., & Rhee, E. (2004). The development of a sense of "we": The emergence and implications of children's collective identity. In M. Bennett & F. Sani (Eds.), *The development of the social self* (pp. 29–76). Hove, UK: Psychology Press.

Ruble, D. N., Taylor, L. J., Cyphers, L., Greulich, F. K., Lurye, L. E., & Shrout, P. E. (2007). The role of gender constancy in early gender development. *Child Development, 78,* 1121–1136.

Rudy, D., Carlo, G., Lambert, M. C., & Awong, T. (2014). Undergraduates' perceptions of parental relationship-oriented guilt induction versus harsh psychological control: Does cultural group status moderate their associations with self-esteem? *Journal of Cross-Cultural Psychology, 45,* 905–920.

Ruedinger, E., & Cox, J. E. (2012). Adolescent childbearing: Consequences and interventions. *Current Opinions in Pediatrics, 24,* 446–452.

Ruff, H. A., & Capozzoli, M. C. (2003). Development of attention and distractibility in the first 4 years of life. *Developmental Psychology, 39,* 877–890.

Ruffman, T., & Langman, L. (2002). Infants' reaching in a multi-well A not B task. *Infant Behavior and Development, 25,* 237–246.

Ruffman, T., Slade, L., Devitt, K., & Crowe, E. (2006). What mothers say and what they do: The relation between parenting, theory of mind, language, and conflict/cooperation. *British Journal of Developmental Psychology, 24,* 105–124.

Runco, M. A. (1992). Children's divergent thinking and creative ideation. *Developmental Review, 12,* 233–264.

Rushton, J. P. (2012). No narrowing in mean Black–White IQ differences—predicted by heritable g. *American Psychologist, 67,* 500–501.

Rushton, J. P., & Jensen, A. R. (2006). The totality of available evidence shows the race IQ gap still remains. *Psychological Science, 17,* 921–924.

Rushton, J. P., & Jensen, A. R. (2010). The rise and fall of the Flynn effect as a reason to expect a narrowing of the Black–White IQ gap. *Intelligence, 38,* 213–219.

Russell, A. (2014). Parent–child relationships and influences. In P. K. Smith & C. H. Hart (Eds.), *Wiley-Blackwell handbook of childhood social development* (2nd ed., pp. 337–355). Malden, MA: Wiley-Blackwell.

Russell, A., Mize, J., & Bissaker, K. (2004). Parent–child relationships. In P. K. Smith & C. H. Hart (Eds.), *Blackwell handbook of childhood social development* (pp. 204–222). Malden, MA: Blackwell.

Russell, S. T., & Muraco, J. A. (2013). Representative data sets to study LGBT-parent families. In A. E. Goldberg & K. R. Allen (Eds.), *LGBT-parent families: Innovations in research and implications for practice* (pp. 343–356). New York: Springer.

Ruthsatz, J., & Urbach, J. B. (2012). Child prodigy: A novel cognitive profile places elevated general intelligence, exceptional working memory and attention to detail at the root of prodigiousness. *Intelligence, 40,* 419–426.

Rutland, A., Killen, M., & Abrams, D. (2010). A new social-cognitive developmental perspective on prejudice: The interplay between morality and group identity. *Perspectives on Psychological Science, 5,* 279–291.

Rutter, M. (2011). Biological and experiential influences on psychological development. In D. P. Keating (Ed.), *Nature and nurture in early child development* (pp. 7–44). New York: Cambridge University Press.

Rutter, M., Colvert, E., Kreppner, J., Beckett, C., Castle, J., & Groothues, C. (2007). Early adolescent outcomes for institutionally deprived and nondeprived adoptees. I: Disinhibited attachment. *Journal of Child Psychology and Psychiatry, 48,* 17–30.

Rutter, M., & the English and Romanian Adoptees Study Team. (1998). Developmental catch-up, and deficit, following adoption after severe global early privation. *Journal of Child Psychology and Psychiatry, 39,* 465–476.

Rutter, M., O'Connor, T. G., & English and Romanian Adoptees (ERA) Study Team. (2004). Are there biological programming effects for psychological development? Findings from a study of Romanian adoptees. *Developmental Psychology, 40,* 81–94.

Rutter, M., Sonuga-Barke, E. J, Beckett, C., Castle, J., Kreppner, J., Kumsta, R., et al. (2010). Deprivation-specific psychological patterns: Effects of institutional deprivation. *Monographs of the Society for Research in Child Development, 75*(1, Serial No. 295), 48–78.

S

Saarni, C., Campos, J. J., Camras, L. A., & Witherington, D. (2006). Emotional development: Action, communication, and understanding. In N. Eisenberg (Ed.), *Handbook of child psychology: Vol. 3. Social, emotional, and personality development* (6th ed., pp. 226–299). Hoboken, NJ: Wiley.

Sadler, T. W. (2014). *Langman's medical embryology* (13th ed.). Baltimore, MD: Lippincott Williams & Wilkins.

Safar, K., & Moulson, M. C. (2017). Facial expressions of emotion in infancy: A replication and extension. *Developmental Psychology, 59,* 507–514.

Safe Kids Worldwide. (2015). *Overview of childhood injury morbidity and mortality in the U.S.: Fact sheet 2015.* Retrieved from www.safekids.org/sites/default/files/documents/skw_overview_fact_sheet_november_2014.pdf

Saffran, J. R. (2009). Acquiring grammatical patterns: Constraints on learning. In J. Colombo, P. McCardle, & L. Freund (Eds.), *Infant pathways to language: Methods, models, and research disorders* (pp. 31–47). New York: Psychology Press.

Saffran, J. R., & Thiessen, E. D. (2003). Pattern induction by infant language learners. *Developmental Psychology, 39,* 484–494.

Saffran, J. R., Werker, J. F., & Werner, L. A. (2006). The infant's auditory world: Hearing, speech, and the beginnings of language. In D. Kuhn & R. Siegler (Eds.), *Handbook of child psychology: Vol. 2. Cognition, perception, and language* (6th ed., pp. 58–108). Hoboken, NJ: Wiley.

Sale, A., Berardi, N., & Maffei, L. (2009). Enrich the environment to empower the brain. *Trends in Neurosciences, 32,* 233–239.

Salihu, H. M., Shumpert, M. N., Slay, M., Kirby, R. S., & Alexander, G. R. (2003). Childbearing beyond maternal age 50 and fetal outcomes in the United States. *Obstetrics and Gynecology, 102,* 1006–1014.

Salmivalli, C. (2010). Bullying and the peer group: A review. *Aggression and Violent Behavior, 15,* 112–120.

Salmivalli, C., & Voeten, M. (2004). Connections between attitudes, group norms, and behaviour in bullying situations. *International Journal of Behavioral Development, 28,* 246–258.

Salmon, D. A., Dudley, M. Z., Glanz, J. M., & Omer, S. B. (2015). Vaccine hesitancy: Causes, consequences, and a call to action. *American Journal of Preventive Medicine, 49,* S391–S398.

Salomo, D., & Liszkowski, U. (2013). Sociocultural settings influence the emergence of prelinguistic deictic gestures. *Child Development, 84,* 1296–1307.

Salomonis, N. (2014). Systems-level perspective of sudden infant death syndrome. *Pediatric Research, 76,* 220–229.

Salvas, M.-C., Vitaro, F., Brendgen, M., & Cantin, S. (2016). Prospective links between friendship and early physical aggression: Preliminary evidence supporting the role of friendship quality through a dyadic intervention. *Merrill-Palmer Quarterly, 62,* 285–305.

Sampaio, R. C., & Truwit, C. L. (2001). Myelination in the developing human brain. In C. A. Nelson & M. Luciana (Eds.), *Handbook of developmental cognitive neuroscience* (pp. 35–44). Cambridge, MA: MIT Press.

Samuelson, L., & McMurray, B. (2017). What does it take to learn a word? *WIREs Cognitive Science, 8,* e1421.

Sanders, O. (2006). *Evaluating the Keeping Ourselves Safe Programme.* Wellington, NZ: Youth Education Service, New Zealand Police. Retrieved from www.nzfvc.org.nz/accan/papers-presentations/abstract11v.shtml

San Juan, V., & Astington, J. W. (2012). Bridging the gap between implicit and explicit understanding: How language development promotes the processing and representation of false belief. *British Journal of Developmental Psychology, 30,* 105–122.

Sann, C., & Streri, A. (2007). Perception of object shape and texture in human newborns: Evidence from cross-modal transfer tasks. *Developmental Science, 10,* 399–410.

Sansavini, A., Bertoncini, J., & Giovanelli, G. (1997). Newborns discriminate the rhythm of multisyllabic stressed words. *Developmental Psychology, 33,* 3–11.

Sarnecka, B. W., & Gelman, S. A. (2004). Six does not just mean a lot: Preschoolers see number words as specific. *Cognition, 92,* 329–352.

Sarnecka, B. W., & Wright, C. E. (2013). The idea of an exact number: Children's understanding of cardinality and equinumerosity. *Cognitive Science, 37,* 1493–1506.

Saucier, J. F., Sylvestre, R., Doucet, H., Lambert, J., Frappier, J. Y., Charbonneau, L., & Malus, M. (2002). Cultural identity and adaptation to adolescence in Montreal. In F. J. C. Azima & N. Grizenko (Eds.), *Immigrant and refugee children and their families: Clinical, research, and training issues* (pp. 133–154). Madison, WI: International Universities Press.

Saudino, K. J. (2003). Parent ratings of infant temperament: Lessons from twin studies. *Infant Behavior and Development, 26,* 100–107.

Saudino, K. J., & Plomin, R. (1997). Cognitive and temperamental mediators of genetic contributions to the home environment during infancy. *Merrill-Palmer Quarterly, 43,* 1–23.

Saunders, B. E. (2012). Determining best practice for treating sexually victimized children. In P. Goodyear-Brown (Ed.), *Handbook of child sexual abuse: Identification, assessment, and treatment* (pp. 173–198). Hoboken, NJ: Wiley.

Saxton, M., Backley, P., & Gallaway, C. (2005). Negative input for grammatical errors: Effects after a lag of 12 weeks. *Journal of Child Language, 32,* 643–672.

Saygin, A. P., Leech, R., & Dick, F. (2010). Nonverbal auditory agnosia with lesion to Wernicke's area. *Neuropsychologia, 48,* 107–113.

Saylor, M. M. (2004). Twelve- and 16-month-old infants recognize properties of mentioned absent things. *Developmental Science, 7,* 599–611.

Saylor, M. M., & Troseth, G. L. (2006). Preschoolers use information about speakers' desires to learn new words. *Cognitive Development, 21,* 214–231.

Scarr, S., & McCartney, K. (1983). How people make their own environments: A theory of genotype → environment effects. *Child Development, 54,* 424–435.

Scarr, S., & Weinberg, R. A. (1983). The Minnesota Adoption Studies: Genetic differences and malleability. *Child Development, 54,* 260–267.

Schaal, B., Marlier, L., & Soussignan, R. (2000). Human fetuses learn odours from their pregnant mother's diet. *Chemical Senses, 25,* 729–737.

Schaal, S., Dusingizemungu, J.-P., Jacob, N., & Elbert, T. (2011). Rates of trauma spectrum disorders and risks of posttraumatic stress disorder in a sample of orphaned and widowed genocide survivors. *European Journal of Psychotraumatology, 2.* Retrieved from www.ncbi.nlm.nih.gov/pmc/articles/PMC3402134

Scher, A., Epstein, R., & Tirosh, E. (2004). Stability and changes in sleep regulation: A longitudinal study from 3 months to 3 years. *International Journal of Behavioral Development, 28,* 268–274.

Scher, A., Tirosh, E., Jaffe, M., Rubin, L., Sadeh, A., & Lavie, P. (1995). Sleep patterns of infants and young children in Israel. *International Journal of Behavioral Development, 18,* 701–711.

Scherrer, J. L. (2012). The United Nations Convention on the Rights of the Child as policy and strategy for social work action in child welfare in the United States. *Social Work, 57,* 11–22.

Schlagmüller, M., & Schneider, W. (2002). The development of organizational strategies in children: Evidence from a microgenetic longitudinal study. *Journal of Experimental Child Psychology, 81,* 298–319.

Schmidt, L. A., Fox, N. A., Schulkin, J., & Gold, P. W. (1999). Behavioral and psychophysiological correlates of self-presentation in temperamentally shy children. *Developmental Psychobiology, 30,* 127–140.

Schmidt, L. A., Santesso, D. L., Schulkin, J., & Segalowitz, S. J. (2007). Shyness is a necessary but not sufficient condition for high salivary cortisol in typically developing 10-year-old children. *Personality and Individual Differences, 43,* 1541–1551.

Schmidt, L. A., Tang, A., Day, K. L., Lahat, A., Boyle, M. H., Saigal, S., & Van Lieshout, R. J. (2017). Personality development within a generational context: Life course outcomes of shy children. *Child Psychiatry and Human Development, 48,* 632–641.

Schmitz, S., Fulker, D. W., Plomin, R., Zahn-Waxler, C., Emde, R. N., & DeFries, J. C. (1999). Temperament and problem behaviour during early childhood. *International Journal of Behavioural Development, 23,* 333–355.

Schneider, B. H., Atkinson, L., & Tardif, C. (2001). Child–parent attachment and children's peer relations: A quantitative review. *Developmental Psychology, 37,* 87–100.

Schneider, D. (2006). Smart as we can get? *American Scientist, 94,* 311–312.

Schneider, W. (2002). Memory development in childhood. In U. Goswami (Ed.), *Blackwell handbook of childhood cognitive development* (pp. 236–256). Malden, MA: Blackwell.

Schneider, W., & Bjorklund, D. F. (1992). Expertise, aptitude, and strategic remembering. *Child Development, 63,* 461–473.

Schneider, W., & Bjorklund, D. F. (1998). Memory. In D. Kuhn & R. S. Siegler (Eds.), *Handbook of child psychology: Vol. 2. Cognition, perception, and language* (5th ed., pp. 467–521). New York: Wiley.

Schneider, W., & Pressley, M. (1997). *Memory development between two and twenty* (2nd ed.). Mahwah, NJ: Erlbaum.

Schoenmaker, C., Juffer, F., van IJzendoorn, M. H., van den Dries, L., Linting, M., van der Voort, A., & Bakermans-Kranenburg, M. J. (2015). Cognitive and health-related outcomes after exposure to early malnutrition: The Leiden longitudinal study of international adoptees. *Children and Youth Services Review, 48,* 80–86.

Schonberg, R. L. (2012). Birth defects and prenatal diagnosis. In M. L. Batshaw, N. J. Roizen, & G. R. Lotrecchiano (Eds.), *Children with disabilities* (7th ed., pp. 47–60). Baltimore, MD: Paul H. Brookes.

Schonert-Reichl, K. A., & Lawlor, M. S. (2010). The effects of a mindfulness-based education program on pre- and early adolescents' well-being and social and emotional competence. *Mindfulness, 1,* 137–151.

Schonert-Reichl, K. A., Oberle, E., Lawlor, M. S., Abbott, D., Thomson, K., Oberlander, T. F., et al. (2015). Enhancing cognitive and social-emotional development through a simple-to-administer mindfulness-based school program for elementary school children: A randomized controlled trial. *Developmental Psychology, 51,* 52–66.

Schoon, I., Jones, E., Cheng, H., & Maughan, B. (2012). Family hardship, family instability, and cognitive development. *Journal of Epidemiology and Community Health, 66,* 716–722.

Schott, J. M., & Rossor, M. N. (2003). The grasp and other primitive reflexes. *Journal of Neurological and Neurosurgical Psychiatry, 74,* 558–560.

Schroeder, R. D., Bulanda, R. E., Giordano, P. C., & Cernkovich, S. A. (2010). Parenting and adult criminality: An examination of direct and indirect effects by race. *Journal of Adolescent Research, 25,* 64–98.

Schull, W. J. (2003). The children of atomic bomb survivors: A synopsis. *Journal of Radiological Protection, 23,* 369–394.

Schulze, C., Grassmann, S., & Tomasello, M. (2013). 3-year-old children make relevant inferences in indirect verbal communication. *Child Development, 84,* 2079–2093.

Schunk, D. H., & Zimmerman, B. J. (2013). Self-regulation and learning. In W. M. Reynolds, G. E. Miller, & I. B. Weiner (Eds.), *Handbook of psychology: Vol. 7. Educational psychology* (pp. 45–68). Hoboken, NJ: Wiley.

Schwanenflugel, P. J., Henderson, R. L., & Fabricius, W. V. (1998). Developing organization of mental verbs and theory of mind in middle childhood: Evidence from extensions. *Developmental Psychology, 34,* 512–524.

Schwartz, C. E., Kunwar, P. S., Greve, D. N., Kagan, J., Snidman, N. C., & Bloch, R. B. (2012). A phenotype of early infancy predicts reactivity of the amygdala in male adults. *Molecular Psychiatry, 17,* 1042–1050.

Schwarzer, G., Freitag, C., & Schum, N. (2013). How crawling and manual object exploration are related to the mental rotation abilities of 9-month-old infants. *Frontiers in Psychology, 4,* Article ID: 97.

Schwebel, D. C., & Brezausek, C. M. (2007). Father transitions in the household and young children's injury risk. *Psychology of Men and Masculinity, 8,* 173–184.

Schwebel, D. C., & Gaines, J. (2007). Pediatric unintentional injury: Behavioral risk factors and implications for prevention. *Journal of Developmental and Behavioral Pediatrics, 28,* 245–254.

Schweinhart, L. J. (2010). The challenge of the High/Scope Perry Preschool study. In A. J. Reynolds, A. J. Rolnick, M. M. Englund, & J. Temple (Eds.), *Childhood programs and practices in the first decade of life: A human capital integration* (pp. 199–213). New York: Cambridge University Press.

Schweinhart, L. J., Montie, J., Xiang, Z., Barnett, W. S., Belfield, C. R., & Nores, M. (2005). *Lifetime effects: The High/Scope Perry Preschool Study through age 40.* Ypsilanti, MI: High/Scope Press.

Schweizer, K., Moosbrugger, H., & Goldhammer, F. (2006). The structure of the relationship between attention and intelligence. *Intelligence, 33,* 589–611.

Schwenck, C., Bjorklund, D. F., & Schneider, W. (2007). Factors influencing the incidence of utilization deficiencies and other patterns of recall/strategy-use relations in a strategic memory task. *Child Development, 22,* 197–212.

Schwier, C., van Maanen, C., Carpenter, M., & Tomasello, M. (2006). Rational imitation in 12-month-old infants. *Infancy, 10,* 303–311.

Scott, L. S., & Monesson, A. (2009). The origin of biases in face perception. *Psychological Science, 20,* 676–680.

Scott, R. M., & Fisher, C. (2012). 2.5-year-olds use cross-situational consistency to learn verbs under referential uncertainty. *Cognition, 122,* 163–180.

Scrimgeour, M. B., Davis, E. L., & Buss, K. A. (2016). You get what you get and you don't throw a fit!: Emotion socialization and child physiology jointly predict early prosocial development. *Developmental Psychology, 52,* 102–116.

Scrutton, D. (2005). Influence of supine sleep positioning on early motor milestone acquisition. *Developmental Medicine and Child Neurology, 47,* 364.

Seburg, E., Olson-Bullis, B., Bredeson, D., Hayes, M., & Sherwood, N. (2015). A review of primary care-based childhood prevention and treatment interventions. *Current Obesity Reports, 4,* 157–173.

Sedgh, G., Finer, L. B., Bankole, A., Eilers, M. A., & Singh, S. (2015). Adolescent pregnancy, birth, and abortion rates across countries: Levels and recent trends. *Journal of Adolescent Health, 56,* 223–230.

Seethaler, P. M., Fuchs, L. S., Fuchs, D., & Compton, D. L. (2012). Predicting first graders' development of calculation versus word-problem performance: The role of dynamic assessment. *Journal of Educational Psychology, 104,* 224–234.

Seibert, A., & Kerns, K. (2015). Early mother–child attachment: Longitudinal prediction to the quality of peer relationships in middle childhood. *International Journal of Behavioral Development, 39,* 130–138.

Seibert, A. C., & Kerns, K. A. (2009). Attachment figures in middle childhood. *International Journal of Behavioral Development, 33,* 347–355.

Seidl, A., Hollich, G., & Jusczyk, P. (2003). Early understanding of subject and object wh-questions. *Infancy, 4,* 423–436.

Sengpiel, V., Elind, E., Bacelis, J., Nilsson, S., Grove, J., Myhre, R., et al. (2013). Maternal caffeine intake during pregnancy is associated with birth weight but not with gestational length: Results from a large prospective observational cohort study. *BMC Medicine, 11,* 42.

Senju, A., Csibra, G., & Johnson, M. H. (2008). Understanding the referential nature of looking: Infants' preference for object-directed gaze. *Cognition, 108,* 303–319.

Senn, T. E., Espy, K. A., & Kaufmann, P. M. (2004). Using path analysis to understand executive function organization in preschool children. *Developmental Neuropsychology, 26,* 445–464.

Serbin, L. A., Powlishta, K. K., & Gulko, J. (1993). The development of sex typing in middle childhood. *Monographs of the Society for Research in Child Development, 58*(2, Serial No. 232).

Sesame Workshop. (2017). *Where we work: All locations.* Retrieved from www.sesameworkshop.org/where-we-work/all-locations

Sevigny, P. R., & Loutzenhiser, L. (2010). Predictors of parenting self-efficacy in mothers and fathers of toddlers. *Child: Care, Health and Development, 36,* 179–189.

SFIA (Sports & Fitness Industry Association). (2015). *2015 U.S. trends in team sports report.* Silver Spring, MD: Author.

Shafer, R. J., Raby, K. L., Lawler, J. M., Hesemeyer, P. S., & Roisman, G. I. (2015). Longitudinal associations between adult attachment states of mind and parenting quality. *Attachment & Human Development, 17,* 83–95.

Sharp, K. L., Williams, A. J., Rhyner, K. T., & Hardi, S. S. (2013). The clinical interview. In K. F. Geisinger, B. A. Bracken, J. F. Carlson, J. C. Hansen, N. R. Kuncel, S. P. Reise, et al. (Eds.), *APA handbook of testing and assessment in psychology* (Vol. 2, pp. 103–117). Washington, DC: American Psychological Association.

Shaul, S., & Schwartz, M. (2014). The role of executive functions in school readiness among preschool-age children. *Reading and Writing, 27,* 749–768.

Shaw, D. S., Hyde, L. W., & Brennan, L. M. (2012). Early predictors of boys' antisocial trajectories. *Development and Psychopathology, 24,* 871–888.

Shaw, D. S., Sitnick, S., Brennan, L., Choe, D. E., Dishion, T. J., Wilson, M. N., & Gardner, F. (2016). The long-term effectiveness of the Family Check-Up on school-age children's conduct problems: Moderation by neighborhood deprivation. *Development and Psychopathology, 28,* 1471–1486.

Shaw, P., Eckstrand, K., Sharp, W., Blumenthal, J., Lerch, J. P., & Greenstein, D. (2007). Attention-deficit/hyperactivity disorder is characterized by a delay in cortical maturation. *Proceedings of the National Academy of Sciences Online.* Retrieved from www.pnas.org/cgi/content/abstract/0707741104v1

Shearer, R. J. B., McWayne, C. M., Mendez, J. L., & Manz, P. H. (2016). Preschool peer play interactions, a developmental context for ALL children: Rethinking issues of equity and opportunity. In K. E. Sanders & A. W. Guerra (Eds.), *The culture of child care: Attachment, peers, and quality in diverse communities* (pp. 179–202). New York: Oxford University Press.

Sheehan, G., Darlington, Y., Noller, P., & Feeney, J. (2004). Children's perceptions of their sibling relationships during parental separation and divorce. *Journal of Divorce and Remarriage, 41,* 69–94.

Shimada, S., & Hiraki, K. (2006). Infant's brain responses to live and televised action. *NeuroImage, 32,* 930–939.

Shin, N., Kim, M., Goetz, S., & Vaughn, B. E. (2014). Dyadic analyses of preschool-aged children's friendships: Convergence and differences between friendship classifications from peer sociometric data and teacher reports. *Social Development, 23,* 178–195.

Shonkoff, J. P., & Bales, S. N. (2011). Science does not speak for itself: Translating child development research for the public and its policymakers. *Child Development, 82,* 17–32.

Shonkoff, J. P., & Garner, A. S. (2012). The lifelong effects of early childhood adversity and toxic stress. *Pediatrics, 129,* e232–e246.

Shriver, L. H., Harrist, A. W., Page, M., Hubbs-Tait, L., Moulton, M., & Topham, G. (2013). Differences in body esteem by weight status, gender, and physical activity among young elementary school-aged children. *Body Image, 10,* 78–84.

Shwalb, D. W., Nakawaza, J., Yamamoto, T., & Hyun, J.-H. (2004). Fathering in Japanese, Chinese, and Korean cultures: A review of the research literature. In M. E. Lamb (Ed.), *The role of the father in child development* (4th ed., pp. 146–181). Hoboken, NJ: Wiley.

Siberry, G. K. (2015). Preventing and managing HIV infection in infants, children, and adolescents in the United States. *Pediatrics in Review, 35,* 268–286.

Sidebotham, P., Heron, J., & the ALSPAC Study Team. (2003). Child maltreatment in the "children of the nineties": The role of the child. *Child Abuse and Neglect, 27,* 337–352.

Seibert, A., & Kerns, K. (2015). Early mother–child attachment: Longitudinal prediction to the quality of peer relationships in middle childhood. *International Journal of Behavioral Development, 39,* 130–138.

Siegal, M., Iozzi, L., & Surian, L. (2009). Bilingualism and conversational understanding in young children. *Cognition, 110,* 115–122.

Siega-Riz, A. M., Deming, D. M., Reidy, K. C., Fox, M. K., Condon, E., & Briefel, R. R. (2010). Food consumption patterns of infants and toddlers: Where are we now? *Journal of the American Dietetic Association, 110,* S38–S51.

Siegler, R. S., & Mu, Y. (2008). Chinese children excel on novel mathematics problems even before elementary school. *Psychological Science, 19,* 759–763.

Silvén, M. (2001). Attention in very young infants predicts learning of first words. *Infant Behavior and Development, 24,* 229–237.

Simcock, G., & DeLoache, J. (2006). Get the picture? The effects of iconicity on toddlers' reenactment from picture books. *Developmental Psychology, 42,* 1352–1357.

Simcock, G., Garrity, K., & Barr, R. (2011). The effect of narrative cues on infants' imitation from television and picture books. *Child Development, 82,* 1607–1619.

Simcock, G., & Hayne, H. (2003). Age-related changes in verbal and nonverbal memory during early childhood. *Developmental Psychology, 39,* 805–814.

Simmonds, M., Llewellyn, A., Owen, C. G., & Woolacott, N. (2016). Predicting adult obesity from childhood obesity: A systematic review and meta-analysis. *Obesity Reviews, 17,* 95–107.

Simpson, E. A., Varga, K., Frick, J. E., & Fragaszy, D. (2011). Infants experience perceptual narrowing for nonprimate faces. *Infancy, 16,* 318–328.

Singer, L. T., Minnes, S., Min, M. O., Lewis, B. A., & Short, E. J. (2015). Prenatal cocaine exposure and child outcomes: A conference report based on a prospective study from Cleveland. *Human Psychopharmacology, 30,* 285–289.

Singleton, J. L., & Newport, E. L. (2004). When learners surpass their models: The acquisition of American Sign Language from inconsistent input. *Cognitive Psychology, 49,* 370–407.

Sirin, S. R., Ryce, P., Gupta, T., & Rogers-Sirin, L. (2013). The role of acculturative stress on mental health symptoms for immigrant adolescents: A longitudinal investigation. *Developmental Psychology, 49,* 736–748.

Skinner, E. A., Zimmer-Gembeck, M. J., & Connell, J. P. (1998). Individual differences and the development of perceived control. *Monographs of the Society for Research in Child Development, 63*(2–3, Serial No. 254).

Slater, A., Quinn, P. C., Kelly, D. J., Lee, K., Longmore, C. A., McDonald, P. R., & Pascalis, O. (2011). The shaping of the face space in early infancy: Becoming a native face processor. *Child Development Perspectives, 4,* 205–211.

Slater, A., Riddell, P., Quinn, P. C., Pascalis, O., Lee, K., & Kelly, D. J. (2010). Visual perception. In J. G. Bremner & T. D. Wachs (Eds.), *Wiley-Blackwell handbook of infant development: Vol. 1. Basic research* (2nd ed., pp. 40–80). Oxford, UK: Wiley-Blackwell.

Slavin, R. E. (2015). Cooperative learning in elementary schools. *Education, 43,* 5–14.

Slonims, V., & McConachie, H. (2006). Analysis of mother–infant interaction in infants with Down syndrome and typically developing infants. *American Journal of Mental Retardation, 111,* 273–289.

Sloutsky, V. (2015). Conceptual development. In L. S. Liben & U. Müller (Eds.), *Handbook of child psychology and developmental science: Vol. 2. Cognitive processes* (7th ed., pp. 469–518). Hoboken, NJ: Wiley.

Smetana, J. G. (2006). Social-cognitive domain theory: Consistencies and variations in children's moral and social judgments. In M. Killen & J. G. Smetana (Eds.), *Handbook of moral development* (pp. 119–154). Mahwah, NJ: Erlbaum.

Smit, D. J. A., Boersma, M., Schnack, H. G., Micheloyannis, S., Doomsma, D. I., Pol, H. E. H., et al. (2012). The brain matures with stronger functional connectivity and decreased randomness of its network. *PLOS ONE, 7*(5), e36896.

Smith, B. H., & Shapiro, C. J. (2015). Combined treatments for ADHD. In R. A. Barkley (Ed.), *Attention-deficit hyperactivity disorder: A handbook for diagnosis and treatment* (4th ed., pp. 686–704). New York: Guilford.

Smith, J. P., & Forrester, R. (2013). Who pays for the health benefits of exclusive breastfeeding? An analysis of maternal time costs. *Journal of Human Lactation, 29,* 547–555.

Smith, L. B., Jones, S. S., Gershkoff-Stowe, L., & Samuelson, L. (2002). Object name learning provides on-the-job training for attention. *Psychological Science, 13,* 13–19.

Smith, T. W., Glazer, K., Ruiz, J. M., & Gallo, L. C. (2004). Hostility, anger, aggressiveness, and coronary heart disease: An interpersonal perspective on personality, emotion, and health. *Journal of Personality, 72,* 1217–1270.

Smyke, A. T., Zeanah, C. H., Fox, N. A., Nelson, C. A., & Guthrie, D. (2010). Placement in foster care enhances quality of attachment among young institutionalized children. *Child Development, 81,* 212–223.

Snidman, N., Kagan, J., Riordan, L., & Shannon, D. C. (1995). Cardiac function and behavioral reactivity. *Psychophysiology, 32,* 199–207.

Snow, C. E., & Beals, D. E. (2006). Mealtime talk that supports literacy development. In R. W. Larson, A. R. Wiley, & K. R. Branscomb (Eds.), *Family mealtime as a context of development and socialization* (pp. 51–66). San Francisco: Jossey-Bass.

Snow, C. E., Pan, B. A., Imbens-Bailey, A., & Herman, J. (1996). Learning how to say what one means: A longitudinal study of children's speech act use. *Social Development, 5,* 56–84.

Snyder, J., Brooker, M., Patrick, M. R., Snyder, A., Schrepferman, L., & Stoolmiller, M. (2003). Observed peer victimization during early elementary school: Continuity, growth, and relation to risk for child antisocial and depressive behavior. *Child Development, 74,* 1881–1898.

Sobel, D. M. (2006). How fantasy benefits young children's understanding of pretense. *Developmental Science, 9,* 63–75.

Sobotnik, R. F., Worrell, F. C., & Olszewski-Kubilius, P. (2016). The psychological science of talent development. In M. Neihart, S. Pfeiffer, & T. L. Cross (Eds.), *The social and emotional development of gifted children: What do we know?* (pp. 145–157). Waco, TX: Prufrock Press.

Society for Research in Child Development. (2007). *SRCD ethical standards for research with children.* Retrieved from www.srcd.org/index.php?option=com_content&task=view&id=68&Itemid=110

Society of Health and Physical Educators. (2016). *Shape of the nation: Status of Physical Education in the USA*. Retrieved from www.shapeamerica.org/advocacy/son/2016/upload/Shape-of-the-Nation-2016_web.pdf

Soderstrom, M., Seidl, A., Nelson, D. G. K., & Jusczyk, P. W. (2003). The prosodic bootstrapping of phrases: Evidence from prelinguistic infants. *Journal of Memory and Language, 49,* 249–267.

Soli, A. R., McHale, S. M., & Feinberg, M. E. (2009). Risk and protective effects of sibling relationships among African American adolescents. *Family Relations, 58,* 578–592.

Solomon, J., & George, C. (2011). The disorganized attachment–caregiving system. In J. Solomon & C. George (Eds.), *Disorganized attachment and caregiving* (pp. 3–24). New York: Guilford.

Somers, M., Ophoff, R. A., Aukes, M. F., Cantor, R. M., Boks, M. P., Dauwan, M., et al. (2015). Linkage analysis in a Dutch population isolate shows no major gene for left-handedness or atypical language lateralization. *Journal of Neuroscience, 35,* 8730–8736.

Soos, I., Biddle, S. J. H., Ling, J., Hamar, P., Sandor, I., Boros-Balint, I., et al. (2014). Physical activity, sedentary behaviour, use of electronic media, and snacking among youth: An international study. *Kinesiology, 46,* 155–163.

Sorkhabi, N., & Mandara, J. (2013). Are the effects of Baumrind's parenting styles culturally specific or culturally equivalent? In R. E. Larzelere, A. S. Morris, & A. W. Harrist (Eds.), *Authoritative parenting: Synthesizing nurturance and discipline for optimal child development* (pp. 113–135). Washington, DC: American Psychological Association.

Soska, K. C., Adolph, K. E., & Johnson, S. P. (2010). Systems in development: Motor skill acquisition facilitates three-dimensional object completion. *Developmental Psychology, 46,* 129–138.

Spangler, G., Johann, M., Ronai, Z., & Zimmermann, P. (2009). Genetic and environmental influence on attachment disorganization. *Journal of Child Psychology and Psychiatry, 50,* 952–961.

Speece, D. L., Ritchey, K. D., Cooper, D. H., Roth, F. P., & Schatschneider, C. (2004). Growth in early reading skills from kindergarten to third grade. *Contemporary Educational Psychology, 29,* 312–332.

Spelke, E. S. (2016). Core knowledge and conceptual change: A perspective on social cognition. In D. Barner & A. S. Baron (Eds.), *Core knowledge and conceptual change* (pp. 279–300). New York: Oxford University Press.

Spelke, E. S., & Kinzler, K. D. (2013). Core knowledge. In S. M. Downes & E. Machery (Eds.), *Arguing about human nature: Contemporary debates* (pp. 107–116). New York: Routledge.

Spelke, E. S., Phillips, A. T., & Woodward, A. L. (1995). Infants' knowledge of object motion and human action. In A. Premack (Ed.), *Causal understanding in cognition and culture* (pp. 4–78). Oxford, UK: Clarendon Press.

Spence, M. J., & DeCasper, A. J. (1987). Prenatal experience with low-frequency maternal voice sounds influences neonatal perception of maternal voice samples. *Infant Behavior and Development, 10,* 133–142.

Spencer, J. P., Perone, S., & Buss, A. T. (2011). Twenty years and going strong: A dynamic systems revolution in motor and cognitive development. *Child Development Perspectives, 5,* 260–266.

Spere, K. A., Schmidt, L. A., Theall-Honey, L. A., & Martin-Chang, S. (2004). Expressive and receptive language skills of temperamentally shy preschoolers. *Infant and Child Development, 13,* 123–133.

Spilt, J., Hughes, J. N., Wu, J.-Y., & Kwok, O.-M. (2012). Dynamics of teacher–student relationships: Stability and change across elementary school and the influence on children's academic success. *Child Development, 83,* 1180–1195.

Spock, B., & Needlman, R. (2012). *Dr. Spock's baby and child care* (9th ed.). New York: Gallery Books.

Spoelstra, M. N., Mari, A., Mendel, M., Senga, E., van Rheenen, P., van Dijk, T. H., et al. (2012). Kwashiorkor and marasmus are both associated with impaired glucose clearance related to pancreatic ß-cell dysfunction. *Metabolism: Clinical and Experimental, 61,* 1224–1230.

Sroufe, L. A., Coffino, B., & Carlson, E. A. (2010). Conceptualizing the role of early experience: Lessons from the Minnesota Longitudinal Study. *Developmental Review, 30,* 36–51.

Stams, G. J. M., Juffer, F., & van IJzendoorn, M. H. (2002). Maternal sensitivity, infant attachment, and temperament in early childhood predict adjustment in middle childhood: The case of adopted children and their biologically unrelated parents. *Developmental Psychology, 38,* 806–821.

Stanovich, K. E. (2013). *How to think straight about psychology* (10th ed.). Upper Saddle River, NJ: Pearson.

Staub, F. C., & Stern, E. (2002). The nature of teachers' pedagogical content beliefs matters for students' achievement gains: Quasi-experimental evidence from elementary mathematics. *Journal of Educational Psychology, 94,* 344–355.

Steensma, T. D., Biemond, R., de Boer, F., & Cohen-Kettenis, P T. (2011). Desisting and persisting gender dysphoria after childhood: A qualitative follow-up study. *Clinical Child Psychology and Psychiatry, 16,* 499–516.

Steensma, T. D., & Cohen-Kettenis, P. T. (2015). More than two developmental pathways in children with gender dysphoria? *Journal of the American Academy of Child and Adolescent Psychiatry, 54,* 147.

Steinberg, L., Blatt-Eisengart, I., & Cauffman, E. (2006). Patterns of competence and adjustment among adolescents from authoritative, authoritarian, indulgent, and neglectful homes: A replication in a sample of serious juvenile offenders. *Journal of Research on Adolescence, 16,* 47–58.

Steinberg, L., & Silk, J. S. (2002). Parenting adolescents. In M. H. Bornstein (Ed.), *Handbook of parenting: Vol. 1. Children and parenting* (pp. 103–134). Mahwah, NJ: Erlbaum.

Steiner, J. E. (1979). Human facial expression in response to taste and smell stimulation. In H. W. Reese & L. P. Lipsitt (Eds.), *Advances in child development and behavior* (Vol. 13, pp. 257–295). New York: Academic Press.

Steiner, J. E., Glaser, D., Hawilo, M. E., & Berridge, D. C. (2001). Comparative expression of hedonic impact: Affective reactions to taste by human infants and other primates. *Neuroscience and Biobehavioral Review, 25,* 53–74.

Stenberg, C. (2003). Effects of maternal inattentiveness on infant social referencing. *Infant and Child Development, 12,* 399–419.

Stenberg, C., & Campos, J. J. (1990). The development of anger expressions in infancy. In N. Stein, B. Leventhal, & T. Trabasso (Eds.), *Psychological and biological approaches to emotion* (pp. 247–282). Hillsdale, NJ: Erlbaum.

Stensland, S. Ø., Thoresen, S., Wentzel-Larsen, T., & Dyb, G. (2015). Interpersonal violence and overweight in adolescents: The HUNT study. *Scandinavian Journal of Public Health, 43,* 18–26.

Sternberg, R. J. (2005). The triarchic theory of successful intelligence. In D. P. Flanagan & P. L. Harrison (Eds.), *Contemporary intellectual assessment: Theories, tests, and issues* (pp. 103–119). New York: Guilford.

Sternberg, R. J. (2008). The triarchic theory of successful intelligence. In N. Salkind (Ed.), *Encyclopedia of educational psychology* (Vol. 2, pp. 988–994). Thousand Oaks, CA: Sage.

Sternberg, R. J. (2011). The theory of successful intelligence. In R. J. Sternberg & S. B. Kaufman (Eds.), *Cambridge handbook of intelligence* (pp. 504–527). New York: Cambridge University Press.

Sternberg, R. J. (2013). Contemporary theories of intelligence. In W. M. Reynolds & G. E. Miller (Eds.), *Handbook of psychology: Vol. 7. Educational psychology* (2nd ed., pp. 23–44). Hoboken, NJ: Wiley.

Stevenson, C. E., Heiser, W. J., & Resing, W. C. M. (2016). Dynamic testing: Assessing cognitive potential of children with culturally diverse backgrounds. *Learning and Individual Differences, 47,* 27–36

Stewart, P. W., Lonky, E., Reihman, J., Pagano, J., Gump, B. B., & Darvill, T. (2008). The relationship between prenatal PCB exposure and intelligence (IQ). *Environmental Health Perspectives, 116,* 1416–1422.

Stiles, J., Brown, T. T., Haist, F., & Jernigan, T. L. (2015). Brain and cognitive development. In L. S. Liben & U. Müller (Eds.), *Handbook of child psychology and developmental science: Vol. 2. Cognitive processes* (7th ed., pp. 9–62). Hoboken, NJ: Wiley.

Stiles, J., Nass, R. D., Levine, S. C., Moses, P., & Reilly, J. S. (2009). Perinatal stroke: Effects and outcomes. In K. O. Yeates, M. D. Ris, H. G. Taylor, & B. Pennington (Eds.), *Pediatric neuropsychology: Research, theory and practice* (2nd ed., pp. 181–210). New York: Guilford.

Stiles, J., Reilly, J. S., & Levine, S. C. (2012). *Neural plasticity and cognitive development.* New York: Oxford University Press.

Stiles, J., Stern, C., Appelbaum, M., & Nass, R. (2008). Effects of early focal brain injury on memory for visuospatial patterns: Selective deficits of global–local processing. *Neuropsychology, 22,* 61–73.

Stipek, D. (2011). Classroom practices and children's motivation to learn. In E. Zigler, W. S. Gilliam, & W. S. Barnett (Eds.), *The pre-K debates: Current controversies and issues* (pp. 98–103). Baltimore, MD: Paul H. Brookes.

Stipek, D., Franke, M., Clements, D., Farran, D., & Coburn, C. (2017). PK–3: What does it mean for instruction? *SRCD Social Policy Report, 30*(2).

Stipek, D. J., Feiler, R., Daniels, D., & Milburn, S. (1995). Effects of different instructional approaches on young children's achievement and motivation. *Child Development, 66,* 209–223.

Stipek, D. J., Gralinski, J. H., & Kopp, C. B. (1990). Self-concept development in the toddler years. *Developmental Psychology, 26,* 972–977.

St James-Roberts, I. (2007). Helping parents to manage infant crying and sleeping: A review of the evidence and its implications for services. *Child Abuse Review, 16,* 47–69.

St James-Roberts, I. (2012). *The origins, prevention and treatment of infant crying and sleep problems.* London: Routledge.

St James-Roberts, I., Roberts, M., Hovish, K., & Owen, C. (2015). Video evidence that London infants can resettle themselves back to sleep after waking in the night, as well as sleep for long periods, by 3 months of age. *Journal of Developmental and Behavioral Pediatrics, 36,* 324–329.

St James-Roberts, I., Roberts, M., Hovish, K., & Owen, C. (2017). Video evidence that parenting methods predict which infants develop long night-time sleep periods by three months of age. *Primary Health Care Research & Development, 18,* 212–226.

Stoner, R., Chow, M. L., Boyle, M. P., Sunkin, S. M., Mouton, P. R., Roy, S., et al. (2014). Patches of disorganization in the neocortex of children with autism. *New England Journal of Medicine, 370,* 1209–1219.

Storch, S. A., & Whitehurst, G. J. (2001). The role of family and home in the literacy development of children from low-income backgrounds. In P. R. Britto & J. Brooks-Gunn (Eds.), *New directions for child and adolescent development* (No. 92, pp. 53–71). San Francisco: Jossey-Bass.

Strang, T. M., & Piasta, S. B. (2016). Socioeconomic differences in code-focused emergent literacy skills. *Reading and Writing, 29,* 1337–1362.

Strapp, C. M., & Federico, A. (2000). Imitations and repetitions: What do children say following recasts? *First Language, 20,* 273–290.

Strasburger, V. C., Wilson, B. J., & Jordan, A. B. (2013). *Children, adolescents, and the media* (3rd ed.). Thousand Oaks, CA: Sage.

Straus, M. A., & Stewart, J. H. (1999). Corporal punishment by American parents: National data on prevalence, chronicity, severity, and duration, in relation to child and family characteristics. *Clinical Child and Family Psychology Review, 2,* 55–70.

Strazdins, L., Clements, M. S., Korda, R. J., Broom, D. H., & D'Souza, R. M. (2006). Unsociable work? Nonstandard work schedules, family relationships, and children's well-being. *Journal of Marriage and the Family, 68,* 394–410.

Strazdins, L., O'Brien, L. V., Lucas, N., & Rodgers, B. (2013). Combining work and family: Rewards or risks for children's mental health? *Social Science and Medicine, 87,* 99–107.

Streit, C., Carlo, G., Ispa, J. M., & Palermo, F. (2017). Negative emotionality and discipline as long-term predictors of behavioral outcomes in African American and European American children. *Developmental Psychology, 53,* 1013–1026.

Striano, T., & Rochat, P. (2000). Emergence of selective social referencing in infancy. *Infancy, 1,* 253–264.

Stright, A. D., Herr, M. Y., & Neitzel, C. (2009). Maternal scaffolding of children's problem solving and children's adjustment in kindergarten: Hmong families in the United States. *Journal of Educational Psychology, 101,* 207–218.

Stright, A. D., Neitzel, C., Sears, K. G., & Hoke-Sinex, L. (2002). Instruction begins in the home: Relations between parental instruction and children's self-regulation in the classroom. *Journal of Educational Psychology, 93,* 456–466.

Strohschein, L. (2005). Parental divorce and child mental health trajectories. *Journal of Marriage and Family, 67,* 1286–1300.

Stronach, E. P., Toth, S. L., Rogosch, F., Oshri, A., Manle, J. T., & Cicchetti, D. (2011). Child maltreatment, attachment security and internal representations of mother and mother–child relationships. *Child Maltreatment, 16,* 137–154.

Stroub, K. J., & Richards, M. P. (2013). From resegregation to reintegration: Trends in the racial/ethnic segregation of metropolitan public schools, 1993–2009. *American Educational Research Journal, 50,* 497–531.

Stroud, C. B., Meyers, K. M., Wilson, S., & Durbin, C. (2015). Marital quality spillover and young children's adjustment: Evidence for dyadic and triadic parenting as mechanisms. *Journal of Clinical Child and Adolescent Psychology, 44,* 800–813.

Sturge-Apple, M. L., Davies, P. T., Winter, M. A., Cummings, E. M., & Schermerhorn, A. (2008). Interparental conflict and children's school adjustment: The explanatory role of children's internal representations of interparental and parent–child relationships. *Developmental Psychology, 44,* 1678–1690.

Suárez-Orozco, C., Abo-Zena, M. M., & Marks, A. K. (2015). Unique and shared experiences of immigrant-origin children and youth. In C. Suárez-Orozco, M. M. Abo-Zena, & A. K. Marks (Eds.), *Transitions: The development of children of immigrants* (pp. 1–26). New York: New York University Press.

Suárez-Orozco, C., Pimental, A., & Martin, M. (2009). The significance of relationships: Academic engagement and achievement among newcomer immigrant youth. *Teachers College Record, 111,* 712–749.

Subrahmanyam, K., Gelman, R., & Lafosse, A. (2002). Animate and other separably moveable things. In G. Humphreys (Ed.), *Category-specificity in brain and mind* (pp. 341–371). London: Psychology Press.

Substance Abuse and Mental Health Administration. (2016). *Results from the 2015 National Survey on Drug Use and Health: Summary of national findings.* Rockville, MD: Author. Retrieved from www.samhsa.gov/data/sites/default/files/NSDUH-FFR1-2015/NSDUH-FFR1-2015/NSDUH-FFR1-2015.pdf

Sullivan, J., Beech, A. R., Craig, L. A., & Gannon, T. A. (2011). Comparing intra-familial and extra-familial child sexual abusers with professionals who have sexually abused children with whom they work. *International Journal of Offender Therapy and Comparative Criminology, 55,* 56–74.

Sullivan, M. C., McGrath, M. M. Hawes, K., & Lester, B. M. (2008). Growth trajectories of preterm infants: Birth to 12 years. *Journal of Pediatric Health Care, 22,* 83–93.

Sullivan, M. W., & Lewis, M. (2003). Contextual determinants of anger and other negative expressions in young infants. *Developmental Psychology, 39,* 693–705.

Sullivan, P. F., Daly, M. J., & O'Donovan, M. (2012). Genetic architectures of psychiatric disorders: The emerging picture and its implications. *Nature Reviews Genetics, 13,* 537–551.

Sunderam, S., Kissin, D. M., Crawford, S. B., Folger, S. G., Jamieson, D. J., Warner, L., et al. (2015). Assisted reproductive technology surveillance—United States, 2012. *Morbidity and Mortality Weekly Report, 64*(SS06), 1–29. Retrieved from www.cdc.gov/mmwr/preview/mmwrhtml/ss6406a1.htm

Sundet, J. M., Barlaug, D. G., & Torjussen, T. M. (2004). The end of the Flynn effect? A study of secular trends in mean intelligence test scores of Norwegian conscripts during half a century. *Intelligence, 32,* 349–362.

Super, C. M. (1981). Behavioral development in infancy. In R. H. Monroe, R. L. Monroe, & B. B. Whiting (Eds.), *Handbook of cross-cultural human development* (pp. 181–270). New York: Garland.

Super, C. M., & Harkness, S. (2010). Culture and infancy. In J. G. Bremner & T. D. Wachs (Eds.), *Wiley-Blackwell handbook of infant development: Vol. 1. Basic research* (2nd ed., pp. 623–649). Oxford, UK: Wiley-Blackwell.

Super, C. M., Harkness, S., van Tijen, N., van der Vlugt, E., Fintelman, M., & Dijkstra, J. (1996). The three R's of Dutch childrearing and the socialization of infant arousal. In S. Harkness & C. M. Super (Eds.), *Parents' cultural belief systems* (pp. 447–466). New York: Guilford.

Supple, A. J., & Small, S. A. (2006). The influence of parental support, knowledge, and authoritative parenting on Hmong and European American adolescent development. *Journal of Family Issues, 27,* 1214–1232.

Suzuki, K., & Ando, J. (2014). Genetic and environmental structure of individual differences in hand, foot, and ear preferences: A twin study. *Laterality, 19,* 113–128.

Swain, M. E. (2014). Surrogacy and gestational carrier arrangements: Legal aspects. In J. M. Goldfarb (Ed.), *Third-party reproduction* (pp. 133–142). New York: Springer.

Swanson, H. L., Harris, K. R., & Graham, S. (2014). Overview of foundations, causes, instruction, and methodology in the field of learning disabilities. In H. L. Swanson, K. R. Harris, & S. Graham (Eds.), *Handbook of learning disabilities* (pp. 3–14). New York: Guilford Press.

Swinson, J., & Harrop, A. (2009). Teacher talk directed to boys and girls and its relationship to their behaviour. *Educational Studies, 35,* 515–524.

Szaflarski, J. P., Rajogopal, A., Altaye, M., Byars, A. W., Jacola, L., Schmithorst, V. J., et al. (2012). Left-handedness and language lateralization in children. *Brain Research, 1433,* 85–97.

T

Tabibi, Z., & Pfeffer, K. (2007). Finding a safe place to cross the road: The effect of distractors and the role of attention in children's identification of safe and dangerous road-crossing sites. *Infant and Child Development, 16,* 193–206.

Taga, G., Asakawa, K., Maki, A., Konishi, Y., & Koizumi, H. (2003). Brain imaging in awake infants by near-infrared optical topography. *Proceedings of the National Academy of Sciences, 100,* 10722–10727.

Tager-Flusberg, H. (2014). Autism spectrum disorder: Developmental approaches from infancy through early childhood. In M. Lewis & K. D. Rudolph (Eds.), *Handbook of Developmental Psychopathology* (pp. 651–664). New York: Springer.

Takahashi, K. (1990). Are the key assumptions of the "Strange Situation" procedure universal? A view from Japanese research. *Human Development, 33,* 23–30.

Talaulikar, V. S., & Arulkumaran, S. (2011). Folic acid in obstetric review. *Obstetrics and Gynecological Survey, 66,* 240–247.

Tamis-LeMonda, C. S., & Bornstein, M. H. (1989). Habituation and maternal encouragement of attention in infancy as predictors of toddler language, play, and representational competence. *Child Development, 60,* 738–751.

Tamis-LeMonda, C. S., & McFadden, K. E. (2010). The United States of America. In M. H. Bornstein & T. Leventhal (Eds.), *Handbook of cultural developmental science: Vol. 4. Ecological settings and processes* (pp. 299–322). New York: Psychology Press.

Tamm, L., Nakonezny, P. A., & Hughes, C. W. (2014). An open trial of metacognitive executive function training for young children with ADHD. *Journal of Attention Disorders, 18,* 551–559.

Tandon, S. D., Colon, L., Vega, P., Murphy, J., & Alonso, A. (2012). Birth outcomes associated with receipt of group prenatal care among low-income Hispanic women. *Journal of Midwifery & Women's Health, 57,* 476–481.

Tangney, J. P., Stuewig, J., & Mashek, D. J. (2007). Moral emotions and moral behavior. *Annual Review of Psychology, 58,* 345–372.

Taras, V., Sarala, R., Muchinsky, P., Kemmelmeier, M., Singelis, T. M., Avsec, A., et al. (2014). Opposite ends of the same stick? Multi-method test of the dimensionality of individualism and collectivism. *Journal of Cross-Cultural Psychology, 45,* 213–245.

Tardif, T., Fletcher, P., Liang, W., Zhang, Z., Kaciroti, N., & Marchman, V. A. (2008). Baby's first 10 words. *Developmental Psychology, 44,* 929–938.

Tarullo, A. R., Balsam, P. D., & Fifer, W. P. (2011). Sleep and infant learning. *Infant and Child Development, 20,* 35–46.

Taylor, C. A., Manganello, J. A., Lee, S. J., & Rice, J. C. (2010). Mother's spanking of 3-year-old children and subsequent risk of children's aggressive behavior. *Pediatrics, 125,* e1057–e1065.

Taylor, M., Carlson, S. M., Maring, B. L., Gerow, L., & Charley, C. M. (2004). The characteristics and correlates of fantasy in school-age children: Imaginary companions, impersonation, and social understanding. *Developmental Psychology, 40,* 1173–1187.

Taylor, M. C., & Hall, J. A. (1982). Psychological androgyny: Theories, methods, and conclusions. *Psychological Bulletin, 92,* 347–366.

Taylor, M. G., Rhodes, M., & Gelman, S. A. (2009). Boys will be boys; cows will be cows: Children's essentialist reasoning about gender categories and animal species. *Child Development, 80,* 461–481.

Taylor, R. D. (2010). Risk and resilience in low-income African American families: Moderating effects of kinship social support. *Cultural Diversity and Ethnic Minority Psychology, 16,* 344–351.

Tecwyn, E. C., Thorpe, S. K. S., & Chappell, J. (2014). Development of planning in 4- to 10-year-old children: Reducing inhibitory demands does not improve performance. *Journal of Experimental Child Psychology, 125,* 85–101.

Temple, C. M., & Shephard, E. E. (2012). Exceptional lexical skills but executive language deficits in school starters and young adults with Turner syndrome: Implications for X chromosome effects on brain function. *Brain and Language, 120,* 345–359.

Temple, J. L., Giacomelli, A. M., Roemmich, J. N., & Epstein, L. H. (2007). Overweight children habituate slower than nonoverweight children to food. *Physiology and Behavior, 9,* 250–254.

Tenenbaum, H. R., Hill, D., Joseph, N., & Roche, E. (2010). "It's a boy because he's painting a picture": Age differences in children's conventional and unconventional gender schemas. *British Journal of Psychology, 101,* 137–154.

Tenenbaum, H. R., & Leaper, C. (2002). Are parents' gender schemas related to their children's gender-related cognitions? A meta-analysis. *Developmental Psychology, 38,* 615–630.

Tenenbaum, H. R., & Leaper, C. (2003). Parent–child conversations about science: The socialization of gender inequities? *Developmental Psychology, 39,* 34–47.

Tenenbaum, H. R., Snow, C. E., Roach, K. A., & Kurland, B. (2005). Talking and reading science: Longitudinal data on sex differences in mother–child conversations in low-income families. *Journal of Applied Developmental Psychology, 26,* 1–19.

ten Tusscher, G. W., & Koppe, J. G. (2004). Perinatal dioxin exposure and later effects—a review. *Chemosphere, 54,* 1329–1336.

Teti, D. M., Saken, J. W., Kucera, E., & Corns, K. M. (1996). And baby makes four: Predictors of attachment security among preschool-age firstborns during the transition to siblinghood. *Child Development, 67,* 579–596.

Thakur, G. A., Sengupta, S. M., Grizenko, N., Schmitz, N., Pagé, V., & Joober, R. (2013). Maternal smoking during pregnancy and ADHD: A comprehensive clinical and neurocognitive characterization. *Nicotine & Tobacco Research, 15,* 149–157.

Thatcher, R. W., Walker, R. A., & Giudice, S. (1987). Human cerebral hemispheres develop at different rates and ages. *Science, 236,* 1110–1113.

Thelen, E., & Corbetta, D. (2002). Microdevelopment and dynamic systems: Applications to infant motor development. In N. Granott & J. Parziale (Eds.), *Microdevelopment: Transition processes in development and learning* (pp. 59–79). New York: Cambridge University Press.

Thelen, E., Schöner, G., Scheier, C., & Smith, L. B. (2001). The dynamics of embodiment: A field theory of infant perseverative reaching. *Behavioral and Brain Sciences, 24,* 1–34.

Thelen, E., & Smith, L. B. (1998). Dynamic systems theories. In R. M. Lerner (Ed.), *Handbook of child psychology: Vol. 1. Theoretical models of human development* (5th ed., pp. 563–634). New York: Wiley.

Thelen, E., & Smith, L. B. (2006). Dynamic systems theories. In R. M. Lerner (Ed.), *Handbook of child psychology: Vol. 1. Theoretical models of human development* (6th ed., pp. 258–312). Hoboken, NJ: Wiley.

Thiessen, E. D., & Saffran, J. R. (2007). Learning to learn: Infants' acquisition of stress-based strategies for work segmentation. *Language Learning and Development, 3,* 73–100.

Thoermer, C., Woodward, A., Sodian, B., & Perst, H. (2013). To get the grasp: Seven-month-olds encode and selectively reproduce goal-directed grasping. *Journal of Experimental Child Psychology, 116,* 499–509.

Thomaes, S., Brummelman, E., Reijntjes, A., & Bushman, B. J. (2013). When Narcissus was a boy: Origins, nature, and consequences of childhood narcissism. *Child Developmental Perspectives, 7,* 22–26.

Thomaes, S., Stegge, H., Bushman, B. J., & Olthof, T. (2008). Trumping shame by blasts of noise: Narcissism, self-esteem, shame, and aggression in young adolescents. *Child Development, 79,* 1792–1801.

Thomas, A., & Chess, S. (1977). *Temperament and development.* New York: Brunner/Mazel.

Thomas, K. A., & Tessler, R. C. (2007). Bicultural socialization among adoptive families: Where there is a will, there is a way. *Journal of Family Issues, 28,* 1189–1219.

Thomas, S. R., O'Brien, K. A., Clarke, T. L., Liu, Y., & Chronis-Tuscano, A. (2015). Maternal depression history moderates parenting responses to compliant and noncompliant behaviors of children with ADHD. *Journal of Abnormal Child Psychology, 43,* 1257–1269.

Thompson, A., Hollis, C., & Richards, D. (2003). Authoritarian parenting attitudes as a risk for conduct problems: Results of a British national cohort study. *European Child and Adolescent Psychiatry, 12,* 84–91.

Thompson, J. M., Waldie, K. E., Wall, C. R., Murphy, R., & Mitchell, E. A. (2014). Associations between acetaminophen use during pregnancy and ADHD symptoms measured at ages 7 and 11 years. *PLOS ONE, 9*(9), e108210.

Thompson, P. M., Giedd, J. N., Woods, R. P., MacDonald, D., Evans, A. C., & Toga, A. W. (2000). Growth patterns in the developing brain detected by using continuum mechanical tensor maps. *Nature, 404,* 190–192.

Thompson, R. A. (2006). The development of the person: Social understanding, relationships, conscience, self. In N. Eisenberg (Ed.), *Handbook of child psychology: Vol. 3. Social, emotional, and personality development* (6th ed., pp. 24–98). Hoboken, NJ: Wiley.

Thompson, R. A. (2013). Attachment theory and research: Précis and prospect. In P. D. Zelazo (Ed.), *Oxford handbook of developmental psychology: Vol. 2. Self and other* (pp. 191–216). New York: Oxford University Press.

Thompson, R. A. (2014). Conscience development in early childhood. In M. Killen & J. G. Smetana (Eds.), *Handbook of moral development* (2nd ed., pp. 73–92). New York: Psychology Press.

Thompson, R. A. (2015). Relationships, regulation, and early development. In M. E. Lamb (Ed.), *Handbook of child psychology and developmental science: Vol. 3. Socioemotional processes* (7th ed., pp. 201–246). Hoboken, NJ: Wiley.

Thompson, R. A., & Goodman, M. (2010). Development of emotion regulation: More than meets the eye. In A. M. Kring & D. M. Sloan (Eds.), *Emotion regulation and psychopathology: A transdiagnostic approach to etiology and treatment* (pp. 38–58). New York: Guilford.

Thompson, R. A., & Goodvin, R. (2007). Taming the tempest in the teapot. In C. A. Brownell & C. B. Kopp (Eds.), *Socioemotional development in the toddler years: Transitions and transformations* (pp. 320–341). New York: Guilford.

Thompson, R. A., Meyer, S., & McGinley, M. (2006). Understanding values in relationships: The development of conscience. In M. Killen & J. G. Smetana (Eds.), *Handbook of moral development* (pp. 267–298). Mahwah, NJ: Erlbaum.

Thompson, R. A., & Nelson, C. A. (2001). Developmental science and the media. *American Psychologist, 56,* 5–15.

Thompson, R. A., Winer, A. C., & Goodvin, R. (2011). The individual child: Temperament, emotion, self, and personality. In M. H. Bornstein & M. E. Lamb (Eds.), *Developmental science: An advanced textbook* (6th ed., pp. 427–468). Hoboken, NJ: Taylor & Francis.

Thompson, W. W., Price, C., Goodson, B., Shay, D. K., Benson, P., Hinrichsen, V. L., et al. (2007). Early thimerosal exposure and neuropsychological outcomes at 7 to 10 years. *New England Journal of Medicine, 357,* 1281–1292.

Thorne, B. (1993). *Gender play: Girls and boys in school.* New Brunswick, NJ: Rutgers University Press.

Thornton, S. (1999). Creating conditions for cognitive change: The interaction between task structures and specific strategies. *Child Development, 70,* 588–603.

Tien, A. (2013). Bootstrapping and the acquisition of Mandarin Chinese: A natural semantic metalanguage perspective. In D. Bittner & N. Ruhlig (Eds.), *Lexical bootstrapping: The role of lexis and semantics in child language* (pp. 39–72). Berlin: Walter de Gruyter.

Tienari, P., Wahlberg, K. E., & Wynne, L. C. (2006). Finnish adoption study of schizophrenia: Implications for family interventions. *Families, Systems, and Health, 24,* 442–451.

Tienari, P., Wynne, L. C., Lasky, K., Moring, J., Nieminen, P., & Sorri, A. (2003). Genetic boundaries of the schizophrenia spectrum: Evidence from the Finnish adoptive family study of schizophrenia. *American Journal of Psychiatry, 160,* 1587–1594.

Tikotzky, L., Sharabany, R., Hirsch, I., & Sadeh, A. (2010). "Ghosts in the Nursery": Infant sleep and sleep-related cognitions of parents raised under communal sleeping arrangements. *Infant Mental Health Journal, 31*, 312–334.

Tincoff, R., & Jusczyk, P. W. (1999). Some beginnings of word comprehension in 6-month-olds. *Psychological Science, 10,* 172–175.

Tishkoff, S. A., & Kidd, K. K. (2004). Implications of biogeography of human populations for "race" and medicine. *Nature Genetics, 36*(Suppl. 11), S21–S27.

Tomasello, M. (2006). Acquiring linguistic constructions. In D. Kuhn & R. Siegler (Eds.), *Handbook of child psychology: Vol. 2. Cognition, perception, and language* (6th ed., pp. 255–298). Hoboken, NJ: Wiley.

Tomasello, M. (2011). Language development. In U. Goswami (Ed.), *Wiley-Blackwell handbook of childhood cognitive development* (2nd ed., pp. 239–257). Malden, MA: Wiley-Blackwell.

Tomasello, M., & Akhtar, N. (1995). Two-year-olds use pragmatic cues to differentiate reference to objects and actions. *Cognitive Development, 10,* 201–224.

Tomasello, M., Carpenter, M., & Liszkowski, U. (2007). A new look at infant pointing. *Child Development, 78,* 705–722.

Tomyr, L., Ouimet, C., & Ugnat, A. (2012). A review of findings from the Canadian Incidence Study of reported child abuse and neglect. *Canadian Journal of Public Health, 103,* 103–112.

Tong, S., Baghurst, P., Vimpani, G., & McMichael, A. (2007). Socioeconomic position, maternal IQ, home environment, and cognitive development. *Journal of Pediatrics, 151,* 284–288.

Torrance, E. P. (1988). The nature of creativity as manifest in its testing. In R. J. Sternberg (Ed.), *The nature of creativity: Contemporary psychological perspectives* (pp. 43–75). New York: Cambridge University Press.

Tottenham, N., Hare, T. A., & Casey, B. J. (2009). A developmental perspective on human amygdala function. In P. J. Whalen & E. A. Phelps (Eds.), *The human amygdala* (pp. 107–117). New York: Guilford.

Tottenham, N., Hare, T. A., Millner, A., Gilhooly, T., Zevin, J. D., & Casey, B. J. (2011). Elevated amygdala response to faces following early deprivation. *Developmental Science, 14,* 190–204.

Tracy, J. L., Robins, R. W., & Lagattuta, K. H. (2005). Can children recognize pride? *Emotion, 5,* 251–257.

Tran, P., & Subrahmanyam, K. (2013). Evidence-based guidelines for informal use of computers by children to promote the development of academic, cognitive and social skills. *Ergonomics, 56,* 1349–1362.

Träuble, B., & Pauen, S. (2011). Cause or effect: What matters? How 12-month-old infants learn to categorize artifacts. *British Journal of Developmental Psychology, 29,* 357–374.

Trautner, H. M., Ruble, D. N., Cyphers, L., Kirsten, B., Behrendt, R., & Hartmann, P. (2005). Rigidity and flexibility of gender stereotypes in childhood: Developmental or differential? *Infant and Child Development, 14,* 365–381.

Trehub, S. E. (2001). Musical predispositions in infancy. *Annals of the New York Academy of Sciences, 930,* 1–16.

Tremblay, R. E. (2000). The development of aggressive behaviour during childhood: What have we learned in the past century? *International Journal of Behavioral Development, 24,* 129–141.

Trentacosta, C. J., & Shaw, D. S. (2009). Emotional self-regulation, peer rejection, and antisocial behavior: Developmental associations from early childhood to early adolescence. *Journal of Applied Developmental Psychology, 30,* 356–365.

Triandis, H. C., & Gelfand, M. J. (2012). A theory of individualism and collectivism. In P. A. M. Van Lange, A. W. Kruglanski, & E. T. Higgins (Eds.), *Handbook of theories of social psychology* (Vol. 2, pp. 498–520). Thousand Oaks, CA: Sage.

Trickett, P. K., Noll, J. G., & Putnam, F. W. (2011). The impact of sexual abuse on female development: Lessons from a multigenerational, longitudinal research study. *Development and Psychopathology, 23,* 453–476.

Trocmé, N., & Wolfe, D. (2002). *Child maltreatment in Canada: The Canadian Incidence Study of Reported Child Abuse and Neglect.* Retrieved from www.hc-sc.gc.ca/pphb-dgspsp/cm-vee

Troilo, J., & Coleman, M. (2012). Full-time, part-time full-time, and part-time fathers: Father identities following divorce. *Family Relations, 61,* 601–614.

Tronick, E., Morelli, G., & Ivey, P. (1992). The Efe forager infant and toddler's pattern of social relationships: Multiple and simultaneous. *Developmental Psychology, 28,* 568–577.

Tronick, E. Z., Thomas, R. B., & Daltabuit, M. (1994). The Quechua manta pouch: A caretaking practice for buffering the Peruvian infant against the multiple stressors of high altitude. *Child Development, 65,* 1005–1013.

Tropp, L. R., & Page-Gould, E. (2015). Contact between groups. In M. Mikulincer & P. R. Shaver (Eds.), *APA handbook of personality and social psychology: Vol. 2. Group processes* (pp. 535–560). Washington, DC: American Psychological Association.

Troop-Gordon, W., & Asher, S. R. (2005). Modifications in children's goals when encountering obstacles to conflict resolution. *Child Development, 76,* 568–582.

Troseth, G. L. (2003). Getting a clear picture: Young children's understanding of a televised image. *Developmental Science, 6,* 247–253.

Troseth, G. L., Saylor, M. M., & Archer, A. H. (2006). Young children's use of video as a source of socially relevant information. *Child Development, 77,* 786–799.

True, M. M., Pisani, L., & Oumar, F. (2001). Infant–mother attachment among the Dogon of Mali. *Child Development, 72,* 1451–1466.

Trzesniewski, K. H., Donnellan, M. B., & Robins, R. W. (2003). Stability of self-esteem across the life span. *Journal of Personality and Social Psychology, 84,* 205–220.

Tsang, C. D., & Conrad, N. J. (2010). Does the message matter? The effect of song type on infants' pitch preferences for lullabies and playsongs. *Infant Behavior and Development, 33,* 96–100.

Tseng, V., Easton, J. Q., & Supplee, L. H. (2017). Research–practice partnerships: Building two-way streets of engagement. *Social Policy Report of the Society for Research in Child Development, 30*(4).

Turiel, E., & Killen, M. (2010). Taking emotions seriously: The role of emotions in moral development. In W. F. Arsenio & E. A. Lemerise (Eds.), *Emotions, aggression, and morality in children: Bridging development and psychopathology* (pp. 33–52). Washington, DC: American Psychological Association.

Turkheimer, E., Pettersson, E., & Horn, E. E. (2014). A phenotypic null hypothesis for the genetics of personality. *Annual Review of Psychology, 65,* 515–540.

Turner, P. J., & Gervai, J. (1995). A multidimensional study of gender typing in preschool children and their parents: Personality, attitudes, preferences, behavior, and cultural differences. *British Journal of Developmental Psychology, 11,* 323–342.

Turner, R. N., Hewstone, M., & Voci, A. (2007). Reducing explicit and implicit outgroup prejudice via direct and extended contact: The mediating role of self-disclosure and intergroup anxiety. *Journal of Personality and Social Psychology, 93,* 369–388.

Tustin, K., & Hayne, H. (2010). Defining the boundary: Age-related changes in childhood amnesia. *Developmental Psychology, 46,* 1046–1061.

Twenge, J. M., & Crocker, J. (2002). Race and self-esteem: Meta-analyses comparing Whites, Blacks,

Hispanics, Asians, and America Indians and comment on Gray-Little and Hafdahl (2000). *Psychological Bulletin, 128,* 371–408.

Twyman, R. (2014). *Principles of proteomics* (2nd ed.). New York: Garland Science.

Tyler, C. P., Paneth, N., Allred, E. N., Hirtz, D., Kuban, K., McElrath, T., et al. (2012). Brain damage in preterm newborns and maternal medication: The ELGAN Study. *American Journal of Obstetrics and Gynecology, 207*(192), e1–9. Retrieved from www.ajog.org/article/S0002-9378(12)00713-2/pdfSummary

U

Uccelli, P., & Pan, B. A. (2013). Semantic development. In J. B. Gleason & N. B. Ratner (Eds.), *Development of language* (8th ed., pp. 89–119). Upper Saddle River, NJ: Pearson.

Ukrainetz, T. A., Justice, L. M., Kaderavek, J. N., Eisenberg, S. L., Gillam, R., & Harm, H. M. (2005). The development of expressive elaboration in fictional narratives. *Journal of Speech, Language, and Hearing Research, 48,* 1363–1377.

Underwood, M. K. (2003). *Social aggression among girls.* New York: Guilford.

Unger, C. C., Salam, S. S., Sarker, M. S. A., Black, R., Cravioto, A., & Arifeen, S. E. (2014). Treating diarrheal disease in children under five: The global picture. *Archives of Diseases of Childhood, 99,* 273–278.

UNICEF (United Nations Children's Fund). (2013). *UNICEF data: Monitoring the situation of children and women.* Retrieved from www.childinfo.org/statistical_tables.html

UNICEF (United Nations Children's Fund). (2017a). *Children in war & conflict.* Retrieved from www.unicefusa.org/mission/emergencies/conflict

UNICEF (United Nations Children's Fund). (2017b). *From the first hour of life: Making the case for infant and young child breastfeeding everywhere.* Retrieved from data.unicef.org/resources/first-hour-life-new-report-breastfeeding-practices

UNICEF (United Nations Children's Fund). (2017c). *Levels and trends in child malnutrition: Key findings of the 2017 edition.* Retrieved from data.unicef.org/wp-content/uploads/2017/06/JME-2017_brochure_June-25.pdf

United Nations. (2017). *World population prospects: Key findings & advance tables.* Retrieved from esa.un.org/unpd/wpp/Publications/Files/WPP2017_KeyFindings.pdf

U.S. Bureau of Labor Statistics. (2017). Employment characteristics of families summary. *Economic News Release*, USDL-17-0444. Retrieved from www.bls.gov/news.release/famee.nr0.htm

U.S. Census Bureau. (2015). *Selected population profile in the United States: 2015 American Community Survey 1-year estimates (American Indian and Alaska Native).* Retrieved from factfinder.census.gov/faces/tableservices/jsf/pages/productview.xhtml?src=bkmk

U.S. Census Bureau. (2016). *America's families and living arrangements: 2015.* Retrieved from www.census.gov/hhes/families/data/cps2015.html

U.S. Census Bureau. (2017a). *American Community Survey (ACS): 2016 data release.* Retrieved from www.census.gov/programs-surveys/acs

U.S. Census Bureau. (2017b). *Fertility of women in the United States: 2017.* Retrieved from www.census.gov/data/tables/2016/demo/fertility/women-fertility.html

U.S. Census Bureau. (2017c). *International data base.* Retrieved from www.census.gov/population/international/data/idb/informationGateway.php

U.S. Department of Agriculture. (2015). *Women, Infants and Children (WIC): About WIC–WIC at a glance.* Retrieved from www.fns.usda.gov/wic/about-wic-wic-glance

U.S. Department of Agriculture. (2016). *Food security in the U.S.: Key statistics and graphics.* Retrieved from www.ers.usda.gov/topics/food-nutrition-assistance/food-security-in-the-us/key-statistics-graphics

U.S. Department of Education. (2016a). *Digest of education statistics: 2015.* Retrieved from nces.ed.gov/programs/digest/2015menu_tables.asp

U.S. Department of Education. (2016b). *The nation's report card: 2015 Mathematics and reading assessments, national results overview.* Retrieved from www.nationsreportcard.gov/reading_math_2015/#reading?grade=4

U.S. Department of Health and Human Services. (2006). *Research to practice: Preliminary findings from the Early Head Start Prekindergarten Follow-Up, Early Head Start Research and Evaluation Project.* Washington, DC: Author.

U.S. Department of Health and Human Services. (2010). *Head Start Impact Study: Final report.* Washington, DC: U.S. Government Printing Office.

U.S. Department of Health and Human Services. (2015a). *Behavioral health trends in the United States: Results from the 2014 National Survey on Drug Use and Health* (HHS Publication No. SMA 15-4927, NSDUH Series H-50). Retrieved from www.samhsa.gov/data/sites/default/files/NSDUH-FRR1-2014/NSDUH-FRR1-2014.pdf

U.S. Department of Health and Human Services. (2015b). *Child health USA 2014.* Rockville, MD: Author. Retrieved from mchb.hrsa.gov/chusa14/dl/chusa14.pdf

U.S. Department of Health and Human Services. (2016). *Health, United States, 2016.* Retrieved from www.cdc.gov/nchs/data/hus/hus16.pdf#060

U.S. Department of Health and Human Services. (2017a). *Child maltreatment 2015.* Retrieved from www.acf.hhs.gov/sites/default/files/cb/cm2015.pdf

U.S. Department of Health and Human Services. (2017b). *What causes Down syndrome?* Retrieved from www.nichd.nih.gov/health/topics/down/conditioninfo/Pages/causes.aspx

Usta, I. M., & Nassar, A. H. (2008). Advanced maternal age. Part I: Obstetric complications. *American Journal of Perinatology, 25,* 521–534.

Uttal, D. H., Meadow, N. G., Tipton, E., Hand, L. L., Alden, A. R., Warren, C., & Newcombe, N. S. (2013). The malleability of spatial skills: A meta-analysis of training studies. *Psychological Bulletin, 139,* 352–402.

Uziel, Y., Chapnick, G., Oren-Ziv, A., Jaber, L., Nemet, D., & Hashkes, P. J. (2012). Bone strength in children with growing pains: Long-term follow-up. *Clinical and Experimental Rheumatology, 30,* 137–140.

V

Vaever, M. S., Krogh, M. T., Smith-Nielsen, J., Christensen, T. T., & Tharner, A. (2015). Infants of depressed mothers show reduced gaze activity during mother–infant interaction at 4 months. *Infancy, 20,* 445–454.

Vaillancourt, T., & Hymel, S. (2006). Aggression and social status: The moderating roles of sex and peer-valued characteristics. *Aggressive Behavior, 32,* 396–408.

Vaillancourt, T., Hymel, S., & McDougall, P. (2013). The biological underpinnings of peer victimization: Understanding why and how the effects of bullying can last a lifetime. *Theory into Practice, 52,* 241–248.

Vaish, A., Missana, M., & Tomasello, M. (2011). Three-year-old children intervene in third-party moral transgressions. *British Journal of Developmental Psychology, 29,* 124–130.

Vakil, E., Blachstein, H., Sheinman, M., & Greenstein, Y. (2009). Developmental changes in attention tests norms: Implications for the structure of attention. *Child Neuropsychology, 15,* 21–39.

Valiente, C., Eisenberg, N., Fabes, R. A., Shepard, S. A., Cumberland, A., & Losoya, S. H. (2004). Prediction of children's empathy-related responding from their effortful control and parents' expressivity. *Developmental Psychology, 40,* 911–926.

Valiente, C., Lemery-Chalfant, K., & Swanson, J. (2010). Prediction of kindergartners' academic achievement from their effortful control and emotionality: Evidence for direct and moderated relations. *Journal of Educational Psychology, 102,* 550–560.

Valli, L., Croninger, R. G., & Buese, D. (2012). Studying high-quality teaching in a highly charged policy environment. *Teachers College Record, 114*(4), 1–33.

Vandell, D. L., Belsky, J., Burchinal, M., Steinberg, L., Vandergrift, N., & NICHD Early Child Care Research Network. (2010). Do effects of early child care extend to age 15 years? Results from the NICHD Study of Early Child Care and Youth Development. *Child Development, 81,* 737–756.

Vandell, D. L., Larson, R. W., Mahoney, J. L., & Watts, T. W. (2015). Children's organized activities. In M. H. Bornstein & T. Leventhal (Eds.), *Handbook of child psychology and developmental science: Vol. 4. Ecological settings and processes* (6th ed., pp. 305–344). Hoboken, NJ: Wiley.

Vandell, D. L., & Posner, J. K. (1999). Conceptualization and measurement of children's after-school environments. In S. L. Friedman & T. D. Wachs (Eds.), *Measuring environment across the life span* (pp. 167–196). Washington, DC: American Psychological Association.

Vandell, D. L., Reisner, E. R., & Pierce, K. M. (2007). *Outcomes linked to high-quality after-school programs: Longitudinal findings from the Study of Promising After-School Programs.* Retrieved from www.gse.uci.edu/childcare/pdf/afterschool/PP%20Longitudinal%20Findings%20Final%20Report.pdf

Vandell, D. L., Reisner, E. R., Pierce, K. M., Brown, B. B., Lee, D., Bolt, D., & Pechman, E. M. (2006). *The study of promising after-school programs: Examination of longer term outcomes after two years of program experiences.* Madison, WI: University of Wisconsin. Retrieved from www.wcer.wisc.edu/childcare/statements.html

van den Akker, A. L. Deković, M., Prinzie, P., & Asscher, J. J. (2010). Toddlers' temperament profiles: Stability and relations to negative and positive parenting. *Journal of Abnormal Child Psychology, 38,* 485–495.

Van den Bergh, B. R. H., & De Rycke, L. (2003). Measuring the multidimensional self-concept and global self-worth of 6- to 8-year-olds. *Journal of Genetic Psychology, 164,* 201–225.

van den Dries, L., Juffer, F., van IJzendoorn, M. H., & Bakermans-Kranenburg, M. J. (2009). Fostering security? A meta-analysis of attachment in adopted children. *Children and Youth Services Review, 31,* 410–421.

van den Eijnden, R., Vermulst, A., van Rooij, A. J., Scholte, R., & van de Mheen, D. (2014). The bidirectional relationships between online victimization and psychosocial problems in adolescents: A comparison with real-life victimization. *Journal of Youth and Adolescence, 43,* 790–802.

van de Vijver, F. J. R. (2011). Bias and real difference in cross-cultural differences: Neither friends nor foes. In F. J. R. van de Vijver, A. Chasiotis, & H. F. Byrnes (Eds.), *Fundamental questions in cross-cultural psychology* (pp. 235–258). Cambridge, UK: Cambridge University Press.

van Geel, M., & Vedder, P. (2011). The role of family obligations and school adjustment in explaining the immigrant paradox. *Journal of Youth and Adolescence, 40,* 187–196.

van Gelderen, L., Bos, H. M. W., Gartrell, N., Hermanns, J., & Perrin, E. C. (2012). Quality of life of adolescents raised from birth by lesbian mothers:

The U.S. National Longitudinal Family Study. *Journal of Developmental and Behavioral Pediatrics, 33,* 17–23.

van Grieken, A., Renders, C. M., Wijtzes, A. I., Hirasing, R. A., & Raat, H. (2013). Overweight, obesity and underweight is associated with adverse psychosocial and physical health outcomes among 7-year-old children: The "Be Active, Eat Right" Study. *PLOS ONE, 8*(6), e67383.

Van Hulle, C. A., Goldsmith, H. H., & Lemery, K. S. (2004). Genetic, environmental, and gender effects on individual differences in toddler expressive language. *Journal of Speech, Language, and Hearing Research, 47,* 904–912.

van IJzendoorn, M. H., & Bakermans-Kranenburg, M. J. (2006). DRD4 7-repeat polymorphism moderates the association between maternal unresolved loss or trauma and infant disorganization. *Attachment and Human Development, 8,* 291–307.

van IJzendoorn, M. H., & Bakermans-Kranenburg, M. J. (2015). Genetic differential susceptibility on trial: Meta-analytic support from randomized controlled experiments. *Development and Psychopathology, 27,* 151–162.

van IJzendoorn, M. H., Bakermans-Kranenburg, M. J., & Ebstein, R. P. (2011). Methylation matters in child development: Toward developmental behavioral epigenetics. *Child Development Perspectives, 5,* 305–310.

van IJzendoorn, M. H., Belsky, J., & Bakermans-Kranenburg, M. J. (2012). Serotonin transporter genotype 5-HTTLPR as a marker of differential susceptibility: A meta-analysis of child and adolescent gene-by-environment studies. *Translational Psychiatry, 2,* e147.

van IJzendoorn, M. H., & Kroonenberg, P. M. (1988). Cross-cultural patterns of attachment: A meta-analysis of the Strange Situation. *Child Development, 59,* 147–156.

van IJzendoorn, M. H., & Sagi-Schwartz, A. (2008). Cross-cultural patterns of attachment: Universal and contextual dimensions. In J. Cassidy & P. R. Shaver (Eds.), *Handbook of attachment* (2nd ed., pp. 880–905). New York: Guilford.

van IJzendoorn, M. H., Vereijken, C. M. J. L., Bakermans-Kranenburg, M. J., & Riksen-Walraven, J. M. (2004). Assessing attachment security with the Attachment Q Sort: Meta-analytic evidence for the validity of the Observer AQS. *Child Development, 75,* 1188–1213.

VanMarle, K., & Wynn, K. (2006). Six-month-old infants use analog magnitudes to represent duration. *Developmental Science, 9,* 41–49.

Varnhagen, C. (2007). Children and the Web. In J. Gackenbach (Ed.), *Psychology and the Internet* (2nd ed., pp, 37–54). Amsterdam: Elsevier.

Vaughn, B. E., Bost, K. K., & van IJzendoorn, M. H. (2008). Attachment and temperament. In J. Cassidy & P. R. Shaver (Eds.), *Handbook of attachment: Theory, research, and clinical applications* (2nd ed., pp. 192–216). New York: Guilford.

Vaughn, B. E., Kopp, C. B., & Krakow, J. B. (1984). The emergence and consolidation of self-control from eighteen to thirty months of age: Normative trends and individual differences. *Child Development, 55,* 990–1004.

Vedova, A. M. (2014). Maternal psychological state and infant's temperament at three months. *Journal of Reproductive and Infant Psychology, 32,* 520–534.

Veenstra, R., Lindenberg, S., Munniksma, A., & Dijkstra, J. K. (2010). The complex relation between bullying, victimization, acceptance, and rejection: Giving special attention to status, affection, and sex differences. *Child Development, 81,* 480–486.

Velez, C. E., Wolchik, S. A., Tien, J., & Sandler, I. (2011). Protecting children from the consequences of divorce: A longitudinal study of the effects of parenting on children's coping processes. *Child Development, 82,* 244–257.

Venables, P. H., & Raine, A. (2016). Impact of malnutrition on intelligence at 3 and 11 years of age: The mediating role of temperament. *Developmental Psychology, 52,* 205–220.

Veneziano, R. A. (2003). The importance of paternal warmth. *Cross-Cultural Research, 37,* 265–281.

Ventola, C. L. (2016). Immunization in the United States: Recommendations, barriers, and measures to improve compliance. *Pharmacy and Therapeutics, 41,* 426–436.

Veríssimo, M., & Salvaterra, F. (2006). Maternal secure-base scripts and children's attachment security in an adopted sample. *Attachment and Human Development, 8,* 261–273.

Vernon-Feagans, L., & Cox, M. (2013). The Family Life Project: An epidemiological and developmental study of young children living in poor rural communities. *Monographs of the Society for Research in Child Development, 78*(5, Serial No. 310).

Vest, A. R., & Cho, L. S. (2012). Hypertension in pregnancy. *Cardiology Clinics, 30,* 407–423.

Viddal, K. R., Berg-Nielsen, T. S., Wan, M. W., Green, J., Hygen, B. W., Wichstrøm, L., et al. (2015). Secure attachment promotes the development of effortful control in boys. *Attachment & Human Development, 17,* 319–335.

Vieites, V., & Reeb-Sutherland, B. C. (2017). Individual differences in non-clinical maternal depression impact infant affect and behavior during the still-face paradigm across the first year. *Infant Behavior and Development, 47,* 13–21.

Vinden, P. G. (1996). Junín Quechua children's understanding of mind. *Child Development, 67,* 1707–1716.

Vinik, J., Almas, A., & Grusec, J. (2011). Mothers' knowledge of what distresses and what comforts their children predicts children's coping, empathy, and prosocial behavior. *Parenting: Science and Practice, 11,* 56–71.

Virant-Klun, I. (2015). Postnatal oogenesis in humans: A review of recent findings. *Stem Cells and Cloning: Advances and Applications, 8,* 49–60.

Visher, E. B., Visher, J. S., & Pasley, K. (2003). Remarriage, families and stepparenting. In F. Walsh (Ed.), *Normal family processes* (pp. 153–175). New York: Guilford.

Vissers, L. E. L. M., Gilissen, C., & Veltman, J. A. (2016). Genetic studies in intellectual disability and related disorders. *Nature Reviews: Genetics, 17,* 9–18.

Vitaro, F., Boivin, M., Brendgen, M., Girard, A., & Dionner, G. (2012). Social experiences in kindergarten and academic achievement in grade 1: A monozygotic twin difference study. *Journal of Educational Psychology, 2,* 366–380.

Vitaro, F., & Brendgen, M. (2012). Subtypes of aggressive behaviors: Etiologies, development, and consequences. In T. Bliesner, A. Beelmann, & M. Stemmler (Eds.), *Antisocial behavior and crime: Contributions of developmental and evaluation research to prevention and intervention* (pp. 17–38). Cambridge, MA: Hogrefe.

Vitrup, B., & Holden, G. W. (2010). Children's assessments of corporal punishment and other disciplinary practices: The role of age, race, SES, and exposure to spanking. *Journal of Applied Developmental Psychology, 31,* 211–220.

Voegtline, K. M., Costigan, K. A., Pater, H. A., & DiPietro, J. A. (2013). Near-term fetal response to maternal spoken voice. *Infant Behavior and Development, 36,* 526–533.

Vogel, C. A., Xue, Y., Maiduddin, E. M., Carlson, B. L., & Kisker, E. E. (2010). *Early Head Start children in grade 5: Long-term follow-up of the Early Head Start Research and Evaluation Study sample* (OPRE Report No. 2011-8). Washington, DC: U.S. Department of Health and Human Services.

Volling, B. L. (2001). Early attachment relationships as predictors of preschool children's emotion regulation with a distressed sibling. *Early Education and Development, 12,* 185–207.

Volling, B. L. (2012). Family transitions following the birth of a sibling: An empirical review of changes in the firstborn's adjustment. *Psychological Bulletin, 138,* 497–528.

Volling, B. L., & Belsky, J. (1992). Contribution of mother–child and father–child relationships to the quality of sibling interaction: A longitudinal study. *Child Development, 63,* 1209–1222.

Volling, B. L., Gonzalez, R., Oh, W., Song, J.-H., Yu, T., Rosenberg, L., et al. (2017). Developmental trajectories of children's adjustment across the transition to siblinghood: Pre-birth predictors and sibling outcomes at one year. *Monographs of the Society for Research in Child Development, 82* (3, Serial No. 326).

Volling, B. L., Mahoney, A., & Rauer, A. J. (2009). Sanctification of parenting, moral socialization, and young children's conscience development. *Psychology of Religion and Spirituality, 1,* 53–68.

Volling, B. L., McElwain, N. L., & Miller, A. L. (2002). Emotion regulation in context: The jealousy complex between young siblings and its relations with child and family characteristics. *Child Development, 73,* 581–600.

von Hofsten, C. (2004). An action perspective on motor development. *Trends in Cognitive Sciences, 8,* 266–272.

Vouloumanos, A. (2010). Three-month-olds prefer speech to other naturally occurring signals. *Language Learning and Development, 6,* 241–257.

Vranekovic, J., Bozovic, I. B., Grubic, Z., Wagner, J., Pavlinic, D., Dahoun, S., et al. (2012). Down syndrome: Parental origin, recombination, and maternal age. *Genetic Testing and Molecular Biomarkers, 16,* 70–73.

Vukasović, T., & Bratko, D. (2015). Heritability of personality: A meta-analysis of behavior genetic studies. *Psychological Bulletin, 141,* 769–785.

Vygotsky, L. S. (1978). *Mind in society: The development of higher mental processes.* Cambridge, MA: Harvard University Press. (Original works published 1930, 1933, and 1935)

Vygotsky, L. S. (1987). Thinking and speech. In R. W. Rieber, & A. S. Carton (Eds.), & N. Minick (Trans.), *The collected works of L. S. Vygotsky: Vol. 1. Problems of general psychology* (pp. 37–285). New York: Plenum. (Original work published 1934)

W

Waber, D. P., Bryce, C. P., Girard, J. M., Zichlin, M., Fitzmaurice, G. M., & Galler, J. R. (2014). Impaired IQ and academic skills in adults who experienced moderate to severe infantile malnutrition: A 40-year study. *Nutritional Neuroscience, 17,* 58–64.

Wadell, P. M., Hagerman, R. J., & Hessl, D. R. (2013). Fragile X syndrome: Psychiatric manifestations, assessment and emerging therapies. *Current Psychiatry Reviews, 9,* 53–58.

Wagenaar, K., van Wessenbruch, M. M., van Leeuwen, F. E., Cohen-Kettenis, P. T., Delemarre-van de Waal, H. A., Schats, R., et al. (2011). Self-reported behavioral and socioemotional functioning of 11- to 18-year-old adolescents conceived by in vitro fertilization. *Fertility and Sterility, 95,* 611–616.

Walberg, H. J. (1986). Synthesis of research on teaching. In M. C. Wittrock (Ed.), *Handbook of research on teaching* (3rd ed., pp. 214–229). New York: Macmillan.

Walden, T., Kim, G., McCoy, C., & Karrass, J. (2007). Do you believe in magic? Infants' social looking during violations of expectations. *Developmental Science, 10,* 654–663.

Waldfogel, J., Craigie, T. A., & Brooks-Gunn, J. (2010). Fragile families and child well-being. *Future of Children, 20,* 87–112.

Waldfogel, J., & Zhai, F. (2008). Effects of public preschool expenditures on the test scores of fourth graders: Evidence from TIMMS. *Educational Research and Evaluation, 14,* 9–28.

Waldorf, K. M. A., & McAdams, R. M. (2013). Influence of infection during pregnancy on fetal development. *Reproduction, 146,* R151–R162.

Walfisch, A., Sermer, C., Cressman, A., & Koren, G. (2013). Breast milk and cognitive development—the role of confounders: A systematic review. *British Medical Journal, 3,* e003259.

Walker, C. (2014). *Early Head Start participants, programs, families and staff in 2013.* Retrieved from www.clasp.org/resources-and-publications/publication-1/HSpreschool-PIR-2013-Fact-Sheet.pdf

Walker, C. M., Walker, L. B., & Ganea, P. A. (2012). The role of symbol-based experience in early learning and transfer from pictures: Evidence from Tanzania. *Developmental Psychology, 49,* 1315–1324.

Walker, O. L., & Henderson, H. A. (2012). Temperament and social problem solving competence in preschool: Influences on academic skills in early elementary school. *Social Development, 21,* 761–779.

Walker, S. M. (2013). Biological and neurodevelopmental implications of neonatal pain. *Clinics in Perinatology, 40,* 471–491.

Wall, M., & Côté, J. (2007). Developmental activities that lead to dropout and investment in sport. *Physical Education and Sport Pedagogy, 12,* 77–87.

Wallon, M., Peron, F., Cornu, C., Vinault, S., Abrahamowicz, M., Kopp C. B., et al. (2013). Congenital toxoplasma infections: Monthly prenatal screening decreases transmission rate and improves clinical outcome at age 3 years. *Clinics in Infectious Disease, 56,* 1223–1231.

Wang, D., & Fletcher, A. C. (2016). Parenting style and peer trust in relation to school adjustment in middle childhood. *Journal of Child and Family Studies, 25,* 988–998.

Wang, M.-T., & Kenny, S. (2014). Parental physical punishment and adolescent adjustment: Bidirectionality and the moderation effects of child ethnicity and parental warmth. *Journal of Abnormal Child Psychology, 42,* 717–730.

Wang, M.-T., & Sheikh-Khalil, S. (2014). Does parental involvement matter for student achievement and mental health in high school? *Child Development, 85,* 610–625.

Wang, Q. (2006). Relations of maternal style and child self-concept to autobiographical memories in Chinese, Chinese immigrant, and European American 3-year-olds. *Child Development, 77,* 1794–1809.

Wang, Q., Shao, Y., & Li, Y. J. (2010). "My way or mom's way?" The bilingual and bicultural self in Hong Kong Chinese children and adolescents. *Child Development, 81,* 555–567.

Wang, S., Baillargeon, R., & Paterson, S. (2005). Detecting continuity violations in infancy: A new account and new evidence from covering and tube events. *Cognition, 95,* 129–173.

Wang, Z., & Deater-Deckard, K. (2013). Resilience in gene–environment transactions. In S. Goldstein & R. Brooks (Eds.), *Handbook of resilience in children* (2nd ed., pp. 57–72). New York: Springer Science + Business Media.

Ward, T. C. S. (2015). Reasons for mother–infant bedsharing: A systematic narrative synthesis of the literature and implications for future research. *Maternal and Child Health Journal, 19,* 675–690.

Warneken, F., & Tomasello, M. (2009). Varieties of altruism in children and chimpanzees. *Trends in Cognitive Sciences, 13,* 397.

Warneken, F., & Tomasello, M. (2013). Parental presence and encouragement do not influence helping in young children. *Infancy, 18,* 345–368.

Warnock, F., & Sandrin, D. (2004). Comprehensive description of newborn distress behavior in response to acute pain (newborn male circumcision). *Pain, 107,* 242–255.

Warren, S. L., & Simmens, S. J. (2005). Predicting toddler anxiety/depressive symptoms: Effects of caregiver sensitivity on temperamentally vulnerable children. *Infant Mental Health Journal, 26,* 40–55.

Warreyn, P., Roeyers, H., & De Groote, I. (2005). Early social communicative behaviours of preschoolers with autism spectrum disorder during interaction with their mothers. *Autism, 9,* 342–361.

Washington, J. A., & Thomas-Tate, S. (2009). How research informs cultural-linguistic differences in the classroom: The bi-dialectal African American child. In S. Rosenfield & V. Berninger (Eds.), *Implementing evidence-based academic interventions in school settings* (pp. 147–164). New York: Oxford University Press.

Washington, T., Gleeson, J. P., & Rulison, K. L. (2013). Competence and African American children in informal kinship care: The role of family. *Children and Youth Services Review, 35,* 1305–1312.

Wasik, B. A., Hindman, A. H., & Snell, E. K. (2016). Book reading and vocabulary development: A systematic review. *Early Childhood Research Quarterly, 37,* 39–57.

Wasserman, E. A., & Rovee-Collier, C. (2001). Pick the flowers and mind your As and 2s! Categorization by pigeons and infants. In M. E. Carroll & J. B. Overmier (Eds.), *Animal research and human health: Advancing human welfare through behavioral science* (pp. 263–279). Washington, DC: American Psychological Association.

Watamura, S. E., Phillips, D., Morrissey, T. W., McCartney, K., & Bub, K. (2011). Double jeopardy: Poorer social-emotional outcomes for children in the NICHD SECCYD experiencing home and childcare environments that confer risk. *Child Development, 82,* 48–65.

Waters, E., de Silva-Sanigorski, A., Brown, T., Campbell, K. J., Goa, Y., Armstrong, R., et al. (2011). Interventions for preventing obesity in children. *Cochrane Database of Systematic Reviews,* Issue 12, Art. No.: CD0011871.

Waters, E., Merrick, S., Treboux, D., Crowell, J., & Albersheim, L. (2000). Attachment security in infancy and early adulthood: A twenty-year longitudinal study. *Child Development, 71,* 684–689.

Waters, E., Vaughn, B. E., Posada, G., & Kondo-Ikemura, K. (Eds.). (1995). Caregiving, cultural, and cognitive perspectives on secure-base behavior and working models: New growing points of attachment theory and research. *Monographs of the Society for Research in Child Development, 60*(2–3, Serial No. 244).

Waters, S. F., & Thompson, R. A. (2014). Children's perceptions of the effectiveness of strategies for regulating anger and sadness. *International Journal of Behavioral Development, 38,* 174–181.

Watrin, J. P., & Darwich, R. (2012). On behaviorism in the cognitive revolution: Myth and reactions. *Review of General Psychology, 16,* 269–282.

Watson, J. B., & Raynor, R. (1920). Conditioned emotional reactions. *Journal of Experimental Psychology, 3,* 1–14.

Waxman, S. R., & Senghas, A. (1992). Relations among word meanings in early lexical development. *Developmental Psychology, 28,* 862–873.

Weaver, J. M., & Schofield, T. J. (2015). Mediation and moderation of divorce effects on children's behavior problems. *Journal of Family Psychology, 29,* 39–48.

Webb, A. R., Heller, H. T., Benson, C. B., & Lahav, A. (2015). Mother's voice and heartbeat sounds elicit auditory plasticity in the human brain before full gestation. *Proceedings of the National Academy of Sciences, 112,* 3152–3157.

Weber, C., Hahne, A., Friedrich, M., & Friederici, A. (2004). Discrimination of word stress in early infant perception: Electrophysiological evidence. *Cognitive Brain Research, 18,* 149–161.

Webster-Stratton, C., & Reid, M. J. (2010). The Incredible Years program for children from infancy to pre-adolescence: Prevention and treatment of behavior problems. In R. C. Murrihy, A. D. Kidman, & T. H. Ollendick (Eds.), *Clinical handbook of assessing and treating conduct problems in youth* (pp. 117–138). New York: Springer Science + Business Media.

Webster-Stratton, C., Rinaldi, J., & Reid, J. M. (2011). Long-term outcomes of Incredible Years parenting program: Predictors of adolescent adjustment. *Child and Adolescent Mental Health, 16,* 38–46.

Wechsler, D. (2012). *Wechsler Preschool and Primary Scale of Intelligence—Fourth Edition (WPPSI–IV).* Upper Saddle River, NJ: Pearson.

Weems, C. F., & Costa, N. M. (2005). Developmental differences in the expression of childhood anxiety symptoms and fears. *Journal of the American Academy of Child and Adolescent Psychiatry, 44,* 656–663.

Weiland, C., & Yoshikawa, H. (2013). Impacts of a prekindergarten program on children's mathematics, language, literacy, executive function, and emotional skills. *Child Development, 84,* 2112–2130.

Weinfield, N. S., Sroufe, L. A., & Egeland, B. (2000). Attachment from infancy to early adulthood in a high-risk sample: Continuity, discontinuity, and their correlates. *Child Development, 71,* 695–702.

Weinfield, N. S., Whaley, G. J. L., & Egeland, B. (2004). Continuity, discontinuity, and coherence in attachment from infancy to late adolescence: Sequelae of organization and disorganization. *Attachment and Human Development, 6,* 73–97.

Weinstein, R. S. (2002). *Reaching higher: The power of expectations in schooling.* Cambridge, MA: Harvard University Press.

Weinstock, M. (2008). The long-term behavioural consequences of prenatal stress. *Neuroscience and Biobehavioral Reviews, 32,* 1073–1086.

Weisgram, E. S., Bigler, R. S., & Liben, L. S. (2010). Gender, values, and occupational interests among children, adolescents, and adults. *Child Development, 81,* 778–796.

Weisman, O., Magori-Cohen, R., Louzoun, Y., Eidelman, A. I., & Feldman, R. (2011). Sleep–wake transitions in premature neonates predict early development. *Pediatrics, 128,* 706–714.

Weiss, K. M. (2005). Cryptic causation of human disease: Reading between the germ lines. *Trends in Genetics, 21,* 82–88.

Weiss, L., Saklofske, D., Holdnack, J., & Prifitera, A. (2015). *WISC-V assessment and interpretation.* San Diego, CA: Academic Press.

Wellman, H. M. (2011). Developing a theory of mind. In U. Goswami (Ed.), *Wiley-Blackwell handbook of childhood cognitive development* (2nd ed., pp. 258–284). Malden, MA: Wiley-Blackwell.

Wellman, H. M. (2012). Theory of mind: Better methods, clearer findings, more development. *European Journal of Developmental Psychology, 9,* 313–330.

Wellman, H. M., & Hickling, A. K. (1994). The mind's "I": Children's conception of the mind as an active agent. *Child Development, 65,* 1564–1580.

Wen, A., Weyant, R. J., McNeil, D. W., Crout, R. J., Neiswanger, K., Marazita, M. L., & Foxman, B. (2017). Bayesian analysis of the association between family-level factors and siblings' dental caries. *JDR Clinical & Translational Research, 2,* 278–286.

Wentworth, N., Benson, J. B., & Haith, M. M. (2000). The development of infants' reaches for stationary and moving targets. *Child Development, 71,* 576–601.

Wentzel, K. R., & Brophy, J. E. (2014). *Motivating students to learn.* Hoboken, NJ: Taylor & Francis.

Werner, E. E. (2013). What can we learn about resilience from large-scale longitudinal studies? In S. Goldstein & R. Brooks (Eds.), *Handbook of resilience in children* (2nd ed., pp. 87–102). New York: Springer Science + Business Media.

Werner, N. E., & Crick, N. R. (2004). Maladaptive peer relationships and the development of relational and physical aggression during middle childhood. *Social Development, 13,* 495–514.

Wessells, M. G. (2017). Children and armed conflict: Interventions for supporting war-affected children. *Peace and Conflict: Journal of Peace Psychology, 23,* 4–13.

Westermann, G., Sirois, S., Shultz, T. R., & Mareschal, D. (2006). Modeling developmental cognitive neuroscience. *Trends in Cognitive Sciences, 10,* 227–232.

Whipple, N., Bernier, A., & Mageau, G. A. (2011). Broadening the study of infant security of attachment: Maternal autonomy-support in the context of infant exploration. *Social Development, 20,* 17–32.

Whiteman, S. D., Solmeyer, A. R., & McHale, S. M. (2015). Sibling relationships and adolescent adjustment: Longitudinal associations in two-parent African American families. *Journal of Youth and Adolescence, 44,* 2042–2053.

Wichmann, C., Coplan, R. J., & Daniels, T. (2004). The social cognitions of socially withdrawn children. *Social Development, 13,* 377–392.

Widen, S. C. (2013). Children's interpretation of facial expressions: The long path from valence-based to specific discrete categories. *Emotion Review, 5,* 72–77.

Widen, S. C., & Russell, J. A. (2011). In building a script for an emotion do preschoolers add its cause before its behavior consequence? *Social Development, 20,* 471–485.

Wigfield, A., Eccles, J. S., Schiefele, U., Roeser, R. W., & Davis-Kean, P. (2006). Development of achievement motivation. In N. Eisenberg (Ed.), *Handbook of child psychology: Vol. 3. Social, emotional, and personality development* (6th ed., pp. 933–1002). Hoboken, NJ: Wiley.

Wigfield, A., Eccles, J. S., Yoon, K. S., Harold, R. D., Arbreton, A. J., Freedman-Doan, C., & Blumenfeld, P. C. (1997). Changes in children's competence beliefs and subjective task values across the elementary school years: A three-year study. *Journal of Educational Psychology, 89,* 451–469.

Willatts, P. (1999). Development of means–end behavior in young infants: Pulling a support to retrieve a distant object. *Developmental Psychology, 35,* 651–667.

Williams, K., & Dunne-Bryant, A. (2006). Divorce and adult psychological well-being: Clarifying the role of gender and age. *Journal of Marriage and Family, 68,* 1178–1196.

Wilson-Ching, M., Molloy, C. S., Anderson, V. A., Burnett, A., Roberts, G., Cheong, J. L., et al. (2013). Attention difficulties in a contemporary geographic cohort of adolescents born extremely preterm/extremely low birth weight. *Journal of the International Neuropsychological Society, 19,* 1097–1108.

Wimmer, M. B. (2013). *Evidence-based practices for school refusal and truancy.* Bethesda, MD: National Association of School Psychologists.

Winkler, I., Háden, G. P., Ladinig, O., Sziller, I., & Honing, H. (2009). Newborn infants detect the beat in music. *Proceedings of the National Academy of Sciences, 106,* 2468–2471.

Winner, E. (1986). Where pelicans kiss seals. *Psychology Today, 20*(8), 25–35.

Winsler, A., Fernyhough, C., & Montero, I. (Eds.). (2009). *Private speech, executive functioning, and the development of verbal self-regulation.* New York: Cambridge University Press.

Witherington, D. C. (2005). The development of prospective grasping control between 5 and 7 months: A longitudinal study. *Infancy, 7,* 143–161.

Witherington, D. C., Campos, J. J., Harriger, J. A., Bryan, C., & Margett, T. E. (2010). Emotion and its development in infancy. In G. Bremner & T. D. Wachs (Eds.), *Wiley-Blackwell handbook of infant development: Vol. 1. Basic research* (2nd ed., pp. 568–591). Oxford, UK: Wiley-Blackwell.

Witte, A. L., Kiewra, K. A., Kasson, S. C., & Perry, K. R. (2015). Parenting talent: A qualitative investigation of the roles parents play in talent development. *Roeper Review, 37,* 84–96.

Wolfe, D. A. (2005). *Child abuse* (2nd ed.). Thousand Oaks, CA: Sage.

Wolff, P. H. (1966). The causes, controls and organization of behavior in the neonate. *Psychological Issues, 5*(1, Serial No. 17).

Wolff, P. H., & Fesseha, G. (1999). The orphans of Eritrea: A five-year follow-up study. *Journal of Child Psychology and Psychiatry and Allied Disciplines, 40,* 1231–1237.

Wood, E., Desmarais, S., & Gugula, S. (2002). The impact of parenting experience on gender stereotyped toy play of children. *Sex Roles, 47,* 39–49.

Wood, J. T. (2009). Communication, gender differences in. In H. T. Reis & S. K. Sprecher (Eds.), *Encyclopedia of human relationships* (Vol. 1, pp. 252–256). Thousand Oaks, CA: Sage.

Wood, R. M. (2009). Changes in cry acoustics and distress ratings while the infant is crying. *Infant and Child Development, 18,* 163–177.

Woolley, J. D., Browne, C. A., & Boerger, E. A. (2006). Constraints on children's judgments of magical causality. *Journal of Cognition and Development, 7,* 253–277.

Woolley, J. D., & Cornelius, C. A. (2013). Beliefs in magical beings and cultural myths. In M. Taylor (Ed.), *Oxford handbook of the development of imagination* (pp. 61–74). New York: Oxford University Press.

Woolley, J. D., & Cox, V. (2007). Development of beliefs about storybook reality. *Developmental Science, 10,* 681–693.

World Health Organization. (2015a). *Levels and trends in child mortality: Report 2015.* Geneva, Switzerland: Author.

World Health Organization. (2015b). *World health statistics 2015.* Retrieved from www.who.int/gho/publications/world_health_statistics/2015/en

World Health Organization. (2017a). HIV/AIDS: *Data and statistics.* Retrieved from http://www.who.int/hiv/data/en

World Health Organization. (2017b). *Immunization, vaccines and biologicals: Data, statistics and graphics.* Retrieved from www.who.int/immunization/monitoring_surveillance/data/en

World Health Organization. (2017c). *Rubella.* Fact sheet No 367. Retrieved from www.who.int/mediacentre/factsheets/fs367/en/

World Health Organization. (2017d). *The World Health Organization's infant feeding recommendation.* Retrieved from www.who.int/nutrition/topics/infantfeeding_recommendation/en/

Worthy, J., Hungerford-Kresser, H., & Hampton, A. (2009). Tracking and ability grouping. In L. Christenbury, R. Bomer, & P. Smargorinsky (Eds.), *Handbook of adolescent literacy research* (pp. 220–235). New York: Guilford.

Worton, S. K., Caplan, R., Nelson, G., Pancer, S. M., Loomis, C., Peters, R. D., & Hayward, K. (2014). Better Beginnings, Better Futures: Theory, research, and knowledge transfer of a community-based initiative for children and families. *Psychosocial Intervention, 23,* 135–143.

Woythaler, M., McCormick, M. C., Mao, W.-Y., & Smith, V. C. (2015). Late preterm infants and neurodevelopmental outcomes at kindergarten. *Pediatrics, 136,* 424–431.

Wright, B. C. (2006). On the emergence of the discriminative mode for transitive inference. *European Journal of Cognitive Psychology, 18,* 776–800.

Wright, B. C., Robertson, S., & Hadfield, L. (2011). Transitivity for height versus speed: To what extent do the under-7s really have a transitive capacity? *Thinking and Reasoning, 17,* 57–81.

Wright, J. C., Huston, A. C., Murphy, K. C., St. Peters, M., Pinon, M., Scantlin, R., & Kotler, J. (2001). The relations of early television viewing to school readiness and vocabulary of children from low-income families: The Early Window Project. *Child Development, 72,* 1347–1366.

Wright, W. E. (2013). Bilingual education. In T. K. Bhatia & W. C. Ritchie (Eds.), *Handbook of bilingualism and multilingualism* (pp. 598–623). Chichester, UK: Wiley-Blackwell.

Wrotniak, B. H., Epstein, L. H., Raluch, R. A., & Roemmich, J. N. (2004). Parent weight change as a predictor of child weight change in family-based behavioral obesity treatment. *Archives of Pediatric and Adolescent Medicine, 158,* 342–347.

Wu, L. L., Bumpass, L. L., & Musick, K. (2001). Historical and life course trajectories of nonmarital childbearing. In L. L. Wu & B. Wolfe (Eds.), *Out of wedlock: Causes and consequences of nonmarital fertility* (pp. 3–48). New York: Russell Sage Foundation.

Wulczyn, F. (2009). Epidemiological perspectives on maltreatment prevention. *Future of Children, 19,* 39–66.

Wuyts, D., Vansteenkiste, M., Soenens, B., & Assor, A. (2015). An examination of the dynamics involved in parental child-invested contingent self-esteem. *Parenting: Science and Practice, 15,* 55–74.

Wyman, E., Rakoczy, H., & Tomasello, M. (2009). Normativity and context in young children's pretend play. *Cognitive Development, 24,* 146–155.

Wynn, K. (1992). Addition and subtraction by human infants. *Nature, 358,* 749–750.

Wynn, K., Bloom, P., & Chiang, W.-C. (2002). Enumeration of collective entities by 5-month-old infants. *Cognition, 83,* B55–B62.

X

Xu, F., Han, Y., Sabbagh, M. A., Wang, T., Ren, X., & Li, C. (2013). Developmental differences in the structure of executive function in middle childhood and adolescence. *PLOS ONE, 8*(10), e77770.

Y

Yang, C.-K., & Hahn, H.-M. (2002). Cosleeping in young Korean children. *Developmental and Behavioral Pediatrics, 23,* 151–157.

Yanovski, J. A. (2015). Pediatric obesity. An introduction. *Appetite, 93,* 3–12.

Yehuda, R., & Bierer, L. M. (2009). The relevance of epigenetics to PTSD: Implications for DSM-V. *Journal of Trauma and Stress, 22,* 427–434.

Yeung, J. W. K., Cheung, C.-K., Kwok, S. Y. C. L., & Leung, J. T. Y. (2016). Socialization effects of authoritative parenting and its discrepancy on children. *Journal of Child and Family Studies, 25,* 1980–1990.

Yirmiya, N., Erel, O., Shaked, M., & Solomonica-Levi, D. (1998). Meta-analyses comparing theory of mind abilities of individuals with autism, individuals with mental retardation, and normally developing individuals. *Psychological Bulletin, 124,* 283–307.

Yong, M. H., & Ruffman, T. (2014). Emotional contagion: Dogs and humans show a similar physiological response to human infant crying. *Behavioural Processes, 108,* 155–165.

Yook, J.-H., Han, J.-Y., Choi, J.-S., Ahn, H.-K., Lee, S.-W., Kim, M.-Y., et al. (2012). Pregnancy outcomes and factors associated with voluntary pregnancy termination in women who had been treated for acne with isotretinoin. *Clinical Toxicology, 50,* 896–901.

Yoshida, H., & Smith, L. B. (2003). Known and novel noun extensions: Attention at two levels of abstraction. *Child Development, 74,* 564–577.

Yoshikawa, H., Aber, J. L., & Beardslee, W. R. (2012). The effects of poverty on the mental, emotional, and behavioral health of children and youth: Implications for prevention. *American Psychologist, 67,* 272–284.

Yoshikawa, H., Weiland, C., Brooks-Gunn, J., Burchinal, M. R., Espinosa, L. M., Gormley, W. T., et al. (2013). *Investing in our future: The evidence base on preschool education.* Ann Arbor, MI: Society for Research in Child Development. Retrieved from fcd-us.org/sites/default/files/Evidence%20Base%20on%20Preschool%20Education%20FINAL.pdf

Youn, M. J., Leon, J., & Lee, K. J. (2012). The influence of maternal employment on children's learning growth and the role of parental involvement. *Early Child Development and Care, 182,* 1227–1246.

Young, S. E., Friedman, N. P., Miyake, A., Willcutt, E. G., Corley, R. P., Haberstick, B. C., et al. (2009). Behavioral disinhibition: Liability for externalizing spectrum disorders and its genetic and environmental relation to response inhibition across adolescence. *Journal of Abnormal Psychology, 118,* 117–130.

Yunger, J. L., Carver, P. R., & Perry, D. G. (2004). Does gender identity influence children's psychological well-being? *Developmental Psychology, 40,* 572–582.

Z

Zachrisson, H. D., & Dearing, E. (2015). Family income dynamics, early childhood education and care, and early child behavior problems in Norway. *Child Development, 86,* 425–440.

Zachrisson, H. D., Dearing, E., Lekhal, R., & Toppelberg, C. O. (2013). Little evidence that time in child care causes externalizing problems during early childhood in Norway. *Child Development, 84,* 1152–1170.

Zadjel, R. T., Bloom, J. M., Fireman, G., & Larsen, J. T. (2013). Children's understanding and experience of mixed emotions: The roles of age, gender, and empathy. *Journal of Genetic Psychology, 174,* 582–603.

Zalewski, M., Lengua, L. J., Wilson, A. C., Trancik, A., & Bazinet, A. (2011). Emotion regulation profiles, temperament, and adjustment problems in preadolescents. *Child Development, 82,* 951–966.

Zaslow, M. J., Weinfield, N. S., Gallagher, M., Hair, E. C., Ogawa, J. R., Egeland, B., Tabors, P. O., & De Temple, J. M. (2006). Longitudinal prediction of child outcomes from differing measures of parenting in a low-income sample. *Developmental Psychology, 42,* 27–37.

Zelazo, N. A., Zelazo, P. R., Cohen, K. M., & Zelazo, P. D. (1993). Specificity of practice effects on elementary neuromotor patterns. *Developmental Psychology, 29,* 686–691.

Zelazo, P. D. (2006). The Dimensional Change Card Sort (DCCS): A method of assessing executive function in children. *Nature Protocols, 1,* 297–301.

Zelazo, P. D., Anderson, J. A. Richler, J., Wallner-Allen, K., Beaumont, J. L., & Weintraub, S. (2013). NIH Toolbox Cognition Battery (CB): Measuring executive function and attention. In P. D. Zelazo & P. J. Bauer (Eds.), National Institutes of Health Toolbox Cognition Battery (NIH Toolbox CB): Validation for children between 3 and 15 years. *Monographs of the Society for Research in Child Development, 78*(4, Serial No. 309), 16–33.

Zelazo, P. D., & Lyons, K. E. (2012). The potential benefits of mindfulness training in early childhood: A developmental social cognitive neuroscience perspective. *Child Development Perspectives, 6,* 154–160.

Zhao, Y., & Castellanos, F. X. (2016). Discovery science strategies in studies of the pathophysiology of child and adolescent psychiatric disorders: Promises and limitations. *Journal of Child Psychology and Psychiatry, 57,* 421–439.

Zhou, X., Huang, J., Wang, Z., Wang, B., Zhao, Z., Yang, L., & Zheng-zheng, Y. (2006). Parent–child interaction and children's number learning. *Early Child Development and Care, 176,* 763–775.

Ziemer, C. J., Plumert, J. M., & Pick, A. D. (2012). To grasp or not to grasp: Infants' actions toward objects and pictures. *Infancy, 17,* 479–497.

Zimmerman, F. J., & Christakis, D. A. (2005). Children's television viewing and cognitive outcomes. *Archives of Pediatrics and Adolescent Medicine, 159,* 619–625.

Zimmerman, F. J., Christakis, D. A., & Meltzoff, A. N. (2007). Television and DVD/video viewing in children younger than 2 years. *Archives of Pediatrics and Adolescent Medicine, 161,* 473–479.

Zimmermann, L. K., & Stansbury, K. (2004). The influence of emotion regulation, level of shyness, and habituation on the neuroendocrine response of three-year-old children. *Psychoneuroendocrinology, 29,* 973–982.

Zitzmann, M. (2013). Effects of age on male fertility. *Best Practice & Research Clinical Endocrinology and Metabolism, 27,* 617–628.

Ziv, Y. (2013). Social information processing patterns, social skills, and school readiness in preschool children. *Journal of Experimental Child Psychology, 114,* 306–320.

Zolotor, A. J., & Puzia, M. E. (2010). Bans against corporal punishment: A systematic review of the laws, changes in attitudes and behaviours. *Child Abuse Review, 19,* 229–247.

Zolotor, A. J., Theodore, A. D., Runyan, D. K., Chang, J. J., & Laskey, A. L. (2011). Corporal punishment and physical abuse: Population-based trends for three-to-11-year-old children in the United States. *Child Abuse Review, 20,* 57–66.

Zosuls, K. M., Ruble, D. N., Bornstein, M. H., & Greulich, F. K. (2009). The acquisition of gender labels in infancy: Implications for gender-typed play. *Developmental Psychology, 45,* 688–701.

Zucker, K. J., & Lawrence, A. A. (2009). Epidemiology of gender identity disorder: Recommendations for the Standards of Care of the World Professional Association for Transgender Health. *International Journal of Transgenderism, 11,* 8–18.

Zukow-Goldring, P. (2002). Sibling caregiving. In M. H. Bornstein (Ed.), *Handbook of parenting: Vol. 3* (2nd ed., pp. 253–286). Hillsdale, NJ: Erlbaum.

Zukowski, A. (2013). Putting words together. In J. B. Gleason & N. B. Ratner (Eds.), *The development of language* (8th ed., pp. 120–162). Upper Saddle River, NJ: Pearson.

NAME INDEX

Italic n *following page number indicates page with an illustration or table.*

C

T

SUBJECT INDEX

Figures and tables are indicated by f *and* t *following page numbers. Notes are indicated by* n *following page numbers.*

D

F

G

H

N

O